WORD BIBLICAL COMMENTARY

VOLUME 18A

Job 21–37

DAVID J. A. CLINES

THOMAS NELSON
Since 1798

NASHVILLE DALLAS MEXICO CITY RIO DE JANEIRO

To my daughter
Miriam

עֹז־וְהָדָר לְבוּשָׁהּ וַתִּשְׂחַק לְיוֹם אַחֲרוֹן

Strength and dignity are her clothing,
and she laughs at the days to come (Prov 31:25).

Word Biblical Commentary
Job 21–37

Library of Congress Cataloging-in-Publication Data
Main entry under title:

Word biblical commentary.

Includes bibliographies.
1. Bible—Commentaries—Collected works.
BS491.2.W67 220.7′7 80–71768

ISBN 10: 0–8499–0217–7 (v. 18A) AACR2
ISBN 13: 978-0-8499-0217-8

Printed in Mexico

Unless otherwise indicated, Scripture quotations in the body of the commentary are the author's own. Those marked RSV are from the Revised Standard Version of the Bible, copyright 1946 (renewed 1973), 1956, and © 1971 by the Division of Christian Education of the National Council of the Churches of Christ in the USA and are used by permission. Those marked NIV are from the New International Version of the Bible, copyright © 1973 by New York Bible Society International. The author's own translation of the text of Job appears in italic type under the heading *Translation.*

The Graeca, Hebraica, and TranslitLS fonts used to print this work are available from Linguist's Software, Inc., P.O. Box 580, Edmonds, WA 98020-0580 USA; tel. (206)775-1130.

4 5 6 7 8 EPAC 16 15 14 13 12

Contents

Abbreviations

Commentaries, Monographs, Journals, Periodicals, Major Reference Works, and Series

AASF	Annales academiae scientiarum fennicae
AAT	Ägypten und Altes Testament: Studien zu Geschichte, Kultur und Religion Ägyptens und des Alten Testaments
AB	Anchor Bible
ABD	*Anchor Bible Dictionary*. Ed. D. N. Freedman. 6 vols. New York: Doubleday, 1992.
AbrN	*Abr-Nahrain*
AcOr	*Acta orientalia*
Aistleitner	Aistleitner, J. *Wörterbuch der ugaritischen Sprache*. Berlin: Akademie, 1963.
AJBI	*Annual of the Japanese Biblical Institute*
AJSL	*American Journal of Semitic Languages and Literature*
Alden	Alden, R. L. *Job*. NAC 11. Nashville: Broadman & Holman, 1993.
Alonso Schökel	Alonso Schökel, L., and J. L. Sicre Díaz. *Job, comentario teológico y literario*. Madrid: Cristiandad, 1983.
ALUOS	*Annual of Leeds University Oriental Society*
ALUOSSup	*ALUOS* Supplements
AnBib	Analecta biblica
Andersen	Andersen, F. I. *Job: An Introduction and Commentary*. TOTC. Leicester: Inter-Varsity Press, 1976.
ANEP	*The Ancient Near East in Pictures Relating to the Old Testament*. Ed. J. B. Pritchard. Princeton: Princeton UP, 1954.
ANET	*Ancient Near Eastern Texts Relating to the Old Testament*. Ed. J. B. Pritchard. 3d ed. Princeton: Princeton UP, 1969.
AnOr	Analecta orientalia
AOAT	Alter Orient und Altes Testament
AS	Alonso Schökel, L. *Diccionario bíblico hebreo-español*. Madrid: Trotta, 1994.
ASTI	*Annual of the Swedish Theological Institute*
ATD	Das Alte Testament Deutsch
Aug	*Augustinianum*
AzTh	Arbeiten zur Theologie
Ball	Ball, C. J. *The Book of Job: A Revised Text and Version*. Oxford: Clarendon, 1922.
Barr, *Comparative Philology*	Barr, J. *Comparative Philology and the Text of the Old Testament*. Oxford: Clarendon, 1968.
BAT	Die Botschaft des Alten Testaments

Bauer–Leander — Bauer, H., and P. Leander. *Historische Grammatik der hebräischen Spraches des Alten Testaments.* Halle: Niemeyer, 1922.
BBB — Bonner biblische Beiträge
BDB — Brown, F., S. R. Driver, and C. A. Briggs. *A Hebrew and English Lexicon of the Old Testament.* Oxford: Clarendon, 1907.
BEATAJ — Beiträge zur Erforschung des Alten Testaments und des antiken Judentum
Beer, BH^2 — Beer, G. Textual notes to Job in *Biblia Hebraica.* Ed. R. Kittel. 2d ed. Stuttgart: Württemburgische Bibelanstalt, 1909. 1062–1112 [only mentioned when it differs from *BHK*].
Beer, *BHK* — Beer, G. Textual notes to Job in BHK^3. 1105–54.
Beer, *Text* — Beer, G. *Der Text des Buches Hiob.* 2 vols. Marburg: Elwert, 1895–97.
BeO — *Bibbia e oriente*
BETL — Bibliotheca ephemeridum theologicarum lovaniensium
BHK — *Biblia Hebraica.* Ed. R. Kittel. 3d ed. Stuttgart: Württemburgische Bibelanstalt, 1937.
BHS — *Biblia Hebraica Stuttgartensia.* Ed. K. Elliger and W. Rudolph. Stuttgart: Deutsche Bibelstiftung, 1966–67.
Bib — *Biblica*
BiBh — *Bible Bhashyam*
BibOr — Biblica et orientalia
BibS — Biblische Studien
BibSem — The Biblical Seminar
Bickell — Bickell, G. "Kritische Bearbeitung des Iobdialogs." *WZKM* 6 (1892) 136–47, 241–57, 327–34; 7 (1893) 1–20, 153–68.
Bickell[2] — Bickell, G. *Carmina Veteris Testamenti metrice: Notas criticas et dissertationem de re metrica Hebraeorum adjecit.* Innsbruck: Libraria Academica Wagneriana, 1882. 151–87.
Bickell[3] — Bickell, G. *Das Buch Job nach Anleitung der Strophik und der Septuaginta auf seine ursprüngliche Form zurückgeführt und in Versmasse des Urtextes übersetzt.* Vienna: Carl Gerold's Sohn, 1894.
Bijdr — *Bijdragen: Tijdschrift voor filosofie en theologie*
BIJS — *Bulletin of the Institute of Jewish Studies*
BKAT — Biblischer Kommentar, Altes Testament. Ed. M. Noth and H. W. Wolff.
Bleeker — Bleeker, L. H. K. *Job.* Tekste en uitleg: Praktische bibelverklaring. Groningen: Wolters, 1935.
Blommerde — Blommerde, A. C. M. *Northwest Semitic Grammar and Job.* Biblica et Orientalia 22. Rome: Pontifical Biblical Institute, 1969.
BMik — *Beth Mikra*
BN — *Biblische Notizen*
Böttcher — Böttcher, F. *Neue exegetisch-kritische Aehrenlese zum Alten Testamente.* Leipzig: Barth, 1863–65.
BR — *Biblical Research*
Brockelmann — Brockelmann, C. *Lexicon Syriacum.* 2d ed. Halle: Niemeyer, 1928.
Brockington — Brockington, L. H. *The Hebrew Text of the Old Testament: The Readings Adopted by the Translators of the New English Bible.* Oxford: Clarendon, 1973.

BSac	*Bibliotheca sacra*
BSOAS	*Bulletin of the School of Oriental and African Studies*
BT	*The Bible Translator*
BTB	*Biblical Theology Bulletin*
Budde	Budde, K. *Das Buch Hiob übersetzt und erklärt.* HAT 2/1. Göttingen: Vandenhoeck & Ruprecht, 1896.
Budde[2]	Budde, K. *Das Buch Hiob übersetzt und erklärt.* 2d ed. HAT 2/1. Göttingen: Vandenhoeck & Ruprecht, 1913.
Buttenwieser	Buttenwieser, M. *The Book of Job.* London: Hodder & Stoughton, 1922.
Buxtorf	Buxtorf, J. *Lexicon Hebraicum et Chaldaicum: complectens omnes voces tam primas quàm derivatas, quae in sacris Bibliis, Hebraeâ, et ex parte Caldaeâ linguâ scriptis extant... Accessit lexicon breve rabbinico-philosophicum.* Basel: J. L. König and J. Brandmüller, 1689. Originally published as *Epitome radicum Hebraicarum et Chaldaicarum* (Basel: Waldkirch, 1607).
BWANT	Beiträge zur Wissenschaft vom Alten und Neuen Testament
BZ	*Biblische Zeitschrift*
BZAW	Beihefte zur *ZAW*
CAD	[*Chicago Assyrian Dictionary*] *The Assyrian Dictionary of the Oriental Institute of the University of Chicago.* Chicago: Oriental Institute, 1956–.
CamB	Cambridge Bible
Carey	Carey, C. P. *The Book of Job Translated... on the Basis of the Authorized Version, Explained in a Large Body of Notes... and Illustrated by Extracts from Various Works.* London: Wertheim, Macintosh, & Hunt, 1858.
CB	Century Bible
CB	*Cultura bíblica*
CBC	Cambridge Bible Commentary
CBQ	*Catholic Biblical Quarterly*
CBQMS	*CBQ* Monograph Series
Ceresko	Ceresko, A. R. *Job 29–31 in the Light of Northwest Semitic: A Translation and Philological Commentary.* BibOr 36. Rome: Biblical Institute Press, 1980.
CJT	*Canadian Journal of Theology*
CML	Driver, G. R. *Canaanite Myths and Legends.* Old Testament Studies 3. Edinburgh: T. & T. Clark, 1956.
CML[2]	Gibson, J. C. L. *Canaanite Myths and Legends.* 2d ed. Edinburgh: T. & T. Clark, 1978.
Cocceius	Cocceius, J. *Commentarius in librum Ijobi.* Franeker, 1644.
Cohen	Cohen, H. R. (C.). *Biblical Hapax Legomena in the Light of Akkadian and Ugaritic.* SBLDS 37. Missoula, MT: Scholars Press, 1978.
ColcTFu	*Collectanea Theologica Universitatis Fujen*
Coverdale	Coverdale, M. *Biblia: The Bible, that is, the Holy Scripture of the Olde and New Testament, Faithfully and Truly Translated out of Douche and Latyn in to Englishe.* Cologne [?]: Cervicornus & Soter [?], 1535.

Cox	Cox, S. A. *A Commentary on the Book of Job, with a Translation.* London: Kegan, Paul, 1880.
CTA	*Corpus des tablettes en cunéiformes alphabétiques découvertes à Ras Shamra-Ugarit.* Ed. A. Herdner. Paris: Imprimerie Nationale, 1963.
CTM	*Concordia Theological Monthly*
CurTM	*Currents in Theology and Mission*
Dahood, *Psalms I*	Dahood, M. *Psalms I: 1–50.* Garden City, NY: Doubleday, 1966.
Dahood, *Psalms II*	Dahood, M. *Psalms II: 51–100.* Garden City, NY: Doubleday, 1968.
Dahood, *Psalms III*	Dahood, M. *Psalms III: 101–150.* Garden City, NY: Doubleday, 1970.
Dalman	Dalman, G. H. *Aramäisch-neuhebräisches Handwörterbuch zu Targum, Talmud und Midrasch.* 2d ed. Frankfurt a.M.: Kauffmann, 1922.
Dalman, *Arbeit und Sitte*	Dalman, G. *Arbeit und Sitte in Palästina.* Gütersloh: Bertelsmann, 1928–42.
Dathe	Dathe, J. A. *Jobus, Proverbia Salomonis, Ecclesiastes, Canticum Canticorum ex recensione textus hebraei et versionum antiquarum latine versi notisque philologicis et criticis illustrati.* Halle: Sumtibus Orphanotrophei, 1789. 1–221.
Davidson	Davidson, A. B. *The Book of Job with Notes, Introduction and Appendix.* CamB. Cambridge: Cambridge UP, 1884.
Davidson–Lanchester	Davidson, A. B. *The Book of Job with Notes, Introduction and Appendix, Adapted to the Text of the Revised Version with Some Supplementary Notes by H. C. O. Lanchester.* CamB. Cambridge: Cambridge UP, 1918.
DB	*Dictionnaire de la Bible.* Ed. F. Vigouroux. 5 vols. Paris: Letouzey & Ané, 1895–1912.
DCH	*The Dictionary of Classical Hebrew.* Ed. D. J. A. Clines. 5 vols. to date. Sheffield: Sheffield Academic Press, 1993–.
DD	*Dor le-Dor*
DDD	*Dictionary of Deities and Demons in the Bible.* Ed. K. van der Toorn, B. Becking, and P. W. van der Horst. 2d ed. Leiden: Brill, 1999.
Delitzsch	Delitzsch, Franz J. *Biblical Commentary on the Book of Job.* Trans. F. Bolton. 2 vols. Edinburgh: T. & T. Clark, 1866.
Delitzsch, Friedrich	Delitzsch, Friedrich. *Das Buch Hiob, neu übersetzt und kurz erklärt.* Leipzig: Hinrichs, 1902.
Dhorme	Dhorme, E. *A Commentary on the Book of Job.* Trans. by H. Knight. London: Nelson, 1967. Originally published as *Le livre de Job* (Paris: Gabalda, 1926).
Dillmann	Dillmann, A. *Hiob.* Leipzig: Hirzel, 1869^3, 1891^4.
DissAb	Dissertation Abstracts
Doederlein	Doederlein, J. C. *Scholia in libros Veteris Testamenti poeticos Jobum, Psalmos et tres Salomonis.* Halle: Curt, 1779.
Dozy	Dozy, R. *Supplément aux dictionnaires arabes.* 2 vols. Leiden: Brill, 1881.
Driver	Driver, S. R. *The Book of Job in the Revised Version.* Oxford: Clarendon, 1908.
Driver–Gray	Driver, S. R., and G. B. Gray. *A Critical and Exegetical Commentary on the Book of Job together with a New Translation.* ICC. Edinburgh: T. & T. Clark, 1921.

Driver, *Tenses*	Driver, S. R. *A Treatise on the Use of the Tenses in Hebrew and Some Other Syntactical Questions.* 2d ed. Oxford: Clarendon, 1881.
Duhm	Duhm, B. *Das Buch Hiob erklärt.* KHC. Tübingen: Mohr, 1897.
DUL	Olmo Lete, G. del, and J. Sanmartín. *A Dictionary of the Ugaritic Language in the Alphabetic Tradition.* 2d ed. Leiden: Brill, 2004.
EB	*Encyclopaedia Biblica.* 4 vols. Ed. T. K. Cheyne and J. Black. London: Black, 1899–1903.
EdF	Erträge der Forschung
Ehrlich	Ehrlich, A. B. *Randglossen zur hebräischen Bibel.* Vol. 6, *Psalmen, Sprüche, und Hiob.* Leipzig: Hinrichs, 1918.
Eitan	Eitan, I. *A Contribution to Biblical Lexicography.* New York: Columbia UP, 1924.
Elberfelder	*Die Heilige Schrift aus dem Grundtext übersetzt.* 2d ed. Wuppertal: Brockhaus, 1988.
Enc	*Encounter* (Indianapolis)
EphLtg	*Ephemerides liturgicae*
ErIsr	*Eretz-Israel*
EstBíb	*Estudios bíblicos*
EstEcl	*Estudios eclesiásticos*
ETL	*Ephemerides theologicae lovanienses*
EvQ	*Evangelical Quarterly*
EvTh	*Evangelische Theologie*
Ewald	Ewald, G. H. A. von. *Commentary on the Book of Job.* Trans. J. F. Smith. London: Williams and Norgate, 1882.
ExpTim	*Expository Times*
FAT	Forschungen zum Alten Testament
Fedrizzi	Fedrizzi, P. *Giobbe: La Sacra Bibbia, traduta dai testi originali illustrata con note critiche e commentata.* Turin: Marietti, 1972.
FF	*Forschungen und Fortschritte*
Fohrer	Fohrer, G. *Das Buch Hiob.* KAT 16. Gütersloh: Mohn, 1963.
FOTL	The Forms of the Old Testament Literature
Freytag	Freytag, G. W. *Lexicon arabico-latinum praesertim ex Djeuharii Firuzabadiique et aliorum Arabum operibus adhibitis Golii quoque et aliorum libris confectum.* Halle: Schwetschke, 1830–37.
FRLANT	Forschungen zur Religion und Literatur des Alten und Neuen Testaments
Galling, *Reallexikon*	Galling, K. *Biblisches Reallexikon.* 2d ed. Tübingen: Mohr, 1977.
Gard	Gard, D. H. *The Exegetical Method of the Greek Translator of the Book of Job.* SBLMS 8. Philadelphia: Society of Biblical Literature, 1952.
Geneva	[Geneva Bible] *The Bible and Holy Scriptvres Conteyned in the Olde and Newe Testament: Translated according to the Ebrue and Greke, and Conferred with the Best Translations in Diuers Langages.* Geneva, 1560.
Gerleman	Gerleman, G., textual notes to Job in *BHS.*
Ges[18]	Meyer, R., and H. Donner, with U. Rüterswörden. *Wilhelm Gesenius Hebräisches und aramäisches Handwörterbuch über das Alte Testament.* 18th ed. 3 vols. to date. Berlin: Springer, 1987, 1995, 2005.

Gesenius, *Thesaurus*	Gesenius, W. *Thesaurus philologicus criticus linguae hebraeae et chaldaeae Veteris Testamenti.* 2d ed. Leipzig: Vogel, 1829.
Gesenius–Buhl	Gesenius, W., and F. Buhl. *Wilhelm Gesenius' Hebräisches und aramäisches Handwörterbuch über das Alte Testament.* 17th ed. Leipzig: Vogel, 1915.
Gibson, E. C. S.	Gibson, E. C. S. *The Book of Job.* WC. London: Methuen, 1899.
Gill	Gill, J. *An Exposition of the Whole Old Testament, Critical, Doctrinal and Practical.* 4 vols. London: George Keith, 1763–65.
GKC	*Gesenius' Hebrew Grammar.* Ed. E. Kautzsch and A. E. Cowley. 2d ed. Oxford: Clarendon, 1910.
Golius	Golius, J. *Lexicon Arabico-Latinum, contextum ex probatioribus orientis lexicographis.* Leiden: Bonaventurae & Abr. Elseviriorum, 1653.
Good	Good, E. M. *In Turns of Tempest: A Reading of Job, with a Translation.* Stanford: Stanford UP, 1990.
Gordis	Gordis, R. *The Book of Job: Commentary, New Translation, and Special Notes.* New York: Jewish Theological Seminary of America, 1978.
Grabbe	Grabbe, L. L. *Comparative Philology and the Text of Job: A Study in Methodology.* SBLDS 34. Chico, CA: Scholars Press, 1977.
Graetz	Graetz, H. "Lehrinhalt der 'Weisheit' in den biblischen Büchern." *MGWJ* 35 (1886) 289–99, 204–10, 544–49 (pp. 402–10, 544–49 often cited as "Register der corrumpierten Stellen in Hiob und Vorschläge zur Verbesserung").
Gray	Gray, J. *The Book of Job.* Sheffield: Sheffield Phoenix Press, 2005.
Greg	*Gregorianum*
Grimme	Grimme, H. "Metrisch-kritische Emendationen zum Buche Hiob." *TQ* 80 (1898) 295–304, 421–32; 81 (1899) 112–18, 259–77.
GSAI	*Giornale della Società Asiatica Italiana*
Guillaume	Guillaume, A. *Studies in the Book of Job with a New Translation.* ALUOSSup 2. Leiden: Brill, 1968.
Guillaume, *Lexicography*	Guillaume, A. *Hebrew and Arabic Lexicography: A Comparative Study.* Leiden: Brill, 1965.
GuL	*Geist und Leben*
Habel	Habel, N. C. *The Book of Job.* OTL. London: SCM Press, 1985.
Hahn	Hahn, H. A. *Commentar über das Buch Hiob.* Berlin: Wohlgemuth, 1850.
HALOT	Koehler, L., W. Baumgartner, and J. J. Stamm. *The Hebrew and Aramaic Lexicon of the Old Testament.* Trans. and ed. by M. E. J. Richardson. 5 vols. Leiden: Brill, 1994–2000.
HAR	*Hebrew Annual Review*
Hartley	Hartley, J. E. *The Book of Job.* NICOT. Grand Rapids, MI: Eerdmans, 1988.
HAT	Handbuch zum Alten Testament
Hava	Hava, J. G. *Al-Faraid Arabic-English Dictionary.* Beirut: Catholic Press, 1964 [original edition 1899].
Heath	Heath, T. *An Essay towards a New English Version of the Book of Job, from the Original Hebrew, with a Commentary, and Some Account of His Life.* London: Millar and Baker, 1756.

Hesse	Hesse, F. *Hiob.* ZBK. Zurich: Theologischer Verlag, 1978.
Hirzel	Hirzel, L. *Hiob erklärt.* KEH 2. Leipzig: Weidmann, 1839.
Hitzig	Hitzig, F. *Das Buch Hiob übersetzt und ausgelegt.* Leipzig: Winter, 1874.
Hoffmann	Hoffmann, J. G. E. *Hiob.* Kiel: Haeseler, 1891.
Hölscher	Hölscher, G. *Das Buch Hiob.* HAT. Tübingen: Mohr (Siebeck), 1937.
Hontheim	Hontheim, J. *Das Buch Hiob als strophisches Kunstwerk nachgewiesen, übersetzt und erklärt.* BibS 9.1–3. Freiburg i.Br.: Herder, 1904.
Horst	Horst, F. *Hiob.* BKAT. Vol. 1. Neukirchen-Vluyn: Neukirchener Verlag, 1960–63.
Houbigant	Houbigant, C.-F. *Biblia Hebraica cum notis criticis.* 4 vols. Paris: Briasson & Durand, 1753.
Houtsma	Houtsma, M. T. *Textkritische Studien zum Alten Testament.* Vol. 1, *Das Buch Hiob.* Leiden: Brill, 1925.
HS	*Hebrew Studies*
HSAT	*Die Heilige Schrift des Alten Testaments.* Ed. E. Kautzsch. 4th ed. by B. Bertholet. Tübingen: Mohr (Siebeck), 1922–23.
HSM	Harvard Semitic Monographs
HTR	*Harvard Theological Review*
HUCA	*Hebrew Union College Annual*
Hufnagel	Hufnagel, W. F. *Hiob neu übersetzt mit Anmerkungen.* Erlangen: Palmische Buchhandlung, 1781.
Hupfeld	Hupfeld, H. *Quaestionum in Jobeidos locos vexatos specimen: Commentatio.* Halle: Anton, 1853.
HvTSt	*Hervormde Teologiese Studies*
IB	*The Interpreter's Bible.* Ed. G. A. Buttrick et al. 12 vols. Nashville: Abingdon, 1951–57.
IBD	*Illustrated Bible Dictionary.* Ed. J. D. Douglas. Leicester: Inter-Varsity Press, 1980.
ICC	International Critical Commentary
IDB	*The Interpreter's Dictionary of the Bible.* Ed. G. A. Buttrick. 4 vols. Nashville: Abingdon, 1962.
IDBSup	*IDB, Supplementary Volume.* Ed. K. Crim. Nashville: Abingdon, 1976.
IEJ	*Israel Exploration Journal*
Int	*Interpretation*
Interp	*The Interpreter*
ISBE	*The International Standard Bible Encyclopedia.* Ed. G. W. Bromiley. Rev. ed. 4 vols. Grand Rapids, MI: Eerdmans, 1979–88.
ITQ	*Irish Theological Quarterly*
JAC	*Jahrbuch für antike und Christentum*
JANESCU	*Journal of the Ancient Near Eastern Society of Columbia University*
Janzen	Janzen, J. G. *Job.* Interpretation. Atlanta: Knox, 1985.
JAOS	*Journal of the American Oriental Society*
Jastrow	Jastrow, M. *A Dictionary of the Targumim, the Talmud Babli and Yerushalim, and the Midrashic Literature.* London: Luzac, 1903.
JBC	*The Jerome Bible Commentary.* Ed. R. E. Brown et al. London: Chapman, 1968.

JBL	*Journal of Biblical Literature*
JBLMS	*JBL* Monograph Series
JBQ	*Jewish Bible Quarterly*
JCS	*Journal of Cuneiform Studies*
JHI	*Journal of the History of Ideas*
JJS	*Journal of Jewish Studies*
JNES	*Journal of Near Eastern Studies*
JNSL	*Journal of Northwest Semitic Languages*
Joüon	Joüon, P. *Grammaire de l'hébreu biblique.* Rome: Pontifical Biblical Institute, 1947.
Joüon–Muraoka	Joüon, P. *A Grammar of Biblical Hebrew.* Trans. and rev. T. Muraoka. 2 vols. Subsidia biblica 14/1–2. Rome: Pontifical Biblical Institute, 1991.
JPOS	*Journal of the Palestine Oriental Society*
JQR	*Jewish Quarterly Review*
JRAS	*Journal of the Royal Asiatic Society*
JSJ	*Journal for the Study of Judaism in the Persian, Hellenistic, and Roman Periods*
JSNTSup	*Journal for the Study of the New Testament,* Supplement Series
JSOR	*Journal of the Society of Oriental Research*
JSOT	*Journal for the Study of the Old Testament*
JSOTSup	*Journal for the Study of the Old Testament,* Supplement Series
JSS	*Journal of Semitic Studies*
JTS	*Journal of Theological Studies*
Kaltner, *Use of Arabic*	Kaltner, J. *The Use of Arabic in Biblical Hebrew Lexicography.* CBQMS 28. Washington, DC: Catholic Biblical Association of America, 1996.
Kamphausen	*Die Bibel, oder, die Schriften des Alten and Neuen Bundes nach den überlieferten Grundtexten übersetzt und für die Gemeinde erklärt.* Vol. 3, *Die Schriften.* Ed. A. Kamphausen. Leipzig: Brockhaus, 1868.
KAT	Kommentar zum Alten Testament
KBL	Koehler, L., and W. Baumgartner. *Lexicon in Veteris Testamenti libros.* Leiden: Brill, 1953.
KEH	Kurzgefasstes exegetisches Handbuch zum Alten Testament
KHC	Kurzer Hand-Commentar zum Alten Testament
King	King, E. G. *The Poem of Job: Translated in the Metre of the Original.* Cambridge: Cambridge UP, 1914.
Kissane	Kissane, E. J. *The Book of Job Translated from a Critically Revised Hebrew Text with Commentary.* Dublin: Browne & Nolan, 1939.
König	König, E. *Hebraisches und aramaisches Wörterbuch zum Alten Testament, mit Einschaltung und Analyse aller schwen erkennbaren Formen, Deutung der Eigennamen sowie der massoretischen Randbemerkungen und einem deutsch-hebraischen Wortregister.* Leipzig: Dieterich, 1910.
König, *Syntax*	König, E. *Historisch-kritisches Lehrgebäude der hebräischen Sprache.* Vol. 3, *Historisch-Comparative Syntax der hebräischen Sprache.* Leipzig: Hinrichs, 1897.
Kroeze	Kroeze, J. H. *Het Boek Job, opnieuw uit de grondtekst vertaald en verklaard.* KVHS. Kampen: Kok, 1960.

KTU	Dietrich, M., O. Loretz, and J. Sanmartín. *Die Keilalphabetischen Texte aus Ugarit.* AOAT 24. Kevelaer: Butzon & Bercker, 1976.
KVHS	Korte verklaring der Heilige Schrift
Lamparter	Lamparter, H. *Das Buch der Anfechtung, übersetzt und ausgelegt.* BAT. Stuttgart: Calwer, 1951.
Lane	Lane, E. W. *An Arabic-English Lexicon.* London: Williams & Norgate, 1863–93.
Larcher	Larcher, C. *Le Livre de Job.* La sainte Bible. Paris: Cerf, 1950.
LD	Lectio divina
Le Hir	Le Hir, A.-M. *Le livre de Job, traduction sur l'hébreu et commentaire, précédé d'un essai sur le rythme chez les juifs, et suivi du Cantique de Debora et psaume CX.* Paris: Jouby & Roger, 1873.
Leigh	Leigh, E. *Critica Sacra, in Two Parts: The First Containing Observations on All the Radices, or Primitive Hebrew Words of the Old Testament, in Order Alphabetical... The Second, Philologicall and Theologicall Observations upon All the Greek Words of the New Testament, in Order Alphabetical.* 3d ed. London: Underhill, 1650.
Leš	*Lešonenu*
Lévêque	Lévêque, J. *Job et son Dieu: Essai d'exégèse et de théologie biblique.* Paris: Gabalda, 1970.
Levy	Levy, J. *Neuhebräisches und chaldäisches Wörterbuch über die Talmudim und Midraschim.* 4 vols. Leipzig: Brockhaus, 1876–89.
Ley	Ley, J. "Die metrische Beschaffenheit des Buches Hiob." *TSK* (1895) 635–92; (1897) 7–42.
Ley[2]	Ley, J. *Das Buch Hiob nach seinem Inhalt, seiner Kunstgestaltung und religiösen Bedeutung, für gebildete Leser dargestellt.* Halle: Waisenhaus, 1903.
Lods	Lods, A., and L. Randon. "Job." In *La Sainte Bible: Traduction nouvelle d'après les meilleurs textes avec introductions et notes.* La Bible de la Centenaire. Vol. 3. Paris: Société Biblique de Paris, 1947.
Löw, *Flora*	Löw, I. *Die Flora der Juden.* Vol. 1, *Krytogamae, Acanthaceae, Graminaceae.* Veröffentlichungen der Alexander Kohut Memorial Foundation 4. Vienna: Löwit, 1928. Vol. 2, *Iridaceae, Papilionaceae.* Veröffentlichungen der Alexander Kohut Memorial Foundation 2. Vienna: Löwit, 1924. Vol. 3, *Pedaliaceae, Zygophyllaceae.* Veröffentlichungen der Alexander Kohut Memorial Foundation 3. Vienna: Löwit, 1924.
Lugt, van der	Lugt, P. van der. *Rhetorical Criticism and the Poetry of the Book of Job.* OTS 32. Leiden: Brill, 1995.
MacKenzie	MacKenzie, R. A. F. "Job." In *The Jerome Bible Commentary.* Ed. R. E. Murphy. Englewood Cliffs, NJ: Prentice-Hall, 1968. 511–33.
MEAH	*Miscelánea de estudios arabes y hebraicos*
Merx	Merx, A. *Das Gedicht von Hiob: Hebräischer Text, kritisch bearbeitet und übersetzt, nebst sachlicher und kritischer Einleitung.* Jena: Mauke, 1871.
MGWJ	*Monatsschrift für Geschichte und Wissenschaft des Judentums*
Michaelis	Michaelis, J. D. "Varianten im Buch Hiob." In his *Orientalische und exegetische Bibliothek* 7 (1774) 217–47; 8 (1775) 179–224.

Michaelis, *Deutsche Übersetzung*	Michaelis, J. D. *Deutsche Übersetzung des Alten Testaments, mit Anmerkungen für Ungelehrte.* 2d ed. Göttingen: Dieterich, 1773–88.
Michaelis, *Supplementa*	Michaelis, J. D. *Supplementa ad lexica hebraica.* 6 parts. Göttingen: Rosenbusch, 1784–92.
Michel	Michel, W. L. *Job in the Light of Northwest Semitic.* Vol. 1. Rome: Pontifical Biblical Institute, 1987. [References without a page number are to his unpublished Vol. 2.]
Moffatt	Moffatt, J. *A New Translation of the Bible.* London: Hodder & Stoughton, 1926.
Murphy	Murphy, R. E. *Wisdom Literature: Job, Proverbs, Ruth, Canticles, Ecclesiastes and Esther.* FOTL 13. Grand Rapids, MI: Eerdmans, 1981.
Mus	*Le muséon: Revue d'études orientales*
MUSJ	*Mélanges de la Faculté Orientale* (Université Saint-Joseph, Beirut)
Muss-Arnoldt	Muss-Arnoldt, W. *A Concise Dictionary of the Assyrian Languages.* Berlin: Reuther & Reichard, 1905.
NAC	New American Commentary
NCB	New Century Bible
Newsom	Newsom, C. "The Book of Job." In *The New Interpreter's Bible.* Ed. L. E. Keck et al. Vol. 4. Nashville: Abingdon, 1996. 317–637.
Nichols	Nichols, H. H. "The Composition of the Elihu Speeches (Job, Chaps. 32–37)." *AJSL* 27 (1910–11) 97–186.
NICOT	New International Commentary on the Old Testament
NIDOTTE	*The New International Dictionary of Old Testament Theology and Exegesis.* Ed. W. A. VanGemeren. 5 vols. Grand Rapids, MI: Zondervan, 1997.
NTT	*Norsk teologisk tidsskrift*
OBO	Orbis biblicus et orientalis
OED	[*Oxford English Dictionary*] Murray, J. A. H. *New English Dictionary on Historical Principles.* Oxford, 1888–1928. Cited from http://dictionary.oed.com/.
Olshausen	Olshausen, J. *Hiob erklärt.* 2d ed. KEH 2. Leipzig: Hirzel, 1852 [first edition by L. Hirzel].
OLZ	*Orientalische Literaturzeitung*
Or	*Orientalia*
OTE	*Old Testament Essays*
OTL	Old Testament Library
OTS	Old Testament Studies
OTS	*Oudtestamentische Studiën*
Payne Smith	Payne Smith, R. *Thesaurus Syriacus.* 2 vols. Oxford: Clarendon, 1879–1901.
Payne Smith, J.	Payne Smith, J. *A Compendious Syriac Dictionary, Founded upon the Thesaurus Syriacus of R. Payne Smith.* Oxford: Clarendon, 1903.
Peake	Peake, A. S. *Job, Introduction, Revised Version with Notes, and Index.* CB. Edinburgh: Jack, 1905.

PEQ	*Palestine Exploration Quarterly*
Perles	Perles, F. *Analekten zur Textkritik des Alten Testaments.* Munich: Ackermann, 1895.
Perles[2]	Perles, F. *Analekten zur Textkritik des Alten Testaments.* Neue Folge. Leipzig: Engel, 1922.
Peters	Peters, N. *Das Buch Hiob übersetzt und erklärt.* Münster: Aschendorff, 1928.
Pope	Pope, M. H. *Job.* AB 15. 3d ed. Garden City, NY: Doubleday, 1973.
Pope[1]	Pope, M. H. *Job.* AB 15. Garden City, NY: Doubleday, 1965.
PrGLM	*Proceedings of the Eastern Great Lakes and Midwest Biblical Societies*
PrIrB	*Proceedings of the Irish Biblical Association*
PTMS	Pittsburgh Theological Monograph Series
QD	Quaestiones disputatae
RAC	*Reallexikon für Antike und Christentum.* Ed. T. Klauser. Stuttgart: Hiersemann, 1950–.
Ravasi	Ravasi, G. *Giobbe, traduzione e commento.* 2d ed. Rome: Borla, 1984.
RB	*Revue biblique*
REAug	*Revue des études augustiniennes*
REG	*Revue des études grecques*
REJ	*Revue des études juives*
Reiske	Reiske, J. J. *Coniecturae in Jobum et Proverbia Salomonis.* Leipzig: Sommer, 1779.
Renan	Renan, E. *Le livre de Job, traduit de l'hébreu.* Paris: Calmann Lévy, 1860.
Reuss	Reuss, E. *Hiob.* Braunschweig: Schwetschke, 1888.
RevExp	*Review and Expositor*
RevQ	*Revue de Qumran*
RGG	*Die Religion in Geschichte und Gegenwart.* Ed. K. Galling. 7 vols. Tübingen: Mohr, 1957–65.
RHPR	*Revue d'histoire et de philosophie religieuses*
RHR	*Revue de l'histoire des religions*
Richter	Richter, G. *Textstudien zum Buche Hiob.* BWANT 3.7. Stuttgart: Kohlhammer, 1927.
RivB	*Rivista biblica italiana*
Rosenmüller	Rosenmüller, E. F. C. *Scholia in Vetus Testamentum: Editio secunda auctior et emendatior.* Vol. 5, *Jobus.* Leipzig: J. A. Barth, 1824.
Rossi, de	Rossi, G. B. de. *Variae lectiones Veteris Testamenti.* Parma: Ex regio typographeo, 1784–98.
Rowley	Rowley, H. H. *Job.* NCB. London: Nelson, 1970.
RS	Ras Shamra
RSP	*Ras Shamra Parallels: The Texts from Ugarit and the Hebrew Bible.* Ed. L. R. Fisher et al. 3 vols. AnOr 51. Rome: Pontifical Biblical Institute, 1972–75.
RTP	*Revue de théologie et de philosophie*
RTR	*Reformed Theological Review*

Saadia	Ecker, R. *Die arabische Job-Übersetzung des Gaon Saadja ben Josef al-Fajjûmi: Ein Beitrag zur Geschichte der Übersetzung des Alten Testaments.* Munich: Kösel, 1962.
SBFLA	*Studii biblici franciscani liber annuus*
SBL	Society of Biblical Literature
SBLDS	Society of Biblical Literature Dissertation Series
SBLMS	Society of Biblical Literature Monograph Series
SBLSCS	Society of Biblical Literature Septuagint and Cognate Studies
SBOT	Sacred Books of the Old Testament
SBT	Studies in Biblical Theology
Schultens	Schultens, A. *Liber Iobi cum nova versione ad hebraeum fontem et commentario perpetuo.* Leiden: Luzac, 1787.
SEÅ	*Svensk exegetisk årsbok*
SEAsiaJT	*Southeast Asia Journal of Theology*
SecCent	*The Second Century: A Journal of Early Christian Studies*
Sef	*Sefarad*
SEL	*Studi epigrafici e linguistici sul Vicino Oriente antico*
Sicre Díaz	Alonso Schökel, L., and J. L. Sicre Díaz. *Job, comentario teológico y literario.* Madrid: Cristiandad, 1983.
Siegfried	Siegfried, C. [G. A.] *The Book of Job: Critical Edition of the Hebrew Text.* SBOT. Baltimore: Johns Hopkins Press, 1893.
SK	*Skrif en kerk*
Skehan	Skehan, P. W. "Strophic Patterns in the Book of Job." *CBQ* 23 (1961) 125–42. Reprinted in *Studies in Israelite Poetry and Wisdom,* CBQMS 1 (Washington, DC: Catholic Biblical Association, 1971) 96–113.
Skehan–Di Lella, *Wisdom*	Skehan, P. W., and A. A. Di Lella. *The Wisdom of Ben Sira: A New Translation with Notes by Patrick W. Skehan; Introduction and Commentary by Alexander A. Di Lella.* AB 39. New York: Doubleday, 1987.
SMSR	*Studi e materiali di storia delle religioni*
Snaith	Snaith, N. H. *The Book of Job: Its Origin and Purpose.* SBT 2/11. London: SCM Press, 1968.
Soden, von	Soden, W. von. *Akkadisches Handwörterbuch.* Wiesbaden: Harrassowitz, 1959–72.
Sokoloff	Sokoloff, M. *A Dictionary of Jewish Palestinian Aramaic of the Byzantine Period.* Ramat-Gan, Israel: Bar Ilan UP, 1990.
Sokoloff, *Targum*	Sokoloff, M. *The Targum to Job from Qumran Cave XI.* Ramat-Gan, Israel: Bar-Ilan UP, 1974.
SOTSMS	Society for Old Testament Studies Monograph Series
SR	*Studies in Religion/Sciences religieuses*
SRSup	*SR* Supplements
ST	*Studia theologica*
Steinmann	Steinmann, J. *Job: Texte français, introduction et commentaires.* Connaître la Bible. Bruges: Desclée de Brouwer, 1961.
Steuernagel	Steuernagel, C. "Das Buch Hiob." In *Die Heilige Schrift des Alten Testaments.* Ed. E. Kautzsch and A. Bertholet. 4th ed. Tübingen: Mohr, 1923. 2:323–89.

Stevenson	Stevenson, W. B. *The Poem of Job: A Literary Study with a New Translation.* London: Oxford UP, 1947.
Stevenson[2]	Stevenson, W. B. *Critical Notes on the Hebrew Text of the Book of Job.* Aberdeen: Aberdeen UP, 1951.
Stier	Stier, F. *Das Buch Ijjob hebräisch und deutsch: Uebertragungen ausgelegt und mit Text- und Sacherläuterungen versehen.* Munich: Kösel, 1954.
Strahan	Strahan, J. *The Book of Job Interpreted.* Edinburgh: T. & T. Clark, 1913.
Strauss	Strauss, H. *Hiob.* BKAT 16.2. Neukirchen-Vluyn: Neukirchener Verlag, 2000.
Str-B	Strack, H. L., and P. Billerbeck. *Kommentar zum Neuen Testament aus Talmud und Midrasch.* 6 vols. Munich, 1922–61.
Szczygiel	Szczygiel, P. *Das Buch Job, übersetzt und erklärt.* HSAT 5.1. Bonn: Hanstein, 1931.
Taylor	Taylor, J. *The Hebrew Concordance, Adapted to the English Bible, Disposed after the Manner of Buxtorf.* London: Waugh & Fenner, 1754.
TBei	*Theologische Beiträge*
TDNT	*Theological Dictionary of the New Testament.* Ed. G. Kittel and G. Friedrich. Trans. G. W. Bromiley. 10 vols. Grand Rapids, MI: Eerdmans, 1964–76.
TDOT	*Theological Dictionary of the Old Testament.* Ed. G. J. Botterweck and H. Ringgren. Trans. J. T. Willis, G. W. Bromiley, and D. E. Green. 13 vols. to date. Grand Rapids, MI: Eerdmans, 1974–.
Terrien	Terrien, S. L. *Job.* CAT 13. Neuchâtel: Delachaux & Niestlé, 1963.
Textual Notes	*Textual Notes on the New American Bible.* Paterson, NJ: St. Anthony's Guild, [1970]. [Pp. 325–451 of some editions.]
Thomas	Thomas, D. W. *A Revised Hebrew and English Lexicon of the Old Testament.* 11 vols. (*aleph* to *kaph*). (Unpublished at the author's death in 1970.)
ThSt	Theologische Studiën
TLOT	*Theological Lexicon of the Old Testament.* Ed. E. Jenni and C. Westermann. Trans. M. E. Biddle. 3 vols. Peabody, MA: Hendrickson, 1997.
TLZ	*Theologische Literaturzeitung*
Torczyner	Torczyner, H. [Tur-Sinai, N. H.]. *Das Buch Hiob: Eine kritische Analyse des überlieferten Hiobtextes.* Vienna: Löwit, 1920.
TOTC	Tyndale Old Testament Commentaries
TQ	*Theologische Quartalschrift*
Tristram	Tristram, H. B. *The Natural History of the Bible: Being a Review of the Physical Geography, Geology and Meteorology of the Holy Land; with a Description of Every Animal and Plant Mentioned in Holy Scripture.* 9th ed. London: Society for Promoting Christian Knowledge, 1898 (original 1867).
TRu	*Theologische Rundschau*
TSAJ	Texte und Studien zum antiken Judentum
TThSt	Trierer theologische Studien
Tur-Sinai	Tur-Sinai, N. H. *The Book of Job, A New Commentary.* Jerusalem: Kiryath-Sepher, 1957.

TVers	*Theologische Versuche*
TynBul	*Tyndale Bulletin*
TZ	*Theologische Zeitschrift*
UBL	Ugaritisch-biblische Literatur
UF	*Ugarit-Forschungen*
Vaccari	Vaccari, A. *Il Libro di Giobbe e i Salmi, tradotti dai testi originali e annotati.* Rome: Pontifical Biblical Institute, 1925.
Voigt	Voigt, C. *Einige Stellen des Buches Hiob.* Leipzig: Drugulin, 1895.
Volz	Volz, P. *Weisheit (Das Buch Hiob, Sprüche und Jesus Sirach, Prediger).* Göttingen: Vandenhoeck & Ruprecht, 1911.
VT	*Vetus Testamentum*
VTSup	Supplements to *Vetus Testamentum*
Wagner, *Aramaismen*	Wagner, M. *Die lexikalischen und grammatikalischen Aramaismen im alttestamentlichen Hebräisch.* BZAW 96. Berlin: Töpelmann, 1966.
Watson	Watson, W. G. E. *Classical Hebrew Poetry: A Guide to Its Techniques.* JSOTSup 26. Sheffield: JSOT Press, 1984.
WC	Westminster Commentaries
Webster	Webster, E. C. "Strophic Patterns in Job 3–28." *JSOT* 26 (1983) 33–60; "Strophic Patterns in Job 29–42." *JSOT* 30 (1984) 95–109.
Wehr–Cowan	Wehr, H. *A Dictionary of Modern Written Arabic.* Ed. J. M. Cowan. Beirut: Librarie du Liban, 1980.
Weiser	Weiser, A. *Das Buch Hiob übersetzt und erklärt.* ATD 13. Göttingen: Vandenhoeck & Ruprecht. 1951.
Westermann, *Structure*	Westermann, C. *The Structure of the Book of Job: A Form-Critical Analysis.* Trans. C. A. Muenchow. Philadelphia: Fortress, 1981.
Whybray	Whybray, N. *Job.* Readings. Sheffield: JSOT Press, 1998.
Wilde, de	Wilde, A. de. *Das Buch Hiob eingeleitet, übersetzt und erläutert.* OtSt 22. Leiden: Brill, 1981.
Witte	Witte, M. *Philologische Notizen zu Hiob 21–27.* BZAW 234. Berlin: de Gruyter, 1995.
WO	*Die Welt des Orients*
Wolfers	Wolfers, D. *Deep Things out of Darkness: The Book of Job: Essays and a New English Translation.* Kampen: Kok Pharos; Grand Rapids, MI: Eerdmans, 1995.
Wright	Wright, G. H. B. *The Book of Job.* London: Williams & Norgate, 1883.
WZKM	*Wiener Zeitschrift für die Kunde des Morgenlandes*
Yellin	Yellin, D. חקרי־מקרא באורים חדשים במקראות. Vol. 1, איוב. Jerusalem: Tarpiz, 1927.
ZA	*Zeitschrift für Assyriologie*
ZAW	*Zeitschrift für die alttestamentliche Wissenschaft*
ZBK	Zürcher Bibelkommentare
ZDMG	*Zeitschrift der deutschen morgenländischen Gesellschaft*
ZDMGSup	*ZDMG* Supplements

ZDPV	*Zeitschrift des deutschen Palästina-Vereins*
Ziegler	Ziegler, J. *Iob.* Septuaginta, Vetus Testamentum graecum 11.4. Göttingen: Vandenhoeck & Ruprecht, 1982.
Zorell	Zorell, F. *Lexicon hebraicum et aramaicum Veteris Testamenti.* Rome: Pontifical Biblical Institute, 1984 (original 1946).
ZRGG	*Zeitschrift für Religions- und Geistesgeschichte*
ZTK	*Zeitschrift für Theologie und Kirche*

Hebrew Grammar

abs	absolute
acc	accusative
adj	adjective, adjectival
adv	adverb, adverbial
consec	consecutive
coh	cohortative
constr	construct
fem	feminine
fut	future
gen	genitive
hiph	*hipʿil*
hithp	*hitpaʿel*
hithpo	*hitpoʿlel*
hoph	*hopʿal*
impf	imperfect
impv	imperative
inf	infinitive
juss	jussive
masc	masculine
neut	neuter
niph	*nipʿal*
obj	object, objective
pf	perfect
pl	plural
prep	preposition
ptcp	participle
sg	singular
subj	subject, subjective
suff	suffix

Textual Notes

Akk.	Akkadian
Aq	Aquila
Arab.	Arabic
Aram.	Aramaic
Assyr.	Assyrian
Eg.	Egyptian
Eng.	English
Eth.	Ethiopic
Germ.	German
haplog	haplography
Heb.	Hebrew
Hitt.	Hittite
K	Kethib, consonantal Hebrew text of OT
Lat.	Latin
LXX	Septuagint
MH	Mishnaic Hebrew
MT	Masoretic Text of the (OT)
NT	New Testament
OG	Old Greek
OL	Old Latin
OT	Old Testament
Pesh	Peshitta, Syriac version of the OT
Phoen.	Phoenician
Q	Qere, Masoretic vocalized Hebrew text of OT
Rashi	commentary printed in rabbinic Bibles
Symm	Symmachus
Syr.	Syriac
Tg	Targum
Theod	Theodotion
Ugar.	Ugaritic
Vg	Vulgate

MODERN TRANSLATIONS

ASV	American Standard Version	NEB	New English Bible
BJ	Bible de Jérusalem	NIV	New International Version
EVV	English versions	NJB	New Jerusalem Bible
GNB	Good News Bible, Today's English Version, Good News Translation	NJPS	*Tanakh: The Holy Scriptures: The New JPS Translation according to the Traditional Hebrew Text*
JB	Jerusalem Bible	NRSV	New Revised Standard Version
JPS	Jewish Publication Society Version	REB	Revised English Bible
KJV	King James Version, Authorized Version	RSV	Revised Standard Version
NAB	New American Bible	RV	Revised Version

BIBLICAL AND APOCRYPHAL BOOKS

OLD TESTAMENT

Gen	Genesis	Cant	Canticles, Song of Songs
Exod	Exodus	Isa	Isaiah
Lev	Leviticus	Jer	Jeremiah
Num	Numbers	Lam	Lamentations
Deut	Deuteronomy	Ezek	Ezekiel
Josh	Joshua	Dan	Daniel
Judg	Judges	Hos	Hosea
Ruth	Ruth	Joel	Joel
1–2 Sam	1–2 Samuel	Amos	Amos
1–2 Kgs	1–2 Kings	Obad	Obadiah
1–2 Chr	1–2 Chronicles	Jonah	Jonah
Ezra	Ezra	Mic	Micah
Neh	Nehemiah	Nah	Nahum
Esth	Esther	Hab	Habakkuk
Job	Job	Zeph	Zephaniah
Ps(s)	Psalm(s)	Hag	Haggai
Prov	Proverbs	Zech	Zechariah
Eccl	Ecclesiastes	Mal	Malachi

APOCRYPHA AND SEPTUAGINT

1–4 Kgdms	1–4 Kingdoms	Ecclus	Ecclesiasticus (Wisdom of Jesus the son of Sirach)
1–2 Esdr	1–2 Esdras	Bar	Baruch
Tob	Tobit	Ep Jer	Epistle of Jeremiah
Jdt	Judith	Sus	Susanna
Add Esth	Additions to Esther	Bel	Bel and the Dragon
Wisd	Wisdom of Solomon	1–2 Macc	1–2 Maccabees

NEW TESTAMENT

Matt	Matthew	1–2 Thess	1–2 Thessalonians
Mark	Mark	1–2 Tim	1–2 Timothy
Luke	Luke	Titus	Titus
John	John	Philem	Philemon
Acts	Acts	Heb	Hebrews
Rom	Romans	Jas	James
1–2 Cor	1–2 Corinthians	1–2 Pet	1–2 Peter
Gal	Galatians	1–2–3 John	1–2–3 John
Eph	Ephesians	Jude	Jude
Phil	Philippians	Rev	Revelation
Col	Colossians		

Old Testament Pseudepigrapha

1 Enoch	*1 Enoch (Ethiopic Apocalypse)*	*Pss. Sol.*	*Psalms of Solomon*
		T. Asher	*Testament of Asher*
4 Ezra	*4 Ezra*	*T. Dan*	*Testament of Dan*
Jub.	*Jubilees*	*T. Jos.*	*Testament of Joseph*

Qumran

1QS	*Community Rule*	1QM	*War Scroll*
1QH	*Thanksgiving Hymns*	11QtgJob	*Targum to Job*

Miscellaneous

al.	*aliter,* otherwise (in text-critical note)	lit.	literally
		m.	Mishnah
b.	Babylonian Talmud	mg.	margin
BH	Biblical Hebrew	MH	Mishnaic Hebrew
cf.	*confer,* compare	MS(S)	manuscript(s)
col(s).	column(s)	n.d.	no date
dittogr	dittograph, dittography	NS	new series
ed(s).	edited by, editor(s)	p(p).	page(s)
e.g.	*exempli gratia,* for example	pl.	plate
ET	English translation	*prb*	*probabiliter,* probably (in text-critical note)
et al.	and others		
frag.	fragment	*prp, prps*	*propositum,* (it has been) proposed (in text-critical note, denotes a reading not adopted by the editor)
frt	*forte,* perhaps (in text-critical note)		
FS	*Festschrift*		
ins	*insere,* insert (in text-critical note)	*q.v.*	*quod vide,* which see
		repr.	reprint(ed)

sc.	*scilicet,* that is to say	v(v)	verse(s)
si v.l.	*si vera lectio,* if the reading is correct	*vel*	*vel,* or (in text-critical note, denotes an alternative reading)
s.v.	*sub verbo,* under that word		
t.	Tosefta	*v.l.*	*varia lectio,* alternative reading
trans.	translated by; translator(s)	vol(s).	volume(s)
Univ.	University	*y.*	Jerusalem Talmud
UP	University Press	§	section or paragraph

The Third Cycle (21:1–27:23)

Job's Seventh Speech (21:1–34)

Bibliography

Alfrink, B. "Die Bedeutung des Wortes רֶגֶב in Job 21, 33 und 38, 38." *Bib* 13 (1932) 77–86. **Aufrecht, W. E.** "Aramaic Studies and the Book of Job." In *Studies in the Book of Job.* Ed. W. E. Aufrecht. SRSup 16. Waterloo, Ont.: Wilfrid Laurier UP, 1985. 54–66. **Bergmeier, R.** "Zum Ausdruck עצת רשעים in Ps 1:1 Hi 10:3 21:16 und 22:18." *ZAW* 79 (1967) 229–32. **Bickell, G.** *Metrices biblicae regulae exemplis illustratae.* Vienna: Libraria Academica Wagneriana, 1879. 32–34 [Job 21 as an example of heptasyllabic meter]. **Dahood, M.** "Chiasmus in Job: A Text-Critical and Philological Criterion." In *A Light unto My Path.* FS J. M. Myers, ed. H. N. Bream, R. D. Heim, and C. A. Moore. Gettysburg Theological Studies 4. Philadephia: Temple UP, 1974. 119–30. ———. "Hebrew-Ugaritic Lexicography II." *Bib* 45 (1964) 393–412. ———. "Hebrew-Ugaritic Lexicography X." *Bib* 53 (1972) 386–403. ———. "Some Northwest-Semitic Words in Job." *Bib* 38 (1957) 306–20. **Guillaume, A.** "A Root שאה in Hebrew [Job 21:12; Isa 42:11]." *JTS* NS 17 (1966) 53–54. **Held, M.** "Rhetorical Questions in Ugaritic and Biblical Hebrew." *ErIsr* 9 (1969) 71–79. **Jacob, B.** "Christlich-Palästinisches." *ZDMG* 55 (1901) 135–45. **Kelly, B. H.** "Truth in Contradiction: A Study of Job 20 and 21." *Int* 15 (1961) 147–56. **Knauf, E. A.** "Zum Text von Hi 21, 23–26." *BN* 7 (1978) 22–24. **Luyten, J.** "Psalm 73 and Wisdom (Job 21:28–34)." In *La Sagesse de l'Ancien Testament.* Ed. M. Gilbert. BETL 51. Gembloux: Duculot; Leuven: Leuven UP, Peeters, 1979. 59–81. **Talstra, E.** "Dialogue in Job 21: 'Virtual Quotations' or Text Grammatical Markers?" In *The Book of Job.* Ed. W. A. M. Beuken. BETL 114. Leuven: Leuven UP, 1994. 329–48. **Witte, M.** *Philologische Notizen zu Hiob 21–27.* BZAW 234. Berlin: de Gruyter, 1995. ———. *Vom Leiden zur Lehre: Der dritte Redegang (Hiob 21–27) und die Redaktionsgeschichte des Hiobbuches.* BZAW 230. Berlin: de Gruyter, 1994. **Wolfers, D.** "Job: The Third Cycle: Dissipating a Mirage." *DD* 16 (1987–88) 217–26; 17 (1988–89) 19–25. **Zolli, I.** "A che forma di sepoltura si riferisce Giobbe XXI, 33." *SMSR* 10 (1934) 223–28.

Translation

1 *Then Job answered and said:*

2 *Listen attentively to my words;*
let that[a] *be the comfort*[b] *you offer me.*
3 *Bear with me*[a] *while I speak;*
and after I have spoken, mock[b] *if you will.*
4 *Is it against another human*[a] *that I*[b] *make my protest?*[c]
Why then[d] *should I not be cramped in spirit?*[e]
5 *Only look at me, and you will be appalled,*[a]
and clap your hand to your mouth.

6 *When I remember,*[a] *I am dismayed;*
my flesh is seized with quivering.[b]

7 *Why do the wicked live on,*
live to be old,[a] *and even increase their strength?*[b]

8 [a]*Their children are established around them,*[b]
their offspring[c] *before their very eyes.*
9 *Their houses*[a] *are safe,*[b] *without fear;*[c]
there is no scourge[d] *of God upon them.*
10 *Their*[a] *bull sires*[b] *without fail,*[c]
their cow gives birth[d] *and does not lose her calf.*[e]

11 [a]*They send their children out*[b] *to play like lambs,*
their young go off to dance.[c]
12 *They sing*[a] *to the timbrel*[b] *and lyre,*
and make merry to the sound of the flute.
13 [a]*They live out*[b] *their days in prosperity,*[c]
and in tranquility[d] *they go down*[e] *to Sheol.*

14 *They say*[a] *to God, "Depart from us;*
we have no wish to know your ways.
15 [a]*What is the Almighty*[b] *that we should serve him?*
What gain shall we have if we pray[c] *to him?"*
16 [a]*Is not their prosperity within their own power?*
Are not the plans[b] *of the wicked*[c] *far*[d] *from him?*[e]

17 *How often*[a] *is the lamp*[b] *of the wicked snuffed out,*[c]
[d]*that calamity*[e] *comes upon them,*
[f]*that he*[g] *apportions*[h] *them destruction*[i] *in his anger?*
18 *How often*[a] *are they like straw before the wind,*
like chaff[b] *swept away*[c] *by the storm?*
19 [a]*Is God*[b] *storing up his punishment for his children?*
Let him requite[c] *the man himself and let him know*[d] *it.*
20 *Let his own eyes see*[a] *his ruin,*[b]
and let him drink[c] *of*[d] *the wrath of the Almighty!*
21 *For what concern*[a] *will he have for his family after him,*[b]
once the number of his months has reached their end?[c]

22 [a]*But who can teach*[b] *knowledge to God,*
to one[c] *who judges even those on high?*[d]
23 [a]*One person dies in perfect health,*[b]
wholly at ease[c] *and untroubled.*[d]
24 *His pails*[a] *are full of milk,*[b]
and the marrow[c] *is juicy*[d] *in his bones.*
25 *And another dies in bitterness of soul,*[a]
never having tasted happiness.[b]
26 *Alike*[a] *they lie in dust,*
and the worms cover them.

27 *Behold,*[a] *I know your thoughts,*
and the schemes[b] *with which*[c] *you would wrong*[d] *me.*
28 *For you say,*[a] *"Where is the house of the prince?*[b]
Where is the tent[c] *where the wicked used to dwell?"*
29 *Have you not asked*[a] *those who travel on the roads?*[b]
Do you not acknowledge[c] *their testimony,*[d]
30 [a]*that on the day*[b] *of calamity*[c] *the wicked is spared,*[d]
that on the day of retribution[e] *he is delivered?*[f]

31 *Who*[a] *denounces*[b] *his conduct to his face?*
And who will requite him for what he has done?
32 [a]*When he is carried to the grave,*[b]
and a watch is kept[c] *over his tomb,*[d]
33 *the clods*[a] *of the valley*[b] *are sweet*[c] *to him,*
[d]*everyone follows*[e] *his funeral procession,*
[f]*and a countless throng goes before him.*
34 *Why then do you offer me empty comforts?*[a]
Only your perfidy[b] *is left in your replies.*[c]

Notes

2.a. זאת must refer to their agreement to listen to him (v 2a; so Dhorme), not to מלתי "my word" (as Terrien).

2.b. תנחומתיכם is "your consolations." The Versions have a sg, but that is no reason to emend to תַּנְחוּמַתְכֶם (as Duhm, Beer [*BHK*]). M. Dahood supposes another noun תַּנְחוּמָה "reply," as also at 15:11; 21:34, from the verb חמה "answer" (also at Zech 10:2; Ceresko adds Job 30:28), cognate with Ugar. *tḥm* "word" ("The Phoenician Contribution to Biblical Wisdom Literature," in *The Role of the Phoenicians in the Interaction of Mediterranean Civilization,* ed. W. A. Ward [Beirut: American Univ. of Beirut, 1968] 123–53 [125–26, 144]; "Hebrew-Ugaritic Lexicography XII," *Bib* 55 [1974] 381–93 [382]); he claims the support of the close parallelism thus created with מלתי "my word" in the first colon.

3.a. This use of נשׂא "bear, endure" with the person as obj is unparalleled (cf. *DCH,* 5:765a §3a); in Jer 15:15; 31:19; Ps 55:12 (13) the obj is a thing ("reproach").

3.b. תלעיג is sg, though the other five verbs in vv 2–5 are pl. Job cannot here be addressing Zophar alone (as Peake, Driver–Gray, Rowley, Habel, Sicre Díaz), so we should emend to pl (as, e.g., Houbigant [*Biblia*], Duhm, Beer [*BHK*], Hölscher, Fohrer, Terrien, JB [Larcher]), regard the form as a defectively written pl (de Wilde), or simply observe that such variations happen (another example in 16:3, where there are two sg forms in a passage plainly addressed to all the friends). Strauss defends MT, taking the verb as impersonal. See also the discussion of a similar problem on 18:2–4. Blommerde supplies the suff ־ני "me" from the first colon.

4.a. האנכי לאדם שׂיחי, lit. "is my complaint to (*or* concerning) a human?" Job's opponent is God, so the weight on his spirit (v 4b) is much greater than if he were simply in disputation with another human being. So understood, the *lamedh* indicates (1) the person addressed, as KJV "As for me, is my complaint to man?," NAB "toward man," NRSV "addressed to mortals," NJPS "directed toward a man," NIV "directed to man," Gordis or perhaps rather (2) the person against whom the complaint is made, as RSV, JB "against man" (Dhorme, Hartley). Less probably, it signifies (3) the subject of the complaint, as REB "about mortals," NJB "just about a fellow-mortal," Driver–Gray, Terrien. Inappropriately, (4) Schultens and Friedrich Delitzsch understood לאדם as "in a human manner."

אדם is almost certainly used in the sense of "a human being" (as NJPS, NJB, Terrien) rather than as a collective, "humankind" (as KJV, RSV, NAB, JB, NIV, REB, GNB, Pope, de Wilde, Hartley, Good, Strauss); on the two senses of אָדָם, see *DCH,* 1:123a–127b. The contrast is between a legal dispute Job could have with another person and the dispute he is engaged in with God.

Among emendations, (1) Ehrlich and Vaccari (presumably) read יִדֹּם "shall [my complaint] be silenced?" (2) J. Reider ("Etymological Studies in Biblical Hebrew," *VT* 4 [1954] 276–95 [291]) emends to האנכי לֹא אָדם שׂיחי ואם מַדּוּעַ לא תקצר רוחי "and as to me, if I should silence my complaint, should I not become impatient because of sickness?," reading אדם as אַדִּים (hiph impf of דמם "be silent") and postulating a new Heb. דוע, cognate with Arab. *d'gh* "be ravaged by sickness" (not דוע "flow," as *DCH*, 2:427a). (3) NEB "may I not voice my thoughts?" reads לֹא אָרִים "shall I not raise?" (4) Szczygiel reads לְאֵד מְשִׂיחִי "have I fallen into calamity because of my lament?," but that does not fit the context well (and אֵיד "calamity" is always spelled with a *yodh*). (5) M. Held ("Rhetorical Questions in Ugaritic and Biblical Hebrew," *ErIsr* 9 [1969] 71–79 [78–79]) reads ואם לֶאֱנוֹשׁ כַּעְשִׂי "or is my vexation to a mortal?," to create a new colon parallel to the first three words of the verse (אנושׁ is parallel to אדם at 25:6, and שׂיח appears with כַּעַס at 1 Sam 1:16). (6) Michel suggests אדם is "the Ground," i.e., the Underworld (for אָדָם "land," cf. Dahood, *Psalms III*, 40), and אם is אֵם, "the Awesome One" (ptcp of an otherwise unattested אים, "be awesome" [though cf. אָיֹם "terrible" and אֵימָה "terror"], as Dahood, *Psalms II*, 213); but the resultant sense is awkward: "Is my complaint against the Ground? Surely against the Awesome One!"

4.b. The emphasis implied by the personal pronoun האנכי "is it I?" may seem misplaced, and it is not surprising that Beer (*BH*² *frt*), followed by Siegfried, read הַאֹמֵר "am I speaking?" (in *Text*, however, he had read הַאָמְנָם "do I indeed?"). However, we should probably take it as emphasizing the suff of שׂיחי (cf. GKC, §135f), thus "is *my* protest against another human?," meaning that the protests of most people will be against other humans, while Job's is particularly distressing because it has to be against God.

4.c. On שׂיח "verbal complaint," see *Note* 7:11.b. See also H.-P. Müller, "Die hebräische Wurzel שׂיח," *VT* 19 (1969) 361–71, defining it as originally meaning "loud, enthusiastic or emotion-laden speech."

4.d. ואם "and if" looks like the beginning of a second question; disjunctive (double) questions usually have the form הֲ... אִם, or sometimes וְאִם for the second member (GKC, §150g; so also Strauss, Witte). But our text is different, for the second colon has an interrogative of its own, מדוע "why?" So we should probably understand ואם as an abbreviated conditional clause, meaning "and if [that is the case]" (so Dhorme, Tur-Sinai, Gordis). Lods read וְאִם בְּדוֹמֶה לִי "or is it against an equal of mine?"; so too Terrien (though the line is missing in his translation, apparently by accident); this offers a neat parallelism, but it is hard to see what לא־תקצר רוחי "my spirit is not cramped" can mean in the context.

4.e. מדוע לא־תקצר רוחי, lit. "why should my spirit not be cramped?," i.e., "why should I not be exhausted?" On the idiom, see *Comment*. Held ("Rhetorical Questions," 78 n. 69), however, maintains the sense "impatience" on the basis of an Akk. idiom.

5.a. If the vocalization is correct, this would be the only example of שׁמם hiph meaning "be appalled" (BDB calls it "inwardly transitive"; cf. GKC, §67v). Usually hiph is "devastate, appall" (transitive), and qal and niph are "be devastated, appalled" (intransitive). Budde, Ehrlich, Beer (*BHK*), Driver–Gray, Hölscher, Fohrer, and Gerleman (*BHS prb*) emend to niph הִשַּׁמּוּ. Stevenson has a good point, that שׁמם "be appalled" is strange between two other words simply calling for attention; yet his proposal of חֲשֹׁבוּ "consider" is weak.

6.a. No obj is expressed, but the prosperity of the wicked is what is in mind (see *Comment*). It is not "When I think of what has happened to me" (GNB). For זכר introducing an account of what is remembered, cf. Ps 42:4 (5).

6.b. ואחז בשׂרי פלצות, lit. "and my flesh seizes quivering"; בשׂרי is the subj (as against BDB, 28a); cf. אחזו שׂער "they are seized with horror," lit. "they seize horror" (18:20). M. Dahood ("Hebrew-Ugaritic Lexicography VIII," *Bib* 51 [1970] 391–404 [397–98]), reads וְאֻחַז "and [my flesh] is seized [by shuddering]," אֻחַז being a qal passive. פלצות "shuddering" (the verb פלץ has been used in 9:6 of the pillars of the earth "quivering") is unlikely to be an allusion to an assistant of Death (as Michel) since Job does not at this point have his own death in view; rather he is expressing his emotion at the thought of the continued existence of the wicked, which serves only to show that God is taking no care for the governance of the universe.

7.a. עתק is "advance," only here (and perhaps Ps 6:8) in the sense "become old" (BDB, 801a), though this is the common meaning of Aram. עתק, and is attested also in Ugar. (cf. D. Pardee, "A Note on the Root *'tq* in CTA 16 I 2,5 (UT 125, KRT II)," *UF* 5 [1973] 229–34). Guillaume (104; "The Unity of the Book of Job," *ALUOS* 4 [1962] 26–46 [29]) saw here a עתק II "thrive, prosper" (cf. Arab. *'ataqa; DCH*, vol. 6, *s.v.*), which would suit the context well.

7.b. גברו חיל, lit. "they become strong in respect of strength," perhaps to be called an adv acc (but cf. GKC, §117z). A similar phrase occurs in Ps 73:12: הִשְׂגּוּ־חיל "they have increased their strength" (also of the wicked).

8.a. Bickell, Duhm, Beer (*BH*[2]), Moffatt, Stevenson, and de Wilde moved this verse to precede vv 11–12, where the topic of the children is resumed (to similar effect, Merx moved vv 11–12 to follow v 8; Siegfried moved v 11 to follow v 8 and reversed the positions of vv 9 and 10). Observation of the chiastic structure of vv 6–13 (cf. also Andersen) obviates this alteration.

8.b. לפניהם עמם "before them, with them" seems a little superfluous; some delete לפניהם (Siegfried [*Hebrew Text*], Budde, Driver–Gray, Beer [*BHK*], Fohrer, Gerleman [*BHS*]), some עמם (Bickell, Duhm, Hölscher, Gordis, Gerleman [*BHS vel*], Strauss). The parallel in Ps 102:28 (29), וזרעם לפניך יכון "and their offspring is established before you," suggests that the latter is preferable. Others conclude the first half of the line with לפניהם (Beer [*BHK*], Dhorme, NAB), though this would mean transferring the *waw* of וצאצאיהם to עמם (though Dhorme thinks not).

Among emendations there is (1) the merely ingenious proposal of Ball to change עמם to עֹמְדִים "are standing" (comparing Isa 66:22), hence Dhorme's "their offspring abide before their eyes," NJB "their offspring secure before their eyes." It is only rarely, however, that עמד means "continue, persist" (e.g., Ruth 2:7; Eccl 8:3). Larcher understood עמד as "come into existence" and translated "increase" (*s'accroissent*); for this sense he could compare Isa 48:13 and Ps 33:9, and perhaps 119:90. BJ has merely "exist" (*subsistent*), but JB follows Larcher with "[their offspring] grow [before their eyes]," whereas NJB has simply "[they see their offspring] secure [before their eyes]." (2) Houbigant, Wright, Hontheim, Beer (*BHK vel*), Kissane, and Gordis (*frt*) moved עמם to the second half of the line and vocalized it עַמָּם "their kinsfolk" (so also NAB). NEB has "their kinsfolk and descendants flourishing," which seems to translate עמם twice, once reading עַמָּם "their kinsfolk" and the second time reading עַמָּם "flourishing" (according to de Wilde, though Brockington does not mention it); REB removes the double translation and has simply "their descendants flourishing"; "flourishing" could reflect the Arab. cognate mentioned by Gerleman (see below). (3) Gerleman (*BHS al*) suggests reading עָמְמוּ צאצאיהם "their progeny spreads out" (from a proposed עמם cognate with Arab. *'amma* "extend oneself" (cf. *DCH,* vol. 6, *s.v.*); similarly Fedrizzi, reading piel עִמּוּ "they multiplied." (4) Szczygiel also emends עמם to a verb in the second colon, reading עָמְמוּ and translating "their offspring are gathered together" (עמם I "join, combine" is recognized by Gesenius–Buhl, 601a, for Ezek 31:8 and probably 28:3; and by KBL, 715b, for Ps 47:10 if emended; cf. also *DCH,* vol. 6, *s.v.*; but it is not acknowledged by BDB or *HALOT*). (5) Not unattractive is the proposal of Mitchell Dahood ("Chiasmus in Job: A Text-Critical and Philological Criterion," in *A Light unto My Path,* FS J. M. Myers, ed. H. N. Bream, R. D. Heim, and C. A. Moore, Gettysburg Theological Studies 4 [Philadephia: Temple UP, 1974] 119–30 [120–21]; Michel, 272 n. 7), that עמם be vocalized עַמִּים, which he understands as "strong, vigorous," from a hitherto unrecognized עַם "strong" (cf. *DCH,* vol. 6, *s.v.*). (6) Less plausible is the emendation of de Wilde to תָּמִים "perfect, unscathed."

Ehrlich thinks לפניהם means "as long as they live" (cf. לפני־שמש "as long as the sun lasts" Ps 72:17), while Dahood thinks לפניהם a term for "ancestors" (as at Eccl 4:16; Ps 80:9 [10]) and translates "their progenitors are with them" ("Hebrew-Ugaritic Lexicography IV," *Bib* 47 [1966] 403–19 [411]; so too Blommerde)—a rather implausible proposal, which he apparently abandoned in favor of the suggestion in the previous paragraph (Michel).

8.c. צאצאיהם "their offspring." This could mean the offspring of their children; so NJPS "they see their children's children," GNB "they have children and grandchildren." But it is more likely that זרעם, lit. "their seed," and צאצאיהם "their offspring" are in synonymous parallelism. The same parallelism is in 5:25.

9.a. בתיהם, lit. "their houses," but in the sense of "descendants," as NEB "families," REB "households."

9.b. בתיהם שלום, lit. "their houses are peace," has provoked various emendations, all questionable, since 5:24, שלום אהלך, lit. "your tent is peace," is sufficient parallel. Siegfried, Duhm, Beer (*BH*[2] *frt*), and KBL read שָׁלְמוּ "are at peace"; Houbigant and Reiske שָׁלוּ "are at ease"; Perles[2], 57 (= "A Miscellany of Lexicographical and Textual Notes on the Bible, Chiefly in Connection with the Fifteenth Edition of the Lexicon by Gesenius-Buhl," *JQR* 2 [1911–12] 97–132 [127]), שְׁלֵוִים "are peaceful." Dahood ("Chiasmus in Job," 128 n. 4) took בתיהם as "in their houses [is prosperity without fear]," the prep *beth* being implied, as often with בית "house" (Michel).

9.c. מפחד "without fear" min privative; cf. Prov 1:33.

9.d. שבט is literally "rod" (as also at 9:34; 37:13), as the means of correction or punishment. NEB expansively renders "the rod of God's justice." Michel sees שבט as effectively "hand," comparing 9:34 (*q.v.*), where it is parallel to אתמו, which he understands, following Dahood, to mean "arm."

10.a. The sg suffs in שורו "his bull" and פרתו "his cow" are being translated here with the pls to harmonize with the prevailing pls in the speech as a whole (sg again in vv 19–21). Merx, Duhm, Beer

(*BH*[2]), and Kissane actually emend to the pl suffs, שׁוֹרָם "their bull" and פָּרָתָם "their cow," in accordance with LXX and Vg.

10.b. The four verbs in this verse are common Heb. words, but used in technical senses not elsewhere attested and thus not very certain. עבר piel "cause to cross (?)" is only here and at 1 Kgs 6:21; it is usually taken to mean "impregnate, i.e., cause to pass over [semen]" (BDB, 718b); but עבר piel, frequent in MH for "impregnate" ("become pregnant" according to Driver–Gray), may be a distinct root (Gordis).

10.c. געל is "loathe," and most take יַגְעִל hiph as "the bull does not allow [the cow] to reject [the semen] as loathsome," or perhaps "shows no aversion [to the cow]" (cf. Driver–Gray).

10.d. פלט piel is usually "deliver," but here apparently "cause to escape, cast forth, give birth to" (BDB, 812a; *HALOT,* 3:931a); it has been proposed as well as a reading for 39:3 (*q.v.*), and for Mic 6:14 (G. R. Driver, "Linguistic and Textual Problems: Minor Prophets. II," *JTS* 39 [1938] 260–73 [267]).

10.e. שׁכל piel is usually "make childless," but technically "miscarry," as in Gen 31:38; Exod 23:26.

11.a. Merx moved vv 11–12, about the children, to follow v 8 on the same theme; see further on v 8.

11.b. שׁלח "send, send out" and often "let go, set free" (BDB, 1019a §3; cf. Isa 32:20), here "send out to play" (Habel; JB "let their infants frisk," NJPS "let their infants run loose"). Not so likely is Pope's "they produce a flock of infants," but it is followed by REB "they produce babes in droves"; cf. Dahood (*Psalms III,* 90), "they give birth to their young like lambs." Driver–Gray want to revocalize (with apparent support from Symm, Vg) to יְשֻׁלְּחוּ "are sent out" merely to provide a closer parallel to the intransitive verb in v 11b (followed by NEB). De Wilde unnecessarily emends to יְסַלְּדוּ "they spring, jump."

11.c. Beer (*BHK*) and de Wilde add (for the meter) כַעֲגָלִים "like calves" on the basis of Mal 3:20 (4:2); Driver–Gray would add כְּאֵילִים "like rams" on the basis of Ps 114:4, 6. Larcher and JB add "like deer" (*comme des cerfs*). Stevenson tamely inserts the inf abs רָקוֹד before the verb, translating "their children are always dancing."

12.a. After ישׂאו "they lift up" we could perhaps understand קוֹלָם "their voice," as also in Isa 42:11 (as Driver–Gray, Fohrer, Fedrizzi, Gordis, Sicre Díaz). But "voice" is not commonly implied with "lift up," and an emendation is not uncalled for. Ehrlich, followed by Beer (*BHK frt*), emends to יָשִׂישׂוּ "they rejoice." Alfred Guillaume, on the other hand ("A Root שׂאה in Hebrew [Job 21:12; Isa 42:11]," *JTS* NS 17 [1966] 53–54; *Studies,* 104), offers a new reading by postulating a new Heb. verb שׂאה, cognate with Arab. *ṣaʾâ* "rejoice" (as also at Isa 42:11). So too apparently NEB, though they read ישׂוֹאוּ (Brockington). This suggestion is adopted in the *Translation* above.

12.b. Most (e.g., Beer [*BHK*], Gerleman [*BHS*]) emend כתף "according to the timbrel" to בְּתֹף "to the accompaniment of the timbrel" (ב as in Pss 149:3; 150:4), as also some MSS. Dahood, reading כְּתִיף "sword" (cf. Ugar. *ktp,* Arab. *katīfun*) saw an allusion to a sword dance supposedly attested at Cant 7:1 ("Northwest Semitic Philology and Job," in *The Bible in Current Catholic Thought: Gruenthaner Memorial Volume,* ed. J. L. McKenzie, St. Mary's Theological Studies 1 [New York: Herder & Herder, 1962] 55–74 [65]); cf. כָּתֵף II "sword," *DCH,* 4:477a; on iconographic evidence, see S. Terrien, "Ezekiel's Dance of the Sword and Prophetic Theonomy," in *A Gift of God in Due Season: Essays on Scripture and Community,* FS J. A. Sanders, ed. R. D. Weis and D. M. Carr, JSOTSup 225 (Sheffield: Sheffield Academic Press, 1996) 119–32 (128–29). In *RSP,* 1:293, Dahood apparently abandoned his view, reverting to the term "tambour."

13.a. Kissane moves vv 30–31 to this place, with little evident improvement.

13.b. K יבלו "they consume, use to the full" (cf. Isa 65:22) is almost universally rejected (though not by Delitzsch, Budde, Hontheim, Beer [*BHK,* though the opposite in *BH*[2]], Fohrer, Gordis, Sicre Díaz, Witte, *HALOT,* 1:132b) in favor of the Q יְכַלּוּ "they complete" (the same phrase יכלו ימיהם בטוב in 36:11); but the meanings are very similar. Most translations have "they spend" (e.g., KJV, RSV, NJPS, NIV), but perhaps the reference is rather to the close of their lives; hence NEB "their lives close," NAB "they live out their days," JB "they end their lives," Kissane "they live out their days."

13.c. טוֹב is the noun, "good thing, benefit, welfare, happiness" (BDB, 375a). KJV "in wealth" means "in weal, happiness," as in Esth 10:3; 1 Cor 10:24 (cf. *OED, s.v.,* §1), not financial wealth. M. Dahood (*Ugaritic-Hebrew Philology: Marginal Notes on Recent Publications,* BibOr 17 [Rome: Pontifical Biblical Institute, 1965] 59–60, and in his review of *Ugaritica V,* by J. Nougayrol et al., *Or* 39 [1970] 375–79 [377]) argues for the nuance "merriment, sweetness"; but there is nothing in the context demanding such a specific sense.

13.d. ברגע ought to mean "in a moment" (KJV, RV, Dillmann, Driver–Gray, Hartley), "quickly" (Pope, Dahood, *Psalms* II, 193). There is, however, a verb רגע II "be at rest" (BDB, 921a), and most modern versions and commentators (e.g., Beer [*BHK*]) read וּבְרֶגַע taking רֶגַע as an otherwise unattested noun, "tranquility, peace" (there *is* an adj רָגֵעַ "restful, quiet" in Ps 35:20; and cf. LXX ἐν ἀναπαύσει "in rest"); see also L. Delekat, "Zum hebräischen Wörterbuch," *VT* 14 (1964) 7–66 (63–64). Similarly Michel, taking ברגע שאול as a constr chain, "to the Tranquility of Sheol," and Tur-Sinai, vocalizing רֹגַע, and taking רגע שאול together as "[to] the peace of Sheol." The idea that the poet had both meanings in mind (Gordis, Hartley [*frt*]) is improbable.

Blommerde translated "into Sheol's perdition," taking a clue from Dahood (*Psalms I,* 29, 182–83) that רֶגַע means "annihilation" or perhaps "place of annihilation, Perdition" (as he claims for Pss 6:10 [11]; 30:5 [6]; cf. also the supposed verb רגע "annihilate" at Job 26:12).

13.e. יֵחַתּוּ seems to be niph of חתת "they are frightened," which cannot be right in the context (but so Reiske, Friedrich Delitzsch). Most read יֵחָתוּ "they go down" from נחת (so, e.g., Beer [*BHK*], Gerleman [*BHS*], *HALOT,* 2:692a, KJV, RSV, NAB, JB, NIV, NJPS, NEB); GKC, §20i, supposes the *dagesh forte* to be *affectuosum.* O. Rössler, "Die Präfixkonjugation Qal der Verba I^{ae} Nûn im Althebräischen und das Problem der sogenannten Tempora," *ZAW* NS 33 (1962) 125–41 (127), followed by Fohrer, derives the word from a חתח "grab" (cf. Akk. *ḫatû*), translating the presumed passive qal as "they are snatched away"; but according to *CAD,* 6:151a, *ḫatû* means "smite," rather than "grab"). A. Guillaume saw here a cognate of Arab. *hatta* "fall (of leaf)" (*Lexicography,* 2:16), but in his translation (*Studies,* 45) reverted to the usual "go down."

14.a. ויאמרו, with *waw* consec, is not, of course, subsequent to the previous verbs, but explanatory of them (cf. Driver, *Tenses,* 99–100).

15.a. The whole verse is lacking in LXX, perhaps in order to shorten the disrespectful speech of the evildoers (Fohrer). It may also be significant that in v 14 LXX has sg in place of MT pl, perhaps to weaken the offensiveness by ascribing it to only one wicked person (Gard, *Exegetical Method,* 74).

15.b. The usual translation of the divine name Shaddai; see *Comment* on 5:17.

15.c. פגע is usually "meet," but sometimes, as here, "meet with a request, entreat, pray" (as Jer 7:16; Ruth 1:16).

16.a. This verse is a considerable crux. The *Translation* above takes the context strongly into account, agrees that the sentence consists of two questions (as in alternative [4] below), and accepts a minor emendation of the last word (as in *Note* 16.e on "from him").

The first line is in MT "Behold (הֵן), their prosperity is not in their hand" (similarly NIV). That is to say, they have no control over their own prosperity, and God can remove it. But how to interpret it? (1) It is a counsel of despair to regard the verse as the comment of a reader scandalized at Job's apparent condoning of the views of the wicked (Pope, Ravasi). Rather than remove the verse by placing it within square brackets, as Pope does, or deleting it as a gloss (Ball, Hölscher, Stevenson, Fohrer, Fedrizzi, Hesse, de Wilde; Siegfried deleted all of vv 16–18), it is better to try to understand it within the context. (2) Job could be speaking in his own voice (so Delitzsch, Hartley), or (3) he could be quoting supposed words of the friends (as he clearly does in v 19, but without any textual indication; RVmg prefixes "Ye say," and it is true that Eliphaz himself actually says the second half of the verse in 22:18; thus Kissane, Newsom; cf. also Tur-Sinai). (4) Alternatively, הֵן may be a hypothetical particle introducing a possibility (cf. BDB, 243b §b), thus "Suppose [= if] their prosperity is not in their own hands" (so NAB); but the analysis of D. M. Stec makes this unlikely (see *Note* 23:8.b). (5) A further alternative is that לא may be the emphatic לָא "indeed" (cf. F. Nötscher, "Zum emphatischen Lamed," *VT* 3 [1953] 372–80, noting as examples 2:10; 8:12; 11:11; 14:16; 21:29; 23:17; 33:14, though not this passage; for bibliography, see Blommerde, 31; and see further on 2:10; *DCH,* 4:495a [לא II], 610a [bibliography]; other examples are proposed for 29:24; 37:24, to which add Hos 10:9; 11:5). (6) To similar effect is the proposal of G. R. Driver, "Affirmation by Exclamatory Negation," *JANESCU* 5 (1973) 107–14 (108), that the negative particle לֹא is sometimes emphatic; his translation, awkwardly expressed, is "lo! is not, that is, their well-being indeed is in their own hands" (similarly NEB). (7) Yet another alternative, rather less plausible, is that of M. J. Dahood ("Ugaritic Lexicography" [review of *Wörterbuch der ugaritischen Sprache* (1963), by J. Aistleitner], in *Mélanges Eugène Tisserant,* vol. 1, *Ecriture sainte—Ancien orient,* Studi e testi 231 [Città del Vaticano: Bibliotheca apostolica vaticana, 1964] 81–104 [92] and review of *Giobbe* [1972], by P. Fedrizzi, *Bib* 55 [1974] 287–88), followed by Blommerde, to see לא as the alleged divine name לָא "the Victor," thus "Behold, the Mighty One, from his hands is their prosperity" (so too Michel, 371). Other alleged occurrences of לָא "the Victor" in Job are at 13:15; 14:4; 21:16; 23:16; 24:1; 27:19; 31:15; 32:14; 33:14; 36:5; 37:23, 24; 41:12 (4), and as "mighty" (of humans) at 29:24; see Blommerde, 28 (bibliography), and *DCH,* 4:495b.

Among emendations, the simplest, which is adopted in the *Translation* above, is (8) to supply the interrogative particle הֲ and to understand "Is not their prosperity within their hand? Are not the plans of the wicked far from him [God]?," i.e., they control their own destiny and God does not concern himself with their plans (Duhm, Beer [BH^2 *vel*], reading הֵן הֲלֹא and מִמֶּנּוּ for מֶנִּי). Alternatively, (9) we could omit לא, thus "their prosperity is in their own hands" (so Merx, Beer [BH^2 *vel*]), which yields the same sense as the previous suggestion. (10) We could try emending בידם "in their hands" to בְּיָדוֹ "in his [God's] hand" (Gordis). (11) Blommerde makes heavy weather of the line by reading בְּיָדַם, the suff being supposedly a northern dual ending, and explaining the *beth* as "from"; thus "from his hands is their prosperity." Or (12) we could emend to הֵן לֹא בְּיָדָיו (בְּיָדוֹ or) טוּבֵנוּ "Indeed, our prosperity is not in his hands" (Yellin, Stevenson, Gordis), taking the line as the conclusion of the speech of the wicked. Or (13) we could emend to בְּיָדִי "in my hand," i.e., within my mental capacity, understanding Job to mean, "I cannot explain the prosperity of the wicked" (as Ehrlich). Or, very improbably, (14) we could read הֲנִלְאָה "is not [their fortune] exhausted [in their hand]?" (Szczygiel).

16.b. עצת רשעים looks very much like "the plans of the wicked," i.e., those made by the wicked (subjective gen), but Ehrlich proposes that the phrase is an objective gen, "[God's] plan for the wicked." In that case, Job would be saying that he cannot understand God's plan (it is רחקה מני "far from me"). Less probably it is "the council, circle, of the wicked" (as Michel).

Duhm suggested reading פְּקֻדַּת "the punishment of" rather than עֲצַת "the plan of," but it is hard to see that the LXX supports this reading as he claims.

16.c. Michel (220) thinks רשעים "wicked ones" is a pl of majesty, which really means "the Wicked One," a name for the king of the Underworld, Mot (as also at 9:23; 10:3).

16.d. NRSV "are repugnant to me" attempts to explain what "far" is; but see next *Note* and *Comment* on v 16.

16.e. מֶנִּי is the pausal form of מִנִּי, itself a poetical form of the usual מִמֶּנִּי "from me." LXX's free translation, ἔργα δὲ ἀσεβῶν οὐκ ἐφορᾷ "and he does not observe the works of the ungodly," seems to presuppose מִמֶּנּוּ "from him," which is read by Dhorme, Beer [*BHK*], Hölscher, Kissane, Fohrer, Hesse (Tur-Sinai and Gerleman [*BHS prb*] read מֶנּוּ = מֶנְהוּ), NAB, NEB ("Are not their purposes very different from God's?"), JB "in their counsels, left no room for God," NJB "God is kept so far from their plans." This emendation is adopted in the *Translation* above, whereas the MT is retained by KJV, JPS, and RSV with "from me" and NJPS with "beyond me"; similarly NIV "I stand aloof from the counsel of the wicked." The same Heb. phrase at 22:18 is translated literally by LXX as βουλὴ δὲ ἀσεβῶν πόρρω ἀπ' αὐτοῦ "the counsel of the wicked is far from him," reading מִמֶּנּוּ for MT מֶנִּי. Szczygiel proposes bringing in כמה from the beginning of the next verse and reading מִנִּי כָּמָה (a new word from מנה "count" or else הֲמוֹנִי) "my portion (or, my wealth) is exhausted," but a comment from Job is out of place here.

Blommerde has argued that we have here one of many examples of the 3d-person suff in *yodh;* see also his *Northwest Semitic Grammar and Job,* 8; L. Sabottka, *Zephanja,* BibOr 25 (Rome: Pontifical Biblical Institute, 1972) 42, 93, 96; W. A. van der Weiden, *Le livre des Proverbes,* BibOr 23 (Rome: Pontifical Biblical Institute, 1970) 83–85, 89, 154; M. Dahood, review of *Il Semitico di Nord-Ovest* (1960), by G. Garbini, *Or* 32 (1963) 498–500 (499). Other alleged examples in Job are: 3:10; 6:13; 9:15, 19, 20, 35; 10:1; 13:17; 14:3, 6; 16:6, 9, 18; 18:13; 19:17, 26, 27, 28; 20:23; 21:16; 22:18; 23:2, 7, 12, 14; 24:15; 27:3; 29:18; 31:18; 33:28; 34:6; 37:4, 11; 37:16; 38:10; 41:10 (2), 11 (3). All these cases are reviewed by L. Boadt, "A Re-examination of the Third-Yodh Suffix in Job," *UF* 7 (1975) 59–72. Since in each case an emendation to the normal 3d-person suff is so slight, it is hard to identify persuasive evidence for this supposed grammatical feature; but it remains a possibility.

17.a. כמה introduces a rhetorical question expecting the answer "Seldom." It is not an exclamation, as KJV has it, for that would convey a completely opposite sense, one quite out of keeping with Job's position.

17.b. ניר "lamp" (more commonly spelled נֵר) is well attested (BDB, 633a). But P. D. Hanson has argued that the term means "(landed) property" ("The Song of Heshbon and David's *nîr,*" *HTR* 61 [1968] 297–320), and McCarter (see *Note* 21:30.c on "calamity") adopts that view.

17.c. דעך is usually "be extinguished" (BDB, 200a). But McCarter renders "confiscated" to suit his interpretation of ניר as "property" (see *Note* 17.b), and of איד as "river ordeal"; in the Code of Hammurabi a person who failed the river ordeal could have his property confiscated. But there is no philological justification for this rendering of דעך.

17.d. NEB adds here לַאֲשֶׁר הֵבִיא אֱלוֹהַּ בְּיָדוֹ, transposed from 12:6, which it translates "bringing it [suffering] in full measure to whom he will"—but the translation cannot be reconciled with the Hebrew, which seems to mean rather "whom God has brought into his own power."

17.e. On איד as "river ordeal" rather than "calamity," see *Note* 21:30.c on "calamity."

17.f. The colon, the last of a tricolon, is thought to be a gloss by Bickell, Hölscher, Fohrer (comparing 20:23), Hesse, de Wilde. Beer (*BH*[2]), on the other hand, thinks a second colon has perhaps fallen out.

Tricola have several functions in Job: (1) Most commonly, in thirty-four places, they serve to mark the close of a strophe, at 9:24; 10:17, 22; 11:6, 20; 12:6; 14:12; 18:4; 19:12, 27, 29; 20:23; 24:12; 26:14, 28:28; 29:25 (but the colon should probably be deleted); 30:15; 34:19, 20 (two lines at the end of a strophe), 29c–30, 37; 37:4 (but 4c is probably to be moved to follow 6); 38:41; 39:25—or with the next line as merely a pendant to the strophe, at 3:9; 5:5 (with a two-verse pendant); 8:6; 13:27; 21:33; 24:24; 31:7; 36:11; 37:12, 23. (2) In nineteen places, they mark the beginning of a strophe, at 7:11; 9:21; 10:1; 12:3–4 (following an introductory line); 14:5 (similarly); 14:7, 13–14; 14:19 (following an introductory line); 15:30 (but 30a is probably to be omitted); 17:1, 11; 21:17; 24:13, 18; 31:35; 32:11, 12 (two lines at the beginning of a strophe). (3) However, in twenty-eight places they do not serve an evident strophic function, at least as strophes have been identified in this commentary: so at 3:4, 5, 6; 4:19; 6:4, 10; 10:3, 15; 15:24, 28; 16:9, 10; 24:15; 28:3, 4; 30:12, 13; 31:34; 33:15, 23–24 (but perhaps the two tricola should be broken up into three bicola), 26, 27; 36:7, 16; 37:6 (if 4c is moved to this point); 42:3. Nevertheless, the analysis of strophes presented here is not an exact science, and most of the examples in this category are evidently at points of beginning or closure even if not formally at the ends of strophes as recognized here. At 24:14, 16 the apparent tricola are probably to be broken up to create bicola; at 37:22b the colon is probably to be deleted, removing the apparent tricolon in 21.

17.g. God is, of course, the subject.

17.h. חלק "divide, apportion," RSV "distribute," NEB "deal out." Dhorme supposes another חלק piel "destroy," on the basis of Akk. *ḫalāqu* (for *ḫulluqu* "make disappear, destroy," see *CAD,* 6:38b; cf. *DCH,* 3:242b); so JB "all his goods destroyed by the wrath of God." So too M. Dahood, review of *Studies in the Text and Theology of the Book of Lamentations* (1963), by B. Albrektson," *Bib* 44 (1963) 547–49 (548); "Hebrew-Ugaritic Lexicography II," *Bib* 45 (1964) 393–412 (408). Larcher and JB (see NJB note) "or the retribution of God destroy his possessions" read יְחֻבַּל חֶלְקוֹ, lit. "his portion is destroyed [חבל pual] [by anger]."

17.i. חבלים is open to several explanations. (1) It has seemed to many to be from חֶבֶל "cord." So some find here the idea of a field that is measured out by line and so allotted; hence "allotted portion in life, fate" (cf. Ps 16:5; Deut 32:9). The connection with חלק "allot" might seem to point in the same direction. Thus NAB "the portion he allots," NIV "the fate God allots" (similarly NJPS; Schlottmann; Terrien *leur dû;* Tur-Sinai "portions" [of chastisement]). Szczygiel suggests חֶבְלָם "their portion." The difficulty with such interpretations is, however, as Driver–Gray remark, that "cords" seems to refer only to parcels of land, not to one's lot in life. Cords in the sense of "snares" can hardly be meant (as Delitzsch).

(2) Others take the word from חֵבֶל "pain, pang" (usually of birth pangs), thus KJV, RV "sorrows," RSV "pains" (so too BDB, 286b; Hitzig, Hölscher, Weiser, Rowley, Fedrizzi, Gordis, Sicre Díaz, Hartley).

(3) More probably we should recognize here a second noun חֶבֶל "destruction" (also at Mic 2:10) (KBL, 272a; *HALOT,* 1:272a; *DCH,* 4:152a; BDB, 287b, also registers this חֶבֶל, but not for our passage), from חבל II "act corruptly, ruin" (KBL, 271a [חבל III]; *HALOT,* 1:285b [חבל III]; *DCH,* 4:149b).

(4) Less convincingly, Dhorme supposes, from the same verb, an adj חַבָּל "wicked," parallel to רשׁע (so too NJBmg); so also Dahood, "Hebrew-Ugaritic Lexicography II," 407, unaware of Dhorme's proposal (for a חַבָּל "wrongdoer"; cf. *DCH,* 3:150b).

Duhm's emendation, חבלים יַחֲזִקֵם באפו "cords [cf. 18:10] take hold of them in his anger" (so too Driver–Gray), has little to recommend it, except that it is preferable to that of Merx and Siegfried (*Hebrew Text,* יֹאחֲזֻם), on the basis of LXX, חבלים יֹאחֲזוּם מֵאפו "pangs seize them because of his anger" (for pangs seizing, cf. Isa 13:8; Jer 13:21).

18.a. The interrogative, explicit in v 17, is implied here (Dhorme, Gordis; against Budde).

18.b. As in 13:25.

18.c. גנב is normally "steal" (BDB, 170a); the sense "remove stealthily" (without theft) is rare (cf., e.g., 2 Kgs 11:2 ‖ 2 Chr 22:11). Something more vigorous seems to be required here, and J. Lust ("A Stormy Vision: Some Remarks on Job 4,1 2–16," *Bijdr* 36 [1975] 308–11 [309]) is probably right that גנב here and at 4:12 and 27:20 means "transport violently"; but that sounds like a different word. גנבתו סופה is a relative clause, with an initial אֲשֶׁר understood.

19.a. Most take this line as a quotation in the mouths of the friends (RSV, NEB, NJPS add "You say," NIV "It is said"; so too Gordis, Newsom). We could, however, read the line as a question (so also Hölscher), expressing a possible objection to Job's line of reasoning (which would equally be the case if these are the friends' words). It can hardly be another rhetorical question in the sequence of "how often" questions beginning at v 17, since vv 20–21 seem to contrast the wicked man himself with his children.

19.b. The explicit subject אלוה "God" is emended by some to the negative אַל "not," i.e., "let him not lay up iniquity for his children" (Ley, Duhm, Peake, Driver–Gray [*frt*], Steuernagel, Beer [*BHK*], NAB).

19.c. "Job is stating what should be the case.... He is not expressing a wish but developing an argument" (Habel).

19.d. וְיֵדָע "and let him know" has the simple *waw* prefixed; it is not a *waw* of purpose (as against Driver–Gray). The word is derived by D. Winton Thomas from his ידע II "be still, be submissive" ("The Root ידע in Hebrew, II," *JTS* 36 [1935] 409–12 [412]; *DCH*, 4:110b; cf. *Note* 9:5.b); hence NEB "and be punished." But the case for this verb is questionable; see e.g., J. A. Emerton, "A Consideration of Some Alleged Meanings of ידע in Hebrew," *JSS* 15 (1970) 45–80; W. Johnstone, "*yd'* II, 'be humbled, humiliated'?," *VT* 41 (1991) 49–62. J. Reider, "Etymological Studies: ידע or ירע and רעע," *JBL* 66 (1947) 315–17 (317), reads וְיֵרֹעַ "so that he is crushed"; but the point in the present context is not that the wicked man should *be* punished, but that he should *know* that he is being punished.

20.a. Duhm reads וראו עינו "and let his eyes see" as יֵרֶא בְעֵינוֹ "let him see with his eye[s]."

20.b. כיד occurs only here (*DCH*, 4:391a); it has been understood in different ways. (1) Traditionally, as "destruction" (as KJV, RSV, NIV; NAB "calamity," JB "ruin," NEB "damnation," REB "condemnation"). Gordis defends the MT as equivalent to Arab. *kaid* "warfare" (so too Pope, comparing Arab. *kayd 'allah,* "divine punishment") and *ka'ada* "be in an evil state" (so too KBL, 433a; *HALOT,* 2:472a [?]; cf. Lane, 2638c, where it is apparent that *kayd* is connected rather with *kyd* "deceive"); de Wilde connects it with Arab. *kadd* "suffering, labour." Schultens thought Arab. *kayd* meant "injury," and at root "fire"; he translates "[let his eyes see] the fire of kindling," which would at least be parallel with חמה "heat," thus "anger," in the next colon. (2) Driver–Gray thought כיד means "craft" (cf. Arab. *kāda* "beguile, circumvent" [Lane, 2638f]). (3) Fohrer and Rowley followed the suggestion of A. F. L. Beeston ("Notes on Old South Arabian Lexicography VI," *Mus* 67 [1954] 311–22 [313–16]) that the word means "condemnation" and is to be connected with Old S. Arab. *kyd* "condemn." (4) Guillaume related it to Arab. *ka'dā'* "calamity, loss."

The word is, however, often emended. The most probable suggestions are (1) that of BDB, Duhm, Driver–Gray, Dhorme, Beer (*BHK prps*), Hölscher, Kissane, and JB (apparently), who read פִּידוֹ "his misfortune" (as in 12:5; 30:24; 31:29), presumably following the ancient versions (LXX τὴν ἑαυτοῦ σφαγήν "his slaughter," Vg *interfectionem suam* "his killing"), and (2) that of Budde and Beer (*BHK prps*), who read אֵידוֹ "his calamity" (as in v 17). Other, less probable, emendations are (3) כְּיָדוֹ "like his hand, i.e., like his deed" (Hoffmann), (4) כּוֹסוֹ "his cup" (Ehrlich), and (5) כידור "the assault" (as in 15:24; Wright). (6) M. Dahood ("Some Northwest-Semitic Words in Job," *Bib* 38 [1957] 306–20 [316]) read כַּדוֹ "his cup, goblet of fate, destiny" (so too Strauss and Pope[1], reading כַּדוֹ "his cup"); see further, Grabbe, 77–79.

20.c. Duhm read, for MT ישתה, the usual juss form יֵשְׁתְּ "let him drink" (as in 1 Kgs 13:18). The long form of the juss is, however, sometimes attested; see GKC, §75t.

20.d. מן partitive ("some of"), as often with verbs of eating and drinking (cf. BDB, 579a §2.b.b).

21.a. חפץ is often "pleasure" (so KJV, RV, JPS; cf. NEB "what joy shall he have?"; similarly REB, JB, NJB), but that is not the point here. It is rather whether the man will be *conscious* of what is happening to his offspring; so we should translate "business," "interest" (so NAB), "care" (cf. RSV "what do they care?"; cf. NIV, NJPS, GNB). For this sense of חפץ, cf. Eccl 3:1, 17; 5:7; 8:6; Isa 53:10; and see *Comment* on 22:3.

21.b. אחריו "after him," i.e., after his death (as in Gen 17:19). Blommerde implausibly renders בביתו אחריו as "[what will be his pleasure] in his final home?," taking the final *waw* of בביתו as a sign of the gen and אחריו as equivalent to אַחֲרִית "end, destiny."

21.c. חצץ is said by BDB, 346a, to mean "divide" ("cut in two [fig. for curtailed]"), and similarly KBL, 325a, *HALOT,* 1:344a, *DCH,* 3:296a, but a better sense is "be at an end" (*DCH,* 3:296a piel). Akk. *ḫaṣāṣû* is "cut, break," though not specifically "break in two" (*CAD,* 6:130b), Eth. *ḫaṣāṣa* is "curtail, diminish" (Rowley), and Arab. *ḫaṣṣa* is "cut, sever" (cf. G. R. Driver, "Problems in the Hebrew Text of Job," in *Wisdom in Israel and in the Ancient Near East,* FS H. H. Rowley, VTSup 3 [Leiden: Brill, 1955] 72–93 [83]); so too Hölscher, Fohrer. But the context shows that Heb. חצץ is not "cut off in the midst" (KJV, RV), or even "cut off" (JB, NJB, RSV) or "snapped" (Moffatt), for Job is arguing that the evildoer does *not* come to an untimely end. Nor is it "if his very months and days are numbered" (NEB; similarly REB) or "determined" (JPS), for Job is not doubting that the evildoer will ultimately die. It is simply: "when his number of months runs out" (NJPS), "is finished" (NAB), "come to an end" (NIV), "when a man's life is over" (GNB), "when his quota of months is spent" (Pope).

Tur-Sinai argues that חצץ always means "wipe off, erase" (as in Prov 20:17; 30:27; Lam 3:16), but the parallels do not support this sense. Emendation to חֹרְצוּ "are cut off" (Ewald [*frt*], Graetz, Budde, Beer [*BHK frt*]; cf. חרץ qal passive at 14:5) does not suit the sense as outlined above.

The pl of חצצו agrees with חדשיו "months" rather than with its grammatical subject, מספר "number" (GKC, §146a; cf. 38:21 ומספר ימיך רבים "and the number of your days is great").

22.a. The verse is deleted by Driver–Gray, Torczyner, and Pope, and removed to follow 22:2 by NAB (cf. Murphy).

22.b. M. Dahood observes that only here is למד "teach" followed by ל of the person, and so proposes that the *lamedh* is asseverative ("will he teach God himself knowledge?") ("Some Northwest-Semitic Words in Job," 316–17); so too Blommerde. However, there is perhaps nothing very peculiar about למד here, since elsewhere it can be followed by the acc of the person (strictly, "my hands") and ל of the thing taught (2 Sam 22:35 ‖ Ps 18:35; Ps 144:1), or the acc of the person and ב of the thing taught (Isa 40:14). The suggestions of Bickell, mentioned by Beer (*BH*[2] *prps*), to read יְלֻמַּד "shall [knowledge] be taught?," and of Beer אֲלַמֵּד־ "shall I teach?" (*BHK*) have little to recommend them (against the former, דעת is usually fem).

22.c. The clause beginning והוא "and he" is to be understood as a circumstantial clause in which "a new subject is introduced in express antithesis to one just mentioned" (GKC, §142d). It seems incorrect to take the subject of ישפט as the same as that of ילמד (thus Pope "Will he judge even the Exalted?"; Dahood, "Some Northwest-Semitic Words in Job," 317; idem, "Hebrew-Ugaritic Lexicography X," *Bib* [1972] 386–403 [390]; Blommerde) and to ignore והוא "and he."

22.d. רמים, pl ptcp of רום "be high," hence "those on high" (in Ps 78:69 it means "the heights" [of heaven]). The reference could be to any "exalted" ones (as in 2 Sam 22:28), but most commentators see here heavenly beings. On the other hand, Dahood ("Some Northwest-Semitic Words in Job," 316–17) thinks we should read רָם־ם or רֹם־ם "the Exalted One," i.e., God, the final *mem* being enclitic; similarly Pope, Gordis (though he translates, strangely, "He judges on high"); but Blommerde, followed by Dahood, "Hebrew-Ugaritic Lexicography X," 389–90, thinks rather that the *mem* is a pl of majesty. On רם as a divine title, see further L. Viganò, "Il titolo divino מרום: 'L'Eccelso,'" *SBFLA* 24 (1974) 188–201; and cf. *DCH*, 5:483b §4.

Emendations are not attractive. However, Merx and Terrien emend to דָּמִים "blood," i.e., spilled blood, acts of violence (as in four Heb. MSS; cf. LXX φόνους "murders"), but this yields a rather feeble sense. Duhm read רְמִיָּה "deceit" and translated "since he judges deceit."

23.a. The verse is absent from the original LXX and also apparently from 11QtgJob. E. A. Knauf, "Zum Text von Hi 21, 23–26," *BN* 7 (1978) 22–24, regards the verse as secondary.

23.b. בעצם תמו, lit. "in the bone of his perfection"; cf. כעצם השמים "like heaven itself," lit. "like the bone of heaven" (Exod 24:10), עצם implying the essence of a thing. תם is here of physical perfection, health; in 4:6 it was of moral perfection. Thus NJPS "in robust health," NIV "in full vigour" (cf. NAB), "robust and hale" (Moffatt). NEB "crowned with success" is perhaps a little loose. An emendation to עֹצֶם "strength" (Stevenson, *Poem*) is improbable.

23.c. שלאנן, occurring only here, is usually thought to be a scribal error for שַׁאֲנָן "at ease, secure" (which some MSS read; cf. Beer [*BHK*]). Dhorme and Gordis think the *lamedh* has been introduced through assonance of that sound in the second half of the line; Guillaume thinks that the form is an Arabism. M. Dahood ("Hebrew-Ugaritic Lexicography XI," *Bib* 54 [1973] 351–66 [358]) defends the reading of MT as a blend of the roots שנן and שלו, both meaning "repose"; he is followed by Strauss.

23.d. שָׁלֵיו "quiet, at ease" is usually spelled שָׁלֵו; the *yodh* is found also at Jer 49:31; Ecclus 41:2. But Beer (*BHK*) regards it as an error and reads שָׁלֵו.

24.a. עֲטִין occurs only here. The main suggestions (see also *DCH*, vol. 6, *s.v.*) can be divided into terms relevant to (A) the person's farm activity, or (B) parts of the body, or (C) abstracts:

(A) (1) *pail, bucket, trough.* So BDB, 742a "pail, bucket," RVmg, JPS "pails," Dillmann, Budde, Peake "milk pails," Driver–Gray, Delitzsch, Duhm, Gerleman (*BHS*), de Wilde "troughs"; cf. MH מַעֲטָן "vessel for olives" (cf. Levy, 3:634–35, 188–89) and Arab. *'aṭana* "put skin into a vat for tanning" (Gordis says there is an Arab. *'atana* "moisten, cause to drip"). (2) *watering places.* So ibn Ezra, Schultens (*pecorosa latifundia* "farms with many cattle"), Reiske, Rosenmüller, Renan (*les parcs de ses troupeaux*); cf. Grabbe. This derives the word from the Arab. cognate *'aṭina* "watering place of camels" or "pens, resting-places, of flocks" (this is not the origin of the translation "pails," as Gordis seems to think). (3) *olives.* So *HALOT,* 2:814a; E. A. Knauf, E. Keller, and A. Schindler, "עטין—Hi 21,24a," *BN* 4 (1977) 9–12; E. A. Knauf, "Zum Text von Hi 21, 23–26," 22–24; so too Strauss, translating "his olives are full of milk." See also below on *testes.* (4) *olive oil.* So Tur-Sinai, reading עָטִין ימלא וְחלב, "he is full of oil and milk" (following *y. Mo'ed Qatan* 2.1.81a).

(B) (5) *breasts* (Geneva, KJV, RV, following Tg ביזוי "his breasts"); so too Guillaume. There is a long tradition supporting this interpretation, and many tales of male lactation exist. For example, J. C. Gray, *The Biblical Museum* (London: Stock, 1871–81) 5:262–63, reports a travelers' tale of men developing breasts and lactating (ascribing it to Alexander von Humboldt, *Personal Narrative of Travels to the Equinoctial Regions of America, 1799–1804* [London: Bohn, 1852–53]); and the Talmud reported a "miracle" of a father suckling his child (*t. Shabbat* 53b). From a medical point of view, the reality of male lactation is not unknown (see R. B. Greenblatt, "Some Historic and Biblical Aspects of Endocrinology," in *Gynecologic Endocrinology,* ed. J. R. Givens [Chicago: Year Book Medical Publishers, 1977] 313–24), but the circumstances are always unusual, and it is hard to believe that such a phenomenon lies behind the depiction here. (6) *sides,* following Pesh *gbwhy,* "his sides." So Larcher (*flancs*). NJB claims this as the source of its translation "his thighs"; but see below. (7) *thighs,* emending to עֲטָמָיו (Dhorme עַטְמָיו; Kissane עֲטִימָיו) "his loins, thighs" (otherwise unattested, but like Aram. עַטְמָא); so Houbigant, Ehrlich (apparently), Beer, (*BHK frt*), Hölscher, Stevenson, Terrien, Fohrer, de Wilde, KBL, 697b, JB, NJB ("thighs"), NEB ("loins"), and Pope ("haunches"). But since Aram. עטם is only the Aram. equivalent of Heb. עֶצֶם "bone" (as Driver–Gray note), which occurs in the second half of the verse, the emendation becomes "precarious, and unnecessary." Cf. Homer, *Odyssey* 17.225: "By drinking milk he may gain thick thighs." (8) *testes,* Gordis understanding "olives" in a transferred sense of the male genitals, filled with "milk," i.e., semen; thus "his vital organs full of milk," or "his testes full of milk" (Hartley; similarly Sicre Díaz). (9) *body* (RSV, NIV) or other similarly vague translations, "figure" (NAB), "powers" (Moffatt), probably depending on the ancient versions that saw here some part of the body (LXX ἔγκατα, Vg *viscera* "entrails"; so too Habel, translating "with intestines full of cream"; the Qumran Tg perhaps had אבוז "buttocks" [B. Zuckerman in Pope]).

(C) (10) *luxury,* emending to עֲדִינָיו "his luxury" (cf. Isa 47:8) (Szczygiel), but the sense is strained.

24.b. Whether we keep MT חָלָב "milk" or revocalize to חֵלֶב "fat" (so LXX στέατος, Vg; Ehrlich, Dhorme, Szczygiel, Beer [*BHK*], Hölscher [חָלָב, but this seems to be a mistake], Kissane, Terrien, Fohrer, Pope, *HALOT,* 1:315b, JB, NAB) depends on the rendering adopted for עטיניו in the same clause (pails and breasts are full of milk, but the other things mentioned in the previous *Note* would be full of fat, except that Strauss thinks that olives could be said to be full of "milk").

24.c. מח "marrow" is a *hapax,* but the rendering is confirmed by ממחים "full of marrow" in Isa 25:6. Tur-Sinai however claims that מח means "fat." Knauf ("Zum Text von Hi 21, 23–26," 22–24) would however emend to the verb וַיְמַח "and he wiped."

24.d. שקה pual "be well watered, fresh, juicy"; the pual occurs only here. In Prov 3:8 the result of right behavior is "drink, refreshment" (שִׁקּוּי) to one's bones.

25.a. בנפש מרה, lit. "with a bitter soul" (cf. 3:20; 7:11; 10:1).

25.b. ולא־אכל בטובה, lit. "and has not eaten of [*beth* partitive, as also at 39:17] good, prosperity." For other examples of *beth* partitive, see Blommerde, 21, and cf. 7:13; 26:14; 39:17.

26.a. יחד is lit. "together," but their togetherness cannot be exactly the point. Perhaps יחד means "entirely, altogether" (as in 3:18; see *Note* 3:18.a), but "alike" seems preferable (BDB, 403a §2c; *DCH,* 3:197a §3b).

27.a. הן is not "if," but a form of הִנֵּה "behold" (as in 13:1). Szczygiel emends to מֵהֶן "because of these things," but the word is not suitable for the context.

27.b. מזמה "plot, scheme," usually with a negative sense (cf. *Note* 17:11.c).

27.c. There is no relative in the Heb.; no doubt בַּאֲשֶׁר "with which" is to be supplied (cf. GKC, §155k).

27.d. חמס hiph "treat violently, wrong" (so, e.g., RSV, NIV, Habel; KJV "wrongfully imagine"; similarly Driver–Gray). Several emendations have been proposed, the first being the most probable: (1) Beer (*BHK*), Hölscher, Kissane (his notation "תַּחְמוֹסוּ, √חמת" must be corrected to "תְּהַמּוֹסוּ, √המס"), Fohrer, Tur-Sinai, Gerleman (*BHS prp*), de Wilde, Fedrizzi, NAB "you rehearse," NEB "you are marshalling," read תְּהַמְסוּ "you consider" from a supposed המס (*DCH,* 2:572b), cognate with Syr. *hms* "meditate" (following B. Jacob, "Erklärung einiger Hiob-Stellen," *ZAW* 32 [1912] 286–87; Dhorme thought חמס a "strengthening" of המס). (2) Duhm, finding the syntax unacceptable, emends to תַּחְפְּשׂוּ "[which] you search out" (as in Ps 64:6 [7]; mentioned in Beer [BH^2]). (3) Beer (BH^2) reads (*frt*) תַּחֲרֹשׁוּ "you devise" (the verb also in Prov 3:29; 6:14; 14:22). (4) Guillaume proposed a new חמס, cognate with Arab. *hamasa* "speak inaudibly" and Akk. *hāmasū* "they spoke secretly together" (*DCH,* 3:256b). (5) Graetz read תַּעַמְסוּ "you load up." (6) Blommerde took תחמסו as a stative, "be violent, unjust," parsing it as 3 fem pl impf and rendering "and your designs against me are unjust" (as Vg *et sententias contra me iniquas*); but there is no parallel to this sense, which is, in any case, weak.

28.a. Ehrlich excises כי תאמרו as "unpoetic," but who is to judge what is "poetic"? Szczygiel proposes an awkward reading, תָּמִירוּ "you change," which he understands to mean "you mix up [the house of the prince with the tent of the wicked]"; but it is hard to see how that could be a way the friends would have of wronging Job.

28.b. On נדיב see *Comment.* There is a slight possibility that we could take "prince" and "wicked" antithetically, and understand the friends' question to mean: what a contrast between the permanence of the fine upstanding prince and the disappearance of the depraved wicked! But the contrast of the two terms is unparalleled, though the contrast between נדיב and נבל "fool" adduced by Tur-Sinai in Isa 32:5 is interesting.

28.c. אהל משכנות רשעים is literally "the tent of the dwelling of the wicked ones"; to some commentators "tent of dwelling" is tautologous, and they have excised אהל "tent" (Budde, Duhm, Peake, Beer [*BHK vel*], Hölscher, Stevenson, Fohrer, Gerleman [*BHS prb*], de Wilde, Sicre Díaz, Hartley, NAB) or משכנות "dwellings" (Beer [*BHK vel*], Houtsma, Fedrizzi). But GKC, §124b, d–f, and König, *Syntax,* §260f, recognize משכנות as a poetically amplificative pl; cf. on 18:21; 39:6. And we can note the phrase אהל ביתי "the tent of my house" in Ps 132:3. Strauss defends MT.

29.a. On the form שְׁאֶלְתֶּם, see GKC, §44d.

29.b. עברי דרך "those who travel the roads" (RSV), "wayfarers" (NAB, NJPS). Less probably, it could perhaps mean the ordinary passerby, "the man in the street" (as Kissane).

29.c. נכר I piel is "recognize" (BDB, 648a; *HALOT,* 2:699b). Pope takes the word from נכר II piel "treat as strange" (*DCH,* 5:694a); thus "Do you not find their tales strange?" But while the friends *would* find the empirical evidence strange if they did not agree with it, this does seem a rather indirect way of Job's posing his question. Hartley likewise takes נכר as "treat as foreign, deny, mistake," and he translates "Have you not denied their evidence?"; similarly Terrien. But this leaves a weaker parallelism, for while "ask" is parallel to "acknowledge," it is not parallel to "not deny"; that is a separate charge on Job's part. Tur-Sinai has "falsify" ("But do not falsify their tokens!"), comparing Deut 32:27, but the same problem with the parallelism remains.

29.d. On אות "sign," see *Comment.* It is not "monuments" (NAB), for wayfarers do not have monuments; nor does "the signs they offer" (NEB) have a very evident meaning (REB revises to "the evidence they bring"). Nor is Guillaume likely to be right that אות is used in the Arab. sense of "words."

30.a. Kissane moves vv 30–31 to precede v 13.

30.b. ליום could well mean "[withheld] *for* the day," but this cannot be the sense here (despite Tur-Sinai). *Lamedh* must have the function of *beth* here (cf. ליום פקדה "on the day of punishment," Isa 10:3). But that is not to say that there is some shadow of Ugaritic here, where *beth* can have a separative idea (cf. Pope, Habel). Dillmann, Siegfried, Budde, Beer (*BHK*), Hölscher, Fohrer read בְּיוֹם "on the day" both here and in the next half-line. Budde and Fohrer think the alteration to "for the day" was made in the interests of orthodoxy. There is certainly no ground for making the sentence negative by inserting לֹא "not" and וְלֹא "and not" before the two occurrences of ליום (Merx), or מִי "who?" before יחשך (Hoffmann). Duhm emended מֵאֵיד "from destruction" for ליום איד "on the day of calamity" (mentioned by Beer [BH^2]).

30.c. אֵיד is common enough for "calamity" (e.g., BDB, 15b). But P. K. McCarter, "The River Ordeal in Israelite Literature," *HTR* 66 (1973) 403–12, has argued that the term means "river ordeal," in which, apparently, the situation of legal judgment and interrogation was viewed as the danger of drowning in deep waters (as, e.g., at Ps 18:16–20 [17–21] ‖ 2 Sam 22:17–21). The word איד in this theory is understood as the same as אֵד in Gen 2:6, and as cognate with Sum., Akk. *id* "river" (*CAD,* 7:8a), as argued originally by P. Dhorme, "L'arbre de vérité et l'arbre de vie," *RB* 4 (1907) 271–74 (274). McCarter finds references to this river ordeal also at 21:17; 31:23. The case for an "ordeal," however, is weak, and there is nothing in the imagery of the Job passages to suggest that the "calamity" is a watery one.

30.d. חשך "spare," as at 2 Kgs 5:20 (Job 33:18, often cited in this connection, is not so relevant).

30.e. עברות, lit. "acts of wrath"; since the pl is rare (only 40:11; Ps 7:7), some prefer עֶבְרָתוֹ "his wrath" (e.g., Beer [*BHK*]). NAB reads וּלְיוֹם קְבָרוֹת יוּבָל "and on the day he is carried to the grave," omitting v 32a as a dittogr.

30.f. יבל is "to lead," so ליום עברות יובלו ought to mean "are led to the day of destruction," which is the opposite of the meaning expected. The nearest parallels to יבל hoph (Ps 45:14 [15]; Jer 11:19; Isa 53:7; 55:12) have no idea of being kept safe. BDB says "lead [in triumph]"; NEB has "conveyed to safety," RSV "rescued," NIV, Pope "delivered," Sicre Díaz "find him absent"; but it is hard to show that the verb can have any of these meanings. So it is perhaps necessary to follow the common conjecture of יֻצָּלוּ "are delivered" or יֻצַּל "is delivered" (נצל pual) (Dillmann, Budde, Driver–Gray, Beer [*BHK*], Fohrer); this emendation is followed in the *Translation*.

Less persuasively, Duhm, Hölscher, Stevenson read יוּכָל "he triumphs," Ball יְפַלֵּט "he is delivered," Dhorme יַבְלִג "he rejoices" (בלג hiph as in 9:27; 10:20). Emendation to the sg יוּבָל "is led," to agree with the sg subj רע "evildoer," is recommended by many (e.g., Merx, Kissane, Larcher, JB), but unnecessary. NJPS has "on the day when wrath is led forth," taking עברות יובלו as a relative clause and "wrath" as the subj of the verb, but the idea of wrath being "led" is strained. The suggestion of Gordis (perhaps KJV's interrogatives point in the same direction) is initially very attractive, that this is another sentence in the mouth of the friends, like v 28, advancing the traditional dogma. But it does not succeed, for it removes any explicit statement of the testimony of the travelers in v 29; there is no point in asking whether the friends have considered the empirical evidence about the fate of the wicked and then failing to tell them (or us) what it is. The same verb is used in v 32, and it has perhaps been mistakenly copied into this verse. Guillaume's proposal for a new Heb. יבל, cognate with Arab. *wabula* "be unhealthy," hence "they are smitten with disease," still leaves the problem of the meaning of the verse as a whole. H. A. Hoffner (*TDOT*, 5:366) sees here a parallel to the Akk. idiom *pānī wabālu* "forgive, spare, show favor" (*CAD*, 1.1:18), but does not attempt a translation of the line.

31.a. For מִי "who?" Beer (*BHK*) reads וּמִי "and who?" moving the final *waw* of the last word of v 30 to this place.

31.b. נגד hiph is usually a more neutral word, "declare" (as in 11:6; 15:18), and KJV, RSV so translate it here; but in Jer 20:10 it seems to have the connotation of "denounce," and that would suit the context here better (so also NEB, NIV; JB has "reproach," NJPS "upbraid," NAB "charge with"). Mic 3:8 and Isa 58:1, often cited as parallels, do not in fact mean "denounce" rather than "declare."

32.a. NEB rearranges vv 32–33 thus: 32a, 33b, 33a, 32b (so also de Wilde), eliminating 33c by adding אין מספר "without number" to the end of 32b and ולפניו "and before him" to the beginning of 33b. This creates a more logical order, with the funeral procession preceding the burial, but the proposal is clever rather than convincing. It is better to see the line as a circumstantial clause (Duhm), i.e., "when he is carried to the grave"; being carried to the grave is of course nothing peculiar to the wicked man.

32.b. קברות pl perhaps signifies the "graveyard" (as קברים in 17:1).

32.c. ישקוד, lit. "he, or one, watches over his tomb." Delitzsch, Driver–Gray, Ball, Dhorme suppose that the effigy of the dead man was imagined to be watching over his own tomb; but the sense is stronger, as well as more natural, if the subject of ישקוד is impersonal (as RSV, NJB, NJPS). KJV's "shall remain" was apparently regarded by the translators as an acceptable metaphorical sense of the word (cf. Leigh, 262a); though it is a weak image, it avoided ascribing a postmortem consciousness to the dead man. Merx and Budde, followed by Duhm (יִשְׁקְדוּ) and Beer (*BH*^{2} *frt*), emend to the plural יִשְׁקֹדוּ "they watch" (JB "men are watching"). Beer (*BHK frt*) reads עָלָיו for על, thus "the burial mound watches over him" (followed by NAB, Stevenson, Kroeze, de Wilde). Emendation to יִשְׁקוֹט "he rests" (Graetz, Ehrlich [יִשְׁקֹט]) is out of line with the visual imagery in these verses (and would he rest על "upon" his burial mound?).

32.d. גדיש is elsewhere "sheaf" (as in 5:26; etc.); what we have here, however, is גדיש II "burial mound," cognate with Arab. *jadat* "grave" (as BDB, 155b; *HALOT*, 1:178b; omitted from *DCH* by oversight), though some prefer revocalizing to גֶּדֶשׁ (Beer [*BHK*], Driver–Gray, NEB [Brockington]). Tur-Sinai maintains, however, that it is "sheaf," translating "while he is ready with a shock of corn," which is supposed to mean when he has amassed many stacks of corn in a ripe old age. But shocks of corn are piled up annually, so the image is unsuitable for the growth of wealth through a lifetime. Strauss thinks "sheaf" could be an ironic image for "grave," which echoes the Geneva Bible translation, "Yet shall he be brought to the grave and remain in the heap."

33.a. Though רגב occurs only here and at 38:38, almost all agree on this meaning. But B. Alfrink ("Die Bedeutung des Wortes רֶגֶב in Job 21, 33 und 38, 33," *Bib* 13 [1932] 77–86) argues, especially on the basis of the ancient versions, that the word means "stone" and not "clod." So too Guillaume, because the winter rains would sweep clods away; however, he continues, in 38:38 "clods" are called "stones," because after rain the sun hardens them; so perhaps they are clods here too. I. Zolli ("A che forma di sepoltura si referisce Giobbe XXI, 33," *SMSR* 10 [1934] 223–28) thinks they are the small stones that lie in the bed of a wadi. But stones could hardly "stick fast together," if that is the meaning of דבק in 38:38.

33.b. נחל is common enough for "valley," but why should the tyrant's tomb be in a valley? Duhm replied, unassailably, that in the author's country that must have been where people were buried ("the favourite position for graves," says Peake, as if he knew something we do not). Hartley thinks of caves along the walls of a dry riverbed. Zolli ("A che forma di sepoltura," 223–28) thinks of the malefactor being buried among the pebbles of a wadi as a form of honorable burial. See, however, *Comment.* Moses was buried in a valley (Deut 34:6), but there seems to be no connection. B. Jacob thought נחל should mean "earth" ("Das hebräische Sprachgut im Christlich-Palästinischen," *ZAW* 22 [1902] 83–113 [102] = "Christlich-Palästinisches," *ZDMG* 55 [1901] 135–45 [141]; cf. נַחַל V, *DCH,* 5:659b), but that weakens the imagery. Hölscher, followed by Fohrer and Strauss, saw here rather grave trenches or shafts (נחל I, *DCH,* 1:659 §3). Among emendations we may mention חול "dust" (Beer [*BHK prps*]) and נַחַת "[clods of] quietness" (Beer [*BHK prps*]).

33.c. Some translations substitute our idea of the earth lying easy (JB) or gently (GNB) on the buried person, but the Heb. idiom expresses delight. Tur-Sinai wants the word מתק "sweet" to mean "suck, suckle" (as Aram., Syr.; *DCH,* 5:573b [מתק II]) and translates "the moistness of the river suckles him." Ball somewhat tamely reads יִשְׁתֹּק בְּמוֹ "he is quiet among [the clods]" (followed by Moffatt "quiet he lies amid the clods"); Stevenson has "[clods] are laid in order," reading תֻּקְּנוּ (pual of תקן) or a piel or pual ptcp, מְתַקְּנִים or מְתֻקָּנִים.

33.d. Driver–Gray find v 33b, c out of place since they seem to describe a funeral procession *after* the reference to the burial in v 32a. They would like to rearrange the text to have vv 32a and 33b together as a description of the funeral pomp and vv 33a and 32b together as an imaginative depiction of the feelings of the wicked after death, v 33c being a later addition. NEB, which follows the rearrangement, has "thousands" keeping watch at the tomb, but for what purpose?

33.e. משך, often "pull," is sometimes, as here, "be drawn," hence "follow behind" (cf. Judg 20:37; Ecclus 14:19, also in a funereal context; cf. *DCH,* 5:524b §14). It is not that everyone will eventually follow him in death (as, e.g., Ball, Hartley).

33.f. This third colon is deleted by Duhm, Ehrlich, Ball, Beer (BH^2), Hölscher, Larcher, JB, Fohrer.

34.a. Lit. "comfort me [with] emptiness (הבל)"; the noun is used adverbially. M. Dahood supposes another noun, תַּנְחוּמָה "reply," and verb, חמה "answer" (see *Note* 21:2.b above), and claims to find a further example here; but the verbal form תנחמוני cannot be derived from a verb חמה, and the verbal and substantival forms seem to have been confused (he cannot be right in saying that the verb תנחמוני is "balanced" by the noun תשובתיכם "your replies" in the next colon).

34.b. מעל "faithlessness," often against Yahweh, but also, more rarely, against humans (of a wife, Num 5:12; of a king, Prov 16:10). Cf. R. Knierim, *TLOT,* 2:680–82. Hölscher insists that it is not here "faithlessness," but "deceit." But see *Comment.* Ehrlich, Stevenson read עָמָל "misery," Stevenson suggesting further יַשְׁאִירוּ "[your replies] leave (only) misery."

34.c. ותשובתיכם נשאר־מעל, lit. "and as for your replies [*casus pendens;* cf. GKC, §143a], there remains [of them] [only] faithlessness."

Form/Structure/Setting

The *structure* of this seventh speech of Job is simple. The poem has only three main elements: exordium addressed to the friends (vv 2–5), a disputation speech about the fate of the wicked (vv 6–33), and a closing address to the friends (v 34). Within the main body of the poem, the friends are consistently in view, though they are addressed directly only in vv 27–30 ("I know your thoughts . . . for you say . . . Have you not asked . . . ?"). The rhetorical questions in vv 16, 17, 19, 31 do not of course necessarily imply the presence of the friends in the speaker's consciousness, but they do suggest it.

The *strophic structure* of the speech is far from clear. The speech contains several major elements that can be identified: vv 2–5: address to the friends; vv 8–15: depiction of the happiness of the wicked, their children and animals; vv 19–21: the wicked themselves should bear their own punishment; vv 28–33: even the death of the wicked is comfortable. But how far the treatment of each theme extends beyond its core is the problem.

Fohrer analyzed the sections (I–III) and strophes (1–8) thus:

	strophe 1	vv 2–5	5 lines
Section I	strophe 2	vv 6–9	4 lines
	strophe 3	vv 10–13	4 lines
Section II	strophe 4	vv 14–18	4 lines (omitting v 16)
	strophe 5	vv 19–22	4 lines
	strophe 6	vv 23–26	4 lines
Section III	strophe 7	vv 27–30	4 lines
	strophe 8	vv 31–34	4 lines

Terrien's analysis largely agrees with Fohrer's, except that he divides the speech into six strophes, each consisting of two substrophes; thus I 2–3, 4–6; II 7–9, 10–13; III 14–15, 16–18; IV 19–21, 22 (he thinks something is missing after v 22); V 23–26, 27–28; VI 29–31, 32–34 (the division by lines is 2, 3, 3, 4, 2, 3, 3, 1, 4, 2, 3, 3).

In Skehan's analysis, only one of these strophes (vv 2–6) coincides with Fohrer's. He divides the stanzas thus: vv 2–6, 7–12, 13–17, 18–20, 21+23–26, 27–29, 30–34 (thus 5, 6, 5, 3, 5, 3, 5 lines), removing v 22 to follow 22:2 (as NAB).

Webster finds nine strophes: vv 2–3, 4–6, 7–10, 11–15, 16–18, 19–21, 22–26, 27–29, 30–33 (with v 34 standing outside the strophic structure). Van der Lugt identifies three main strophes (vv 5–15, 16–26, 27–33), with a preface in vv 2–4 (but v 5 must surely be connected with vv 2–4, since the focus is still upon the friends).

RSV has the major breaks before vv 17 and 27, NEB before vv 7, 16, 23, and 27 (REB dispenses with the one before 16), JB before vv 14, 17, and 27, NIV before vv 4, 17, 22, 27, 34, NJPS before vv 7 and 27, and GNB before vv 4, 7, 14, 17, 19, 23, 27, 34.

A comparative table of the beginnings of strophes shows that only at one place is there complete agreement about a strophic division (v 27), though vv 7 and 17 (or 19) are also quite strongly supported. (See table on facing page, Strophe Beginnings in Job 21.)

The firmest points in a strophic analysis are these: v 6 must be attached to what follows (see *Comment*), and v 27 marks a major division in that the description of the evildoer is supplanted at this point by direct address to the friends. Clearly vv 8–10, 11–13, 14–15, 17–18, 19–21, 23–26, 28–30, and 31–33 are unbreakable units, and vv 6–7 must be a preface to 8–13, and 27 to 28–34; but how these units should be grouped and how vv 16 and 22 are to be attached are uncertain. There are no significant changes of subject or orientation from v 6 to v 33, but the following movements in the argument can be discerned: (1) the wicked do not live unhappy lives, as the friends have argued (vv 7–13); (2) their godlessness goes unpunished (vv 14–18); (3) the argument that retribution is visited on the descendants of evildoers undermines the doctrine of retribution itself (vv 19–21); (4) even if it were true it would be irrelevant, for everyone has a common fate in death (vv 22–26); (5) the evidence from experience is contrary to the doctrine of retribution, for even notable sinners flourish and are respected after their death (vv 27–33). The *Translation* suggests the following division: vv 2–5, 6–7, 8–10, 11–13, 14–16, 17–21, 22–26, 27–30, 31–34, i.e., nine strophes of 4, 2, 3, 3, 3, 5, 5, 4, 4 lines, respectively.

Throughout this poem there are regular bicola, interrupted only by the tricola at v 19

Strophe Beginnings in Job 21

	Fohrer	Terrien	Skehan	Webster	v. d. Lugt	RSV	NEB	REB	JB	NIV	NJPS	TEV	Clines
3				•									
4		•								•		•	
5					•								
6	•			•									•
7		•	•				•	•			•	•	
8													•
10	•	•		•									
11													•
13			•										
14	•	•		•					•			•	•
15													
16		•			•		•						
17						•			•	•		•	•
18			•	•									
19	•	•										•	
21			•	•									
22		•								•			•
23	•	•		•			•	•				•	
26													
27	•	•	•		•	•	•	•	•	•	•	•	•
29		•		•									
30			•										
31	•												•
32		•											
34										•		•	

(at the beginning of the second major section of the speech) and at v 33 (the last verse of the subject matter proper, v 34 being a pendant of address to the friends).

The *genre* of the poem is that of the *disputation speech.* All its elements derive from the *wisdom instruction,* and as a whole it has the character of an argument, picking up the opinions of other speakers already expressed and attempting to refute them. Typical of the exordium in the wisdom instruction is the demand to be heard (vv 2–3; cf. 15:17) and the request for silence (v 5; contrast 6:24). We note also the speaker's prefatory account of the strong emotion that his subject matter inspires in him (v 6; cf. 4:12–15). Rhetorical questions are particularly frequent (vv 7, 16, 17–18, 19, 21, 22, 29–30, 31, 34; plus those within quoted speech in vv 15, 28).

Perhaps we should recognize here also *parody* of a traditional form of wisdom instruction, the poem on the blessedness of the pious (Fohrer); such a parody, applying the language of blessedness to the wicked, is of course met with frequently in the Psalms (cf. Pss 10:5–6; 73:3–7, 10). The features of such blessedness are long life, strength (v 7), offspring (v 8), security (v 9), abundance of possessions (v 10), innocent (!) happiness (vv 11–12), prosperity, and a peaceful death (v 13). Unlike the Psalms, however, the parody is encountered in the context not of the lament but of argument.

Not a parody but a *readaptation* of traditional language is found in vv 23–26, where a *topos* on the annihilation of distinctions in Sheol is drawn upon (cf. 3:17–19) for a new purpose: here the material functions to support the argument that the doctrine of retribution is invalid and that death is not a "punishment."

The *citation of words* of opponents (in this case, of the wicked and of the friends) is a common feature of the wisdom instruction. In vv 14–15 the wicked say to God, "Depart from us," and ask rhetorically "What is the Almighty that we should serve him?" (similar citations in Pss 10:11; 14:1; 53:1 [2]; 73:11). In v 28 the friends say, "Where is the house of the prince?" (RSV attributes v 19 also to the friends, but see *Note* 19.a). The citation of the friends is not verbatim, and of course the citation of the evildoers' words is wholly fictive (see *Comment* on vv 14–16).

The *argument form* is most evident in vv 19–21, where a hypothetical objection to Job's position is put forward as a question, "Is God storing up his punishment for his children?" and answered by a series of futures with jussive force ("let him requite, let his own eyes see, let him drink") that function as a critique of the traditional doctrine, and by a motive clause introduced by כי "for."

Finally, the wisdom instruction is sustained by the *appeal to experience* (vv 29–33). Usually such an appeal takes the form of an account of the speaker's own experience (as in 4:12–17; 5:27; cf. 13:1) or of traditional experience (cf. 8:8–10; 15:17–19; 20:4–5), but here it is an invitation to glean knowledge from contemporaries of the speaker, namely travelers. Job has of course always been arguing from his own experience, but this is the first time (13:1 notwithstanding) that he has used such a form of words. He has not previously said, "This is what I (or others) have experienced; therefore I know it is true," but in this speech he imitates the friends much more closely than in his other speeches.

The *function* of the speech is to support in a more logical fashion the view of the doctrine of retribution that Job has already arrived at more instinctively. In previous speeches he had denied the validity of the doctrine in that he, as a righteous man, was suffering; now he denies the doctrine by arguing that the unrighteous do *not* suffer. In a wider horizon, then, we could say that the function of the speech is to further defend his innocence, or, indeed, to prepare for the oath of innocence he will swear in chap. 31 (so Fohrer).

The *tonality* of the speech is to be discerned from the exordium of vv 2–5 and the peroration of v 34. There is a distinct harshness here, not of course unparalleled by previous criticisms of the friends by Job (cf., e.g., 6:15, 27; 13:4; 16:2) but all the more striking because the speech is as a whole comparatively low-key, impersonal, and unemotional. In fact, the strongest emotional language in the whole speech concerns Job's attitude to the friends, rather than, as previously, his own suffering and his obloquy of God. To the friends he says here that the only consolation they could offer would be to be silent (v 2; cf. v 5b)—which is a contradiction in terms and so completely undermines their value and significance (they are nothing if they are not "comforters"; why else are they there in Uz?). But sharper than that is Job's assumption that when he has finished speaking they will resume their "mockery" (v 3); that means to say that that is all he can hear in their speeches. In tune with that sentence is his closing thrust (v 34): their consolations are "nugatory" (הבל) since they contain no acceptance of him as an innocent man, but not quite empty of significance, for what they do contain is a residue (שׁאר) of impiety or faithlessness (מעל) inasmuch as they tell lies about God and his governance of the world.

The *nodal verse* must be the opening rhetorical question of the speech proper, "Why do the wicked live . . . ?" (v 7). This stands in headline position, and from it devolves the speech as a whole. The answer to the question, though it is never explicitly stated, is evident throughout the speech. It is: "Because there is no moral order in the universe, no principle of retribution and no divine justice."

Comment

2–34 In this seventh speech of Job, there is a different note from the others, something a little anticlimactic. From his first, self-pitying, speech in chap. 3 to his sixth, vigorous and forward-looking, speech in chap. 19, there has been a crescendo of decisiveness, of mounting determination to take things into his own hands and not to bow meekly before the onslaughts of fate, the personal animus of the Almighty. In chap. 19 we saw him, at the height of his self-confidence, expressing his belief in the certainty of his vindication, "I know that my champion lives" (19:25), no matter how long that outcome may take, and no matter whether it will eventuate before his death or not. Throughout, he has been wrapped up in his own misery, struggling with the tension between his innocence and his suffering. And his speeches have given slight recognition to the arguments and even the presence of the friends. In every one of the speeches he has lapsed from response to his interlocutors into soliloquy or address to God. But here in this speech he enters into direct dispute with the friends, addressing them and them alone from the beginning to the end of the speech. He actually refers to their arguments—something he has rarely done before. And his language is cooler, less aggressive.

The ostensible issue in the speech is whether the friends have been right in their portrayal of the fate of the wicked. Eliphaz in chap. 15 has depicted the wicked as "in torment all his days" (15:20); Bildad in chap. 18 has focused on the last days of the typical wicked man: "Truly, the lamp of the wicked will be snuffed out" (18:5); Zophar in chap. 20 has emphasized the contrast between the "triumph cry" (20:5) of the godless and the annihilation that eventually befalls him. But what is Job's interest in engaging in this disputation? He is not one of the wicked, and he resents every implication that he is. Can it be that he speaks only in the interest of objective truth, that he cannot let his interlocutors get away with a false opinion? That is certainly an element in his motivation. But there is more to it than that. There is a hidden implicate of this argument about the fate of the wicked that affects him personally. If the wicked are not punished, it can only mean that there is no correlation between deed and consequence. But then, if recompense is not meted out for the wicked, why should we expect it to be granted to the righteous?

By force of his moral conviction of his innocence, Job reached by chap. 19 a point of equilibrium over the question of his righteousness despite the evidence of his suffering; now it is time when he can support that same position on grounds of logic and publicly observable facts. He is not personally concerned in the least about the fate of the wicked; but the fate of the righteous is an issue that he has to ventilate with all the thoroughness he is capable of. "His own relation with God belonged to those things of which people say 'I must settle it or go mad.' The question of God's moral government looms up behind it, and is a question of far more radical significance, but it is more abstract, and does not touch him on the raw" (Peake).

In short, Job's argument is this: if the wicked are not recompensed, neither are the righteous. *That* is the simple meaning of his suffering: there is no meaning to it at all. (Fohrer takes it all quite differently: he thinks it is a further argument for Job's innocence. If the wicked lead successful and happy lives, and Job's is so miserable, Job cannot be one of the wicked. But Job does not argue that he is *not wicked,* just that he is *innocent.*)

2–5 Job's address to the friends is more bitter than it has been previously.

2 How do friends usually offer consolation? Various rituals of consolation are attested (e.g., sharing a meal, 42:11; cf. Jer 16:7), but presumably acts of consolation are normally accompanied by comforting words (for the combination of נחם and words, cf. Isa 40:1; Gen 50:21; see also H. J. Stoebe, *TLOT,* 1:734–39). See also, especially on the role of consolation as a combating of grief through rational argument, C. A. Newsom, "'The Consolations of God': Assessing Job's Friends across a Cultural Abyss," in *Reading from Right to Left,* FS D. J. A. Clines, ed. J. C. Exum and H. G. M. Williamson, JSOTSup 373 (London: Sheffield Academic Press, 2003) 347–58. Job ironically observes that the biggest consolation his friends could offer him would be to say nothing at all. Their speeches defending the doctrine of retribution have made them into "torturer-comforters" (16:2), even though they themselves (or Eliphaz at least) have represented their words as "God's encouragements" (15:11). It would not of course *be* a consolation for them to keep silence; it would be less than a consolation, as the turn of phrase shows: "let *that* [your silence] be the comfort you offer me." But the mere absence of their persistent putting him in the wrong would almost seem a consolation in itself. Job knows he is right, of course, and he does not want to be gainsaid any longer. Whatever they say will be wrong, and their "consolation" is bound to be, at the end of the day, "vanity, emptiness" (הבל) and "deceit" (מעל, perhaps meaning "infidelity to God") (v 34).

3 The language of this exordium is very conventional, and quite artificial to boot. Given the rhythm of the dialogues, there is no likelihood that his interlocutors will fail to "bear with" him or let him speak until he has finished. No one has interrupted anyone so far, and none of the speakers has any reason to think it will be otherwise. What else, in any case, are they all doing in Uz, or in this book, except sitting there speechifying? (For similar promises and requests to be silent, see 6:24; 13:13; 33:31.) And the invitation to "mock on" after he has finished is not only ironic (for he wishes no such thing) but unjust, for we have heard no mockery in their speeches, nothing worse than dogmatism, wrongheaded advice, and well-meant criticism. Zophar indeed has accused Job of "mockery" (לעג, 11:3), by which he means mockery against God; if Job does not accept that God is right to punish him, he mocks God's justice. And Elihu will say of Job that he "drinks up mockery like water" (34:7, לעג), meaning that mockery of God is meat and drink to Job. But the friends do not themselves "mock" Job, and Job is being petulant here if he thinks that is their attitude or if he needs to ask for their forbearance before he launches himself upon another speech.

We might wonder why Job asks the friends not to "mock" him until he has finished speaking. Alonso Schökel observes that he could mean that once he has been allowed to speak the truth as he sees it he doesn't care whether they mock or not, for they cannot cancel out what has been said; or he might mean, We'll see then who will be doing the mocking, you or me, or, See if you'll be able to mock then. It seems more likely that Job assumes that nothing he can say will make any difference to their dogmatism, *and* that to disagree with him is to despise him and make sport of him.

4 Why should the fact that Job's complaint is not addressed to mortals be a reason or excuse for his "impatience"? "Impatience" might reasonably result from not yet having his complaint heard, but not from the identity of the person addressed (so Peake cannot be right that he means, "Why should *you* be so vexed? I fly at higher game"). Job's "protest," his legal complaint (שׂיח) for a hearing of his grievance in court, has of course been directed entirely against God (7:11, 13; 9:27; 10:1; cf. too 23:2) as the author of his suffering. But God has not responded, and the effect on Job is a deep psychic weakness. He says he is "impatient," but that does not mean that he is fretting at the delay in settling his complaint. For the term קצר רוח, lit. "short of breath, spirit, cramped in spirit," like its near synonym קצר נפש, goes deeper than that; it must here have the connotation of "weak, exhausted" (as in Judg 16:16; cf. R. D. Haak, "A Study and New Interpretation of *qṣr npš*," *JBL* 101 [1982] 161–67 [164], followed by Strauss; Newsom, however, interprets the phrase as describing the "psychological state of a person immediately before some decisive word is spoken or action taken"). "It is as though one's energy is derived in part from the future viewed in hope . . . impatience [is] to be understood as the desire to give up on life, to give up the ghost (or *ruaḥ* or *nepeš*), to resign oneself to one's fate" (Janzen). If his claim had been against mortals, he might have become tetchy or impatient; but the failure of *God* to answer robs him of strength.

5 Presumably the friends have been looking at Job throughout the dialogues, so how can they now heed Job's demand, "Look at me, turn to me"? He means that if they were not just to see him physically but to recognize what is before their faces—an innocent man who is being made to suffer by God like one of the wicked—they would be "appalled" or "dumbfounded" (JB) and "clap [their] hand[s] to [their] mouth[s]"; the silence that would strike them then would be the silence that Job requires of them (v 2a), a silence that would count as consolation (v 2b).

The term שׁמם "devastate, appall" seems to be used here, not in its subjective sense of the feeling of horror or amazement, but in a more objective sense of the speechlessness that results (cf. F. Stolz, *TLOT,* 3:1372–75; and cf. *Comment* on 17:8). The gesture of clapping the hand to the mouth (as in 29:9; 40:4; Mic 7:16) then corresponds exactly to the silence of amazement (not exactly that "to speak would be useless or unwise," as NJB). The gesture is illustrated on a Mesopotamian seal cylinder (*ANEP,* no. 695); cf. also M. J. Dahood, "Northwest Semitic Philology and Job," in *The Bible in Current Catholic Thought: Gruenthaner Memorial Volume,* ed. J. L. McKenzie, St. Mary's Theological Studies 1 (New York: Herder & Herder, 1962) 55–74 (64); B. Couroyer, "'Mettre sa main sur sa bouche' en Egypte et dans la Bible," *RB* 67 (1960) 197–209.

6–13 This long strophe of eight lines should probably be regarded as a single unit since it appears to be arranged in a roughly chiastic pattern (so too Andersen), with the focus on the wicked themselves in the outmost verses (7, 13), on their children in the circle within (8, 11–12), and on their houses and cattle in the center (9–10).

Job here takes up the opposite view about the fate of the wicked from that persistently advanced by the friends. For him, the wicked do not live unhappy lives in anxiety and they are not cut off early; rather, they enjoy comfortable lives, with their children and cattle safe about them, and they even die in peace. With generalizations of this magnitude, who is to say which speaker is in the right? All that is interesting is that by advancing his deviant view Job merely demonstrates that there is no truth to be had on this subject; there is nothing but assertion. And of course Job does not have to be very much in the right for the damage to be done to the orthodox line of the friends; it is enough that some color can be given to the very opposite view for the reader to recognize that here we are hearing not about realities but about wishful thinking. The fact is, if Job is even only half right, that the wicked and the innocent are neither rewarded or punished—not, that is, in any measure that makes a general rule deducible, not to any degree that entitles theologians to draw inferences about the moral quality of those who suffer or prosper—then the friends' case is doomed. Even a single case of a prosperous wicked man would destroy the friends' dogma.

The conflict between the friends and Job is not a novel one; it is the conflict between the wisdom tradition and the psalmic tradition. Wisdom teaches that wickedness is punished; the psalms lament, Why do the wicked prosper? The book of Job makes trouble by planting an innocent sufferer from out of the Psalms into the world of the orthodox wisdom teachers. But the conflict is also not just an ancient one. We tell our children that bad behavior will have harmful consequences, and we tell our friends who are suffering for no apparent reason that there is no necessary connection between their deeds and their experience of life. The conflict lies within us all.

6 This verse is connected by most commentators (except Duhm, Peake, Fohrer, Tur-Sinai) and versions with what precedes, but to do so is to misunderstand the text. What is it that Job "remembers" (זכר) that causes him dismay (בהל) and shuddering (פלצות)? It cannot be something about his own condition, his own suffering, or the wrong that is being done to him, because he is conscious of that all the time, and so he can hardly "remember" it. It is something that he knows from experience and observation, something that is not constantly in the forefront of his mind but that causes him mental distress whenever he thinks about it. It can only be the happy life of the wicked and "God's immoral government of the world" (Peake), the very subject of this speech as a whole. Their lot, as he pictures it, troubles him because it proves that there is no justice in the world if the wicked are not punished, and also, no doubt, because he would like to see the kind of retribution in play that would punish evildoers and reward him for his piety instead of leaving him to suffer at the hands of a cruel God.

What usually causes distress in the beholder is some calamity: Job is "dismayed" (בהל), says Eliphaz, when his bereavement and illness strike him (4:5; cf. *Note* 4:5.d). He is "dismayed" by the presence of God (23:15, 16), or by sudden terror (22:10). But here, strangely enough, it is not calamity but prosperity that dismays him; that is to say, the world has turned topsy-turvy when the wicked live comfortably, and the effect on the moral onlooker like Job is to shake his equilibrium (the verb פלץ has described in 9:6 the quivering of the earth's pillars when God "shakes the earth from its place").

7 The question, Why do the wicked live? does not mean, as Davidson rightly saw, just "How can your theology account for the fact?" but a larger question, "Why in the government of a righteous God do the wicked live?" This is not just a debating point for Job; he is "not seeking a dialectical triumph over the friends" (Peake). The "dismay" and "quivering" of v 6 signal that the prosperity of the wicked is a reality that fills him with horror. Nevertheless, he is not in the position of a lamenting psalmist who raises to heaven the cry, Why do the wicked prosper? meaning thereby to urge God, Stop them prospering, and let me prosper instead. Unlike the psalmists, Job is not suffering at the hands of the wicked, he is not being victimized by their prosperity. Where their prosperity touches him is that, if they are prospering, the God with whom he deals is an absentee landlord of an amoral universe. Job desperately wants the doctrine of retribution to be true, not so that the wicked will get their just deserts but so that he, the innocent man, will get his. His experience has taught him now that the doctrine is false, but he does not rejoice in his discovery; he is appalled by the consequences.

As for these evildoers, he says, they not only go on living (חיה could refer to bare existence), they live to ripe old age (עתק), not losing their powers as they grow older but acquiring even more strength and wealth (חיל can mean both physical health and material prosperity). There could even be the implication that the strength of these wicked men is not purely personal and domestic, but has a social dimension also. The very phrase גברו חיל *gābᵉrû ḥayil* "they increase their strength" is reminiscent of the common term גבור חיל *gibbôr ḥayil* "mighty man of valor, member of the landed aristocracy," who uses his wealth both to determine the affairs of the society and to wage war (so Hartley). For the theme of the prosperity of the wicked, cf. Jer 12:1–4; Mal 3:15; Hab 1:13; Eccl 7:15; 8:14; Ps 73:3.

8 The friends have of course maintained that the wicked either have no offspring or else lose them: Eliphaz in 15:34 has said that the godless as a group are "sterile"; Bildad in 18:19 has represented the wicked as leaving no posterity; and Zophar in 20:26 has pictured the destruction by fire of the evildoer's progeny. Job, on the other hand, portrays the wicked as surrounded by his children, who are "established" or "secure" (נכון; cf. also Prov 12:3; Ps 102:28 [29]). An awareness of the presence of the children in the life of the wicked is emphasized by "with them" (עמם), "before their eyes" (לעיניהם). The phrase is "a pathetic touch from the hand of the man whose sons [!] had been taken from him" (Davidson). But it is not only galling to Job to see the wicked enjoying the company of their children (and the status that comes from having descendants); it is a refutation of the friends' claim. (For a similar depiction of the burgeoning of life in children and cattle, cf. Ps 144:12–14, and especially the future Eliphaz promises Job in 5:19–26.)

9 Children and houses are not so very different; בנים *bānîm* "children" and בתים *bāttîm* "houses" are both derived from the verb בנה *bānâ* "build," and "houses" can sometimes mean "families." And the language of this verse could even be taken as referring to children (as NEB and REB believe, though the parallel with 5:24 makes that unlikely). Job may even be ironically borrowing the words Eliphaz addressed to him in 5:24, when he assured him that his "tent" would be "safe" (lit. "peace," שלום). It is the wicked who, in reality, know this security, not the innocent man, says Job. It is the wicked who are "without fear" (מפחד), not the one who listens to wisdom as in Prov 1:33 (cf. also Prov 3:25, where sudden פחד is associated with the downfall of the wicked). It is the wicked who do not feel the "rod" (שבט) of God, i.e., God's avenging justice; it is not Job, for he is suffering under that very "hand" of God that wields the scourge (19:21) and in dread of that very "rod" (שבט, 9:34; cf. also 37:13; Isa 10:24–26). The "rod" of God is not simply a metaphor for God's punishment but some physical manifestation of it, like destruction or illness (as God's "hand" is in 19:21). What happens to the houses of the wicked, according to the friends, is quite the opposite: fire consumes them (15:34), fire lodges in them (18:15), a flood sweeps them away (20:28).

10 Though the friends have never happened to mention the fecundity of animals as a sign of divine pleasure in an individual, the idea is common enough (cf. Deut 28:4; Ps 144:13–14). The bitterness of a man who was once richer in cattle than all the other Easterners is very visible.

11 The picture of children at play inevitably conjures up feelings of joy, peace, freedom from anxiety, and even innocence (cf. Zech 8:5, where the play of children in the city streets symbolizes Jerusalem's happiness). Their insouciance is that of lambs gambolling (the point of the metaphor is not the *number* of the children or lambs, as Duhm, Budde, Davidson, Peake). In Pss 29:6 and 114:4, 6, mountains "skip" (רקד, as here) like lambs or rams, but in terror. Here "the joy of the children [shows] that the merrymaking is not a facade, as is often the case at a feast put on by the rich" (Hartley). Zophar had of course maintained that the "happiness" (שמחה) of the wicked lasts only a moment (20:5).

12 Those who celebrate with timbrel, harp, and flute are not just the children of the happy evildoers but the evildoers themselves. The worst of it is, for Job, not that the wicked are as wicked as they can possibly be, but that they can enjoy perfectly innocent family festivities when their wrongdoing should have made it impossible for them. Perhaps we should be thinking of the dark counterpoint to this text in chap. 1, where the festivities of Job's family were interrupted by tragedy. Here the singing is accompanied by three folk instruments: a percussion instrument (תף "timbrel"), a stringed instrument (כנור "lyre"), and a wind instrument (עוגב "flute"; also in 30:31). The timbrel and harp accompany joyful occasions in Gen 31:27; Isa 5:12; 24:8; cf. also *IDB* 3:474–75.

13 Even the death of the wicked, its time and its manner, declares their good fortune. They are not cut off before their time, as Eliphaz has asserted (see on 15:32), for they live out the full measure of their days and die like patriarchs, old and full of days (cf. 42:17). Their prosperity (טוֹב) lasts their whole life long (as against Zophar, who said their prosperity [טוֹב] does not endure, 20:21). And when the natural end of their life is reached, they suffer no lingering death but suddenly slip away, "in a moment" (ברגע, see *Note* 13.d), to Sheol (see 7:9; 14:13; 17:13, 16). Job, by contrast, longs for a death that never comes (cf. 3:20–21).

14–16 After the depiction of the prosperity of the wicked in vv 6–13, a second theme in Job's speech emerges here: the godlessness of the wicked that goes unpunished. Here it becomes apparent that evildoers are not simply fortunate despite their wrongdoing; they live happy lives despite their express blasphemy against God. We should not infer that these people are not really godless, since they do speak of God (as Hesse); what makes them godless is not that they deny his existence but that, accepting that there is a God, they believe it is not he that brings them weal or woe (as v 16 will say plainly).

This is of course a pious man's depiction of the impious; these are not the words of the impious themselves. The ungodly are hardly to be found, for example, addressing themselves to God, even with dismissive words like "leave us." They might perhaps say, What gain shall we have if we pray to him? But it is still more likely that these are the words Job ascribes to such people. To whom in actuality would they be addressing such words? Who would be urging them to pray to God, that they feel obliged to resist, with their appeal to utility?

14 "Leave us," they say, "turn aside," "leave us alone" (NRSV), as though God were an unwelcome companion (cf. the imperative of סור "turn aside, depart" in 2 Sam 2:22; Pss 6:8 [9]; 119:115; Isa 30:11; the same phrase in Eliphaz's next speech, 22:17). Their attitude is the polar opposite of the pious, who desire (חפץ) to know God's ways (דרכים) (Isa 58:2); in not wishing to know his ways they declare their unwillingness to follow his commands (cf. Pss 25:4; 27:11; 86:11; 119:27, 32, 33; 143:8). Isa 58:2 shows, however, that it is possible to desire knowledge of God's ways and nevertheless be disobedient to his will.

15 The wicked have no respect for God. "What maner of felowe is the Almightie that we shulde serve him?" (Coverdale), they say. A question formed on the pattern of "Who am I that I should . . . ," "Who is he that I should . . . ," challenges the status or ability of the person referred to. Cf. Judg 9:28, 38, "Who is Abimelech . . . that we should serve him?" and Exod 5:2; 1 Sam 17:26; and cf. 1 Sam. 25:10; Prov 30:9. The construction expresses contempt, says BDB (566b), or modesty (which is a form of self-contempt; see George W. Coats, "Self-Abasement and Insult Formulas," *JBL* 89 [1970] 14–26). Here we have "what?" (מה) rather than "who?" (מי), but the sense is the same; cf. also 2 Kgs 8:13.

Their challenge is no merely generalized antipathy to religion, however. They ask why they should "serve," using one of the basic terms for religious duty (cf. Jer 2:20), the "Almighty" (שַׁדַּי Shaddai; see on 5:17), for they know no evidence that he *is* Almighty. Or if he is, he does not act as if he is. To their knowledge, the Almighty metes out no retribution, and he seems to be indifferent to human behavior. Any religious observances they perform will have no discernible effect upon their lives and happiness; there will be no "profit" (יעל hiph) in them. Neither have they any call to "pray" to the Almighty, for they lack nothing, and they have nothing to gain from prayers of entreaty (which are what פגע signifies).

From the standpoint of utility, their view of religion can hardly be faulted by Job. His own scrupulous piety has not prevented the death of his children and the destruction of his well-being. There has been no "profit" in *his* prayer. The question was long ago raised by the Satan whether Job served God gratuitously (1:9), without reward. The irony of the question is that if Job does receive accurate recompense for his piety it calls his piety into question; and if he does not, it calls God's governance of the world into question and lends support to the impious speech of the wicked.

Religious people are often in a double bind over this question of the utility of their religion. On the one hand, they cannot allow that religion is useful, or else they turn it into a mechanism, rather than an end in itself. On the other hand, they cannot accept that it is useless, or else adherence to it seems irrational. It is said of idols that they cannot profit or save (1 Sam 12:21) and that following the Baals is a going after "things that do not profit" (Jer 2:8, 11). The implication is that serving the true God *does* profit. And the people of Israel are reproached by the prophets for claiming that "there is no profit in keeping his commands" (Mal 3:14); the implication must be that, in the prophet's view, keeping God's commands *is* profitable. But the moment anyone says there is a utility in religion, the theologians and commentators (at least) are up in arms. Is this not an example of "bad faith" if such religious leaders are not willing to accept the implications of what they affirm and deny?

16 Job does not begrudge anyone a happy life, not even the wicked. It is not that his own tragedy has embittered him too deeply to rejoice when others are successful and enjoy seeing their children at play and their cattle thriving. What he hates to see about the prosperity of the wicked is the proof it affords that God cares nothing for the moral order of the world. The prosperity of the wicked is "in their own power"; it lies under no threat from a just God. And their plans for their continuing success, indeed for their perpetration of further wickedness, is outwith the scope of the divine concern; the "counsel of the wicked is far from him," and God has not the remotest interest in their plans. So Job's animus is not against the wicked, but against God; and it is not so much that God allows the wicked to prosper (Job never expresses hatred for the Sabeans and Chaldeans that have brought him into misery), but that a God who allows the wicked to prosper is inevitably a God who allows the righteous to suffer.

There are some intertextual references here. Job's word טוב "prosperity," the prosperity of the wicked that they have in their own control, is Eliphaz's word in 20:21, where he affirmed that the "prosperity, produce" of the wicked cannot last (cf. also on 22:18). And "the counsel of the wicked" (עצת רשעים, also in 10:3) may be an allusion to Ps 1:1. There is no verbal allusion to Deut 8:17, where Israel is warned not to say, "My power and the might of my hand have gotten me this wealth," but it is moral exhortation like that, and the idea of divine reward on which it depends, that Job is resisting here.

17–21 What the friends assert as the rule about the fate of the wicked is no more than an occasional occurrence, says Job; so the principle of retribution, which claims a regularity in the moral order of the world, is overturned.

17 Now Job seems to be questioning the assertion of Bildad in 18:5–6, that "the lamp of the wicked will be snuffed out" (Bildad in fact said אור "the light [of the wicked]," in v 5, but in the next verse he spoke of נרו "his lamp"). But Job is not alluding only to Bildad; the phrase is a commonplace in wisdom texts (the same wording in Prov 13:9; 24:20). "Disaster" (איד) is again Bildad's word, from 18:12, where he had personified Disaster as one of the Terrors that wait for the wicked to drag him down into the underworld. How often do the wicked come to an untimely end? asks Job—not denying that it sometimes happens, but implying it is too seldom for any moral principle in God's dealings to be inferred.

18 As in v 16, there seems to be an allusion here to Ps 1, where also the wicked are like chaff (מץ) swept away by the wind (רוח) (1:4). And "the storm sweeps him away" (גנבתו סופה) is a phrase that we will hear again, probably from the mouth of Zophar, in 27:20. In 13:25 Job had compared himself to a "withered straw" (קש) blown by the wind; but what he is, the wicked are not.

The term for straw (תבן) refers to the chopped pieces of straw used as fodder, and in Exod 5:7–18 for reinforcing bricks; elsewhere in metaphorical contexts it represents what is weak (41:19 [27]) or what is worthless (Jer 23:28). Chaff (קש) is finer still, the dust of straw left behind on the threshing floor, a symbol of what is insubstantial and fleeting (cf. 13:25; Isa 17:13; Jer 13:24; Ps 35:5; etc.; see also *Note* on 41:28). Cf. Dalman, *Arbeit und Sitte,* 3:138.

19 Job has been denying that the principle of retribution is valid; but perhaps the friends might reply that the doctrine never said that it was always the wrongdoers themselves that suffered the consequences of their misdeeds; sometimes, at least according to popular versions of the doctrine, the fathers could eat sour grapes and the teeth of the children be set on edge (Jer 31:29; Ezek 18:2; cf. also Exod 20:5; Deut 5:9; 24:16; 2 Kgs 14:6). None of Job's friends has actually advanced this view, indeed; for when Eliphaz in 5:4, Bildad in 18:19, and Zophar in 20:10 (if the text is sound) spoke of the suffering of the wrongdoer's children, they thought of it as an *additional* calamity that befalls the ungodly, not as a substitute for his own suffering. But suppose that someone should attempt to deflect the force of Job's argument by claiming that it is sometimes the children who suffer, not the evildoers themselves; then, says Job, anticipating such an objection (Peake), that is unjust, for it is the evildoer himself who should pay the penalty for his wrong, and should "know" that he is paying it (it is not so much a question of his "experiencing" or "feeling" the punishment, as Driver–Gray thought).

20 We are speaking here of the most elemental moral values, of "tit-for-tat" justice and "fair's fair," so the language becomes the basic, concrete, language of "seeing" and "drinking," first the observation of the disaster as it approaches, and then the full internal experience of it. For Zophar, the fate of the wicked is to become invisible (20:7b–9), for the eye that saw him to see him no more; for Job, the fate of the wicked should be to be fully conscious of all that is happening to him. The idea of drinking God's anger is found also in the image of the cup of the divine wrath in Isa 51:17; Jer 25:15; Ps 75:8 (9); *Pss. Sol.* 8:14; Rev 16:19 (cf. also Job's drinking of the poison on the divine arrows, 6:4). On the image of drinking from a cup, see H. A. Brongers, "Der Zornesbecher," in *The Priestly Code and Seven Other Studies,* by J. G. Vink et al., OTS 15 (Leiden: Brill, 1969) 177–92.

21 Once the wrongdoer is dead he does not even know what is happening to his children (cf. 14:21–22), so their suffering can be no punishment for him. Justice demands that the person who has committed wrong be personally punished for it. The phrase "number of his months" has occurred in 14:5, and "number of years" in 15:20, in neither case with the idea of a predetermined span of life but simply in reference to a whole life as a finite period.

22–26 Any theology that does not take account of the facts is a form of patronizing God. For if we assume that what happens in the world is, broadly speaking, the will of God, any theological schema like the doctrine of retribution that differs from the facts makes God out to be secondary to the schema. What happens in the world must be, according to Job, more or less what God intends, and anyone who pretends to have a better way of running the world is setting out to "teach God knowledge" (v 22).

The fact is that death does not separate the wicked from the righteous. If the doctrine of retribution were true, we would expect to see some differences in the manner of human deaths. All that happens, however, is that people die, regardless of their wealth and happiness or otherwise, and, once dead, there is nothing to distinguish a wicked person from a righteous; alike they lie in dust (v 26). It is noteworthy that Job does not claim that the prosperous of vv 23–24 are the wicked and the bitter of v 25 are the righteous. He is not maintaining that the doctrine of retribution is wholly invalid, and it does not affect his argument if some of the prosperous are also the righteous. What he wants to say here is not so much that the doctrine of retribution is wrong, but that even if it were right it would be irrelevant; for ultimate human fate has nothing to do with morality. "In life no moral differences explain their diversity of fortune; in death as little do they explain their common fate" (Rowley). Death likewise is not a punishment for wickedness, and all the assertions of the doctrine of retribution about the fate of evildoers are false (Fohrer, remarking on *1 En.* 103–104 as an attempted refutation of this section of Job).

22 Some think that the verse is a citation of the friends' view (as has also been claimed for v 19; cf. v 28). Gordis, for example, takes it as meaning that, in the friends' view, Job cannot presume to criticize God and so to teach him knowledge (cf. 4:17; 15:8–14; 11:5–9). To that supposed riposte of the friends Job would be replying that he can in fact teach God something, that the world, with its evident discrepancy between deeds and fate, is not the world God claims it to be. However, it seems preferable to take the sentence as Job's own defense of God against the purely human doctrine of retribution. According to Job, we must assume that God knows what he is doing in not punishing the wicked as they deserve; any dogma that asserts that he does execute retributive justice is really telling him how he should be behaving, and so is "teaching" him "knowledge."

Not only do logic and experience stand opposed to the idea of giving God lessons in theology; such an undertaking would also be an error of proportion. For if God is himself the sovereign disposer of the fortunes even of heavenly beings, it is hardly right for mortals to attempt to give him instruction. For the picture of God as the heavenly judge, cf. Pss 58 and 82:1, where he sits in judgment over those other heavenly beings who are supposed to have judicial powers. שׁפט "judge" may be used here in its more general sense of "decide, dispose affairs" rather than more specifically of legal judgment (cf. also G. Liedke, *TLOT,* 3:1392–99). He is the "highest" God, with lesser deities ranged beneath him. Such a God cannot be "taught" by humans (cf. Isa 40:14).

23–26 These twin pictures of the fate of humans are meant to be as different as possible. The first is of a person whose life is perfection (תם), not in the moral sense like Job himself in 1:1, but in the sense of a full enjoyment of life that yields peace and quiet and security (שלאנן and שליו). Its perfection is the very quintessence of perfection (בעצם תמו, lit. "in the bone of his perfection"). In the antique world of the Job story, such perfect well-being is symbolized by physical qualities: fatness (חֵלֶב, if the text is emended; see *Note* 24.a) and vigor (literally, moistness of one's marrow, מח). On fatness as a sign of physical health, see on 15:27, and contrast Job's own emaciation (19:20; cf. also Ps 73:4, 7). The moistening of the marrow apparently means that "he is refreshed and strengthened" (Peake).

The point is that no matter what human experience of life has been, no matter how diverse, human encounter with death is always the same. If the ultimate fate of humans is the same, and it does not matter in the end whether one has been fortunate or unfortunate, how can there be a principle of retribution at work in the world? Cf. also Eccl 2:15–16. (But this is not a picture of *premature* death, as Hartley thinks.)

26 "Lie down" (שכב) is in Job a common term for death; cf. 3:13; 7:21; 14:12; 20:11 (differently in 7:4; 11:18; 27:19). In 20:11 (Zophar) we have the same phrase "lie down in the dust" (על־עפר שכב; similarly לעפר שכב in 7:21). For the "dust" as the grave, see also 7:21; 17:16; 20:11; 34:15 (and cf. Michel, 97, 113). For worms as the inhabitants of Sheol, see 17:14; Isa 14:11 (Michel thinks the "Worm" is an epithet for Mot, the god of death, or even Leviathan, as supposedly at 7:5).

27–34 In his assault on the doctrine of retribution Job has now argued that the wicked do not live unhappy lives, as the doctrine teaches (vv 7–13), that their godlessness goes unpunished (vv 14–18), that the apparent invalidity of the doctrine of retribution cannot be evaded by arguing that it is the descendants of the evildoer who suffer (vv 19–21), and that even if the doctrine were true it would be irrelevant to most of human life, since everyone has a common fate in death (vv 22–26). Now he asks where the evidence comes from for this traditional doctrine, and whether the testimony of those with experience of life does not point altogether in the opposite direction.

In fact, says Job, if you ask those who travel around and have a wide knowledge of human destinies, you will find that everywhere wrongdoers come to no harm; rather, they prosper, in life and in death, and they gain great reputations.

This long strophe is framed by two sentences, which enclose two substrophes of three lines each, directly addressed to the friends and their intentions (vv 27, 34). The closure of these two principal substrophes is marked by the tricolon in v 33, to which the final verse of the speech (v 34) is attached as a pendant.

27 Job's thought here needs a little unraveling. The friends of course do not think they are using violence (חמס) against Job with their speeches, and they would not accept that their arguments are "schemes" or "plots" (מזמות) they are devising against him. Each has his own distinctive position, and they do not all think that Job is a great sinner; Eliphaz in particular is more determined to give Job encouragement than to accuse him. But Job maintains that so long as they advance the doctrine of retribution—even if they do not go so far as to draw from it the conclusion that Bildad does, that Job is a great sinner, suffering at this moment for his deeds—they put him in the wrong. No matter how you modulate it, the dogma says that the wicked are punished and the innocent rewarded. Job is certainly not being rewarded, and the dogma can therefore only mean that in some degree or other he is a sinner. And that inference, he says, is an act of violence against his innocence. Moreover, anyone who adopts that line of reasoning can only do so out of spiteful motives as part of a hostile plot against him. Job is being paranoid about the friends' motives, of course, and the complexity of thinking that the term "schemes" (מזמה) implies is not all on the friends' side. But he is not wrong about the logical implications of their teaching.

How can he be so sure about what they are thinking ("I know your thoughts")? Only because he himself has had the very same thoughts in his time. He too has belonged to the company of the wise and has been an adherent of the traditional dogmas; all that was included in the opening panegyric about him, that he was a perfect man who feared God and eschewed evil (1:1). In the world of the story, at least of the story of the prologue, there is no other way of doing that than to subscribe to orthodox opinion. Since his experience has led him to assail orthodoxy, he is not a pious man any longer in the traditional sense, and the misgivings of the friends are in a way fully justified.

28 To get to the point: the friends have always implied that evildoers come to an unhappy end. That is one of the primary implicates of their doctrine of retribution. They have never said the exact words that Job puts in their mouth here, "Where is the house of the prince?" but that is a fair enough paraphrase of their argument. Bildad has said that the "dwelling of the evildoer" becomes the dwelling place of fire (18:15; cf. Eliphaz in 15:34), and Zophar that a flood sweeps away his house (20:28). Asking "where" (איה) the house or tent is implies of course that it has disappeared (cf. איה in 14:10; 20:7), which is to say, through an act of divine retributive justice.

At first sight it is strange that the "wicked" (רע) in the second half of the line should be paralleled by the "prince" (נדיב) in the first half. Are "princes" necessarily wrongdoers? And, for that matter, are not Job and his friends rather in the class of princes themselves? It is true that "prince" is not used elsewhere in such a pejorative sense; princes are nobles of the Israelite people (Num 21:18) and of other godfearing nations (Ps 47:9 [10]), honored rulers (1 Sam 2:8; Ps 113:8; cf. Prov 17:26) who are given their position by God (Prov 8:16). Of course, like all powerful people, they are prey to temptation, and their power is sometimes contrasted with the superior might of Yahweh, who "pours contempt upon princes" who happen to get in his way (12:21; Ps 107:40). And compared with taking refuge in Yahweh, it is not recommended to put one's trust in princes (Pss 118:9; 146:3). The world of the Job story is not, however, the workaday world of ancient monarchic Israel. It is rather a fairy-tale world, of rustic charm and simplicity, a patriarchal world where the best a man can aspire to is old age surrounded by numerous descendants (v 8), an untroubled agricultural existence with the certainty that the bulls will breed without fail and the cows will not cast their calves (v 10). In that world, the figure of the "prince" is somewhat alien. He is the independent leader and master of men, whose life is played out in the public domain (Fohrer), the grand seigneur (de Wilde). If he is here said to live in a "tent" (אהל), that is only because the archaic story world of the book requires that everyone be depicted as seminomads (see on 5:24); in reality, he is the kind of ruler who rebuilds famous ruins for himself (3:14). The military aspects of the function of the "prince" (see on 12:21) are probably in mind also, so he represents something of an antithesis to a pacific pastoralist like Job. He is the kind of man who is followed about by retainers (v 33), the kind of man for whom, when he is carried to his grave, watch is kept over his tomb (v 32). Job is of course no nonentity himself, he is not without his own form of authority in his community (chap. 29); but it has been earned not by military prowess and lavish spending but by social compassion (29:12–27).

29 It is typical of Job that he wants to bring dogma to the bar of reason. There is no point in pontificating about the fate of the wicked in general terms if the empirical evidence does not support it. In a largely preliterate society, recourse cannot be had to books for knowledge of the world of humans; travelers are the source of knowledge about the world outside one's own little community, the "news service of antiquity" (de Wilde). Such travelers will be the unprejudiced observers, who bring "signs" (אות) home with them, either souvenirs from strange places or, more probably, their travelers' tales about monuments and memorials to famous tyrants, stories of successful villainy (Ball); Duhm imagines, for example, the effect of a report to postexilic Jews of the splendid tomb of Nebuchadnezzar in Babylon despite the fact that he was the destroyer of the temple in Jerusalem. Such travelers will be the ones to confirm or deny the friends' assertions about evildoers. Cf. Lam 1:12, where travelers are invited to say whether they have ever seen so great a disaster as the fall of Jerusalem, and Ecclus 34:10 "he that has traveled acquires much cleverness" (cf. also Ecclus 34:11–12; 43:24; and cf. Odysseus's experience acquired by travel, in *Odyssey* 1.1–3; Eliphaz seems to have expressed a more xenophobic attitude to travelers in 15:19). The term "signs" or "marks" reminded Dhorme, rather romantically, of the graffiti to be seen on rocks beside roads in the Sinai, on which "tramps or wandering labourers, who go from town to town . . . [would] write their names and their thoughts." But it is hard to see how Job's friends would "recognize" (נכר piel) these marks, and equally doubtful that the fate of the wicked would be the subject of such graffiti.

30 Has Job himself been questioning passing travelers and tinkers, we wonder, that he knows what they have to report? Or is all this counterclaim of his no less rhetorical and fictive than the dogma of the friends? No matter; Job maintains that the evidence is that notorious wrongdoers do not succumb to divine punishment, but are spared, as if they were themselves the righteous under the watchful eye of the deity. The day of "wrath" must be the day of divine wrath, not some eschatological day but a time of natural catastrophe such as an earthquake, famine, warfare, or the like. For a "day of calamity" (יום איד), cf. Deut 32:35; Jer 18:17; and for the "day of wrath" (יום עברה), cf. Ezek 7:19; Zeph 1:15, 18; Prov 11:4.

31 Not only is the wicked man not brought to a sudden end by God, he is not even disapproved of by his fellows. He is a tyrant, and no one has dared to reproach him "to his face" (cf. Ps 73:10 RSV; and contrast Job in 13:15, who proposes defending himself "to his [God's] face").

32–33 This is a grandee, who is being buried in a richly decorated tomb. The burial mound raised above him, formed of clods of earth taken from a nearby wadi, is a sign to acquaintances and passersby alike that this was a man of significance. Rather than having his memory obliterated, as Bildad had affirmed of the evildoer, he achieves a perpetual memorial (contrast the humiliation of not being buried, in Isa 14:19–20; Jer 22:19). Life has been so comfortable for him, it has to be assumed that death will be as pleasant. Such a wrongdoer will not disgorge his gains nor fail to find pleasure in the fruit of his wrongdoing (as Zophar had said in 20:18). For such a man as this, even the soil that covers him will be "sweet" (מתק). The usual human condition after death, as Job has said in 14:21–22, is that one "feels only one's own pain"; for this man, however, the only postmortem feeling is delight. He will lie in death in pleasant fertile soil beside a river (Gordis); in life too he had never had to wrest a living out of stony uplands. "May the earth lie light upon you" (*sit tibi terra levis*), the Romans said at a burial (cf. Euripides, *Alcestis* 463). But this man has no need of such good wishes; his fate is assured, that after his death he will enjoy an underworld existence of peace and quiet. So does everyone, of course, according to Job (3:17–19), but he will have more than mere absence of trouble; he will find the afterlife positively pleasant. By a strange twist of fate, this sentence about the postmortem existence of the evildoer became part of the liturgy of the festivals of the first Christian martyr Stephen, "The stones of the brook are sweet to him; all just souls follow after him" (cf. A. Vaccari, "Ad 'Carmina Scripturarum' symbolae," *Bib* 3 [1922] 50–52 [51]; F.-M. Abel, "Lapides torrentis," *RB* 32 [1923] 598–601).

Why does his tomb need a watch to be kept over it? It is perhaps not so much an act of honor, like the guarding of the tomb of the unknown warrior or Lenin's tomb (Delitzsch refers to the Muslim custom of appointing servants to tend the tomb of a honored man), but as a protection against grave robbers. This is a wealthy man, and everyone will know that there are precious objects buried with him. Many tombs in antiquity carried an inscription invoking curses on grave robbers (cf. the elaborate invocations on the sarcophagus of Eshmunazar, *ANET,* 662), but this former tyrant has made better arrangements for the security of his tomb: he has left money for guards to be posted. For an earlier reference to grave robbing, cf. on 3:21. Hölscher, however, thinks the reference is to the performance of offerings and libations at the tomb. See also A. Musil, *Arabia Petraea* (Vienna: Hölder, 1908) 414.

On burial practices, see W. L. Reed, *IDB,* 1:474–76; E. Bloch-Smith, *Judahite Burial Practices and Beliefs about the Dead,* JSOTSup 123 (Sheffield: JSOT Press, 1992), and cf. Eccl 8:10. It is a little strange that the picture of the funeral procession (v 33b, c) follows the reference to the soil in which he is buried being sweet to him. But it is understandably one conglomerate image. There is little merit in the view of Peters, that the crowds accompanying the deceased man were denizens of the underworld. Fohrer thought there might be a reference to a practice like the Indian suttee, when wives and servants of the dead ruler are put to death along with him (cf. A. Scharff and A. Moortgat, *Ägypten und Vorderasien in Altertum* [Munich: Bruckmann, 1950] 45, 249–51). Not in the least probable is the idea that reference is made to people who follow his way of life (Renan, *il entraine le monde entier à sa suite;* Pope: those who "imitate the defunct one's mode of life") or to the fact that everyone must ultimately follow him in death (Le Hir, Hartley).

34 Finally, Job turns again to the friends, to whom he addressed himself directly in the opening verses. There he had said that the best comfort they could offer him would be to "listen to [his] words." That would not itself be a consolation, but it would be better than ramming their dogma down his throat. So, now that we have got to the end of the speech, and they have let him have his say, why does he round on them, and demand, "Why do you offer me empty consolations?" Is he not being churlish?

It must be that all that they have said still rankles with him. They have said, all of them, in one way or another, that he is a wrongdoer. But they have no evidence for that; their judgment of him is based solely on a theory about the way the world works, the dogma of retribution. Now that he has argued that the dogma is proved false by the countervailing evidence from the life-history of the typical evildoer, it follows that everything they have said is nugatory, which is exactly what הבל "vanity, emptiness" means. They thought they were offering him comfort because, while assuming that he was a wrongdoer in some degree or other, they were assuring him that he was redeemable and reformable. But he does not call their words "comfort" at all; the friends call their speeches "consolations," but Job calls them lies. The phrase "comfort with emptiness" occurs also at Zech 10:2.

No, it is not quite right that their speeches are entirely nugatory (הבל). However devoid of real "consolation" they have been, there is a residue (שׁאר) in them of what Job here calls "faithlessness." He could mean by that term that he feels let down by the friends, as in 6:14–21, where he accuses them of lack of loyalty (חסד) and of "treachery" (בגד). But it is perhaps more likely that he means they are being irreligious, for the term "faithlessness" (מעל) is commonly used elsewhere of disloyalty to God (R. Knierim, *TLOT,* 2:680–82; H. Ringgren, *TDOT,* 8:460–63). If they have been misrepresenting the ways of God with humans, and claiming that he rules the world according to a principle of strict and exact retribution when the opposite is the case, they are guilty of disloyalty to him, of the kind of breach of religious obligation that worshipers of foreign deities are often accused of elsewhere in the Bible. (It is not so much that "their interpretation is disloyal to the facts," as Dhorme puts it, but rather that their answers are "an act of faithlessness against the truth and by that token against God" [Gordis].) It is ironic that these paragons of religious orthodoxy should be, by Job's lights, no better than syncretists and Baal worshipers. But that is all that remains of their "responses" (תשׁובה) when their professed "consolations" (נחם) have been discounted: a deep strain of impiety!

Explanation

This has been a disappointing speech, coming from Job, for it has lacked the fire of his earlier speeches, and it has taken on the timbre of the friends' lamer, less passionate, more didactic speeches. It has so little color compared with his picture of God's loving nurture and sinister design in chap. 10, or with the contrast between human hopelessness and the hope of the tree in chap. 14. Nothing comes to life here except perhaps, for a moment, the image of the evildoer surrounded by his dancing children (v 11) or the pompous ceremony of his burial (vv 32–33). Job has determined, for the first time, to answer the friends according to their folly, and he has of necessity taken up their windy rhetoric and dreary didacticism.

But if the poetry is tame, the ideas are not. In this speech Job (and the author of the book) shows us that he still has some ideas to shock us with. The first is the primary subject of the speech: the fact that evildoers do not receive punishment for their wrong but rather prosper. This is not a completely new idea for Job, for in 12:6 he has inferred from his own dismal experience as a righteous man that "the tents of robbers are at peace, and those who provoke God are secure"—presumably since not everyone is in the kind of trouble Job is experiencing and evidently it is righteous people who are doing the suffering in the world. But that verse is the only time Job has focused upon the fate of the wicked. His almost exclusive concern has been himself, and the meaning of the suffering that he as an innocent man is experiencing. What he has decided about that is that there are two facts that cannot be subordinated to one another: he is righteous and he is suffering—at God's hand, for no one else is ultimately responsible for what happens. The existence of those facts proves that the traditional dogma of retribution is in error, for the righteous man that he is should, according to the dogma, be rewarded with prosperity and not with suffering.

But that is only one side of the doctrine. Now, for the first time, he considers the situation of the wicked. Here is no passing allusion to the topic (as in 12:6), but a thorough investigation of it. If you consider what happens to the wicked, says Job, leaving aside the fate of the righteous, what you find is that the wicked prosper. This is not Job's invention. The psalmists knew it was true, and they complained about it and asked God to stop it being true. Job, however, is concerned not to *change* the way things are but rather to *understand* them. He is not appealing to God to give the unjust their deserts; rather, he is drawing the implications of the facts for his theology.

If it is true, he means to say, that the wicked do not live unhappy lives (vv 5–13), that their godlessness goes unpunished (vv 14–18), that the visitation of retribution on the descendants of evildoers is not a confirmation but a denial of the doctrine (vv 19–21), that even if the dogma were true it would be irrelevant, since everyone has a common fate in death (vv 22–26), and above all that the evidence from experience is contrary to the doctrine of retribution, for even notable sinners flourish and are respected after their death (vv 27–33)—if all of that is true, then the doctrine of retribution collapses on that front also, just as it has already collapsed on the side of the fate of the innocent. And if there is no retribution, we live in an amoral universe where act has no relation to consequence and where nothing can be justified in terms of its outcome.

No one these days wants a doctrine of retribution as simplistic as that advocated by Job's friends, but what Job puts in its place is scary. If Job is right, there is no moral order at all and your moral behavior or otherwise will have no effect on your well-being. This is the challenge Job's speech brings, not just to the religious believer, but to any person with moral values. Inculcated in all of us is the belief that certain behavior is not just right in itself but beneficial, and even that the rewards that certain moral behavior entails constitute some kind of authentication of the value of that behavior. If Job is correct, there is indeed a right and a wrong, but no one should imagine that doing the right and eschewing the wrong is going to yield any benefit; if anything, it is wrongdoing that yields the greatest benefits.

Can we evade the force of Job's position by observing that he, no less than the friends, is trading entirely in generalities, casting everything entirely in black and white? Not really, for it is quintessential to the doctrine of retribution that it has general applicability. If it cannot be relied on but is only sometimes, or even often, true, it loses its meaning, for it claims to be an account of necessary relations between act and consequence. If, on the other hand, Job is right that there is no necessary relation between act and consequence, it does not matter for his theory that sometimes good deeds have good results and bad deeds bad, for his theory can always maintain that those results are coincidental. There is, of course, available to us a way of evading Job's position that he could not have dreamed of: we can say that the mismatch between act and consequence that he observed is correct, but that the doctrine of retribution is not thereby challenged, for acts will all have their proper consequences ultimately, namely *in the afterlife*. The fact that such a revision of the theory cannot be tested empirically will not worry some people, but it will damn it for others.

The second point at which this speech of Job addresses a fundamental question about ethics and religion is the sentence ascribed to the evildoers in v 15b, "What gain shall we have if we pray to him?" (see also on 22:2). The text presents this as a cynical and self-regarding utterance of those who do not "desire the knowledge of your [God's] ways" (v 14b). But the question resonates beyond the context of the quoted speech and provokes the further question whether it would be *good* to believe that some "gain" results from piety. We recollect that Job himself does not seem to have benefited from all his scrupulous piety, rather the reverse; and we recall that the whole story of Job takes its rise in the question whether Job's piety is in fact gratuitous. If the pious person wants to insist that prayer is not offered for the sake of "gain" and piety is an obligation regardless of any profit, why are the evildoers being castigated here for their question, "What gain shall we have?" And especially if the evildoers are constituted as evildoers just because they say such things (any actual wrongdoing on their part is conspicuous by its absence from this chapter), what is the difference between the righteous and the wicked?

Job's speech does no more than allow these questions to be raised. They are tangential to the primary purpose of the book, which concerns the problem of the injustice Job is suffering. But as the obverse of the issues the figure of Job raises, perhaps they deserve a sequel to the book of Job all to themselves.

Eliphaz's Third Speech (22:1–30)

Bibliography

Berger-Lutz, R. "Hart beschuldigt—doch nicht verstummt: Elifas und Hiob (Hiob 22 und 23)." In *Hiob: Ökumenischer Arbeitskreis für Bibelarbeit.* Ed. R. Berger-Lutz. Bibelarbeit in der Gemeinde 7. Basel: Reinhardt, 1989. 244–60. **Bishai, W. B.** "Notes on HSKN in Job 22.21." *JNES* 20 (1961) 258–60. **Caquot, A.** "Traits royaux dans le personnage de Job." In *Maqqēl shâqēdh, La branche d'amandier.* FS W. Vischer. Montpellier: Causse, Graille, Castelnau, 1960. 32–45. **Chajes, H. P.** "Note lessicali a proposito della nuova edizione del Gesenius-Buhl." *GSAI* 19 (1906) 175–86. **Dahood, M. J.** "The Metaphor in Job 22, 22." *Bib* 47 (1966) 108–9. ———. "Northwest Semitic Philology and Job." In *The Bible in Current Catholic Thought: Gruenthaner Memorial Volume.* Ed. J. L. McKenzie. St. Mary's Theological Studies 1. New York: Herder & Herder, 1962. 55–74. ———. "Punic *hkkbm 'l* and Isa 14,13." *Or* 34

(1965) 170–72. **Gordis, R.** "Corporate Personality in Job: A Note on 22:29–30." *JNES* 4 (1945) 54–55. Reprinted in *The Word and the Book: Studies in Biblical Language and Literature* (New York: Ktav, 1976) 133–34. **Guillaume, A.** "Metallurgy in the Old Testament." *PEQ* 94 (1962) 128–32. **Hermisson, H.-J.** "Von Gottes und Hiobs Nutzen: Zur Auslegung von Hiob 22." *ZTK* 93 (1996) 331–51. Reprinted in *Studien zu Prophetie und Weisheit: Gesammelte Aufsätze,* ed. J. Barthel, H. Jauss, and K. Koenen, FAT 23 (Tübingen: Mohr Siebeck, 1998) 300–319. **Jirku, A.** "Eine Renaissance des Hebräischen." *FF* 32 (1958) 211–12. **Kuhl, C.** "Neuere Literarkritik des Buches Hiob." *TRu* NS 21 (1953) 163–205, 257–317. **Morrow, F. J.** "11 Q Targum Job and the Massoretic Text." *RevQ* 8 (1972–75) 253–56. **Redditt, P. L.** "Reading the Speech Cycles in the Book of Job." *HAR* 14 (1994) (= *Biblical and Other Studies in Honor of Reuben Ahroni, on the Occasion of His Sixtieth Birthday,* ed. T. J. Lewis [Columbus: Melton Center for Jewish Studies, Ohio State Univ., 1994]) 205–14. **Sarna, N. M.** "A *Crux Interpretum* in Job 22:30 'ימלא אי־נקי'." *JNES* 15 (1956) 118–19. **Thexton, C.** "A Note on Job xxii. 30." *ExpTim* 78 (1966–67) 342–43. **Wieder, A. A.** "Three Philological Notes." *BIJS* 2 (1974) 102–9. **Witte, M.** *Philologische Notizen zu Hiob 21–27.* BZAW 234. Berlin: de Gruyter, 1995. ———. *Vom Leiden zur Lehre: Der dritte Redegang (Hiob 21–27) und die Redaktionsgeschichte des Hiobbuches.* BZAW 230. Berlin: de Gruyter, 1994. **Wolfers, D.** "Job: The Third Cycle: Dissipating a Mirage." *DD* 16 (1987–88) 217–26; 17 (1988–89) 19–25.

Translation

1 *Then Eliphaz the Temanite answered and said:*

2 *Can a human*[a] *be profitable*[b] *to God?*
  [c]*Can*[d] *even a sage*[e] *benefit*[f] *him?*[g]
3 *Is it an asset to the Almighty if*[a] *you are righteous?*
  Does he gain if your conduct is blameless?[b]
4 *So is it because of your piety*[a] *that he reproves you,*
  and enters into judgment with you?
5 *Is it not for your great wickedness,*[a]
  for your endless iniquities?

6 [a]*You must have been taking*[b] *pledges from your kinsfolk*[c] *without cause,*
  stripping them naked of their clothing.[d]
7 *You must have even been refusing water*[a] *to the weary,*[b]
  denying bread to the hungry,
8 [a]*as if the land belonged to the powerful,*[b]
  as if only the privileged[c] *should occupy it.*
9 *You must have sent widows away empty,*
  you must have let the strength of orphans be crushed.[a]
10 [a]*That is why snares are all about you,*
  and sudden terror[b] *affrights*[c] *you,*
11 *why darkness*[a] *so that you cannot see,*[b]
  why a flood of waters covers you.

12 [a]*Is not God in the heights of the heavens?*[b]
  Does he not look down[c] *on the topmost stars,*[d] *high as they are?*[e]
13 [a]*Yet you say,*[b] *"What does God know?*
  Can he see through thick cloud to govern?

[14]*Thick clouds veil him, and he cannot see*
as he goes his way on the vault of heaven!"[a]
[15]*Will you keep to*[a] *the ancient*[b] *path,*
which[c] *evildoers have trodden,*
[16]*who were shriveled up*[a] *before their time,*[b]
whose foundations were swept away by a flood?[c]
17 [a]*They had said to God, "Depart from us,"*
and "What can the Almighty[b] *do for us?"*[c]
18 [a]*Yet he had filled their houses with prosperity,*
though the plans of the wicked[b] *were far from him.*[c]
[19]*When the righteous saw*[a] *it, they were glad;*
the innocent laughed at them with scorn:
20 [a]*"See how*[b] *their possessions*[c] *have been destroyed!*
See how their wealth[d] *has been consumed by the fire!"*

[21]*Come to terms*[a] *with him, and*[b] *be at peace;*[c]
prosperity[d] *will come to you thereby.*[e]
[22]*Receive instruction from his mouth,*
and lay up[a] *his words in your heart.*
[23]*If you will turn to*[a] *the Almighty,*[b] *you will be restored,*[c]
[d]*and wickedness will remove far*[e] *from your tent.*
24 [a]*You will regard*[b] *gold*[c] *as*[d] *dust,*
gold of Ophir[e] *like the stones*[f] *of the wadi.*
[25]*And the Almighty will be your gold,*[a]
and he will be a mound[b] *of silver for you.*[c]
26 [a]*Then*[b] *you will take delight*[c] *in the Almighty,*
and you will be able to lift your head in God's presence.[d]
[27]*You will pray to him, and he will hear you,*
and you will be able to pay[a] *your vows.*
[28]*Once you decide*[a] *a matter, it will succeed for you,*
and light will shine on your paths.
29 [a]*For God humbles the one who speaks boastfully,*
but he saves[b] *the lowly.*[c]
[30]*He delivers the innocent,*[a]
and by the cleanness of your hands[b] *you will be delivered.*[c]

Notes

2.a. גבר is usually "man" as distinct from "woman" (cf. *DCH,* 2:313), but a gendered term is inappropriate here; we should understand it as "human" (for other examples of גבר as "one," cf. 34:9; Prov 28:21; Lam 3:1), thus NJB "a human being," NRSV "mortal," REB "anyone." It is sometimes said to mean specifically humans in opposition to God (so, e.g., Budde, Fohrer, comparing 16:21), but any word for "human" can be used in such a sense. Terrien wants it to mean a "strong man, a superman, the most vigorous specimen of virility" (cf. H. Kosmala, *TDOT,* 2:377–78), but that too goes far beyond what the term itself can convey. See *Comment* on 3:3.

2.b. E. Lipiński ("*skn* et *sgn* dans le sémitique occidental du nord," *UF* 5 [1973] 191–207 [191–92]) claims that סכן in four occurrences in Job (15:3; 22:2; 34:9; 35:3) means "run a danger" (cf. Aram. סכן; such a סכן II is acknowledged by BDB, 698a, for Eccl 10:9, though *HALOT,* 2:755a, surprisingly reckons it just another sense of סכן "be of use"; see also *DCH,* vol. 6, *s.v.*) and translates "Can a man endanger God?" (followed by Habel).

2.c. This second colon could perhaps be taken as RSV "Surely he who is wise is profitable to himself"; cf. NJB "when even someone intelligent can benefit only himself," NAB "Though to himself a wise man be profitable!" Similarly Duhm, Driver–Gray, Dhorme, Fohrer. But NRSV prefers the alternative, "Can even the wisest be of service to him?"; similarly NJPS, NIV, Sicre Díaz, and this certainly suits the parallelism better.

2.d. The double question is prefaced by הֲ in the first colon and כי in the second (an anomaly, since it is usually ה and אם; see GKC, §150h). But כי could also be a "strengthening particle" (de Wilde; cf. BDB, 472a §1d).

2.e. For "sage" as an intensification of "human," see also 37:24.

2.f. סכן occurs in both cola of the line. Gordis (followed by Hartley) argues that in the second colon it is another סכן, equivalent to postbib. Heb. סכם "agree," and translates "is in harmony [with God]" (cf. *DCH*, vol. 6, *s.v.*). But the supposition of a Heb. verb not attested elsewhere in Semitic and only as a "metaplastic form" of a later Heb. word is not strong. The parallel with Job 34:9, where Elihu quotes Job, and the use of the verb in v 21 do not amount to evidence of this claimed meaning. The sense "gain control, gain an advantage," proposed by B. A. Levine, *Numbers 21–36*, AB 4A (New York: Doubleday, 2000) 158, for סכן qal, does not seem appropriate here.

2.g. עלימו, usually "to them," must be a form of עָלָיו "to him, to himself" (as at 20:23 [*q.v.*]; 27:23; cf. GKC, §103f n. 3; Gerleman [*BHS*]). Some actually emend to עליו (Bickell [עלו], Duhm, Hölscher, Fohrer, NAB); it is no solution to emend יסכן to יִסְכְּנוּ "they profit" (Merx). The על must be equivalent to the ל in the first colon. Habel reads עוֹלָם "the Eternal One," taking the ל in the first colon as a double-duty prefix implied before this term also.

3.a. כי is represented lit. by KJV "Is it any pleasure to the Almighty, that thou art righteous?" (cf. JPS), and perhaps NJB "Does Shaddai derive any benefit from your uprightness?" But while Eliphaz is not denying that Job is righteous, his point here is not to stress that general truth but to insist that Job has committed wrongs; so כי is best taken as the "when" that amounts to an "if" (cf. BDB, 473a §2b; *DCH*, 4:386b §5).

3.b. כי־תתם דרכיך, lit. "if you make your ways perfect." The idiom is unique in the Hebrew Bible (though תם דרך "perfection of way" is found at 4:6 and תם דרך "perfect of way" at Prov 13:6), but it is well attested at Qumran, at 1QS 8:25; 10:21; 11:7; 1QH 12:32; etc. On the form תַּתֵּם, impf hiph of תמם "be perfect," see GKC, §67g. The doubling of the first consonant of double *ayin* verbs is often called an Aramaism, but even if it is, no dating consequences should be drawn. Hartley thinks this a declarative hiph, and translates "you claim that your ways are blameless."

4.a. יראתך "your fear [of God]"; I do not find here a double entendre with the meaning "[God's] fear of you" (cf. KJV "Will he reprove thee for fear of thee?"), as Habel suggests, a meaning, he says, "fraught with bold sarcasm."

5.a. הלא רעתך רבה, lit. "is not your wickedness great?" The *Translation* aims to display v 5 as the antithesis of v 4 (Dhorme, arguing that מן "from, because of" in v 4 in a causal sense enables כי to be understood in v 5, i.e., "is it not because your wickedness is great?").

6.a. The initial כי indicates that what follows in vv 6–9 is epexegetical of v 5; it is כי *explicativum* (BDB, 473b §3c).

6.b. תחבל is an ordinary impf, and the modal verb in the translation ("must be taking"), as with the other verbs in vv 6–9, attempts to reflect the exegesis suggested in the *Comment*. The verbs are all impfs, except in v 9a. The impf no doubt expresses repeated action in the past.

6.c. Lit. "your brothers." Some MSS, followed by Budde, read the sg אָחִיךָ "your brother," but the meaning is the same.

6.d. Lit. "you are stripping off the garments of the naked," proleptically, for they must be naked *after* their garments are stripped off (cf. Hos 2:5 [3]). It is true that "naked" can mean "without the usual outer garments" (as may be the case in Isa 20:2–3; 58:7; Ezek 18:7), and so the line could possibly refer to taking off the undergarments of those who are already "naked," i.e., without their cloak (סִמְלָה) (so Rosenmüller, Delitzsch, Budde, Duhm, Fohrer), but this is an unnecessary refinement.

7.a. Lit. "not water you make the thirsty drink," מים "water," being before the verb by way of stressing how slight a gift is being denied (GKC, §152e).

7.b. עיף is properly "weary" (KJV, JPS, RSV, Moffatt, NEB, NIV), though most prefer "thirsty" here (though even in Isa 29:8 and Prov 25:25, the nearest examples, it does not certainly mean "thirsty," despite Gordis; Esau's "weariness" calls out for food, not water, in Gen 25:30; in Jer 31:25 it may be for food or water). צָמֵא is the normal word for "thirsty" (as at 5:5).

8.a. The line certainly seems out of place. Not only does it break the flow of the accusations, all framed similarly in the 2d person, but it is very hard to interpret. Siegfried, Budde, and Peake regard it as a gloss. Kissane moved it to follow v 14. The "as if" at the beginning of the line in the *Translation* follows NAB, which thus links v 8 with v 7. More commonly, v 8 is regarded as a separate charge against Job, e.g., NJB "[you have] handed the land over to a strong man, for some favoured person to move in" (cf. RSV, NJPS, Dhorme). Others find here a reference to Job as himself the "strong man" who has seized the land of the poor (Delitzsch, Davidson, Dillmann, Duhm, Strahan, Driver–Gray, Habel); but does this not put God in the wrong for allowing it to happen (Budde)? NIV takes the line rather differently, in reference to Job himself: "though you were a powerful man, owning land—an honoured man, living on it" (cf. JPS). And NEB makes it an independent rhetorical question: "Is the earth, then, the preserve of the strong and a domain for the favoured few?"

Gordis took the verse as a quotation of supposed words of Job: "For you believe, 'The man of violence owns the land...'" (cf. also Hartley). This has effectively the same meaning as the rendering proposed in the *Translation* (similarly Fohrer). Coincidentally, the Qumran Tg begins the verse with ואמרת "and you say," which may lend Gordis some support (but see Pope). De Wilde thinks the verse

WORD
BIBLICAL
COMMENTARY

noun, "height," with a ב understood before it; it would then be an accus of place (GKC, §118g; Gordis), like מָרוֹם "[on] high" in Isa 40:26. M. Dahood saw here a divine title, גבה שמים "the Lofty One of Heaven" ("Punic *hkkbm 'l* and Isa 14,13," *Or* 34 [1965] 170–72 [171]; *Psalms I*, 62), reading גְּבֹהַּ for MT גֹּבַהּ.

12.c. Reading רְאֵה "see!" as יִרְאֶה (e.g., Beer [*BH*² *vel*], Kissane, NAB) or רֹאֶה ("the see-er of," ptcp, constr; Michaelis, Siegfried) or רָאֹה (inf abs; so Ehrlich, Stevenson) or רָאָה (Graetz), "he sees" (cf. LXX μὴ οὐχὶ ὁ τὰ ὑψηλὰ ναίων ἐφορᾷ "does not the one who dwells in the heights see?"), or וְרָאָה "and he sees" (Beer [*BH*² *vel*]); so Peake, JB, NEB. Dhorme, however, retains the MT (as KJV, RSV, NJPS, NAB, NIV). Dahood ("Punic *hkkbm 'l*," 171) finds another divine title here, רֹאֶה "the One Who Sees" (see *Note* 12.b on "heights of the heavens").

12.d. Lit. "the head of the stars" (ראש כוכבים), an unparalleled expression. Gordis suggested it was the "troop of stars," comparing ראש in 1:17 for "band, troop." Budde thought it was perhaps the "pole star," the axis of the heavens, but he wondered if ראש were not simply a mistaken dittograph of ראה, the previous word; similarly Driver–Gray, Hölscher, Sicre Díaz. Beer (*BHK*) proposed reading ראש as שׁוּר "see!" and deleting וראה.

12.e. רָמּוּ, with *dagesh affectuosum* (GKC, §20i). JB, NJB (but not BJ), following Larcher (who, however, decides that the clause is a gloss), read כִּי־רָמּוּ "that they are high" as כִּי רָם הוּא "because he is up there" and attach the clause to the beginning of v 13; this is very unconvincing, for it would require the deletion of the ו of ואמרת, and it would make v 13 far too long.

13.a. Vv 13–16 are missing from LXX, perhaps in order to portray Job in a more favorable light (Fohrer).

13.b. ואמרת, with *waw* consec and frequentative force, "you are in the habit of saying" (cf. GKC, §112m).

14.a. חוג שמים is an adv acc.

15.a. NEB "Consider the course of the wicked man" takes שמר, usually "keep," in the sense of "observe," which is hard to parallel (observing prudence, justice, etc., as in Hos 12:7, Isa 56:1, is a different sense of "observe"; cf. BDB, 1037a).

15.b. H. P. Chajes ("Note lessicali a proposito della nuova edizione del Gesenius-Buhl," *GSAI* 19 [1906] 175–86 [182–83]), Tur-Sinai, de Wilde, and NEB suggested emending עולם "eternity" to עַוָּלִים or עַוָּלָם (Chajes) or עֲוִלִים (Ball) "the wicked."

M. J. Dahood ("Northwest Semitic Philology and Job," in *The Bible in Current Catholic Thought: Gruenthaner Memorial Volume*, ed. J. L. McKenzie, St. Mary's Theological Studies 1 [New York: Herder & Herder, 1962] 55–74 [65–66]), however, found here another Heb. word, עלם "darkness" (which he did not vocalize), comparing Ugar. *ǵlm* "be dark" (so too Blommerde [vocalizing עוֹלָם], Pope "the dark path," and Hartley "the hidden path"; cf. *DCH*, vol. 6, *s.v.*); Dahood originally connected the word with עלם "conceal" as well as with Ugar. (as also in "Canaanite-Phoenician Influence in Qoheleth," *Bib* 33 [1952] 30–52, 191–221 [206]), but it seems rather to be a distinct word. Dahood saw the same word also in Eccl 3:11 and a verb עלם "be dark," possibly to be found in 6:16 and 42:3 (cf. *HALOT*, 2:835a; *DCH*, vol. 6, *s.v.*); but see further on 6:16. J. J. Scullion ("Some Difficult Texts in Isaiah cc.56–66 in the Light of Modern Scholarship," *UF* 4 [1972] 105–28 [115]) suggested the same word for Isa 58:7. The existence of a Ugar. *ǵlm* "be dark" remains questionable, however; cf. D. J. A. Clines, "The Etymology of Hebrew צֶלֶם," *JNSL* 3 (1974) 19–25 (24); reprinted in *On the Way to the Postmodern: Old Testament Essays, 1967–1998*, JSOTSup 293 (Sheffield: Sheffield Academic Press, 1998) 2:577–84 (583).

15.c. Chajes, "Note lessicali," 178 (אֲשֻׁר), Pope, Blommerde (אֲשֻׁר), de Wilde read אשר as אָשׁוּר or אֲשֻׁר "path," parallel to ארח "way" in the first colon.

16.a. On this sense for קמט, see *Note* 16:8.a (so NJPS). But most versions have "snatched away" (RSV, NAB), "carried off" (NEB, NIV), "borne off" (JB). Gordis thinks it a separate root, meaning "cut off."

16.b. ולא־עת, lit. "and without time," is a phrase that occurs nowhere else and should perhaps be emended to בְּלֹא־עֵת, which would more naturally signify "and before time," as it does in Eccl 7:17 (so also some MSS, and Beer [*BHK*]).

16.c. The "by" is to be understood (NJB "swamped by a flood"), perhaps as a 2d accus, "in a flood" (KJV "with a flood"; cf. GKC, §121d). Many take it as an accus of result (GKC, §121d[c]), meaning "their foundation was poured out as a river, viz. so that it formed a river" (so Dillmann, Budde, Driver–Gray, Sicre Díaz; cf. RV "whose foundation was poured out as a stream"; NEB "their very foundation flowing away like a river"). Dhorme, however, understands "a river poured itself over their foundations," יסודם being an acc of place (similarly Hölscher, Gordis). RSV does not appear to translate נהר "river" at all, but NRSV has "by a flood."

17.a. Vv 17–18 are deleted by Budde, Duhm, Driver–Gray, Beer (*BH*[2]), Moffatt, Hölscher, Fohrer, de Wilde as a gloss formed from elements of 21:14–16. Only v 18 is so regarded by Pope, NAB.

17.b. The usual translation of the divine name Shaddai; see *Comment* on 5:17.

17.c. למו is "to them," which is possible if we think v 17b has changed into indirect speech (as Delitzsch). But more probably we should emend to לָנוּ "to us," as almost all commentators and modern versions do (as Beer [*BHK*], Gerleman [*BHS prp*]; contrast KJV "do for them" [but RV "for us"], JPS; and cf. NJPS "What can Shaddai do about it?"); the Qumran Tg, LXX, and Pesh also read "to us." If we compare the verse with 21:14–15, to which it alludes, לנו is likely to mean "for us" rather than "to us," since the issue is the matter of profit (so too Delitzsch). Cf. also KJV "what can the Almighty do for them?" and Terrien "Qu'est-ce que le Tout-Puissant peut bien nous faire?" But most do not see this nuance, which is confirmed by the use of פעל ל in Pss 31:19 (20); 68:28 (29); Isa 26:12.

18.a. Kissane transposes the verse to follow v 8, which he moves to follow v 14.

18.b. עצת רשעים "the counsel of the wicked." R. Bergmeier, "Zum Ausdruck עצת רשעים in Ps 1:1; Hi 10:3; 21:16 und 22:18," *ZAW* 79 (1967) 229–32, has argued that עצה here means, rather than "counsel," "company," a frequent sense in Qumran (cf. also *DCH*, vol. 6, *s.v.*). It seems more likely, however, that the verse means that the intention of the wicked was remote from God (see *Comment*).

18.c. מני is "from me" (the colon is identical with 21:16b; see *Note* 21:16.e). But here, as there, we should no doubt read מִמֶּנּוּ "from him" (so LXX, Dhorme, Beer [*BHK*], Hölscher, Kissane, Fohrer; as also apparently NJB "although excluded from the plans of the wicked," and the prosaic rendering of the NEB "although their purposes and his were very different"). But MT is kept by Driver–Gray, Rowley, Pope, Gordis, Hartley, KJV, JPS, RSV, NJPS, NIV, NAB (and by de Wilde, regarding it as a pious ejaculation of a copyist). This understanding obviates the suggestion that the pf רחקה may have an optative force, "may it be far from me," Vg *procul sit a me* (Joüon–Muraoka, §113k). Blommerde and others find here the supposed 3d-person *yodh* suff, on which see *Note* 21:16.e.

19.a. יראו, past frequentative; emendation to the historic past רָאוּ "they saw" (Duhm, Beer [*BHK*]) and of the next verb to a *waw* consec וַיִּשְׂמְחוּ "and they rejoiced" is no improvement.

20.a. Dillmann suspected the verse was secondary.

20.b. אם־לא, lit. "is it not [the case that]."

20.c. As it stands, קימנו would have to be a sg noun, "our hostility," perhaps as a collective for "our enemies" (recently defended by van der Lugt). Most, however, read קָמֵינוּ "those who rise up against us, our enemies" (cf. Ps 18:40), making the verb pl also, נִכְחֲדוּ (Siegfried, Duhm, Beer [*BH*[2]], Ball, Rowley). But Merx, Wright, Graetz (יְקוּמָם), Beer (*BHK*), Driver–Gray, Dhorme, Fohrer, Pope, de Wilde, NAB read יְקָמָם (also suggested are קִנְיָנָם [Beer (*BHK vel*), NEB], קִיּוּמָם [Hölscher], קִימָם [Kissane, Gordis, Hartley]) "their possessions" (יְקוּם; cf. BDB, 879b), parallel to יתרם in the next colon, noting that the ancient versions all have a 3 pl suff (LXX ἡ ὑπόστασις αὐτῶν "their possessions") (and note that נו is often mistaken for ם; see Gordis); so JB "their wealth," NEB "their riches," NJPS "their substance" (KJV also had "our substance," but RV "they that did rise up against us"). NAB "these have been destroyed where they stood" is a strange translation, considering that its reading is יְקָמָם "their possessions." Guillaume proposes a new Heb. word קִים "possession" on the basis of Arab. *qiwām* "sustenance" and *qiyām* "subsistence" (as also in his *Lexicography,* 3:7).

The reading יְקָמָם "their possessions," adopted in the *Translation,* is perhaps to be preferred to קָמֵינוּ "our enemies" because the wicked are not here being represented as the enemies of the righteous, persecuting them, for example. Both for Job and for Eliphaz, the wicked are those who reject the knowledge of God.

20.d. יתר is "remainder, excess," but probably not here in the sense of "the remnant of them" (KJV), "their remnant" (NJPS), "such as were left" (NAB), their descendants (Fohrer), what was left to them (Peake) or even "what they left" (RSV), but rather "wealth" or "riches" (as BDB, 452a §2c ["abundance, affluence"], JB, NEB ["the profusion of their wealth"], NIV; similarly Delitzsch, Driver–Gray, Dhorme, Kissane, Gordis, Sicre Díaz). M. Dahood ("Hebrew-Ugaritic Lexicography III," *Bib* 46 [1965] 311–32 [325–26]) has also drawn attention to this sense of יֶתֶר, which he finds also in Hab 2:8 (cf. *DCH,* 4:344b).

21.a. סכן may be derived from several distinct roots: (1) Usually, it is thought to be סכן qal "profit," as in v 2; in hiph as here it seems capable of meaning "behave carefully," as in Num 22:30, "be familiar with," as in Ps 139:3, and "acquaint oneself with," as here (so KBL; cf. KJV, JPS, NJPS "be close to"; cf. Driver–Gray "accustom thyself"). But BDB, 698a, says "shew harmony with" (hence RSV "agree with," JB "make peace with," NEB, NAB "come to terms with"; cf. *HALOT,* 2:755a, "be reconciled with," Dhorme's "reconcile yourself"). Friedrich Delitzsch rendered "join oneself." (2) NIV's "submit to" seems to depend upon Pope's parallel to Ugaritic (*UT* 51.i.21); he translates "yield" (so also Hartley). Pope evidently depends on the argument of W. B. Bishai, "Notes on HSKN in Job 22:21," *JNES* 20 (1961) 258–60 (258–59), that סכן is "be quiet, acquiesce" (as Arab. *sakana*; cf. *DCH*, vol. 6, *s.v.*) and שלם means "submit" (as Arab. *sallama*). (3) Guillaume (also in his *Lexicography*, 4:18) sees here Arab. *thakama* "be occupied in, remain in a place," and translates "accustom yourself to him." (4) Given the attested range of meanings of סכן, Gordis's suggestion of another verb סכן "agree" (see *Note* 22:2.b, and cf. *DCH*, vol. 6, *s.v.*) becomes unnecessary.

21.b. The two imperatives joined by "and" are probably successive (Dhorme), or perhaps even simple equivalents, rather than the latter being the consequence of the former; the בהם in the next colon seems to refer to the two verbs as injunctions of equal standing. It does not seem to be a case of the hypothetical impv, i.e., "if you come to terms with him, you will be at peace" (as at 40:32 [41:8]; cf. GKC, §110f).

21.c. שלם is, according to BDB, 1023b, from the denominative verb שָׁלַם "be at peace" rather than from שָׁלֵם "be complete, safe," as is the case in 9:4 (see *Note* 9:4.d). *HALOT*, 4:1533b, does not acknowledge the existence of two separate verbs, but takes שלם here as "keep peace" nevertheless. Beer (*BHK*) reads hiph וְהַשְׁלֵם, with the same meaning. Pope thinks it should mean "submit," like the idea of "submission" in the word *Islam* (from the same root), or like the Sumerian idea of submission to fate (cf. S. N. Kramer, "'Man and His God': A Sumerian Variation on the 'Job' Motif," in *Wisdom in Israel and in the Ancient Near East, Presented to Professor Harold Henry Rowley . . . in Celebration of His Sixty-Fifth Birthday*, ed. M. Noth and D. W. Thomas, VTSup 3 [Leiden: Brill, 1995] 170–82; idem, "Sumerian Theology and Ethics," *HTR* 49 [1956] 45–62 [59–60]). But there is no evidence that Heb. שלם has this connotation. The *athnach* should be moved from עמו to ושלם (as Gerleman [*BHS*]).

21.d. תבואתך is called by Driver–Gray a "grammatical *monstrum*." Probably intended is the verb תְּבוֹאֶךָ, 3 sg impf of בוא with suff, "shall come to you" (GKC, §48d; so too Budde, Fohrer), with direct object, as rarely (BDB, 98a). Others explain the verbal suff as datival, i.e., "to you." For other examples of supposed datival suffs in Job, see Blommerde, 8 (with bibliography) (for Psalms, see Dahood, *Psalms III*, 376–78), and note, in addition to the present case, 3:25; 6:4, 13; 9:31; 10:2, 14; 15:12, 18, 21; 20:22; 28:17, 19; 29:11, 16; 31:18, 37; 41:29 (21); 42:5.

But the consonantal text could equally well be vocalized תְּבוּאָתְךָ "your increase, gain" (so LXX ὁ κάρπος σου "your fruit," Pesh, Tg; followed by Dillmann, Duhm, Driver–Gray ["Thereby will thine increase be good"], Beer [*BHK*], Dhorme, Kissane ["thy gain"], JB ["your happiness"], Pope [though he translates "good will come to you"], Gerleman [*BHS*], Hartley, NAB, NJPS). Blommerde, following Dahood, *Psalms II*, 296, and *Psalms I*, 187, entertains the fanciful notion that טובה is a divine title, translating "then your gain will be the Good One."

21.e. בהם "by them" must refer to the two verbs of the first colon; the masc for neut is unusual since fem is normal (GKC, §122q).

22.a. שים "set" with "in the heart" (usually על־לב or אל־לב), meaning "remember, treasure up," is best paralleled by Isa 42:25; 47:7; 2 Sam 13:33; 19:20 (19). M. Dahood's claim ("The Metaphor in Job 22, 22," *Bib* 47 [1966] 108–9), that שים here means "write, inscribe" (as he also suggests for 38:33; Prov 8:29; Ps 56:8 [9]), is an attractive one (see *Comment*); he is followed by Strauss.

23.a. עד "as far as" with שוב "return" is unusual (אֶל or לְ is normal), but is attested in the phrase שוב עד־יהוה "return to Yahweh" in Amos 4:6; Hos 14:2; etc. (cf. BDB, 997b §6c).

23.b. Bickell and Duhm arbitrarily emended שדי to אֵל "God" on the ground that שדי will appear in v 26.

23.c. תבנה, lit. "you will be built up" (so the older Eng. versions and NJPS, NAB, NIV; Gordis, Sicre Díaz, Hartley "reestablished"), a perfectly satisfactory rendering, which is adopted in the *Translation* above; see also *Comment*. But the text has been questioned because the note of restoration would otherwise first clearly appear in v 25, and, moreover, LXX did not apparently have תבנה before it, since it reads καὶ ταπεινώσῃς σεαυτόν "and [if] you humble yourself," implying presumably תְּעָנֶה (as also Ewald, Dillmann) or וְתְעָנֶה (Bickell, Duhm, Driver–Gray, Dhorme, Beer [*BHK vel*], Hölscher, Fohrer, Guillaume, de Wilde), or perhaps וְתִכָּנַע (Merx, Siegfried [תִכָּנַע], Graetz [תִכָּנַע], Beer [*BHK vel*], Hölscher [*vel*], Terrien), all with the same meaning. This proposal is followed by RSV "humble yourself," GNB "you must humbly return to God" (cf. Moffatt, JB); presumably NEB "in true sincerity" follows the same reading, though the translation is loose. The emendation to וְתִפְנֶה "and you turn yourself" (Reiske, Hitzig, Torczyner, Ball) gives an equally satisfactory sense, but it does not have the support of LXX. Likewise Kissane's reading וְתִבָּנֶה "and be restored," which makes Job's restoration another condition Job must fulfill. Dahood's understanding of בנה as "heal," a sub-sense of בנה "build" ("Northwest Semitic Philology and Job," 66; followed by Pope and Habel "rehabilitated"), is both strained and needless.

23.d. Most regard this colon as continuing the "if" at the beginning of the verse, and find a sequence of "if" clauses in the verses that follow. It is by no means agreed that the apodosis should begin after these various protases, whether at the beginning of v 24 (Dhorme, Gordis), v 25 (as JB, NEB, NAB, NIV, Terrien, Rowley, de Wilde, Hartley), v 26 (JPS, Moffatt, RSV, Andersen), or v 27 (NJPS). Quite a lot depends on whether v 24 is taken as an invitation to Job to have no regard for wealth, or, as seems more probable, an assurance that he will have again abundant wealth (see *Comment*). If the former, it is a condition he has to fulfill, but if the latter, there is no cause to take it as an "if" clause.

23.e. Taking תרחיק as 3 fem sg, "it will be far" (as hiph of רחק can mean), not 2 masc sg "you shall make far."

24.a. Vv 24–25, following Bickell's deletion, were regarded by Duhm as intrusive, "a dilly-dallying poem, such as commonly arises from a one-sided concern with religious affairs." Fohrer also deletes the verses as a gloss that disturbs the connection between v 23 and v 26. Beer (*BH*^{2}) thinks that either they are an addition or else should be moved to precede v 23. Strauss regards v 24 alone as a gloss.

24.b. Lit. "set" (שִׁית), probably not in the literal sense, as JPS "lay thy treasure in the dust" or RSV "lay gold in the dust" (similarly Pope, NJB) or NIV "assign your nuggets to the dust" (cf. GNB "throw away, dump," Driver–Gray, Terrien, Gordis, Habel), or even "safely place your gold in the dust" (Gordis), but "treat" (NAB), "regard" (NJPS), "reckon" (JB), or "esteem" (Dhorme; cf. de Wilde). ושית is impv, "and set!"; but most prefer, following LXX θήσῃ "you will set," an emendation to תָּשִׁית "you will set" (Merx, Beer [*BHK vel*]) or, better, וְשַׁתָּ "and you will set" (Budde, Beer [*BHK vel*], Driver–Gray, Dhorme, Gerleman [*BHS prp*], de Wilde; Hartley retains MT). NEB emends to וְתַעֲשֶׂה "you treat [lit. make] your precious metal as dust."

24.c. בצר "gold, gold ore" occurs only here (but the form בְּצָר occurs in 36:19, and can perhaps be restored in Ps 68:30 [31]); we are in no position to say that it is more specifically "a fragment or nugget of gold" (Driver–Gray), "precious ore, ingot" (BDB, 131a), "gold ore" (*HALOT,* 1:149a), "the gold as it leaves the crucible" (Dhorme), or "lumps of refined metal" (A. Guillaume, "Metallurgy in the Old Testament," *PEQ* 94 [1962] 128–32 [132]), comparing Arab. *baṣrat* (Lane, 211a), which he defines as "stones or clay containing pebbles, and so small fragments or nuggets of ore containing metal," which could be either gold or silver (cf. F. Rundgren, "Hebräisch *bäṣär* 'Golderz' und *'āmar* 'sagen': Zwei Etymologien," *Or* 32 [1963] 178–83 [178–81]; Pesh thought it was silver). All these suggestions depend upon Semitic cognates that may or may not be relevant. If we rely solely on Heb., we could relate the term to בצר I "cut" and thus pieces of gold, "nuggets"; or to בצר II "test" (*DCH,* 2:247a; בצר IV, *HALOT,* 1:148), thus "refined gold."

24.d. על־עפר is lit. "on the dust" or, as we would say, "in the dust" (the uses of the phrase in 19:25 and 41:25 [33] are not helpful here). Those who take שִׁית "set" as "regard, esteem" generally prefer to read לֶעָפָר "to the dust" (Dhorme, Hölscher [לֶעָפָר]), and Larcher apparently reads כֶּעָפָר "like the dust"; but the MT can stand, and על can be taken as "beyond," indicating excess (cf. BDB, 755a), i.e., "you will regard gold as more than [= more common than] dust."

24.e. The Heb. has simply the place name Ophir rather than the usual phrase "gold of Ophir" (כתם אופיר, 28:16; Ps 45:9 [10]; Isa 13:12; זהב אופיר, 1 Chr 29:4).

24.f. צור is normally "cliff." Though it may perhaps refer to a single rock in 2 Sam 21:10; Prov 30:19; Judg 6:21; 13:19 (BDB, 849b; I doubt it, however), it can hardly refer to the "pebbles" or "stones" (as the modern versions have) that abound in the beds of wadis. We would have to suppose that it is a dialectal byform of צֹר "pebble, flint" (so *HALOT,* 3:1017a), or else emend to צוֹר (so, e.g., Kissane), or else translate "deposit [thy] gold in the rock of the wadys" (BDB, 849b). Many MSS have וכְצור "and like the rock," and so also Theod, Vg, Pesh, Tg, de Wilde (Beer [*BHK*] mentions the reading וּבְצוּרֵי "and in the rocks of"). Tur-Sinai saw here a noun בְּצוּר "strength, wealth, treasure" (cf. בֶּצֶר "gold"), as also in 28:10, thus "the treasure of the rivers."

25.a. Since בצר is here pl, but sg in v 24, Dhorme argues that here it is "ingots," as distinct from "gold" in v 24, just as כְּסָפִים "coins" is pl of כֶּסֶף "silver."

25.b. תועפות "mounds, hills," as in Num 23:22; 24:8; Ps 95:4, or perhaps rather "heaps" (BDB). KJV has "plenty of silver," JB "silver piled in heaps," and GNB "silver, piled high," Habel "mound of silver." Others think כסף תועפות "silver of eminences" must be "excellent silver" (so RV, RSV, NJPS "precious silver," NIV "choicest silver"; similarly KBL; Fohrer "exquisite silver"). Guillaume thinks rather of "mountain" silver (from Armenia) as superior to other ores ("Metallurgy in the Old Testament," 132). Ecclus 45:7 has בתועפות תואר "in eminences of splendor, in outstanding splendor," but the phrase is not exactly parallel since it is not "splendor of eminences." Others again connect it with יפע "shine" and translate "sparkling silver" (NAB, Delitzsch). F. Rundgren (*AcOr* 21 [1953] 316–25) derived it from a root *אעף and translated "doubling"; hence presumably NEB "your silver in double measure." Emendations are hardly likely: Duhm has טוֹטָפוֹת "headbands, frontlets" (mentioned by Beer [*BHK*]) and Budde, Driver–Gray, feebly, תּוֹרָתוֹ "his instruction" (Beer [*BHK*] notes תּוֹרָתְךָ). Wright's עוֹפֶרֶת "lead" (i.e., "silver will be lead to you") implies an exegesis that is not probable (see *Comment*); equally implausible is the proposal noted by Beer (*BH*[2]), וְאוֹפִיר "and Ophir" (in view of the mention of Ophir in the preceding verse).

25.c. De Wilde proposes the wooden emendation of לך "to you" to אֱלוֹהַּ "God," making the second colon exactly balance the first.

26.a. Beer (*BH*[2]) thought the line should perhaps be deleted, or else be moved to follow v 23.

26.b. כי is perhaps best taken as an "emphatic" or "asseverative" particle, strengthening אז "then." On the supposed "emphatic" כי, see Blommerde, 30 (with bibliography); it has been seen also at 29:11; 30:23; 31:12; 34:11, 23, 31; 36:18; 37:20; 38:5, at 11:15 (in the combination כי עז), and at 3:13; 4:5; 6:3, 21; 7:21; 8:6; 13:19 (in the combination כי עתה). See further, *DCH,* 4:388a; *HALOT,* 2:470a §A1; M. Dahood, *Psalms III,* 277, on Ps 138:2.

26.c. ענג hithp is usually understood as "take one's delight in" (BDB, 772a, "take exquisite delight"; *HALOT,* 2:851a; *DCH,* vol. 6, *s.v.*), with Yahweh as the obj, preceded by על at 27:10; Isa 58:14; Ps 37:4. But other examples of ענג mean "pamper oneself" (Deut 28:56) and "make fun about" (Isa 57:4), and Gordis, thinking "take delight" inappropriate when God is the object, proposes another root ענג (or perhaps another sense of ענג), "implore, importune" (similarly NJPS "When you seek the favor of Shaddai"), parallel with what he regards as the sense of the second half of the verse. An Arab. cognate would be (with metathesis) *naja'a* VIII "seek a favor or present," while V is "play the coquette, use amorous gestures" (Lane, 2299; Dozy, 2:228b); but perhaps more probable would be a connection with Arab. *ghanaja* "be impudent." G. R. Driver ("Problems in the Hebrew Text of Job," in *Wisdom in Israel and in the Ancient Near East, Presented to Professor Harold Henry Rowley . . . in Celebration of His Sixty-Fifth Birthday,* VTSup 3 [Leiden: Brill, 1955] 72–93 [84]) suggested an ענג II cognate with Arab. *'anaja* "draw, support" (cf. *DCH,* vol. 6, *s.v.*), hence "thou basest thyself upon" or "dost depend on the Almighty" (so NEB, REB "with sure trust," perhaps also GNB "then you will always trust in God"), but the parallelism does not support it, and it seems contrary to the general sense that Job should "depend" on the Almighty when the issue is rather when he can depend on his own sense of innocence.

26.d. ותשא אל־אלוה פניך, lit. "and you will lift your face before God"; see *Comment.*

27.a. The impf has a modal sense, "be able to" (as JB, NJB); cf. NEB "you will have cause to."

28.a. This and the following verb form a pair of jussives, paralleled as a way of expressing a hypothetical (cf. Driver, *Tenses,* §152; GKC, §159d).

29.a. The line is very difficult, perhaps lit. "when they are low, you will say, Pride" (taking גוה as גַּאֲוָה "pride"). Thus NJPS "When others sink low, you will say it is pride" (similarly NRSV); but it is hard to see why Eliphaz should at this point be ascribing such an expression of strict retribution to Job. Others think גוה should mean "lifting up"; thus KJV "When men are cast down, then thou shalt say, There is lifting up" (similarly Habel, Hartley), NIV "When men are brought low and you say, 'Lift them up!' then he will save the downcast" (followed by Newsom), RV "When they cast thee down, thou shalt say, There is lifting up," Pope "When they abase, you may order exaltation." But these renderings strain the sense of גאוה.

Most adopt an emendation, usually reading the verb as sg and understanding God as the subj: (1) הִשְׁפִּיל אֱלוֹהַּ גַּאֲוָה "God humbles pride" (Budde, Driver–Gray, RSV, GNB), (2) הִשְׁפִּיל אֱלוֹהַּ גֵּאֶה "God humbles the proud" (Stevenson [reading אֵל], de Wilde), (3) הִשְׁפִּיל רוּמַת גֵּאֶה (or גֵּוֶה) "he casts down the pride of the arrogant" (Beer [*BHK frt*], Fohrer, Terrien, Sicre Díaz, JB, NJB, NAB, NEB), (4) הִשְׁפִּיל רוּמַת גֵּוָה "he humbles the pride of arrogance" (Hölscher). Less plausible are (5) הִשְׁפִּיל אֶת־רָם וְגֵוֶה "he humbles the proud and arrogant" (Beer [*BH*[2] *frt*]), (6) הִשְׁפִּיל אֹמֶר גַּאֲוָה "he humbles the word of pride" (Duhm, Beer [*BH*[2] *vel*]), or with an alternative noun אֵמֶר "word" (Gerleman [*BHS frt* אֵמֶר]), (7) הִשְׁפִּיל אֹמֵר גֵּוָה "he humbles the one who speaks proudly" (Richter, Weiser); (8) הִשְׁפִּיל אֶת־גֵּוָה "he humbles pride" (Dhorme). (9) Perhaps the best emendation, adopted in the *Translation* above, is הִשְׁפִּיל מִתְאַמֵּר גֵּוָה "he humbles the one who boasts in pride" (Kissane, Larcher, Rowley) since אמר hithp itself means "boast" (as in Ps 94:4; Isa 61:6; 4Q488.2.1). It is improbable that we should understand השפילו as "[when your ways] go downwards" (Rosenmüller, Dillmann, Delitzsch, Davidson, Peake), even though דרכיך "your ways" has been the last noun that could function as the subj of השפילו. See M. Dahood, "Some Rare Parallel Word Pairs in Job and in Ugaritic," in *The Word in the World,* FS F. L. Moriarty, ed. R. J. Clifford and G. W. MacRae (Cambridge, MA: Weston College Press, 1973) 19–34 (24).

29.b. It is most natural to regard "God" as the subj of יושע "he saves," but Pesh, Vg took the verb as a passive (= יִוָּשַׁע) (so too Gordis, Habel); alternatively, the subj could be indefinite (cf. Gordis).

29.c. שח עינים "lowly of eyes," שח from שחח "be bowed down," occurring only here; the contrasting phrase is גבה עינים "lofty of eyes" (Ps 101:5).

30.a. אי נקי seems to mean "the non-innocent," "the guilty"—if אי is a negative; the only other possible attestation of this particle in biblical Heb. is in the name איכבוד "Ichabod," which may however mean "Where [אי] is the glory?" אי "not" is common in postbib. and modern Heb., a common negative in Eth. and known also in Phoen. A possible occurrence in pre-exilic Heb. is in Lachish ostracon 2.6 (cf. *DCH*, 1:204a [אִי III]). Such is the understanding of RV, NJPS, NIV ("even one who is not innocent"), NRSV, Davidson, Pope, Gordis, Habel, Hartley, Good, Grabbe, 83–86, and Thexton ("A Note on Job xxii. 30." *ExpTim* 78 [1966–67] 342–43, in reference to Job himself; see *Note* 30.c on "you will be delivered").

Most, however, think that the context will not allow this rendering (see *Comment*) and adopt one of the following emendations: (1) Read אִישׁ "man" for אי (so Reiske, Dhorme, Beer [*BHK vel*], Hölscher, Kissane, Fohrer, de Wilde, NAB); G. R. Driver, followed by NEB, achieves the same result, not by emending the text but by regarding אי as an abbreviation of אִישׁ "man" ("Once Again Abbreviations," *Textus* 4 [1965] 76–94 [81]). However, נקי is never used with איש attributively (cf. *DCH*, 5:750b). (2) Omit אי (we cannot tell which of these emendations most Eng. versions follow, e.g., RSV, JB, NJB, NAB). Theod (ῥύσεται ἀθῷον "he will deliver the harmless man") and Vg (*salvabitur innocens* "the innocent will be saved") are sometimes called in support for this reading, but it is impossible to divine the text they read from their translations. Less probable are the readings (3) אֵל "God" (Merx, Beer [BH^2 *prps*], Ball, Stevenson); (4) אֱלֹהִים "God" (Gerleman [*BHS prb*]); (5) אֱלוֹהַּ "God" (KBL, 35b); (6) אִי, understood as "whoever," as perhaps also אִי in Prov 31:4; so N. M. Sarna, "A *Crux Interpretum* in Job 22:30 ימלא אי־נקי," *JNES* 15 (1956) 118–19, comparing *ajumma* (*CAD* 1.1:236a; Sarna writes it *ayyu*[*m*]), Arab. *'ayya*, Ugar. *'ay* "whoever" (Terrien, Strauss, van der Lugt; similarly A. Guillaume, "The Arabic Background of the Book of Job," in *Promise and Fulfilment*, FS S. H. Hooke, ed. F. F. Bruce [Edinburgh: T. & T. Clark, 1963] 106–27 [115]; also *Studies*, 107), thus "[he will deliver] whoever [is innocent]"; (7) אֶת־ (sign of direct obj) (Beer [*BHK vel*]). (8) More radically, Duhm, Beer (BH^2 *vel*) read יְמַלֵּא תַּאֲוַת נקי . . . כַּפָּיו "he shall satisfy the desire of the innocent, [and he shall be delivered by the cleanness of] his hands." (9) There is no probability that אי here means "island" (so ibn Ezra, KJV, Tur-Sinai), for where is the "isle of the innocent," and what has it to do with Job? (10) No less implausible is the proposal of M. Dahood that it is the Ugar. *'ē* "not" ("Hebrew-Ugaritic Lexicography VI," *Bib* 49 [1968] 355–69 [363]).

30.b. LXX and Vg have "his hands" (= כַּפָּיו), which some (Duhm, Ball, Hölscher, Kissane, Stevenson [*Poem*], Fohrer) want to read here.

30.c. ונמלט "and he is delivered" is intelligible only if the idea is of Job's intercession for others (so KJV ["it"], RV, NJPS, NRSV; see *Comment*), or if "your hands" is changed to "his hands"; so most read וְנִמְלַטְתָּ or תִּמָּלֵט "[and] you will be delivered" (as Theod; so RSV, JPS, JB, NJB, NAB, NEB [וְנִמְלָט]), Merx, Siegfried, Driver–Gray, Beer [*BHK*], Terrien [וְנִמְלָט], Guillaume, de Wilde, Sicre Díaz). Dhorme unnecessarily proposes וְנִצַּלְתָּ "and you will escape" to avoid the repetition of מלט. Duhm's יְמַלֵּא תַּאֲוַת נָקִי "he fulfills the desire of the innocent" is more clever than convincing. The suggestion of Thexton ("Job xxii. 30," 342–43) that the second half of the sentence is a rhetorical question (cf. GKC, §150a)—thus "He [God] delivers the man who is not innocent; And wilt thou be delivered by the cleanness of thy hands?"—does not fit with Eliphaz's general affirmatory stance toward Job as here understood; moreover, it seems a weak note for Eliphaz to conclude on, that Job will not be delivered by his innocence, since in Eliphaz's opinion he has none.

Form/Structure/Setting

With this speech begins the third cycle of speeches in the book of Job. The reader, who has become accustomed to a rigid pattern of speeches in the first two cycles, each of the friends speaking in turn and Job answering each friend, may well feel disoriented by the third cycle, where the pattern largely disappears. Here there is, as the text stands, (1) a speech by Eliphaz (chap. 22), (2) a long response by Job (chaps. 23–24), (3) a very short speech by Bildad (chap. 25), and (4) a very long speech by Job (chaps. 26–31). There is no speech of Zophar at all, and many of the sentences of Job sound strange in his mouth (e.g., 24:18–15; 26:5–14; 27:7–23). For these reasons some have argued that the original book of Job did not contain a third cycle. Others have thought that the assignment of verses to Job is correct and that the variant positions he appears to adopt are merely evidence that he is wavering in his convictions and pondering whether to accept the views of his friends (so P. L. Redditt, "Reading the Speech Cycles in the Book of Job," *HAR* 14 [1994] [= *Biblical and Other Studies in Honor of Reuben Ahroni, on the Occasion of His Sixtieth Birthday,* ed. T. J. Lewis (Columbus, OH: Melton Center for Jewish Studies, Ohio State Univ., 1994)] 205–14). More commonly, however, commentators have attempted to reconstruct the third cycle by reassigning elements of these chapters to other speakers. For details of the many such proposals, see G. A. Barton, "The Composition of Job 24–30," *JBL* 30 (1911) 66–77; Driver–Gray, xl; A. Regnier, "La distribution des chapitres 25–28 du Livre de Job," *RB* 33 (1924) 186–200; P. Dhorme, "Les chapitres XXV–XXVIII du Livre de Job," *RB* 33 (1924) 343–56; Dhorme, xlvi–li; R. H. Pfeiffer, *Introduction to the Old Testament* (London: A. & C. Black, 1948) 671–72; C. Kuhl, "Neuere Literarkritik des Buches Hiob," *TRu* NS 21 (1953) 163–205, 257–317 (277–78); R. Tournay, "L'ordre primitif des ch. XXIV–XXVIII de Job," *RB* 64 (1957) 321–34.

In this commentary, the view has been taken that 24:18–24 belongs to Zophar, not Job, that 26:2–14 belongs to Bildad, not Job (vv 2–4 preceding Bildad's 25:2–6), and that 27:7–23 belongs to Zophar, not Job (24:18–24 fitting in after 27:17). In this way, speeches that are roughly equal (except for Job's last) can be reconstructed for the interlocutors: 23:2–24:17 (Job, thirty-three lines), 26:2–4 + 25:2–6 + 26:5–14 (Bildad, eighteen lines), 27:2–6, 11–12 (Job, seven lines), 27:7–17 + 24:18–24 + 27:18–23 (Zophar, twenty-two lines). The last speech of Job is much shorter than usual, but when we consider its content, which is nothing but a solemn declaration of his innocence, its succinctness may seem quite meaningful. According to the view taken in this commentary, what followed this third cycle of speeches was originally the whole of the Elihu speeches, i.e., chaps. 32–37 + chap. 28. Once Elihu has spoken, all the friends have had their say, and it remains only for Job to deliver his final climactic speech (chaps. 29–31), whereupon Yahweh speaks from the tempest (chaps. 38–41), and the book moves toward its conclusion.

The distribution of third-cycle speeches above resembles that of JB, which ascribes to Bildad 26:5–14 and to Zophar 27:13–24. Terrien also allots to Bildad 25:2–6 + 26:5–14, and to Zophar 24:18–24 + 27:12–23. Pope gives to Bildad 25:2–6 + 26:5–14, to Job 26:2–4 + 27:2–7, and to Zophar 27:8–23 + 24:18–25. Among those who take an interest in such matters, a consensus seems to be developing around such an analysis, even if there is disagreement over some details.

The *structure* of this speech of Eliphaz clearly is of two unequal parts: vv 2–20 devoted to an accusation of Job, and vv 21–30 devoted to advice and encouragement. Within the first part there is a further clear distinction, between vv 2–11, where the theme is Job himself and particular presumed wrongdoings of his, and vv 10–20, where the theme moves from the supposed general godlessness of Job to the fate of the wicked in general.

The *strophic structure* may then be suggested to be (so also Habel, Hartley):

Part 1a	strophe 1	vv 2–5	4 lines (3 + a pendant)
	strophe 2	vv 6–8	3 lines
	strophe 3	vv 9–11	3 lines
Part 1b	strophe 4	vv 12–14	3 lines
	strophe 5	vv 15–17	3 lines
	strophe 6	vv 18–20	3 lines
Part 2	strophe 7	vv 21–25	5 lines
	strophe 8	vv 26–30	5 lines

Skehan's analysis (followed by NAB) is very similar, though he makes some adjustments to the text, inserting 21:22 after v 2 and deleting vv 8 and 18. He thus obtains six strophes, each of five lines except the third, of three lines. The resulting strophes (vv 2–5, 6–11, 12–14, 15–20, 21–25, 26–30) nevertheless coincide closely with the pattern in the table.

Terrien's structure is not very different: he finds six main segments, each with two strophes: I: vv 2–3, 4–5; II: vv 6–8, 9–10; III: vv 11–12, 13–14; IV: vv 15–16, 17–20; V: 21–22, 23–25; and VI: 26–28, 29–30. But it is not plausible to separate v 10 from v 11 since they are parallel in wording and both addressed to Job.

Fohrer marks out six regular strophes, each of four lines, given that vv 12, 17–18, 24–25 are to be omitted, in his view, as glosses: vv 2–5, 6–9, 10–14, 15–20, 21–26, 27–30. This neat pattern does not, however, satisfactorily display the disjunction between v 11 and v 12.

Webster marks out six strophes: vv 2–5, 6–9, 10–14, 15–20, 21–25, 26–30. But at one point this analysis is questionable: the focalization of vv 6–11 (Job's alleged behavior and its punishment) is so different from that of vv 12–14 (God and his awareness of human actions) that a major disjunction must occur between vv 11 and 12.

Van der Lugt identifies the same three major strophes mentioned above, dividing strophe I into five two-line substrophes, II into a one-line substrophe (v 12) followed by four two-line substrophes, and III into two three-line substrophes and two two-line substrophes (vv 21–23, 24–25, 26–28, 29–30). The only difficulty with this analysis is that v 8 connects rather with what precedes than with what follows.

The speech is in its *genre* of course yet another example of the *disputation speech*. The frequent rhetorical questions, especially in the first section (vv 2–5, 12, 15), are markers of that genre, whether they are argumentative (as in vv 2–3) or more accusatory (vv 4–5). The *wisdom* elements are strongly marked, especially the language of receiving instruction in v 22 and the imperatives that convey advice (vv 21–22). The instruction to "turn" to the Almighty is also a wisdom motif (cf. Prov 1:23; 9:4); the term does not here mean "repent."

There are *prophetic* elements here too, noticeably the "therefore" (על־כן) that follows the catalogue of sins and introduces the punishment. Neglect of the widow and orphan is a specially prophetic theme (Isa 1:17, 23; 10:2; Jer 7:6; 22:3; Ezek 22:7; Zech 7:10; Mal 3:5), as is also the exacting of pledges (Ezek 18:7, 12, 16; Amos 2:8; Hab 2:6); and the listing of accusations also suggests a derivation from prophetic announcements.

Psalmic elements appear in the depiction of the triumph of the righteous who laugh the wicked to scorn (vv 19–20; cf. Pss 52:6 [8]; 58:10 [11]; 107:42), in the language of the salvation of the pious (vv 29–30), and of paying of vows when prayer has been heard (v 27; cf. Pss 22:26; 50:14; 61:6, 9).

The *function* of the speech seems to be ultimately to encourage Job to believe in a future restoration to his wealth and status. But before he offers such encouragement, Eliphaz first attempts to disabuse Job of some misconceptions he believes he holds, such as the idea that God's punishment is due to some loss God fears he suffers when humans sin and the idea of Job that he is perfectly innocent and undeserving of any suffering at all.

The *tonality* of the speech is as ambiguous as its argument. On the one hand, Eliphaz addresses language to Job that suggests he is severely critical of him: "Is it not for your great wickedness . . . ?" (v 5); "That is why snares are all about you . . ." (v 10). Newsom finds in v 4 a tone of "exasperated incredulity." On the other hand, the last section (vv 21–30) sounds more like the Eliphaz we have heard in his previous speeches (chaps. 4–5, 15). Here there is little demand laid upon Job (only v 23aα), but many promises and much encouragement. Although the last verse (v 30) raises the specter of indeterminacy, most readers find it wholly supportive of Job ("by the cleanness of your hands you will be delivered") and, in view of its position at the close of the three speeches of Eliphaz, likely to be determinative of how the speech as a whole is to be read.

The *nodal verse,* it may be suggested, is v 23: "If you will turn to the Almighty, you will be restored"—for here the advice of Eliphaz, and thus the whole purpose of his intervention in the dialogue, is put in a nutshell.

Comment

22:1–27:23 The third cycle of the dialogues now begins. Especially in its latter chapters, the text is in some disarray, to the extent that at some points we cannot be sure who is the speaker. There have consequently been those who have doubted whether the original book of Job even included a third cycle. The view is taken in this commentary that it is not difficult to reassign material to the various speakers and so to reconstruct all the original speeches of the third cycle. See further under *Form/Structure/Setting.*

22:2–30 Now, for the first time, one of the friends seems to add to the dynamic of the book, move the argument in a new direction, disclose new facts that bid fair to change all established positions. Job seems temporarily to have lost the initiative, with his more reflective and mainly rational speech in chap. 21. Here, to our surprise, Eliphaz suddenly speaks with more passion and conviction than Job.

What disturbs the flow of the book here is not Eliphaz's speech as a whole, which comes to rest on the selfsame note with which his first speech opened. For here he concludes that "you will be delivered through the innocence of your hands" (v 30); there too he had begun his encouragement with the words, "Is not your piety your source of confidence? Does not your blameless life give you hope?" (4:6). What is disturbing in this speech is rather the fact that Eliphaz also accuses Job of being a great sinner, speaking not just generally but with many instances of Job's wrongdoing (vv 5–9).

If Eliphaz is telling the truth, and if his words mean what they say, we have to revise everything we know about Job (and about Eliphaz too, for that matter). If indeed there is "no end to [Job's] iniquities" (v 5b), if it is true that he has given no water to the weary to drink and has sent widows away empty (vv 7a, 9a), then he is not the righteous man we were introduced to in 1:1—and that means that he no doubt deserves some at least of what is happening to him, and that there can be in the book no question of injured innocence. And further, Eliphaz's own assurances to him, even in this chapter, ring hollow. How can such a sinner as this Job be "delivered through the cleanness of [his] hands" (v 30b), if he has been "keeping to the old way, which wicked men have trod" (v 15)?

The commentators evidently do not know how to handle this enormous change in Eliphaz's attitude from his mild and encouraging stance in chaps. 4–5. Gordis correctly observes that "No more sweeping charge against Job has been lodged by any of the Friends, including the impolitic Zophar," and Andersen that "Eliphaz now openly brands Job a sinner more bluntly than anyone has so far dared to do." Terrien finds Eliphaz to be losing his sangfroid: "At first he had shown himself a master of composed courtesy, but now has thrown overboard all restraint. He plunges brusquely into sarcasm, and tries to give color to his accusations by gross lies." And Hartley opines that "A complete turnabout has taken place in Eliphaz's attitude toward Job." Some indeed believe that Eliphaz's account of Job's wickedness is inferred from his knowledge of Job's suffering, and not from any personal observation of Job's wrongdoings that he has been able to make, Hölscher, for example, suggesting that Eliphaz's charges are nothing more than "postulates of the doctrine that Job must have acted thus and thus" (similarly Rowley). Nevertheless, almost no one seems to take seriously the possibility that Eliphaz's three speeches are consistent, even if their emphases differ. Tur-Sinai indeed attempts to find such consistency when he denies vv 2–11 to Eliphaz by representing them as his quotation of Job, with vv 5–11 being God's words embedded in Job's speech; the convolution this reading demands is unpersuasive. However, the commentary on the following verses will argue for the possibility of consistency in Eliphaz's three speeches. See further, D. J. A. Clines, "The Arguments of Job's Three Friends," in *Art and Meaning: Rhetoric in Biblical Literature,* ed. D. J. A. Clines, D. M. Gunn, and A. J. Hauser, JSOTSup 19 (Sheffield: JSOT Press, 1982) 199–214 = *On the Way to the Postmodern: Old Testament Essays, 1967–1998,* JSOTSup 293 (Sheffield: Sheffield Academic Press, 1998) 2:719–34, for an attempt to profile the distinctive positions of the friends and to display their coherence.

2–5 Eliphaz's logic takes some fathoming, mainly because there are a couple of elements in it that remain only implicit. But this seems to be what he means: God stands to gain nothing from human behavior, for how can a deity be affected one way or the other by how his creatures behave? So if he brings suffering upon a human, we need not look to God for any explanation of its reasons, as if God had something to gain or lose. The only explanation for human suffering must lie in the humans themselves; "the root of the matter" lies there (19:28). And, since God is not immoral, he cannot be making a human like Job suffer for his *piety;* if Job is suffering, it can only be for his *impiety.* The implicit elements assumed by Eliphaz's argument are these: (1) Not only is it no gain to God if Job is innocent; it is no loss either if he is wicked. (2) Suffering is always in proportion to wickedness; great suffering presupposes great wickedness, and temporary suffering presupposes wickedness that can be repented of and eradicated.

Eliphaz here announces the premise on which the whole speech depends: if Job is suffering (and he is) and God has nothing to gain or lose personally from Job (and he hasn't) and God is just (and he is), then Job is suffering for his sins. And if he is suffering much (as he is), it follows that he has offended much. And if there is no evidence of Job's sins, then all his sins must be secret and unobservable ones. However, what undermines Eliphaz's logic is something he does not know, but that we readers know: that God indeed has much to gain (or lose) from Job's behavior; for Job is a test case for the gratuitousness of piety. If Job does not remain pious when all his blessings have been taken away, it proves that humans serve God only for the sake of the rewards and it shows religion up as a self-seeking practice of humans.

Eliphaz has not been listening to Job in chap. 21. For Job has argued that there is not a moral order in the universe that brings retribution to the wicked (nor, by implication, to the innocent). If Job is right, he can say that if there is no evidence of his sins, then he has not sinned, and not, as Eliphaz must argue, that his sins must be secret sins, sins without visible evidence. Fohrer, incidentally, seems to be incorrect in taking Job to mean that since the wicked lead happy and successful lives, he himself cannot be one of the wicked. Job's argument is more complex. It is that the happiness of the wicked is a sign of the invalidity of the doctrine of retribution; and if there is no retribution there is no reason to infer Job's guilt from his suffering and every reason to believe his own account of his innocence.

2–3 Eliphaz opens his speech with a string of questions (vv 2–5). These rhetorical questions are a symbol of his surprise and dismay at the assault Job has been mounting on the traditional theological doctrines. After Job's denial in chap. 21 of God's moral government of the world, Eliphaz cannot move immediately into his usual instructional mode; he has to express his outrage.

To begin with, Eliphaz picks up the concept of "profit" from Job's speech in 21:15 (Job had said יעל, but Eliphaz speaks of סכן, "profit," as at 15:3, where he had also used יעל), but he uses it in his own distinctive way. Job had had the wicked remark that there is no "profit" in prayer—by which Job implied that the wicked live only for profit and judge religion by results. That is not in the least Job's own view, for he has had less profit out of his godliness than most, but it has not brought him to leave off speaking to God (which might well be called a kind of "prayer"). Eliphaz, on the other hand, appears to ascribe this sentiment of the wicked to Job himself, and ripostes that, if we are going to talk about utility in religion, it is not only human utility we had better have in mind. There is also the matter of what is useful *to God*. Human righteousness, says Eliphaz, is of no profit to God—presumably because God is so self-sufficient and detached that no human action can bring him benefit or otherwise. But this is not in any way a reply to Job or even to the wicked whom Job quotes; it is no more than a debating point to say, You claim religion is not beneficial to humans, I claim it is not beneficial to God either. The only relevance of the point here is that it can reinforce what all the friends have all the time been insisting: that it is for his sin that Job is suffering. If God gets no benefit from Job's piety, then he comes to no harm from Job's lack of piety (Elihu will say that explicitly in 35:6–7, and Job has already argued that himself in 7:20). So he cannot be punishing Job for any personal loss Job has caused him; he can only be punishing Job for, and in accord with, Job's own wrongdoing.

Three terms are used for "profit" here. The verb סכן, in both bicola of v 2, is "be of use, service" (as also 15:3; 34:9; so NRSV, Terrien here). חפץ in v 3a is often "pleasure" (as indeed it is translated in KJV, RSV, NIV), but that rendering would be misleading here. Eliphaz is not asserting that human goodness does not bring *pleasure* to God, but, as the context shows clearly, *benefit*. חפץ sometimes, especially in later Biblical Hebrew, means "business" (so Eccl 3:1, 17; 5:7; 8:6; Isa 53:10) or, as here, the result of business, "gain" (so NJPS; JB "benefit," NEB "asset," REB "advantage"); it is a little different from its sense of "interest, concern" in 21:21 (so it is not a case of God's being "indifferent" to human behavior, as Andersen thinks, nor that he is impassible, as Terrien thinks). בצע in v 3b is also "profit, gain." The language of these two verses is distinctively from the world of business and trade, and its very distance from the moral and religious vocabulary of the book points up how inappropriate the whole idea is that it attempts to express.

Eliphaz begins with a general statement about human utility (v 2), but then immediately applies it to Job ("if you are righteous," v 3)—which shows us that he is not so much interested in the principle as in the argument against Job. Why then should he ask, "Can even a *wise* man benefit him" (v 2b NEB)? We might expect him to ask whether even a *righteous* person could benefit God, and we must presume that for him here the "wise" (משׂכיל) is identical with the "righteous." The משׂכיל is the sage, endowed with mental superiority and prudence (Terrien). משׂכיל is used of the wise son, speaker, or servant in Prov 10:5, 19; 14:35; etc.

The possibility that Job's "conduct" could be "blameless" (lit. "if you make your ways perfect," תתם דרכיך) reminds us of Eliphaz's assurance in his opening speech that Job's "blameless life" (the same terms, תם דרכיך) should give him hope (4:6). Eliphaz is not here denying what he has said in chap. 4, but his focus now is not upon the wide sweep of Job's life but upon the sinfulness within it that Job seems bent on ignoring. The wrongdoing that in chap. 4 could be regarded as marginal has now come to occupy the whole stage.

Eliphaz is essentially a deist. As Weiser says, "On the one hand God is here depersonalized, reduced to a mechanistic conception of righteousness as an impartial norm; and on the other hand, as in all law-oriented religion, what remains of human piety is only a utilitarian ethics of obedience that is ultimately motivated by egocentric considerations despite its religious framework." No doubt, deism is the safest theology, and the tidiest; but Job operates with a highly personalistic view of God as his rival and enemy, a being who can be addressed, challenged, and changed. Whether that is the deity of the divine speeches in chaps. 38–41 or the author's conception of the divine is another matter. (Terrien compares the *ataraxia* or carefreeness of the Greek gods, citing A. H. Krappe, "L'indolence des dieux," *REG* 39 [1926] 351–54, who finds these verses in Job to be essentially Epicurean in tone, and thus probably an addition to the book.)

It is of course an irony that Eliphaz's theology of the divine detachment stands in unrecognized contradiction to the narrative framework of the book (though not to the claim of v 4 that God is punishing Job, as Terrien thinks, for Eliphaz does not deny the involvement of God in human affairs). For in the prologue it is patent that God stands to gain (or lose) a great deal by Job's reaction to the suffering that Satan encourages God to inflict on him. And it is precisely, though Eliphaz would not be able to believe it, because of his piety that Job is experiencing the divine "reproof." And, for that matter, we readers, who know the prologue to the book, might even agree with Eliphaz that there is "no end" to Job's iniquities, but only because there is no beginning to them!

Cf. John Milton: "God doth not need / Either man's work or his own gifts" (Sonnet 19 "When I consider how my light is spent"); Acts 17:25: "The God who made the world and all that is in it . . . is not served by human hands, as if he needed anything."

4 Eliphaz has not changed his view of Job since chaps. 4–5; he still allows that Job *is* righteous. But Job's righteousness is irrelevant to the present debate, he believes, which concerns his suffering. Suffering implies sin, and it is his sin that Job must acknowledge if he is to understand the meaning of his suffering. It is not his piety (יראתך "your fear," of God; cf. *Note* 4:6.a and *Comment* on 15:4) that brings him into suffering, but his sin. The discipline or reproof (יכח hiph) he is experiencing at God’s hand is meted out as just retribution for guilt; in 5:17 Eliphaz had said Job should count himself lucky to be reproved (יכח also) by God since God’s chastening leads to recovery and healing—but only if the person does not “despise” it. Job’s refusal to acknowledge his errors, to allow that his suffering is in fact divine discipline for them, is exactly what is meant by despising the chastening.

In chaps. 4–5 Eliphaz had represented Job’s suffering as a kindly disciplining by a fatherly deity who was interested only in Job’s well-being. If he wounds, Eliphaz had said, he also binds up, and his ultimate purpose for Job is deliverance (5:18–19). In chap. 15 also, though he speaks more forthrightly to Job, he still wants to represent God as essentially offering Job “encouragements” and “speech that deals gently with you” (15:11) through the words of the friends. But there is a harder underlying edge in Eliphaz’s attitude to Job, and it comes to the fore once he adopts Job’s perception that what is going on is nothing less uncomfortable, impersonal, and confrontational than a lawsuit. It is Job who has introduced the idea of the lawsuit, though he regarded it as being initiated by himself as the injured party (cf. on 13:3, 18–19). Not so, says Eliphaz; it is not you who have been summoning God to court, it is he who has summoned you (יבוא עמך במשפט “entered into judgment with you”; cf. 9:32; 14:3) and has, moreover, already judged you guilty and set in train your punishment. On the language of the lawsuit, see S. H. Scholnick, “Poetry in the Courtroom: Job 38–41,” in *Directions in Biblical Hebrew Poetry,* ed. E. R. Follis, JSOTSup 40 (Sheffield: JSOT Press, 1987) 185–204 (= *Sitting with Job: Selected Studies on the Book of Job,* ed. R. B. Zuck [Grand Rapids: Baker, 1992] 421–40).

Eliphaz’s question here seems unassailable: surely it is inconceivable that a person could be suffering like Job just because he is pious. But it is the fact! “[The] rhetorical question is subverted by the ironic undertow set in motion by the prologue” (Janzen). And the question, though expecting the answer No!, is only properly answered with a Yes!

5 Can Eliphaz really mean what he says, that Job’s wickedness is great and his iniquities without end? Unless he is totally contradicting his position in chaps. 4–5, he cannot mean that Job is thoroughly wicked, or even that his wickedness outweighs his righteousness. The issue is, How great is “great,” how limitless is “without end”? Eliphaz, as an adherent of the doctrine of retribution, must believe that Job’s sin is as great as his suffering. He does not adopt Zophar’s view, that God is not even punishing Job as much as he deserves (11:6); he simply reasons that if Job is suffering badly, he must have offended badly. If Job does not allow that his suffering is as great as his deserts, he must be overlooking some of his faults. Eliphaz’s self-imposed duty then is to bring to Job’s attention areas of his life in which Job must have been defective.

There is another factor in Eliphaz’s view of Job’s “great wickedness.” Even when his speech to Job has been encouraging, and has stressed his piety and social beneficence (as in 4:3–6), he has expressed the most pessimistic views about human goodness. In 4:17 he denied that humans can be righteous or pure in the sight of God, and he sounded as if he meant that without qualification. In 15:14–16 he asked, “What is humankind, that it could be blameless, one born of woman, that such a one could be innocent?” and he concluded that humanity is “loathsome and foul, that drinks wrongdoing like water.” No matter whether this is merely rhetoric, or his statement of the unbridgeable distance between the divine purity and human taintedness, it still needs to be laid alongside his assessment of Job's "limitless iniquities." Which is to say, if Eliphaz calls Job a sinner of "great wickedness," we need to remember that Eliphaz would on principle probably call anyone that, even the saintliest person on earth. And moreover, that he could at the same time allow that Job is essentially righteous, even "blameless" in general.

6–11 What sins exactly does Eliphaz attribute to Job? It is not any misdemeanor on the strictly religious front; "Job is not charged with any failure in his duty to God" (Andersen). But neither has he obviously broken any of the social laws we are familiar with from the Hebrew Bible in general. His sins are mostly sins of omission, and, even in the case of taking pledges, it is not the act as such that is wrong but its circumstances. There is a stereotypical character to this list of faults. They are not, I would argue, the observed sins of the real man Job but the kinds of sins a person in his position can be imagined as committing, "such sins as a powerful Oriental ruler naturally falls into, inhumanity, avarice, and abuse of power" (Davidson). Natural or not, such sins are no more than what Eliphaz infers Job must have been committing (regularly, since the imperfect verb denotes repeated action) if his punishment is commensurate with his wrongdoing. For Job, being a righteous man, by and large, such sins would no doubt amount to "great wickedness," but not by normal human standards. There is no murder nor false witness nor idolatry here, nothing against the Ten Commandments, nothing indeed except a hardheartedness and a failure of social conscience. They are not, in fact, sins committed by the man Job, and readers are not supposed to imagine they are anything other than Eliphaz's desperate attempt to find reason in Job's experience of suffering (the accusations are "patently false," as Habel says). They are the sins that Eliphaz thinks he "must have been" committing; hence the *Translation:* "You must have been taking pledges from your kinsfolk without cause. . . . You must have even been refusing water to the weary. . . . You must have sent widows away empty" (vv 6, 7, 9).

Job himself will take care to reject these accusations of Eliphaz in his concluding speech (31:16–21), though he does not there specifically mention the taking of pledges or even giving a cup of water to the thirsty. He sees, apparently, no call to refute Eliphaz's charges line by line.

6 The two halves of the line have to be taken together: taking pledges consists of stripping off the clothes of the poor. The pledge that a creditor would take as collateral for a debt would, in the case of a very poor person, be clothing. According to the law of Exod 22:25–26 (26–27) (cf. also Deut 24:6, 10–11), which the author of Job may or may not be referring to, a garment taken in pledge must be restored before nightfall. Eliphaz is, however, not accusing Job of acting against such a law (against Rowley). What he thinks wrong is that Job should have been taking pledges of everyday garments, that he should have been taking them from his kinsfolk, and that he should have been taking them without good cause. If debtors are so poor that they have no possessions apart from the clothes on their back, it is disproportionate for a man in Job's position, the wealthiest of the Easterners (1:3), to be taking pledges of them at all. They should rather be the objects of his charity. What is more, if his debtors are members of his extended family, his "brothers" (אחיך), he should not be treating them as mere fellow citizens (Exod 22 envisages loans on pledge to "neighbors" [רעים], not "brothers"). And furthermore, whoever his debtors are, he should not be taking pledges "without cause" (חנם). We cannot tell whether this means excessive pledges, or deceitful (fictitious or dubious debts, says de Wilde); it can hardly mean "without reason" since the question of pledges can only arise when there is a debt, which is itself a good reason; nor is it likely to mean "giving nothing real or substantial in return for his pledge" (Gordis), or foreclosing on the debt too early for the debtor to have had a chance to work off his debt (Hartley). Perhaps Eliphaz means that, being a rich man, Job should not need to take pledges (Fohrer), but it would be wrong of him to mean that pledges as a rule are unreasonable. In any case, חנם "gratuitously" is a leitmotif of the Job story (cf. 1:9; 2:3), and it would be ironic if the man who is being made to suffer gratuitously should come to grief on an allegation of gratuitous behavior himself.

7 A cup of water for an exhausted (or thirsty, if that is what the adjective means; see *Note* on עיף) person costs the donor little, but it is all important to the receiver. It is "the most primary of all gifts," says Dhorme, comparing Matt 10:42 (cf. also *TDNT,* 2:226–27, on the general oriental custom). Refusal of water is not illegal; it is simply mean-spirited, to the extent of being antisocial. Withholding food (לחם may have the wider connotation, and not be restricted to bread alone here) is equally no infringement of law. Sharing one's food with the underprivileged is of course a moral virtue urged by prophets (Isa 58:7; cf. Prov 25:21, sharing with enemies) and can even be incorporated in a definition of "righteousness" (Ezek 18:7, 16; cf. Matt 25:42), but it is hard to see that not doing so constitutes "great wickedness" by the standards of the book.

8 The relevance of this verse at this point is hard to justify. Vv 6–7, 9 refer clearly to matters Job was responsible for. But how is it his fault if "the man with power possessed the land" (RSV)? If he is the chief of his village (as in chap. 29), perhaps he has some say in who should own the surrounding land, but is there such injustice, within the world of the text, in people of power owning land that Job must be blamed for it? If, as de Wilde suggests, the verse really belongs after v 9 (cf. also Fohrer, who makes the same connection but does not change the order of the verses), so that it is the land of widows and orphans that is being seized by powerful men, it makes more sense, but it is still unclear how Job is responsible for their actions. He will indeed boast of delivering the poor and making the unrighteous drop his prey from his teeth (29:12, 17), but again we wonder whether failing to achieve such deliverance can count as "wickedness." For that reason I have adopted the rendering of the NAB, "As if the land belonged to the man of might, and only the privileged were to dwell in it." This translation does not make of the verse another accusation against Job but suggests the mindset of a haughty member of the ruling classes who has no interest in the fortunes of the lower orders, neglecting their claims on his generosity (v 7).

9 According to the law of Exod 22:21 (22) (cf. Deut 24:17), widows and orphans are not to be "afflicted" (ענה) or oppressed. "Widow" (אלמנה) and "orphan" (יתום) are very commonly linked together, since orphans are not, as with us, children who have lost both parents but the children of widows (cf. 24:3, where the "orphan" seems still to have a widowed mother, and 31:17, where what the "orphan" seems to lack is just a father; cf. also Exod 22:23 [24]; Ps 109:9). A "widow" seems to be defined as a woman without a male protector (cf. H. A.

Hoffner, *TDOT,* 1:288). To “send away” (שׁלח) the widow implies that she has appealed to Job for protection, just as the widow does in Luke 18:3. It is not simply a question of charity (as we had in v 7), but of ensuring that the widow gets what she has a right to, and that she is not “empty-handed” (ריק) of possessions of her own (cf. Gen 31:42; Deut 15:13). Assuming that the Hebrew text is correct, Job himself is not being accused of “crushing the arms” of orphans (for the phrase, cf. 38:15); the complaint is that by sending impoverished widows away without assuring them of a livelihood Job has allowed the strength of their children to be destroyed. Perhaps the metaphor is still a live one, conveying the picture of children too weak to be able to glean in the fields to support their family (Hartley). On the responsibility of the wealthy for widows and orphans in the ancient Near East generally, see F. C. Fensham, “Widow, Orphan and the Poor in Ancient Near Eastern Legal and Wisdom Literature,” *JNES* 21 (1962) 129–39, and compare what is expected of the Ugaritic rulers Danel and Keret (Keret 2.6.30–32, where the prince Yassubu accuses his father Keret: “you have let your hand fall down in slackness: you do not judge the case of the widow, you do not try the case of the impatiently waiting”; cf. also Aqhat 2.5.7–8).

10 The “therefore” (על־כן) with which this verse opens marks out vv 10–11 as the punishment of God; there is a hint of the prophetic judgment speech here, with the accusations introduced by כי “because” and the judgment by על־כן “therefore” (Newsom). The snares (פחים) that surround Job are those described by Bildad as lying in wait for the wicked (18:10; cf. Job’s own reference to God’s net, 19:6), and the “terror” (פחד) that affrights (בהל; cf. B. Otzen, *TDOT,* 2:3–5) reminds us of the terrors (בלהות) that dismay the wicked in the immediately succeeding verse (18:11), but also of the fear that Job himself gives voice to in 3:25 and 7:14. As so often, the terror here is not the internal feeling so much as the objective reality that inspires terror.

11 The allusion to Bildad’s speech continues, with reference to the “darkness” that comes when the light in the evildoer’s tent is extinguished (18:5–6, 18; cf. also Job’s own allusion to the darkness that God has set on his paths, 19:8; also 23:17). Eliphaz himself has earlier spoken of the darkness that lies ahead of the sinner (15:22, 23), and Zophar too has spoken of the darkness that lies in wait for the treasures of the wicked (20:26), and of the “flood” (נבל, emended text) that sweeps away his house (20:28). Here the flood is an “abundance of waters” (שׁפעה־מים, as also at 38:34; for “flood” as an image of destruction, cf. 27:20; 2 Sam 22:17; Jonah 2:6; Pss 32:6; 69:1–2 [2–3]), which “covers” (כסה piel, as also at 38:34; Exod 14:28; Ps 78:53; and elsewhere). The phrase “a flood of waters shall cover you” occurs again at 38:34, but in an apparently totally different context (cf. also Isa 60:6 “a flood of camels [!] shall cover you”). The two images of darkness and drowning give wrongdoers a foretaste of Sheol, universally known in antiquity as shadowlands and as watery chaos (Hartley). Dalman, *Arbeit und Sitte,* 1:190, gives an account of Palestinian waterfloods.

12–20 In this section of the speech, Eliphaz continues his suppositions about Job’s sins that have brought him into the present straits. Whereas in vv 6–9 he had alleged particular misdemeanors against Job, here he attributes to him a general attitude of godlessness that he must assume if he is to account for God’s present punishment of Job. But the speech loses its way a little in the middle of this section; for by v 16 Eliphaz has lost sight of Job and has begun to expatiate yet again on the fate of the wicked in general. And in v 17 the words of the wicked, "Depart from us," are not in any way ascribed to Job himself, while the scornful laugh of the righteous at the discomfiture of the wicked has even less to do with the case of Job himself.

Eliphaz certainly has his difficulties in trying to bring Job to a recognition and confession of his undoubted sins (as they must be in Eliphaz's reckoning) and, at the same time, in attempting to maintain his fundamental stance that Job is a righteous man who deserves encouragement. In this section he brings to an end his accusations against Job more or less by letting them peter out; all the dreadful charges fade away like a bad dream, and in the succeeding section of his speech (vv 21–30) he will have almost nothing but hope to offer Job.

12 The relevance of this verse to Eliphaz's argument is not very evident. In vv 13–14 he will be claiming that Job's attitude is that God in heaven is too remote to take notice of human doings. Why then would he be assuring him in v 12 that God is indeed "in the heights of the heaven"? There does seem to be a satisfactory way of construing it, however. It is to understand v 12 as meaning that God is so high that he can of course see everything that takes place on earth, so it is very foolish for Job or anyone to say that God does not know (v 13) or see (v 14). "And you say" at the beginning of v 13 then contrasts the evident truth of v 12 with the folly of Job's supposed claim in vv 13–14. The claim that God is prevented from seeing human affairs by the thick cloud that surrounds him is a perverse way of evading the truth of God's omniscience.

It must be admitted, however, that the distinction between Eliphaz's position and the one that he ascribes to Job is not strongly marked in the text, and it is tempting to adopt Gordis's supposition, that v 12, equally with vv 13–14, are Job's supposed words as quoted by Eliphaz.

13–14 When is Job supposed to have said this? The nearest Job has come to these ideas is in chap. 21, where he has said that God does not in fact make the wicked pay for their wrongdoing. Not for a moment did Job suggest that God was unaware of what was going on among humans, that he did not "know"; he simply said that God did not care (cf. also 19:7). Job has always been very confident that God knows exactly what is happening to *him* at least (see 7:19; 10:6, 14; 14:3, 6). Eliphaz is perverting Job's position; yet his defense must be that God cannot know of human wrongdoing and yet do nothing about it. If he believes that, and it is likely that he does, he will have to argue that Job's denial of God's interest in human affairs must be a denial that God knows what is going on. And that is the position of the practical atheist, the one who thinks his deeds are unobserved, the one who says, "What can God know?" (for such a sentence in the mouth of the wicked, cf. Isa 29:15; Ezek 8:12; Pss 10:11; 73:11; 94:7). It is with such a one that Job is aligning himself, thinks Eliphaz. But such views can easily be disproved by the untimely death of the wicked (v 16a), says Eliphaz. He is still in the business of inferences (as he was in vv 6–9), and he quotes not what Job has actually said but what he takes him to have implied.

The idea of God being shrouded in cloud (ערפל, "thick cloud" or "thick darkness"; cf. M. J. Mulder, *TDOT,* 11:371–76) is common in Israelite traditions (Exod 20:21; Deut 4:11; 2 Sam 22:10; 1 Kgs 8:12). But elsewhere the function of the cloud is to conceal him from human gaze. It is a rather ingenious twist to this traditional conception of the deity to argue that the clouds prevent *him* from seeing and separate him from earthly affairs; and one cannot imagine wrongdoers seriously thinking themselves safe from the divine scrutiny because of the traditional encompassing cloud. Wrongdoers of whatever time do not bother with fine theological details like this, and if they ever say, What can God know? they mean only that they have no anxiety about possible reprisals. Only a theologian trying to double guess the mind of a practical atheist could have invented such a subtle angle. Equally subtle is the problem v 13b raises of God's attempting to govern (שׁפט in this general sense, no doubt, as NJPS, rather than specifically "judge"; cf. *HALOT,* 4:1624a §I i.6.c.β) "through" (בעד) the barrier of the deep cloud. The clouds are a veil (סתר) covering his face and preventing him from seeing (cf. 9:24 where the faces of judges are covered so that they cannot see wrongdoing). In theological mode, in Lam 3:44 the lamenter complains that the cloud surrounding God prevents prayers reaching him, while in Ecclus 35:16 the prayer of the humble pierces the clouds.

How God spends his time, since he cannot know anything of what is happening on earth, says Job (according to Eliphaz), is to "walk about, roam" (התהלך), like the Satan of the prologue roaming about the earth (1:7; 2:2), "on the vault [חוג] of heaven." This "vault" (RSV, NAB, NEB) or "dome" (NRSV), lit. "circle," is hardly likely to be the horizon, God being pictured as walking "on the confines of the world, at the spot where the vault of the heavens rests on the earth and the waters" (Dhorme; similarly Duhm and Fohrer, thinking of such a place as the earthly paradise; cf. JB "rim," GNB "the boundary between earth and sky"). It is rather the vault of heaven, "that inverted Bowl we call The Sky" as the *Rubaiyat* of Omar Khayyam has it (*Rubaiyat* 52; cf. also Isa 40:22; it is not the "circle" [חוג] on the face of the waters in 26:10 and Prov 8:27 [against Hartley]). The vault or firmament of heaven, pictured in Gen 1 as a thin but solid covering (רקיע "thing beaten out"), thus separates God from his creation.

15 Eliphaz seems to have misunderstood Job's speech in chap. 21 about the fate of the wicked. He seems to be thinking that Job recommends the practice of wickedness for imitation since he charges Job with intending to keep to the way of the wicked (v 15) and attributes to him the skeptical question he has put in the mouth of the wicked (v 13; cf. 21:15). An "ancient way" (ארח עולם) in Eliphaz's language might be expected to be a good path since he is a great believer in the wisdom of the fathers (cf. 15:18), and it is perhaps a little ironic that here it is the way wicked men have trodden. Presumably the wicked have been around as long as the good (which of course makes the antiquity of an idea less valuable than Eliphaz would normally allow), and there is a characteristic "way" they have of behaving. Since Eliphaz is now talking about ideas and attitudes and words rather than actual deeds, we have to assume that the "way" of the wicked is to deny that God knows what is happening in the world. Eliphaz's question is a way of warning Job not to associate himself with the typical language of the wicked, not to "keep" (שׁמר) to their path (for the language, cf. Prov 2:20; Job 23:11 and Ps 18:21 [22] contain also the image of keeping the commandments). On the metaphor of the path in wisdom thinking, see N. C. Habel, "The Symbolism of Wisdom in Proverbs 1–9," *Int* 26 (1972) 131–57 (135–39). R. Girard ("'The ancient trail trodden by the wicked': Job as Scapegoat," *Semeia* 33 [1985] 13–41) has discerned in this language of Eliphaz the tendency of the friends to turn Job into a scapegoat by aligning his way of life with that ancient trail of the wicked.

16 The old way of the wicked has only ever led to one destination: the divine punishment of a premature death, "before their time" (lit. "and it is not [the] time"). It is a standard feature of the fate of the wicked as portrayed by the friends that they are cut off in their prime (8:12; 15:32; and cf. Pss 55:23 [24]; 102:24 [25]; Prov 10:27). The idea of premature annihilation belongs to both the images of this verse, that of the plant that is "shriveled" (קמט, as in 16:8) and that of the house whose foundations are swept away by a stream (another reference to the torrents of the Palestinian wadi, as in v 11). The language is reminiscent of the curse of Esarhaddon upon those breaking treaties: "May a flood, an irresistible deluge, rise from the bowels of the earth and devastate you" (*ANET,* 539). Some have seen here an allusion to Noah's flood, noting נהר "river, flood," יצק pual "pour out," and קמט in the first colon, which some think means "sweep away" (so Dhorme; cf. Davidson, Hölscher, Terrien); but the suggestion has little probability.

17–18 These verses sit awkwardly here, since the scornful laughter of the righteous in v 19 might be expected to follow directly on the description of the premature end of the wicked in v 16. Not a few commentators delete the verses as an erroneous repetition of the material of 21:14–15 (see *Note* 17.a). If the verses are original, they have to be seen as Eliphaz's quotation of Job's words in chap. 21 "in order to show that those whose good fortune he has vaunted are the very ones who were the victims of the catastrophe" (Dhorme). On the phrase "Depart from us," see *Comment* on 21:14. Job has not had the wicked saying, "What can the Almighty do to us?" (RSV), but he did have them sneering that there was no profit in praying to him (21:15b), so the line here most probably means, "What can the Almighty do *for* us?" They are denying not his power to punish them (though they dismiss that possibility) but his power to aid them.

Despite their denial of his profitability for them, God nevertheless has "filled their houses with prosperity" (cf. also 3:15)—according to Job, that is, of course, who has drawn such a picture of the prosperity of the wicked in 21:7–13 and has claimed that their prosperity (טוּב; it is טוֹב here, with no real difference in meaning) is something they can rely on without any threat from an avenging God (21:16). Their prosperity is in their own hand, Job had said in 21:16a, meaning that they have it in secure possession; here the words that Eliphaz puts into Job's mouth are that God has filled their houses with good things, meaning that their prosperity is real and by God's design. The meanings are not the same, but Eliphaz is not misrepresenting Job. Job would agree, though he did not say so himself in chap. 21, that God fills the houses of the wicked with good things. There he had said that there is no scourge of God upon them (v 9) and that God does not apportion them suffering in his anger (v 17); in portraying their prosperity as a simple fact, he had not meant that it was uncaused or even the mere result of their own labors or their own wickedness. His very question, "Why do the wicked live?" implied that it was God who was sustaining the wicked in their continued existence.

When Job had said in 21:16 that the "counsel of the wicked is far from [God]," he had meant that God takes no interest in the deserts of the wicked but allows them to "live out their days in prosperity" (21:13). Now when Eliphaz quotes Job's words, "and the counsel of the wicked is far from him," he means the same thing: despite the blasphemy of the wicked, God showers abundance on them and takes no notice of their "counsel" (עצה) or plans or thoughts that they entertain about him. Their willful ignorance of him is "remote" (רחק) from him, a matter of no significance to him. It is much the same idea as Eliphaz has ascribed to Job in vv 13–14: God dwells in a remote heaven, wrapped in thick clouds that hinder his gaze upon human affairs. From such a distance, and separated from the world by a "deep darkness," he cannot "rule" it, and the plans of the wicked—and no less the plans of the righteous—are beyond either his ken or his concern.

19 Vv 19–20 link back to vv 15–16. That is to say, what the righteous see that causes them to laugh with scorn is the destruction of the wicked who are shriveled up and swept away. If the language Job uses puts him on the path of the wicked, doubting whether God has any interest in ruling the world with justice (vv 13–14), he may expect to become the laughingstock of the righteous when an inevitable disaster overtakes him. For the idea of laughing with scorn at the downfall of the wicked, see *Comment* on 12:4, 5; and cf. Pss 52:6 (8); 58:10 (11); 107:42; Prov 1:26 (of Wisdom). It is what God himself does in Ps 2:4.

20 These are most probably the words of the righteous; though there is nothing in the Hebrew corresponding to the "saying" of RSV, REV, and NIV, the opening phrase אם־לא, lit. "if not," seems to introduce their rhetorical question. They are glad to see the possessions of the wicked destroyed and all their wealth consumed, not because they have been suffering at the hands of the wicked like the righteous in the Psalms, but because the punishment of the wicked confirms that the doctrine of retribution is in good working order; they as the righteous can have all the more confidence in their own reward if they can see retributive justice being meted out to wrongdoers.

21–30 It is entirely in character for Eliphaz to conclude his speech by painting a picture of the happy future in store for Job. From the beginning of his first speech, Eliphaz has affirmed Job's essential innocence, and, despite the charges of vv 5–9, he does not really believe that Job is a dreadful sinner. Those accusations were no more than inferences Eliphaz felt compelled to draw from the fact of Job's suffering (see on vv 2–30 above); if they had been the result of his knowledge and observation of Job, he could never have said in 4:6 that Job's fear of God was reason for him to have confidence, or have pronounced Job happy at the very moment he is enduring the discipline of the Almighty (5:17). Nor could he be concluding his final speech, in this chapter, with the words, "by the cleanness of your hands you will be delivered" (v 30).

The truth is, Eliphaz knows of nothing wrong that Job has done. He is as much in the dark as Job himself about the reason for Job's suffering. He can guess and he can speculate, but in the end he finds there is no sin he can urge Job to forswear, no amendment of life he can encourage. All he can say, in the most generalizing way, is that Job should "come to terms with" God (v 21) and "return" to him (v 23). And even so, the accent in this final strophe is not upon what Job must do to restore himself to God's favor, and certainly not upon any difficulties this program of repentance may hold for Job (as it would for a truly wicked person); Eliphaz wants to stress rather the blessed future that he can confidently predict for Job. By the end of the strophe the language of future delights has taken over, and the conditions that Job must first fulfill have effectively dropped out of sight. The balance we observe between the conditions Job has to meet and the blessedness that awaits him depends somewhat upon how many of the lines in vv 23–26 we decide are conditional clauses. But if the *Translation* above is correct, the only conditions are those of vv 21aα, 22, and 23aα, and all the rest of vv 21–30 (with the exception of the proverb-like sentence of v 29) is assurance to Job.

What of Eliphaz's theology then? Do his exhortations bear "the stamp of the most materialistic utilitarianism" (Dhorme)? "Decidedly not," says Newsom, correctly, despite NIV's rendering of v 21: "Submit to God . . . in this way prosperity will come to you." Well-being (טובה) is multidimensional: it includes restoration to a comfortable life, with an abundance of wealth (v 24), underwritten by God himself (v 25), and the exercise of personal autonomy (v 28), but it equally includes a renewed relationship of trust between Job and God, and even of delight in God (v 26).

21 What troubles Eliphaz about Job is, evidently, not that he is a dreadful sinner in imminent danger of annihilation but that he continues a fruitless disputation against God that only prolongs his agony. If he thought Job were a truly wicked man, Eliphaz would not be urging him to "agree with" (סכן) God; this is the language one uses for friends who have fallen out with one another. No doubt Eliphaz expects Job to accede to God's treatment of him. He does not encourage Job to hammer out a compromise with the Almighty; but neither, we observe, does he use the language of defeat or resignation. His hope for Job is not that he should win his case against God, nor that he should lose, but that he should be reconciled with his divine opponent.

In urging Job to "agree with" God (הַסְכֶּן־נָא *hasken-nāʾ*, with the particle *nāʾ* for politeness' sake and encouragement), Eliphaz makes a wordplay with his opening line (v 2), where he had denied that a human can be "profitable" (יִסְכָּן *yiskon*, יִסְכֹּן *yiskōn*) to God. Job cannot hope to bring any gain to God by his piety (or damage him by his sin), but he can come to terms with him and live in harmony with him. God is not threatened by Job's hostility, but he has no wish that Job and he should remain unreconciled. Being at peace (שלם) is a state Eliphaz esteems highly: in 5:23–24 he had envisaged a restored Job being at peace (שלם) with the wild animals and his dwelling being secure, or rather, literally, peace itself (שלום). He was dismayed at Job, as a wise man, not being at peace in himself but racked with "violent notions" (15:2), and he laid before Job the portrait of the wicked man, Job's mirror image, as a man without a moment's peace, in torment all his days (15:20). Eliphaz himself is a peaceable person who recoils from expressions of anger (cf. 15:12–13); his ideal is "gentle" and rational speech (15:11). For Eliphaz, being set at peace is the best thing that could happen to Job.

Job both needs Eliphaz's advice and cannot afford to take it. If Job were to dampen his anger at the injustice of his lot, his integrity would suffer. Job's maturity, human worth, and dignity all hang on his taking charge of his own experience and not resigning himself to letting it all wash over him. On the other hand, in the end will it not be a coming to terms with God and letting himself be reconciled to his suffering that will be the resolution Job reaches? When he lays his hand on his mouth (40:4–5; cf. 42:3) and abandons his case against God, it is all over, as they say, bar the shouting. But what will have happened to Job then? Will he not have suffered a kind of death in bowing to the force of an inscrutable omnipotence? He needs Eliphaz's advice to live at peace with God, for otherwise he will go on tearing himself to pieces (18:4); but if he takes the advice, he will be submitting his intelligence, his integrity, and his worth to the rule of an unknowable deity. The "happy" resolution of the book, corresponding exactly to Eliphaz's sincerest hopes for Job, that sees Job restored to his former prosperity, will not tell us the whole truth about Job. It will not breathe a word of the headache Job will endure for the rest of his life, the agony of having experienced a disaster for which there never has been, and never will be, any explanation. "By submitting to God one finds inner harmony and a sense of well-being," says Hartley (whether in Eliphaz's voice or in his own I do not know). But at what price, Job must ask. Is inner harmony worth a lobotomy?

"Good will come" to Job "thereby," promises Eliphaz, meaning by "thereby" (בהם, lit. "by them") the two acts of coming to terms with God and being at peace. Who says there is no profit in religion? It might even be that he says, "Your increase, or, income (תבואה) will be good," using a word for harvest from the field (Exod 23:10; Job 31:12; etc.), a term often encountered also in the wisdom literature for "gain, profit" (e.g., Prov 3:14; 8:19); see *Note* 21.d. In any case, Eliphaz clings to the idea that there is material benefit in piety, despite Job's best endeavors in chap. 21 to sever the link altogether between morality and prosperity.

22 Eliphaz is nothing if not the teacher of wisdom. In this sentence his vocabulary is almost entirely that of Proverbs. Being an instructor in wisdom himself, he wants to represent God as essentially the heavenly teacher whose ambition is to warn and guide the foolish and impressionable by his wisdom. The *torah* of God is not of course the law in the Pentateuchal sense; God is pictured rather as the fatherly author (cf. on v 4 above) of teaching or guidance like the *torah* in Proverbs that comes from one's father (3:1; 4:2; 7:2) or mother (1:8; 6:20), or from the wise (13:14). "Receiving" or "accepting" (לקח) is the term for the pupil's imbibing of the teacher's wisdom (cf. Prov 1:3; 2:1; 4:10; 8:10; 10:8; 21:11; 24:32; and the term לֶקַח "learning, teaching" [lit. "what is received"] in Job 11:4; cf. also Prov 1:5; 4:2; etc.). Even the idea of oral instruction "from the mouth of" the teacher is Proverbs language (cf. Prov 2:6 [מפיו "from his mouth," of God's wisdom]; 4:5; 5:7; 7:24; 8:8). And the "words" (אֵמֶר) of the teacher are equally a pointer to the wisdom location of Eliphaz's speech (cf. the noun in Prov 1:2, 21; 2:1; 4:5, 10, 20; 5:7; 7:1, 24; 8:8; etc.); Job for his part, being a wise man himself, will use the same language in 23:12 in affirming that he has treasured the words of God's mouth. Only the term "lay up" (שׂים) in the heart is not Proverbs language; there we hear of applying or setting (שׁית) the heart to knowledge (22:17; 24:32; cf. 27:23), or bringing (בוא hiph) the heart to knowledge (23:12), of the heart taking hold (תמך) of the teacher's words (4:4) and of the parents' commands and *torah* being "bound" (קשׁר) upon the heart (3:3; 6:21; 7:3). But the idea of internalizing the instruction is similar enough; and the idea of wisdom or wise words being treasure that is stored up is quite common (cf. the comparison with silver and gold and jewels [Prov 3:14–15; 8:10, 19; 10:20] and the image of treasure [2:1, 4]). Perhaps M. J. Dahood has correctly discerned here the language of scribal dictation: "at his mouth" denotes "at dictation" in Jer 36:17–18, while setting (שׂים) words on or in the heart is reminiscent of writing words on the "tablet of the heart" (Prov 3:3; 7:3) ("The Metaphor in Job 22, 22," *Bib* 47 [1966] 108–9).

And what *are* these words from the divine teacher? It is not the suffering itself that is God's instruction (as against Duhm), for it is specifically a teaching with "words" and from the "mouth." No doubt Eliphaz means the kind of promises of a blessed future that he will himself be offering in the next verses, the rewards that the doctrine of retribution can guarantee for a life of virtue. But he does not here hold himself out as the channel of divine revelation (as against Driver–Gray); what he has to recommend to Job is nothing mysterious, no personal communication from the supernatural world like his night vision of 4:12–17, but the everyday teaching of the wise that is attributed to God as its source (cf. "God's encouragements" in 15:11, which are nothing but the orthodox theology Eliphaz teaches).

23 The Proverbs language continues in the demand to Job that he "turn" (שׁוב) to the Almighty. Though the verb is often translated "repent" elsewhere in the Hebrew Bible (e.g., Jer 18:11; cf. BDB, 997a, §6d; J. A. Soggin, *TDOT,* 3:1312–17), it never means that in Job (so it is not an echo of the prophetic call to repentance, as Fohrer thinks). It is not even that Job should "return" to God (as RSV, JB, NIV), as if he had wandered away or departed from God, but that he should "turn" himself and his attention to God as a pupil does to his teacher when receiving instruction. It is the same language as in Prov 1:23, where the simple are urged to "turn" to Wisdom's reproof. Despite his extravagant words in vv 5–9, Eliphaz does not really believe that Job needs to make a radical amendment of his life or to repent of his crimes. What Job needs is not more righteousness but more wisdom.

There are not many conditions Eliphaz is laying upon Job. It is a simple paying of attention to the conventional teaching that will inevitably have its effect on a rational and essentially pious man like Job. Simply turn your face to the truth, says Eliphaz, and you will be "established," "built up" (בנה). The thrust of Eliphaz's speech is constantly toward encouragement and promise, not toward the prescription of a regime of acts of contrition. But the translations and commentaries cannot let Job off the hook so lightly. They want him, many of them, to "humble" himself (so Moffatt, RSV, JB, GNB), adopting an emendation of the quite intelligible text (see *Note* 23.c; but not so NAB, NIV). And they think Eliphaz must surely be wanting to impose more conditions on Job's restoration than simply a "turning" to God, so they make into conditional sentences vv 23b–25 (RSV, NJPS) or at least 23b–24 (JB, NEB, NAB, NIV). The Hebrew will allow any of these suggestions, but it is more likely that the only conditional clause is that introduced by the particle אם "if": "if you turn to Shaddai." For otherwise it would be necessary to suppose that the "if" at the beginning of v 23 is to be understood also at the beginning of v 23b, even though the main clause "you will be built up" has intervened; and it would be necessary also to suppose that, after a simple "if" clause in v 23a and a one-word main clause, we then embark upon a long sequence of "if" clauses in v 23b that is not concluded until v 25 or 26. And there is the further question of the best interpretation of v 24 (see below).

Everyone assumes that letting, or making, wickedness be far from his tent is another condition that Job must fulfill if he is to enjoy the favor of the Almighty (v 26). But it is equally possible that this absence of wrongdoing is part of the benefit that will come to Job if he will simply "turn" himself to the Almighty: iniquity will be far from his tent, and he will not suffer any of the punishments that have hitherto resulted from the presence of wrongdoing in his family. It is not only Job's personal wrongdoing that may be in view, but the kinds of sin his children must have been involved in that brought about their deaths. There is no doubt an allusion to Zophar's line in 11:14: "If there is wrongdoing in your hand, renounce it [רחק hiph, as here, lit. "put it far"], and do not let iniquity [עולה, as here] dwell in your tent." But whereas Zophar formed these words as commands, Eliphaz shapes them as promises for the restored state of Job and his family. The image, as in 11:14, is of wickedness having no house room in Job's dwelling; and Job's "tent" (אהל) is nothing but archaic language for his house (cf. also 5:24; 8:22; 19:12; 29:4).

24–25 There is more than one way of taking these verses, and it is very revealing of the prejudices of commentators to see what they choose. The prevailing view is that Job is being encouraged by Eliphaz to abandon his trust in material wealth and put his hopes in Shaddai instead: "Let Job no more place his confidence in gold . . . , but rather throw it away as worthless" (Driver–Gray); he should "make God his portion" (Peake). "When Job thus casts from him temporal things, by the excessive cherishing of which he has hitherto sinned, then God himself will be his imperishable treasure, his everlasting higher delight" (Delitzsch). Job may give expression to his change of heart either by assigning his nuggets to the dust (NIV) and dumping his finest gold in the dry stream bed (GNB, if not flinging it in the stream [Moffatt]) or shipping his gold back to Ophir (Newsom)—metaphorically, no doubt—or by simply treating his precious metal as dust (NEB), regarding it as dirt (NJPS). On this reading, Job would be affirming in 31:24 that he has not indeed made his gold the ground of his confidence.

The alternative view, which is to be preferred, is that Job is here being promised by Eliphaz that if he "returns" to the Almighty (v 23), he will regain his former wealth. Either he will become so rich that he will regard gold as no less common than dirt (or rather, even more common than dirt or dust, the על signifying excess), or else he will "lay up" (KJV) his gold like dust in piles as if it were as plentiful as stones in the wadi, or (improbably) he will be so secure that he will be able to leave his gold lying about on the ground without risk of losing it (Gordis). The Almighty would then have "become" his gold and silver in the sense of having been the provider of it. This is a less "religious" interpretation but a more concrete one; the alternative idea of God becoming Job's "gold" and "silver" in the sense that Job will esteem God as the highest good is quite banal, since Job has little doubt about the supremacy of the divine.

An initial objection to this second view is that gold and silver in the book of Job are usually the sign of the despot (as they were in 3:15) and Job himself measures his wealth in cattle and servants, not precious metals. But in view of v 25, Eliphaz must be using "gold" metaphorically for wealth in whatever currency, as Job does in 31:24–25, and in any case Eliphaz cannot be taking a negative view of these precious metals if Shaddai is going to be Job's gold and silver.

The problem with the first and more common view is that, if Eliphaz means that Job has relied overmuch on his wealth instead of putting his trust in God, this would be a new accusation of Job, a charge not previously made by Eliphaz in his criticisms of Job's supposed sins in vv 5–9. And it would be strange for a new charge to be introduced in the present strophe, which on the whole is trying to offer Job assurance (similarly Gordis). Perhaps we should think that all of

Job's crimes in vv 5–9 are instances of his having esteemed his wealth too highly; but it is hard to believe that the reason he has withheld a cup of water from the exhausted (v 7) is because he has been trusting in his riches. A more serious difficulty with the view that Job should trust in God rather than his wealth is that Job now has no wealth to divest himself of (as Rowley remarks), and in any case Eliphaz himself can hardly envisage Job's restoration as anything other than a restoration of his possessions. What would it mean for Shaddai to "be" Job's silver if no actual wealth is in view? How will Job be able to employ servants again, and how will he manage to pay his vows (v 27) if he lives the life of a penniless pietist?

The wordplay in v 24 suggests that we may be dealing with a proverbial saying: "dust" in the first colon (עָפָר *ʿāpār*) is in assonance with "Ophir" (אוֹפִיר *ʾôpîr*) in the second, and "gold" (בֶּצֶר *beṣer*) in the first with "in, or with, the rock, or pebble" (בְּצוּר *bĕṣûr*) in the second. The reference to Ophir, a traditional home of fine gold, as well as the use of "Ophir" alone rather than "gold of Ophir" (as in 28:16; Isa 13:12; Ps 45:9 [10]; Ecclus 7:18), points in the same direction. Ophir is thought to lie either in the south Arabian peninsula, by the shores of the Red Sea (modern Yemen) and near Sheba, or on the East African coast, the Egyptian land of Punt (modern Somalia). See G. A. van Beek, *IDB,* 3:605–6; E. M. Cook, *ISBE,* 3:607–8; D. J. Wiseman, *IBD,* 2:1119–20; M. Görg, "Ofir und Punt," *BN* 82 (1996) 5–8.

There is perhaps another, more hidden, wordplay here as well. As Eliphaz nears the end of his last speech, can it be accidental that he assures Job that God will be his gold, when he, Eliphaz, bears a name that sounds as if it means exactly that—"My God is gold" (cf. *Comment* on 2:11)?

26–27 Eliphaz continues his depiction of the happy future that awaits a Job who has fulfilled no more onerous condition than to "turn" to God (v 23). Job will "delight" in Shaddai, the verb (ענג hithp) suggesting exquisite and refined delight (in Deut 28:56 it is used of a woman so exquisite that she "does not venture to set the sole of her foot on the ground"); in 27:10, Ps 37:4, and Isa 58:14 also it is used of the delight of the pious in the Lord, a *jouissance mystique* (Terrien). And Job will be able to "lift up [his] face" toward God with confidence in his own innocence. The phrase, which is quite rare in the OT, means not "pray" or "entreat" (for which the Hebrew idiom is "lift up the hands"), but rather "not be ashamed," "feel innocent" (as in 2 Sam 2:22), or perhaps "be happy" (cf. on 11:15), in parallel to "delight."

It is not a condition for but a consequence of Job's restoration that he will be able to "make supplication" (עתר) for God's blessing on any matter at all (not for recovery from his illness, as Peake) and be heard; and that for Job would be a restoration worth the name since he has more than once expressed his desire for a reciprocal "calling" and "answering" (cf. 13:22; 14:15; see also 9:16; 12:4; 19:16; 30:20). He will be "able to pay" his vows because what he has been seeking from God has been given him (cf., e.g., Deut 23:22 [21]; 2 Sam 15:7; Pss 22:26; 50:14; 61:6, 9; Eccl 5:4 [5]). It is not that Eliphaz promises him that he will be so pious that he "will" in fact pay his vows, but that he will be given everything he asks for so that he "will be able," "will have good cause," to present the offerings he has vowed. On conditional oaths of this kind, see C. A. Keller, *TLOT,* 2:719–22; and on vows in general, see T. W. Cartledge, *Vows in the Hebrew Bible and the Ancient Near East,* JSOTSup 147 (Sheffield: JSOT Press, 1992).

Further, Job's decisions will be "established." This sounds like legal decisions he makes (the verb גזר occurs in the sense of "decide" elsewhere only at Esth 2:1), which will not be controverted because he is so evidently enjoying God's favor that his judgments have an almost divine authority attaching to them. To "establish" (קום) a word is to ensure that it takes effect, is successful (cf., e.g., 1 Sam 1:23; 1 Kgs 2:4; Isa 14:24; Jer 44:29). In short, all that he does will prosper; that is the sense of the metaphor of light shining on his paths (in 19:8 his path was veiled in darkness).

29–30 To conclude his speech, Eliphaz resorts to a conventional wisdom antithesis. God humbles boasters, he says, and delivers the lowly (cf. Prov 3:34; 29:23; Ps 18:27 [28]). But there is more than mere sententiousness here; though he does not say so, explicitly, we are to understand from him that Job's failing is pride and that Eliphaz is recommending to him a healthy dose of humility. In so doing, he returns to the theme with which this strophe (vv 21–30) opened: Job should humbly accept the instruction God is offering him. And God's "instruction" (v 22) is nothing more nor less than the assurance that by simply "turning" to God (v 23)—that is, by a pious concentration on divine intentions rather than upon his own sense of injustice—every aspect of his life will be restored. Insisting upon his own righteousness is pride, and it has to be beaten down by God.

Despite all the inferences Eliphaz has been earlier drawing about Job's "great wickedness" (cf. on vv 6–9), but which he has been unable to substantiate, he cannot deny at the end of his speech that Job is innocent; his hands are clean. Job's problem has been that, in trumpeting his righteousness and protesting against God's treatment of him on grounds of his deserts, Job has been putting himself in the camp of the haughty, who think they know better than God.

Eliphaz's last sentence (v 30)—which is quite important for understanding his speech as a whole—suffers from some textual uncertainty. As it stands in the Hebrew, it seems to say that "[God] delivers the guilty, and it is by the cleanness of your hands that he will be delivered." R. Gordis has fastened on this text as an expression of what he calls "horizontal collective responsibility" ("Corporate Personality in Job: A Note on 22:29–30," *JNES* 4 (1945) 54–55 = *The Word and the Book: Studies in Biblical Language and Literature* [New York: Ktav, 1976] 133–34). When Job has been restored to God's favor, Gordis thinks, he will be able to intercede for others, who are less righteous than himself, and to enable them to evade the consequences of their sin. Interestingly, it is exactly this that turns out to be the case when at the end of the narrative Job, now publicly acknowledged as a righteous man, makes intercession for the friends so that they escape the punishment their folly deserves (42:7–9). And "it is quite in the poet's manner to let the speakers drop unconscious prophecies of the final issue" (Peake; similarly Delitzsch).

There are some problems with this reading, however. There is a textual difficulty, in that the word for "guilty" is an otherwise unknown compound (אי־נקי, lit. "not innocent," if indeed אי can mean "not"; see *Note* 30.a), and there seems to be no reason for the construction of such an awkward compound when there are plenty of words for "guilty" and "wicked" available. There is a general theological difficulty, in that it is hard to imagine the character Eliphaz or the author of Job stating so baldly that "God delivers the guilty" (the prayer of Job for his friends in chap. 42 is not a proper analogy since they are not "non-innocent" but merely "foolish"). And there is a contextual difficulty in that, so understood, the verse would bring Eliphaz's speech to a strange conclusion, focusing on the deliverance of others through the merits of Job rather than on the question of Job's innocence or otherwise, with which it has been concerned as a whole.

This reading is nevertheless not impossible, though the language of "collective responsibility" could well be dispensed with. It could be that Eliphaz is representing the peak of Job's restoration to divine favor by promising him that he will so enjoy the divine favor that because of his innocence, "through the cleanness of [his] hands," his prayers on behalf of others will not fail to have their effect, and he will have acquired the "status of a patriarchal hero or mediator with the capacity to redeem the condemned by his powerful word" (Habel). If that is what Eliphaz means, it is an irony that he promises Job what Job already knows to be problematic. For the innocence of Job's hands in chap. 1 did not ensure that his prayers on behalf of his children, guilty or otherwise, were successful.

On balance, however, I prefer to accept an emendation of the text (see *Note* 30.a), mainly because of the linguistic difficulty of אִי־נָקִי, which apparently means "not innocent." Eliphaz would then be concluding: "He delivers the innocent; by the cleanness of your hands you will be delivered." The idea is as banal as the rhetoric. The repetition of "deliver" (מלט) seems weak, and even as circumspect a scholar as Dhorme wished to emend it to "escape" simply to avoid the limp ending to the speech. But perhaps this flat-footed conclusion matches the thought well: Eliphaz has progressed not an inch from the moment he first opened his mouth in chap. 4; he has learned nothing from Job and Job's experience, and he knows nothing except that "God delivers the innocent."

What that has to do with Job remains unclear. Does Eliphaz mean that the only way anyone is "delivered" is by being innocent, and that Job will only be able to apply the foregoing assurances to himself if he can give himself a clean bill of health morally speaking, even after that acerbic list of crimes Eliphaz has ascribed to Job (vv 5–9)? Or does he mean that he believes that Job actually is, all things considered, an innocent man, and that the cleanness of his hands, which Eliphaz has never really doubted despite the evidence of Job's sufferings to the contrary, will lead sooner or later to his deliverance? The latter seems to be the more likely if we recall the opening of Eliphaz's first speech to Job: "Is not your piety your source of confidence? Does not your blameless life give you hope?" (4:6). The most encouraging of the friends, Eliphaz has always taken Job's general righteousness and piety as a datum, and has assured Job that the sufferings of a pious man cannot be long-lasting. It would be wholly in keeping with this outlook that his very last words to Job should be "the cleanness of your hands."

And yet there is always the possibility of a less positive reading of Eliphaz's peroration. He does not need to pose explicit conditions in order to leave the whole outcome still hypothetical. For if deliverance is "through" the cleanness of Job's hands, then everything *depends upon* the cleanness of his hands. And if there is any question about just how clean Job's hands are, whether indeed there are any proper inferences to be drawn about Job's morals from his present state (and we cannot forget that Eliphaz has been stridently drawing such consequences just a few minutes ago), then there is no comfort in these closing words for Job, just a tame and ultimately unfeeling reiteration of the old doctrine of impersonal retribution, a "sterile legalism of salvation for the righteous alone" (Andersen).

So the end, the conclusion, perhaps the point, of all this speech of Eliphaz, and perhaps of all Eliphaz's speeches, is caught in an indeterminacy. Eliphaz is a moderate man, who does not hold with the categorical claims of a Job to perfect innocence (see on 15:5–6, 14); even the angels are imperfect (4:18), the heavens themselves are not clean in God's sight (15:15), and so much less humankind, which is loathsome and foul, and drinks wrongdoing like water (15:14, 16). From Eliphaz's point of view, Job is pious but not perfect; even within the dialogue itself Job has allowed himself to be drawn into profitless, irreverent, crafty, wild talk (15:2–6). Combine that commonsensical moderation with a doctrinaire belief that everything has its exact and just reward, and you find that Eliphaz after all has nothing to offer Job. Everything depends on the degree of Job's innocence, which is to say, on the degree of his culpability. If the moderate man says, It is through the cleanness of your hands that you will be delivered, *and* humankind is loathsome and foul, what comfort is to be taken by the sufferer, who shows no signs of being delivered?

There is another problem with Eliphaz's conclusion. He makes a naive and paradoxical statement on the question of causality; but he has not worked through it. It is God who delivers the innocent, he says; but it is through, or by, the cleanness of a person's hands that they are delivered (the phrase "cleanness of hands" is elsewhere only in 2 Sam 22:21 [= Ps 18:20 (21)]; Ps 18:24 [25]; cf. also Pss 24:4; 73:13). If innocence is what delivers, where is the need for God, in Eliphaz's theology? And if it is God that delivers, but only on the basis of the individual's innocence, what is God but the mechanism for executing retribution in general? It is a feature of OT talk about God's salvation that it is extended to those who are needy, not to those who deserve it; the human requirement is trust (e.g., Pss 22:4 [5]; 37:40), or reverence (e.g., Ps 33:18–19), not innocence (cf. G. G. O'Collins, "Salvation," *ABD*, 5:907–14 [909]). God saves the righteous, indeed (e.g., Ps 7:10 [11]), but not "according to their righteousness"; he may "judge" them according to their righteousness (e.g., Ps 7:8 [9]), but he saves them according to his mercy. "Salvation" is in any case not part of the wisdom vocabulary: the verb ישע "save" occurs in Proverbs only at 20:22 and 28:18, the latter perhaps not in reference to God's saving, and the noun יֵשַׁע "salvation" never; and in Job the verb occurs elsewhere only at 5:15; 26:2; 40:14, and the noun at 5:4, 11. Only here and at 5:15 (and perhaps 5:11) do the terms refer to God's salvation, and they are in Eliphaz's mouth there too. And as for "deliverance" (verb מלט), it is found in Job elsewhere only in the sense of "escape" (as in 1:15, 16, 17, 19; 19:20; 20:20; 41:11 [19]) or of human rescue (6:23; 29:12), never of divine deliverance. So what is the wisdom teacher Eliphaz (cf. on v 22) doing with prophetic or psalm-like promises (not commonplaces of wisdom teaching, as Andersen) of divine salvation (ישע) for the humble (v 29) and divine deliverance (מלט) for the innocent (v 30)? And why has he denatured the notion of divine salvation by making it hang upon the cleanness of Job's hands? All in all, there is something very odd about this conclusion to the sequence of Eliphaz's fine and interesting speeches (Driver–Gray: "not a very forcibly expressed conclusion"; Alonso Schökel: "an ironic distance on the author's part"), and we need not doubt that the poet was well aware of what ideas and what rhetoric his character was taking refuge in.

Explanation

The mild, moderate man Eliphaz has thrown something of a bombshell into the stately procession of speeches, each in its turn, each of much the same length, each followed by a Joban speech. Eliphaz, the most encouraging and understanding of the friends, here accuses Job of "great wickedness," or rather, he has asked a rhetorical question, as if the answer were inevitable and everywhere known, "Is not your wickedness great?" (v 5).

This is a charge that is as much out of character for Eliphaz as it is unimaginable for Job. It drives commentators to desperation. Here is one such reaction, sympathetic and intelligent but, ultimately, too sentimental:

> In this speech Eliphaz, since nothing else is left for him to do, roundly accuses Job of such sins as were only too common in the East among men of his social standing.... It is remarkable that Eliphaz should close this speech, which has gone beyond all the others in its bitter and unjust charges, with so highly coloured a description of Job's happiness if he will turn to God. It is not quite easy to see why. Perhaps the poet wanted to represent Eliphaz as conscious of the harshness of his speech, feeling, it may be, that he had gone too far. But more probably, as he utters his last speech, the wish to save his friend becomes uppermost, and after the terrors of the Law he would utter the consolations of the Gospel, seeking to win if he could not alarm. (Peake)

Eliphaz's accusation against Job is not something that he first utters and then withdraws. It has to be understood within the context of a speech as whole that ends with Eliphaz assuring Job of God's salvation and affirming that he will be "delivered" through the cleanness of his hands (vv 29–30). And it has to be understood within the framework of Eliphaz's speeches as a group, which began with his question, "Is not your piety your source of confidence? Does not your blameless life give you hope?" (4:6).

It is not impossible that Eliphaz, having now experienced at first hand Job's intransigence and unequivocal insistence on his perfect innocence, should abandon his initial softsoaping, and in this closing speech deliver against Job something of a coup de grâce. But it is inconceivable that, having done so, he should then resume his optimistic predictions of a blessed future for Job. In some way, then, the charges of Eliphaz against Job have to be understood differently from their face value.

In the *Comment,* I have argued that all that Eliphaz means is that Job's wrongdoing "must have been" great if he is suffering so badly, and that, knowing nothing of which to accuse him in detail, he is reduced to imagining the kinds of misdeeds a man in Job's position must have been guilty of—callous disregard of the needs of the poor and underprivileged. These are charges, which, as Davidson says, "furnish a singular illustration of the length to which good men will suffer their theoretical opinions in religion to carry them." If I am right in thinking that there is no substance in them at all, that they are figments of Eliphaz's imagination or inferences from his dogma, it casts an unwelcome light upon the character of this most congenial of Job's friends, and therewith upon the power of religious ideas to turn humans into monsters.

There is something positive to be said about the Eliphaz of this chapter, though. If I have rightly understood the syntax of vv 23–28, and am right in thinking that there is only one condition that Eliphaz imposes upon Job for a full restoration to divine favor, Eliphaz is a lot more humane and less legalistic than many of his commentators. For his sole condition seems to be that Job should "turn" to God (v 23), which is a demand not for repentance but for a reverent and trustful commitment of his cause to God. If Job will do that, and forswear his aggressive and confrontational legal dispute that he has been preoccupied with ever since chap. 13 (13:18–23), there is nothing to stand in the way of his restoration to intimacy with the divine, Job making his prayer to God and God responding (v 27), Job finding his delight in the Almighty and the Almighty restoring him to his position of power and authority (v 28). Repentance is not the issue; despite his presumptive great wickedness, Job is in essence an innocent man, whose only real fault is to be facing the wrong way. If he would turn *to* God instead of *against* him, he would find deliverance.

Who can dispute with Eliphaz? How can "turning" to God be anything but pious and altogether desirable? Only Job knows how dishonest such an act would be; "turning" to God and abandoning his grievance against him would be to bow submissively to the dictates of a tyrant, to stifle his sense of outrage, and to negate his own personal experience. Not all the promises that Eliphaz can hold out of restoration to health and wealth and divine favor can bribe Job into abandoning his cause against the maltreatment he has received at God's hand.

The "exhortations and promises by which Eliphaz . . . seeks to lead Job back to God are in and of themselves true and most glorious," writes Delitzsch. "But even these beauteous words of promise are blemished by the false assumption from which they proceed, . . . that Job is now suffering the punishment of his avarice. . . . Thus do even the holiest and truest words lose their value when they are not uttered at the right time, and the most brilliant sermon that exhorts to penitence remains without effect when it is prompted by pharisaic uncharitableness." The question is, whether words spoken "out of season" have any right to be called true, glorious, and beautiful, and not simply malapropisms; whether there is ever any truth in words or only in words in situations; whether Eliphaz, in short, has anything wise or profound to say or whether his speech as a whole should simply be labeled "not right" and "folly"—which is, at the end of the day, the divine evaluation according to the narrator (42:7–8).

At the least, even if Eliphaz's theology is not to be judged cruel, it is, for all its piety, poverty-stricken. Duhm, for one, evidently despised it: "Humility and purity are . . . for Eliphaz the essential elements in religion and the sure foundation for good fortune; both are within the capacity of humans to achieve. . . . Theology makes salvation depend on the deeds of humans, religion on the heart of God." What is the worst of it for Duhm is hard to tell from this succinct account, whether the elevation of moral virtues above theological realities, the bureaucratic certainty about reward for good behavior, or the prominence of works-righteousness. Whatever its greatest weakness, Eliphaz's theology cannot meet the situation of the man Job; as in his first speech, Eliphaz's theoretical position cannot allow the possibility of a Job, and, now that he confronts a man who is suffering grossly when any sins he can possibly have committed are sins of hard-heartedness rather than illegality, he does not know where to turn. The confusion in his speech is a sign in itself that a further more drastic resolution of the case of Job is still awaited.

Job's Eighth Speech (23:1–17; 24:1–17, 25)

Bibliography

Balentine, S. E. "Job 23:1–9, 16–17." *Int* 53 (1999) 290–93. **Berger-Lutz, R.** "Hart beschuldigt—doch nicht verstummt: Elifas und Hiob (Hiob 22 und 23)." In *Hiob: Ökumenischer Arbeitskreis für Bibelarbeit.* Ed. R. Berger-Lutz. Bibelarbeit in der Gemeinde 7. Basel: Reinhardt, 1989. 244–60. **Burns, J. B.** "Support for the Emendation *rĕḥōb mĕqōmô* in Job xxiv 19–20." *VT* 39 (1989) 480–85. **Byington, S. T.** "Some Bits of Hebrew: IV. Texts in Job." *ExpTim* 57 (1945–46) 110–11. **Clines, D. J. A.** "Quarter Days Gone: Job 24 and the Absence of God." In *God in the Fray.* FS W. Brueggemann, ed. T. Linafelt and T. K. Beal. Minneapolis: Fortress, 1998. 242–58. Reprinted in *On the Way to the Postmodern: Old Testament Essays, 1967–1998,* JSOTSup 293 (Sheffield: Sheffield Academic Press, 1998) 2:801–19. **Dahood, M. J.** "Northwest Semitic Philology and Job." In *The Bible in Current Catholic Thought: Gruenthaner Memorial Volume.* Ed. J. L. McKenzie. St. Mary's Theological Studies 1. New York: Herder & Herder, 1962. 55–74. **Deuel, D. C.** "Job 19:25 and Job 23:10 Revisited: An Exegetical Note." *The Master's Seminary Journal* 5.1 (1994) 97–99. **Driver, G. R.** "Problems in Job." *AJSL* 52 (1936) 160–70. **Geyer, J. B.** "Mythological Sequence in Job xxiv 19–20." *VT* 42 (1982) 118–20. **Guillaume, A.** "The Arabic Background of the Book of Job." In *Promise and Fulfilment.* FS S. H. Hooke, ed. F. F. Bruce. Edinburgh: T. & T. Clark, 1963. 106–27. **Humbert, P.** "Le mot biblique ébyôn." *RHPR* 32 (1952) 1–6. Reprinted in *Opuscules d'un hébraïsant,* Mémoires de l'Université de Neuchâtel 26 (Neuchâtel: Secrétariat de l'Université, 1958) 187–92. **Kopf, L.** "Arabische Etymologien und Parallelen zum Bibelwörterbuch." *VT* 8 (1958) 161–25. **Kuhl, C.** "Neuere Literarkritik des Buches Hiob." *TRu* NS 21 (1953) 163–205, 257–317. **Labuschagne, C. J.** "The Emphasizing Particle *gam* and Its Connotations." In *Studia biblica et semitica Theodoro Christiano Vriezen qui munere professoris theologiae per XXV annos functus est, ab amicis, collegis, discipulis dedicata.* Ed. W. C. van Unnik and A. S. van der Woude. Wageningen: Veenman & Zonen, 1966. 193–203. **Loretz, O.** "Philologische und textologische Probleme in Hi 24,1–25." *UF* 12 (1980) 261–66. **Martin, G. W.** "Elihu and the Third-Cycle in the Book of Job." Diss., Princeton, 1972. **Michel, W. L.** "*Slmwt,* 'Deep Darkness' or 'Shadow of Death'?" [Job 24:17]. *BR* 29 (1984) 5–20. **Morrow, F. J.** "11Q Targum Job and the Massoretic Text." *RevQ* 8 (1973) 253–56. **Reider, J.** "Some Notes to the Text of the Scriptures." *HUCA* 3 (1926) 109–16. **Rignell, L. G.** "Comments on Some *cruces interpretum* in the Book of Job." *ASTI* 11 (1978) 111–18. **Selms, A. van.** "Motivated Interrogative Sentences in the Book of Job." *Semitics* 6 (1978) 28–35. **Sutcliffe, E. F.** "A Note on Job xxiv 10, 11." *JTS* 50 (1949) 174–76. **Tournay, R.** "L'ordre primitif des chapitres xxiv–xxviii du livre de Job." *RB* 64 (1957) 321–34. **Vermes, G.** "'The Torah Is a Light.'" *VT* 8 (1958) 436–38. **Wilde, A. de.** "Eine alte Crux Interpretum, Hiob xxiii 2." *VT* 22 (1972) 368–74. ———. "Vervreemding in Job 24:10, 11." *NTT* 28 (1974) 165. **Witte, M.** *Philologische Notizen zu Hiob 21–27.* BZAW 234. Berlin: de Gruyter, 1995. ———. *Vom Leiden zur Lehre: Der dritte Redegang (Hiob 21–27) und die Redaktionsgeschichte des Hiobbuches.* BZAW 230. Berlin: de Gruyter, 1994. **Wolfers, D.** "Job: The Third Cycle: Dissipating a Mirage." *DD* 16 (1987–88) 217–26; 17 (1988–89) 19–25.

Translation

1 *And Job answered and said:*

2 *Surely*[a] *my complaint is rebellious*[b] *today,*[c]
[d]*even though I lay a heavy hand upon my groaning.*

[3]*Oh, that I knew*[a] *how*[b] *I might find him,*
that I might come to his dwelling.[c]
[4]*I would set out*[a] *my case*[b] *before him,*
and fill my mouth with arguments.[c]
[5]*I would learn what answers he would have for me,*
and consider what[a] *he would say to me.*
[6]*Would he use his great power*[a] *to contend*[b] *with me?*
No![c] *he would surely*[d] *listen to me.*[e]
[7]*There*[a] *it would be an upright man in dispute*[b] *with him,*[c]
and I would escape[d] *once and for all*[e] *from my judge.*[f]

8 [a]*If*[b] *I go to the east,*[c] *he is not there;*
or to the west, I cannot see him.
[9]*In the north I seek him,*[a] *but I see*[b] *him not;*
I turn to the south,[c] *but I behold him not.*
[10]*For*[a] *he knows*[b] *what is my way;*[c]
should he assay me,[d] *I should come forth*[e] *pure as gold.*
[11]*My feet*[a] *have kept to*[b] *his path,*
I have followed[c] *his way without swerving.*[d]
12 [a]*From the commands*[b] *of his lips I have not departed;*
in my heart[c] *I have treasured the words of his mouth.*

[13]*If*[a] *he has decided,*[b] *who*[c] *can dissuade him?*
Whatever he desires, he does.
14 [a]*What he has planned for me,*[b] *he will surely*[c] *carry out;*
and there are many such plans[d] *in his mind.*[e]
[15]*Therefore*[a] *I am terrified before him;*
when I take thought, I am in dread of him.
[16]*God has made my spirits*[a] *weak;*[b]
the Almighty has dismayed me.
[17]*For*[a] *I am annihilated by darkness,*[b]
and thick darkness covers my face.[c]

24:1 *Why*[a] *are days of assize*[b] *not kept*[c] *by*[d] *the Almighty?*
Why do those who know him[e] *not see his judgment days?*[f]
2 [a]*The wicked*[b] *remove*[c] *boundary stones,*
they carry off[d] *flocks and pasture them*[e] *as their own.*
3 [a]*They drive away the donkey of the fatherless,*
and take the widow's bull as a pledge.[b]
[4]*They force the needy off*[a] *the road,*
and the poor of the land are utterly[b] *driven into hiding.*[c]

[5]*Like*[a] *onagers of the steppe country,*[b]
they go out[c] *to their work,*[d]
[e]*foraging*[f] *for provisions,*[g]
and the desert[h] *yields*[i] *them*[j] *food for their children.*[k]
6 [a]*They reap*[b] *in a field*[c] *that is not their own,*[d]
[e]*and glean*[f] *in the vineyard of the wicked.*[g]

7 [a]*They pass the night naked,*[b] *without clothing;*
they have no covering against[c] *the cold.*
8 *They are drenched by the mountain rain,*
and for lack of shelter take refuge among the rocks.[a]

9 [a]*The wicked*[b] *snatch the fatherless child from the breast,*[c]
and seize the child[d] *of the poor as a pledge.*
10 [a]*And the poor go about naked*[b] *and unclothed,*[c]
starving[d] *even as they carry the sheaves.*[e]
11 *Among*[a] *the olive rows*[b] *of the wicked they press oil;*[c]
[d]*they tread*[e] *the wine presses, but suffer thirst.*[f]
12 *From the towns*[a] *comes the groan*[b] *of the dying,*[c]
[d]*and the souls*[e] *of the wounded*[f] *cry out for help.*
[g]*But God charges no one with wrong.*[h]

13 [a]*They are among those who*[b] *are rebels against the light;*[c]
they do not know its ways,
and they do not frequent[d] *its paths.*
14 [a]*The murderer rises at daybreak*[b]
to kill[c] *the poor and needy.*[d]
15 *The eyes of the adulterer*[a] *watch for*[b] *the twilight,*
thinking,[c] *"No one will see me*[d] *then;"*
[e]*and he masks his face.*[f]
14c [a]*At night the thief prowls.*[b]
16 [a]*In the dark he breaks*[b] *into houses.*
By day they shut themselves in,[c]
[d]*for they do not know the light.*
17 *To all of them,*[a] *morning*[b] *is the darkness of death;*[c]
[d]*for they make friends*[e] *with the terrors*[f] *of death's shadow.*[g]

[24:18–24 transferred to Zophar's Third Speech, after 27:17][a]

25 *If this is not so, who can prove me wrong?*[a]
Who can reduce[b] *my argument to nothing?*[c]

Notes

2.a. גם must here be emphatic, though not of היום "today," which follows it, but of the whole sentence (cf. C. J. Labuschagne, "The Emphasizing Particle *gam* and Its Connotations," in *Studia biblica et semitica Theodoro Christiano Vriezen . . . dedicata*, ed. W. C. van Unnik and A. S. van der Woude [Wageningen: Veenman & Zonen, 1966] 193–203). A translation "today also" has led to unpersuasive speculations that the dialogue is represented as continuing into a second (? or third) day (so Duhm, Driver–Gray, de Wilde). היום "today" may be used like כַּיּוֹם "at today," i.e., "now" (1 Sam 9:13 [כהיום]; Isa 58:4; cf. *DCH*, 4:182 §b). Beer (*BH*[2]) notes the proposal to read אָמְנָם "surely" instead of גם־היום. NAB adds יָדַעְתִּי after גם, thus "surely I know" (cf. LXX καὶ δὴ οἶδα "and I surely know").

2.b. מרי, lit. "rebelliousness," from מרה "be contentious, rebellious" (as RV, JB, NEB "resentful," Pope "defiance," Gordis "defiant," Terrien "my complaint is a revolt"; cf. BDB, 598a; *DCH*, 5:485b), not from מרר "be bitter" (as Pesh, Vg, Tg, KJV, RSV, NAB, JPS, NJPS, NIV, REB "embittered," Driver–Gray, Andersen, Hartley, Good), such a noun not being recognized by the standard dictionaries. Beer (*BHK*) and NAB, following Tg (מריר), Pesh, Vg (*in amaritudine*), read מַר "bitter." Beer

(*BH*[2]) proposes מִשַּׁדַּי "from Shaddai" (*frt*), but it is hard to see how Job's complaint can be *from* Shaddai. De Wilde emends the colon rather drastically to עַל־שַׁדַּי מַר שׂחי "bitter is my complaint against Shaddai" (for a full discussion, see his "Eine alte Crux Interpretum, Hiob xxiii 2," *VT* 22 [1972] 368–74); the sense is, however, unobjectionable.

2.c. היום "today" is transposed by NAB to follow ידעתי in v 3, thus "oh, that today I might find him."

2.d. Lit. "my hand is heavy upon my groaning." Elsewhere a heavy hand is always an oppressor's (Judg 1:35; God's at 1 Sam 5:6, 7, 11; Ps 32:4; for the hand as oppressive, cf. also Job 13:21; 19:21), so Job probably means that he attempts to repress his groaning (Peake; similarly Kissane, Hartley). The best way this reading can be combined with the first half of the verse is by taking it as a concessive clause ("even though [I lay a heavy hand upon my groaning]"). KJV, RV have "my stroke is heavier than my groaning"—which seems to mean that he would be justified in complaining more that he does; but it is hard to see a connection with the first half of the verse. "My stroke" follows Tg מחתי "my blow" and perhaps Vg *manus plagae meae* "the hand that strikes me," both rather forced interpretations. Dhorme thinks "Job would like to suppress his groaning, but the hand which checks his sobs seems to weigh too heavily," but the meaning of his sentence remains elusive. NJPS's "My strength is spent on account of my groaning" and Good's "my hand is heavy from my groaning" (that is, he is so discouraged that he feels it too difficult even to lift a hand) are attractive, but there seem to be no parallels to such an understanding of "heavy hand." Terrien's "It is the weight of my hand that forces me to groan" is hard to justify from the Heb., and is not a very meaningful sentence anyway.

Most emend ידי "my hand" to יָדוֹ "his [God's] hand" (so LXX, Pesh, RSV, JB, NEB, NAB, NIV, Duhm, Beer [*BHK*], Hölscher, Larcher, Fohrer, Pope, Ravasi, Sicre Díaz, Habel, Newsom, Strauss), but that does not necessarily make better sense. For how are we to understand God's hand being upon (על) Job's groaning? Taking על as "in spite of" (as RSV) is a questionable move (BDB quotes only Job 10:7; 34:6, and, as a conjunction, 16:17 and Isa 53:9; in all these, however, the sense "because of" is preferable; see the *Comment* on the Job passages), as is also "in" (NAB "his hand is heavy upon me in my groanings"; similarly NEB, REB), for this is a quite rare sense of על (BDB, 754b), and in the main used with seasons or occasions (e.g., על ריב, "upon occasion of a lawsuit," Exod 23:2). Gordis thinks על must be "more than" (BDB, 755a), but it is rarely used in this sense except with numerals and plurals, and "heavy" (כבד) is not elsewhere used of "groaning" (אנחה) (though it is of מִסְפֵּד "lamentation" and אֵבֶל "mourning" in Gen 50:10–11). Nor can על mean "upon," for Job can hardly mean that God tries to repress his groaning, or aggravates his groaning (Driver–Gray). M. Dahood ("Northwest Semitic Philology and Job," in *The Bible in Current Catholic Thought: Gruenthaner Memorial Volume,* ed. J. L. McKenzie, St. Mary's Theological Studies 1 [New York: Herder & Herder, 1962] 55–74 [62]), Blommerde, Andersen, van der Lugt (*frt*) improbably think that the *yodh* suff is a 3d-person suff (for other examples of this alleged form, see *Note* 21:16.e). Szczygiel emends to יָדְךָ "your [Eliphaz's] hand." De Wilde arbitrarily reads אָזְנוֹ "his ear," i.e., God's ear is deaf to my groaning. Beer (*BHK*) reads עוֹד (*frt*) "still it is heavy," but I do not know what the subj is; it cannot be שׂחי, which is masc.

3.a. Exceptionally, a pf follows מי־יתן "oh that," lit. "who will give that" (similarly Deut 5:29; see GKC, §151b; *DCH*, 5:800b). Probably it is the semantics of ידע that determines the tense (cf. GKC, §106g), and we need not think of emending to דַּעְתִּי "my knowledge" or deleting ידעתי (Beer [*BH*[2]], Driver–Gray, with the support of one MS).

3.b. The two verbs ידעתי and ואמצאהו, "I knew" and "I may find him," are coordinated but not in the same tense (cf. GKC, §120e). There is not perhaps much difference between knowing "how" (so NEB, REB, NJPS) and knowing "where" (so KJV, RV, RSV, NRSV, JPS, NIV, GNB) he might find God.

3.c. תְּכוּנָה is elsewhere "arrangement" or "preparation"; only here of a place (BDB, 467b; *HALOT,* 4:1730b), and equivalent to מָכוֹן, which is well attested for the dwelling place of God, whether on earth or in heaven, his "seat" (KJV, RV, RSV) or "court" (NEB), though not in the legal sense, not "judgment seat" (NAB), "tribunal" (Davidson), or "throne" (Moffatt, Hartley).

4.a. The coh form shows that the verbs in this verse are not governed by מי־יתן (v 3).

4.b. משפט, lit. "a case" (for the sense, cf. *DCH*, 5:558a §1c), not necessarily understanding the suff of פי "my mouth" as doing double duty for משפט (as Dahood, "Northwest Semitic Philology and Job," 66; Blommerde). The משפט is evidently Job's own, so the emendation of Beer (*BHK*) and NAB to מִשְׁפָּטִי "my case" is otiose.

4.c. תוכחות "legal arguments"; the root יכח has been commonly used of Job's lawsuit (9:33; 13:3, 15; 16:21).

5.a. מה in an indirect question as at 23:5; 34:4, 33 (BDB, 552b).

6.a. Tur-Sinai reads רַב־כֹּחַ (or רַב־כֹּחַ), which he understands as "attorney, plenipotentiary" (followed by Pope, de Wilde, Good), but the evidence is very weak. ברב־כח cannot mean that in Ps 33:16.

6.b. It is still the language of the lawcourt, so ריב is to be translated "contend" (so RV, JPS, RSV, NRSV, NJPS, NAB), or "plead" (KJV); more general terms like "oppose" (NIV), "browbeat" (NEB), "meet" (Moffatt), or "use all his strength against me" (GNB) miss something of the flavor. It is not a "debate" (JB, NJB) but a legal contest (Hartley: "would he oppose me with great legal power?").

6.c. Some read לֹא as לֻא "would that [he would heed me]" (so Budde, Beer [*BHK*], Gerleman [*BHS frt*], NAB), but the suggestion is not necessary.

6.d. לא אך־הוא "no; certainly he . . ." is odd, but J. Reider's suggestion may be safely dismissed, that אך is an abbreviation for אַכְזָר, translating "He is not cruel that he should attack me" ("Contributions to the Scriptural Text," *HUCA* 24 [1952–53] 85–106 [104]). NEB reads אֵיךְ "how" for אַךְ "surely," but it is hard to see what difference that makes for its translation, "God himself would never bring a charge against me"—difficult to justify from the Heb.

6.e. ישׂם בי, lit. "would he set on me?" is a problem. If it is elliptical for ישׂם לִבּוֹ בִּי "would he set his mind on me?" (so Driver–Gray, Gordis, Pope, Rowley, Habel, van der Lugt; Duhm and Beer [BH^2 *frt*] actually insert לִבּוֹ), it is strange that we have בִּי and not לִי or עָלַי. But שׂים does seem to be elliptical for "set one's mind to" in 4:20 (*q.v.*; see also 24:12; 34:23). RV and JPS, reading the MT, have "he would give heed to me," but it is hard to see how some other versions derive their translations: NIV and Hartley have "he would not press charges against me," NJPS "He would not accuse me," NEB "would never bring a charge against me," and REB "would never set his face against me." Eitan, 61–62, argues that שׂים here has the sense of "attack," as does its synonym שׁית "set" at Isa 22:7; Ps 3:6 (7) (followed by Reider, "Some Notes to the Text of the Scriptures," *HUCA* 3 [1926] 109–16 [115]).

Others emend to יִשְׁמַע "he would listen to me" (Dhorme, Beer [*BHK frt*], Kissane, Larcher), but שמע is not followed by בְּ of person except in one unusual case (Ps 92:11 [12]; see Driver–Gray); Graetz avoided that problem by drastically emending אך־הוא ישׂם בי to יִשְׁמָעֵנִי "he would [not] hear me."

7.a. שׁם "there" must refer to God's dwelling (תכונה, v 3), though it is awkward that its antecedent is so distant. Delitzsch, Budde, Gordis, Habel think it should mean "then, in that case," i.e., at the time of Job's lawsuit with God, while W. L. Moran ("Amarna *šumma* in Main Clauses," *JCS* 7 [1953] 78–80), M. Dahood ("Some Northwest-Semitic Words in Job," *Bib* 38 [1957] 306–20 [306–10]; "Hebrew-Ugaritic Lexicography VIII," *Bib* 51 [1970] 391–404 [397]), A. Jirku ("Eine Renaissance des Hebräischen," *FF* 32 [1958] 211–12 [212]), and C. F. Whitley ("Has the Particle שׁם an Asseverative Force?" *Bib* 55 [1974] 394–98 [395]) think it is "if" like Ugar. *tm* or Akk. *šumma* (cf. also on 35:12); the word is suggested also for 35:12. So too Blommerde and Gerleman (*BHS prb*). Friedrich Delitzsch, Hontheim, Beer (BH^2) read שָׂם "he sets" with four MSS and the apparent support of Vg, which has a verb (*proponat* "let him set"); but this would yield only a sententious thought, "He has set right and justice with him [Beer עִמִּי 'with me']."

7.b. נוֹכָח is vocalized as the niph ptcp, "one in dispute"; so it is not exactly that "an upright man could reason with him" (as RSV) but that the one contending with him would be an upright man, "it would be an upright man arguing with Him" (Gordis), which means that "it would be satisfactorily proved that an upright man may contend with Him" (Delitzsch). NJPS "would be cleared" does not offer an appropriate meaning for יכח niph, and NEB "There the upright are vindicated before him" (similarly REB), by putting it in the pl, fails to connect the sentence closely enough with Job himself. Beer (BH^2) inserts "and" before the word (as also LXX, Tg, Vg), thus וְנֹכַח "he has set right and justice [with me]."

7.c. Beer (BH^2) reads עִמִּי "with me" (cf. Vg *contra me,* Tg עמי).

7.d. פלט piel is elsewhere always "deliver," not "escape"; and it is never used of acquittal at law but only of deliverance from an enemy or a disaster, so "be acquitted" (RSV; cf. Terrien, Gordis) is hard to justify above "be delivered" (KJV, JPS, NIV) or "escape" (NJPS). Dhorme thinks that "my soul," "myself" (נַפְשִׁי) is implied (followed by Hartley); but that is not the case elsewhere (21:10 is too strange for any weight to be placed on it). נֶפֶשׁ, however, can be used as the obj of the similar verb מלט piel "deliver" (1 Kgs 1:12; Jer 48:6; 51:6, 45). Others say אפלטה is intransitive (Budde, Gordis), though there are no parallels; less likely still is the claim that the piel is intensive of the qal, and so "I should be free" (Delitzsch).

Even if we read אֶפְלְטָה (qal) "I would escape" (Driver–Gray, G. R. Driver [see below], Beer [*BHK frt*], Hölscher, Blommerde, van der Lugt), it would still not be the language of legal acquittal. If מִשְׁפָּטִי is read as the obj (see *Note* 7.f), וַאֲפַלְּטָה could perhaps mean "I will succeed in my cause," lit. "I will deliver my cause"; so NAB "I should preserve my rights," JB "I should win my case" (similarly de

Wilde). Tur-Sinai understood פלט, as in 21:10, to mean "bring forth, give birth" (hence Pope "I could bring justice to successful birth"; similarly, Janzen, Good); but unlike in 21:10, here there is nothing in the context to suggest such a sense for פלט. Habel attractively translates "I would be free of my suit," i.e., free from the burden of the impending court case; but מִשֹּׁפְטִי could hardly be the obj of פלט piel in that case, and he would need to read מִמִּשְׁפָּטִי "from my case."

G. R. Driver ("Problems in Job," *AJSL* 52 [1936] 160–70 [160]) proposed שם יָשֹׁר וְנוֹכַח עִמִּי "there he would affirm [his case] and argue with me, [but I should escape (אֲפַלְּטָה) successfully from my judge]."

7.e. לנצח, usually "for ever," is reasonably thought to mean here (and, e.g., in Prov 21:28) "wholly, successfully" by G. R. Driver, "Problems in Proverbs," *ZAW* 50 (1932) 141–48 (144–45), and D. Winton Thomas, "The Use of נֵצַח as a Superlative in Hebrew," *JSS* 1 (1956) 106–9 (109); cf. L. Kopf, "Arabische Etymologien und Parallelen zum Bibelwörterbuch," *VT* 8 (1958) 161–215 (185); P. R. Ackroyd, "נצח—εἰς τέλος," *ExpTim* 80 (1968–69) 126; so too NEB "an absolute discharge," REB "an outright acquittal," Good "successfully" (cf. *DCH*, 5:739b). But "for ever" seems at least equally plausible.

7.f. מִשֹּׁפְטִי "from my judge" (as KJV, RSV, NIV, NEB, NJPS) is revocalized by many to מִשְׁפָּטִי "my case, my cause" (so some MSS, LXX, Pesh, Vg, KBL, 1003a, JB, NAB, Hitzig, Duhm, Strahan, Beer [*BH*²], Kissane, Larcher, Fohrer, Pope, Gerleman [*BHS frt*], de Wilde, Sicre Díaz, Habel, Good, understanding "I will succeed in my cause," lit. "I will deliver my cause"). But God is elsewhere always the subj of פלט piel "deliver." Stevenson² attractively proposed מִמְּשֹׁפְטִי "from my adversary, my opponent at law" (as in 9:15), on the undeniable ground that in the context "God is a litigant against Job and not his judge." This emendation is accepted in the *Translation* above. Blommerde's reading מִשְׁפָּטִי "his judgment," the suff being 3d person, is strained; for other examples of the alleged *yodh* 3d-person suff, see *Note* 21:16.e.

8.a. Vv 8–9 are omitted by Budde, Siegfried, Duhm, Driver–Gray, Beer (*BH*²), Hölscher, Fohrer, Fedrizzi, de Wilde as a gloss on v 3, and as spoiling the connection between v 7 and v 10. The original LXX omits v 9.

8.b. הן, usually "behold," but probably to be translated here as "if." D. M. Stec, "The Use of *hēn* in Conditional Sentences," *VT* 37 (1987) 478–86, has shown that in certain syntactic settings "behold" can have this significance; it is not that the word "means" "if," as a cognate of some other Semitic particles like Ugar. *hm* and Arab. *'in* (as, e.g., Guillaume; Blommerde, 28 [bibliography]). This is an example of the sentence type where the first clause begins with הן and the second with *waw* (as also at 9:11; 12:14, 15; 19:7; 40:23, though the *waw* is lacking here). Other examples of הן "if" may be found at 4:18; 9:12; 13:15; 15:15; 21:16; 25:5; 36:30.

8.c. קדם, lit. "forward." The four directions in vv 8–9 could be in reference to movement of the body (forward, backward, to the left, to the right) (as KJV, RSV, NEB) but is more probably in reference to the four points of the compass (east, west, north, south) (as NAB, JB, REB, NIV, NJPS, GNB); as usual, when directions are indicated, the speaker is thought of as facing east.

9.a. שמאול בעשתו, lit. "left [i.e., north] in his working" (KJV, RV, JPS "where he doth work," NIV "when he is at work in the north"; so too Terrien, Hartley, Good). There is conceivably some allusion to the north as the seat of the gods (cf. O. Eissfeldt, *Baal Zaphon, Zeus Kasios und der Durchzug der Israeliten durchs Meer* [Halle: Niemeyer, 1932]; W. F. Albright, "Baal Zaphon," in *Festschrift Alfred Bertholet zum 80. Geburtstag gewidmet von Kollegen und Freunden,* ed. Walter Baumgartner [et al.] [Tübingen: Mohr, 1950]). On שמאול "north" rather than "left hand," see *Note* 8.c. But a reference to God's "working" in the north, rather than dwelling or even sitting in judgment there, seems out of place. So some emendation is called for.

The usual emendation is of בעשתו "in his working" to בִּקַּשְׁתִּיו or בִּקַּשְׁתּוֹ "I seek him" (so Pesh; followed by Merx, Budde, Duhm, Beer [*BHK* (בִּקַּשְׁתִּי(ו], Driver–Gray, Dhorme, Hölscher [בִּקַּשְׁתִּי], Kissane, Larcher, de Wilde, RSV, JB). This emendation is accepted in the *Translation* above.

Other philological approaches, not requiring emendation, include (1) the proposal of a new verb עשה "turn" (cf. Arab. *ghaša* "come to"), thus "when he turns [to the left]." So G. R. Driver, "Difficult Words in the Hebrew Prophets," in *Studies in Old Testament Prophecy Presented to Professor Theodore H. Robinson,* ed. H. H. Rowley (Edinburgh: T. & T. Clark, 1950) 52–72 (54); A. Guillaume, "The Arabic Background of the Book of Job," in *Promise and Fulfilment,* FS S. H. Hooke, ed. F. F. Bruce (Edinburgh: T. & T. Clark, 1963) 106–27 (115–16); idem, *Studies,* 107; Pope, Fedrizzi. Cf. *DCH,* vol. 6, *s.v.* But it is hard to see why Yahweh would be turning to the left, and not surprisingly NEB emends to בַּעֲשֹׂתִי "in my turning," thus "when I turn left [REB north]," which would then be parallel to Job's "going" to the east and west in v 8. In any case, there is the problem that the Arab. cognate *ghaša* usually means "cover" (see below) and, although a sense "come" is attested by lexica (Freytag, 3:277b;

Lane, 2261b, 2262a; Wehr–Cowan, 674b), quotations in the lexica show "come, come upon" (as of an event) as a mere translation equivalent for the normal sense "cover." In any case, there is no evidence that it means "turn." (2) Yellin and Eitan, 57–58, followed by Gordis and Habel, suppose another עשׂה "cover," cognate with Arab. *ghaša* (Lane, 2261b), as also at Prov 13:16; Isa 32:6; Obad 1:6 (Tur-Sinai suggested a noun עשׂתו "covering," as also in Cant 5:14, which Gerleman [*BHS frt*] seems to follow) (cf. *DCH,* vol. 6, *s.v.*). NRSV "on the left he hides," NJPS "since He is concealed, I do not behold Him," and NAB "where the north enfolds him" adopt this suggestion. These proposals, however, are more strained than the simple emendation of one consonant that is adopted in the *Translation.*

9.b. אָחַז, pausal form of אַחַז, which is the apocopated form of אֶחֱזֶה "I see." Fohrer, NAB insist on reading the full form, אֶחֱזֶה.

9.c. יַעְטֹף "he turns aside," from עטף I (BDB, 742a; KBL, 698a; *HALOT,* 2:814b [both KBL and *HALOT* attribute to עטף both the senses "turn aside" and "cover"; *DCH,* vol. 6, *s.v.*). Many read אֶעְטֹף "I turn" (BDB, *HALOT,* Pesh, Vg, RSV, JB, NEB ["I face right"], Budde, Duhm, Driver–Gray, Dhorme, Beer [*BHK*], Hölscher, Kissane, Larcher, Fohrer, Pope, de Wilde); this emendation is adopted in the *Translation* above. Others take it from עטף II "envelop oneself" (as in Pss 65:13 [14]; 73:6); so KJV, RV "he hideth himself," NJPS "He is hidden," NAB "he is veiled," NJB "invisible as ever," Terrien, Gordis, Good; but it can hardly be that the reason why God cannot be found in the other quarters is that he is hiding himself in the south (as Good); for why would he do that?

10.a. כִּי is most naturally taken as "for" (JPS) rather than "but" (KJV, RV, RSV, NEB), "yet" (NAB), "and yet" (JB), or than the asseverative "surely" (Gordis). What is introduced is the reason why Job is unable to find God: it is because of what is said in vv 10–13; see *Comment.*

10.b. Beer (*BHK*) unnecessarily emends to יֵדַע "he knows" (impf rather than MT pf).

10.c. דרך עִמָּדִי, lit. "the way that is with me," i.e., my habitual way of life. But the expression is unusual, and several suggestions have been made: (1) Pesh led Houbigant, Graetz, Beer (*BH*[2]), Dhorme, Larcher, de Wilde to emend to דַּרְכִּי וְעָמְדִי "my way and my standing," "my going and my standing," like אָרְחִי וְרִבְעִי "my walking and my resting" in Ps 139:3. Thus NEB "he knows me in action or at rest," and JB "every step I take," lit. "my walking and my stopping." (2) Steuernagel, Budde, Hölscher, S. T. Byington ("Some Bits of Hebrew: IV. Texts in Job," *ExpTim* 57 [1945–46] 110–11 [110]), Fohrer, Hartley unconvincingly emend to דֶּרֶךְ עָמְדִי "the way of my standing" (inf constr of עמד "stand"), i.e., where I stand (cf. Ps 1:1), and where therefore God could look for me. But what would the *way* of *standing* be? (3) Alternatively, we could emend to עָמַדְתִּי "[where] I stand" (Budde), but the same problem exists. (4) Houbigant offered an alternative suggestion, דַּרְכּוֹ "his way," which Merx also follows ("his dealings [against me]"), but that destroys the parallelism with the next colon. (5) Reider ("Some Notes to the Text," 115) reads דרך עָמְרִי "the way of my life," postulating a new Heb. noun עמר on the basis of Arab. *ʿmr* "life, religion." (6) G. R. Driver's emendation to אֲשֻׁרַי "[the way of] my steps" ("Problems in Job," 161) is tautologous. (7) M. Dahood (*Ugaritic-Hebrew Philology: Marginal Notes on Recent Publications,* BibOr 17 [Rome: Pontifical Biblical Institute, 1965] 60) reads עַמּוּדַי "my pillars," which he understands to be "[the way of] my legs," a hugely improbable suggestion; he finds the same sense of עַמּוּד at 29:6.

10.d. בחנני, pf in a hypothetical clause, with impf in apodosis (see GKC, §§106p, 159h). NEB "when he tests me, I prove to be gold" suggests more than one test, which is not the point. It is not refining itself that is the image here but "testing, assaying" (בחן); presumably, however, the same process has to be used.

10.e. R. C. Van Leeuwen, "A Technical Metallurgical Usage of יצא," *ZAW* 98 (1986) 112–13, explains יצא "come out" in reference to the molten metal that flows out of the smelter refined and ready to cast (cf. Exod 32:24; Isa 54:16). G. R. Driver ("Problems in the Hebrew Text of Proverbs," *Bib* 32 [1951] 173–97 [190]), however, postulated a new Heb. יצא "be bright, clean" at Prov 25:4, comparing Akk. *(w)aṣû* "go forth" (*CAD* 1.2:356a; used *inter alia* of the bright rising of the sun) and Arab. *waḍuʾa* "be fair, clean." But, as Van Leeuwen points out, the Akk. verb itself does not denote brightness. Dahood, apparently without being aware of Driver's view, also finds a יצא III "shine" ("Northwest Semitic Philology and Job," 67; "The Linguistic Position of Ugaritic in the Light of Recent Discoveries," in *Sacra Pagina: Miscellanea biblica Congressus Internationalis Catholici de re biblica,* ed. J. Coppens, A. Descamps, and E. Massaux, BETL 12–13 [Gembloux: Duculot, 1959] 1:267–79 [1:274 n. 24]). The suggestion of a יצא "shine" is followed by R. B. Y. Scott, *Proverbs and Ecclesiastes: A New Translation with Introduction and Commentary,* AB 18 (Garden City, NY: Doubleday, 1965) 153; cf. also *DCH,* 4:265a, and see further on 28:1.

11.a. רגלי "my foot" (as KJV, JPS, RSV, NAB), but the Eng. idiom is perhaps rather "feet" (as NEB, NIV); JB "footsteps."

11.b. אחזה "has held fast to" (as RSV; NEB "kept to," NIV "closely followed," similarly NJB). NAB "my foot has always walked" and NJPS "I have always followed" represent the Heb. less successfully.

11.c. שׁמר, lit. "kept," as most modern versions.

11.d. So JB, NJPS; lit. "and I have not turned aside."

12.a. Lit. "the commandment of his lips and I have not departed." מצות שׂפתיו could be taken as a *casus pendens* and the *waw* as the *waw apodosis* (GKC, §143d; so Delitzsch, Driver–Gray, Dhorme, Gordis, Hartley); cf. Ps 115:7 and perhaps Job 4:6. Emendation to מִמִּצְוַת שׂפתיו לא אמישׁ "from the commandment of his lips I have not departed" (so Siegfried, Beer [*BH*[2]], Kissane; מִמִּצְוֹת "from the commandments of," Merx, Budde, Beer [*BHK*]) is tempting, but Dhorme suggests that the *casus pendens* obviates the need for the prep. Beer (*BHK*) deletes the *waw* of ולא, with the support of many MSS; likewise Gerleman (*BHS*) and NAB, but strangely without any alteration to מצות. Duhm reads מִמִּצְוָתוֹ "from his command," omitting "lips" with LXX.

12.b. Lit. "command" (מצות); LXX, Vg have pl, but there is no need to emend to מִצְוֹת "commands" (as Merx, Siegfried, Budde, Beer [*BHK*]). Unlikely is Blommerde's proposal that מצות שׂפתיו "the command of his lips" is a further obj of שׁמרתי "I have kept" (v 11).

12.c. מֵחֻקִּי is, at it stands, "from my statute," the prefixed מן being sometimes understood as comparative *min* "more than" (BDB, 582a §6; *DCH,* 5:340b §5), but even so the meaning is not obvious: Davidson has "more than my own law," Habel "beyond that required of me," Good "within my limits," van der Lugt "beyond my statute." An alternative is to take חק as "portion" (as in Prov 30:8, לֶחֶם חֻקִּי is "my prescribed portion of food"); hence KJV, RV, JPS "more than my necessary food," NJPS, NIV "more than my daily bread."

But most emend, following LXX ἐν κόλπῳ μου "in my bosom" (H. M. Orlinsky, "Studies in the Septuagint of the Book of Job: V," *HUCA* 35 [1964] 57–78 [75]; and cf. Ps 119:11 for words laid up in the heart), to בְּחֵקִי (Reiske, Merx, Budde, Duhm, Peake, Driver–Gray, Dhorme, Beer [*BHK*], Hölscher, Kissane, Larcher, Fohrer, Terrien, Gerleman [*BHS frt*], de Wilde, Sicre Díaz, Hartley, Strauss) "in my bosom" (RSV, NRSV) or "in my breast" (JB), even though they are hardly contemporary words, or "in my heart" (NJB, NEB [בְּחֵיקִי], NAB). The "bosom" may seem a strange place to keep words, since it is really the fold of the garment at the chest, used normally as a pocket (thus for carrying a lamb [2 Sam 12:3], or, metaphorically, for Moses carrying the people [Num 11:12] or for carrying insults [Ps 89:50 (51), emended] or for keeping sins concealed in [Job 31:33, where the term is חב]); cf. *DCH,* 3:216a. It is not usually metaphorical for some internal part of the body, and yet 19:27 seems to provide a clear analogy. Here it must be the idea of keeping safe the words, as if they were precious, a treasure.

M. Dahood ("Hebrew-Ugaritic Lexicography V," *Bib* 48 [1967] 421–38 [427]) attempts to salvage the MT by taking מן as "in" (so too Blommerde, Pope "in my bosom," reading מֵחֵקִי); Dahood elsewhere argued that the *yodh* suff of מחקי is a 3d-person suff (*Psalms I,* 11), but the resultant meaning is obscure. On the 3d-person *yodh* suff, see further *Note* 21:16.e. Gordis proposes, but does not adopt, כְּחֻקִּי "as my law."

13.a. This is no doubt a conditional clause without an introductory conditional particle (cf. GKC, §159b); the apodosis is a rhetorical question, as in 9:12; 11:10; 34:29 (Driver–Gray).

13.b. והוא באחד is lit. "and he is in one," which is taken to mean (1) "he is in one mind" (KJV), i.e., "he is unchangeable" (RSV), "he never changes" (GNB), "he is determined, unchangeable" (Gordis, similarly Terrien, Sicre Díaz) (a rather strained reading of the phrase); (2) "he is at one with Himself" (JPS) (does this mean that he has no second thoughts?); (3) "he stands alone" (NIV, NRSV) (it is hard to see what this means in the context, whether it is followed by "who can oppose him?" [NIV] or "who can dissuade him?" [NRSV]); (4) "He is one" (NJPS, Hartley) (but what has the fact that "there is no other God" [Hartley] to do with God's execution of his plans?; the idea of the existence of other gods likely to sabotage his plans seems entirely out of place); or (5) "he is one, i.e., sovereign, absolute in his decisions" (Habel); "The statement that 'He is One' carries with it an affirmation of God's sole sovereignty" (Andersen; but is it true that "one" implies "sovereign," and, if so, why not say so?). (6) C. H. Gordon, "His Name is 'One,'" *JNES* 29 (1970) 198–99, made the curious suggestion that "One," the numeral 1, is regarded as "the official name of God" (as also at Zech 14:9), but he does not explain how this could fit with the present context.

The *beth* is often said to be *beth essentiae* (GKC, §119i, Strauss), but that too is not very convincing; it is hardly a parallel to the classic case of *beth essentiae,* Exod 6:3. See Dahood, "Northwest Semitic Philology and Job," 67, followed by Blommerde, who thinks אֶחָד means "only ruler," the *beth* being an "emphasizing particle" (he sees other examples of אֶחָד "the Unique" at 14:4; 31:15, in his review of *Job et son Dieu: Essai d'exégèse et de théologie biblique,* by J. Lévêque, *Bib* 52 [1971] 436–38 [438]). But in the same place he argues rather that in the present text באחר means "when he seizes," אחר being a Canaanite form of אחז "seize."

In view of these difficulties, an emendation to והוא בָחַר "and he has chosen" seems plausible (so Budde, Duhm, Peake, Beer [*BHK*], Driver–Gray, Hölscher, Kissane, Larcher, Fohrer, Pope, de Wilde, NEB "he decides" [reading בְּאַחַר = בָּחַר], JB "has decided," NJB "once he has made up his mind," NAB). It is adopted in the *Translation* above. The resulting parallelism of בחר "choose" with אוה piel "desire" is attested in Ps 132:13 also.

13.c. ומי "and who?"; Gerleman (*BHS prb*) omits the *waw*, with some MSS.

14.a. ויעשׂ, the apodosis of the conditional sentence being with *waw* consec and the impf (GKC, §159h).

14.a. The verse is lacking in the original LXX and is deleted by Duhm as incomplete and prosaic. So too Hölscher, Fohrer. Beer (*BH*[2]) would either delete it or move it to follow v 17.

14.b. חקי "my decree" is a little odd, though it can be understood as "the decree concerning me" (so Rowley), "my sentence" (JB). NJPS "He will bring my term to an end" does not fit the context. Gordis glosses חקי as "my limit" but strangely translates "what he has decreed for me." Good's "he will come to terms with my sentence" is hard to understand. Not surprisingly, some emend to חֻקּוֹ "his decree" (Dhorme, Hölscher, NEB "What he determines"), which makes good sense. M. Dahood thinks the *yodh* suff to be a 3d-person suff anyway (review of *Il Semitico di Nord Ovest,* by G. Garbini, *Or* 32 [1963] 499). On the suff, see further *Note* 21:16.e.

14.c. The opening כי "for" is difficult to connect with the preceding; it could be the reason why no one is able to dissuade him, but מי ישיבנו have not been the immediately preceding words. It is probably best to take כי as an asseverative, "surely" (so also Gordis; cf. BDB, 472b; GKC, §159ee; *DCH,* 4:388a §9), rather than emend it to כֵּן "thus" (as Siegfried, Budde, de Wilde).

14.d. כהנה רבות, lit. "like these things, many things," i.e., "many such things" (as כאלה רבות in 16:2). Hoffmann, followed by de Wilde, read רִבוֹת "lawsuits" instead of רַבּוֹת "many things," i.e., "so are lawsuits with him."

14.e. עמו is lit. "with him." For the use of עם to suggest purpose, cf. 10:13; 27:11.

15.a. על־כן "therefore" gives as the reason for his terror his awareness that God will carry out his hostile purposes against him (on the other hand, Dhorme thinks that it answers the על־כן of Eliphaz in 22:10).

16.a. לבי is lit. "my heart."

16.b. רכך hiph "make tender, weak, soft," thus "languid, lacking in energy," just as its opposite, "make the heart strong" (usually סעד) means to gain energy and good spirits from food (סעד at Judg 19:5, 8; Ps 104:15; cf. Heb 13:9; כון "make firm," metaphorically, Ps 10:17).

17.a. כי is again a problem, as in v 15. Much depends on how the verse as a whole is understood. If Job means that it is not his sufferings as such that frighten him, but God's involvement in them, then the thought can be: God terrifies me, "for" it is not by the darkness that I am annihilated ("yet," as in NEB, NIV, NJPS, is less likely). But if he means that he *is* annihilated by darkness, or if he is wishing that he could be annihilated, כי will have to be asseverative, "surely" (so Gordis, Hartley, NAB).

17.b. On the meaning of צלמות, lit. "darkness of death," see *Note* 3:5.a. See now also C. Cohen, "The Meaning of צלמות 'Darkness': A Study in Philological Method," in *Texts, Temples, and Traditions,* FS M. Haran, ed. M. V. Fox, V. A. Hurowitz, and A. Hurvitz (Winona Lake, IN: Eisenbrauns, 1996) 287–309.

This verse is a true *crux interpretum.* Its difficulties revolve about (1) the meaning of צמת, (2) the particle לא, and (3) the sense of the second colon in relation to the first (on which see the next *Note*).

(1) צמת niph is variously understood as: (a) "Be exterminated" (BDB, 856a; Gesenius–Buhl, 687a; Zorell, 695b, "lose, destroy, oppress"). This seems to lie behind NRSV "If only [see below on לא] I could vanish in darkness," and NJB "the darkness having failed to destroy me." (b) "Silence" (König, 390b; KBL, 807b), comparing Arab. *ṣamata* "be silent"; so NEB "I am not reduced to silence by the darkness"; similarly NIV, Fohrer, Newsom. But it is far from clear how *darkness* could have *silenced* Job. (c) Both "destroy" and "silence" (*HALOT,* 3:1035b). (d) "Dry up," thus "be silent"; so Dhorme, followed by Fohrer, Good, translating נצמתי as "I have been silent" on the ground that in 6:17 צמת means "dry up," and "[o]n the plane of the mind and heart 'to become dry' means to cease to speak, to be silent." But "dry up" is no more than a translational equivalent in 6:17, where wadis "dry up" but only in the sense "are annihilated." So there is no case for extending the meaning "dry up" to other contexts such as this. (e) "Hem in," as RSV, in accord with cognates in MH, Aram., meaning "press together" or "gather together" (Jastrow, 1289b; Dalman, 365a; Sokoloff, 467a); this however does not appear to be a suitable rendering in any other of the fifteen occurrences of the verb (Leigh, 206a,

however, recognized this as a meaning in 1650, citing Lam 3:53). (f) "Cut off"; so KJV (no doubt following Buxtorf, 652; similarly Taylor, no. 1602; so too NJPS). (g) "Dismay" (RVmg) is not generally acknowledged as a meaning, but may be found in Leigh, 206a. (h) "Flee" (Friedrich Delitzsch). (i) "Complete"; so J. Barth, *Etymologische Studien zum Semitischen, insbesondere zum hebräischen Lexicon* (Berlin: Itzkowski, 1893), comparing Arab. *ṣatama* "complete"; but this suggestion requires also the supposition of a metathesis of the letters *mem* and *taw*.

Only one emendation seems to have been suggested, that of Siegfried, who emended נצמתי to נִצְפַּנְתִּי "I was [not] hidden."

(2) לא "not" is a difficulty, because the first half of the line, which has it ("I am not annihilated by darkness"), seems to mean much the same thing as the second half of the line, which lacks it ("darkness covers my face"). KJV handled the problem by applying לא "not" to both halves: "I was not cut off before the darkness, neither hath he covered the darkness from my face" (similarly JPS); but this is improbable. NJB tries hard (too hard) to make the first clause negative and the second positive by translating, "The darkness having failed to destroy me, I am plunged back into obscurity by him!" Driver–Gray make a desperate attempt at sense by taking the last two words (כסה־אפל "thick darkness covers") as a relative clause: "I am not undone because of the darkness, or because of my own face which thick darkness covereth" (meaning that Job feels overwhelmed neither by the calamity itself nor by his "face," i.e., his face as disfigured by his sufferings); similarly Fohrer.

Another route to a solution is to revocalize לא "not" as לֻא "would that"; so NAB "would that I had vanished in darkness, and that thick gloom were before me to conceal me," Pope "Would that I could vanish in darkness, and thick gloom cover my face," Sicre Díaz, and NRSV "If only I could vanish in darkness, and thick darkness would cover my face!" (but here too it is hard to match the translation with the Heb. syntax unless ומפני is emended to ופני, which NAB for one is not proposing to do).

Another suggestion is that of Kissane, who read לא as לוֹ "to him" and translates, "to Him I am blotted out by the darkness, and from me the gloom hath veiled Him," which is ingenious (so too Larcher, and JB "darkness hides me from him"); but it is hardly consistent with God's knowing Job's way (v 10), and in any case being invisible to God does not seem to be something Job would be complaining about.

Yet another suggestion is that of Gordis, followed by Habel and van der Lugt, to take לא as an emphatic: "Indeed, I am destroyed by the darkness." To similar effect, Strauss argues that the sentence (though he must mean the colon) is a rhetorical question, rendering "Am I not annihilated before the darkness? blackness covers (everything) before me." But the evidence for לא emphatic is tenuous in the extreme, and it strains the Heb. to take the first colon as a question. Neither suggestion is more probable than a straightforward deletion of the troublesome word.

Such a deletion is proposed by Bickell, Budde, Duhm, Peake, Beer (*BH*[2]; *BHK frt*), Hölscher, Terrien, Rowley, and followed by RSV "I am hemmed in by darkness" (see above, however, on the meaning "hem in"). The deletion is adopted in this *Translation*.

17.c. ומפני "and from my face," emended to וּפָנַי "and my face" (obj of כסה "covers") by Budde, Duhm, Beer (*BH*[2]; *BHK frt*), Hölscher, Terrien, Sicre Díaz; the emendation is adopted in the *Translation* above. Dhorme gave the forced explanation that "because of my face which darkness has veiled" is a hypallage for "because of darkness which has veiled my face"; he is apparently followed by NIV "by the thick darkness that covers my face" (similarly Newsom). Kissane reads כִּסָּהוּ "[from me the gloom] hath veiled Him," and so too Larcher, followed by JB "the gloom veils his presence from me," but the difficulty with this interpretation has been outlined above. Good reads מִפְּנֵי כִּסֵּה־אפל "from before the throne of gloom"; but כִּסֵּא "throne" is rarely spelled with a *he* and is never in construct with an abstract noun (except "judgment" in Prov 20:8 and "honor" in Isa 22:23). De Wilde arbitrarily emends the colon to כִּי־הוּא צָמַם פָּנַי חֹשֶׁךְ "for he it is who has wrapped my face (in) darkness" (although צמם does not occur in classical Heb.).

Another possibility is that we should read וּמִפְּנֵי as equivalent to וּמִפְּנֵי אֲשֶׁר "and because [deep darkness covers (me)]" (so Gerleman [*BHS prp*]). NEB also reads וּמִפְּנֵי, but its translation "nor from the mystery which hides him" is unexplained, unless perhaps it renders אפל as "mystery" and reads וּמִפְּנֵי אפל כִּסָּהוּ "and from the mystery [that] hides him" (though this reading is not mentioned by Brockington).

24:1.a. מדוע "why?" is omitted by NEB, for no apparent reason.

1.b. עתים, lit. "times," and in the context, "times for judgment" (NIV, NJPS), "sessions of set justice" (Moffatt), "proper times" (Good), not "the day of reckoning" (NEB) since it is plural.

1.c. צפן "hide, treasure up." Gordis wants it to mean "are hidden from" the Almighty (as in Jer 16:17), and since that does not make any sense in the context, he has recourse to a syntactic oddity attested in Isa 5:4, where the opening "why" relates only to the second half of the line, the first half being a subordinate conditional clause; O. Loretz ("Philologische und textologische Probleme in Hi 24,1–25," *UF* 12 [1980] 261–66 [262]) also thinks it is "hidden." If that were parallel to this verse, we could translate "Since the times of judgment are not hidden from the Almighty, why do those who love Him never see the days of retribution?" (so also KJV, Habel, Hartley, Newsom, Strauss; similarly NEB "is no secret to the Almighty")—which is not preferable to the usual reading (for it is hard to see what times of judgment being "hidden" from God might mean). The meaning "treasure up, keep" for צפן is in fact quite acceptable (as most recently in 23:12); and so RV, JPS "laid up," RSV "kept," NJPS "reserved," NIV "set." NJB "Why does Shaddai not make known the times he has fixed?" (cf. JB "Why has Shaddai his own store of times?") is explained in the margin as lit. "not have times in reserve," i.e., a "store of times from which to lengthen a human life and so provide opportunity for punishment." I cannot see how "make known" can be equivalent to "not have times in reserve," and the idea of a "store of times" is strange.

Beer (BH^2) deletes לא, with the support of two MSS, but not of LXX, which he claims. Dhorme follows with his rendering "Why have times been hidden from Shaddai?" explaining that "Times, that is to say, the great events which are unfurled in the course of ages, seem to escape His attention"; but that seems to have nothing to do with the present argument of Job. Terrien's explanation of "Why are certain moments not hidden from the Almighty?" as Job's attempt to safeguard the justice of God by wishing that his omniscience were limited is extremely strained.

1.d. The מן of "efficient cause (or personal agent)" (GKC, §121f).

1.e. ידעו "those who know him," i.e., "his friends" (Pope, Habel, NAB), "those close to him" (NJPS), "his followers" (Moffatt), "his faithful" (JB), "those who serve him" (GNB), "those who love Him" (Gordis). The variety of renderings confirms that the term seems not entirely suitable: why should it be those who "know" him who would be interested in his judgments, and not humans generally? See further, *Comment.* The proposal of Beer (BH^2 *frt*), however, to read רָעִים "the wicked," does not solve the difficulty.

1.f. NEB "though those who know him have no hint of its date" is hard to justify from the Heb. Duhm and Beer (BH^2 *frt*) read יוֹמוֹ "his day" for ימיו "his days," thinking of an eschatological day of judgment; but then why are "times" (עתים) in the pl?

2.a. Kissane moved vv 2–4 to follow 23:15 on the ground that they interrupt the connection between vv 1 and 5; but between 23:15 and 23:16 they are even more poorly located, changing the focus from Job to the poor and back again to Job.

2.b. The Heb. lacks an explicit subj; hence KJV "some remove," RV, JPS "there are that remove," RSV, NIV, GNB, Hartley "men," Habel "there are some who," NJPS "people." The first half of the line is unusually short (only two words), and LXX has an explicit subject, ἀσεβεῖς "the impious," so many insert רְשָׁעִים "the wicked" (so Moffatt, JB, NAB, NRSV, Merx, Dhorme, Beer [*BHK vel*], Hölscher, Larcher [presumably], Kissane) or רָעִים "the wicked" (NEB, Beer [*BHK vel*]); emendation to רְשָׁעִים is adopted in the *Translation* above. Driver–Gray prefer the order גבולות רשעים ישיגו. Budde read הֵמָּה "these" as having dropped out after ימיו, i.e., "some," with a correlative הן at the beginning of v 5 (so too Habel, and also Gordis, but he translates "the wicked").

2.c. ישיגו "they remove," שׂוג apparently being a byform of סוג hiph "remove" (BDB, 962a; *HALOT,* 4:1311b).

2.d. On the pf of "experiences frequently confirmed" in connection with *waw* consec, see GKC, §111s.

2.e. LXX has ποίμνιον σὺν ποιμένι "a flock with its shepherd," which leads Merx, Siegfried, Budde, Beer (*BHK*) to emend וירעו to וְרֹעוֹ "and its shepherd." So too Dhorme, Pope, NEB "carry away flocks and their shepherds" (but REB "pasture flocks they have stolen"). KJV "and feed thereof," i.e., eat the flocks they have stolen, is unlikely, because רעה usually means "pasture (animals)," and in the few cases where it means "feed oneself (on something)" the subj is usually depicted as an animal (e.g., death in Ps 49:14 [15]; the poor in Isa 14:30 [parallel to "lying down"; similarly Zeph 3:13]; Israel feeding on Carmel in Jer 50:19); here such an image is not explicit.

3.a. NEB rearranges vv 3–9 in the sequence vv 6, 3, 9, 4, 5, 7, 8.

3.b. This is a normal meaning of חבל, though BDB, 286a, regards the senses "bind" and "pledge" as belonging to the one verb; *DCH,* 3:149b, on the other hand, distinguishes חבל I "pledge" and חבל IV "bind." The proposal of Yellin (followed by NEB) that it means "lead by a rope" (from חֶבֶל "cord") is unnecessary.

4.a. Most take יטו as hiph of נטה "thrust aside" (so RSV "thrust off," NIV "thrust from," NJPS "chase off," Good "shove off"). But Dhorme takes the verb as intransitive: "The needy turn aside from the road," as if they realize that there is no room for them on the high road; certainly the hiph of נטה is attested as intransitive (cf. *DCH,* 5:675b §8). Similarly Terrien, who, by making the poor the subj of v 4, is able to link v 5 with it in the same strophe.

4.b. יחד, often "together" (so KJV, JPS, NEB), must here have the sense of "altogether, utterly" (as in 3:18; see *Note* 3:18.a, and cf. *DCH,* 4:197b §3d). It is not as though there is a community of the poor, "huddl[ing] together in obscure haunts" (Davidson). Most translations represent יחד by "all [the poor]" (RSV, NJPS, NAB, NIV).

4.c. חבאו, lit. "have hidden" (RSV "hide themselves"), i.e., presumably, "have been forced to hide" (similarly NIV, NAB, NJPS), in fear (Driver–Gray), NJB "have to keep out of sight." Driver–Gray and Beer (*BHK*) would prefer to read יִתְחַבְּאוּ (hithp) "they hide."

5.a. הֵן is presumably (so Gordis, Habel) "they" (3 masc pl pronoun, equivalent to הֵם and הֵמָּה, as perhaps also in 13:1) and not "if" (as in 4:18; 9:11; and so on) or "behold" (as in 8:20; though Good translates "See the wild asses"; similarly Duhm). Emendation to הֵם or הֵמָּה (as Budde) is unnecessary. Dhorme, claiming the support of LXX, Vg, Pesh, emends to הֵיךְ, equivalent to אֵיךְ "like" (followed by Hölscher, Kissane, Terrien, de Wilde, Hartley, and probably JB).

5.b. מדבר, traditionally translated "wilderness" (NJPS, NEB, GNB), "desert" (KJV, RSV, NAB, JB), is better rendered "steppe, grazing land" (cf. *HALOT,* 2:547a; *DCH,* 5:139b).

5.c. יצאו "they go out" could in principle have פראים "onagers" as the subj (cf. NEB "The poor rise early like the wild ass, when it scours the wilderness for food"), but in view of Ps 104:23 (יצא אדם לפעלו "humans go out to their work") it is more likely to be the poor. Gerleman (*BHS*) took the verb with במדבר, i.e., "they go out in the steppe." Fedrizzi moved the verb to before ערבה in the next colon: "they go out into the desert."

5.d. בפעלם, lit. "in their work," i.e., daily labor (cf. *DCH,* vol. 6, *s.v.*), the prep being different from Ps 104:23, but there is no need to delete (as Peake, Strahan, Stevenson) or to emend to לְפעלם "to their work" (as some MSS, Driver–Gray, Beer [*BH*[2] *frt*], Hölscher, Fohrer, Sicre Díaz). Beer (*BHK frt*) conjectured בַּפֹּעֲלִים "among the workers." Duhm replaced it with בָּעֲרָבָה "in the steppeland" (followed by Strahan). Peake simply omitted it, as also de Wilde (as a reminiscence of Ps 104:23). Larcher, followed by JB, moves לֶחֶם לַנְּעָרִים "bread for their children" from the end of the next colon, translating "driven by the hunger of their children," but it is not clear how he understands בפעלם. Dhorme unconvincingly transferred בפעלם to follow לטרף, and read עַד־עֶרֶב instead of ערבה, translating "[although they work] until the evening" (followed by NEB "though they work till nightfall"; similarly NJB "and at evening"). Gerleman (*BHS*) moved בפעלם to the next colon, which would yield the unsatisfactory sense "in their work they forage for provisions."

5.e. De Wilde transfers this colon to follow v 12b.

5.f. On the sense of שחר piel "seek earnestly," see *Comment.* NJB reads מִשַּׁחַר "from morning [for food]," translating "searching from dawn for food"; Terrien has a similar rendering without changing the text. Kissane reads שִׁחֲרוּ (?) "they search." Beer (*BHK frt*) proposed נִשְׂכְּרוּ "they hire themselves out."

5.g. Rather than "prey" (KJV, RSV), which is the food of animals. Fohrer thinks they are being forced to eat cattle food (cf. Hartley "the meager food the poor find by scavenging"), but elsewhere טרף seems to mean regular human food; see *Comment,* and cf. BDB, 383a; *DCH,* 3:376b. On the syntax of משחרי לטרף, a constr followed by *lamedh,* cf. GKC, §130a.

5.h. ערבה, "steppe, desert," is emended by Beer (*BHK*) to עָבְדוּ "they work [for food among the young men]" (*frt*). Hölscher, Fohrer, Gordis, de Wilde, and Hartley would put the *athnach* here, reading "searching for food in the desert"; but this weakens the second half of the line. Dhorme emended to עַד־עֶרֶב "[although they work] until the evening," Terrien and NEB to עֶרֶב "(in) the evening." NJB presumed עֶרֶב לַלֶּחֶם "(at) evening for food." The proposal of Beer (*BHK frt*) and Kissane, עָבְדוּ לַלחם "they work for food," sounds a bit lame.

5.i. Lit. "the desert [is] food." Others take ערבה as an adv acc (Hartley).

5.j. For examples of a sg suff when the reference is to the pl, cf. GKC, §145m.

5.k. Lit. "the desert is food for him for (his) children" (similarly JPS, NJPS "The wilderness provides each with food for his lads," Habel). לו "for him" is anomalous, in view of the pl verb יצאו "they go out," but it is easily enough intelligible. Many translations do not attempt to render it (so RSV, NIV); KJV "for them and for their children" is not quite accurate. Some would prefer to delete it (so Merx, Driver–Gray, Gordis, Pope, Habel). Guillaume ("Arabic Background," 116; *Studies,* 108) strains after a better sense by reading לו as לֻו "would that," translating "to see if there be food" (followed by Hartley, translating "even bread"); cf. *DCH,* 4:522a §2b. Beer (*BHK*), Hölscher, Fohrer, and Good emend לו לחם to לַלֶּחֶם (Beer [*BH*[2] *frt*]) and NAB to לְלֶחֶם "for food," rendering "the steppe provides food for the young among them." Beer (*BHK frt*) changes לנערים to בַּנְּעָרִים "among the young men" (Duhm over-imaginatively proposes לַנְּנֻעָרִים or לַנֻּעָרִים "for the shaken ones," from נער as in 38:13; Beer [BH^2 *frt*] לָרְעֵבִים "for the hungry"). Budde, Duhm, Peake, Strahan, Dhorme, Beer (BH^2 *al*) read לו as לֹא "no [bread for the children]"; so too Terrien, NEB "their children go hungry."

6.a. NEB moves this verse to follow v 2.

6.b. K יקצירו appears to be hiph, "they cause to harvest" (?); more probable is Q יִקְצוֹרוּ "they harvest."

6.c. NAB "in the untilled land" is a possible translation of שׂדה (more commonly, "field"), but it does not square with "harvest"—which can only be of cultivated land, unless the verb is used metaphorically.

6.d. בלילו "his fodder" (as in 6:5; Isa 30:24) does not seem appropriate here, though Driver–Gray have "the mixed fodder (of cattle)" and JPS "provender," RSV, NIV "fodder" (KJV "corn" means "grain"); it is defended also by Newsom. Since the term is not elsewhere used of human food, it would be strange to speak of reaping "mixed" fodder, and the parallelism suggests that they are reaping what they do not own. It would of course make perfectly good sense if the poor were having to eat food more properly suitable for cattle. Hitzig's suggestion, however, following LXX, Vg, Pesh, Tg, that the term is really בְּלִי־לוֹ "not theirs" fits much better (so too Kissane [בְּלִי לָמוֹ], Gordis, Sicre Díaz, GNB "They have to harvest fields they don't own," less satisfactorily NEB "they reap what is not theirs"). We may compare בְּלִי־מָה "nothingness," lit. "not anything" (26:7), בארץ לא להם "in a land that is not theirs" (Gen 15:13), רִיב לֹא־לוֹ "a dispute that is not his" (Prov 26:17), and משכנות לא־לו "dwellings that are not his" (Hab 1:6) (and see GKC, §155e). Improbable is Tur-Sinai's rendering "a field without yield," i.e., a field that has nothing (followed by de Wilde).

Others emend to בַּלַּיִל (Merx, Duhm, Peake, Strahan, Beer [BH^2]) or בַּלַּיְלָה "in the night" (Budde, Dhorme, Beer [*BHK*, בלילה], Fohrer, Terrien, Moffatt, NAB), but this supposes that the picture is that the poor are reduced to pilfering food from the rich (see *Comment*). Beer (*BHK*) notes the reading adopted by Larcher (*vaurien*), JB, and Pope, בִּשְׂדֵה בְלִיַּעַל "in the field of a scoundrel"—which makes a neat but rather tame parallelism with "the vineyard of a wicked man."

6.e. NAB transposes the colon to follow v 11a.

6.f. לקשׁ piel occurs only here, and there are several suggestions for its meaning: (1) BDB, 545b, suggests "despoil," as a denominative from לֶקֶשׁ "aftergrowth," thus "take everything," which seems a little forced. (2) Gesenius–Buhl, 390b, and *HALOT*, 2:536a, have "grab in a hurry," comparing Arab. *laqaṭa*; so NEB "filch," NJB "pilfering" (similarly Fohrer; A. Guillaume, "A Contribution to Hebrew Lexicography," *BSOAS* 16 [1954] 1–12 [7, 10], "hurried reaping in the dead of night"). (3) "Be late" (cf. MH "retard, do late" [Jastrow, 719b]; Arab. *laqasa* [Lane, 2668]; and perhaps לֶקֶשׁ "aftergrowth" and מַלְקוֹשׁ "latter rain"); thus Rosenmüller, Delitzsch, Driver–Gray, and Newsom "gather the late-ripe fruit" (Driver–Gray regard the verb as a privative piel). Gordis understands rather "toil late," while Strauss has "drudge" (though he seems to conflate Arab. *laqaṭa* and *laqasa*). (4) לקשׁ may, however, be no more than a variant for the similar-sounding verb לקט, the common word for "glean." The translation "glean" satisfies most (RV, RSV, NIV; NAB "harvest"; *DCH*, 4:576b). NJPS seems to combine both לקט "glean" and לקשׁ II "be late" in its translation "glean the late grapes"—which is not really acceptable.

6.g. Some (Budde, Duhm, Peake, Beer [BH^2; *BHK al*], Fohrer, NEB) read עָשֹׁר or עָשִׁיר "rich" for רָשָׁע "wicked"; see *Comment*. Guillaume ("Arabic Background," 116; *Studies*, 108) ingeniously made רשׁע actually mean "rich" by comparing Arab. *rassagha* "provide handsomely for one's family" (so too Sicre Díaz). Ehrlich read כֶּרֶם רֶשַׁע "vineyard of wickedness" (like לֶחֶם רֶשַׁע "bread of wickedness" in Prov 4:17 and אוֹצְרוֹת רֶשַׁע "treasures of wickedness" in Prov 10:2). De Wilde improbably emends to וכרם רָשׁ "and a hungry, unproductive vineyard," to match his understanding of שׂדה בלי לו.

7.a. The verse is deleted by Duhm, the first half as repetitious of v 10a and the second as a makeweight. BH^2 would delete either v 7a or v 10a. Larcher, followed by JB and NJB, moves vv 10–11 to precede v 7, explaining the displacement as due to the similarity of the beginning of v 7 and v 10.

7.b. ערום "naked" is sg, while its verb ילינו "they pass the night" is pl; we have had such an interchange of number in v 5, with יצאו and לו, and in v 6, with יקיצרו and בלי לו (see GKC, §145, and §118o on the sg adj expressing a state). De Wilde deletes ערום as intrusive from v 10a.

7.c. Lit. "in" (ב).

8.a. צור is "rock," but Kissane, comparing Lam 4:5, where the defeated "cling to" (חבק, as here) ashheaps (אַשְׁפַּתּוֹת), suggested we read צֹר "flint, gravel," i.e., they must lie on the bare ground.

9.a. Most commentators and some translations regard the verse as displaced (as NJPS) and move it to follow v 3 (Driver–Gray, Dhorme, Terrien, Moffatt, NEB) or v 4 (Strahan) or v 12 (Kissane) or omit it altogether as repetitious (so Budde, Beer [BH^2], Hölscher, Stevenson, Fohrer, NAB).

9.b. MT has nothing corresponding to "the wicked," but the situation seems the same as at the beginning of v 2. If the order of the verses is correct, the text reverts here to a focalization on the wicked, and in the next verse makes the same move as in v 4b to a focalization on the poor. This focalization is also expressed by JPS "There are that pluck," RSV "There are those who snatch." NIV preserves the focalization on the poor in vv 4b–8 by translating יגזלו and יחבלו as passives, "[the fatherless child] is snatched" and "is seized" (similarly JB). Sicre Díaz also adds "the wicked."

9.c. שֹׁד is usually "destruction" and שַׁד is "breast," so some emend to מִשַּׁד "from the breast" (e.g., Duhm, Beer [BH^2], Kissane). But שֹׁד is clearly "breast" in Isa 60:16; 66:11 (שֹׁד II, BDB, 994b), and must be so here too. Beer [*BHK*] read מִשְּׂדֵה "from the field of [the orphan]"; perhaps Larcher's translation "they take from the fatherless his field" and JB "fatherless children are robbed of their lands" follow the same reading; similarly too M. Dahood, "Hebrew-Ugaritic Lexicography X," *Bib* 53 (1972) 386–403 (399), reading מִשְּׂדֵי "from the fields of [the orphan]."

9.d. MT is "and over [עַל] the poor they take pledges" (so KJV, JPS). But most agree that עֻל "infant" should be read here (as, e.g., Duhm, Beer [*BHK*], Kissane, Gerleman [*BHS prp*], NEB [עָל, though that form never occurs elsewhere]). Larcher attractively reads (presumably) וּמְעִיל "and the mantle of [the poor]" (as also JB "and poor men have their cloaks seized as security"), which would further confirm his translation of the first colon (see previous *Note*). M. Dahood retains the MT reading by understanding על as "from" (the so-called Phoenician sense) ("The Phoenician Contribution to Biblical Wisdom Literature," in *The Role of the Phoenicians in the Interaction of Mediterranean Civilizations,* ed. W. A. Ward [Beirut: American University in Beirut, 1968] 123–52 [138]), but the emendation is superior.

10.a. Beer (BH^2) transposed vv 10–11 to follow v 6. Gray thought that the original order was vv 10a, 11a, 10b, 11a. NAB omits v 9 and v 10a and moves v 10b to follow v 11.

10.b. ערום "naked" is emended to עֹרְגִים "longing" by A. de Wilde ("Vervreemding in Job 24:10, 11," *NTT* 28 [1974] 165).

10.c. It may seem a little strange that they are both "naked" (ערום) and "unclothed" (בלי לבוש); surely the two terms mean exactly the same thing? S. T. Byington proposed reading בִּכְלֵי לְבוּשׁ "[naked] with articles of clothing," i.e., belonging to others, just as in the second colon they are hungry as they carry the sheaves ("Some Bits of Hebrew: IV. Texts in Job," *ExpTim* 57 [1945–46] 110–11). But the proposal is forced. E. F. Sutcliffe prefers מִבְּלִי לבוש "for lack of clothing" ("A Note on Job xxiv 10, 11," *JTS* 50 [1949] 174–76), which is perhaps a marginal improvement on the MT.

10.d. On the adj of state or condition, with a verb, cf. GKC, §118n–o.

10.e. On עמר as "ears" rather than "sheaves," see *Comment,* and *DCH,* vol. 6, *s.v.*

11.a. Lit. "between" (בֵּין), but olive oil presses are not literally located "between" the rows of olive trees, only in the general vicinity.

11.b. שׁורתם "their walls" (from שׁוּר II, according to BDB, 1004a), the antecedent presumably being the wicked who are implied at the beginning of v 9 (so also RSV). Peters, Fohrer, *HALOT,* 4:1453b, understand it of the supporting walls of the terraces. Perhaps, however, we should argue that שׁוּר here means "row" (cf. Gordis), or derive it from a שׁוּרָה "row" (as BDB, 1004b). Many read the dual שׁוּרֹתַיִם "two rows" (Beer [*BHK vel*], Hölscher, Kissane [שׁוּרֹתַיִם], Fedrizzi; NJB "two little walls," NEB imaginatively but unconvincingly "in the shade where two walls meet") or simply שׁוּרוֹת "rows" (Beer [*BHK vel*]) or שׁוּרִם "rows" (Duhm). Dhorme, followed by Pope, thought the word meant "millstone," reading שׁוּרֹתַיִם, but there is no parallel. He is followed nevertheless by JB "They have no stones for pressing oil," presumably reading אֵין "there are no" for בין "between."

Among more substantial emendations, de Wilde read בְּצָרוֹתָם "in their distresses." Bickell, 153–54, reads בֵּין שִׁירֹתָם "among their songs," explaining that the workers were forced to sing to prevent them eating the crops they were harvesting (!). By comparison, Sutcliffe's proposed reading, בְּאֵין־שִׁירֹתָם "without their songs," i.e., deprived of the usual harvest and vintage-time songs ("A Note on Job xxiv 10, 11," *JTS* 50 [1949] 174–76), seems a lot more plausible; but the deprivations of these farmworkers are a lot more serious than that. Byington, in line with his rendering of v 10 (see above), wanted to see here some contrast between the lot of the poor and the commodity they were producing, as there is in the second colon of v 11 also; so for בין־שורתם he read בְּנִשְׁרֹתָם "with their hard skin" (i.e., unsoftened by oil), supposing a new Heb. noun cognate with Arab. *nšr* "frog of a hoof," but that seems very unlikely.

11.c. צהר hiph "press oil," from יִצְהָר "oil," occurs only here (BDB, 844a; KBL, 796a; *HALOT,* 3:1008a). A less suitable possibility is that צהר is derived from צָהֳרַיִם "midday," hence "spend the noon time"; so Vg *meridiati sunt,* Hontheim "they work in the noonday sun," Tur-Sinai, Larcher, NJB "their shelter at high noon"; cf. Gesenius–Buhl, 675b.

11.d. NAB replaces v 10a by this colon, and follows it with v 6a (its sequence is vv 7, 8, 11a, 6b, 11b, 10b).

11.e. דרך "tread" is used of treading olives in Mic 6:15, but elsewhere of treading grapes, which must be in view here (because of יקב "wine vat"), although grapes are not specifically mentioned. For the perfect of "experiences frequently confirmed," see GKC, §111s.

11.f. Duhm, convinced that we are still reading about pilfering from the fields, reads וַיִּגְמְאוּ "and they swallow down" instead of יצמאו "they thirst" (so too Beer [BH^2 *frt*]).

12.a. MT מעיר מתים, according to the accents, is to be taken as one phrase, meaning "out of the city of men" (see *Note* 12.c on "dying"). But most modern authors take מתים as subj of ינאקו. De Wilde emends to מְעֵי מְתִים "the bowels, inward parts, of men" as subj. Steuernagel, Beer (*BHK*), Hölscher, and Fohrer emend to מֵעֲבֹדָתָם "from their work," on the ground that it is not the city but the countryside that is in view (but see *Comment*). Tur-Sinai, Gordis, and Strauss think it is the word עִיר "terror" (BDB, 735b), as in Jer 15:8, but terror seems the wrong emotion here. NEB "far from the city" attempts to keep the focus on the countryside, as also NAB, which emends to מֵעָפָר "from the dust."

12.b. ינאקו, lit. "they groan," not to be emended with Bickell, 154, Duhm, and Strahan to יָנֻדוּ "are chased away" or יִנָּדְחוּ "are thrust away," following LXX ἐξεβάλλοντο. Less plausible still is the proposal of Beer (BH^2), נָקֹאוּ "they are vomited out" (קיא elsewhere never in niph, and LXX can hardly be claimed in support); in Lev 18:25 the land vomits out its inhabitants because of their defilement, which is irrelevant here.

12.c. מְתִים is "men" (so KJV, RV "the populous city," JPS, NJPS, Habel "grown men"), but most emend to מֵתִים "the dying" (the ptcp can mean "dying" [as in Zech 11:9] as well as "dead"; cf. GKC, §116d) (so RSV, JB, NEB, NAB, NIV, Beer [*BHK al*]), parallel to חללים "the wounded." Bickell, 154, Duhm, Strahan, Beer (BH^2) uninterestingly emend to וּבָתִּים "[from the city] and houses," following LXX οἱ ἐκ πόλεως καὶ οἴκων "those from the city and houses."

12.d. This colon is deleted by Fohrer.

12.e. Gordis, Pope, de Wilde, and Ravasi suggest that the physical sense of "throat" is in view here.

12.f. חֲלָלִים "wounded" is not to be emended to עֹלָלִים "children" (Merx [עֹלְלִים], Duhm, Beer [BH^2] [עֹלָלִים], de Wilde), following LXX νηπίων.

12.g. Surprisingly, NAB wants to omit this key colon, on the improbable ground that it is a dittogr of v 25b. Kissane moves vv 12c–13 to follow v 16.

12.h. ואלוה לא־ישים תפלה, lit. "and God does not set wrong, folly," implying either "does not impute wrong *to them* (the wicked)" (viz. supplying בָּם "to them"; cf. *Note* 4:18.c) or "does not set it to his heart" (viz. supplying אֶל־לִבּוֹ "to his heart" or עַל־לִבּוֹ [Duhm]). שׂים is used elliptically also at 4:20. So KJV "God layeth not folly to them," JPS "God imputeth it not for unseemliness" (RV "to folly"), NJPS "God does not regard it as a reproach," NIV "God charges no one with wrongdoing," Peake "taketh no heed of the wrong," Habel "Eloah seems to consider nothing wrong." Emendation to יִשְׁמַע "hears" (as Budde, Ehrlich, Dhorme, Beer [*BHK*], Hölscher, de Wilde, JB "remains deaf to") is unnecessary. So too (against *Note* 1:22.b) is the emendation of תִּפְלָה "folly, wrongdoing" to תְּפִלָּה "prayer," i.e., God does not set his mind to, pays no attention to, their prayer (as two MSS, Pesh, RSV, JB, NEB, GNB, Budde, Dhorme, Beer [*BHK*], Hölscher, Larcher, Terrien, Fohrer, Gerleman [*BHS frt* תְּפִילָה], de Wilde, Sicre Díaz). Newsom, however, thinks that "both translations are required for one to hear the text in all the fullness of its meaning"—which is open to doubt. Duhm emended, taking נֶפֶשׁ as "hunger," וֶאֱלֹהַּ לֹא יֵשׁ מִתְפַּלֵּל "and about it no one prays," which is hardly attractive Heb.

13.a. Duhm and others regard vv 13–18 as secondary. V 13 is transferred by Dhorme to follow v 16b.

13.b. המה היו במרדי־אור "they are among those who are rebels of, i.e., against, the light." As Driver–Gray rightly say, המה points "commonly to persons mentioned before" (see *Comment*). They themselves, however, though translating "Those are of them that," think, as most do, that here the pronoun "points to persons whom the poet is thinking of or has in his mind's eye"; similarly Gordis: "introducing a new subject"; cf. NJB "In contrast, there are those."

The *beth* is ignored by many; thus RSV, NAB, NIV "there are those who," NJPS "They are rebels," NEB "Some there are who." It can hardly be a *beth essentiae* (GKC, §119i), as Strauss. KJV was better: "They are of those that" (cf. JPS); similarly Dhorme, but he transferred v 13 to follow v 16b. For a parallel to היה ב, cf. Judg 11:35 (היית בעכרי "you have become one of those who trouble me").

13.c. NEB does not do well to translate "the light of day," for the term must include the symbolic and moral dimensions of light also; REB has simply "light." It would be a great loss to accept the emendation of Beer (*BHK prps*) and Hölscher from אוֹר "light" to אֵל "God."

13.d. יָשְׁבוּ, lit. "dwell," "abide" (KJV). It is strange to "dwell" on paths, even stranger to "sit" on them (Good), and Isa 58:12 (משובב נתיבות לשבת "the restorer of streets to dwell [in]") is not an exact parallel. RSV, NIV "stay [in its paths]" is a brave attempt at making sense of ישב "dwell," but it is hard to find a case where the verb means "stay" other than in the sense of "live, dwell" (Judg 6:18; 1 Sam 20:38 may perhaps be exceptions). Some MSS have יָשׁוּבוּ "they return" (cf. Vg *reversi sunt*), which is no improvement (against Ehrlich and Kissane, reading יָשֻׁבוּ); "they have not returned by its paths" (Dhorme) stands in need of explanation itself. Emendation to הָלְכוּ "have walked" (cf. Driver–Gray) or יֵלְכוּ "walk" (Beer) on the basis of LXX ἐπορεύθησαν (cf. Pesh) is hard to defend. Kissane also contemplates an emendation to יַחְשְׁבוּ "they do [not] consider [his paths]," comparing Ps 144:3.

14.a. Vv 14–18a were not to be found in the original LXX and have been supplied from Theod. This omission does not, however, necessarily mean that their Hebrew text lacked it. Gard, 64, argued that the reason was simply "to avoid the minutiae of criminal action"; or possibly the translators could not see the relevance of these verses to the broader context.

14.b. לאור, lit. "at light," hence "with the light" (KJV), "at dawn" (GNB), "at daybreak" (Dhorme; similarly Sicre Díaz), "at twilight" (Hartley, meaning "dawn"). Many think the murderer should be about his business only in the dark, so emend to לֹא אוֹר "not light, i.e., before the light," "before daylight" (NEB) (cf. לֹא עת "before time" at 22:16, but it is doubtful that the clause וְלֹא עת is strictly parallel to what we have here); so Wright, Budde, Strahan, Driver–Gray, Beer [*BHK*], Kissane, Fedrizzi, de Wilde, RSV. But some treat the phrase as simply meaning "in the dark" (RSV, Moffatt), "at dusk" (NRSV), "when there is no light" (NAB, Peake), "when daylight is gone" (NIV), and לֹא אוֹר would be a strange way of saying that. Hölscher emends to בְּלֹא אוֹר "when there is no light" (followed by Larcher, JB). Duhm and Beer (*BH*[2]) forthrightly emended to לָעֶרֶב "in the evening." Gordis, followed by NJPS, reckoned לאור itself to mean "nightfall," comparing Aram. אורתא "evening"; but this is a specialized use of the normal word for "light," to mean the beginning of a day that commences with the evening (cf. Jastrow, 32b, *s.v.* אוֹר II; 35a, *s.v.* אוּרְתָּא), so there is no real parallel with our text. Pope thought the *lamedh* of לאור was used in the "separative sense 'from,'" thus "away from the light" and so "twilight" (followed by Habel "in the evening"), but the evidence of such a sense is feeble.

14.c. For other examples of a subordinate (purpose or consequence) clause without the particle *waw,* cf. GKC, §120c. Dhorme, however, does not recognize this use. For the juss as impf, cf. GKC, §109k.

14.d. Duhm, followed by Strahan, Beer (*BH*[2] *prps* אֹיְבוֹ וְצָרוֹ), emended עני ואביון "poor and needy" to צָרוֹ וְאֹיְבוֹ "his opponent and his enemy," on the ground that a murderer would not be wanting to kill the poor; see *Comment.*

15.a. Is NEB's translation, "the seducer," intended to make his action appear more hostile and self-centered than perhaps "adulterer" would sound?

15.b. שמרה, lit. "keeps," but here "watch for" (as in 10:14; 39:1; Ps 130:6; etc.; cf. BDB, 1036b, §1c).

15.c. אמר, usually "say," sometimes can be understood as "think" (as NEB, NJPS, NIV, Pope), but JB, for example, is very definite that "he mutters."

15.d. תשורני "will see me." Dahood, however, followed by Blommerde, reads תְּשׁוּרֶנִּי "will see him," the suff being a 3d-person *yodh* (review of *Il Semitico di Nord Ovest,* by G. Garbini, *Or* 32 [1963] 499); on the supposed 3d-person *yodh* suff, see further *Note* 21:16.e.

15.e. The colon is moved by NEB to follow v 14c. But why would the burglar need to mask his face in the night? The covering of the face fits the adulterer in the shadowy twilight better.

15.f. סתר פנים ישים "he sets a covering of the face." For שׂים of putting clothing on, see BDB, 963b, §1b. Duhm suggests that עַל פָּנָיו "over his face" is implied.

14c.a. Many move this colon to prefix v 16a (as in the *Translation* above), making the burglar follow the adulterer (so Peake, Dhorme, Hölscher, Pope, Hartley, NEB), especially with the emendation of יהי; see next *Note* 14c.b. NAB moves this colon together with v 15c to precede v 16a, so that it is the burglar who puts a mask over his face. Others move v 16a to follow this colon, making the burglar precede the adulterer (so JB, de Wilde, Sicre Díaz).

14c.b. Lit. "and at night let him be like a thief." If the colon is left in its place, at the end of v 14, and it is still the murderer who is in view, it is banal to say that he is like a thief (NRSV; similarly RSV); the banality is evident in GNB's "At dawn the murderer gets up and goes out to kill the poor, and at night he steals." But equally, if we have now moved on to the image of the thief, it is odd too that he should be said to be "*like* a thief." Gordis, followed by Hartley, takes the *kaph* as *kaph* asseverative (as he claims to find in 3:5 also, *q.v.*), but such a particle is very dubious (despite R. Gordis, "The Asseverative Kaph in Ugaritic and Hebrew," *JAOS* 63 [1943] 176–78).

The juss יְהִי is odd, though there seems to a perfectly sound parallel at 18:12. Merx, Budde, Duhm, Peake, Driver–Gray, Beer (*BHK*), Dhorme, Hölscher, Kissane, de Wilde, NAB emend to יְהַלֵּךְ גַּנָּב "the thief goes about, roams"; so too NEB "the thief prowls," REB "prowls about," NJB "goes on the prowl"; this emendation is adopted in the *Translation* above. Others (e.g., Sicre Díaz) read יְהָךְ גַּנָּב, with the same meaning, an Aram. impf of הלך "go" (as in Ezra 5:5), but it is not clear why we should suddenly have an Aram. verb form. Fedrizzi proposes יְחַכֶּה גַּנָּב "the thief waits for [the night]," but חכה does not elsewhere take ב.

16.a. Very probably to be moved to connect with v 14c. It is the thief, not the murderer or adulterer, who breaks into houses. It does not matter much whether the thief (vv 14c, 16a) is described after the murderer (v 14ab) or after the adulterer (v 15).

16.b. חתר, lit. "he digs," usually with ב "into" following (Ezek 8:8; Amos 9:2). If it is the same person(s) throughout this verse, there is an anomaly of number between חתר "he digs" and חתמו "they seal." Beer (BH^2) and Dhorme emend to חִתֵּם "he marked" (NEB חָתַם), to preserve the sg for the burglar (as in v 14c). KJV, RSV, NJPS, NIV have the pl. Duhm, thinking it is still the adulterer, translates "breaks out."

16.c. חתמו למו, lit. "seal themselves up" (RV "shut themselves up"), so as not to be seen. KJV "which they had marked for themselves in the daytime" took חתם piel as "place a seal, a mark." So too Beer (BH^2), Dhorme, Gordis, and NEB, but the idea seems implausible. What burglar worth his salt will need to mark the house he proposes breaking into in case he should forget it by evening? The burglar in *Ali Baba and the Forty Thieves*, whom Peake calls in evidence, is a different kettle of fish. And as Rowley remarks, a seal identifies the person it belongs to, and thieves are hardly likely to be leaving their signature on houses they intend to burgle. The "marking" cannot refer, either, to a mental note the burglar has made of promising houses to rob, for חתם does not mean that. Good can hardly be right that "houses" is the subj of "are sealed around him."

16.d. Dhorme, followed by de Wilde, NEB, NAB, moves this colon to follow יחדו at the beginning of v 17. Beer (BH^2), on the other hand, inserts here (*frt*) כִּי יַחְדָּו "for altogether" from v 17.

17.a. יחדו is here probably "together" (as in 2:11; 9:32), hence "all of them" (e.g., RSV), "one and all" (NEB), though it could mean "altogether" (as in v 4; see *Note* 24:4.b). If it is an asseverative, it is more likely that it modifies the whole sentence (like גם; see *Note* 23:2.a) rather than "morning" (as Gordis "every morning is like darkness"). Pope omits כי יחדו as overloading the colon; Beer (*BHK*), Fohrer, NEB move יחדו to v 16c. Not very probable is the suggestion of Byington, "Some Bits of Hebrew," 110, to read יחדו בקר לָם וְצלמות "alike to them are morning and gloom" (why would לם "to them" come between בקר "morning" and צלמות "gloom"?).

17.b. Duhm, followed by Strahan, read בָּחֲרוּ "they have chosen" for בֹּקֶר "morning." Kissane proposed בקר "examine," i.e., if God examined the wicked. Beer (BH^2), following Pesh, reads בָּקְרוּ "they seek," but this misses the point of the depiction.

17.c. Kissane deletes צלמות "darkness of death" because it is repeated in the second colon.

17.d. NAB omits this colon.

17.e. יכיר "he makes friends with" (or simply "know," as RV, or "discern," as Habel) is to be understood as having the "rebels against the light" as subj, even if it is not emended to יַכִּירוּ "they make friends with" (as Driver–Gray, Beer [*BHK*], Hölscher, Fohrer). REB, to similar effect, has "amid the terrors of night they are at home." NEB "in the welter of night" apparently tries to reproduce the idea of turmoil in בלהה ("welter" is "upheaval" or "rolling, tumbling" of waves). KJV has the awkward translation "if one know them, they are in the terrors," attempting to represent the sgs and pls (but it has "they dig" in v 16 for a sg). NJB "since that is when they know what fear is" apparently attempts to render the MT, with the omission of the second צלמות. Gordis has a fanciful notion that כי יכיר "when one recognizes" (another possible meaning for נכר hiph) is an idiom for "morning" because that is the time one recognizes one's neighbor (as in Ruth 3:14; *m. Berakot* 1.2); similarly Hartley "a time when one recognizes the terrors of deep darkness." Dhorme attractively emends יכיר to יָאִיר "[when] its light shines."

17.f. בלהות "terrors" is emended by Duhm, Strahan, and Beer (BH^2 *frt* [הֲלִיכוֹת]) to הֲלִכוֹת "the paths of" (cf. דרכיו "its ways" in v 13).

17.g. It is strange that צלמות "shadow of death" is repeated in this verse (for the translation, cf. *Note* 3:5.a). Dhorme emends this second occurrence to עָלֵימוֹ "[terrors are] upon them" (the form also in 6:16; 21:17); Duhm, Beer (*BHK*), and Fohrer to עֲלָטָה "thick darkness," Stevenson to מָוֶת "death," and Hölscher to (?) לַיְלָה "night." Larcher, followed by JB, deletes it.

24:18–24.a. For *Notes* and *Comment* on 24:18–24, see after 27:17.

25.a. כזב hiph "prove me wrong" (NEB) (factitive, declarative [GKC, §53c], as רשע hiph in 9:20;

10:2; 15:6), as also RSV, NJB "prove me a liar," but not "make me lie, make me be wrong" (KJV "make me a liar" no doubt also means "show me to be a liar," "claim I am a liar"). NJPS, NAB, Pope "confute" is not the same thing. At 34:6, it is כזב piel that has the declarative sense (*HALOT,* 2:468a; *DCH,* 4:379a).

25.b. Driver–Gray, Beer (*BHK*), and Hartley read the more normal form וְיָשֵׂם, for וְיָשֵׂם (two MSS have יָשִׂים).

25.c. לְאַל is apparently "to nothing," but אַל is not elsewhere used as a noun (cf. BDB, 39a §c; *HALOT,* 1:48a §3; *DCH,* 1:253a §3). Driver–Gray and Beer (*BHK*) read לְאַיִן "to nothing." NJPS "or prove that I am wrong" (cf. GNB) is a rather loose translation; it is rather "show that there is nothing in what I say" (RSV), "make nonsense of my argument" (NEB), "show that my words have no substance" (JB), or even "show that what I urge is idle talk" (Moffatt).

Form/Structure/Setting

The *structure* of this eighth speech of Job is in essence twofold. In chap. 23 his concern is with himself and the recognition of his own innocence; in chap. 24 his concern is with others and the absence of justice in the world generally. The speech as a whole is a soliloquy, addressed at no point either to the friends or to God. Nevertheless, there seems to be a consciousness in Job that he has an audience. The closing sentence, "If this is not so, who can prove me wrong?" (24:25), is in form at least a challenge to hearers, and the rhetorical questions (23:6, 13; 24:1, 25), while not necessarily implying an audience, keep before the readers a certain awareness of Job's hearers.

The *integrity* of this speech, as also of the remainder of the third cycle of the dialogue, is open to question. Together with most commentators, I regard 24:18–24 as not properly part of this speech but wrongly transposed to this place during the course of the transmission of the text (against, e.g., D. Wolfers, "The Speech-Cycles in the Book of Job," *VT* 43 [1993] 385–402). The *order* of the verses in chap. 24 has also been thought by many to have been damaged; in this commentary, however, only two changes have been adopted: (1) the transposition of v 14c to follow v 15, and (2) the assignment of vv 18–24 to Zophar, probably to follow 27:17.

A more radical view of chap. 24 was taken by Duhm and Fohrer, who regarded it as consisting of four independent poems, not originally parts of a speech of Job (O. Loretz similarly argues that the whole chapter is secondary and that there are no genuine tricola in the speech ["Philologische und textologische Probleme in Hi 24,1–25," *UF* 12 (1980) 261–66]). According to Duhm, the poems are vv 1–4, 5–12 (plus 30:2–8), 13–18a, 18b–24, all of them consisting exclusively of tricola. But his reconstruction of tricola is often very strained, and he proposes numerous arbitrary emendations of the text. Fohrer has no interest in identifying tricola, but he does find four poems: vv 1–4, 10–12, 22–23 (on the powerful wicked and their victims), vv 5–8 (on the poor who live in the desert), vv 13–17 (on the rebels against the light), and vv 18–21 (on the end of the wicked). Van der Lugt assigns the chapter as a whole to Bildad.

Following is an index of alterations of order and deletions proposed for chap. 24 by modern English translations and some representative scholars:

vv 1–12, 25—after 25:6, as a ninth speech of Job (de Wilde).
v 5c—after v 12b (de Wilde).
v 6—after v 2 (NEB).
v 8—followed by 30:2–8 (Moffatt).
vv 9–12—after v 4 (Fohrer).
v 9—after v 3 (Moffatt, NEB, Driver–Gray, Dhorme, Terrien, Pope, Fedrizzi, de Wilde); after v 4 and omitted (Fohrer); omitted by NAB, Hölscher; said by NJPS to belong to vv 2–4a.

vv 10–11—after v 6 (NJB).
v 10a—in small type as probably out of place or corrupt (Driver–Gray).
v 11—after v 8 (NAB).
v 11a—in small type as probably out of place or corrupt (Driver–Gray).
v 12—after v 14 (Moffatt).
v 12c—in square brackets (NAB).
v 13—after v 16b (Dhorme).
v 14c—after v 15b (NEB); after v 15c (Moffatt, NAB, Driver–Gray, Dhorme, Pope, Clines).
v 15a–b—after v 14b (Hölscher); after vv 14, 15c, 16a, 18a (the burglar) (Fedrizzi).
v 15c—after v 14c (Hölscher, Fedrizzi).
v 16a—after v 14 (NJB), Fohrer, de Wilde, Alonso Schökel–Sicre Díaz, Hartley.
v 17b—omitted (NAB); after v 14b (de Wilde).
vv 18–25—after 27:23 (Pope); attributed to Zophar (Terrien).
vv 18–24—after 27:13 (NJB, Dhorme); after 27:17 (Clines); after 27:7 and assigned to Zophar (Alonso Schökel–Sicre Díaz); assigned to Zophar (GNB); vv 18b–24 assigned to Bildad or Zophar (Fedrizzi).
v 18a—omitted (NAB); after v 16a (Hölscher, Fedrizzi).
vv 18b–19—after 27:13 (de Wilde).
v 18c—omitted (NAB).
vv 19–21—in double square brackets, as not Job's (Moffatt).
v 19—omitted (NAB).
v 20—omitted (NAB); after v 24 (de Wilde).
v 20b—after v 18aα (Fohrer).
v 20c—after v 24a (Hölscher).
v 21—omitted (NAB); after v 9 (Pope).
vv 22–23—after v 12 (Fohrer).
v 22a—after v 23a (NAB).
vv 24–25—omitted (Fohrer).
v 24—in double square brackets, as not Job's (Moffatt).

Rather than attempting a detailed examination of these proposals, I shall try to offer in the *Comment* a coherent exegesis that renders most of them unnecessary.

The *strophic structure* that one discerns depends of course upon prior decisions about the order of verses and possible deletions, so a comparison among the commentators is not always meaningful. I find it best to reckon with nine strophes, as in the pattern shown:

Strophe 1	23:2	1 line
Strophe 2	23:3–7	5 lines
Strophe 3	23:8–12	5 lines
Strophe 4	23:13–17	5 lines
Strophe 5	24:1–4	4 lines
Strophe 6	24:5–8	4 lines
Strophe 7	24:9–12	4 lines
Strophe 8	24:13–17	6 lines (including two tricola)
Strophe 9	24:25	1 line

This schema assumes that 24:18–24 is to be removed from this speech (as noted above). The speech shows unusual opening and closing strophes of one line each, a regular pattern of five-line strophes in chap. 23 and of mostly four-line strophes in chap. 24. It would be possible to divide chap. 23 differently, viz. vv 2–7, 8–9, 10–14, and 15–17. But vv

8–12 are best regarded as belonging together since they focus upon Job's experience, whereas with v 13 the focus changes to God (and then, of course, in vv 15–17, again to Job and his reaction to what has been said of God in vv 13–14).

For chap. 23, NIV and van der Lugt find the same five-line strophic structure; so too Terrien: vv 2–7 (four lines plus two), 8–12 (two lines plus three), and 13–17 (two lines plus three). RSV, NJB, and NJPS note only the strong disjunction between vv 1–7 and 8–17. NAB has strophes of 23:2–7, 8–14, 15–17 (recognizing the disjunction between God's intentions in vv 13–14 and Job's reactions in vv 15–17). Webster, following MacKenzie, identifies five strophes, vv 2–4, 5–7, 8–10, 11–14, and 15–17; but is strange to make a separation between vv 4 and 5, which both concern Job's envisaged court case with God, and between vv 10 and 11 since both have the theme of Job's path.

For chap. 24 NRSV agrees with the analysis proposed above, except that it joins vv 1–8 as a single strophe. NIV displays as strophes vv 1–12, 13–17, and 18–24. Terrien's strophic divisions are: vv 1–5, including v 9 after v 4 (four lines plus two), 6–11, excluding v 9 (three lines plus two), and 12–17 (two lines plus four)—and then, assigned to Zophar, two strophes, vv 18–20 (three lines plus two; but the first two lines are missing!), and 21–25 (three lines plus two). But linking v 5, where the focalization is the poor, to what precedes (vv 1–4), where the focalization is the wicked, is unpersuasive (see *Note* 24:4.a). RSV's divisions after v 17 and v 20 reflect its decision that vv 18–20 are a quotation by Job of the friends' words.

NAB despairs of making sense of chap. 24, and displays as strophes vv 1–3, 4–10, 12, 13–17a, 18–20, 22–24, and 25. Skehan explains the NAB's strophic structure for 23:2–24:11 as consisting of strophes of 3, 3, 3, 4, 3, 3, 3, 4 verses; but that pattern cannot be meaningful since the major disjunction (at 24:1) falls after the fourth three-line strophe. Moreover, the omission of 24:11 is hard to justify, and to dismember the strophe about the suffering farm laborers with its climactic line "From the dust the dying groan and the souls of the wounded cry out[,] yet God does not treat it as unseemly" (NAB) is unforgivable. Webster finds the strophes to be vv 1–3, 4–5, 6–8, 9–12, 13–17, 18–21, and 22–24 with a pendant (v 25); the one point of difficulty here is that vv 4 and 5, with quite different themes, can hardly form a single strophe. Van der Lugt analyzes the strophic structure as vv 1, 2–4, 5–6, 7–9, 10–12, 13–14, 15–16, 17–18, 19–20, 21–22, and 23–24, thus strophes of 1, 3, 3, 3, 3, 2, 2, 2, 2, 2, 2, 1 lines, respectively. But it is inexplicable how vv 7–8 can be said to describe the wicked and so be linked with v 9, while v 17 must surely be connected with the preceding picture of the "light-shy," and it is hard to accept that v 21 is a tricolon rather than two bicola. V 25 is separated off as a strophe in its own right by NIV, NJB, NJPS (as also in my analysis).

The *genre* of the speech is a complaint (as against Murphy, 35, who regards it as a disputation speech, while acknowledging that "the tone is more reflective and less polemical than usual"). Like chap. 3, this is a soliloquy, addressed neither to God nor to the friends. It expresses in its first half Job's longing for a personal encounter with God, using the *form* of the *wish*, "who will grant that . . . ?" (23:3), and in its second half Job's complaint that God does not give the wicked the punishment they deserve, using the *form* of the *rhetorical question*, "Why are days of assize not kept by the Almighty?" (24:1).

Other *forms* that are drawn upon are the *disputation*, especially in 23:4–5, where the language of the lawsuit is prominent (cf. "set forth a case," "arguments," "answer," "understand"); the *certainty of success* in the legal dispute (23:7; cf. 16:19, 21; 19:25), and the *avowal of innocence* (23:10–12; cf. 6:10; 13:16, 18). Fohrer points out a similar combination of these three elements in 13:13–19. In vv 13–14 we have the echo of a hymnic form expressing God's *self-determination* (cf. 9:12; Pss 33:9; 132:13–14). There is also the *accusation* (of God, 23:16), with its proof (23:17). In 24:5–8, 10–12 we find the *pathetic* description, of poor farmworkers (cf. 30:2–8).

The language of chap. 23 is especially influenced by *psalmic* models, especially in the depiction of Job's piety in vv 10–12 (cf. "way," "test," "feet holding fast to paths," "depart," "hiding in one's heart," "the words of his mouth"). In chap. 24 there are reminiscences of both Deuteronomic and prophetic texts (cf. removing boundary stones [v 2], the widow and fatherless [vv 3, 9], taking of pledges [24:3, 9]), and a probable allusion to the Ten Commandments in particular (in the sequence of depictions of the murderer, the adulterer, and the thief in vv 14–16a, reflecting the sixth, seventh, and eighth commandments, respectively). There is probably a wisdom connection also in these pictures, with a reminiscence of the portrait of the woman of Prov 7:5–21 who encounters her young man "in the twilight" (7:9).

The *function* of the speech is twofold: on the one side, a more subjective and personal one, it heightens Job's demands for a legal disputation with God by the idea of his making a journey to God's own dwelling, only to dash his hopes still further by the recognition that this is no more than an unrealizable fantasy. On the other side, a more intellectual one, it constitutes a charge against God (though it is not couched in the second person) that, in doing nothing to punish the wicked, he has abdicated his responsibility for world order. Job's own case of injured innocence was the first proof, and the escape of the wicked from divine censure is now the second. By the end of the speech Job may be psychologically "annihilated by darkness" (23:17), but that does not preclude his being intellectually convinced that there is no principle of just order anywhere to be found in the world.

The *tonality* of the speech ranges widely. As he considers his own case, Job moves from candor (23:2) to longing (23:3–5), from desperation (23:8–9) to self-assurance (23:10–12) and then immediately to utter despair (23:15–17). But the moment he turns from his own case to the wrong that God does humanity at large by his carelessness for justice, Job is powerful again, driven by a strong sympathy for the oppressed, and by a stronger sense of outrage against their oppressors; he is moved by the irony of the laborers' lot, who starve among plenty (24:10–11), and above all by indignation at the God who connives at wrongdoing. No more withering attack on the divine can be imagined (not even his catalogue of divine assaults in 16:11–14) than his lapidary conclusion to the narrative of social injustice (24:2–12b)—a single clause says it all, "But God charges no one with wrong" (24:12c). Evil roams the land, and takes ever new forms; but God arrests no one, brings no evildoer to book. There is almost a bitter playfulness in the portrait of the three "light-shy" evildoers (vv 14–16a); but they are not the butt of Job's anger. For he sees that the real problem in human society is not the out-and-out criminals but the powerful who defraud and destroy by force of law, the unnamed mighty who must themselves be ranked among "the rebels against the light" (24:13). There is no dying fall in this speech, as in so many of Job's speeches; the final note is defiance: "Who can prove me wrong? Who can reduce my argument to nothing?" (24:25). There is substance here, and Job knows the weight of it.

The *nodal* verses of the speech are two: "Oh that I knew how I might find him" (23:3) and "Why are days of assize not kept by the Almighty?" (24:1). On these two key sentences, each in headline position, hangs the whole matter of the speech, its first half concerned with Job's fruitless quest for justice for himself, and the second with the evidences of God's failure to keep order in the moral universe.

Comment

2–7 With a magnificent disregard for everything Eliphaz has just now said, Job launches into a powerful expression of his own urgent desire for a settlement of his dispute with God. There is a compelling mixture here of confidence and despair. He believes that if he could find the occasion to present his case to God he would be given a fair hearing and would emerge triumphant. But he knows also that there is no chance that he can stand in court with God; the wish, "Oh that I knew where I might find him" (v 3), is a hopeless one. God cannot be compelled to court, so Job has recognized already (9:19); but neither can any wistfulness or yearning bring about the showdown that Job deserves. He does not want to call God unjust, and it is brave of him to insist that, given the right circumstances, an upright man could reason with God and be acquitted. But since the circumstances do not exist, and never can, so far as Job knows, holding the belief is, practically speaking, no different from not holding it.

But perhaps Job alludes to something in Eliphaz's speech? Eliphaz has urged him to "turn" to God (22:23), not in repentance but by way of fixing his attention upon him rather than upon the injustice that is embittering Job. Does Job then reply, though not explicitly to the language, by saying, Turn to God? I want not just to "turn" to him but to travel the path, no matter where it lies or how long it is, to be able to present my case before him in person.

2 If Eliphaz has been counseling acceptance of the will of God, Job signals that he will have none of it. Against every palliative, Job insists that he is still in rebellion against the fate that has befallen him. It is not so much that he is "bitter" (as RSV and others; see *Note* 2.b), though he is that; rather, he remains determined, "today" as on every day since disaster struck, to confront the author of his misfortune. That may be called "rebellious" (JB) and "resentful" (NEB), and that is how Job is determined to be. He could be even more aggressive than that, if he were to give full vent to his feelings, "too fierce to be expressed" (Handel, *Solomon*); for he is even now repressing much of his anger and pain: his hand is "heavy upon [his] groaning"—as if he were an enemy to himself, subduing and keeping under control his own instinct to protest (elsewhere too the heavy hand is always that of the oppressor, in Judg 1:35; 1 Sam 5:6, 7, 11; Ps 32:4). And why is he repressing his resentment? It is not that he is trying to be brave, to wear a stiff upper lip, to play the man; it must be that if he were to say what is really in his mind he might find himself saying, God is unjust; he might be a blasphemer. It is not out of bravery but out of fear that he restrains himself, and his recourse to the metaphor of contention with God according to the rules of legal debate is a way of channeling the anger that makes him want to hit out at his enemy.

Fohrer finds a reminiscence here of the opening of Job's second speech: "If only my anguish could be weighed" (6:2); but the similarity of the language should not disguise how different Job's standing place is here. There he was uttering a cry for understanding, for allowances to be made for his "unrestrained words" (6:3), and his dearest wish there was that God would "let loose his hand and cut me off" (6:9). Here he apologizes for nothing, recognizes his rebellion and resentment, and determines upon an aggressive carrying of his case forward, as far as to the heavenly courts.

On "groaning" or "sighing" (אנחה), see on 3:24, where it is his daily bread.

3 Job's rebellion is by no means an abandonment of religion; it is precisely a determination to press home his cause with God. It is in envisaging a journey to the seat of his heavenly persecutor and a disputation with him on his own home territory that he recognizes himself as "rebellious." A more docile believer might have let the matter rest, now that God has not responded to the challenges to a lawsuit that Job has thrown out to him (13:22–24; cf. 9:16); but Job is not ashamed to admit he is in no mind to be submissive. If he has called and not been answered (19:7), if God has hidden his face from him (13:24) even though he has a cause against him, Job has no alternative but to carry his dispute into the redoubt (מכון, "established place, seat") of his enemy (13:24). His cry for justice has already preceded him into the divine presence, and stands there permanently as his "witness" (16:19) and "champion" (19:25), a thorn in God's side until his case is settled. But even that is not good enough for Job; to "find" him, that is, "to see him for myself, to see him with my own eyes, not as a stranger"—that is Job's deepest desire; for that his "inmost being is consumed with longing" (19:27). It is not the beatific vision that Job desires, not communion with the divine, not some placid sinking into the everlasting arms, but a face-to-face confrontation with the heavenly bully who maltreats him.

What is meant by "finding" (מצא) God? The expression is (perhaps surprisingly) quite rare (only elsewhere in 37:23; Deut 4:29; Jer 29:13; 1 Chr 28:9; 2 Chr 15:4; cf. Acts 17:27; and see G. Gerleman, *TLOT,* 2:682–84); as with the related term, to "seek" (בקש) God, the context is usually prayer or some other activity of the cult (cf., e.g., Dan 9:3 "seeking him with prayer and supplications and fasting and sackcloth and ashes"; see S. Wagner, *TDOT,* 2:236–39). The language, reverential though it is, implies the absence of God; whether the distance has been created by human guilt or divine indifference, seeking and finding is necessary only if there is a separation. Here the metaphor is more alive than it is in the traditional language of piety; for Job is not speaking of prayer or worship, but of a journey he contemplates, of a knight pursuing his quest for the grail of a denied innocence into the castle of an angry giant.

It is a forlorn quest; the language shows that (מי יתן, "Oh that!" lit. "who will give that?" always introduces a hopeless wish, as in 6:8; 11:5; 13:5; 14:4, 13; 19:23). Vv 8–9 will spell out the impossibility of tracking down the god who will not let himself appear. When God does appear out of the tempest, it will be on his own terms, and Job will hardly have his wish even then, to hear and be heard.

4–5 If only he could confront God with his lawsuit, everything would turn out well. All would proceed according to due order: Job would "arrange" (ערך; see on 13:18) his case, like an army drawing up its lines of battle before the enemy (as ערך in Judg 20:22; 1 Sam 4:2). He would fill his mouth with arguments, so as never to be short of a charge or a response no matter how the case proceeded. Bildad had envisaged Job's mouth being filled with laughter at his restoration (8:21; as in Ps 126:2), but Job has serious work to do first. Instead of being in the dark about God's intentions, and having to guess what charges he might have against him, he would be able to understand all that was going on, and prepare himself to respond in every detail, filling his mouth with arguments.

In this disputation with God, the man Job would be alone. "The friends are not wanted in this discussion" (Dhorme). In 13:7–12 Job had envisaged the friends' presence at the lawsuit, functioning as witnesses to the facts, though not as partisans on behalf of God. That thought has dropped away now, as Job imagines a brave, not to say reckless, encounter of himself alone with God.

6–7 Now Job does not fear such a legal encounter with God. If he could find his way to God's dwelling, Job does not believe that God would resort to the use of naked power to win the case against him; he would be amenable to rational arguments. Even though God could not be expected himself to initiate a trial, he would not be averse to Job's case; God would listen to him, and recognize him as an upright man who was arguing fairly and on good grounds. Job lays claim to nothing that the narrator of the book has not certified of him: when he depicts himself as an "upright" (ישׁר) man, he only echoes the first description we read of him in 1:1. And the acquittal he expects, as Andersen reminds us, is "not the pardon of a guilty man by grace, but the vindication of a righteous man by law."

What has happened to Job that he can speak so fearlessly and optimistically? When he first imagined a lawsuit with God (9:3–4), he immediately recognized that in such a dispute one could not answer him once in a thousand times: "who ever argued with him and succeeded?" (9:4). Even if he were in the right, he could not defend himself against such an adversary; even if God were to respond to Job's summons, he could not be sure that he was really listening to him (9:14–16). God cannot be brought to court as if he were merely another human being (9:32). If it is a matter of strength (כח, as here), he is the mighty one; if it is a matter of justice, who can arraign him (9:19)?

Nothing of course has happened. God has not spoken or given any sign of encouragement to Job; the friends' speeches have not emboldened him to confront God. It is simply that, having once launched himself upon the idea that his suffering is ground for a lawsuit against God, he becomes more and more attached to the idea; the more he considers it, the more it becomes a reality. So in his next speech, even though he has no hope of success (13:15), he says straight out, "It is to the Almighty that I would speak; it is with God that I crave to enter into dispute" (13:3). And he addresses God with two preconditions for a legal disputation: that God should cease to assault him and that he should not threaten him (13:20–21). In his next speech, his fifth, he affirms that he already has a "witness" stationed in heaven, his "cry" that is his "spokesman" in God's presence (16:19–20). He has spoken in the presence of God and now sleeplessly waits for God's reply (16:20b). Then in his sixth speech he voices his conviction that sooner or later—perhaps even after his death—his case will be heard; nevertheless what he really wants is to confront God in person, "to see him for myself" (19:27).

Once Job has realized that what he most wants is God's personal acknowledgment of his innocence, the fear that he cannot possibly be justly treated by God recedes, and he convinces himself that anyone, even God, must respond favorably to so obvious a case of injured innocence. But the reader cannot forget everything that Job has so plausibly charged God with in the previous speeches, and must wonder whether Job's conviction here that God will not use violence with him, that he will actually listen to him, and, above all, that he will acknowledge him as innocent, has any likelihood about it. Job's experience of God has been only of an enemy (e.g., 19:6–12); and the rightness of his cause can be no guarantee that it will succeed when his opponent wields his power so arbitrarily. So it is not that "Job's thought of God has softened" (Peake), that "he has gradually acquired new confidence in God" (Delitzsch), or that "he is suddenly possessed by something like euphoria" (Good); it is rather that his conviction of his own integrity has hardened.

Job's language in v 7 shows that he is thinking more of his own innocence than of God's reasonableness (as against Hartley: "Job rests his hope for a favorable decision on the Judge's just character"). And here there is no "gleam of hope in the justice of God left by the poet in the soul of his hero" (Terrien). Job is not expressing a generalized confidence that in God's court any upright person could reason with him and gain a favorable verdict (as RSV and NIV suggest); rather, he says that if he, Job, were at the divine court, that would be a case of "an upright man arguing with [God]" (see *Note* 7.b). Such a case would be bound to prevail, Job means to say—not because God is fair but because the case is unassailable. As in 13:16, what he "takes refuge in" is not the goodness or the justice of God but the fact that "a godless man dare not approach him"—and that is what he, Job, is not.

It is not "acquittal" as such that Job desires (despite RSV) but "escape"—escape from his perpetual adversary (if Stevenson's emendation of משפטי, "from my judge," to מִמְּשֹׁפְטִי, "from my adversary at law," is accepted; cf. on 9:15) or from the lawsuit that weighs so heavily upon him (if the common emendation to מִשְׁפָּטִי, "from my case, my cause," is adopted). As the Hebrew text stands, it is strange that Job should here call God his "judge" (שֹׁפֵט) since throughout the speeches—and especially in this very context—he has represented God as an opponent rather than a judge. God is never called "judge" in Job, and in the only places the verb "judge" (שפט) is used of him it probably means "govern" in general rather than "decide a case" (in 21:22 he "governs" the heavenly beings, and in 22:13 he is said not to be able to "govern" the world because of the thick cloud that intervenes between him and humans).

On God's "power" (כח), see also 9:4, 19; 24:22; 26:12; 36:5, 22; 37:23.

It does not matter, in the end, whether Job is confident of a fair hearing from God or not, for he can set forth his case before him only if he can reach God's dwelling place—and that is an impossible dream, as Job himself recognized when he started out on this train of thought at the beginning of v 3: "Oh, that I knew how I might find him" means, first and last, that there is no chance whatever of finding him and having one's case heard.

8–9 The thought loops back to v 3. There Job wished that he knew how to find God (v 3); now he says that he has not just idly expressed a wish. "If he fails to find God it is not for want of effort" (Peake). He has, in fact, sought him vainly in every direction (vv 8–9). Shorn of the metaphor, this is nothing other than his reiterated desire to speak face to face with God and to lay the blame for his suffering at God's door. But with the metaphor Job portrays a superhuman quest that has taken him far from Uz: to the four points of the compass (which means everywhere) he has searched for this elusive and unresponsive God. "Forward" and "backward," "to the left" and "to the right" is his language, but these are also terms, especially when all four occur together, for the four quarters of the earth; the speaker is imagined facing east, with the north on the left and the west behind. קדם for "east" and אחור for "west" both occur in Isa 9:11 (12), שמאל for "north" in Gen 14:15 and ימין for "south" in 1 Sam 23:19.

It has seemed to many that the verses are intrusive, and that his expectation of "escape" from his lawsuit in v 7 should have been followed directly by vv 10–13, which spell out Job's conviction that he is an upright man and must therefore emerge with honor from any celestial trial (so Budde, Siegfried, Duhm, Driver–Gray, Beer [*BH*[2]], Hölscher, Fohrer, Fedrizzi, de Wilde). Others, who leave the verses in their place, want to establish a close connection between v 9 and v 10, since the opening "for" (כי) of v 10 encourages us to do so. Thus vv 10–13 are said to explain "why God eludes the searches of Job" (Dhorme) or to "state the reason why God will not let himself be found by Job: he knows that he is innocent (10–12), but yet will not be diverted (13–14) from his hostility towards Him" (Driver). It would indeed be bitter of Job to say that the reason that God will not enter into dispute with him is because he well knows that Job is innocent, and that he does not want to be called to account for persecuting a righteous man unjustly. But that is no reason to deny that this is what Job means (as Budde and Peake do). This is not a speech, after all, of longing for the divine, but a speech of frustration at not reaching any conclusion to his case (vv 3–10), of continuing terror at what the next onslaught of the Almighty might be (v 16), and of a life-denying wish to "vanish in darkness" (v 17)—which strikes a note we have not heard since 6:8–9. Job has earlier depicted God as a spy upon humans (7:17–20), as sustaining Job's life simply in order to pay him the more close and cruel attention (10:13–17), and as a vicious enemy (16:7–14). It is no surprise now if Job portrays God's elusiveness as a sign of bad faith, suggesting that "the god avoids the sufferer precisely because he knows that the trial will turn out in Job's favor" (Good).

10–14 The train of thought seems to be this: Despite my desire to find God and present my case to him (vv 3–7), I am unable to find him (vv 8–9). And he is elusive just because (כי, "for," v 10)—although I am a righteous man who has always kept God's commands (vv 10–12)—he is determined to make me suffer as long as he wants (vv 13–14). If I were to find him now, and he were to listen to my defense, he would have to admit my innocence, and forthwith desist from his persecution of me; but he is more committed to his plan of harassment than he is to the execution of justice. That is why he will not let me find him.

10–12 This is an assertive expression of his self-consciousness as a righteous man, such as we have heard on several occasions before (e.g., 9:20–21; 13:16, 18). But it is not an expression of confidence in the outcome of his confrontation with God (against Peake), for which he here utters no hopes but only fears (vv 15–17). It is not that "God's distancing himself from Job's consciousness reflects his trust in Job" (Hartley), but rather that Job remains in despair of being treated justly by his heavenly opponent.

God cannot have any doubt or ignorance about Job's innocence. Being God, he must well know what Job's way of life (his דרך) is, his habitual behavior—even humans know that. This is not so much an expression of God's omniscience (as is suggested perhaps by translations like "he knows every step I take" [JB, GNB] or "the way I take" [KJV, RSV, NJPS, NIV]) as an assertion that God knows Job is righteous despite treating him as a sinner. If God were to test Job's innocence—in a lawsuit, Job means, but he uses the metaphor of refining gold in a crucible—Job would emerge triumphant. Job is not referring to his present experience of suffering as a "trial" or a "testing," for from his point of view it is no such thing, but an unprincipled and unmotivated attack. No, he is saying that if God would have the courage to put Job to the test, in the future—as he would if Job could find his seat and lay his case before him—God would find that he has been altogether misjudging Job. God imagines that Job is a mixture of good and bad, of base metal with gold, and were he to "prove" (NAB) or "assay" (NJPS) Job "in the crucible" (JB) (the verb is בחן, "test, examine," as in 7:18; Pss 11:4, 5; 17:3; 26:2; 66:10), there would be a great deal of base metal to be absorbed by the porous crucible before the residue of gold appeared (on the technology implied, see R. J. Forbes, *Studies in Ancient Technology* [Leiden: Brill, 1955–64] 7:90; and for the idea of testing a person like gold, cf. Prov 17:3; Plato, *Gorgias* 486d; *Republic* 3.20 §413e; J. P. Brown, "Proverb-Book, Gold-Economy, Alphabet," *JBL* 100 [1981] 169–91 [182]). But such an estimation is a mistake, says Job, for there is no dross in his life; he is pure gold.

There are no words for the upright life of Job other than the language of psalmic piety. We are dealing here not so much with obedience to specific divine commandments as with conformity to a pattern of life prescribed by instruction or teaching. The way (usually דרך) of the Lord is the psalmic language for the way of life for humans enjoined by God; see Pss 18:21 (22); 25:9; 27:11; 37:34; 119:3, 15 (cf. G. Sauer, *TLOT,* 1:343–46). It is unusual here, though, that the term אשר "step" is used, since elsewhere it always refers to the steps of humans, not of God (Pss 17:5; 37:31; 40:2 [3]; 44:18 [19]; 73:2; Prov 14:15). And the thought of Job's foot holding fast (אחז) to God's way may seem rather odd; a similar phrase in 17:9, "the righteous maintain [אחז] their way," had a different meaning, since it was the way of the righteous themselves rather than God's way that was in view. Carey explains that "The oriental foot has a power of grasp and tenacity, because not shackled with shoes from early childhood, of which we can form but little idea." Ah, the rich tapestry of oriental life! But Ps 17:5 provides a good parallel, though the verb is תמך "hold fast to, support": "My steps (אשר, as here) have held fast to your paths (מעגלות)." Opposite is the idea of "restraining" (כלא) or "withholding" (מנע) the feet from a wicked path (Ps 119:101; Prov 1:15). "Keeping" (שמר) the way of the Lord (Gen 18:19; Ps 37:34; cf. Ps 119:33; Prov 2:20) means observing the commands for one's own way of life and not "turning" (נטה) from them (cf. Ps 44:18 [19]; with סור "turn aside," cf. Job 34:27; Prov 22:6; Deut 9:16; 11:28; 31:29; 2 Kgs 22:2; 2 Chr 20:32; 34:2). Job is the embodiment of psalmic piety: he has not "departed" (מושׁ) from the "commandment of his lips"; the phrase "commandment of his lips" does not recur, but Ps 17:4 has "by the word (דבר) of your lips (שׂפתיך, as here) I have kept (שׁמרתי, as in v 11b) [? myself from] the ways of the violent." The term for "depart" (מושׁ) is not used again in this moral sense, but the related מוט "depart, be moved" is another psalmic term that expresses the opposite of the pious person's steadfastness (as in Pss 15:5; 16:8; 21:7 [8]; 62:2 [3], 6 [7]), though not, admittedly, in reference to adhering to the law. "Hiding" or "treasuring" God's words in one's heart is likewise a psalmic idea; see Ps 119:11 (cf. Prov 2:1; 7:1; the verb צפן is used differently in Job 10:13; 17:4; 21:19). The idea of hiding God's word in one's "bosom" (חיק) is, admittedly, unparalleled; the normal language is rather of hiding or "putting" (שׂים) words into one's "heart" (לב), as in 22:22; Ps 119:11 (cf. Job 10:13; Deut 4:39; 11:18; 32:46). A final psalmic idiom is "the words of [his] mouth" (usually אמרי פי), frequent in the Psalms and wisdom texts (Job 8:2; Pss 19:14 [15]; 36:3 [4]; 54:2 [4]; 78:1; 138:4; Prov 4:5; 5:7; 6:2; 7:24; 18:4; Eccl 10:12, 13) but rare elsewhere (only Deut 32:1; Jer 9:20 [19]; Hos 6:5).

This last phrase, to "treasure the words of his mouth" in the bosom or the heart, corresponds closely to the admonition of Eliphaz to Job in 22:22, that he should "receive instruction from his mouth, and lay up his words in your heart." But it is not clear that Job is in any sense "answering" Eliphaz (as Dhorme, Terrien), since his general stance throughout the speech is to ignore what his friends have been saying and to press forward rather with the logic of his own position.

13–14 I am perfectly innocent, says Job (as in 9:21), but that does not make any difference to the way God treats me. He is determined upon his persecution of me, and there is no deflecting him from his purpose. We have heard this language before: if God were to commit an act of theft, Job has said in 9:12, "who could dissuade him?" And Zophar has said the same (11:10): if God shuts someone up in prison, or if he calls a person to account, "who can dissuade him?" (in both places the same word ישׁיבנו "turn him back," "dissuade him," as here). This can be called an expression of God's sovereignty if you will (so Andersen, Hartley); but for Job it is an exercise of God's arbitrary power. Job himself believes in a world where piety is rewarded and wrongdoing punished, where the upright could enter into dispute with a celestial lord in the hope of winning acquittal (v 7). But God operates according to his own whim, without regard for justice: "whatever he desires, he does" (v 13). This phrasing, נפשׁו אותה "[whatever] his soul desires," sounds like that of Qoheleth in his hedonist days: "Whatever my eyes desired I did not keep from them" (Eccl 2:10), or like the merry carnivore of Deut 12:15: "slaughter and eat flesh within any of your towns, as much as you desire" (בכל־אות נפשׁך "with all the desire of your soul"), or like the greedy sluggard of Prov 13:4: "the soul of the sluggard craves but gets nothing" (cf. also 2 Sam 3:21). There is something in Dhorme's comment that "in the נֶפֶשׁ resides the strength of passion and desire," so that Job is suggesting that God's "decree," for all its formality and fixity, is nothing more than an appetite. "How striking the contrast of [Job's] steadfastness with the incalculable waywardness of God's own dealing with men!" (Peake). "There is no space between the god's desire and his deed, no thoughtful reflection, no canvasing of implications" (Good). We cannot save face for Job's God by suggesting that he is "not . . . charging God with acting capriciously. Rather his distress is that since God is not bound to a mechanistic application of his own laws, he does not have to execute exact retribution immediately" (Hartley). No, caprice ("absolute caprice," Delitzsch) is the name of the divine game, in which Job is inexorably the loser.

What is it that God has "planned" for Job, that he will "carry out" (v 14)? It is not exactly his death (as Davidson; cf. Driver–Gray), for it seems to Job that death is the one thing that God is bent on denying him (6:8–9; 13:15 seem only to mean that God *may* slay him). It is rather an interminable assault on his body, his dignity, and his innocence that God evidently has planned for Job. Job can of course only know what he has experienced; and if his experience is of unrelenting suffering, he has no choice but to suppose that such is God's malign intention for him. That intention, which, being God's, is no mere wish but a settled and determined "decree" (חק), will no doubt be carried through (שׁלם hiph, "complete," as in Isa 44:26, 28) to the bitter end, "mak[ing] the realization fully correspond to the intent" (Driver–Gray). And when it has come to an end, even that will not be the end of Job's pain, for the ever inventive and permanently malign deity will readily enough devise "many such things." Job does not, as some commentators think (e.g., Davidson, Duhm, Driver–Gray, Terrien, Gordis, Habel), here look outward from himself to the suffering fate of other humans; nothing in this chapter moves beyond the horizon of his own experience (things will be different in chap. 24).

15–17 So far in this speech Job seems to have been in control. All the initiative has been his: his novel imagining of a journey to the seat of God and of a face-to-face encounter with his heavenly assailant. He has lacked nothing in confidence, being as convinced as ever of his perfect innocence and, now, of God's willingness to listen to reason and not overwhelm him with his power. The only emotion we have noticed in Job has been a burning desire, a reckless desire, to have done with the intolerable situation he suffers daily. He is conscious that his attitude could be called "rebellious" (v 2), but he is not ashamed of that, for he thinks he has good reason for rebellion. He stifles his "groaning" (v 2), whether it conveys his pain or his anger, because he has work to do and he has plans to resolve matters, not to capitulate to them (contrast 42:6). His head is bloody but unbowed.

But now suddenly his language moves into a different register. In a moment he begins to speak entirely of the feelings of terror that beset him, and the words come tumbling out: he is "dismayed" (בהל niph), "in dread" (פחד), God has "made him soft, limp, weak" (רכך hiph) and "terrifies" (בהל hiph) him; he has been "annihilated" (צמת) by darkness, deep darkness "covers his face" (on the text, see *Note* 23:17.c). How to explain this sudden transition from self-assertion to collapse? It can only be a renewed recognition that, do what he may, Job is unable to stay God's hand. Whatever God desires, he does (v 13), and nothing that Job desires is of any consequence. All that talk of a civil confrontation with his opponent, of a stately going to law with him, of an upright man in dispute with a listening God (vv 6–7)—all that was an impossible dream, every bit as much as the hope for a resurrection in 14:14–17. The reality is that God has a "decree" (חק, v 14) out against him; Job is the victim of a malign power, and even when that decree has been fully executed (שלם hiph) there are others of the same violence waiting in the wings to be unleashed against him (v 14b). The sheer experience of his suffering is not what terrifies Job; it is when he "considers" (בין hithpo), that is, turns his mind to his state and thinks out its implications, that the terror starts up. The object of his terror is not to be mistaken: it is God personally. The emphasis is strong and explicit: Job is dismayed "at his presence" (מפניו), he is in dread "of him" (ממנו), it is "God" (אל) who has made him weak, it is "the Almighty," "Shaddai" (שדי), who has terrified him. So much for the dream of a listening God: it is a heartless tyrant, who acts only on the basis of his impulses and appetites (נפש, v 13), and not at all in accord with law or justice, with whom Job has to do.

It is a pity that the closing sentence of the chapter is so problematic. Does Job mean that he is "not annihilated by darkness," that it is not his sufferings as such that frighten him, but God's involvement in them? Or is it a wish, "Would that I could vanish in darkness, and thick gloom cover my face" (Pope)? Or does he mean that he now feels that he *is* annihilated by darkness, that deep darkness covers his face, that he feels he has now in actuality entered the world of darkness that he once called down upon the day of his birth (3:3, 4, 5, 6, 9), the land of deep darkness to which he knows he is bound (10:21–22), the darkness that already has lain on his eyes (16:16), the darkness that has already veiled his path (19:8)?

What is clear, despite the exegetical problems, is that his thought, as so often, has taken a downward turn, a dying fall. The language of longing with which the speech opened has given place to a depressive language that entertains no future. There is something worse than all his sufferings: the darkness that covers him is "not only his suffering, but his complete helplessness in the face of reality" (Budde). This powerful depiction of a legal encounter with God has in the end only served to sharpen his sense of God's injustice in his own case and total irresponsibility in the governance of the world. For it was all a falsity, that longing for being listened to and treated fairly, and the darkness means precisely that there is nothing to be seen, no end to his own suffering, no pattern for the universe, no contours, and no meaning.

24:1–8 Job is not the only sufferer from God's abdication of responsibility for the world's moral governance. His theme hitherto in this speech has been the impossibility of wringing justice for himself from an inaccessible God, but there are others also who desperately need justice. In his previous speech (chap. 21) he had argued from the prosperity of the wicked ("How often is the lamp of the wicked snuffed out?" v 17) that the doctrine of retribution for wrongdoing is false. Though he does not say so explicitly, in that speech he is effectively arguing that the prosperity of the wicked proves that God has abandoned governing the world in justice. Here that conclusion is extensively illustrated by the effects of human wickedness on the poor. The wicked can dispossess others of their livelihoods with impunity; there is no retribution for them, and there is no justice for the dispossessed any more than there is for Job.

1 In a properly governed world, there would no doubt be immediate retribution for the pious and for wrongdoers alike. Clearly God is not disposed to keep short accounts; but if he has not the inclination to mete out instant retribution, why does he at least not settle the score with humans on a regular basis, appointing assize days when he will weigh up their merits and demerits and apportion to them their rewards? Why are there no fixed "days" (as there were "Quarter Days" in England for the settling of accounts: Lady Day, Midsummer, Michaelmas, and Christmas), no days for judgment when God as a magistrate would pay a visit to outlying parts of his territories and settle outstanding cases and suits? Those who "know" God, i.e., who recognize his rights to rule, would then at least be able to look forward to justice that is not unreasonably delayed. It is an old legal principle, in England at least, that justice delayed is injustice, and Magna Carta (1215 C.E.) enshrined the principle that "To none will we sell, or deny, or delay right or justice." And Job would play well the role of the barons attempting to wrest from the unjust and extortionate King John such a safeguard for gentry like himself and for hungry peasants alike. See further, David J. A. Clines, "Quarter Days Gone: Job 24 and the Absence of God," in *God in the Fray*, FS W. Brueggemann, ed. T. Linafelt and T. K. Beal [Minneapolis: Fortress, 1998] 242–58 (= *On the Way to the Postmodern: Old Testament Essays, 1967–1998,* JSOTSup 293 [Sheffield: Sheffield Academic Press, 1998] 2:801–19).

In asking "why" (מדוע) God does not keep assize days, Job is not seeking a reason, but uttering a lament that he does not (cf. the "why" questions in 3:11, 12).

We might have expected Job to wish that everyone, not just those who "know" God, should "see his days," i.e., experience retribution, whether by way of reward or punishment. He would agree with that, of course, but he focuses here on the satisfaction that pious people would get from knowing that their piety is being recognized and rewarded. To "know God" is a rare expression in the wisdom literature (in Job only elsewhere at 18:21; in Psalms only at 36:11 [10]; 79:6; perhaps 87:4; and in Proverbs only at 2:5). It is a mainly prophetic term (see on 18:21), and it is perhaps natural that it should occur here in a passage so reminiscent of prophetic condemnation of the wicked rich. To "know" God is essentially to recognize him and his rights; it is not so much to know or acknowledge that there is a God as to esteem him as God.

2 God's failure to provide regular days for judgment both dismays the pious who suffer oppression and—more to Job's present point—encourages wrongdoers in their belief that they will never be called to account. Job goes on to give some striking examples. So negligent is God indeed that the wicked can rob and dispossess with impunity. Removing one's neighbor's landmark or boundary stones (גבולה; cf. M. Ottosson, *TDOT,* 2:361–66 [366]), that is, in order to increase the size of one's own property by including the neighbor's within one's own, is commonly prohibited, and the offender lies under a curse (Deut 19:14; 27:17; cf. also Prov 22:28; 23:10; Hos 5:10; CD 5:20; 8:3). As a marker of ancestral property, boundary stones are spoken of as set in their place by the fathers (Prov 22:28), and presumably protected by the patriarchal landowner, since it is the fatherless who are particularly in danger of having their claim to ancestral property negated (cf. vv 2–3; Prov 23:10; and from Egypt, *Amenemope* 6 [*ANET,* 422b]; for Babylonian boundary stones (*kudurru*), often with inscriptions, see *ANEP,* plates 519–21; *IDB,* 3:66). Protection of the landmarks is sometimes made a divine responsibility (as with the widow's boundary in Prov 15:25). We need to observe that people do not get up in the middle of the night and move a neighbor's boundary stone, to the consternation of the landholder the next morning. When landmarks are moved, there is at least a tacit approval by the community, and those responsible believe they are within their rights in so doing, and may in fact have the law on their side. It is a typical move of upper-class moralists (like the author of Job) to make out that such oppression of the underprivileged is an example of the wickedness of individuals when it is rather structurally determined and legitimated by the social system that gives the moralists their own status and livelihood. On the practice of acquiring estates (latifundism), see Mic 2:2; Isa 5:8; and cf. D. N. Premnath, "Latifundialization and Isaiah 5.8–10," *JSOT* 40 (1988) 49–60 (= *Social-Scientific Old Testament Criticism,* ed. D. J. Chalcraft, Bib Sem 47 [Sheffield: Sheffield Academic Press, 1997] 301–12); J. L. Sicre Díaz, "Diversas reacciones ante el latifundismo," in *Simposio bíblico español, Salamanca, 1982,* ed. N. Fernández Marcos, J. Trebolle Barrera, and J. Fernández Vallina (Madrid: Universidad Complutense, 1984) 393–412.

Seizing flocks is a different crime; it is hardly likely to mean that the wicked steal animals and then openly pasture them on the fields they have taken possession of (as Hartley). Pasturing flocks cannot in itself of course be a crime, so it is not appropriate to translate "they seize flocks and pasture them" (as RSV, for example); it is necessary to adopt some such translation as NIV, "they pasture flocks they have stolen." They openly pasture the stolen flocks as if they were their own (Duhm). "Flocks" or "herds" (עדר) are generally sheep (e.g., Gen 29:2) and, less commonly, goats (e.g., Cant 4:1), but they may also include cattle (as Gen 32:17 [16]); here we have no doubt sheep (and goats) in v 2 and ass and ox in v 3.

3 It is a particularly heinous, and cowardly, crime to steal from the poor, who have few possessions and no opportunity for legal redress. The "orphan," or rather "fatherless" (יתום), is the child of a widow, that is, a woman without male relatives (see on 22:9), who therefore has difficulty in gaining her rights or assuring herself of legal protection. The "fatherless" and "widow" are here depicted as having only one ass and only one bull (cf. the poor man of 2 Sam 12:3 who has only one sheep). That is, they are represented as poor peasants, not as the urban poor. And they are perhaps not the poorest of the poor if they own an ass and a bull (the very poorest must give as a pledge the clothing from off their back, having no possession more valuable; cf. on 22:6). The "ox" (שׁור) is not, as Duhm sentimentally thought, the widow's last cow, whose milk is her only nourishment, since שׁור is always used of a male animal (except in Lev 22:28).

The ass has been simply "led off" (נהג is to "drive off" or "lead away") by the wicked (presumably it too, like the ox, has been taken in payment for a debt; so Hartley), and the ox has been taken in pledge (חבל), that is, as collateral for a debt (see on 22:6). In the Code of Hammurabi (§241; *ANET,* 176b), taking an ox as security could be punished by a fine of one-third of a mina of silver, no doubt because to retain the pledge in the event of default on the loan is to rob the owner of the ox of any future means of earning a livelihood; the ox and the ass are the "indispensable instruments of agricultural activity" (Ravasi). We recollect that Eliphaz has not long ago inferred that Job himself has been "taking pledges from [his] kinsfolk without cause" (22:6), but Job does not deign to deny it or to reply to Eliphaz, and here calmly alludes to one of the stereotypical crimes of the wicked as if Eliphaz's finger had never been pointed at him. For taking an ox or ass as a typical act of theft or fraud, cf. Num 16:15; 1 Sam 12:3.

Who are being depicted in these verses as the perpetrators of crimes against the poor? They are not professional thieves or brigands who make their living from theft, for such people might do better robbing from the rich than from the poor. And they do not make off with what they have stolen, for landmarks have little resale value, and the flocks they have stolen they pasture under the noses of their victims. So they are people of the same community as the poor, people who are careless of ancestral custom, public opinion, and divine displeasure. They have the wealth to lend money at pledge, and they have the power and authority to remove landmarks. They must be the chieftains and ruling class in the kind of feudal society depicted as Job's, "powerful and wealthy landowners" (Strahan). And the portrayal of them in these verses must be from the point of view of their victims, since they themselves would be describing their actions not as theft or oppression but as the enforcing of their legal rights (Davidson speaks of "forms of law little different from violence"). All the actions in vv 2–3 are probably to be taken as resulting from peasant debt.

4 What is the injustice against the poor here? Some think that we have a general statement of how the wicked rob the needy of their rights, as in Amos 5:12, where they "turn aside" (נטה hiph, as here) the poor in the gate. But "in the gate," i.e., at the place where justice is dispensed (or denied), is not the same as "from the road," and even in the Amos passage what is in mind is probably a physical "thrusting aside" of the poor from access to justice rather than a general denial of justice. So what we have here is probably the idea that the wicked, adding insult to injury, arrogantly or violently (Gordis) thrust the poor off the public path, where anyone has a right to walk (Dillmann). Andersen thinks that "something more culpable than 'jostle' (NEB) is required," but perhaps the reality of life for the poor is portrayed more graphically by such an image than by any number of facts and figures and accusations. (It is unlikely to mean that they are afraid to walk on the worn paths lest they be robbed and beaten [as Hartley], since the poor are less in fear of thugs that roam the streets than of their properly constituted rulers.) On the "poor" (אביון), see on 5:15; and cf. also P. Humbert, "Le mot biblique ébyôn," *RHPR* 32 (1952) 1–6 (= *Opuscules d'un hébraïsant,* Mémoires de l'Université de Neuchâtel 26 [Neuchâtel: Secrétariat de l'Université, 1958] 187–92).

And why do the poor need to hide themselves? It is for safety's sake (as חבא also suggests in 5:21; cf. Gen 31:27; Amos 9:3), as if to say that their very presence in society is a standing inducement to their oppressors to fasten upon them. It may also be a sign of self-effacement, as if they had internalized the scorn of their oppressors for them and had come to feel themselves unworthy members of society (like the young men who in ceremonious respect for the grandee Job "hide" [29:8; also חבא]) from him when he takes his seat in the gate of the city).

With v 4b the focalization changes from that of the wrongdoers to that of their victims, where it remains almost to the end of the next strophe but one (v 12b).

5–12 We can hardly deny that Job evinces a deep sympathy with these miserable people (Hölscher). But his purpose, we should recall, is not to bewail their lot or to urge that some action should be taken on their behalf. He is not even principally concerned to charge society at large with cruelty or their oppressors with injustice. The sufferings of the poor are depicted not for the sake of the poor but for the sake of Job's theological program: their misery is the evidence he needs to show that God has abandoned the moral government of the universe. So we cannot put it to the credit of the character Job or of the author of the book that they have a sensitive "prophetic" conscience about social injustice. No doubt they do, but they are not suggesting that anyone should do anything about it; rather they are complaining that God does not.

In fact, the depiction of the poor in this chapter, as elsewhere in Job, is not perhaps wholly realistic. The author (or at least, his character) does not seem to know very much about systemic poverty, or lifelong and inherited poverty, a poverty that has never known anything else, but can only portray a poverty that arises from the loss of possessions. The poor here are essentially those who have lost, along with the man of the household (for they are widows and fatherless), the possessions they once had: flocks and ass and bull and land protected by boundary stones (vv 2–3). They are, in other words, Job himself, on a small scale; they are the impoverished, not the long-term poor. They of course have not, like Job, been thrown into poverty by the raids of Sabeans and Chaldeans (1:15, 17), but their unhappy state has come about through the operation of the loan system that has obliged them to put up their possessions as pledges (vv 3, 9). And, further, lest we should treat this text as a piece of social realism, we need to notice that, despite the privations they suffer, they are evidently working for a wage. They would not be carrying sheaves, pressing oil, and treading the wine presses if they were not earning something, and, callous as it may sound, it must be in their interest to be hard at work in agriculture and industry; otherwise, why would they be there? And if they are literally slaves (as some think), and not wage slaves, their masters are not going to let them literally starve, for it is not in *their* interests to do so. It is a colorful portrait, and it is affecting, but it is not *fact.*

5 The poor who are here described as "scavengers of the wilderness" (Habel) have as their chief priority in life finding food for themselves and their families. When they "go out to their work" (יצאו בפעלם, the same language as in Ps 104:23), it is not to some productive or rewarding labor; their one concern is to seek enough food for survival. All they can find, so it is said, is the produce of the steppe, plants and roots (cf. 30:3–4), which are properly the food of animals. The verb for "seek" (שחר piel) is often said to mean "seek early in the morning" because it is apparently connected with שַׁחַר "morning" (KJV "rising betimes"; cf. NEB), but it seems rather to mean "seek earnestly" (as in 7:21; 8:5; Prov 11:27; etc.). What they seek is mere sustenance or "provisions" (the term טרף commonly denotes the "prey" of animals, but is used also of food for humans in Ps 111:5; Prov 31:15; Mal 3:10); but because they have no land of their own, they are forced to seek their food in the wasteland (ערבה, the steppeland), which is the home of the onager, according to 39:6 also.

The onager (פרא, *Equus hemionus hemihippus,* commonly "wild ass") is an undomesticated member of the horse family. It was to be found in the wildernesses of the ancient Near East in antiquity (Xenophon, *Anabasis* 1.5.2) and into modern times (see A. H. Layard, *Nineveh and Its Remains,* 2d ed. [London: Henry, 1849] 1:324–25; Tristram, *Natural History,* 41–43). In biblical imagery, the onager is noted for its untameability (cf. 11:12), its independence and solitariness (cf. Gen 16:12; Hos 8:9), and its lust (Jer 2:24) (see also W. S. McCullough, *IDB,* 4:843). In 39:5–8 (*q.v.*) the onager is one of the wild animals useless to humans but described in loving detail as one of the creatures God is proud to have created. One of the key elements in the depiction there is of the onager's ceaseless search for food, even in unlikely places, ranging over the mountains as its pasture and searching after any green plant (39:8). In 6:5 also the onager's life is centered on the quest for "green grass" (דשא; similarly the hind in Jer 14:5–6), and it brays no longer when it has found it. This is the point of comparison with the poor: their total concentration on the quest for survival.

This is a powerful picture, but it does not seem to sit well with what follows. How can those foraging for provisions in the desert be at the same time reapers in the field and gleaners in the vineyard (v 6) and be engaged in various agricultural processes (vv 10–11)? Obviously they cannot. The key to a coherent interpretation of vv 5–11 lies in the phrase "to their work" (בפעלם). If they are literally scavenging for food in the wilderness, they are not doing "work," however tiring and demanding their search may be. For although the noun פֹּעַל can refer to any activity or deed, when it is a matter of "going out" (יצא) to one's work, it is specifically one's daily work or occupation (cf. BDB, 821b). The parallel in Ps 104:23, "People go out to their work [פעל] and to their labor until the evening" (NRSV), is very close (cf. also the use of פֹּעַל for "wages" for daily work in 7:2 [of a day laborer like those here]; Jer 22:13). What we have here, therefore, is not a literal foraging in the wilderness, but a metaphorical depiction of the hard work required to earn an inadequate living as a farm laborer: it is no better, the poet says, than scavenging for roots in the steppe.

6 There are linguistic difficulties in this verse too, though it clearly depicts the struggle of the dispossessed poor to find food. Some versions have them gathering animal fodder to eat (so RSV, NJPS, NIV), or pilfering food from the fields of the rich in night-time forays (so JB). Some even suggest that the verb לקש (is it "glean" or "despoil" or "work late hours"?; see *Note* 24:6.f) has the idea of stealing the late-ripe fruit, "the poorest and scantiest of the year" (Driver–Gray). But it is perhaps preferable to understand the picture as that of the former landholders of v 2, who have lost their land when their boundary stones were removed, and are reduced, like the landless Ruth, to gleaning in the fields of others (Ruth 2:2–3; cf. Judg 8:2). "Harvesting" (קצר) in a field that is not theirs could mean that they are employed as day laborers and simply paid each day with no security of work (Dhorme; but that image seems to be reserved for v 11); or they could be gleaners, not contributing to the landowner's harvest but reaping for themselves the edges and corners of the field left by the employed workers, as is prescribed by Lev 19:9; 23:22; Deut 24:19. If they are actually "gleaning" (assuming that is the meaning of לקש) in a vineyard, they are picking up grapes that have fallen on the ground or picking the occasional cluster that has been left deliberately on the vines by the workers (Lev 19:10). The idea found in many commentaries that these poor people actually live in the steppe country and pilfer from the cultivated land at night (Peake: "Hounded from civilization, they steal by night, since they dare not show their faces to beg by day") has little to support it from the text. Less likely still is the idea that those described are the survivors of war who try to keep their freedom by decamping to the mountains (Terrien).

The fields in which they harvest and glean are said to belong to the "wicked" (רשע). Some emend "wicked" to "rich" (see *Note* 24:6.g), on the ground that "the ethical character of the landowner is not here in question" (Driver–Gray). But the term serves to remind us that it is those who own land who are functioning as the wicked in this depiction of injustice. The especial social wrong that lies unpunished because of God's failure to observe days of judgment is not so much that people are robbed of their cattle and their land but that they are dispossessed by members of their own community, who enjoy the regard of society and are not ostracized by them. It is not that Job means that the rich are always wicked; it is just that it is a wickedness that the rich should be able to oppress the poor.

7–8 Dispossessed of their land, these wronged people lose their warm clothing and their houses also. Even in the cold weather, they sleep "naked" (ערום), which probably means not stark naked but rather without an outer garment, a mantle (מעיל) or cloak (שמלה), as the term seems to mean in 22:6, Isa 58:7, and Ezek 18:7. Cf. the picture in *King Lear:* "Poor naked wretches . . . that bide the pelting of this pitiless storm" (3.4.31–32). They have to sleep outdoors, subject to the elements. The mountain rain (זרם) is the heaviest and most violent rain (for Yahweh as a shelter [מחסה, as here] from it, cf. Isa 25:4). The "rock" (צור) where they shelter will not be a lone rock but the hilly rocky country, where there are caves; it is not a question of "wretches caught by a terrible shower and clutching desperately the rocks because they have no hole or corner in which to take refuge" (Dhorme) or of "crouch[ing] by boulders for a little shelter" (Hartley).

Isa 2:10 speaks of "entering" the rock (צור) to hide from the Lord's glory, and Ps 71:3 of Yahweh as "a rock of habitation," i.e., presumably, a rock with caves where one can take refuge and dwell. They "embrace" (חבק) it as if it were a friend, as the survivors of Jerusalem's downfall in Lam 4:5 "embrace" ash heaps.

9–12 The main subject of this strophe is the lot of the poor who work as day laborers (or perhaps, as slaves) but do not enjoy the fruit of their work. Though they spend their days on the land, they have no ownership of the grain, olive oil, and wine they are producing, but are starving in the midst of plenty. They are a classic case of what Marx called the alienation of the workers from their production, and Job the character, and therewith the author of the book, is sensitive to the social injustice involved, even if the blame is fastened on some few "wicked" and not upon the social and economic system that legitimates such an abuse.

Job, however, is not a prophet, inveighing against the ills of his society, or, like an Amos, announcing a forthcoming destruction because of long-standing social injustices. On the contrary, it is Job's point that such injustices prevail and God does nothing about them, charging no one with wrongdoing (cf. NIV), and not treating the injustice as unseemly (cf. NAB). The key to the whole of his social comment is the complaint, "Why are days of assize not kept by the Almighty?" (v 1).

The opening verse of this strophe (v 9) is not easy to harmonize with the flow of the chapter, since from v 4b onward we have been hearing about the lot of the poor, and that will continue to be the theme as far as v 12b. V 9, which concerns those who "seize the fatherless child from the breast," then seems to be out of place, and many move it to a different place in the chapter or omit it altogether (see *Note* 24:9.a). But it is possible, and preferable, to parallel the flow of the two sections, vv 2–8 and vv 9–12. In both, we begin with a focalization on the wicked, which then gives place to a focalization on their victims, the poor—in the first section at v 4b, where we move from the haughty wicked pushing the poor aside from the path to the poor's experience of hiding themselves, and in the second section at v 10a, where we move from the wicked taking children in pledge to the experience of the poor at work in the fields.

If that is how the text is structured, we shall need to indicate at the beginning of v 10 the shift in focalization, either with a phrase like "There are those who . . ." (as RSV, though it puts the whole verse in parentheses, as if its authenticity were doubtful) or with a resumptive subject, "The wicked." There is in fact a good deal of similarity between those who are acting here in v 10 and those who have acted in vv 2–4a, for the essence of the wrongdoing of both groups is that they are oppressing poor people from whom they have extracted pledges: in v 3 pledges of cattle and (probably) in v 2 pledges of land, and in v 9 pledges of children (though there is nothing to say that they are lacking clothes in vv 7, 10 because they have pledged them).

9 The injustice of which Job complains, the injustice that God does nothing about, is not of course a literal snatching of fatherless children from the breast. Familiar though we ourselves may be with "tug-of-love" stories in which a separated parent snatches a child, that is not the case here, for it is in no one's interest literally to take an unweaned child from its mother. The second half of the line makes it clear (on the principle of the "parallelism of greater precision"; cf. D. J. A. Clines, "The Parallelism of Greater Precision: Notes from Isaiah 40 for a Theory of Hebrew Poetry," in *New Directions in Hebrew Poetry,* ed. E. R. Follis, JSOTSup 40 [Sheffield: JSOT Press, 1987] 77–100 [= *On the Way to the Postmodern: Old Testament Essays, 1967–1998,* JSOTSup 292–93 [Sheffield: Sheffield Academic Press, 1998] 314–36) that in the whole verse it is a matter of taking children as pledges, and so treating them as chattels, since they are the only property of the poor (cf. Habel). That is to say, in Israel, as elsewhere in the ancient Near East, loans of money were secured by pledges, usually of property, which became the lender's if the debtor defaulted, but sometimes of persons, especially the children or slaves of the debtor. If children were pledged for a debt and then the debtor was unable to pay, the value of the labor of the child could be credited against the debt (see G. A. Barrois, *IDB,* 1:809–11). We do not need to take very literally the image of the child at the breast or to understand the word for "child" (על) as "infant" (as RSV). The economics of debts and pledges make clear that we must be dealing with children who are old enough for their labor to be productive and valuable (it is not so likely that the child is intended by the creditor to be sold as a slave or brought up as a slave, as Davidson, Rowley, de Wilde). For a case of parents pledging their children for debts, see Neh 5:2 (reading, with NEB and others, ערבים "pledging" for רבים "many"). The action of the pledge holder is described as "snatching" (גזל), as in v 2, but we need to recall that the practice is regarded as socially, if not legally, legitimated, so that Job's complaint is against the system that permits such a practice and not simply against the pledge holders themselves.

10–11 These day laborers (or, slaves) are so poor that they cannot clothe themselves properly—which means, in the rhetoric of the poem, that they are "naked" (cf. on v 7). That some people should be able to starve in the midst of plenty is an especial injustice in the social structure. In similar vein, Joseph Addison (1672–1719) wrote of the Italian poor: "The poor inhabitant beholds in vain / the red'ning orange and the swelling grain; / joyless he sees the growing oils and wines, / and in the myrtle's fragrant shade repines; / starves, in the midst of nature's bounty curst, / and in the loaden vineyard dies for thirst" (*A Letter from Italy to the Right Honourable Charles Lord Halifax in the Year MDCCI,* lines 113–18). It is indeed "a torture of Tantalus to have to carry sheaves when one suffers from hunger," as Dhorme says—but that puts it entirely from the victims' point of view, when Job is at least as much concerned with the issue of social justice and the responsibility of the society that has allowed such a state of affairs to develop as with the feelings and experience of the poor.

The poor are engaged in the production of the three staples of Palestinian life: grain, wine, and oil (for the combination, cf., e.g., Deut 7:13; 11:14; 18:4; Neh 5:11; Joel 2:19; Hag 1:11; always in that order [except Num 18:12: oil, wine, grain]—which is the sequence in which they are harvested—and not, as here, grain, oil, and wine). The grain (barley in April–May, wheat in May–June) was cut with a sickle, a handful at a time; these handfuls were bound into sheaves (אלמה "bundle" or עמר, as here; cf. Gen 37:7; Ps 129:7; Jdt 8:3), and then carried by cart (Amos 2:13; cf. Mic 4:12) or beast of burden (cf. on 1:3) to the threshing floor. Here the laborers seem to be doing the backbreaking work of carrying the sheaves themselves (though perhaps the verb נשא means literally "lift up," i.e., into the carts). Fohrer and others insist that here we have the term עמר, "ears" rather than "sheaves," because the stalks of grain were cut directly under the ears (cf. KBL, 717a, "ears of grain cut off"; contrast BDB, 771a, "sheaf," *HALOT,*

2:849b, "small heap of cut corn"). See also D. M. Howard, *ISBE,* 4:455; and cf. Dalman, *Arbeit und Sitte,* 3:46–53.

Olive oil production, in October or November, was an important industry of ancient Palestine, and those engaged in its production could perhaps be better regarded as factory workers than farm laborers. The olives were shaken or beaten from the trees with poles (Deut 24:20) and carried in baskets to the olive press (for an illustration, see *IDB,* 3:596); the press would not be exactly "between" (בין) the rows of olive trees, as the Hebrew text has it, but, more loosely speaking, in its vicinity. The olives could be trodden by foot (Mic 6:15), pounded in a mortar, or crushed by a stone wheel (see also *ISBE,* 3:585). Whatever the method used, olive oil extraction is a physically demanding activity, and the picture of undernourished laborers engaged in it is a particularly effective one. See also Dalman, *Arbeit und Sitte,* 4:201.

The grape harvest occurred in Palestine in August and September. Wine presses consisted of two connected pits, often dug out of rock; the upper pit was the wine press (גת) proper, in which the grapes were trampled (דרך) by foot. The juice then flowed through a channel to the lower pit, which was the wine vat (יקב) in which the wine fermented. Here, as also in Isa 16:10, the term for "wine vat" is used loosely for the wine press.

Deut 25:4 prohibits a landowner from muzzling an ox when it treads out the grain, but here the farmworkers are depicted as being treated worse than oxen. The Talmud applied the law of the ox to an agricultural worker (*t. Baba Metzia* 87b). The farmworkers here do not even have the status of neighbors who visit a farmer's field and are allowed to pluck ears or eat grapes (Deut 23:24–25 [25–26]). They are the embodiment of the oppressed and disregarded wage slave. For the perspective of the slave or day laborer who has nothing to look forward to apart from the day's wages, cf. 7:2; 14:6. And for defrauding farmworkers of their wages, cf. Jas 5:4.

Once again (as in v 9), we are dealing with rhetoric rather than social reportage. It is difficult to imagine that such a cruelty regularly figured in the world of the author; for one thing, it is hardly in the interests of any landowner for his laborers to be too weak to carry out their physical work. It is not the simplistic picture given in the text that is the real injustice—though such a picture may have been from time to time literally true, since every culture has no doubt had its share of sadists and monsters—but the socially approved practice of denying workers, especially farmworkers, a realistic living wage. The matter of Job's complaint could easily be turned to social critique; Isa 58:7 expresses such a prophetic challenge to the presence of the hungry and the naked in the community. But Job's point is different: he is urging not that society should change its ways but that God should change his. This is the way the world is, says Job, and the real injustice is that God does nothing about it, neither avenging the oppressed nor punishing their oppressors.

12 Here is the nub of the matter: "God charges no one with wrong." Throughout the chapter the weight of Job's argument has been upon the wrongdoing of the oppressors rather than upon the experience of the oppressed, even though it has been their unhappy lot that has figured most prominently in the description. And here the argument comes to a climax: the wrongdoers are able to get away with their wickedness.

Their victims have no future before them except death; we translate "the dying," but the Hebrew is "the dead" (מתים) since those who are destined for death or on the point of death can in Hebrew be called "dead" (e.g., Moses as destined to die in Transjordan, Deut 4:22; Jacob about to die, Gen 48:21). Their "groaning" (נאק) is that of the oppressed (as in Exod 2:24; 6:5; Judg 2:18; of the poor in Ps 12:5 [6], with the noun אנקה) or the wounded (as in Ezek 30:24). They are "slain" or "wounded" (חלל) metaphorically since the word properly implies death (e.g., 1 Sam 31:1; Jer 14:18) or fatal wounding (e.g., Lam 2:12) in battle. In Jer 51:52 and Ezek 26:15 also the "wounded" are said to "groan" (the verb is אנק, a byform of נאק). It is the "soul" (נפש *nephesh*) that cries out since "in the נֶפֶשׁ resides the strength of passion and desire" (Dhorme); in Job it is especially the *nephesh* that experiences bitterness and pain and weariness (cf. 3:20; 7:11; 10:1; 14:22; 30:25). The cry that comes from the *nephesh* is not, however, here a cry of pain, but specifically a cry for help (שׁוע piel, as in 19:7, where it is perhaps rather a cry for legal aid; Pss 30:2 [3]; 88:13 [14]; etc.).

Some versions alter the focalization of the chapter by translating, like RSV, "God pays no attention to their prayer" (so also JB, NEB). That fixes the reader's gaze on the poor, as if it is the injustice they suffer that is the substance of Job's complaint. But that rendering depends on an emendation of the Hebrew (reading תְּפִלָּה "prayer" for תִּפְלָה "folly, wrongdoing"). Translators are perhaps inclined to this rendering because of their sympathy with the affecting picture of the poor (this is the most poignant verse in the book, according to Terrien); but Job's argument has a harder edge to it. In the prologue of the book, Job refused to charge God with "wrongdoing" (this same word, תפלה), despite the evidence of his maltreatment of Job. Here now he describes a pervasive social wickedness, one to which God conspicuously refuses to bring a charge of "wrongdoing" (תפלה). Is that refusal in itself not an act of "wrongdoing," and is not Job's real criticism against God's failure to recognize his own "wrongdoing"?

It has surprised some that Job should here seem to turn to the fate of city dwellers after his concentration on the fate of farm laborers (vv 10–11). NEB even tried to make this verse refer to country people by translating מעיר, lit. "from the town, city," as "far from the city," and NAB also, by emending עיר "town" to עפר "dust" and translating "from the dust." Others connect v 12 with what follows rather than seeing it as the climax of vv 2–11 (so Hartley). It can hardly be that reference to the city shows that this injustice is universal, in city and country alike (Davidson). The solution to the difficulty is that in ancient Israel there was not the same distinction between town and country that many of us are now familiar with. Most people will have lived in towns, and had their houses there, and have gone out to their fields each day to work (cf. Ruth 2:2, 18). So everyone is a town dweller, and many of the town dwellers are landholders, peasants, and agricultural workers also.

13–17 We have here a set of three vignettes (in the style of Rembrandt, says Ravasi) depicting the enemies of the light: the murderer, the adulterer, and the thief—violators of the sixth, the seventh, and the eighth commandments (for stereotypical lists of criminals, see also Hos 4:2; Jer 7:9). The three wrongdoers may also be linked by the time of their activity: the murderer before the light dawns, the adulterer at twilight, and the burglar at night. The framing verses (13, 16b–17) speak generally of all three groups, and the three vignettes would be neater if we made a simple rearrangement of the lines, putting v 14c after v 15 (as Moffatt), or v 16a after v 14c (as JB, Fohrer). (Good is one of the few who does not recognize a separate picture of the burglar in this strophe, and attributes both v 16 and v 17 to the adulterer.)

The important question is: What is this picture of the enemies of the light doing in this context, where Job's purpose is to criticize God's failure to keep days of assize (v 1), and where his constant theme has been the victimization of the poor by the wealthy and powerful (vv 2–12)? It might be thought that these too are wrongdoers, "a new class of malefactors" (Davidson), who deserve God's judgment but are allowed to escape by his negligence. But then there would be no connection with the preceding verses. It is preferable to translate the beginning of v 13 literally, "They are among those who rebel against the light"; the preposition *beth,* "in, among," before "those who rebel" is a crucial one. The theme of this strophe is still, as it has been hitherto, the wealthy oppressors of the poor, who are now said to be fellows of those who flagrantly breach the law, the "rebels against the light." The rich, as we have seen, are pillars of the community, who rely on social custom and law for their legitimation and would be horrified at being classed with lawbreakers. So Job's complaint against God is, not that he does not call murderers and adulterers and thieves to account—for in most cases, he does not need to do so; society has already identified them and brought them to book—but that he does not carry out the judgments that he alone is responsible for: determining that social injustice, even when it is according to law, is an evil, and punishing those, even when they are in power in society, who take advantage of an unjust system.

In view of this connection of the strophe with what precedes, it is incorrect to label it an independent poem (as, e.g., Fohrer).

13 To the company of "rebels against the light," the "light-shy" as the Germans can say, belong all those who are wrongdoers. The phrase is unique in the OT, though the moral sense of "light" is widespread (see G. Aalen, *TDOT,* 1:147–67 [162–63]). In addition to many references to darkness as the hiding place of the wicked (e.g., 34:22; Isa 29:15), we find occasional references to darkness as a kind of metaphysical entity (e.g., to the "ways of darkness" in Prov 2:13; a further ethical development in John 3:20; Eph 5:8; 1 Thess 5:4–7). Elsewhere in Job "light" (אור) is the symbol of life (3:16, 20; 33:30), the sign of success and divine favor (22:28). Here there is an obvious reference to the light of day since all the activities of these wrongdoers are carried out in the darkness (see on v 14); but "the light" must have the wider, symbolic, sense also (so Pope, Gordis, Habel, against Duhm, Driver–Gray, Hölscher, Fohrer, NEB), if for no other reason than that these wrongdoers "rebel" against the light. No one "rebels" against daylight!

This is the only place where the term "rebel" (מרד) is used metaphorically; normally it refers to rebellion against a king (e.g., Gen 14:4; 2 Kgs 18:7) or against God (e.g., Num 14:9; Jos 22:16), and the breach of authority, whether that authority is legitimate or imposed by force. מרד signifies especially attempted but unsuccessful rebellion (cf. R. Knierim, *TLOT,* 2:684–86). The implication here is both that "light" has the right to rule the lives of humans and that wrongdoers' opposition to it is ultimately futile. Tur-Sinai had the idea of an allusion here to a myth of a primeval underworld king rising up against the light as a murderer, but he has gained no following.

14a–b The murderer (רוצח) is pictured, if the Hebrew text is correct, as rising from his bed before dawn (see *Note* 24:14.b), so as to be busy with his nefarious work (the obverse to the doughty woman of Prov 31:15 who rises "while it is still night" to provide for her household). The objects of his evil intent are the "poor and needy" (עני ואביון), whom we meet with often in the Psalms (e.g., 35:10; 37:14), in Proverbs (e.g., 31:9), in Deuteronomy (15:11; 24:14), and in the prophets (e.g., Isa 41:17; Jer 22:16; Ezek 18:12). There is no recognizable difference between the two terms, which equally denote the oppressed, that is, the underprivileged, persons in Israelite society. They are of course typically the economically poor, but they include other types of oppressed persons, such as the chronically ill and prisoners (see further, E. Gerstenberger, *TLOT,* 1:15–19; R. Martin-Achard, *TLOT,* 2:931–37; G. J. Botterweck, *TDOT,* 1:27–41; Humbert, "Le mot biblique," *RHPR* 32 [1952] 1–6 [= *Opuscules d'un hébraïsant,* Mémoires de l'Université de Neuchâtel 26 (Neuchâtel: Secrétariat de l'Université, 1958) 187–92]; R. J. Coggins, "The Old Testament and the Poor," *ExpTim* 99 [1987] 11–14; R. N. Whybray, *Wealth and Poverty in the Book of Proverbs,* JSOTSup 99 [Sheffield: JSOT Press, 1990]).

Why would anyone want to murder the poor and needy? Duhm found the idea so implausible that he wanted to emend the text (see *Note* 24:14.d). The usual grounds for murder are hatred (e.g., Num 35:20–21), revenge, and greed (cf. Hos 6:9), but none of these seems applicable in the case of the poor. It does not solve the problem to observe that in Ps 94:6 also the wicked are said to slay the widow and murder (רצח) the fatherless and to claim that this was therefore an attested practice in Israel (cf. also Pss 10:8–9; 37:14). Nor can we simply remark with Dhorme, "The murderer kills to kill, not to rob or avenge himself. He is the professional criminal." For what kind of a living can a "professional" make out of killing the poor?

The answer can only be that those who are killed by a murderer are *ipso facto* "poor and needy." Regardless of one's prior wealth or social status or moral quality, anyone whose life is brought to an end by violence is an oppressed person. The murderer does not leave his bed in order to look for poor people to kill; rather, those who fall victim to him are thereby unfortunate people, poor and needy. (It is not relevant to the present question to note that רצח is used both of intentional and unintentional killing [cf. Exod 20:13; Num 35:6], for the issue here is entirely of intentional killing that the murderer plans.) In the context of the present chapter, the point is that those who oppress the actual poor put themselves in the company of real murderers, as "rebels against the light."

15 A second type of "rebel" is the adulterer. He belongs with the murderer and the burglar since his activity is viewed as an attack on the property rights of another, the husband of his lover. He is a more nervous man than the brazen murderer, it seems, for he takes precautions that he should not be recognized, leaving his wrongdoing till the darkness of evening twilight, and even then putting a "covering" (סתר) on his face to avoid recognition. Though we may call this "masking" his face, we are not to think of a face mask (as NEB "his face covered with a mask"; cf. NAB), or of "disguising" (RSV) his face, and still less of his dressing himself in women's clothes with the oriental veil over his face (Wetzstein, quoted by Delitzsch; so too Strahan, and Peake, "to slip into the harem"); it is simply that "he keeps his face concealed" (NIV). The "ample, all-purpose garment could serve to conceal the face of a man or a woman" (Pope). Though he is technically liable to the death penalty (Lev 20:10; Deut 22:22–24), it does not seem to be that that worries him; it is more the fear of public exposure. The situation is more that of Prov 7: the woman seduces the young man while her husband is away, and no danger of capital punishment seems to hang over them (and when her house is called "the way to Sheol" [7:27] it is because of the moral, rather than the legal, consequences that can be envisaged).

It is a nice irony that while the adulterer's offense takes its rise from his "eye" (עין), which is the seat of his lust, his overriding concern is that no "eye" should see him. He will give full license to his own eye and its demands, but will attempt to cover the eyes of others with his own cover-up (סתר). "Twilight" (נשף) appears in Prov 7:9 also as the time of sexual misdemeanors.

14c, 16a There is much to be said for rearranging the lines in this strophe, so as to re-create a unified picture of the third of the wrongdoers, the burglar. It makes sense for the thief of v 14c to be a different person from the murderer, and Dhorme is quite right that "'to be like a thief' does not amount to much where a murderer is concerned!" It is more intelligible too if it is the thief (v 14c) who is "digging" into houses (v 16a) and not the adulterer, "creating," as Driver–Gray charmingly put it, "the need for awkward explanations when the husband returned" (cf. *Note* 24:16.b). And it helps with the overall flow of the thought if we can distinguish the act of the thief ("digs," in the singular, v 16a) from those of the rebels against the light in general ("shut themselves up," "do not know," in the plural, v 16b, c). But we need to adopt an emendation of the text, for the Hebrew has "and in the night let him be like a thief"; an emendation of one letter, together with a different division of the words, yields the sense: "In the night the thief roams about" (similarly JB, NAB, NEB). Cf. Shakespeare, "When the searching eye of heaven is hid, / Behind the globe, that lights the lower world, / Then thieves and robbers range abroad unseen / In murders and in outrage" (*King Richard II* 3.2.36–40).

Housebreaking, or burglary, is known in the OT by the verb חתר, lit. "dig" (as also in Exod 22:2 [1]; Jer 2:34; Ezek 8:8; cf. Matt 6:20; and in the Code of Hammurabi, §21 [*ANET*, 167a]), presumably from the time when houses were made of clay or mud bricks; but it does not necessarily imply that it is by this method that burglars normally gained entrance to houses. It is sometimes said that "An Eastern burglar would hesitate to break into a house through the door because of the sanctity of the threshold" and the danger of calling down the vengeance of the house god (Peake; similarly Fohrer).

16b–17 We now resume the depiction of the "rebels against the light" as a group, who say, as in Schiller's "Robber-Song": "The moon is our sun" (*Der Mond ist unsere Sonne*). They love darkness rather than light because their deeds are evil (John 3:19); as if photophobic, they shut themselves up securely (lit. "seal themselves," חתם piel) in their houses during the day. They do not "know" the light, that is, the right and God-ordained ways for humans to live; and that ignorance of the moral "light" is displayed by their unwillingness to walk abroad during the day.

V 17 may mean that "morning is the shadow of death," in the sense that the criminal sleeps by day, or, better, is frightened by the light (cf. JB "morning is a time of shadow dark as death, since that is when they know what fear is"), so that the morning "is to them what the death-shade of midnight is to others, a season of peril" (Peake). Or the clause may be read the other way round: "deep darkness is morning" (as RSV; similarly NEB), meaning that the wicked, like wild beasts (Ps 104:20–22), are up and about during the night: "midnight gloom is their morning, the work-time when they are fullest of energy" (Peake). In either case, there is the implication here that the wrongdoer turns day into night, in a metaphorical sense, pervertedly (cf. Isa 5:20; Amos 5:8). But the former is perhaps preferable, in view of the sequel in v 17b: they are friends with the terrors of darkness but afraid of the light (cf. GNB "They fear the light of day, but darkness holds no terror for them"). As Peake says, the term "terrors" is "spoken rather from the poet's point of view, theirs is the familiarity which breeds contempt." In v 13 they are said to be no friends of the light (נכר hiph), and here we learn that is because they are friends of the terrors of deathly darkness.

This vignette has come to a somewhat surreal conclusion, in which the literal and the symbolic are collapsed. These rebels against the symbolic light naturally enough carry out their crimes under cover of literal darkness; they prefer the darkness of night to the light of day and feel more at home with it (v 17). They go so far as to shut themselves in their houses during the day because they do not "know" or recognize the light (v 16)—but it must be the symbolic light that they reject by shutting themselves away from the literal light. There is, of course, nothing as banal here as the idea of the burglar, for example, sleeping in of a morning after his nocturnal excursions; there is a profound correspondence between deeds of darkness and crimes committed at night. But it is nevertheless a rhetorical correspondence, for, in reality, more crimes—in any society—are committed during the day than at night (since far more people are awake then!), and night can be as pleasant and safe and moral as day. There are certain fears specific to the night, of course, and the rhetoric plays on them by linking crime with darkness. The real enemies of the light, however, are not those who cover their crimes with darkness, but those who cover them with light: the powerful and esteemed in society, with whom this chapter has been principally concerned, who use publicly legitimated law and custom for their own aggrandizement and to the oppression of the weak.

18–24 For *Comment* on these verses, see after 27:17. They seem to have belonged originally to the third speech of Zophar.

25 Even if, as is argued in this commentary, the previous seven verses (vv 18–24 of the present chapter) did not belong here originally but were part of Zophar's third speech in chap. 27, this last verse certainly belongs with Job's speech in 23:2–24:17. Job is sure that he cannot be contradicted ("Who can prove me wrong? Who can reduce my argument to nothing?"), for he has described social reality, shorn of theological explanations. Whatever the meaning of his observations, what cannot be gainsaid is that landmarks are indeed removed, widows are robbed, and the poor suffer want—and the fact that such evils continue to happen is all the proof one needs that God does nothing about it. Who can put Job in the wrong (כזב hiph is "prove me a liar")? In form, his closing sentence is a challenge (Habel), but he expects no refutation, no riposte. It is a rhetorical affirmation of the strength of his conviction.

That is surely Job's meaning, but, it must be admitted, it is a strange way of saying so. We would use Job's formulation, "If that is not true, who will prove me a liar?" only when what we have said is open to question but we cannot see how we can be refuted. By itself, the question "Who will (or, can) prove me a liar?" is an assertion of our belief in what we have said, and equally so the question "Since that is true, who can prove me a liar?" What we have here is a somewhat anomalous blend or contamination of (a) an oath formula like "if that is not true, may I be punished" and (b) a simple rhetorical question "who can prove me wrong?" (cf. Joüon–Muraoka, §165g, on the mutual contamination of imprecation and oath).

Explanation

After his lackluster speech in chap. 21, Job is back on form in this, his eighth speech, a monologue that addresses the reader all the more directly because it faces neither toward Job's interlocutors nor toward God. Here there is color and pace and drama; here there is passion, despair, and defiance. But, above all, here there is the outworking of an inexorable logic that gathers up all that Job has earlier argued and presses beyond it to a new and conclusive argument about theodicy—or rather, about the disturbing and culpable absence of theodicy, of divine government, in the world. In a way, this is the climax of Job's speeches; for though he has yet to utter one of the most powerful and most polished of his speeches (chaps. 29–31), in that final speech he will come to focus again exclusively on himself, his past and his present, and, finally, upon the grand, master theme of his innocence. In the present speech, by contrast, he makes a move we have seen before but never to more dramatic effect: beginning with himself, his own experience, his own desires, his own resistance to the lies his suffering tells about him, he moves outward to the experience of humankind and, beyond that, to the nature of the divine. We saw this move before in chaps. 12–14, when his sense of the disproportion of the divine surveillance of him and his demand for justice gave place to a meditation on the fleeting life of humans and the hopelessness of any dream of a life beyond the grave. Here too the movement of the speech as a whole is outward from his own conviction of the impossibility of gaining justice from God to his settled conclusion that God has abandoned the moral government of the world. What sets out as Job's plea for vindication comes to an end as a savage and telling indictment of God.

And this is the way it goes. Long ago, in the bitterness of his undeserved suffering, he imagined (9:3–4) a lawsuit with God, his tormentor, in which he could declare his innocence and have it publicly recognized. But with the imagination of it came the realization that such a debate was futile, for "who can arraign him?" (9:19). No one could answer him once in a thousand times; "who ever argued with him and succeeded?" (9:4). Even if God were to respond to him, he could not be sure that he was really listening to him (9:14–16). For God cannot be compelled into a court as if he were some human being (9:32).

And yet, once the idea has been given life by Job's words, it comes to take on a reality of its own. So in his next speech, even though he realizes that the case is a hopeless one (13:15), the desire for confrontation with God has seized hold of him: "It is to the Almighty that I would speak; it is with God that I crave to enter into dispute" (13:3). By the time of his next speech, the idea has taken on yet more definite contours: here he claims that he already has a "witness" stationed in heaven, that is to say, his "cry" that is his "spokesman" in God's presence (16:19–20). In the next speech that cry has become his "champion" that will plead his cause, even if Job himself should die before his case is heard. But that would be a second best, for what Job most desires is to confront God in person, "to see him for myself" (19:27), to gain God's personal acknowledgment of his innocence.

But nothing happens. The speech of chap. 21 makes no allusion to the idea of a lawsuit with God, and we might be tempted to imagine that Job is now content to let his heavenly champion prosecute his cause. Not so. The moment this speech of chaps. 23–24 opens, Job is intent upon carrying his case forward. The image of the witness or champion has dropped away, and the desire, already expressed in chap. 19, for a personal, face-to-face encounter with God, has overwhelmed everything. Since God is evidently not going to make any move toward Job, it is for Job to search him out, to find the way to his dwelling, to beard the giant in his lair. This is the drama of this speech.

The quest for personal vindication from God is, of course, not a new idea for Job. In a way, he has been set upon it ever since the four messengers arrived on that fateful day. He has been seeking God east, west, north, and south (23:8–9). But, like every other of his plans for vindication from the deity, like every other conceptualization of the conflict between reality and dogma, it is a hopeless quest. Not only can God not be found, but it is pointless to bring to the bar of rational judgment a being who acts solely on whim and impulse. "Whatever he desires, he does" (23:13), that is the key to the truth about God. This is not some cry of faith in praise of divine freedom and unfettered omnipotence; it is a bitter and hopeless conclusion that the moral governor of the universe is a giant Id, unaccountable and unarraignable. All that can be said of him with any certainty is that whatever he has planned he will carry out (23:14), for he pleases none but himself.

There are two directions Job can now move in, and he takes them both. One, a more subjective one, is to retreat further into himself and experience again his feelings of terror and hopelessness before the meaninglessness of the moral universe. The other, a more intellectual one, is to project his own experience upon the world of humans generally and to ask what his own experience signifies for religion and theology; to ask also whether his own experience coheres with that of other humans of his own kind.

In 23:15–17 he makes the first move, and from our experience of the dying fall in so many of Job's speeches we might well think that with the line "I am annihilated by darkness, and thick darkness covers my face" (23:17) he has relapsed into the hopelessness of his first monologue (chap. 3). But he has not, for the second half of the speech opens with a rousing challenge, "Why are days of assize not kept by the Almighty?" (24:1), and a wonderful and terrifying arraignment of the God of justice unfolds. Job is no prophet, and the kaleidoscope of images of how the poor are victimized by the powerful in society does not serve as a cry for sympathy for the poor, still less as a condemnation of the oppressors; rather, it is the gravamen of his charge against God, that not only he, Job, the innocent man, is suffering unjustly at the hands of an angry God, but that the weakest of humanity generally are the victims of God's refusal to bring oppressors to book.

What is a charge like this against the Almighty doing in the sacred Scriptures?

If it is refuted, by the divine speeches or by the outturn of the narrative itself, it is refuted in such a different voice that Job's savagery remains undiluted. Heinrich Heine called the book of Job "the Song of Songs of skepticism"—for its seductiveness, its powerful entrancement of the reader to share its vision of the world. Who can dispute Job's vision? *Can* God be charmed or inveigled by humans into answering their prayers—even if they are prayers for justice long delayed? *Does* God indeed rule the world, or does the evidence of oppression and misery all around us not show him up as feckless—and so himself unjust?

Still, we must ask, what does Job want of God? What does he imagine happening on these famous days of assize that God has defaulted on, and why does he think that management of the universe is essentially a matter of settling accounts, and why does he seem so constrained to think in absolute terms, about riches and poverty, about the righteous and the wicked, about the presence and absence of God? So long as Job is permitted to construct the discourse about God and divine rule, or about ethics, his position seems well nigh unassailable. But Job too, as much as the friends, needs to be read against the grain, to have his underlying assumptions questioned and perhaps unmade.

Job wants the wicked to be judged and punished by God. That is the only way he knows of dealing with human wickedness. The ideas of the repentance, reform, forgiveness, understanding, or education of wrongdoers does not occur to him. This, it must be confessed, is in the end a moral bankruptcy, to have no resources for dealing with wrong except punishment; and Job misjudges any God worth the name if he thinks that God in his wisdom is shut up to this petty principle of tit for tat.

Likewise, Job's hard and fast distinction between the wicked and the righteous, according to which a person is ranged definitively in one camp or the other, is a mark of moral immaturity. It is the morality of the school playground, of the Western B movie, to divide everyone into goodies and baddies. What of the good ruler who is sometimes selfish and careless, whose neglect can amount to cruelty but whose conscience can soon be pricked? What of the bad widow, whose ill temper and self-righteousness makes her a torment to family and neighbors alike, but who nevertheless suffers real poverty and perpetual frustration?

And in any case, why does he think the rectification of social injustice to be God's problem? By what right does he displace the responsibility for equity and justice among humans from society to God? If there are rich and poor in a community, and if that is an injustice, to appeal to God to do something about it is to absolve humans of responsibility, of the rich to care for the functioning of the whole community that sustains their wealth and of the poor to unite in action against a system from which they are suffering. Job is very concerned about those who remove the landmarks of the widows' property, for example, but to put the problem on God's doorstep is to evade the issue. God actually has fewer resources for dealing with the problem than do humans: he can bring the life of the landowner to an untimely end, but he cannot restructure the system of loans or institute social welfare programs or rebuild a sense of family solidarity or engineer a social system in which women are not dependent on men for their livelihood and so do not need special support when their partners die. Religion becomes the opiate of the people when it is used to sidestep issues of social justice, and Job, for all the passion of his speech and the bravery of his resistance to traditional dogma, is an enemy of the people so long as he insists on making God's business everything that needs amendment in the world.

His complaint against God in this speech has been twofold: that he cannot win from God a declaration of his innocence, and that God himself has given up on governing his world. Stepping outside the ideology of the text for a moment (commentators rarely permit themselves the privilege), we could say, in response to Job's first complaint, that however uncomfortable it is for Job in his particular society to be suffering and poor, he is on a hiding to nothing if he thinks that God is going to do anything about it. If his society believes that prosperity and health are signs of divine approval and certificates of moral integrity, the society is laboring under a vast illusion, and the best thing God can do is to let lots of excellent people suffer dreadfully until the dogma withers away of its own accord. Job himself had better not be "restored," for that will only mean further support for the illusion. If Job does get his health and wealth back, it will mean that God is conniving at the illusion society has wrapped itself in.

As for Job's second complaint, we could respond that there are more ways of managing an enterprise than being an accountant. Job wants God to hold days of assize, days in which bills can be settled, fines can be levied, punishments meted out. This is all accounting, after the event. A good manager will be at least as concerned with developing a vision for the enterprise, a sense of identity and worth for the workers, good personal interrelationships, and cooperative management structures. The manager whose eye is constantly on the bottom line is a monster. If Job is to be allowed in this book to construct for the world's management the discourse according to which God is going to be assessed, God will need to watch out. No need to worry, though, because we know that when the time comes for God's (forced) self-appraisal he will simply ignore the discourse Job has elaborated, and offer his own rationale for his management style.

Bildad's Third Speech (25:1–26:14)

Bibliography

Cyss-Wittenstein, C. "Reading Job 26–31 with Bakhtin." *Gravitas* (Graduate Theological Union) 1.2 (2000). **Daiches, S.** "Job XXVI 12–13 and the Babylonian Story of Creation." *ZA* 25 (1911) 1–8. **Dhorme, P.** "Les chapitres xxv–xxvii du Livre de Job." *RB* 33 (1924) 343–56. **Driver, G. R.** "Problems in Job." *AJSL* 52 (1936) 160–70. ———. "Problems in the Hebrew Text of Job." In *Wisdom in Israel and in the Ancient Near East.* FS H. H. Rowley. VTSup 3. Leiden: Brill, 1955. 72–93. **Fuchs, G.** *Mythos und Hiobdichtung: Aufnahme und Umdeutung altorientalischer Vorstellungen.* Stuttgart: Kohlhammer, 1993. **Gross, H.** "Die Allmacht des Schöpfergottes: Erwägungen zu Ijob 26,5–14." In *Die alttestamentliche Botschaft als Wegweisung.* FS H. Reinelt, ed. J. Zmijewski. Stuttgart: Katholisches Bibelwerk, 1990. 75–84. **Habel, N. C.** "He who stretches out the heavens" [Isa 40:21–23; 42:5; 44:24; 45:12; 48:13; 51:13; Job 26; Pss 18; 104; 144]. *CBQ* 34 (1972) 417–30. **Hermisson, H.-J.** "Ein Bibeltext für Fortgeschrittene (Hiob 26)." *TBei* 27 (1996) 137–44. **Herrmann, W.** "Philologica hebraica." *TVers* 8 (1977) 35–44. **Jenks, A. W.** "Theological Presuppositions of

Israel's Wisdom Literature." *HBT* 7 (1985) 43–75. **Löhr, M.** "Die drei Bildad-Reden im Buche Hiob." In *Beiträge zur alttestamentlichen Wissenschaft Karl Budde zum siebzigsten Geburtstag am 13. April 1920 überreicht von Freunden und Schülern.* Ed. K. Marti. BZAW 34. Berlin: Töpelmann, 1920. 107–12. **Martin, G. W.** "Elihu and the Third-Cycle in the Book of Job." Diss., Princeton, 1972. **Michel, W.** "Hebrew Poetic Devices in the Service of Biblical Exegesis: Illustrated in a Discussion of Job 25:1–6." In *Proceedings of the Eleventh World Congress of Jewish Studies: Division A. The Bible and Its World.* Ed. D. Assaf. Jerusalem: Magnes; World Union of Jewish Studies, 1994. 151–58. **Prado, J.** "La creación, conservación y gobierno del Universo en el Libro de Job." *Sef* 11 (1951) 259–88. **Regnier, A.** "La distribution des chapitres 25–28 du Livre de Job." *RB* 33 (1924) 186–200. **Roberts, J. J. M.** "*ṢAPÔN* in Job 26,7." *Bib* 56 (1975) 554–57. **Tournay, R.** "L'ordre primitif des chapitres XXIV–XXVIII du livre de Job." *RB* 64 (1957) 321–34. **Witte, M.** "Die dritte Rede Bildads (Hiob 25) und die Redaktionsgeschichte des Hiobbuches." In *The Book of Job.* Ed. W. A. M. Beuken. BETL 114. Leuven: Leuven UP, 1994. 349–55. ———. *Philologische Notizen zu Hiob 21–27.* BZAW 234. Berlin: de Gruyter, 1995. ———. *Vom Leiden zur Lehre: Der dritte Redegang (Hiob 21–27) und die Redaktionsgeschichte des Hiobbuches.* BZAW 230. Berlin: de Gruyter, 1994. **Wolfers, D.** "Job: The Third Cycle: Dissipating a Mirage." *DD* 16 (1987–88) 217–26; 17 (1988–89) 19–25. ———. "Job 26: An Orphan Chapter." In *The Book of Job.* Ed. W. A. M. Beuken. BETL 114. Leuven: Leuven UP, 1994. 387–91. ———. "The Speech-Cycles in the Book of Job." *VT* 43 (1993) 385–402.

Translation

25:1 *And Bildad the Shuhite answered and said:*

26:1 [a] *[Then Job answered:]*
2 *How well you have aided the one without power!*[a]
How well you have saved[b] *the arm*[c] *without strength!*
3 *How well you have counseled one without wisdom,*
and revealed your insight in abundance![a]
4 *With whose help*[a] *have you uttered these words?*
Whose inspiration has issued from you?[b]

25:2 *A dreadful dominion*[a] *is his;*[b]
he imposed[c] *peace*[d] *in the height of his heavens.*[e]
3 *Is there any number to his troops?*
On whom does his light[a] *not arise?*[b]

4 [a]*How then can a human be righteous before God?*[b]
How can one born of a woman be innocent?
5 *Behold, even*[a] *the moon is not bright,*[b]
and the stars are not clean in his sight.
6 *How much less a mortal, who is a maggot,*[a]
a human, who is a worm?

26:5 [a]*The shades tremble*[b] *in terror*[c]
[d]*beneath*[e] *the waters and those who live in them.*[f]
6 *Sheol is naked before him,*
Abaddon lies uncovered.

[7]*He it is who stretched out*[a] *the North*[b] *over chaos,*
and suspended the earth from[c] *nothing.*[d]
[8]*He wrapped up the waters in his clouds,*
but the clouds did not burst under their weight.
[9]*He covered*[a] *the sight of his throne;*[b]
he spread[c] *his cloud over it.*
[10]*He drew a circle*[a] *upon the face of the waters,*
as[b] *the boundary between light and darkness.*

[11]*The pillars of heaven trembled;*[a]
they were aghast[b] *at his rebuke.*[c]
[12]*By his power*[a] *he stilled*[b] *the sea;*[c]
by his skill[d] *he crushed Rahab.*
[13]*By his wind the heavens became clear;*[a]
his hand pierced[b] *the twisting*[c] *serpent.*
[14]*But*[a] *these are but the fringes*[b] *of his ways,*[c]
and what[d] *do we hear of him*[e] *but a whisper,*[f]
[g]*and*[h] *who can conceive the thunder of his might?*[i]

Notes

26:1.a. In this commentary, chap. 26 is assigned to Bildad, and this heading is regarded as secondary; see further, *Comment* and *Form/Structure/Setting*. Moffatt has the same rearrangement as in the *Translation* above. JB, following Larcher, moves 26:1–4 to follow 26:14.

2.a. ללא־כח "to the one without strength." For the use of עזר with ל in the sense of "come to the aid of," cf. 2 Sam 21:17 and *HALOT,* 2:811a §2; *DCH,* vol. 6, *s.v.* Against the majority of translators, NJPS "You would help without having the strength" (similarly Habel)—and similar translations for v 2b, 3a—is hard to justify from the Heb.

2.b. הושעת "you have saved." Beer (*BHK*) and Hölscher read וְהוֹשַׁעְתָּ "and you have saved."

2.c. Saving an arm seems a little strange (though it seems acceptable to KJV, RSV, NIV); Andersen suggests that since the arm "is always that of the deliverer," the prep *beth* is to be understood; he translates "with your arm" (NJPS differently "you would deliver with arms that have no power"). It is surprising, however, that there are no parallels to saving (ישׁע hiph) with an arm. And the parallel would suggest that the arm belongs to the one who is aided. NAB tries to avoid the oddity with "what strength to the feeble arm!"; similarly JB "for the arm that is powerless, what a rescuer!," NEB "what deliverance you have brought to the powerless!"

3.a. לרב "according to abundance, abundantly," often "for multitude"; see BDB, 914a. To create a more exact parallelism, various speculative proposals, all unnecessary, have been made. (1) Graetz read לְבַעַר "to the fool"; (2) Reiske, Beer (*BH*[2] *frt*), Kissane לְרַךְ "to the tender, feeble" (the form לָרֵךְ must be an error, since the word is not in pause); (3) Beer (*BHK*), Terrien לְבַר (de Wilde לְבֹר) "to the uncultivated person" (as MH; see Jastrow, 148b), or "boor" (G. R. Driver, "Textual and Linguistic Problems of the Book of Psalms," *HTR* 29 [1936] 171–95 [172], followed by NEB "to the foolish," REB "to the simple"; Brockington's note of NEB's reading as לְרָב is unintelligible); and (4) Gordis לְרַב or לְרֹבֶה "to the youth, the inexperienced" (though the word does not occur elsewhere in the OT). (5) Tur-Sinai sees here a רֹב "helpless," as at 4:3 (*q.v.*).

4.a. את־מי "with whom?" i.e., with the help of whom?; so JPS, RSV, NIV, NAB; NEB "who has prompted you?" This instrumental use of את is rare but well enough established (cf. *DCH,* 1:452b, §6a). KJV, NJPS (and Driver–Gray, emending to אֶל־ "to") have "to whom" (cf. JB "For whom are these words of yours intended?")—which would suggest that Job has been presumptuous in addressing those who know better than he does; but the thought is rather tortuous, and this interpretation spoils the parallelism. Beer (*BHK*) makes the same emendation, to אֶל־ "to."

4.b. ונשמת־מי יצאה ממך, lit. "and the breath of whom has issued from you?" KJV has "whose spirit came from thee," NAB better "whose is the breath that comes forth from you?," NEB more prosaically "whose spirit is expressed in your speech?" NJB has more loosely "whence comes that wit you are now displaying?"

25:2.a. המשל ופחד, lit. "dominion and dread." On the use of "dominion" (המשל) and "fear" (פחד) together as a hendiadys, see *Comment.* The usual translations, such as "dominion and fear" (RSV), "authority and awe" (NEB), "dominion and awe" (NIV), and "what sovereignty, what awe" (JB), are inappropriate, since while "dominion" is with God, "dread, fear, awe" is with his subjects. NAB has "awesomeness" for פחד, which is something that *can* be said to be "with" God; but פחד never means "awesomeness." המשל is hiph inf abs used as a noun (GKC, §85c). For פחד, the Qumran Tg has ורבו "and grandeur."

2.b. The absence of the referent "God" for the pronoun "his" (suff of עמו) does not necessarily imply that something is missing prior to this verse; for parallels, see *Note* 24:22.b.

2.c. עשה is a ptcp, and is translated as a present tense by most Eng. versions (except NEB "has established [peace])." But the ptcp when used as a verb (as here) signifies "a single and comparatively transitory act, or related to particular cases, historical facts and the like," whereas the ptcp used as a noun indicates "repeated, enduring, or commonly occurring acts, occupations, and thoughts" (GKC, §116f); there are several more examples in 26:7–10. It is not that "he keeps his heavenly kingdom in peace" (GNB), as if he were a pacific and beneficent ruler; Moffatt's "he keeps the peace in heaven" does at least carry the suggestion of ongoing conflict.

2.d. The older emendation of שלום to שִׁלּוּם "retribution" (cf. Rosenmüller [*Scholia*], Wright, Tur-Sinai) is not now favored.

2.e. במרומיו "in his heights." Emendation to בְּמֹרְדָיו "[he takes vengeance] on his rebels" (Wright) is not impressive; "*his* rebels" sounds implausible.

3.a. אורהו "his light" would normally be vocalized אוֹרוֹ. NJB thinks it is "lightning," but would lightning "arise" (קום)? A quite different reading is offered by Michaelis, Duhm, Strahan, Beer (*BH*[2] אָרְבּוֹ), Dhorme, Hölscher, Kissane, Larcher, and Gerleman (*BHS prp*), following LXX ἐπὶ τίνας δὲ οὐκ ἐπελεύσεται ἔνεδρα παρ' αὐτοῦ "and upon whom will there not come a snare from him?" (perhaps supported by the Qumran Tg; see Pope), who emend אורהו "his light" to אֹרְבוֹ "his ambush, ambush party" (*DCH,* 1:366b), translating "against whom will his ambush not arise?" (for אֶרֶב as the subj of קום, cf. Josh 8:19); Fohrer reads אָרְבּוֹ "his ambush." Hence NEB "at whom will they not spring from ambush?," JB "can anyone . . . boast of having escaped his ambushes," and presumably Moffatt "Whom cannot he surprise and seize?" This is a good emendation (though the Heb. makes perfectly satisfactory sense; but see next *Note*), especially compared with Siegfried's תּוֹרָתוֹ "his law" and Ehrlich's אִמְרָהוּ "his word" (followed by Beer [*BHK*] and Gerleman [*BHS al*]), both of which are boring and unsuitable to the context. De Wilde implausibly conjectures מַטֵּה "staff" or שֵׁבֶט "scepter." Tur-Sinai sees here a new word אֹור "condemnation," from ארר "curse," as also in 36:30; 37:3, 11, 15, 21. For contextual reasons, the MT reading is to be preferred (it is retained also by Pope, Gordis, Habel, van der Lugt).

3.b. קום "arise" does not elsewhere have אור "light" as the subject (זרח "shine" is the normal way of saying that light "arises"). This makes the text a little questionable, it must be admitted. Usually קום with על "against" has a hostile sense (e.g., Deut 19:11; Judg 9:18), so in this regard also our verse is abnormal (on JB "against whom," see *Comment*).

4.a. Peake finds vv 4–6 to be a gloss.

4.b. עם־אל "with God," i.e., in his presence (עם is used similarly at 12:13, 16). Terrien wants this "with" to signify a single combat, even a theomachy; but there is no word of *conflict* here.

5.a. הן עד־ירח is lit. "behold, even the moon[, and it is not bright]"; עַד, as rarely, can be taken as "even" (BDB, 724b, §3; cf. also *HALOT,* 2:787a, §5; *DCH,* vol. 6, *s.v.*). For the *waw* after the *casus pendens,* see GKC, §143d. But G. R. Driver, "Problems in Job," *AJSL* 52 (1936) 160–70 (161), and "Hebrew Notes," *JBL* 68 (1949) 57–59 (58), reads עָד, i.e., עוד II qal (BDB, 728b; piel at Ps 119:61; cf. *DCH,* vol. 6, *s.v.*), "goes round," thus NEB "if (הֵן) the circling moon [is found wanting]." On הן "behold," meaning translationally "if," see D. M. Stec, "The Use of *hēn* in Conditional Sentences," *VT* 37 (1987) 478–86, who analyzes a sentence type beginning with הן and followed by אף כי or אף; for other examples, see *Note* 23:8.b, and cf. *DCH,* 2:572b. Gordis sees in עד a contracted form of יָעַד "he orders," translating "he commands the moon and it does not shine." J. Reider ("Contributions to the Biblical Text," *HUCA* 24 [1952–53] 85–106 [105]) proposes to read עִדֵּר "he makes [the moon] grow small," but the point is no longer God's power but the impurity of all created things.

5.b. יאהיל as it stands looks like a hiph of אהל "pitch tent." But this does not make any sense, and the form is usually said to be an error (or, byform, or "extreme plene spelling" [Gordis]) for יָהֵל, hiph impf of הלל "shine," which Beer (*BHK*) reads. BDB, 14b, and *HALOT,* 1:19a, propose rather a

אהל II "be clear, shine." The sense "be bright, shine" appears in KJV, RSV, NAB, JB, NIV. But Driver ("Problems in Job," 161), following a suggestion of Ehrlich, supposes a verb אהל hiph "be worthy" (cf. Arab. *'hl*) and translates "shows herself not worthy"; thus NEB "is found wanting."

6.a. Relative clause without אשׁר (cf. on 24:19).

26:5.a. The passage 26:5–11 was lacking in the original LXX, and has been supplied from Theod.

5.b. יחוללו is, according to BDB, 297b, polal of חיל/חול I "writhe, whirl," thus "be made to writhe," or better, according to *HALOT,* 1:311a, and *DCH,* 3:212b, polal of חיל I "be in pain," thus "be brought to trembling." KJV "are formed" is "a misrendering due to Ḳimchi" (Driver–Gray). Beer (*BH*[2] *prps,* יָחוּלוּ לוֹ; *BHK prps*) and de Wilde strain after a new interpretation by reading יָחִילוּ לוֹ "writhe before him."

5.c. Ball and Fohrer add מִפָּנָיו "from before him," on the ground that the colon is too short. The sense is not wrong even if the emendation is unnecessary.

5.d. Dhorme, Larcher, JB, NAB, NEB transfer מתחת to the first colon, as "beneath, under the earth," or "in the underworld" (NEB). This leaves room for a verb in this second colon, which many fill with יֵחַתּוּ "are terrified" (so Beer [*BH*[2] *prps*], Dhorme, Hölscher, Larcher, Fohrer [*frt*], Pope, Rowley [apparently], Fedrizzi, de Wilde, NEB "the waters and all that live in them are struck with terror," JB), but it is not very likely that the "waters" should be in fear. Blommerde strained for a novel interpretation by attaching the *mem* of מתחת to the preceding verb, יחוללו, as an enclitic, and then taking תחת as תֵּחַת, i.e., 3 fem sg niph of חתת with a collective (pl) subj, "are crushed."

5.e. MT accentuation prescribes that we connect "beneath" (מתחת) with the second colon; so NIV "those beneath the waters," NJPS "[tremble] beneath the waters." Many, however, connect "beneath" with the first colon (so Hölscher, Fedrizzi, Gordis, de Wilde, Good, RSV, NAB "The shades beneath," JB "The Shadows tremble underneath the earth," NEB "In the underworld the shades writhe"). But the image of Sheol beneath the sea (as in the MT accentuation) is preferable to the idea of the waters and the fish trembling, along with the shades. GNB wrongly has the shades "in" the waters: "The spirits of the dead tremble in the waters under the earth"—and it leaves the fish out of it altogether. Pope, however, also maintains that it is the underworld itself that is meant by the "waters."

5.f. ושכניהם "and their dwellers" is emended to מִשְׁכְּנֵיהֶם "[who have] their dwellings [under the water]" by Duhm, Strahan, Beer (*BH*[2] *al*), thinking it rather stupid to have the giant Rephaim living beneath the fish.

7.a. נטה "stretching out." As throughout vv 7–10, the ptcp used as a verb refers to a single past action (cf. on עשׂה, 25:2); they are not "participles of recurrent divine action" (Driver–Gray). The ptcp is in "loose apposition to the suffix" of נגדו "before him" (v 6), as in 12:19 (Driver–Gray).

7.b. צפון "north" may be the terrestrial north (as Schultens, Ewald, Hitzig, Dillmann, Budde, Duhm) or the northern part of the sky, perhaps conceived of as the highest heaven (so Rosenmüller, Driver–Gray, Dhorme). See further, *Comment.*

7.c. תלה על is "suspend from," "hang upon" (as Gen 40:19; Isa 22:24; Ps 137:2; Esth 2:23); so KJV, Pope, de Wilde (BDB, 1067b; *HALOT* 4:1738a, "hang, hang up"). It is not "suspend over"; 2 Sam 4:12 is no parallel, for there the על with תלה means "beside" (against Driver–Gray). But the latter view is taken by Fohrer, Habel, JPS "hangeth the earth over nothing," NJPS "suspended earth over emptiness," JB "poised the earth on nothingness," NEB "suspends earth in the void," NAB "over nothing at all," NIV "over nothing." It is the view of classical cosmology that the earth is suspended over empty space; cf. Lucretius 5.534–49; Ovid, *Fasti* 6.269–70.

7.d. בלי־מה "nothingness," lit. "without anything," occurs only here.

9.a. The piel of אחז occurs only here, as ptcp מְאַחֵז. The verb generally means "seize, grasp," but most agree that here it must mean "cover" (so BDB, 26b; *DCH,* 1:187b); thus NJPS "shuts off [the view]"). It would seem preferable, however, to suppose a second verb אחז II "cover," as F. Perles[2], 83; idem, "Übersehenes akkadisches Sprachgut im Alten Testament," *AfO* 4 (1927) 218–20 (218); KBL, 29b; *HALOT,* 1:32b); the verb would occur also at 1 Kgs 6:10 and 2 Chr 9:18. However, the Akk. *uḫḫuzu* (from *aḫāzu*) means not "cover" but "mount an object in precious metals" (*CAD,* 1.1:79b), so the supposition of such a verb becomes questionable. Beer (*BHK*) and NAB emend to אֹחֵז "holds back [the appearance of the moon]," but it is more likely that deeds at creation are spoken of here, not recurrent heavenly phenomena.

9.b. כִּסֵּה, a variant spelling, apparently, of כִּסֵּא "throne" (so BDB, 490b; *DCH,* 4:439b). Emendation to כִּסְאוֹ or כִּסְאֹה "his throne" (Duhm, Beer [*BH*[2] *vel* כסה]) is unnecessary. The MT reading is supported here (as also by Driver–Gray, Gordis, Habel, van der Lugt). Many, however, following ibn Ezra and Houbigant, emend to כֶּסֶה (= כֶּסֶא) "full moon" (so KBL, 446a; *HALOT,* 2:487a; cf. RSV "he covers the face of the moon"; similarly NAB, NIV, JB, NEB, Moffatt, Budde, Ehrlich, Beer [*BHK*],

Dhorme, Hölscher, Larcher, Fohrer, Fedrizzi, Gerleman [*BHS prp*], Ravasi, de Wilde, Sicre Díaz, Good, Newsom, Strauss [כִּסֶּה; the first vowel appears to be an error]). In its two other occurrences, כסא once means the full moon itself (Prov 7:20, יום הכסא "the day of the full moon") and once "the day of the full moon" (Ps 81:3 [4]). If, as seems likely, we are still dealing here with events of creation (as in vv 7–8), spreading a cloud over the full moon would not be appropriate, whereas hiding the divine throne from view would be. Kissane unnecessarily emended to סֻכּוֹ "his tent" (as in Ps 27:5). Duhm more plausibly suggested changing פְּנֵי "the face of" to פִּנֵּי "[he makes fast] the pillars of [his throne]" (so too Strahan, Beer [*BH*²]); the pl פִּנִּים is attested at Zech 14:10. However, פנה usually means "corner" rather than "pillar," though perhaps sometimes "corner pillars" (cf. *DCH*, vol. 6, *s.v.*).

9.c. פרשז is an anomalous form (some MSS have פַּרְשֵׁז), perhaps best explained as a combination (*forma mixta*) of פָּרַשׂ and פָּרַז, both meaning "spread," though פרז does not occur in Biblical Hebrew (but cf. MH פרז hiph "extend, exceed," and perhaps Arab. *faraza* "remove, separate"); see also G. R. Driver, "Problems in the Hebrew Text of Job," in *Wisdom in Israel and in the Ancient Near East,* FS H. H. Rowley, VTSup 3 (Leiden: Brill, 1955) 72–93 (84). Budde reads פָּרֹשׂ (inf abs; so too Beer [*BHK*], Fohrer) or פֹּרֵשׂ or פָּרַשׂ; Beer (*BH*²), Hölscher, Kissane פֹּרֵשׂ; Fedrizzi פָּרַשׂ.

10.a. חֹק is "something prescribed, statute" and so, according to BDB, 349a §5, is several times "prescribed limit, boundary" (38:10; Isa 5:14; Jer 5:22; Prov 8:29; Ps 148:6; Mic 7:11; of time, Job 14:5, 13). *HALOT,* 1:346a, however, recognizes only "appointed time" (for Mic 7:11, and the doubtful Zeph 2:2) and "limit" (for Jer 5:22; Isa 5:14); at Prov 8:29, Ps 148:6 it understands the word as "law, regulation"; at Job 14:5, 13 as "portion" (reading חֻקִּי); for the present passage it adopts the emendation to חָקַק חָג "inscribed a circle" mentioned below, and likewise reads חֻקִּי at 38:10. חָג, as it stands, is 3 masc sg of חוג "draw round, describe a circle" (BDB, 295a; *HALOT,* 1:295b; *DCH,* 3:169a). חק־חג is then "he hath described a boundary" (RV), "he drew a boundary" (NJPS), "he marks out the horizon" (NIV), or "he has fixed the horizon" (NEB).

However, many emend to חָג חָק (or חָקַק) "he has drawn a circle," חקק being "carve, inscribe, decree" (BDB, 349a; *HALOT,* 1:347b; *DCH,* 3:303b), and חוג being "circle" (*HALOT,* 1:295a; *DCH,* 3:169a; BDB, 295a has "vault, horizon") as at 22:14; Isa 40:22; Prov 8:27; Ecclus 43:12 (MS M), 1QM 10:13. This reading is adopted by RSV "he has described a circle," NAB "he has marked out a circle," JB "traced a ring," Budde, Duhm, Driver–Gray, Dhorme, Beer (*BHK*), Hölscher (חָקַק), Kissane, Larcher, Fohrer, Terrien, Rowley, Fedrizzi, de Wilde (חָקַק), Sicre Díaz, and Good, noting the similar wording in Prov 8:27, בְּחֻקוֹ חוּג עַל־פְּנֵי תְהוֹם "when he decreed a circle on the face of the deep."

10.b. עד "as far as," is a little strange. KJV "until the day and night come to an end" can hardly be what is meant, but at least it attempts to take עד seriously. RSV, JB, REB have "at the boundary," NEB "at the farthest limit," NJPS "at the extreme," NAB "as the boundary," and NIV "for a boundary"; such seems to be the sense, but there is something to be said for the emendation to יָעַד "he appointed, designated" (Beer [*BH*² *prps*]).

11.a. רפף "shake, rock" only here (in polal); MH רפף is "vibrate, vacillate," and in pilpel "move, shake, flutter" (Jastrow, 1491a); Arab. *raffa* is "quake, convulse." The form is no doubt preterite, in reference to a simple past action.

11.b. תמה "be astounded" expresses emotion (as also, e.g., Gen 43:33; Ps 48:5 [6]).

11.c. NAB replaces מגערתו "at his rebuke" with מֵרַעַם גַּעֲרָתוֹ "at the thunder of his rebuke," transferring to this point from v 14c the phrase ורעם גבורתו "and the thunder of his power."

12.a. בכחו, lit. "by his power." NEB has "with his strong arm," but it is hard to see how God's "arm" would have been used to still the sea.

12.b. רגע may be one of five different verbs: (1) רגע I "disturb" (BDB, 920b), as also in Isa 51:15 (= Jer 31:35) with the sea as the obj. KBL, 874a, and *HALOT,* 3:1188a, recognize only one verb and translate the term here "arouse." So too Duhm, Hölscher, Fohrer, Fedrizzi, JB "he has whipped up the Sea," NAB "stirs up" (similarly JPS), NIV "churned up"; but how can that be parallel to "has crushed Rahab," and can it be an expression of his "rebuke"? It is too strained to think that God is supposed to have "stirred up" the sea only in order to quell it (as Duhm), and in any case stirring up the sea is not much of an exercise of power (כח). (2) רגע II "be at rest, repose" (BDB, 921a); thus "come to rest," with the sea as the subj (de Wilde). Many, however, prefer to regard the verb as transitive, with God as the subj; thus LXX κατέπαυσεν "stilled," "still" (Peake, Sicre Díaz, Good; similarly RVmg, RSV, NJPS "stilled," Moffatt "quelled"). For a transitive sense, however, an emendation may be called for, to הִרְגִּיעַ "he stilled" (as Beer [*BHK*]). (3) רגע III (not recognized by the modern lexica, but cf. Buxtorf, 715, *fissus fuit* "was divided") "cleave, divide"; so too KJV "divideth," NEB "cleft." So also Dhorme (followed by Ravasi), thinking to find a parallel in Marduk's splitting open Tiamat's heart (*Enuma elish* 4.102; *ANET,* 67a). Dhorme finds the same meaning for רגע in Isa 51:15 (= Jer 31:35), but it is improbable that dividing the sea or the sea monster is what makes its waves roar; in any case, the likely meaning in those passages ("stir up") need not be determinative here, since there we are not dealing with creation mythology. "Divided" gives a good sense and suits the parallelism, but since there is no other attestation of a verb with this meaning, it is perhaps better to settle for "stilled." (4) M. Dahood (*Psalms I*, 29, 182–83) claimed that the verb means "annihilate" (cf. the noun רֶגַע, which he explains as "annihilation" or perhaps "place of annihilation, Perdition" (Pss 6:10 [11]; 30:5 [6]; found also at Job 21:13 by Blommerde). (5) A fifth רגע "harden, congeal" (BDB, 921b) does not seem appropriate here (against *Note* 7:5.c).

12.c. NEB "the sea-monster," understanding ים "sea" as the name of the Canaanite deity Yam, the sea god.

12.d. K ובתובנתו is probably merely a miswriting of the form offered by Q, וּבִתְבוּנָתוֹ. NAB emends to וּבִגְבוּרָתוֹ "and by his power," creating a more exact but uninteresting parallelism.

13.a. Lit. "were clearness, beauty" (שִׁפְרָה, a noun); the phrase is intelligible but awkward (it is retained by Fohrer, van der Lugt). Driver–Gray spoke for many when they said that "Neither the Heb. nor any of the emendations leaves the impression of being exactly what the poet wrote." KJV, ASV "garnished" follows Vg *ornavit* "he adorned" (cf. Buxtorf, 841: *pulchros effecit, ornavit* "made beautiful, adorned" for this passage), understanding שפרה as a (piel) verb, though it should not be fem if God is the subj (Vg, reading רוחו for ברוחו, had the fem "his spirit, breath" as subj; similarly Kissane). JPS has "are serene," NJPS "calmed," RSV, NIV "fair," NEB, GNB, Moffatt "clear." T. H. Gaster had the wonderful idea that "the movement of winds across the sky is [here] represented as God's breathing on its surface in order to polish it" (*IDB*, 2:270a); but the image of the sky as a mirror is absent here, though attested at 37:18.

Several small emendations have been suggested: (1) to שָׁפְרוּ I "became fair" (qal, as at Ps 16:6) (BDB, 1054b), an attractive proposal of Beer (*BH*[2]). (2) Alternatively, Dhorme, followed by Hölscher, Larcher (apparently), Terrien, de Wilde, JB "made the heavens luminous," and *HALOT*, 4:1635b, emended to רוּחוֹ שמים שִׁפְּרָה, which he understood as "His breath has swept the heavens clean," taking שפר II piel as equivalent to Arab. *safara* "shine," but also "sweep [the clouds away]" (Lane, 1370a, c), as perhaps also at 38:37 (*q.v.*); and cf. ספר II "disperse" (*DCH*, vol. 6, *s.v.*). This Arab. verb was also appealed to by Driver, "Problems in the Hebrew Text of Job," 92, as cognate with שפר "be fair," but at 38:37 he associates it rather with ספר II "disperse," and it would seem better to suppose also a שפר II "disperse"; NEB "at his breath the skies are clear" reads שָׁפְרָה (Brockington), from this verb, but since it translates ברוחו as "at his breath," it is not clear what it understands as the subj of the verb. (3) Hölscher[2], followed by *HALOT*, 4:1635b, reads בְּרוּחוֹ שמים שִׁפֵּר "by his breath he swept the heavens bare," i.e., invoking the same שפר II but making God the subject.

Less plausible emendations are: (4) Gordis, following S. Daiches, "Job XXVI 12–13 and the Babylonian Story of Creation," *ZA* 25 (1911) 1–8 (3), proposes a שפר III "spread out" (Rashi already compared שַׁפְרִיר [Q] at Jer 43:10, apparently "canopy"; cf. also Akk. *šuparruru* "spread out") and reads שִׁפְּרָה "[his breath] stretched out [the heavens]" (followed by Habel). This suggestion has the advantage of relating the colon to the moment of creation, but it is difficult to see what the image is; how can breath stretch out heavens? (5) NAB emends to מַיִם פֵּרַשׂ "[by his (angry) breath] he scatters the waters," and inserts 27:22a ("and he hurls against it relentlessly") after it, and 27:22b ("from his hand it flees") after v 13b; but again the image is hard to detect, and there is no obvious parallel to scattering waters. (6) Tur-Sinai made the ingenious suggestion that in שפרה we have a Heb. cognate of Akk. *sapāru* "bag, net" (cf. Aram. שְׁפִיר "bag, act [of fetus]"; Arab. *zufra* "water-bag"), and that there is an allusion here to Marduk's attack on Tiamat with a net (*Enuma elish* 4.95; *ANET*, 67a). Tur-Sinai supports his proposal with the claim that סִפְרָה in Ps 56:8 (9) means "bag" (though most think this *hapax* means "book," it *is* parallel to נאד "skin-bottle, skin"; on the other hand, perhaps נאד is "parchment" [Dahood, *Psalms II*, 46]). An emendation of the colon then becomes necessary, to ברוחו שָׂם יָם סִפְרָה "by means of his wind he put the sea (in) a bag" (though שׂם ים is hard to believe in). This is little more than a string of philological conjectures; there is the difficulty that in *Enuma elish* it is not Tiamat but her helpers who are bagged by Marduk (4.110–12); and the whole proposal depends upon the Babylonian myth being known in its details among the Hebrews. It is not wise to follow Tur-Sinai, as do Pope, M. Fishbane ("Jeremiah iv 23–6 and Job iii 3–13: A Recovered Use of the Creation Pattern," *VT* 21 [1971] 151–67 [163]), and Cohen, 50.

13.b. KJV "formed" assumes the verb is חול polel "writhe in travail with, bring forth" (cf. on יחוללו in v 5); but "his hand" (ידו) is not a suitable subject, and in any case the context suggests strongly that we are dealing with the primeval conflict. The verb is rather חלל III poel "pierce" (*DCH*, 3:235b; *HALOT*, 1:320a חלל II polel), as most moderns recognize (and probably also NEB "breaks," REB "slays").

13.c. Various suggestions for the meaning of בָּרִחַ have been made. (1) It has usually been connected with ברח "flee" and understood as "fleeing" (so RSV, JB; NJPS "elusive," NIV "gliding"); cf. *HALOT,* 1:156b (ברח); *DCH,* 2:263b (בָּרִחַ I). (2) But in Isa 27:1 the בריח serpent Leviathan is also (some say, associated with) the "twisting" (עקלתון) serpent; so some have thought that בריח should mean the same thing (so NEB). (3) Alternatively, since it is parallel to "twisting," it might mean the opposite, "straight" (Gordis), perhaps as derived from בְּרִיחַ "bar, pole." A straight serpent would, however, be something of a zoological marvel. (4) C. H. Gordon thought it was "evil" ("Near East Seals in Princeton and Philadelphia," *Or* 22 [1953] 242–50 [243–44] ["3. The Vanquished Dragon of Evil"], and *UT,* 376, following Izz-al-Din Al-Yasin, *The Lexical Relation between Ugaritic and Arabic,* Shelton Semitic Series 1 [New York: Shelton College, 1952] 45, 152, and comparing Arab. *barḥ* "evil"; cf. *DCH,* 2:263b [בָּרִחַ II]; M. Dahood, "Ebla, Ugarit and the Bible," in *The Archives of Ebla: An Empire Inscribed in Clay,* by G. Pettinato [Garden City, NY: Doubleday, 1981] 271–321 [288]). The translation "evil" is adopted by Habel, E. Zurro ("La raiz *brḥ* II y el hápax **mibrāḥ* [Ez 17,21]," *Bib* 61 [1980] 412–15), and A. Schoors, in *Ras Shamra Parallels: The Texts from Ugarit and the Hebrew Bible,* ed. L. R. Fisher, Analecta orientalia 49 (Rome: Pontifical Biblical Institute, 1972–75) 1:34–36. (5) W. F. Albright wanted it to mean "primeval" ("Are the Ephod and the Teraphim Mentioned in Ugaritic Literature?" *BASOR* 83 [1941] 39–42 [39 n. 5]), on the shaky ground that ברח and Arab. *baraḥa* mean "pass," for it is a long way from "pass" to "primeval," even if there is an Arab. *bâriḥ* "past, of time." But NEBmg acknowledges this proposal, which is also noted by *DCH,* 2:263b (בָּרִחַ IV). (6) W. Herrmann ("Philologica hebraica," *TVers* 8 [1977] 35–44 [36–39]) thought it meant "dangerous, destructive" (cf. Arab. *barḥ* "difficulty"; cf. *DCH,* 2:263b [בָּרִחַ III]). (7) C. Rabin, having considered the possibility that it means "hairless, slippery," decided that it properly means "convulsive, tortuous," comparing Arab. *bārīḥ* "twisted" ("*BĀRIᴬḤ,*" *JTS* 47 [1946] 38–41). The term is used of Leviathan in Ugar., *ltn btn brḥ* (*UT* 67.1.1–4), where also it is parallel with *'lqtn* "twisting," but that does not advance our understanding of the term. (8) T. H. Gaster, "Folklore Motifs in Canaanite Myth," *JRAS* (1944) 30–51 (47), argues that it means "sinister, ill-omened" (cf. Arab. *barīh, barūḥ*).

14.a. הֵן, lit. "behold"; the contrast is implied. Dhorme takes הן as "if," but it is difficult to see that this colon can be taken as an agreed thought between the speaker and his audience, so enabling the next colon to be drawn as a consequence.

14.b. קְצָה (unlike קֵץ, which is usually "end" in a temporal sense) is "end, extremity, border, outskirts" (outskirts of a city, 1 Sam 9:27; 14:2; Josh 4:19). KJV has "parts," NAB, Dhorme "outlines," GNB "hints," JB "fraction," NEB "fringe," NIV "outer fringe," JPS, RSV "outskirts."

14.c. Reading Q דְּרָכָיו "his ways" (as Pesh, Tg, Vg, Dhorme, de Wilde), for K דרכו "his way" (as LXX, Good, NEB). An alternative proposal is that of many scholars who identify a דֶּרֶךְ II "dominion, power," cognate with Ugar. *drkt* (cf. *DCH,* 2:472b, 633a [bibliography]; *HALOT,* 1:232b §7). So, e.g., W. F. Albright, "The Oracles of Balaam," *JBL* 63 (1944) 207–33 (219 n. 82); M. Dahood, "Some Northwest Semitic Words in Job," *Bib* 38 (1957) 306–20 (320); idem, "Hebrew-Ugaritic Lexicography II," *Bib* 45 (1964) 393–412 (404). This view is followed by Pope with "bits of his power," and Andersen with "these are only the boundaries of his realm." NEB "the fringe of his power" does not accept this suggestion, despite appearances (cf. Brockington), and probably NJPS "glimpses of His rule" does not either; Moffatt, long before Albright, had "the mere fringe of his force" and GNB, probably not drawing on this proposal, has "hints of his power"—all of them reasonable, if somewhat loose, translations for דרכיו "his ways." Fohrer compares the use of דרך "way" for "work" in 40:19, while Habel regards the "way" as virtually synonymous with God's "design" (עצה) for the cosmos (as in 38:2).

14.d. The מה is exclamatory, like the מה with which Bildad began this speech (26:2) (see also 6:25; cf. Dhorme; BDB, 553b, §2b), though I have chosen to translate the colon as a question.

14.e. בּוֹ is said to be *beth* partitive (Driver–Gray); for other examples, see *Note* 21:25.b. שמע with ב is rare (but see 37:2 and Gen 27:5; Job 15:8, however, is not an analogy since it means "listen *in* [the council]"; 1 Sam 14:6 is an erroneous reference in BDB, 1033b, §1a). Dhorme has "How small is the whisper we hear of them [his works]," but it is hard to see how that is explained by his comment, "The complement בּוֹ refers to the understood relative אשׁר implied before נִשְׁמַע."

14.f. Lit. "and what [is] the portion of a word [that] we hear of him?" שמץ דבר is usually understood as "a whisper of a word," though שמץ is probably (cf. on 4:12) rather "portion" (as KJV) or "fraction" (JB; Gordis "echo")—but that is much the same as "whisper" anyway.

14.g. Duhm, Beer (BH^2), and Hölscher delete this colon. NEB puts the colon in square brackets, as if of doubtful authenticity; NAB removes the first two words to v 11b and deletes the others as a dittogr. A closing tricolon is, however, quite acceptable (see *Comment*).

14.h. Duhm objected against this colon that if Bildad says that we can only hear a whisper of God he cannot continue, "Who considers the thunder of his might?" For how can anyone consider what they cannot know? We might add an introductory "for," as if to say: It is because we cannot conceive or comprehend the full reality that we are reduced to hearing or knowing only the whisper or the fringes. With NIV "Who then can understand the thunder of his power?" it is hard to see how if we hear only a whisper of him the *consequence* can be that we cannot understand his power. Beginning the colon with "but" (as KJV, JPS, RSV, JB) is unsatisfactory because it implies the rather illogical sequence (1) Here are some mighty acts of God (vv 5–13); (2) But they are marginal compared with his ways as a whole (v 14a–b); (3) *But* we cannot understand the totality (v 14c). Perhaps it is best to have simply "and" or no connective at all, understanding the colon as closely in parallel with the two preceding, as if to say: These mighty acts are only the margin of his works, and (putting it another way) we cannot know the totality.

14.i. Keeping K גברותו "his might" (so LXX, Pesh, Tg, Vg, KJV, RSV, NEB, JB, NIV, Dhorme) rather than Q גְּבוּרֹתָיו "his mighty acts" (so JPS, NJPS, NEB [גְּבוּרֹתָו], Driver–Gray, de Wilde) since the theme of the whole speech is God's power (cf. 25:2). The "thunder of his might" could mean "his mighty thunder" (as Hölscher insists), but not here, where the theme is not the thunder but God's power.

Form/Structure/Setting

The question of the *integrity* of the text at this point is crucial both for exegesis and for the matters of form and structure that are to be treated in this section. The decision has been made in this commentary that the third speech of Bildad, although it occupies only 25:1–6 in the Masoretic text, should have assigned to it also 26:1–14, and that the *order* of the verses should be: 25:1; 26:2–4; 25:2–6; 26:5–14. That way of putting it makes the rearrangement look more complicated than it actually is; we could just as well say that it is simply a matter of moving the three verses 26:2–4 to the beginning of chap. 25, while deleting the heading at 26:1, which makes the chapter Job's. For an explanation and justification of the arrangement, see *Comment*.

The *structure* of the speech is, first, a proemium in which Job is addressed (26:2–4), then a doxology in praise of God as the mighty creator (25:2–6; 26:4–14). Within the doxology, three main themes appear in sections of unequal length: the rule of God in the heavens (25:2–6), the control of God over the underworld (26:5–6), and the power of God in creation (26:7–13). The unifying theme throughout is the power of God. Despite the focalization on God, the structure of the speech does not allow us to lose sight altogether of its role as address to Job, for at two points the speech contains rhetorical questions, the former at the end of the first section of the doxology (25:4, 6) and the latter—with questions that include both speakers and interlocutors, as well as Job—at the very end of the speech (26:14).

The *strophic structure* of the speech as reconstructed here is of a sequence of short strophes consisting of two, three, or four lines. Some of the strophes are clearly marked out: 26:2–4 (three lines) as the proemium, 25:4–6 (three lines) as an argument about the impossibility of human righteousness, and 26:11–13 (three lines) as a small narrative about the primordial conflict. The structure may then be displayed as shown here:

Strophe 1	26:2–4	3 lines
Strophe 2	25:2–3	2 lines
Strophe 3	25:4–6	3 lines
Strophe 4	26:5–6	2 lines
Strophe 5	26:7–10	4 lines
Strophe 6	26:11–14	3 lines + a pendant

We could create more regularity in the strophic structure by regarding 25:5–10 as two strophes of three lines each; but there is little direct connection between vv 5–6, about the underworld, and v 7, about creation. More satisfactorily, we could combine strophes 2 and 3 and strophes 4 and 5 as strophes of five and six lines, respectively.

It is hard to compare the above strophic structure with those of other commentators and of the English translations, since there are not many who agree that Bildad's speech has the content and order that have been proposed here. Most versions indicate no strophic divisions in this material other than between chapters (so REV, JB); but NEB and NJPS mark off 26:2–4 as a strophe. NAB delimits as strophes 26:2–6 (thus recognizing the disjunction between v 6 and v 7 noted above) and 26:7–9. Terrien's analysis agrees with much of the above (though he does not rearrange or reassign the material of chaps. 25–26), but he makes a disjunction between v 11 and v 12 of chap. 26 even though both concern the primeval conflict. Fohrer surprisingly makes a strong division between v 9 and v 10 of chap. 26 (so too Terrien, Habel); but vv 7–10 are clearly to be taken together as depicting the creation (note the sequence of participles for God's activity) and as separated from vv 5–6 as the account of the world of the dead and from vv 11–13 as the account of the primordial battle. Hölscher and de Wilde discern throughout strophes of two lines each, but their scheme connects 26:13 with v 14 when it clearly belongs with v 12 (Hölscher furthermore moves 25:2 to follow 26:4; de Wilde moves 25:4–6 to follow 26:14, allowing, however, that it is a three-line strophe). Webster, who regards all of chap. 26 as Job's, identifies strophes as vv 2–4, 5–9, and 10–14; but it seems better to keep vv 4 and 5 together.

The *genre* of the speech is again the *disputation speech,* as the opening address to Job, quite sharply phrased (26:2–4), makes clear. In the proemium, the exclamations with מה "how!," here of feigned amazement at the failure of the other speaker to carry conviction (26:2–3), are an element of this genre (cf. 6:25; 26:14b), as are the rhetorical questions (26:4), here to deny that Job has had supernatural assistance in preparing his speech—though of course Job has never claimed to have such (rhetorical questions in proemia at 8:2–3; 11:2–3; 15:2–3; 16:3; 18:2–4; 19:2; 20:4–5; 21:4; 22:2–5). Rhetorical questions appear again in 25:3, 4, 6 and 26:14b, c, marking this speech as strongly disputatious. The argument *a fortiori* ("how much less?" vv 5–6) is another element of the disputation speech.

Even so, elements of other *forms* predominate in the speech. Principal among them is the *hymn* or *doxology,* which appears first in 25:2–6, intertwined with rhetorical questions (vv 3, 4, 6), v 4 having the ring of a *wisdom saying* (Fohrer) in the form of a rhetorical question. The whole of 25:2–6 bears a decidedly wisdom cast. More strictly exhibiting the hymnic form is 26:5–13, which is concluded by a more wisdom-like exclamation and a rhetorical question (v 14b, c) expressing a response to the depiction of the power of God by means of the hymn. The participial style characteristic of the hymn is prominent here (vv 7–10), and the focalization is principally upon the figure of God (vv 7–10, 12, 13b).

The intended *function* of the speech, as its sarcastic proemium already announces, is to refute the argument of Job in his previous speech (chaps. 23–24). It addresses, however, only the first theme of Job's speech, his desire to force God into a court of law that will declare Job's innocence. And it picks up only the issue of whether Job's desire to compel God has any legitimacy. That is a side issue, of course; the principal issue for Job personally is whether or not he is innocent; the means by which that innocence can be recognized is secondary. And of course also, Bildad completely ignores the main thrust of Job's last speech, his charge against God that he has abandoned moral governance of his world. That is what has been truly new about Job's argument, and if Job is right, all that Bildad has to say is only whistling in the dark.

The *tonality* of the speech is established by the three exclamations (26:2–3) and the two rhetorical questions (v 4) with which it opens. If anything, the exclamations are even more sarcastic than the rhetorical questions that have featured so commonly in the openings of the speeches (see above on *genre*). Bildad's sarcasm implies that Job's intention in his speech has been to be helpful and wise, which is a jibe perhaps at the reputation of Job that Eliphaz had at the beginning described (4:3–4). To say ironically "How helpful you have been" when one means the opposite is sharper criticism than simply to deny one's opponent's helpfulness. What adds to the sharpness is the recognition that Job's purpose has by no means been "helpful." In attacking God's disregard of social injustice in the world (chap. 24) he has not in the least been trying to "save" or "counsel" anyone, and it is cruelly dismissive of the radicality of Job's program to pretend that his aim is simply to be a pair of helping hands.

By comparison with the opening of the speech, the doxology that constitutes its greater part seems rather neutral in tone, objectively portraying, it appears, a universe far removed from Job and human concerns. Bildad seems to distance himself from feeling in focusing upon the heavens, the underworld, and the events of creation. There is, indeed, a note of awe in his depictions, and they are not free of the language of emotion (cf. "writhe" in 26:5, "tremble" and "be aghast" in v 11). But it is noteworthy that these are the reactions of bystanders to the divine power: those who writhe in Sheol (26:5) are by no means at the receiving end of any divine punishment, but are simply conscious of the naked power of God, just as their dwelling place is naked before him (v 6); and those who trembled and were aghast at the moment of creation were not God's foes but the pillars of heaven, normally noted for their stability, which witnessed the great primordial conflict between God and the forces of chaos. The enemies of God are denied subjectivity: the sea is simply "stilled," Rahab is "crushed," the serpent is "pierced" (vv 12–13)—as if they were mere objects (the syntax that makes them objects grammatically serves the larger program). The whole doxology, then, for all its apparent objectivity, serves as an intimidation of Job, who, according to Bildad, is—despite his professed helpfulness (26:2–4)—a creature helpless before the divine might.

The *nodal verse* of the speech is evidently 25:2a: "A dreadful dominion is his." This is the underlying theme of the doxology: the power of God that instills fear. See further, *Explanation.*

Comment

By the standards of previous speeches in the book, the third speech of Bildad in the Masoretic text (25:2–6) is exceedingly short. It has sometimes been thought that Bildad's brevity is a deliberate sign on the part of the author that the friends have begun to run out of steam (so, e.g., Andersen; against this, see K. Fullerton, "The Original Conclusion to the Book of Job," *ZAW* 42 [1924] 116–35 [121]). Newsom thinks that the disarray is "the author's attempt to represent the interruptive and even overlapping speech of the parties to a conversation that has irretrievably broken down." But the evidences of general disarray in the attribution of speeches from 24:18 through to chap. 28 suggests rather that the text has been subjected to some damage in the course of transmission. We can never be sure, of course, whether our modern rearrangements of the order of the text successfully restore the attributions of speeches in the original text in its final form, especially when the speeches of the three friends have so much in common; but it is necessary for the sake of the exegesis to make decisions, right or wrong, about who is speaking at any point.

Here is an index of views various scholars have taken of how Bildad's third speech is to be reconstructed. If we label the verses attributed by the text to Bildad (25:2–6) as A, the ironic introduction to the speech attributed to Job (26:2–4) as B, the account of God's creative work in the same speech (26:5–14) as C, and the description of the fate of the wicked in Job's subsequent speech (27:13–23) as D, we can see that several different combinations of these four units have been proposed.

A 25:2–6 (Fohrer, Fedrizzi, Andersen, Good)
AC 25:2–6 + 26:5–14 (JB, Siegfried, Ball, Dhorme, Stevenson, Terrien, Pope, Rowley, Gordis, Ravasi, Alonso Schökel–Sicre Díaz, Habel, Newsom; Peake deletes 25:4–6; de Wilde makes 25:4–6 follow 26:5–14)
AD 25:2–6 + 27:13–23 (Hartley)
BCA 26:2–14 + 25:2–6 (Strahan)
BAC 26:2–4 + 25:2–6 + 26:5–14 (Löhr, Steinmann; Duhm and Hölscher delete 26:7–10)
CA 26:5–14 + 25:2–6 (Lefèvre, *SDB,* 4:1078–79)
CAB 26:5–14 + 25:2–6 + 26:2–4 (Tournay, "L'ordre primitif des chapitres XXIV–XXVIII du livre de Job," *RB* 64 [1957] 321–34)

We should not conclude from the variety of these suggestions that none of them is convincing (as does Andersen, who will not entertain them—"if only because the number and variety of competing solutions leave the student quite dizzy"); better to start again when one's head is clear and recognize that there is something of a consensus about what belongs to Bildad, but no consensus about what order the verses should be in—and that it doesn't matter.

As it stands in the present form of the book, Bildad's speech begins abruptly at 25:2; abrupt though he may be in manner, he has previously begun his speeches with an address to Job (8:2; 18:2), and we may suppose that some such proemium once belonged here too (so Rowley, Habel). M. Löhr thought 26:2–4 constituted the missing verses, and these verses certainly have the right air of irony and aggression about them (M. Löhr, "Die drei Bildad-Reden im Buche Hiob," in *Beiträge zur alttestamentlichen Wissenschaft Karl Budde zum siebzigsten Geburtstag am 13. April 1920 überreicht von Freunden und Schülern,* ed. K. Marti, BZAW 34 [Berlin: Töpelmann, 1920] 107–12; so too Hölscher). Although most scholars want to preserve those verses for Job himself, the view is taken here that they are best assigned to Bildad and form the opening of his speech (so too Duhm, Strahan, Hölscher, Kissane).

Though Job does not generally deign to reply to the friends' speeches (cf. on 23:2–7), the friends themselves do take up Job's claims. And here Bildad is responding to Job's continued assertion of his innocence. To be sure, that has not really been the main point of Job's argument in chaps. 23–24. There he had been taking his own innocence for granted, indeed, but his theme had been much more radical and subversive than Bildad has heard. If you have just declared that God is not fit to be the governor of the universe, it is not very shocking to pronounce yourself innocent of the crimes for which you are being punished.

But Bildad's only concern is with the question whether Job, or, indeed, any human being, can possibly be called "righteous" or "clean" in God's sight. And he thinks he can answer that question by scorn and by appeal to the power of God. Neither line of argument is likely to be very effective, for, in the first place, there is nothing foolish about Job's claim; there is no reason in logic why a perfect God should not have created perfect creatures, or *some* perfect creatures at least; and it is not the slightest derogation of divine righteousness to maintain that humans too can be righteous. And in the second place, no amount of appeal to the omnipotence of God can make any contribution to the question of morality, whether human or divine. Dominion and dreadfulness may well be his (25:2), as Job would be the first to agree; but by what standard of reckoning does that make God righteous and Job a maggot (25:6)?—not unless of course you believe that might is right after all.

26:1 The whole of chap. 26 is ascribed to Job in the present form of the book. Most commentators, however, believe that in chaps. 24–28, at the end of the third cycle of speeches, there has been some damage to the text in the course of its transmission. Not only does the orderly succession of speeches break down, but, as the text stands, Job speaks twice (cf. 26:1; 27:1) without any intervening speech from one of the friends, and, more importantly, presents positions (especially on the fate of the wicked, 27:13–23) quite at odds with his consistent views throughout the rest of the book. For these reasons, I have regarded the present verse as an addition to the book, introduced by a copyist after the damage to the sequence had occurred.

2–4 In this proemium, a single person is consistently addressed in all the verbs. Job himself has never addressed any of the friends individually but has spoken to them collectively using plural verbs and pronouns. The exceptions to this rule have been only apparent: in 12:7–8 and 16:3 it seems that Job is putting a sentence in the friends' mouths rather than addressing them himself, and in 21:3 the singular verb seems to be a scribal error, sitting awkwardly as it does in a passage addressing the friends in general, with five other verbs in the plural. The friends of course always address Job in the singular (Eliphaz at 4:2–7; 5:1, 17, 19–27; 15:4–13, 17; 22:3–7, 9–11, 13, 15, 21–28, 30; Bildad at 8:2, 4–8, 10, 21–22; 18:4 [perhaps also in vv 2–3]; Zophar at 11:3–8, 13–19; 20:4), and it seems plain that these lines too must belong to a speech of one of the friends, even if we cannot be certain it is Bildad. (For a defense of the assignment of these verses to Job, see Peake, Driver–Gray, Fohrer, Gordis, de Wilde, Hartley.)

2–3 The strophe, with its two exclamations ("how!") and its rhetorical question ("with whose help?"), is quite sharply ironic in tone and scornful of the previous speaker's abilities. It seems to be a general-purpose denigration of an interlocutor, denying the helpfulness and wisdom of what has just been said. It is unnecessary to look for specific attempts by the previous speaker to "help" or "save" or "counsel"—for such are the general purpose of any speaker. We do not need to understand Bildad as taunting Job that he has represented God as weak and ignorant and himself as offering God support and counsel (as Strahan and Driver–Gray, for example, think). If Job himself is the speaker in vv 2–4, it is he who is the weak and foolish one—though not by his own admission, only in the eyes of the friends; his words would be in that case equally ironic (or at least half ironic and half in earnest, say Fohrer and de Wilde) as if the speaker were Bildad. For a minority view that Job's words are in earnest, and a genuine confession of his powerlessness, cf. P. L. Redditt, "Reading the Speech Cycles in the Book of Job," *HAR* 14 (1994) (= *Biblical and Other Studies in Honor of Reuben Ahroni, on the Occasion of His Sixtieth Birthday,* ed. T. J. Lewis [Columbus, OH: Melton Center for Jewish Studies, Ohio State Univ., 1994]) 205–14.

"Help" (עזר) is what one needs to become "strong" (as in 2 Chr 26:15; Pss 28:7; 46:1 [2]; Nah 3:9) and when one is not strong (Job 35:9); for the association of "save" (ישׁע hiph) or "salvation" (ישׁועה) with strength, cf. Pss 21:1 [2]; 86:16; Isa 30:15; 63:1. On the arm as a symbol of strength, cf. 22:8, 9; 38:15. On "insight" or "effective counsel" (תושׁיה), see *Note* 5:12.a (the term is also at 6:13; 11:6; 12:16).

4 If Job's words had been effectual and wise, one might have supposed him to speak with divine inspiration, as Elihu declares: "It is the spirit in a man, the breath [נשׁמה, as here] of the Almighty, that makes him understand" (32:8; cf. Prov 20:27)—as well, of course, the principle that keeps one alive (33:4). But the ironic rhetorical question here implies that Job has had no inspiration, human or divine, for his speech. It is doubtful that there is any reference to the claim of Eliphaz to divine revelation (4:12–19; so Gordis). But readers will recall that long ago Job was depicted by Eliphaz as famous for his support for others, instructing, giving vigor, lifting up, strengthening (4:3–4). Not now, says Bildad; whatever the past abilities of Job may have been, now he has no gifts of wisdom, empowerment, or counsel.

25:2–6 After Job's rebarbative speech (chaps. 23–24), Bildad will try to raise the tone of the dialogue by declaiming a hymn in the classic style of the doxology (Terrien). But first, in this strophe (vv 2–6), following the proemium of 26:2–4, he announces the topic sentence of the whole speech, "A dreadful dominion is his" (v 2), and declares, with rhetorical questions that are even harder to challenge than naked assertions, that humans cannot be righteous in the sight of God. This theological conviction is, however, uttered not for its own sake but strictly for its applicability to Job and its capacity to deny everything that motivates him—his sense of injured innocence and his craving for vindication.

2 As befits the style, Bildad's language is as lapidary and indeterminate as a haiku: "Rule and fear are with him; he makes peace in the heights." What *exactly* does that mean? Does it mean anything, exactly?

"Rule" and "fear" sit together uneasily. For "rule" (המשׁל) is what is "with" (עם) the one who rules, whereas "fear" (פחד) is not "with him" but with those he rules by his power. פחד can indeed mean "object of dread" (as in Gen 31:42, where it is God himself; Ps 31:12 [11]), but it can hardly mean that here, since the "fear" is "with" God. The phrase must form a hendiadys; i.e., it has the sense of "a dominion of dread, a rule that inspires fear" (so also Duhm, Gordis "awesome dominion," Good "dreaded rule," Moffatt "he wields a dread authority").

The second half of the colon must be an example, a specification, of God's "dreadful dominion" (on the parallelism of greater precision, see on 24:9), for presumably Bildad does not think God's rule is confined to heaven. Peace through terror is God's style, according to Bildad, peace through force of arms (Job, more humanely, had made a *contrast* between "terror" [פחד] and "peace" [שׁלום] in 21:9). To "make peace" (עשׂה שׁלום) is an unusual phrase (only Isa 27:5 and, by emendation, Prov 10:10; normally שׁלם hiph is used). It suggests here the imposition of peace upon warring factions, rather than simply victory over opponents. There are ample references in the OT to a mythological tale of a primeval conflict, especially against a monster of chaos sometimes called Rahab (cf. 9:13; 26:11–13; Ps 89:10; Isa 51:9; and for war in heaven, cf. also Isa 24:21–22; Dan 10:13, 20; so Davidson, Peake, Strahan). If the allusion here is to that myth (and there will be repeated references to it in the remainder of the speech, at 26:11–13), Bildad suggests by his term "makes peace" that it was no matched conflict of equals in which there was any danger to the rule of God; it was not a struggle between two great powers but the suppression of a rebellion by the supreme ruler, whose rule was never seriously in doubt. Though the present tense, "he makes peace," is used by most of the English versions, the reference of the participle is clearly to a single action (cf., e.g., "creating" [בורא], of the act of creation, in Isa 42:5; 45:18; and the participles of 26:7–10); it would be better to use a past tense, as in the *Translation* above, "he imposed peace." It is not so likely that his "peace" refers more generally to "the celestial order" (Habel), still less to the stilling of the atmospheric elements (cf. Davidson).

If the traditional wisdom about God is that he rules in awe-inspiring might, imposing his iron will even upon supernatural powers who may be fractious—and Bildad knows an old story that supports this wisdom—it follows that humans cannot hope to match God's standards and cannot be righteous and "clean" (v 4). "Bildad does not appear to touch Job's argument as to God's rule of the world. He only seeks to subdue the immeasurable arrogance of Job in thinking that he would be found guiltless if placed before the judgment-seat of God" (Davidson). Such is Bildad's argument. It is not that "no person can hope to comprehend God's enterprises" (Andersen), or that it is improper that Job should criticize him (Driver–Gray), or that this is a rejection of Job's assertion that there are many cases of injustice on earth (Hartley). The issue is simply Job's claim of innocence, as the climactic sentences in vv 4 and 6 make plain.

3 Plainly, for Bildad, God governs by force. Even "making peace" (v 2) is for him an act of power, a matter of imposing one's will, not of negotiating an end to a conflict. So a large standing army is essential for God's rule to be effective, and of course in Hebrew thought it is the stars that are the army of God, the "host (צבא, army) of heaven," his troops (גדוד) that he holds in readiness (not "the angels," as GNB); see also Judg 5:20; Isa 40:26; Ecclus 43:9–10. In 19:12 God's troops (גדוד) that Job felt ranged against him were of course diseases and misfortunes; but Bildad is speaking here not of them (as against Fohrer), but in cosmic terms, and the "innumerable" troops he refers to must be the stars. For the idea of their uncountability, cf. Gen 15:5; Deut 28:62; 1 Chr 27:23; Heb 11:12.

"Upon whom," he asks, "does his light not rise?" meaning that there is no creature in all God's dominions to whom the light of the stars is invisible; since the stars are God's army, all creatures therefore must reckon themselves as under the surveillance of God's army. This is a more concrete understanding of the text than one that sees the "light" as simply "the sign *par excellence* of the divine power" (Terrien), and a more probable one than finds in "light" a reference to the sun (Davidson) or a symbol of "warmth, joy, and life" (Hartley). The language does not mean that no one is hidden from God, that "no-one can secretly withdraw himself from His dominion" (Driver–Gray), all his creatures being "open and laid bare to the eyes of him with whom we have to do" (Heb 4:13; cf. Peake). Since it is the stars that are the troops, it does not make sense to ask "to which of them does not his light extend" (as NAB), as if he had some other source of light (the sun is of course not in view here). And it is not a question of "Against whom does his lightning not surge forth?" (JB; similarly Terrien), since not everyone is subject to the assaults of God, though all are in his power. It is simply a matter of the inescapability of creatures from the dread rule of their creator, the world being a giant panopticon and its denizens being supervised by the innumerable company of God's heavenly troops.

4 "It is hard to escape the feeling that for Bildad the power of God was equated with his purity" (Rowley). Indeed, the only way this verse can be connected with what precedes is to assume that Bildad believes that because humans are much weaker than God they must also be less morally strong, moral fallibility being a correlate of physical frailty (it is less certain that human mortality is thought of as the cause of human corruption, as Terrien). This is no different, of course, from what we have already heard from Eliphaz in 4:17 and 15:14. It may sound similar to Job's words in 9:2 and 14:4, but Job has a different thought in mind in both places (as against Fohrer, Terrien, Pope): in 9:2 he means that it is impossible to gain vindication from God—which is a mile from meaning that no one is just in God's sight, since it signifies only that God will not make any acknowledgment of their innocence. And in 14:4 he assumes, for the sake of argument, the view of the friends that human beings are as a class "unclean," and uses that as a reason that God should not persecute them for their wrongdoing; again, this is a far cry from affirming the impossibility of human innocence, for his own righteousness is a cardinal point of Job's whole position.

The first colon is exactly Job's in 9:2, and the second takes all its language from Eliphaz's line in 15:14. The issue for Bildad is not, of course, as it was for Job, whether humans can be *declared* innocent by God but whether they can in fact *be* so. So it is not a matter of whether one can "be in the right before God" (NJPS, Terrien) or "be cleared of guilt" (NJPS) or "How can a man be justified in God's sight?" (NEB) or "Could anyone think God regards him as virtuous?" (JB). Nor is it a matter of "having a righteousness independent of God's" (Driver; cf. Terrien). It is simply whether in comparison with God's standards any mortal can in any degree *be* "righteous." The term used for "human person" (אנוש) is often said to have connotations of weakness, but that is probably incorrect. For the term "clean" (זכה) and its normal ethical connotations, see on 15:14. For the phrase "one born of woman" (ילוד אשה), and whether it implies human weakness or simply mortality ("That which is born also must die" [Newsom]), see on 14:1.

5 Here moral purity is linked not with power but with physical brightness. The brightness of the moon and stars is no certificate of their moral cleanness (both הלל "shine" and זכה "be clean" are of course being used metaphorically). In 4:18 and 15:15 it is God's servants, the angels, who are not "trusted" by God, and in 15:15 it is the heavens that are not "pure" (זכה) in his sight.

6 Bildad is nothing if not brutal. Humans, he says, are so impure—which is to say, ethically unclean—that compared with God they are "maggots" and "worms," which are literally unclean, being associated with things that are dead; these are terms that "have the smell of death about them" (Hartley). In the OT, "maggots" (רמה), the larvae of various beetles, are always denizens of the grave (17:14; 21:26; 24:20; Isa 14:11; also *1 En.* 46:6; Jdt 16:17; Ecclus 7:17; Mark 9:48; רמה in Job 7:5 is probably "pus") or at least agents of decay (Exod 16:24) (see W.

S. McCullough, *IDB,* 4:878). "Worms" (תולעה) appear with the same connotation in Isa 14:11 and 66:24, though in some other places they connote merely insignificance (Ps 22:6 [7]; Isa 41:14). Here the association with "maggots," as well as the sense of vv 4–5, suggests that humanity is being labeled as positively unclean, not merely insignificant (as Fohrer, Rowley). The term בן־אדם "son of man" for a human being occurs in Job elsewhere only at 16:21. On Bildad's perspective on humanity, see also the incisive article of S. Lasine, "Bird's-Eye and Worm's-Eye Views of Justice in the Book of Job," *JSOT* 42 (1988) 29–53, and the *Explanation* below.

26:5–14 If these verses are rightly attributed to Bildad (see at the beginning of this *Comment*), their purpose is to develop further the idea of God's "fearful dominion" in 25:2. Bildad's response to Job's indictment of God as an irresponsible governor of the universe has been, in 25:2–6, to hymn God's power and denigrate human goodness by comparison with it. The doxology functions as an avoidance technique for the uncomfortable criticisms of a Job. Now Bildad continues, in a more elaborated doxology, the theme of God's power over the natural world, especially as revealed at creation—though, perhaps surprisingly, without any concomitant obloquy upon the human race.

5 Having cast his gaze upon the moon and stars, God's troops—which keep humans mindful of their subordinate role but which themselves are not free from contamination—Bildad looks to the lowest parts of the earth to see how God's writ runs there. There too, in the underworld of Sheol, God's "fearful dominion" (25:2) reigns (it is not that God is *present* there, as Dhorme and Terrien suggest). The dead themselves, though they are for the most part incapable of normal human emotions (cf. 14:21–22) and experience only an "attenuated half-life" (Rowley), nevertheless writhe (חול) in terror before the naked power of the deity. Not for Bildad the Joban picture of tranquillity and ease in the afterlife (3:13; cf. 3:17–18; 7:21). Amos (9:2) and the Psalms (139:8) indeed depict the power of God as reaching as far as Sheol, but Bildad's is the most comprehensive statement in the OT of God's fearsome control of the underworld.

The inhabitants of Sheol are here called Rephaim (רפאים). The term is used several times in the OT for the dead in general (as in Ps 88:11 [10], in parallel with מתים "the dead"; and in Isa 26:19, where the underworld is called "the land of the Rephaim"; also Prov 2:18; 9:18; 21:16). In Isa 14:9, however, the Rephaim are specifically dead kings (they are parallel to "rulers of the earth), and the same may be true at Isa 26:14 (where the Rephaim may refer to the "lords" of v 13); in Ugaritic the term also occurs, to denote a line of dead kings and heroes (RS 34.126 = *KTU* 1.161; perhaps cf. also Ezek 32:27, though the term is not used). And in Deut 2:11; 3:11, 13 the Rephaim are a race of giant inhabitants of pre-Israelite Moab (cf. also Gen 14:5; 15:20). See further, M. S. Smith, *ABD,* 5:674–76; S. B. Parker, *IDBSup,* 739; O. Loretz, "'Ugaritic and Biblical Literature': Das Paradigma des Mythos von den *rpum*—Rephaim," in *Ugarit and the Bible: Proceedings of the International Symposium on Ugarit and the Bible, Manchester, September 1992,* ed. G. Brooke, A. H. W. Curtis, and J. F. Healey, UBL 11 (Münster: Ugarit, 1994) 175–224. With that complex background to the term, here in Job the meaning could be that even mighty kings, now dead, remain in awe of God (so LXX, Pesh, Vg, Tg, Duhm, and Strahan translate with "giants," Symmachus with θεομάχοι "those who fought with God," and Moffatt "Before him the primaeval giants writhe"); but it is perhaps more likely that it is all the inhabitants of Sheol, the "shades," who are in mind (so too Strauss). The word is connected, if only by way of folk etymology, with the verb רפה "sink, relax," and is applied to the underworld shades as insubstantial versions of their former selves.

The cosmology presupposed here is of the earth floating on the cosmic sea, which is connected with the ordinary sea since it has "inhabitants" (שׁכניה), fish and sea monsters, no doubt. Beneath that sea is the underworld, Sheol, where the shades live (see T. H. Gaster, *IDB*, 1:703, 787–88). Sheol is the deepest place of all (cf. 11:8; according to 38:16–17, its gates lie in the region of the "springs of the sea" and the "recesses of the deep").

6 Deep though Sheol may be within the earth (the idiom "deep as Sheol" is in Isa 7:11; cf. Amos 9:2), and hidden from the sight of humans, it is not hidden from God. It is "naked" (ערום is metaphorical only here), and by its other name, Abaddon, "destruction," it is "without covering" (אין כסות, the phrase used of the poor in 24:7 and 31:19). Cf. Prov 15:11, where Sheol and Abaddon are "before" (נגד), i.e., open before, God. Abaddon is also in Job at 28:22 (parallel with "death") and at 31:12 (the fire that consumes as far as Abaddon). In Ps 88:11–12 (12–13) God's faithfulness is not recounted in the grave or in Abaddon, for it is "the land of forgetfulness." In 1QH 3.32 the rivers of Belial break through to Abaddon, and in 1QM 14.18 a burning fire is kindled "in the dark places of the Abaddons, in the Abaddons of Sheol."

Sheol's openness to God means not just that he can see what is going on there but, more to the point of the present speech, that the lower world is not outside the divine jurisdiction (Terrien), and his dominion is known and feared there—as it is in the heavens (25:2). Cf. similarly, Homer, *Iliad* 20.61–66.

7–13 If Job wants to take the measure of God's power, let him consider the facts of creation, says Bildad. They are primordial acts that we seem to be hearing of here, not the regular maintenance of the cosmic order (as against, e.g., Dhorme). Though participles are used throughout vv 7–10 ("stretching out," "hanging" [v 7], "binding" [v 8], "covering," "spreading out" [v 9], "drawing a circle" [v 10]), it is plain that these are works of creation, the participles being used, as is normal, to replace verbs of a single past action (see *Note* 25:2.c on "imposed," and cf. 9:8–9; among English versions, only NJPS uses past tenses consistently throughout these verses). And all creation, as it is here described, tends toward a single significance: all of it demonstrates the power of God, which causes trembling and astonishment in all who witness it (v 11). This is what Bildad means by God's "dreadful dominion" (25:2), and this is what Job, in his selfish demand for personal justification, has woefully neglected. If Job is to speak properly of God, he will speak respectfully of him and without presumption, in fear and trembling; he will not attempt to storm heaven with his cry of innocence (23:3–7).

7 The sky is here viewed as a tent that is stretched out over its poles; נטה "stretch out" is commonly used in connection with a tent (e.g., Gen 12:8; Jer 10:20) as well as with the heavens (Job 9:8; Isa 40:22; 44:24; 45:12; 51:13; Jer 10:12; 51:15; Zech 12:1; Ps 104:2; 1QH 1.9); see further N. C. Habel, "He who stretches out the heavens" [Isa 40:21–23; 42:5; 44:24; 45:12; 48:13; 51:13; Job 26; Pss 18; 104; 144], *CBQ* 34 (1972) 417–30. There are "pillars of the heavens" at the four corners of the earth (see on v 11), but what supports the "tent" across the vast expanse of the sky, from one horizon to the other? Nothing! There is no center pole to the tent that is the sky. Here then is an example of the power of God, that he can spread out the skies with nothing to hold them up. The "north" (צפון) is presumably heaven itself (so too Fohrer), the "canopy of the sky" (NEB); it is "not a direction but a spatial term for the high heavens, the place of God's throne" (Hartley; cf. also Hartley, *ISBE,* 3:550–51). Others have thought that the "north" was the northern part of the heavens, containing the great constellations (so Davidson, Dhorme), perhaps the *stella polaris,* the axle of the Wain around which the constellations seem to revolve (Terrien) or (less probably) the heaven of clouds (as E. Vogt, "*Ṣāfôn = caelum nubibus obductum,*" *Bib* 34 [1953] 426; J. de Savignac, "Note sur le sens du terme *ṣāphôn* dans quelques passages de la Bible," *VT* 3 [1953] 95–96, as also in Isa 14:13; Pss 48:2 [3]; 89:12 [13]; Ezek 1:4). Others still have suggested that the reference is to the great mountain of the north, known as Zaphon (i.e., "north" [צפון]), and attested as the dwelling place of the gods (cf. the mount of assembly in the far north, Isa 14:13) and so a part both of earth and of heaven (so Fohrer), and others, less probably, that it refers to the northern part of the earth, naming the part instead of the whole (Duhm, Strahan). J. J. M. Roberts ("*ṢAPÔN* in Job 26,7," *Bib* 56 [1975] 554–57) argued that the mountain of the "north" is synonymous with "the earth," the image being of a mountain whose peak is visible but whose base is shrouded by clouds, as if it were hanging in the air. But this is to ignore the fact that the "north" is "stretched out" while the earth is "suspended."

8 The clouds are conceived of as "the waterskins of the sky" (as in 38:37). At creation, God wrapped up all the rain waters in the clouds, but—so great is his power—they did not burst, for all the weight of the water. See E. F. Sutcliffe, "The Clouds as Water-Carriers in Hebrew Thought," *VT* 3 (1953) 99–103. In Prov 30:4 also, God at creation "wrapped up" (צרר, as here) the waters, but in a garment. A comparable act is God's gathering the waters of the sea into a bottle (Ps 33:7). In Gen 1:6–7, of course, it is the firmament that is thought to hold back the rain from falling on the earth.

The verb "wrap up" (צרר) has been used in 18:7 of a vigorous stride being "hobbled" (also in 20:22); in 14:17 iniquity is thought of as being sealed up in a "bag" (צרור). It is used of wineskins in Josh 9:4. The verb "burst, crack open" (בקע) is used also in Gen 7:11 of the breaking open of the fountains of the great deep at the flood. We may distinguish, strictly speaking, between individual "clouds" (עב, here in the plural) and the cloud mass (ענן, here in the singular) (so R. B. Y. Scott, "Metereological Phenomena and Terminology in the Old Testament," *ZAW* 64 [1952] 11–25 [24–25]); but since the image throughout the verse is entirely of individual clouds as containers of the rain we should not press the distinction here. But v 9 is different.

9 The control room for this mighty operation of God's power is hidden from human eyes: the throne of God is separated from the world of humans by cloud. This arrangement is part of God's creation design—to cover the "face," i.e., the outside front, of the divine throne with cloud. God is often said to dwell in clouds (see on 22:14; 2 Sam 22:12 = Ps 18:11 [12]; Ps 97:2), and the cloud on Sinai is an earthly counterpart to the heavenly cloud (Exod 19:9; 24:16); so fixed is the association of God's dwelling place with cloud that there is even, surprisingly, a cloud in the Jerusalem temple (1 Kgs 8:10–11 || 2 Chr 5:14), where also

God dwells. Here in Job the precise term for a cloud mass (ענן) is used; for the divine throne is not concealed behind a single cloud but by cloud in general (as also in Ps 97:2). The cloud is "his cloud" also at 37:15.

10 The cosmology implied here is not entirely clear. The general Near Eastern conception was of the earth as a disk floating on an ocean. The furthest horizon therefore lies upon the oceans, and the solid firmament of Gen 1 will rest upon those waters all around that horizon (even in ancient times it was of course known that the horizon recedes as one approaches it, and so the reference must be to the "furthest" horizon, i.e., the rim of the earth's surface). In Prov 8:27 we find God at creation drawing a circle—which must be that horizon—on the face of the deep. In Gen 1:2 there was, before creation, darkness over the whole face of the deep water, and God's creative act was to separate light and darkness, as day and night, two realities that alternate in the same physical space. Here, on the other hand, it appears that the horizon is also the dividing line between light and darkness and that beyond the horizon there is a permanent area of darkness: "within the circle is the region of light, without it the region of darkness" (Peake). Thus the "confine" (חק) that is "drawn as a circle" (חג) is "as far as" (עד) the "completeness, end" (תכלית), which means to say "boundary," of light and darkness (lit. "light with darkness," אור עם־חשך). Cf. also on 38:19.

Again it is evident that it is creation that is being spoken of, not the regular procession of day and night (against, for example, de Wilde). It is evidence of the creator's might that he was able to establish these fundamentals of cosmology.

11–12 When—in primeval times, since we are hearing consistently about creation here—did God rebuke anyone so violently as to astound the pillars of heaven? It can only have been when he smote the cosmic monster Rahab, for that battle was the only hostile event at creation. The pillars of heaven themselves had no role to play in that conflict; they were innocent bystanders, witnesses to the wrath of the creator god (he did not rebuke *them* [as against Rowley], for we know of nothing they did wrong). The term for God's "rebuke" (גערה) does not signify so much a moral judgment as an expression of anger (as A. A. Macintosh, "A Consideration of Hebrew גער," *VT* 19 [1969] 471–79; S. C. Reif, "A Note on גער," *VT* 21 [1971] 241–44; A. Caquot, *TDOT,* 3:49–53) or even "explosive blast" (see especially J. M. Kennedy, "The Root *GʿR* in the Light of Semantic Analysis," *JBL* 106 [1987] 47–64; cf. also P. J. van Zijl, "A Discussion of the Root *gāʿar,*" in *Biblical Essays: Proceedings of the 12th Meeting of De Ou Testamentiese Wekgemeenskap in Suid Afrika* [Pretoria: Pro Rege & Pers Beperk, 1969] 56–63). In a cosmic context the word occurs also at Ps 18:16 (15) (|| 2 Sam 22:16), but there it is not exactly creation that is referenced; rather, the psalmist envisages God replaying creation by way of delivering him from his enemies. There his "explosive blast" is parallel to "the blast of the breath of your nostril" (נשמת רוח אפך); here too the breath or wind (רוח) of God seems to play some part in the rebuke (v 13). In Isa 50:2 and Nah 1:4 God's "blast" (גערה) dries up the sea and turns rivers into a desert; in Ps 106:9 it dries up the Red Sea. So it is evidently a strong, hot wind (NJPS translates "blast"; in Ps 104:7 it is parallel to thunder, but that does not mean that it itself is a thunderclap, as Gordis thinks). If the "blast" is conceived of as something physical, like a mighty wind from God, rather than as a (verbal ?) "rebuke," it makes better sense of the pillars of heaven trembling under its onslaught. It is interesting that in the Babylonian creation myth, *Enuma elish* (4.96–102; *ANET,* 67a), the creator god Marduk uses, as one of his forms of attack upon the chaos monster Tiamat, the stratagem of blowing a hot wind into her mouth, thus distending her and enabling him to shoot an arrow into her. But the parallel with the Hebrew image of the hot wind is probably coincidental.

The "pillars of heaven" (עמודי שמים) are referred to only here in the OT (but commonly in Egyptian texts; cf. H. Grapow, *Die bildlichen Ausdrücke des Ägyptischen: Vom Denken und Dichten einer altorientalischen Sprache* [Leipzig: Hinrichs, 1924] 26–28), but they must be the same as the "foundations of the heavens" (מוסדות השמים) at 2 Sam 22:8 (parallel Ps 18:8 has מוסדי הרים "the foundations of the hills"). Like the pillars of the earth (see on 9:6), the pillars of heaven support it from beneath. They are presumably conceived of as mountains near the rim of the world (the very edge of the world is ocean, according to v 10, and so there cannot be mountains there). Cf. in classical mythology the Atlas mountain (cf. Silius Italicus 1.22) or Etna (cf. Pindar, *Pythia* 1.39 [2]).

The stilling of the sea as an act of creation implies a tempestuous ocean, perhaps as preexisting material for the creation. In any case, it plainly needed to be subdued, and the stilling of the sea is the sign of God's victory. (In Gen 1:2 a wind moving over the face of the waters also implies a turbulent sea, but there is no thought there of a divine conflict with it.)

On the sea monster Rahab, see on 9:13. In Ps 89:11 she is "crushed" (דכא) by God, and in Isa 51:9 (1QIsa[a]) she is "shattered" (מחץ), as here. מחץ seems to be a general poetic term for destroying (used absolutely in Deut 32:39); the object can be heads (Num 24:17; Judg 5:26; Pss 68:21 [22]; 110:6; Hab 3:13) or loins (Deut 33:11) or enemies in general (Ps 110:5 [perhaps also v 6]; 2 Sam 22:39 || Ps 18:38 [39]; cf. Job 5:18). The only weapons connected with the verb are arrows (Num 24:8), but that need not mean that the verb means specifically "pierce," and we do not know that it means "cut to pieces" (NIV).

To defeat the primordial sea monster, God used more than sheer force, though simple power continues to be the overarching theme of the whole speech. His "understanding" (תבונה) or "wisdom" has frequently been glossed (e.g., by Fohrer, Pope, de Wilde, Habel) by reference to the craft employed by Marduk, called "wisest of the gods," in defeating Tiamat (*Enuma elish* 4.93–104; *ANET,* 67a); but it is a natural enough idea in any culture to represent the work of creation as demanding extraordinary wisdom (cf. also Jer 10:12 where God made the world "by his power" and "by his understanding" [בכחו and בתבונתו, as here]). "His victory is due not simply to his might, but also to his intelligence, which chaos lacks" (Duhm).

13 We are still in the same mythological picture here (as against Duhm, for example, who thinks the text is now dealing with the present); the slaying of the serpent shows clearly enough that the setting is still primordial times. But the idea of the primeval conflict being played out under dark clouds and of victory for the deity being announced by the clearing of the sky is an unparalleled one. The fleeing serpent (נחש בריח) is known also from Isa 27:1, where it is called Leviathan, the "twisting" (עקלתון) serpent, and associated with the sea "dragon" (תנין). There these mythological beings are identities for Egypt and Assyria, but here of course the reference is to the conquest of chaos that is effected by the acts of creation. As everywhere in this chapter, the theme is the power of God, and the vignettes of creative acts since v 7 have all earned their place in the speech as illustrations of the topic sentence of 25:2: "A dreadful dominion is his."

14 But even these acts of power are far from displaying the full sovereignty of God. They are only the edges (קצת) of his power, as if its outward expressions were somehow less potent than the thing itself. What is heard by humans, what survives in the reports the old myths tell about God, is not the full force of his rebuke (v 11) but only a whisper or echo of it. The quintessential "thunder" (רעם) of his power, the naked force, is beyond human conceiving (בין hithpo "consider diligently," as in 11:11; 23:15). For Bildad, God's power is no quiet influence, not a settled control or an infallible design, but the exercise of a strident and rumbustious force. *Allah akbar,* God is great, says Bildad, and that is the end of every matter. It is not so much that a contrast is being drawn between the acts of God in creation and his acts in the life of humans and peoples, "infinitely greater and moreover less comprehensible than his creative acts" (Fohrer), nor that there is a contrast between natural and revealed theology, with "the universe only a mirror of the divine magnificence and not the transcription of his commandments" (Terrien). The contrast is wholly between the power that is visible in the tradition of the creative acts of God and the unseen power that can be assumed to lie at the center of his being and that drives these acts of force and violence.

With the tricolon of this verse, Bildad's third speech, as it has been reconstructed here (consisting of 26:2–4; 25:2–6; 26:5–14), comes to a close. It is the only tricolon in the speech, and a tricolon is not infrequently a marker of closure (see *Note* 21:17.f). The doxology has run its course, objectively (so to speak) rehearsing marvelous acts of divine power; how can it ever end? Only by closing the album of fading snapshots of great deeds long past and addressing the audience with a "Lo!" (הן), only by turning to the human response. Without the human acknowledgment of the divine power, these acts are somewhat nugatory. No one can conceive the full force of his power, but it is enough for Job to acknowledge that it exists for him to see the error of demanding from such a God a certificate of innocence—or indeed anything at all, for that matter. A doxology is not just a praise of God—at least a doxology that is spoken in the presence of others or written in a text; it makes a demand upon its hearers or readers, even if it is only to join in the praise or to acknowledge it. In Job, doxologies have a sharper point than that (cf., e.g., 12:13–25); and here too Bildad's doxology has the goal of putting Job in his place and denying him the right to vindication. Fine words about God, even true ones, may be instruments of human power—but that is no more than what we have seen over and over again throughout this book of Job.

Explanation

Bildad's speech has here been taken to be not only the few verses assigned to him in the Masoretic text (25:2–6) but also chap. 26, which has been traditionally ascribed to Job. The materials of these chapters have been rearranged in this order: 26:1–6; 25:2–6; 26:5–14. For an explanation of these proposals, see at the beginning of the *Comment* and on 26:1.

Bildad's speech professes to reply to Job's speech of chaps. 23–24, just concluded. Its tone seems at first oddly disjointed, beginning as it does with sarcastic depreciation of Job and then continuing with a high-sounding doxology about the power of God. But that is only an appearance, for Bildad's single-minded purpose from beginning to end is to deflect the force of Job's arguments and to expose Job as a pretentious man incapable of accepting his own creatureliness.

Job's last speech has had two main thrusts: the first is Job's desire to win vindication for himself from an inaccessible God (chap. 23), the second to merge his own fate as an innocent man who can never find vindication with that of humanity at large, which lives its life out without attracting the divine attention, whether for punishment or reward (chap. 24). The outcome of that speech has been that Job has charged God with cosmic negligence—and ultimately as being himself effectively one of those rebels against the light pictured in 24:13–17.

It is only against the background of that speech that Bildad's can be properly understood and evaluated. His move is to pour scorn on Job as an unclean and powerless being compared to the divine purity and might. For him, Job's speech has been hopelessly unsuccessful (26:2–4) because he has not taken stock of God's holiness (25:4–6) and power (25:2–3; 26:5–14). How can Job hope to win vindication from God when no human can be righteous or innocent before him (25:4)? How can Job envisage an assault on heaven, a carrying of his case to the heavenly court, a wresting of justice from his persecutor, when God rules his universe with a "dreadful dominion" (25:2)?

It matters nothing to Bildad that, by the end of his speech, Job's concern has no longer been with himself and his own vindication but with a much more serious cause, the question of whether God, if he will not even keep days of assize (24:1), is fit to govern. To respond that God's power is absolute, that even the most spectacular exhibitions of his might that we know of are but the "fringes of his ways" (26:14), does not touch the issue at all.

We have had plenty of opportunity before to observe the friends speaking at cross purposes, but things have become very much more serious here. For the place Bildad's absolutism has led him to is a complete denial of human worth and an affirmation that power is at the center of the divine essence. These are ugly theologies, and if they are the best that can be said against Job's critique of the divine rule it is a sorry world we live in.

Bildad's speech is the *reductio ad absurdum* of absolutism. Every complaint about the world order, every criticism about justice delayed, every doubt about divine integrity, is ruled out of order, if divine power fills the whole horizon. If all questions about the evils that beset humans are subordinated to affirmations about divine might—which consists essentially of works of cosmic dimensions and deeds of violence against enemies—the result is Bildad's twin assertions: the universe is ruled with a dread dominion, and humans are no better than maggots (cf. Calvin's famous description of a human as a "worm five feet in length" [*Institutes,* 1.5.4, though not in the standard translation by Henry Beveridge]).

This is how we know Bildad is in the wrong—not because he does not address the points that Job has made nor because of some logical flaw in his arguments, but because of the conclusions his position leads him to. He tells lies about God, for no God worth the name will want to rule by terror, nor to be the god of a race of maggots. He tells lies about humans too, for humans know of a God who can be delighted in (22:26), a God who saves the lowly (22:29), a God of encouragements (15:11), a God who does not reject the pious (8:20). And humans know too that they are not worms and maggots: the Bildad who addresses Job in this speech, with sarcasm and self-assurance, is no maggot either, but a powerful and self-determining man who thinks he must damn humanity in order to defend God.

Job's Ninth Speech (27:1–6, 11–12)

Bibliography

Dhorme, P. "Les chapitres XXV–XXVIII du Livre de Job." *RB* 33 (1924) 343–56. **Giesebrecht, F.** *Der Wendepunkt des Buches Hiob, Capitel 27 und 28.* Diss., Greifswald, 1879. **Reventlow, H. G.** "Tradition und Redaktion in Hiob 27 im Rahmen der Hiobreden des Abschnittes Hi 24–27." *ZAW* 94 (1982) 279–93. **Tournay, R.** "L'ordre primitif des chapitres XXIV–XXVIII du livre de Job." *RB* 64 (1957) 321–34. **Witte, M.** *Philologische Notizen zu Hiob 21–27.* BZAW 234. Berlin: de Gruyter, 1995. ———. *Vom Leiden zur Lehre: Der dritte Redegang (Hiob 21–27) und die Redaktionsgeschichte des Hiobbuches.* BZAW 230. Berlin: de Gruyter, 1994. **Wolfers, D.** "Job: The Third Cycle: Dissipating a Mirage." *DD* 16 (1987–88) 217–26; 17 (1988–89) 19–25.

Translation

1 *And Job answered and said:*[a]

2 [a]*By the life of God,*[b] *who*[c] *has denied*[d] *me justice,*[e]
as the Almighty lives, who has made my life bitter,
3 [a]*I swear,*[b] *so long as*[c] *there is life in me,*[d]
and God's breath is in my nostrils,
4 *my lips surely*[a] *speak no wrong,*
my tongue utters[b] *no deceit.*
5 *Far be it from me*[a] *to reckon*[b] *you right;*
until I die[c] *I shall not abandon my claim to innocence.*[d]
6 *I maintain my integrity and shall not give it up;*
my heart does not reproach me[a] *for any of my days.*[b]

11 [a]*I will teach you*[b] *what is in God's power;*[c]
the purpose of[d] *the Almighty I will not conceal.*
12 [a]*If*[b] *all of you have seen them,*[c]
why do you speak this empty talk?[d]

Notes

1.a. ויסף איוב שאת משלו ויאמר "And Job took up his discourse and said." This would be an appropriate introduction to a speech of Job's that followed immediately on a prior speech of Job's, as is the case in the MT (see the heading at 26:1). But it is a consequence of the decision in this commentary to assign chap. 26 to Bildad that the present verse should be emended to וַיַּעַן אִיּוֹב וַיֹּאמַר

"And Job answered and said" (as also Beer [*BHK*]), to match previous speech openings such as 21:1; 23:1. The Eng. versions in the main translate the MT, but NAB and GNB delete the verse altogether, simply indicating that Job begins to speak at this point. The verse is deleted or regarded as secondary also by Duhm, Peake, Dhorme, Hölscher, Fohrer, Terrien, Pope, Gordis, de Wilde, Sicre Díaz, and Hartley. For comment on the verse, cf. *Notes* and *Comment* on 29:1, where it also occurs.

2.a. NAB prefixes this verse with 27:11.

2.b. The oath formula חי "as [he] lives" is found only here with אל as the name of God (it is usually יהוה, but in 2 Sam 2:27 it is האלהים). The form is חַי when God is referred to, חֵי when it is humans (cf. M. Greenberg, "The Hebrew Oath Particle *Ḥay/Ḥē*," *JBL* 76 [1957] 34–39 [35]). The *Translation* above follows the view of Greenberg, that the formula means "by the life of" God, חי being a noun, not the adj חַי "living." See also G. Giesen, *Die Wurzel* šbʿ "*schwören*," BBB 56 (Bonn: Hanstein, 1981) 27.

2.c. The relative pronoun אֲשֶׁר "who" is understood here and in the next colon (cf. GKC, §155f).

2.d. סור hiph is "remove" or "set aside" or "deny" (JB, NAB, NIV) or "refuse" (GNB) or "take away" (KJV, RSV, JPS) or "deprive" (NJPS) or "withhold" (NAB); see *DCH*, vol. 6, *s.v.*

2.e. משפטי could be "my justice" in the abstract sense (cf. JB, NJPS, NEB, NIV, GNB), "my right" (JPS, RSV, Pope) or, more concretely, "my case" (cf. Habel "deprived me of litigation").

3.a. The verse is moved to follow v 5 by Duhm, Moffatt. It is deleted altogether by Hölscher.

3.b. There is no word for "swear," but the conjunction כי (probably an asseverative) is normal for introducing an oath (BDB, 472a). Does Job mean that so long as he lives he will not lie (so RSV, JPS, NJPS, JB, NAB, NEB, NIV, GNB, Dhorme, Terrien), or that as long as he lives he *swears* he is no liar (so KJV)? And if the latter, does he swear that he *will* not lie (as KJV) or that he *does* not lie, now (as Davidson, Peake)? Though few adopt this view, Job must surely be speaking about his whole position in all his speeches, not just about his future speaking (of which there will not be much, since he has come almost to the end of his speeches); i.e., he swears that he *does* not lie. And so we should understand that it is his *swearing* that lasts as long as he lives. RV (followed by Rowley) regarded v 3 as a parenthesis, but no good sense can be made of saying that he swears *because* the spirit of God is in his nostrils.

3.c. כל־עוד נשמתי בי apparently means "all the while that my breath is in me," עוד being a noun, lit. "all the duration of" (so Driver–Gray). A closely parallel phrase (כל עוד נפשי בי) occurs at 2 Sam 1:9, though the text there has sometimes been thought to be a little corrupt (see Driver–Gray). It is improbable that כל־ should be taken adverbially as "wholly" (cf. GKC, §128e; and cf. RV "my life is yet whole in me"). Curiously, BDB, 728b, 482a (§1f) does not recognize it as a noun, and, like Duhm, regards כל as being "severed from its genitive"; but the meaning cannot be "all my breath," for Job would maintain his integrity even when almost all his breath had left him! *HALOT*, 2:796a, also seems to regard עוד as an unproblematic adv, translating "as long as (something) is still present," even though it acknowledges the use of עוד as a noun, "duration." "The idiom כָּל עוֹד as 'so long as' has entered modern Hebrew from these verses and under the influence of the Israeli national anthem, 'Hatiqvah,' which begins with the words, 'so long as within the heart'" (Gordis).

3.d. Blommerde unnecessarily maintains that the suff of נשמתי is 3d person, thus "his breath is in me," parallel to "God's breath is in my nostrils"; on the supposed 3d-person *yodh* suff, see *Note* 21:16.e.

4.a. The אם at the beginning of the colon is the asseverative negative particle with which vows and oaths commonly begin (see *DCH*, 1:304 §2b); implied is a self-imprecation such as "thus may God do to me, if . . ." (as in 1 Sam 25:22; etc.).

4.b. Some read תֶּהְגֶּה, the fem form, to agree with לְשׁוֹן "tongue," rather than masc יֶהְגֶּה (so some MSS, Duhm, Driver–Gray, Beer [*BHK*]). But לשון is masc at Prov 26:28 and Lam 4:4, so others (Dhorme, Fohrer, Gordis) retain the masc verb here.

5.a. Lit. "a profaned thing may it be from me אם," the אם being an asseverative (cf. on v 3), or perhaps rather the sign of a curse formula (cf. Joüon–Muraoka, §165k).

5.b. אצדיק, declarative hiph of צדק (GKC, §53c).

5.c. Against the Masoretic punctuation, this phrase (עד־אגוע) is to be attached to the second colon (so Driver–Gray, Gordis). עד־אגוע is deleted as a gloss by Hölscher.

5.d. Lit. "I shall not turn my innocence away from me." The last word, ממני "from me," is deleted by Duhm, seeking support from LXX, which does not represent it; but Dhorme rightly observes that אסיר "I will turn away" demands ממני "from me" as a complement.

6.a. Lit. "does not reproach any of my days," the initial *mem* of מימי being the מן partitive. חרף "reproach" requires an obj, which is supplied by the "days" within the form מימי. Blommerde strangely argues that "me" is the implied obj on the principle of the "double duty suffix"; but the suff of לבבי "my heart," on a noun, can hardly do double duty for a verbal suff. Gordis, not entirely persuasively, maintains that חרף here means "blaspheme," God being understood as the obj; so too Habel (and cf. Terrien). Beer (*BHK*) wanted to read (*frt*) the piel יְחָרֵף, which is, admittedly, more common; so too NEB. H. A. Fine ("The Tradition of a Patient Job," *JBL* 74 [1955] 28–32 [30]) argued that חרף intransitive (as here) means "blaspheme" (as in MH; see Jastrow, 505a), and translates "my mind shall not be blasphemed (future perfect, as in 1 Sam 25:28) from the beginning of my days" (on the latter phrase, see 38:12; cf. 1 Kgs 1:6; 1 Sam 25:28).

Duhm, followed by Dhorme, Kissane, de Wilde, Hölscher, prefers to read יֶחְפַּר "[my heart] is [not] ashamed [on account of my days]." Guillaume sees here a new verb חרף cognate with Arab. *ḥarafa* "change" and translates "My mind will not change as long as I live" (*Lexicography,* 3:3–4; *Studies,* 109).

6.b. Gordis interestingly suggests that מִימַי "from my days" means "since I was born," as seems to be the case at 38:12 and 1 Kgs 1:6 (1 Sam 25:28 is not an analogy, however).

11.a. Vv 11–12 are assigned to Job by, e.g., Beer (*BHK*) and of course also by those who think that the whole chapter or at least vv 1–12 are Job's, e.g., Dhorme, Terrien; v 12 alone is regarded as Job's by Duhm, Strahan, and Beer (*BH*[2]), who keep v 11 for Zophar. NAB transfers v 11 to precede v 2.

11.b. אתכם is "you" pl, which makes sense if Job is addressing the friends. Some who think that Zophar is here speaking want to emend to אִתְּךָ "you" (sg), as if he is addressing Job (so Strahan, Beer [*BH*[2] *frt*]). But the two pl verbs and אתם כלכם "all of you" in v 12 are strong support for the pl here, no matter who is understood to be the speaker.

11.c. Lit. "[I will teach you] about the hand of God" (for ב "about," cf. BDB, 90b §IVe); KJV "by the hand of God" (cf. JPS) is inappropriate. Gordis, thinking that Job (whom he takes to be the speaker here) has nothing to say to the friends about God's *power,* understands ביד "in the hand of" as equivalent to בְּעַד "on behalf of God, in God's stead." Beer (*BH*[2] *frt*) reads מַה־בְּיַד־אֵל "what is in the hand of God," following LXX τί ἐστιν ἐν χειρὶ κυρίου. Duhm, followed by Strahan, reads אוֹרְךָ אֲשֶׁר "I will teach you [sg] what."

11.d. Lit. "what is with" (which is how RSV, NJPS translate [similarly KJV, JPS], though perhaps not very helpfully). For the use of עם specifically to suggest purpose, cf. 10:13; 23:14 (JB "making no secret of Shaddai's designs," NEB "purpose"); and cf. BDB, 768b §4a. It is not exactly "the truth about Shaddai" (Habel), nor even "the ways of the Almighty" (NIV) or his "dealings" (Moffatt), still less "what Shaddai has" (Good).

12.a. Transferred to follow v 6 by Duhm, Strahan.

12.b. הן could be "behold" (as KJV, JPS, RSV, NAB, Driver–Gray, Fohrer, Pope) or "if" (as JB, NEB, Dhorme). Gordis takes it as an emphatic, "indeed." The "if" is no doubt equivalent to "since," for Job assumes that the friends already know as much as they need to in order to agree with his point of view. JB, however, takes the "if" as a true hypothetical: "if you had understood them [God's designs] for yourselves, you would not have wasted your breath in empty words."

12.c. The obj of חזיתם "you have seen" is not expressed, but must be the "power" and "purpose" of God in v 11.

12.d. הבל תהבלו, lit. "you are empty in respect of emptiness," a cognate acc serving the function of an inf abs (GKC, §113w). NJPS sees that the "futility" or "emptiness" lies in what the friends say ("So why talk nonsense?"; similarly Moffatt, JB, NEB, NAB, NIV, GNB) rather than in their becoming "altogether vain themselves" (as RSV; cf. KJV, JPS).

Form/Structure/Setting

As throughout the third cycle of speeches as a whole, the *integrity* of the speech is crucial to its interpretation. The view is taken in this commentary that Job's ninth speech properly contains only 27:1–6, 11–12, and that the remainder of chaps. 27–28, which in the Masoretic text are also assigned to Job, belong to other speakers. As will become apparent, the argument advanced here is that 27:7–23 (apart from vv 11–12), on the fate of the wicked, is what remains of the third speech of Zophar, which is otherwise entirely missing from the book; and that chap. 28 is the closing element in the speech(es) of Elihu, if chaps. 32–37 are moved to follow chap. 27.

There are very many views of how these speeches should be rearranged, if at all. Everyone agrees that 27:1–6 is Job's, and very many scholars believe that chap. 28 is certainly not his. There is less agreement about the assignment of what intervenes, 27:7–23, though the majority think that most of it is not Job's. See further on 27:7–23.

Rowley agrees that Job's speech is only 27:1–6. Pope and Alonso Schökel–Sicre Díaz add v 7, and others add v 12 (Duhm, Strahan), or vv 11–12, where the speaker addresses the friends in the plural, as Job himself has been in the habit of doing (Peake, Driver–Gray, Fohrer). Dhorme, Terrien, Gordis, Habel, Hartley, Skehan, 112 (cf. NAB), JB, GNB think the whole of 27:1–12 to be Job's, and assign 27:13–23 to Zophar (Hartley to Bildad); Terrien prefaces 27:1–12 with 24:18–25 (Zophar).

Others want to connect with the present speech (27:1–6), which is indubitably Job's, other material from the third cycle. So Peake, Dhorme, Fohrer, Pope, de Wilde, Alonso Schökel–Sicre Díaz, and Habel preface Job's speech with 26:1–4 (de Wilde moves it to follow Zophar's third speech [27:7–23]). MacKenzie thinks the original place of this speech was at the beginning of Job's great oath, and so between chap. 30 and chap. 31. Among those who do not recognize the presence of any other speaker but Job in this chapter are Davidson, Andersen, Good, and Murphy, 36.

Since the speech is so short, the issue of *structure* hardly arises: the speech as a whole is addressed to the friends, who are explicitly mentioned in v 5. As for *strophic structure,* the speech can be analyzed as one strophe of five lines, or two of three and two, respectively, since there is a break between v 4, where the oath proper concludes, and v 5, where the friends are addressed.

The *genre* of the speech, despite the marked presence of the oath in vv 2–4, is nevertheless a *disputation speech,* since it is addressed to the friends, strongly resisting their positions. Formally speaking, it is a denial that they are in the right (the declarative use of צדק hiph).

Among the elements of other *forms,* the most prominent is the *oath,* which is marked by the formula "as God lives" (v 2) and by the introductory כי and אם in vv 3 and 4 (see *Comment* on vv 3–4 and *Note* 27:4.a). The oath is surprisingly reticent and inexplicit, since it is an oath that he does not lie, and not specifically that he is innocent of the sins he is presumed to have committed. Incorporated within the oath, unusually, are elements from the *accusation* or *complaint*: the one by whom the oath is sworn is the one who "has denied me justice" (cf. 34:5) and "has made my life bitter" (v 2), the language of the lament in 3:20; 13:26; 23:2. Other forms are the *negative wish,* an expression of sacrilege (חלילה "far be it from me") in v 5 (cf. Joüon–Muraoka, §§105f, 165k), and the *assertion* (vv 5b–6).

The *function* of the speech is to affirm Job's intention of not surrendering his position of innocence—and that in opposition to the friends who in one way or another have urged him to accept that he is deserving of what he is suffering.

The *tonality* of the speech is resolute and solemn (but not exactly "confident" and "calm," as Duhm has it). The repeated reference to "as long as I live" (vv 3, 5b) marks Job's determination, while the phrase "my heart does not reproach me for any of my days" (v 6b) shows that Job intends his statement here to be total and comprehensive; he has taken everything into account, and weighed the consequences of what he is saying. The oath is the sure sign of the high seriousness of this speech, for he has never before sworn an oath, and to swear by the life of God is the most solemn manner of oath taking he could use. There is a solemnity too in his negative wish (v 5a), abjuring the invitation of the friends to agree with their assessment of him.

The *nodal verse(s)* must of course be vv 5b–6a, which are the essence of the speech, viz. his affirmation that he intends to maintain his innocence against all opposition.

Comment

2–6 If the assignment of verses to speakers adopted in this commentary is correct, this speech is by far the shortest of all Job's speeches. It is vigorous and to the point: Job's only purpose is to affirm his innocence as strongly as he can, which he does by swearing an oath, for the first time in the book.

The time is past for reasoning and for argument. All that remains for Job is to state the position he has finally arrived at through the course of his speeches. In chaps. 29–31 he will review the course of his life, from the "months of old" (29:2) to the present, but now he wants to utter nothing but his central affirmation: he is an innocent man. Here he does not even stop to say that his present suffering is unjust, that some guilt must not be inferred from it, or that the God who has sent the suffering is acting as his enemy. Here it is enough to say: "I maintain my integrity" (v 6).

Habel sees Job's oath as an oath before the court to which he has been denied access, an oath as if the heavenly court to which he longed to present his case were already in session. If this were the setting, then the drama of Job would have progressed even beyond the point reached in chaps. 23–24; but it is not clear that the oath has any connection with the legal controversy that Job has envisaged, and is not rather a displacement of the controversy by an autonomous and one-sided affirmation.

2 Job prefaces the central sentence of this speech (v 6) first with an oath (vv 2–4) that what he will say is no lie. Not only is he innocent, but he will invoke God's life in support of his claim. This is a very serious undertaking, and it is noteworthy that Job has not taken the step of swearing by God before this climactic speech. To say "as God lives" does not simply mean that as surely as God lives so surely is my utterance true (cf. Dhorme). Rather, and much more radically, it expresses a desire that God should not live if the utterance is untrue (Fohrer)—and so the oath is a potential curse against God. Hence, swearing is a hugely risky business. Swearing "by" someone or some thing implies a curse upon that thing if the promise or statement sworn to turns out to be wrong or invalid. (It is not so much a curse upon oneself [as Habel, Hartley], for the form for that curse is, "May the Lord do so to me and more also," as in 1 Sam 25:22; 2 Kgs 6:31.)

"Old Testament *oaths* basically consist of a *promise* [we might add, or statement] that is strengthened by the addition of a *curse*, usually in conjunction with an appeal to the deity or king who could carry out the curse.... Oath statements seem conditional, but *it is the curse, not the promise, that is conditional*" (T. W. Cartledge, *Vows in the Hebrew Bible and the Ancient Near East*, JSOTSup 147 [Sheffield: JSOT Press, 1992] 15 [Cartledge's emphasis]). That is to say, the execution of the implied curse comes into effect only if the promise or the statement falls. Uttering an oath is of course a very impressive way of guaranteeing what one says, since it could involve the utterer in cursing what is precious or divine property (cf. Matt 5:34–36) or, as in this case, God himself. On the oath, see further, J. Hempel, "Die israelitischen Anschauungen von Segen und Fluch im Lichte altorientalischer Parallelen," *ZDMG* 4 (1925) 20–110; S. H. Blank, "The Curse, Blasphemy, the Spell, and the Oath," *HUCA* 23 (1950–51) 73–95.

It is an irony that Job swears by the God he believes has treated him unjustly. If he proves not to be innocent, then he has cursed God; but the only person who can disprove his innocence is God himself, since Job himself knows beyond a shadow of doubt that he has done nothing to deserve his suffering. If God does not declare Job innocent, then God has brought Job's curse upon himself. So long as God refuses to clear Job's name, in fact, he leaves himself open to the possibility of being cursed by Job.

The irony is not exactly that Job affirms and denies the justice of God at the same time (as Strahan, Terrien, Andersen, and others), for in swearing by God Job is not calling upon his justice but laying a curse upon God in the event that he, Job, is telling a lie.

They are no light charges that Job lays against God in these parenthetical clauses that, formally speaking, do no more than specify the God by whose life Job is swearing. It is part of Job's bitterness that he disclaims all knowledge of traditional reverential titles for God used by communities of worshipers and names him simply by reference to himself as "the one who has denied me justice," "the one who has made my life bitter." To deny justice (הסיר משפט, lit. "turn aside justice"), with the suggestion of deflecting it from those who deserve it and giving its benefits to others, is expressly forbidden in Deuteronomic law (Deut 24:17; 27:19; cf. 1 Sam 8:3 [נטה is the verb in all three places]; Isa 40:27 [the verb is עבר "pass over"]); it is the mark of the arrogant and careless judge, such as Job has made God out to be in chap. 24. And God has made Job's life, his inner personality (נפש), bitter, not only by making him suffer, but by making him suffer unjustly. "Bitter" (מר; the verb is מרר, as here) is a key word for Job (see 3:20; 7:11; 10:1; 13:26; 21:25; 23:2).

3–4 These verses contain the oath itself. Though the term "I swear" is not used, the phrase "[as] God lives" in v 2, followed by the introductory particle כי "assuredly," makes certain that we are dealing with the words of a solemn oath. In v 3 (which is not a parenthesis, as against RV, Peake, Rowley) he swears that the oath is of lifelong validity, and in v 4 he states the content proper of the oath: that he does not say anything wrong. He means "about my claim to innocence"; but he does not say anything so specific here, for he is reserving to the last lines of the speech (vv 5b–6) what it is to which he is swearing, "my integrity" (תמתי), "my righteousness" (צדקתי).

So long as he is alive, he will tell no untruth about his innocence. He means even more that he will not deny the innocence he has than that he will not lay claim to an innocence he does not have. It would be a sin against his integrity to collude with the divine judgment on him, accepting that the evidence is against him and that he must be a sinner after all. For Job, maintaining his integrity means continuing to claim it and assert it, and not merely continuing to have it.

So long as he is alive: that is, so long as there is "breath" (נשמה) in him. The term נשמה (see T. C. Mitchell, "The Old Testament Usage of *nᵉšāmâ*," *VT* 11 [1961] 177–87; H. Lamberty-Zielinski, *TDOT,* 10:65–70) is elsewhere used in Job of the breath of God, especially as the life force imparted by God to humans (as in 4:9; 32:8; 33:4; 34:14; and by implication 26:4), and the parallel here with "the spirit of the Almighty" no doubt suggests a similar sense for "breath." But it is not that נשמה itself means that; it is the context in each case that is determinative. The "spirit" (רוח) of a human being is the life or vitality of that person (as in 6:4; 10:12); in calling his life-breath the spirit of the Almighty in his nostrils, Job is no doubt alluding to the creation narrative of God breathing into the nostrils (אפים, as here) of the first man the "breath of life" (נשמת חיים; here רוח). "Breath" is, not surprisingly, often viewed as the animating principle (cf. Gen 7:22; Isa 42:5). Calling his life God's breath that has been breathed into him makes the oath more solemn, but it does not mean anything more than Job's own life; it is not specifically the spirit of life and the spirit of wisdom (as Dhorme).

The oath is essentially that he tells no lie; he uses the terms עולה "falsehood" and רמיה "deceit" as in 13:7. עולה perhaps suggests what is objectively wrong (the word also means "wrongdoing"), whereas רמיה suggests rather a subjective intention to lie. Job does not of course mean that he tells no lie on any subject whatsoever, though of course he would make that claim if the subject arose; he means rather that in the matter of his innocence, of his claim to be suffering undeservedly at God's hands, he is telling the truth—no matter what the appearances may be against him. For Job, his standing is very closely bound up with words and appearances, and the visualization here of the breath, the nostrils, the lips, and the tongue stresses the facial aspect of truth and innocence.

5–6 It is because he will not lie that he cannot agree with the friends. He is not being cantankerous in sticking to his last, he is not trying to refute their arguments one by one, he is not even denying that they have reason and evidence on their side. It is just, he says, that if he were to agree with them, he would be denying what he knows to be true about himself. That would be to lie; that would be to abandon his integrity. He uses the strong idiom "far be it from me!" (חלילה לי), a phrase that implies "there is something sacrilegious or profane in the idea that is repudiated" (Rowley). The term means "[may it be] a profane, defiled thing," and it is perhaps better translated as "God forbid" (so KJV, NEB) than by a simple emphatic (as NIV "I will never admit"). Though Bildad has insisted that no human can be innocent before God (25:4), Job regards such a conclusion in his own case as religiously defiled. Until his dying day Job will not abandon his innocence (תמה). God may have denied (סור hiph, lit. "turn aside") Job justice (v 2), but Job will not deny (the same word, סור hiph) his innocence—and not just in the service of his self-esteem, but rather in the service of truth. If God will not rule the world with justice, if he fails to keep days of assize (24:1), if he deflects justice (27:2), Job himself will uphold justice. In 2:3, 9 maintaining (חזק) his righteousness had meant that he did not sin by cursing God as the author of his suffering; here, on the other hand, it means maintaining that he is in the right (so also Peake). "The egoism of the passage—'my' occurs eight times in six verses—is, all things considered, not only pardonable but heroic" (Strahan).

Job's "righteousness" (צדקה) is not to be distinguished from his "innocence" (תמה); in 6:29 he has said that his "righteousness" or "integrity" (צדק) is still intact, and in 29:14 he speaks of "putting on" righteousness (צדק) as his clothing. In 31:6 he asks that God should test his "innocence" (תמה), and in 2:3, 9 he has been said by God and by his wife to "hold fast" his integrity (תמה). In all these passages his righteousness is his guiltlessness of anything for which his suffering could be a recompense, rather than a claim to absolute perfection (though such language is sometimes to be found, as also here in v 6b). He is unaware of any sin that could account for his suffering, and so he says that his "heart" (לבב) does not reproach him. Sometimes the "heart" has a more moral sense and corresponds to what we might call the conscience (and it is so translated by Pope,

NIV); so in Ps 7:10 (11) "the upright in heart"; Ps 24:4 "the pure in heart"; 1 Sam 24:6 (5) "David's heart smote him" (cf. F. Stolz, *TWHAT,* 1:861–67 [864]). But it may here mean simply the consciousness (as in Exod 7:23; 1 Sam 4:20; etc.). "My heart does not reproach me for any of my days"—that is the inscription Job would like to have engraved on his tombstone, says Ravasi; that is his alternative autobiography, perpetually in opposition to the lies of God and his friends about him.

11–12 In this commentary it is argued that this speech of Job's originally concluded with vv 11–12 of the present chapter, before the disarrangement occurred that chaps. 25–28 have been subjected to. Somehow they have become embedded in material that properly belongs to Zophar.

These two verses fit badly in the mouth of Zophar (who in this commentary is assumed to be the speaker of the rest of vv 7–23), since they address the hearers as "you" in the plural. Elsewhere in the dialogue it is Job, not the friends, who uses the plural form of address (Pope and Alonso Schökel–Sicre Díaz are alone in apparently finding no problem here). There are two ways of solving the problem: we could suppose that here, exceptionally, Zophar addresses both Job and the two other friends, or that these verses belong to Job and have been misplaced. The difficulty with the former view is that Zophar is unlikely to be saying that the other friends have been speaking "empty talk" (הבל, v 12), at least in the same sense as Job has. As far as the content of the verses go, of course, they could well belong to any of the speakers in the dialogue, Job or any of the friends, for all of them alike claim to know the power and the purpose of God.

So we should probably assign these verses to a speech of Job (so Peake, Driver–Gray; Strahan and de Wilde give only v 12 to Job); those who think that Job has not ceased to speak since the beginning of the chapter (as Dhorme, Hölscher, Terrien, Gordis, Ravasi) of course have no problem with the assignment of the verses. There is no obvious place to which they belong since they could fit well in the opening of any speech of his. De Wilde transfers v 12 to follow 24:25, at the end of Job's eighth speech—which is quite a tempting possibility except that it does not cope with v 11 (de Wilde leaves that for Zophar, in its present place). Perhaps the best solution is to regard these verses as the conclusion of Job's ninth speech, that is, as following v 6 of this chapter (so also Fohrer; Strahan does the same with v 12 only, leaving v 11 within Zophar's speech); there is a close connection of thought and mood with v 5, where Job has said it would be a sacrilege for him to accept the views of the friends. On the other hand, if these words are really Job's, the remainder of this speech is apparently missing, for v 11 seems to foreshadow some further elaboration about the power of God ("I will teach you"). Habel, it may be noted, attractively interprets these verses as the conclusion of Job's speech and translates "I have been teaching you about El's hand; I have not concealed the truth about Shaddai."

If then these verses are Job's, they show him in a defiant and belligerent mood. Not only does he intend not to abandon his claim to innocence (vv 5b–6), he also puts himself in the role of the teacher of his less intelligent friends (vv 11–12). What Job has personal experience of, that will be the first subject of his instruction: the power (יד, lit. "hand") of God (see on 19:21; and cf. 6:9; 10:7; 13:21 for the image of God's hand as destructive or terrifying). And the second will be the inference he draws from God's exercise of his might: the purpose of the Almighty (אשר עם־שדי, lit. "what is with the Almighty"); for a more ample exposition of the perverted purposes of God, see on 10:13–14. By saying that he will not "hide" (כחד) his knowledge of God's purposes, he speaks a little more emphatically than if he said merely that he will declare what he knows (a similar trope at 13:20; 15:18; Pss 40:10; 78:4).

It is not that Job announces some new knowledge. The friends have already had before their eyes all the evidence they need of both God's might and of his intentions. It is Job himself in person that is the best testimony to both, not the histories of creation and the slaying of the ancient dragon (as Bildad had claimed in 26:5–13). To proclaim themselves teachers of wisdom (cf. 15:17) and yet not to accept the truth that stares them in the face is futility; it is to become "altogether vain" (הבל תהבלו, lit. "you are empty in respect of emptiness," the duplication of the verb with the cognate noun serving as an intensification). הֶבֶל *hebel,* as in 7:16 and in Ecclesiastes, is literally a "breath," and then metaphorically what is empty, nugatory (as in 21:34), insubstantial, futile (as in 9:29), or absurd. The verb הבל, derived from the noun, can mean "be full, fill with vain hopes" (Ps 62:11 [10]; Jer 23:16), but the sense here is more probably simply "be empty," that is, of intelligence (as in Jer 2:5; 2 Kgs 17:15). "Why vapour so vainly?" translates Moffatt; "why do you puff a wind-gust?" (Good).

Explanation

If it has been correctly discerned in this commentary that this ninth speech of Job concludes with 27:6, with the addition of vv 11–12 (see *Form/Structure/Setting*), we see that the book still has something to surprise us with in its dramatic development. Here it seems that Job himself has almost run out of words, for this has been by far the shortest of all Job's speeches. It is as if he is saving for his final, climactic speech in chaps. 29–31 all he still has to say—and even that will be a recapitulation, of his life story, of the injustice of God's assaults on him, and of his declaration of innocence. In this speech, on the other hand, though he has no more arguments to develop, and no more criticisms of God, he reaches a new dramatic point when he formulates almost his whole speech (vv 2–6) as a single comprehensive oath. This is not the language of rationality, of narrative or description or accusation; it is the language of cursing, of binding oneself by an affirmation. If what Job affirms is untrue, then he will have cursed God, for the oath is by God's life.

Now the oath that he takes, and that he imagines himself committed to as long as he lives (v 3), is not about something he might perform in the future, as oaths often are, but about something that he swears is true even now: that is, that he tells no lie. And on what subject does he tell no lie? He does not mean, on any subject whatever—though if he were pressed, he would doubtless say that too. It is simply that he does not lie when he asserts his innocence, that he tells no untruth when he maintains that he knows of nothing in his life for which his present suffering could possibly be a punishment. That is worth swearing an oath about, worth the risk of having laid a curse upon God, because that is the only way Job can create order out of his experiences. If it should turn out, after a lifetime of scrupulous piety, that he was a sinner all the time, rightly subject to God's chastisement, then his life would have been an absurdity.

For that reason, he finds himself saying to his friends that it would be a sacrilege for him to agree with them (v 5). That is not the desperation of someone who finds himself talking to a brick wall, the petulance of someone who cannot get his own way; it is not Job at his coolest when he says, "It would be a profanity, a sacrilege, for me to agree with you," for if he were to agree with them, he would be denying what he knows to be true about himself. That would be the ultimate lie, that is what it would be to abandon his integrity. If he agreed with the friends that he deserved what he suffered, he would not only acknowledge that he had been a sinner all along, but his whole moral universe would have fallen apart.

His language in this speech is very simple; there is no imagery in it, and not a lot of poetic imagination. But it is very measured and very serious—much more than appears at first sight. He binds himself and his destiny to his own construction of himself; if his self-understanding falls, he falls—he curses God and he dies. In some ways, this is the climax of his speeches; and Job is all alone as he reaches it. He has nothing to rely on but himself: God is nothing but the "one who has denied me justice" (v 2) and the friends offer words that only threaten to dissolve all meaning in his life. He has nothing to cling to but his innocence, and to that he "holds fast" and "will not let it go" (v 6).

Nevertheless, the modern reader cannot help raising a quizzical eyebrow at anyone, ancient or modern, who can entertain such a naive faith in their own innocence. Surely self-doubt did not originate with Paul or with Freud. What of the psalmist of Ps 19, caught up in reverent adoration of the God of creation and the law, and then bursting out with, "But who can detect their errors? Clear me from hidden faults" (Ps 19:13 [12])? Or of Ps 139, full of devout praise for the creator's wonderful works (139:14), but calling on God nevertheless to search the heart to see if there remains any "hurtful way" within the psalmist (Ps 139:23–24). There is something very antique about the book of Job, its characters moving with the stiffness of the protagonists in an Aeschylean tragedy—and it is no doubt quite a bad mistake to read the book as a psychologically realist novel. Here there is played out before us, not the true history of an individual but a truth about the tolerance limits of humans for absurdity, and it is not surprising perhaps if the issues are presented in sharp and extreme forms.

There is another point, too, at which the reader might part company with Job: it is his assumption that there should indeed be a correlation between act and consequence. Everything in the book so far takes for granted that the just should be rewarded and the unjust punished; Job and the friends are united in that. But what right has Job to suppose that innocence of life should be any safeguard against poverty or physical suffering? What is the point of railing at God for unjust treatment if the very idea of just treatment is nothing but a human construction, a piece of wishful theological thinking? It will be interesting, to say the least, to hear what the character God has to say about this assumption when he at last breaks his silence.

Zophar's Third Speech (27:7–10, 13–17; 24:18–24; 27:18–23)

Bibliography

Burns, J. B. "Support for the Emendation *rᵉḥōb mᵉqōmô* in Job xxiv 19–20." *VT* 39 (1989) 480–85. **Dhorme, P.** "Les chapitres XXV–XXVIII du Livre de Job." *RB* 33 (1924) 343–56. **Giesebrecht, F.** *Der Wendepunkt des Buches Hiob, Capitel 27 und 28.* Diss., Greifswald, 1879. **Guillaume, A.** "The Arabic Background of the Book of Job." In *Promise and Fulfilment.* FS S. H. Hooke, ed. F. F. Bruce. Edinburgh: T. & T. Clark, 1963. 106–27. **Reventlow, H. G.** "Tradition und Redaktion in Hiob 27 im Rahmen der Hiobreden des Abschnittes Hi 24–27." *ZAW* 94 (1982) 279–93. **Tournay, R.** "L'ordre primitif des chapitres XXIV–XXVIII du livre de Job." *RB* 64 (1957) 321–34. **Witte, M.** *Vom Leiden zur Lehre: Der dritte Redegang (Hiob 21–27) und die Redaktionsgeschichte des Hiobbuches.* BZAW 230. Berlin: de Gruyter, 1994. **Wolfers, D.** "Job: The Third Cycle: Dissipating a Mirage." *DD* 16 (1987–88) 217–26; 17 (1988–89) 19–25. ———. "The Speech-Cycles in the Book of Job." *VT* 43 (1993) 385–402.

Translation

[a]*[And Zophar the Naamathite answered and said:]*

7 *May my enemy be like*[b] *the wicked,*
may my assailant[c] *be like the wrongdoer!*
8 *For what is the hope of the godless when he is cut off,*[a]
when God requires[b] *his life?*
9 *Will God hear his cry*
when trouble comes upon him?
10 *Will*[a] *he delight himself*[b] *in the Almighty,*
and call upon[c] *God at every moment?*[d]

11–12 [a][transferred to follow 27:6, as part of Job's Ninth Speech]

13 [a]*This is the portion of the wicked*[b] *from*[c] *God,*
the heritage of oppressors[d] *that*[e] *they receive*[f] *from the Almighty.*[g]
14 *Though their*[a] *children be many,*[b] *they are destined for the sword;*[c]
their offspring will never have enough to eat.
15 *Those who survive*[a] *will be brought to their grave*[b] *by plague,*[c]
and their widows[d] *will be unable to bewail them.*[e]
16 *Though they heap up silver like dust,*
lay up fine clothing like piles of clay,
17 *they may lay it up, but the righteous will wear it,*
and the innocent will divide their silver.

24:18 [a]*The wicked*[b] *are a fleck*[c] *on the face of*[d] *the waters,*[e]
their portion[f] *in the land is accursed,*

[g]*and no one turns*[h] *to their vineyards.*[i]
19 [a]*As drought*[b] *and*[c] *heat snatch away*[d] *the snow waters,*[e]
so[f] *Sheol*[g] *snatches away sinners.*[h]
20 [a]*The womb*[b] *forgets them,*
the worm sucks[c] *on them;*
they are no longer remembered,
[d]*and wickedness is shattered*[e] *like a tree.*
21 [a]*They wrong*[b] *the barren woman,*[c]
and do no good[d] *to their widows.*[e]
22 [a]*God*[b] *drags away*[c] *the mighty*[d] *by his power;*
even when[e] *they are prosperous*[f] *they can have no assurance of life.*[g]
23 *He allows*[a] *them to rest*[b] *in security,*[c]
but[d] *his eyes*[e] *keep watch over their ways.*[f]
24 *They are exalted*[a] *for a moment, and then are gone;*[b]
they are brought low,[c] *and shrivel*[d] *like mallows;*[e]
they wither[f] *like the heads of grain.*

27:18 *The house they build is like a bird's nest,*[a]
like a booth made by a watchman.[b]
19 *They go to bed rich,*[a] *but for the last time;*[b]
when they[c] *open their eyes, their wealth*[d] *is all gone.*
20 *The Terrors overtake*[a] *them like a flood;*[b]
in the night a tempest carries them off.[c]
21 *The east wind seizes them, and they are gone;*[a]
it whirls them away, out of their place.
22 [a]*It hurls itself*[b] *against them without mercy;*
they flee headlong[c] *from its force.*
23 [a]*It claps*[b] *its hands*[c] *at them*[d] *in derision,*
and hisses[e] *at them from*[f] *its*[g] *place.*[h]

Notes

7.a. The line is conjecturally restored on the basis of 20:1, the opening of Zophar's previous speech.

7.b. There is no call to follow Gordis in taking the *kaph* here and in the next colon as *kaph* asseverative.

7.c. Habel translates "my adversary at law," taking this to be Job speaking of God, his legal opponent (so too Good). But it makes little sense to wish that God's offspring should die and that God should not be heard when he prays to God.

8.a. As the text stands, God must be the subj of יבצע "cuts off." But בצע in the sense of "cut off" seems to be always piel, so Budde, Beer (*BHK*), and Hölscher emend to יְבַצַּע "he cuts off" (so RSV and perhaps Habel "Eloah drains his life away") or יְבֻצַּע "is cut off" (so too Driver–Gray, NEB, NAB, NIV; NJPS "is cut down"). Gordis (followed by Hartley) strains after interpreting the qal as meaning "he is cut off," but Joel 2:8 is not a helpful parallel. The qal sense, "gain by violence," is not very suitable (as KJV "though he hath gained," JPS "though he get him gain"), for כי concessive ("although") is not well attested (but cf. BDB, 473b, §2c); similarly Gerleman (*BHS*), understanding it as "he finishes [his life]"; and so too Fohrer, reading the piel יְבַצַּע. G. R. Driver takes יבצע qal as meaning "he comes to an end" ("Problems in Job," *AJSL* 52 [1936] 160–70 [162]); so too Kissane, and apparently Gerleman (*BHS*), who identifies it as "finish [life]." An interesting but conjectural emendation was made by S. Mandelkern (*Veteris Testamenti concordantiae hebraicae et chaldaicae,* 2d ed. [Leipzig: Margolin, 1925] 228b), and followed by Dhorme, JB, and Rowley (apparently): יִפְגַּע "when he prays," which fits well with v 9; but why should a "godless" (חנף "impious") man be praying? It is presumably when adversity smites him. Duhm, Strahan, Moffatt, Fohrer, Fedrizzi, and de Wilde omit the clause כי יבצע.

8.b. ישל has been variously understood. (1) According to BDB, 1017b (with some support from Gordis), it is from שלה II "draw out, extract" (not otherwise attested in Heb.; it is not acknowledged by *HALOT*); hence RSV "takes away" (similarly KJV, JPS, NJPS, NIV, Fedrizzi). (2) Others take it from שלל II "spoil, plunder" (BDB, 1021b; *HALOT*, 4:1531a); Dillmann (followed by Kissane, Gerleman [*BHS prp*], Sicre Díaz, Hartley "despoils," Good) proposes יָשֹׁל "carries off [his life] as booty." (3) The most favored emendation, adopted in the *Translation* above, is that of Siegfried, Budde, Duhm, Strahan, Driver–Gray, Beer (*BHK*), Gordis, Moffatt, and GNB ("demands"); NEB (Brockington, *Hebrew Text*) and NAB to יִשְׁאַל "requires."

Less probable are the following suggestions: (4) Perles, Hölscher, Rowley, and de Wilde emend to יִשָּׂא לֶאֱלוֹהַּ נפשו "when he lifts up his soul to God" (de Wilde לֶאֱלוֹהַּ); so too *HALOT*, 4:1504a, translating "if his soul longs after God." Rowley quotes Confucius, *Analects* 3.13: "he who offends against Heaven has none to whom he can pray." (5) Fohrer reads יִשָּׂא אלוה "[when] God takes away [his life]." (6) A. Guillaume ("The Arabic Background of the Book of Job," in *Promise and Fulfilment*, FS S. H. Hooke, ed. F. F. Bruce [Edinburgh: T. & T. Clark, 1963] 106–27 [117]; *Studies*, 109) finds a new Heb. word, cognate with Arab. *yisalu* (= *yis'alu*) "draw out, take away." (7) Strauss derives the form יַשֵּׁל from שלה I "have rest, be at ease" (BDB, 1017a; *HALOT*, 4:1503b), which has occurred at 3:26; 12:6. He translates "[when God] brings [his life] to rest"; but qal means "be at rest," niph apparently "give oneself up to rest," and hiph "set at ease, lead to false hope," so it is hard to see how it could be "bring to rest." It is also strange to have the cutting off of the life of the wicked being referred to as bringing the life "to rest."

10.a. The אם introduces the second question, as at 6:12 (cf. GKC, §150c; *DCH*, 1:304b §3b). Strangely, NJPS makes vv 9–10 into a single complex question: "Will God hear his cry when trouble comes upon him, when he seeks the favor of Shaddai, calls upon God at all times?" (similarly Habel). JB puts the second question into the past, "Did he make Shaddai all his delight?" but this is not very likely.

10.b. On ענג hithp "delight oneself," but perhaps better "implore," see *Note* 22:26.c. Here the parallelism with קרא "call upon" would support the sense "implore."

10.c. Though it is not normal, קרא "call upon" can have a direct obj (as also in Isa 43:22; Ps 14:4). Some MSS indeed have a more expected phrase, אֶל־אלוה "upon God" (which Beer [*BHK*], Hölscher, and de Wilde read). Beer (*BH*[2] *vel*) and NAB read אֵלָיו "to him" (corresponding to LXX). Ehrlich (and apparently Good "meet") reads יִקְרַב אֶל־אלוה "does he approach God?"

Gordis translates "Is he free to implore the Almighty—can he call upon God at any time?" meaning "is God accessible to him at all times and not merely at specially propitious hours?" But it is hard to see that the question here should be whether God is *accessible*; it is rather whether God is going to respond to him.

10.d. For אלוה בכל־עת "God at every moment," Duhm read אֵלָיו הֲיִפְגָּעֶה "will he welcome him?" He took his lead (cf. also Strahan) from LXX, making the verse consist of further questions about the unlikelihood of the wicked being heard by God. Thus LXX has μὴ ἔχει τινὰ παρρησίαν ἔναντι αὐτοῦ; ἢ ὡς ἐπικαλεσαμένου αὐτοῦ εἰσακούσεται αὐτοῦ; "has he any confidence before him? or will Job hear him when he calls upon him?" Also following the LXX, Beer (*BHK*) and Hölscher emended to יֵעָתֶר־לוֹ "[when he calls upon God] will he allow himself to be supplicated by him?"

11–12.a. Vv 11–12 are transferred in this commentary to follow v 6, and thus form part of the ninth speech of Job. Kissane, regarding them as part of Bildad's speech, moves them to precede v 7.

13.a. V 13 is deleted by Hölscher.

13.b. אדם רשע "wicked person," אדם having no specific gender reference. Good, translating "this lot of evil humankind," seems to be the only commentator who recognizes the proper force of אדם. Duhm deletes it as a gloss to ensure that the following word is pronounced רָשָׁע "wicked" and not רֶשַׁע "wickedness" (as also in 20:29; cf. Beer [*BHK*]).

13.c. עם, lit. "with," not here in the sense of "in the purpose of" (as in v 11) but rather as "in the presence of, laid up with" (cf. עמדי in Deut 32:34); cf. the sense "in the custody *or* care of" (BDB, 768a §3c). M. Dahood (review of *Ugaritica VI*, *Or* 41 [1972] 135) argued that עם here actually means "from," on the basis of Ugar. *'mn*; so also Pope and Hartley, though the Ugar. can be well explained in accord with the Heb. usage. Driver–Gray, Dhorme, Beer (*BHK*), Fohrer, Rowley (perhaps), Fedrizzi, Gerleman (*BHS prp*), and NAB emend עם־אל "with God" to מֵאֵל "from God," on the basis of the parallel in 20:29.

13.d. The pl עריצים "oppressors" is parallel to the sg רשע "the wicked (person)" in the first colon; there is no need to emend the text (as Duhm, Peake, Strahan, Beer [*BHK*]; Stevenson to עָרִיץ "oppressor" and to יִקַּח "will receive"), since the sg and the pl are alike generic. For other cases of parallelism of a sg in the first colon with a pl in the second, cf. 16:11; 24:24; Isa 5:23 (for the reverse, cf. Isa 53:9).

13.e. The relative pronoun אֲשֶׁר "that" is understood after the phrase נחלת עריצים "the heritage of oppressors."

13.f. יקחו "they receive" is omitted by Hartley as overloading the line (and there is no verb in the parallel 20:29). Beer (*BHK*) reads the sg יִקַּח "he receives" in order to harmonize with the sg עריץ "the oppressor" emended earlier in the colon.

13.g. Dhorme and Rowley follow this verse with 24:18–24, de Wilde with 24:18b–19.

14.a. Here and throughout vv 14–23 the sg is used of the wicked person (אדם, following the use of that term in v 13); but in order to preserve the gender-free language of אדם "person," I have used the pl, in conformity with the pl of עצירים "oppressors." Habel and GNB also have the pl throughout, though whether for the same reason is not apparent.

14.b. רבה is "be many" rather than "become great," "grow up" (as Moffatt), as at 39:4.

14.c. The last clause in the translation is in the Heb. simply למו־חרב "for the sword."

15.a. K שרידו is "his survivor"; Q שְׂרִידָיו "his survivors" (followed by Hartley). K is to be preferred since its suff corresponds to that of אלמנתיו "his widows"; the sg is of course generic or distributive (cf. GKC, §145l–m).

15.b. יקברו, lit. "will be buried." Merx, Beer (*BHK frt*), Pope, NAB read לא יקברו "they will not be buried," which would explain why their widows cannot mourn them. But see *Comment* for the idea that being "buried" by plague effectively means not being buried properly; in fact it would make no sense to say they are "*not* buried by plague" (by what *are* they buried, then?). Fedrizzi, sensing something amiss in the idea of *death* "burying" the wicked, emends to בַּקְרָב יָמוּתוּ "they will die in battle"—which does at least form a parallel to v 14a; but the image of pestilence burying them (see next *Note*) is more striking.

15.c. Most agree that מות here does not have its usual sense of "death" (as KJV, Fohrer), but the specific sense of "plague" or "pestilence" (as in Jer 15:2; 18:21; 43:11; so JPS, Moffatt, NJPS, RSV, JB, NEB, NIV, GNB ["disease"], and Habel ["death"], but in the sense of plague, as in "the Black Death," Good "[buried with] Mot"); cf. NJPS "will be buried in a plague." W. F. Albright, following S. Iwry, wanted to read בָּמוֹת "(in) burial mounds," which he understood as "in pagan graves" ("The High Place in Ancient Palestine," in *Volume du Congrès, Strasbourg 1956*, VTSup 4 [Leiden: Brill, 1957] 242–58 [246]); so too Pope "will not be buried in a tomb."

15.d. אלמנתיו "his widows" is not likely to mean that he is polygamous (see *Comment*); more probably it refers to each individual of the "survivors" (שרידים; cf. GKC, §145m). The same form occurs in the parallel text at Ps 78:64, where also "their widows" is expected. Alternatively, we might emend to וְאַלְמְנֹתָם "and their widows" (as Duhm [אַלְמְנֹתֵיהֶם], Strahan, Driver–Gray, Beer [*BHK*], Kissane, Fedrizzi, de Wilde [wrongly אַלְמְנֹתָם]; LXX has χῆραι δὲ αὐτῶν "and their widows," admittedly "not decisive as to the translator's *reading*" [Driver–Gray]).

15.e. NAB, following Beer (*BH*²), reads לא תְּבָכֶינָה "will not be mourned."

24:18.a. On the place of vv 18–24 in Zophar's last speech, see *Comment*. Among other suggestions, de Wilde moves vv 18b, 18c, and 19 to follow 27:13. Hölscher moves the colon to follow v 16a, while Duhm attaches v 18a to the end of v 17. NAB simply deletes v 18a.

18.b. Lit. "he." Those spoken of in this strophe (vv 18–24) are sometimes in the sg (vv 18a, 18c [?], 20a, c, 21a, b, 22b, 23a, 24aβ), sometimes in the pl (vv 18b, 22a, 23b, 24aα, b, c). I have used "they" consistently in the translation, but I do not think it is necessary to emend the text in order to create only pl forms. The subject "the wicked" is supplied in the *Translation* (as also at v 9), since the strophe is concerned with wicked persons in general and not just those types of the wicked (murderer, adulterer, thief) mentioned in the previous strophe. Good strangely thinks "he" refers to God, translating "He, on the contrary, is swift across the waters"—like the divine wind of Gen 1:2; and for him the whole of vv 18–24 is about this god of chaos.

18.c. קל הוא, lit. "he is light." קל usually implies "swift" (see *Comment*), so many see here a picture of a light object being carried off "swiftly" by water (so RSV "They are swiftly carried away," Moffatt "swept off by the flood," GNB "swept away by floods"), or of something skimming over the water (RV, JPS "he is swift upon the face of the waters"; similarly Sicre Díaz), or of something swift like water (KJV "he is swift as the waters"). But it is more likely that the image is rather of a light and insubstantial object floating on the water (NJB "a straw floating on the water," NIV "foam on the surface of the water," NJPS "flotsam," perhaps even NEB "scum," since the idea of something contemptible is also present). Gordis's "perish" is too loose. Some of course want to read קַלּוּ "are light" for the sake of harmony with the pl of חלקם (so Budde, Beer [*BHK prps*], Fohrer, Gerleman [*BHS prp*]), while others read כָּלוּ "they come to an end" (Beer [*BHK al*]).

18.d. Gordis wants על־פני to mean "like," as לִפְנֵי occasionally does, but such an idiom is unparalleled.

18.e. Beer (*BHK prps*) and Fohrer read לִפְנֵי יוֹמָם "before their day," i.e. (apparently), "in their day," instead of עַל־פְּנֵי־מָיִם "upon the face of the waters." Kissane suggests עַל־פְּנֵיהֶם "upon them," but translates "upon the face of the waters." Fedrizzi has לִפְנֵי יוֹם "before the day," and moves the colon to follow v 16a.

18.f. Duhm, Beer (BH^2 *frt*), and de Wilde, want to keep the wrongdoer as sg, so emend to חֶלְקָתוֹ "his portion."

18.g. NAB deletes this colon.

18.h. Duhm and Beer (BH^2 *prps*) read יַאַסְפֶּנָּה (it should be יַאַסְפֶנָּה) "[drought and heat] consume it [their portion]" for לא־יפנה "does not turn" and delete "to their vineyard."

18.i. Lit. "he does not turn by way of the vineyards" (similarly JPS). NJPS "may none turn aside by way of their vineyards" sounds as if no one will take a shortcut through their vineyards—a strained rendering.

As it stands, the text seems to have the "light" man as the subj (so KJV, JPS, Davidson; GNB "he no longer goes to work in his vineyards"); most, however, think the subj is "one, anyone" (so RSV, NJPS, NJB "nobody goes near his vineyard"). פנה can also mean "look," hence KJV "he beholdeth not the way of the vineyards"; but it is hard to see what such a statement would signify.

Peake, Beer (BH^2; דֹּרֵךְ in *BHK* seems to be a mistake), Driver–Gray, Dhorme, Hölscher, Fohrer, Fedrizzi, Gordis, Habel, Strauss read לא יפנה דֹּרֵךְ כַּרְמָם "no treader [of grapes] will turn toward their vineyard" (so too presumably NEB "no labourer will go near their vineyards"). Ehrlich protests that one cannot "tread" a vineyard, but כרם "vineyard" is connected with פנה "turn," not with דרך "tread." LXX, with its τὰ φυτὰ αὐτῶν "their plants," seems to support the 3 masc pl suff of כַּרְמָם. De Wilde has דֹּרֵךְ כַּרְמוֹ "treader... towards his vineyard." Kissane proposes לֹא יִפְרֶה כַּרְמָם מִצִּיָּה "their vineyard would not bear fruit because of drought."

19.a. NAB deletes the whole line as corrupt.

19.b. Pope omits ציה "drought," while Kissane removes it to the end of the previous colon.

19.c. גם, lit. "also," but merely "and" here (Dhorme). Good tries to represent the גם with "dryness, like heat, seizes snow waters," but the English is not very intelligible. Kissane makes the ingenious proposal that for גַּם־חֹם "also heat" we read גַּנָּתָם "their garden(s) the snow-waters would sweep away," parallel to v 18c in his rendering.

19.d. Dhorme moves יגזלו to follow שלג and reads יִגְזֹל שְׁאוֹל חוֹטֵא "[the drought and the heat carry away the snow waters, and] Sheol carries away the sinner." Duhm and Beer (BH^2 *prps*) emend to יִגְזְלוּהָ "[snow waters] snatch it [the portion] away"; hence NJB "so does Sheol anyone who has sinned." Hölscher proposes צִיָּה וָחֹם יִגְזְלוּם וּמֵי שֶׁלֶג שְׁאוֹל יַנְחִיתוּ "May drought and heat despoil them, and may snow-waters lower (them) into the underworld." Guillaume ("Arabic Background," 116–17; *Studies,* 108) finds in יגזלו a new word גזל "be large" (cognate with Arab. *jazula*) and in שאול not "Sheol" but a verb שלה "flow" (cf. Arab. *sāla*) or a noun שְׁאוֹל "watercourse, torrent" (cf. Arab. *sayl*), thus "When drought and heat are great, the snow waters fail to flow." But, quite apart from the doubtfulness of these linguistic proposals, we expect something of the fate of sinners, not of jejune meteorological observation.

19.e. De Wilde reads מֵימָיו "his water" as obj of יגזלו, and יִשָּׂא שֹׁאָה לְחִטָּתוֹ "brings destruction to his wheat," more ingeniously than convincingly. Peake, Beer (*BHK frt*), Fohrer, Pope, and O. Loretz ("Philologische und textologische Probleme in Hi 24,1–25," *UF* 12 [1980] 261–66 [265]) omit מימי, as overloading the colon. NEB reverses the order of מימי and שלג and translates "so the waters of Sheol make away with the sinner."

19.f. The clauses are comparative clauses, unusually without *waw* (GKC, §161a).

19.g. Instead of שאול "Sheol," Kissane proposes שָׁאַל אֵל "[if] God examined the sinner." Beer (BH^2 *frt*) deleted שאול חטאו.

19.h. Lit. "those who have sinned," the relative pronoun being understood before חטאו. LXX ἀνεμνήσθη αὐτοῦ ἡ ἁμαρτία "his sin is remembered" seems to have understood the Heb. as שָׁאוּל חֶטְאוֹ "his sin is asked for." Driver–Gray suggested שְׁאוֹל חַטָּאִים תַּחְטֹף "Sheol snatches away sinners" (cf. Ps 10:9) (so too Beer [*BHK prps*]) or שְׁאוֹל חַטָּאִים יֵחָתּוּ "sinners go down to Sheol." Along similar lines, Beer (BH^2 *prps*) has יֵחָתּוּ, understanding the second colon as "snow waters go down." Good offers the strained rendering "[snow waters,] which never flow down to Sheol," understanding

חטא as "miss," i.e., having evaporated, the water cannot reach down as far as Sheol. Kissane emends to חֹטֵא "the sinner," NEB to חַטָּא "the sinner."

20.a. NAB deletes v 20a–c.

20.b. Duhm, Beer (*BH*[2]), Budde[2], Strahan, Driver–Gray, Beer (*BHK frt*), Hölscher, Fohrer, Rowley, de Wilde, KBL, 583b, and *HALOT,* 2:655b, emend רחם מתקו "the womb, [the worm] feasts" to רְחֹב מְקֹמוֹ (or רְחוֹב מְקוֹמוֹ) "the square of his place," i.e., native place (as Ruth 4:10 שער מקומו "the gate of his [native] place"); hence RSV "the squares of the town" (but NRSV "the womb forgets them"), Moffatt "the streets of his native place [forget him]," and J. B. Burns, "Support for the Emendation *r*[e]*ḥōb m*[e]*qōmô* in Job xxiv 19–20," *VT* 39 [1989] 480–85. But Sicre Díaz justly complains that this trivializes the image, and it is certainly more prosaic; J. B. Geyer, "Mythological Sequence in Job xxiv 19–20," *VT* 42 [1992] 118–20, also defends the MT.

20.c. מתקו רמה "the worm feasts on (?) him" has a fem subj and masc verb, which is anomalous but by no means unparalleled (cf. GKC, §145o). מתק is also a problem since it is usually "be sweet" (as in 21:33), but here it would have to mean "suck" (like מתק in Aram.); so BDB, who think the sense dubious nevertheless. It is no doubt best to suppose two distinct verbs, מתק I "be sweet" and מתק II "suck" (as *DCH,* 5:573b). NJPS "may he be sweet to the worms" and NRSV "the worm finds them sweet" favor the former, while NIV "feasts" and NEB "the worm sucks him dry" prefer the latter (as also in the *Translation* above); KJV "shall feed sweetly on him" combines the two senses in one verb. Terrien understands מתקו as "his sweetness" (? reading מָתְקוֹ), and takes רחם מתקו together as "the womb of his sweetheart, lover," i.e., his wife or concubine, not his mother; but there are no parallels to such a meaning for מֹתֶק or מֶתֶק "sweetness," and the suggestion is improbable. It is tempting to see some connection with Job's speech in 21:33, where the earth that covers the wicked man is "sweet" (מתק, as here), but it is hard to see what the significance of the verbal parallel can be.

Dhorme proposes emending to פִּתְּקוֹ "[that] formed him," assuming a new Heb. root פתק cognate with Akk. *patâqu* "make, create, form"; hence JB "the womb that shaped him." Bickell, Budde, Duhm, Strahan, Beer (*BH*[2]; *BHK al*). Kissane connected מתקו with the previous phrase and read רָמֹה עוד לא יזכר "his height is not remembered," a curious subj for "remember" (Dhorme) and altogether an emendation that cannot be counted a great success compared with MT, if it has been correctly understood. Driver–Gray, followed by Dhorme, Beer (*BHK* רָמֹה), Hölscher, Fohrer, Terrien, Rowley, de Wilde, and Burns ("Support for the Emendation," 482), preferred שְׁמֹה "his name"; hence RSV, JB "his name is recalled no longer." Kissane read וְיִנָּתֵק וְ "and he would be plucked out and," but the principle of *lectio difficilior* suggests we should keep to the MT.

20.d. Fohrer moves the colon to follow v 18a, NAB to follow v 18b, Hölscher and NEB to follow v 24a. Davidson interestingly attaches it closely to the following verse, rendering "And wickedness shall be broken like a tree—even he that devoureth . . . And doeth no good."

20.e. שבר niph is unproblematically "be broken," but it may not seem a natural word to use of a tree. However, in Exod 9:25 hail "shatters" (שבר) every tree (an allusion to the same event in Ps 105:33, with the same language), so the traditional understanding is acceptable. NEB "iniquity is snapped like a stick" attempts to overcome the perceived difficulty, but שבר is not a natural word for "snapping" a stick (שבר is used of a "rod" [מטה] in Isa 14:5 and Jer 48:17, but a translation "is broken, shattered" is appropriate). NAB "is splintered" is too precise a term.

Good translates "is bought like wood," deriving the verb from שבר II "sell." But שבר II is used only of buying food (grain, Gen 41:57; food, 42:7; wine and milk, Isa 55:1), and it is not used in the niph. Duhm rewrites the colon as כְּעֵץ רֹעֵעַ יֵעָקֵר "like a rotten tree he is uprooted," following LXX ἴσα ξύλῳ ἀνιάτῳ "like an incurable [!] tree."

21.a. NAB omits this verse as too obscure for translation.

21.b. רעה is properly "he grazes on"; the verb may occasionally be used in a pejorative sense of enemies "depasturing" (Mic 5:6 [5], though RSV has "rule"; and the wind can be said to "feed" on people [Jer 22:22, RSV "shepherd"], and so can fire [Job 20:26]). Hence RV, JPS "devoureth," RSV "feed on," NIV "prey on," Habel "feed on," Good "he pastures on." But a simple emendation to הֵרַע "ill treat, wrong" (Budde, Dhorme, Beer [*BHK*], Hölscher, Kissane, Rowley, de Wilde) is attractive also; so KJV "He evil entreateth," NEB "He may have wronged," NJB "He used to ill-treat"; so too the *Translation* above. Does this verse perhaps give the reason why he has come to such an end—as GNB: "That happens because he ill-treated widows and showed no kindness to childless women"?

NJPS "may he consort with" derives the word from רעה II "associate with" (similarly Fohrer, Fedrizzi, Terrien; cf. Prov 13:20 רעה כסילים "one who associates with fools"; 28:7; 29:3), but in all these cases it is a group of people whom one associates with, not an individual (though רעה hithp is used in Prov 22:24 with a sg). Andersen takes רעה as "female companion" (like רֵעָה in Ps 45:14 [15]), and Hartley follows this lead, reading רֵעָה and understanding "let his female companion be barren." Gordis thinks רעה is a hitherto unrecognized verb, a byform of רעע II "break, crush" (also at Mic 5:5).

21.c. Lit. "the barren woman [who] does not give birth." Avoiding the apparent redundancy, Gordis interestingly proposes "the barren woman so that she cannot give birth," but the presence of "barren" (עקרה) is no less strictly unnecessary. The phrase is, however, paralleled in Isa 54:1: עקרה לא ילדה "the barren woman, who did not give birth." Fedrizzi thinks this a quasi-proverbial expression of evildoing: he associates with prostitutes. Duhm offers an emendation to וְעוּלָהּ לֹא רִחֵם "and he did not have pity on her child," incorporating עולה from the end of v 20.

21.d. On the unusual form יְיֵטִיב, see GKC, §70c; some recommend to read the normal יֵיטִיב (Driver–Gray). On the ptcp followed by a finite verb, see GKC, §116x.

21.e. Not to widows in general, but to the wrongdoer's own widow (see *Comment*).

22.a. NAB rearranges vv 22–23 in the order vv 22b, 23a, 22a, 23b.

22.b. The subj is supplied in the *Translation* above. For other cases where the name of God is to be supplied (often as the subj), cf. 3:20; 12:13; 16:7; 20:23; 22:21; 25:2; 30:17 (perhaps), 19. Budde[2] and Beer (*BHK frt*) want to emend the name of God into the text, and propose וְאֵל מֹשֵׁךְ אַבִּיר בכחו "and God, the mighty one, prolongs by his power." Duhm, following LXX ἀδυνάτους "the powerless" and Bickell, suggests ומשך אֹבְדִים בכחו "and he (the wicked) snatches away the (financially) ruined by his might"; cf. Driver–Gray. Gordis too thinks the evildoer is still the subj, translating "The mighty man may continue in his strength" (similarly Habel), but משך is not used absolutely except in the sense of "walk, go" (21:33; Judg 4:6; 20:37), and Gordis needs to explain away the pl suff of אבירים as an enclitic or a dittogr. De Wilde also takes the wicked as the subj but finds an obj in אבירים (see *Note* 22.d on אבירים "mighty"). NJPS also takes the wicked as the subj but understands משך differently (see next *Note*).

22.c. The verb משך has a very wide range of meanings (cf. *DCH,* 5:522a). There are two that have been favored to explain this passage: (1) "prolong"; thus BDB, 604b, "prolong the life of" (hence RSV and Davidson "continueth," Driver–Gray "maketh the mighty to continue," NAB "sustains the mighty"). However, there are no parallels with persons as the subj; in Isa 13:22 days are "prolonged," in Ezek 12:25, 28 the word of Yahweh (i.e., its execution) will not be "delayed," and in Jos 6:5 the priests "prolong" with the sound of the ram's horn. And in this meaning of "draw out, prolong, continue," משך usually has as its direct obj the thing prolonged (except in Neh 9:30). Kissane creates such an obj with the proposed reading אַבִּיר יָמָיו "the tyrant [prolongeth] his days." (2) "draw, drag off," more common a sense. Hence KJV "draweth," JPS "draweth away," NIV "drags away," NEB "carries off," Good "draws out." This is the sense adopted in the *Translation* above, but with some misgiving since we might expect the text to say what the mighty are dragged away *from.* Pope has "He lures the mighty with his power," and Hartley "allure," but there is no evidence for this sense, and it is hard to see what it could refer to in the context.

Possibly we should connect the passage with a new verb משך II "seize" (cf. Arab. *masaka*; *DCH,* 5:525a). So Dhorme, Hölscher, NJPS, emending to מֹשֵׁךְ "seizing," and translating "He who by His power seizes the mighty"; hence JB "he who lays mighty hold on tyrants." But again we should expect something more explicit about the purpose or result of this seizing. Terrien goes further, with "he has the power to tame [bulls]," but there is no evidence that משך means "tame."

22.d. Terrien takes אבירים from אַבִּיר "bull" and translates "he has the power to tame bulls"; NJPS also finds "bulls" here: "Though he has the strength to seize bulls." De Wilde and Strauss (אֶבְיֹנִים) emend אבירים "the mighty" to אֶבְיוֹנִים "the poor," and Duhm and Beer (BH^2) to אֹבְדִים "those who are perishing," claiming the support of LXX ἀδυνάτους. But that is probably an inner-Greek corruption of δυνάτους = אבירים (Dhorme). Beer (*BHK*) reads, with some MSS, the sg אַבִּיר "the mighty one."

22.e. A circumstantial clause (cf. 42:3; GKC, §156f). Others see a contrast here; so Gordis "he may survive, but has no faith in life" (similarly Habel).

22.f. יקום "he rises up," which is presumably a case of sg for pl since the subj is אבירים "the mighty." Driver–Gray are inclined to emend to the pl, יָקוּמוּ "they rise up." Dhorme makes the subj God ("he rises up"), but then the subj of the next verb has to be the wicked and the whole rendering becomes too convoluted. JB, following Dhorme, does a good job of smoothing the sentence: "rises up to take away that life which seemed secure," but the underlying interpretation is still awkward. LXX has "when he [the wicked] has arisen, a man will not feel secure of his own life" (ἀναστὰς τοιγαροῦν, οὐ μὴ πιστεύῃ κατὰ τῆς ἑαυτοῦ ζωῆς)—which makes an attractive sense but also is convoluted, having different subjs for the verbs יקום and יאמין. NJPS "May he live with no assurance of survival" strains the meaning of יקום "he arises" to make it mean "he lives" (and the sequence of thought in vv 22–23 in NJPS is hard to explain). NAB has "to him who rises [? from his bed] without assurance of his life he gives safety and support"; but there is no call here to mention those lacking in assurance since the focus is exclusively upon the wealthy wicked. Terrien tries hard with "but [one fine morning] he arises with no confidence in life!" Duhm wants the sequence of verbs to be passive, so he reads יֻקַם "he is made to arise," and in v 23 יֻתַּץ "he is broken down" for יתן. Beer (*BH*² *frt*) reads יִמַּק (מקק niph) "he rots, moulders away," which at least creates a parallelism with the remainder of the colon.

22.g. האמין בחיין, lit. "believe in life," i.e., have assurance of life, is a phrase found also in Deut 28:66. Driver–Gray are inclined to read the pl, יַאֲמִינוּ "they do [not] rely." Pope omits the לא "not," or else regards it as an asseverative. חיין would be an Aramaizing pl (GKC, §86e), but many read חַיָּיו "his life" (so LXX, some MSS, Duhm, Driver–Gray, Dhorme, Beer [*BHK*], Hölscher, Kissane, Fedrizzi, de Wilde, and Hartley).

23.a. The subj must be God, especially in view of v 23. But Terrien translates "who will lend him support?" supposing that the verse is a question. Rather than יתן "he gives, grants, [to him]," Beer (*BH*²) reads יֻתַּץ "he [the mighty] is broken down" (from נתץ), which conceivably represents LXX μαλακισθεὶς or, less probably, יְדֻכֶּה "is crushed" (from דכא).

23.b. שׁעַן, lit. "lean."

23.c. לבטח is a little odd, lit. "[he gives him] in security [and he leans]." We could understand לִהְיוֹת לבטח "[he grants him] to be in security" (or לָשֶׁבֶת לבטח "to dwell in safety" [Gordis]), or emend to לִבְטֹחַ "to trust, feel secure" (so Beer [*BHK*], Gerleman [*BHS prp*]; בטח is abs also at Isa 12:2). But Dhorme's interpretation is surely correct: לבטח belongs with וישען, thus "he allows him to rest in security." An excellent parallel is 19:23 מי־יתן בספר ויחקו "who will grant that they should be inscribed in a book?" lit. "who will grant in a book that they should be inscribed?" Rearrangement of the verse to יתן לו וישען לבטח (Hölscher) is unnecessary. Duhm and Beer (*BH*²) have לא יִבְטַח "he does not trust," which seems supported by LXX. De Wilde arbitrarily suggests יִתְהַלֵּל בְּטוֹבָה "he congratulates himself on his good fortune."

23.d. Most take the two cola as parallel, but KJV has attractively "yet his eyes are upon his ways" (similarly JPS, JB, NEB, NIV, GNB), Dhorme "but His eyes were watching."

23.e. עֵינֵיהוּ is an unusual form of the 3 masc suff (see GKC, §91l). Rather than accept that "nonform," Duhm reads מְעַנֵּהוּ "his oppressor," i.e., God. Beer's proposal (*BHK*), wisely qualified with a question mark, to read עֵינֵי יָהוּ "the eyes of Yahu (Yahweh)," may be discounted (יָהוּ does not appear in the Hebrew Bible as an independent form).

23.f. Lit. "their ways" (דרכיהם). Dhorme wants the references to the wicked to be in the sg (though he accepted אבירים in v 22), so he emends דרכיהם "their ways" to דְּרָכָיו "his ways" (so too Beer [*BHK*], Hölscher, Fedrizzi, Sicre Díaz). De Wilde would like to read וְאוֹנוֹ הוּא עַל־דַּרְכּוֹ "and his misfortune is already upon his path."

24.a. רוֹמּוּ is a strange form, perhaps a qal passive, "they are exalted" (GKC, §67m)—a grim pun on רמה "maggot" (v 20), thinks Good. Because איננו is sg, Duhm (רָמוּ), Beer (*BH*²), Hölscher, de Wilde read רוֹמוֹ "his exaltation," which is perhaps supported by LXX. Dhorme reads יָרוּם "he was high, exalted"; and Beer (*BHK*), Fohrer, and NEB have רָמוּ "they were high." Gordis claims that רומו is the impv of a רום II "wait" (so "wait just a little"), which he thinks occurs also in Isa 30:18 in parallel to חכה piel; so too Moffatt "Have patience! they will soon be gone." But the rendering seems forced. Ehrlich's proposal that God's eyes are the subject of רָמוּ is no better.

24.b. איננו is sg, whereas רמו was pl; most versions use the pl (KJV, JPS, etc.), and Beer (*BHK*), Kissane, Fohrer, Gerleman (*BHS prp*), Hartley, NEB actually emend to אֵינָם "they are not, i.e., they are gone." Davidson translated "in a moment they are not," but מעט belongs rather with רמו.

24.c. מכך "be low, humiliated," elsewhere only at Ps 106:43; Eccl 10:18. On the so-called Aramaizing form הֻמְּכוּ, cf. GKC, §67y. Dhorme, wanting all the verbs about the wicked to be in the sg, reads וְהֻמַּךְ "and he has collapsed" (so too Duhm, Beer [*BH*²], Hölscher). But it is not abnormal to find a sg in the first colon parallel to a pl in the second (cf. 16:11; 27:13).

24.d. קפץ is "draw together, shut," of hand (Deut 15:7) or mouth (Job 5:16); this will hardly refer to "contraction in death" (cf. BDB, 891b), but perhaps will justify "shrivel" (NJPS, Hartley). Olshausen (with one MS) proposed יִקָּבְצוּן "are gathered [for burial]"; cf. NAB, NIV "are gathered up." Siegfried read יִקָּטְפוּן (so too Beer [*BHK*; *BH*² יִקָּטֵף *prps*], Fohrer, Gerleman [*BHS prp*]) "are plucked off" (in 8:12 of papyrus and reeds; in 30:4 of mallows, interestingly enough). Dhorme, reading the qal יִקְטְפוּן, lamely translates "[he has collapsed like the orach] that one gathers" (similarly Hölscher). RSV "fade" seems to have reversed the positions of יקפצון and ימלו. Duhm and Beer (*BH*²) want the sg יִקָּפֵץ.

L. Kopf ("Arabische Etymologien und Parallelen zum Bibelworterbuch," *VT* 8 [1958] 161–215 [200]) proposed a קפץ II "snatch away" (cf. Arab. *qubida* [Lane, 2482a]; cf. *HALOT*, 3:1118a). Guillaume (*Lexicography,* 3:7; *Studies,* 109) compares rather Arab. *qabaṣa* "pluck," but somewhat strangely translates "are taken out of the way."

24.e. כְּכֹל "like the totality" does not fit here (KJV "as all other"; similarly JPS, Moffatt, NAB, NIV, Fohrer, Fedrizzi). RSV and JB have "mallow," JPS "mallows," NEB "mallow-flower," NJB "saltwort," and GNB "a weed," but it is hard to tell what they are reading. The possibilities are:

(1) כֹּל is the name of a plant, as Ehrlich supposes and J. Reider argues ("the umbel of a plant, the melilot or honey-lotus," in "Contributions to the Hebrew Lexicon," *ZAW* 53 [1935] 270–77 [273–75], comparing Aram. כלילא; cf. also Grabbe, 88–89; and Gordis, proposing a כל "grass," parallel to Arab. *ka'lun* "forage, herbage"; cf. also *DCH,* 4:413b).

(2) We should emend, following the lead of LXX ὥσπερ μολοχή and reading כְּמַלּוּחַ "like mallows, saltwort" (BDB, 572a; *HALOT,* 2:587b; *DCH,* 5:291b; so too Beer [*BH*² כְּמַלַּח; *BHK*], Hölscher, Kissane [כְּמַלַּח], Terrien [כְּמַלַּח], Pope, Habel), a desert plant (genus *Malva*) growing in salt marshes, with edible fruit, leaves, and seed. Dhorme insists that מלוח is the orach (*Atriplex halimus*), a plant related to spinach, protein rich, and used as animal feed (see R. K. Harrison, *ISBE,* 3:230; J. C. Trever, *IDB,* 3:233). On another word for "mallows" (חַלָּמוּת), see *Note* 6:6.c.

(3) The Qumran Tg has כיבלא "like dog grass" (Pope), which Hartley follows to restore כִּיבוּל "like grass" to the Heb. (for יְבוּל "produce," cf. BDB, 385a; *DCH,* 4:73a).

(4) De Wilde reads for the colon וַהֲמוֹנָיו כַּפּוֹל יִקָּפְצוּן "and his riches shrivel like beans" (a marvelous image, he says). Good leaves a gap in his translation, wanting reference to a plant but being unsatisfied by the emendation to כמלוח.

24.f. ימלו from מלל "languish, wither, fade," NEB "droop," NAB "shrivel" (BDB, 576b [מלל III]; *HALOT,* 2:593b [מלל I]; *DCH,* 5:327b [מלל I]). RSV, NIV "cut off" is hard to justify; there is another verb מלל "cut" (BDB, 576b [מלל IV]), a byform of מול, but it seems restricted to the meaning "circumcise" (though it may be simply "cut" in 14:2; Ps 58:8; see *DCH,* 5:328a [מלל IV]). Duhm, Beer (*BH*²), Dhorme, Hölscher read the sg יִמַּל "he fades."

27:18.a. כעשׁ is apparently "like a moth," as in 4:19; 13:28. This is odd, since moths are not elsewhere spoken of as building, but it is the rendering of KJV, JPS, Sicre Díaz, Good. NIV "like a moth's cocoon" attempts to explain the metaphor. Schultens, Ehrlich, Dhorme, Fedrizzi, and Gordis, however, find a different עָשׁ "bird's nest" (comparing Arab. *'uššun;* cf. also Akk. *ašāšu* A "a bowerlike reed cover used by water fowl" (*CAD,* 1.2:422b); so too G. R. Driver ("Difficult Words in the Hebrew Prophets," in *Studies in Old Testament Prophecy,* FS T. H. Robinson, ed. H. H. Rowley [Edinburgh: T. & T. Clark, 1950] 52–72 [67]), NEB, NJPS; mentioned by Barr (*Comparative Philology,* 333; cf. *DCH,* vol. 6, *s.v.*); Ehrlich finds the word also at 4:19. Pope doubts that עשׁ can be cognate with the Akk., and proposes as a cognate Arab. *'āš* "night watchman" (ptcp of *'ass* "keep night-watch"); he is followed by Habel. This proposal creates a very close parallel with נצר in the second colon, but it would be odd to have a comparison with a watchman in the first colon and with a hut in the second.

LXX translates the term twice over, ἀπέβη δὲ ὁ οἶκος αὐτοῦ ὥσπερ σῆτες καὶ ὥσπερ ἀραχνή "his house has gone away like moths and like a spider." The latter translation suggests to many an emendation to כְּעַכָּבִישׁ "like a spider" (as in 8:14; Isa 59:5); so Merx, Budde, Duhm, Peake, Strahan, Driver–Gray, Beer (*BHK*), Hölscher, Fohrer, Terrien, Rowley, Gerleman (*BHS prp*), Andersen, de Wilde; and thus "like a spider's web" (RSV, JB, GNB, Hartley), "as of cobwebs" (NAB). But עכביש does not mean "spider's web," and it would be very awkward if the verse were to mean "he builds, like a spider, his house, and [it is] like a booth [that] a watchman makes"; it is more natural if כסכה "like a booth" is parallel to some flimsily built object represented by עשׁ. See also the full discussion in Grabbe, 89–91.

18.b. Lit. "like a booth [that] a watchman makes," the relative pronoun אֲשֶׁר being understood.

19.a. עשׁיר "rich" is acc of state and in emphatic position (as ערום "naked" in 1:21).

19.b. ולא יאסף "and he shall not be gathered" (so KJV; cf. JPS, Davidson) is not very plausible in the context. Some have explained it as gathered for proper burial (as in Jer 8:2; Ezek 29:5), but it would be strange to read of the death of the wicked before, in the next colon (v 19a), they open their eyes. Good "but has no harvest" apparently reads יֶאֱסֹף "he gathers." Most, including the *Translation* above, accept an emendation (or perhaps just the recognition of an "aberrant vocalization and orthography" [Gordis]) to וְלֹא יוֹסִף (perhaps written as יֹאסִף) "and he does not add," i.e., to do so again (so RSV, NIV "but will do so no more," NAB, GNB "one last time," JB, NEB "but never again"); so too (with the support of LXX, Pesh) Duhm, Strahan, Driver–Gray, Beer (*BHK*), Dhorme, Hölscher, Fohrer, Pope, Rowley, Fedrizzi, Gerleman (*BHS prp*), de Wilde, Sicre Díaz, Habel, Hartley. The idiom "and [he] does not add" can be seen also at 20:9; 34:32; 40:5. The proposal of M. Dahood (review of *Job et son Dieu: Essai d'exégèse et de théologie biblique,* by J. Lévêque, *Bib* 52 [1971] 436–38 [438]) and Blommerde, that לא is a divine title, לֵא "the Mighty One," and that אסף means "snatch away," suffers from the same difficulty as the MT, that v 19a cannot easily refer to death if v 19b speaks of them opening their eyes. For other supposed examples of לָא "the Victor, Mighty One," see *Note* 21:16.a.

19.c. Some have thought that the subj is impersonal ("when one opens one's eyes, the wicked is gone," i.e., is dead). But it is more probable that the subj is the same as in the first colon.

19.d. The subject is implied (as RSV, JB, NEB, NAB, NJPS, NIV, GNB), though a noun for "wealth" has not been previously used (it is the adj עָשִׁיר "rich" in the first colon). ואיננו "and he/it is not" could mean, at a pinch, that when the wrongdoer wakes up he is dead (cf. 2 Kgs 19:35 || Isa 37:36), but that is most unlikely.

20.a. Sg verb with pl subj (GKC, §145k); for other examples, cf. *Note* 22:9.a. Duhm however thought it would be better to vocalize as a pl, תַּשִּׂיגֻהוּ "they overtake."

20.b. כמים is really "like water," a phrase that usually refers to the availability or cheapness or drinkability or pourability of water (as in 3:24; 15:16; 34:7), and not to water as a destructive force. RSV, NEB, NJPS, NIV, and GNB ("sudden flood") hope with the translation "flood" to make water into a sufficiently powerful parallel to "tempest" in the second colon, but there are few, if any, real analogies to this sense, not even Job 22:11 and Isa 28:2 with a "flood [זרם, שׁפעה] of waters," 2 Sam 5:20 with the "bursting forth [פרץ] of waters," Ps 66:12 "through fire and water," or Ps 32:6 "the rush [שׁטף] of great waters." Perhaps the best analogy is Isa 28:17, where "waters" (מים) "sweep away [שׁטף] a shelter." And it is a question whether "overtake" (נשׂג hiph) can be thought of as something water can do. Nevertheless, "like waters" is accepted by Driver–Gray and de Wilde; in the absence of a better solution, perhaps we should stay with this translation.

However, because the parallel to כמים is לילה "by night," many propose reading בַּיּוֹם "by day" (Merx, Graetz, Beer [*BHK vel*], Gerleman [*BHS prp*]) or יוֹמָם (Wright, Budde, Strahan, Beer [*BHK vel*], Dhorme, Hölscher, Pope, Gerleman [*BHS vel*], Sicre Díaz, NAB; so too Moffatt, NAB, JB "in broad daylight"). But this emendation does not commend itself unequivocally, for the context of vv 19–20 seems rather to be of the loss of wealth and life in a *night,* and it is a little odd to have the terrors in the day and the tempest later on, in the night. The phrase in 5:14, "by daylight they meet with darkness," is no real parallel (against Dhorme), though the Terrors may be thought of as, properly speaking, creatures of the night.

20.c. גנב is the ordinary word for "steal" (BDB, 170a). M. Dahood ("Hebrew-Ugaritic Lexicography VII," *Bib* 50 [1969] 337–56 [342]) translated the colon, "Night will kidnap him like a tempest," regarding "Night" as a term for the underworld. But this requires recourse to Dahood's view of the prep *kaph* as "double-duty," and agreement that "like a tempest" is a suitable adverbial phrase for "kidnaps." J. Lust ("A Stormy Vision: Some Remarks on Job 4, 12–16," *Bijdr* 36 [1975] 308–11 [309]) has correctly seen that גנב here and at 4:12 and 21:18 means "transport violently"; it sounds like a different word, but no alternative etymology is propounded.

21.a. On the pausal form יֵלַךְ, see 7:9, and GKC, §§29q, 69x.

22.a. NAB combines this verse with 26:13.

22.b. וְיַשְׁלֵךְ is unaccountably juss; perhaps it should be vocalized וַיַּשְׁלֵךְ "and it casts" (as, e.g., Beer [*BHK*]; one MS has וישליך). Most modern versions take the east wind (קדים) of v 21 as the subj and assume that שׁלך hiph is to be understood as reflexive (Gordis), though there seem to be no parallels. Duhm supplies as the obj "missiles," Fohrer "stones" or "sand," Strahan "thunderbolts." Dhorme, Hölscher, and Fedrizzi think the subj of שׁלך is impersonal ("Men hurl themselves at him"), while KJV, RV had "God" (so too Moffatt "God pelts him without pity," Duhm, Strahan, Driver–Gray, Terrien). According to Brockington, NEB adopts the emendation to וְיֻשְׁלַךְ "and it is driven"; but NEB itself has "it [the east wind] flings itself on him."

22.c. ברוח יברח, the inf abs before the verb to emphasize "either the certainty . . . or the forcibleness or completeness of an occurrence" (GKC, §113n). G. R. Driver proposed that a second verb ברח "wound" should be postulated for Heb., cognate with Arab. *baraḥa* (not *baraha*) "bruise" and attested in the pual here (reading יְבֹרַח "he shall be sorely bruised [by its force]") and at 41:28 (20), and in the qal at Prov 19:26; Job 20:24. See G. R. Driver, "Proverbs xix. 26," *TZ* 11 (1955) 373–74; idem, "Problems in the Hebrew Text of Job," in *Wisdom in Israel and in the Ancient Near East,* FS H. H. Rowley, VTSup 3 (Leiden: Brill, 1955) 72–93 (81); *HALOT,* 1:156b; *DCH,* 2:263a. For an argument against this proposal, see D. J. A. Clines, "Were There a ברח II 'vex' and ברח III 'wound, bruise, pierce' and ברח IV 'bar' in Classical Hebrew?" (forthcoming in Sara Japhet Festschrift).

23.a. NAB deletes this verse as merely a variant form of v 21.

23.b. שׂפק "clap" is elsewhere spelled ספק (BDB, 706b).

23.c. The מוּ־ suff of כפימו is usually pl, thus "their hands"; so some emend the verb to יִשְׂפְּקוּ "they [indefinite] clap" (Driver–Gray, Beer [BH^2 *frt*]; cf. KJV, RV) or the noun to כַּפָּיו "his hands" (Duhm) or כַּפָּיִם "hands" (Beer [*BHK*], Hölscher [*frt*], Kissane, Fohrer [כַּפָּיִם], Gerleman [*BHS prb*]). But the suff seems to be sg at 20:23 (see also GKC, §103f, n) and may be allowed to stand here also. Peake, Hölscher, Fohrer, Terrien, Rowley, Fedrizzi, Gordis, Ravasi, and Sicre Díaz also regard the subj as impersonal ("men"), but do not emend the text. Duhm, Strahan, and Andersen think the subj is God, as in v 21.

23.d. The suff of עלימו also may be regarded as sg (as, e.g., Gerleman [*BHS*]), and the word need not be emended to עָלָיו "against him" (as Duhm, Driver–Gray, Beer [*BHK*], Hölscher, Fohrer). In both כפימו and עלימו we may be dealing with consciously archaic forms (cf. GKC, §91l: "these [suffixes] are revivals of really old forms. That they are consciously and artificially used is shown by the evidently intentional accumulation of them"). At the very least they are chosen for their sound (Sicre Díaz).

23.e. Beer (*BH*[2] *frt*) would make the sg verb וישרק into pl in conformity with the emendation of the previous verb.

23.f. Gordis thinks the *mem* should mean "in [his former place]." NEB "wherever he may be" likewise takes the *mem* as "in." One MS (cf. *BHS*) has מקמו "his place," which would then be the subj of ישרק "hisses"; this is adopted by Beer (*BHK*) and is followed also by Sicre Díaz, who thinks it is equivalent to "the men of his place." It is much more natural, however, to translate "from its place." Beer (*BH*[2]) notes alternative emendations, to מִמָּרוֹם "from on high" or, most unlikely, מִתְקֹמְמוֹ (which must be an error for מִתְקֹמְמָה) "[and] rising up [they (indefinite) hiss at them]."

23.g. It is the wind's place (as RSV, NJPS, Habel, Good) and not the wicked's place (as KJV, JPS, NIV) or God's (Duhm, Strahan; Moffatt "hisses scorn at him from heaven").

23.h. JB, Pope, and Ravasi follow this verse with 24:18–24 (Pope and Ravasi add v 25).

Form/Structure/Setting

Once again, the question of the *integrity* of the speech must be treated. The view that has been preferred in this commentary is that, although the Masoretic text ascribes 27:7–23 to Job, these verses (with the exception of vv 11–12) in fact constitute the last speech of Zophar, which is otherwise entirely missing from the book (so also, e.g., Beer [*BHK*]). H. G. Reventlow ("Tradition und Redaktion in Hiob 27 im Rahmen der Hiobreden des Abschnittes Hi 24–27," *ZAW* 94 [1982] 279–93) thinks that vv 7–10 and 13–23 have been inserted at a late date from a wisdom psalm on the fate of the wicked, but it is preferable to assign the material rather to a final speech of Zophar.

The other main element of Zophar's third speech, as here reconstructed, is the strophe 24:18–24, which has been retrieved from Job's eighth speech, and located after 27:17. The passage fits poorly within Job's speech in chaps. 23–24, but here it is entirely suitable, continuing Zophar's depiction of the wicked in 27:13–17 with a strophe of eight lines. For further discussion of the reasons for the transference of this strophe from Job's eighth speech, see *Comment* below on 24:18–24. Two verses of chap. 27 have been transferred from their traditional place to follow 27:6, as part of Job's ninth speech.

The *strophic structure* of the speech is of four strophes of unequal length, all of them devoted to the theme of the wicked. The first strophe (27:7–10) concerns the hopeless future of the godless wicked, the second (27:13–17) the reversal of the expectations of the wicked, the third (24:18–24) the downfall of the wicked as brought low by God, and the fourth (27:18–23) the downfall of the wicked as the victims of cosmic forces that tear them from their dwellings.

The three strophes of chap. 27 that are here assigned to the third speech of Zophar are of four lines, five lines, and six lines, respectively; and the strophe that we should probably insert (after 27:17) from 24:18–24 contains eight lines, perhaps consisting of two substrophes of four lines (24:18–20, with closure at v 20d; and 24:21–24, with closure in v 24). Within the strophic structure there are some two-line units, notably vv 14–15 about the offspring of the wicked, vv 16–17 about the possessions of the wicked, and vv 18–19 about the instability of the wealth of the wicked. Hölscher and de Wilde as usual find everything to be composed as two-line strophes, but Hölscher needs to omit v 13 and de Wilde v 12 to make this system work. Almost all the lines are bicola, except for the tricola in 24:18, 24, framing the strophe 24:18–24.

Terrien notices the same three strophes in the text of chap. 27 as it stands (though he assigns vv 7–10 to Job); the second strophe he divides quite reasonably into vv 13–15 and 16–17, but his two substrophes of vv 18–21 and 22–23 are hard to justify since the violence of the east wind is the subject both in v 21 and in vv 22–23 (though the objection does not apply if Terrien's own understanding of God as the subject of vv 22–23 stands). Fohrer likewise recognizes three strophes, but he attaches v 13 to vv 7–10 (perhaps because the "This is . . ." sentence functions elsewhere as a mark of closure), and he connects v 18 with vv 14–17 (similarly NAB); it is better though to connect it to what follows, since it announces the theme of instability and uncertainty, which is developed summarily in v 19 and more extensively in vv 20–22. Webster finds five strophes in the chapter, which he regards as a unity: vv 2–6, 7–11, 12–15, 16–19, and 20–23, a scheme that has no evident difficulties if the reassignment of verses proposed here is not accepted. The disjunction between v 12 and v 13 is quite commonly recognized, by RSV (not NRSV), JB, NEB, NAB, NIV, GNB (but not NJPS), Gordis, and Habel. Good marks a break only between v 13 and v 14.

The *genre* is again the *disputation speech,* of which the four *rhetorical questions* in vv 8–10 are a typical feature (e.g., 21:27–31; 22:2–5; 26:4).

Among elements of *forms* drawn on in the speech there is principally the *wisdom instruction,* which prevails in vv 13–23 and 24:18–24 (which is here seen as part of this speech of Zophar); motifs encountered in the wisdom literature and the Psalms are frequent. The *headline* form, a noun clause opening with "This is . . . ," is a feature of the wisdom teaching (cf. Ps 49:13; in Job 8:19 and 20:29 it serves to introduce a closing summary appraisal). The form of the *contrast* is repeated, between the good fortune of the wicked in their children and the fate of the those children (vv 14–15), between their acquisition of wealth and clothes and use of them by others (vv 16–17), between their exaltation and their humiliation (24:24). The *topos* of the fate of the wicked (as already in 5:12–14; 8:13–19; 15:20–34; 18:5–21; 20:5–29) is a familiar one in the book of Job.

The other distinguishable form is the *wish*: the speech probably lacks, because of disturbance in the course of transmission, its original proemium, and, in its present form, it opens with a wish (v 7), apparently against the enemy of the speaker, which is comparable with psalmic wishes against enemies (e.g., Pss 5:10 [11]; 12:3 [4]; 31:17b–18 [18b–19]); but here the wish is directed against the wicked rather than against the person with whom the speaker is in disputation.

The *function* of the speech cannot be established from the internal evidence of the text, for it is almost entirely descriptive and gives no clues about its intention. However, in the light of the other speeches of Zophar (chaps. 11, 20), it seems most likely that its function is to encourage Job to avoid the fate of the wicked that is here depicted. Though there are some points at which the language reflects, rather cruelly, the life experiences of Job (as in the references to the many children of the wicked being destined one and all for death [vv 14–15], and to the role of the east wind in bringing the wicked to their doom [vv 21–23; cf. 1:19]), it does not seem that Zophar claims that Job is himself one of the wicked. On the contrary, the depiction in this speech is precisely of what Job must avoid becoming.

The *tonality* of the speech is likewise difficult to determine, since Zophar distances himself so sharply from the subject matter of his speech and employs an objective reportorial style. But the language, with its many rhetorical flourishes, suggests that Zophar is savoring the description of the downfall of the wicked, elaborating traditional material to a fanciful degree (e.g., with the trope of the threefold agents of death [vv 14–15; cf. Zophar also at 20:24–25] or with the picture of the personified east wind that does not spare [v 22] and that plays the role of the passing traveler who mocks at the signs of the ruin of the wicked [v 23]). The tone of the speech has a distinct element of *Schadenfreude* in it, which overwhelms the professed didacticism ("This is the portion of the wicked . . .") and any ulterior motivation that may be to Job's benefit.

The *nodal verse* may be said to be v 8, "What is the hope of the godless?" For the theme of the speech is that the future of the wicked is established and fixed: they have a "portion," a "heritage" from God (v 13), from which there is no hope of escape. And they can have nothing positive to hope for, since their posterity is already marked down for death, and they themselves can expect only a sudden and irreversible removal from the stability of their life.

Comment

27:7–10, 13–17; 24:18–24; 27:18–23 This sequence of verses is here taken as Zophar's third speech (see on *integrity* under *Form/Structure/Setting*), its theme being evidently the fate of the wicked. It is not a lot different from chap. 20, Zophar's previous speech, except that the focus here is entirely on the fact of the destiny of the wicked, and not at all on the behavior that marks them out as wicked. In this speech there is hardly a word of what the wicked have done wrong (apart from wronging barren women and widows [24:21, if this strophe is correctly transposed to this point]; heaping up silver and fine clothes [v 16] is not represented as a crime).

Parallels of language and thought between this speech that is here presumed to be Zophar's and the previous speech that was indubitably his, are these: the survivors (27:14–15; cf. 20:26); he is overtaken by a flood (27:20; cf. 20:28); he is swept out of his place (27:21; cf. 20:9b); he is forgotten (24:20; cf. 20:7–9).

We might well suppose that Zophar's speech once began (before the damage to the text in the course of transmission) with the conventional opening, "And Zophar the Naamathite answered and said" (as in 20:1), and perhaps also with some personal address to Job (as in 11:2–6; 20:2–4; cf. also Duhm).

7 Zophar is appalled at the thought of what lies in store for the wicked man. His destiny is to be abandoned by God (v 9), to see his children fall to the sword, to famine, or to plague (vv 14–15), to lose his wealth overnight (v 19), to be swept away from the security of his home (vv 20–22), and to be ultimately forgotten (24:20). Zophar wishes no one any harm—any harm, that is to say, that they do not deserve—and he shudders to think of such a fate befalling anyone, unless perhaps they had assaulted him personally ("rose up against" him). We ourselves might say we wouldn't want it to happen to our worst enemy, and there is perhaps only a difference in rhetoric when Zophar wishes it *would* happen to his enemy (for the language, cf. 2 Sam 18:32). It is not that Zophar is thinking of any particular enemy of his, or even that he is conscious of having any enemies at all (any more than we are when we speak of our worst enemy). His emphasis is entirely on the wicked (as Davidson sees), rather than upon any hypothetical enemy he might have.

So how is Job connected with this depiction? We may be sure that by his "enemy" Zophar does not in the least mean Job. Job is his friend (even if Job will not believe it), and Zophar wishes Job no harm. In 11:13–19 he had offered Job his prescription for how he could be restituted to his former happiness and security, and had painted a glowing picture of future hope, safety, and rest for Job. The purpose of this third speech of his is no doubt the same as that of his second speech (chap. 20): it was the grimmest picture Zophar knew how to paint of the fate that awaits the wicked, and he set it before Job in order to frighten him, in all kindliness, into amendment of life. Not for a moment does he regard Job as a wicked (רשׁע) man or a wrongdoer (עול)—though Job has no doubt sinned in some way and is being punished for it, and that less than he deserves (11:5–6). What Zophar does not seem to realize is that Job has in fact already suffered the fate of the wrongdoer, having lost all his offspring and being overturned by a flood of disasters. It is an irony that what Zophar wishes for his enemy is reality for his friend.

8 One might think that when anyone, righteous or wicked, is "cut off," they do not have a lot of hope; there is certainly no hint here that the righteous *do* have hope when the wicked do not (cf. Driver–Gray), and it is not a matter of recovery from sickness (as Strahan). The only hope anyone can have at the end of their days is that they may somehow survive in their descendants and in the property they leave behind them for their descendants—and that, says Zophar, is the hope that is denied the wicked (the thought will be developed in vv 14–17).

9–10 Even the "impious" (חנף, previously at 8:13; 13:16; 15:34; 17:8; 20:5) may be constrained by calamity to approach God with prayers. But God of course—for (we must remember) Zophar knows what God will and will not do (cf. 11:5–6)—will have no regard for the prayers of the wicked. If the situation of vv 14–15 is already in view, of the loss of the wicked's offspring, that has already happened before the wicked man is being "cut off"—so it is not for their survival that he is praying. The logic of Zophar's position leaves something to be desired.

On the "cry" (צעקה) for help, see on 19:7. On "delighting" (ענג hithp) in God, see on 22:26–27, where also it appears in the context of prayer. By asking whether the wicked will call upon God "at all times," Zophar asks whether the wicked will become a pious person, constant in prayer (cf. de Wilde "Can he have his delight in the Almighty, so that he can call on God at any time?"). He is not suggesting that "it is useless to cry to God in the crises of life, if he is ignored at all other times" (Rowley). Nor is it that v 10 strays from the track of the fate of the wicked to the question of his character, whether he acts as a pious man (as J. Strahan). For the sequence of thought seems to be: Will he be heard by God? Will he be continuously in prayer, as the pious are, and so be sure to be answered?

These sentences contain a hidden message for Job, no doubt. Since he is not one of the "impious" and the "wrongdoers," he could conclude—and Zophar wants him to make this inference—that he *will* be heard by God in his extremity. This is no more than the obverse of Eliphaz's cameo in 22:26–27 of how Job may expect God to listen to his prayer.

11–12 These verses are assigned in this commentary to Job's ninth speech (27:1–6, 11–12); for *Comment* and *Notes* see after 27:6.

13–23 The fate of the wicked person (אדם is "human being" and not "man" specifically) is here described in terms of the fate of the offspring. The end of the wicked is here not to be cut off in their prime but, worse than that, to live to see the death of their children, who are brought to an early grave. Rhetorically, it heightens the disaster that befalls the wicked person if others of the family are drawn into the same fate; but ideologically also there comes to the surface an important theme in Hebrew ethics, that of the solidarity of the family and the difficulty of escaping the consequences of one's parents' wrongdoing (cf. Jer 31:29; 18:21).

Though the Hebrew uses the singular forms throughout vv 13–23 to speak of the wicked (except in v 13b), it also has, unusually, described the wicked in v 13 as an אדם, a "person," without specifying the gender. So in the translation and commentary I have used plural forms consistently since it appears that the text does not want us to regard the wicked here as necessarily male.

13 The remainder of this third speech of Zophar's, on the fate of the wicked, begins with a sentence that is almost a trademark of his. At the end of his second speech he has concluded "Such is the fate God allots to the wicked" (20:29a), using identical language to that of v 13a here—except that it is "with God" (עם־אל) here and "from God" (מאלהים) there, and "this, such" (זה) looks backward there and forward here.

On the meaning of "portion" (חלק) as life as a given totality and of "inheritance" (נחלה) as life as something in process of becoming, see on 20:29. The doctrine of exact retribution is combined in these terms with a kind of predestination.

14–15 The unfortunate fate of the children of the wicked is now the theme; it is a common *topos* in wisdom texts (cf. 5:5; 18:19; 20:10; Prov 13:22). Having many sons, or children of either sex (the Hebrew is rarely specific, the term בנים meaning either "sons" or "children"), is usually a mark of divine favor (cf. Pss 127:3; 128:3). For them to die early, before their parents, is a mark of signal divine displeasure (cf. 5:4; 20:10; and cf. Ps 37:25). The misfortune of the wicked will be to lose their children to an unavoidable disaster; the text invokes the familiar sinister trio of death—war, famine, and plague (so too in Jer 14:12; 15:2; Ezek 5:12; 6:11–12; 14:12–20 [with wild beasts]; Rev 6:8 [also with wild beasts]; in Job 5:20 we have simply famine and war, and in Lam 1:20 war and plague). The image is of some children surviving the first disaster only to be carried off by the second, and so on (cf. 20:24); for "those who survive" (שׂריד) in v 15 cannot be those children who outlive the wicked person, since the death of the wicked person is not in view at that point.

If the children of the wicked have become many, it is not a mark of divine blessing, says Zophar; it is only to provide food for the sword (for the image of the sword as "devouring," cf. Deut 32:42; 2 Sam 2:26; 11:25; 18:8; Isa 31:8; Jer 2:30; 12:12; 46:10, 14; Hos 11:6; Nah 2:14 [13]; 3:15; 1QM 6:3; 12:12; 19:4). The sword is implicitly personified, as the plague is explicitly—and, later, the east wind (vv 22–23). Those of them that escape death in war will starve; if they are "not satisfied with food," that does not mean that they are hard to please; rather, it is a litotes for not having enough to live on (cf. Amos 4:8; Mic 6:14). Those who escape the first two disasters will be brought to their death by the third, plague; and if they are buried by the plague (במות יקברו), it means that they lie where they fall and they are not really buried at all; so to the fact of their death is added the bitterness that they lie unburied, a terrible fate (cf. 1 Kgs 13:22; 2 Kgs 9:10; Jer 7:33; 8:2; 9:21 [22]; 14:16; 22:19).

But who are "his widows" (אלמנתיו), who do not weep? If we take the word at its face value, they must be the widows of the wicked person, who is generally referred to in the singular throughout vv 13–23 (though in v 13b it is the plural "oppressors"). In that case, the wicked person is a polygamist (so Hölscher, Fohrer, Gordis, Andersen, Sicre Díaz, Good). That makes sense, of a sort, since in most societies it is only the wealthier who can afford to be polygamous, and the wicked one here is plainly a person of means (cf. vv 16–17, 19). But it seems a little strange that the reference to polygamy should be dropped into the text so casually; it is alluded to nowhere else in the book of Job, and it is not as though there is anything "wrong" with the practice, since in the Hebrew Bible it is mostly attested to among the ancestors and rulers of the people, not among evildoers. And it is strange too that the wicked person here being described should have been called in v 13a an אדם, a "person," and not an איש, a "man," if the wicked one in question is so clearly a male as to have wives. It is odd too to find here a reference to widows of the wrongdoer when there has been no sign hitherto that the wrongdoer has died; indeed the very point of vv 14–15 seems to have been that the wrongdoer outlives his or her children, and has the misfortune of seeing their premature deaths.

All of these difficulties disappear if we regard the widows as the wives of the wrongdoer's children. These offspring of the wicked have been said to be "many" (v 14a), so that is why "widows" is in the plural; and if they are killed by the sword they are perhaps more likely now to be adults than children. So they will have been married, and it is *their* widows who will not mourn their death. And why will they not? The same clause occurs at Ps 78:64b, where the priests of Yahweh have fallen by the sword. Are these widows "unmoved" by their husbands' death (Dhorme)? Or are they "glad to be rid of him [the wicked man]" (Andersen)? Or is it that death by plague becomes so common that even mothers will not weep for their children (Gordis), or that they are facing such hardship themselves that they cannot weep over the loss of their own children (Hartley)? Or is it that "their widows are too stricken to think of the customary rites of mourning" (Strahan)?—which is to say, no doubt, that they are at the point of death themselves, since plague is nothing if not contagious. Or is it not rather that, if they are not buried, their widows cannot carry out the solemn rituals of mourning for them, and do not even have the consolation of laying them to rest (Davidson, Duhm, Hölscher)?

The picture of the premature deaths of adult children is cruelly reminiscent of the personal history of Job himself, and it might be thought that Zophar is implying that, with such an event in his life, Job must belong to the company of the wicked. But it is more likely that this is no more than another example of the callousness of the friends, and that Zophar's point, just as in his second speech (chap. 20), is not to threaten Job but to bring him, by portraying the fate of the unrepentant sinner, to abandon any guilt in his own life.

16–17 The evildoers' conspicuous wealth now becomes the subject. Even if their children are many, the wicked do not get the benefit of them, for they die before their time (vv 14–15). And now we find that even if the possessions of the wicked accumulate, they are not left to the children to live on, and the wicked have no enjoyment of them themselves. Rather they are distributed to the righteous. Nothing is said here explicitly of the *death* of the wicked; but it is hard to see how the innocent can divide the wrongdoers' silver among themselves if not after the wrongdoers' death. Though nothing is said explicitly of God's involvement here either, it is no doubt implied that it is his doing that the righteous find themselves rewarded for their piety out of the proceeds of the evildoers' activities.

The clause "he heaps up silver like dust" occurs also at Zech 9:3b (though with a variant word order); it is doubtful, however, whether there is any literary relationship between the texts. Unusually, it is not gold that is here paired with silver (as in 3:15; 22:25; 28:1) but clothing (מלבוש), another commodity of high value (cf. Gen 24:53; Josh 7:21; 2 Kgs 7:8; Zech 14:14; Matt 6:19). Hartley notes a similar parallel in Ugaritic texts (*UT* 1115:3–5; 2101:14–17 [= *RSP,* 1:248, no. 329]). The parallelism of dust (עפר) and clay (חמר) as substances without value is met with also at 4:19; 10:9 (cf. 30:19). There is a hidden order of things alluded to here: "dust is not only a symbol of what is abundant (Gen 13:16; 28:14) but also one with the world of death and decay" (Habel).

The two cola of v 17 correspond in inverse order to the two cola of v 16 (a rare example of "mirror chiasmus," as at Isa 22:22; cf. Watson, 203): the righteous wear the clothing the impious have amassed (vv 16b, 17a), and the innocent share out the silver the wicked have heaped up (vv 16a, 17b). For the idea of others acquiring one's wealth, cf. 5:5; Ps 39:6 (7); Eccl 2:18–21; and especially Prov 13:22 "The sinner's wealth is laid up for the righteous." It must be said, however, that the idea that, in the real world, the righteous fall heirs to the wealth of the wicked is a piece of wishful thinking, no more.

24:18–24 This strophe has been transferred from its usual place in chap. 24 because it appears to belong to a speech of Zophar rather than of Job. It forms one of the most difficult sets of verses encountered in the book. There are many textual and philological problems; NAB, for example, does not even attempt to translate most of vv 18–21 but simply offers an English version of the Vulgate in a footnote. The worst problem, however, is that, in its present position in the book, it is so hard to see what these verses have to do with Job's argument in this speech, indeed with Job's argument at any point in the book. If they are really saying that the wicked get their just deserts, that is not only the position of the friends and not of Job, but it is also the very opposite of what Job has been arguing in this very speech in chaps. 23–24.

For this reason, it would not be surprising if the theory that the strophe has been misplaced were correct; for we are at the end of the third cycle of speeches where by all accounts there has been serious textual corruption. In the Hebrew text as it stands, Zophar has no speech at all in the third cycle, and there are good grounds for assigning 27:7–10, 13–23 to one of the friends rather than to Job. Perhaps the present strophe (24:18–25) belongs with that passage and helps to restore Zophar's missing speech.

Many commentators and some translations believe that the strophe is misplaced in its present position in chap. 24, and remove it to some other speech. Larcher, followed by JB and Pope, for example, places vv 18–24 after 27:23, and Dhorme after 27:13, attributing the verses to Zophar. GNB also assigns this speech (perhaps vv 18–25) to Zophar. Alonso Schökel–Sicre Díaz transpose the verses to follow 27:7, and regard them as the opening of Zophar's speech. The passage might equally well serve as part of Bildad's speech, after 25:6, just a few verses away. Peake thinks only vv 18–21 are not Job's, but it is just as hard to imagine v 24 in Job's mouth as vv 18–21.

There are three possible ways for salvaging this strophe for Job's speech, which are worth reviewing, though none of them is ultimately successful. One is to regard vv 18–24, affirming the eventual downfall of the wicked, as words Job puts in the mouth of the friends. The passage could then be prefaced with "You say" (as RVmg; so too RSV, Gordis, regarding the quotation as extending from v 18 to v 24; NRSV, however, does not have "You say"). This is the view of Davidson, who thought that vv 18–21 might be Job's parody of the popular view of the fate of the wicked, while vv 22–24 are his own depiction of the actual truth. It is an attractive interpretation, especially if we understand vv 22–23 as God's continuing support for the wicked; but it is hard to see how v 24 can mean that "it is natural death that overtakes them, like that of all others [Davidson reads the MT ככל]. . . . And they are cut off . . . not prematurely, but having attained to full ripeness." For the emphasis seems rather to be upon the brevity of their exaltation (רומו מעט "they are exalted for a moment")—which makes the verse into a rather conventional statement of the fate of the wicked. And there are other problems, too: the meaning of משך (v 22) and the sense of "his eyes are upon their ways" (v 23; see *Note* 24:22.c and *Comment* on v 23).

The second method of understanding these lines as genuinely Job's is to take them as a curse that he puts on the evildoers. Thus NJPS "May they be flotsam on the face of the water; may their portion in the land be cursed." Similarly Hartley, Newsom. This interpretation follows the LXX, which translates several of the verbs in vv 18–20 as wishes (optatives). The difficulty with this approach is that there are no clear jussives among the Hebrew verbs here, i.e., there are no grammatical markers to show that we are dealing with wishes (we have, for example, קל הוא "he is light" and not קַל יְהִי הוּא "let him be light," and we find יִפְנֶה "he turns" and not יִפֶן "let him turn").

A third approach is to see vv 18–24 as an argument that, though the wicked do in fact suffer disasters, in the end things turn out well for them. That would account for apparently categorical statements about the fate of the wicked, such as "their portion is cursed in the land." Job could be perhaps be meaning that although their portion may be cursed, nevertheless . . . The verbs could be used in a modal sense (cf. *Note* 4:20.b; NEB adopts such a view in v 21: "He may have wronged . . . yet God in his strength . . ."). This line of interpretation would depend on finding some strong positive statement about the success of the wicked, and vv 22–23 seem to provide such a statement. If we are to follow the RSV, for example, it would seem that God "prolongs the life of" the wicked and "gives them security," even when they themselves are in despair. That would fit well with Job's general point of view in this speech, where he is arguing that the wicked are able to persevere in their nefarious deeds without any intervention by God. Here he would be saying, at the climax of his speech, that not only does God not bring wrongdoers to justice on days of assize (v 1) but he even supports and encourages them in their wickedness. The strophe could then be translated:

[18]They may be carried off swiftly on the face of the waters,
their portion in the land may be accursed,
and no one may turn to their vineyard.
[19]Drought and heat may snatch away the snow waters,
Sheol may snatch away sinners,
[20]The womb may forget them,
the worm may feast on them;
they may no longer be remembered,
and wickedness may be shattered like a tree;
[21]they may wrong the barren woman,
and do no good to the widow—
[22]yet God prolongs the life of the mighty by his power;
they rise up even when they have despaired of life;
[23]he allows them to rest in security,
and his eyes keep watch over their ways.

But there are problems with this approach. The first is that it cannot cope with the verse that follows, which can only mean that the wicked come to a bad end:

[24]They are exalted for a time, and then are gone;
they are brought low, and shrivel like mallows;
they wither like the heads of grain.

Vv 18–21 can indeed be concessive, but v 24 cannot—partly because it is the sequel to the "positive" verses (22–23) and partly because the fate that it portrays is so final: the wicked "are no longer," they "shrivel" and "wither."

The second problem is that even the apparently "positive" verses may not be such. A lot hangs on the verb משך in v 22: does it mean that God "prolongs" the life of the mighty (i.e., the wicked), or, since there is nothing in the Hebrew corresponding to "the life of," may it perhaps not mean what it usually does, "he drags off" the wicked? If that is the meaning of the verb, then vv 22–23 could be rendered:

[22]God drags away the mighty by his power;
if they rise up, they can have no assurance of their life.
[23]He allows them to rest in security,
but his eyes keep watch over their ways.

All in all, it seems most satisfactory to regard vv 18–24 as descriptive of the downfall of the wicked, and, moreover, as belonging to a speech of Zophar rather than of Job, as it does in its present place. See further the *Comment* on v 23.

The theme of this strophe is the end of the wicked; we can compare Bildad's depiction in 8:11–19 and 18:5–21, and Zophar's in 20:4–29. The main themes of the account are that the wicked, when their time comes, are swiftly and utterly removed from the world of human life (vv 18–19); they are soon forgotten (v 20); their security and ease are only apparent (vv 22–23); their power is temporary; and their end is as final as the death of a plant (v 24). The whole strophe has the air of certainty we have come to expect from the friends.

18 The controlling idea in this whole depiction of the fate of the wicked (vv 18–23) seems to be the contrast between the disastrous reality that has overwhelmed them and the appearance they have given of solidity and strength. Their appearance is that they are "the mighty" (v 22), who are "at ease" (v 23) and "exalted" (v 24). But what this opening line says of them, now that they have met their end (or, at least, now that their end is known to the wisdom teacher who speaks these words), is that they are nothing but "light" (קַל) and insubstantial. קַל is normally used of a swift runner (2 Sam 2:18; Eccl 9:11; Isa 18:2; Jer 46:6; Amos 2:14, 15), but since one cannot run "on the face of the waters" the image must be of something light on the surface of the water, like the twig on the face of the waters in Hos 10:7; NJPS and Habel think of "flotsam" on the waters, NIV of "foam," and NEB of "scum." The verb קלל, with which the adjective קַל "light" is connected, means "to be trifling, of little account, contemptible" (e.g., 40:4; Gen 16:4; 1 Sam 2:30; but also "to be swift," as in Job 7:6; 9:25). So the "mighty" are in reality as light as a leaf, and "contemptible"—if only a God's eye view of them could be taken.

Furthermore, to be "light" or "contemptible" (קַל) is also in a way already to be "cursed"; קלל piel is a normal word for "curse" (as in 3:1), and the next line plays on the connection between "light" and "cursed" with its phrase "their portion is cursed (קלל) in the land." Their "portion" (חלק) is obviously their portion of ground, their parcel of land (as in 2 Sam 14:30 [RSV "field"]; Amos 7:4 [RSV "land"]) since it is "in the land" (בארץ). Being "cursed," presumably by God (as in Gen 8:21), it will be barren. Likewise their vines yield no grapes, so no one turns down the path to their vineyard. Less probably, the idea may be that the curse that lies on the vineyards frightens off farmworkers, so that the crops of the wicked cannot be reaped; so NEB "their fields have a bad name throughout the land, and no laborer will go near their vineyards." Fields and vineyards are, as Ravasi says, the outward signs of a socioeconomic position of well-being. To have one's productive land cursed means annihilation (cf. Deut 28:16).

19 If v 18 has pictured the wicked as cursed, v 19 has their actual death in view, snatched away from life by Sheol. The verse must contain a comparison, between the effect of heat on snow waters and the effect of Sheol on sinners. To "snatch away" or "rob violently," the usual meanings of גזל (as already in vv 2, 9; also in 20:19), is strange language for what heat does to snow water, and Sheol itself is not elsewhere said to "seize" its victims, though the wicked is "torn" (נתק) from his tent by the underworld terrors in 18:14, and the snares of Sheol encompass (אפף) the pious in Ps 116:3 (cf. Ps 18:4 [5]). The point of the comparison may be the rapidity of the disappearance both of the snow and of the sinners: as we have read in 6:15–17, the wadis are in their season "swollen with thawing snow," but "no sooner are they in spate than they dry up; in the heat (חם, as here) they vanish away." But it is perhaps more likely that the idea is that both the snow waters and the wicked disappear without trace; there would then be a connection between this verse and the following, where the wicked are "forgotten" and "no longer remembered."

20 The images of the fate of the wicked here become increasingly random and incoherent (contrast 8:11–19; 15:2–35; 18:5–21; 20:4–29). Their mothers forget them, the worm eats them, they are forgotten (by humanity generally, apparently), their wickedness is broken like a tree. Three or four unrelated images (if the text is sound) are clumsily (so it seems) lumped together; or perhaps the text is becoming surrealistic.

The wicked are soon forgotten. In a society in which it is important to have one's name "kept in remembrance" (cf. 2 Sam 18:18), it is a dreadful end that one should be forgotten. Cf. Jer 11:19, where the prophet is threatened with being "cut off," so that his name is no longer remembered. This forecast of the fate of the wicked is very different from that given by Job in 21:32–33, where watch is kept over the evildoer's burial mound. Usually, of course, it is offspring that keep one's name alive; here it is, strangely enough, the mother of the wicked. The womb is not elsewhere said to "forget" (שׁכח), but cf. Isa 49:15: "Can a woman forget her nursing child, or show no compassion for the child of her womb?"

And the wicked are nothing but food for the worms (רמה). Job himself has spoken of addressing the worms as "mother" and "sister" (17:14; cf. also Isa 14:11), as if he already belonged to their company, and he has seen the fate of humanity, prosperous and miserable alike, to be covered by worms (21:26). Zophar's picture here is grosser, one of an infernal gastronomy, as the wicked are "snatched" from the upper world by Sheol (v 19) in order to be fed to its worms as juicy tidbits to be sucked at (מתק).

For the image of a tree being "broken" or "shattered" (שׁבר), cf. Exod 9:25; Ps 105:33. We have already had images of a tree being "cut down" (כרת, 14:7) and of hope being pulled up (נסע) like a tree (19:10).

21 Here is another oddity about this strophe. While its prevailing subject is the fate of evildoers, at this point it seems to veer off into a description of their wrongdoing, not their eventual end. Whatever they do or do not do to the barren woman and the widow seems at this point irrelevant to the depiction of their ultimate fate. Some indeed think that this verse too must recount one of the punishments in store for them, namely, that they should "consort with a barren woman who bears no child" (NJPS), and so fail to produce offspring who will keep their name alive. But it would be strange if a reference to the barrenness of their wives should follow the reference to their death (v 20), and in any case there are some difficulties with the translation of רעה as "associate with, consort with" (see *Note* 24:21.b).

The Hebrew text has the wicked "feeding" or "preying" (רעה) on the barren woman, but what have they to gain from preying on such a person? Habel thinks the wicked man is trying to extract the last ounce of life from her and finds this "another example of the poet's brilliant combination of incongruous elements." Somewhat preferable is the small emendation to הרע, which will yield the translation, "he wrongs" the barren women. But is that any more meaningful? However unhappy the situation of a childless woman in a patriarchal society (cf. Ps 127:3; Isa 51:18; 54:1), how can it be the fault of the wicked man? It can only be that the childless woman is his own wife, and that in his lifetime he is already being punished by having no offspring, which not only hurts him but is a matter of him "doing wrong" (רעע) to his wife by being the indirect cause of her barrenness. And he "does no good" to his widow (again, his own wife, not widows in general) by leaving her childless, without sons and daughters to support her.

However the verse is understood, it seems to have no connection with what precedes or follows it.

22 There are two main ways in which the Hebrew of this verse may be taken. (1) RSV: God prolongs the life of the wicked, giving them security even when they are despairing (v 23), but then bringing them to destruction (v 24). There would be a conflict then between the extending of life in v 22 and the brevity (מעט "[for] a moment") of the exaltation of the wicked in v 24; and there is a problem with rendering the verb משך as "prolong" (see *Note* 24:22.c). (2) NIV, NEB: God drags away the mighty; even if they feel secure, they can have no assurance about their life (v 22). God lets them rest in a feeling of security (v 23), but their power soon comes to an end.

"Dragging" (משך) is something done with cords or ropes (Jer 38:13; presumably Gen 37:28; with a fishhook, Job 40:25 [41:1]; metaphorically, Isa 5:18). In Ps 28:3 also it is the fate of the wicked to be "dragged away" by God to destruction. The metaphor is from hunting (cf. 18:8–10): the prey is caught with ropes and dragged off by the hunter. When do the wicked "rise up," then? In Job, קום "rising up" is most commonly used of rising from sleep (7:4; 24:14; from the sleep of death, 14:12) or of rising to one's feet (1:20; 19:18, 25). Here it seems to be the latter, "standing up" in the metaphorical sense of being prosperous, successful (as Ps 20:8 [9]; cf. BDB, 877b). Even when things seem safe for the wicked, says Zophar, they can have no certainty (lit. "he does not trust in life, or, his life"); the phrase is found also in Deut 28:66, among the curses for disobedience to Yahweh: "your life shall hang in doubt before you; you shall be in dread night and day, and you will have no assurance of your life."

23 If v 22 has said that no matter how mighty the wicked may be, they can be taken away by God, and that even when they feel they are in possession of their power, they can have no assurance of their life—then in this verse also there is a contrast between their apparent security and their underlying insecurity. God grants them to live untroubled lives of ease (שען "be at ease," לבטח "in safety"), as he leaves the tents of brigands in peace (12:6)—but his eyes are "on" (על) their ways. This latter phrase is taken by some as a further indication of God's protection of them (so RSV "and his eyes are upon their ways"; cf. Peake, NAB, Moffatt), but the phrase is elsewhere always used in a negative sense: in 2 Sam 22:28 God's eyes are on the proud to bring them down; in Jer 16:17 his eyes are on the wicked people of Israel, whose iniquity is not concealed from him; and in Job 34:21 his eyes are upon the ways of a man, and there is no darkness where an evildoer can hide (Job has himself suffered from the over-watchful eyes of God; see 7:20; 10:14; 13:27). It is different when "our eyes are upon you" (in prayer, 2 Chr 20:12), and different again when the preposition is אֶל "unto, towards," as in Ps 34:15 (16), where the eyes of the Lord are toward the righteous (quoted in 1 Pet 3:12; cf. also Job 33:18), or when it is בְּ "on," as in Job 7:8, when God is looking for Job. So it seems that there is in this verse a contrast between the ease that God grants the wicked and his searching examination of their doings that never ceases (GNB "but keeps an eye on him all the time"). It is the contrast between appearance and reality that we have met with also in v 18, at the beginning of the strophe.

To "rest" is literally to "lean" (שען), as when a man leans upon his house (8:15) or upon a spear (2 Sam 1:6) or "relies" on God (2 Chr 16:7; Isa 50:10) or upon horses (Isa 31:1). Here, exceptionally, the verb is used absolutely, of resting, being at ease, feeling secure. The sense is strengthened by the word לבטח "in safety," which is commonly used of dwelling in safety (e.g., 11:18; Lev 25:18).

24 The theme of appearance versus reality is here transposed onto the temporal plane; that is, the contrast is now not between two concurrent states of affairs but between the high standing of the wicked that is swiftly overtaken by their sudden humiliation. They are “high” (רום) for a little, but then they are suddenly “low” (מכך); for a moment they are very visible, and then they have disappeared (איננו “he is not”; cf. 7:8, 21). The picture cannot be of a swift and painless death (cf. Peake), of their being harvested when they are fully ripe (as in Eliphaz’s picture in 5:26 of the sheaf of grain coming up to the threshing floor at its season), for the language is of the contrast between elevation and humiliation, and that cannot be a positive picture.

“Mallow” (מלוח, emendation of כל “totality”; see *Note* 24:24.e) is a desert plant that grows in salt marshes. Whether or not there is a backward reference to the “drought and heat” of v 19 as the cause of the shriveling of the mallows and the withering of the heads of grain, the wicked are destined for the same withering away, drooping, and ceasing to exist. The image of the withering of plants for the death of the wicked has been used previously in 8:12 of papyrus and reeds (which wither even when they are not “cut” [קטף, which some read here instead of קפץ, which apparently means “shrivel”; in 30:4 קטף is used of cutting mallows]). We cannot tell whether the heads of grain are thought of as withering on the stalk because of dryness or because they have been cut off. “Heads of grain” (ראש שבלת) is the natural term for what is harvested, since “corn was reaped by cutting off the tops of the stalk a little below the ear” (Driver–Gray; others, however, say that the stalks of grain were cut off a few inches above the ground; so J. A. Patch and C. E. Armerding, *ISBE,* 1:74). Wetzstein, quoted by Delitzsch, reports that bedouin will make raids on standing grain, cutting off the heads of grain with their knives, since they obviously do not carry sickles on raids. It would be interesting if this idea of violent plundering by death lay behind the picture of the heads of grain here.

27:18–23 Finally in this last speech of Zophar, the personal fate of the wicked becomes the subject. The fragile house that the wicked build (v 18) is a symbol for the insecurity of their existence, and the strophe as a whole focuses on the sudden (vv 19–20) and inescapable (vv 21–22) devastation that awaits them, concluding with a picture of the final triumph of death over the wicked (v 23). The language of death, however, is never used, and the disappearance of the wicked is portrayed rather as a violent dislocation by a hurricane. It is as if they were trees that are uprooted from soil where they believe themselves to be planted permanently, from their “place” (v 21).

18 The wicked do not of course recognize that the houses, or lives, they make for themselves have no more permanence than a bird’s nest (some versions make it a spider’s web) or a flimsy hut (סכה) built in the fields during the summer for a watchman who will guard a vineyard or field of crops (as in Isa 1:8, where Zion after an assault on it has no more security than such a booth, and 24:20, where earth sways like a booth). J. G. Wetzstein, quoted by Delitzsch, gives an interesting description of the watchman’s hut in nineteenth-century Syria: it was built for the protection of vineyards and melon and maize fields against thieves, herds, or wild beasts; in its commonest form, the hut was a cube of about eight feet, with four corner poles and a roof of planks on which the watchman’s bed lay. Three sides of the hut were hung with a mat or with reeds or straw, and the watchman would sit in its shade during the day and sleep on its roof at night. Once the crops were gathered, the hut would be dismantled. See further, Dalman, *Arbeit und Sitte,* 1:161–63; 2:55–63; 4:316–19, 333–34.

19 In a night, the wealth of the wicked can disappear. They can go to bed rich, and wake up poor. And once their wealth is gone, it is gone forever; it simply "is not" (איננו). It does not seem to be the wicked themselves who disappear (as against Dhorme) at this point, but their wealth. Nevertheless, this loss of their wealth is the beginning of the end, and death itself follows hard on its heels; it is more of a punishment, and it suits Zophar's moral audit better that the wicked should personally experience during their lifetimes the loss of all that is valuable to them.

20 The "Terrors" (בלהות) we have met with before at 15:21 (פחדים), 18:11, 14, and 20:25 (אמים) as personified spirits of vengeance, denizens of the underworld; they hunt their prey down, surround them, and drag them off to Sheol. The Terrors overtake the wicked "like water" (כמים); the image may seem a little tame since water is not usually an image for sudden destruction (see *Note* 27:20.b); perhaps the best analogy is Isa 28:17, where "waters" (מים) "sweep away (שטף) a shelter," and the image here may be of travelers caught in the bed of a wadi by a sudden rush of water from a cloudburst (Fohrer). Job himself has spoken of the wicked being "stolen away" (גנב) by a tempest (סופה) in 21:18, but to very different effect: there he questioned whether that conventional language (cf. Ps 1:4) is borne out by reality, but here Zophar expresses no doubts, only certainties. It might be doubted whether tempests can do anything as secretive as "stealing"; the point then must be not any secretiveness but the fact that the tempest robs the wicked from life and from their dwellings where they have seemed to belong. The onset of destruction in the night only makes it all the more fearful, of course.

21 The picture of the wicked being carried off by a tempest is now elaborated throughout vv 21–23 in a fantastical and baroque style. Though the wicked are not said to "die," it would seem that being "seized" (נשׂא) and "whirled away" (שׂער) by a tempest can mean only that (so Fohrer, as against Dhorme, who finds in vv 20–21 only that the wicked are victimized by the Terrors and condemned to wander through the world like Cain, and Hölscher, who thinks that the death of the wicked is nowhere in view in vv 20–23).

The sirocco, the hot violent wind from the desert that blew down the house of Job's children (1:19), is here the "east wind" (קדים; cf. on 15:2). It sweeps the wicked from their "place" (מקום), their habitation viewed as their stable and fixed location; and, as we have heard before, once they are driven out, their "place" does not see them again (20:9), does not know them any longer (7:10), but disowns them, saying, "I never knew you" (8:18). J. G. Wetzstein, quoted by Delitzsch, reports that in Syria and Arabia the east wind or sirocco is mostly experienced in the winter and early spring. "The east wind is dry; it excites the blood, contracts the chest, causes restlessness and anxiety, and sleepless nights or evil dreams. Both man and beast feel weak and sickly while it prevails." Here the east wind is connected with a "tempest" (סופה, v 20), and Wetzstein's reports are once again a propos: "Storms are rare during an east wind. . . . But if an east wind does bring a storm, it is generally very destructive, on account of its strong gusts; it will even uproot the largest trees."

22 The focus is still upon the tempest as this verse opens, and it is represented as a "demonic enemy" (Habel), a vicious assailant who "does not spare" (as of God as Job's enemy in 16:13, and as of pain in 6:10), and who assaults the wicked with its "hand" (יד) or force. Then, for a moment, by way of portraying the effect of the tempest upon its victims, the wicked are focalized as they desperately seek to escape from it; the infinitive absolute in the phrase ברוח יברח ("fleeing he flees") "emphasizes the flight as hasty and inevitable" (Dillmann).

Dhorme thinks we are still reading of the wicked who have been uprooted from their homes and have been "abandoned to public vengeance"; so too Hölscher and de Wilde, who think that it is the oppressed who now turn on the wealthy wicked and throw (שלך) stones at them. So too JB, translating "Pitilessly he is turned into a target, and forced to flee from the hands that menace him. His downfall is greeted with applause, he is hissed wherever he goes." (Hartley manages to combine the east wind with human enemies by having the wicked hear "the taunts of the community in the howling of the wind.") But there is no explicit mention in the text of human opponents, and it is perhaps unlikely that the populace in general would be said to act "without pity" (since it is usually a very much superior opponent, who could in principle show mercy, to whom such a phrase is applied), and above all, once the underworld Terrors have entered the scene (in v 20), we are surely reading about the ultimate fate of the wicked and not their hounding by a disgruntled public. The tempest and the east wind are not mere meteorological phenomena: they are cosmic agents of vengeance, and their intervention also signals that the wicked are now *in extremis*.

23 Finally, there is attributed to the tempest a human-like gloating over the fate of the wicked, perhaps specifically over "the deserted ruins where the wicked once lived in splendor" (Habel), a calling to attention of the shame of the wicked in their downfall. The tempest claps its hands (שפק כף) at them, a mark, not of approval as it is with us, but of anger, grief, or horror, either genuine (Num 24:10; Nah 3:19) or in derision (Lam 2:15). Hissing or whistling (שרק) is a way of expressing scorn (Jer 49:17; Ezek 27:36; Zeph 2:15; Lam 2:15). And the tempest, which might have been thought to be always in motion, with no fixed "place" of its own, on the contrary stands securely in *its* place (מקומו), jeering at the wicked who have been driven from *their* place (מקומו, v 21; strangely, Pope thinks this interpretation "insipid and much too tame for the context"). The tempest and the east wind are depicted as malevolent autonomous forces, but just below the surface Zophar means that they are agents of the divine retribution.

Zophar is at the top of his bent as he draws his depiction to a close. If the art of the poet is to suggest rather than to describe, he has excelled himself in never explicitly mentioning the death of the wicked (so successfully as to lead some commentators to deny that their death is even in view!) and in making his only reference to it the reaction of the east wind: it claps its hands and hisses at them—which it could not do if their fate were not sealed. In this closing verse, moreover, he implicitly invokes the authority of the past with the archaic language he presses into service (see *Note* 27:23.d). And he has a fine sense of an ending, leaving to the very last the word for stability (מקום "place"), which the wicked lose but the east wind keeps. And the whole comes packaged with rhythm, assonance, and rhyme: *yišpōq ʿălêmô kappêmô, wĕyišrōq ʿālāyw mimmĕqōmô.*

Explanation

This speech is the nearest the poet of Job comes to automatic writing. There is nothing new in this speech of Zophar's. It is hard to see what its point is, and what it seems to be saying is profoundly unrealistic.

Its starting point is that there is a category of humans who are the "wicked." It is not the purpose of this speech, however, to tell us how they come to be wicked or in what their wickedness consists; its concern is solely with what they may expect, what is their destiny, their "portion" or "heritage" appointed by God (v 13).

What the wicked may expect, one and all, is that they will be "cut off" (v 8), which means that in a night (v 19) all their wealth may be taken from them and they themselves may be snatched away from life as by a violent wind (vv 20b–22). It means also that they will not even succeed in living on in the person of their children, for they will see them die premature deaths (vv 14–15); nor will they leave property behind them as a memorial of their dignity, for it will be shared out among others more righteous than they (vv 16–17). Perhaps, as they see such disasters coming upon them, they will in remorse cry out for help to God; but they can expect no hearing from God (v 9). After all, they have proved by their way of life that they are not the kind of people who "delight in the Almighty" (v 10), so there is little likelihood that they will be found at their prayers. In short, there is no "hope" (v 8) for these people, and their destiny is fixed.

But why is Zophar saying all this to Job? Either Job is one of these people or he is not. Since there is no hope for the wicked, there is no point in preaching to them about their guilt. So if Zophar is preaching to Job, he must believe (as we are encouraged to think from his previous speeches in chaps. 11 and 20) that Job himself is not one of the wicked. Job is of course not perfect, in Zophar's opinion, for he is being punished by God, and no one is punished without due cause (11:11). But that is not the same thing as belonging to the company of the wicked, so everything that Zophar says about them is in principle irrelevant to Job.

Perhaps Zophar means not to warn Job against becoming like one of the wicked but rather to assure him that there is no danger of that happening, and that the future he can expect is the very opposite of theirs? That seems to have been the line Zophar was taking at the end of his first speech: "You [Job] will be secure, because there is hope; you will be protected and lie down in safety. . . . But the eyes of the wicked will fail, escape there will be none for them, their only hope very despair" (11:18, 20). If that is still his line in this speech, then perhaps by reiterating that there is no hope for the wicked (v 8), he means to say that by contrast there *is* hope for Job. All one can say is, if that is his intention, it is a strange way of expressing it. For throughout his second and third speeches (20:2–29; 27:7–23) Zophar has addressed not a word to Job personally, has held out no encouragement to him, and has said nothing with a shred of hope in it, but has made his unwavering theme the fate of the wicked. He is expecting a lot of good will from Job if he expects him to hear all of this as indirect support, as constant affirmation that Job may expect in every detail the very opposite of what is laid up for the wicked.

If we take all of Zophar's three speeches together, their logic does seem to be that Job has nothing to fear since he is essentially a righteous man who has only to "direct [his] mind toward God and spread out [his] hands to him" (11:13) for his life to become "brighter than the noonday" (11:17). But where stands logic if Zophar does nothing (in his second and third speeches) but harp on doom and gloom? Communications have effects beyond their logical force and sometimes to the contrary of what their utterers intend. And the airtime Zophar gives to the wicked suggests that it is with them rather than with Job that his interests lie. If Job is not disposed to take comfort from Zophar's words, we can hardly be surprised.

But the worst of it is that Zophar's theology is without a hint of realism. All his depiction of the fate of the wicked can only be what *ought* to happen, not in the least a report of what *does* happen. Perhaps we should assign his speech to the genre of "magic realism" so common today in the novel and the cinema. There are, to be sure, literally wicked people in the world, there are oppressors and godless, there are children and widows. But the Terrors and the Tempest, the Plague and the East Wind, of which Zophar speaks (and which we must capitalize, as abstractions personified), belong to a world of magic, of make-believe and wish fulfillment. For these beings have the capacity to discriminate between godly and godless, to sweep away only the oppressors and their offspring, and to leave the pious dividing the silver and wearing the fine clothes of the wicked (v 17). There are terrors and plagues and tempests in the real world, of course, but their effect is entirely indiscriminate—and that is what Job knows, Job who has lost his children and his wealth and his hope of life, and what Zophar knows too, since he has traveled through a real world to visit a real-life Job. But his theology has gotten the better of him.

Elihu's Speeches (32:1–37:24; 28:1–28)

Bibliography

Althann, R. "Elihu's Contribution to the Book of Job." *OTE* 12 (1999) 9–12. **Bakon, S.** "The Enigma of Elihu." *DD* 12 (1984) 217–28. **Barton, G. A.** "Some Text-Critical Notes on the Elihu-Speeches." *JBL* 43 (1924) 228. **Beeby, H. D.** "Elihu—Job's Mediator?" *SEAsiaJT* 7 (1965) 33–54. **Boelicke, M.** *Die Elihu-Reden nach ihrem Zusammenhange mit dem übrigen Theil des Buches Hiob und nach ihrem sprachlichen Charakter.* Inaugural Diss. Halle: Karras, 1879. **Brolley, J. D.** "The Importance of Being Elihu: A Consideration of Bilateral Aspects of *riv* and Elihu as Literary Event on the Book of Job." Diss., Candler, Atlanta, 1995. **Clines, D. J. A.** "Putting Elihu in His Place: A Proposal for the Relocation of Job 32–37." *JSOT* 29 (2004) 115–25. **Cox, C.** "Origen's Use of Theodotion in the Elihu Speeches." *SecCent* 3 (1983) 89–98. **Curtis, J. B.** "Why Were the Elihu Speeches Added to the Book of Job?" *PrGLM* 8 (1988) 93–99. ———. "Word Play in the Speeches of Elihu (Job 32–37)." *PrGLM* 12 (1992) 23–30. **Dennefeld, L.** "Les discours d'Elihou (Job XXXII–XXXVII)." *RB* 48 (1939) 163–80. **Deutsch, I.** *De Elihui sermonum origine atque auctore: Commentatio philologico-critica.* Diss., Bratislava, 1873. **Evans, J. M.** "Elihu and the Interpretation of the Book of Job." Diss., Glasgow, 2000. **Finnan, A. P.** "A Rhetorical Critical Analysis of Job 32–37." Diss., Southern Baptist Theological Seminary, 1988. **Fohrer, G.** "Die Weisheit des Elihu (Hi 32–37)." *AfO* 19 (1959–60) 83–94. Reprinted in *Studien zum Buche Hiob, 1956–79,* 2d ed., BZAW 159 (Berlin: de Gruyter, 1983) 94–113. **Freedman, D. N.** "The Elihu Speeches in the Book of Job: A Hypothetical Episode in the Literary History of the Work." *HTR* 61 (1968) 51–59. Reprinted in *Pottery, Poetry, and Prophecy: Studies in Early Hebrew Poetry* (Winona Lake, IN: Eisenbrauns, 1980) 329–37. **Gelzner, A.** "קובץ אליהוא" [The Elihu Collection]. *BMik* 78 (1979) 283–94. **Gordis, R.** "Elihu the Intruder: A Study of the Authenticity of Job (Chapters 32–33)." In *Biblical and Other Studies.* Ed. A. Altmann. Studies and Texts (Philip W. Lown Institute of Advanced Judaic Studies) 1. Cambridge, MA: Harvard UP, 1963. 60–78. **Gore, K. W., Jr.** "The Unifying Force of the Identity and Role of Elihu within the Book of Job." Diss., Southwestern Baptist Theological Seminary, 1997. **Habel, N. C.** "The Role of Elihu in the Design of the Book of Job." In *In the Shelter of Elyon: Essays in Palestinian Life and Literature.* FS G. W. Ahlström, ed. W. B. Barrick and J. R. Spencer. JSOTSup 31. Sheffield: JSOT Press, 1984. 81–98. **Hemraj, S.** "Elihu's 'Missionary' Role in Job 32–37." *BiBh* 6 (1980) 49–80. **Johns, D. A.** "The Literary and Theological Function of the Elihu Speeches in the Book of Job." Diss., St. Louis, 1983 (Ann Arbor: University Microfilms 8325382, 1983). **Kroeze, J. H.** "Die Elihu-reden im Buche Hiob." *OTS* 2 (1943) 156–70. **Leder, A. C.** "Job 32–37: Elihu as the Mouthpiece of God." In *Reading and Hearing the Word from Text to Sermon.* FS J. H. Stek, ed. A. C. Leder. Grand Rapids: Calvin Theological Seminary; CRC Publications, 1998. **Martin, G. W.** "Elihu and the Third-Cycle in the Book of Job." Diss., Princeton, 1972. **McCabe, R. V., Jr.** "Elihu's Contribution to the Thought of the Book of Job." *Detroit Baptist Seminary Journal* 2 (1997) 47–80. ———. "The Significance of the Elihu Speeches in the Context of the Book of Job." Diss., Grace Theological Seminary, 1985. **McKay, J. W.** "Elihu—A Proto-Charismatic?" *ExpTim* 70 (1978–79) 167–71. **Mende, T.** *Durch Leiden zur Vollendung: Die Elihureden im Buch Ijob (Ijob 32–37).* TThSt 49. Trier: Paulinus, 1990. **Michel, W. L.** "Job's Real Friend, Elihu." *Criterion* (Chicago) 21.2 (1982) 29–32. **Montgomery, J. A.** "The Hebrew Divine Name and the Personal Pronoun *Hū.*" *JBL* 63 (1944) 161–63. **Nichols, H. H.** "The Composition of the Elihu Speeches (Job, Chaps. 32–37)." *AJSL* 27 (1910–11) 97–186. **Pfister, X.** "Leiden als Bewährungsprobe: Die Reden Elihus (Hiob 32–37)." In *Hiob: Ökumenischer Arbeitskreis für Bibelarbeit.* Ed. R. Berger-Lutz. Bibelarbeit in der Gemeinde 7. Basel: Reinhardt, 1989.

261–76. **Posselt, W.** *Der Verfasser der Eliu-Reden (Job Kap. 32–37): Eine kritische Untersuchung.* BibS 14.3. Freiburg i. Br.: Herder, 1909. **Staples, W. E.** *The Speeches of Elihu: A Study of Job 32–37.* [A revised Hebrew text with introduction, notes, and a translation into English.] University of Toronto Studies Philological Series 8. Toronto: Univ. of Toronto Press, 1924. **Tate, M. E.** "The Speeches of Elihu." *RevExp* 68 (1971) 487–95. **Viviers, H.** "Elihu (Job 32–37), Garrulous but Poor Rhetor? Why Is He Ignored?" In *The Rhetorical Analysis of Scripture: Essays from the 1995 London Conference.* Ed. S. E. Porter and T. H. Olbricht. JSNTSup 146. Sheffield: Sheffield Academic Press, 1997. 137–53. ———. "Die funksie van Elihu (Job 32–37) in die boek Job." *SK* 16 (1995) 171–92. **Wahl, H. M.** "Ein Beitrag zum alttestamentlichen Vergeltungsglauben am Beispiel von Hiob 32–37." *BZ* 36 (1992) 250–55. ———. "Elihu, Frevler oder Frommer? Die Auslegung des Hiobbuches (Hi 32–37) durch ein Pseudepigraphon (TestHi 41–43)." *JSJ* 25 (1994) 1–17. ———. "Das 'Evangelium' Elihus (Hiob 32–37)." In *The Book of Job.* Ed. W. A. M. Beuken. BETL 114. Leuven: Leuven UP, 1994. 356–61. ———. *Der gerechte Schöpfer: Eine redaktions- und theologiegeschichtliche Untersuchung der Elihureden—Hiob 32–37.* BZAW 230. Berlin: de Gruyter, 1994. ———. "Seit wann gelten die Elihureden (Hi 32–37) als Einschub? Eine Bemerkung zur Forschungsgeschichte." *BN* 63 (1992) 58–61. **Waters, L. J.** "The Authenticity of the Elihu Speeches in Job 32–37." *BSac* 156 (1999) 28–41. ———. "Elihu's Theology and His View of Suffering." *BSac* 156 (1999) 143–59. ———. "Elihu's View of Suffering in Job 32–37." Diss., Dallas Theological Seminary, 1998. **Whedbee, J. W.** *The Bible and the Comic Vision.* Cambridge: Cambridge UP, 1988. 242–45. ———. "The Comedy of Job." In *Studies in the Book of Job (Semeia 7).* Ed. R. Polzin and D. Robertson. Missoula, MT: Society of Biblical Literature, 1977. 1–39. Reprinted in *On Humour and the Comic in the Hebrew Bible,* ed. Y. T. Radday and A. Brenner, JSOTSup 92 (Sheffield: JSOT Press, 1990) 217–49. **Wilson, L.** "The Role of the Elihu Speeches in the Book of Job." *RTR* 55 (1996) 81–94. **Witte, M.** "Noch einmal: Seit wann gelten die Elihureden im Hiobbuch (Kap. 32–37) als Einschub?" *BN* 67 (1993) 20–25. **Wolfers, D.** "Elihu: The Provenance and Content of His Speeches." *DD* 16 (1987–88) 90–98.

Elihu's First Speech (32:1–33:33)

Bibliography

Dahood, M. J. "The Dative Suffix in Job 33,13." *Bib* 63 (1982) 258–59. ———. "Hebrew-Ugaritic Lexicography I." *Bib* 44 (1963) 289–303. ———. "Love and Death at Ebla and Their Biblical Reflections" [Job 33:22]. In *Love and Death in the Ancient Near East.* FS M. H. Pope, ed. J. H. Marks and R. M. Good. Guilford, CT: Four Quarters, 1987. 93–99. ———. "Northwest Semitic Philology and Job." In *The Bible in Current Catholic Thought: Gruenthaner Memorial Volume.* Ed. J. L. McKenzie. St. Mary's Theological Studies 1. New York: Herder & Herder, 1962. 55–74. ———. "The Phoenician Contribution to Biblical Wisdom Literature." In *The Role of the Phoenicians in the Interaction of Mediterranean Civilizations.* Ed. W. A. Ward. Beirut: American Univ. in Beirut, 1968. 123–52. ———. Review of *The New English Bible. Bib* 52 (1971) 117–23. ———. "Some Northwest-Semitic Words in Job." *Bib* 38 (1957) 306–20. **Driver, G. R.** "Once Again Abbreviations." *Textus* 4 (1965) 76–94. **Gammie, J. G.** "The Angelology and Demonology in the Septuagint of the Book of Job." *HUCA* 56 (1985) 1–19. **Gevirtz, S.** "Phoenician *wšbrt mlṣm* and Job 33:23." *Maarav* 5–6 (1990) 145–58. **Ginsberg, H. L.** "עיונים בספר איוב" [Studies in the Book of Job (4,17–20; 5,14–23; 16,2–9; 33,1–11)]. *Leš* 21 (1956–57) 259–64. **Guillaume, A.** "The Arabic Background of the Book of Job." In *Promise and Fulfilment.* FS S. H. Hooke, ed. F. F.

Bruce. Edinburgh: T. & T. Clark, 1963. 106–27. ———. "An Archaeological and Philological Note on Job xxxii, 19." *PEQ* 93 (1961) 147–50. **Jenkins, R. G.** "Hexaplaric Marginalia and the Hexapla-Tetrapla Question" [Job 32:11–15; 39:22]. In *Origen's Hexapla and Fragments: Papers Presented at the Rich Seminar on the Hexapla, Oxford Centre for Hebrew and Jewish Studies, 25th [July]–3rd August 1994.* Ed. A. Salvesen. TSAJ 58. Tübingen: Mohr-Siebeck, 1998. 73–87. **Leibel, D.** "עבר בשלח" [Job 33:18; 36:12]. *Tarbiz* 33 (1963–64) 225–27. **Reider, J.** "Etymological Studies in Biblical Hebrew." *VT* 4 (1954) 276–95. **Ross, J. F.** "Job 33:14–30: The Phenomenology of Lament." *JBL* 94 (1975) 38–46. **Rouillard, H.** "Le sens de Job 33,21." *RB* 91 (1984) 30–50. **Sauer, A. von Rohr.** "Masters in the Making" [Job 32–33]. *CTM* 43 (1972) 338–45. **Skehan, P. W.** "'I Will Speak Up' (Job 32)." *CBQ* 31 (1969) 380–82. ———. "The Pit (Job 33)." *CBQ* 31 (1969) 382. **Trendelenburg, C.** כפר מלאכה מליץ, *i.e. Elihu descriptio Messiae prophetici et sacerdotalis ex Job.* XXXIII, *v. 23. 24, praeses Nicolai Köppen . . . respondens Christopherus Trendelenburg.* Greifswald: Adolphus, 1705. **Wehrle, J.** "Zur syntaktisch-semantischen Funktion der PV *k'=mᵉaṭ* in Ijob 32:22." *BN* 55 (1990) 77–95. **Weingreen, J.** "The Construct-Genitive Relation in Hebrew Syntax." *VT* 4 (1954) 50–59. **York, A. D.** "11 Q tg Job XXI, 4–5 (Job 32, 13)." *RevQ* 9 (1977) 127–29.

Translation

1 *Then these three men ceased answering Job, because he was righteous in his own*
eyes.[a] 2 *Then Elihu,*[a] *the son of Barachel,*[b] *the Buzite, of the family of Ram,*[c] *became*
angry;[d] *he was angry with Job because he considered himself rather than God*[e] *to be in*
the right;[f] 3 *and he was angry also at the three friends of Job because they had not found*
an answer,[a] *and because*[b] *they had not shown Job to be in the wrong.*[c] 4 *Elihu had*
waited to speak to Job[a] *because they were older than he.* 5 *But when Elihu saw that there*
was no answer in the mouth of these three men,[a] *he became angry.* 6 *Then Elihu, son of*
Barachel, the Buzite, gave answer and said:

I am young in years,[a]
  and you are aged;[b]
therefore I was timid[c] *and afraid*
  to declare[d] *my opinion*[e] *to you.*[f]
7 *I said,*[a] *"Let days*[b] *speak;*
  let the multitude of years[c] *teach*[d] *wisdom."*

8 *But surely*[a] *it is the spirit*[b] *in a human being,*
  the breath[c] *of the Almighty, that*[d] *gives understanding.*
9 *It is not only*[a] *the old*[b] *who are wise,*
  or the gray-haired[c] *who understand justice.*[d]
10 [a]*So I say,*[b] *"Listen*[c] *to me;*
  let me also declare[d] *my opinion."*[e]

11 *Behold, I waited*[a] *for your words;*
  I listened[b] *for*[c] *your wise sayings*[d]
  [e]*while you searched out*[f] *your responses.*
12 *I gave you my attention,*[a]
  but behold there was none who confuted[b] *Job,*
  or answered his words, among you.

13 *So*[a] *do not say,*[b] *"We have found wisdom;*
God may rout him,[c] *but no human."*
14 *He has not*[a] *marshalled*[b] *his words against me,*
and I shall not reply to him with your speeches.

15 *They are dismayed;*[a] *they answer no more;*
words have deserted them.[b]
16 *Am I to wait*[a] *because they cannot speak,*
because they stand still[b] *and answer no more?*
17 *I too will take my part in reply;*[a]
I too will offer my opinion.[b]
18 [a]*For I am full of words;*[b]
the breath[c] *within me*[d] *constrains*[e] *me.*

19 *Behold,*[a] *my belly is like wine without a vent;*[b]
like new wineskins,[c] *it is*[d] *ready to burst.*[e]
20 *I must speak*[a] *so as to get relief,*[b]
I must open my lips and answer.
21 *I will surely*[a] *show partiality*[b] *to no one;*
I will use no flattering names[c] *for anyone.*[d]
22 *For I cannot give*[a] *flattering titles,*
or else[b] *my Maker would soon*[c] *put an end to me.*[d]

33:1 *But now,*[a] *hear*[b] *my speech, O Job;*
give ear to all my words.
2 [a]*Behold, I open my mouth;*
the tongue in my mouth[b] *speaks.*[c]
3 [a]*My words*[b] *are*[c] *the uprightness*[d] *of my heart,*
and what my lips know they speak sincerely.[e]
4 [a]*The spirit of God has made me,*
and the breath of the Almighty gives[b] *me life.*

5 *Answer me*[a] *if you can;*
set your words in order[b] *before me; take your stand.*[c]
6 *Behold, I am in God's sight the same as you;*[a]
I too was pinched off[b] *from a piece of clay.*
7 *Behold,*[a] *no fear of me should*[b] *terrify*[c] *you;*
there will be no heavy pressure[d] *from me upon you.*[e]

8 *Now,*[a] *you have said in my hearing,*[b]
and I have heard the sound of your words:[c]
9 *"I am pure, without transgression;*
I am innocent;[a] *there is no wrong in me.*
10 *Behold,*[a] *he finds occasions*[b] *against me;*
he regards me as his enemy.
11 [a]*He puts*[b] *my feet in the stocks;*[c]
he watches all my paths."

12 *Behold, in this*[a] *you are not right; I will answer you.*[b]
God is greater than[c] *humans.*
13 *Why do you contend with*[a] *him, saying,*[b]
"He answers none of my words"?[c]
14 *For God speaks in one way,*
and in another[a]*—though mortals may not perceive him.*[b]

15 *In a dream, in a vision*[a] *of the night,*
[b]*when deep sleep*[c] *falls on mortals,*
while they sleep[d] *upon their beds,*
16 *then he opens*[a] *the ears of mortals,*
and dismays[b] *them with apparitions,*[c]
17 *so as to turn humans away*[a] *from their deeds,*[b]
and to cut away[c] *pride*[d] *from mortals.*[e]
18 *So he keeps them*[a] *back*[b] *from the Pit,*
their life[c] *from crossing the river of death.*[d]

19 [a]*Humans*[b] *may also be chastened*[c] *by pain upon their beds,*[d]
and by unending[e] *strife*[f] *in their bones,*[g]
20 *so that their life*[a] *loathes*[b] *food,*[c]
and their appetite[d] *dainties.*[e]
21 *Their flesh is so wasted*[a] *that it cannot be seen,*[b]
and their bones, once hidden,[c] *are laid bare.*[d]
22 *Their life draws near*[a] *to the Pit,*[b]
their being to those who bring death.[c]

23 *But if*[a] *there is by them*[b] *an angel,*[c]
a mediator,[d] *one of the Thousand,*[e]
[f]*who declares*[g] *to humans what is right for them,*[h]
24 [a]*and he takes pity*[b] *on them and says,*
"Deliver[c] *them from going down to the Pit!*
I have found a ransom;[d]
25 [a]*let their flesh become fresher*[b] *than in youth,*[c]
let them return[d] *to the days of their vigor,"*[e]
26 [a]*then they entreat*[b] *God and he favors*[c] *them,*
they behold[d] *his face with joy.*[e]
[f]*He restores*[g] *their righteousness*[h] *to them.*[i]

27 *They sing*[a] *before*[b] *others, saying,*[c]
"I sinned, and perverted what was right;[d]
and there was no profit in it for me.[e]
28 *He has redeemed*[a] *my life*[b] *from passing into the Pit,*[c]
and my being shall enjoy light."[d]
29 *Behold, such are the things God does,*
twice, three times,[a] *with mortals,*
30 [a]*bringing back*[b] *their life from the Pit,*
that they may be illumined[c] *with the light*[d] *of life.*[e]

31 [a]*Be attentive, Job; listen to me;*
be silent, and I will speak.
32 *If you have anything to say, let me hear it;*[a]
speak, for my desire is to justify[b] *you.*
33 [a]*But if not, listen to me;*
be silent, and I will teach you wisdom.

Notes

32:1.a. NEB "he continued to think himself righteous," JB "was convinced of his innocence," Moffatt "he considered himself in the right." For בעיניו "in his eyes," one MS, with LXX and Pesh, has בְּעֵינֵיהֶם "in their eyes" (similarly Symm); but it would not make much sense to say that Job was righteous in their eyes, since that is not the impression we (or Elihu!) have received hitherto. Nevertheless, Dhorme, Hölscher, and Kissane accept this reading.

2.a. On the "meaning" of the name, see also *Comment.* Some have argued that the הוא element in the name is a divine name or title (cf. J. A. Montgomery, "The Hebrew Divine Name and the Personal Pronoun *Hū*," *JBL* 63 [1944] 161–63), but it is more normal to regard the name as meaning "he is my God" (as J. D. Fowler, *Theophoric Personal Names in Ancient Hebrew: A Comparative Study,* JSOTSup 49 [Sheffield: JSOT Press, 1988] 129).

2.b. On the name, see *Comment.* For evidence of the name in the Murashu documents, see H. V. Hilprecht and A. T. Clay, *Business Documents of Murashû Sons of Nippur, Dated in the Reign of Artaxerxes I (464–424 B.C.),* The Babylonian Expedition of the University of Pennsylvania, Series A: Cuneiform Texts 9 (Philadelphia, 1898) 52; M. D. Coogan, *West Semitic Names in the Murašû Documents,* HSM 7 (Missoula, MT: Scholars Press, 1976) 16–17.

2.c. It is a curious fact, but probably entirely without significance, that the phrase הבוזי ממשפחת "the Buzite, of the family of . . ." is very similar to בוז־משפחות "the contempt of families" in 31:34 (noticed by Hoffmann, Peake). Interesting, but also probably equally without significance, is the identification of Ram as Abraham by the Tg.

2.d. ויחר אף "and his wrath became hot." Some versions evidently have found the repetition of this language (חרה אפו in vv 2, 3; ויחר אפו in vv 2, 5) tedious and have rung the changes on it: NIV combines the first two occurrences as "became very angry," then has "was angry" and "his anger was aroused"; NAB has "the anger of Elihu was kindled," "he was angry" twice, and "his wrath was inflamed"; JB has "was infuriated," "fumed with rage," "was equally angry," and "his anger burst out." But it is arguable that an Eng. translation should, on the contrary, represent the wooden style of the original.

2.e. In מאלהים, the *min* should perhaps be taken as "rather than" (as also in Jer 3:11); so too RSV, Pope. "In the presence of" is possible (so NEBmg "had justified himself with God," NJPS "thought himself right against God"; similarly Davidson, Dhorme, Hölscher, Terrien). It is arguable, however, that the most appropriate translation is "more than" (as NEB "made himself out more righteous than God," Moffatt "for making himself out to be better than God"; cf. JB "for thinking that he was right and God was wrong," Delitzsch "at the expense of God"; so also Duhm, Peake, Strahan, Andersen, Good); for by arguing that he is innocent and that God has been treating him unjustly Job is surely claiming that he is more "in the right" than God (cf. צדק מן in Gen 38:26).

2.f. צַדְּקוֹ, inf constr piel of צדק, "be righteous, right," the piel (as also in 33:32; Jer 3:11; Ezek 16:51–52) having the same declarative force as the hiph of רשע in v 3 and commonly; thus "declared, considered himself to be in the right" (as NAB), more exactly than "justified himself" (as KJV, RSV, NIV).

3.a. לא־מצאו מענה "they had not found an answer," i.e., a satisfactory answer, as NAB "had not found a good answer" (they had found plenty of "answers"!), NIV "had found no way to refute Job," JB "giving up the argument." מענה is used here and in v 5 for "answer," though elsewhere in Job it is תשובה "response" (21:34; 34:36) or מלים "words" (8:10; 23:5). Some see here further evidence of different authorship for the Elihu speeches, but it is a small point.

3.b. וירשיעו את־איוב could be (1) "and because they condemned Job," or (2) "and yet they condemned Job," or (3) "and (therefore) they did not condemn Job," or (4) "and (so) had not shown Job to be in the wrong." (1) The first possibility has Elihu taking up Job's cause and being angry because Job did not deserve their condemnation.

(2) The second possibility has Elihu angry at the friends because they could not show why Job was in the wrong even though they maintained that he was. It is adopted by KJV, NIV "and yet," RSV "although," NJPS "but merely condemned Job," Good "while condemning Job."

(3) The third possibility has Elihu angry with the friends because they could not refute Job's position and therefore drew back finally from denouncing him as wicked. It assumes that the negative particle לֹא "not" from the first clause is to be understood here also; thus NAB "and had not condemned Job," and Driver–Gray, Andersen; Davidson explains: "found no answer wherewith to condemn Job." A somewhat awkward variant on this view is that the *waw* is *waw explicativum*, i.e., the clause explains what a satisfactory "answer" would have been, viz. that they would have found Job to be in the wrong (so Blommerde; on *waw explicativum*, cf. *Note* 29:12.b).

(4) The fourth possibility has him angry with them because they had not been able to refute Job and thus prove him to be in the wrong. It is adopted by NEBmg, Gibson, Rowley, as well as in the *Translation* above.

3.c. וירשיעו, a declarative hiph; KJV "condemned," RSV "declared Job to be in the wrong."

The Masoretic marginal note (*tiqqun sopherim*) is that איוב "Job" is a "correction" for הָאֱלֹהִים "God," that is, a way of avoiding the apparent blasphemy of declaring God wrong. NEB translates the "uncorrected" text with "had let God appear wrong" (noting this as the probably original reading), Gordis "had placed God in the wrong," Moffatt "for compromising God by failing to refute Eyob"; so too Strahan, Dhorme, Kissane, Fohrer, Terrien, Gordis, de Wilde. JB "[giving up the argument and] thus admitting that God could be unjust" (NJB "and thus putting God in the wrong") is an ingenious rendering of the same Heb. text. NIV merely notes the uncorrected reading as "an ancient Hebrew scribal tradition."

4.a. חכה את־איוב בדברים, lit. "waited for Job with words" (RVmg, Good), an unparalleled use of חכה piel "await." Driver–Gray judge the translation of RV, "had waited to speak unto Job" (similarly RSV, NIV), no more than a paraphrase. NEB has "had hung back while they were talking with Job," NAB "bided his time before addressing Job," Moffatt "Elihu had waited for them to argue with Eyob."

Some versions and commentators think that the phrase means that Elihu had waited for Job to finish all his speeches; thus KJV "had waited till Job had spoken," NJPS "waited out Job's speech"; so too Delitzsch, and Habel: "After Job had completed his speeches, then he and Elihu waited some time for a reaction." But the sequel, "because they were older than he," can only refer to the friends (who are the subj of the two verbs in the preceding verse), so it is clear that Elihu's deference is to the friends, not to Job.

Emendations have been offered: Some emend דברים "words" to בְּדַבְּרָם "in their speaking"; thus Dhorme "Elihu had waited, while they were speaking to Job"; so too Ehrlich, Beer (*BHK frt*), Gordis, Habel, and NEB, understanding חכה as "waited with, beside [Job] for their speaking," i.e., for them to speak. Wright, followed by Kissane, Fohrer, Hesse, and Hartley, reads בְּדַבְּרָם אֶת־איוב "while they spoke with Job," and so too NJB "while they and Job were talking." Duhm, following LXX, emended to חכה לְהָשִׁיב את־איוב "waited to respond to Job," and Hölscher deleted את־איוב "with Job" (following Steuernagel) and read בְּדַבְּרָם "in their speaking"; so too Pope, Larcher, and JB "While they were speaking, Elihu had held himself back." Hitzig read חכה לְרֵעֵי איוב "he waited for the friends of Job."

5.a. JB "had not another word to say in answer," NJPS "that the three men had nothing to reply."

6.a. צעיר לימים, lit. "small in days"; JB has "still young" (similarly Fohrer), NJPS "I have but few years."

6.b. יָשִׁישׁ is just "old" (as in 12:12; 15:10; 29:8), not especially "very old" (as KJV, NAB) nor "decrepit" (Good); Pope has "venerable." Duhm was inclined to add כֻּלְּכֶם "all of you" at the end of the colon for the sake of the meter; he is followed by Beer (*BHK*).

6.c. Some take זחל as "withdraw, hold back," comparing זֹחֵל in Deut 32:24 and Mic 7:17 as a term for (poisonous) snakes or worms, presumably as those who "shrink back" or "crawl away" (so too RV, NEB, NAB, Moffatt, JB "was shy," Budde, Fohrer, Good "crawled about," and Pope "recoiled"). But most now see a זחל II "be afraid" (as Aram. דחל; used in Dan 5:19; 6:27), attested in the Old Aram. inscription of Zakir, king of Hamath (ninth century B.C.E.); so, e.g., *HALOT,* 1:267b; *DCH,* 3:101a. Duhm remarks that the poet of the rest of the book of Job, though he often speaks of being afraid, never uses this word; but it is a small point, not at all decisive for the question of authorship.

6.d. חוה III "declare," sometimes said to be an Aramaism, is common enough in Job (15:17; 32:10, 17; 36:2; also Ps 19:3).

6.e. דֵּעַ "knowledge" (as NAB; NEB "displaying my knowledge," NIV, JB "to tell you what I know," NJPS "to hold forth"), but also "opinion" (RSV, Moffatt, REB ["expressing my opinion"]); cf. *DCH,* 2:455b. The term is used only by Elihu in the OT (32:10, 17; 36:3, 4; 37:16), but it is attested also at

Ecclus 16:25 and perhaps 1Q418 177.7a. Fohrer observes that Elihu uses the more normal term דֵּעָה for "knowledge" only when he is saying something negative about it (34:35; 35:16; 36:12), but that may be no more than coincidental (and it is not true of 33:3, which Fohrer has to emend). D. W. Thomas thought דֵּעַ was a different word for "word" in all these places, as also at Prov 24:14 if דְּעֶה "know" is emended to דֵּעַ "word of" (review of *The Legend of King Keret: A Canaanite Epic of the Bronze Age,* by H. L. Ginsberg, *JJS* 1 [1948–49] 63–64 [64]; and cf. *DCH,* 2:456a).

6.f. אֶתְכֶם is a second direct obj of חוה piel "declare"; but Beer (*BHK frt*) and Hölscher suggest reading אִתְּכֶם "to you."

7.a. For similar usages of אמרתי "I said (to myself)," cf. 7:13; 9:22; 32:10. NEB actually translates "I said to myself," JB "I told myself," NJB, NJPS "I thought," Moffatt "I felt."

7.b. ימים "days"; NEB, NIV, NJB, NJPS more idiomatically in English "age," JB "old age," Moffatt "the word lay with a long life."

7.c. NEB "length of years," NIV, NJPS "advanced years," JB "advancing years," NAB "many years," Moffatt "years entitled men to instruct wisely."

7.d. ידיעו, plural *ad sensum,* the subj being רב שנים "multitude of years."

8.a. אכן "surely"; see *Comment.* NJPS has "but truly." JB "but now I know" suggests a change of mind rather than a counterargument Elihu has put to himself; NJB has "There is, you see, a spirit."

8.b. The parallelism suggests that the "spirit" (רוח) in a human is the spirit of God; cf. Num 27:18 איש אשר־רוח בו "a man in whom is the spirit" (so here NIVmg "the Spirit"). But it is perhaps more likely (see *Comment*) that the spirit is a possession of a human being, no doubt as a divine gift. Thus REB "it is a spirit in a human being," NAB, NJB "a spirit," JB "a breath."

It is needless to emend to רוח־היא "it is the spirit" to רוח־אֵל "the spirit of God" (as Bickell, Budde, Beer [*BHK prps*], NEB "the spirit of God himself") or to רוח־אֱלוֹהַּ "the spirit of Eloah" (as Hölscher, de Wilde), or even less probably to רוח־יהוה "the Spirit of Yahweh" (cf. Beer [*BHK*]); the support of Symm is no doubt only for the sense, not for the reading. Moffatt "God inspires a man" follows the emendation of Duhm, תָּאִיר אֱנוֹשׁ, lit. "enlightens a man" (perhaps preferably אֲנָשִׁים "men," he says).

8.c. KJV, JB "inspiration," but most have "breath" (so RV, RSV).

8.d. The relative pronoun is understood.

9.a. There is no word for "only" in the Heb., but we need to prevent the sentence from sounding too categorical. KJV has "great men are not *always* wise" (the italics indicating the insertion of the word), NEB, NIV "it is not only the old who are wise," Moffatt "it is not always seniors who are sage." Pope expresses it more subtly: "seniors may not be sage." Andersen proposes that רבים "many" and זקנים "old," though in different cola, are to be taken together, thus "not many old men are wise"; but that hardly seems to be Elihu's point.

9.b. MT is רבים "the many" (RSVmg, NIVmg "many") or perhaps "great ones" (KJV "great men," RV, NIVmg "the great"). This term by itself can hardly mean "aged" (as RSV, NEB, NIV "old," NJPS "aged," NAB "those of many days," JB "great age," and similarly Dillmann, Hitzig, Delitzsch, Strahan, Gordis; cf. LXX πολυχρόνιοι, Vg *longaevi* "aged"), for even in Gen 25:23 רב יעבד צעיר may be "the greater will serve the lesser" rather than "the older will serve the younger." Pope, de Wilde, Habel refer to the רבים in the Qumran community, conventionally translated as "the elders"; but that evidence does not prove the point. Dhorme argues that the presence of רב שנים "multitude of years" in v 7 prevents any ambiguity in רבים.

Budde and Beer (*BHK prps*) emend to שָׂבִים "the gray-haired" (as in 15:10, where it is parallel to יָשִׁישׁ "aged"); the suggestion is followed by Driver–Gray and is adopted in the *Translation* above. Duhm, Beer (*BHK*), Hölscher, Fohrer read רֹב יָמִים "multitude of days," but that does not make for a good parallel with זקנים "elders" in the second colon. Better would be רַבֵּי יָמִים "the great/many of days" (Gerleman [*BHS frt*]; cf. Pope). G. R. Driver suggested that an original רַבֵּי יָמִים had been abbreviated to רב׳ ימ׳, which was then misread as רַבִּים ("Once Again Abbreviations," *Textus* 4 [1965] 76–94 [91]).

9.c. REB, NIV "not only the aged," NJPS "the elders," JB "longevity," NJB "seniority."

9.d. משפט is "judgment" (KJV; as in 9:32) or "justice" (as in 8:3); NEB, NIV "what is right," JB "sound judgement," NJB "fair judgement," NJPS "who understand how to judge." Duhm says it has its "proper sense," "what is right."

10.a. Duhm, followed by Beer (BH^2), Strahan, Moffatt, Hölscher, de Wilde, removed vv 15–17 to this place, and deleted v 10.

10.b. אמרתי is lit. "I said" (as KJV), but is more naturally translated "I say (now)" (so RVmg, RSV); JB has "and so I ask you for a hearing."

10.c. שמעה is sg, as if addressed solely to Job; but elsewhere in this passage Elihu is addressing Job and the friends, in the pl (vv 6, 11–14). So many emend to שִׁמְעוּ "hear" (pl), with two MSS, LXX, Pesh, Vg, JB, Hitzig, Budde, Driver–Gray, Larcher, and de Wilde. Gordis defends the sg.

10.d. Or "I shall declare" (similarly KJV).

10.e. NEB "will display my knowledge," NAB "set forth my knowledge," NIV "will tell you what I know," REB "I too want to express an opinion," JB "it is my turn to tell you what I know," NJPS "I also would hold forth." As in v 6, Ginsberg and Thomas (see *Note* 32:6.e), followed by Pope, see here a דֵּעַ "word, utterance" (cf. *DCH,* 2:456a), connected with a verb דעו "call." The Qumran Tg has מלי "my words," but that may simply be a translation *ad sensum,* and cannot be used as philological support for a word דֵּעַ.

11.a. Gordis, followed by Habel, thinks that יחל hiph has the sense here (and in v 16) of "be silent"; he is probably right that that is what "wait" here *implies,* but not that it *means* it. JB interprets: "There was a time when I hoped for much from your speeches"; NJB "Up to now, I was hanging on your words." NIV differently, "I waited while you spoke," implies his waiting in silence.

11.b. אָזִין is a contracted form of אַאֲזִין (GKC, §68i), which is read by a few MSS. M. Dahood, *Proverbs and Northwest Semitic Philology,* Scripta Pontificii Instituti Biblici 113 (Rome: Pontifical Biblical Institute, 1963) 38, proposed a root וזן "weigh" (cf. Arab. *wazana* [Lane, 3052a]), as also in Prov 17:4 (*DCH,* 2:598b).

11.c. עד suggests "as far as" and not merely "unto"; it may be an ironic emphasis. Dhorme thinks it suggests "listening to something which one finds it difficult to catch."

11.d. תבונתיכם, lit. "your understandings," i.e., "words or speeches in which your understanding would declare itself" (Driver–Gray); thus "your reasons" (KJV), "your reasoning" (NIV, REB), "the conclusions of your thoughts" (NEB). The term תְּבוּנָה usually signifies the faculty of comprehension or the act of understanding, here the object or content of wisdom (as Prov 5:1; 19:8; Ps 49:4); so Gordis.

11.e. Duhm, Beer (*BH*[2]), Strahan, Moffatt, and NAB transpose v 11c to follow v 12a. Dhorme and Hölscher find three bicola in vv 11–12 rather than two tricola, taking v 11c as the beginning of a colon and v 12b as its end.

11.f. חקר "search out" sometimes implies "to the limit" (as 5:9; 9:10; 34:24; 36:26; Isa 40:28; Ps 145:3), but that is not to say that חקר means "finish [your speeches]" (as Gordis implies). Good has "digging for words," NEB "sought for phrases," REB "picked your words," NIV "were searching for words."

12.a. NEB "I have been giving thought to your conclusions" is overprecise.

12.b. אין לאיוב מוכיח might be "there was no one for Job (to act as) a confuter" (so Driver–Gray), or simply "there was no one confuting Job," the ל being the sign of the obj as in Prov 9:7; 15:12; 19:25 (so Dhorme). יכח hiph is "reprove," "convict" (NAB, REB), "confute" (Moffatt, RSV, Pope), "refute" (NEB, Delitzsch, Hartley), thus "gave Job the lie" (JB), "proved Job wrong" (NIV), "disproved what Job has said" (GNB); "convince" and "confound" (NJB) wrongly suggest, as against the Heb., that the issue was whether Job accepted their reproof (in KJV "convince" has its seventeenth-century sense of "overcome, confute"). "Criticises" (Dhorme) is inappropriate, for the friends have certainly been criticizing; what they have not been doing is proving anything. "Job has no arbiter" (Good) begs the question of whether we are dealing with legal language here (see *Comment*).

13.a. NRSV has "yet do not say."

13.b. פן "lest" is elliptical for "beware, lest" (as also in 36:18; Deut 29:18 [17]; Isa 36:18; Jer 51:46); so RV; NEB "take care then," REB "see then," JB "so do not dare to say," NJB "so do not say," Moffatt "say not." M. Dahood, however, argued that פן is sometimes the simple negative "not," as also in Ps 28:1 ("Hebrew-Ugaritic Lexicography VIII," *Bib* 51 [1970] 391–404 [398–99]).

13.c. ידפנו, from נדף, "drives him away." One MS has יִרְדְּפֶנּוּ "pursues him" (so too Graetz), and another has יֶהְדְּפֶנּוּ "thrusts him away." It is probably best to retain the strong metaphor, thus "rout" in the *Translation* above. Since the verbs have similar meanings, we cannot always be certain which reading the versions are adopting. KJV has "thrusteth him down," Good "drive him off," RV, RSV, NAB "may vanquish," Delitzsch "smite," NEB "will rebut," NIV "refute," Pope "rebuke," Moffatt "It must be God, not man, who puts him down."

Dhorme, followed by Hölscher and Larcher, emended to יְלַפֵּנוּ "[God] instructs us, not a man" (אלף piel, with the omission of the *aleph,* as at 35:11); hence JB "[do not dare to say] that your teaching is from God not man," NJB "Our teaching is divine and not human."

14.a. Gordis and NAB read ולא as וְלוּא "and if." M. Dahood and Blommerde read לְא אערך "I will assuredly prepare my own discourse," with לְא emphatic. Dahood further reads לא as לְא "the Almighty," rendering "The Almighty has prepared arguments against me" (review of *Job et son Dieu: Essai d'exégèse et de théologie biblique,* by J. Lévêque, *Bib* 52 [1971] 436–38 [438]); for other supposed occurrences of לְא "the Victor," see *Note* 21:16.a.

14.b. ערך is "draw up in order," in a military sense in 6:4, and in a transferred sense referring to words and arguments in 13:18; 23:4; 33:5; 37:19. KJV, RSV have "directed," KJVmg "ordered"; Pope offers "He has not matched words with me," Good more literally "he has not arranged words to me" (whatever that means). The translation "marshalled" that is adopted above retains the military metaphor. Guillaume wants a more intense meaning, translating "he has not attacked me" and invoking the acknowledged Arab. cognate *'arika* "be vehement in altercation" to strengthen the military sense (Lane, 2023b, though *'araka* normally means "rub").

Among emendations may be mentioned: (1) NAB "For had he addressed his words to me, I should not have answered him as you have done" makes good sense, involving only the minor emendation of וְלֻא "and if" for וְלֹא "and not." (2) Driver–Gray, followed by Dhorme, Beer (*BHK frt*), Hölscher, Larcher, Terrien, Fedrizzi, de Wilde, NEB, read לֹא אֶעֱרֹךְ כָּאֵלֶּה "I will not set forth [such words] as these"; so too JB "I am not going to follow the same line of argument." (3) Similarly Bickell, with לֹא־אָעִד "I will not testify" (cf. Pesh "I shall not speak against words").

15.a. KJV thinks this refers to the past ("they were amazed"), but most take it as the present situation with the friends. חתת is "be shattered, dismayed"; KJV has "amazed," NRSV, NAB, NIV, Pope "dismayed," NEB "confounded," JB "nonplussed," Moffatt "dumbfounded," Gordis "beaten"; RSV has the obsolescent "discomfited." P. Joüon, "Notes de lexicographie hébraïque (suite)," *MUSJ* 5.2 (1912) 416–46 (428–29), argued that חתת means not only "be frightened" but also "be ashamed, confused" and also "be weak" (as in 1 Sam 2:4; Prov 10:15); here the weakness of the friends who are powerless to respond may be rendered "were speechless." The word is obviously in need of further precisions.

The 3d-person verbs in reference to the friends suggest that Elihu is now addressing Job; GNB is explicit on that point with "Words have failed them, Job."

15.b. עתק is "move" both in qal and hiph according to BDB, 801a, thus "words have moved away from them" (similarly Good), an internal hiph with an intransitive sense (Driver–Gray). But KJVmg "removed speeches from themselves" takes the hiph as a causative (against Buxtorf, 593, but perhaps with the support of Leigh, 184a mg). KJV "left off speaking," RV, Gordis "have not a word to say," NAB, NEB, Moffatt "words fail them" (similarly NIV, JB, GNB, *HALOT,* 2:905a) all lose the metaphor. Pope's "words have forsaken them" retains something of the idea, as does Fohrer's "have abandoned them, left them in the lurch (*im Stich gelassen*)."

16.a. Many find here the use of *waw* consec with the pf to introduce a question (GKC, §112cc); so RV, RSV "and shall I wait?," NRSV, Moffatt "am I to wait?," NAB, NIV "Must I wait?," Pope "Should I wait?," Driver–Gray, Fohrer. For Gordis's thought that יחל hiph is "wait silently," see *Note* 11.a above. P. W. Skehan thought it was "resumptive" ("'I Will Speak Up' [Job 32]," *CBQ* 31 [1969] 380–82).

Not recognizing this idiom, KJV had to offer a strained rendering: "When I had waited, (for they spake not, but stood still, *and* answered no more;) *I said,* I will answer also my part." Dhorme contests the alleged question idiom, observing that the very same form (הוחלתי, "I have waited") has been used in v 11 in its normal sense. So he construes vv 16–17 thus: "And I have waited! But since they do not speak . . . I too will reply for my part." He is followed by JB, Terrien; similarly Delitzsch, Good.

Emendation can be ruled out, for either of the interpretations mentioned already is satisfactory. Beer (*BHK prps*) and Ehrlich wanted to read וְהַהִלּוֹתִי "and I have begun," and Tur-Sinai וְהוֹאַלְתִּי "and I have decided" (יאל hiph).

16.b. עמד "stand," is occasionally "stand still, remain inactive" (as also at 2 Chr 20:7; Neh 7:3; perh. Isa 46:7; cf. BDB, 764a; *DCH,* vol. 6, *s.v.,* §9a; G. R. Driver, "Forgotten Hebrew Idioms," *ZAW* 78 [1966] 1–7 [5]); cf. RSV, NIV, NEB "they stand there," KJV "stood still."

17.a. Lit. "I also will answer (as for) my portion." אַעֲנֶה is apparently vocalized as a hiph (otherwise poorly attested), perhaps suggesting that חלקי "my portion" is the obj. It could of course be the obj of ענה qal (as KBL, 806a). But most think that חלקי is a kind of adv acc (Driver–Gray, Dhorme) and that the vocalization is equivalent to אֶעֱנֶה (so Gerleman [*BHS*], Gordis; against GKC, §63f), or else actually emend to אֶעֱנֶה (Duhm, Beer [*BHK*], Hölscher, Fohrer). KJV has "I will answer also my part," NAB "I will speak my part," Pope "I will say my piece," RSV "I also will give my answer." NIV "I too will have my say" (similarly JB), and Moffatt "I will offer my own answer" are tamer. NEB "I too have a furrow to plough" supposes an ענה "plow" (cf. *DCH,* vol. 6, *s.v.* ענה X; from this comes מַעֲנָה "field for plowing" [BDB, 776a] or "furrow, plough furrow" [*DCH,* 5:409a]).

Emendation of חלקי "my portion" to לִקְחִי "my teaching" (Graetz, Ehrlich) is unsuccessful since the verb ענה "answer" is inappropriate (Dhorme).

17.b. Or "show my knowledge"; see *Comment* on vv 6–10.

18.a. Some have found the colon too short, and read כי פי מלאתי "for my mouth is full" (Beer [*BHK al*]), or אָנֹכִי "I" (Beer [*BHK frt*]), or כִּי אֲנִי or כִּי אָנֹכִי "for I" (Duhm, Beer [*BHK frt*]). Beer (*BH*[2]) moves the verse to follow v 14.

18.b. KJV "matter" (mg "words"), NAB "matters to utter." NEB "bursting with words" introduces into this colon the image of the next.

18.c. It is doubtful that we should connect the physical רוח "breath" here very closely with רוח "spirit, breath" in v 8; so it is best to avoid "spirit" (which KJV, RV, RSV, NAB, NIV have); Duhm mischievously inquired what kind of a spirit it would be one would have in one's belly. Good has "the wind in my belly."

18.d. רוח בטני, lit. "the breath of my belly, innards" (cf. RVmg); NAB "my bosom is ready to burst" tames the metaphor somewhat.

18.e. צוק is "constrain" (so too KJV, RSV), i.e., compel to speak (the image of wind bursting out appears only in the next verse), NIV "compels," Moffatt "my mind urges me to speech," Gordis "presses upon me," Good "pushes on me." NEB "a bellyful of wind gripes me" and Pope's "Wind bloats my belly" are graphic; but "gripes" and "bloats" are not what צוק means, and the issue is not how Elihu is feeling but how he feels compelled to enter the conversation; REB improves matters only somewhat with "as if wind in my belly were griping me." JB "choked by the rush of them [words] within me" is too loose a rendering, and NJB returns to a more traditional translation, "and forced to speak by a spirit within me."

19.a. Beer (BH^2; *BHK prps*) reads הֵן, the short form of הִנֵּה "behold" for the sake of the meter.

19.b. לא־יפתח, lit. "[that] is not opened" (as KJVmg), i.e., that has no vent (so KJV, RSV), rather than "unopened wine" (Good); NAB "like a new wineskin with wine under pressure" is no doubt accurate but a bit too technical even for Elihu. NIV "inside I am like bottled-up wine" is not a very good translation, for it does not hint at what "bottled-up wine" does. Moffatt "My mind is like wine bottled up, ready to burst out, like new bottles" is better, but is it not wine rather than the bottle that "bursts out"? JB "I have a feeling in my heart like new wine seeking a vent" is attractive, except for "in my heart," which is too bland, and suggests emotion. NJB is better, translating "within me, it feels like new wine seeking a vent." NEB "My stomach is distended as if with wine" is a loose translation *ad sensum.*

M. Dahood, "The Phoenician Contribution to Biblical Wisdom Literature," in *The Role of the Phoenicians in the Interaction of Mediterranean Civilizations,* ed. W. A. Ward (Beirut: American Univ. in Beirut, 1968) 123–52 (134–35), and in his review of *The New English Bible, Bib* 52 (1971) 117–23 (119), infers that the verb is not פתח "open" but a form of פוח "breathe, below" (with infixed *-t-*), thus "wine not aerated." His interpretation is correct, but the MT is capable of the same sense, it would appear.

Sicre Díaz understands the whole verse to mean: "Behold, my belly is like new wineskins that are burst by unvented wine," rearranging the order to הנה־בטני כאבות חדשים כיין לא־יפתח יְבַקֵּעַ (correcting his form *yᵉbaqqe'*)—but his rendering still effects a smoothing of the Heb. Beer notes the proposal to read וְאֹבוֹת "and wineskins" together with יְבַקֵּעַ piel "bursts," i.e., "like wine that is not vented and that bursts new wineskins"—which is more logical than the belly being like wine *and* like wineskins, but not necessarily how the text originally ran.

On the imagery of the verse, see *Comment.*

19.c. אוֹב in the sense "skin-bottle," "wine-skins" (RVmg; not "bottle," as KJV), occurs only here (it is a different word from BDB's אוֹב "necromancer, ghost," as *HALOT,* 1:20a, and *DCH,* 1:148b, recognize). A. Guillaume, however, thinks it is "wine-jar" ("An Archaeological and Philological Note on Job xxxii, 19," *PEQ* 93 [1961] 147–50 [= *Studies,* 141–44]), comparing Arab. *wa'b* "wide vessel" (Lane, 2913b), thus also KBL, 18a, Fedrizzi, and cf. KJV "bottles," NJPS "jugs"; it is hard to identify this Arab. *wa'b;* while KBL's citation is of Arab. *'āba* as "turn inside out," Lane, 123b, does not mention this sense for the verb that usually means "return," and there is no Arabic noun corresponding to Heb. אוֹב. There are, moreover, other words for jar in Heb. (כַּד, נֵבֶל), and the belly is more naturally compared to a wineskin than to a pottery jar. Little is gained by reading וְאֹבוֹת "and wineskins" (Beer [*BHK*]) rather than כְּאֹבוֹת "like wineskins." On waterskins (not wineskins), see *Comment* on 26:8.

19.d. The sg suggests that it is his belly that is ready to burst; it is not very surprising that the verb יבקע, which should be fem to agree with the subj בטני, is masc, since it is so far removed from its subject; and we could always emend it if we thought it so important (so Duhm, Beer [BH^2; *BHK al*] reading תִּבָּקֵעַ). But it could perhaps be "wine-skins which are ready to burst" (so RV; similarly NIV, Terrien, Pope, Gordis). Dhorme, Beer (*BHK prps*), Sicre Díaz read יְבַקֵּעַ (piel rather than niph) "bursts," seeking support from Vg *disrumpit* and rendering "like a wine which bursts new wineskins"; the point is presumably that the fermentation is so advanced that even pliable new wineskins would be in danger of being burst. Dhorme's emendation is followed by Larcher, JB "[like new wine} bursting a brand-new wineskin," NJB "bursting out of new wine-skins."

Gordis thinks it possible that the negative לא applies also to the second colon, thus "like new wine skins that are not opened"; but בקע "break open" would be a strange verb to use for that.

19.e. LXX has ὥσπερ φυσητὴρ χαλκέως ἐρρηγώς "like the bursting bellows of a coppersmith," reading חָרָשִׁים "smiths" rather than חֲדָשִׁים "new"; there is no evidence elsewhere that אוב can mean "bellows." This reading is, however, followed by Tur-Sinai and by NEB "bulging like a blacksmith's bellows"; but such a rendering again draws attention to Elihu's physical condition, whereas the context is rather of the compulsion Elihu feels to speak. Dahood reproves the translators of the NEB for the mixed metaphor of its translation "distended as if with wine, bulging like a blacksmith's bellows," opining that biblical poets were "very congruent in their use of metaphors" (review of *The New English Bible,* 119). But it is probably not for that reason that REB abandons the emendation, translating "about to burst open like a new wineskin."

20.a. אדברה coh "let me speak" (as Driver–Gray, Gordis, Good, NAB), or perhaps better, the modal sense of "must" (as RSV, NEB, NIV, NJB, Pope); similarly JB "Nothing will bring relief but speech." Some translations, however, have a simple future, "I will speak" (as KJV).

20.b. רוח "be spacious, be relieved" is recognized by BDB, 926a, and *HALOT,* 3:1196a, for this place and for 1 Sam 16:23; Jer 22:14—a distinct verb from ריח "breathe, smell." RVmg, RSV, NEB, NIV have "find relief" (similarly NAB), Moffatt "I must relieve myself by speaking." Terrien (cf. Strahan) hints that the term may be a euphemism, as if Elihu were obeying a call of nature; but the parallel in 1 Sam 16:23 tells against that idea. The contrast of this relief and spaciousness with the constriction of צוק in v 18 (noted by Duhm) is perhaps no more than accidental. An alternative, but less appropriate, philological interpretation is adopted by KJV "that I may be refreshed" (mg "breathe"), taking רוח as "breathe" (the verb of רוּחַ "breath"), in accord with some lexicographers of its time (Buxtorf, 721; against Leigh, 226b), as well as now by KBL, 877a; *HALOT,* 3:1195b.

21.a. אל is the emphatic particle, reinforced by the particle נא, thus "surely." It is not "Let me not, I pray you" (as KJV), nor, weakly, "I would not be partial" (NAB), "I would show favour to no man" (Moffatt), "Let me be partial to no one" (Pope).

21.b. אל־נא אשא פני־איש, lit. "I will surely not lift up the face of a man"; so KJV "accept any man's person," RV "respect any man's person," Dhorme "side with any one."

21.c. כנה piel "give an epithet," "give a title of honor" (*DCH,* 4:4343b "grant title, give honorary name"); so JB "heap on fulsome flatteries." Gordis observes that in rabbinic Heb. כנה piel means "modify, disguise an expression"; hence Ehrlich understood "I shall call things by their right names," but it is hard to see how that connects with the first colon.

21.d. One Heb. MS has וְאֵל "and God" for וְאֶל "and unto," which could be rendered, though with some strain, "and, being a human, I will not flatter God." NEB "I will flatter no one, God or man" reads וְאֵל ואדם "whether God or human," appealing to Vg *et Deum homini non aequabo* "and I will not equate God and man." אדם is "human being," not "man, male" (see D. J. A. Clines, "אדם, the Hebrew for 'Human, Humanity': A Response to James Barr," *VT* 53 [2003] 297–310), but strangely both Hölscher and Fohrer insist that here it means "man." Good curiously has "to Adam would not give honor." Beer (*BH*[2] *prps*) mentions the suggestion to read simply וְאַף אַל "and I will certainly not [use flattering names]."

22.a. Lit. "I do not know (how) to give flattering titles" (as KJV); RSV "do not know how to use flattery," NAB "I know nought of flattery," NEB "I cannot use flattering titles," JB "I have no skill in flattery."

22.b. The logical connective between the bicola has to be supplied: KJV "*in so doing,*" NAB "if I did," RV, RSV, Pope "else," JB "otherwise," NRSV, NEB, NJB, Moffatt "or." Gordis and Habel vocalize לא as לֻא "if," thus "if I were skilled in flattery, my Maker . . ."; perhaps this is followed by NIV with the same translation.

22.c. כמעט, lit. "like (in) a little." J. Wehrle, "Zur syntaktisch-semantischen Funktion der PV *kᵉ=mᵉaṭ* in Ijob 32:22," *BN* 55 (1990) 77–95, connects the word with what precedes, i.e., "even if I were to flatter a little"; but it is improbable that אכנה should do double duty, once with לא ידעתי "I do not know" and once with מעט.

22.d. נשׂא "carry off" is not a very specific verb, but it probably suggests to carry off and away like the wind, as we have seen at 27:21 (Dhorme and Gordis have "carry me off"). Other renderings are: "take away" (KJV, NAB, NIV), "put an end to" (RSV), "make an end of me" (Moffatt), "do away with me" (NEB), "would make short work of me" (NJB), "dispatch" (Pope), "lift me up" (Good), and JB, perhaps too loosely, "silence me."

33:1.a. אולם "but," a sign of a new topic ("but now," NJPS). It is not a logical connective, such as "wherefore" (KJV), "therefore" (NAB), or "howbeit" (RV).

1.b. The verb is followed by the particle נא, conventionally regarded as a polite softening of an impv, "please," "pray." Some translators try to represent it; thus Dhorme "Be good enough, then, O

Job, to hear my words," JB "be kind enough," NJB "please listen," KJV "I pray thee," NEB "Come now." But almost anything in English seems too forceful.

2.a. Driver–Gray remark that "The poverty of this v. seems to Bu[dde] to be cured by making it hypothetical: If I have opened my mouth"—but it is not to be cured.

2.b. בחכי "in my palate" (KJVmg). The palate is the organ of speech in Prov 5:3; 8:7; but it is only here where anyone says that their tongue is "in" their palate. Usually when "tongue" and "palate" are mentioned together the tongue is cleaving to the palate in thirst (e.g., Ezek 3:26; Ps 137:6). Could this then be another metaphor that has gone somewhat awry, like that of the wineskins in 32:19? NEB makes a good effort in "the words are on the tip of my tongue" (similarly NIV, Hartley), but that is not of course what the Heb. says. NAB "my tongue and my voice form words" seems a rather labored translation. JB makes an even more determined effort to represent the Heb.: "my tongue shapes words against my palate"; similarly Pope, Habel "My tongue forms words on my palate," NJPS "my tongue forms words in my mouth." But these attempts go beyond the Heb.

Ehrlich offered the conjectural emendation to בְּחֻבִּי "in my bosom" (as in 31:33 [*q.v.*]), but the "bosom" (חֹב or חֵק) is not properly a part of the body but more or less equivalent to "pocket"; and Elihu's tongue can hardly have spoken in his pocket.

2.c. Though the two verbs פתחתי "I have opened" and דברה "has spoken" are pfs, they do not refer to the past but to Elihu's present speaking (as against KJV). Fohrer, however, sees the pfs as signifying that Job should listen to Elihu because he has already begun to speak. It is hard to justify NIV "I am about to open my mouth" (similarly Terrien).

3.a. Kissane transfers the verse to precede 32:21, where indeed it would fit well.

3.b. Duhm read אמרי ודעת "my words and knowledge" (in separate cola in the MT) as אִמְרֵי דַעַת "words of knowledge" (as in Prov 19:27; אִמְרֵי בִינָה "words of understanding" in 1:2; אִמְרֵי־יֹשֶׁר "words of uprightness" in Job 6:25); so too Beer (*BH*[2]), Strahan, Driver–Gray, Dhorme, Beer (*BHK frt*), Hölscher, Kissane, Fohrer (reading דֵעַ, as in 32:6), Terrien, Guillaume, Gordis, Hesse, de Wilde, and NEB "I speak with knowledge."

3.c. There is no verb in the Heb.; "my words are the uprightness of my heart" no doubt means that they embody it. NIV and Hartley have "come from an upright heart," Pope "are from an upright heart," KJV "shall be of the uprightness of my heart," RV "shall utter," RSV "declare," NJPS "bespeak," Budde "mirror," Moffatt "my heart uttering what is right and true." Andersen and Habel think that the verb מללו "speak" will do duty for both cola. Good unconvincingly takes "straightforwardness" of mind, words, and knowledge of lips as three subjects of מללו "speak." Habel regards ישר "uprightness" and דעת "knowledge" as adv accs, rendering "With uprightness my heart states my case; with knowledge my lips argue clearly"; but this seems rather awkward, especially in the first colon.

Emendations are plentiful. (1) Duhm, Driver–Gray, Beer (*BHK vel*), Fohrer, de Wilde read יָשֹׁק "overflows" (from שׁוק II "be abundant," as in Joel 2:24; 3:13 [4:13], of wine and oil vats). (2) Beer (*BHK frt*) reads רָחַשׁ "is astir" (which occurs elsewhere only in Ps 45:1 [2], where also לב "heart" is the subj; it is proposed also for Job 20:2 [*q.v.*]). (3) Dhorme suggests יָשֵׁר "will repeat" (from a new word שׁור "repeat," which he identifies also in vv 14, 27, and Hos 14:9. (4) Hölscher, followed by Hesse, proposes another new word, שׁרר "speak truly" (cf. Syr. *šar* "affirm" [J. Payne Smith, 595a]), vocalized יָשֵׁר "[my heart] speaks truly." Similarly, G. R. Driver, "Difficult Words in the Hebrew Prophets," in *Studies in Old Testament Prophecy Presented to Professor Theodore H. Robinson,* ed. H. H. Rowley (Edinburgh: T. & T. Clark, 1950) 52–72 (68), compares Akk. *šarāru* "affirm" as well as Syr. *šar,* and finds the verb also at vv 14, 27, and Hos 14:9; so too NEB "My heart assures me that I speak with knowledge," reading יָשֹׁר or יָשֵׁר (Brockington). (5) Kissane suggests yet another new word שׁרר, vocalized יָשַׁר and meaning "shall reveal" (cf. Arab. *šarra,* usually "be evil" but also apparently sometimes "make known" [Lane, 1524b]; Kissane connects it also with the Syr., but that seems to be a different verb); he is followed by Rowley. (6) Gordis suggests יָשִׁיר or יָשׁוּר, from שׁור "sing" (similarly Terrien, apparently); but Elihu is not proposing to sing his speech, and Gordis actually translates "proclaim," which is not a meaning of שׁור. (7) JB "my tongue shall utter sayings full of wisdom" and NJB "I shall utter words of wisdom from the heart" claim to emend to *yishereh,* which is perhaps יְשָׁרֶה "shall utter" from שׁרה "let loose." The MT, though awkward, is preferable to these conjectures, and is followed by Budde, Weiser, Tur-Sinai, Fedrizzi, and Sicre Díaz.

3.d. NAB "I will state directly what is in my mind" and Good "my straightforward mind" apparently think of the use of ישׁר for the "straightness, evenness" of paths (as Prov 2:13; 4:11). But even in those places there is a strong moral sense, and "honest, upright paths" would be an appropriate meaning; so there is no real evidence that the term can mean "directness." JB has "my lips speak the honest truth," NJB "my lips will speak in all sincerity."

3.e. ברור is an adj, "pure, sincere"; this is an adv acc. RV, RSV, NIV, NAB have "sincerely," NEB "with sincerity," Moffatt "my speech utterly sincere," NJPS "honestly." KJV "clearly" may mean "brightly, luminously" (though *OED* says it means "plainly"); the Heb. never means "clearly" in the sense of "plainly" or "intelligibly." Dhorme also has "clearly," but says it retains its original meaning of "clean, sparkling"; it is hard to see how that is possible. Habel too translates "clearly."

4.a. Budde, Duhm, Beer (*BH*²), Hölscher delete the verse as inappropriate here, and as a gloss based on v 6 and 32:8. Dhorme, more persuasively, removes it to follow v 5 (following Budde), Strahan, Peake, and de Wilde to follow v 6, and Kissane to follow 32:13.

4.b. תחיני is apparently impf, and so generally translated as a present, "gives me life" (as RSV, NIV, NJPS "sustains"), as distinct from the pf עשׂתני "made me." KJV ignored the distinction, translating both verbs by pfs (so also JB, Good), and NEB also has two pfs, perhaps understanding תחיני as a preterite (as in v 8 אשׁמע is a preterite in parallel with the pf אמרת).

5.a. השׁיבני, lit. "return (to) me," "answer me" (BDB, 999b). Beer (*BHK*) inserts, following LXX πρὸς ταῦτα "to these things," לְזֹאת "to this"; in *BH*² he read rather אֵלֶּה "these things."

5.b. The Heb. has simply ערכה "set in order," with no obj. The implied obj may be מִלִּין "words" (as in 32:14; so too KJV, RSV, NAB "arguments," Hölscher) or מִשְׁפָּט "cause" (as in 23:4), or even, since ערך is often used in a military context, מִלְחָמָה "warfare, battle" (as in, e.g., 1 Sam 17:8; 2 Sam 10:8; in Judg 20:22, 33 the obj is omitted, as here). NEB "marshal your arguments" represents the metaphor well, and JB more loosely "Prepare your ground to oppose me." NIV, NJB "prepare yourself" and NJPS "argue against me" avoid a definite obj, but these are not exact translations of ערך. Fohrer and Gordis insist that ערך is not used in a military sense, but forensically; it is unwise, however, to draw a strong distinction between the two.

5.c. יצב hithp "take one's stand" is used in a military sense in 1 Sam 17:16; 2 Sam 23:12. NEB continues the military metaphor with "confront me" (so too NIV); similarly NAB "stand forth" and NJB "take up your position."

6.a. הן־אני כפיך לאל, lit. "I am to God like your mouth," כְּפִי "like a mouth" being used in the sense of "in proportion to" (as in Exod 16:21; Lev 25:52; BDB, 805b), thus "I am in the proportion of you as far as God is concerned," which is to say, "In God's sight we are equals," "In God's sight I am just what you are" (NEB, similarly NIV), "You and I before God are the same" (Moffatt, similarly NJPS), "I am your like (*ton semblable*)" (Terrien), RV "I am toward God even as thou art" (similarly RSV), NRSV "before God I am as you are." KJV, RVmg "I am according to thy wish in God's stead" suggests wrongly that Elihu in some way considers himself to be God's representative. NAB does not improve matters by combining the two cola: "Behold I, like yourself, have been taken from the same clay by God." Sicre Díaz has "I am the work of God, the same as you," understanding the ל as *lamedh* of origin or ownership. There is no good reason to regard the ל as meaning "from" (as Habel "I am from God"). Pope, unconvincingly, thinks לאל is an oath formula, "By God!" NEBmg "in strength" nods to the understanding of אֵל as "power, strength" (*DCH*, 1:259b; *HALOT*, 1:48b; contrast BDB, 43a).

M. Dahood's proposal to find here a new word פִּיךְ "jar, drinking bowl," on the basis of the term βῖκος "(Phoenician) jar, drinking bowl," is nothing if not ingenious, especially because of its fit with "pinched off from a piece of clay" in the second colon ("The Phoenician Contribution to Biblical Wisdom Literature," 127). He is followed by Blommerde and Good. "A jar from God," understanding the *lamedh* of לאל as "from," is, however, weak; it would be stronger to understand "I am an earthen pot in God's sight." However, though humans were made from clay, they were not fired in an oven, and there is no good reason why Elihu should call himself, and Job, a clay pot. Beer (*BHK*) and Ehrlich emend to כָּמוֹךָ "like you."

Beer (*BH*² *frt*), Ehrlich, and Ball (*frt*), following Symm οὐκ εἰμὶ Θεός "I am not God," emended לאל "to God" to לא אֵל "not a god." Hence Larcher, Terrien, JB "See, I am your fellow man, not a god," and NJB "Look, I am your equal, not a god."

6.b. קרץ is lit. "nip, pinch," as a potter nips off a piece of clay for working, as Pope and Habel "I, too, was nipped from clay" (similarly Hartley, NJPS). Most versions have the more general term "form" (KJV, RSV). KJVmg "cut" no doubt incorrectly suggests "with a knife." NEB "I too am only a handful of clay," JB "I was fashioned out of clay" (NJB "moulded" is better), NIV "I too have been taken from clay," and Moffatt "formed of clay" needlessly abandon the metaphor. Hölscher is alone in denying that קרץ means "nip" and claiming that its sense is rather "form" (e.g., a dumpling); he compares *m. Kil'ayim* 15.2, Arab. *qaraṣa* (Lane, 2514a), and Akk. *qarāṣu*, together with Dalman, *Arbeit und Sitte*, 4:101, 108 (cf. 46, 82). But Arab. *qaraṣa* certainly means "pinch," and it is evident that "forming" is no more than the result of "pinching off" a piece of clay; the Akk. verb is now written *qarāšu*, and the sense "make dough into loaves" carries a question mark in *CAD*, 13:128a.

7.a. Dhorme thinks that הנה "behold" signifies the "logical conclusion to the preceding verses" and translates "thus then," but it seems rather to mark the transition from the statements of fact in vv 4, 6 to the encouragement in v 7.

7.b. A modal use of the impf, as RSV "need terrify you" (similarly NEB), NIV "should alarm you," NAB, Pope "should dismay," JB "need disturb," Moffatt "need scare," Habel "need dismay." Less appropriate is a simple future, as, e.g., KJV "my terror shall not make thee afraid," or even a present "You are not overwhelmed" (NJPS).

7.c. בעת is, as far as we can tell, a forceful verb, meaning "terrify, frighten, overwhelm" (BDB, 129b; *HALOT,* 1:147a; *DCH,* 2:244b), which should not be softened into NEB's "abash."

7.d. אֶכֶף "pressure" occurs only here, but the verb אכף "press" (Prov 16:26; BDB, 38b; KBL, 45a) is well attested in Aram. and Syr., and there appears to be a noun אַכְפָּה "pressure" at Ecclus 46:5, 16 (*DCH,* 1:249a). A. Guillaume, "The Arabic Background of the Book of Job," in *Promise and Fulfilment,* FS S. H. Hooke, ed. F. F. Bruce (Edinburgh: T. & T. Clark, 1963) 106–27 (121), advocates the sense as "weight, burden," comparing Arab. *'ikāf* "pack-saddle" (Lane, 71a; also mentioned by BDB, *s.v.* אכף "press"). This rendering is also supported by Tg טוני "my burden." So too Beer (*BHK*) (rendering "burden," "authority"), Hölscher, Gordis, Hartley. Driver–Gray say that the sense is "urgency" rather than "pressure" (RV, NJPS), but they do not mean "urgency" in a temporal sense but rather "compulsion."

Older lexicographers, following LXX ἡ χείρ μου, understood אכף as a form of כַּף "palm, hand" (Leigh, 10b; Buxtorf, 67); among modern lexica, *HALOT,* 1:47b, offers this interpretation also; so too Larcher. KJV had "my hand," and among modern translations NIV and JB "my hand will not lie heavy over you." Some emend the form to וְכַפִּי (Duhm, Beer [BH^2], Peake, Dhorme, Fedrizzi), but it might stand as it is written in the MT. M. Dahood, followed by Habel, saw the א as "prothetic *aleph*" (Hebrew-Ugaritic Lexicography I," *Bib* 44 [1963] 289–303 [293]). Strictly speaking, if the word is a form of כף "hand," the verb should be fem; thus Duhm, Beer (BH^2), Dhorme emended to תִּכְבַּד "is heavy."

7.e. ואכפי עליך לא־יכבד, lit. "and my pressure upon you will not be heavy," i.e., "nor should my presence weigh heavily upon you" (NAB). NEB is somewhat looser, with "nor any pressure from me overawe you"; similarly Moffatt "I will not be hard on you."

8.a. If אך is "only" (i.e., אך restrictive), Dhorme could be right that אך אמרת is "you have merely said," i.e., "You have done nothing but talk." But such a rendering does not seem to represent Elihu's attitude to Job, and it is better to take אך as a general emphatic "surely, no doubt" (so too Delitzsch), NJPS "indeed."

8.b. אמרת באזני, lit. "you have said in my ears." NEB "You have said your say" imports an impatient tone here that is lacking in the Heb.

8.c. מלין is simply "words," but the pronoun suff is to be understood. Some emend, with the claimed support of LXX[NA] and Pesh, to מִלֶּיךָ "your words" (Duhm, Beer [BH^2], Strahan, Hölscher [*frt*], Kissane, Hartley). Pope avoids the pronoun suff with "I heard the very words."

9.a. חף "clean, innocent" (BDB, 342b) occurs only here, but the meaning is not uncertain; the verb חפף is "wash" in Aram. and later Heb.

10.a. "Behold" (הנה) "announc[es] an observed fact such as occasions surprise" (Dhorme). Beer (BH^2) replaces it with הוּא "he."

10.b. תנואה "opposition" ("displeasure" in Num 14:34), thus "occasion for hostility" (BDB, 626a), from נוא "restrain"; thus KJV, RSV, "occasions," RVmg "causes of alienation," NEB "occasions to put me in the wrong," NIV "fault," JB "grievances," NJPS "reasons to oppose me," Moffatt "picks a quarrel with me," which was Coverdale's idiom too: "he hath pyked a quarell agaynst me"; Fohrer also retains the MT. Good takes it very literally with "he finds frustration over me," but it would be very surprising if that was what Job means.

On the other hand, Wright, Budde, Beer (*BHK* תּוֹאֲנוֹת), Dhorme, Kissane, de Wilde (as also Rashi), NEB read תֹּאֲנוֹת "occasions, opportunities," "pretexts" (Driver–Gray, Larcher, Pope, Habel, NAB), "excuses" (NJB), from אנה "be opportune" (cf. Arab. *'anā* [Lane, 118c]), the noun at Judg 14:4 (a ground of a quarrel with Samson) and the verb at 2 Kgs 5:7 (of Naaman seeking a quarrel with the Israelite king). Gordis claims, without much justification, that the latter meaning "may well inhere in the Masoretic reading."

11.a. Bickell, Duhm, Beer (BH^2) unreasonably delete the verse as a extension of Elihu's original citation made by a reader. The verse is a repetition of 13:27, but that is not a problem since Elihu is professedly quoting Job.

11.b. יָשֵׂם is apparently juss "let him set," which does not fit the context; more suitable would be

יָשֵׂם "he sets" (Driver–Gray, Beer [*BHK*], Gerleman [*BHS* (?)], Fedrizzi, NEB). But the use of a juss for an impf is not uncommon (Driver, *Tenses*, §§170–74; GKC, §109k), so the text does not need to be emended. Fohrer, following a hint from ibn Ezra, thought the same phrase at 13:27 meant that God coated Job's feet with white chalk so as to track his every movement, וְתָשֵׂם being from a new שׂים "paint, coat (with paste)" (of Jezebel painting her eyes at 2 Kgs 9:30), with a byform סמם "paint"; KBL, 661b, was in accord (*s.v.* סמם). Curiously, neither KBL nor Fohrer proposes this view for the present passage, even though the language is almost identical with 13:27. *HALOT,* 2:760a, explicitly rejects this view for both 13:27 and the present passage. The difficulty with this suggestion is that chalk on Job's feet would wear off before long, so that God would not be able to track him. See further, next *Note.*

11.c. סַד, occurring elsewhere only at 13:27, is traditionally rendered "stocks" (so KJV, RSV, NAB, JB, Driver–Gray, BDB, 690a; KBL, 650a), though NIV has "shackles," Pope "fetters," and Moffatt "fastens logs to my feet." See further, *Comment* on 13:27. There is a problem, however; for how can God be watching Job's paths if his feet are in the stocks? KBL, 655b, *HALOT,* 2:743b, and Fohrer (235, 238–39, 253) think to solve the conundrum by finding at 13:27 a new word סִיד "quicklime, lime mortar" (a byform of שִׂיד "mortar" at Deut 27:2, 4 and "lime" at Isa 33:12; Amos 2:1), but strangely they do not propose the same for the present verse. Quicklime is calcium oxide, formed by burning bones, wood, or limestone, and used in the ancient world for making mortar. It destroys flesh, so putting Job's feet in quicklime would be a cruel punishment, which would probably have the effect of preventing him from ever walking again. Once again, God cannot be watching his paths if he cannot walk.

12.a. זֹאת, acc of respect, "in regard to this" (as also in Ezek 20:27; 36:37; perhaps Neh 13:22).

12.b. This isolated word, אֶעֶנְךָּ "I will answer you," is something of a problem. It can hardly mean: "In this you are not right is what I will answer" (NEB "Well, this is my answer: You are wrong"; similarly REB, JB, NAB "in this you are not just, let me tell you," Davidson, Good), since there are no parallels to such a phrase. KJV has "I will answer thee, that God is greater than man"; so too NRSV "I will answer you: God is greater than any mortal" (similarly NJPS). Some think that the word should be deleted because Elihu does not in fact answer this allegation of Job (so Driver–Gray); but the whole of his speech could be seen as an answer (so Gordis).

Gordis resists the face value of the colon on the ground that it is no answer to Job to say that God is greater than humans; he thinks that Elihu is quoting Job, thus "You are wrong when you declare, God is stronger than man." But Elihu cannot believe that God is *not* stronger than humans, and in any case he is not using this sentence as an *answer* to Job.

There is really nothing wrong with the text—as the *Translation* above shows—and conjectural emendations are uncalled for. Duhm, scorning the mildness of Elihu's reproach, proposed הִנֵּה אִם אֶצְעַק לֹא עָנָה "behold, if I cried out, he does not answer" (reflecting 19:7); similarly Moffatt. Beer (*BHK*) unashamedly retroverts the LXX πῶς γὰρ λέγεις δίκαιός εἰμι, καὶ οὐκ ἐπακήκοέν μου into הֵךְ תֹּאמַר צָדַקְתִּי וְלֹא אֵעָנֶה "how do you say, I am righteous but I am not answered?"—which is not strong logically speaking. Job can complain because he calls upon God and is not answered or because he is righteous and is not declared innocent; but not for a combination of the two. The alternative reading noted by Beer (*BH*² *vel*), צָעַקְתִּי "I cry out," is more probable, though it does not correspond to LXX.

12.c. רבה "be great"; cf. *Note* on 39:4. Beer (*BHK*) reads כַּבִּיר "mightier than" (of God also at 36:5), allegedly following LXX αἰώνιος "eternal." Much less successful was Duhm's suggestion, reported in *BH*² (*prps* ?), and followed by Moffatt, מַעְלִים "[God] hides [his eyes from humans]," on the basis that LXX read מֵעוֹלָם "from eternity." עלם hiph may indeed mean "hide oneself" in Ps 10:1; but Elihu cannot be arguing here that God hides himself if in the remainder of the chapter he is explaining how God communicates with humans.

13.a. אליו ריב "charge him" (Pope), "rail at him" (JB), "complain against Him" (NJPS).

13.b. The word is supplied, interpreting the second colon as the content of Job's charge (so RSV, NAB). KJV "For he giveth no account" took the second colon as the reason why Job should not be contending with God.

13.c. דבריו "his words," but it is hard to make sense of the line. KJV "for he giveth not account of any of his matters" means that he does not justify to others what he does; so too NAB "that he gives no account of his doings" (similarly Delitzsch, Davidson, Sicre Díaz), and NIVmg "he does not answer for any of his actions." But ענה "answer" can hardly mean "answer for," "give an account of." At a stretch, it could mean "[God] gives no answer to his [humanity's] words" (so Delitzsch, Dhorme, Gordis, Hartley, NIV "he answers none of man's words"; similarly NJPS), but the issue is not that God does not answer human prayers or complaints in general, but that he has not responded to Job. NEB "for no one can answer his arguments" renders the Heb., but Job's main contention is not that one cannot adequately respond to God's arguments (though he does make that point, e.g., in 9:16) but that God will not respond to his.

Many therefore emend to דְּבָרַי "my words" (so RSV, Duhm, Strahan, Driver–Gray, Beer [*BHK*], Fohrer, de Wilde, Habel), regarding this as a free quotation of some of Job's complaints. This emendation is followed in the *Translation* above. Others read דְּבָרֶיךָ "your words" (so Beer [*BHK vel*], Terrien, Pope, Fedrizzi), i.e., continuing the address of Elihu to Job; similarly Larcher, JB "for not replying to you, word for word," Moffatt "for never answering your cry." M. Dahood reads דֹּבְרָיו "[he does not answer] those who speak to him" ("The Dative Suffix in Job 33,13," *Bib* 63 [1982] 258–59); but the qal of דבר is comparatively rare (42 of its 1,137 occurrences), and in any case at this point we are not hearing about generalities but about Job.

14.a. באחת . . . בשתים is "in one way . . . in two ways" (or, "in a second way") (so too RVmg, RSV, NIV "now one way, now another," Delitzsch, Peake, Terrien, de Wilde, Sicre Díaz, JB "first in one way and then in another," Moffatt "God has one mode of speech, yes, and another"), not "once . . . twice" (as KJV, NEB, NAB, Fohrer, Fedrizzi, Gordis "time and time again," NJPS "time and again," Habel, Good), which would be אחת and שתים alone (as in 40:5; 2 Kgs 6:10; Ps 62:11 [12]; cf. Neh 13:20 [שתים ,פעם]). The phrase does not, however, mean that God has only two ways of communicating with humans, for שתים effectively means "more than once" (as also at 40:5). A quite different interpretation is offered by Hölscher, translating "God speaks only once; he does not consider a second time"; similarly NEB "once God has spoken he does not speak a second time to confirm it," though the translation of the second clause depends on a different understanding of the verb שור (see next *Note*).

14.b. לא ישורנה "without perceiving him, or, it"; on the idiom, cf. Driver, *Tenses*, §162. Dhorme took שור as "repeat" (as in v 3), but this is a verb not known to the lexica (Dhorme cites Vg *repetit* here in support and finds the verb also in Hos 14:9); similarly NEB "once God has spoken he does not speak a second time to confirm it." Fedrizzi thinks it is שיר "sing" and thus "repeat with singing"; but the verb does not seem to mean "repeat," even in Ps 59:16 (17), which he cites. In any case, 33:29 says explicitly that God does repeat his warnings; L. Dennefeld rightly argues that it must mean "take notice" ("Les discours d'Elihou [Jb XXXII–XXXVII]," *RB* 48 [1939] 163–80 [175 n. 14]).

The obj of ישורנה may be "it," i.e., the fact that God is speaking (so KJV, NJPS), or "him," i.e., God. The subj must be אנוש "humans" (v 12b), though it must be admitted that, since God is the explicit subj of the first clause, it is a little odd to have humans as the inexplicit subj of the second (so Dhorme). Hölscher thinks the subj is God ("God speaks only once; a second time he does not consider"). Similarly Fedrizzi, and Good "and twice he does not regard it." If humans are the subj, the verb must be used modally ("*may* not perceive," as NIV; NAB "though one perceive it not"), for Elihu is not insisting that humans *never* perceive that it is God who is speaking. Peake inserts אִם "if [humans do not perceive it]"; so too Moffatt. It could of course be "when man regardeth it not" (Davidson), i.e., when they are asleep—but that would be to anticipate v 15.

Among emendations, (1) Siegfried and Budde change the person of the verb, reading תְשׁוּרֶנָּה "you [do not] perceive it." (2) Houbigant (ישננה), Michaelis (יְשַׁנֶּה), Beer (*BH*², יְשְׁנֶה) read a form of שׁנה "repeat" (cf. 40:5 where אחת "once" and שׁתים "twice" are joined with דבר "speak" and אסף hiph "continue, repeat"; and note Vg *repetit* "he repeats"); this suggestion yields the same sense as Dhorme's proposal for שׁור (see above). (3) Houbigant (*vel*), Duhm, Beer (*BH*² *vel*) read לֹא יְשִׁיבֶנָּה "does not reverse it," taking a hint from Symm οὐκ ἀκυρώσει αὐτόν "he will not settle it." (4) Less probably, Graetz has יִשְׁמָעֶנָּה "one [does not] hear it"; it is not a difficulty with the MT that one usually "hears" a word rather than "sees, perceives" it (against Dhorme). (5) Kissane makes a tiny alteration to וְלֹא ישורנה, which perhaps makes a concessive sense of the clause, "though one perceiveth Him not." (6) Gordis vocalizes לא as לֻא "if only [man would perceive it!]." (7) Blommerde reads לא as לֵא, allegedly "the Mighty One [appears]" (for other examples, see *Note* 21:16.a), but Elihu is not speaking of divine appearances, only of indirect warnings from God. (8) NEB's "he does not speak a second time to confirm it" reads יְשֹׁרֶנָּה or יְשַׁרְנָה (Brockington, 114). The former would be from a verb שׁוּר, though not presumably שׁוּר "see" (BDB, 965a) or other possible roots spelled שׁור meaning "struggle" or "rule" or "turn aside" or "install officials" or "saw apart" (all mentioned by *HALOT*, 3:1313ab). The latter perhaps invokes Syr. *šar* aphel "affirm" (see *Note* 33:3.c above).

15.a. חזיון is simply "a vision," but six MSS have בְּחֶזְיוֹן "in a vision," and so do Pesh Vg (but we cannot tell if that was in their text), Beer (*BH*²). חזיון לילה "vision of the night" can no doubt be understood simply as in apposition to חלום "dream" (as Dhorme).

15.b. Since the colon is identical with 4:13b, many think it should be deleted as a gloss (Bickell,

Budde, Duhm, Beer [*BH*[2]], Strahan, Driver–Gray, Hölscher, Fohrer, Fedrizzi, de Wilde, NAB). But since Elihu has quoted 4:13a in the first colon, there is no reason whatsoever why he should not quote 4:13b in the second.

15.c. תרדמה "deep sleep," i.e., normal sleep, as at 4:13 (see *Comment* on 4:13), rather than "trances" (Moffatt).

15.d. בתנומות, lit. "in [their] slumbers."

16.a. גלה, lit. "uncovers" (KJVmg), "reveals" (Moffatt). See *Comment.* NEB loosely "God makes them listen," but REB "imparts his message." JB thinks it must be "whispers," no doubt because they are asleep. NJB reverts to "speaks." NIV rightly sees that this verb also may be understood modally: "he may speak in their ears."

16.b. The colon is very difficult, and the translation of the verb and noun impinge upon one another. The verb יַחְתֹּם is "seals," explained by BDB, 367b, as God putting his seal upon discipline, i.e., ratifying it. KJV "sealeth their instruction" suggests that God first opens the ear, then pours instruction into it, and then closes or seals the ear of the recipient so that the message is retained (so Renan *et y scelle ses avertissements* "and there he seals up his warnings," Davidson; cf. Peake). Alternatively, the image could be of "impress[ing] the instruction on the recipients as an impression is stamped on a seal" (cf. Peake); he "stamps it on their minds" (Gibson), as we would say. Habel ingeniously renders "by warning them leaves his signature" (similarly NJPS); but it is hard to see what the meaning of that would be in the ancient world context. Delitzsch thought of the dreams as putting God's seal upon the warning, which otherwise they might take little notice of, and thus too Driver–Gray, that God "puts the seal to, or confirms, their moral education."

In view of the difficulties with "seal," it may be preferable to adopt (as in the *Translation* above) the emendation to יְחִתֵּם "dismays them" (Driver–Gray), "terrifies them" (RSV, NAB, NIV, Peake, Kissane, Pope), "frightens" (JB, Hartley), or "strikes with terror" (NEB), from חתת (cf. LXX ἐξεφόβησεν "he frightened"; similarly Aq; so too Wright [יְחִתֵּם], Bickell[2], Hoffmann, Budde [יְחִתֵּם], Duhm, Strahan, Dhorme, Beer [*BHK*], Hölscher, Fohrer, Terrien, Fedrizzi, de Wilde, Sicre Díaz), yielding the sense "by their punishment [the punishment they receive] he terrifies them"; thus too NEB "his correction strikes them with terror," Moffatt more loosely "sends them awful warnings." It is not a strong objection that the object of God's punishment according to Elihu is not to terrify but to restrain humans from contemplated wickedness; that may well be so, but the punishment is terrifying all the same.

M. Dahood suggested an emendation to יַחְתֵּם, from חתה "snatch," thus "he snatches them from their bond," the bond (see next *Note*) referring either to distress, as in Ps 116:16, or to the "bond of the body" from which people are delivered through sleep ("Some Northwest-Semitic Words in Job," *Bib* 38 [1957] 306–20 [311]). But such an interpretation is unsuited to the context, for there is no sense here that the mortals receiving divine warnings have been "bound" in any way. In his "Hebrew-Ugaritic Lexicography VI," *Bib* 49 (1968) 355–69 (360), however, Dahood preferred to emend to יֵחְתֵם, understood as impf of נחת "descend" with a dative suff (as with other verbs of motion, according to M. Bogaert, "Les suffixes verbaux non accusatifs dans le sémitique nord-occidental et particulièrement en hébreu," *Bib* 45 [1964] 220–47 [239–40]), thus "and for their instruction descends to them." Apart from the questionable dative suff, God's "descending" is strange, and the rendering leaves unstated what exactly it is that God does to turn humans away from their deeds.

16.c. The noun מֹסָרָם (equivalent to מֻסָרָם, according to Gerleman [*BHS*]) is apparently "their discipline," i.e., the discipline meted out to them, "their correction," i.e., the correction they receive from God (thus NEB "his correction"), or perhaps "their warning," i.e., the warnings they receive (Beer [*BHK al* בְּמֻסָרָם], NAB, Habel [בְּמוּסָרָם], REB "as a warning," Sicre Díaz [בְּמוּסָר]). But it is not easy to conceive how God could seal with "their discipline" or "their warning" those who are asleep (as Good "seals up with chastisement"). Graetz prefers לְמוּסָרָם "for their discipline."

Alternatively, מֹסָרָם could be read as מֹסֵרָם "their bond, fetter" (מוֹסֵר from אסר), but it is hard to find meaning for this in the context; Fedrizzi reads "terrifies them with chains," comparing the bonds of affliction in Ps 116:16—but that seems rather strained. Rather than emend the consonantal text, Dahood implicitly proposes a new word מֹוסָר "bond" ("Some Northwest-Semitic Words in Job," 311; cf. *DCH*, 5:177a). Alternatively, the word could be revocalized to מֻסָרִם "disciplines, instructions," "admonishments" (Driver–Gray), perhaps "warnings" (RSV, NIV, Kissane, de Wilde), though the noun does not elsewhere occur in the pl. Or it could be emended to וּבְמֻסָר "and by a warning" (Fohrer).

An attractive emendation is that of Dhorme, who reads וּבְמַרְאִים "and by apparitions," which is supported by LXX ἐν εἴδεσιν "in visions"; cf. Job's words in 7:14, "you terrify me with dreams, affright me with visions." This solution is adopted in the *Translation*. So too Beer (*BHK vel*), Larcher, Terrien, Pope (but he translates "warning"), and Hartley. JB "with fearful sights" seems to translate both מַרְאִים "sights" and מוֹרָאִים "terrors," as also LXX may have (ἐν εἴδεσιν φόβου τοιούτοις "in such visions of terror"); NJB has simply "with apparitions." Less probable are the emendations of Duhm, Beer (*BH*[2] *frt* בְּמוֹרָיִם; *BHK frt* בְּמֹרָיִם), and Hölscher, וּבְמוֹרָאִים "and by terrors [he frightens them]," or Beer (*BH*[2] *vel*) וּבְמַעֲרָצִים "and by terrors" (מַעֲרָץ is not attested elsewhere, but has been proposed also for Isa 8:13; see *DCH*, 5:415b, where the reference should be corrected to 8:13), or Nichols, 156, מַרְאֵי מוֹרִים (for מַרְאֵי מוֹרָאִים) "appearances of terrors," thus "fearful forms."

17.a. סור hiph "turn aside," "deter" (Pope), "withdraw" (KJV), "draw back" (Moffatt). NEB strains somewhat to connect this verse with the following: "To turn a man from reckless conduct . . . at the edge of the pit he holds him back" (similarly NAB).

17.b. להסיר אדם מעשה, lit. "to turn aside human(s) deed," is not a possible reading since סור hiph "turn aside" does not take two objects (KJV has "*from his* purpose," since both italicized words are supplied). RVmg "That man may put away his purpose" takes אדם as the subj of להסיר (supported by GKC, §115i; cf. Delitzsch, Peake). This interpretation is improbable, since God is the subj of the main verbs in v 16, and so should be of this inf of purpose also.

Most therefore accept an emendation: (1) most commonly to מִמַּעֲשֵׂהוּ "from his deed" (so Driver–Gray, Beer [*BHK*], Hölscher, Fohrer, Rowley, Gerleman [*BHS prp*], and van der Lugt; adopted in the *Translation* above), though Delitzsch, Larcher (apparently), Gordis, Habel, Hartley, Sicre Díaz propose simply מִמַּעֲשֶׂה "from a deed," i.e., the deed(s) they intended to do. Others simply translate as "wrongdoing" (NIV) or "evil-doing" (JB), without apparently emending the text. (2) Since such deeds are obviously evil deeds (for God would not be restraining people from good deeds), some have emended into the text a word for wickedness, such as מֵעַוְלָה "from evil" (Bickell, Duhm, Strahan, Terrien, Pope, probably Peake, Moffatt), or (3) מֵרֶשַׁע "from evil" (NAB), or (4) מֵעֹשֶׁק "from oppression" (Graetz, Beer [*BH*[2]], Terrien; cf. LXX ἀπὸ ἀδικίας "from wickedness"), or (5) מִפֶּשַׁע "from sin" (Beer [*BH*[2] *vel*]), or (6) מִמַּעֲקָשֵׁהוּ "from his crooked ways" (de Wilde). (7) Ehrlich reads לְהַסְתִּיר מֵאָדָם מַעֲשֵׂהוּ "to turn aside their deed from humans" (cf. Ps 81:6 [7], where the shoulder is turned aside from the burden rather than the burden from the shoulder). (8) Kissane read, but rather forcedly, אֵד מִמַּעֲשֶׂה "[to avert] a calamity from his handiwork." (9) Bickell[2] and Beer (*BH*[2]), on the basis of LXX τὸ δὲ σῶμα αὐτοῦ ἀπὸ πτώματος ἐρρύσατο "and he saved the body from disaster," read וְגֵוֹה מִשֶּׁבֶר יִפְצֶה "and his body he rescued from breaking" (פצה as in Ps 144:7, 10, 11; perhaps a different word from פצה "open"; cf. *DCH*, vol. 6, *s.v.*). (10) Or perhaps the retroversion yields יִפְדֶּה "ransoms" (Beer [*BH*[2] *vel*]).

Good takes מעשה וגוה "deed and pride" as a hendiadys, translating "an arrogant deed"; but it is hard to gain a sense from the resultant sentence. NEB "reckless conduct" and REB "evil deeds" read, according to Brockington, עֲשֶׂה, presumably a new word meaning "evil deed" cognate with Arab. *'iša'* "evil conduct" (cf. Guillaume). But such a word does not seem to be attested in the standard Arab. lexica (*'iša'* is "nightfall" according to Lane, 2056a). J. Reider ("Etymological Studies in Biblical Hebrew," *VT* 4 [1954] 276–95 [291–93]) proposes מַעֲשֶׂה "[to remove man] from a thing hidden," a new noun עֲשֶׂה, cognate with Arab. *ghašiya* "hide" (Lane, 2261b; see *DCH*, vol. 6, *s.v.* עשה III); he is followed by Fedrizzi, rendering "from his (hidden) deeds"; for the verb, see *Note* 23:9.a. Guillaume read מֵעֲשָׁה "[to remove humans] from blindness," though he translates more conventionally "that he may remove man's blindness."

17.c. יכסה "hides," but what can "he hides pride from a man" (as KJV) mean? Delitzsch thought it meant "withdraw, wean from," but that is a strained sense. Gordis, followed by Hartley, understands "hide" as "separate," Pope as "keep from," NJPS, Habel as "suppress," and Fedrizzi and Sicre Díaz as "protect," but none of them offers any parallel for such senses. NRSV, NIV also have "keep from pride"; NEB "check the pride."

Many emend to יְכַסֵּחַ "cuts away" (as with a knife; cf. Ps 80:16 [17]; Isa 33:12); thus RSV, Bickell, Duhm, Peake, Strahan, Driver–Gray, Beer (*BHK*), Hölscher, Fohrer, Terrien, Gerleman (*BHS prp* יִכְסַח qal), de Wilde; followed also by Larcher (apparently), JB "make an end of," NJB "put an end to," and probably by Moffatt "make them give up pride," as well as in the *Translation* above. An alternative emendation is יְכַלֶּה "puts an end to, destroys" (Dillmann [*vel*], Budde, Duhm, Peake, Beer [*BHK vel*], Hölscher, Rowley) or יְעַנֶּה "humble" (Dillmann [*vel*]).

Dhorme makes the ingenious proposal to change the places of מעשה "deed" and גוה "pride," reading "to turn man away from pride (מִגֵּוָה), He hides from man His action (מַעֲשֵׂהוּ)"—but why God should hide his action is entirely unclear.

17.d. גֵּוָה "pride" is often said to be an Aram. form for גַּאֲוָה (it does occur in Dan 4:34), but it is also in Job 22:29; Jer 13:17; NEB reads נַאֲוָה. Gordis calls it merely a defective spelling of נַאֲוָה. Kissane makes the ingenious proposal to read וְגֵוֹה מִשֶּׁבֶר "and [to cover, i.e., save] his back from wounding"; but שֶׁבֶר is "breaking" rather than "wounding," and saving one's back from wounding sits rather awkwardly here. Reider ("Etymological Studies," 292) reads וְגֵוֹה "and his body" (cf. *DCH,* 2:328b), following LXX, he says.

17.e. Reider ("Etymological Studies," 292–93) finds here, not the usual גבר "man," but a new word גֶּבֶר "pride, insolence" (cf. Arab. *jabār* "proud," *jabariyya* "pride" [Lane, 374a, c]), thus "[that He may hide his body] from pride."

18.a. נפשו, lit. "his life," i.e., the life of the humans (אדם) and men (גבר) of v 17; RSV, NIV, NAB, JB "his soul"; NIVmg "him."

18.b. יחשׂך "spares" (Habel), "keeps back" (KJV), "withholds" (NAB), "save" (JB, Moffatt). It is not clear whether the verb is in sequence with יכסה (v 17): "to turn aside," "and to cover," "[and] to keep back" (as RVmg, NIV, JB, Delitzsch, Driver–Gray), or whether it begins a new sentence (as KJV, RSV, NJB).

18.c. חַיָּה is usually "living thing, animal," but occasionally (as also in vv 20, 22, 28; 36:14; Pss 74:19; 78:50; 143:3; Ezek 7:13) "life," "his soul" (RSV). NEB "stops him from crossing" is probably just a loose rendering.

18.d. מעבר בשלח is apparently "from passing away, dying, through [God's] weapon, missile" (so Driver–Gray), rendered as "from perishing by the sword" (KJV, RSV, NIV, Fohrer "from running upon the spear," Strahan "from rushing upon the weapon"). But עבר probably never means "die" (the only plausible example is at 34:20, where it is parallel to מות "die"; in Ps 37:36 the text should be emended). And שׁלח is a general term for weapon (as RVmg), not specifically "sword" (KJV). A variant of the phrase occurs in 36:12, בשלח יעברו "they perish by the weapon." Duhm, followed by Peake, Beer (*BHK prps*), Hölscher (*frt*), de Wilde, emended to בִּשְׁאֹלָה "[from passing over] to Sheol" in both places. Perhaps NAB "from passing to the grave" follows this emendation; JB "[save his life] from the pathway to Sheol" and Moffatt "their lives from rushing on their doom" apparently do.

Others argue that שׁלח here must be a parallel to שחת "the Pit," especially because in v 18 we find a very similar phrase, מעבר בשחת "from passing into the Pit." Hence Dhorme sees the noun שֶׁלַח "conduit, canal, channel" (Joel 2:8; perhaps Cant 4:13), of which byforms occur in the place names Shiloah (Isa 8:6) and Shelah (Neh 3:15), interpreting it of the vertical canal, like the well of souls, which enables the spirit of the dead to pass into the underworld; he translates "[He saves] his life from passing through the Canal"; thus NJB "his life from passing down the Canal." The phrase is similarly understood by Terrien, Fedrizzi, and Andersen, but more plausibly of crossing the underworld river (see *Comment*); so NRSV "their lives from traversing the River," NIVmg "from crossing the River," NEB "crossing the river of death," Sicre Díaz "crossing the frontier of Death," and D. Leibel, "עבר בשלח," *Tarbiz* 33 (1963–64) 225–27 (English, p. i). From a European perspective, Pope's rendering in the same vein, "to spare his life from crossing the Channel" (similarly Habel, Hartley), unfortunately strikes a false note!

Guillaume's proposal for a new word שֶׁלַח "sudden death" (a metathetical form of Arab. *ḫalasa* "seize, carry off" [Lane, 784c]) is rather weak.

19.a. Sicre Díaz inserts "at other times," rendering the disjunctive *waw.*

19.b. The sg is used throughout vv 19–28, though no subj is expressed, except for אדם "humanity" in v 23; the last suitable subjs have been אדם and גבר "man" in v 17. For the sake of inclusive language, all the sgs in these verses have been rendered in the *Translation* by pls, as also in NRSV.

19.c. יכח hiph can be "reprove" or "correct." The former is of the nature of punishment, the latter of instruction. Elihu is likely to be thinking of the latter, so "chasten" (KJV, RSV, NAB, NIV), "is reproved" (NJPS; similarly Duhm, Fohrer, Hartley, Good), and "corrects" (Terrien), in the sense of "discipline or correct by punishment," may be less suitable than "instruct." JB takes the more educational option with "he corrects man on his sick-bed," NJB "he corrects by the sufferings of the sick-bed"; so too NEB "man learns his lesson on a bed of pain"; similarly Fedrizzi. Habel's "indicted" arises from his view of the prominence of a legal conceptuality here. The pf with *waw* consec (והוכח) describes what is likely to happen often (Driver–Gray).

Since a major new section of the speech begins here, some commentators are disappointed at not finding a clear marker of transition, and consequently emend the text. Thus Duhm גַּם יֻכַּח "also, one is chastened," Budde וְהוּא הוכח (*frt*) "and he chastens," Beer (*BH*[2]) אוֹ יוֹכִחֶנּוּ "or he chastens one" (claiming support from LXX, Pesh, Vg).

Dhorme emends to וְהוֹכִחַ אתוֹ "and he corrects him," following LXX, Pesh, Vg, which all have God as the subject. So too Larcher, JB, Terrien, Fedrizzi, de Wilde (without אתוֹ).

19.d. Bickell, Beer (*BHK*), Hölscher read מִשְׁכָּב, deleting the suff, on the doubtful grounds that it is not present in the parallel in v 15 and that it is not represented in LXX, Vg.

19.e. אתן, usually spelled אֵיתָן, is "firm, reliable, continuous," thus RV, RSV "continual strife in his bones." KJV took it as the adj of an implied noun, "strong pain."

Duhm reads אִטֵּר "are lamed," following LXX (from Theod) ἐνάρκησεν "have become numb, rigid" (Dhorme's view that Theod took איתן from יָשֵׁן "sleep" is not very probable); hence Moffatt "his limbs are all benumbed."

19.f. רִיב "strife" is the reading of K and is followed by Hitzig, Delitzsch, Budde, de Wilde. Thus too NIV "constant distress" and NAB "unceasing suffering" (omitting ו "and" before ריב "strife" [*Textual Notes*], though this is not reflected in the translation), which Dhorme thinks has been influenced by the similar phrase in 4:14. Peake thought that meant that it was as though his bones were being pulled apart by two warring parties, but that is a little forced. Pope and Sicre Díaz have "agony" and Hartley "aching," but neither is really the meaning of ריב. Good "his bones constantly on trial" thinks of them in conflict not with one another but, apparently, with God.

Q has רוֹב "multitude," which is followed by LXX πλῆθος, Pesh Tg Vg, KJV, Dillmann, Duhm, with some such rendering as "when the multitude of his bones are firm," which would mean, while he is still young (Gibson). Guillaume ("Arabic Background," 121) proposed a new word רֹב "tumult" (cf. Arab. *rāba* "churn" [Lane, 1175b "churn (milk), confuse"]). Later, however, he compared Arab. *rāba* "be tired," and proposed a new Heb. word רֹב "aching, weariness" (*Studies*, 118); but this *rāba* (Lane, 1197c) seems attested rather in the sense of "be doubtful, suspicious, disquieted," rather than "be tired, aching."

Others find here a new noun רִיב "shaking," cognate with Akk. *rîbu* "earthquake." Hence Dhorme "shaking," NJPS "trembling," JB "his bones keep trembling with palsy," NJB "someone's bones tremble continuously," NEB "tormented by a ceaseless ague" (similarly Larcher, Terrien), Fedrizzi "torture." Rowley comments that such a rendering is not strong enough for the context, but it may also be thought too specific.

Emendation to רְקַב "rottenness of" (Beer [*BH*^{2}, *BHK prps*]) (of bones also at Prov 12:4; 14:30; Hab 3:16), to כְּאֵב "the pain of" (Siegfried), or to דּוּב "wasting of" (Hölscher) are other possibilities, but not especially plausible.

19.g. NAB takes עצמיו "his bones" as his whole body, "within his frame," as עצם clearly means elsewhere (cf. *Note* 30:30.b); so too de Wilde.

20.a. Perhaps חיה "life" is used here in the specialized sense "appetite" (as BDB, 312b; *HALOT,* 1:310b; *DCH*, 3:209b), exactly parallel with נפש "life, appetite" in the next colon (cf. NAB "to his appetite food becomes repulsive"). But perhaps not.

20.b. זהם "make loathsome" occurs only here (BDB, 263b; *HALOT,* 1:265b), though some see it also in 6:7 (*q.v.*; cf. *DCH,* 3:93a), but there are close cognates in Aram., Syr., Arab. (*zahima* "stink" [Lane, 1263c]). The lit. sense is "his appetite makes food loathsome," i.e., treats it as loathsome. Thus he "detests" (NJPS) or "loathes" (Gordis, Hartley) or "is revolted by" food (JB), "turns from food" (Moffatt), "turns from his food with loathing" (NEB), "turns away in disgust" (Dhorme), "finds food repulsive" (NIV), or "makes bread loathsome" (Good), or else the food itself "becomes repulsive" (NAB) or even "the thought of food revolts him" (NJB). The suff on זִהֲמַתּוּ must be regarded as anticipatory of לחם "food"; but this idiom (called "permutation" by GKC, §131k) is rare, and some prefer to delete the suff, reading זִהֲמָה (Duhm, Beer [*BHK*], Hölscher, de Wilde). Gordis and Habel, not very persuasively, regard it as an ethic dative: "his soul loathes food for itself."

20.c. לחם is traditionally translated "bread," but it is also a general term for "food" (as in 3:24; 6:7; 15:23; 20:14; 24:5; 27:14; 28:5; 42:11; perhaps at 22:7 it has the more specific meaning of "bread").

20.d. נפש "life, vitality," in the sense of "appetite" (so JB, Strahan, Terrien, Fedrizzi, Gordis, Hartley), as in Ps 107:9; Prov 27:7; חיה in the same sense in Job 38:39; NAB "senses." Less probable is the sense "throat" (as Good).

20.e. מאכל תאוה, lit. "food of desire"; KJV "dainty meat," KJVmg "meat of desire," KJV "dainty meat," RSV, Hartley "dainty food," Moffatt "dainty dishes," JB "dainties," Gordis "the daintiest food," NEB "the choicest meats," REB "the choicest dishes," NAB "the choicest nourishment," NIV "the choicest meal," Pope "choice dishes," NJPS "fine food." NJB differently, "the thought of food revolts him, however tasty it is."

21.a. יִכֶל is juss of כלה; the juss with the same meaning as a regular impf (GKC, §109k; Driver, *Tenses*, §§170–74) is well attested, especially at the beginning of a clause. There is no reason to emend to the impf יִכְלֶה (Beer [*BHK*]). The meaning is "is complete, at an end," thus "is wasted" (NAB), "wastes away" (NJPS), "wastes from sight" (Pope, Hartley), "disappears from view" (Dhorme), "vanishes from sight" (Good). NIV "wastes away to nothing" is a reasonably equivalent Eng. idiom. JB "his flesh rots as you watch it" is graphic but not what the Heb. says. NEB "his flesh hangs loose upon him" is unexplained.

21.b. מֵרֹאִי, lit. "away from seeing," i.e., so that it cannot be seen (as מִן in Gen 23:6; 27:1; Isa 23:1); see also J. Weingreen, "The Construct-Genitive Relation in Hebrew Syntax," *VT* 4 (1954) 50–59 (56–57). Perhaps, however, it is not the inf constr but the noun רֳאִי "sight, fine appearance" as at 1 Sam 16:12 (רֹאִי in pause), thus "without fair appearance" (so Budde); cf. the noun מַרְאֶה with the same sense (Isa 53:2; 2 Sam 23:21). De Wilde proposes לְרֹאִי "to the sight."

G. R. Driver, "L'interprétation du texte masorétique à la lumière de la lexicographie hébraïque," *ETL* 26 (1950) 337–53 (351), sees here a new noun רֹאִי "saturation," from a ראה that is a byform of רוה "saturate"; he does not suggest a translation but presumably intends "without moisture." Guillaume follows him, taking ראי as a form of רִי "moisture" (BDB, 924a; elsewhere only at 37:11 [*q.v.*]).

Duhm and Beer (*BH*[2]) read מֵרָזִי "from leanness," hence Moffatt "his flesh grows lean and foul"; almost identically, Beer (*BHK frt*) and de Wilde read מֵרָזוֹן (claiming support from LXX σαπῶσιν "become putrid, rotten"), with the same meaning.

21.c. Taking לֹא ראו "were not seen" as a relative clause, "which had not been seen" (NIV "once hidden," NAB "once invisible"). It might of course be a gloss on שפו "are bare." This is the only occurrence of ראה in pual, but it is improbable that the phrase means that his bones "do not offer a beautiful appearance" or "are unlovely" (Dillmann). Budde and Beer (*BHK prps*) arrived at the same sense by emending to לֹא נָאוּ "are not beautiful" (an emendation in bad taste, says Dhorme); but while the poet Theodore Roethke's mother was "lovely in her bones" ("I Knew a Woman," in *The Collected Poems of Theodore Roethke* [London: Faber & Faber, 1968] 127), the idea of attractive bones seems outside the world of the ancient poet.

Guillaume, translating "unrefreshed," appears to invoke the verb רוה "be saturated" (BDB, 924a), perhaps with a piel form. Duhm, followed by Moffatt and Strahan, and reported by Beer (*BHK al*), deletes the phrase.

21.d. שפי K would seem to be שְׁפִי "bareness of [his bones]." Q is שֻׁפּוּ (pual) "[his bones] are laid bare" (so Beer [*BH*[2]], Gerleman [*BHS*]), or JB "his bare bones begin to show," NAB tamely "appear," that is, without flesh (Larcher, de Wilde).

KJV, NIV, Hartley "stick out" (Habel, van der Lugt "protrude") depends on the idea of a hill (שְׁפִי) being something that sticks up and is high (so too Leigh, 259; Buxtorf, 837); and Gordis has "protrude" (but "are bared" or "are crushed" in the commentary proper). In fact שפי may not perhaps mean "hill" at all but some other kind of "wind-swept place" (BDB, 1046a; see also *HALOT*, 4:1628a).

Others invoke new words: (1) שׁפה, meaning "polish, rub away" (cf. Aram. שׁוּף "rub" (Jastrow, 1539a; Sokoloff, 541b; this may, however, be the same word as שׁפה "make bare"); thus NJPS "his bones are rubbed away till they are invisible." (2) Hölscher thinks of a new word שׁפה "become thin," understanding עצמיו as "his limbs," and comparing Arab. *šaffa* "be thin" (Lane, 1568b). But although עצמיו may not mean "his bones" literally, it is unlikely that a verb that is inappropriate for bones should be used here; although bones can and do become thin, that is by no means evident to the naked eye. The same Arab. cognate is appealed to by Dhorme, translating "are emaciated," but it is not bones that become emaciated. (3) A. S. Yahuda, "Hapax legomena im Alten Testament erklärt und erläutert," *JQR* 15 (1902–1903) 698–714 (712), also compares Arab. *šaffa* in its meaning "be transparent," thus "[his bones which had not been seen] become seen," but being seen is very different from being transparent (the Arab. is used of a gem that is transparent). This view is, however, adopted by H. Rouillard, "Le sens de Job 33,21," *RB* 91 (1984) 30–50. (4) Guillaume proposes a שׁפה "dry up" (he compares Arab. *saffa,* which he glosses as "took dry medicine" [cf. Freytag, 2:320b; Lane, 1367c]), and renders "and his bones are dried up unrefreshed" (on this last word, see previous *Note*). But Arab. *saffa* means "take" and thus "take into the mouth, eat"; it often has as an obj something dry (food, medicine, and the like) since it means "eat," not "drink," but it is not a word for "be dry," and it will not serve for that sense in this passage. (5) NEB "his bones are loosened and out of joint" apparently depends on yet another verb שׁפה.

Among emendations, Beer (*BH*[2] *vel*) proposed וְשָׁחֲפוּ "and [his bones] waste away"; though שׁחף is not attested, there is a noun שַׁחֶפֶת "wasting disease, consumption" (BDB, 1006b; *HALOT*, 4:1463a). The *waw* consec with the pf is something of a problem, it must be admitted.

22.a. To conform to the norms of the *waw* consec, Beer (BHK) reads וַתִּקְרַב.

22.b. More prosaically, Moffatt "his life is on the verge of death."

22.c. ממתים, though it is the only occurrence of the hiph ptcp of מות "die," is perfectly clear as "those who cause death" (Vg *mortiferi* "bringers of death"), thus KJV "the destroyers," RSV "those who bring death," NIV, Hartley "the messengers of death," NEB "the ministers of death," Moffatt "the destroying angels," Gordis "the emissaries of death," Good "the executioners"; NJPS less correctly has "death," and Fedrizzi, strangely, "the dead."

Among emendations, none of them compelling, are: (1) לְמוֹ מֵתִים "to the dead," as Hoffmann (or לַמֵּתִים), Perles, 48, Budde, Beer (*BHK frt*), Hölscher (*vel*), Kissane, Gerleman (*BHS prp*), van der Lugt. LXX ἐν ᾅδῃ "in Hades" is probably no more than a paraphrase. (2) Pope, followed by Andersen, has לְמֵי מָוֶת־מוֹ with enclitic *mem* emphatic; REB perhaps follows this in translating "to the waters of death." (3) Beer (*BHK frt*) noted the emendation to לִמְקוֹם מֵתִים "to the place of the dead," which is followed by Ball (*vel*), Dhorme, Hölscher, Larcher (apparently), Rowley, de Wilde, JB and apparently NAB ("to the place of the dead"), though the *Textual Notes* say it reads למו מֵתִים "to the dead." G. R. Driver thought the MT represented an abbreviation for לִמְקוֹם מֵתִים "to the place of the dead" ("Once Again Abbreviations," 91). (4) M. Dahood, followed by Habel, read לְמוֹ מֹתִים "to Death," arguing that the plural מֹתִים, also at Ps 88:6, is an alternative form for מוֹת "death" ("Hebrew-Ugaritic Lexicography V," *Bib* 48 [1967] 421–38 [435–36]).

23.a. Duhm emends אם "if" to אָז "then" in the interest of his interpretation (see *Comment*).

23.b. עליו, lit. "by him"; for this use of על with עמד "stand," cf. 1 Kgs 22:19; NEB has "stands by him"; a positive sense for על can be paralleled in Judg 9:17; 1 Sam 25:16; 2 Kgs 10:3; Neh 4:8; Ezek 13:5. It is not "an angel over him" (Good). Hitzig and Wright understand the angel to be standing "beside" God, but this seems improbable since God has not been mentioned since v 18.

23.c. מלאך is "messenger" (as KJV, RVmg; similarly Rowley) or heavenly messenger, "angel" (RV, RSV, NEB, JB, NAB, NIV, Habel, Hartley), "representative" (NJPS), "spokesman" (Gordis).

23.d. For מליץ KJV, Driver–Gray, and Good have "interpreter," RSV, JB, NAB, NIV, Larcher, Hartley "mediator," NEB "a mediator between him and God," Pope "spokesman," NJPS, Gordis, Habel "advocate." We have had the term in 16:20, of Job's cry as his "spokesman" in the heavenly court. It is strange that the LXX represents the angels here as "death-bearing" (θανατόφοροι), though it may simply be because the term has been used in the previous verse; on the role of the angels here, cf. J. G. Gammie, "The Angelology and Demonology in the Septuagint of the Book of Job," *HUCA* 56 (1985) 1–19 (5); S. Gevirtz, "Phoenician *wšbrt mlṣm* and Job 33,23," *Maarav* 5–6 (1990) 145–58 (145–48).

23.e. אחד מני־אלף is rendered variously: KJV, Habel, and Hartley have "one among a thousand," RVmg, REB "one of a thousand," NAB, NIV, Good "one out of a thousand," NJB "one in a thousand," NEB "one of thousands," JB "chosen out of thousands," NJPS "against a thousand." Gordis thinks "one among a thousand" means "however rare, however difficult to find" (comparing Eccl 7:28). But more probably what is envisaged is a troop of one thousand angels; thus RSV "one of the thousand." Pope "one out of the thousand," Moffatt "one of God's thousand angels." The colon is deleted by Budde and Siegfried.

23.f. Sicre Díaz transposes this colon to follow v 26c. NAB and NEB move v 26c to follow this colon (see further, *Note* 23.h below).

23.g. להגיד "to declare," meaning that the angel has the function of declaring. Duhm and Beer (BH^2 *frt*) read וְיַגִּיד "and he shows," on the basis of LXX ἀναγγείλῃ "he should announce," a finite verb.

23.h. ישרו "his uprightness" (ישר has a suff only elsewhere at Prov 14:2) (as KJV, RVmg); though "what is right for him" makes good sense (so RV, RSV, NAB, NIV, Fedrizzi, Hartley), it is hard to parallel (cf., however, Prov 11:24; 17:26). Dhorme adopts the same interpretation, with "to reveal to man his duty"; so too JB "to remind a man where his duty lies" (and perhaps similarly Good "to tell a human his morality").

The other two main interpretations of the clause are represented by (1) REB "to expound God's righteousness to man," and (2) NEB "to expound what he has done right," NJPS "to declare the man's uprightness," and Gordis's "to vouch for a man's uprightness" (similarly Habel), making the angel into a defender of the suffering person in the divine court.

Among emendations, Duhm, Beer (*BHK*), and Strahan read מוּסָרוֹ "his instruction, punishment," taking a lead from LXX τὴν ἑαυτοῦ μέμψιν "his blame." Thus Moffatt "he tells the man his faults, and then in pity intercedes for him." Beer, following LXX τὴν δὲ ἄνοιαν αὐτοῦ δείξῃ, adds וְחַטָּאתוֹ יוֹדִיעֶהוּ "and he makes known to him his sin."

NAB transposes to this point v 26c, "and bring the man back to justice" (reading וְיָשִׁיב "and he will return, bring back"; similarly NEB, reading וְיָשֵׁב); but to bring to justice suggests the infliction of punishment, and this cannot be what is in mind, since v 24 concerns the person's deliverance. NEB also brings v 26c to this point, rendering, in line with its translation of v 23c, "and to secure for mortal man his due" (REB has the same rendering, but it does not fit with its different translation of v 23c).

24.a. This clause could be a further conditional clause, like the "if" of v 23a (RVmg, RSV, NEB; similarly JB, NIV, Peake, Hartley), or the apodosis, "then [he takes pity]" (as KJV, NAB, Gordis).

24.b. The implied subj is either God (Hitzig, Davidson, Delitzsch, Dillmann, Steuernagel, Strahan, Gordis, NJPS) or, much more probably, the angel (NEB, NAB, NIV, Budde, Duhm, Peake, Hartley). G. R. Driver, "Some Hebrew Roots and Their Meanings," *JTS* 23 (1921–22) 69–73 (72), proposes a new Heb. verb חנן "supplicate" (not in *DCH*), to which all the examples of חנן hithp should be ascribed (now twenty-two occurrences, including one in Ecclesiasticus and four in Qumran texts; cf. *DCH,* 3:273b); hence NEB "speaks in the man's favour" and REB "speaks on behalf of him." Budde reads וִיחננו וְיאמר with simple *waw,* Beer (*BHK frt;* his reading וְיחֻנֶּנּ׳ seems to be an error) and NAB יְחָנֶּנּוּ וְיֹאמַר, but a change is not necessary (cf. Driver, *Tenses,* §138).

24.c. A verb פדע is not otherwise attested (BDB, 804b, pronounces it dubious, and *HALOT,* 3:914a, thinks it should be emended; cf. also *DCH,* vol. 6, *s.v.*). Grabbe, 105–7, discusses whether it could be cognate with Arab. *fada'a* "break" (Lane, 2352b), which seems unlikely. We could simply assume from the context that it must mean "redeem" (as NJPS, Good). Otherwise, we could emend to פְּרָעֵהוּ "let him loose [from going]" (so some MSS, Budde, Duhm, Beer [*BHK*], Kissane, Fohrer, Gerleman [*BHS frt*], Gordis, Habel, NAB, NEB); the problem with this is that פרע is elsewhere always used in a bad sense. In the end, it seems best to emend to פְּדֵהוּ "redeem him" (as Dillmann [פְּדָאֵהוּ], Bickell [פְּדֵה], Beer [*BHK al*], Hölscher, Terrien), perhaps in the general sense of "deliver him" (as KJV, RSV, NAB), "spare him" (NIV, NJB), "reprieve him" (NEB), "exempt him" (Dhorme, Larcher), or "release him" (JB). This emendation is adopted in the *Translation* above.

Guillaume ("Arabic Background," 121; *Studies,* 119) sees here the particle *pa-* with the impv of ודע (= ידע) "allow, let off" (cf. Arab. *wada'a* [Freytag, 4:449b; Lane, 3051a]) and so "deliver"; he is followed by Pope. This is highly improbable on two counts: (1) the questionable and not exactly "irrepressible" (Guillaume) particle *pa-* (see on 9:12, 20; 16:14; 30:12; and cf. Blommerde, 32–33 [bibliography], and *DCH,* vol. 6, *s.v.*; on its use in Ugar., see now W. G. E. Watson, "The Particle *p* in Ugaritic," *SEL* 7 [1990] 75–86); and (2) the doubtful appeal to a supposed ידע or ודע "be quiet, humiliated" (D. W. Thomas, "The Root ידע in Hebrew," *JTS* 35 [1934] 298–306; "The Root ידע in Hebrew, II," *JTS* 36 [1935] 409–12; "More Notes on the root ידע in Hebrew," *JTS* 38 [1937] 404–5; cf. *DCH,* 4:110b, 586a), the existence of which has been challenged by J. A. Emerton, "A Consideration of Some Alleged Meanings of *yd',*" *JSS* 15 (1970) 145–80, and W. Johnstone, "*yd'* II 'be humbled, humiliated'?" *VT* 41 (1991) 49–62.

24.d. KJVmg "an atonement"; NEB "the price of his release." Obviously the ransom is *for the life,* but some think that must have been explicit, and read כֹּפֶר נַפְשׁוֹ "the ransom of his life" as at Exod 30:12 and similarly Prov 13:8 (so Bickell[2], Budde, Dhorme, Beer [*BHK vel*], Hölscher, Fohrer, de Wilde, Hartley, JB), or כֹּפֶר לְנַפְשׁוֹ "a ransom for his life" (Duhm, Beer [*BHK vel*], Hölscher [*vel*]); so too, apparently, Moffatt "a ransom for the man."

25.a. Is this still the speech of the angel? If we observe the sequence of verbs strictly, it seems that it is, for the sufferers should regain their vigor (v 25) only after they have entreated God (v 26); so the reference at this point to new vigor must be the wish of the angel, not a report of the regaining of vigor (so Duhm, Hölscher, de Wilde, RSV; NJPS thinks the speech of God that began in v 24 continues). Among those who confine the angel's words to v 24 are JB, NEB, NAB, NIV, Peake, Strahan, Driver–Gray, Dhorme, Terrien, Pope, Fohrer, Hartley.

25.b. רֻטֲפַשׁ occurs only here and is very problematic. *HALOT,* 3:1223a, does not make a choice among the suggestions it mentions. BDB, 936a, thinks it is "grow fresh"; thus too RSV, Gordis, Hartley "become fresh," NIV "is renewed," NAB "become soft," Moffatt "turns fresh," NJPS "be healthier."

Driver–Gray think it an error for a form of טפשׁ "be fat" (as at Ps 119:70; BDB, 382a; *DCH,* 3:373b); "fatness" may be a token of strength or of softness. Budde, Duhm, Beer (*BHK*), Hölscher, Kissane, KBL, 888a, Fohrer, Pope[1], Fedrizzi, Gerleman (*BHS prp*), de Wilde, NEB read the impf יִטְפַּשׁ; similarly NEB "grow sturdier." NAB prefers the pual יְטֻפַּשׁ "shall become soft." Thus originally M. A. Altschüller "Einige textkritische Bemerkungen zum Alten Testamente," *ZAW* 6 (1886) 211–13 (212), though he read the pf; so too Delitzsch, Pope, Good "is plumper." Similarly Gordis, explaining the form as a metathesis of טְרֻפַּשׁ, which is טפשׁ with infixed ר. Pope[2] thinks it is rather an adj with an infixed *-t-,* meaning "plump," cognate with Akk. *rapāšu* "be wide."

Dhorme, followed by Larcher and Terrien, reads יִרְטַב "becomes moist, fresh" (from רטב, as at 24:8); thus JB "recovers the bloom of its youth" and NJB "its childhood freshness." Similarly Guillaume, followed by Habel, translating "becomes fresh." Less plausibly, Nichols, 158, reads יֵרַךְ "grows soft."

25.c. מִנֹּעַר, lit. "from youth." נֹעַר is elsewhere "the time of youth" (Job 36:14; Prov 29:21; Ps 88:15 [16]), not the abstract "youthfulness" (as against Delitzsch, Budde), so it would have to mean "more than [in] youth" (Hitzig), "as in the days of his youth" (Duhm), "[fresher] than a child's" (KJV), or "than he was in youth" (NEB; similarly NJPS), and not just "than childhood" (KJVmg), "fresh with youth" (RSV), "recover its childhood freshness" (NJB), "as in youth" (Habel). More loosely, and missing the comparative sense of the *mem*, NIV has "like a child's," NAB "as a boy's," and JB, even more loosely without any gain in sense, "he lives again as he did when he was young." "[Plump] as a boy's" (Pope), "[plumper] than a boy's" (Good), and "fresher than a child's" (Moffatt) convey the comparative force, but it is questionable whether the Heb. can refer to any person other than the sufferer.

LXX ὥσπερ νηπίου "as of a youth" apparently read כְּנֹעַר "like a youth," a reading that is perhaps assumed by some of the translations mentioned above.

25.d. יָשׁוּב "he will return" is read by Bickell[2] (יָשׁוּב), Duhm, and Beer (*BH*[2]) as a juss יָשׁוֹב "let him return," continuing the address of the angel that began in v 24; this small emendation is adopted in the *Translation* above. "He returns" is transformed by some into a statement about the person's flesh; thus NIV "it is restored."

25.e. עלומים is "youth" (KJV, *HALOT*, 2:831b) or "youthful vigor" (BDB, 761b) or "vigor" (Habel) or "prime" (NEB) or "lustihood" (Driver–Gray), presumably both of a young man (עֶלֶם) and of a young woman (עַלְמָה) (cf. *DCH*, vol. 6, *s.v.*). Since one cannot literally return to one's youth, some want to modify the Heb. in translation; thus NAB "he shall be again as in the days of his youth," NIV "it [his flesh] is restored as in the days of his youth." But NJB is content to translate literally: "he will return to the days of his youth" (similarly Good); similarly NJPS "Let him return to his younger days" and Gordis "he returns to the days of his vigor."

26.a. NEB makes vv 26–27 a chain of conditional clauses, with an apodosis beginning at v 28: "If he entreats God . . . then he saves himself." But it seems preferable to see here the beginning of a narrative sequence that continues to v 28. "Then" is introduced into the *Translation* to make clear that the protasis of vv 23–25 has ended and the apodosis of vv 26–28 now begins.

26.b. יעתר is "prays" (KJV, RSV, NIV, NJPS; similarly NAB), "entreats" (NEB). It will be the sufferer, not the angel (against NEB), who prays to God, since it is the sufferer, not the angel, who is "accepted."

Budde, trying to normalize the verbs to the rules of the *waw* consec, reads וַיִּרְצֵהוּ וַיַּרְאֵהוּ . . . וַיָּשֶׁב "and he favors him and makes him see [his face] . . . and he restores."

26.c. וירצהו: KJV "will be favourable," RV "is favourable," RSV "accepts," NJPS "is accepted," NAB "will favor him," Dhorme "delights in him," NIV "and finds favour with him." JB "He prays to God who has restored him to favour" reverses the sequence of events in the Heb., where first the person prays, and then God shows favor. Beer (*BHK*) and NAB, NEB read וְיִרְצֵהוּ, an impf with simple *waw* rather than *waw* consec.

26.d. וַיַּרְא qal "and he [the sufferer] sees." Beer (*BHK*) reads וְיִרְאֶה impf with simple *waw* rather than *waw* consec (NAB reads יִרְאֶה, without the *waw*; NEB has וְיַרְא). To see God's face is of course to worship, as Moffatt translates. The form וַיַּרְא could also be hiph "and he [God] shows" (so Sicre Díaz, Habel "reveals his face"; see also *Comment*), the implied suff being supplied from the previous verb, or, with a small emendation, to וַיַּרְאֵהוּ "and he [God] lets him see" (so Budde [וַיַּרְאֵהוּ], Beer [*BH*[2] *frt*], Fedrizzi). Tur-Sinai took וירא as a form of רוה "satiate, fill," translating "he shall saturate his face with joy"; but while it is possible to "fill (מלא) the mouth with laughter" (8:21), one can hardly "fill" a face.

26.e. תרועה is properly a "shout," often of joy; so some have "and shouts for joy" (NIV; similarly NEB, NJPS), Driver–Gray "with (the sound of Temple) music," Habel "amid festal shouting." JB, on the other hand, has merely the word for the feeling, "in happiness"; similarly Gordis "joyfully."

26.f. The colon is removed to follow v 23c by Dhorme, NEB, NAB.

26.g. Perhaps the most natural way of taking this colon is that of RV "he restoreth unto man his righteousness" (so too Davidson, Hartley, Good); similarly NIV "he is restored by God to his righteous state." God is clearly the subject of וישב "and he returns, restores." It is not clear how KJV "for he will render unto man his righteousness" is to be understood, nor Terrien's "[God] will confer his justice on a mortal man." NJPS "For He requites a man for his righteousness" is perhaps a possible translation of the Heb. (the sense appears in just one place, 1 Sam 26:23; in 2 Sam 16:12 the same idiom concerns the reward, not the ground for the reward; W. L. Holladay, *The Root Šubh in the Old Testament with Particular Reference to Its Usages in Covenantal Contexts* [Leiden: Brill, 1958] 95, does not properly discriminate between these senses). Gordis, translating "recounts," argues that שׁוב hiph can have this meaning, but he can offer no parallel.

Many emend the text, thinking that the depiction of the public assembly in v 27 begins with this colon. The possibilities are: (1) וַיְסַפֵּר "and he recounts" (Duhm, Strahan, Driver–Gray [*vel*], Beer [*BHK vel* וִיספר], Hölscher [וִיסַפֵּר], RSV), and (2) וַיְבַשֵּׂר "and he brings the good tidings" (cf. Strahan, Driver–Gray; so Duhm, Beer [*BHK vel* וִיבשׂר], Hölscher [וִיבַשֵּׂר], Larcher [apparently], Fohrer, de Wilde [וִיבַשֵּׂר]; Moffatt "he tells men how God saved him," Pope "announces," JB "he publishes far and wide the news of his vindication"; but NJB less theatrically "He will tell others how he has received saving justice").

Fedrizzi makes the interesting proposal to reverse the places of וישׁב "and he returns" in v 26 and ישׁר "he sings," thus "he celebrates before men" and "he turns to men, saying." But that does not appear to be a possible meaning of שׁוּב.

26.h. צדקה makes good sense as the former "righteousness" of the sufferer to which he is restored. But if the verb is emended to mean "recounts" or "announces," the alternative well-attested sense of "salvation" (NJB "saving justice") would be more appropriate; so also Pope. Gordis more loosely has "[God's] goodness."

26.i. Sicre Díaz transposes v 23c to this point, rendering "he will restore to the man his salvation, by showing to the mortal his uprightness." The inf להגיד is, however, not well accounted for on this view.

27.a. There are two possible interpretations of יָשֹׁר. (1) It could be from שׁיר "sing," as the impf (שׁוּר is inf in 1 Sam 18:6 K); many, however, prefer to revocalize to יָשִׁיר or יָשֹׁר "he sings"; thus NAB, JB, Moffatt, Beer (*BHK*), Hölscher, Fohrer, Terrien, Gerleman (*BHS prp*), de Wilde, Hartley, Good, and Dahood ("Northwest Semitic Philology and Job," in *The Bible in Current Catholic Thought: Gruenthaner Memorial Volume,* ed. J. L. McKenzie, St. Mary's Theological Studies 1 [New York: Herder & Herder, 1962] 55–74 [69–70]). Dhorme maintains, without adequate evidence, that it is "sing" in the sense of "repeat" (as he claims also for vv 3, 14). Nor is there good cause to render the verb as "declare" (NEB, NJPS) or "proclaim" (Gordis); NIV's "then he comes to men" is a quite unjustifiably loose rendering.

(2) יָשֹׁר is, as far as the form goes, more naturally derived from שׁוּר, thus "he looks" (so Vg *respiciet,* KJV, RVmg); KJV understands "He looketh upon men, and if any say, I have sinned... he will deliver his soul," but it is not natural to have different subjects for ישׁר "looks" and ויאמר "says" (two words later).

J. Reider ("Contributions to the Hebrew Lexicon," *ZAW* 53 [NS 12] [1935–36] 270–77 [275]) reads יָשֵׁר ("or rather יָשֵׁר," i.e., hiph) "he confesses," deriving his new word from Arab. *sarra* IV "keep or disclose a secret" (Lane, 1337b). This is the source of the reading noted by Gerleman (*BHS*), יָשֵׁר, from a new word שׁרר hiph "confess" cognate with Arab. *'ašarra.* But *šarra* means "be bad" (Lane, 1524a); although Lane gives an example of *'ašarra* (Form IV) apparently meaning "reveal, make known," he prefers to derive it from *sarra* IV, meaning both "conceal" and "reveal" (Lane, 1337b); perhaps that is the word intended by Gerleman. G. R. Driver, "Glosses in the Hebrew Text of the Old Testament," in *L'Ancien Testament et l'orient: Etudes présentées aux VIes Journées Bibliques de Louvain (11–13 septembre 1954),* Orientalia et biblica Lovaniensia 1 (Louvain-Leuven: Publications Universitaires/Instituut voor Orientalisme, 1957) 23–61 (32), translates "the rare *yāšōr*" as "he asserted," apparently on the basis of the same cognate; hence probably NEB "he declares." It is the Arab. *sarra* (Lane, 1337a) to which Guillaume appeals for a Heb. שׂרר "rejoice, say joyfully," as also at 36:24 ("Arabic Background," 122; *Studies,* 119).

27.b. If ישׁר is derived from שׁיר "sing" (see *Note* 27.a), על "upon" must mean "before"; BDB, 756a §6c, allows the sense "by" (of location), but only in reference to verbs of standing; the fuller treatment in *DCH,* vol. 6, *s.v.* §1.c.1 shows a plentiful number of cases with other verbs as well as in nominal clauses. It is unnecessary to appeal to Ugar. *'al* as does Dahood, "Northwest Semitic Philology and Job," 70, though his appeal to Prov 25:20 is very apposite (שׁר בשׁרים על לב־רע "one who sings songs in the presence of a sad heart").

27.c. Beer (*BHK*) and NAB read וְיֹאמַר, simple *waw* rather than *waw* consec.

27.d. ישׁר העויתי leads to a wide variety of renderings: "turned right into wrong" (NEB), "falsified the right" (Dhorme), "perverted the right" (Pope, Gordis, Habel), "perverted what was right" (NIV, NJPS), "perverted morality" (Good), "made crooked that which was straight" (Driver–Gray), "left the path of right" (JB), "went astray" (Moffatt), or simply "did wrong" (NAB).

27.e. ולא־שָׁוָה לי is probably to be taken as RV "and it profited me not" (as also Guillaume). So too Gordis "but it was not to my advantage," comparing שׁוה qal in Esth 3:8; 5:13; 7:4; he is followed by Habel, Hartley.

The phrase is, however, often taken as "it was not requited to me" (Delitzsch, Dillmann, RVmg), "I was not paid back for it" (NJPS), "I did not get what I deserved" (NIV), "he has not punished me accordingly" (NAB; similarly JB, Moffatt, Sicre Díaz, Good); but שוה qal is "be equal, be like," and it is never used for "be requited." RVmg "and it was not meet for me" does not fit the context very well. It is equally difficult to find a good parallel for שוה piel as "requite," which is an objection to the emendation of Duhm, Beer (*BHK*), Hölscher (*vel*), Larcher, de Wilde, ולא שִׁוָּה לי כַּעֲוֹנִי "and it was not made equivalent to me according to my sin," JB "God has not punished me as my sin deserved" (Bickell and Hölscher [*vel*] have כְּחַטָּאתִי "according to my sin" rather than כַּעֲוֹנִי; NAB reads simply ולא שִׁוָּה לי "he has not punished me") and to that of Budde and Beer (*BHK vel*), who have אֵל לֹא שִׁוָּה "God did not requite" (Budde's alternative reading, שִׁלַּם "he paid, requited," certainly has the appropriate sense; it is followed by Fohrer, de Wilde). Reading ולא־שִׁוָּה הוא לי "and he did not requite me" (Beer [BH^2 *vel*]) is tame; equally tame is Siegfried's proposal of הֵשִׁיב "he returned to me, made requital to me" (as in Prov 24:12, 29). NEB "and thought nothing of it" (REB "without a thought") is unexplained.

28.a. פדה "redeem" (as NIV, NJPS), not in the strict sense of paying a ransom but simply of "deliver," "spare" (JB); cf. *DCH*, vol. 6, *s.v.* NEB "he saves himself" is a possible meaning of the Heb., but it is hard to believe that it is what Elihu could have been meaning.

28.b. נפשי...חיתי K "my life . . . my life" (similarly KJVmg, NAB, NIV, Duhm, Gibson, Beer [*BHK*], Hölscher, Fohrer, Gordis, Gerleman [*BHS*], de Wilde, Hartley, Good). Q נַפְשׁוֹ...חַיָּתוֹ "his life . . . his life" (thus KJV; similarly NJPS) can make sense if the sufferer's speech has concluded with v 27. K could perhaps be taken as another example of the 3d-person *yodh* suff (see further *Note* 21:16.e).

28.c. מעבר בשחת, lit. "from going over into the Pit," "from passing to the pit" (NAB; similarly NJPS, Good), which makes a certain sense, but is a phrase not found elsewhere (it varies from the similar phrase at v 18 and 36:12 in having שחת "pit" rather than שלח "river, canal"). Many translate *ad sensum* "from going down to the pit" (as JB, NEB, NIV, Gordis; similarly Habel), though this is not what the Heb. says. Pope loosely "saved my soul from the Pit." Dhorme's translation (in the original edition of 1926 as well as the translation of it in 1967) "from passing through the Canal" seems to be an error, since in his commentary proper he has "pass through the Pit."

Budde reads מֶרֶדֶת שַׁחַת "from going down to the Pit" (which he had removed from v 24), or else the same phrase as we had in v 18, מֵעֲבֹר בַּשֶּׁלַח, now to be translated, in all probability, as "from crossing the underworld river."

Driver–Gray, Beer (*BHK frt*), and de Wilde think the whole phrase was originally מִשַּׁחַת "from the pit" and that עבר ב has been wrongly added under the influence of v 18.

28.d. ראה ב "look upon" is no doubt used in the special sense of "enjoy," as at 20:17 (*q.v.*). NAB "I behold the light of life" (similarly Gordis), NIV "I shall live to enjoy the light," JB "allowing my life to continue in the light," NJB "making my life see the light," Moffatt "let me see the dear light of the living," NJPS "he will enjoy the light."

29.a. פעמים שלוש "two times (or) three," i.e., several times, a case of "ascending numeration" (Gordis) or "number parallelism" (Watson, 144–49); cf. the example in 5:19. For the omission of the article, cf. שנים שלשה "two or three" (Isa 17:6).

30.a. Kissane transfers the verse to follow v 25, which is plausible but not really called for.

30.b. להשיב "to bring back" seems unobjectionable, but Beer (BH^2) reads the finite verb הֵשִׁיב "he brought back" (claiming the support of Pesh) or the ptcp מֵשִׁיב "bringing back."

30.c. לאור is for לְהֵאוֹר niph inf of אור "enlighten," thus "to be enlightened" (KJV), "become light" (Delitzsch). NJPS and Habel translate more loosely "bask in," Terrien "cause him to enjoy." NJB "to make the light of the living still shine" is quite hard to interpret; Good "to shine with" can hardly be justified from the Heb. Hartley and Sicre Díaz understand the verb as niph but nevertheless translate "to light him." Driver–Gray understand ראה ב as "see his fill of (the light of life)" (as also in v 28; BDB, 908a, §8a5 "gaze at with pleasure").

Some have not been content with the Heb. and have proposed emendations, e.g., לָאִיר "to enlighten" (Wright), לְהָאִיר בּוֹ "to make shine upon him" (Duhm [לָאִיר], Driver–Gray, apparently also Pope, "to light him with the light of life" and NIV "that the light of life might shine on him," but perhaps these translations are merely putting the passive of לאור into the active). Beer (BH^2 *frt*) suggests לָאִיר (= לְהָאִיר) בּוֹ אור "to make light shine upon him." There is no good reason to accept emendations such as לִרְאוֹת "to see" (thus apparently RSV, following Budde, Ehrlich, Beer [*BHK*], Hölscher, Fohrer, de Wilde, supported by Pesh) or בְּאֶרֶץ החיים "in the land of the living" (Reiske, Ehrlich, and NAB, with a question mark) or בָּאָרֶץ "on the earth" (Beer [*BHK*?]).

30.d. Dahood (*Psalms I*, 222) saw אור not as "light" but as a different word "field" (cf. Ugar. *ur*), which he finds also at Pss 36:10; 56:14; 97:11; and Isa 26:19, thus "that he might be resplendent in the field of life."

30.e. Is אור חיים "the light of life" (RSV, NJPS, NIV, Delitzsch, Driver–Gray, Pope, Gordis, de Wilde, Habel, Hartley) or "the light of the living" (KJV, NAB, NJB, Dhorme, Terrien, Tur-Sinai)? It is hard to say.

31.a. Vv 31b–33 are not found in the original LXX, and vv 31–33 are deleted from this place by Duhm, Beer (*BH*[2] *frt*), Hölscher, Fohrer. Duhm, Hölscher, and de Wilde regarded them as the introduction to another speech, Duhm and Beer (*BH*[2] *frt*) moving them to precede 34:16, Kissane to precede 34:2, Fohrer to precede 35:2, and de Wilde to precede 35:4 (his order is 35:1; 33:31–25; 35:4, 2, 3). Strahan remarked that Elihu's request here "serves less as the conclusion of the first speech than as the exordium of the second," but by that he may only have meant that the passage is a bridge between the two speeches (similarly Weiser, and Peake: "Exhortation to Job to listen to his next speech").

32.a. השׁיבני, lit. "return (answer to) me," as in v 5.

32.b. צדק qal "declare to be in the right," as in 9:2; 13:18; cf. 27:5 (hiph), "find you in the right" (Habel), "I wish to see you right" (Good). Some prefer to vocalize as a noun, צִדְקֶךָ "(I desire) your righteousness" (as Beer [*BHK*?]).

33.a. The repetition is a bit cloying, and Budde understandably omits the line. But, as Dhorme says, "Elihu is not at all afraid of repeating himself, and it would be unkind of us to rob him of v. 33."

Form/Structure/Setting

The *structure* of this first speech of Elihu is plainly twofold, though where the division between the two unequal parts comes is not easy to determine. After the prose preface to the speech (32:1–6a), Elihu is obviously addressing the friends in 32:6b–14 and Job in 33:1–33. The question is, whether 32:15–22 is a soliloquy or is addressed to the friends or to Job. The view taken here (see *Comment* on 32:15–22) is that at 32:15 Elihu turns his attention to Job, and so the major structural division of the speech comes at that point.

The *strophic structure* displays a set of strophes of three or four lines in length:

Part 1	strophe 1	32:6b–7	3 lines (v 6b two bicola)
	strophe 2	32:8–10	3 lines
	strophe 3	32:11–14	4 lines (vv 11, 12 tricola)
Part 2	strophe 4	32:15–18	4 lines
	strophe 5	32:19–22	4 lines
	strophe 6	33:1–4	4 lines
	strophe 7	33:5–7	3 lines
	strophe 8	33:8–11	4 lines
	strophe 9	33:12–14	3 lines
	strophe 10	33:15–18	4 lines (v 15 tricolon)
	strophe 11	33:19–22	4 lines
	strophe 12	33:23–26	4 lines (vv 23, 24, 26 tricola)
	strophe 13	33:27–30	4 lines (v 27 tricolon)
	strophe 14	33:31–33	3 lines

RSV shows a similar pattern, in Part I combining strophes 2 and 3, and in Part II combining strophes 1 and 2, 3 and 4, 6 and 7, 8 and 9 and part of 10 (vv 27–28), as well as part of 10 (vv 29–30) with 11. Its strophes are thus: 32:6b–10, 11–14, 15–22; 33:1–7, 8–11, 12–18, 19–28, and 29–33 (but the summarizing sentences vv 29–30 can hardly belong to the same strophe as the concluding address to Job, vv 31–33). NEB marks strophe divisions only after 32:22, 33:11, and 33:30. REB is more like RSV, except that it regards as strophes 33:12–22, 23–25, and 26–30; but it must be wrong to make a division after 33:18, i.e., between the communications by dreams and by illness, and it is questionable whether

33:26 is to be attached to what follows rather than to what precedes (see *Note* 33:26.a). NIV resembles RSV, except that it has 32:6b–9 (taking לכן in v 10 as a transition marker), 33:12–22 (but it does not make much sense to have a division between the illness and the angel passages if there is none between the dreams and the illness passages, i.e., after v 18), and 33:29–30, 31–33 (rightly separating between the summary verses, 29–30, and the final address to Job, 31–33). NAB also is like RSV, except that it divides 33:1–7 into vv 1–4 and 5–7, and 33:19–28 into vv 19–22, 23–24, 25–26, and 27–28; strangely, it does not separate vv 29–30 from 31–33. P. W. Skehan offered a different structure for chap. 32: an opening couplet (v 6), followed by strophes of 4, 7, and 4 lines (vv 7–10, 11–16, 17–20), and a concluding couplet (vv 21–22) ("'I Will Speak Up' [Job 32]," *CBQ* 31 [1969] 380–82). NJB has only four large strophes, of very unequal length—32:6b–14, 15–22; 33:1–30, 31–33—but they do indicate the important divisions of the speech.

Fohrer's analysis differs from RSV only in connecting 33:12 with the preceding strophe, in seeing 33:25–30 as a strophe (but this cannot be if v 25 is understood, as here, to be part of the speech of the angel), and in removing 33:31–33 from this chapter altogether (he also makes 33:15 a bicolon, deleting v 15b). De Wilde analyzes regular strophes of two bicola throughout the speech, but at some cost: he moves 32:15–17 to follow v 9 and 33:5 to follow v 3; he allows no tricola; and he deletes 33:31–33 from the chapter. Terrien identifies nine main strophes, each with two substrophes: thus 32:6b–10 (containing 3+3 bicola), 11–14 (2 tricola + 2 bicola), 15–22 (3+5 bicola), 33:1–7 (4+3 bicola), 8–13 (4+2 bicola), 14–18 (1 bicolon and 1 tricolon + 3 bicola, 19–24 (4 bicola + 3 tricola), 25–28 (1 bicolon and 1 tricolon + 1 tricolon and 1 bicolon), 29–33 (2+3 bicola). This corresponds exactly to RSV, except that he (with some justification) connects 33:12–13 with what precedes and (also against the interpretation given here) makes a break between 33:24 and 25.

In *form,* these chapters contain a prose *narrative* (32:1–6a), followed by an *apology for intervention* (32:6b–22) and another *disputation speech* (33:1–33).

The *narrative* is in form an introduction to the speeches that will follow, in just the same manner as the narrative of the arrival of the friends in 2:11–13. The materials of this introduction are for the most part formed on the basis of the narrative prologue to the book: e.g., the specification of the speaker's family descent (cf. 32:2 with 2:11); the initial silence (cf. 32:4 with 2:13); the reason for the silence (cf. 32:4b with 2:13b); and the reason for the breaking of silence (cf. 32:2–3, 5b with 2:12a).

The *apology,* which is addressed first to the friends (vv 6b–14) and then, apparently, to Job (vv 15–22), contains these elements: reason for not having entered the debate previously (his youth and timidity, vv 6b–7; his expectation that one of the friends would confute Job, vv 11–12), justification for entering the debate now (his possession of the divine breath that inspires understanding, vv 8–9; his incapacity to restrain himself from speaking, vv 18–20), reproach of the friends for their defeatist attitude (v 13), assertion of his intention to develop new arguments not previously deployed (v 14), verdict on the failure of the friends' arguments (v 15), assurance that he will speak candidly, without flattery (vv 21–22).

The *disputation speech* is evidently the principal genre of chaps. 32–33. Elihu sees his project as "confuting" (יכח hiph) Job, which the friends have failed to do (32:13; cf. 32:5, 15), as "answering" (ענה, שוב hiph) the arguments Job has put forward (32:12, 14, 16, 17, 20; 33:12). He demands that Job "answer" (שוב hiph) him, that he set his words in order (ערך) and "take his stand" as if in a court hearing represented as a military engagement (33:5; cf. 33:32). The language of "justification" (with the verb צדק) also points to the setting of the law court or its analogue in the nonlegal disputation such as we have here: thus Elihu is angry at Job because he "justified himself" (32:2), he tells him forthrightly that he is "not right" (33:12), and he declares that his intention is in the end to "declare [Job] to be in the right" (33:32).

The materials of the apology are principally derived, not surprisingly, from the sphere of *wisdom teaching*. The language includes חכמה "wisdom" (32:7, 13), חכם "be wise" (v 9), שׁמע "hear" (imperative) (v 10), דע "knowledge" (vv 6, 10, 17), דבר "word" (v 11), מלה "word" (vv 11, 14, 15, 18), אמר "word" (vv 12, 14), תבונה "wise saying" (v 11), and ענה "answer" (vv 12, 15, 16, 17, 20). Elihu cites a wisdom saying in v 7, he makes use of the traditional sapiential idea that wisdom is a gift from God (v 8), and he professes himself "full of words" (v 18). Typical of the exordium in the wisdom instruction is the demand to be heard (32:10; 33:1; and cf., as a virtual exordium to chap. 34, 33:31, 33; and cf. also 15:17; 21:2–3), the request for silence (33:31, 33; cf. 21:5), and the reference to the strong emotions inspired in the speaker (32:18–20; cf. 21:6). Other common features of the wisdom instruction are the use of rhetorical questions (32:16; 33:13), and the citation of words of the opponents (32:13, against the friends; 33:9–11, 13, against Job; there are also two self-citations, in 32:7, 10). The appeal to experience (cf. 8:8–10; 15:17–19; 20:4–5; 21:29–33) is a further element in the wisdom instruction: here it appears in the cameos of the dream warnings (33:15–18) and of the angelic deliverance from illness (33:19–28).

There is *psalmic* language as well: he "waits" (יחל hiph, eight of its sixteen occurrences being in Psalms and Lamentations), and he imagines the friends leaving the "routing" (נדף) of Job to God (cf. Pss 1:4; 68:2 [3]). And there is *prophetic* language also: his opponents are "dismayed" (חתת, thirty-eight of its sixty-eight occurrences being in prophetic texts), God is his "Maker" (עשׂה, participle of God five times in prophetic texts, three times in Proverbs, twice in Psalms, and only twice elsewhere), he will not "surname" anyone with honorific titles (כנה piel appears elsewhere only in Isa 44:5; 45:4), and he likens his fullness with words in v 19 (even if unconsciously) to Jeremiah who also was "full" (מלא) of Yahweh's fury and weary of holding it in (Jer 6:11).

The *rhetoric* of the Elihu speeches as a whole has been carefully analyzed by H. Viviers ("Elihu [Job 32–37], Garrulous But Poor Rhetor? Why Is He Ignored?" in *The Rhetorical Analysis of Scripture: Essays from the 1995 London Conference,* ed. S. E. Porter and T. H. Olbricht, JSNTSup 146 [Sheffield: Sheffield Academic Press, 1997] 137–53), using the theory of argumentation developed by C. Perelman and L. Olbrechts-Tyteca, *The New Rhetoric: A Treatise on Argumentation* (Notre Dame: Notre Dame UP, 1969). He concludes that the character Elihu deserves to be ignored within the book as a whole, since he is not presented as a "good person," which the classical rhetoricians postulated as the essential quality of an effective speaker. It is questionable, however, whether Elihu can be judged on such a narrow basis, and it seems better to work with the evidence from the speeches themselves. The analysis of Elihu's modes of argument is nevertheless valid, even if the evaluation of his intervention is one-sided.

The *function* of the speech as a whole is to instruct Job, to enable him to consider truths he has not fully recognized previously, truths that the friends have failed to convince him of. There are other motivations expressed in the speech: in 32:2–3, 5 his speech arises from Elihu's anger, both at Job and at the friends; in 32:18–20 it is necessary for him to give vent to his words in order to gain some relief from the pressure they have built up in him; in 33:32 his own motivation is to "justify" Job. All these motives lie behind the speech, but its function proper is to teach Job wisdom, as Elihu announces he will also do in the subsequent speech (33:33).

The *tonality* of the speech is not easy to determine. There is a good deal of anger in Elihu when he opens his speech, as the narrative prologue warns us: he "became angry... angry at Job... angry also at Job's three friends... he became angry" (32:2–3). He is so full of words that he feels he will burst if they are not let loose (32:18–20). And he is clear that Job is in the wrong, and he makes no bones about saying so to his face (33:12). Yet he goes out of his way to stress to Job that "no fear of me should terrify you; there will be no heavy pressure from me upon you" (33:7). This may be felt to be patronizing (though see *Comment*), but that is the worst it can be; his words plainly mean that he is trying to be supportive of Job, and indeed the closing remark of this speech, "My desire is to justify you" (33:32), should not come as any surprise. If it does surprise, the reader needs to survey the whole of the speech again from that perspective, and recall how positive Elihu's attitude to Job indeed is. After all, the highlight of the speech has been the lively depiction of the man in mortal danger whose life is redeemed through angelic intervention (33:19–28), a man with whom Job must be intended to identify. Job's suffering, according to Elihu, is a means of God's communication with him, not a punishment—a more supportive position than that of any other of the friends.

The *nodal* sentence in the speech comes, as not infrequently (cf. under *Form/Structure/Setting* on chap. 28), at its close: "My desire is to justify you" (33:32). Job will of course have to confess his fault (cf. 33:27b–c), will have to modify his protestation of perfect innocence (33:9), and will have to withdraw his charges against God (33:10–11) for Elihu to be able to take his side fully. We know that Job cannot agree to any of these conditions, but Elihu does not, and his speech is nothing but well intentioned.

Comment

32:1–37:24 The Elihu material is divided up in the Masoretic text in this way: (1) preface (in prose) (32:1–6a), (2) first speech (32:6b–33:33), (3) second speech (34:2–37), (4) third speech (35:2–16), and (5) fourth speech (36:2–33). To the fourth speech may be added the poem on wisdom (28:1–28), in accordance with this commentary's assignment of that chapter to Elihu. But the speeches could be divided up differently on thematic lines (following Terrien): (1) introduction, addressed to the three friends and perhaps a wider audience (32:6–22); (2) part 1: God's silence not signifying his injustice (33:1–33), response to Job's attack on divine retribution (34:1–37), and Job's misjudgment about his innocence (35:1–16); and (3) part 2: the purpose of human suffering (36:1–25) and praise of God as sovereign of the three seasons (36:26–37:24), the divinely appointed means for humans to gain wisdom.

It is commonly thought that the Elihu material is a secondary addition to the book. H. M. Wahl ("Seit wann gelten die Elihureden [Hi 32–37] als Einschub? Eine Bemerkung zur Forschungsgeschichte," *BN* 63 [1992] 58–61) and M. Witte ("Noch einmal: Seit wann gelten die Elihureden im Hiobbuch [Kap. 32–37] als Einschub?" *BN* 67 [1993] 20–25) have discussed who began the trend; Gersonides may have been the first and, among modern scholars, one Elias Busitas in 1772. Some of the reasons put forward are these: (1) Unlike the other speakers in the book, Elihu has not been referred to in the narrative prologue, and will not be mentioned in the epilogue. (2) The speeches of Elihu could be omitted without loss to the book, and it can even be said that "the dramatic power of the book is heightened by the omission of his speeches" (Strahan). (3) The style of the Elihu speeches and narrative differs from that of the book elsewhere: it is "prolix, laboured and tautological; the power and brilliancy which are so conspicuous in the poem generally are sensibly wanting" (Driver–Gray).

These arguments are not strong. It can be replied that (1) an editor capable of inserting the Elihu speeches in an existing book of Job would be capable also of making minimal adjustments to prologue and epilogue to incorporate his character within the framework of the book. The absence of Elihu from the framework is a problem for any view of the composition of the book. (2) A judgment of the dramatic dynamics of the book is a matter of opinion. Many have found the delay between Job's final speech and the reply of Yahweh from the tempest exceedingly effective and tantalizing. And on the theory advanced in this commentary, that the speeches of Elihu belonged originally after the third cycle of speeches (i.e., after chap. 27) and before Job's final speech (chaps. 29–31), the Elihu collection can be viewed as integral to the book and at the same time no rein on the movement from Job's last speech to Yahweh's first. (3) The point is conceded that Elihu is differently portrayed from the other friends; but the poet is capable enough to have managed to create a distinctive figure in the young man Elihu, and there is no argument here in favor of another author. Elihu is indeed prolix, but in his mouth are also set some of the poet's finest lines (see *Explanation* to chaps. 36–37), so debate over authorship seems rather futile.

There has been indeed in recent years something of a backlash against the almost universal relegation of the Elihu speeches to the realm of the secondary intrusion. See Habel (36–37), Janzen (218), Gordis (xxxi–xxxii, 546–52), D. N. Freedman ("The Elihu Speeches in the Book of Job: A Hypothetical Episode in the Literary History of the Work," *HTR* 61 [1968] 51–59; reprinted in *Pottery, Poetry, and Prophecy: Studies in Early Hebrew Poetry* [Winona Lake, IN: Eisenbrauns, 1980] 329–37), and Good (7–9, 321). Even if the secondary character of the Elihu material can be sustained, the speeches still merit a full examination, for they would represent the second thoughts on the problem of Job by a later age. Its author would be representing a new approach to the issue raised by Job's suffering: he argues that suffering, rather than being a punishment sent from God, is best regarded as one of God's means of communicating his will to humans.

Another critical issue is the question of the original location of the Elihu speeches. In this commentary the new view is proposed that these speeches (chaps. 32–37) originally followed chap. 27 and were followed by chap. 28, the poem on wisdom, which is also here assigned to Elihu (in volume 1 of this commentary [WBC 17], I had earlier suggested it might be Zophar's [p. lix]). In the course of scribal transmission, I argue, chaps. 32–37 were displaced to their present position, thus severing the link between Job's final demand to be heard by God (31:35) and Yahweh's immediate reply in chaps. 38–41.

How is Elihu portrayed? Many comment on the prolixity of his style, on his pompousness (Andersen) and self-importance (Rowley). W. Whedbee ("The Comedy of Job," in *Studies in the Book of Job [Semeia 7]*, ed. R. Polzin and D. Robertson [Missoula, MT: Society of Biblical Literature, 1977] 1–39) has even argued that Elihu plays the role of the *alazon* of Greek drama, the buffoon, "a comic figure whom the author exposes and ridicules." Similarly, N. C. Habel ("The Role of Elihu in the Design of the Book of Job," in *In the Shelter of Elyon: Essays on Palestinian Life and Literature*, FS G. W. Ahlström, ed. W. B. Barrick and J. R. Spencer,

JSOTSup 31 [Sheffield: JSOT Press, 1984] 81–98) assesses him an "opinionated fool." Terrien calls him a pedant (225), Good "insufferably pompous" (326) and "a pompous, insensitive bore" (321). According to Gordis (554), "his truculence is in part a mask for his embarrassment and insecurity in the presence of his elders." C. A. Newsom offers a series of more subtle reasons for why, as she puts it, people loathe Elihu. Following a lead from Gordis, who referred to him as "Elihu the Intruder" ("Elihu the Intruder: A Study of the Authenticity of Job [Chapters 32–33]," in *Biblical and Other Studies,* ed. A. Altmann, Studies and Texts [Philip W. Lown Institute of Advanced Judaic Studies] 1 [Cambridge, MA: Harvard UP, 1963] 60–78.), Elihu intrudes, she says,

> into an intense moment, not just among the characters in the book, but also between the reader and the book. He breaks the dramatic spell and spoils the integrity of an aesthetic, emotional, and religious encounter at the climax of the book.... By the end of chap. 37, Elihu has distanced the reader from the immediacy of Job's passion and has changed the nature of the reader's experience of the book, so that ideas dominate over passions.... Elihu's need to control—to control the reader's perception of God and perhaps even to control God—is amply on display when he speaks. This dynamic, coupled with Elihu's unconcealed conviction that he alone understands what is said and can point out and remedy its defects is what earns Elihu the undying resentment of generations of readers.

All this hostility is overblown. None of Elihu's critics gives, in the end, an adequate account of what harm he does, or can say why he is so much worse than the other friends. J. W. McKay ("Elihu—A Proto-Charismatic?" *ExpTim* 70 [1978–79] 167–71) is one of the few with a positive view of Elihu. He sees him as "young and full of vitality," making a sincere appeal to the heart as well as the mind. It is his role to focus Job's attention on God rather than on his sufferings, and so his speeches form a necessary prelude to the entry of Yahweh into the conversation. Whether or not that particular approach is adopted, the important questions about Elihu are not about his character but about his ideas, and, in the commentary that follows, a reassessment of his theology, which goes well beyond those of the other friends, will be attempted.

On Elihu's character, cf. also the *Comments* on 32:6–10, 15–22; 33:2.

1–5 The primary function of these verses is to explain the intrusion of a new speaker into the dialogue. Elihu's intervention is accounted for as irresistible: he has listened to the speeches both of Job and of the friends with mounting anger, and he is unable to contain himself any longer. Without question, this introduction of a new character into the book gives the narrative an unexpected dramatic twist, for which the reader has been wholly unprepared.

But who is to say what might have been expected to happen next in the book of Job if we read it in its traditional Masoretic sequence? Job himself has delivered his final speech. Its contents have a note of finality about them, with a comprehensive survey of his life and a detailed self-examination of his behavior. And the speech has concluded by his proffering a signed document attesting his innocence and appealing to the Almighty to respond with a counteraccusation of his own (31:35). And the narrator has confirmed that our instincts were correct and that with this speech "the words of Job are (well and truly) ended" (31:40c). On the other hand, when Job called for someone to give him a legal hearing, and demanded the document that God as his legal adversary had written, he used one of his favorite locutions, "O that" (מי יתן, lit. "who will give that ...?"), which always introduces wishes he believes are hopeless. So what are we readers to think will happen next? Will the impossible wish turn, this time, into reality, and will God himself enter the debate? Will the friends take the opportunity of the ending of Job's protests to browbeat him (and the readers) into submission to their own theologies, in yet another round of speeches? Will the book now draw to a close, the issues as much unresolved at the end as they were at the beginning? Whatever we imagine, none of us—Job, the friends, or the reader—is prepared for what next happens: the entry of a fresh interlocutor, about whom we have had no hint in all the preceding narrative.

This Elihu will call into question all that has been said hitherto, on both sides; it is as if he were preparing the way for a new dialogue to start up. And at the same time he will defer, perhaps even deflect, the intervention of the prime actor in the drama, the Godot for whom all have been waiting, without hope, the figure of whom all speak but who has remained determinedly offstage. Readers will have to contain their curiosity yet further.

So far I have been giving an account of the narrative structure of the book as it lies before us in the Masoretic text. If the argument of this commentary is correct, however, the sequence of the Masoretic text at this point is defective, the result of a major scribal corruption. Here it is being argued that the speeches of Elihu, an original part of the book, were by the author designed to be read after the other three friends had reached the end of their arguments. (Fohrer also argues that the introduction in 32:1 takes us back to the situation where the third cycle of speeches has concluded and Job's final speech has yet to be uttered.) In the third cycle of speeches, the three friends had not been able to sustain the vigor or even the length of their previous speeches; thereupon Elihu had felt free to intervene. Between the last speech of Zophar (chap. 27) and the last speech of Job came the speeches of Elihu, including, as the end of his peroration, the famous poem on the finding of wisdom (chap. 28). Then when Elihu had had his say, Job launched into his final speech, more or less ignoring everything all the friends, including Elihu, had said. The moment he called for a divine response, and finished his words (31:40c), at that moment came the voice from the tempest (38:1). But in the course of transmission of the scroll of Job, chaps. 32–37 became dislocated from their original place preceding chap. 28. The dynamics of the resolution of the book were drastically disturbed, but perhaps no great harm was done by the new shape of the book. We might even derive some pleasure from the deferment of the divine response in that new shape of the book while we listen to six chapters' worth of wordy and sententious utterances from Elihu (Terrien speaks of the Elihu material as a kind of liturgical "gradual").

1 The fact that this introduction to the Elihu speeches opens with the words "these three men ceased to answer Job" is prima facie evidence that it once stood at the end of the speeches of the friends, namely, after chap. 27 (Zophar's last speech) rather than in its present position in the Masoretic book, after Job's speech. Some have urged that the phrase "these three men" (שלשת האנשים האלה) is the sign of another author from that of the rest of the book, where the other interlocutors are always known as "friends" (2:11; 42:10 in the narrative framework; 19:21 within the dialogues); here they seem to "become personages almost foreign to the rest of the prose narrative" (Dhorme). In Ezek 14:14, 16 the same formula is used to speak of persons remote from the time of the author and of the surrounding narrative (curiously, Job is there one of the persons). There is indeed a distancing note in the authorial voice, but that need not evidence a different author; in any case, we should also notice that already in v 3 they are being referred to as "his three friends" (שלשת רעיו). What is more, Habel has pointed out how the narrator of the Job story typically uses an allusive "this" and "these" as markers of closure and transition (cf. 1:22; 2:10; 42:7, 16).

There is something strange about the reason given by the narrator for the friends' lapsing into silence: it is "because [Job] was in the right in his own eyes." He means of course that this was the reason they gave themselves, not the reason he infers for them. What is odd about this reason is that throughout the dialogues the friends have always known that Job has been in the right in his own eyes, and it has not stopped them before. It could even be argued that his certainty of his own righteousness is the very reason why they engage with him in dialogue in the first place. The meaning can only lie in an unexpressed middle term, that they have run out of patience for arguing with a man who continues to maintain his innocence in the face of all the evidence to the contrary.

We cannot believe that the friends have now come to side with Job, and that their desisting from argument is "a recognition of the rectitude of Job" (as Dhorme, reading with one manuscript and some of the ancient versions "because he was justified in their eyes"; see *Note* 32:1.a). Nor can we infer from the phrase "because he was in the right in his own eyes" that the author of the Elihu chapters shared the opinion of the friends that Job was not truly righteous (as Strahan), for it is their reason rather than his that he proffers.

2 Elihu is provided with an impressive lineage, as "son of Barachel, the Buzite, of the family of Ram," as if he were an important historical personage (Duhm). None of the other participants in the book bears more than his own personal name and the name of his town, Job the Uzite, Eliphaz the Temanite, Bildad the Shuhite, and Zophar the Naamathite. We might infer, with Gordis, that the elaborate introduction of Elihu is to show that though he was young he had enough family status to entitle him to speak (cf. the lineage of the young Diomedes in Homer, *Iliad* 14.113–27). One might argue that the different form of noting his lineage is the sign of a different author, but it is normal in Hebrew prose narratives to give the name of a man's father, even though that has not been done in the case of the three friends (2:11), nor in the case of Job himself (1:1).

Elihu is a not uncommon Hebrew name, borne by at least four other individuals in the Hebrew Bible: an Ephraimite, ancestor of Samuel (1 Sam 1:1), a brother of David, otherwise known as Eliab (1 Sam 16:6; 1 Chr 2:13; 27:18), a Manassite chief in the time of David (1 Chr 12:21), and a Korahite gatekeeper (1 Chr 26:7); cf. *DCH*, 1:290b. From the point of view of its etymology, the name "means" "He is (my) God"; but names have reference rather than sense, and unless we can establish some wordplay with the name, there is not much value in identifying its supposed etymological meaning (see further, *Note* 32:2.a). Duhm whimsically suggested that Elihu may be named after Eliphaz, since he borrows so many of his ideas.

The name Barachel is not attested elsewhere in classical Hebrew, but we can compare names like Berechiah (known for twelve individuals), Barchi, Beracah, Baruch, and Jeberechiah (see *DCH,* 2:271–74), all formations from the verb ברך *bārak* "bless." The related name Barakilu is attested in the Murashu family of Jewish bankers in Babylonia in the fifth century B.C.E. (see further, *Note* 32:2.b). The clan or phratry name of Ram, etymologically connected with the verb רום *rûm* "be high," is known as that of an ancestor of David (Ruth 4:19; cf. 1 Chr 2:9, 10, 25, 27); perhaps it is a short form for some such theophoric name as Eliram, "God is exalted." So we learn nothing about the character Elihu from the personal names of himself and his family (and certainly not that Elihu is an Israelite, as Hartley thinks)—except that Elihu is no unknown interloper but a member of the world of Job and his friends (Habel).

The place name Buz, on the other hand, is more significant. While it is attested in Gen 22:21 as the personal name of a cousin of Abraham, and brother of Uz, more to the point it appears in Jer 25:23 as a place name associated with Dedan and Tema (the land of Uz has appeared in v 20). These are names that we found also in Jer 49:7–8, in an oracle about Edom, and the Edomite Tema has already occurred in Job as the home of Eliphaz (cf. on 2:11; it is not a matter of northwest Arabia, as many claim). So it would seem that Elihu too, like the other three friends of Job, is being portrayed as an Edomite.

If there is any significance in the names themselves, it may be that Elihu, "he is God," could suggest that this speaker will be the one who best upholds the divine honor, the wisdom equivalent perhaps of his near prophetic namesake Elijah, "Yahweh is God." His father's name Barachel may suggest "God blesses" or "may God bless!" perhaps an implicit denial of the cruel and unjust character of the God whom Job has been depicting. His clan name Ram suggests "high," perhaps meaning that Elihu's high birth entitles him to speak despite his youth. But his place Buz can only suggest "disgrace" or "despising" (cf. the verb בוז "despise"), and it would be straining things to see in that a sign of the apparently unimpressive arguments of a young man. In fact, the "meanings" conjured up by all the proper names are of such generality that it is hard to think that they have been chosen designedly (against Fohrer). It is merely a curiosity of exegesis that one nineteenth-century translator of Job, believing that Elihu's language is too sublime for merely human lips, identified him with the second person of the Trinity, translating his titulature as "Elihu, the blessed Son of God, the Despised One, of the lineage of the Most High" (J. N. Coleman, *The Book of Job, the Most Ancient Book in the Universe . . . Translated from the Hebrew with Notes Explanatory, Illustrative, and Critical* [London: Nisbet, 1869]).

The anger of Elihu is obviously a key motif here, since it is explicit four times in these five verses of introduction. Fohrer explains it as the "righteous, holy anger that represents God's cause over against any injury done to his claim to lordship or any disregard of his holiness" (following J. Fichtner, *TDNT,* 5:392–409); Elihu is not God, however, and has little right to any indignation God may be feeling. Hartley thinks of it as "righteous indignation, for [Elihu] sees the whole dialogue between Job and the three friends as having been poorly argued on both sides." De Wilde thinks the anger of Elihu is an expression of the author's anger at what Job was allowed to get away with in the original book! There may be a truth in these views, but the text deserves to be probed yet deeper. What is surprising is that it is *anger* that drives Elihu into this theological debate. All the participants, including Elihu, are in agreement about almost every religious idea, and the whole argument of the book hangs upon very fine distinctions over one doctrine, that of retribution. It is strange therefore that there should be cause for anger among the disputants, and we are driven to seek a more psychological or social explanation. The anger we read of here is intellectualized by the author as an anger that arises *because of* the arguments of Job and the friends—but that term "because of" very probably signals a displacement of the source of the anger. For one does not become *angry* because someone else holds a different view from oneself on esoteric points of theology; it is in cases where one's own identity is in some way threatened by that view or its expression that intellectual disagreement connects with the emotions.

Perhaps the best interpretation of Elihu's anger is that he resents the way his opinions are suppressed by the custom that keeps the young silent, that is, that the text is transparent to the social anger between the generations (see D. J. A. Clines, "Why Is There a Book of Job and What Does It Do to You If You Read It?" in *The Book of Job,* ed. W. A. M. Beuken, BETL 104 [Leuven: Leuven UP; Peeters, 1994] 1–20 [10]; reprinted in Clines, *Interested Parties: The Ideology of Writers and Readers of the Hebrew Bible,* JSOTSup 205; Gender, Culture, Theory 1 [Sheffield: Sheffield Academic Press, 1995] 122–44 [131–32]). Elihu's hostility to the friends is explicable: they are older and more authoritative men who have kept him in the background (Newsom refers to Ps 119:99–100, where meditation on the Torah gives the speaker more understanding than the elders, to the wisdom of the young man Joseph in Gen 41, to that of Daniel and his three friends in Dan 1:17–20, and to the contrast between the clever youth Daniel and the wicked elders in Sus 44–64). But why is Elihu angry with *Job?* Presumably because Job has argued in his own defense instead of immediately adopting what is apparently God's point of view, that Job is a sinner. We for our part, since we know that Job is innocent, are no doubt in favor of Job's defending himself and might at this point even start to become angry with Elihu!

3 Elihu is angry with the friends because "they did not find an answer." They of course thought that they had found perfectly adequate answers to Job's accusations against God. But because they had not silenced Job, still less had brought him to admit the error of his ways, they had in Elihu's eyes failed to find an answer. He is angry also because, apparently, "they condemned Job" or "put Job in the wrong." But why exactly should that make him angry? It is not that he is so attracted to the rightness of Job's cause that he resents their condemnation of a righteous man (it will not be until Yahweh speaks in 42:7–8 that they are compelled to accept the rightness of the way Job has spoken about God, as Habel notes). Nor is it that he is such a reasonable fellow that he dislikes their condemning him without finding good reasons for doing so (against Hölscher). It seems rather that he is angry because they have not been able to find such good reasons as to be able to overcome him with the condemnation he deserves (so Davidson), and thus "had not shown Job to be in the wrong."

There is a Masoretic marginal note (*tiqqun sopherim*), that איוב "Job" is here a "correction" for הָאֱלֹהִים "God"; that is, the Masoretes attempted, by changing the traditional text, to avoid the apparent blasphemy of declaring God to be in the wrong (one of eighteen such corrections; see Carmel McCarthy, *The Tiqqune*

Sopherim and Other Theological Corrections in the Masoretic Text of the Old Testament, OBO 36 [Freiburg: Universitätsverlag; Göttingen: Vandenhoeck & Ruprecht, 1981] 115–20; we should note that in 40:8 the same verb is used of putting God in the wrong, and there is no correction). NEB translates the "uncorrected" text with "had let God appear wrong" (noting this as the probably original reading); Gordis "had placed God in the wrong"; and Moffatt translated "for compromising God by failing to refute Eyob." Among those who restore the original uncensored reading are Duhm, Strahan, Dhorme, Hölscher, Fohrer, Pope, Andersen, Hesse, de Wilde, Habel, and Hartley. The thought must be this: By failing to refute Job's claims to innocence and by failing to show that he has in fact been a sinner, they give the impression (however unintentionally) that Job is in the right and that therefore God, his opponent, is in the wrong.

But it is a little hard to see what more the friends could have done. If Job insists on maintaining his innocence, how can the friends prove his guilt other than by making allegations against him—which he will forthwith deny? Does that really put God in the wrong? Tur-Sinai, followed by Rowley, did not think so and preferred the Masoretic text with its alleged scribal correction (so too Gibson). And, as Delitzsch pointed out, it is not principally the friends who have put God in the wrong but Job himself, much more directly.

If the present form of the book of Job is original, in which Job's last speech (chaps. 29–31) is not answered by any of the friends, we might find an answer in the procedures of law. It is often thought that a Hebrew lawsuit was won when one side or the other admitted defeat by not speaking again; so perhaps the fact that the three friends have not silenced Job or brought him to acknowledge defeat means that Elihu believes that, unless he intervenes, Job has won the debate. Cf. on 19:25–27; and see H. Richter, *Studien zu Hiob: Der Aufbau des Hiobbuches, dargestellt an den Gattungen des Rechtslebens* (Berlin: Evangelische Verlagsanstalt, 1959) 40–41, 104–10, followed by Hartley. But Elihu's anger with the friends' failure to convince Job is equally well explicable if, as argued in this commentary, he is speaking immediately after the end of the third cycle of speeches: since the faults in Job's position are so evident to him, he is astonished that the other friends have not been able, after all this time, to make them plain to Job.

4 As we have seen already in Job's last speech (30:1), in a patriarchal society it is not only women who are oppressed by the system, but younger men also. It is taken for granted that a young man must wait his turn to speak until his elders have finished all they want to say (cf. also v 6; 15:10; Ecclus 32:9). Elihu then is not just "chafing under the restraints imposed by etiquette upon youth" (Strahan), or deferring to the social custom of the time (Hartley), but speaking up against a kind of inverse ageism, which will not listen to ideas on their own merits but makes the age of their propounder the principal thing.

Gordis thinks that Job expected a further reply from the friends after his speech in chaps. 29–31 and that Elihu, who had been a silent and impatient listener to the dialogue, when he found that the friends had nothing more to say (vv 1, 5) now joined in the conversation.

5 Nothing new is added by this verse, but, as Dhorme says, "If this preamble seems prolix, it resembles . . . the style of Elihu in the whole ch. 32." Some commentators would like to excise vv 2–5 (e.g., Hoffmann), but the elaborate style can well be understood as an intentional introduction to the character of Elihu, as a kind of inverse "represented speech" (*erlebte Rede;* cf. G. Goldenberg, "On Direct Speech and the Hebrew Bible," in *Studies in Hebrew and Aramaic Syntax,* FS J. Hoftijzer, ed. K. Jongeling, H. L. Murre-van der Berg, and L. van Rompay, Studies in Semitic Languages and Linguistics 17 [Leiden: Brill, 1991] 79–96). In that mode, the speech attributed to a character is contaminated by the knowledge or language of the narrative in which that speech is embedded; here it would be the narrative that is contaminated by the language of the character.

6–22 In this first phase of Elihu's first speech (32:6b–33:33) he offers three justifications for joining the conversation. In vv 6b–10 he argues that he is entitled to speak, in vv 11–14 that he needs to speak, and in vv 15–22 that he must speak. (Fohrer labels the strophes somewhat differently: I want to speak, I can speak, I must speak.) He is entitled to speak because as a human being he has all the wisdom necessary to have an opinion, even though he is young; he needs to speak because the friends have so obviously failed to refute Job; and he must speak because he finds silence in the face of such a situation intolerable.

6–10 After the introductory formula of the narrator's (v 6a), Elihu explains why he has not intervened in the debate hitherto, and why he is intervening now. It is assumed that he has been present throughout the speeches of Job and the three friends. He is younger than the other interlocutors, but, since one of them at least is said to be a generation older than Job (15:10), we cannot tell whether Elihu is represented as fifteen or twenty-five or thirty-five years of age. Throughout their dialogues, so he says, he was too timid to interject his own opinions, since his society so privileged the ideas of older men that he felt it necessary to keep silence out of pure respect for their seniority. However, this respect is not inhibiting him now, and he will feel free to speak uninterruptedly for longer than anyone else in the book. So there is something rather formal, if not insincere, about his reason for having waited till now to speak.

The narrator has said that Elihu's reason for intervening is his anger at the ineffectualness of the other friends. Elihu himself, however, is not so impolite as to express that anger in so many words; rather, he here gives as his reason for speaking merely the fact that he believes he is capable of adding to the debate. Yet there is something a little disingenuous in his statement; for he does not suggest that the thought has just occurred to him that it is the "breath of the Almighty" in a mortal that gives understanding. If he has always known or thought that, it cannot be the reason why he has waited until now to join in, nor indeed why he joins in now.

On the broader issue of Elihu's character, it makes something of a difference whether we think he is offering to display his knowledge (as NEB has it) or merely proffering his opinion (as RSV has it; see further *Note* 32:6.e). Are we to find in him an opinionated and patronizing bore, or a hesitant and cautious thinker whose language is long-winded because he is lacking in confidence? Unfortunately, we really cannot tell. Many commentators think they can, picking up on phrases that sound insensitive and arrogant. Some rabbis spoke of him as "Balaam in disguise," while many of the Fathers scorned him as a type of the false wisdom. Herder called him "a pert braggart boy," "a mere shadow." Among the modern commentators we read, for example, of "a combination of deference and cocksureness" (Andersen), or that "[h]is professed modesty is belied by his self-importance and pomposity" (Rowley). Good finds Elihu a "pompous, insensitive bore: an opaque thinker and an unattractively self-important character." But it might be better to recognize that Elihu's character may be much more indecipherable, and to keep an open mind about his motivation as well as his theology until we have heard him out. Terrien finds him a remarkable mixture of timidity and boldness, and it will be important to savor the contradictions in his portraiture. It is probably true that ancient Hebrews spoke not of holding opinions but of "knowing" things; if that is so, it would be hard to blame Elihu for not speaking more reservedly than anyone in his social world. On Elihu's character, cf. also *Comment* on 32:1–37:24 above.

6 It is interesting that age should be such an important element in the characterization of Elihu. These days, we would be more interested in knowing if his ideas have any merit in them than in his comparative age, and we are inclined to be impatient at his elaborate justification for a young man intruding in the conversations of older men. It would be different for us if Elihu spoke *as a young man,* and offered some more youthful perspective on the problem of the book; as it is, we are more than tempted to regard him as a young fogey rather than as a representative of a youth culture. Typical of wisdom language is the call to "hear" (the imperative of שׁמע occurs twelve times in Proverbs, fourteen in Job; but it is also frequent in the prophets: seventy-seven times in Isaiah, Jeremiah, and Ezekiel). The term for "declare" (חוה piel) is a rare one (only six occurrences, five of them in Job). The actual noun for "opinion" used here (דע) occurs only in Job, but the more usual form דעת is clearly typical of wisdom writing (of its ninety occurrences, forty are in Proverbs and ten in Job).

7 When he was not intervening in the debate, he had justified his silence by saying (to himself, obviously, since he remained silent!), "Days should speak, many years should teach wisdom." This was never his own view, of course; he only learned it from other people, which is to say, from older men, who taught it to him in their own interest. But he mouthed it, since it was safer to abide by the etiquette of his world. See also the speech of Diomedes asking that his hearers should not become angry because he is the youngest to make a speech (Homer, *Iliad* 14.111–12).

We have encountered this view already, especially in 12:12: "Wisdom is found with the aged, understanding comes with length of days." Though the sentence is found in a speech of Job's, there is good reason to think that he is not there speaking in his own voice, but ironically mouthing what he thinks the friends have been saying, or would say, to him (see on 12:7–12). Eliphaz has tried to put Job in his place by reminding him that "Among us is one [probably Eliphaz himself] who is gray-haired and aged, older indeed than your father!" (15:10), with the implication that Job's understanding cannot possibly be superior to that of the older man (cf. v 9). Cf. also Ezek 7:26, where counsel perishes from the elders, and Ecclus 25:4–6, where wisdom is becoming to the aged, and the crown of old men is wide experience.

When we hear "wisdom is with the aged" used against Job, most readers naturally resist it (cf. the comments of Peake cited on 15:10); but when we hear Elihu's refusal of it, commentators become tart. Rowley, for example, remarks: "In his youth Elihu denies wisdom to the aged. In old age he might less readily agree that he had lost the wisdom of which he now boasts." The commentator shows clearly enough that he does not rank himself with the young!

8 His own opinion was far different: he prefaces it with the particle אכן "surely," which is defined by Driver–Gray as "a strong asseverative, often used to introduce emphatically the statement of a *fact,* after what had been, mistakenly[,] 'said' or thought (Zeph 3:7; Jer 3:20; 8:8; Isa 49:4; 53:4; Ps 31:22 [23]; 82:7)."

Elihu is apparently arguing that what gives intelligence to humans, enabling them to "understand" (בין), is the life "spirit" (רוח) that is in humans, namely the "breath of Shaddai, the Almighty" (נשמת שדי), breathed into humanity at its creation (cf. Gen 2:7); so, e.g., Davidson, Habel. On this reasoning, all humans have their portion of God's breath, which is their own vitality, and so all have the necessary precondition for wisdom. Elihu cannot of course mean that because all humans are equally dependent on the divine breath for their life, all humans are equally wise. His interest is solely in denying that length of life is the *sine qua non* for wise judgment; everyone who is alive has the same capacity for it, he says. How the distinction between the wise and the foolish comes about is not his concern.

Some think it better to regard the divine wisdom-bestowing spirit as a special gift that Elihu lays claim to; other references to such a "spirit" are Gen 41:38; Exod 28:3; 31:3; Num 27:18; Deut 34:9; 1 Sam 10:6; Isa 11:2; Dan 5:11–12. Elihu himself speaks of a revelation by dreams in 33:15–18, but he does not claim dreams as the source of his own inspiration. Peake thought that Elihu means that he is speaking by a divine inspiration, not vouchsafed to the other friends; similarly too Strahan, Terrien, Hesse, Janzen, de Wilde, and J. W. McKay ("Elihu—A Proto-Charismatic?"). Others, such as Driver–Gray, think that even the distinction between the common human endowment of life-breath and the special inspiration of the wise and the prophets is unreal: it is "the same spirit in less or greater measure, working for and achieving different ends." And here too it seems preferable to see Elihu referring to the life-spirit common to all humans. See further, R. Dussaud, "La néphesh et la *rouaḥ* dans le 'Livre de Job,'" *RHR* 128 (1945) 17–30; T. C. Mitchell, "The Old Testament Usage of *nešāmâ,*" *VT* 11 (1961) 177–87.

It goes too far to find here, with Fohrer, a hint of the later wisdom ideology, which stressed, more than ancient wisdom, the concept of the divine origins of wisdom. We do not have here in the "spirit" of God a "supernatural element enabling humans to stand before the divine majesty in order to receive auditions and visions" (P. Volz, *Der Geist Gottes und die verwandten Erscheinungen im Alten Testament und im anschliessenden Judentum* [Tübingen: Mohr (Siebeck), 1910] 45). There is more in the thought of Alonso Schökel that we have here the revolutionary idea that wisdom is a charismatic gift rather than an acquisition, implying that "God does not submit to monopolies" and that when he pours out his spirit he does away with discrimination (Joel 2:28–29 [3:1–2]). But Elihu is not a radical theologian, and in this verse, we may be sure, he has set his sights no higher than to justify his own intervention in the debate.

9 If we translate the verse literally, we perhaps make Elihu sound too categorical, and even absurd. He says, "It is not the great [or perhaps, the old] who are wise, nor the aged who understand justice [or, judgment]." Many translators and commentators have rightly attempted to soften such a statement, from KJV "Great men are not *always* wise" (the italics indicating the insertion of the word), to NEB and NIV "it is not only the old who are wise," and Moffatt, more melodiously, "it is not always seniors who are sage" (see further, *Note* 9.b).

What of the word for "great" (רבים), which can also mean "many," but never "old" (though that is what RSV, NEB, and NIV have)? The parallelism with "the aged" in the second colon would suggest that here too we have a word for the old, but the only way to achieve that is to emend the text. In the *Translation* above, the emendation is accepted to שָׂבִים "the gray-haired."

It is not to Elihu's point to deny wisdom to the friends or to the elderly in general; he is only concerned to make room for himself in the dialogue, as the transition with "so" (לכן) to the next verse shows.

10 In v 7 Elihu had reported what he used to say when he was just parroting the words of his elders and betters: "Let days speak." In vv 8–9 he reports some general ideas, about wisdom deriving from the divine spirit that is in every human, that had changed his opinion. And now in v 10, he draws the conclusion for the present moment: he will speak anyway, despite the social pressures against him.

Strangely, it is only Job whom Elihu here intends to address, "hear" (שמעה) being in the singular. Elsewhere in this passage Elihu is addressing Job and the friends, in the plural (vv 6, 11–14), so perhaps the verb is an error for the plural (see *Note* 32:10.c). Yet since Elihu speaks of the friends in the third person in vv 15–16 (which implies that there he is speaking to Job alone), and addresses only Job throughout the whole of chap. 33, it is not impossible that here in v 10 he turns from the friends to Job, and back to the friends in v 11.

The last words of the verse (which are the last words also of his opening strophe, vv 6–10) are in emphatic position: "I too." He does not at this moment want to negate the words of the other friends, but simply to insert himself into the dialogue.

11–14 Elihu's first motivation for intervening in the debate was that he felt he had something of his own to say despite his comparative youth (vv 6–10). His second reason, in these verses, is that the three friends have in his eyes failed to confute Job and his position. He agrees essentially with the views of the friends and is angry with them only because they have not succeeded against Job; their cause is better than their advocacy of it (Davidson).

11–12 Elihu had waited silently, out of necessity (cf. vv 6–7), for all his seniors to complete their speeches; perhaps he hints also, with this term "wait" (יחל), that he had waited expectantly for them to utter the words that would defeat Job—as if he somehow knew what they would be. Ironically, he calls the friends' speeches their "understandings" (תבונה), for now he will make plain that he thinks them all a dismal failure. What the friends should have been doing was "reproving" or "convicting" (יכח hiph) Job for the wrongness of his views, but despite their best endeavors, "searching out" or "digging out" (חקר) arguments as if they already existed somewhere and had only to be found by eager inquiry (Duhm notes the irony, though Hesse sees only politeness), they have not succeeded. Job remains unmoved, maintaining his integrity.

Though the term for "confuting" (מוכיח) is the same word as that for "arbiter" (as in 9:33), it is not the absence of an arbiter that Elihu laments here, nor that Elihu offers himself as arbiter and for the defense of God (as against Habel, Good). It is not the formal legal language that is being spoken here, but the language of debate and disputation. Elihu of course takes for granted that Job is in the wrong; for a young man, he is remarkably conformist to the traditional theology, as Alonso Schökel observes.

It is interesting, but perhaps of no special consequence, that the friends never mention Job's name but Elihu does so frequently (32:12; 33:1, 31; 34:5, 7, 35, 36; 35:16; 37:14).

13 The friends are at risk of admitting defeat in the struggle with Job, according to Elihu. Well, they may have failed, but that need not mean that everyone must. They should be on their guard against allowing that Job is cleverer than they are, or saying, "We have found wisdom"— that is, a wisdom in Job that outranks theirs. They are implicitly adopting a defeatist tone, as if they were thinking, Only God can refute Job; no human can.

The sentence attributed to the friends, "We have found wisdom," is unlikely to refer to their own claim to be wise (as Fedrizzi, Gordis), as if they laid claim to wisdom on the ground of their age (as vv 7, 9). For then the connection with the second line would be hard to discern. It could be that the second colon is the content of the wisdom they have discovered, as if to say: The only sensible thing is to give up arguing with Job and let God deal with him (Sicre Díaz, de Wilde; cf. Gordis). But a better interpretation seems to be that they are disconcerted by having found wisdom in Job. As Moffatt puts it, "We found him too clever for us," or Renan, "This man is wisdom personified"; similarly Delitzsch, Duhm, Gibson, Ehrlich, Strahan, Driver–Gray, Fohrer, and Hesse. It is interesting to contrast this sentence Elihu attributes to the friends, "We have found wisdom," with 28:12, which probably comes from Elihu himself, and which asks whether it is possible that the place of wisdom should be "found"; perhaps he means to say that any claim to have found wisdom is ruled out in advance as false—how much more if they claim to find it in Job, when we all know it cannot be found in the land of the living, and even the deep and the sea disclaim all knowledge of where it can be found (28:13–14).

Elihu's response to their defeatism is to proffer himself as champion of logic and justice. "No need to call in God, is Elihu's retort, I am quite equal to the task of overcoming him" (Peake). But it is going too far to see these lines as "a direct polemic against the poet, a strong assertion that the Divine speeches which follow had been better omitted" (Peake)—for we may suspect that the poet of the Elihu speeches did not share all the views of his creature Elihu.

14 Elihu has the advantage, so he claims, of being able to start afresh the dispute with Job. Job has not arrayed (ערך), as if in battle order, since it is a military term, his arguments against Elihu, and Elihu hopes to shift the discussion onto quite other grounds. Whatever he says in response to Job, the words will be his own; he will not be borrowing the arguments of the friends—which, he implies, have now exhausted their usefulness. "You need not give up the conflict as lost," Peake paraphrases, "for he has still to debate with me."

15–22 Elihu makes a third sweep among his reasons for intervening in the conversation. It is not just that he feels entitled to speak because of his own wisdom (vv 6b–10), nor that the friends have failed to give an adequate answer to Job (vv 11–14), but that he cannot forbear from speaking. He is so full of words that he feels he will explode if he does not speak; he must find relief in speech.

Up to this point Elihu has plainly been addressing the friends, as the pronouns and verbs in vv 6, 10 (if emended), 11–14 show. Now in vv 15–16 he speaks of the friends in the third person and does not address them again until 34:2. Perhaps we may think of vv 15–22 as a soliloquy (as Peake, Driver–Gray), or as an address to an imaginary audience (Dhorme), or to real bystanders (Rowley on vv 15–16), or even half to himself and half to bystanders (Gibson). But it is more probable that in v 15 Elihu turns to Job (Rowley, Andersen). For his question, "Am I to wait because they cannot speak?" would seem to be addressed to someone present rather than spoken into thin air, and in 33:1, immediately after this strophe, we know for sure that he is addressing Job, for he does so by name. GNB wants its readers to understand that Job is being addressed from v 15 onwards, for it inserts his name at that point. (Budde omitted vv 11–17, with the result that the whole of the speech in chap. 32 is addressed to the friends.)

There is no denying that Elihu speaks at length, but in this book, who doesn't? What is more interesting is the depth of feeling Elihu rouses in his commentators by his wordiness: Terrien, for example, says that Elihu becomes "grotesque" in repeating himself; Andersen on vv 16–17 comments "Once more bombast," and sneers at vv 19–20 as "a fancy image." Strahan had remarked that a "Western audience . . . would overwhelm [a speaker] with ridicule if he were to compare himself to a fermenting wine-sack" (and Strahan does not think the Western audience would be in the wrong). Fedrizzi thinks the style grotesque or at least ironic. Hölscher scorns Elihu as an "armchair scholar" (*Stubegelehrte*); Hölscher, Professor at the University of Heidelberg, should know. Duhm, always free with his scorn, uses terms like "impertinent," "smug," "bombastic," "theatrical," and "self-important," is reminded of Horace's *parturiunt montes, nascetur ridiculus mus* (the mountains are in labor; a ridiculous mouse is born), remarks that the only thing for which Elihu is remarkable is his unintentional humor, and wonders what would be left of the Elihu speeches if all the puerilities were removed. Peake thought that "Elihu's conceit would be less insufferable to an Oriental than to us" (whoever "we" are, not "Orientals" at any rate). And Habel complains that "To boast of one's integrity comes with ill grace from a youth who has experienced none of the sufferings of Job and yet pretends to gainsay his arguments" (but integrity is a virtue whether or not one has suffered, or even whether or not one is in the right; and that word "youth" is inescapably pejorative!). It cannot be, can it, that these academics recognize in Elihu what they most fear to see in themselves?

Davidson tries to bring balance to the debate: "There are some things in his manner of introducing himself and in the way in which he speaks of his own arguments, which seem to offend against modesty and almost shock our sense of decorum. We must not, however, apply Western standards of taste to the East. There was nothing further from the intention of the author of these Chapters than to make Elihu play a ridiculous part." And Hartley cautiously observes that Elihu's wordiness "may be a sign of uncertainty," that he is very aware of the risk he runs in challenging the tradition, and in these lines he may well be expressing "his deference to his elders in a sincere though wordy apology."

15 Elihu is of course offering his own reading of the friends' feelings. They would hardly agree that they have become "dismayed" or "terrified" by their lack of success with Job. The word Elihu uses is a strong one (חתת): Job has used it of the frightening dreams God has sent him (7:14), of the fear he might have felt, but did not; of the social pressure of his kinsfolk, of the fear of contagion he imputes to the friends (6:21), while in 39:22 it is used of the fear the wild horse knows nothing of. It is in raillery that Elihu alleges that they are afraid to continue the debate, "the once redoubtable Three, who, as exhausted combatants, have retired from the fray" (Strahan); and by implication he casts himself as the brave hero who is willing to take Job on when the others have lost their nerve. Piling on the irony, he says that "words have deserted them"—a newly minted phrase, though a cliché to us—as though speech itself of its own accord has abandoned them as men beyond help (in 9:5 עתק was used of God removing mountains). If words have shown a clean pair of heels to the friends, it is all too easy to see where they have been headed: it is to Elihu, who now finds himself with almost a surfeit of the most excellent arguments.

17 By taking his "part" (חלק) in reply, Elihu is not so modest as to mean that his contribution will form only part of the case against Job or that he will be engaged in any communal enterprise with the friends. He thinks, as we have seen, that he will succeed where the friends have only failed (v 14); while of course he will be but one of the interlocutors, his intervention will be the decisive one, he feels sure.

18–19 Elihu, unlike the friends, is not short of words. In fact, he is so full of them that he will burst if he does not speak, somewhat like Jeremiah who is "full" (מלא) of Yahweh's fury and weary of holding it in (Jer 6:11). Elihu's image is that his body is filled with words, which are also breath (since they come out of the mouth with one's breath). The words themselves generate air, as new fermenting wine generates gas. If a wineskin is not vented, the new wine will burst it; and if he is not allowed to speak out, he will explode. (Gordis thinks that the wineskins are ready to burst just because they have been filled to the brim, but that ignores the idea of venting.) Prov 22:18 has the idea of the words of the wise being kept within one's "belly" (בטן), and Prov 20:30 that of the "chambers of the belly," the repository of thoughts, being "cleansed by disciplinary blows." On wineskins, typically containing circa fifteen liters, see Dalman, *Arbeit und Sitte,* 4:378; 5:194.

The Hebrew is a little compressed. Elihu says in v 18 that the *wind* of his "belly" (בטן) compels him, but he means that the unexpressed *words* that are "within" him (since "belly" can mean any of the internal organs or all of them together) are forcing themselves out of him. Then he says in v 19 that his "belly" is like wine, but what he means is that the *words* in his belly are like wine. And he says that his belly will burst like *new wineskins,* when he means like wineskins (probably old wineskins) with *new wine* in them. *New* wineskins are of course the least likely to burst from the fermenting new wine (Matt 9:17). This is the only simile Elihu uses in his speeches of chaps. 32–37, so it is a pity that it is not better thought through, that it is "more striking than fitting" (Fohrer). Can the poet be deliberately making Elihu falter?

It is important to distinguish the semantic worlds of vv 18 and 19: though the term "belly" appears in both, the "breath" or wind in his belly that impels him in v 18 is not the gas of fermenting wine to which his belly is likened in v 19. For the "breath" drives him forward, to speech, while the fermenting wine threatens to explode or burst out, to his destruction, no doubt. So it is unfair to Elihu to say that he "inadvertently calls himself a windbag . . . characteriz[ing] himself in terms typical of the brash fool" of 15:2 (Habel). The analogy with that passage is only superficial. Eliphaz there protested that a wise man would not fill his belly with the east wind—but his point was that turbulent outbursts are unbecoming to the sage. We can hardly make Elihu an offender for a similar phrase that has to do with motivation more than emotion.

Though Elihu is no prophet, and does not fancy himself as one (against Fedrizzi), his experience of an inner breath or spirit that "constrains" or "compels" (צוק) him is reminiscent of the prophetic experience of inner compulsion; so the prophet in Jer 20:9 speaks of a fire in the bones, a "more dignified, if not more forcible, simile," according to Strahan. In Walter Scott's epic poem *Lord of the Isles,* the bard's inspiration has echoes of Elihu's: "A power that can not be repressed. / It prompts my voice, it swells my veins, / It burns, it maddens, it constrains!"

20 Elihu describes the prospect of speech as a "relief" of inner tension (ירוח־לי, lit. "it would be a relief for me," the same idiom as in 1 Sam 16:23, where Saul was relieved by David's music; cf. ינוח לי "rest for me" in Job 3:13). Wordsworth speaks of the same experience of a "thought of grief": "A timely utterance gave that thought relief, / And I again am strong" (*Intimations of Immortality from Recollections of Early Childhood,* ll. 23–24). Elihu need not worry so much; he will not die of holding his peace. He would do well to take Ben Sira as his mentor: "Have you heard a rumor? Let it die with you," says that worthy; "never fear, it will not make you burst" (Ecclus 19:10).

21 Despite the strength of his desire to speak, Elihu is not going to let himself be carried away by emotion. He is going to impose a correct degree of objectivity upon his declarations, by refusing to show favor to any party in this dispute. In so saying, Elihu manages in one verse to be both obscure and less than candid. To say that he will show no partiality to anyone, not "side with" anyone (Dhorme), lit. "lift up the face" (נשׂא פנים; see on 13:8), seems less than honest when he has plainly decided that Job is in the wrong. The other colon is less than intelligible, for what title would Elihu imagine he could confer, and on whom? What would "flattery" in this context be? The term כנה (piel) means properly "bestow an honorable title upon," as Yahweh does to Cyrus in Isa 45:4 or to the nation of Israel in Ecclus 36:17, or as Israelites might do themselves with the name of Israel in Isa 44:5.

Rowley, among others, thinks that this self-certification of impartiality only makes Elihu look ridiculous, Terrien that it is a labored caricature. Nevertheless, Peake stresses that "[t]he parade of impartiality is sincerely meant," and Rowley that "[h]e is doubtless deadly sincere, for he takes himself so seriously." Strahan is more to my taste: "No man can be always so serious and virtuous, without being sometimes an unconscious humorist. Elihu declares that he will show respect to no man's person . . . else his Maker will soon take him away! It must be difficult to breathe on these heights. To give honorific titles to any poor human beings (Rabbis, Doctors, and suchlike) is no doubt a very foolish and reprehensible practice, but a death-sentence for it is somewhat too severe."

22 Why does Elihu imagine that his Maker would be so very interested if he bestowed flattering titles on people—even to the extent of bringing Elihu to an untimely end? There must be more here than meets the eye. Duhm thought he meant that he is so important a person that he stands under the very gaze of God. Pope suggests that he thinks that in the dialogues the friends have been too polite to Job. Perhaps (following a hint from Andersen) it is the Leveler in Elihu that is speaking, and what he is insisting is that he will speak courageously, without deference to the snobbery of age or class (it is unfair to say with Habel that this contradicts his attitude of deference to the aged in v 6, for there he reports that attitude precisely as something he has given up). If he then invokes divine wrath against any who are cowed by social distinctions, perhaps he is more of a radical than we think (cf. Alonso Schökel on v 8). He needs to be, of course, if he is oppressed by the presumption that the opinions of old men carry more weight.

We cannot tell at this point whom Elihu has most in his sights, whether Job or the friends. It is too sharp to say with Hitzig that here Elihu "intimates his intention of being rude to Job."

We might have hoped at this point that the elaborate exordium of Elihu had drawn to a close. But it is not to be, for the first seven verses of the next chapter contain a supplementary exordium addressed more explicitly to Job himself.

33:1–7 Elihu has in all probability turned from the friends at 32:15 and begun to address himself to Job. So it would perhaps have been better to have begun chap. 33 with that verse. At any rate, by the time we reach the present verse, there can be no doubt that Elihu's attention is toward Job. Here he embarks on a rather elaborated proem, inviting Job to listen to him (vv 1–3) and to respond if he can. He does his best to assure Job that he speaks to him on equal terms and that Job need have no fear of what he is about to say (vv 6–7, and perhaps this is also the import of v 4).

1 Only Elihu of all the friends actually uses Job's name (also at 33:31; 37:14; cf. also on 32:12). We can hardly tell whether it signifies some closer or familial relation in which Elihu stands to Job (so Fohrer). Pope speculates that it is in the nature of Elihu's temperament that he expresses greater familiarity with Job in his use of his name. Gordis comments: "Feeling insecure, [Elihu] seeks to hold Job's attention by calling him by name." Others think that the use of the simple name, without for example mentioning the father's name, is impolite or else the sign of the lower status of the one addressed; cf. 1 Sam 1:8; 17:55; 22:16; 2 Sam 9:6; 2 Kgs 2:4; 5:25; 9:22, and I. Lande, *Formelhafte Wendungen der Umgangssprache im Alten Testament* (Leiden: Brill, 1949) 28. But the evidence is very complicated (see further, D. J. A. Clines, "X, X *ben* Y, *ben* Y: Personal Names in Hebrew Narrative Style," *VT* 22 [1972] 266–87 [273–74]; reprinted in *On the Way to the Postmodern: Old Testament Essays, 1967–1998,* JSOTSup 292–93 [Sheffield: Sheffield Academic Press, 1998] 1:240–62 [257–59]). Hartley suggests that in calling Job by his simple name Elihu is being as good as his word in the previous two verses (32:21–22), where he has promised not to use any flattering titles. What would they be? Could they be something as straightforward as "my lord"?

2 If we take this verse literally, Elihu is inviting Job to listen to his speech because he has now opened his mouth and "his tongue is already in motion" (Delitzsch)—which would be a bit of a waste if words were not to proceed from the mouth and a listener to those words were not to be available. That would indeed be a droll line of reasoning, but it is more probable that these are simply conventional lines of introduction to a speech, more in the nature of phatic communion than of actual communication (cf., e.g., Ps 78:2; Prov 8:6–8). We are dealing here not with a "formal summons to appear in court for a public trial"

(Habel) but with a rather old-fashioned rhetoric signifying a "grave and deliberate utterance" (Cox); for the phrase "open the mouth" (פתח פה), cf. Isa 53:7; Pss 51:15 (17); 78:2; Job 3;1; Dan 10:16.

Commentators quickly lose patience with Elihu. Bickell deletes the verse as "too prosaic even for Elihu." Dhorme, allowing the authenticity of the verse, can only explain that the banality of it must have been intended by the author as signaling a man who talks for the sake of talking; he is *un phraseur intarissible,* a tireless speechmaker, while Rowley speaks of his "interminable prolixity." De Wilde calls the verse the height of banality. There is no denying that lines like this are not very interesting, but even much finer Hebrew poetry can contain ballast lines, especially in a proem like this (cf. Deut 32:1–2; Ps 49:2–5).

For some a verse like this is further evidence, if such were needed, that the Elihu speeches are from a different, and inferior, poet than those of the rest of the book. "It would show a strange lack of literary tact to credit the great genius to whom we owe the poem with such bathos as this," remarks Peake. Duhm outdoes himself in irony over this verse. "How beautiful is that phrase, 'tongue in palate,'" he writes, "and what particular effect that 'behold' has, especially if accompanied by an appropriate gesture." But it is not for a commentator who writes a million words about the thousand verses of the book to take Elihu to task for prolixity.

3 In saying that his words are sincere (ברור), Elihu can hardly be taking a sideswipe at Job, implying that he by contrast has spoken out of a sinful heart (as Fohrer suggests). It is rather that his words are neither insincerely flattering (cf. 32:21) nor malicious. Elihu aims not at Job's defeat (though he does want to correct him) but only at establishing the truth about the meaning of Job's afflictions. If anything, Elihu is contrasting his intentions of honesty and sincerity with that of the three friends, whose speeches Job had found insincere and false (e.g., 6:25; 13:7–10; 16:2–5; 19:2–5; 21:27, 34).

Habel has pointed out the many coincidences of language between Elihu's speech here and that of Wisdom in Prov 8:6–8: שמע "hear," דבר "speak," and פתח פה "open mouth" here and פתח שפה "open lips" in Proverbs; חך "palate" and אמרי "my words" here and אמרי־פי "words of my mouth" in Proverbs; ישר "uprightness" here and מישרים "right things" and צדק "rightness" in Proverbs. We should not conclude that Elihu therefore "claims to exemplify the sincerity and candor characteristic of Lady Wisdom in her public role," and far less that as a spokesman for Wisdom Elihu "claims the right to adjudicate the trial of Job" (Habel), but simply that Elihu is drawing upon a repertory of public speech, equally at home in the lawcourt, the wisdom school, and the council of elders.

4 Why is this verse here? If it has been accidentally misplaced (from following v 5, for example; see *Note* 33:4.a), it could be connected with either what precedes or what follows. It could be that Elihu is promising to speak sincerely (v 3) because he intends to act responsibly as befits a creature of God; or it could be that because he is no more than a mortal fashioned by God, he can challenge Job to a contest of equals (v 5). In the latter case this verse will have the same effect as v 6: to assure Job that he will be put at no unfair disadvantage in Elihu's forthcoming speech.

If the verse is in its right position, it is the first substantive remark that Elihu actually makes after all the introductory matter. But it can hardly be the essence of his speech, and we would need to regard it as an anticipation of his statement in v 6 that he regards himself, despite his desire to confront Job in argumentation, as laying claim to no authority over him and as being no more than a fellow creature with Job.

It is commonly said that Elihu, in referring to the spirit of God and the breath of the Almighty, is casting himself as one of the wise. Thus Strahan: "Elihu's prolix and somewhat turgid exordium amounts to a claim of inspiration. It is his sense of having received the breath of the Almighty . . . that constrains him to break his silence,—that changes his modest deference to the authority of age and experience into indifference to human opinions,—that makes him positive and dogmatic, ready to set all parties right, impetuous, self-confident, eloquent." And Davidson: "Elihu feels that this spirit of God is within him in a powerful degree and gives him a higher wisdom than ordinary" (similarly Rowley, Pope). But this does not seem to be correct: whether or not there is a direct reference to the narrative of Gen 2:7, Elihu's words refer unambiguously to the moment of creation (as also Peake, de Wilde), when the divine life force was imparted to all humans without differentiation. On the "breath" (נשׁמה) of the Almighty, see *Comment* on 32:8.

5 Elihu challenges Job to prepare for debate. The language is of course that of conflict, as argument must necessarily be. Job is called upon to "draw up" or "marshal" (ערך) his arguments as one draws up warriors in line of battle (as at 1 Sam 17:8; 2 Sam 10:8) and to "take his stand" (יצב hithp) as soldiers do in battle array (1 Sam 17:16; Jer 46:4). This could be thought very hostile language, as if a fight to the death is about to ensue. Or one could detect a sharp sarcastic edge; the phrase "if you can" might imply "but of course you cannot," as Duhm thought. Or it could be a legal summons to present a case before an assembled court (Habel). But it is more likely that all we have here is the rather tame and conventional language for an invitation to debate.

6–7 It is important to Elihu to establish a commonality with Job. In 32:8 he had used the common creation of humankind as his justification for entering the conversation. If all humans have a share in the divine breath, all have some kind of wisdom, some entitlement to participate in dialogue and debate, he said. Here he is aligning himself with Job as a fellow human being, both equally created by the one God. Though there is a contention between them, they are essentially on the same side, both on the same footing.

In saying "no fear of me should terrify you," Elihu is not pretentiously, patronizingly (Habel), or arrogantly (Hesse) implying that Job, his elder and better, might have good cause to fear him. At the beginning of his speech, Elihu had been apologizing (in whatever spirit) for intervening in the debate at all, and that attitude of deference is still in evidence here. It is possible that, if he had judged Job to be a great sinner fully deserving of God's wrath against him, he might have felt himself so superior to Job that he could offer him a patronizing reassurance that his "pressure" would not be heavy upon him. But it seems that Elihu makes no such categorical judgment against Job (despite 36:17–21). Though he thinks Job has drawn the wrong inferences from his sufferings, and though he is determined to set Job's thinking straight, he is not against Job himself, and his avowed interest is to "justify" Job (v 32), that is, to get him to a position where Job can be in the right again.

Elihu, it seems, in stressing his common creatureliness with Job and in saying that Job has no cause for alarm is making allusion to Job's fear in 9:34 and 13:21. There Job had said that if he were to come into legal confrontation with *God* he would not get a fair hearing for he would be "terrified" (בעת, as here) by his presence. Elihu means precisely to say that, unlike the God whom Job envisions, he does not intend to be patronizing or superior or threatening to Job; even though he believes passionately in the value of what he has to say and in his right to say it, he does not lay claim to more than human wisdom, and he certainly has no supernatural authority (for אימה as the divine terror, cf. Exod 15:16; 23:27).

We have only to assume that Elihu finds it awkward to put himself forward in the conversation, and that his wordiness is a sign of his hesitation, and his words to Job here become unexceptionable. He wants to have a good argument with Job, inviting him to deploy all his arguments and strengthen all his defenses (v 5), but in the end it can only be an intellectual debate. He has no rights over Job. Nothing he can say will deflect God's attention from Job, none of his arguments will settle matters between Job and God. The prospect of debate with a fellow creature can be no threat to a Job (v 7). Elihu, in other words, apologizes for himself by calling himself harmless. There is no "irony" here (against Dhorme, Fohrer, Pope). (Good has this interesting translation, "After all, fright of me does not terrify you, and my pressure on you is not heavy"—as if Elihu were reminding Job that in fact Job does not fear anything from Elihu.)

Elihu uses an expressive word for the creation of humans from clay. They have been "pinched off" (קרץ) from a lump of clay, as a potter nips off with the fingers the piece of clay to be worked into a pot or plate. The verb is elsewhere used in Prov 16:30 of pursing the lips and in Prov 6:13; 10:10; Ps 35:19 of winking the eyes, and, more to the point, in Mishnaic Hebrew of the baker nipping off dough (*m. Kelim* 15:2). The same image appears famously in the Gilgamesh Epic when the female creator deity Aruru "nipped off clay" to create Enkidu—interestingly enough, in order that he should be the equal of Gilgamesh (*Gilgamesh* 1.2.34; *ANET,* 74a). On the language of kneading humankind from clay, see further J. C. Greenfield, "The Root 'GBL' in Mishnaic Hebrew and in the Hymnic Literature from Qumran," *RevQ* 2 (1960) 155–62. On the idea of "clay" (חמר) as the native substance of humanity, see on 4:19; 10:9. There does not seem to be a direct allusion to the creation of Adam out of the mud of the earth in Gen 2:7 (the term חמר "clay" is not used in the creation narrative).

It is far fetched to see here criticism of the poet of the original book of Job for introducing the divine speeches (cf. Rowley), as if the author of the Elihu speeches "felt that Job's enigma could be solved without the theophany" (Strahan; similarly Peake).

8–33 Elihu sets about his task in polite (Duhm) but businesslike fashion. He is going to state Job's position as he understands it, and then offer his arguments against it. Of course, this is poetry, and this is rhetoric, so nothing will be precise or strictly logical or sequential enough to satisfy a legalist.

According to Elihu, Job's position is that (1) he is faultless (v 9), and that (2) God's afflictions of him are therefore expressions of groundless hatred and enmity (vv 10–11), and that (3) God refuses to answer his complaints of unjust treatment (v 13). Any response Elihu makes to the first two points are made very indirectly; his attention is concentrated on the third issue. Even here his reply is not a direct one, for he responds to Job's complaint that God does not answer *him* by showing how God does indeed speak to humans generally.

Elihu's argument will be that God has various ways of speaking to humans (and, implicitly, that therefore it is wrong to accuse him of not responding). One such mode is the dream, when God puts warnings into human minds (vv 15–17), and another is suffering (vv 19–28), which can be accepted as sent from God to bring people to their senses, acknowledging their sin. By either means, God's intention is not to punish but to rescue humans from their sin.

8 "At last Elihu gets down to his self-appointed and much advertised task. He is going to take Job's arguments to pieces" (Rowley). This is the first of Elihu's several quotations of Job's arguments, whether verbatim or more general; others are at 34:5–6, 9; 35:2–3. Free and summary quotation, rather than exact citation, is the accepted norm in the OT; we should not often conclude that a variation in wording is intentional. Fedrizzi suggests that we consider in this light Gen 2:17 and 3:3, 18:12 and 18:13.

9 Elihu is not quoting Job directly here but representing his position on the issue of his innocence. Job's claims in 9:21; 10:7; 13:18; 16:17; 23:7, 10–12; 27:4–6; and chap. 31 as a whole are the substance of this claim.

It seems incorrect to accuse Elihu of misrepresenting Job (as Driver–Gray, Rowley, Gordis, Pope, Andersen, and de Wilde claim)—even marginally. Hartley, for example, says, "Elihu has chosen words that have Job claim moral perfection whereas Job has asserted that he is innocent or blameless." Though Job has never protested his innocence in exactly the words Elihu is using, there is no difference between his own claims and Elihu's account of them, and he would not dissent from this statement of his attitude. Throughout his speeches he has always claimed to be without fault (which is no more than the narrator of the prologue has assured us is the case in 1:1). So it is not true that "Job has made frequent references to his errors and transgressions" (Gordis). For all the passages that are thought to show this are to be explained differently. In 7:21 "my sin" means "my sin as you reckon it." In 10:6 "my sin" means "some supposed sin in me." In 19:4 in referring to "my error" Job is arguing that his punishment is out of all proportion to "any error I can possibly have committed." In 13:26 he does indeed refer to the "sins of my youth," but he means by that sins or faults for which he is not morally responsible since he does not think he should be punished for them.

There are four terms here for the guiltlessness of Job, corresponding rhetorically to the fourfold accusation of God by Job in vv 10–11 (Habel). There is a pair of adjectives, "pure" (זך) and "innocent" (חף), and there is a pair of phrases, "without sin" (בלי פשע) and "without guilt" (לא עון לי).

"Pure" (זך, with its associated verbs זכה and זכך) or "clean" is used several times in the book, always in a moral sense (except 9:30, of hands washed clean in soap and lye). Job has said his prayer is clean in 16:17. In 11:4 Zophar has said that Job thinks his way of life is pure, but in this he is wrong. In 8:6 Bildad encouraged Job to be "pure and upright," which implies that he thinks such a state is possible for a human. On the other hand, Eliphaz has denied in 15:14 that any human could be "clean," saying that the heavens themselves are not "clean" in God's sight (v 15). And in 25:5 Bildad has supported him, saying that the stars are not "clean" in God's sight. It does not appear that Elihu is here denying Job's claim to be "pure."

The term "innocent" (חַף) occurs only here in the Hebrew Bible. The term for "sin" (פשׁע) has been used several times by Job for sin he has *not* committed or sin he is alleged to have committed (7:21; 13:23; 14:17; 31:33). Apart from Bildad's reference to the presumed sin of Job's children (8:4), all the other uses of the word are in the mouth of Elihu (34:6, again of Job's claim to innocence; 34:37, the presumption Elihu attributes to the "wise" that Job adds rebellion to his "sin"; 35:6, a hypothetical "sin" of Job; and, most interestingly, 36:9, where God informs the *righteous* of their "sin"). It is a similar pattern with "iniquity" (עון): mostly it occurs in Job's own references to his alleged sins (7:21; 10:6, 14; 13:23, 26; 14:17; 31:33), in 11:6 of Zophar's charge of iniquity against Job, and in 15:5 and 22:5 of Eliphaz's (the only other uses are in 19:29; 20:27; 31:11, 28).

Habel observes that Elihu's synopsis of Job's claims to innocence "virtually ignores Job's complex and detailed oath of clearance (ch. 31) and reduces Job's position to the blunt assertion that Job claims to be innocent of any sin at all." It is indeed interesting that Elihu, who has listened carefully to Job's speeches, and who cites and alludes to him throughout his own, shows no knowledge of Job's final speech in chaps. 29–31. This fact is another little argument in favor of seeing the Elihu speeches as having their original place after the friends had finished theirs—that is, at the end of chap. 27—and before Job concludes the dialogues with his own final speech.

10–11 Job's complaint is that his sufferings have no cause in himself but result from a studied hostility on God's part. Though he is without fault, God treats him as his enemy! The man Job (אִיּוֹב *ʾiyyôb*) has become an enemy (אוֹיֵב *ʾôyēb*) to God. Though we should not turn the language of poetry into a legal document, it seems that, according to Elihu, Job has been making a fourfold accusation against God. (1) God finds pretexts against him, i.e., unreasonable grounds for assaulting him. He has been framed. (2) He treats him as an enemy, not as a creature, still less as a pious man. (3) He puts Job's feet in the stocks, i.e., limits his freedom of movement, constrains him to suffer and to be humiliated. (4) God spies on all his doings, so that Job feels oppressed and perpetually under scrutiny.

10 In the first line, Elihu summarizes Job's attitude as expressed in 9:17; 10:13–14, for example, that God finds fault with him without cause. In the second line, Elihu quotes Job exactly. At 13:24 Job had said to God, "Why do you count me your enemy?" and at 19:11 he had complained, "He counts me his enemy" (cf. also 30:21). At several other places also Job has depicted the hostility of God to him, assailing him as if he were a wild beast (perhaps 6:4), a target (7:20; 16:12), a chaos monster (7:12), an enemy warrior (16:13–14; 19:11–12), or an opponent in wrestling (30:21–22).

11 The verse is an exact quotation of 13:27, with only a couple of changes in the number of the persons: "he sets" (ישׂם) here for "you set" (תשׂם) there, and "he keeps" (ישמר) here for "and you keep" (ותשמר) there (and 13:27 has an extra colon at the end). If Job's feet are in the stocks, however, he will not be walking on any paths that God can watch over; so perhaps the suggestion (see *Note* 33:11.c) that the word is סִיד "quicklime" rather than סַד "stocks" is to be accepted.

12 Why does Elihu want to remind Job that God is greater than humans, a very obvious fact that Job would be the first to agree with (cf. 9:1–13)? Some think it means that, since God is so much greater than humans, it makes no sense for Job to complain that God is not answering his charges; for God is not accountable to humans, he "does not fit man's measure" (JB), he "cannot be expected to vindicate His ways to man" (Gibson). Others think that Elihu means that "God is above the petty feelings that Job has attributed to him" in vv 10–11 (Rowley; similarly Duhm "above all arbitrary, unreasoning hostility"; so too Davidson). It is less likely that he means that, because God is more powerful than humans, they cannot successfully argue with him (as Pope). Elihu is very fond of the thought that God is greater than humans (cf. also 36:5, 26)—his God is always a God of power (Fedrizzi)—and for him this is an explanation of practically everything.

Habel takes an independent line in understanding "God is greater than humans" as a quotation by Elihu of Job's words. That is to say, if Job himself acknowledges that God is so great, why does he bring a suit against him, since he knows that God answers none of his charges? The logic in this interpretation is a little complex, in that there are two reasons why Job should not be bringing a complaint against God: the facts that he is great and that he does not answer. It is not clear how the two reasons are related. It would be simpler to think that God's greatness (v 12b) is connected with Job's earlier complaint of being unjustly made his enemy (vv 10–11), and that his refusing to answer (v 13b) is not a reason why Job should not bring a complaint, but rather the substance of the complaint itself.

13 Why do you have a grievance against God that he does not answer? says Elihu, "still preserving his accent of surprise" (Cox). It all depends on what you mean by "answer." God is by no means silent: he does speak to humans, in more than one way (v 14).

Less probable is the interpretation of Dhorme: since God is greater than humans, why has Job made it a matter of complaint that God does not reply to all the words of humans? He speaks once (v 14) and that is enough (Dhorme).

Job's complaint that God does not answer him has been rehearsed in 9:16; 19:7; 30:20.

14 God has various modes of communication with human beings: he can speak "in one way" (באחת) or "in another way" (בשתים) or (implicitly) in yet other ways. The two examples that Elihu will cite (and he does not mean that they are God's only means of addressing humans) are dreams (vv 15–18) and suffering (vv 19–28). (Habel finds a third means of communication in cultic experience [vv 23–28], and Good both a third and a fourth means of communication in angels [vv 23–24] and through prayer [vv 25–29]; but the whole unit of vv 19–28 is so closely bound together that it is impossible to find more than one kind of communication here.) It is not that God speaks "once" and then "twice" (as KJV, NEB, NAB) or "time and time again" (Gordis), or that "twice" signifies the doubling of a dream that is proof of divine origin according to Gen 41:32 (Andersen); see *Note* 33:14.a. There might be more to be said for the interpretation that God speaks in one way, then, if humans do not hear the message, he uses another form of communication (so Peake; cf. Moffatt "God has one mode of speech; yes and if man heeds it not, another").

Because these are indirect revelations, humans do not necessarily recognize God's voice in them: "mortals may not perceive him." But if they do not, that is their fault, not God's.

15–18 Elihu's point is that God uses dreams in order to speak to humans. The kind of message he conveys through the medium of dreams is a warning, to prevent a person continuing in a wrong course of action. So God's intention is salvific: if wrongdoing leads to premature death, restraining a person from sin is equivalent to holding them back from falling into Sheol.

And this disquisition on dreams is meant to answer Job's complaint that God will not answer him: God does speak to humans, responds Elihu, even if they do not always recognize it (v 14b). Nonetheless, it does not really address Job's complaint, since he is troubled not about whether God engages in communication with humans in general but about why God refuses to answer his own particular charge of injustice. Auditions in dreams are not the kind of communication Job has been seeking (Andersen), but some kind of public announcement of his innocence, some demonstrable restoration of his good name.

It is interesting that for Elihu divinely sent dreams do not seem to be an extraordinary occurrence, as Eliphaz had made out, with all his rhetoric about his waking vision in 4:12–21. For Elihu, the dreams that we all have may well be divine revelation, if only we would "perceive" them (v 14). It does not occur to Elihu that these indirect forms of divine communication that he so highly thinks of are indeed rather inefficient. If it is possible for humans not to recognize (v 14b) in their nightmares or in their sufferings the sound of a divine message trying to get through to them, perhaps a deity who really cared about making himself plain to his creatures could conceive of another vehicle for his communications.

15 Elihu quotes Eliphaz in 4:13 almost verbatim. In the so-called *Babylonian Job,* known from its first words as *Ludlul Bēl Nēmeqi,* the sufferer likewise discerns in his dreams a message of restoration to health (III.1–53; *ANET,* 598b–99a).

16 Job already has some experience of God's use of dreams. He has been terrified by dreams sent from God and frightened by visions (7:14). He thought of these dreams as part of his torture by a monster god, but Elihu wants him to believe that God has sent them to thwart some evil enterprise he is engaged in, to prune his pride, or to warn him against some future transgression (it is not clear whether the sin from which dreams hinder one are actual rather than potential, as Strahan suggests). When he wakes up screaming in the night, he should be glad to know that the god behind his nightmares is not some distant silent deity but the Great Communicator who is ever near at hand. Job, for his part, will know all about that; has he not given us the classic depiction of the god who is too close for comfort in 7:16–20?

The term "warning" (מוסר) in v 16—if that is indeed the correct reading and the correct rendering—suggests that it is not punishment that is the function of the dreams. They may be "terrifying" (if we revocalize the verb in the second line; see *Note* 33:16.c), but that is of the nature of apparitions and nocturnal auditions, perhaps because their recipients are aware of their supernatural dimension; that is not their purpose, however.

For revelations of God (or his angel) in dreams, cf. Gen 20:3, 6; 28:11–15; 31:11, 24; 41:25–32; 46:2–4; Num 12:6; 1 Kgs 3:5. See *Comment* on 4:13, and on the present passage cf. E. L. Ehrlich, *Der Traum im Alten Testament,* BZAW 73 (Berlin: Töpelmann, 1953) 146–48. To "uncover the ears" (גלה אזן) is a common phrase (e.g., 1 Sam 9:15; Ruth 4:4) for "inform" (it is going too far to say that it always signifies vital information, as Pope, or information that closely concerns the hearer, as Driver–Gray). In Job it occurs only in the speeches of Elihu (here and at 36:10, 15); an alternative idiom is to "open the ears."

17 God's purpose in sending dreams is that he should divert (סור hiph "turn aside") humans from their deeds or, perhaps, that humans should divert themselves from their deeds. Unless the text has been corrupted (see *Note* 33:17.d), it is interesting that it speaks of diverting humans not from their *sin,* but from their "deed" or "action" (מעשׂה), a neutral term. Hartley infers that the deed is not in itself a sin, but that "the potential sin for the doer resides in his becoming proud of his accomplishments."

Gordis observes that the singling out of "pride" (גוה) as "a surrogate for generic 'evil'" is significant, that pride being hybris, "the arrogance to which men, particularly good men, are prone." And Terrien writes that "hybris is the crime of the man who is morally pure." But whether Elihu thinks that hybris is the sin that Job, in his titanic resistance to God, is especially drawn to (so Habel) is hard to tell—though obviously he does feel it needful to remind Job from time to time that God is greater than humans (v 12; 36:5, 26), and that it is pride that prevents the oppressed from directing their cries to God (35:12). It is more likely that "pride" serves here merely as one example of a sin that can be corrected through a dream audition.

"Pride" (גוה, more usually גאוה or גאון) is not necessarily a fault; it is attributed to God (Deut 33:26; Ps 68:34 [35]), the produce of the land is the pride of future Israelites (Isa 4:2), and Jerusalem is an eternal source of pride (Isa 60:15), while wild animals are called "sons of pride" (שׁחץ) in Job 28:8. Though in the OT pride is sometimes clearly enough an internal disposition (as Prov 29:23, where it is contrasted with humility; Isa 9:8, parallel with גדל לבב "greatness, stubbornness, of heart"), as it is with us, it seems also to be a course of conduct, as when the wicked "in their pride" persecute the poor (Ps 10:2), and when it is parallel to "violence" (חמס, Ps 73:6). See further, H.-P. Stähli, *TLOT,* 1:285–87; D. Kellermann, *TDOT,* 2:344–50; J. A. Wharton, *IDB,* 3:876; and on the word field, P. Humbert, "Demesure et chute dans l'Ancien Testament," in *Maqqél shâqédh, La branche d'amandier: Hommage à Wilhelm Vischer* (Montpellier: Causse, Graille, Castelnau, 1960) 62–82. It is hard to see what kind of a dream would restrain a person from pride as an internal disposition or self-estimation, but perhaps easier to think of some nightmare frightening a person off committing an act of violence or arrogance against another.

It is unsurprisingly "men" (גבר), males, who exhibit pride in ancient Israelite culture. Though Elihu and his poet are no doubt not intending to confine pride-destroying dreams to males, they choose a word that refers to men as distinct from women and children (cf. on 3:3). Good thinks of an arrogant deed of a "hero," but the inclusive-language version NRSV removes the reference to males altogether. The term has occurred previously at 3:3, 23; 4:17; 10:5; 14:10, 14; 16:21; 22:2—mostly as a general term for humans (3:3; 16:21 are more specifically to do with males), and sometimes, as here, the demands of parallelism and of variety in vocabulary (we have had אנשׁים "men" in v 16 and אדם "humans" in v 17a) may have influenced the choice of the term. All the same, the juxtaposition is telling.

18 Nightmares may be very unpleasant, but God has to be cruel to be kind. His gracious intention is to prevent a person from incurring a fatal penalty for some dreadful sin. If those into whose ears these nocturnal warnings are poured will realize their significance, they will abandon their evil ways and so be "spared" or "restrained" (חשׂך, as in 7:11; 16:5, 6; 21:30; 30:10) from the Pit (שׁחת), that is, delivered from descending into the underworld (on the Pit, see on 17:14). Elihu perhaps has in mind not the dyed-in-the-wool villains of whom the other friends had spoken but basically good people who run a risk of sin and can be restrained from it by a quiet word in the ear, so to speak. In 36:7–11 he will speak in similar fashion of the righteous who are temporarily transgressing and behaving arrogantly; God opens their ears to instruction, and if they respond they complete their days in prosperity.

It is common now to understand שׁלח (translated in the older versions as "sword" or "weapon") as the subterranean canal, like the river Styx of the Greeks and the river Ḫubur in Mesopotamian mythology, which the dead must cross in order to reach Sheol. Thus NEB has "the river of death," NRSV "the River" (so M. Tsevat, "The Canaanite God *Šälaḥ*," *VT* 4 [1954] 41–49 [43]; Gordis, Pope, Good). Less probably, this waterway may be thought of as a vertical canal down which the dead pass on their way to the underworld (Dhorme). See also O. Loretz, "Der Gott *šlḥ*, *he. šlḥ* I und *šlḥ* II," *UF* 7 (1975) 584–85; B. Becking, *DDD*, 762–63; and Grabbe, 103–4. It is not a term for the underworld as such (as S. Rin, "Ugaritic-Old Testament Affinities," *BZ* 7 [1963] 22–33 [25]). This would be the only place in the OT where such an underworld river is alluded to, but in the *Babylonian Theodicy* there is similar language: "Our fathers so indeed give up and go the way of death. It is an old saying that they cross the river Hubur" (lines 16–17; *ANET,* 602a). And Habel suggests that the titles Šaḥat and Šelaḥ, Pit and Channel, may be reminiscent of the names of the Canaanite deities Šaḥar and Šalim, Dusk and Dawn.

Keeping alive is the ultimate good in Elihu's book: not to descend to the Pit is what humans most desire, if we are to believe his reiterated references to it (vv 18, 22, 24, 28, 30), and to hold humans back from the Pit is what God himself spends his energies upon. For Job, however, though Elihu will never understand this, it is all one whether he lives or dies (much of the time in fact he thinks death is a preferable state to life [3:20–21; 6:8–9]). The one thing he wants is justice, whether in this life or after he is dead (16:18; 19:25–26).

19–28 God's second language (Alonso Schökel) is suffering. It is a more drastic mode of divine speech, for it can lead to the brink of death or beyond. Whether or not it is designed as a second string to God's bow, to be called upon if the first method of communication fails (as Peake, Strahan), is hard to tell. (Terrien insists that the suffering itself is not an instrument of divine revelation, but it prepares a person who is in the grip of his own hybris to receive such a revelation; but the distinction is difficult to accept.)

This is a very fluent section of Elihu's speech, and its material is by no means hackneyed. But its import is harder to discern than at first appears. For as we begin the strophe, we believe we are going to hear about a mode of God's communication. But when we come to the end, we feel we have been hearing more about God's saving care, since the note on which it concludes is not that God has spoken to the sufferer but that God has brought the sufferer back from the edge of death. This impression is reinforced by the following summary sentences (vv 29–30), which say that God "does all these things" in order to "bring a person back from the Pit." Certainly the stress in Elihu's presentation of God lies on his beneficence. For Elihu, God is not the adversary of humans, not the persecutor of Job, not even primarily a judge of human deeds—but a savior. But he seems to have wandered somewhat from his main point: how God communicates with humans.

Elihu's understanding of suffering as divine education is not dissimilar from that of Eliphaz as he develops it in 5:17–26. There Eliphaz stresses that the same God who "reproves" with afflictions is the one who restores: "he may smite, but his hands heal" (5:18). Here, in a slightly different vein, it appears not just that the one who smites later heals but that he has healing as his purpose from the very beginning. This is a different view from that of most of the book, where the friends see suffering only as punishment—and Job too concurs with them, except that he believes that in his case it has been misdirected.

19 The illness that can fall on humans by way of divine enlightenment can be long and severe. The sufferer is obviously bedridden and experiences the pain as a conflict (ריב) in the bones, as if they were at war with one another.

In his depiction of suffering, Elihu is clearly drawing upon Job's own account of his afflictions. "No one can well doubt whence all these details were drawn who remembers how Job had sighed, 'I *waste* away!', 'My *limbs* are a shadow' . . . 'I *loathe* my life'" (Cox).

20 The implication seems to be that the sickness the person experiences upon their bed makes them feel nauseous, so that even the tastiest foods appear disgusting to them. But a strong connection between v 19 and v 20 may not be intended, for there are not so many illnesses that could be called "strife in the bones" that also induce nausea. For other depictions of loss of appetite, cf. Pss 102:4 (5); 107:18.

The phrase "food of desire" appears also in Dan 10:3, though the wording is different (לחם חמדות instead of מאכל תאוה).

21 As between v 20 and v 21, there does seem to be a clear connection: if the suffering person loses their appetite, they lose weight also. It may not be literally true that a sick person can lose all their flesh or that their bones can become visible, but for all practical purposes it is as if they had. The sufferer is not only deprived of pleasures, like tasty food (v 20), but in danger of losing grip on the fundamentals of existence.

The verb "waste away" (כלה) has already been used of the wicked (4:9), of days (7:6), of a cloud (7:9), of eyes (11:20; 17:5), and of the kidneys as signifying the inner being (19:27).

22 On the brink of the abyss, when the sufferer is almost in the grip of the angels (or demons) of death, the supernatural intervention takes place. Destroying angels are encountered elsewhere at 2 Sam 24:16 || 1 Chr 21:15; 2 Kgs 19:35; Ps 78:49; *T. Asher* 6, *b. Ketubot* 104a: "When a wicked man is destroyed, three bands of destroying angels meet him; one cries, No peace, saith God, for the wicked; another, Ye shall lie down in pain; and a third, Go down and lie with the uncircumcised." The demons of death are known by the same term in Mesopotamian texts as Akkadian *mušmīrûti*. The LXX saw the destroying angels also in v 23, and expanded the text: "Even if there should be a thousand messengers of death, not one of them shall wound him, if he should determine in his heart to turn to the Lord."

23–28 When the sick are at death's door, an angel may take up the cause of the sufferers and beg God to spare them from death. The sufferers would then be restored to their youthful health and strength, turn to God in prayer, and publicly acknowledge both their wrongdoing and their thankfulness for deliverance. It seems clear (as Duhm stresses) that those in view here are basically good people, not the thoroughly godless, who are presumably beyond redemption.

There is no agreement among commentators over the role of the angel. Some, understanding the term מליץ as "interpreter," think the angel is interpreting to the sufferer the meaning of his illness as a message from God. This view is supported by the rendering of v 23c as "to declare to man what is right for him" (as RSV), i.e., where his duty lies. Others, however, more convincingly, regard the angel as an advocate in heaven rather than a messenger on earth (so Habel), pointing to the clear role of the angel in v 24 as an intercessor with God on behalf of the sufferer, and render v 23c "to declare the man's uprightness" (as NJPS), i.e., to act as attorney for the defense. On the מליץ, see also M. A. Canney, "The Hebrew מֵלִיץ," *AJSL* 40 (1923–24) 135–37. Such an angel would be a counterpart to the Satan of the prologue, whose task is to act as the adversary of humans (cf. 1:6).

If this latter understanding is correct, the nice question arises whether Elihu thinks that what he describes is the situation of Job himself. It seems that it is, for three reasons: Elihu never brands Job an evil man; he uses language very reminiscent of Job's when he describes the illness of the sufferer (see on v 19); and he avers in v 32 that his desire is not to condemn but to "justify" Job.

23 Clearly, deliverance of the sick from death does not always take place. Not everyone has the good fortune to be the object of an angel's ministrations. Duhm thought Elihu's argument would not stand unless one could be sure that God always sent such an angel to communicate with humans; and so he changed the "if" (אם) to a "then" (אז). Needless to say, the emendation is arbitrary.

Not a word is said of the angel being dispatched by God; the text reads as if the kindly angel takes up the cause of the sufferer of his own accord. But in the context, where Elihu is arguing that God has more than one way of communicating with humans, we must be meant to assume that the angel is carrying out God's bidding.

We have heard of such beings previously at 5:1, where Eliphaz warned Job that there was no point in calling out to such a heavenly being for deliverance from the web of sin and punishment in which he was now caught. There too the angel was envisaged as a mediator between humans and God who would seek mercy from God for the suffering human. The angel is an "interpreter" or "mediator" (מליץ), apparently meaning that its function is to interpret "the foreign and unintelligible language (Gn. 42:23) of God's dealings with them" (Driver–Gray), to explain God's purpose in the infliction of suffering (Peake). We have had the term also in 16:20, of Job's cry as his "spokesman" in the heavenly court, and in Isa 43:27 it is used of the prophets as mediators between God and humans. The idea of mediation by an angel is compared by Pope with the Mesopotamian belief in personal gods who defended in the divine assembly the interests of individuals (S. N. Kramer, "Sumerian Theology and Ethics," *HTR* 49 [1956] 45–62 [59]).

On the protective angel, see Ps 34:6–7 (7–8); Dan 12:1; Tob 12:12, 15; 1 *En.* 9:3, 10; 15:2; *T. Dan* 6; *T. Asher* 6; *T. Joseph* 6; Matt 18:10; Acts 12:15.

Such an angel would be "one of the Thousand," apparently a term for the band of mediating angels (though Fohrer thinks all the angels would have the same function). In Dan 7:10 there are 10,000 times 10,000 (100 million) angels before the divine throne, but here the Thousand are more reminiscent of the Israelite military grouping by the same name (Num 10:4; Josh 22:14; 1 Sam 10:19; Mic 5:2 [1]). Alonso Schökel compares David's band of warriors known as the Thirty (2 Sam 23:23–24). In uncharacteristically sentimental vein Gray (in Driver–Gray) writes: "No sick man need fear that there are not enough angels deputed for this service to serve all needs." Hartley thinks of a single angel, like the angel of Yahweh in Gen 16:7–13 and Num 22:35, who is closely identified with Yahweh himself.

What is the function of this mediating angel? The Hebrew apparently has "to declare to a human his right." This could mean to declare God's righteousness to humans (REB "to expound God's righteousness to man"), but that would be a convoluted way of saying, To tell them that God is rightly disciplining them with suffering. Others think it means "what is right for him," i.e., for the sufferer (so, e.g., Driver–Gray, RV, RSV, NAB, NIV), where his duty lies (in a moral, not a cultic sense), but the moment of death seems a rather inappropriate time for lectures on one's duty. Yet others think it is "the right means to remedy the sin or sickness" (Andersen) or "the way that will lead him out of suffering and back to God" (Hartley), "the way of repentance and faith" (Delitzsch). Others again see the angel as defending the sufferer, and as declaring "in regard to the human" (לאדם) his righteousness, and thus pleading with God that he does not deserve to die (so NEB "to expound what he has done right," NJPS "to declare the man's uprightness" and Gordis's "to vouch for a man's uprightness"). NEB transfers to this point the seemingly similar line in v 26c, "and to secure for mortal man his due." But it is then a mystery how all this is a communication of God to humans. It is no improvement to follow the LXX, which had the angel declaring the sufferer's "blame."

It may be better to understand this clause as describing the usual function of the mediating angels, representing them as essentially conveying God's will to humans, like prophets. The angel would then be described as "one whose function is to inform humans of their duty." Like prophets also, they may sometimes represent humans before God (as do the angels in Tob 12:12, 15; *T. Dan* 6; *Jub.* 30:20; *1 En.* 15:2). Job himself will act later in the book as an intercessor for his friends (42:8, 10). See also S. Mowinckel, "Hiobs *gō'ēl* und Zeuge im Himmel," in *Von Alten Testament: Karl Marti zum siebsigsten Geburtstage gewidmet von Freunden, Fachgenossen und Schülern,* ed. K. Budde, BZAW 41 (Giessen: Töpelmann, 1925) 207–12; H. N. Richardson, "Some Notes on ליץ and Its Derivatives," *VT* 5 [1955] 163–79 [169]; W. A. Irwin, "Job's Redeemer," *JBL* 81 (1962) 217–29; R. S. Wallace, "Intercession," *ISBE,* 2:58–59; J. Behm, *TDNT,* 5:809–10.

This mediating angel is reminiscent of figures alluded to by Job in earlier chapters, but it is not the same. In 9:33 he had wished for a mediator (מוכיח, one who judges or reproves), who is either a negotiator between himself and God, or an arbitrator superior to them both. This is in a legal context where there is a dispute between two parties. In 16:20 his "spokesman" (מליץ, as here) has been his "cry" that now sounds in heaven on his behalf; there his personified appeal for justice played the role of an advocate for him. In 19:25 he affirmed his confidence in his "champion" (גאל) who would defend his case in a courtroom struggle between himself and God—and it seemed that the only champion Job could have would be his affirmation of innocence, the same entity as his spokesman in 16:20. Now Elihu has no interest in supporting Job's case against God; his notion of a mediator is not someone who will prove to God that Job is in the right, but someone who will prove to Job that God is in the right.

24 Apparently the angel has a choice about whether to be gracious or not; that is, the "if" clause is continued (RVmg, RSV, NEB; similarly JB, NIV). Less probably, this verse could be regarded as the consequence of the angel's taking up the cause of the human; we could translate "then he is gracious" (as KJV, NAB, Gordis). No doubt it is the angel who is gracious (as NEB, NAB, NIV) rather than God (NJPS); for to whom would God say (in the singular) "release him from going down to the pit"? Not to the angel (as Delitzsch), for this is an intercessory angel, not an angel of destruction.

The angel then addresses God, asking him to spare the human who is at the point of death. Less probably he addresses a particular angel of death (as Duhm, Peake, and Hartley think, as also Driver–Gray, comparing the dispute of the angel Michael with Satan over the body of Moses in Jude 9).

A ransom (כפר) is usually money paid to release a guilty person from punishment. Ransom money is paid by the guilty person in Exod 21:30; 30:12; Num 35:31–32; Prov 13:8; Job 36:18, or is paid for him in Job 6:23; Isa 43:3; Prov 21:18; Ps 49:7 (8). Obviously, there is no question of a money payment here, so what is the ransom? Peake thinks it is the suffering, Dhorme that it is suffering and repentance, de Wilde repentance and a vow, while Dillmann, Strahan, Kissane, Fohrer, Hesse, and Fedrizzi think it is the repentance alone. Habel is inclined to see it as "the pleading of the advocate and his willingness to stand surety for the sufferer based on his past record." Driver–Gray, however, rightly say that the "sentence implies that the sick man has confessed and repented" but not exactly that the ransom is the repentance. Hartley also resists the temptation to specify what the text does not; it is enough that the ransom "compensates the divine justice for that person's failures." Davidson too believes that "the words may mean nothing more than that God is pleased of His goodness to hold the sinner as ransomed."

What is striking is that repentance is not a precondition for deliverance. Although the sufferer has indeed sinned, and publicly acknowledges in v 27 that he has, it is not some confession of his that brings about the change in his fortunes, but entirely a heavenly act of pity (so too J. F. Ross, arguing that the entreaty and the confession are the consequence and not the cause of God's restoration ["Job 33:14–30: The Phenomenology of Lament," *JBL* 94 (1975) 38–46]). Many commentators indeed think that the protecting angel has been advising the sufferer to repent (so Fohrer, Hesse), but not a word is said of that. Peake too infers that the angel has been "finding the sufferer amenable to his instruction." But Terrien rightly recognizes that the sufferer's prayer (v 26) is not for deliverance, since that has already been granted, but an act of thanksgiving that is accompanied by joy. Especially those commentators who have been nurtured in the Christian tradition find it inconceivable that there could be restitution for sinners without a preceding repentance; but the prophets also not infrequently suggest that repentance (which is not a mental decision but a series of acts) is something that *follows* forgiveness.

So what is the ransom? It may be that there is nothing that can be strictly called a ransom at all, and that the term, like "redeem" in v 28 (and in v 24 if that is what the Hebrew has; see *Note* 33:24.c), is no more than a metaphor for deliverance. Thus "I have found a ransom" may be a poetical way of saying, "Deliver him; there is no good reason for him to die." In the same way, in 5:20 God will "redeem" (פדה) the righteous from death, but there is no question of any ransom money being paid (similarly Hos 13:14).

25 It makes some difference if we think that the angel's words continue in this verse, with his prayer to God that the sufferer be restored to health (as RSV "let his flesh become fresh with youth"), or if we have here a report that in such a case the sufferer will indeed be restored (thus NAB "Then his flesh shall become soft as a boy's"). The sequence of verbs ought to settle matters. It would seem illogical that the sufferers should first regain their vigor (v 25) and then later entreat God (v 26); so we should see the restoration to health here as the wish of the angel, not as a report of the restoration. It is God who has sent the illness, and we may presume that it is only he who can remove it.

Since this is a divine restoration, it goes well beyond what might have been expected. The sufferers may well have been content to regain their health, but God insists that they should regain the health and strength of their youth or, rather, that they should be even more vigorous than they were in youth (the sense of the comparative *min* in מנער). The language is reminiscent of the healing of Naaman, whose "flesh returned like the flesh of a little child" (נער קטן, 2 Kgs 5:14; cf. נֹעַר "childhood" here). On the idea of the vigor of youth, cf. Isa 40:31; Pss 103:5; 110:3; 144:12; Eccl 11:9.

26 The language is of a visit of the restored sufferer to a temple to make a thanksgiving offering. While it is of course possible for a Hebrew to pray to God anywhere, the combination of prayer, of being "accepted" (which would normally require a priestly oracle), of seeing the face of the deity, and of the cultic cry of triumph points clearly to a setting in a temple. That is to say, the picture is of a visit to a temple; but such an image may well of course be a metaphor in itself (similarly Fohrer). It is no objection to say that the book of Job is not set within Israel (as Rowley), since it is not necessarily an Israelite temple that is in view.

The term עתר "make supplication" occurs also at 22:27; while the term does not necessarily point to the cult, such is its natural home (as in 2 Sam 24:25; Ezra 8:23). There is little reason to agree that the word suggests an offering with incense (as Terrien, comparing Arabic *ʿiṯr*, "perfume" [Lane, 2078a]).

If God "accepts" (רצה) the worshiper, it usually means that a sacrifice has been offered and a priest has confirmed that the offering is acceptable; cf. 2 Sam 24:23; Isa 60:7; Jer 14:12; Ezek 20:40–41; 43:27; Hos 8:13.

To see the face (ראה פנים) of God is an unusual expression (Gen 33:10 is not really about God; Exod 33:20 says it is fatal; Ps 11:7 is open to other interpretations; Ps 17:15 is a metaphor). The normal idiom is more commonly "to appear before (the face of) God" (Exod 23:15; 34:20; Isa 1:12) or to "seek the face of God" (Ps 24:6; 1 Chr 16:11). See F. Nötscher, *"Das Angesicht Gottes schauen" nach biblischer und babylonischer Auffassung* (Würzburg: Becker, 1924) 63–76; A. R. Johnson, "Aspects of the Use of the Term פָּנִים in the Old Testament," in *Festschrift Otto Eissfeldt zum 60. Geburtstage 1. September 1947, dargebracht von Freunden und*

Verehrern, ed. J. Fück (Halle an der Saale: Niemeyer, 1947) 155ff. Seeing the face of a king signifies admission to his presence in order to find favor; cf. Gen 32:21; 44:23, 26; 2 Sam 3:13; 14:24, 28, 32. Seeing or being seen by God probably implies presenting a gift, whether vowed or freewill, since there is an injunction that one should not approach God empty handed (Exod 23:15; 34:20). It is possible that it is not a matter of the worshiper seeing the face of God or even being seen by God, but of God revealing or manifesting himself to him (taking וַיַּרְא as hiph, "and he reveals [his face]"), thus signifying his acceptance of the sufferer.

The cultic ambience of the verse is confirmed by the last word of the second line, "with a shout of joy" (תרועה), the cry that accompanied various ritual acts (cf. Pss 27:6, where "sacrifices of a shout" are mentioned; 33:3; 47:5 [6]; 107:22, where the cry is רנה); Duhm thought the term referred to cultic music. In 8:21, however, the shout of joy is not in a cultic context, and some think that it is just the emotion of joy that is intended (Dhorme, Rowley). See further, P. Humbert, *La "Terou'a": Analyse d'un rite biblique* (Neuchâtel: Secrétariat de l'Université, 1946).

God's response to the sufferers who pray to him is to restore them to their former righteousness. Though the Hebrew has some difficulties, and many want to emend the text (e.g., RSV "he recounts to men his salvation"), what we probably have here is an anticipation of Job's own restoration in chap. 42. With the acceptance of his sacrifice (in Job's case, of his prayer, 42:8, 10), he is publicly declared to enjoy God's favor, and so has his state of righteousness restored to him. "All suspicion of wrongdoing that has been raised against him during his affliction fades into the dusk" (Hartley).

27 The public setting of this scene is evident here too, where the restored sufferer "sings" to others (אנשים "people"), making public confession of his sin and a public thanksgiving for God's graciousness. It is all very like the scene in Ps 40:9–10 (10–11), where the psalmist "announces" (בשר, as here if one emendation is followed) God's "deliverance" (צדק and צדקה, like צדקה in v 26) in the "great assembly," or like Ps 22:21–25 (22–26), where the erstwhile sufferer praises God in the midst of the congregation.

We can take the term "sing" (שיר) quite literally. Even if the restored worshiper does not personally sing a psalm of thanksgiving such as we have in the Psalter, but engages a priest to perform the song for him, it is plainly some such song as we find, for example, in Pss 30, 40, 92, 116. What follows in the present verse is a compressed example of such a thanksgiving, with the elements of confession, salvation, and proclamation.

The sufferers' confession is that they "perverted" (עוה) what was right (cf. Jer 3:21; and Prov 10:9, Mic 3:9, and Isa 59:8, where the verb is the synonym עקש). In saying that there was no profit in it for them (לא־שוה לי) they are making a understatement; they mean that it was nothing but loss. Because of their wrongdoing, they suffered terrible pain and came near to losing their lives. Such a rendering is more acceptable than the usual one, that their wrongdoing was not requited to them (see *Note* 33:27.e). Quite apart from the difficulty with the Hebrew, it does not seem to be true that the suffering was not a requital for the sin; and in any case it is strange to find one of Job's friends urging the claims of a theology in which exact retribution is not central.

There is an apparent contradiction between the sufferers' confession that they have sinned and perverted the right (ישר) and the mediating angel's defense of their "uprightness" (ישר) before God (v 23c). Clearly the angel is pleading that the general good character of the sufferers be allowed to weigh more heavily than the act of transgression that the sufferers are now confessing. Of course, if Elihu thinks he is going to get Job to confess to anything, he is much mistaken. But his message to Job must be that he should take heart from the possibility that some heavenly being will adopt his cause. In so saying, we observe, Elihu directly contradicts the view of Eliphaz that there is none among the heavenly beings to whom Job may call for release from the nexus of sin and punishment in which he is now caught (5:1).

28 It is God who is now the subject, of course, of the act of redemption (Dhorme); the angel has been only a mediator. Strictly speaking, a redemption requires a price; but, just as in v 24 with the ransom, the language of ransom and redemption may be purely metaphorical, and equivalent to "deliverance." It is hard to believe that we should render, with NEB, "then he saves himself." Though the Hebrew is capable of that meaning, it does not fit with Elihu's idea of divine communication with humans.

To "see the light" (ראה אור) is to be alive (cf. Isa 9:1 [2]; 53:11 [emended]; Pss 36:9 [10]; 49:20; Job 3:16); here some think (e.g., Driver–Gray) that the slightly different idiom ראה באור "to look upon the light" means to behold it with joy; ראה ב has such a sense in Pss 27:13; 37:34; 54:7 (9); 59:10 (11); 106:5; 112:8; 118:7 (though it hardly signifies as well "the quality of inner clarity that accompanies communion with the divine" [Terrien]). The light is the light of day, which is symbolic of life, and implicitly is contrasted with the darkness of Sheol. See further, J. Hempel, "Die Lichtsymbolik im Alten Testament," *Studium Generale* 13 (1960) 352–68; S. Aalen, *TDOT,* 1:147–67.

29–30 These summarizing sentences maintain the positive note that Elihu has been determined on striking in this chapter. The purpose of suffering, in short, is not to punish, and certainly not to bring the life of erring humans to a close, but to restore sufferers to health. That means not only bringing them back from the edge of the Pit, so that they do not die, but also, more creatively, ensuring that they are "enlightened with the light of life."

29 The phrase "all these things," which God does, refers no doubt both to the dreams of vv 15–18 and to the illness of vv 19–28 (Alden), since both prevent a person from going down to the Pit (vv 18, 22, 24, 28); God's words of communication (דבר, v 14, in reference to both) are themselves deeds (פעל) of salvation (Weiser). It is interesting that, when all is said and done, all the deliverance is ascribed to *God* ("God does all these things"), the work of the mediating angel (vv 23–25) being subsumed into the divine activity. And as an educational process, it is necessarily iterative, with repeated deliverances ("twice, three times" means "repeatedly"), just as we had in v 14 the sequence "in one way, in another" for the repeated means of God's methods of communication with mortals.

30 To be enlightened with the light of life (לאור באור חיים), i.e., the light that betokens life, is to be surrounded by it, bathed in it, so that those who have been delivered "bask in it" (NJPS, Habel).

31–33 This closing address to Job has at first sight something of the exordium about it, as if Elihu were beginning, rather than ending, his speech. Duhm and others regarded it as the introduction to another speech. But it is preferable to take it as simply preparing for the second speech, which will immediately follow. Elihu is not bringing his words to a conclusion, but announcing that he has not yet finished. He asks Job to continue listening to him (v 31). If Job has something he must say now, let him do so (v 32), but if not, Elihu intends to develop further his teaching of wisdom (v 33). Whichever way Elihu will proceed, Job should know that Elihu's fundamental desire is for Job's vindication (v 32b)—not, needless to say, that he should be proved right in his complaint against God, but that he should emerge from his experience of suffering with his righteousness fully upheld.

31 For a parallelism between קשׁב hiphil "hearken" and שׁמע "hear," cf. 13:6 (Job), though there, as is usual, שׁמע is the term in the first colon (the A-word) (as also, e.g., at 1 Sam 15:22; Isa 28:23; 34:1; 49:1). Only at Jer 18:19 is קשׁב the A-word in strict parallelism (though cf. Isa 42:23; Jer 8:6; 23:18). A summons to "hear" (שׁמע) him is one of Elihu's trademarks: he says the same thing to Job at 33:1, 33 and 34:16 and to the friends at 32:10 and 34:2, 10.

32 It is not a contradiction that Elihu says in v 31 "be silent" and in v 32 invites Job to speak, nor is it that he changes his mind (Dhorme). It is rather that he asks Job to hear him, but is willing for Job to interject if he has any reply to make, lit. "if there are words" (אם־ישׁ מלין), i.e., if there are words ready to be spoken in Job's mouth or mind.

It may come as something of a surprise that Elihu should be motivated by a desire for Job's vindication, such a surprise that several commentators think he must be speaking ironically (e.g., Dhorme, Tur-Sinai, Gordis), while Rowley drily remarks that "of this Elihu has given little indication." Strahan disparagingly thinks Elihu "merely desires to ingratiate himself with his hearer." But what would he mean if his professed desire to justify Job were ironic? That his true desire was to prove him a wicked man? Elihu certainly thinks Job is not right in what he says (לא־צדקת "you were not justified," v 12), but why would he be offering Job all this instruction in wisdom if he did not think he could improve Job by so doing, or if his only purpose was to humiliate Job still further? Habel thinks Elihu "brazenly asserts that he would be delighted to find Job 'in the right,'" but Elihu's language is more positive than that: he "desires" Job's vindication, and there is nothing "brazen" about that, or even "pompous" (Terrien). To "desire" (חפץ) is a very strong and deliberate act in the book of Job: Job desires to argue his case with God (13:3), and he has withheld nothing that the poor desired (31:16), while the wicked desire not the knowledge of God's ways (21:14); cf. also 9:3; 21:21; 22:3. It is certainly stronger than, for example, Delitzsch allows: "he would gladly be in the position to be able to acknowledge Job to be right." It is, in a word, the ultimate motivation Elihu has for his intervention in the debate: the anger that propels him into the conversation is no more than his authorization for opening his mouth. He was angry with Job "because he justified himself rather than God," i.e., justified himself at the cost of God's integrity, and that is plainly unacceptable. But if he, Elihu, can justify both God and Job, bringing Job to a point where he can acknowledge his sin and forthwith be restored to his former state of uprightness, he will have achieved his heart's desire.

33 Elihu's undertaking to "teach wisdom" means no more than what every one of the wise would have offered, though the combination of "teach" (אלף) and "wisdom" (חכמה) occurs only here. It is not that he will teach his own wisdom as distinct from what he has learned (as Tur-Sinai). Some, however, have thought this an arrogant boast on Elihu's part; thus Whybray remarks that Elihu "makes the extraordinarily presumptuous claim that he is fully qualified . . . to do what his elders had not been able to do: *he* will teach Job wisdom—that is, he claims to possess a knowledge which all have sought and which, as Job had discovered (chap. 28), is the possession of God alone." On the contrary, it had been a commonplace that "wisdom is with the aged" (12:12); though Job does not agree with that, Elihu's claim that wisdom is with the young (like himself) is no more scandalous. No doubt there are senses in which wisdom is God's own possession, but "wisdom" is also the common property in which the "wise" trade, and Elihu is only being true to the manners of his class.

Explanation

As far as we can judge, there has been plenty of persiflage in this opening speech of Elihu's, and—although it is hard for us to assess another culture's norms—he does seem to be a self-important young man. And the narrator's introduction in vv 1–6a has warned us that Elihu enters the discourse full of fury (his anger is mentioned four times in those verses). Elihu is, to say the least, not immediately a sympathetic character, though it is harder to answer Newsom's pointed question, Why does everyone loathe Elihu?

Certainly, none of the friends makes such a distinct impression upon us, and readers are bound to react to the character the poet has created. But to form a balanced assessment of Elihu, we need to linger over the motives he says drive him to speech. He is angered at the course the dialogue has taken (32:11–12), and he feels he must intervene if he is not to explode with frustration (32:18–20). But these are not his fundamental reasons for speaking; by his own account, as he states in the penultimate, climactic line of this opening speech, his desire is to "justify" Job (33:32). His goal is Job's restoration, not to prove Job is in the wrong. A key element in his speech has been the cameo depicting the righteous man in danger of his life who is redeemed by the intervention of an angel (33:19–28); Job must surely be intended to identify with such a person, and to believe that his future will be as fortunate. For that to happen, Job will of course have to confess that he has been in the wrong (cf. 33:27b–c), will have to reconsider his claim to perfect innocence (33:9), and will have to withdraw his charges against God (33:10–11). Nevertheless, this is the most supportive address to Job we have heard so far in the book. Beside that, the matter of Elihu's pomposity or prolixity is of little account.

The character of Elihu is one thing, his attitude to Job another. But neither is as important, in the design of the book as a whole, as the arguments he advances, the theological position he represents. The key to his position in this speech, and what marks him out from the other interlocutors, is his conviction that suffering is a means of divine communication with humans. He does not abandon the concept of suffering as retribution, but he displaces it with the idea of education. God, he says, has more than one way of communicating with mortals: he may use dreams, to warn people against sins they may be tempted to (33:15–18); and he may use physical suffering (33:19–28) to bring home to them the effects of their sins. The suffering in such a case is not a requital; it is in order that they might acknowledge their wrongdoing (v 27) and be restored to God's favor (vv 26a, 28). There is, let it be noticed, nothing automatic about this process; it depends on the good offices of a mediating angel who begs for the sufferers' release (vv 23–25). On the other hand, sufferers have no need for self-flagellation in order to attain redemption: it is plain that it needs only the sufferers' appeal (v 26a), along with the support of the angel, for God to restore their righteousness to them (v 26c); though they will subsequently confess their sins (v 27b–c), confession is not a prerequisite to restoration.

All of this is very different from what the other friends have been saying, and Elihu earns his place in the book for this speech alone. Nevertheless, it still leaves Job somewhat in the lurch. If Job is one of these sufferers, what is he to do? Stay on his ash heap hoping for a passing angel? If this suffering is God's way of warning against future sins, has not Job already got the message? God may have his various ways of communicating with humans, but what ways have they of communicating back? And is that not exactly the problem that Job has been complaining about?

So despite Elihu's professed good intentions towards Job, he has not helped him any more than the other friends have, even if he has broadened the more theoretical discussion about the nature of suffering. And, in any case, how much benefit to sufferers comes from the claimed theological insight that suffering may not be punishment but education? They are still suffering, and powerless, on Elihu's reckoning, to do anything about it.

Elihu's Second Speech (34:1–37)

Bibliography

Boadt, L. "A Re-Examination of the Third-Yodh Suffix in Job." *UF* 7 (1975) 59–72. **Cox, C. E.** "Elihu's Second Speech according to the Septuagint." In *Studies in the Book of Job.* Ed. W. E. Aufrecht. SRSup 16. Waterloo, Ont.: Wilfrid Laurier UP, 1985. 36–53. **Dahood, M. J.** "Northwest Semitic Philology and Job." In *The Bible in Current Catholic Thought: Gruenthaner Memorial Volume.* Ed. J. L. McKenzie. St. Mary's Theological Studies 1. New York: Herder & Herder, 1962. 55–74. ———. "Qoheleth and Northwest Semitic Philology." *Bib* 43 (1962) 349–65. ———. Review of *Job et son Dieu: Essai d'exégèse et de théologie biblique,* by J. Lévêque. *Bib* 52 (1971) 436–38. ———. "Ugaritic-Phoenician Forms in Job 34,36." *Bib* 62 (1981) 548–50. **Driver, G. R.** "Difficult Words in the Hebrew Prophets." In *Studies in Old Testament Prophecy.* FS T. H. Robinson, ed. H. H. Rowley. Edinburgh: T. & T. Clark, 1950. 52–72. ———. "Hebrew Poetic Diction." In *Congress Volume, Copenhagen 1953.* VTSup 1. Leiden: Brill, 1953. 26–39. **Gelzner, A.** "איוב ל״ד: הספר שכתב אליהוא" [Job 34: The Book Eliahu Wrote]. *BMik* 80 (1979–80) 9–24. **Girard, R.** "The Ancient Trail Trodden by the Wicked: Job as Scapegoat" [Job 34:24–26]. *Semeia* 33 (1985) 13–41. **Goodman, L. E.** "Baḥya on the Antinomy of Free Will and Predestination" [Job 34:11, 29]. *JHI* 44 (1983) 115–30. **Lipiński, E.** "*skn* et *sgn* dans le sémitique occidental du nord." *UF* 5 (1973) 191–207. **Michel, W. L.** "*Ṣlmwt,* 'deep darkness' or 'shadow of death'?" [Job 34:22]. *BR* 29 (1984) 5–20. **Sutcliffe, E. F.** "Notes on Job, Textual and Exegetical: 6, 18; 11, 12; 31, 35; 34, 17. 20; 36, 27–33; 37, 1." *Bib* 30 (1949) 66–90. **Weil, H. M.** "Exégèse de Jérémie 23, 33–40 et de Job 34, 28–33; (Jérémie 44, 9)." *RHR* 118 (1938) 201–8. **Wilde, A. de.** "Job

34:16–37, proeve van tekstrestauratie." *Theologie en Praktijk* 24.2 (1969). **Wolfers, D.** "Sire! (Job xxxiv 36)." *VT* 44 (1994) 566–69. **Zuckerman, B.** "Two Examples of Editorial Modification in 11QtgJob" [Job 36,14; 34,31]. In *Biblical and Near Eastern Studies.* FS W. S. La Sor, ed. G. A. Tuttle. Grand Rapids: Eerdmans, 1978. 269–75.

Translation

1 [a]*Then Elihu continued and said:*

2 *Hear my words, you wise men;*
give ear to me, you men of learning![a]
3 [a]*For the ear tests words*[b]
as the palate tastes the food in the mouth.[c]
4 *Let us choose*[a] *for ourselves what is right;*[b]
let us decide among us[c] *what is good.*
5 *Job has said, "I am innocent,*
but God has taken away my rights.[a]
6 *As for*[a] *the judgment against me, I call it a lie;*[b]
though I am innocent, an arrow has wounded me incurably."[c]
7 *Who*[a] *is there like Job,*
who drinks scoffing like water,
8 *walks in company with evildoers*
and goes along[a] *with the wicked?*[b]
9 [a]*For he says, "It is of no profit*[b] *to a man*
to take pleasure in God."[c]

10 *Therefore,*[a] [b]*you men of understanding,*
listen to me.
Far be it[c] *from God to do wickedness!*[d]
Far be it from the Almighty[e] *to do wrong!*[f]
11 *Surely*[a] *he repays*[b] *humans according to their deeds,*[c]
and brings upon them[d] *what their conduct deserves.*
12 *Assuredly,*[a] *God does no wrong,*[b]
the Almighty does not pervert justice.
13 *Who put the earth*[a] *in his charge?*[b]
Who gave him rule[c] *over the entire world?*
14 [a]*If he were minded,*[b]
he could withdraw his spirit and his breath,
15 *and all that lives*[a] *would utterly*[b] *expire;*
humanity would return to mud.[c]

16 [a]*If you have understanding,*[b] [c]*hear this, O Job,*[d]
listen to the words I have to say.[e]
17 *Can*[a] *one who hates*[b] *justice govern?*[c]
Will you condemn[d] *the Righteous One,*[e] *the Almighty,*[f]
18 *who can say*[a] *to a king,*[b] *"You are a scoundrel,"*[c]
and to nobles,[d] *"You are wicked men,"*[e]

19 *who shows*[a] *no partiality to princes,*
and does not favor[b] *the high-ranking*[c] *above the poor,*
since they are all alike the work of his hands?[d]
20 [a]*In a moment they may die,* [b]*in the middle of*[c] *the night.*
[d]*The nobles*[e] *are shaken,*[f] *and they pass away,*[g]
and the mighty[h] *are taken away*[i] *without effort.*[j]

21 *For his eyes are on the ways of mortals,*
and he sees every step they take.
22 *There is no gloom or deep darkness*[a]
where evildoers may hide themselves.[b]
23 [a]*Indeed,*[b] *he does not set a time*[c] *for anyone*
to go before him for judgment.[d]
24 *He shatters*[a] *the mighty without inquiry,*[b]
and sets[c] *others in their place.*
25 [a]*Thus*[b] *he knows*[c] *their deeds;*[d]
he can overthrow[e] *them by night*[f] *so that they are crushed.*[g]
26 [a]*He strikes them down*[b] *for*[c] *their wickedness,*[d]
[e]*where all can see,*[f]
27 [a]*because*[b] *they turned aside from following him,*[c]
and had no regard for[d] *his ways,*
28 [a]*so that they caused the cry of the poor*[b] *to come*[c] *to him*[d]—
[e]*and he heard the cry*[f] *of the afflicted.*
29 [a]*If he is quiet,*[b] *who can condemn him?*[c]
If he hides his face,[d] *who can see him?*[e]
[f]*Yet he rules*[g] *over nations and individuals*[h] *alike,*[i]
30 [a]*so that*[b] *the godless*[c] *should not govern,*[d]
[e]*and a people should not be ensnared.*[f]

31 *Indeed,*[a] *you should say*[b] *to God,*[c]
"I was misguided,[d] *I will not offend*[e] *again;*[f]
32 *what*[a] *I do not see,*[b] *do teach me;*[c]
if[d] *I have done wrong, I will do it no more."*
33 *Will he then requite you*[a] *as you see fit*[b]
when you have rejected him?[c]
You need to decide;[d] *I*[e] *shall not;*
[f]*but do say what*[g] *you believe.*[h]
34 *What men of understanding*[a] *are saying to me,*[b]
and any wise person who hears me, is:
35 *"Job is not speaking with knowledge,*
and his words are without insight.
36 *Would that*[a] *Job were thoroughly*[b] *examined*[c]—
for he gives replies[d] *like those of the wicked.*[e]
37 *For he adds*[a] *to his sin,*[b]
questioning[c] *his transgression*[d] *in our presence,*[e]
and he multiplies[f] *his words*[g] *against God."*

Notes

1.a. Beer (BH^2) questions whether this line should not be deleted. Kissane moves it to precede 33:31, where he sees Elihu's second speech beginning.

2.a. ידעים, lit. "[you] knowers," i.e., "you learned men," REB "you master-minds." NEB's "men of long experience" is too specific.

3.a. Hölscher and de Wilde delete the verse, which was absent also from LXX (the present text in LXX editions is supplied from Theod), as a gloss. Duhm moved it, along with 33:31–33, to precede v 16. Beer (BH^2) thought it should perhaps be moved to follow 33:33, but at 34:16 moves 33:31–33 + 34:3 to that point.

3.b. אזן מלין תבחן is a crisp proverbial phrase; Moffatt's "A man's mind tests what he is told" is an attempt to reproduce the style rather than the exact wording.

3.c. There is a slight verbal variation here (וחך יטעם לֶאֱכֹל "and the palate tastes in order to eat" or "tastes in eating"; Pope "as the palate tastes by eating") from the same proverb at 12:11 (וחך אכל יטעם־לו "and the palate tastes food for itself"). But it is hardly necessary to emend, as Budde does, to יטעם לו אֹכֶל "tastes food for itself" (followed by Beer [*BHK vel*], NAB, Ehrlich, Driver–Gray, Hölscher, Fohrer, Hesse, Gerleman [*BHS vel*], van der Lugt), לְאֹכֶל "[tastes] for food" (Beer [*BHK*], Gerleman [*BHS prp vel*]; so too NEB, Kissane, Tur-Sinai, Good), or לאֹכֶל "food," with the *lamedh* as the sign of the acc (Gray). Nor is it necessary to follow Dahood ("Qoheleth and Northwest Semitic Philology," *Bib* 43 [1962] 349–65 [350]) and Blommerde in seeing the *lamedh* as equivalent to causal *min* and translating "by eating."

4.a. בחר is usually "choose" (BDB, 103b). But here בחר is thought by some to mean "examine" (so Hölscher, Tur-Sinai, de Wilde, Gray, NEB), as it apparently does in Isa 48:10, Ecclus 4:17, and perhaps also Job 36:21 (if emended); of refined or tested silver in Prov 10:20. This would be בחר III, cognate with Aram. בחר, according to *DCH,* 2:139, and Gesenius–Buhl, 1:138, but merely another meaning of the usual verb בחר according to *HALOT,* 1:119b. Good, exceptionally, takes נבחרה and נדעה as "declaratives," translating "we will decide," "we know," and appealing to GKC, §108b, in support.

4.b. The phrase מה־טוב "what is good" occurs seven times in the Hebrew Bible, but without any distinctive sense (against G. Brin, "The Significance of the Form *mah-ṭṭôb,*" *VT* 38 [1988] 462–65); the meaning of "good," as one would expect, varies according to the context.

4.c. Instead of בֵּינֵינוּ "among us," Beer (*BHK frt*) reads וְנָבִינָה "and let us understand"; so too Hesse. But there is nothing wrong with בֵּינֵינוּ since בין is not only "between" two persons or things, but also "among" three or more (as Cant 2:2, 3; Ezek 19:2; 31:3).

5.a. משפטי, lit. "my justice, my right"; on the term, cf. on 27:2; 40:8.

6.a. על, when it is not "upon" or "concerning" or "as for," is usually "because," and it is more than doubtful that it can ever mean "although" (despite RSV, NAB, NIV, Moffatt, Budde, Tur-Sinai, Gordis, Hartley, de Wilde, Sicre Díaz); see on 10:7 and 16:17, where that meaning has been alleged. Ibn Ezra took על־משפטי as "because I demand my justice." It could be "against my right" (Dillmann, Delitzsch) if אכזב means "I am made out to be a liar." But על־משפטי cannot mean "despite my honesty" (as M. Dahood, review of *Job et son Dieu: Essai d'exégèse et de théologie biblique,* by J. Lévêque, *Bib* 52 [1971] 436–38 [438]) since על is not concessive and משפט does not mean "honesty" as an ethical quality (as *DCH,* 5:556b–64b will show).

6.b. The *Translation* follows Rashi ("concerning my judgment, I declare it a lie"), who presumably regarded the piel as declarative or factitive (cf. Joüon–Muraoka, §52d); similarly NJPS "I declare the judgment against me false." אֲכַזֵּב is otherwise to be translated as "I am lying" or (though there is no interrogative particle) "Am I lying?" or, taking the verb as modal, "Should I lie?" (so KJV, RVmg). Gordis can hardly be right that we have here a "virtual indirect quotation," viz. "[they say that] I am a liar."

Since כזב piel is simply "lie," the verb as it stands can hardly mean "I am thought to be a liar" (as Renan, Strahan; and Habel, calling it a delocutive). To get that meaning, we should need to revocalize the verb, with Duhm and Beer (BH^2 *prps*), to niph אֶכָּזֵב "I am shown to be false," as of hope in 41:9 (1) or the person reproved by God in Prov 30:6 (Duhm rendered "I am deceived," which is not really the point). This revocalization is apparently adopted silently by RV ("I am accounted a liar"), RSV ("I am counted a liar"), NIV ("I am considered a liar"), Moffatt ("God makes me out a liar"), and explicitly by NAB "I am set at nought" (*Textual Notes,* 378) and Hesse. M. Dahood (review of *Job et son Dieu,* by J. Lévêque, 438) similarly revocalizes to אֻכְזַב "I am declared a liar."

Elihu claims to be quoting Job, but Job has not actually used this language; so is there some problem with the text that needs more than a simple revocalization? LXX has ἐψεύσατο "he lied," which would correspond to יְכַזֵּב "he [God] lies" (so Dhorme, arguing that MT represents a correction to avoid the blasphemy of the original text, and comparing 32:3 [*q.v.*], though it is open to question whether the supposed Masoretic correction [*tiqqun sopherim*] there is genuine). This revocalization was further adopted by Hölscher, Terrien, and Pope. NEB too, with "he has falsified my case," accepts the emendation and sees the piel as declarative. G. A. Barton accepts the emendation but understands the implied subject as Job, not his case; thus "concerning my just case he counts me a liar" ("Some Text-Critical Notes on the Elihu-Speeches," *JBL* 43 [1924] 228).

Another approach is to emend אכזב to a different verb. Ehrlich read אֶכְאַב "I am in pain," followed by Beer (*BHK*), de Wilde, Gray, and by Driver–Gray, comparing Jer 15:18, where כאבי "my pain" is paralleled to מכתי אנושה "my incurable wound," with אנוש as here. What then is על? Not "notwithstanding my right" (Driver–Gray), for the reasons given in *Note* 6.a; nor "against my right" (Ehrlich) or "despite my just cause" (Gray) since it seems implausible that על־משפטי should mean "in contradiction to what I deserve." No, it would need to be read as an ironic "because I am in the right, I am in pain."

Yet another possibility is to find here the term אַכְזָר "cruel," but only if we emend the colon to עָלַי מְשֹׁפְטִי אַכְזָר "against me my judge is cruel" (so Kissane, Larcher, NJB "my judge is treating me cruelly"). Very implausible is Tur-Sinai's emendation to the less than euphonious אַךְ זַךְ "(my cause) is quite pure."

6.c. Lit. "my arrow is incurable," an odd expression not completely explained by Gordis's suggestion that the epithet is "transferred," since it is neither the arrow nor the sufferer that is "incurable" but the wound caused by the arrow (cf. NIV "his arrow inflicts an incurable wound"). It is no improvement to read חִצָּיו "his arrows" (Pope, Hesse [apparently]) or to accept with Blommerde (reading חִצַּי "his darts") and L. Boadt ("A Re-Examination of the Third-Yodh Suffix in Job," *UF* 7 [1975] 59–72 [64–65]) that the final *yodh* is really a 3d-person suff (for other examples, see *Note* 21:16.e).

An attractive emendation is ready to hand in מַחְצִי "my wound" (so Duhm [*frt*], Dhorme, Beer [BH^2 *prps*], Hölscher [*frt*], Kissane, Larcher, Fohrer, Rowley, de Wilde, Gray, NJB), the noun occurring elsewhere only at Isa 30:26, and in one or two places in the Qumran texts (*DCH*, 5:227b). Not so attractive, because more remote from the MT, is the proposal reported by Beer (BH^2 *prps*), חָלְיִי "my sickness."

Among philological proposals, there is (1) the idea of I. Eitan that חץ means "lot, luck" (comparing Arab. *ḥazz* "fate, lot" [Lane, 595b]) and that it is Job's lot that is incurable ("Studies in Hebrew Roots," *JQR* NS 14 [1923–24] 31–52 [41–42]); similarly Guillaume, though he translates "my state [is desperate]," which seems to differ somewhat from the meanings of the Arab., which he gives as "fate, lot, portion." But we should note that the Arab. seems to mean "good fortune, a portion of something good or excellent," which makes it a dubious support for a Heb. word signifying bad fortune. Eitan's idea is followed, however, by NEB "my state is desperate," and toyed with by Andersen. (2) S. Iwry saw here "lot, fortune" as a secondary meaning of חץ "arrow" ("New Evidence for Belomancy in Ancient Palestine and Phoenicia," *JAOS* 81 [1961] 27–34 [30]; noted in *HALOT*, 1:342b). (3) Another possibility is offered by Tur-Sinai, suggesting a חץ cognate with Syr. *ḥaṣ* "loin, back" (J. Payne Smith, 154a; Tur-Sinai finds the word also in Num 24:8), thus "my loins are wounded"; but אנוש means "incurable," not "wounded," so there is no real improvement.

The term אנוש is normally translated "incurable, *unheilbar*," but "disastrous, *unheilvoll*" might well be preferable. BDB, 60b, offers only the former, but *HALOT*, 1:70a, allows the second meaning for Jer 17:16. AS, 77b, suggests "incurable, chronic, enflamed (*enconada*)," the last for Jer 30:15.

7.a. Instead of מי "who?" Beer (*BHK frt*) reads the emphatic מִי אֵפוֹ "who indeed?" because the first colon was thought to be too short; Driver–Gray too thought a word parallel to something in the second colon had dropped out.

8.a. ללכת, lit. "to go"; the use of the inf (rather than a *waw* consec) to continue the thought of a finite verb is unusual but not without parallel (cf. GKC, §114p).

8.b. אנשי־רשע "men of wickedness." It is interesting, though perhaps not very significant, that Elihu is the only speaker who uses the term אנשי "men of" (34:8, 10, 34, 36; 37:7) or אנשים "men" (33:16, 27; 36:24; 37:24; but it does occur at 4:13 and at 32:1, 5 in the preface to the Elihu speeches), the other speakers using מתי (11:11; 19:19; 22:15; 24:12; 31:31) or מתים (11:3). This variation could of course be evidence of a different author for the Elihu speeches.

9.a. Budde and Hölscher delete the verse as inappropriate at this point.

9.b. E. Lipiński ("*skn* et *sgn* dans le sémitique occidental du nord," *UF* 5 [1973] 191–207 [191–92]) reads "a man runs no danger in putting his trust in God" (on this sense for סכן, see *Note* 22:2.b).

9.c. ברצתו, lit. "in his taking pleasure." רצה is "be pleased with," "take delight in," as of a father in his son (Prov 3:12), of Esau in Jacob, surprisingly (Gen 33:10), and of Rehoboam in the people (2 Chr 10:7). But these occurrences have the person delighted in as a direct obj of the verb. Only Ps 50:18 has the exact idiom found here, with עם before the person delighted in; it is usually translated "you make friends with [a thief]." The idea of friendship is appropriate there, because the context is of a person taking pleasure in someone not previously known; the verb רצה nowhere else has anything to do with friendship, and the idea of friendship is altogether too specific for our context, despite Duhm ("is a friend of God"), Fohrer ("makes friends with God"), de Wilde ("lives in friendship with God"), Hesse ("maintains friendship with God"), Moffatt ("to be the friend of God"), and Delitzsch ("entering into fellowship with God"); similarly "enjoying the company of God" (NJB). The most satisfactory translations are the more general "delight oneself with God" (KJV) and "delight in" (so RSV; similarly Hölscher); "being well pleased with God" (Driver–Gray) has the same idea, but it seems strange to say that a human is "well pleased" with God. "Seek his joy in communion with God" (Terrien) tries to combine the ideas of delight and of friendship, but the result is a bit overblown. Gray suggests interestingly that the sense is "fulfill one's obligations," as in 14:6 (cf. also Isa 40:2; Lev 26:34, 43; 2 Chr 36.21).

Unsatisfactory are those translations that imply that the pleasure is on God's part, for God cannot be pleased (רצה) "with" (עם) God, and in any case it is hard to see Job affirming that God can take pleasure in someone without their benefiting from it. Such translations are, for example, "find favour with God" (NEB), "being in favor with God" (Gordis; similarly NJPS), "pleasing to God" (NAB, Pope), "when he tries to please God" (NIV), "when he pleases God" (Hartley), "compliant with God [i.e., trying to please him]" (Tur-Sinai), "to try to follow God's will" (GNB). Likewise "court God's favor" (Habel) and "seek the favor of God" (Fedrizzi) incorrectly regard it as God's pleasure that is in view. "Take delight in God's favor" (Sicre Díaz) unfortunately tries to combine both translations.

The proposal of Lipiński ("*skn* et *sgn*," 193) that סכן means "run a danger" (as in Talmudic Heb. [Jastrow, 991b]; cf. *DCH*, vol. 6, *s.v.*) has found no following; for his other examples, see *Note* 22:2.b).

10.a. לכן in the great majority of cases means "therefore" (see *Comment*). Occasionally it seems to mean "surely, assuredly" (*DCH*, 4:548b), which could be appropriate here. Less likely is Dhorme's suggestion that it means "but" (on the analogy of Arab. *lākinna*); cf. also *Note* 34:25.b.

10.b. Bickell[2], Duhm, Beer (*BHK*), Fohrer, Hesse, de Wilde, and Gray inserted חֲכָמִים הַאֲזִינוּ "hearken to me, you wise men," on the ground that the line is too short; still, as Driver–Gray say, the short line may have been intended to make the summons more emphatic. Rather than fill out the line, Bickell and Hölscher simply deleted what was there.

10.c. חללה is usually spelled חלילה; see *Comment* on 27:5, its only other occurrence in Job.

10.d. חללה is often followed by an inf, so many emend the noun מֵרֶשַׁע "from evil" to מֵרְשֹׁעַ "from doing evil" (so Budde, Duhm, Beer [*BHK*], Driver–Gray, Hölscher, Fohrer, de Wilde, Gray). Gordis is probably right, however, that the (obvious) verb is simply implied; so too Hartley. It can hardly be that רשׁע is a "verbal noun" (Fedrizzi).

10.e. Some want to read וּלְשַׁדַּי "and from Shaddai" to match לָאֵל in the first colon (so Houbigant, Bickell, Duhm, Beer [*BHK*], Hölscher, Fohrer, Hesse, de Wilde, Gray), but the prep is so easily understood that it is not necessary to supply it in the text (so Delitzsch, Budde, Driver–Gray, Gordis, Hartley).

10.f. Again, following חללה, many emend the noun מֵעָוֶל "from iniquity" to מֵעַוֵּל "from doing iniquity" (so Duhm, Beer [*BH*[2]], Driver–Gray, Hölscher, Fohrer, de Wilde, Gray). Others prefer מֵעַוֵּת צֶדֶק "from perverting justice" (Beer [*BHK*]) or מִפְּעֹל עָוֶל "from doing iniquity" (Budde). LXX ταράξαι τὸ δικαιόν "to subvert what is just," with an inf and an obj, may lend some support (ταράξει in Beer [*BHK*] is an error).

11.a. כי will hardly be "for," since this sentence does not supply the reason why the friends should listen to Elihu. Rather, we have the well-attested use of כי as an emphatic particle; for other examples, see *Note* 22:26.b.

11.b. שׁלם piel "repay, reward," as at v 33; 21:19, 31; 41:11 (3).

11.c. פעל אדם ישלם־לו, lit. "he repays the deed of a human." Reiske, Beer (*BHK*), Gerleman (*BHS prp*), and Fedrizzi, following LXX and Pesh, read כְּפֹעַל "according to the deed of" (so too Gray), but the MT is perfectly acceptable (Prov 7:14 is a good analogy). Blommerde's suggestion that the *kaph* of the second colon does duty also in the first is unlikely (though followed by Hartley); see also on 41:18 (10).

11.d. מצא hiph "cause to overtake, befall," not "cause to find" (as KJV, RV, Tur-Sinai "and cause every man to find according to his ways"; see *DCH,* 5:441b). Though מצא is usually "find," the qal means "overtake" at 31:29.

12.a. אַף־אָמְנָם, a double asseverative, "indeed, in truth" (Gordis).

12.b. Budde, Duhm, Beer (*BHK*), Driver–Gray (perhaps), and Gray read יִרְשַׁע qal "does evil," but ירשׁיע hiph "act wickedly" is perfectly acceptable (cf. GKC, §53d).

13.a. אַרְצָה would usually be "to the earth," with *he locale,* which will not suit here. Most agree that it (and the same form at 37:12) is a misvocalization of אַרְצֹה "his earth," an alternative form of אַרְצוֹ, which one Heb. MS reads (so, e.g., Beer [*BHK*], Gerleman [*BHS prp*]); cf. תֵּבֵל אַרְצוֹ "his habitable world" at Prov 8:31 and תֵּבֵל אַרְצֹה at Job 37:12 (emended). Possibly, however, we have here a use of the acc ending (so GKC, §90f, Gerleman [*BHS*], Gordis; Sicre Díaz), meaning simply "the earth" (cf. also on 37:12). Duhm's proposal simply to delete the final *he* is too cavalier.

13.b. For פקד with the administrative sense of "entrust with a task," cf. W. Schottroff, *TLOT,* 2:1023, 1028; and cf. *DCH,* vol. 6, *s.v.*

13.c. שָׂם is "has set," presumably with עָלָיו "upon him" implied from the previous colon (so too Dhorme, Hölscher, Fohrer, Rowley, de Wilde, Sicre Díaz, Good); Beer (*BH*[2]) inserts the word. "Set upon him" is rather cryptic, nevertheless (as is RSV "laid on him the whole world"), and its meaning can only be inferred from what precedes. Some have thought that שׂם should mean "founded" (Beer [*BHK*], NJPS "Who ordered the entire world?"; cf. NAB "who else set all the land in its place?" NEB "Who but he established the whole world?" KJV "who hath disposed the whole world?"; similarly Dillmann, Delitzsch, Hesse), but the difficulty with that, as Driver–Gray pointed out, is that then the reply expected to the first colon would be "no one" but to the second "no one but him," which is awkward. The same objection applies to the emendation of Duhm and Beer (*BH*[2] *al*), who transferred לִבּוֹ "his heart" from v 14 to become the object of "set" and inserted a ב before תבל, thus rendering "Who has attended to the whole world?" (so too Peake). NJB, following Larcher, avoids the difficulty by translating "Did someone else entrust the world to his care[;] was he given charge of the universe by someone else?"

14.a. De Wilde inserts here 12:7–10, which are admittedly difficult verses, but which can nevertheless be satisfactorily explained; see *Comment* on 12:7–12.

14.b. Lit. "if he should set his mind to himself." שׂם לִבּוֹ אל is at 2:3 "consider" (and at 1:8, with על instead of אל). NEB took that to mean "if he were to turn his thoughts inwards," i.e., were to neglect his universe (similarly Dillmann, Renan "if he considered only himself," Fohrer, Hesse, Fedrizzi), but that seems an overinterpretation for the more straightforward "If it were his intention" (NIV), "If he plans in his heart" (Habel), "If he took it in his mind" (Pope), or "If he decided on his own (*por su cuenta*)" (Sicre Díaz). So too was ibn Ezra's rendering "If God pays attention to man in order to kill him" (similarly Rosenmüller). KJV, following Vg, "if he set his heart upon man" makes the thought even more difficult by understanding the "him" of עליו as "man."

For ישׂים "should set," Beer (*BHK*) reads, with LXX, Pesh, two Heb. MSS, and the Kethib of five oriental MSS, יָשִׁיב "should bring back," and deletes לבו "his heart," thus yielding "if he should take back his spirit to himself" (so too RSV, NAB, NJB, GNB, Moffatt, Houbigant, Budde, Duhm, Peake, Strahan, Driver–Gray, Dhorme ["the correction is almost irresistible"], Beer [*BHK*], Hölscher, Kissane, Larcher, Fohrer [though he retains ישׂים as meaning "think"], Terrien, Tur-Sinai, Guillaume, Rowley, Gordis, de Wilde, Hartley, Gray). "His spirit" would then end the first colon rather than begin the second. This is an attractive and well-supported emendation, but the traditional reading is here found more acceptable (see also *Comment*).

Little benefit, incidentally, comes from the feeble emendation of Budde and Beer (*BH*[2] *vel*), שָׁמַר "has kept."

15.a. כל־בשׂר, lit. "all flesh," which may or may not include animals. NEB "all that lives," like "all flesh" (which is, however, archaic, despite its use not only by KJV but also by RSV, NAB, NJB, NJPS, REB [!]), leaves the options open (as does Dhorme), whereas NIV "all mankind" and Moffatt "the human race" have settled for one of the possible interpretations.

15.b. On יחד meaning "altogether," see *Note* 3:18.a; *DCH,* 4:197b §3d.

15.c. On עפר as *wet* earth, see *Note* 10:9.c; *DCH,* vol. 6, *s.v.*

16.a. Beer (*BH*[2] *frt*), followed by Moffatt, moves to this place 33:31–33, which is also a direct address to Job to listen to Elihu's words. Beer (*BH*[2] *frt*) also moves v 3 to this point.

16.b. Since בינה, accented on the first syllable, is the impv of בין "understand," the אם can hardly be the usual "if." We could regard אם, following Gordis and Hartley, as an emphatic particle "indeed" (cf. Arab. *'inna*) and translate "Assuredly [not 'therefore,' as Gordis], understand this." I accepted this sense for 6:13 but rejected it for 8:4; 14:5; 17:2, 13, 16, the other places where Gordis claimed it occurred, and it does seem a rather forced way of preserving the MT. Even more forced is Tur-Sinai's view that אם is effectively אם כן "and if so." A much more suitable reading comes from moving the accent to the second syllable, so making בינה the noun "understanding"; thus "If [you have] understanding" (so Duhm, Dhorme, Sicre Díaz, Habel).

It makes no difference to the translation, but most prefer to adopt the emendation to בִּינוֹתָ (or בִּנוֹתָ or בִּינֹתָה) "[if] you understand" (so Budde, Hölscher, Fohrer, Beer [*BHK*], Driver–Gray, Fohrer, Hesse, Gerleman [*BHS prp*], de Wilde, Gray). It is incorrect to claim the support of the ancient versions for this emendation, however, as *BHK* does; although they have a verb, they may well be translating somewhat freely (Driver–Gray).

Good translates "If understanding hears this, gives ear to the sound of my words," improbably taking בינה as the subj of the two fem verbs in v 16, revocalizing them to שְׁמְעָה and הַאֲזִינָה, and of תרשׁיע "condemns [fem.]" in v 17. A conjectural emendation of אם־בינה to וְאַתָּה אִיּוֹב "and you, Job" is accepted by NAB.

NEB "if you have the wit" and JB "If you have any intelligence" sound rather ruder than they need. "If you have understanding" (RSV, NIV) is all that we need. NJPS "if you would understand, listen to this" suits the context well, but the pf tense does not have that modal sense.

16.c. NAB inserts וְעַתָּה אִיּוֹב "and now, O Job."

16.d. Job's name is not present in the Heb., but the sg verb shows that he is now being addressed. NEB also supplies his name.

16.e. קול מלי "the voice of my words," Moffatt "my lesson," Habel "the force of my argument."

17.a. האף, the אף strengthening the interrogative, always introduces an "inadmissible hypothesis" (Dhorme); it occurs elsewhere only at 40:8; Gen 18:13, 23, 24; Amos 2:11.

17.b. Parallels to "hating" (שׂנא) an abstract like "justice" are Mic 3:2 (hating what is good) and Prov 1:22 (hating knowledge).

17.c. חבשׁ (see also on 28:11) is "bind" (an ass, Gen 22:3; a headband, Exod 29:9; in piel and pual a wound, e.g., Ps 147:3; Isa 1:6), but nowhere "govern," which is what the sense requires (so *HALOT,* 1:289b; *DCH,* 3:157b; and most versions). BDB, 290b, and Ges[18] think this is a metaphorical sense, "restrain, control." Isa 3:7, where a man refuses to be a "ruler" (קָצִין) or a "healer" (חבשׁ), is no real help, though often quoted in this connection; for, although a ruler might heal, "heal" does not become a word for "rule" (so also G. Münderlein, *TDOT,* 4:199). Nor is it likely that חבשׁ here means "imprison" (T. D. Alexander, *NIDOTTE,* 2:19), despite Syr. *ḥebhaš* "shut up" (J. Payne Smith, 125a) and Arab. *ḥabasa* "confine" (Lane, 500b).

Dhorme's idea that חבשׁ means "bind on the yoke" is unsupported by the verb's usage, as is the variant of Fohrer and de Wilde, "hold the reins" (similarly NEB, but REB "is in control"). No better is the proposal of E. F. Sutcliffe, to translate "Can he even heal one who hates justice?" ("Notes on Job, Textual and Exegetical: 6, 18; 11, 12; 31, 35; 34, 17, 20; 36, 27–33; 37, 1," *Bib* 30 [1949] 66–90 [75]), which would explain why Job is suffering but would not advance Elihu's argument at this point. Tur-Sinai had suggested "Would he, if he hated right, heal?" meaning "Can he who heals be called a hater of justice?" but that would be a strange note on which to begin his address to Job, since it has hardly been in Job's mind whether God is a healer (that was Eliphaz, 5:18).

M. Dahood attractively sees here חבשׁ, a byform of חפשׂ "enquire, search out," with the nuance "make judicial enquiry" ("The Phoenician Contribution to Biblical Wisdom Literature," in *The Role of the Phoenicians in the Interaction of Mediterranean Civilizations,* ed. W. A. Ward [Beirut: American University in Beirut, 1968] 123–52 [126–27]; cf. *Comment* on 28:11 and *Note* 28:11.b, and see *DCH,* 3:157a). But unfortunately there is no question about holding an inquiry here.

17.d. תרשׁיע "you will condemn" is emended by Hölscher, Larcher (but not BJ), Fohrer, Hesse, de Wilde (with two MSS, Tg) to יַרְשִׁיעַ "he will condemn," i.e., "shall the almighty righteous one do iniquity?" the verb being an internal hiph. Beer (*BH*[2] *prps*) mentions the suggestion to read qal יִרְשַׁע, with the same sense.

17.e. Kissane reads מַצְדִּיק "judging," i.e., "And dost thou condemn Him that judgeth the mighty?" So too Pope, but he withdrew his support in the third edition of his commentary.

17.f. כביר "mighty," as at 8:2. צדיק כביר "the righteous, mighty one"; the asyndeton is unusual, but cf. 37:16, Gen 37:27, and, arguably, Ps 31:18 [19] (and cf. Joüon–Muraoka, §177s). Strahan compares the Roman title *Jupiter optimus maximus,* in which also two titles are joined asyndetically. M. Dahood (review of *Job et son Dieu,* by J. Lévêque, 438) saw here a divine title "the Aged One" (as also at 36:5), taking כַּבִּיר as a new word cognate with Arab. *kabīr* "aged" ([Lane, 2586c]; like עַתִּיק "ancient, old," which he finds in Pss 31:18 [19]; 75:6; cf. *DCH,* vol. 6, *s.v.*).

18.a. MT הַאֹמַר is apparently the interrogative ה with the inf constr, an anomalous construction that could only mean "Is one to say?" So KJV, RV "Is it fit to say to a king?"; NJPS "Would you call a king a scoundrel, great men, wicked?"; Tur-Sinai "Doth one say to a king?"; and perhaps also Andersen, understanding Elihu's argument to be that "the government of human rulers cannot be questioned or opposed" (see further *Comment*). KJV and RV continue with "How much less to him that accepteth [RV respecteth] not the persons of princes," but that "how much less" is, as Driver–Gray say, "obviously illegitimate."

Most prefer to vocalize (with one Heb. MS) הָאֹמֵר (or הָאוֹמֵר) "who says," corresponding to אשר "who" in the next verse; so Beer (*BHK*), Gerleman (*BHS prb*), and most English versions and commentators. Obviously, God is not making such judgments of all rulers, so we should translate "who *can* say, who *may* say" (on the attributive ptcp with the nuance "can, may," see Joüon–Muraoka, §121i).

18.b. מלך is conventionally translated "king," but NEB "prince."

18.c. בליעל is translated "worthless one" (RSV, similarly NIV), "knave" (Moffatt), "scoundrel" (NRSV, NJB, NJPS, Habel), "good for nothing" (JB), "vile" (RV, Tur-Sinai), or "*vaurien* (worthless)" (Terrien). The prevailing assumption is that it is a compound of בלי "without" and יעל "profit" (so BDB, 116a; AS, 120b; Zorell, 114a; *DCH*, 2:178a; Gordis; not mentioned in *TLOT*). But there is little to recommend this suggestion, not least because there is no noun יַעַל "profit" (there is a verb יעל "profit, avail"). Ges[18], 152b, says "etymology unknown," and *HALOT*, 1:133b, that the etymology is uncertain, with four suggestions being noted, but the key translation given is "worthlessness" all the same. F. M. Cross and D. N. Freedman suggested (see below), most improbably, that it means a place from which no one comes up, i.e., the underworld (a compound of בל "not" and עלה "come up"). Perhaps the most satisfactory proposal is that of D. W. Thomas (see below), that the word is derived from בלע "swallow," thus "the swallower" as a name for Sheol; "sons of Belial" would then be deadly or destructive persons, though with no necessary reference to the underworld itself.

Whatever the etymology of the word, its use suggests that בליעל is no more than a general word for "wicked," with a more specific meaning, if any, of "destructive." It is used in all kinds of contexts, juridical, cultic, and social.

Literature: W. von Baudissin, "The Original Meaning of 'Belial,'" *ExpTim* 9 (1897–98) 40–45; F. M. Cross and D. N. Freedman, "A Royal Song of Thanksgiving: II Samuel 22 = Psalm 18," *JBL* 72 (1953) 15–34 (22 n. 6); G. R. Driver, "Hebrew Notes," *ZAW* 52 (1934) 51–56 (52–53) (from בלע II "be confessed"; cf. *DCH*, 2:180b); J. A. Emerton, "Sheol and the Sons of Belial," *VT* 37 (1987) 214–18; V. Maag, "*Belīja'al* im Alten Testament," *TZ* 21 (1965) 287–99; P. Joüon, "בְּלִיַּעַל Bélial," *Bib* 5 (1924) 178–83; D. W. Thomas, "בְּלִיַּעַל in the Old Testament," in *Biblical and Patristic Studies in Memory of Robert Pierce Casey*, ed. J. N. Birdsall and R. W. Thomson (Freiburg: Herder, 1963) 11–19; B. Otzen, *TDOT*, 2:131–36; P. D. Wegner, *NIDOTTE*, 1:661–62.

18.d. נדיבים is "nobles," but NEB has "magnates" (REB "nobles"). The word is pl, but, strangely, God says to them, "You wicked man (רשע)." Gordis (followed by Hartley) suggests that נדיבים is "distributive," i.e., "to each noble," or else (much less likely) the final *mem* is enclitic. More probably, רשע is sg because בליעל in the preceding colon is sg.

18.e. NEB's "and [will] call his magnates blackguards to their faces" improves nothing by avoiding the direct speech; רשע "wicked" may be turned as "villain" (Moffatt) or "criminals" (JB). Habel has "condemned," thinking of the legal nuances here.

19.a. נשא פני, lit. "has [not] lifted up the face of," the pf denoting an action that continues into the present (GKC, §106g; Joüon–Muraoka, §112c).

19.b. נכר is either niph pf, i.e., "the rich is not recognized before, i.e., above, the poor," or, more probably, piel pf, i.e., "he [God] does not recognize the rich above the poor" (so Gordis, Hartley). Duhm and Beer (*BH*[2] *frt*) read הִכִּיר hiph, the piel being rare (only elsewhere at 21:29; Deut 32:27; 1 Sam 23:7; Jer 19:4), but that is not reason enough for a change.

19.c. שׁוֹע seems to be a term for class ("high-ranking") rather than for wealth ("rich"), though of course the same people tend to be both (also in Isa 32:5); cf. P. Joüon, "Notes de lexicographie hébraïque: XIII. שׁוֹעַ 'grand' (socialement)," *Bib* 18 (1937) 205–6; V. Sasson, "Ugaritic *ṯ'* and *ǵzr* and Hebrew *šôwa'* and *'ōzēr*," *UF* 14 (1982) 201–8; M. Dietrich and O. Loretz, "Ugaritische *ṯ'/ṯ'y* und hebräisch *šw'*," *UF* 19 (1987) 33–36; K. T. Aitken, *NIDOTTE*, 4:66; and cf. Isa 32:5.

19.d. De Wilde transposes v 25a to this point to create a bicolon and make some sense of the difficult לכן that begins v 25a. Gray, however, moves vv 29c–30 to this point.

20.a. De Wilde moves v 20a to follow v 25 since they both concern the death of the wicked.

20.b. ימתו "they may die," a modal use of the impf, recognized also by NEB and Habel; cf. *Note* 4:20.b. NJPS "some die suddenly" also reflects an understanding that this is not a sentence of universal validity. Dhorme, followed by Larcher, Terrien, and Rowley, moves to this position ויעברו, yielding "In a moment they die and pass away." Thus also JB "They die, they are gone in an instant." Sutcliffe ("Notes on Job," 75–76) also feels that the line is too short and adds at the end יִגְוָעוּ "[and in the middle of the night] they perish."

20.c. MT וְחָצוֹת "and the middle of," which could perhaps be "and [that in] the middle of the night" (Hesse "und [das] mitten in der Nacht"), but Gerleman (*BHS frt*), de Wilde, Sicre Díaz delete rather the ו "and" as a dittograph of the preceding letter.

20.d. De Wilde removes v 20b, c to precede v 26.

20.e. עם "people" was brilliantly emended by Budde to שׁוֹעִם "the nobles, high-ranking" (see *Note* 19.c above), presuming haplography of the last two letters of the preceding word (followed by Peake, Strahan, Driver–Gray, Hölscher, Kissane, Larcher, Fohrer, Rowley, Hesse, de Wilde, Gray, Gerleman [*BHS prp*], Moffatt, JB, NAB, NEB "great though they are, they perish," as well as by the *Translation* above). The emendation has the advantages of removing the (not very serious; cf. GKC, §145b) anomaly of a sg subj and two pl verbs, and, more importantly, of concentrating the focus of the verse on the high-ranking rather than diffusing it to both them and the general populace. Less probable is Ehrlich's emendation to שָׂרִים "princes."

Pope, Gordis, Sicre Díaz, Habel, Hartley argued against any change on the ground that עם means the upper classes, but that view appears to rest solely on 12:2, which is much better explained quite differently (see *Note* 12:2.a).

Another approach is to question whether we do have here the common word עם "people." H. J. van Dijk (*Ezekiel's Prophecy on Tyre [Ez 26,1—28,19]: A New Approach,* BibOr 20 [Rome: Pontifical Biblical Institute, 1968] 102) and Blommerde suggested that we see here, parallel with אביר "mighty," a new word עַם "strong" (first proposed by M. Dahood, *Psalms III,* 112, 283–84, 286; cf. *DCH,* vol. 6, *s.v.* עם IV), from the supposed verb עמם "be strong," thus "even the strong one is shaken" (reading יְגֹעַשׁ). Tur-Sinai made the attractive suggestion that the word is עֲמִי "dusk, evening" (cf. MH, Aram. עמי "be dark," עֲמְיָא "darkness" [Jastrow, 1087b; Dalman, 315b]; and cf. *DCH,* vol. 6, *s.v.*), thus "they pass away in the dark"; see too *Note* 36:20.d and *Comment* on 36:20, where עם may also be parallel to לילה "night."

20.f. יגעשו "are shaken." Terrien interestingly translates "se révolte," which enables him to render the third colon "and God deposes a tyrant without lifting a hand" (similarly Fedrizzi, JB "it costs him no effort to remove a tyrant"; Ravasi "tyrants are overturned without a hand being lifted"). For יגעשו, Driver–Gray (*vel*) read יְגֹרְשׁוּ "are driven out" (so too apparently Moffatt "are torn away"), followed by מֵעָם "from a people" (as also Duhm), i.e., they are driven out from their people and pass away. But Driver–Gray (*vel*), Rowley, Hesse preferred יִנָּגְעוּ שׁוֹעִים "the opulent are smitten." Beer (*BHK*), Kissane (שׁוֹעִם), Larcher, de Wilde, Good read יִגַּע שׁוֹעִים "he smites the wealthy" (cf. NEB "at his touch the rich are no more," JB "it costs him no effort to remove a tyrant"). Hölscher (*frt*) and Fohrer read יִגְוָעוּ "they perish" (Gerleman [*BHS prp* יִגְוְעוּ]), Guillaume יִגְוַע "perishes" (sg verb with pl subj). Tur-Sinai reads יָנִיעַ "he drives out." NAB, according to its *Textual Notes,* read יַגִּיעַ hiph "he touches (?)" (*yâggîaʿ* must be a misprint for *yaggîaʿ*), but translates "he brings on (nobles)," which is hard to decipher.

As the MT stands, there are two pl verbs (יגעשו and ויעברו) with a sg subj (עם), but since the subj is a collective ("people"), there is no problem (GKC, §145b), and it is quite unnecessary to suggest that the verb endings are old indicatives (Blommerde).

20.g. וְיַעֲבֹרוּ "and they pass away." NAB reads hiph וְיַעֲבִיר "and he takes (them) away." Blommerde deletes the final *waw* as a dittograph, in order to make his new word עם "strong" the subject of the verb (he vocalizes the word as עָם).

20.h. Beer (BH^2), Ehrlich, de Wilde, and Moffatt emend אביר "the mighty one" to אֲבִירִים "the mighty ones" (with one MS), to parallel the emended pl שׁוֹעִים "wealthy."

20.i. ויסירו is hiph impf "and they remove," which can be explained as an indefinite subj (GKC, §144g; Delitzsch, Blommerde, Gordis, Hartley), translated by the passive "and are taken away." One Heb. MS (cf. *BHK*), however, reads וְיָסוּרוּ qal "and they depart" (which Beer [BH^2] adopts, as also NEB "and the mighty vanish"). However, since the subj is sg (אביר), some would emend the verb also to the sg: thus וְיָסוּר "and he [the mighty] departs" (Hölscher, Kissane, Fohrer, Hesse, Sicre Díaz [*prb*], Gray), or וְיָסִיר "and he [God] removes" (Beer [*BHK,* with one Heb. MS], REB, JB, NAB, Duhm, Terrien, de Wilde, Hartley [*weyāsûr* is an error]), or וְיוּסַר pual "and (the mighty) is removed" (Budde, Driver–Gray, Sicre Díaz [*prb*]). Some translations suggest a stress upon the term אביר, thus "even great men are removed" (NJPS), "great though they are" (JB).

For סור hiph "depose, remove (from royal rule)," cf. 1 Kgs 15:13 (*DCH,* vol. 6, *s.v.,* §9).

20.j. The destruction of these rulers is said to be "without hand" (לא ביד). Many think this means "without human agency," i.e., by divine intervention (so Peake, Strahan, Hölscher, Fohrer, Fedrizzi, Gordis, Andersen, Habel, Moffatt "the mighty disappear mysteriously," NJPS "not by human hands," similarly RSV, NIV), as with Dan 2:34 and 8:25, where a stone is cut "but not with hands" (די־לא בידין) and a king is broken "without a hand" (באפס יד); cf. also οὐ χειροποιητός "not made with hands" in Mark 14:58; Heb 9:11, 24. But there is a closer parallel in Lam 4:6, where Sodom was overthrown in a moment, no hand being laid on it (ולא־חלו בה ידים "and no hands whirled over it"), i.e., without anyone's having to use force, which would yield the translation here "though no hand is laid on them" (NEB), or "without lifting a finger" (REB), "without lifting a hand" (NAB) (so too Dhorme, Terrien).

Gray suggests that יָד here may mean "[without] memorial," like the memorial set up by Absalom (2 Sam 18:18). Friedrich Delitzsch emended ולא ביד "and not by hand" to לְאַבְּדוֹ "by destroying him," which yields a rather weak sense.

22.a. On the meaning of צלמות, lit. "darkness of death," see *Note* 3:5.a. KJV has "shadow of death" and NJB "shadow dark as death"; but the "death" element is avoided by most modern versions.

22.b. Though the subj פעלי און "evildoers" is separate from the inf, it is a nominative (GKC, §115f).

23.a. Dhorme, followed by NAB and NEB, removes v 25 to this point because of the connection of "night" (v 25) with the darkness (v 22) that does not hide evildoers from God (so too Gray). But he still cannot make sense of לכן as "wherefore" (see *Note* 25.b below).

23.b. כי is hardly "for" here (as, e.g., RSV), since the verse does not provide the reason for what precedes, but "indeed" (as in v 11); thus Terrien *en effet* and Habel "indeed"; for other examples, see *Note* 22:26.b.

23.c. לא על־איש ישים עוד, lit. "he does not set again upon a man," which is barely intelligible (KJV "for he will not lay upon man more than right"). Attempts to sustain the MT, usually implying that God already knows all human deeds, are difficult to justify from the Heb.; thus Tur-Sinai "he need not further lay it upon man," RV "For he needeth not further consider a man," NIV "God has no need to examine men further," Hitzig "investigate." Le Hir understood "God does not look at man twice" (similarly Renan "God has no need to look at man twice to impose his judgment on him"). We might wonder whether שים means "attack" as in 1 Kgs 20:12, but it seems more likely that שים there means "set (yourself), take up position" (cf. RSV, NJB). Delitzsch thought it was לִבּוֹ "his heart" that was implied as the object of "set," thus "He needeth not long to regard a man (i.e., before he knows the truth about a man's deeds)." So too Good, but, not too convincingly, he takes that to mean "give permission."

Because of the difficulty with the MT, most (including the *Translation* above) gladly adopt the old emendation by Reiske of מוֹעֵד "time" for עוד "again" (assuming a haplography), thus "he has not appointed a time" (RSV), "he has no set time for man to appear" (NJPS), or, more loosely, "he forewarns no man of his time to come before God" (NAB), "he serves no writ on anyone" (NJB), "God has not to fix sessions" (Moffatt); so too Wright, Budde, Duhm, Peake, Strahan, Driver–Gray, Dhorme, Beer (*BHK*), Hölscher, Kissane, Larcher (but not BJ), Fohrer, Terrien, Pope, Fedrizzi, Gerleman (*BHS prp*), and Hesse. Beer (*BH*^{2}) reads the verb as a passive יוּשַׂם "is set" (or else he would read יֵשׁ מוֹעֵד "there is a time"); perhaps NEB takes a hint from this reading in its use of the passive in "There are no appointed days." For שים מועד "set a time," cf. Exod 9:5. Gray less satisfactorily omits the verb, translating "not on any man's account is there an appointed time."

Gordis has offered an important variation on this emendation, by reading שִׂים (or לָשִׂים) for ישים, thus "It is not for man to set the time to go to God for judgment," which would be a direct rebuttal of Job's complaint that times of judgment are not observed by God (24:1); so too Sicre Díaz, Hartley, and Newsom (similarly Habel). This reading makes better sense of הלך "go"; if God is setting the time, we might rather expect "come" (בוא), since the movement would more naturally be from his perspective. Furthermore, a good sense is obtained for the word על, which would then mean "incumbent, proper" (as in 2 Sam 18:11; Ezra 10:12).

Reiske's emendation is to be preferred, nonetheless, for the sake of the flow of thought: v 23 would be affirming that God does not need to wait for an assize day to reach a judgment but can execute it immediately, while v 24 would be saying that he does not need to carry out a lengthy process of investigation since he already knows all there is to be known about the crime.

Guillaume attempts to retain the MT by postulating a new Heb. noun עוֹד "time" (cf. Arab. *'īd* "time,"); but *'īd* means "festival" (Lane, 2190c) rather than any appointed time.

23.d. הלך במשפט is unmistakably "go for judgment," but the normal idiom is, nevertheless,

בוא במשפט עם "come to judgment with" (as in 14:3; 22:4; Isa 3:14; Ps 143:2 [with את]; Eccl 11:9; 12:14 [without עם in the last two references]). Ehrlich read לְהַלֵּךְ אֶת־אֵל בְּמִשְׁפָּט "to go to judgment with God," את "with" as in Ps 143:2; perhaps it does not matter that the verb there is בוא "come" rather than הלך "go" (against Driver–Gray).

24.a. רעע "break" is usually said to be an Aramaism (Heb. רצץ), but it is well established in Heb. (five occurrences).

24.b. לא־חקר "without inquiry," a circumstantial clause in which אין would be more normal as the negative (Driver, *Tenses*, §164), though לא־חקר is also to be found at 36:26. In 5:9, 9:10, and 36:26 the phrase means "without the possibility of inquiry"; here it is "without the need for inquiry" (Driver–Gray), though not precisely "without a trial" (Moffatt, NAB). Good rather improbably translates "unscrutinized," as if it were God who was the object of inquiry. KJV "without number" presumably took its lead from 5:9 and 9:10, where אין חקר "without inquiry" was parallel to אין מספר "without number"; but no modern translations or commentators follow this possibility. RV has "in ways past finding out."

24.c. עמד hiph is normally "make to stand," but commonly enough also "set in position, set up" (*HALOT,* 2:841b; *DCH,* vol. 6, *s.v.*). Normal syntax would require that the verb be prefixed with simple *waw,* not *waw* consec (as MT); hence Beer (*BHK*) וְיַעֲמֹד, Gerleman (*BHS* [?]) וְיַעֲמִיד.

25.a. Budde deletes vv 25–28, while Beer (BH^2 *frt*) deletes only v 25 as a variant on vv 20–21, and Dhorme, Kissane, Gray, NAB, NEB move v 25 to precede v 23.

25.b. לכן is usually "wherefore," "therefore," but here nothing has preceded to which it can be logically attached (though Terrien translates "that is why"). And it "seems to invert the logical relation" (Peake). Delitzsch rightly saw that it introduces not the "real consequence" but "a logical inference, something that directly follows in and with what precedes" (citing 42:3; Isa 26:14; 61:7; Jer 2:33; 5:2; Zech 11:7). The most suitable translation is "thus" (as RSV).

Less probable is the sense "indeed"; so Gordis (similarly Habel), citing Isa 26:14, Jer 5:2, and perhaps Gen 4:15 as parallels (cf. also Arab. *lakinna*); this sense is also acknowledged by *HALOT,* 2:530b, citing 1 Sam 28:2, Jer 2:33, and *DCH,* 4:548b. Others suggest "but"; so Dhorme (followed by Gray) and Guillaume, also adducing Arab. *lakinna,* though in the sense "but"; Dhorme cites v 10 and 42:3 as parallels, neither very convincing.

It might seem rather obvious to translate it "because," the first colon being then the reason for the second; so Moffatt "because he marks what they are doing," Tur-Sinai "because he knoweth their deeds." But that seems to be one thing לכן cannot mean.

For the meaning "and now then," see W. Eugene March, "*Lākēn:* Its Functions and Meanings," in *Rhetorical Criticism,* FS J. Muilenburg, ed. J. J. Jackson and M. Kessler, PTMS 1 (Pittsburgh: Pickwick Press, 1974) 256–84.

Strahan thought that לכן must be changed to כי or else omitted, as in LXX.

25.c. יכיר, lit. "recognizes"; others translate "consider" (Fohrer [*achtet*]), "discern" (NAB), or "take note of" (NIV). Gordis unnecessarily emends to יַעְכֹּר "disturbs, troubles," which he thinks also means "destroys" (as at Josh 7:25, 26; Judg 11:35; 1 Kgs 18:17–18; similarly *HALOT,* 2:824b "entangle, put into disorder, bring disaster"), in order to create a parallelism with הפך "overturn." But, if לכן were to mean "because," there would be no need to seek a parallel in the verse.

F. Zimmermann ("Notes on Some Difficult Old Testament Passages," *JBL* 55 [1936] 303–8 [306–7]) proposed a new Heb. נכר hiph, "repudiate" (cf. Arab. *nakara* IV [Lane, 2849b], Syr. *nkr* [J. Payne Smith, 340b]); he is followed by NEB, Terrien, and Fedrizzi (cf. נכר IV, *DCH,* 5:694b). Guillaume advanced the same proposal, with the sense "disapprove of" (the Arab. cognate is the same as in Zimmermann's proposal, and the entry for a זכר V in *DCH,* 5:694b, should be deleted).

25.d. מעבדיהם "their deeds" is often called an Aramaism (Dan 4:34). To avoid the Aramaism, Ehrlich reads יַכִּירֵם מֵעֲבָדֵיהֶם "recognizes them from their servants" (which seems improbable), assuming haplography of the *mem;* but there are many other examples of alleged Aramaisms in Job (the previous in v 24), and the present word is no cause for concern. Guillaume suggests that we have here a new Heb. word מַעְבָּד "way" (cf. Arab. *mu'abbad;* cf. *DCH,* 5:379a); but *mu'abbad,* though it can mean "beaten, trodden" (of a road), does not seem to mean the road itself (Lane, 1936b).

25.e. Siegfried, Dhorme, Beer (*BHK*), Hölscher, Larcher, Weiser, Fedrizzi, and Gray read וַיַּהַפְכֵם "and he overthrows them," with the obj expressed rather than implied as it is in MT. Delitzsch thought that without the suff the word might well mean "causeth an overthrow," i.e., "creates a new order of things." But the suff can easily be inferred from the suff of מעבדיהם "their deeds," the preceding word.

הפך is "turn, overturn, overthrow"; NEB "he turns on them" plays with the meaning, but it is not an attested sense. NAB "he turns at night and crushes them" is improbable since הפך is used intransitively only with a qualifying adv phrase or another verb (in battle, Judg 20:39 [and 20:41 in that context]; on the day of battle, Ps 78:9; from a chariot, 2 Kgs 5:26; to one's way, 1 Sam 25:12; followed by "and went," 2 Chr 9:12; see *DCH,* 2:580b).

25.f. לילה "(in) the night," acc of time (GKC, §118i). Good is the only person who thinks that "night" is the obj of the verb: "[he] overturns the night."

25.g. Beer (*BH*[2]) moved וידכאו "and they are crushed" to the beginning of v 26 (as also Pesh). But, as Dhorme points out, "they are crushed" is the result of being overthrown in the night. The form וִידַּכָּאוּ is hithp, with elided *taw,* as at 5:4. NAB reads (*Textual Notes,* 378) וַיְדַכְּאֵם "and he crushes them." It is hard to see what image NJB has in mind with its rendering "He overthrows them at night, to be trampled on."

26.a. NAB omits, comparing 34:24b, 27a; 27:21, 23; but the repetition of phrases found also in those verses can hardly be called a "dittography" (*Textual Notes,* 378). G. R. Driver, "Difficult Words in the Hebrew Prophets," in *Studies in Old Testament Prophecy,* FS T. H. Robinson, ed. H. H. Rowley (Edinburgh: T. & T. Clark, 1950) 52–72 (62), inserts at the beginning of the verse יְחִתֵּם "he terrifies them"; this is the origin of NEB's "he strikes them down" (cf. Brockington).

26.b. ספק is usually "slap, strike" (hands in Num 24:10 and Lam 2:15; without an explicit obj, Isa 2:6 [hiph]; and doubtfully in Job 34:37; the obj is the thigh in Jer 31:19; Ezek 21:12 [17]). Jer 48:26 (?) "fall with a splash" (BDB, 706b) is problematic, and may be a separate root, as *HALOT,* 2:765b. It is never "smite," which is the sense needed here, so the text may be questionable; nevertheless, KJV has "strikes," NEBmg "chastises them," NIV "punishes." Good translates "jeers," on the ground that to clap the hands is a gesture of derision in Lam 2:15, but it is doubtful that כַּפַּיִם "hands" is to be understood as the object of the verb. On the use of the pf tense here, cf. *Note* 19.a on נשׂא.

Tur-Sinai and others see here another ספק "be full, sufficient," a byform of שׂפק II (BDB, 974a; *HALOT,* 3:1349a), which is well attested in Ecclesiasticus (cf. *DCH,* vol. 6, *s.v.*). Hence Tur-Sinai renders "He investeth those (others) instead of the wicked," i.e., empowers them to be rulers. But, though this would give a normal sense to תחת "instead of," it is unlikely that the obj of the verb should be אחרים from as far back as v 24.

G. R. Driver ("Difficult Words," 62) put forward another sense for the same verb ספק, viz. "empty out, vomit up" (as also at Jer 48:26; perhaps it should be regarded as a separate word, as *DCH,* vol. 6, *s.v.*; it is also registered by *HALOT,* 2:765b). He moves the verb to the second colon and translates "he emptieth them out in place of their satiety"; hence NEB, reading סִפְקָם "makes them disgorge their bloated wealth." However, the evidence for the sense "vomit" is weak (only in a lexical list in Syr.; cf. Payne Smith, 2705a).

26.c. תחת, lit. "under," often "instead of," but that will not suit here. It can hardly mean "like" (contra KJV "[as] wicked men," Vg *quasi impios* "as if they were wicked," NJB "like criminals," Dhorme, Terrien "like malefactors," Fedrizzi *come empi*). Such a sense for תחת is poorly attested, if at all (see BDB, 1065b; though at Ecclus 30:25 [33:13] "good *like* delicacies" it does seem to have that sense [Dhorme]). But it is perhaps not an insuperable objection that they cannot be "like" the wicked since they themselves have been called "wicked" (v 18)—for the sense could well be that they, the kings and princes, are "like common criminals."

Pope sees here תחת "among" (rendering "as criminals"), and J. C. Greenfield argues for the sense "among" at Isa 57:5 on the basis of Ugar. *tḥt* ("The Prepositions B . . . Taḥat . . . in Jes 57 5," *ZAW* 32 [1961] 226–28); similarly M. J. Dahood, "Northwest Semitic Philology and Job," in *The Bible in Current Catholic Thought: Gruenthaner Memorial Volume,* ed. J. L. McKenzie, St. Mary's Theological Studies 1 (New York: Herder & Herder, 1962) 55–74 (71). For other examples of תחת "among," see *Note* 30:7.b. Watson, 345, sees this as a case of "reversed ballast preposition," i.e., ב in the second colon being the key prep and תחת in the first colon acquiring its sense from the ב (another example of the phenomenon appears at 37:8). Guillaume finds here a new Heb. תַּחַת cognate with Arab. *'al-taḥt* "people of low class" (Lane, 298b).

The best solution is to take תחת as "because of, for" (so also RSV, NEB, NIV, Gordis, de Wilde, Habel, Hartley), as in 2 Sam 19:22 and Jer 5:19 (a sense not acknowledged by the lexica, though *HALOT,* 4:1723a §3c, allows "as recompense for"), with the following noun revocalized to רִשְׁעָם "their wickedness." Gray, however, offers an attractive possibility by understanding תחת in a "locative" sense, "on the scene of their crime," as in Ugar. *tḥt 'adrm dbgrn* "in the place of the notables who are in the public place" (*KTU* 1.17 V 6). Yet such a sense of *tḥt,* only once attested in Ugar., really means "among" (*DUL,* 866), which is not so suitable here.

26.d. רשעים "wicked ones"; but, following Houbigant, Beer (*BH*[2] *prps; BHK*), Larcher, Gordis, de

Wilde, Habel, Hartley, Gray, RSV, JB, NEB, and NIV, as well as the *Translation* above, read רִשְׁעָם "[because of] their wickedness."

Other emendations include: (1) יִדְעֲכוּ רשעים "the wicked are extinguished" (Bickell); (2) תְּחַת רשעים חֲמָתוֹ "his wrath shatters the wicked" (Bickell[2], Budde, Moffatt "he breaks the villains in his wrath"); (3) יְדַכְּאוּ מִתַּחְתָּם רשעים "they crush the wicked from their place" (מִתַּחַת as in Exod 10:23; Zech 6:12); (4) רְסִיסִים "fragments," as in Amos 6:11 (Duhm [רְסָסִים], Beer [BH^2 *al*]); (5) על־כן חִתַּת רשעים "therefore [transposing על־כן from v 27] hath He smitten the wicked" (Kissane, followed by Rowley; Kissane's חִתַּת seems an error for חִתַּת).

26.e. The colon is "too short and strange" (de Wilde); for אשר (v 27) במקום ראים "in the place of those who see, who," he reads לִמְקוֹם רְפָאִים אָשְׁרוּ "to the place of shadows they go" (for rulers as underworld shades, cf. Isa 14:9), which is clever but not very strong (אשר occurs only once elsewhere in the qal, which is presumably what de Wilde means by *'ašarû*). Beer (*BHK*) and Gerleman (*BHS frt*) insert a verb, הִכָּם "he smote them" or יַכֵּם "he smites them." Dhorme fills out the colon by moving back the troublesome אשר from the beginning of v 27 to follow במקום (revocalized בִּמְקוֹם), thus "in the place where there are spectators"—which makes no difference to the translation. Gray adds simply עֲלֵיהֶם "[where men may gloat] over them," ראה על being equivalent to the common ראה ב "see one's desire upon" (as Mic 7:10; Ps 22:17 [18]). Ehrlich reads במקום רָעִים, which he takes to mean "like common criminals."

NEB, following G. R. Driver ("Difficult Words," 62), offers for the colon "and makes them disgorge their bloated wealth," but REB returns to a more traditional rendering, "he strikes them down as a public spectacle." In place of אשר, the first word of the next verse, Larcher reads אֲסָרָם "he chains them," comparing 36:13; hence NJB "chained up for all to see."

26.f. במקום ראים "in the place of those seeing" is admittedly a strange phrase, though it can be rendered into acceptable Eng.; thus RV "in the open sight of others," NRSV "while others look on," Hartley "in a public place" (similarly Pope), Good "in the onlookers' place," Moffatt "before the world." Terrien translates the phrase twice over: "in the public place in view of all."

For ראים "those seeing," Driver ("Difficult Words," 62–63) reads רְאָיָם "their satiety," from a new word רְאִי, derived from רוה "be saturated," sometimes spelled ראה, like the verb "see"; hence NEB "their bloated wealth" (though Brockington gives the form as רְאָיִם). Tur-Sinai alleges that the word means "impure" (as also in 33:21; he thinks רֳאִי in Nah 3:6 is "filth," parallel to שִׁקֻּצִים "filth").

27.a. Duhm, followed by Beer (BH^2), deletes the verse as a gloss; it is admittedly a bit dull.

27.b. אשר על־כן must mean "because" (so too Dhorme, Gordis), but it is an awkward phrase (Ps 45:2 [3] may be a parallel). Delitzsch attempted to preserve the Heb. by understanding that they are struck down "because they therefore, i.e. to suffer such have turned aside" from God—but this is overly subtle. Gordis compared כי על־כן "because" (Num 10:31; Gen 18:5 is different), which is, however, not the same phrase. Good is alone in insisting that the phrase should mean "therefore," referring back; thus "that is why they turn from following him." But it would be a little perverse to say that the reason the wicked turn from following God is that he has jeered at them (which is how Good understands ספק).

De Wilde reads על־כן אשר "on account of the fact that." Beer (*BHK*), Fohrer, Gray, NAB read על־אשר "on account of the fact that, because," deleting כן. Hölscher reads על־כן "since," deleting אשר. Bickell read אשר "who," deleting על־כן. Larcher translates "if one replies" (so too BJ, JB "you may say"), but it is hard to see what Heb. he is reading.

27.c. For the phrase סור מאחרי "turn from following" (Habel "were disloyal to," NEB "have ceased to obey him"), cf. Deut 7:4.

27.d. שׂכל hiph may be (1) "understand" (Dhorme, NJB), "recognize" (Terrien *méconnu*), or (2) "ponder" (BDB, 968a), "consider" (KJV), "have regard for" (RV, RSV, NIV), "pay heed to" (NEB, similarly NAB), "attend to" (Good), "were reckless of his rules" (Moffatt), the latter alternative being the more probable (similarly Habel).

28.a. LXX omits vv 28–33, though whether because of their extreme difficulty is hard to say.

28.b. דל is conventionally translated "poor" (cf. *Comment* on 20:19), but NJB has "weak."

28.c. להביא, lit. "so as to cause to come," expressing purpose (GKC, §114f); it has to be ironic to say that they disregarded God's ways *so that* they would cause the cry of the poor to rise to God (cf. BDB, 775b, *s.v.* למען: "sometimes, in rhetorical passages, the issue of a line of action, though really undesigned, is represented by it ironically as if it were designed"). This is a more interesting rendering than taking the inf as equivalent to a gerund, "by causing to come to him" (as Dhorme; cf. GKC, §114o). Presumably it is the wicked who cause the cry of the poor to come to God, though Davidson thought that it was God who, by smiting the wicked down, caused the cry of the poor (similarly Habel

"Thus he lets the cry of the poor reach him"). But this would be to confuse cause with consequence. Good can hardly be right that the wicked rulers "fail 'to bring to him the outcry of the poor,'" for it is not the responsibility of rulers to bring the grievances of the oppressed to God but to correct them themselves.

28.d. עליו must be equivalent to אליו "to him," as Beer (*BH*[2]) noted, and two MSS read; for the interchangeability of אל and על, see BDB, 41a, 758a; so too Gordis. Dahood ("Northwest Semitic Philology and Job," 69–70) suggests that על has a special sense of "into his presence" (as also at 29:13; 33:27); cf. *DCH,* vol. 6, *s.v.* §1.c.1.

28.e. Good also sees that this colon is syntactically disjunct from the previous. It is not another aim (or consequence, read ironically) of the wicked's failure to follow after God (contra Dhorme).

28.f. To avoid the repetition, for this second צעקת Duhm and Beer (*BHK*) read the synonyms וְצְוָחַת "and the cry of" or וְשַׁוְעַת "and the cry of" (so too NAB "plea"). Blommerde suggests, not unreasonably, that repetition of a word from the first colon as the first word of the second colon, prefaced with emphatic *waw,* is a normal feature of Heb. poetry (cf. also 3:17; 17:15 [though an emendation may well be required here]; 38:17, 22; 41:24 [16]).

29.a. NEB (but not REB) encloses vv 29–30 in brackets, as if they were secondary.

NJB understands the syntax thus: "if he is silent and no one can move him... he is taking pity on nations and individuals, is setting some wrong-doer free"; apart from the detailed difficulties with this rendering, such a complex syntactic construction of the five cola is not very probable.

The first two cola begin with conditional clauses without introductory conditional particles (cf. GKC, §159b); the apodosis is a rhetorical question, as in 9:12; 11:10; 23:13 (Driver–Gray).

29.b. שקט hiph is "be quiet" in all but one of its ten occurrences (e.g., Isa 7:4; 30:15); thus "rests" (Dhorme), "remains tranquil" (NAB). Only in Prov 15:18 is it "make quiet" (BDB, 1053b, thinks it has this sense here; similarly KJV "giveth quietness," Habel "silences," Delitzsch "maketh peace" [improbably, by overthrowing the tyrant]). Budde (יִשְׁקֹט), followed by Gray, and Beer (*BHK*), however, read יִשְׁקוֹט qal (with one Heb. MS).

Among philological proposals, (1) A. S. Yahuda ("Hapax legomena im Alten Testament erklärt und erläutert," *JQR* 15 [1902–1903] 698–714 [713]) found here a new Heb. verb שקט "fall down" (cf. Arab. *saqaṭa* [Lane, 1379c]), thus "casts down" (hiph). Perhaps this should rather be regarded as simply a new sense of BH שקט "be quiet," which BDB, 1052b, already related to Arab. *saqaṭa.* (2) A. Guillaume ("The Arabic Background of the Book of Job," in *Promise and Fulfilment,* FS S. H. Hooke, ed. F. F. Bruce [Edinburgh: T. & T. Clark, 1963] 106–27 [122]), transposing the first two letters of the root, found here a קשט "declare just," as in Arab. *qasaṭa* "act justly" (Lane, 2522c); so too Tur-Sinai, but the case is strained.

29.c. Seeking a closer parallel to שקט "be quiet" (as there is in the next colon), Hitzig, Beer, *Text,* Dhorme, Hölscher (*frt*), Larcher (followed by BJ), and Gray (יַרְעִישֶׁנּוּ), transposing two letters of the verb, read יַרְעִשׁ "can cause disquiet, stir up" (as in Isa 14:16) for MT ירשע "condemns," yielding "who can stir Him?" (Dhorme, NJB "move him"). Ehrlich emends to יִוָּשֵׁעַ "[who] can be saved?" Gordis retains the MT at the cost of proposing another Heb. רשע, meaning "stir up," comparing Arab. *rasa'a* "be loose (of limbs)," but the analogy fails to convince, and the Arab. is questionable: there seems to be no *rasa'a,* and *rassagha* is either "reach to the ankles" or "be abundant," though there is a noun *rasagh* meaning "laxness in the legs of a camel" (Lane, 1081a), which is perhaps what Gordis is thinking of. It is a long way semantically from "stir up."

KJV's "who can make trouble?" follows Buxtorf, 756, in allowing "disquiet" as a sense for רשע hiph; Leigh, 236b, goes further in regarding רשע itself as a byform of רעשׁ "quake," a view that would find no favor today.

29.d. For a judge to "hide the face" might refer to the taking of bribes, but this is clearly not what is in mind here (cf. on 9:24). Delitzsch, unlike other commentators, takes the reference here to be to God's anger, while to behold him would be to make him visible and thus show his favor again. The parallel with שקט "be quiet" makes clear enough that סתר פנים "hide the face" refers to inactivity. Dahood has well argued, however, that the phrase, in all its occurrences in the Psalms at least, involves not the verb סתר "hide" but rather a form of סור "turn aside," with an infixed *-t-,* and thus means "turns his face away" (so, e.g., at Pss 10:11; 13:2; 19:7; 19:13; 22:25; 27:9; 30:8; 38:10; 44:25; see his *Psalms I,* 64, 76, 123, 124, 142, 169, 183, 235, 268; and cf. *DCH,* vol. 6, *s.v.*). If that were the case here, the sense would be of God ignoring injustice in the world. Gray also derives the verb from סור, as an iphteal (as in Mesha and Ugar. [*DUL,* 770]), or as hithp with metathesis of *t* and *s.*

29.e. For ישורנו "shall see him," Budde, Beer (*BHK frt*), Peake, de Wilde, Moffatt ("blame"), and perhaps NEB "who can find fault?" read יְיַסְּרֶנּוּ "who will correct him?" Wright and Beer, *Text,* ingeniously but unpersuasively emended to יִשְׁרֶנּוּ "will release" (from שׁרה), i.e., "when he removes the condemned (lit. hides the face [of the prisoner]), who can release him?" Gray suggests יְשִׁיבֶנּוּ "who can make him turn again?" which would fit well with סתר in the first colon, understood as "turn aside."

29.f. Budde thought this colon a gloss, explaining that the previous two cola relate to Job personally and not just to nations; similarly Fohrer and Hesse. Gray moved vv 29c–30 to follow v 19; NAB omitted them as "obscure" (*Textual Notes*, 378). Duhm removed אדם חנף "a godless person" as a gloss on מקשׁי עם "snares of the people" and created a couplet from vv 29c and 30: (or יָעֻר) ועל־גוי ועל־אדם יער "and over a people and over humans he watches [so that no snare of the people might reign]"; so too *BHK* (*prps*).

The syntactical understanding in the *Translation* is the same as that in NIV: "Yet he is over nation and man alike, to keep a godless man from ruling." Gordis also connects v 29c with v 30, translating: "When over both a nation and all its people He permits a godless man to rule"; but it is hard to accept that גוי "nation" and אדם "people" can have the same referent when they are linked by... ועל ועל "both... and."

NEB "What though he makes a godless man king over a stubborn nation and all its people" implies something like מַמְלִךְ חנף ועל־גוי מְקֻשֶּׁה ועל־אדם, מקשׁה being pual ptcp (not elsewhere attested). According to Brockington, NEB read מִמְּקֻשֵׁי, which hardly clarifies things, since there is no word מְקֻשֶּׁה connected with קָשֶׁה "hard, stubborn"; LXX ἀπὸ δυσκολίας λαοῦ "because of the discontent of the people" suggests only that LXX read some form of קָשֶׁה but does not specify what exactly.

29.g. Lit. "he is over" (על). Habel can hardly be right in taking the colon as epexegetic of the subj of the verb ישׁורנו "sees him": "who can see him—Be it one nation or all humanity?" For this takes no account of the על. KJV "whether it be done against a nation or against a man only"; RV (awkwardly) "whether it be done unto a nation, or unto a man, alike." The difficulties here show the need to understand the syntax differently.

29.h. אדם is "humankind" or "person" (ungendered); cf. D. J. A. Clines, "אדם, the Hebrew for 'Human, Humanity': A Response to James Barr," *VT* 53 (2003) 297–310. Here על־גוי ועל־אדם could be "over a nation and over an individual human" (similarly NRSV, NIV, NJB) or "over a nation and over humanity (generally)"; less probably "over a nation and all its people" (NEB). "An individual" seems the better option.

29.i. יחד "alike" is felt by many to be odd and in need of emendation. It can hardly mean "all humanity" (as Habel). Without emendation, M. Dahood (review of *Job et son Dieu,* by J. Lévêque, 438; "Hebrew-Ugaritic Lexicography II," *Bib* 45 [1964] 393–412 [407–8]; *Psalms III,* 203, 298, on 33:15; 49:11) understands יָחַד as a dialectal form of יָחֲז "he sees, watches"; but חזה על never means "watch over," only "see concerning" (*DCH,* 3:181b). Blommerde followed this proposal, revocalizing to יֶחֱד (with omission of the final *he*), and Gray, reading יֶחֱדֶה. Hartley too thinks this suggestion the best, though he offers "alike" in his translation. Guillaume thinks rather of a new word cognate with Arab. *ḥadda* "set a limit to, restrain, punish" (Lane, 524b), thus "he sets a limit to a nation or a man to prevent a profane man from reviling."

Among proposed emendations are the following: (1) Beer (*BHK prps*) reports the suggestion יִפְקֹד "he punishes" (but פקד על usually has an obj). (2) Duhm, followed by Beer (*BHK vel*), has יָעֻר or יָעִר "he watches" (see *Note* 29.f). (3) Ehrlich, Dhorme, Hölscher (*frt*), and Terrien read יָחֲז "he sees, watches"; the difficulty with that has been noted above, and the evidence is equally weak for ראה על "watch over" (Exod 1:16; 5:21, adduced by Dhorme, are really irrelevant, and BDB, 907b, seems to acknowledge this sense only for the verb used absolutely). (4) Kissane, followed by Larcher (and BJ), emends to יָחֹן "he is compassionate," or with the sequel, "delivering a miscreant from the snares of affliction." Similarly NJB "he is taking pity." (5) Kissane offers an alternative possibility, יָחֹס "he takes pity." (6) De Wilde reads יִחַר "he is angry." (7) Fedrizzi makes the improbable proposal to read יָרַד, lit. "go down (in order to bless)," which is supposed to mean "watch diligently."

30.a. RSV connects v 30 with v 28, making v 29 a parenthesis (so too Rowley, de Wilde). But it seems inappropriate that God's control of earthly rulers should only be in response to the cry of the oppressed; Elihu's stress in this chapter is rather on God's proactive role in managing his subordinate rulers (cf. vv 18–19, 21, 24). Pope creates a logical sequence that extends from v 29c to v 32—which is far from persuasive. Fohrer and Hesse deleted the whole verse as an explanatory gloss on vv 24–26.

30.b. מן with inf "so as not to, so that not" (BDB, 583a).

30.c. Dhorme (followed by Hölscher) removes חנף "godless" to follow האמר in v 31, and renders "so that no one of those who ensnare the people should reign." It is hard to see why Habel translates חנף "godless" as "the condemned." KJV's "hypocrite" follows Theod ὑποκριτής and Vg *hominem hyp-*

ocritam, with support from Buxtorf, 246. Beer (*BH*[2] *frt*) is inclined to delete אדם חנף "a godless person" as a gloss. Larcher deletes אדם "person" as a repetition from v 29.

30.d. Rather than מִמְּלֹךְ "so as not to rule," Budde (מַמְלִךְ), Gordis, and de Wilde read, with Tg and Vg, מַמְלִיךְ "causing to rule," thus "He permits a godless man to rule" (Gordis), "and he makes a wicked man to rule because of the crooked paths of the people" (de Wilde). So too NEB "he makes (a godless man) king" (מַמְלִךְ). Kissane, followed by Larcher, BJ, JB, emends to מֹלִךְ "causing to go, leading," which he translates "delivering [a miscreant]," though there are no parallels to this sense of הלך hiph.

30.e. Several commentators are unhappy with the alleged shortness of this colon (though, since it has two stresses, it is hard to see why). Budde thus proposed beginning the colon with מֹשֵׁל "ruler," i.e., "When he makes a godless man king, (even) a ruler out of the snares (sc. destroyers) of the people"—a forced solution, if ever there was one. Gray more attractively adds וּמְעַקְּשָׁם "[those who would ensnare the people] and wrong them," creating "such an assonance as the writer of Job favoured."

30.f. ממקשי עם is lit. "from, or of, snares of a people," either (1) parallel to אדם חנף "a godless person," which is to say, "that is, one from among those who ensnare a people" (cf. GKC, §119w), or, (2) parallel to ממלך "so as not to reign," taking the מן in a negative or privative sense, i.e., "so as not [to be] a snare for the people" (cf. GKC, §119x–y, the *mem* being equivalent to מִהְיוֹת "so as not to be" [Delitzsch]). In either case, the sense must be "lest the people be ensnared" (KJV; RSV "that he should not ensnare the people," NIV "from laying snares for the people"), perhaps, with Good, "from being the snares of a people." Terrien translates "from setting traps for the people." עם "the people" is an obj gen (Hartley).

Among emendations may be noted the following: (1) Houbigant emends to ממעקשי עם "on account of the perverters of a people." (2) Similarly, de Wilde emends to מִמַּעֲקַשֵּׁי "because of the crookednesses of" (cf. Vg *propter peccata*, though מַעֲקַשׁ occurs in only one other place [Isa 42:16] and not in this moral sense). It is hard to believe that Elihu thinks that a wicked ruler is the fault of the people. (3) Likewise for the emendation of Nichols, 180, to מִפִּשְׁעֵי עם "because of the sins of the people." (4) Beer (*BHK prps*) notes a similar emendation to מְעַקֵּשׁ "perverting"; either is tame and "removes an essentially Biblical image" (Dhorme). (5) Rowley suggested (perhaps) מִטְּמֹן מֹקְשֵׁי "so as not to hide snares [for the people]" (טמן מקשים "hide snares" in Ps 64:5 [6]). (6) Kissane reads עֳנִי "[from the snares of] affliction"; Larcher and NJB "[he] is setting some wrong-doer free from the meshes of affliction" evidently follow the same reading, while "setting free" may perhaps be presuming מְשַׁלֵּחַ "sending out, setting free" (שלח piel ptcp). (7) Tur-Sinai read מַמְקְשֵׁי עם, lit. "from among the hardeners of the people" (קשה hiph ptcp), i.e., those among the people who harden themselves against God (though קשה hiph usually has an obj, it does not at 9:4, but perhaps we do not have the usual קשה there [see *Note* 9:4.c]).

It is improbable that the people are at fault in this context, since the theme is very certainly that of the wickedness of rulers. Hence Gordis "When . . . He allows a godless man to rule, it is because of the sins of the people" is intrinsically unlikely, as well as difficult to substantiate from the Heb.

31.a. כי "indeed"; for other examples, see *Notes* 34:11.a, 34:23.b, and 22:26.b.

31.b. הֶאָמַר is "has he said?" (NJPS) or "has one said?" (so Dillmann, Delitzsch, KJV "surely it is meet to be said unto God," RV "hath any said unto God?" RSV, Driver–Gray, Pope, Good "can one say?"). Tur-Sinai improbably sees Job as the subj (but Elihu is directly addressing Job!). The colon may of course be taken as the apodosis of a conditional sentence (so NEB, NIV "suppose . . . ," NJB "when such a one says," Dhorme "if a man says"; similarly Newsom). The interrogative ה need not be the first word of its clause (cf., e.g., Neh 13:27; Jer 22:15). A revocalization to הֵאָמֵר (niph inf) yields "(to God) it should be said" (Ehrlich), but this leaves the meaning too vague.

The most plausible reading, adopted in the *Translation* above, results from a simple revocalization to אֱמֹר qal impv, "say" (omitting the initial ה), making vv 31–32 into an address to Job (so Reiske, Dathe, Ley, Gordis, Sicre Díaz, Habel, Hartley, Whybray, Moffatt).

Less convincing is the proposal of Beer (*BH*[2] *vel*), Dhorme, Hölscher, Kissane, Larcher (followed by BJ, JB), to read אָמַר "has said," taking the subject to be חנף "a godless man," which they remove to this point from v 30. NAB also reads אָמַר "when anyone says to God," but then they need their subj אִישׁ "a man" to be conjecturally inserted. Gray follows a similar line, reading כִּי אֶל־אֱלוֹהַּ אָמַר "If one were to say to God." Van der Lugt's proposal to read הָאֹמֵר "the one saying" presumably implies "if one says . . . would God actually punish him?"

Least probable of all is the suggestion of Beer (*BHK*) to take vv 31b–33 as spoken by God, emending (*frt*) to הֲיֹאמַר אֵל אֵלֶיךָ "will God say to you?" (so too Weiser, Fohrer, de Wilde). This would involve a quite remarkable speech by God, ironically confessing to Job that *he* has sinned and will try to do better in future!

31.c. If אמר is read for MT האמר, the initial *he* may be attached to אֶל־אֵל "to God," thus אֶל־אֱלֹהַּ "to Eloah" (Beer [*BH*² *vel*], Dhorme, Hölscher, NAB; אֱלוֹהַּ Kissane [misspelled אֱלוֹהַ], Larcher, Gordis, Sicre Díaz, Habel, Hartley), with no change in meaning.

31.d. MT נָשָׂאתִי is "I have lifted up, borne," which of itself makes little sense here. Some have suggested that "guilt, sin" (עון or חטא, חטאה) is understood as the obj (so Guillaume, Gordis, Hartley, KJV, RSV, NJPS, NIV "I am guilty," Moffatt "suffered"), but there are no parallels. G. R. Driver supplies רֹאשׁ "head" as the implicit obj (expressed at Judg 8:28; Ps 83:2 [3]), thus "I have lifted up my head, i.e., I have presumed" ("Hebrew Poetic Diction," in *Congress Volume, Copenhagen 1953*, VTSup 1 [Leiden: Brill, 1953] 26–39 [39]). Good thinks that "lift" means "I accept, show favor," but offers no parallels (נשׂא פָּנִים "lift up the face" would mean this, but no obj is expressed here). Delitzsch translated "I have been proud," without any alteration to the text, comparing Hos 13:1; Ps 89:9 (10).

A simple revocalization, adopted in the *Translation* above, may solve the problem: נִשֵּׁאתִי (from נשׁא II "beguile") would yield "I have been led astray, beguiled" (Dhorme, Beer [*BHK frt*], Hölscher, Kissane, Larcher, Fohrer, Terrien, Pope, Rowley, Sicre Díaz, Habel, de Wilde, Gray), "I was misled" (NJB), "I was misguided" (NAB), though not exactly "I was mistaken" (Pope), since some element of an act of leading astray should perhaps be retained.

Less probable is the revocalization to נִשֵּׂאתִי (נשׂא niph "be lifted up, lift oneself up"), "I have exalted myself," as in Isa 33:10; Ps 94:2 (Duhm, NEB "I have overstepped the mark" [cf. Brockington]). An emendation to the same effect is הִתְנַשֵּׂאתִי (נשׂא hithp "be lifted up"), "I have revolted" (Beer [*BH*² *frt*]).

Tur-Sinai's novel approach to these verses was to take נשׂאתי as נשׁאתי "I have lent" (נשׁא I), אחבל as "I will take in pledge, as a surety" (as in 22:6; 24:3, 9), אחזה (34:32, *q.v.*) as אֲחֻזָּה "take a pledge!" (אחז "take"), הרני (34:32, *q.v.*) as "give as a pledge," and ישלמנה (34:33, *q.v.*) as "make payment (of a pledge)," thus creating a unifying metaphor throughout vv 31–33. The difficulty is to know what it is that Job may have lent to God, and why he is not demanding a pledge for it. Tur-Sinai imagines both parties in a lawsuit putting up security for the claims made against them before the case itself could take place; Job would have been declaring, according to this view that Elihu is representing, that although he has a claim against God, he is not demanding any surety in advance of having his case heard. Elihu would then be scornfully asking in v 33 whether God is to pay his fine, if he should be found guilty, out of the surety that Job has put up. The whole idea is lent some color by the two key terms in v 31 (נשאתי and אחבל), but the allusions to the metaphor in the following verses are strained (see the *Notes* below). H. M. Weil ("Exégèse de Jérémie 23, 33–40 et de Job 34, 28–33 [Jérémie 44, 9]," *RHR* 118 [1938] 201–8 [207]) advanced a similar understanding, though entirely on the moral plane: these would be the words of a "hypocrite" (חנף, v 30), who undertakes not to make further loans at interest; but it is hard to see how such a sense can be integrated with the argument of the speech.

31.e. חבל II "act corruptly" (in 17:1 it is pual "be destroyed"); cf. Neh 1:7 for another use of the word in its moral meaning. Unusually, Driver–Gray take לא אחבל as "without offending," comparing Ps 26:1; Lev 1:17 (RVmg "though I offend not"; see Driver, *Tenses*, §162)—which would make the colon a complaint of unjust punishment. But this does not harmonize with the next verse, though it is true, as Driver–Gray stress, that v 32b has אם "if," which v 31b does not. Gray proposes reading אֵחָבֵל "I shall [not] be liable," from חבל I "take in pledge," the niph meaning "bind oneself by a pledge," i.e., be liable. This fits with Gray's general understanding, that "the sinner is palliating his sin, alleging that he has been seduced . . . and is therefore not liable," which leads to angry riposte from Elihu; but this differs from the view taken here.

31.f. There is no word for "again" in the MT, but it may be easily supplied from the sense (as in KJV, RSV, NJPS). Dhorme, Hölscher, Larcher (followed by BJ, JB), Pope, de Wilde, NAB, NEB (Brockington), however, would actually add עוֹד "again," which they think was lost by haplography (with בלעדי in v 32).

32.a. בלעדי "apart from," a prep in the constr followed by a relative clause (GKC, §130d). בלעדי אחזה "apart from I see" must mean "what I do not see" (RSV). It can hardly be "not for me, far be it from me" (as Tur-Sinai; Gen 14:24 is no parallel).

Beer (*BHK*) deletes בלעדי from its present place, as a dittograph of the last two letters of אחבל, and uses the letters עד from it to restore עוֹד "again" at the end of v 32 (followed by Fohrer, de Wilde). Dhorme (followed by Pope) also dispenses with the letters בל of בלעדי and makes use of the letters עד twice, once to create עוד for the end of v 31, the second time to read עֲדֵי "until" at the beginning of v 32, i.e., "until I see, do Thou instruct me" (Pope "that I may see"); similarly Gray עַד אֶחֱזֶה "that I may see." Habel reads עֲדֵי "until," but does not apparently restore עוֹד "again" in v 31 (though he does translate "If I have done iniquity, I will no more"). Driver, "Hebrew Poetic Diction," 39, apparently deleted בלעדי altogether.

32.b. אחזה "I see." Moffatt has "teach me what I am blind to."

Driver, "Hebrew Poetic Diction," 39, found here a new Heb. חזה (חזה III in *DCH,* 3:182a), "be vile" (cf. Arab. *ḫaziya* [Lane, 735a]), thus "I am vile"; so NEB "vile wretch that I am," REB "I am contemptible." Terrien related it rather to חזה II "be opposite," thus "I have revolted" (on חזה II, cognate with Arab. *ḥaḏâ,* see G. R. Driver, "Studies in the Vocabulary of the Old Testament VI," *JTS* 34 [1933] 375–85 [381]; "Problems in Job and Psalms Reconsidered," *JTS* 40 [1939] 391–94 [391]; "Hebrew Poetic Diction," 38–39; *DCH,* 3:181b). Tur-Sinai, developing his thesis that we have here an extended metaphor from the realm of the pledge, read אֶחֱזָה "take a pledge!" (אחז "take"), but there is no evidence that אחז, a common verb for "hold, take," can mean "take a pledge" if no obj is expressed (in fact an obj is missing only at Isa 13:8 [*DCH,* 1:186b], and it can easily be supplied from the context).

The verb is emended by Beer (*BHK*) to חָטָאתִי (אם) "if I have sinned" (cf. Vg *si erravi*); Beer is followed by Hölscher (*frt*), Larcher, Fohrer, de Wilde, NAB "teach me wherein I have sinned," NJB "although I have sinned."

32.c. הרני is "teach me," but NEB "be thou my guide," REB "grant me guidance" evoke the alleged etymology of ירה "teach" from ירה "throw, shoot" (as in BDB, 434b–35a). It is more likely, however, that the two are separate verbs (as in *HALOT,* 1:436; *DCH,* 4:290–91). Tur-Sinai, in accord with his thesis of the metaphor of the pledge throughout vv 31–33, read הָרְנִי, as if from the MH רהן hiph "give as a pledge" (Jastrow, 1454b; cognate with Arab. *rahana*); but it is hard as see how the translation "take thou my pledge" can be sustained if the verb means "give as a pledge."

32.d. אם is "if" for most translators, but "although" for NJB (on "concessive" אם, see GKC, §160a).

33.a. ישלמנה (the MS followed by *BHS* omits the *dagesh* in the *lamedh* that most MSS have) "he will requite it," *sc.* "to you" (the fem sg suff serves as neut, referring to the guilt in vv 31b, 32b). Not all accept that "you" is the implied obj of the verb: NJB, for example, has "should he punish such a one?" and Delitzsch and Gordis think it is human actions in general that are being recompensed. Good translates cryptically, "Does he repay out of what is yours because you despise?" Difficult also is NEB "Will he, at these words, condone your rejection of him?" as also is Moffatt "leave him to deal with you, as he may please."

Beer (*BHK*), continuing his perception of vv 31c–33 as the words of God, emends (*frt*) to שַׁלֵּם אֲשַׁלֵּם "I will assuredly requite"; similarly Fohrer and de Wilde, reading simply אֲשַׁלֵּם. Beer (*BH*[2] *frt*), not regarding these verses as being in the mouth of God, read יְשַׁלֵּם "he will requite." Gray reads יְשַׁלֶּמְךָ "[that] he should requite you," assuming corruption of the final *kaph* to *nun* in the paleo-Heb. script.

Tur-Sinai, in line with his notion that the metaphor of a pledge runs through vv 31–33, translates "Shall he pay it out of what is thine?" i.e., "Is he to pay his fine, if he should be found guilty—out of what you have put up, since he has not given security for himself?" But this cannot be harmonized with the following מאסת, which Tur-Sinai attempts to understand as "any security that God may have given."

33.b. המעמך, lit. "is it from with you?" i.e., originating with you, conforming to your standards or notions of propriety (cf. מֵעִם in Gen 41:32; 1 Sam 20:7; 2 Sam 3:28; and עם in Job 10:13; 27:11), thus "as you see fit" (NJPS) or "to suit you" (RSV); similarly "by your leave" (Gordis), "according to thy judgment" (Rowley), "in your opinion" (Dhorme, NJB), "on your terms" (Pope, NIV), "according to thy mind?" (KJV), or "as thou wilt" (RV).

33.c. כי מאסת "when you have rejected [him]"; it is perhaps not exactly "Should he requite you on your terms when you reject his?" (Habel), since the contrast is not between two sets of *terms.* The "him" is understood (as by Terrien, NJPS "But you have despised [Him]!"). Less meaningful is RSV "[Will he then make requital to suit you,] because you reject it" (God's requital), which would be an awkward way of saying "because you reject it if *it does not suit you*"; cf. RV "Shall his recompence be as thou wilt, that thou refusest it?" NAB "Would you then say that God must punish, since you reject what he is doing?" is a brave attempt to make sense, but the "since" clause seems to hang upon the "say," which is not really in the Heb. (i.e., the כי clause cannot depend on המעמך).

This passage and 42:6 (*q.v.*) are probably the only places where מאס is used absolutely (in 7:16 the obj "my life" is present as a concept in the verse [explicit in 9:21]; in Ps 89:38 [39] the obj "my anointed" is also present in the verse, though not as the direct obj of this verb). NIV fills out the sense with "(when you refuse) to repent," but apparently without emending the text. Beer (*BHK*) and de

Wilde agree that some obj for the verb has been omitted, and supply מִשְׁפָּטִי "my justice," which will of course be meaningful only if the prior decision, that vv 31c–33 are the words of God, is accepted. Dhorme thinks some word for "teaching" has fallen out, while Bickell[2] supplies דַּרְכֵי אֵל "the ways of God," and Hölscher "what he decides"; it is not clear what word Larcher, BJ, NJB would supply in rendering "his decisions." Beer (*BH*[2] *prps*) mentions a suggestion to read מָאַס תַּאֲוָתוֹ "he has rejected your desire," but decides that the MT is probably preferable after all. To make the obj explicit, Gray reads מְאַסְתּוֹ "you have rejected him." Kissane transfers to here from v 37b the phrase בינינו יספוק, which he emends to בְּדִינוֹ יספוק, translating "[If thou reject] His decision, must He smite?"; this would be another example of ספק in this sense, which otherwise appears only in v 26. Merely ingenious, without a shred of plausibility, is Ehrlich's translation "because you hate (to say), 'You [God] choose, not I.'"

It is a little tempting to find a parallelism between מאס "refuse" and בחר "choose" (as in KJV "he will recompense it, whether thou refuse, or whether thou choose," Gordis "depending on whether you reject or approve"), but then it is very hard to make sense of "and not I" at the end of the verse.

33.d. תבחר looks like a modal use of the impf, "you should, must, decide" (GKC, §107m–n); cf. NEB "it is for you to decide," NJPS "You must decide." בחר is usually glossed "choose," but elsewhere it has an obj, except for 23:13, where an emendation to בחר (of God) is widely accepted and the meaning "decide" is the most appropriate.

33.e. Pope thinks it should be "he," i.e., "Shall you choose and not he?"; similarly Moffatt "are you to choose the terms, not God?" and Gray, reading ולא־הוא "the choice (of your course) was yours not his."

33.f. Gray thinks this colon is possibly to be omitted as a gloss.

33.g. מה "what?" in an indirect question; cf. 34:4; 23:5; BDB, 552b; *DCH,* 5:151b §1.

33.h. ידעת is of course "you know," but Job often has said he "knows" when we would say we "believe"; see D. J. A. Clines, "Belief, Desire and Wish in Job 19:23–27: Clues for the Identity of Job's 'Redeemer,'" in *'Wünschet Jerusalem Frieden': Collected Communications to the XIIth Congress of the International Organization for the Study of the Old Testament, Jerusalem 1986,* ed. M. Augustin and K.-D. Schunk, BEATAJ 13 (Frankfurt: Lang, 1988) 363–70; reprinted in *On the Way to the Postmodern: Old Testament Essays, 1967–1998,* JSOTSup 293 (Sheffield: Sheffield Academic Press, 1998) 2:762–69. NJB has "so kindly enlighten us!" Good takes מה "what" as an interrogative and דבר as the inf, thus "what do you know to speak?"; similarly NEB "but what can you answer?" Moffatt, not too convincingly, connects the colon with the next verse, rendering "Say what you like, but thinking men will say with me."

34.a. אנשי לבב, lit. "men of heart," i.e., understanding; NJB "ordinary sensible people."

34.b. KJV understands the colon as "Let men of understanding tell me," not regarding v 35 as what they will say. Most take יאמרו as fut, which is natural, but it is quite legitimate to see it as the impf of repeated action (GKC, §107g), "are saying," as in the *Translation* above; so too NIV "declare."

36.a. אבי is a problematic word occurring only here (אָבִי at 1 Sam 24:12; 2 Kgs 5:13 has sometimes been thought to be the same word). It is traditionally translated "would that" (RV, RSV, NJPS), "Oh that" (Moffatt, Hartley), "my desire is that" (KJV), "if only" (NEB), or "kindly [examine him]" (NJB); Pope, though taking it as expressing a wish, translates "Job ought to be tried" (similarly Habel).

Many take it as an otherwise unattested noun with suff, "my desire" (so Gordis), derived from the verb אבה "wish"; A. M. Honeyman, "Some Developments of the Semitic Root *'by*," *JAOS* 64 (1944) 81–82, thought it an impv of that verb. Guillaume thinks it an adj "willing" from אבה "be willing." *HALOT,* 1:4a, suggests it may be connected with the verb בעי "entreat" (BDB, 106a; cf. Arab. *bayya* "come as suppliant"), thus "O that" (so too de Wilde). Others call it an optative particle (Duhm, Zorell, 3b, Sicre Díaz). Perhaps it would be simplest to regard אבי as a byform of בִּי "please, O that!" (BDB, 106b; the fact that בי is elsewhere always followed by אֲדֹנִי "my lord" or אֲדֹנָי "my Lord" may be coincidental since a "particle of entreaty," as BDB calls it, is very naturally used in address to a superior). On no account can it be אָבִי "my father" (Vg *pater mi*), despite the demurral of D. Wolfers, "Sire! (Job xxxiv 36)," *VT* 44 (1994) 566–69, who takes it as an address to Eliphaz as the foremost of the friends (supposed parallels are at 1 Sam 24:12; 2 Kgs 5:13).

M. Dahood ("Ugaritic-Phoenician Forms in Job 34,36," *Bib* 62 [1981] 548–50) sees here a form אֹבִי "my foe," thus "as my foe let Job be tested," but Elihu is not portrayed as Job's foe (Habel).

Hitzig, Dhorme, and Kissane (*vel*) read אֲבָל "but" (as LXX οὐ μὴν δὲ ἀλλά; similarly Pesh); the meaning would then be "not a wish that Job's trial might be continued, but the reason why Elihu must still further expose his errors" (Rowley); cf. Terrien "So (*donc*) it is desirable that Job should be examined." Bickell reads אולם "but" (אלם, which he vocalizes *lam*), Graetz אָמְנָם "truly," Fedrizzi אַךְ

"certainly," and Kissane (*vel*) אַף "also." Hoffmann emends to אֲבִי or אֲבוֹי "alas, woe" (cf. Duhm), Tur-Sinai regarding אבי as simply a defective spelling of אבוי.

Beer (*BHK*), Budde, Hölscher, Fohrer, Gray, NAB would delete the troublesome word altogether (as a dittograph of איוב).

36.b. עד־נצח can mean "forever" (Good "constantly"), but also, as is more appropriate here, "thoroughly" (NJB; similarly KJV "unto the end," RSV, Gordis "to the end," NJPS, NRSV "to the limit," NIV "to the utmost"). Cf. *Note* 4:20.c; D. W. Thomas, "The Use of נֵצַח as a Superlative in Hebrew," *JSS* 1 (1956) 106–9; and *DCH*, 5:739b §1.3; 5:740 §c2. NEB "once and for all" is hardly suitable to the Heb.

36.c. יבחן "will be tested." De Wilde, following Duhm and Beer (*BH*² *prps*), reads יִזָּהֵר "should be warned" (זהר niph impf does not happen to occur elsewhere), which he thinks best suits "Elihu's pedagogical tone." Tur-Sinai proposed here a new בחן "perish" (cognate with Arab. *ibhânna*), rendering "Woe, Job will perish for ever," which seems greatly out of line with the tone of the speech.

36.d. De Wilde feels that the term תשובה "answer" suggests not reasoned response but simple opposition; but there is nothing to confirm that (the term means "answer" only elsewhere at 21:34; in its six other occurrences it is "return"). Gordis thinks it means "confidence," but that is hardly the issue here in Elihu's speech. Habel's "testifies" derives from his emphasis on legal language.

Tur-Sinai reads תְּשָׁבַת "(because of his) dwelling (among the wicked)," though such a noun does not occur in biblical Heb. Graetz proposes, following Pesh, וְאַל־יִתְחַשֵּׁב "and let him not be reckoned [among the wicked]," though this does not cohere well with the next verse and remains conjectural. Dahood ("Ugaritic-Phoenician Forms") reads עֲלַת שֶׁבֶת "because he sits [with impious men]," עלת being a Phoenician form of על "upon" and the *beth* of באנשי־און meaning "by" (as in Gen 13:18 וישב באלני ממרא "and he dwelt by the oaks of Mamre"). However, quite apart from the philological oddities involved, the proposal fails on the ground that it is Job's words that are here being criticized, not his behavior (such as "sitting with impious men").

36.e. באנשי־און, lit. "among men of iniquity." Many emend (with some Heb. MSS) to כְּאַנְשֵׁי "like men of" (Beer [*BH*² *frt*], Driver–Gray, Dhorme, Hölscher, Kissane, Larcher, Fohrer, de Wilde, Habel, Hartley, van der Lugt), similarly RV, NEB "[answers] that are meant to make mischief," REB "like a mischief-maker," NJB "his answers imply that he is a criminal," NJPS "answers which befit sinful men," NIV "for answering like a wicked man." KJV "because of his answers for wicked men" does not solve the problem. Gordis counters with the sense "because of his confidence in evil men," which accounts for the ב at the expense of proposing an unparalleled sense for תשובה. Good's way of maintaining MT is to translate "about his returning among bad men," which does not carry conviction. Sicre Díaz also retains the MT, yet translates it "worthy of an evildoer." As Driver–Gray note, the *beth* could be *beth essentiae* (BDB, 88be; *DCH*, 2:84b) (Delitzsch calls it a "*beth* of association"), but the minor emendation to *kaph* seems preferable.

37.a. יסיף "add" is without an expressed obj also at 2 Chr 28:13.

37.b. Transferring פשע into the second colon, as the obj of יספוק, with Dhorme, Tur-Sinai, Pope, Hartley, NJPS. The word is omitted by Bickell, Duhm, Hölscher, Fohrer.

37.c. Identifying ספק, with Dhorme, *BHS* (*frt*, יְסַפֵּק), Larcher (followed by JB "calling justice into question"), as another Heb. ספק, like Aram. ספק "doubt" (cf. *DCH*, vol. 6, *s.v.*), and reading יְסַפֵּיק "casts doubt on," with פשע as the obj; so too Pope "denies his transgression" (similarly Gray), i.e., maintaining his innocence, and Hölscher, but he deletes the clause nevertheless. Terrien accepted Dhorme's understanding of ספק, but absolutely, and so rather too intellectually: "he creates doubts among us" (leaving פשע in the first colon). Gerleman (*BHS frt*) reads יְשַׂפֵּק, which is presumably intended as a byform of ספק, though it is not acknowledged by BDB or *HALOT*.

ספק might otherwise be "clap"; see *Note* 26.b. Thus NIV "scornfully he claps his hands," Sicre Díaz "taunts" (*burla*), and Good "jeers" (as in v 26). If it is that verb, its obj would have to be understood. Beer (*BHK frt*), Budde, Driver–Gray make it explicit by supplying כַּפָּיו "his hands." Ehrlich emended בינינו "among us" to פָּנֵינוּ "[he slaps] our faces."

Tur-Sinai and Gordis took ספק as "suffice" (as also at 34:26; cf. שפק at 20:22; BDB, 974a, has a שפק II "suffice" for 1 Kgs 20:10, and *HALOT*, 3:1349a, notes it also for Ecclus 15:18 and perhaps [hiph] Isa 2:8), hence in hiph "have a surplus," thus "multiplieth transgressions among us" (Tur-Sinai, followed by de Wilde), "increases impiety" (Gordis), "increases rebellion" (Hartley, similarly NJPS, Habel). Difficult to understand is NAB's "[he is adding rebellion to his sin] by brushing off our arguments," no emendation of the text being implied.

Larcher added חק "law," as omitted by haplography, thus "putting law in doubt among us." NJB adopted this proposal, and also changed יספוק to יָסִיף חֹק, thus "he makes an end of law" (סוף hiph). Peters reads פֶּשַׁע בנינו יספוק "rebelling, he mocks among us," an awkward sentence. Driver ("Difficult Words," 63) made the far-fetched suggestion that בֵּינֵינוּ יִסְפּוֹק means "between ourselves, it's enough," "a gloss inserted *extra metrum* by a clerkly admirer of Job to express his feeling that Elihu has decried his wisdom and sense quite enough."

Duhm, Beer (*BH*[2] *frt*), Hölscher, Fohrer, Moffatt, NEB delete בינינו יספוק as a gloss.

37.d. Dhorme and Beer (*BHK frt*) read פִּשְׁעוֹ for MT פֶּשַׁע "transgression," but the MT will comfortably yield the same sense.

37.e. בנינו "among us" (on בין, not just "between" but also "among," see *Note* 4.c). Kissane ingeniously reads בְּדִינוֹ יספוק and transfers the phrase to the end of v 33b, thus "[If thou reject] His decision, must He smite?"

37.f. וירב "and he multiplies," the juss as at 33:21 (*q.v.*). Beer (*BHK*) therefore reads a verb with simple *waw:* וְיַרְבֶּה "and he multiplies" (so too Gray). NEB translates loosely "with his endless ranting against God," Moffatt "heaping blasphemies on God"; NJB "heaping abuse on God," Habel "inundates El with speeches."

37.g. For אמריו "his words" Tur-Sinai (followed by NJPS) reads מֶרְיוֹ "his rebellion," thus creating of v 37 a very regular tricolon, with the three verbs "adds," "increases," and "multiplies" and the three noun objects "sin," "iniquity," and "rebellion"—"perhaps too much of a good thing" (de Wilde).

Form/Structure/Setting

The *structure* of Elihu's second speech is plain. There are two parts to it, distinguished by the addressees. In vv 2–15 he is addressing the friends, as wise men, men of learning (v 2), and calling upon them to form a collective decision about the merits of Job's case (v 4), and to listen to his arguments (v 10). In vv 16–37, on the other hand, he is addressing Job, whom he summons to hear him (v 16), questions (v 18), dictates the terms of a confession to (vv 31–32), and questions again (v 33).

The *strophic structure* is equally obvious. A first analysis suggests five strophes, of 8, 7, 5, 10, and 6 lines, respectively. But within each of these strophes it is not hard to discern smaller substrophes. So doing, we may outline the strophic structure thus:

Strophe 1	vv 2–9		8 lines
		vv 2–4	3 lines
		vv 5–6	2 lines
		vv 7–9	3 lines
Strophe 2	vv 10–15		7 lines
		vv 10–12	4 lines (v 10 four cola)
		vv 13–15	3 lines
Strophe 3	vv 16–20		5 lines
		vv 16–18	3 lines
		vv 19–20	2 lines (both tricola)
Strophe 4	vv 21–30		10 lines
		vv 21–22	2 lines
		vv 23–24	2 lines
		vv 25–26	2 lines
		vv 27–28	2 lines
		vv 29–30	2 lines (vv 29c–30 a tricolon)
Strophe 5	vv 31–37		8 lines
		vv 31–32	2 lines
		v 33	2 lines (four cola)
		vv 34–35	2 lines
		vv 36–37	2 lines (v 37 a tricolon)

It is noticeable how the tricolon is used as a marker of closure (in vv 19–20, 29c–30, 37).

The macrostructure outlined above corresponds exactly with that of RSV (vv 2–9, 10–15, 16–20, 21–30, 31–37). Webster notes the same two main divisions, though he finds nine strophes in all (not further specified) in the speech. NAB is broadly comparable with strophes of vv 2–6, 7–9, 10–15, 16–21, 22–28 (though omitting v 26), 29–33 (though omitting a translation of v 30), and 34–37; it would seem better, however, to connect v 21 with what precedes, since its opening כי "for" suggests a new beginning.

Van der Lugt's analysis shows variances from the above outline at these points: (1) He divides between vv 3 and 4, but v 4 is most closely connected with v 2, and the כי "for" that opens v 5 suggests that a new beginning is being made here. (2) He takes v 10 as a tricolon, whereas I take it (with Fohrer) as two bicola. (3) He takes v 33 as a tricolon, which is also possible. As it stands, the line is a bit too long for a tricolon and a bit too short for two bicola. (4) He analyzes vv 16–22 and 23–30 as major strophes, which is as plausible as the analysis given above.

Fohrer identifies five major strophes: vv 2–9, 10–15, 16–22, 23–29b (he omits vv 29c–30), and 31–37 (omitting vv 33c, 37b), with 8, 7, 8, 7, 7 lines, respectively (he takes vv 19–20 as three bicola). Terrien has seven main strophes (vv 2–6, 7–11, 12–17, 18–22, 23–28, 29–33a, 33b–37), an analysis that seems driven to some extent by a desire to identify, within those strophes, regular substrophes with three lines each. It is highly unlikely that there should be a single strophe (vv 12–16) that includes both address to the friends and address to Job.

In *genre* the speech is another *disputation speech,* of which the main materials are *address to the hearers, quotation,* and *wisdom instruction.* The coloration of *dispute* is especially signaled by the many rhetorical *questions* (vv 7–8, 13, 17–19, 29, 33), but also by the rejection of other opinions, e.g., with the particle אף־אמנם "assuredly" (v 12). The *address to the hearers* element contains a command to listen (v 2), which is then motivated (v 3), and followed by a call to decide (v 4). The demand to the friends to listen is reiterated in v 10, and a further call to Job to listen is made in v 16.

The element of *quotation* is a notable feature of the speech. In vv 5–6 and v 9 Elihu quotes what Job is alleged to have said, in v 18 what God says in criticism of certain rulers, in vv 31b–32 what he urges Job to say by way of confession, and in vv 35–37 what other people are saying about Job. These quotations, which constitute nearly a quarter of the speech, lend it a certain lecturelike quality, as Fohrer has noted, with their implicit appeal to authority (cf. Westermann, classing the speech as "a lecture by a teacher of wisdom in a circle of the wise" [*Structure,* 140]). Even if the authority happens to be the opponent, Job, it is important to Elihu to source his accusations of Job correctly.

Wisdom instruction is the material of vv 11–12, on the justice of God, and of vv 13–15, on the divine breath in the animate creation. The wisdom orientation is evident also in the judgment of the wise in v 35 that Job is without insight.

There are also, interestingly, several other kinds of material in the speech. The *hymn* is evoked in the participial style of vv 18–19a, where God is depicted as the one who makes judgments of the rulers of the earth. The language of *legal procedure* is drawn upon in vv 23–24, where the questions of an appointed time for legal judgment and of pretrial investigation are raised. The quotations may also have their presumed setting in the legal sphere. *Psalmic language* is in the background of vv 31–32, where Elihu stipulates words of confession for Job to use, and as well in the idea of the sudden moment (v 20).

The *function* of the speech is essentially to instruct Job about the justice of God, and thus to correct his misunderstanding of the divine government of the universe. Formally, it may seem that the speech is designed to gain agreement from the friends about the case of Job (cf. esp. v 4), but Elihu can hardly doubt that he has their agreement already and his address to them may be something of a smokescreen. His business is with Job, and his motivation remains a desire to justify him (33:32), even though, we must say, he has a strange way of going about it.

Supporting this view of the function of the speech, its *tonality* is perhaps more positive toward Job than many have supposed. No one could call Elihu delicate in his manner of speech, though it is wrong to think, for example, that v 16, "if you have understanding . . . ," is at all rude. We may allow that his quotation of Job in v 9 is plainly misrepresentation if not downright mischievous, and there is more than a hint of impatience in his exclamation, "Who is there like Job, who drinks scoffing like water?" (v 7). Nevertheless, at two points his reserve is marked, and he draws back from belittling Job. The first is in his stipulation of how Job should confess his wrongdoing: though his offer of advice may be a little presumptuous, nevertheless he demands only that Job should say he was "misguided" or "misled" (v 31) and should promise that *"if"* he has done wrong he will not offend again (v 32), which would amount to a remarkably low-key confession. The second point is that he puts his rather negative summing up of Job's position in the mouth of others, fictional though they may be (vv 35–37). It is of the essence of Elihu's position that he is right and Job is wrong, so it would not be surprising if Elihu were to say in his own voice, "Job speaks without knowledge; his words are without insight" (v 35). But he does not (though contrast 35:16), and we may well be right to think he is pulling his punches. As a whole, the speech may rightly be thought harsher in tone than his first one, but it is not offensive or haughty.

The *nodal* verse is surely v 17, "Can one who hates justice govern?," for the issue of the speech is the very question of what it means to be a governor, arising as it does from Job's assertion that God has taken away his rights (v 5).

Comment

1–37 Elihu's first speech (chaps. 32–33), notwithstanding the anger that motivates his intervention in the dialogue, was remarkably emollient toward Job. Though he intends to be businesslike with Job, and to refute his errors in due order, he has assured him that there will be no heavy pressure from him and that Job has nothing to fear from his speeches. His self-professed desire is to justify Job (33:32). This second speech (chap. 34) is of a rather different character. Here the theme is no longer the educative role of suffering, and Elihu's manner has lost some of its expository tone. The theme becomes rather the rebelliousness of Job against the divine justice, and the manner becomes correspondingly more assertive and dogmatic. No doubt it is too severe to say, with Andersen, "He is no longer reasoning with Job with a view to helping him; he is attacking Job in order to score a point." But Job, and the readers, could be forgiven if they sense a colder atmosphere in this speech.

Elihu signals a growing distance between himself and Job by deliberately appealing for support from the other friends. In the first speech he had begun by justifying his intrusion to the friends but had before long turned his attention to Job personally, addressing him by name at the beginning and end of chap. 33 (33:1, 31), quoting him to his face (33:8–11), addressing him with twelve imperative verbs, four second-person verbs, and four "beholds" (הן, הנה). True, in the central section of the chapter (vv 14–28) Elihu was expounding his views, and there were no second-person verbs of address to Job; but it was clearly marked that it was to Job he was speaking and not into the thin air: his peroration was explicitly introduced as an "answer" to Job (33:12), and it concluded with a "behold" (הן) invoking Job's attention (33:29) and an insistent appeal to Job to pay heed to his opinions (33:31–33). Things are different in this second speech: Elihu begins with a lengthy address not to Job but to the friends (34:2; contrast 33:1), uses Job's name only in the third person (34:5, 7, 35, 36), directs to him only four imperative verbs (34:16, 31 [if emended], 33) and four second-person verbs (34:17, 33), and eschews the interlocutor-involving "behold." When he quotes Job (34:5–9), it is not to debate Job's utterances with him face to face but to remind the friends of the scandal of Job's theology, making of Job a moral outlaw whose claim to innocence will be decided for him by a court of his superiors. Above all, the ultimate alienating effect Elihu indulges himself with is to side with the friends against Job, inviting them to join with him in determining what is "right" and "good" in the case of Job (34:4)—all this from a young man who, a speech ago, had been seething with anger at Job's friends (32:3; cf. 33:11–12) and had moreover been offering Job his sympathetic support (33:7, 32).

The speech has two movements, corresponding to the separate addressees envisaged in it. In vv 2–15 Elihu is speaking to the friends, whom he calls "wise men" and "learned men" in v 2 and "men of understanding" in v 10. At v 16 he turns to Job, and the rest of the speech is addressed to him, as the second-person verbs in vv 16–17 and again in v 33 show. The argument in both movements is the same: God, as the supreme governor of the universe, cannot do wrong by failing to requite good and bad behavior appropriately, whereas Job, who is claiming that God has treated him unjustly, is doing wrong by implying that God has perverted justice.

All Elihu's criticism of Job, it should be noted, is about what Job has been saying in his speeches to the friends. Despite occasional appearances (especially v 8), Elihu does not condemn Job for any deed, nor for anything Job may have said before his troubles came upon him. In this speech, Elihu is concerned solely with Job's reaction to his suffering and the allegations he is making against God. He wants of course to affirm that the world is governed according to the principle of retributive justice (v 11), and that must mean that Job deserves what is happening to him; but explaining why Job is suffering is not Elihu's main point here, for his focus is on the infamy of Job's complaints against God.

1–9 In this speech, Elihu's first move is to ensure that he has the friends of Job on his side. He proposes to co-opt them in order that collectively they might decide upon Job's condition: "let us decide among us what is good" (v 4b) is the theme of his project here. And for that project he will use the words of Job against him (vv 5–6, 9), holding them out before the friends again as a dreadful example of rebellion against God (cf. v 37), while at the same time prejudicing any fair discussion of Job's case with a couple of sentences of character assassination (vv 7–8).

1 The second speech begins with the notation "and Elihu answered and said" (ויען אליהוא ויאמר), but the verb usually translated "answer" (ענה) does not necessarily imply any previous speech; it must mean here "respond to an occasion, speak in view of circumstances" (so BDB, 773a). There has to be some significance in the fact that all the other speakers speak once and then wait for a reply (there is one apparent exception, at 27:1), whereas Elihu makes four speeches in sequence without any intervening response (perhaps five speeches in all if we allow that chap. 28 is also Elihu's and that it should have a caption like the present one). But it is not at all clear what the significance is; perhaps it is just the author's way of representing Elihu as an insistent, almost unstoppable, orator once he gets going. But why then are his six (perhaps seven) chapters of discourse broken into separate speeches?

2 The "wise men" (חכמים) and "knowing ones" or "learned ones" (ידעים) whom Elihu addresses (without irony, contra Dhorme, Terrien) must be the other three friends (so too Duhm, Strahan), who are very definitely in view at the opening of the Elihu episode (32:3, 5). Some have thought that he may have in mind as well a wider audience of listeners (so, e.g., Budde, Delitzsch, Peake, Terrien, Gordis, Whybray); Rowley too thought it hardly likely that Elihu can be addressing the friends as "wise men" after what he has said of them in 32:11. Habel, following a hint from B. Gemser ("The *rîb*- or Controversy Pattern in Hebrew Mentality," in *Wisdom in Israel and in the Ancient Near East,* FS H. H. Rowley, ed. M. Noth and D. W. Thomas, VTSup 3 [Leiden: Brill, 1955] 120–37 [124]), finds a "forensic" sense in the very common verb ידע "know." This leads to the translation "judges" rather than "learned ones" and to the view that Elihu is addressing the judges of the community, assuming the role of chief judge and arbiter for himself, and constructing his audience as "a legal assembly exercising critical discernment in the judging of Job's case." But these are views difficult to sustain, since there is no hint of an audience of bystanders in the book (as Peake allows), and we seem to be hearing the language of debate and disputation rather than formal legal language, which is conspicuous by its absence from this chapter. There has certainly been a change in Elihu's attitude to the friends from that of chap 32: there he had set himself over against both Job and the friends, while here he ranges himself alongside the friends. There he had said he had lost patience waiting for the friends' wisdom (תבונת, lit. "understandings," 32:11), while here he flatters them as wise and learned men. That is a conflict, to be sure, but it is of the essence of the characterization of Elihu that he is something of a trimmer. He is something of a young fogey, too, conventional in thought and word alike (cf. on 32:11–12): addressing them he uses the most jejune language of "hearing" (שמע) and "giving ear" (אזן hiph), the very same terms in which he had summoned Job in 33:1.

3 We have heard this proverb before, at 12:11, from Job's mouth. But it was not Job's proverb; it was a thought he was attributing, by way of parody, to the friends—a blindingly obvious observation that just as the mouth serves not just for eating but also for tasting and rejecting unwholesome food, so too the ear is not just for receiving words but for judging and discriminating among the words that reach it. If Job, in irony, thinks this is the deepest wisdom his friends can come up with, then Elihu proves how right he is. Elihu is of course so cocksure about his own access to wisdom that he invites the others to listen to him *because* (כי) ears are discriminating organs—and when they are his words that are bombarding the friends' ears, the ears will be in for a real treat.

4 Elihu intends to set the other friends entirely at their ease again, after the hostility he initially expressed toward them (32:11–12, 15–16), by implying that they and he together are the men of wisdom who know what's what. He does not mean that they should arbitrarily decide for themselves what is right and good in all cases of moral uncertainty, but simply that they should decide, in the case of Job, whether the view to be sustained is that of Job or that of the conventional wisdom (which he represents). It is a fraud, of course, to suggest that there is any future choosing to be done; the matter is already settled. As Strahan says, the verse has the same ring as Paul's "Choose all things; hold fast that which is good" (1 Thess 5:21).

5 Out of his own mouth Job will be condemned, thinks Elihu. Beyond question, Job has said, and said repeatedly, that he is innocent; Elihu's citation "I am in the right" (צדקתי) is near enough to Job in 13:18, "I know that I am in the right" (אצדק), the perfect tense here being indistinguishable in meaning from the imperfect tense there. In 9:21 Job has said "I am blameless" (תם־אני); in 19:7 that he is "not guilty"(לא ארשע); in 16:17 that on his palms there is nonviolence; and in 27:5–6 that until he dies he will not abandon his claim to innocence (תמה), that he maintains his integrity (צדקה), and that his heart does not reproach him for any of his days. And as for God having "taken away" (סור hiph), or denied him, his right (משׁפט), these are exactly Job's words in 27:2 (*q.v.*), where he has gone so far as to devise for God the unhappy sobriquet of The One Who Has Denied Me Justice.

6 But in v 6 it is hard to match the words with anything Job has actually said. He has never said that the case or judgment (both possible meanings of משׁפט) against him is a lie; on the only occasions he has used the term "lie" (כזב), it has been to assert that he will not lie to the friends (6:28) and to throw out the challenge that he be proved a liar for his analysis of the social injustices that God does nothing about (24:25). He has never used the term "my judgment" (משׁפטי) to mean the judgment of God against him, either.

The translation of v 6 is problematic, to be sure (see *Notes*). Some revocalize the verb to yield "I am counted a liar" (RSV), "I am considered a liar" (NIV). But that is not something that Job has said either, quite apart from the facts that the Hebrew cannot mean "in spite of my right I am counted a liar" (RSV) since the preposition על ought to mean "because of" rather than "in spite of" and that Job has never complained that he is being punished *because of* his righteousness.

Others emend the Hebrew slightly, to read "he [God] lies concerning my case," which is equally hard to parallel in the speeches of Job. He did say in 19:6 that God has "put [him] in the wrong," destroying his reputation for innocence by making him suffer, which might be thought to amount to much the same thing—but the language is very different.

Nor is the second half of the verse the language of Job. Literally it says, "My arrow is incurable, without sin," meaning presumably that his wounds caused by God's arrows are fatal, though he has not sinned and so does not deserve to be so afflicted. At 6:4 he has spoken of the poisoned arrows of the Almighty that have stuck fast in him, at 9:17 of God raining blows or wounds on him, and at 16:13 of God's archers surrounding him; but in none of the depictions of God's assaults on him (e.g., 9:17–18; 16:7–17; 19:6–12) has his theme been the incurability of his pains, but rather their extreme severity. This is not to say, nevertheless, that he expects healing for his ills (cf. his despair in 17:11–16). Perhaps, however, the term אנוש means not strictly "incurable" but just "disastrous," as may well be the case in its other occurrences (Isa 17:11; Jer 17:9, 16; 30:15; Mic 1:9). And Job has always contrasted his suffering with his innocence, to the same effect as the phrase here, בלי־פשע, lit. "without sin," i.e., though I have not sinned. So while the language may be the language of Elihu, the thoughts are identifiably the thoughts of Job.

7–8 Elihu has not yet finished citing Job (he will continue in v 9), but now that he has brought himself to utter two Joban sentences he cannot restrain himself from delivering an evaluation of Job's character. Eliphaz had said in 15:16 that humans are naturally disposed to "drink iniquity like water," but for Elihu Job is a man apart ("Was ever a fellow like Job? He gulps mockery like water" [Pope]; more prosaically NEB "Was there ever a man like Job with his thirst for irreverent talk?"): for him it is as natural a need to "scoff" (לעג) as to slake his thirst. The metaphor is a little strange, no doubt, since mockery of the divine design is what Job gives voice to rather than what he drinks in (it cannot be, as Lamparter thought, that vv 7–8 continue Job's words, as if Job were complaining how much mockery he has endured).

Now what counts as "scoffing" (לעג) is very much a matter of opinion. Job thinks he is being objectively descriptive of his own situation when he says that he is in the right and that God has deprived him of justice. To Elihu, however, that sounds like blasphemy, since he cannot admit that the Almighty could in any way do wrong (cf. v 10). Elsewhere in Job "mockery" or "scoffing" (לעג) is mockery among the disputants in the Joban drama (11:3; 21:3; 22:19; though 9:23 is different, being about God's "mockery" of innocent sufferers); but elsewhere in the wisdom literature mockery is often within the religious realm (e.g., Ps 1:1; Prov 1:22), as blasphemy against God or as the typical behavior of the godless against the godly (e.g., Pss 10:1; 35:16; 39:8 [9]; 42:3 [4]). "The evildoer is always a scoffer; in scoffing the evildoer's sinful nature is disclosed" (Fohrer). That is what Job's "scoffing" is, for Elihu. But, we should note, all Job's fault is still nothing but words, words that are in fact religious language, discourse about theology; Job has *done* nothing wrong, as far as Elihu is concerned at this point.

8 Job has not in fact been consorting with wicked men, and Elihu does not for a moment think he has. What he means by saying that Job walks in company with, or goes about with (ארח), evildoers and goes along (הלך) with the wicked, a "fellow-traveller with wicked men" (NEB), is that Job's questioning of the divine justice puts him in bad company, intellectually speaking. "One who is perplexed in faith *must* be impure in deeds," thinks Elihu (Strahan). According to Psalm 1, the righteous do not walk in the counsel of the ungodly nor go in the way of sinners nor sit in the company of scoffers (the term there is לץ), but Elihu has determined that Job has been ranging himself with evildoers (פעלי־און, one of Job's terms [31:3]) and not with the righteous. This company of the wicked is known elsewhere in the book as "men of worthlessness" or "hollow men" (מתי־שוא, lit. "men of emptiness," 11:11), "men of iniquity" (מתי־און, 22:15). Some have thought that the "workers of iniquity" (פעלי־און) in the Psalms may be workers of magic (so, e.g., S. Mowinckel, *Psalmenstudien,* vol. 1, *Åwän und die individuellen Klagepsalmen* [Kristiana: Dybwad, 1921] esp. 33–67), but there is little reason to suppose that such is the specific identity of the evildoers here (or, indeed, anywhere; cf., e.g., K.-H. Bernhardt, *TDOT,* 1:144–47).

Elihu uses of Job the term גבר "male" (as also in v 34 of wise men he is likely to agree with). In certain contexts it signifies an adult man as distinct from a woman or a child (though in 3:3 it is of the infant Job), but mostly in Job it has no special meaning beyond "man" (e.g., 3:23; 16:21). Contrary to common opinion, the term does not refer to male strength (though the verb גבר does mean "be strong," and the adjective גבור certainly means "mighty"); cf. *DCH,* 2:313a–14b. This rather spoils Terrien's proposal that Elihu views Job as no common criminal but a superman (גבר) who is protesting against heaven.

9 The clinching example of Job's harmful theology is, according to Elihu, his statement that there is no profit in religion. It is true that Job has said, in two classic passages at least, that there is no reward for good or punishment for evil: in 9:22 he has said that God destroys both righteous and wicked alike, and in 21:7 that the wicked live to a ripe old age and are not cut off for their sins. In the one place, that sounds as if there is no profit in religion because there is no profit anywhere, in the other as if there is no profit in religion because there is no retributive punishment anywhere. Either way, Elihu's report of Job's theology seems fair. Yet it is this same Job who has also described the *wicked* as those who say, "What gain shall we have if we pray to him?" (21:15). On this matter of profit Job has been in a double bind: if he says religion is profitable, it means that his piety is not disinterested (as well as contradicting his own experience); but if he says religion is unprofitable, he aligns himself with the wicked who have no time for God (see further on 21:15). For Elihu it is obvious that Job's language is impious (as also talk of the unprofitability of religion is in Mal 3:14), but for Job it is the language of a God-obsessed man wrestling with the problems of theodicy.

The term Elihu uses for "profit" (סכן) is not Job's; he had used יעל "benefit" in 21:15 when reporting the views of the wicked. It was Eliphaz who had used סכן (22:2), but he was asking, not whether God can be profitable to humans but whether humans can be profitable to God (answer: no). Still, it raised the question whether the language of the marketplace can be at all appropriate to the realm of religion. Religion is defined here as "delighting" in God (רצה; see *Note* 9.c), rather than finding favor with God (NEB) or trying to please God (NIV); it is for Job his gratuitous devotedness to God that roused the Satan's interest in him in the first place (1:9).

10–15 Continuing his address to the friends, Elihu reiterates that God cannot be conceived of as acting unjustly. In vv 5–9 Elihu has let the error of Job's opinions be manifested by mere citation of them; now in vv 10–12 he will state in his own voice the truth about the divine character. God, being God, cannot do wrong—which means, in the present context, that he cannot fail to implement retributive rewards and punishments. Job has alleged that he himself is both innocent and punished; Elihu calls that statement a wickedness, since for God not to award due recompense would amount to a perversion of justice.

The next verses (13–15) go in an apparently unexpected direction, however. They affirm that God is solely responsible for the governance of the universe, and that all living things depend for their breath, which is their life, on God's goodwill. How do these unexceptionable truths support the argument of the preceding verses? we may well ask. They cannot be stated just for their own sake (as Driver–Gray, for example, seem to believe). Whybray is right that if Elihu means only that God cannot do anything unjust because he has absolute power, it is "an extremely feeble argument." But is that what Elihu means?

Perhaps the best line of approach is this: if life, which depends entirely on God's decision, continues as it does, it shows that God is not perverting the justice due to the righteous. You have only to assume, says Elihu, that there are righteous people and that they deserve to live. The fact that they continue to live shows that God is not acting wickedly; if he were, they would be dead. He has only to withdraw his breath, and they would meet their fate.

This is not the same interpretation as that of Gordis, for example: he writes that God's creation of the world and his giving of life "testify that God, far from being cruel and malevolent as Job has declared, loves His creatures and is free from injustice in His dealings with them" (similarly Budde, Dillmann, Fohrer, and Peake ["that man still lives on proves His benevolent care"]). For whether God is cruel is not the question on Elihu's agenda here: it is whether he is just. And the issue cannot be whether God loves his creatures in general, for some of those creatures are suffering, and dying, at this very instant—and justly so, according to Elihu. Only those who deserve to live are alive, so Elihu believes. Ergo, God does not pervert justice.

It is equally incorrect to understand Elihu as meaning that almightiness and justice are inseparable from one another (as Terrien). At this juncture, Elihu is far from arguing that it is because God is almighty that he is necessarily just; rather, his position here is that being almighty he has every opportunity to be *unjust* if he should choose. If God were simply to have the mind to it (v 14a), he could wipe out all that lives; but that would be wicked, for it would not be rendering to each according to their deeds (v 11).

10 Reiterating his address to the friends, Elihu now states his own position on the matters Job has been debating. Job has asserted that he is innocent and yet being punished by God, but Elihu must set the record straight. God does not do wickedness, and it would be wickedness if he were to act as Job claims, denying Job what is justly due to him.

His opening word in this strophe, לכן "therefore," gives at least the impression of a logical development from what precedes, but what logic there is remains a little obscure. Is it that since Job has been allowed to have his say, in the words that Elihu has quoted or paraphrased from him, *therefore* a refutation is in order? Or is it that since he has called on the friends to determine with him what is right in this matter (v 4), *therefore* a positive statement of theological truth must now be made? Whatever the "therefore" means, it is clear that Elihu intends to pontificate, not to discuss or enter into the proffered joint decision making he had promised in v 4. All the friends, these "men of understanding" (לבב, lit. "heart," in the sense of brain; cf. on 12:3), need do is "listen" to him, and their part in the dialogue will be adequately fulfilled.

In saying "far be it from" (חלילה מן) God that he should do wickedness, he uses a very solemn and emphatic idiom, which almost amounts to a curse; it designates an unthinkable action, one that is totally out of character for the person (it is usually in the context of dialogue, designating what is unthinkable for "me" or "us" or "you"; cf. 27:5; Gen 44:7; Josh 22:29; 1 Sam 12:23). It is the same response as Paul's: "Is there injustice with God? By no means (μὴ γένοιτο)!" In the only other use of the phrase in the OT in reference to God, Abraham is protesting that God cannot possibly destroy the righteous along with the wicked (Gen 18:25). The idiom implies that "there is something sacrilegious or profane in the idea that is repudiated" (Rowley on 27:5), not (against Tur-Sinai) that it would be a shame for humans to attribute wickedness to God. And of course, to all right-thinking people it is very shocking to conceive that God might not be, in every particular, just; Job, though he believes it, is no less shocked by the thought. There is no special distinction here between the terms "God" (אל) and "the Almighty" (שדי), nor between "wickedness" (רשע) and "wrongdoing" (עול); Elihu feels very secure with synonymous parallels that say the same thing again and again.

11 The essence of justice in God, for Elihu, is that he operates a policy of strict retribution, rendering to everyone according to their deeds. This is why (so says the initial כי "for") it is unthinkable that he should act unjustly. No matter that this is a very mechanical view of justice, which does not differentiate among people, evaluate intention and motivation, or recognize that different circumstances create different moral values for the same deed. All that matters is that the world is at bottom a very simple and straightforward place. And Elihu has many supporters: Bildad had said in 8:3 that God cannot pervert justice, and Pss 28:4; 62:12 (13); Prov 12:14; 19:17; 24:12; Isa 3:11; Jer 25:14; Ecclus 16:14; Matt 16:27; and Rom 2:6 unite in affirming that all will be judged according to their works.

The sentence is couched in a rather aphoristic style, as if from the book of Proverbs. The rule is of universal application, for all humans: the first colon shows that it is humanity (אדם) that is in view, not just males; and while the parallel term is איש, which is the normal word for "man, male person," it can often mean "person," without distinction of gender, and, quite commonly "each," distributively, which would suit the present context well (cf. *DCH,* 1:221b–22a). The term ארח for "way," "conduct" in a metaphorical sense, is typical of the wisdom literature (twenty times in Proverbs, eleven in Job, fourteen in Psalms, out of sixty-three occurrences in total).

12 Elihu repeats the substance of v 10, though couching it in more legal terms (רשע "act wickedly" and משפט "justice") than those of the oath formula there. Since he can think of no more emphatic way of stating it, he opens with a double asseveration אף־אמנם "indeed, assuredly" (which occurs elsewhere only at 19:4; Gen 18:13). But his emphases are platitudes; the second colon is nothing but Bildad's language at 8:3. All the same, the thought is perhaps rather more precise than the language, for Elihu is thinking not of any and every kind of wickedness that must not be ascribed to God but of the particular case of wrongdoing that consists in declaring an innocent person guilty, condemning someone unjustly.

13 The rhetorical question "Who put the earth in his charge?" plainly expects the answer "No one." There is no one who has "assigned, entrusted" (as פקד means at, e.g., Num 4:27; 27:16; Jer 15:3; 51:27) the world to God's charge, since he is its sole creator. The second colon, though harder to interpret, is likely to have a parallel meaning (the previous three lines have all been in synonymous parallelism), "Who gave him rule over the entire world?" (see *Notes*). It is true that in the face of such authority Job's challenge is a disparagement of God's person (Hartley), but there is more to it than that. The sentence can make sense in the context only if we understand that God's undisputed sovereignty over the world ensures that whatever he wants to happen does happen, and thus, implicitly, that if some humans are rewarded and some are punished, that is God's implementation of his ruling principle of retribution.

It is not, as Strahan, Peake, and de Wilde think, that it is God's independence that guarantees his justice; if he were some subordinate, he could perhaps enrich himself at his master's expense, but, as things stand, everything is his property (cf. Moffatt "he is no viceroy lording it on earth!"). For it is possible that he could be both independent *and* unjust, as a tyrant is—and as Job himself is arguing. Nor is it likely to mean, as Rowley thinks, that God is "subject to no pressures to be unjust," for that does not guarantee his justice either: he could easily be irrationally or whimsically or determinedly, but certainly unconstrainedly, unjust.

14–15 As the sole governor and sustainer of the universe (v 13), God would find it very easy to destroy all his creation (vv 14b–15), if he set his mind to it (v 14a). But he does not do so because that would be unjust to those who deserve to live, and he would not be true to himself if he did not uphold the rights of the righteous.

V 14 begins with a key clause, which is variously interpreted (for the details, see *Note* 14.b). As it stands, the Hebrew says, "If it were his intention" (NIV), "If he plans in his heart" (Habel), which suggests that God has the capacity to bring life to an end but that he does not choose to exercise that power. Other translations and commentators emend the text to read "if he should take back his spirit to himself" (so RSV, NAB, NJB, GNB), but the emendation seems unnecessary. The sense is not greatly altered, nevertheless.

The main idea is that all living things live through the breath given them by God. Since he is the giver of breath (also at Isa 42:5), he has the right also to be the taker, so the thought runs (cf. 1:21). A quite similar text is Ps 104:29: when God takes away the breath (רוח) of creatures, they die and return to their dust. But in this Joban passage there is a novelty: the breath of living creatures is not just their own breath but the breath of God. It is *his* spirit (רוחו) and *his* breath (נשמתו) that sustain life. Another intertext is Gen 2:7, where the human has breathed into it God's breath (נשמה) of life and so becomes a living being (cf. also Job 27:3; 33:4 for God's breath in the human being). But here it appears to be all living creatures, "all flesh" (כל־בשׂר), that are imbued with the divine breath. For "all flesh" as a term that explicitly includes the animal creation, cf. Gen 7:21 "All flesh died that moved upon the earth, birds, cattle, beasts, all swarming creatures that swarm upon the earth, and every human." In a few places "all flesh" does seem to be restricted to humans (Isa 40:5; 49:26; 66:23; Jer 25:31; Ezek 20:48 [21:4]; 21:5 [10]; Joel 3:1 [2:28]; Zech 2:13 [17]; Pss 65:2 [3]; 145:21), but mostly it is either clearly or possibly all living beings. "All flesh" is parallel here to אדם "humanity," but that does not mean that the two terms are equivalent; a similar parallelism of כל־חי "all that lives" (see also on 28:21) with איש "humankind" can be seen in 12:10. On the idea of God "gathering" (אסף) his breath to himself, cf. Ps 104:29; in Eccl 12:7 the spirit "returns" (שׁוב), more of its own volition, to God who gave it. On עפר "mud" as well as "dust," see *Comment* on 30:19.

There are many unsatisfactory ways of understanding these verses. Taken by themselves, and out of their context, they have been called one of the most beautiful and striking passages in the OT (Budde), teaching that "the transcendent

God is also the immanent God, sustaining all life by his animating breath" (Strahan). On the contrary, in the context of Elihu's argument they take on a darker hue, speaking not so much of the animation of life as of its precariousness, the existence of human and beast alike hanging by the thread of a divine thought. Delitzsch too argued that since "by the impartation of His living creative breath" God sustains the universe, and does not "allow them to fall away into nothingness," there must be "a divine love which has called the world into being and... as the perfect opposite of sovereign caprice, is a pledge for the absolute righteousness of the divine rule." But it is difficult to see how it is divine love for the universe that ensures that the wicked are punished, and it is negative retribution for sinners that Elihu is defending just as much as the positive form for the righteous.

Rowley, for his part, thought that these lines meant that since all humans are equally dependent on God, "there can be no reason why he should favour one more than another," but the issue of divine impartiality is not being raised by Elihu before v 19. De Wilde saw the argument as being that since God freely created humanity, he must therefore treat it well and justly; but that neither follows nor is it appropriate to Elihu's position, which does not concern humanity in general but rather the differing experiences of the righteous and the wicked. Andersen thinks that Elihu is arguing that with God might is right, but this can hardly be correct since Elihu is above all concerned to affirm that God acts according to principles of justice and not arbitrarily.

Elihu's words must be viewed in the context of Elihu's argument as a whole. He is well aware that God does from time to time "gather in his breath to himself" and returns certain humans to their original clay. The fact that he does not treat all humans in that way, though he has the power to do so, is proof that he discriminates between humans, which is to say that he operates according to the law of retribution. Of course, we might add, it is possible in theory that his sustaining of one life and cutting another life short could be pure whim, but Elihu does not consider that possibility. It is a weak point in his argument but it is perhaps not fatal to it—not unless, that is, one's opponent is a Job, who has determined that the rule by which God operates is indeed caprice, pure caprice (see on 23:13–14).

16–20 Now in the second movement of the speech Elihu turns to Job, and will address him directly until the end. The theme is the same as in the first movement: God, as the universal ruler, cannot act wrongly, and any suggestion by Job that he does is itself a wickedness.

In the first strophe of this address to Job, Elihu argues that just rule is of the essence of God's sovereignty. Deciding cases, discriminating between suppliants, ordering the social framework, impartially dispensing justice, that is the very business of a ruler. Anyone who does not care for that line of work does not become a sovereign: does an enemy of justice govern (v 17a)? Elihu's thought is not so crass as some of his commentators make out: he is far from arguing that might is right or that God's power in itself is all the guarantee needed for the rightness of his judgments. And Elihu is not much concerned here with the case of tyrants and unjust rulers (except insofar as they lie under God's judgment, v 18), though as limiting cases they are not a little damaging to his position. The center of his thesis is this: rectitude is bound up in the notion of sovereignty.

His chief argument in this strophe is that a supreme sovereign must of necessity judge, and adjudicate impartially among his subordinates. If such a ruler cannot reprimand inferiors (v 18), he is no sovereign. If he shows partiality to one group over another (v 19ab), he is in the pocket of that group and not his own person. When God is the ruler in question, his sovereignty has a special quality that other sovereignties lack: all his subjects have an identical relation to him, as his creatures (v 19c), and that further safeguards his objectivity and critical distance.

So it is not a simple matter of Elihu's begging the question, as a stream of commentators, from Duhm onward, have argued. Here is Duhm's reasoning: "Since God rules the world, it follows that he also must have the capacity to rule; if he hated justice and order, everything would necessarily fall apart. This is a veritable *petitio principii*: the question is precisely whether or not in the moral realm things have fallen apart, whether God does in reality rule the world if the wicked are on top and innocence is laid low." Elihu could well answer that the mere raising of a doubt by Job cannot undermine a whole moral universe; his charges do not merely concern the character and the attitude of the divine ruler to one particular individual, but the very nature of sovereignty, which cannot be called government if it does not have at its heart a drive for justice.

Peake, who represented Duhm's challenging biblical criticism to the English-speaking world, put the point like this: "The fact that God governs means that His rule is righteous, a strange begging of the question .... [T]he righteousness of God's rule ... is the very point to be proved." Driver–Gray too outline Elihu's case in similar words: "God actually governs, and is *ipso facto* a lover and securer of right within His dominion; for (17a) hatred and rejection of right brings government to naught: injustice and government are incompatible; similarly (v 17b), God is the mighty just one: therefore he is not unjust." On this their comment is: "Since whether the government of God and perversion of right, God and injustice are incompatibles, is the question that Job has raised, Elihu's questions imply assertions which ... are really a *petitio principii*" (this language of begging the question is repeated by Strahan, Rowley, and de Wilde, among others). To be sure, Elihu is not answering Job; no one in the whole book does. And he cannot confront the case that Job is making. But from Elihu's own perspective, Job's allegations are simply unacceptable, for if you claim that the supreme governor of the universe is without moral sense you have an amoral universe—and that, Elihu could argue, is far from the world *he* knows. In a way, then, Elihu is appealing to experience no less than Job is, though of course it is an experience refracted through his theological education.

For Gordis, Elihu's argument, that it is inconceivable that an enemy of justice should rule and that those who rule are righteous, is a reflection of the upper-class orientation of the wisdom literature; it is this very assumption that Job is calling into question. There may be something in this, and yet Elihu is quite well aware that kings and princes can be wicked (v 18) and deserve to be overthrown (v 24).

16 The imperative verbs "hear" (שמע) and "give ear" (אזן hiph) in the singular show that Elihu is now addressing Job directly. His language is of the most conventional. In 33:8 he says he has heard (שמע) the sound (קול) of Job's words (מלין), and here he will reciprocate, with just the same terms; he does not much vary his formulae, as Dhorme remarks. There is no reason to think Elihu is being rude to Job in summoning him to listen, or that he is insulting his intelligence (as NEB "if you have the wit" and JB "If you have any intelligence") or being ironic (Whybray). To be sure, the young man Elihu believes he has truths to impart to his senior, Job, but this is hardly impertinence (as Duhm thought); Hartley for one sees here politeness on Elihu's part.

17 Can an "enemy of justice" (JB) govern? The issue is not whether states are ever in the grip of tyrants who care nothing for justice (they are envisaged in the next verse, in fact) but whether the rule of such tyrants can properly be called *governing*. For Elihu, governing implies fair dealing, and the supreme governor of the universe, the "mighty one" (כביר, of God also at 36:5, of wind at 8:2, age at 15:10, wealth at 31:25), is almost by definition the "just one" (צדיק). "Whoever will rule must lay down rules, and whoever lays down rules must himself be bound by them" (de Wilde). Hartley interestingly remarks that, unlike modern democracies where the judicial system is separate from the executive, the ancient world tended rather to conflate the two. The issue here then is not so much whether with God injustice and government are incompatible (Driver–Gray) or whether in God right and might form a unity (Fohrer), but whether the governing of the universe is possible on any other basis but order and justice. It is not for Job, says Elihu, to put that universal governor in the wrong (רשע, declarative hiph); the question form suggests the astonishment of Elihu that such could be Job's undertaking. If declaring the innocent guilty is a matter for reproach in law and prophets and writings (Exod 23:7; Isa 5:23; Prov 17:15), how much worse it must be when the innocent is himself the mighty just one!

18 God is far above criticism himself, for he is the one who makes criticisms. It is his role to evaluate others, even rulers, not to be evaluated himself. His rank as supreme governor entitles him to judge (when necessary, of course) even kings as scoundrels (בליעל). The term בליעל is commonly translated "worthless," on the assumption that it is a compound of בלי "without" and יעל "profit." But this is most unlikely, not least because there is no noun יַעַל "profit" (though there is a verb יעל "profit, avail"). It seems rather that it is a general term for "wicked," perhaps with an overtone of "destructive" (it is parallel to "death" in 2 Sam 22:5; and cf. Ps 41:8 [9]). To apply it to a king would be a great insult, since very often it seems to be low-class persons who are thus designated (e.g., Judg 19:22; 1 Kgs 21:10; 2 Chr 13:7).

The translation "who says" or "who can say," offered by almost all the English versions and the commentators, rests upon a revocalization of the Hebrew to the participle (הָאוֹמֵר "the one who says"). The MT, which is grammatically anomalous and can hardly be correct, interestingly seems to say "Is one to say?" So KJV, RV "Is it fit to say to a king?," NJPS "Would you call a king a scoundrel, great men, wicked?," Tur-Sinai "Doth one say to a king?" The implication would be that Job is out of order in alleging that God is unjust, since not even of a human ruler should such a criticism be made. If this is what Elihu really says, it would certainly make his dismay at Job's accusation of God even more intelligible. But the reading comes to grief finally on the opening word of v 19: the "who" there must refer back to the mighty just one of v 17, and it can hardly do that if v 16 also does not concern God, being introduced with "who says."

For a parallel, and a much more extensive treatment of the responsibilities of kings and judges, see Wis 6:1–8, where they are reminded that their dominion was given them from the Lord, who, while being merciful to low-ranking persons, will carry out a "strict inquiry" into the deeds of rulers. He "will not stand in awe of anyone, or show deference to greatness; because he himself made both small and great" (v 7 NRSV). On righteousness and wisdom as a mark of rulers, cf. also Prov 8:15–16; 16:10, 12–13; 20:8.

19 A further mark of God as supreme governor is that he shows no favoritism: high-ranking officials are not preferred above ordinary people (on the meaning of שׁוע "high-ranking," see *Note* 19.c). On showing partiality, lit. "lifting up the face" (נשׂא פנים), see on 13:8; God's impartiality in judgment is the topic also in Deut 10:17; 2 Chr 19:7; Wis 6:7; Acts 10:34–35; Rom 2:11; Eph 6:9; Col 3:25; 1 Pet 1:17. It is not a self-denying ordinance by which God resists showing favoritism to high-ranking members of society, says Elihu; God is impartial because from his perspective all humans are on a common footing, as equally his creatures (the reference in the third colon is probably to all humans, rather than to rulers, as Peake suggested). And again, it is not their creatureliness that disposes God to act kindly toward them; it is that their common status as the "work of his hands" makes the social distinctions they have engineered among themselves entirely insignificant.

20 The picture of how God, far from being unjust himself, calls his subordinate rulers to account because of their wrongdoings is continued from v 18. There he named and shamed them, here he brings their life to an end in retribution for their wickedness. They are not of course all kings and princes who are here in view, but only those who have not executed their responsibility for righteous government. In a sense, this verse answers the rhetorical question posed in v 17a: "Shall an enemy of justice govern?" If one who is in a position of authority turns out to be an enemy of justice, that person is soon and effortlessly (לא ביד, lit. "without hand") dispatched. And the universal order is reestablished, that enemies of justice do not govern.

The rulers are variously named: in v 18 they have been "kings" (מלך) and "princes" or "aristocrats" (Good) (נדיב, also at 12:21, where it is parallel to אפיק, probably "warrior," and at 21:28, where it is parallel to רשׁע "wicked"). In v 19 they have been "princes" (שׂר, a term used for the rich at 3:15, for Job's peers at 29:9, and for military leaders at 39:28), and "high-ranking" (שׁוע; see *Note* 19.c). Here it appears that שׁוע "high-ranking" is used again (if we accept the common emendation of the MT עם "people"), along with "mighty" (אביר, also at 24:22, where they are wicked). All these terms are obviously interchangeable, and no special significance should be seen in the use of one word rather than another; collectively they denote those who govern.

The image of these unjust rulers being cut off from life "at midnight" (חצות לילה) inevitably recalls another biblical occasion of sudden midnight death, at the hands of the angel of the Lord: the slaying of the Egyptian firstborn (Exod 11:4; cf. the slaughter "in the night" of 185,000 Assyrian troops, also by the angel of the Lord, in 2 Kgs 19:35). Destruction "in a moment" (רגע) is a common trope (Exod 33:5; Num 16:21; 16:45 [17:10]; Isa 47:9; Jer 4:20; Pss 6:10 [11]; 73:19).

Some have seen here a depiction of unjust rulers or tyrants being overthrown by a popular rebellion; thus Terrien translates: "in the middle of the night, a people revolts, and God deposes a tyrant without even lifting a hand" (similarly JB,

Fedrizzi, Ravasi). But this interesting proposal does not give full force to "and they pass away" (ויעברו), which Terrien removes to the first colon, and, more tellingly, it makes the improbable suggestion that popular revolt is God's preferred means of dealing with unrighteous rulers.

On the question whether לא ביד means "without force" or "by no human agency," as it is more commonly understood, see *Note* 20.j.

21–30 This long strophe is no more than an elaboration of the point Elihu had attained to in the previous strophe. There (in vv 16–20) he had argued that God's sovereignty is bound up with rectitude, and a testimony to that is the freedom he has to call his subordinates to account, even cutting off their life if they deserve it. Now he deals in some detail with the way God disposes of those high-ranking officials he has called scoundrels and villains in v 18.

Although the language of vv 21–30 may seem to apply to humans generally, it becomes plain that Elihu is thinking primarily, if not exclusively, of the "mighty" who have offended against the divine will. Thus we read of "a man" (איש) in vv 21 and 23 and of "evildoers" (פעלי־און) in v 22, but it is not humanity at large that is Elihu's focus: it is rather the "mighty" (כבירים), visible in v 24, that are his concern, the mighty as contrasted with the "poor" (דל) and the "afflicted" (עניים) of v 28. And the "godless reprobate" of v 30, whom God prevents from ensnaring a whole people like a wild animal in a trap, is not just any evildoer, but specifically one of God's subordinate rulers who has disregarded God's ways (v 27).

If any of these governors appointed by God behave unjustly, God knows (v 25a), and acts immediately, without any need for a long-drawn-out inquiry (v 24a), striking them down for their wickedness (vv 24a, 26) and replacing them with others more compliant with divine standards of justice (v 24). Even if he appears to be unaware of what is going on in the world of humans (v 29a–b), we may be sure that he is taking care that unjust rulers should not reign (v 30).

Significantly, Elihu includes in his depiction of God's judgment on these unjust rulers the fact that he "sets others in their place" (v 24b). For God's purpose is not only to punish the unjust by removing their authority; it is equally to supply alternative rulers, worthier and more honest, in order to ensure that good government is restored.

21 Despite appearances, it is not to Elihu's purpose to turn his attention to the fate of evildoers in general. His theme in the speech as a whole is the justice of God's universal governorship (vv 10, 12), and one of his proofs of it has been God's readiness to bring to book subordinate rulers who deviate from his standards (vv 18–19). They have been the focus in v 18, where God evaluates kings and high-ranking officials; in v 19, where he is beyond partiality; and in v 20, where his execution of judgment against the "mighty" removes them from their office. Continuing the theme here, the "man" (איש) whose steps are under perpetual assessment by heaven is the typical ruler.

Whether deliberately or not, in this verse Elihu is borrowing the words of Job. In saying that God's eyes are upon the ways of humans, he virtually cites Job at 24:23, though there Job had been speaking of God's apparent concern for the prosperity of the wicked (Job has been much occupied with God as the "Human-Watcher," as he calls him in 7:20). In saying that God sees all the steps of humans, he is again using Job's language, at 31:4 (cf. also 34:21; 14:16), where they were Job's steps that were being scrutinized by God, in the same sense as

Elihu has in mind here. On human steps as watched by God, a wisdom motif, cf. Pss 33:13; 69:5 (6); 94:11; 119:168; 139:1–4; Prov 5:21.

22 Such rulers, if they become evildoers, cannot hope to hide their iniquity from God. It is a familiar trope in the Hebrew Bible that darkness cannot conceal wicked deeds from God's gaze and there is no hiding from God (Ps 139:11–12; Jer 23:24; Amos 9:2–3; cf. Ecclus 23:19).

23–24 When one of these rulers offends against justice, not only is there no escaping the divine scrutiny (vv 21–22), but also retribution is swift (vv 23–24). Since God knows their deeds already (v 21), he has no need, like a human judge, to investigate whether they are criminals or not, so "without inquiry" (v 24a) and without awaiting a stated assize day (v 23a) he can proceed immediately to "shatter" (רעע) them and install others in their place. "God does not need to use the formalities of legal procedure, He acts by sovereign authority" (Dhorme).

Job has made it a particular point of complaint against God that he does not hold regular days of assize at which the wicked can be sure to be held accountable (24:1). Elihu may be alluding to Job's charge (it is an indirect rebuke of Job, thinks Whybray), though Job is speaking there of wrongdoers in general and not just of rulers. In any case, Job's real objection to the way God is governing the world is not that he does not hold regular court sessions (rather than meting out punishments on an ad hoc basis) but that he does not hold the guilty to account even after long periods have passed.

For a depiction of the transfer of an official's authority to another, see Isa 22:19–24; and for a poetic wish in a similar context, see Ps 109:8; cf. also 1 Sam 2:7–8; Pss 75:7 (8); 113:7–8.

25–28 Little new is added in these verses, which are essentially a recapitulation of the content of vv 20–24. God knows their works (v 25a = v 21), he overturns them (v 25b = shaken, v 20b, shattered, v 24a), in the night (v 25b = at midnight, v 20b), they are crushed (v 25b = shattered, v 24a). He strikes them (v 26a = shattered, v 24a) for their wickedness (v 26a = evildoers, v 22; cf. v 18), in public view (v 26b = they are replaced by other rulers, v 24b). They turned from following God and had no regard for his ways (v 27 = evildoers, v 22). Only in v 28, where the wicked rulers are viewed as oppressing the poor, who then call upon God for redress, do we find new material.

25 If they are "crushed" (דכא), they are completely annihilated, incapable of coming back into power (Hartley); the verb has been used literally of arms being broken (22:9) and, metaphorically, of humans being destroyed by death (4:19; of Job 6:9; 19:2; of the fool's sons, 5:4). The term "overthrow" (הפך) is especially reminiscent of the overthrow of Sodom and Gomorrah (Deut 29:22; used elsewhere of the cataclysmic overthrow of thrones, Hag 2:22, and of mountains, Job 9:5; 28:9).

26 The punishment of official wrongdoing must be public, not just because its perpetrators have thought they could hide themselves (v 22; so Hartley), but because the wrong has affected society, and God must restore public confidence in the process of just government.

27 The phrase סור מאחרי "turn aside from after" is used elsewhere of literal turning away from following someone (2 Sam 2:21, 22) and, more metaphorically, of turning away from God (Deut 7:4 [hiph]; 1 Sam 12:20; 2 Kgs 18:6; 2 Chr 25:27). It is obviously the opposite of the common phrase הלך אחרי "go after" (literally in, e.g., Gen 24:5; frequently of going after other gods in, e.g., Deut 4:3; 6:14; sometimes of going after Yahweh, in Deut 13:4 [5]).

28 Here is the specific point in which these unjust rulers have disregarded God's ways: their actions have caused the cry of the poor to ascend to heaven, which means that they have been wronging the poor. Their chief departure from divine principles has been in their oppression of the needy. The Hebrew implies that the rulers disregarded God's ways *in order to* cause the cry of the oppressed to rise to God for redress. Clearly, the cry of the poor is in reality the *result* of the unjust governing by their rulers. It is of course an ironical turn of phrase to express a result as an intention, as if all the consequences of their action were foreseen and deliberate (see *Note* 28.c). For the "cry" (verbs צעק, זעק; nouns צעקה, זעקה) for justice, see also 16:18; 19:17; 27:9; 31:38; 35:9, 12.

29 In v 26 Elihu has affirmed that God deals with high-ranking malfeasance in a very public way; but at times it seems rather that God is not managing the world's governance very visibly. Nonetheless, says Elihu, behind the scenes he is constantly at work. He may be "quiet" (שׁקט), apparently at ease (the verb is often used of the land, e.g., Judg 3:11; 8:28; of a people, Judg 18:7; of Yahweh as an inactive spectator, Isa 18:4; of Yahweh being called upon not to stand idly by, Ps 83:1 [2]). He may "hide his face" (סתר פנים hiph, of God also at Deut 32:20; Isa 8:17; 54:8; 64:6; Mic 3:4; but perhaps the phrase means "turn aside his face"; see *Note* 29.d), which is to say, not allow himself to be seen as active, as if he had no interest in earthly affairs, just as Job had already alleged (13:24). The phrase "hide the face," when used of God, can sometimes signify his displeasure (as in 13:24; Deut 32:20; Isa 54:8; 57:17), sometimes merely his absence (e.g., Pss 10:11; 22:24 [25]; 104:29), and sometimes, as here, rather his forgetfulness (e.g., Ps 44:24 [25]). Nothing can be done—or, more to the point, need be done—about such apparent divine indifference: since he is God, no one can "condemn" (רשׁע hiph) him for inaction (or, if the text is to be emended, "stir him up" [NJB]; see *Note* 29.c), no one can "see" him if he chooses to hide himself. Nor *need* anyone condemn him or strive to see what he is doing.

What we may be sure of, says Elihu, is that behind such appearances God remains "over" (על) nations and individuals alike. We might have expected some verb in the third colon to signify that he is watching or ruling over his world; one suggestion is that the word יחד "alike" should be emended to יחז "he watches," but see *Note* 29.i.

30 Since the theme of God's assured control of his subordinate governors is what animates this strophe, it is only proper that at its end the purpose of his ever-watchfulness over both nations and persons (v 29c) should become explicit: it is in order that unjust rulers should not survive or treat their peoples like the prey of a wild animal.

The text is awkwardly expressed, and may well be defective, but as it stands it seems to mean that God rules over nations and individuals (v 29c) "so that a godless person should not reign, and so be a snare for a people." For parallels to the term מוקשׁ "snare" used metaphorically, cf. Exod 10:7 (of Moses), Judg 2:3 (of foreign gods), and 1 Sam 18:21 (Michal). Such rulers become a snare to the people, not in some vague moral sense (e.g., their "evil example and bad government become the ruin of the community," Delitzsch), but in the specific sense that they regard their subjects as prey to be caught in a trap, for the use and pleasure of their rulers. When rulers are hunters (or, more precisely, the trap itself) and their people are the prey, the people are oppressed and have reason to appeal to God about something (v 28).

31–37 The theme of this speech has been the right of God to govern his world, its keynote being the rhetorical question, "Can one who hates justice govern?" (v 17). In concluding the speech, Elihu encourages Job to recognize God's rightful rulership by forswearing his hostility to God.

Elihu has been addressing Job directly since v 16, but from v 18 onward he has slid into a discursive mode in which it may well have seemed that Job himself had been forgotten. Now, in the peroration of his speech, Elihu turns to Job again with his advice on what Job should be saying, formulating for him, a bit presumptuously, the very words he should use by way of confession of his wrongdoing. For Elihu the only way forward is for Job to acknowledge his sin and to promise he will not offend again (vv 31–32). He cannot expect that God will adopt his standards of justice and reward him as Job himself sees fit, especially when Job has declared himself so violently in opposition to God (v 33ab). Though Elihu can offer advice, it is of no value unless Job makes up his own mind about how he will act: he needs to sort out where he stands now, and make an open confession of what he really believes (v 34cd).

Elihu would like to envisage himself as being truly on Job's side, but he is aware, so he says, of a groundswell of opinion against Job. The view among thinking people is that, in his assaults on God, Job has taken up the position of the godless (v 36b), getting himself deeper and deeper into sin by the tone of his speeches (v 37). Others are saying that such a stubborn Job needs to suffer even greater trials (v 36a). Elihu himself, so he professes, is not saying anything so harsh: he is encouraging Job to give up his recalcitrance and take the penitent's stool, but he cannot hide the fact that others are being far less sympathetic (these others are no doubt mere bogeymen whom Elihu is inventing to frighten Job with).

There have been other interpretations of these extremely difficult verses that are very different. Rowley, for example, thought they were asking whether, "if any man should repent and confess his sin under divine correction, ought not God to spare him without first consulting Job?" If Job agrees, then, that God forgives the penitent, then Elihu has caught Job: Job is plainly not forgiven, ergo he is not penitent. If such is Elihu's intention, it seems a very roundabout way of arriving at it, since the question of whether God needs to consult Job is entirely beside the point.

31–32 As the Hebrew stands, the strophe opens with a question, apparently whether anyone has confessed their guilt to God and has promised amendment of life (so, e.g., RSV). Such a question is not only absurdly obvious, it is irrelevant to the situation of Elihu and Job. Since, moreover, by v 33 Elihu is directly addressing Job, it is much more likely that vv 31–32 also are to be read as his advice to Job. So the opening colon should be translated, "Indeed, you should say . . ." (see *Note* 31.b).

The issue is whether the first verb (האמר), usually translated "has anyone said?," can make sense. Driver–Gray, understanding the last words of the colon (לא אחבל) as referring to the past, "I did not offend," take it to mean that no one before Job had asserted he had suffered without having committed some offense. That is true of Job's position in general, but it seems much more probable that לא אבחל in v 31b refers to the future ("I shall not offend"), parallel to the plain words לא אסיף, "I shall do so no more," in v 32b.

The first word Job should utter is, in the Hebrew, "I have borne," but there is no object to signify what it is he has borne. According to KJV, RSV, NJPS, NIV, and others, it is his guilt, or its punishment, but there are no parallels to such an idiom, and it is preferable to adopt a small revocalization of the text to yield "I was misguided" (see *Note* 31.d). Elihu will allow Job some dignity: he does not have to denigrate himself before God, but simply to concede that he has been "misled, misguided, beguiled" (נשא II, niph only elsewhere at Isa 19:13), and to promise that "*if* I have done wrong, I will do it no more" (v 32b). He has only to seek instruction or enlightenment ("teach me what I do not see"), like a pious psalmist inviting God's "teaching" (Pss 27:11; 86:11; 119:33) or a pupil in a wisdom school (Prov 4:4, 11), though without the irony of Job's use of הורוני "teach me" at 6:24; for חזה "see" as a term for intellectual knowledge, cf. on 15:17. Even proud persons might find themselves capable of making such a low-key confession without violating their conviction of their own innocence.

33 Though all the words in this verse are rather straightforward, together they form one of the most cryptic verses in the book. What would suit Elihu's position, as well as properly reflecting the wording, would be for him to affirm that God must be free to execute justice according to his own standards, and not in accord with what Job happens to think he deserves. Thus I translate, "Will he then requite you as you see fit?," lit. "Is it from with you that he will requite it?" The issue is the justice of God's retribution or "repayment" (שלם piel, as at v 11; 21:19, 31; 41:11 [3]), and it is already a foregone conclusion that it operates strictly according to deeds (v 11) and not according to claims of desert, as Job would have it.

Job is in no position to decide matters for God since he has made himself God's opponent (מאסת "you have rejected him"). But he does need to decide matters for himself (אתה תבחר "you choose"), i.e., whether he will persist in his hostility to God or acknowledge his sin. It is a choice between penitence and defiance (Driver–Gray's thought, that it is a choice of what alternative system of retribution Job would like God to invoke, is strained). No one can make that decision for him; however pressing Elihu's advice may be, it is not he (לא אני "not I") who can choose Job's future. And Job himself, if he is to regain the confidence of others, must make public any newly acquired convictions (ומה־ידעת דבר "and what you know, say," i.e., "do say what you believe"). Job has often said he "knows" when we would say we "believe" (see *Note* 33.h): he knows (ידע) that God will not hold him innocent (9:28), that fastening guilt upon him was always God's purpose (10:13), that he will be vindicated (13:18), that his champion lives (19:25), that God will bring him to death (30:23). Where do all these beliefs or knowledges stand now?, Elihu is asking. Now that he has had the chance to hear Elihu's disquisition on universal governance, what does he "know"? Many are waiting to hear him "declare" (דבר piel) it.

34 Who are these "men of understanding" (אנשי לבב) and the "wise man" (גבר חכם) to whose opinions Elihu makes appeal? They do not seem to be the other friends of the dialogue, whom Elihu has indeed called "wise men" (חכמים) and "men of learning" (ידעים) in v 2. Neither are they a wider audience than that of the three friends (Strahan). They stand rather for right-thinking persons in general, beyond the intimate circle that is represented in the dialogues of the book. They are the reference group from which Elihu and the friends—and Job himself—derive their norms. The most natural way of understanding the words of theirs that Elihu quotes in vv 35–37 is, admittedly, that they are words that will be spoken in the future. But that does not fit very well with Elihu's advice in the preceding verses; for if Job heeds his advice, repents, promises to amend his ways, and makes known his change of attitude (vv 31–33), then the criticism of the "men of understanding" will no longer be valid, and will not in fact be made. Some have thought that Elihu pauses at the end of v 33 to see what effect his speech is having on Job (so Rowley [possibly], Hartley, Dhorme "Elihu considers he has won the debate since Job does not reply") and, finding Job unmoved, ratchets up his animus against Job by appealing to this example of hostile public opinion. The speeches in the book of Job are not scripts for the theater, however, and it is quite out of place to imagine some intervening event. It is much more plausible to locate the speeches of the "men of understanding" in the present (taking יאמרו as "they say," the imperfect of repeated action [GKC, § 107g]), and so as the framework within which Elihu sees himself operating: on every side he must perforce hear these damning criticisms of Job, but he himself has hit upon the key to Job's full restitution by God and in the eyes of the populace: acknowledgment of guilt.

35–37 Translators and commentators are divided over whether we are to hear in these three verses the verdict of the shadowy "men of understanding" (v 34) (so NEB, JB, Hölscher, Fohrer, Gordis, Hesse, Alonso Schökel–Sicre Díaz, Habel, Good), or whether only v 35 is quoted from them, Elihu speaking again in his own voice in vv 36–37 (so RSV, NJPS, Moffatt, Delitzsch, Peake, Dhorme, Terrien, Pope, Rowley, Fedrizzi, Ravasi, de Wilde, Hartley). It makes a good deal of difference whether we ascribe v 36, with its cruel demand that Job should continue to be "tried," and that "to the utmost," to Elihu or not. The wording, however, suggests strongly that vv 36–37 continue to cite the "men of understanding," since it is they who refer to Job by his name and in the third person both in v 35 and v 36, and it is improbable that Elihu, who has been addressing Job in the second person in vv 31–33, should now use third-person language of him ("would that Job were tried," "he adds to his sin"). On the other hand, it is a little strange that these "men of understanding" should speak of Job clapping (v 37), if that is what he is doing, "among us" (בינינו), since Job is not among *them,* but among the interlocutors in the dialogue. The text, however, is so uncertain at this point that little weight should be placed on this argument.

35 It is hard to know which is the most stringent condemnation of Job: that he is not wise (v 35) or that he is speaking like a wicked person (v 36b). Plainly, we are in the world of the wisdom teachers, where lack of "knowledge" (דעת) or "insight" (השׂכיל; for the combination of the two terms, cf. Jer 3:15 [דעה]) is morally culpable, and where folly and wickedness are almost interchangeable ideas. For the idea of Job's words being "without knowledge," cf. 35:16 (Elihu); 38:2; 42:3 (God).

36 The term for "test, examine" (בחן) has been used in v 3 of the ear testing words (as also in 12:11), but, more to the point, it has been Job's term for God's perpetual scrutiny of humans (7:18) and, metaphorically, for the process of assaying that Job expects God to subject him to in 23:10. Now the opinion of the "men of understanding" is that Job should be "thoroughly examined" (the same בחן). This is the unkindest cut of all, the suggestion that so far Job has not suffered enough! If Elihu does not speak in his own voice but in that of others, it does palliate the severity somewhat, even if the "men of understanding" are no more than a front for Elihu's inner thoughts. (Habel's suggestion that the further "testing" might be "more relentless argumentation by Elihu and his companions" [similarly Weiser], though daunting, does not seem to be what is in mind.)

37 There is more than one way of conceiving of the structure of this verse. As the Hebrew stands, there are three cola: "For he adds to his sin rebellion / among us he claps (?) / and multiplies his words to (or, against) God," the cola being arranged in an ABA pattern as a marker of the close of the speech (Watson, 182, 183). The first colon would be reminiscent of Isa 30:1, "to add sin to sin" (though the verb may be not exactly the same; for יסף על hiph "add to" with "sin," cf. Ezra 10:10; 2 Chr 28:13). Some have wondered if "rebellion" (פשׁע) is presented as a worse fault than mere "sin" (חטאת), but there seems no good reason to think so.

The word translated "claps" (ספק) is very problematic, having no expressed object, and it is preferable to understand it as a different verb, meaning "cast doubt on" (see *Note* 37.c). In that case, פשׁע "rebellion" from the first colon will be the object, and the first two cola will read: "For he adds to his sin / questioning his transgression in our presence," i.e., denying that he is at fault (not in general "creating doubts," though Terrien cannily remarks that creating doubts among theologians is the real fault in Elihu's eyes). Others (e.g., Duhm, Hölscher, Fohrer, Moffatt, NEB), in despair at making sense of the second colon, have deleted it altogether, leaving just two cola for the verse.

It does seem ironic, as Habel says, that "Elihu, the brash and verbose know-it-all, should condemn Job for being ignorant and garrulous," but, to be fair to Elihu, it is not the quantity of Job's words that he takes exception to, but the fact that so many of them are "against" (אל) God; neither has he any fault to find with Job's wisdom in general, for the issue is solely whether Job accepts the truth about God's just government of the universe.

Explanation

In his first speech, Elihu had argued that suffering was one of God's ways of communicating with humans (cf. especially 33:14–30), and that therefore Job should recognize that his own experience is not the result of divine hostility so much as of a divine desire for his education. In this speech, on the other hand, his interest is not in suffering as such, but in debating one of Job's key themes, that God has been treating him unjustly. Against Job's claims, Elihu develops this speech around the nodal sentence, "Can one who hates justice govern?"

This speech is no work of analytic philosophy and the writing is, frankly, rather dull—by the standards of the book as a whole. The Hebrew, too, is often quite cryptic, though that is more likely to be the fault of its textual transmission than a weakness in its author. Yet in the speech Elihu explores the question of God's justice in a quite thoughtful way. No one can of course equal the power of Job's fierce diatribes against the dogma of divine justice in the face of the realities of human existence. But Elihu in reply does not simply throw up his hands in horror (he does in vv 5–9), as the other friends have been inclined to do. Without seeking to resolve the problems of retributive justice or to explain the many contradictions to it that are empirically encountered, he asks rather what it means for God to be the supreme governor of the universe, and what sense a charge of injustice could make in reference to such a one.

Though he refers to God as "the Righteous Mighty One" (v 17), his point is by no means that for the universal governor might equals right. Rather, he is affirming that the very business of governing is the dispensing of justice, and that it makes no sense to envisage an unjust ruler of the world. The special supporting case Elihu takes up is of God's authority over human subordinates, kings and princes, who can be judged and deposed by him without fear or favor (vv 18–20). That is what it means to be a governor: controlling those with power in one's realm. The evidence from human history and society shows that God is running a tight ship, says Elihu: mighty rulers fall in a moment and are replaced by others, a testimony to the divine system of justice that keeps all power holders under perpetual scrutiny (vv 21–22), executes instant and public judgment (vv 23–26), and ensures that the people they rule are protected from unjust government (v 30). Indeed, the dispensing of life and death across the whole creation (vv 14–15) is a signal that the divine writ runs everywhere, requiting to everyone according to their deeds, whether for weal or for woe (v 11). Even if God appears to be inactive in just rulership, behind the scenes he is controlling the fate of nations and individuals alike (vv 29c–30).

There are just two flaws in Elihu's argument. First, the evidence of history is against it. Tyrants *may* fall in an instant, but *do* they, as a matter of course? Secondly, he does not allow for the possibility that the supreme governor of the universe is himself an arbitrary tyrant. If the second rung of world governors, kings and princes and the like, can include evildoers who should be deposed, who is to say that the very top rung is not occupied by the ultimate malign force? It is not a question that very often arises, for most of those who do not believe in an all-just God do not believe in any God at all. But it is precisely Job's question, for while he does not for a moment doubt the existence of God, he deeply questions God's integrity. And so Elihu, like all the other friends, talks right past Job.

Elihu's Third Speech (35:1–16)

Bibliography

Althann, R. "Syntax and Meaning in Job 35,15." *JNSL* 24 (1998) 71–74. **Haggai, Y.** "נתן זמרות הלילה 'He gives zemirot at night' (Job 35,10)." *BMik* 111 (1986–87) 373–80. **Verheijen, L.** "'Sapientior a uolatilibus caeli' (Job 35,11): Une réminiscence biblique non remarquée dans les Confessions VI, 1 (1) et X, 17 (26)." *Aug* 17 (1977) 541–44.

Translation

[1]Then Elihu continued and said:

2 [a]Do you count[b] it[c] justice[d]
when you say, "I am more righteous than God," [e]
3 when you ask,[a] "How does it profit[b] me?,"[c]
"How[d] am I better off than if I had sinned?"[e]
4 [a]I will answer you
and your[b] friends[c] with you.

5 Look up to the heavens and see;
regard the clouds high above you.[a]
6 If you have sinned, what harm have you done[a] him?[b]
If[c] your offenses are many, how do you affect him?[d]
7 If you are righteous, what do you give him?
What does he receive from your hands?
8 It is your fellows who suffer[a] from your wickedness;
it is other humans who benefit from your righteousness.

9 [a]People cry out[b] because of many[c] oppressions;[d]
they call for help because of the power[e] of the mighty,[f]
10 but no one says,[a] "Where is God my Maker,[b]
who gives songs[c] in the night,
11 who teaches us[a] more than[b] the beasts of the earth,
makes us wiser than the birds of the heavens?"
12 [a]Though[b] they cry out, he does not answer,
because of[c] their pride and wickedness.[d]

13 God does not of course listen to an empty plea;[a]
the Almighty pays it no attention.[b]
14 How much less[a] when you say[b] that you cannot see him,[c]
that your case lies before him[d] and you are still[e] waiting for him[f]—
15 [a]and, what is more, that his anger never[b] punishes,[c]
and that he cares little about[d] wickedness.[e]
16 When Job opens his mouth, it is empty talk;[a]
he multiplies words without knowledge.[b]

Notes

2.a. Fohrer, de Wilde, Ravasi, Gray transfer to the beginning of this speech the closing verses of Elihu's first speech, 33:31–33. De Wilde further transfers v 4 of this chapter to precede v 2. Fedrizzi brings the proem of 36:2–4 to this place, deleting the heading for that speech (36:1).

2.b. חשב with ל is "consider as," as at 13:24; 19:15; 33:10 (cf. *DCH*, 3:327b, for other examples).

2.c. זאת "this," referring to what follows in v 3 (Rowley), not to Job's verbal attacks on God mentioned by Elihu in the previous verse (34:37) (Whybray).

2.d. הזאת חשבת למשפט is "Do you think this according to justice?" (Pope). Justice is the issue, as it was in chap. 34, so it is not a simple matter of "Do you think you are right?" (as Terrien, Fohrer), "Do you think it right to say?" (NAB; similarly NIV), "This thinkest thou to be right?" (Driver–Gray), "do you presume to maintain that you are in the right?" (JB), or even "Is it fair?" (Moffatt). Still less is it a question of wisdom (as Dhorme's translation "Did you consider this to be wise?"). We need at least "Do you think it just to say?" (NJPS).

NEB thinks the legal sense of משפט is in play: "Do you think that this is a sound plea?" (cf. Habel: "Job contends that he has a just claim for litigation [*mišpāṭ*]"). But the issue does not seem to be Job's position in a lawsuit so much as whether Job knows what justice itself is. NJB understands the syntax thus: "Do you think you can prove yourself upright... by daring to say to him, 'What does it matter to you?'" The objection to this translation is that no one, not even Job, would think that questioning the value of piety to God would be a likely way of proving one's own uprightness.

2.e. צדקי מאל is lit. "my righteousness is from God." The *mem* is understood here as the מן of comparison (as also Delitzsch, Ewald, Gordis); cf. Vg *iustior Deo sum*; NAB "I am just rather than God," KJV "my righteousness is more than God's." NJPS "I am right against God" (similarly Habel), NEB "in the right against God," and Tur-Sinai "justice is with me against God" perhaps adopt the same understanding.

NIV renders "I shall be cleared by God," understanding the injustice to lie in Job's belief that God will vindicate him while at the same time asking what profit there is in not sinning. It is difficult, however, to see that holding these two views constitutes an *injustice*, whereas saying one is more just than God is clearly doing him an injustice.

Others understand the phrase to mean "my justification before God" (so Dhorme; similarly Terrien), or "Do you call it 'my rights before God'?" (so Moffatt; similarly Fohrer), "And callest it my righteousness before God" (Peake), "It is my right from God" (Pope). Fedrizzi has "my right is independent of God," which seems to lay rather too much weight on the prep מן. RSV "Do you say, 'It is my right before God,' that you ask, 'What advantage have I?'" is virtually unintelligible.

Some think that the ancient versions read צָדַקְתִּי "I am righteous," and Graetz, Beer (BH^2), and Kissane emended to this form. But the change is unnecessary.

3.a. תאמר is the frequentative impf, "you keep saying" (as Driver–Gray). It is translated "ask" here because "say" has been used in the previous line, and also because it is followed by a question. Watson, 171, identifies כי־תאמר as an "introductory monocolon," prefacing two normal cola.

3.b. E. Lipiński, "*skn* et *sgn* dans le sémitique occidental du nord," *UF* 5 (1973) 191–207 (191–92), renders "how does that make you run a danger?" For this supposed sense of סכן (cf. *DCH*, vol. 6, *s.v.*), see *Note* 22:2.b.

3.c. לך "you" (sg), if it is direct speech, must be God, as addressed by Job (thus Dhorme "What does it matter to Thee?," Kissane, Pope, JB). But it is much more likely that we have here indirect speech, i.e., "you ask how it profits you (Job)," followed by a clause in direct speech. In translation it is smoother to make both clauses direct, and thus to translate "How does it profit me?" (so RSV, NEB, NAB, Moffatt); NJPS keeps the first colon as indirect speech, and has the second in direct speech. It must be admitted that it is more normal to have direct followed by indirect speech (as in 19:28). Emendation to לי "to me" (Graetz, Beer [*BHK*], Hölscher, Fohrer, de Wilde, NEB [Brockington]) is unnecessary. Habel renders "When you admit your own self-interest: 'What is my gain if I avoid sin?'"

3.d. מה "what, in what respect" is emended to כַּמָּה "by how much?" by NEB, using the *kaph* of the preceding word לך, which they have emended to לי.

3.e. מחטאתי, lit. "from my sin," i.e., more than my (hypothetical) sin = more than if I had sinned (Driver–Gray), "from not sinning" (NJPS; similarly NIV), or, more complexly, "how does it benefit me, whether I have sinned or not?" (NJB). Gordis renders "what good if I avoid sin?" regarding the *mem* as the "*mem* of separation," thus "by my being removed from sin." Unacceptable is Pope's "What would I profit from my sin?," and NEB "how much should I gain from sinning?," since Job would not be allowing that he had ever sinned or be contemplating sinning in the future. Improbable too is the idea that it is privative *mem*, thus "(What do I profit) without sin?" (so Hölscher, Weiser, Gray). NJB "how does it benefit me, whether I have sinned or not?" is logically very odd, for the question *whether* one has sinned cannot be a benefit or otherwise.

Tur-Sinai saw here not the noun חטאה "sin" but a noun (not otherwise attested) from a presumed חטה or חטא "propitiate" attested in Aram., thus "what profit shall I have from my appeasing (thee)." But since God does not appear to be the referent of לך, God cannot be understood as the obj of the verb here, which undermines the proposal. As for the meaning of the word itself, Dalman, 142b, recognizes a second verb חטא, meaning in the piel "enjoy good living" (*Wohlleben genießen*), and in the hithp (1) "take one's pleasure," (2) "show oneself friendly," (3) "behave familiarly." Jastrow, 1:448b, offers for חטי hithp, nithp (which, strange to say, it does not distinguish from חטי "sin") (1) "enjoy, be gratified," (2) "show oneself a nobleman, be generous, proud," (3) "be imperious, lord it, ask petulantly." None of these senses is equivalent to "propitiate," and none of them would be appropriate in the present context. Tur-Sinai also finds the supposed verb at 41:25 (17) (*q.v.*), where he is joined by Gordis.

Ehrlich, followed by Dhorme, Kissane, Larcher, Terrien, BJ, JB, emended to מָה אֶפְעַל אִם חָטָאתִי "what do I do (to you) if I sin?," analogously to 7:20, and following LXX τί ποιήσω ἁμαρτῶν. Graetz thought to improve matters by reading מִתֻּמָּתִי "by my innocence," but the effect is weaker.

4.a. Budde omits the verse, which he would locate after v 8 if it is retained.

4.b. Beer (*BHK frt*) suggests adding שְׁלֹשֶׁת "three" on the basis of the LXX; so too Gray, NAB "and your three companions" (*Textual Notes,* 378), NEB.

4.c. רעיך is almost universally understood as "your friends," from רֵעַ II "friend." Beer, *Text,* 222, however, derived it from רֵעַ III "purpose, thought" (BDB, 946b).

5.a. שחקים גבהו ממך, lit. "the clouds, (which) are higher than you."

6.a. תִּפְעָל is vocalized as if the impf were normally יִפְעֹל, but it is always יִפְעַל, which many read here (so Beer [*BHK*]; Driver–Gray [*prb*]).

6.b. בו "against him," is stronger than לו "to him" (Driver–Gray), not just a desire for variation from the לו in the second colon (Dhorme). NEB "how does it touch him?," JB "what do you achieve against him?"

6.c. A second אם "if" is understood at the beginning of the second colon (so too Gray).

6.d. מה־תעשה־לו, lit. "what do you do to him?," or, more loosely, "what does it mean to him?" (NEB). Beer (*BH*[2] *frt*) would perhaps delete לו "to him."

8.a. לאיש־כמוך רשעך, lit. "to a man like yourself is your wickedness." לאיש־כמוך "to a man like yourself" is in emphatic position, as is ולבן־אדם "and to a human" in the next colon. The point is that, while God may be untouched by human behavior, humans are indeed affected by wickedness and righteousness in others; so it is wrong to translate "Your wickedness touches only men" (as NEB; similarly NAB, NIV, NJB, Moffatt, Pope). JB rightly has "Your fellow men are the ones to suffer from your crimes, humanity is the gainer if you are good." It would be technically possible to take "a man like yourself" as meaning "you yourself" (as Fohrer notes), but Elihu can hardly be arguing that Job's behavior has consequences for himself, since that would contradict v 3.

9.a. Duhm and Beer (*BH*[2]) remove v 16 to follow v 8, and v 9 to follow v 11; so too Strahan. Moffatt also puts v 16 after v 8, but he deletes v 9 altogether. Both changes make Job the one who never asks, "Where is God my maker?" (which does at least explain the sg of אמר "says" and עשי "my maker" in v 10).

9.b. זעק hiph is usually understood as "cry out" (so BDB, 277b; *HALOT,* 1:277b; *DCH,* 3:128b), though KJV translated "they make [the oppressed] to cry." Beer (*BHK*), followed by Gray, would read the qal, יִזְעָקוּ "they cry out."

9.c. רב is lit. "the multitude of." Two other possible readings are suggested: (1) NJPS "because of contention" reads רב as a byform of ריב "contention, conflict," but it is surely because of their oppression rather than because of conflict in general that the oppressed are crying out. (2) Tur-Sinai saw here again another רֹב "weakness, fear" (cf. Arab. *rāba* "disquiet, alarm" [Lane, 1197c]), as also at 4:3, 14; 26:3; 29:16.

9.d. עשוקים "oppressions" occurs also at Amos 3:9 and Eccl 4:1, but not surprisingly emendations are also offered: to עוֹשְׁקִים (Peters, Fohrer, Gerleman [*BHS prp*], de Wilde), עֲשׁוּקִים (Beer [*BHK*], NAB), or עָשׁוֹקִים "oppressors" (Hölscher), as in עָשׁוֹק in Jer 22:3; for either reading, cf. LXX MSS and Vg.

9.e. זרוע, lit. "arm."

9.f. If רבים means "great ones, mighty," it is a rather rare sense of רבים, which usually means "many" in the pl (though it is parallel to עצומים "mighty ones" at Isa 53:12). It is therefore emended to כַּבִּרִים "mighty ones" by Beer (*BH*[2] *vel; BHK*) or perhaps רָעִים "wicked" by Budde and Beer (*BH*[2]), or else רְשָׁעִים "wicked" or עָרִיצִים "terrifying" (Beer, *Text*).

10.a. ולא־אמר, lit. "and one does not say." The changes from the pl verbs of v 9 to the sg אמר "says" and עשי "my maker," and back to the pl in v 11, are not too difficult to explain: v 9 concerns the oppressed in general while v 10 represents what an individual would say in prayer, and v 11 shows that individual in association with other oppressed persons. Budde, Dhorme, Beer (*BHK*), Gray adopt the Pesh reading that implies אָמְרוּ "they say" and עֹשֵׂינוּ (or עֹשֵׂנוּ) "our maker," but this easier reading is not to be preferred. NAB emends ולא־אמר "and one does not say" to לֵאמֹר "saying," which would make an important difference: it would mean that the oppressed *do* cry out to God, and that he does not hear them—which seems to be more Job's view than Elihu's. No good sense comes from regarding Job as the subj (as Tur-Sinai). ולא־אמר is another "introductory monocolon" (Watson, 171; cf. on v 3).

10.b. עֹשָׂי is curiously pl, lit. "my makers," perhaps on the analogy of other words for the deity such as אלהים, a kind of pl of majesty (GKC, §124k). The word appears as a pl in Isa 22:11; 54:5; Ps 149:2; and as a sg in 4:17; 40:19; Isa 44:2; 45:18; 51:13; etc.

10.c. זמרות is apparently "songs," as in six other places in the OT and four in the Qumran texts. But the image, though striking, is unexpected, so some have suggested that it is a different word. S. E. Loewenstamm's paper has no more in it than the assertion that "the notion of praise in cultic music [which is how he understands זמרה] becomes reduced to that of glory, pure and simple" ("'The Lord Is My Strength and My Glory,'" *VT* 19 [1969] 464–70 [468]); he is followed, however, by E. M. Good ("Exodus xv 2," *VT* 20 [1970] 358–59; see further, Parker's remarks, mentioned below).

Philological proposals are: (1) On the basis of Ugar. *dmr* and Arab. *ḏamara* "be violent, courageous, mighty" and *damīr* "courageous," Tur-Sinai, Pope, Sicre Díaz, Gray ("courage") postulate a זִמְרָה "strength" (as KBL, 260a; *HALOT,* 1:274a; Ges[18], 305a); so too NJPS. BDB, 275a, and *DCH,* 3:119b, note זִמְרָה II "choice produce," which may be the same word. Cf. also Tg לנצבתנא "for our strength" (see Sokoloff, 136). But Ugar. *dmr* is "protect, guard" (*DUL,* 287), and Arab. *ḏamara* is rather "excite, urge, be angry, blame" (Freytag, 2:294b; Lane, 977c). There is no sense of "strength" about the word in either language. Grabbe, 108–10, doubts the existence of such a word in Heb.

(2) Relying on another sense of the same Arab. word *ḏamara* "protect," which for the present purpose may be regarded as a separate word, T. H. Gaster ("Notes on 'The Song of the Sea' [Exodus xv]," *ExpTim* 48 [1936–37] 45; "Exodus xv. 2: עָזִּי וְזִמְרָת יָהּ," *ExpTim* 49 [1937–38] 189) suggested the meaning "protection" (as also in Exod 15:2), which is followed by Kissane, Habel, and NEB, and defended at length by S. B. Parker ("Exodus xv 2 Again," *VT* 21 [1971] 373–79). I. Zolli had proposed the same sense, comparing Arab. *ḏamara* ("Note esegetiche: Es. xv. 2," *GSAI* 48 [1935] 290–92 [290]). But *ḏamara* means nothing like "protection," and *HALOT,* 1:274, notes more appropriate cognates, viz. Old S. Arab. *ḏmr* "protect" and Amorite *zmr* "protect"; see also *DUL,* 287, for Ugar. *dmr* "protect, guard." (3) Yet another cognate is invoked by Fedrizzi, Syr. *dmr* ethpa "wonder" (J. Payne Smith, 95a), thus "marvels [in the night]"; but he does not explain what kind of marvels these might be.

Among emendations, there are: (1) NAB adopts the emendation to מַרְאוֹת "visions." (2) Ehrlich proposed מְאֹרֹת "lights," thinking of the lights of Gen 1:16, but there is unfortunately only one such light in the night (Dhorme). (3) LXX φυλακάς "watches" presumably read שְׁמֻרוֹת "watches" (BDB, 1037b); Bickell followed. (4) Wright, followed by Graetz, offers מַזָּרוֹת "the Hyades" (cf. on 38:32), which is, according to Gray, "graphically the most feasible," but it stretches the imagination to think what nocturnal comfort might be derived from a glimpse of the Hyades (Gray thinks of a grateful peasant asleep with the assurance of God's provision of the vital rain).

11.a. מַלְּפֵנוּ is a (perhaps defective) writing of מְאַלְּפֵנוּ "who teaches us" (as Beer [*BH*[2]]). Klostermann proposed מַפְלֵנוּ "who distinguishes us," following LXX ὁ διορίζων με; Driver–Gray thought this reading "may be right." Tg פי פרשנא פרשנא seems to understand the word in the same way (Sokoloff, *Targum,* 136). Graetz offers מַפְלִיאֵנוּ "who makes us marvel," but it is hard to see how that fits with the "beasts of the earth," and it effaces the parallel with "makes us wiser," even though it would fit with the proposal of Fedrizzi for זמרות, mentioned in the preceding *Note.*

11.b. The מן of מבהמות and מעוף is most often taken as the comparative מִן, i.e., "more than [the beasts, the birds]," i.e., God teaches humans more than he teaches animals (so KJV, RSV, JB; cf. NJB "has made us more intelligent than wild animals"). This idea seems too obvious, however, and there is much to be said for translating it as "by" (so Delitzsch, Dhorme, Tur-Sinai, Pope, Fedrizzi, Sicre Díaz, Habel, Hartley, Whybray, NIVmg). The resultant problem of what it is that is taught by God by means of the animal creation, and what in any case "teaching" has to do with the situation of the oppressed, is discussed in the *Comment.*

12.a. Tur-Sinai takes the verse as a quotation from Job, which Elihu then rejects in v 13. Kissane moves the verse to follow v 9.

12.b. שׁם is normally "there" in a local sense, which is inappropriate here. Some think a temporal sense "then" as with the Arab. *ṯumma* (cf. Delitzsch, Hölscher, Gordis, Gray, NJPS) is preferable, but v 12 does not seem to be subsequent to the preceding verses. Others speak of an inferential sense (cf. Driver–Gray), presumably "thus" (similarly NAB) or "so" (NEB). Or we could suppose the sense "in that case" as in 23:7 (as Budde). All of these senses are poorly attested, if at all, for the word. Less probably, it means "if," as is supposed for 23:7 (*q.v.*); thus M. Dahood ("Some Northwest-Semitic Words in Job," *Bib* 38 [1957] 306–20 [307]), C. F. Whitley ("Has the Particle שׁם an Asseverative Force?" *Bib* 55 [1974] 394–98 [395]), Terrien (perhaps), Blommerde; cf. also on 23:7. "Though" in the *Translation* above does not attempt to render שׁם but merely reflects the contrast between יצעקו "they cry out" and לא יענה "he does not answer," a contrast that is expressed with the particle *waw.*

12.c. מפני is most naturally "because of," though NAB has "against [the pride of the wicked]." The sequence suggests strongly that "because of the pride of the wicked" explains why God does not answer, not why the oppressed cry out; so NEB "he does not answer, because they are self-willed [REB proud] and wicked" (similarly GNB). Less probably it is seen as the reason why the oppressed cry out; thus NIV "He does not answer when men cry out because of the arrogance of the wicked"; similarly Elberfelder, Gordis, de Wilde, Andersen, Newsom.

12.d. מפני גאון רעים, lit. "because of the pride of the wicked." On the question whether it is the oppressed themselves, or their oppressors, who are proud and wicked, see *Comment.*

Gray thinks גאון is a form of, or corruption of, a Heb. גָּו "voice," cognate with Ugar. *g* "(loud) voice, shout" (*DUL,* 90; cf. *DCH,* 2:328b), thus "shouting"; other examples may be 30:5; Isa 16.6; Jer 49:29. NEB emends רָעִים "wicked" to רֵעִים (Brockington, 116), but it is hard to see what that means (NEB translates "they are self-willed and proud").

13.a. Taking שׁוא "emptiness" as the obj of ישמע "listens to." Some, however, take אך שׁוא as an independent clause referring to the cry of those who are proud and wicked: "it is indeed empty"; thus "All to no purpose" (NEB), "It is a pure waste of words" (Dhorme). Alternatively, it has been understood as a clause that introduces the next: "Surely it is false [that God does not listen]" (NJPS; similarly Tur-Sinai, Gordis), or "But it is idle to say God does not hear" (NAB), "How idle to maintain that God is deaf" (JB). What an "empty" plea may be is discussed in the *Comment;* it is hardly "trivialities" (as NJB).

13.b. The obj suff in ישורנה "regards it" is fem, while its antecedent שׁוא "emptiness" is masc. This is not a great problem, but it is for this reason that Gordis and others take אך שׁוא as an independent clause (see *Note* above). To remove the difficulty, Gray takes it as an energic ending, while Duhm (*frt*) reads יְשׁוּרֶנּוּ "regards it [masc]" (noted also by Beer [*BHK*]), and Bickell, Duhm (*frt*), and Beer (*BH*[2] *frt*) read שְׂפַת שׁוא "a lying lip," like שפת און "a wicked lip" in Prov 17:4, while Budde reads שַׁוְעַת שׁוא "an empty cry."

14.a. אף כי usually means "how much more" or "how much less." Delitzsch takes it as "although," RVmg, Gordis as "even if." BDB, 65b, affirms that here and in Neh 9:18 אף כי means simply "yea, when."

14.b. תאמר "you say" is emended by Kissane to אָמַר "he [Job] said," Elihu on his view contrasting Job in his former days with the Job of today (vv 15–16). He translates "Nay, when he said: 'He doth not behold it,' / He was silent before Him."

14.c. This line is understood in the same way as RSV. NIV spells out the implication with its "How much less, then, will he listen when you say that you do not see him." An alternative explanation is that of NJPS "Though you say, 'You [God] do not take note of it,' the case is before him."

Some prefer to read יְשׁוּרֶנּוּ "he does [not] see it," with possible support from Vg and Tg (so Kissane), or יְשׁוּרֵנִי "he does [not] see me" (Bickell); NEB claims support for this reading from some Heb. MSS, but Brockington's note does not make clear that the reading of such MSS is תשורני, with a 2d-person verb (as MT; cf. de Rossi); REB reverts to "you do not see him" (so too KJV, RSV, NAB, NIV), which is indirect speech for direct speech "I do not see him" (as NJB). Gray reads תְּשׁוּרֵנִי "you see me."

14.d. It seems better to understand this as what Job says (according to Elihu) about his lawsuit (דין) against God than as Elihu's own statement of the facts ("The case is before him," NJPS, NAB). Larcher makes the small emendation to דִּינִי "my case" (followed by BJ, JB "my cause is exposed before him").

NEB "Humble yourself in his presence" follows the proposal of a new Heb. word דין, cognate with Arab. *dāna* "be low" (Lane, 918c); so B. Jacob ("Erklärung einiger Hiob-Stellen," *ZAW* 32 [1912] 278–87 [287]); G. R. Driver ("Problems in the Hebrew Text of Job," in *Wisdom in Israel and in the Ancient Near East,* FS H. H. Rowley, VTSup 3 [Leiden: Brill, 1955] 72–93 [89]); cf. *DCH,* 2:426b, *s.v.* דון II. So too Guillaume, Gordis "yield to him," NEB "humble yourself."

Alternatively, the text is emended: (1) Perles, 69, Duhm, Peake, Strahan, Beer (*BHK*), Hölscher, de Wilde, Gray emend דִּין "judgment, cause" to דּוֹם "be silent," as at Ps 37:7, where דום is also followed by חול "wait patiently" (though hithp in Ps 37 and polel here). (2) Kissane followed Perles's lead with דָּם "he waited," i.e., the more patient Job of former times.

14.e. Added to express the sense that his waiting has been too long; cf. JB "and yet I wait and wait."

14.f. The root of ותחולל is חול according to BDB, 297b, where it is given as one of the senses of חול I "whirl." In *DCH,* 3:213a, on the other hand, it is derived from חיל II "wait," which is registered as a separate root (similarly van der Lugt). In either case, it is quite rare in the sense of "wait" (only here in polel and only at Ps 37:7 in hithp; three occurrences in qal). Gordis thinks the verb may be a denominative from תּוֹחֶלֶת "hope," and may thus mean "trust" (KJV also has "trust in him").

The *Translation* above assumes that it is Job who says he is waiting for God; others take the verb as Elihu's advice to Job (NAB "you should wait upon him," NJPS "So wait for Him," NEB "wait for his word," KJV "therefore trust thou in him," Moffatt "Hush! Only wait for him," Gordis "trust in him").

Others emend, to (1) וְהֹחֵל "and wait (impv)" (Beer [*BHK* וְהוֹחֵל], Fohrer, Pope, Gerleman [*BHS prp*], de Wilde, Gray, *HALOT,* 1:310b; 2:407a), or (2) וְהִתְחוֹלֵל (Budde, Beer [*BH*²], Hölscher [*frt*]); cf. the impv of חיל in Ps 37:7. (3) Kissane reads וַיִּתְחוֹלֵל "and he [Job] was silent before him, and waited for him." (4) Larcher (followed by BJ, JB, NJB) reads "I await," presumably וְאֶתְחוֹלֵל (which would be hithpo of חול or חיל).

15.a. The *Translation* assumes that the verse continues Elihu's representation of Job's position (so too NJB, NIV), with two parallel statements of Job's view: (a) God does not punish the wicked, and (b) he does not even care much about wickedness. Davidson, exceptionally, thinks v 15b the conclusion drawn from v 15a: "But now because his anger visiteth not, Therefore he careth nothing for transgression!"

Others think that Elihu is speaking for himself; thus RSV "And now, because his anger does not punish . . . ," NJPS "But since now it does not seem so, He vents his anger," NAB "but now that you have done otherwise [*sc.* not wait upon God], God's anger punishes," Gordis "For now, if you do not [trust in God], He keeps his wrath alive." Hölscher deletes vv 15–16 on the grounds that their connection with what precedes is unclear.

15.b. כי־אין פקד אפו can apparently be understood as "his anger does not punish anything" (Dhorme, followed by Pope); for פקד with transgression as the obj, cf. Ps 89:32 (33). Most, however, think the words cannot be satisfactorily explained as they stand. אַיִן cannot negate the verb פקד "visited," both because the punctuation is against it and because neither אַיִן nor its construct form אֵין can modify a finite verb. אֵין can modify a ptcp, but if that were the case here one would expect the noun אפו "his wrath" to precede the ptcp. Tur-Sinai avoids the difficulty by splitting the colon into two clauses: "Even now that there is none [i.e., no chastisement of the wicked], he keepeth his wrath"; but there is no evident referent for "none." Gordis translates כי אין as "if you do not [yield to God]," but that understanding of v 14b is questionable.

Others have recourse to emendation: (1) Siegfried, Budde (אין פֹּקֵד), Beer (*BH*² אין פֹּקֵד), Driver–Gray, Beer (*BHK*), Fohrer, Gray, NEB read אֵין אַפּוֹ פֹּקֵד "his anger does not punish"—which makes fair sense in the context and is adopted in the *Translation* above. (2) De Wilde emends to אֵין פְּקֻדַּת אַפּוֹ "there is no visitation of his wrath." (3) Kissane interestingly reads אָוֶן "iniquity," i.e., "But now, because his wrath is visiting iniquity, And he hath not held back his soul from calamity, Job with vanity openeth his mouth"; but this depends on Kissane's overall view of these verses as contrasting the former Job with the Job of the present.

15.c. פקד is often "visit," whether for blessing or, as here, for punishment (as Jer 6:15; 49:8; Ps 59:5 [6]), but usually with an obj or with על "on account of," not absolutely as here (it was absolute at 31:14, but in the sense "inquire"). Tur-Sinai's "he keepeth in mind his wrath" forces the sense of פקד.

15.d. Lit. "he does not know much about." Exceptionally, Gordis claims that לא does not mean "not" but is the "interrogative-emphatic particle," i.e., "does he not know? = he surely knows." Driver–Gray are worried that MT qualifies לא ידע "he does not know" with מאד "much" since, they think, what is expected is "he does not know at all." But Elihu cannot be charging that Job thinks that God does not *know* about wickedness; the issue is solely whether God *does* anything about it, i.e., whether he cares. It is quite plausible that Elihu should allege that Job believes that God does not *care* about wickedness "very much" (מאד). Beer (*BHK prps*) and Hölscher suggest, quite attractively, that we read פֶּשַׁע אָדָם "the wickedness of humans." Tur-Sinai ingeniously reads ולא יִדְעַךְ "and it [God's wrath] is not extinguished" (for ולא ידע ב), but the emendation will not work unless it is agreed that the line is Elihu's and not Job's as quoted by Elihu. Kissane, more persuasively, reads גָּרַע נַפְשׁוֹ מֵאֵד "He hath [not] held back his soul from calamity" (though אֵיד is always spelled with a *yodh*).

15.e. פש is an otherwise unknown word, variously explained: (1) Since Cocceius, it has been compared with Arab. *fāsīs* "weak," *fasfās* "foolish" (Freytag, 3:347b), thus "silliness, folly" (Gesenius–Buhl, 664b; cf. BDB, 832b; *HALOT,* 3:979b); so too Budde, Guillaume, Fedrizzi, and NEB (cf. *DCH*, vol. 6, *s.v.*). (2) The translation "arrogance" by RV, Davidson, and Terrien (cf. *DCH*, vol. 6, *s.v.*) depends on an Arab. cognate *fašša* "belch, utter calumnies," perhaps also with the meaning "be proud" (though this may be a separate *faša'a* or *fāša;* cf. Freytag, 3:348b; Lane, 2399c, 2400a, c), as suggested by Delitzsch; but Arab. *š* does not usually correspond to Hebrew שׂ. (3) Others relate it to פושׁ "charge along, frisk about" (for the verb, cf. BDB, 807b; *HALOT,* 3:921a; it is no doubt a different verb from פושׁ "scatter," as BDB, and *DCH,* vol. 6, *s.v.*); a noun from such a verb could perhaps mean "arrogance" (cf. Dhorme). (4) KJV "yet he knoweth it not in great extremity" apparently depends on the view of medieval Jewish lexicographers that there was a פֶּשׂ "abundance, multitude" from פוש "increase" (so too Buxtorf, 601); similarly Tur-Sinai, reading וְלֹא יְדַעֵךְ פֶּשׂ מְאֹד and translating "that it [the wrath] is not extinguished, it waxeth strongly" (though he does not vocalize פשׂ). NJPS "He does not realize that it may be long drawn out" probably depends on the same root. (5) R. Althann, "Syntax and Meaning in Job 35,15," *JNSL* 24 (1998) 71–74, thinks פשׂ is a phonetic variant of בֹּשׁ "shame," thus "he does not care about being very much shamed"; but the idea of God being shamed seems odd.

Most, however, since Houbigant, and following LXX (Theod), Symm, Vg, regard it as a scribal error for פֶּשַׁע, i.e., "[he does not take note of] transgression" (BDB, 807b; Zorell, 673a; KBL, 784a; RSV, similarly NJB, NIV), "he is not serious about sin" (Moffatt); so, e.g., Beer (*BHK*), Gerleman (*BHS prp*); this proposal is adopted in the *Translation* above. Among other emendations are: (1) Larcher quite attractively proposes בְּפֶשַׁע אָדָם "the revolt of humanity" (so too BJ; JB "men's rebellion"). (2) NAB "nor does he show concern that a man will die" depends on an emendation וְלֹא־ידע בְּנֶפֶשׁ אָדָם, lit. "and he does not know concerning the life of a human" (cf. Pesh). (3) Gray reads וְלֹא־ידע בְּפֶשַׁע מְאֹדוֹ "and his might takes no note of transgression," understanding מאד as a noun (as also BDB, 547a; *DCH*, 5:106b §3), with a suff.

16.a. ואיוב הבל יפצה־פיהו, lit. "and Job opens his mouth (with) emptiness," הבל being in effect adverbial (de Wilde). KJV renders הבל "in vain," NAB "to no purpose," NJB "nonsense," NEB "windy nonsense."

16.b. בבלי־דעת "without knowledge" is circumstantial, not cause ("for lack of knowledge," as Gordis). It is more freely translated by NJB "ignorantly babbling on and on," NEB "makes a parade of empty words," REB "babbles a stream of empty words," Moffatt "lavishing words thoughtlessly."

Form/Structure/Setting

The *structure* of this third speech is straightforward. It has two parts, corresponding to the two main points Elihu is making. The first part is also distinguished from the second by its being couched entirely in the second person as an address to Job; in the second part, only vv 14–15 are addressed to Job (and even then only v 14 contains second-person verbs).

The *strophic structure* can be analyzed thus (so too Terrien, van der Lugt):

Part 1	strophe 1	vv 2–4	3 lines
	strophe 2	vv 5–8	4 lines (3 + a pendant)
Part 2	strophe 3	vv 9–12	4 lines
	strophe 4	vv 13–16	4 lines

NAB and Webster identify the same strophes. NRSV and NJPS mark only two strophes, corresponding to the two parts of the speech (strangely, RSV marks no strophes). NIV divides the first part into vv 2–3 and vv 4–8 and takes the second part (vv 9–16) as a single strophe. NEB has vv 2–8 as the first strophe but divides the second part into two strophes, vv 9–13 and vv 14–16. This division is acceptable, since v 13 can be regarded either as the conclusion of one strophe or the beginning of the next. JB and NJB divide vv 2–4 and vv 5–16, but perhaps they are not considering these segments technically as strophes. Moffatt sees two major segments, but he deletes v 9 and moves v 16 to precede v 10, so his second part is vv 16, 10–15.

Because Fohrer transfers to the beginning of this speech the closing verses of Elihu's first speech, 33:31–33, his strophic divisions differ. He also deletes 36:1 and regards 36:2–26 as belonging to this third speech of Elihu; the result is: (1) 33:31–33; 35:2–3 (five lines), (2) vv 4–8 (five lines), (3) vv 9–14 (six lines), (4) 35:15–16; 36:2–4 (five lines). De Wilde also brings in 33:31–33 to the beginning of this speech, and moves v 4 to precede v

2, thus connecting together four lines about Elihu's intentions in his speech; de Wilde then sees in the chapter only regular strophes of two lines each: 33:31–32; 33:33 + 35:4; 35:2–3, 5–6, 7–8, 9–10, 11–12, 13–14, 15–16. This neat pattern is disturbed, however, if it is not agreed that v 4 stands outside the system of chap. 35; it is unthinkable also that vv 10 and 11 should not lie within the same strophe since they form a single sentence. The interpretation offered below in the *Comment* would tell against separating v 15 from v 14, for it is argued there that both lines are an indirect quotation of Job.

The *genre* of the chapter, like that of chap. 34 and much of chaps. 32–33 before it, is that of the *disputation speech.* Its main materials are *address to the hearer* (vv 2–8, 14–15), containing quotations, mostly of alleged sayings of Job (vv 2a, 3, 14–15) but also a hypothetical quotation in the mouth of the oppressed (v 10). The only sentence of *wisdom instruction* is v 13. The note of *dispute* is signaled by the numerous *rhetorical questions* (vv 2, 3 [two questions embedded in a question], 6–7, 10), an *exclamation* ("how much less," vv 14–15), and the logical and emphatic particles אך "surely," אף כי "how much less," and ועתה "and now."

The only other genre that is drawn upon is that of the *hymn,* which appears in the quotation hypothetically ascribed to those calling for deliverance from oppression: the participial forms describing the deity's activity (making, giving, teaching, vv 10–11) are typical of the hymn.

The *function* of the speech is to convince Job of the two points about justice that Elihu advances (see *Comment* on 35:1–16). Its *tonality* is not easy to infer. The unrelenting sequence of questions may be felt aggressive, but there is no overt reference to feelings or tone until the last sentence, where Elihu judges that Job's utterances have been "empty talk" and "words without knowledge." This language may be seen as quite hostile, but it is no different from many such remarks by all the friends and by Job himself (see on v 16), and it would be unwise to develop a portrait of Elihu's attitude to Job on such a foundation. We should note that not all the questions addressed to Job concern him personally. While it is Job himself who is asked, "Do you count it justice when you say, 'I am more righteous than God'?" (v 2), it is rather more Job as an example of humanity who is asked, "If you have sinned, what harm have you done him?"—and so also with all the questions and statements of vv 6–8.

The two *nodal verses* reflect the twin interests of Elihu in this speech: v 8 communicates the theme of justice as a human-to-human relation: "It is your fellows who suffer from your wickedness; it is other humans who benefit from your righteousness," and v 13 addresses the theme of suffering that does not deserve deliverance: "God does not of course listen to an empty plea; the Almighty pays it no attention."

Comment

1–16 There are two roughly equal parts to this speech (vv 2–8, 9–16), and we would expect them to be related. The connection is, however, quite subtle, and not usually recognized.

In the first part, Elihu takes up Job's complaints, (a) that he is no better off than if he had sinned (v 3b) and (b) that there is no benefit in righteousness (v 3a). There are two ways of reading Elihu's response. Either, he regards Job's first complaint as an impious statement, since it implies that God is not operating the principle of retributive justice, and thus that God is unjust. Naturally, if you say that God is unjust, it means that you think you are more just than God (v 2b). Or,

Elihu is simply arguing that talk about *my* rights and *my* benefit is not how we should speak about justice: a truly pious person would not be so self-centered. Indeed, piety should not even be focused on the question of its value to God (vv 5–7). The mark of true piety is whether it brings benefit to others, while justice is not a matter of my getting what I deserve but of others benefiting from my virtue. This seems the preferable reading.

In the second part (vv 9–16), Elihu explains why God does not always answer cries for help, and why therefore Job is not receiving any response to his case. When a sufferer remains unanswered by God, it is not because God is unjust, as Job alleges, but because there is some fault in the person who is calling for help. Those victimized by powerful oppressors may not be answered because they are proud or evil themselves (v 12) or because their cry is "empty" (v 13), whatever that means. Job too is not being answered, despite his conviction that he has laid his case before God and is awaiting a decision (v 14), because there is something wrong with Job himself—which Elihu does not further specify here.

The connection between the two parts of the speech hangs on the initial clause, lit. "Do you consider this for justice?" (v 2a). In the first part, the issue is the more theoretical one whether there is any injustice in the working of the principle of retribution, in the second it is a general question why sufferers are not always delivered, which develops into the more practical question of whether there is any injustice in Job's not being answered by God.

Most commentators have had a great deal of difficulty with the logic of this chapter. Driver–Gray felt that "much is awkwardly expressed; and the argument is none too clearly articulated." Whybray agrees that it is "not easy to follow" and that it may be "rather futile to try to make sense of this chapter." But in fact Elihu's thought is largely intelligible and, more than that, quite original.

2–8 From Elihu's point of view, Job has still a lot to learn about justice. Job has been worrying about the benefit (or rather, lack of benefit) to himself of his pious life, asking how he, in all his suffering, can possibly be better off than if he had been a great sinner. Elihu's significant move in this chapter is to open up the issue—as none of the friends nor Job has—of the benefits of right living. Job has been asking about the benefits to himself, and while Elihu does not negate Job's question, he is concerned rather with the benefits of piety to God and to other humans. In Elihu's view, the key point is that God does not benefit from human goodness (nor does he suffer because of human wickedness), but other mortals do. In so saying, Elihu is advocating an interestingly utilitarian ethics that, on the one hand, dispenses with the (theological) theory of retribution and, on the other, makes ethics not so much a duty toward God as a duty toward one's fellow humans.

2 The issue in the previous speech (chap. 34) has been whether God perverts justice (v 12), which means whether he fails to execute retribution, as Job alleges. In that chapter, Elihu has been concerned with the justice of God; here it is rather human justice. The term משפט "justice" is a key link back to chap. 34, where it occurs six times, most notably in the nodal verse 34:17, "Can one who hates justice govern?"

It may be that Elihu is addressing Job's implicit claim to be more righteous than God, to adhere to a higher standard of justice. Job has not himself said that he is more righteous than God (as Rowley notes), but in claiming that God is unjust he implies it. And to say that God is unjust is of course, from Elihu's perspective, a wrong done to God, itself an injustice that must be called into question: "Do you count it justice when you say, 'I am more righteous than God'?"

A preferable way of interpreting Elihu, however, is to take "Do you consider this to be justice?" as a denial that the issue of one's own vindication is the proper or the primary question about justice. Are assertions like "I am more righteous than God" and questions like "What value is there for me?," Elihu says, the right assertions to be making, the right questions to be asking? His answer will be that this line of thinking will not lead to an understanding of justice as right behavior; the key question should rather be, "What value for others is there in my actions?"

Less convincing is the interpretation that Elihu is asking, "Do you really think that you are placed in the right before God by your repeated assertions that humans get no advantage from being righteous?" (so Driver–Gray). This could be a good debating point, an ironic statement that it will do Job no good to be joining swords with God. But if it is meant seriously, it is unthinkable that Job, or anyone else, would think that questioning the principle of retribution is any way to gain God's approval.

3 Job had quoted the wicked as asking, "What gain shall we have if we pray to [the Almighty]?" (21:15). Job was not in the least approving of their sentiment, but complaining that although they say such wicked things they are not punished for it.

4 Elihu undertakes to answer both Job and the friends at the same time because he is trying to move the dialogue along from the impasse into which they have brought it. They have been complicit with Job in discussing only the question of his innocence and have left out of the discussion what Elihu believes to be the real question in ethics, which is how one's behavior impacts on others.

The reference to the friends is unmistakably to the three friends of the dialogue, not to any supposed group of bystanders (as against Dhorme, Pope); see further on 34:2. It is no more than we have been led to expect from the beginning of Elihu's speech that he will undertake to refute both Job and the friends (32:2–3), but nevertheless his words here are another opportunity for commentators to express their scorn for him. Peake writes: "That Elihu proceeds to appropriate the thoughts of the friends is no proof that he cannot be professing to instruct them; such conduct would be characteristic of him." And Rowley: "Elihu in his vanity would be ready to include [the bystanders]." And Andersen: "His claim to be able to answer everybody (4) is not borne out. What he says in verses 5ff. is largely drawn from earlier speeches, and affirms commonplaces about the greatness of God not in dispute." All this is somewhat gratuitous abuse of Elihu, whose theological skills are second to none among the friends, and who deserves a patient hearing.

5–7 Let Job not imagine that God is affected by Job's behavior, good or bad. The very distance from earth to the skies is symbol enough for the differing scales of values between the earthly and the divine, and token of the necessity to judge the matter of Job's innocence in terms of his impact on his fellow humans.

5 Eliphaz has already asked, "Is not God in the heights of the heavens? Does he not look down on the topmost stars, high as they are?" (22:12). But Eliphaz's purpose there was to affirm that God is so high that he can easily see everything that happens on earth; here Elihu means rather that God is so far removed from the realm of humans that their goodness or badness can have no effect on him. Elsewhere the height of the heavens above the earth has been used, to different purpose, as a symbol of the unknowability of the divine mind, which is "higher than heaven" (Zophar, 11:8).

As Habel notes, "'Look at' and 'behold' are pedagogical injunctions; the perceptive wisdom student discerns truth through the observation of nature."

6 Job himself has already asked, "If I have sinned, how do I injure you, O Human-Watcher?" (7:20), but his meaning was not the same as Elihu's. There Job was arguing not that human sin is trivial but, very specifically, that any wrong he may have done is hardly worth retribution since he will very soon be dead. Elihu for his part is not trivializing sin either, or saying that it is beneath God's notice (though in v 15 he will allege that such is Job's view). He means rather that what is important is the impact of sin and righteousness upon other humans rather than their effect upon God.

7 Eliphaz has already asked, "Is it an asset to the Almighty if you are righteous? Does he gain if your conduct is blameless?" (22:3). But his purpose there differs from Elihu's here. Eliphaz appears to say that no human action can benefit God because he is self-sufficient and detached from the human realm. Eliphaz's purpose has been to respond to the alleged view of Job that there is no benefit in religion, and he does so by saying, You claim that religion is not beneficial to humans, I claim it is not beneficial to God either. Elihu goes further: while piety is of no benefit to God (as in v 6), it is most certainly of benefit to other humans.

If Elihu's doctrine were one of the impassivity of God to human actions, it would hardly be in accord with the program of the book of Job as a whole, in which God stands to gain or lose a great deal from the response of Job to his suffering. But it is not divine impassivity that Elihu is urging, nor does he imply a cosmology in which "the earthly domain is a self-contained universe where human actions are restricted in their influence to fellow humans in that world" (Habel). No, Elihu everywhere sees God as actively involved with human affairs, communicating with humans in various ways (33:14), delivering mortals from destruction (33:29–30), requiting evil (34:11), sustaining creaturely life (34:14–15), judging rulers (34:17–19), investigating wrongdoing (34:21–22), and visiting it with punishment (34:25–28). In what he says here his theme is that the justification of right behavior must be its effects in the world of humans, not its influence upon the divine, whom he represents as unharmed by human evil, unblessed by human goodness (note the interesting parallel in Rom 11:35). We should not, however, take the further step and argue that "Self-interest is accordingly not present in God as a disturbing influence to entice Him from the path of justice" (Peake), since it is not the issue of God's justice but of Job's that is on Elihu's agenda in this passage. Nor is it Elihu's point that "Job's attempts at forcing God to descend in person and vindicate Job's innocence are therefore ludicrous" (Habel), since the issue here is the theoretical question of justice, not so much Job's personal circumstances.

8 Here we find in a nutshell the point of the whole speech from v 2 onwards. For Elihu, the purpose of right living is not to secure rewards for oneself, not to influence the deity, but to help other human beings. That is where profit or benefit in righteousness lies. Job's concentration upon his own benefit (v 3) is therefore wrongheaded, and not in accord with justice (v 2).

9–16 The justice that Job seeks would lie in a response from God, justifying Job and declaring his innocence. It is agreed between Job and Elihu that such a response has not been forthcoming, and in this second phase of the speech, Elihu argues that the absence of a response from God does not mean, as Job thinks it does, that God cares nothing about what happens in the world of humans. Job needs to recognize that God will respond to the cries of the oppressed only if they deserve justice. If there is something amiss with those who call for justice, they cannot expect to receive it at God's hand. Oppression of the weak by the strong is an injustice, but what if the oppressed are themselves unjust or in some way wicked? It would itself be an injustice to relieve them of oppression if that is their desert. And none of this is mere theoretical theology. It all ultimately concerns the case of the man Job, upon whom the panoramic sweep of Elihu's rhetoric will come to rest in the last verses of the speech (vv 14–16).

9–13 Being oppressed is no proof of innocence, says Elihu, and crying out in pain is a far different thing from appealing to God for deliverance. When Job spoke of the cry of the poor oppressed not being heard by God (24:12), he blamed God; but he left out of account, suggests Elihu, the possibility that the blame lay with the poor oppressed themselves. Oppressed people may themselves be "proud" or "evildoers" (v 12), and therefore undeserving of deliverance. Or they may be innocent enough, but neglect to make a deliberate and explicit address to God (vv 10–11). Such a cry is "empty" because it is bereft of any recognition of God's role as deliverer.

And this will be for Elihu no mere theoretical debating point about theology. For, as we shall soon see (vv 14–16), the general point has a direct bearing on Job: Job is suffering, he allows, but is he innocent? Job is crying out, but is he directing himself towards God?

9 Elihu paints a picture that is not meant to be true of all who cry out in distress. It focuses simply on the case of those who cry out but are not delivered. Of course, people may cry out in distress for other reasons too: they may be ill or frightened, for example. But this is a typical case, expressed in stylized language and using a verb common for the cry of the poor or distressed (זעק, also spelled צעק), as also in v 12. Using this verb, Job himself has spoken of his cry in 19:7, and in 31:38 has envisaged his land crying out for justice against him.

10–11 The cry of the oppressed is not heard. And that is because it is a cry that has not been addressed to God. These victims of oppression have responded with a kind of instinctive cry of pain, their cry the "natural voice of suffering" (Davidson); what they have not done is turn their natural response into a prayer that seeks God's aid. Their vision has lifted them no higher than their own bitter circumstances (it is a bit harsh to say that their cries are merely expressions of self-interest, as does Habel). Elihu offers a model prayer for such sufferers, using language typical of the hymn (the participial forms descriptive of the deity, "making, giving, teaching," and the reference to singing).

What, in particular, they have not said, is "Where is God my Maker?" Rhetorical questions that begin "Where is . . ." are often negative in tone: so, for example, when the Judeans are threatened by famine, the prophet Joel envisages the nations saying, "Where is their God?" (2:17); an enemy says to a pious person in distress, "Where is your God?" (Mic 7:10). In Jer 2:6, however, such a question is something to be encouraged: the ancestors of Israel are in the wrong for not saying, "Where is Yahweh who brought us up from the land of Egypt?," and in 2:8 the priests are reproached because they did not say, "Where is Yahweh?" This must be the significance here. The question is a question of the pious, who typically "seek after" God (e.g., Isa 65:1; Jer 29:13; Pss 14:2; 24:6; 78:34).

Why should they have said, "Where is Yahweh *my Maker*?" In distress would the oppressed not be expected to call upon Yahweh as *savior* or *deliverer*? In Job the language of God as Maker has referred variously to his superior moral purity (4:17), in Elihu's mouth to God's power to unmake his created beings if they misbehave (32:22), and in the second divine speech to his sole power to control Behemoth (40:19), though even he needs to approach the monster with a sword! None of this seems at all appropriate here.

Even more puzzling is that God should be described as one who "gives songs in the night." Assuming that the night is, as so often, figurative for a time of sorrow and suffering (cf. Isa 17:14; 21:11; Ps 30:5 [6]), and that songs in the night are for keeping the spirits up (cf. Ps 42:8 [9]; Acts 16:25) until the morning when God's deliverance may be expected (cf. Pss 46:5 [6]; 90:14; 143:8), would the oppressed not have been better off appealing to God for deliverance rather than for fortitude in suffering? Dhorme has the fascinating suggestion that the divine songs in the night are the crash of thunder, by which God speaks to humans; but however meaningful God's thunder may be, it is not going to help the oppressed out of their misery. Gordis and Whybray think the songs are the music of the heavenly spheres (cf. Ps 19:2–5; Job 38:7), but they do not consider how such music could be of value to the oppressed. Some have suggested that the term for "song" (זמרה) should be understood as a different word spelled alike, meaning "strength" (see *Note* 10.c), but strength is what is needed for endurance, and it is not as desirable as actual deliverance, one would have thought.

The final epithet of Yahweh, that he "teaches us more than the beasts of the earth, makes us wiser than the birds of the heavens," is even harder to explain, for how is human superiority to animals relevant to what those oppressed by tyrants should be praying? It is no better if the alternative rendering is adopted, that God "teaches us *by means of* the beasts of the earth, makes us wise *by means of* the birds of the air" (see *Note* 10.c). It seems equally irrelevant to the situation of those who are oppressed. It is unsatisfactory simply to remark that these lines are commonplace (Dhorme) or "not very profound" (Alden) or "too banal even for Elihu" (Pope), since the problem with them seems rather their apparent total irrelevance.

Job has ironically represented the friends in 12:7–9 as believing that the mysteries of God's workings are evident even to beasts and birds and plants, and the wording is very similar to what we have here. Perhaps Elihu is presented as alluding to Job's words, even as attempting to refute him; but there is little commonality in thought between the passages.

Perhaps the puzzles outlined above can find some solution along the following lines. What these verses show is how Elihu thinks of God: though God is deeply involved in human affairs (see above on v 7), he is not primarily a savior but a creator ("my Maker"), who is the author and sustainer of life (e.g., with "songs in the night") and a teacher (cf. 36:22 "Who is a teacher like him?")

whose blessings for humans are above all on the intellectual and cognitive plane (teaching and making wise, v 11). If you are in distress, he means to say, it would be better to understand that distress than merely to escape from it. The victims of oppression would find their prayers answered if they saw their suffering as a learning opportunity, first for endurance ("songs in the night") and secondly for wisdom about its meaning as intended by God ("teaches us," "makes us wise"). Simply to cry out in pain is to align oneself with the animals, who lack understanding. Alternatively, if we adopt the translation "by means of the beasts and birds," the meaning will be that since even animals cry to God when they are in need (cf. Pss 104:21; 147:9; Joel 1:20), humans should imitate them and not just cry out for sheer pain (so Pope, Habel).

What attitude toward animals is shown is this passage? If the translation "by means of the beasts and birds" is adopted, they are evidently highly valued, for in crying to God for their food they display their knowledge of how to behave toward the deity, a knowledge that humans can well learn from. Even if the translation "who teaches us more than the beasts of the earth" is followed, though the wisdom of the animal creation would be compared unfavorably to that of humans, it is not entirely effaced; for why would the wisdom taught by God to animals be mentioned at all if it were nonexistent? A similar allusion to animal wisdom is made in 28:7, where the way to wisdom is "a path no bird of prey knows, and the falcon's eye has not seen it"—the implication being that such birds have their own remarkable wisdom and insight. In the first divine speech the ostrich is said to have been made to forget wisdom by God (39:17), which implies that she would otherwise have possessed it, and in Proverbs ants, badgers, locusts, and lizards are credited with wisdom (6:6; 30:24–31). The reference in Job 12:7–9 to animals (beasts, birds, fish) and plants teaching humans is rather more difficult to evaluate: Job means that the friends assume that God's ways of working are so straightforward that they are known even to the lowliest forms of life, animals and plants. There is undoubtedly present the idea that animals can teach humans, but it is implied that only the most ignorant of humans could be so instructed, so that particular text does not esteem animals as highly as might at first appear.

12 We come to the nub of the matter here: deep down, the reason why some oppressed people fail to get divine deliverance is that they themselves do not deserve it. Not only have they not explicitly addressed themselves to God (vv 10–11), they may themselves be "proud" and "wicked." This is somewhat surprising language to use of the oppressed: it is usually oppressors, rather than their victims, who show pride (גאון; cf., e.g., Isa 13:11; Prov 8:13), and it is decidedly unusual for those who are oppressed to be called wicked (רע). But it fits with Elihu's purpose, which is to explain how it could possibly be just of God to ignore the cries of oppressed and apparently innocent people. His answer is that they may well be oppressed, but they are not necessarily innocent. In the next chapter, Elihu argues that even the "righteous" may have committed sins and be behaving "arrogantly" (36:9). If that can be true of the truly righteous, who are able to repent and so be delivered (36:10–11), how much more can it be true of those of whom no more is known that they are "oppressed."

Are their "pride" and "wickedness" further sins, which, in addition to the omission of God from their cries, account for God's refusal to hear them? It is hard to say, but the context would suggest the opposite, namely that "pride" and "wickedness" are how Elihu describes their failure to call explicitly to God. Otherwise, there is a conflict between reasons why their cries are not heard: vv 10–11 would say it is because they do not call upon God; v 12 because they are proud and wicked. It is more likely that Elihu means that the very act of ignoring God (which is how he views their unfocused cries) is itself "pride"—and who can deny that pride is "wicked"? On "pride," see further on 33:17. His language is extreme, no doubt, but what he is feeling after is the difference between a religious and an irreligious view of life. The litmus test is: Does oppression call forth a prayer or a groan?

Newsom observes that the distinction Elihu depends on, between a mere cry and a prayer, is hard to parallel in the Hebrew Bible. When the Israelites are in Egypt, for example, they "groaned under their slavery, and cried out. Out of the slavery their cry . . . rose up to God. God heard their groaning, and . . . God looked upon the Israelites, and God took notice of them" (Exod 2:23–25 NRSV). It seems there as if the mere cry is enough to attract God's deliverance; nothing is said of a prayer directed to God. On the other hand, Elihu is not denying that God can respond to a mere cry of pain; he is only setting out to explain why such a cry may well not be enough. In any case, he would not feel himself bound by the language of the book of Exodus.

13 A cry that does not address itself to God is an "empty" (שׁוא) cry, and it stands to reason that God will not answer words that are not addressed to him. Others understand the sentence differently, as for example "Surely it is false that God does not listen" (NJPS; see *Note* 13.a); but Elihu can hardly be saying in v 12 that God does not listen and in v 13 that he does. Gordis's explanation is that in v 12 God does not answer, but that does not mean he does not "hear" ("But it is not true that God does not hear," v 13). It is true that שׁמע can mean either "listen, i.e., respond" or merely "hear," but would Job be satisfied with an argument that although God does not always respond, he has been hearing (and seeing) what is done by humans, and therefore God cannot be called unjust? No, Job would say that not addressing situations of injustice is exactly what he means by being unjust, and he would not be impressed by a subtle distinction between "hearing" and "listening." More plausible is the suggestion that the first line of the verse means that what the wicked sufferers cry is "a pure waste of words" (Dhorme; cf. NEB "All to no purpose!").

14–15 Now for the first time since v 8 Elihu turns to Job (as against Davidson, who thinks Elihu is still speaking generally). In vv 9–13 he has been considering the general case of those who suffer and cry out but are not answered by God; but how does that apply to Job? Job can hardly be accused of failing to address himself to God directly (as against Terrien), so he is not like these sufferers in that respect. What Job can be accused of, however, is pride and wickedness. His faults lie in his reproaches of God, claiming, according to Elihu, that he cannot see God, and that although his case has been before God he is still awaiting an answer (v 14), and as well that in general God does not punish wrongdoers and cares little about wickedness (v 15).

Elihu's representation of Job's position in these indirect quotations at least does no injustice to Job, for Job has certainly said that he cannot "see" God (23:8–9; cf. also 13:24; 30:20), that his case is before God awaiting resolution

(10:2; 13:18–23; 23:4; 31:35–37), and that God does not much care about wrongdoing (cf. 12:6; 21:17–26).

What is the connection of vv 14–15 with what precedes? It seems to be that if God does not respond to the misery of the oppressed merely because they have omitted to address themselves explicitly to him (vv 9–13), "how much less" (אַף כִּי) can Job expect to be heard when he treats God with insolence and denigrates his governance of the world (vv 14–15).

Others take it that vv 14–15 are not all words put into Job's mouth by Elihu but that after "you say that you do not see him" it is Elihu himself who speaks. In such a case, he would be assuring Job that his case against God is still awaiting adjudication, and that he should be patient (v 14), and (perhaps) he would also be attributing to God's reticence in punishment Job's continuing meaningless words (vv 15–16). Thus RSV "And now, because his anger does not punish, and he does not greatly heed transgression, Job opens his mouth in empty talk"; similarly Fohrer, Pope, de Wilde, Hartley; cf. KJV, RVmg.

It seems unlikely, however, that Elihu should be giving Job advice at this point, since his whole effort in this speech has otherwise been to argue through the theological views taken up by Job. And it would be strange to find Elihu admitting that God's anger does not punish; even if all that he means is that it does not do so as yet in Job's case, and that that is the reason why Job continues unchecked in his ignorant talk, he puts himself in danger of sounding self-contradictory.

Another way of understanding v 15 is suggested by Gordis: "But now, if you do not [trust in God, as urged in v 14b], He keeps his wrath alive." But it has been argued above that v 14b should not be read as an exhortation to Job, but as Elihu's account of his position. Yet another interpretation is that of Duhm, who removes v 16 to follow v 10 and omits 36:1: And now, [as for your claim] that God's anger never punishes, and that he is not much troubled by iniquity (v 15), wait for me a little and I will show you (36:2)—which he proceeds to do in 36:6, 13–14. But the best solution, all things considered, is that vv 14–15 as a whole are words attributed by Elihu to Job.

16 This is a summary sentence in which Elihu evaluates Job's arguments. "When Job opens his mouth, it is empty talk; he multiplies words without knowledge." This is standard fare for the academic debates of the wise, and it mainly serves to assert Elihu's own opinion that he has satisfactorily disposed of all Job's views on alleged divine injustice. For similar language addressed to Job earlier, cf. 8:2; 11:3; 15:2; 18:2; and for Job's own use of it, see 21:34; 27:12 (both with הבל).

It is a little strange that Elihu, in addressing Job, as he has been throughout this speech (explicitly in vv 2–6, 14), should in conclusion refer to him in the third person ("Job opens his mouth"). Such seemed to be the case also at the end of the previous speech, but there it was possible to argue that the third-person references to Job were all placed in the mouth of the "men of understanding" whom Elihu imagined sitting in judgment, metaphorically speaking, on Job's case. They are not in view here, however, so it is perhaps the three friends whom he is addressing at this point. Elihu has claimed in v 4 that, in this speech, presumably, he will answer not only Job but the friends; and although his reference here to Job can hardly count as any "answer" to them, it is clear that he has the friends in view (similarly Rowley), even if they do not appear on the surface of the text until now.

When Job speaks, judges Elihu, it is nothing but windy emptiness (הבל), Qoheleth's term for aimless vanity, without worth or substance. Talk without knowledge (בלי־דעת) is anathema to Elihu, since he is so committed to rationality and sound learning. The wicked, he will shortly affirm, come to the grimmest of ends by dying without knowledge (36:12), so it is a rather shocking judgment to make of the wise man Job that he "multiplies words without knowledge" (cf. also the fate of humans who die "without wisdom" [ולא בחכמה, 4:21]). Ironically, this will be the judgment that is delivered not once but twice by God (38:2; 42:3), and in which Job acquiesces. Can the author be "creating the impression that God is endorsing Elihu's judgment" (Newsom)?

Explanation

In his previous speech (chap. 34), Elihu had probed the meaning of "justice," asking whether a charge of injustice against a supreme ruler could make any sense. The language was far from brilliant, but the idea was original and thoughtful. In this speech he treats two further questions about justice: first, whether justice is best understood as what is due to a person and, second, whether justice in God demands that he deliver victims of oppression from their suffering. Like Socrates in the first book of Plato's *Republic,* who is also occupied with the question of justice, he aims to show that the immediate responses of the casual thinker to such questions are unsatisfactory, and in so doing introduces some finesse into the discussion of a key theme in the book of Job—even if his exposition is more than a little awkward and uncertain. Job and Job's claims are always before him, but he shows a true theological impulse to broaden the scope of the issues from the lone individual Job, and to study them in the general.

His speech marks a progress, even if a small one, in the thought of the book when it questions the apparently obvious assumption that justice such as Job seeks must mean being treated as one deserves. Job assumes he is being treated badly by God, and cries for a justice that will restore to him what has been taken from him. Elihu, however, believes that to focus on what is due to oneself is to narrow the scope of justice, which should rather concern the benefit of others. Right living, he argues in a quite startling manner, has no effect upon God (he means not that God does not know or care about human behavior but that he himself is unchanged by it), and its worth is therefore to be found entirely in its effects upon other humans. In so saying, he takes up an unusual ethical position for a Hebrew sage. Right behavior, including justice, is in his view not a theological but a humanistic virtue. Job's fixation on what is due to him neglects the social dimension of the practice of justice.

Elihu's second point in this speech is that the usual pious assumption that God should and will deliver those who are suffering needs refinement. His argument is that it needs more than the mere fact of suffering to call forth the divine mercy: there must be some desert in the sufferer, or at least no contraindication against deliverance. Just because people are suffering they do not necessarily deserve to be released from their suffering; they may be wicked people, or they may be innocent enough sufferers who neglect the religious dimensions of their suffering: they cry out in pain, but they do not cry to God. This practical atheism may be called a kind of "pride," a wickedness in itself. Elihu's argument is very different from the simple faith of the psalmists, for example, that God will deliver them just because they are suffering. They do not stop to consider whether their suffering is deserved.

Under the cloak of yet another disputation among the wise, and even at this late stage in the dialogue of interlocutors, the author of the book of Job has here raised important questions that remain troubling. Elihu's first point, about the redefinition of justice to mean something like "what I can give" rather than "what I can get" amounts to a question of values. In an age of the "re-valuation of all values" (Nietzsche), it is a pressing question whether justice is a supreme value or whether it must struggle with other values for its place in a ethical system. This very question of value-pluralism will emerge again with the divine speeches of chaps. 38–41, where Job's quest for justice is decidedly downgraded, while other values are said to occupy God's attention.

Elihu's second point, that God discriminates among candidates for deliverance—not so much saving those who deserve to be saved, as refusing to save those who do not deserve to be saved—may seem a harsh and unpleasant one, but it remains a real issue in theology and public policy alike. Does an all-loving God redeem all those who need redeeming, or must he have their cooperation? Does an ethical and caring government make welfare payments to all who are in need, or only to those who will not squander them and will put something back into the community?

But what of Elihu as a disputant with Job, or as his self-professed instructor in wisdom? Elihu may have the germ of some valuable theological ideas, but what have they to do with Job? With his first point, that justice has to do more with others than with oneself; he has nothing to say to Job. In the first place, Job has always lived for others, whether for his family and domestics, or for the people of his town—at least by his own account. In the second place, Job has certainly been treated unjustly—at least that is plain to all readers of the prologue to the book—and where can the blame be in demanding justice for himself? The facts that Yahweh will not give him justice, that he will declare implicitly that he has higher values than justice on his agenda, and that Job will capitulate to the divine wisdom—will they remove the justice of his cry for justice? The irrelevance of Elihu's response to Job is no worse than the irrelevance of the divine response, so perhaps Elihu should not be too sharply criticized.

Elihu's second point, that God does not deliver sufferers if they happen to be proud and wicked or even just negligent, is partly appropriate for Job, and partly inappropriate. Job is certainly not in the camp of those who merely cry out in pain and do not cry to God, for his whole response to his suffering has been to approach God with it as its inevitable cause. On the other hand, Job has been far less respectful toward God than those who merely neglect to say, "Where is God my Maker?" If they are not answered, how much less, says Elihu, may Job expect to be when he complains that his case is unforgivably delayed, and that God has given up ruling the world with justice (vv 14–15). It is a reasonable point in itself. But there is an important difference between Job and the undeserving sufferers:

they are expecting deliverance and relief from their suffering, which is to say, a boon. Job, on the other hand, is calling for what he believes is owed to him, and God cannot refuse to answer Job without damaging himself.

Elihu's Fourth Speech (36:1–37:24)

Bibliography

Brown, J. P. *Israel and Hellas.* BZAW 276. Berlin: de Gruyter, 2000. **Clifford, R. J.** *The Cosmic Mountain in Canaan and the Old Testament.* HSM 4. Cambridge, MA: Harvard UP, 1972. **Cross, F. M.** *Canaanite Myth and Hebrew Epic: Essays in the History of the Religion of Israel.* Cambridge, MA: Harvard UP, 1973. **Curtis, J. B.** "On Job's Response to Yahweh." *JBL* 98 (1979) 497–511. ———. "Some Jewish Interpretations of Job 37:6—Midrash or Ancient Cosmogony?" *PrGLM* 9 (1989) 113–23. **Dahood, M.** "Congruity of Metaphors." In *Hebräische Wortforschung.* FS W. Baumgartner. VTSup 16. Leiden: Brill, 1967. 40–49. ———. "Eblaite *ì-du* and Hebrew *ʾēd,* 'Rain Cloud.'" *CBQ* 43 (1981) 534–38. ———. "Hebrew-Ugaritic Lexicography II." *Bib* 45 (1964) 393–412. ———. "Hebrew-Ugaritic Lexicography VII." *Bib* 50 (1969) 337–56. ———. "Is the Emendation of *yādîn* to *yāzîn* Necessary in Job 36,31?" *Bib* 53 (1972) 539–41. ———. "Northwest Semitic Philology and Job." In *The Bible in Current Catholic Thought: Gruenthaner Memorial Volume.* Ed. J. L. McKenzie. St. Mary's Theological Studies 1. New York: Herder & Herder, 1962. 55–74. ———. Review of *Giobbe,* by P. Fedrizzi. *Bib* 55 (1974) 287–88. ———. Review of *Job et son Dieu: Essai d'exégèse et de théologie biblique,* by J. Lévêque. *Bib* 52 (1971) 436–38. ———. Review of *The New English Bible. Bib* 52 (1971) 117–23. **De Wilde-Uitentius, A.** "Twee OT Tekstemendaties." *Theologie en Praktijk* 32 (1972) 28–32. **Dhorme, P.** "Un mot aryen dans le livre de Job" [Job 37:11]. *JPOS* 2 (1922) 66–68. **Diewert, D. A.** "Job xxxvi 5 and the Root *m's* II." *VT* 39 (1989) 71–77. **Driver, G. R.** "Hebrew Homonyms." In *Hebräische Wortforschung.* FS W. Baumgartner. VTSup 16. Leiden: Brill, 1967. 50–64. ———. "Problems in the Hebrew Text of Job." In *Wisdom in Israel and in the Ancient Near East.* FS H. H. Rowley, ed. M. Noth and D. W. Thomas. VTSup 3. Leiden: Brill, 1955. 72–93. **Esh, S.** "Job 36,5a in Tannaitic Tradition." *VT* 7 (1957) 190–91. **Gammie, J. G.** "The Angelology and Demonology in the Septuagint of the Book of Job." *HUCA* 56 (1985) 1–19. **Gold, S. L.** "Making Sense of Job 37.13: Translation Strategies in 11Q10, Peshitta and the Rabbinic Targum." In *Biblical Hebrew, Biblical Texts: Essays in Memory of Michael P. Weitzman.* Ed. A. Rapoport-Albert and G. Greenberg. JSOTSup 333. Sheffield: Sheffield Academic Press, 2001. 282–302. **Houtman, C.** *Der Himmel im Alten Testament: Israels Weltbild und Weltanschauung.* OTS 30. Leiden: Brill, 1993. **Jacob, B.** "Erklärung einiger Hiob-Stellen." *ZAW* 32 (1912) 278–87. **Jenssen, H.-H.** "Die Polarität von Zeitnähe und Offenbarungstreue in der Naturpredigt: Vergleich von vier Predigten [including Fritz Dosse (1929), "Unser Gott ist ein Gott des Wetters" (Job 37,2–13)] im Lichte der Strukturtheologie Otto Haendlers." *TLZ* 105 (1980) 331–38. **Komlós, O.** "אַף־בְּרִי יַטְרִיחַ עָב" [Job 37:11]. *VT* 10 (1960) 75–77. **Kopf, L.** "Arabische Etymologien und Parallelen zum Bibelwörterbuch." *VT* 8 (1958) 161–215. **Leibel, D.** "עבר בשלח" [Job 33:18; 36:12]. *Tarbiz* 33 (1963–64) 225–27. **Niccacci, A.** "La conclusione di Elihu (Giobbe 37, 19–24)." In *Studia Hierosolymitana.* Vol. 3, *Nell'ottavo centenario francescano (1182–1982).* Ed. G. C. Bottini. Studium Biblicum Franciscanum, Collectio maior 30. Jerusalem: Franciscan, 1982. 75–82. **Perles, F.** "The Fourteenth Edition of Gesenius-Buhl's Dictionary." *JQR* 18 (1906) 383–90. **Reider, J.** "Etymological Studies in Biblical Hebrew." *VT* 4 (1954) 276–95. **Skehan, P. W.** "Job 36, 16 Vulgate." *CBQ* 16 (1954) 295–301.

Sutcliffe, E. F. "Notes on Job, Textual and Exegetical: 6, 18; 11, 12; 31, 35; 34, 17. 20; 36, 27–33; 37, 1." *Bib* 30 (1949) 66–90. **Thomas, D. W.** "Hebrew עֲנִי 'Captivity.'" *JTS* NS 16 (1965) 444–45. ———. "Job xxxvii 22." *JJS* 1 (1948–49) 116–17. ———. "Note on לְדַעַת in Job xxxvii. 7." *JTS* NS 5 (1954) 56–57. **Viganò, L.** *Nomi e titoli di YHWH alla luce del semitico del Nord-ovest.* BibOr 31. Rome: Biblical Institute Press, 1976. **Wolfers, D.** "Science in the Book of Job." *JBQ* 19 (1990–91) 18–21. ———. "The Stone of Deepest Darkness: A Mineralogical Mystery (Job xxviii)." *VT* 44 (1994) 274–76. **Zuckerman, B.** "Two Examples of Editorial Modification in 11QtgJob" [Job 36:14; 34:31]. In *Biblical and Near Eastern Studies.* FS W. S. La Sor, ed. G. A. Tuttle. Grand Rapids: Eerdmans, 1978. 269–75.

Translation

36:1 [a]*Then Elihu added and said:*

2 [a]*Be patient a little and let me explain;*[b]
there is yet more to be said on God's behalf.[c]
3 *I will range*[a] *far and wide for knowledge*[b]
to[c] *ascribe justice*[d] *to my Maker.*[e]
4 *Truly,*[a] *nothing I say will be deceptive;*
a man sincere in his ideas[b] *stands before you.*[c]

5 [a]*Though*[b] *God is mighty in strength,*[c]
he will not reject the pure of heart.
6 *He does not let the wicked*[a] *live long,*[b]
and he gives justice to the humble.
7 *He does not take his eyes*[a] *off the righteous,*[b]
[c]*but with*[d] *kings on a throne he seats them,*[e]
and they are exalted[f] *on high.*[g]

8 *Then if*[a] *they are bound*[b] *with fetters,*
and held fast with the bonds of affliction,[c]
9 *he declares*[a] *to them what they have done*[b]
and their transgressions, that[c] *they are behaving arrogantly.*[d]
10 *He opens*[a] *their ears*[b] *to instruction,*[c]
and commands[d] *that they turn*[e] *from iniquity.*
11 *If then they hearken and serve*[a] *him,*
they complete[b] *their days in prosperity,*
[c]*and their years in contentment.*[d]
12 *But if they do not hearken,*[a] *they cross the river of death,*[b]
and have died without knowledge.[c]

13 [a]*The godless*[b] *lay up*[c] *anger for themselves;*
they do not cry out when he binds[d] *them.*
14 *Their life comes to its end*[a] *in their youth,*
their existence at the hands of the Holy Ones.[b]
15 *He delivers the afflicted by*[a] *their affliction,*
[b]*and opens their ears*[c] *by their distress.*

16 [a]*He has removed you*[b] *also*[c] *from the mouth of distress,*[d]
into a broad place[e] *where, instead,*[f] *there was no constraint*[g]
and your table was weighed down[h] *with an abundance of fatness.*
17 *But you are full of*[a] *the judgment*[b] *due to the wicked;*[c]
judgment[d] *and justice lay hold of you.*[e]
18 [a]*Beware*[b] *that it*[c] *does not draw you into mockery,*[d]
and do not let your ample ransom money[e] *lead you astray.*[f]
19 *Will your wealth*[a] *defend you*[b] *from distress,*[c]
or all your strong exertions?[d]
20 [a]*Do not long for*[b] *the night,*[c]
when nations[d] *are cut off*[e] *where they stand.*[f]
21 [a]*Take care that you do not turn to iniquity,*
for that is why[b] *you are being tested*[c] *by affliction.*[d]

22 *Behold, God is exalted*[a] *in his power;*[b]
who[c] *is a teacher*[d] *like him?*
23 *Who prescribed*[a] *for him his conduct?*[b]
Who said to him, "You have done wrong"?[c]
24 [a]*Remember to extol*[b] *his work,*
which mortals have praised in song.[c]
25 [a]*Every person has seen it;*[b]
humans have gazed on it from afar.[c]

26 [a]*Behold, God is great,*[b] *and we know him not;*
the number of his years is beyond finding out.[c]
27 [a]*For he draws up*[b] *drops*[c] *of water,*
and distills[d] *rain from the mist,*[e]
28 [a]*which*[b] *the clouds*[c] *pour out*[d]
and trickle down[e] *on humans*[f] *as showers.*[g]
31 [a]*For by these*[b] *he nourishes*[c] *peoples,*
and gives food[d] *in abundance.*[e]

29 [a]*Who indeed*[b] *can understand*[c] *the spreading*[d] *of the clouds,*
the thunderings[e] *from his pavilion?*[f]
30 [a]*When*[b] *he spreads*[c] *his light*[d] *over it,*[e]
he exposes[f] *the roots*[g] *of the sea.*[h]
32 [a]*He fills*[b] *his hands*[c] *with lightning,*[d]
and bids[e] *it*[f] *strike its mark.*[g]
33 *His thunder*[a] *declares*[b] *his wrath,*[c]
the passion[d] *of his anger*[e] *against iniquity.*[f]

37:1 *At this indeed*[a] *my heart*[b] *trembles,*
and leaps[c] *from its place.*
2 *Only listen*[a] *to the raging*[b] *of his voice,*[c]
the growling[d] *that comes from his mouth.*
3 *Across*[a] *the whole heavens he flashes*[b] *his lightning,*[c]
and to[d] *the corners of the earth.*

4*After it*[a] *a sound*[b] *roars;*[c]
he thunders[d] *with his majestic voice.*[e]

5 [a]*[God thunders*[b] *with his voice.]*
He does wonderful things,[c]
great things that we cannot know.[d]
6*For to the snow*[a] *he says,*[b] *"Fall*[c] *on the earth,"*
and to the downpour of rain,[d] *"Be strong."*[e]
4c [a]*Once*[b] *his voice is heard, he does not delay them.*[c]
7*He shuts everyone indoors*[a]
[b]*so that all*[c] *may recognize that he is at work.*[d]
8*Then the beasts*[a] *enter*[b] *their lairs*[c]
and take shelter in their dens.[d]

9 [a]*Out of its chamber*[b] *comes the tempest,*[c]
and cold from the scattering winds.[d]
10*At the breath of God, ice*[a] *forms,*[b]
and the broad waters are frozen hard.[c]
11*As well,*[a] *he loads*[b] *the clouds*[c] *with moisture,*[d]
and makes them overflow[e] *with torrents.*[f]
12 [a]*They*[b] *wheel round and round*[c] *at his direction,*[d]
to fulfill[e] *all his commands*[f]
upon the face of the earth.[g]
13 [a]*Whether for correction,*[b] *or for his land,*[c]
or for loyalty,[d] *he dispatches*[e] *them.*

14*Hear this,*[a] *O Job;*[b]
stop[c] *and consider*[d] *the wonderful deeds of God.*
15 [a]*Do you know how God arranges his works,*[b]
how he makes lightning[c] *flash*[d] *from his clouds?*[e]
16*Do you know*[a] *the spreading*[b] *of the clouds,*
the marvels[c] *of one who is perfect in knowledge?*[d]
17 [a]*You, whose clothes are hot*[b]
when the earth lies still[c] *under the south wind,*[d]
18 [a]*will you, with him,*[b] *hammer out*[c] *the sky,*[d]
hard[e] *as a metal*[f] *mirror?*[g]

19 [a]*Teach us*[b] *what we shall say to him;*[c]
we cannot order our thoughts[d] *because of the darkness.*[e]
20 [a]*If I speak,*[b] *will he learn?*[c]
If[d] *anyone says anything, will he be better*[e] *informed?*[f]
21 [a]*At one moment*[b] *the sunlight*[c] *is not seen;*[d]
it is overcast[e] *with clouds;*
[f]*then the wind blows and clears them*[g] *away,*
22*and out of the north comes a golden glow.*[a]
[This refers to[b] *God, awesome*[c] *in majesty.]*

23 [a]*As for the Almighty, we cannot*[b] *find*[c] *him.*
Supreme in power, mighty[d] *in righteousness,*
he does not pervert[e] *justice.*
24 [a]*Therefore mortals fear him,*[b]
and the wise in heart are afraid of him.[c]

Notes

36:1.a. The line is deleted by Hölscher, Fohrer, Ravasi, Gray. Duhm also regards it as secondary. See *Comment.* Beer (BH^2) moves it to follow 35:14, linking 35:15 with 36:2 (without indicating what is to be done with 35:16).

2.a. Fedrizzi moves vv 2–4 to form the proem of chap. 35, i.e., following 35:1.

The whole colon is composed of Aram. words: (1) כתר is "wait" in Aram. but "surround" or "be crowned" in Heb., where three separate roots should probably be distinguished (as in *DCH*, 4:477b). Guillaume finds a different כתר "leave alone" (cf. Arab. *taraka* [Lane, 304c], one of Guillaume's many examples of *badal*, interchange of consonants), which he translates "give me a little time, suffer me a little" (*Lexicography*, 2:19–20). (2) זעיר "little" is common in Aram., but only here and at Isa 28:10, 13 in Heb. (in those places it is in a quantitative sense, but here in a temporal [Gray]; the form זְעִיר occurs at Ecclus 11:6; see *DCH*, 3:125b; there is also a מִזְעָר "little"); Heb. is usually מְעַט. (3) חוה piel "show" is normal Aram., but reasonably well attested also in Heb. (six times in Heb. Bible, five of them in Job; two times in Ecclesiasticus; perhaps once in DSS); Heb. would normally be נגד hiph.

Blommerde adopts the usual Heb. meaning of כתר "surround" (piel at Judg 20:43; Ps 22:12 [13]) and understands זעיר as "young man," thus yielding "form a circle around me, a young man" (it being older men who usually stand in the center of a circle of interlocutors). But he has no followers.

2.b. ואחוך, lit. "and I will show you," with direct obj of the person (as in 15:17; 32:6). RSV has "show," NAB "instruct," JB, NJB "explain," NEB "enlighten," Moffatt, Habel "convince."

2.c. עוד לאלוה מלים, lit. "there are yet words for, or belonging to (ל), God." Most take them as words Elihu will speak, but they could be words God will speak (so Friedrich Delitzsch, and Tur-Sinai, who understands that God has yet more ways of speaking to humans than through dreams). Since Elihu will be speaking on behalf of God, the two senses amount to much the same thing (Gordis). Graetz, Duhm, and Beer (BH^2 *frt*) thought it necessary to add לי "to me" after עוד "yet more," to make clear that the words will be Elihu's, not God's; but that seems plain enough already (Bickell added בי "in me"). Blommerde less plausibly thought the לי of the first colon served also for the second, and that לאלוה meant "from God," like למרחוק "from afar" in v 3.

3.a. On נשׂא "bring, bear," see *Comment.* Fedrizzi renders "I will raise my knowledge to the height," but it is not clear what that means.

3.b. אשׂא דעי למרחוק, lit. "I will bring my knowledge from afar." KJV, RSV have "from afar," JB "I shall range far afield for my arguments," NEB "I will search far and wide," Moffatt "from a wide survey of the truth." למרחוק "from afar" occasionally means "from of old" (2 Kgs 19:25 ‖ Isa 37:26), a sense that perhaps determined the Vg rendering *a principio* "in the beginning." Whybray understands it in this sense, of traditional teaching. Ibn Ezra thought the term referred to God, and so does Fohrer.

Some argue that למרחוק means "to the far distance" (Hölscher, Tur-Sinai), Dhorme citing 39:29, where the eagle sees its prey "far away" (cf. NJPS "I will make my opinions widely known," i.e., to the far distance). But it could equally well be that the eagle sees its prey "*from* far away," and there seems little reason why Elihu should announce that he is about to broadcast his views to a wide audience; surely he is addressing just Job and the other friends. In Ezra 3:13, when the noise of shouting is heard עד־למרחוק, the phrase must mean "from as far as far away," not "to far away" (cf. Hartley). It does not seem necessary to invoke Ugar. *l* "from" (as M. Dahood, review of *The New English Bible, Bib* 52 [1971] 117–23 [120]; Blommerde, Gray; cf. *DUL*, 477, §1b) to arrive at the appropriate sense.

3.c. The two cola of this verse are linked with a simple *waw;* but the second seems to contain the intention of the first.

3.d. נתן צדק "give justice," i.e., "justify, declare in the right," which is normally represented by צדק hiph. See further, *Comment.* Andersen has the original but somewhat labored proposal that דע "knowledge" and צדק "righteousness" form a single phrase, "authentic knowledge," translating "I will bring authentic knowledge from afar, and from my Maker I will give authentic knowledge [to Job]," the ל both in למרחוק and in לפעלי meaning "from"; similarly Blommerde and M. Dahood ("Congruity of Metaphors," in *Hebräische Wortforschung,* FS W. Baumgartner, VTSup 16 [Leiden: Brill, 1967] 40–49 [41 n. 4]).

3.e. פעלי is presumably the ptcp of פעל "make, do," hence "my Maker"; but "Maker" in reference to God is elsewhere always עֹשֶׂה. Some therefore suggest the word is פָּעֳלִי "my deed," especially because LXX has ἔργοις μου "my deeds" (so Ehrlich); but is hard to think what Elihu's "deeds" might be. Dahood (followed by Blommerde, *NW Semitic*) understood the prep *lamedh* as "from" and rendered "and [I shall] report the truth from my Maker" ("Congruity of Metaphors," 41 n. 4; review of *The New English Bible,* 120).

4.a. אמנם "truly," as in 9:2.

4.b. The pl noun is no doubt intensive (GKC, §124e), signifying Knowledge with a capital letter (Dhorme). Fedrizzi thinks תמים was originally כַּבִּיר "mighty," which then changed places with the כביר of v 5b (it is a problem for his view that he thinks vv 2–4 properly follow 35:1). Terrien even transforms the line into a wish, "May the God of perfect knowledge be with you!," in order to avoid the apparent extravagant self-praise. M. Dahood even regards the term תמים דעות as a divine epithet ("Hebrew-Ugaritic Lexicography XII," *Bib* 55 [1974] 381–93 [388]).

4.c. עמך, lit. "[is] with you." Gray thinks that עם has an adversative sense, as in Ugar. (not, however, recognized in *DUL,* 161) and with certain verbs in Heb. (e.g., נלחם "fight," ריב "contend"), but there is no verb here to suggest such a connotation.

5.a. The verse is one of the most difficult in the chapter, and no doubt the text is corrupt. There are three main problems: (1) The verb ימאס "rejects" needs an obj. (2) The repetition of כביר "mighty" in the second colon is suspicious. (3) The phrase כח לב "power of understanding" does not occur elsewhere and is difficult to understand, especially in combination with כביר. Does it really mean "mighty in power of understanding," as it seems to? All these problems must be considered together.

As for ימאס "rejects," it is unlikely (see also on 42:6) that the word can be used absolutely, as in NJPS "He is not contemptuous," Tur-Sinai "God is a judge and despiseth not," J. B. Curtis "he does not feel loathing revulsion" ("On Job's Response to Yahweh," *JBL* 98 [1979] 497–511 [505 n. 26]). Some versions supply an obj they think is understood; thus KJV "despiseth not any," RSV "does not despise any," NIV "does not despise men." Others assume the obj has been lost in transmission, and on the basis of LXX (which is Theod at this point) οὐ μὴ ἀποποιήσηται τὸν ἀκακόν "he does not reject the blameless," insert תָּמִים as the obj, and usually read just הן אל לא ימאס תמים; thus Beer (*BHK al*), Larcher, JB "God does not spurn the blameless man," NJB "God does not reject anyone whose heart is pure," Driver–Gray, Hölscher. Rowley's objection, that תמים might then wrongly seem to refer to Elihu, is not very weighty since its opposite, רשע "wicked," appears in the next line.

Against this view, it could be argued that LXX did not read a better Heb. text but has filled the gap as best it could (Gordis), and that other emendations, including changes of word order, should be considered. Nichols, 162, followed by Dhorme, Pope, Rowley, Sicre Díaz, Hartley, Gray, moves כח "strength" from the second colon to the first, and emends כביר "strong" in the second colon to בָּבָר "[to] the pure" (cf. Pesh), translating "Behold, God is mighty in strength and he will not despise the pure of heart." This is the proposal that is adopted in the *Translation* above, though with the suggestion that the first colon is concessive ("though") (and ימאס is vocalized יִמְאָס because it is no longer in pausal position); cf. *Comment.* It is partly supported by the Tannaitic tradition, attested in Sifre to Numbers §135, that the line should read הן אל כביר לב לא ימאס תם "behold, God is mighty in understanding; he does not reject the pure" (cf. S. Esh, "Job 36,5a in Tannaitic Tradition," *VT* 7 [1957] 190–91). Gray makes a small adjustment, to בָּרֵי לֵב "the pure of heart."

Duhm's solution (followed by Beer [*BHK*], Strahan) is to read the whole line as הן אל ימאס כְּבַד לֵב "behold, God rejects the hardened in heart," i.e., the obstinately wicked (כְּבַד לֵב, as in Exod 9:7)—which is attractive textually but does not fit the thought too well, since the emphasis at the beginning of this strophe should be on the righteous (who are its principal theme), not the wicked. But perhaps the "hardened of heart" here are not in fact the wicked but those from among the righteous who do not learn from God's instruction (cf. vv 9, 12); nevertheless, this would still be a far from clear way of beginning the strophe, since the term "hardened of heart" does not point immediately to any such group among the righteous.

Among other approaches are these: Fohrer and de Wilde read simply הן אל ימאס כביר "behold, God rejects the mighty" for the whole line, NEB הן אל ימאס כביר כח וָלֵב "God, I say, repudiates the high and mighty" (lit. "the one mighty in strength and will"), and Kissane הן אל לא ימאס בְּבַר לֵב "Lo, God rejecteth not the pure of heart," making a second colon of כביר כח לא־יחיה רשע "mighty in strength He will not let the wicked live." Fedrizzi proposes אל כביר כח לב ולא ימאס תמים "God is mighty (by) the power of (his) heart, and he does not reject the innocent," but the sense is not very plausible.

The problematic כח לב "power of understanding" (somewhat loosely translated by NIV as "firm in purpose") is addressed by Budde's emendation of the second colon to כביר כח וַחֲכַם לב "mighty in strength and wise in heart" (similarly Terrien "he does not despise a great man with a pure heart"); but, as Driver–Gray remark, this would create a line of 4+4 stresses, which is very rare in Job. Gordis emends it to the common phrase בַּר לֵב "pure of heart," and translates "Behold, God is mighty, but does not despise—the Mighty One [does not despise] the pure of heart"; but the verse he cites as parallel in structure, Ps 29:1 "Give to Yahweh, O sons of the gods, give to Yahweh glory and strength," is not very similar (nor are his other examples, Num 23:7; Cant 3:9).

Approaching the problems of the verse from the standpoint of comparative Semitic philology, Dahood (review of *Job et son Dieu: Essai d'exégèse et de théologie biblique,* by J. Lévêque, *Bib* 52 [1971] 436–38 [438]; *Psalms II,* 213), followed by Blommerde, takes לא as the title לֵא "the Victor" and כביר as a divine epithet, "the Old One" (as also at 34:17), translating "Though El is the Old One, he is still the Victor; the Old One detests stubbornness"—which makes little sense in the context. For other examples of the supposed לֵא "Victor," see *Note* 21:16.a. Habel, who also sees כביר as a divine epithet, "the Champion," suggests that מאס has the connotation of מסס "melt" (*DCH,* 5:367a) and translates "does not waver." Similarly, D. A. Diewert suggests that the verb is מאס II "melt," hence "he does not cower" ("Job xxxvi 5 and the Root *m's* II," *VT* 39 [1989] 71–77); cf. *DCH,* 5:121b *s.v.* מאס II "flow, waste away"; but that too has little relevance to the context; for why might it be thought that God should "cower"? Perhaps we should consider whether it is not מאס III "err" (*DCH,* 5:122a = מאס II in *HALOT,* 2:541a).

Radical rearrangement of the order of the verses may be seen, for example, in NAB: there v 5 becomes a statement about the wicked ([5a] God rejects the obstinate [reading הן־אל כִּבְדֵי לב ימאס], [5b = MT 6a] and does not preserve their life), while vv 6–7 are about the righteous ([6a = MT 7a] God does not withhold their rights from the just [reading ולא־יגרע מצדיק דִּינוֹ], [6b] but gives vindication to the oppressed, [7] and sets them on thrones with kings). Moffatt similarly has "[5a] The stubborn God disdains, [6a] he will not spare the wicked, he rights those who are wronged, and gives the just their due"; he then inserts 35:9, 12, further description of the plight of the righteous.

5.b. הן is here perhaps not "behold" (as KJV, RSV, NAB; NJPS "See"), but "although" (cf. C. J. Labuschagne, "The Particles הֵן and הִנֵּה," *OTS* 18 [1973] 1–14 [13]; so too Curtis, "On Job's Response," 506). See also on 40:4.

5.c. Reading כַּבִּיר כֹּחַ "mighty in strength," like אמיץ כח "powerful in strength" (9:4) and שַׂגִּיא־כח "great in might" (37:23).

6.a. רשע "wicked" is sg, but ענוים "humble" is pl; some think we should read רְשָׁעִים "wicked [pl]" (Hölscher), but such variations in number occur quite frequently (cf. צדיק in v 7).

6.b. חיה hiph is "cause to live"; "keep the wicked alive" (RSV, NIV) does not perhaps quite capture the point, which is that God ensures that they meet an early death. NEB "does not let the wicked prosper" is too loose. BJ, JB, NJB "or let the sinner live on in all his power" depend on Larcher's transfer of כביר כח "mighty in strength" from v 5 to this point.

7.a. Arguing that גרע properly means "pull down, curtail, suppress," Bickell, Budde, Beer (*BHK*), Peake, Dhorme, Hölscher, Terrien, de Wilde emend עיניו "his eyes" to דִּינוֹ "his judgment, right" (which is admittedly more prosaic [Sicre Díaz]); so too Larcher, JB "and upholds the good man's rights," NJB "he does uphold what the upright deserve." Some support for this emendation comes from the reading of LXX at v 17 (where it translates our v 7a): οὐχ ὑστερήσει δὲ ἀπὸ δικαίων κρίμα "he will not delay justice to the just." However, "diminish" and "withdraw" are equally possible senses of גרע (see *HALOT,* 1:203b; *DCH,* 2:376b).

7.b. צדיק is sg; we might expect a pl, in view of the pls ענוים "humble" in v 6 and אסורים "bound" in v 8 and pl verbs in vv 7–12. So Budde (צַדִּיקִם) and Driver–Gray read צַדִּיקִים "righteous ones." But such a shift in number can easily be paralleled (cf. Gordis).

Duhm and Beer (*BHK vel,* in the order צֶדֶק מֵעָנוֹ) offer the emendation מֵעָנוֹ צֶדֶק "[he does not withdraw] justice from the lowly." They are followed in principle by NEB "he does not deprive the sufferer of his due [REB sufferers of their due]" (reading מִצֶּדֶק עָנָו or מִצִּדְקוֹ [Brockington]).

7.c. Dhorme and others take it that a new couplet begins here: "He has placed kings on the throne, and has seated them there forever. But they have exalted themselves, [8] and behold them now bound with fetters," reading with Perles[2], 41, וְשָׁת "and he set" instead of וְאֵת (so too Hölscher, de

Wilde, Gray). For a parallel use of שית, cf. Ps 132:11 אשית לכסא "I will set on a throne." Larcher, BJ, JB, NJB read בְּשְׂאֵת "when he raises," yielding a fluent rendering: "When he raises kings to thrones, if they grow proud of their unending sway [NJB rule], then he fetters them with chains."

NEB has "look at kings on their thrones: when God gives them sovereign power, they grow arrogant"; but REB has "but on the throne with kings he seats them in eminence, for ever exalted," reverting to a more traditional and probably more correct interpretation, which sees the text as still speaking of the righteous.

Tur-Sinai thinks a line parallel to v 7a is missing here.

7.d. את "with" is emended by Beer (BH^2) to וְאִם "and if [he seats kings on a throne]."

7.e. וישיבם, i.e., ישב hiph (not שוב, as Habel), lit. "and he set them," but most translations effectively ignore the *waw;* thus RSV, NIV, NJPS, REB, and explicitly Beer (*BHK*), NAB, Fohrer, and Sicre Díaz; Kissane actually deletes it. Some parallels to such a use of the *waw* consec are mentioned, however, by GKC, §111b. Blommerde thinks it an emphatic *waw* that throws the verb to the end of the clause; the final *mem* then is enclitic, and the obj is sg throughout. Most agree that the Masoretic accent at לכסא "on a throne" is misplaced and should go rather with וישיבם "and he set them." Larcher perhaps reads יֹשְׁבִים "those who sit"; he is followed by BJ and JB. NJB "if they grow proud of their unending rule," lit. "who hold unending rule," is hard to decipher, but perhaps it also reads יֹשְׁבִים, i.e., "who sit enthroned," followed by ויגבהו "and they are exalted, proud."

7.f. ויגבהו is qal, "and they are high, i.e., exalted," but some would rather it were a hiph, וַיַּגְבִּהוּ (so, e.g., Blommerde, with sg suff in agreement with צדיק). If the previous verb is corrected from a *waw* consec to an impf, this also should be an impf; hence Beer (*BHK*) reads וְיִגְבָּהוּ "and they are exalted."

7.g. לנצח is usually "for ever," but since the next verse envisages them being subsequently imprisoned, that makes no sense (despite all the versions), and we must have recourse to the other well-attested meaning of נצח, "utterly" (cf. *DCH*, 5:739b)—i.e., in the present context, "on high" (similarly already Duhm, who translated "in glory"; followed by Strahan; and so too Gray). Even if we translate לנצח "for ever," its link with וישיבם "and he set them" in the MT is less than ideal; many translators connect it rather with ויגבהו "and they are exalted," whether on the basis of a formal emendation or not is hard to say (so NAB, NIV, REB, Pope).

Duhm, Beer (BH^2), and Strahan replace שאת with וְאִם "and if," thus "And though kings were on the throne, whom he seated [יְשִׁיבֵם without ו] in glory, so that they became proud, though they were bound in fetters (and) were taken in cords of affliction, he would declare . . ."

8.a. ואם, lit. "and if"; Dhorme argues that this is an inappropriate place for the hypothetical clause to begin, since it is in vv 11–12 that the alternatives are set out. Hence he reads וְהִנָּם "and behold, they . . ." But there is no reason why both v 8 and vv 11–12 should not contain hypotheticals. On the view taken here (see *Comment*), this verse depicts a new situation in the life of the righteous; hence the translation above, "then if."

8.b. אסורים "bound"; one might expect the subj to be expressed, so some read אסורים הֵם "they are bound" (Beer [*BHK*], de Wilde); the result seems rather unpoetic. Alternatively, Budde, Driver–Gray, Beer (*BHK vel*), Larcher, JB, Gordis read אֲסָרָם "he has bound them" (as in v 13). Less plausibly, Tur-Sinai suggests וְאִם מָרוּ אֲסָרָם "and if they rebel, he binds them."

8.c. D. W. Thomas ("Hebrew עֳנִי 'Captivity,'" *JTS* NS 16 [1965] 444–45) argues that עֳנִי here does not mean "affliction," as most think, but is a separate word cognate with Arab. *ʿanā* "become a captive" (Lane, 2178b; the verb actually means "be lowly, submissive," and only in certain contexts has the idea of captivity), thus "ropes of captivity." He finds the noun also at Ps 107:10 and the verb ענה piel "imprison" at Ps 105:18 (cf. *DCH,* vol. 6, *s.v.* עֳנִי II). Similarly L. Kopf, "Arabische Etymologien und Parallelen zum Bibelwörterbuch," *VT* 8 (1958) 161–215 (190), adding Exod 3:17 as a further possible example of the verb.

9.a. ויגד "and he declared"; Beer (*BHK*), followed by Gray, reads וְיַגֵּד "and he declares" and NAB יַגִּיד "he declares," to avoid the *waw* consec, since the continuing thought is of an ongoing or repeated action.

9.b. פעלם is lit. "their work." Delitzsch thinks the term here means "evil deed." But in no case does פעל itself carry a pejorative meaning; it is the combination with חמס "violence" (Isa 59:6) or רע "wickedness" (Mic 2:1) or רשע "wicked" (Ps 9:17) that creates a negative tone in some contexts.

9.c. כי יתגברו "that they behave arrogantly," i.e., "explaining wherein פעלם and פשעיהם consist" (Driver–Gray), rather than "when they are guilty of pride" (Gordis). כי is understood as "how" by Blommerde, followed by Habel ("how they too became arrogant"), but it is questionable whether כי could mean "how" in this sense (examples from Gen 1:4 and Isa 22:9 are not convincing).

9.d. REB attempts to inject some drama into the translation of a basically prosaic verse: "he denounces their conduct to them, showing how, puffed with pride, they lapsed into sin" (NEB "showing how insolence and tyranny was their offence").

גבר qal is "be strong," hithp "show oneself strong, behave proudly" (as here); some translations suggest the meaning rather "be many, excessive," with פשעיהם "transgressions" as the subj (NJPS "and that their transgressions are excessive"; cf. KJV "and their transgressions that they have exceeded"). Gray, translating "they have sinned defiantly in their tyranny," thinks of גבר as a denominative from גִּבּוֹר "tyrant."

10.a. ויגל "and he opened"; Budde reads וְיָגֶל "and he opens" (Beer [*BHK*] וְיְגַלֶּה, NAB יְגַלֶּה "he opens") to avoid the *waw* consec (as in v 9).

10.b. אזנם "their ear" is vocalized by Blommerde as אָזְנַם "ears," supposedly a contracted dual, with the suff understood.

10.c. ויגל אזנם למוסר, lit. "and he opens their ear to instruction"; NJB has, more loosely, "in their ears he sounds a warning."

10.d. The verb ויאמר "and he says" seems remarkably feeble in the context, but "command" is well attested as a sense of אמר "say" (cf. BDB, 56b; *HALOT,* 1:66b §6; *DCH,* 1:323 §5; Guillaume compares Arab. *'amara* "command" [Lane, 95b], but recourse to the Arab. is unnecessary). Translations attempt to put some color into it: RSV, NIV "commands," NAB "exhorts," NJB "ordering," NEB "[his warnings] summon," NJPS "ordering them back from mischief," REB "he directs them back from their evil courses." Rather than the *waw* consec form וַיֹּאמֶר, Budde and Beer (*BHK*), followed by NAB, Gray, read וְיֹאמַר "and he says" (as also in v 9).

10.e. שוב is "turn" rather than "return," and not (as more frequently in the prophets) "repent." See further, *Comment.*

11.a. ויעבדו "and serve (him)," the obj being understood. It is very rare for עבד in the sense of "serve" to be used absolutely; Isa 19:23, used of worship, is the nearest parallel (cf. also Exod 21:2). It is unnecessary to see here an Aramaism "(if they listen) and do so" (Tur-Sinai). Kissane, troubled by the absence of an obj for the verb, reads, following a suggestion of Duhm, וְיַעַבְרוּ "and they shall pass," continuing with words from v 16, where he thinks them out of place: מפי־צר רחב לא־מוצק תחתיה "from the mouth of distress, Freedom unrestrained shall be instead thereof."

11.b. יכלו "they complete" is omitted by NEB (cf. Brockington), which has the reading "they spend (their days)" even though they read no verb here. REB "they will live out their days" seems to revert to the MT reading. Many MT MSS have יְבַלּוּ "they wear out, use to the full, enjoy" (cf. BDB, 114b). The colon is closely parallel to 21:13, where יְבַלּוּ is actually the K to יכלו (see *Note* 21:13.b). As at 21:13, the reference is to the close of their lives (thus "they complete their lives") rather than to the remaining days (as NJB "the rest of their days are prosperous," NIV "they will spend the rest of their days in prosperity," NAB "they spend their days in prosperity," NJPS "they shall spend their days in happiness").

11.c. The colon is omitted by Beer (*BH*²), Hölscher, Fohrer, de Wilde, on the ground that it makes the line too long.

11.d. נעמים is pl of נָעִים "pleasant," thus "pleasant things, pleasantness (as an abstract)," hence NAB "happiness," NIV "contentment," NEB "comfort," NJPS "delight," KJV "pleasures"; cf. JB "their closing years are full of ease," NJB "the years pass pleasantly."

12.a. ישמעו "they hearken" is open to question, according to Beer (*BH*² *frt*).

12.b. שלח seems at first to be the word for "weapon," a general word, and not specifically "sword" (as KJV, RSV, NIV, NJPS). Beer (*BHK*), Hölscher (*frt*), Fohrer, de Wilde, Gray, NAB omit בשלח "by the sword" as a dittograph of the phrase in 33:18. Understanding שלח as "sword" is supported by Tg בחרבא יפלון "by the sword they shall fall." JB "a thunderbolt destroys them" perhaps thinks of the thunderbolt as God's weapon. Moffatt's "they die a violent death," though unexplained, anticipates Guillaume (*Studies,* 118), who proposes a new שֶׁלַח "sudden death," a cognate, by metathesis, he alleges, of Arab. *ḫālis* "death" (Lane, 785b; the word means properly "one who carries off," from *ḫalasa* "seize, carry off").

But if שלח is "weapon," it does not sit well with the verb עבר "pass over." Contrary to some opinion, this verb does not usually mean "die," and the argument has already been made for the same phrase in 33:18 (*q.v.*) that it refers rather to crossing the underworld river (שלח) that separates the land of life from the land of death. Thus NEB "they cross the river of death," NIVmg "cross the River," GNB "cross the stream into the world of the dead" (similarly Terrien, Gordis, Hartley). Less likely is an understanding of that stream as a vertical channel, as NJB "they go down the Canal."

12.c. כבלי־דעת "(?) as without knowledge" appears in *BHS* (Codex Leningradensis); we should probably read, with other MSS, בִּבְלִי "without" (so too Beer [*BHK*], Gerleman [*BHS*]) with the *beth* of accompaniment, as in NEB "they die, their lesson unlearnt," NJB "and perish in their stupidity," Moffatt "and perish in their folly." It is not likely that the ב is equivalent to the מ of cause, "for lack of understanding" (which is not what the phrase means at 35:16, against Gordis, Hartley; מבלי־דעת, lit. "from without knowledge" [Isa 5:13; cf. Hos 4:6], is a different matter). Nor will it mean "without being aware" (as for example Terrien, JB "death comes on them unawares"), for whether they are aware they are dying or not seems beside the point. And it can hardly mean "without others being aware" (Fohrer; cf. Gordis) or "without others knowing how it happened" (Tur-Sinai). To die without being noticed may be unfortunate, but what is relevant here is dying without gaining wisdom, which is culpable (just as at 4:21); Gray has more or less the same view in translating "without themselves paying heed," *sc.* to what their conduct involves. Duhm reads בִּשְׁאֹלָה "[they pass over] to Sheol," as at 33:18 (*q.v.*), an emendation that has lost its raison d'être since the correct sense of שלח has emerged.

13.a. Budde deletes vv 13–14.

13.b. On the precise meaning of חנף "(?) godless," see *Comment.* On the proposed homonym חָנֵף II "haughty," see Thomas, 8:300 (and cf. *DCH,* 3:277). It is another matter how "stubborn" (JB) is to be justified.

13.c. ישׂימו is from שׂים "set," and there are no parallels to the phrase שׂים אף "set anger." Beer (*BHK*) thinks it probably means "store up" (his note is "= reponunt?"). Duhm added בְּלִבָּם "in their heart" (cf. Ps 13:2 [3] שׁית בנפשׁ). Michaelis, following Heath (יָשִׂימוּ "cast forth [fury]"), read יַשִּׁימוּ "they stir up" (hiph of נשׁם, though that means "breathe" and occurs only once, in the qal); furthermore, it does not suit the context well, for the idea of stirring up the divine anger seems inappropriate here. Nevertheless, Beer (*BH*[2] *prps*) acknowledges this emendation, while Gerleman in *BHS* reads the qal form (*frt*); so too Lévêque, 586; NEB has the same understanding, reading יַשִּׁימוּ or ישׁמו (Brockington) and translating "rage against him."

Dhorme suggests יִשְׁמְרוּ "they keep," translating "they nourish spite" (followed by Hölscher [*frt*], Larcher, Gray, JB "cherish"). שׁמר and נטר "keep," used absolutely, appear to be used for "keep (anger)" in Jer 3:5. However, it seems more probable that there is a separate verb נטר II for "be angry" (see *DCH,* 5:679a), and the same may well be true for שׁמר. Here, nevertheless, the obj אף "anger" is expressed, and though the only parallel seems to be Amos 1:11, where עברה "wrath" is the obj of שׁמר, the sense appears plausible. It is another matter why anger in particular should be ascribed to these godless persons or hypocrites (see *Comment*).

Guillaume translates "hide (their anger)," proposing a new שׂים cognate with Arab. *šāma* "hide" (Lane, 1634a). Gray is tempted by this possibility, which he would translate "assume the appearance of anger," or perhaps "scowl," though he settles for Dhorme's emendation.

13.d. אסר "bind" is unproblematic, except perhaps that here it concerns the wicked whereas in v 8 it concerned the righteous. Guillaume suggests not implausibly, however, that it may be another אסר "chastise," a byform of יסר.

14.a. תמת בנער נפשׁם, lit., "their life dies in youth." תמת is juss in form, but it must be impf in meaning (cf. GKC, §109k). There is no need to emend to תָּמוּת "dies," as Beer (*BHK*). The meaning of this unusual phrase is discussed in the next *Note.*

14.b. וחיתם בַּקְּדֵשִׁים, lit. "and their life is among the prostitutes," the word חיה being used for "life" in this colon, whereas it was נפשׁ in the previous colon.

קָדֵשׁ is usually understood as "male prostitute," and "cult prostitute" at that, in view of the apparent connection of קדשׁ with the root קדשׁ "be holy." On the question whether cult prostitution existed in ancient Israel, and if so, how it is to be defined, see *Comment.* Most translations and commentators have this understanding of the term, but many hesitate to express it and resort to periphrases and euphemisms. NJB has, candidly, "live among the male prostitutes of the temple," whereas the earlier JB more timidly translated "live a life despised by all" (following Larcher; BJ wrongly says *méprisée* is a "[textual] correction" of the Heb., when it is actually a bowdlerization of it). NIV uncompromisingly has "they die in their youth, among male prostitutes of the shrines" (similarly NJB); NEB "they die in their prime, like male prostitutes, worn out," REB "short-lived as male prostitutes," Pope "their life among the sodomites." KJV, on the other hand, had "their life is among the unclean," and RSV and even NRSV followed suit with "their life ends in shame" (though RSVmg has "among the cult prostitutes," NRSVmg "among the temple prostitutes"). NAB says "they perish among the reprobate," NJPS "expire among the depraved," and Habel "their life is spent among perverts" (which he understands as a "broader sense" than the specific "male prostitutes"), while GNB has "worn out by a life of disgrace," Hartley "they lose their life in youthful shame." In a rather individual move, Dhorme translates "their life ends in adolescence," explaining that קדשים must be an abstract noun like נעורים "youth" (so too JB), and thus "the age of the youthful prostitutes"; similarly Hölscher and Fohrer, as if the word meant only "youth," with no direct reference to prostitutes—but that is most improbable.

While one caveat must be entered about the rendering "temple prostitute" or "cult prostitute" since the evidence is thin that prostitutes had anything to do with temples (which are not plentiful in the world of Job anyway), a second caveat concerns the translation "male prostitute." It is true that קדשים is a masc noun, but that does not mean that all of those referred to by it are male. Not all the רשעים "wicked" are male and not all the נביאים are "male prophets," so why should not קדשים mean "male and female prostitutes"? 2 Kgs 23:7 has Josiah destroying the houses of the קדשים "where the women did weaving for Asherah." Why are there women in the houses of male prostitutes? J. Gray agrees that the קדשים are "prostitutes of both sexes" (*I and II Kings: A Commentary,* 2d ed. [London: SCM Press, 1970] 734; and also in his Job commentary).

Not many aver that the text is likely to be corrupt, yet it does have a number of serious problems. (1) It is very strange to have "their life" as the subj of "die" (מות). מות has a recognizably inanimate subject only twice: ארץ "land" (Gen 47:19, an odd example with "we and our land" as the combined subj) and חכמה "wisdom" (Job 12:2, wisdom being personified) (cf. *DCH,* 5:194b; מרבית "increase" [1 Sam 2:33] is technically an abstract subj, but it refers to people). (2) קדשים, if it means "male prostitutes," is an improbable parallel to "youth" (נער) in the first colon. (3) If the first colon means that they die in their youth, why does the second colon speak of their life? If the verb תמת "dies" is to be understood in the second colon, with חיה as its subj, the problem of its having an inanimate subj is doubled. If, on the other hand, the second colon means "and their life is among the prostitutes," it is hard to explain why that should follow the first colon, which is about their death.

An apparently strange reading of LXX may provide an important clue. It has ἡ δὲ ζωὴ αὐτῶν τιτρωσκομένη ὑπὸ ἀγγέλων "and their life is wounded by angels." This reading suggests the LXX's Heb. text had a verb in the second colon and that they read קדשים as קְדֹשִׁים "holy ones," the angels we have met with already at 5:1; there are destroying angels at Ps 78:49 (Gray sees in the "wounding" a reference to the castration of male prostitutes, but he does not undertake to explain the role of the angels). The Qumran Targum בממתין "by the killers" might also be thought an allusion to such angels (though, it must be noted, Tg has היך מרי זנו "like masters of prostitution," i.e., keepers of brothels [Jastrow, 1:406a], not male prostitutes [Terrien, Pope]). The LXX understanding of קדשים is adopted in the *Translation* above ("their existence at the hands of the Holy Ones"), but there is still no acceptable suggestion for the missing verb of the second colon (if indeed it is missing), nor a satisfactory emendation for the first colon.

In the second colon, NEB adds תִּתַּם after וחיתם (Brockington); this would appear to be 3 fem sg impf of תמם "be perfect, complete," though the form in its only occurrence elsewhere is תִּתֹּם (Ezek 24:11); or, by analogy with יִתֹּם in Ezek 47:12, it could be תִּתֹּם. NEB translates וחיתם תִּתַּם, lit. "their life is completed," with "worn out." REB presumably makes the same addition for its translation "short-lived." Beer (*BHK*) inserts (*frt*) חָלְתָה "(their life) becomes weak"; so too de Wilde (*ḥālitā* is an error).

The ב of בקדשים is "among," but Tg has כ "like," and de Wilde proposes we read "like prostitutes" (he is incorrect, though, that Beer [*BHK*] recommends that reading).

15.a. ב is "by," not "in" or "from" (as Fohrer, NJPS). For חלץ ב "deliver by," cf. Prov 11:9 (מן is "from" in Prov 11:8). M. J. Dahood, however, argued that ב does mean "from" (cf. Vg *de angustia* "from narrowness"), and pointed out that in 5:19 also ב is "from" in the first colon and "in" in the second ("Northwest Semitic Philology and Job," in *The Bible in Current Catholic Thought: Gruenthaner Memorial Volume,* ed. J. L. McKenzie, St. Mary's Theological Studies 1 [New York: Herder & Herder, 1962] 55–74 [71]).

15.b. Dhorme judged vv 19–20 to be alien to the context and omitted them from his translation.

15.c. ויגל אזנם, lit. "and opens their ear," is connected with simple *waw* to the preceding impf verb חלץ, since it takes place at the same time as the delivering (cf. the suggested emendations in vv 9, 10a, 10b). Since there is no call for a juss here, some would read וַיְגַלֶּה "and he opens" (so Beer [*BHK*]). The idiom is rendered variously by the Eng. versions: KJV, RSV have "openeth [opens] their ear," NAB "instructs them," NJB "warning him," NIV "speaks to them," NJPS "opens their understanding," NEB "teaches them," JB, following Larcher, "uses distress to open their eyes" [!].

Those who believe that number and gender should agree in a Heb. sentence read אָזְנוֹ "his ear," to agree with עני "the afflicted one" (so Budde, Duhm, Beer [BH^2], Hölscher, Kissane, de Wilde, sometimes appealing to Vg, though its translation may be purely *ad sensum*). Dahood thinks the *mem* is enclitic ("Northwest Semitic Philology and Job," 71), and Blommerde that it is a contracted dual (as at v 10).

16.a. Beer (*BHK*) comments that the whole verse is doubtful, while NAB does not offer any translation of vv 16–20 on the ground that "the Hebrew text is in disorder."

16.b. הסיתך, lit. "he has enticed you," from סות, usually "incite, instigate," but apparently also "entice" (cf. also 2 Chr 18:31); so RVmg, RSV "allured," NIV "wooing." Dhorme argued that both there and here it means "remove." Driver–Gray think it unlikely that a verb used normally with negative connotations ("seduce, entice") would be used with God as the subj (but it is used in 2 Chr 18:31 of God luring the enemy away from Jehoshaphat; cf. also Gordis). But it is no more likely that רחב "a wide place" should be the subj (as Ewald "and thee also hath led astray more than biting need the wide place"). Duhm, followed by Beer (*BH*[2] *frt*) and Strahan, moves רחב from v 16b and ונחת from v 16c to follow הסיתך and translates "But freedom has led you away and ease before the mouth of distress." Kissane takes a lead from Duhm (see *Note* v 11.a), and reads here אַף הֲסִיתְךָ נחת "Indeed, comfort hath seduced thee," נַחַת "comfort" being from נוח "rest" (BDB, 629a; the entry in *DCH*, 5:671a, should not be preceded by an asterisk).

Emendations include הֱסִירְךָ "he withdrew you" (Hitzig, Hölscher [*frt*]) and הִסִּיעֲךָ "he snatched you" (Beer [*BH*[2] *frt*]).

16.c. ואף "and also" at the beginning of the colon. Some add אַתָּה "you" (Bickell[2], Budde, de Wilde) or replace ואף with אַתָּה (Duhm, Beer [*BH*[2]], Beer [*BHK frt*], apparently NEB); the sense would be, "and as for you, [he has removed you]." Gray reads אַךְ "but."

16.d. The phrase מפי צר, lit. "from the mouth of narrowness," is quite unparalleled, and almost certainly corrupt, even though no satisfactory alternative has been proposed. *HALOT*, 3:1052a, offers "from the jaws of need." Driver–Gray mention, only to reject, the improbable interpretation of "mouth of confinement" as referring to the prayer of a pious sufferer. Conceivably, צר is "enemy" (cf. Driver–Gray) as in 6:23; 16:9; 19:11 (Theod has ἐκ στόματος ἐχθροῦ "from the mouth of the enemy"). Enemies (אֹיֵב) open their mouths in Lam 2:16; 3:46, and the mouth of the wicked pours out evil in Prov 15:28. But there is no parallel to the phrase "the mouth of the enemy." Habel understands צר as "the Adversary," i.e., Death (so also in v 19), comparing פי שאול "the mouth of Sheol" in Ps 141:7 and Ugar. references to Baal entering the mouth of Mot (Baal I.ii.1–6 = *CML*, 105a; *KTU* 1.5; *CTA* 5). The problem here is that Elihu should not be suggesting that God is wanting to lure Job from the jaws of death, but rather is wanting Job to make up his mind about where his allegiance lies.

Guillaume proposes a new זור "starve" (cf. Arab. *ḍāra*), thus "has enticed you from the mouth of the starving" (זָר being ptcp); but it is hard to know what he refers to since *ḍāra* (Lane, 1812a; Wehr–Cowan, 547b) means "injure, harm," *ḍarra* (Lane, 1775c; Wehr–Cowan, 537b) has the same meaning, with its noun *ḍarr* being "harm, hurt, disease, leanness," but not specifically "starvation," and *taḍawwara*, from *ḍwr* (Lane, 1809c), means "writhe, cry out (from pain or hunger)," but is not a word for "starve."

Among emendations, (1) Beer (*BHK frt*), followed by Gray, notes מִפֶּרֶץ, a new noun "wealth" (not in *DCH*), derived from פרץ "break through" and in Gen 30:43 "increase beyond limit" (of Jacob); but this is a most unusual sense of פרץ, and the noun is not otherwise attested. However, Rowley adopts it, translating "wealth hath enticed thee" (similarly Gray). (2) Lévêque, 586, read מפי צְרִיחַ "[he will deliver you] from the mouth of the tomb" (צריח "vault, crypt" [BDB, 863b; *HALOT*, 1055b], however, is never attested elsewhere in poetic texts). (3) Duhm thinks צר would be better read as צָרָה "distress."

(4) Bickell[2] adds at the end of the first colon לִרְוָחָה "for respite, relief" (elsewhere only Exod 8:15 [11]; Lam 3:56); NEB follows and translates the whole colon "Beware, if you are tempted to exchange hardship for comfort," presumably reading וְאִם for אף and understanding the colon as "if one has seduced you from the mouth of distress to relief." (5) De Wilde adds לְנַחַת "for rest" (his transliteration *linḥat* must be an error), removing the questionable נחת from v 16c to here. (6) Kissane moves the phrase מפי־צר "from the mouth of distress" and the following clause, רחב לא־מוצק תחתיה, from this place to v 11 (see *Note* 11.a).

16.e. רחב is locative, "to a broad place" (Delitzsch). Pope translates רחב לא־מוצק "(in) unconfined expanse," Sicre Díaz "(to) a place that is spacious and open." For the idea, cf. Ps 31:8 (9) "you set my feet in a broad place (מֶרְחָב)."

16.f. תחתיה is lit. "beneath it [fem.]," which is hard to interpret and is generally ignored in translations. Dhorme plausibly understood it as "instead of that," i.e., the distress in the previous colon. Emendations: (1) Some read תַּחְתֶּיךָ "beneath you" (so Vg, Bickell[2], Dillmann [*frt*], Budde, Beer [*BHK prps*], Hölscher, Fohrer, Rowley "unlimited abundance beneath thee [i.e., behind you]," de Wilde "is your place," Gray "plenty and no pinch where you are placed," and NEB "unlimited plenty spread before you"). (2) Duhm and Beer (*BH*[2] *al* הַחִתְּךָ) emend to הַחִתְּךָ "(no trouble) frightens you" (reading the colon as לא־מוצק החתך). (3) Pope reads נְחָתְךָ "he set you," presumably as 3 masc sg of נחת piel; but נחת piel, occurring only three times, apparently means "press down," which is inappropriate here (cf. Ps 65:10 [11]; at 2 Sam 22:35 ǁ Ps 18:34 [35] the verb may not even be נחת I "descend," but rather נחת II "be strong" or נחת IV "fashion, hew" [cf. *DCH,* 5:671a]).

16.g. מוצק may be explained as a noun "narrowing," thus "distress" (like צר in the previous colon), or as יצק hoph ptcp "narrowed, hemmed in." As a noun, it will be from צוק "constrain"; the מוצק in 37:10 (*q.v.*) is more probably a different noun, from יצק "pour out, cast."

16.h. נחת שלחנך מלא דשן, apparently "the rest, calm, of your table was full of fat." נַחַת (from נוח "rest"; cf. BDB, 629a) is often understood as "the comfort of [your table]," in reference to the excellent food provided on it (cf. NIV "to the comfort of your table laden with choice food"). But one senses that there is something not quite right here. Alternatives are: (1) Perhaps נחת is a separate word from נוח, or a separate sense of נַחַת, meaning "what is set down, spread" (cf. Gordis, Hartley, *DCH,* 5:671b); cf. KJV "that which should be set on thy table," RSV "what was set on your table." (2) Gray proposes a new word נַחַת "level place, level board," thus "top" of a table, translating "and your table-top [full of fatness]" (cf. Ugar. *nḫt* "dais [?]" ["divan" in *DUL,* 630], Arab. *nāḫa* "level" [though *nāḫa* seems to mean rather "lie down," as Lane, 2864b]). (3) Some take נחת as the subj of מלא "is full" (so RSV "what was set on your table was full of fatness"); in that case the masc verb would have a fem subj, so some emend to מָלְאָה "is full."

(4) Alternatively, שלחן could be the subj of מלא, i.e., "the comfort of your table, which was full of fat" (so Ewald, Dillmann). Translations often give just a general sense: NJB "with rich food piled high on your table," NJPS "your table is laid out with rich food," NEB "and a generous table." (5) Budde, Hölscher, Dhorme, Larcher (followed by JB, NJB), Fohrer, Rowley, Habel omit נחת as a mistaken dittograph of the previous word תחתיה, Pope as a dittograph of his נחתך. *HALOT,* 2:692b, thinks נחת is what remains of a lost colon. (6) Lévêque, 586 n. 5, reads וְנִחַת שלחנך מְלֹא דשן "and an abundance of fatness weighed down (נחת piel) your table," a modest and attractive suggestion, adopted in the *Translation* above.

17.a. מלאת "you are full" is deleted by Dhorme, Hölscher, Tur-Sinai, Pope, Rowley, Gordis, as a dittograph of מלא in v 16c; Kissane's emendation also dispenses with מלאת. See *Note* 17.c.

17.b. דין is usually recognized as "judgment," as in the next colon. But Guillaume, followed by Gray, sees here a *tauriya,* the word having different meanings in the same sentence. The first דין, Guillaume suggests, is a new word, "food" (cf. Arab. *zuwān;* see *DCH,* 2:435a; but on the Arab., cf. *Note* 13.c and *Note* 36:31.c), translating "you are full of a rich man's food" (see further, *Note* 17.c).

17.c. ודין־רשע מלאת should be, straightforwardly enough, "and (with) the judgment of the wicked you are full." This could mean that instead of the security and ease that Job once enjoyed (or perhaps, could at this moment be enjoying if only he adopted the right attitude to his suffering), he is experiencing the judgment of punishment that is usually meted out to the wicked (so Driver–Gray, Peake). Thus Moffatt "you meet the full doom of the wicked," and thus, one presumes, RSV "you are full of the judgment on the wicked," and NIV "you are laden with the judgment due the wicked" (though why change the image of being full to being laden?). KJV "thou hast fulfilled the judgment of the wicked" perhaps intends the same sense.

Many, however, are not content with this sense. (1) NRSV, for example, has "you are obsessed with the case of the wicked," which is true enough of Job, but there are no parallels to this sense of מלא "be full," and it is not easy to see what the meaning of the second colon "judgment and justice seize you" can then be; is it that the idea of judgment, or a concern for judgment, overwhelms Job? That too is true enough, but how can that be a criticism of Job, and what does Elihu think he should be doing about it? The translation seems rather cerebral, and is no clear improvement on the RSV. (2) NJPS had earlier translated the first colon "You are obsessed with the case of the wicked man," but had continued "but the justice of the case will be upheld." What does that mean? If there is any "case" about the wicked in Job's eyes, it is a case against God, that he is not punishing them; Job is certainly obsessed about this issue, but Elihu cannot be meaning that Job's case against God will be upheld, so the translation is unacceptable. (3) Habel thought, rightly enough, that the case that obsessed Job was his own case against God and translated "But you are full with the suit of a guilty man [i.e., yourself], lawsuit and litigation obsess you." But this is a rather too intellectual understanding of דין ומשפט יתמכו, which should mean that Job is on the receiving end of justice rather than that the idea of justice absorbs him.

Among emendations we find: (1) וְדִין רְשָׁעִים לֹא תָדִין (Tur-Sinai); though Tur-Sinai translated "But do not judge as the wicked judge" (which is irrelevant in this context), the words would be better translated "the case of the wicked you did not judge" (so Kissane, Pope, Rowley, Sicre Díaz). This reading is adopted by Larcher and followed by JB "you did not execute justice on the wicked" (so too NJB "you did not bring the wicked to trial"). The objection to this reading is that this is not the place for Elihu to be reproving Job for alleged sins in his past life, for the issue here is entirely how Job should be responding to the instruction God is offering him by means of his suffering. The same words could be translated "do not plead the cause of the wicked" (Lévêque, 587), but why should Elihu be urging this at this point? Less plausibly, they could be rendered "Do not judge (according to) the judgment of the wicked" (Fedrizzi), but the same criticism of the relevance of such words applies.

(2) Gordis develops Tur-Sinai's proposal with an emendation to וְדִין רָשֵׁי עָם לֹא תָדִין "and the cause of the poor you did not plead," רָשׁ being a frequent term in wisdom literature. The phrase רשי עם does not occur elsewhere, but עניי־עם "poor of the people" is in Ps 72:4 and אביני עמך "the poor of your people" in Exod 23:11. The reading is, however, open to the same objection as that of Tur-Sinai's followers, as well as flatly contradicting Job's own affidavit (29:16).

(3) Dhorme and Hölscher read וְדִין רָשָׁע תָּדִין "and the judgment of the wicked you will judge," meaning that Job will be restored to his role as magistrate. The suggestion founders on the unlikelihood that we are reading here about Job's future restoration; it is much more probable that the subj is the choice before Job of how he will here and now respond to God's instruction.

(4) De Wilde reads וְעִם רֶשַׁע מלאת דין ומשפט יִתְמְכוּךְ "and though you are full of wickedness judgment and justice hold you fast," which does not seem well connected to the previous verse, where there is no hint of anything improper in Job.

And among philological proposals we find: (1) G. R. Driver's suggestion ("Problems in the Hebrew Text of Job," in *Wisdom in Israel and in the Ancient Near East*, FS H. H. Rowley, ed. M. Noth and D. W. Thomas, VTSup 3 [Leiden: Brill, 1955] 72–93 [89–91]) of a דִּין II "food" (cf. Arab. *dāna* V "enjoy abundance" [Freytag, 2:73–74; Lane, 938b]; cf. *DCH,* 2:435a). Thus NEB "if you eat your fill of a rich man's fare." But this is a dubious proposal, since *dāna* usually means "be low, vile," the sense "enjoy abundance" being restricted to Form V, and since in any case a noun for "abundance" (not attested in Arab.) would not necessarily suggest "food" in a cognate language. (2) Guillaume ("The Arabic Background of the Book of Job," in *Promise and Fulfilment,* FS S. H. Hooke, ed. F. F. Bruce [Edinburgh: T. & T. Clark, 1963] 106–27 [122]; *Studies,* 127) also found the meaning "food" here, by postulating a דִּין III (not in *DCH*) on the basis of Arab. *zuwān,* which he allows usually means "the refuse in food that is discarded," and which must therefore be explained here as an *'aḍdād* (reversal of meaning) with the sense "food." On the difficulties with this view, see *Note* 36:31.c. (3) Without subscribing to the view of either Driver or Guillaume, Gray also understands דִּין as "food," arguing that the poet played on the phonetic variation between *z* and *d* in Semitic, having in mind the verb זון "feed" with its noun מָזוֹן (BDB, 266a). (4) Guillaume ("Arabic Background," 116) also argued that there is a רֶשַׁע "rich, copious" (as also at 24:6, and, famously, at Isa 53:9; cf. Arab. *rassagha* "he provided handsomely for his family" [Lane, 1080c, but "for his family" is not part of the meaning of the word]); so NEB "if you eat your fill of a rich man's fare," and Blommerde "You were filled with food, being rich." This suggestion is considered, but finally rejected, by Gray. The difficulty with this whole line of interpretation is that advice to Job, should he eat his fill of a rich man's fare, not to be led astray with lavish gifts of wine, seems singularly inappropriate at this point, and the translation cannot be deemed credible.

17.d. דין "judgment" is omitted by Duhm and Beer (BH^2), as a variant on משפט "justice."

17.e. תמך is "lay hold of, grasp," the idea being that Job has been caught hold of by the divine justice (so, e.g., Fohrer), the subj being דין ומשפט "judgment and justice," which is perhaps a hendiadys for "right judgment" (Hartley). Job would be the understood obj (it is hardly that "judging and judgment lay hold on one another," as Delitzsch), and some actually add the suff to the verb, reading יִתְמְכוּךְ "seize you" (so Driver–Gray, de Wilde, NEB [Brockington]) or תְּמְכוּךְ (Beer [*BHK frt*]), or, if דין has been removed from this second colon, תְּמָכֶךְ (מִשְׁפָּטוֹ) "his judgment has seized you" (so Duhm, Beer [BH^2]). Hartley translates "just judgment will be upheld," but תמך means "support," not "be supported," and we would need to emend to the niph, יִתָּמְכוּ. The weakness with this view is that there is no motivation in the present context for Elihu to assert that divine justice will be maintained, and it is better to see the colon as a further statement of Job's present condition (as in the *Translation* above). Gray suggests that the verb may have the nuance "manipulate [a case at law]," but there is no parallel to such a sense. NEB "when you are occupied with the business of the law" apparently understands "seize" in the sense of "seize the attention," though there is no parallel for such an interpretation.

The text has of course attracted emendations. (1) Taking דין into the first colon as token of a verb (e.g., תדין "you will judge") produces a second colon that is too short for some. Dhorme and

Hölscher, for example, then add יָדֶיךָ "your hands" as subj, translating "your hands will seize justice," meaning that Job will once again be able to dispense justice in Uz. This reading is improbable, because these verses are not about Job's restoration to happiness but about the choices that are currently before him (note "beware!" [חמה] at the beginning of v 18). Moreover, the idiom "seize justice" seems strange, and the alleged parallel in Deut 32:41 (ותאחז במשפט ידי "and my hand will seize judgment") may be more apparent than real (some think אַשְׁפָּה "quiver" should be read there for מִשְׁפָּט; so, e.g., *HALOT,* 2:652a).

(2) The verb יתמכו itself has also been emended. Gordis reads וּמִשְׁפַּט יְתֹמִים "or the suit of the orphans." In general, those who see an accusation of Job in the first colon, that he did not judge the cause of the poor, are inclined to see a similar charge in the second colon. JB has "you cheated orphaned children of their rights" (NJB "and did not give fair judgement to the orphan"). All these proposals take "the justice of the orphans" as a second obj of the emended לֹא תָדִין "you did not judge." (3) Lévêque, 587, accommodates both orphans and the verb "support," reading ומשפט יָתֹם תְּמֹךְ "and support the right of the orphan" (the letters תמ having been lost by haplography); this is a good suggestion, apart from the fact that such generalized advance is not a propos. (4) Kissane, followed by Rowley, reads יָתוֹם מֻסָּר "[and the right of] the orphan was taken away," מֻסָּר being pual of the rare and perhaps questionable verb מסר "deliver up, offer" (BDB, 588a; *HALOT,* 2:608b, understands it rather as "select"; cf. also *DCH,* 5:376b, *s.v.* מסר II "hand over," III "deliver up," IV "select"); "taken away" is not a probable sense of any verb מסר. (5) Fedrizzi reads יִתְמַכֵּךְ "shall become low," i.e., "[a decision] will be obvious (*una decisione cadrà da sè*)." מכך is, however, not elsewhere attested in the hithp, and the idiom is not known in Heb. Blommerde also invokes מכך hithp, reading יִתְמַכּוּ "[right and justice] collapsed."

(6) The line is, however, still too short for the taste of some. Pope adds at the end כִּזַּבְתָּ "[the orphan's justice] you have falsified." But כזב piel never has a direct obj; it is either used absolutely (e.g., Num 23:19; Prov 14:5) or with ב (e.g., 2 Kgs 4:16) or ל "(lie) to" (e.g., Ps 78:36), and it does not mean "falsify" or "belie." This may also be the reading adopted by Larcher, who translates "you disappointed the right of the orphan," and is followed by JB "you cheated orphaned children of their rights" (similarly NJB).

18.a. Terrien thinks this verse may be a marginal note wrongly inserted into the text, and he sets it within square brackets. Kissane moves to this point v 21.

18.b. כי is emphatic "indeed"; for other examples, see *Note* 22:26.b. It is deleted by Beer (*BHK frt*), Hölscher, Larcher, Fohrer, and Pope as a dittograph of the last letters (כו) of the previous verse.

חמה seems to be the noun "wrath," but the syntax is odd (כי־חמה פן "indeed wrath lest"), and the verb should not be masc when the subj is fem and precedes the verb. RSV "Beware lest wrath entice you into scoffing" (similarly RVmg, Driver–Gray, Fohrer, de Wilde, Gray) translates פֶּן, lit. "lest," as "beware" (unlike the explanation mentioned below), effectively moving חמה to the פן clause. The anger would be Job's anger at being treated like the wicked. KJV, RV "Because there is wrath, beware lest he take thee away with his stroke" (similarly Strahan) attempts to make a whole clause out of the word חמה "wrath," which would in this case be God's wrath that Job must guard himself against. NJPS has "Let anger at his affluence not mislead you," the פן "lest" presumably being absorbed into the "let not," but the translation here depends on that of v 17, "You are obsessed with the case of the wicked," which seems improbable.

Most, however, agree that the word should be vocalized חֲמֵה, as the impv of the Aram. חמי "see," thus "beware" (so Beer [*BHK frt*], Hölscher, Kissane, Larcher, Terrien, Pope, Gordis, Gerleman [*BHS prp*], Sicre Díaz, Hartley, JB, NJB, NIV). This is the view adopted in the *Translation* above.

Among other philologically based proposals may be mentioned: (1) G. R. Driver argued that חמה means not only "hot anger, fury" but also "fiery wine," and translates "(Beware) lest fiery wine in plenty incite thee" ("On *ḥēmāh* 'hot anger, fury' and also 'fiery wine,'" *TZ* 14 [1958] 133–35), explaining the lack of congruence between subj and verb as "due to the intervening particle." It remains unexplained, however, why Elihu should be lecturing Job on the dangers of strong drink. Driver's suggestion is adopted in NEB, but in an even more implausible form: "do not be led astray by lavish gifts of wine." It is one thing to warn a person *not to drink so much wine* as to cloud his judgment; it is another to advise him *against accepting gifts* of wine (why wine in particular?).

(2) Guillaume relates חמה to Arab. *ḥimā'* "ransom" (Lane, 652a) and proposes a Heb. verb חמה "pay a ransom." Arab. *ḥamā,* however, is a general verb for "protect" (Lane, 651a), and provides little evidence for such a Heb. verb. (3) Dhorme connects חמה with Arab. *ḥmy* "defend, protect, keep safe" (Lane, 651a), thus "beware," similar to the השמר "keep yourself, beware" of v 21. (4) Bickell[2] and Budde implausibly saw here חם "heat," in reference to the heat of God's wrath, translating "That

things get hot should not mislead you to mockery." Fedrizzi is inclined to this reading, translating "Let no anger lead you to mockery," but it is hard to see what merit the emendation has over the reading חמה.

Among emendations, Beer (*BH*[2]) mentions לְחֵמָה "for heat, anger," כִּי־חֵמָה "for heat," and כְּחֻמָּה "when it is hot."

18.c. Understanding the judgment (דין) that Job is suffering (v 17a) as the subj of יסיתך. Others think the subj is impersonal and translate with a passive; so Dhorme "Take care lest a generous gift lead you astray," Gordis "lest you be seduced by your wealth."

18.d. סֵפֶק is variously understood: (1) BDB takes it as "mockery" (from ספק "slap, clap"; see further *Notes* 34:26.b, 37.c, and *Comment* there); thus RSV "scoffing" (similarly Delitzsch, Driver–Gray, Fohrer, de Wilde; cf. *DCH,* vol. 6, *s.v.* סֶפֶק I). (2) Others think it is a different word, meaning "chastisement" (Dillmann, Duhm, Peake, Moffatt), sometimes comparing Arab. *ṣafaqa* (Gerleman [*BHS al*]; cf. *DCH,* vol. 6, *s.v.* סֶפֶק III; for *ṣafaqa* "slap, clap," cf. Lane, 1700a). (3) Tur-Sinai thinks ספק strictly means "clench the fist" (as also at 20:22; Lam 2:15), and translates "For neither shall anger induce thee with the (clenched) fist," but this does not connect with the second colon "nor shall great ransom mislead thee."

(4) Commonly, but inappropriately, ספק is regarded as a byform of שֶׂפֶק "sufficiency" (at 20:22; cf. *DCH,* vol. 6, *s.v.* סֶפֶק II); so *HALOT,* 2:765b, and RV "lest thou be led astray by thy sufficiency," JB "In future beware of being led astray by riches," NJB "Beware of being led astray by abundance," NIV "Be careful that no one entices you by riches," NJPS "let anger at his affluence not mislead you." Similarly NEB "do not be led astray by lavish gifts of wine." Pope has "Beware, lest he entice by abundance," but it is not clear who "he" is; Gray's "lest one entice you with satiety" resolves that issue. The subj is taken as impersonal also by Dhorme, with "Take care lest a generous gift cause you to err," followed by Rowley "Beware lest one entice you by a generous gift" (similarly Sicre Díaz, Hartley). Such advice could only be meant as a warning against the corruption of justice once Job is returned to prosperity, but it must rather be that Elihu's focus is on Job's situation here and now. (5) Least plausible of all is Guillaume's proposal (*Studies,* 125) of a new סֶפֶק "meanness" (cf. Arab. *ṣafiqa* "be mean, stingy"), translating "[pay a ransom lest you be tempted by] meanness." But it is not possible to identify this Arab. word since it is not to be found in Lane or Wehr–Cowan (*ṣafaqa* is "slap, clap" [Lane, 1700a]).

Emendations: (1) Beer (*BHK frt*) deletes the prep ב prefixing ספק, thus suggesting that ספק may be the subj of יסיתך. Similarly Peake, rendering "Let not chastisement entice thee to wrath" (but the word order would be strange); so too Hölscher, Terrien. (2) Budde reads לְשֹׂפֶק "to scorn," (3) Bickell suggests בְּשֹׂפֵק "against the chastiser," and (4) Duhm and Beer (*BH*[2] *prps*) מִשְּׂפֹק "[lest] chastising [lead you into anger]," though the noun does not occur elsewhere.

18.e. כפר "ransom," as at 33:24 (the verb פדה "ransom, redeem" is used in a similar sense at 5:20; 6:23; 33:28). Hölscher thinks it is a bribe, bakshish, given to corrupt justice (similarly NIV, NJPS, NEB); it is at least money Job would use to buy himself out of difficulties in the past. רב כפר is lit. "greatness of the ransom" (Driver–Gray, RSV). Another sense to that adopted in the *Comment* is that Job should not let the greatness of the ransom he has to pay (i.e., his severe sufferings) turn him from the right path (so Peake; cf. Moffatt "let not the cost of discipline deter you"). But Elihu does not seem to be arguing that suffering is itself the ransom paid for deliverance from punishment; it is more that obedience to God's instruction is the ransom.

18.f. נטה hiph is "incline, turn aside," and thus, in a moral sense, "entice, deceive, lead astray"(cf. BDB, 640b; *DCH,* 5:675a §5 "pervert [justice]").

19.a. שׁוּעַ has three possible meanings: (1) "Cry, cry for help" (from שׁוע "cry out"), as in 30:24 (which is, however, not without problems). So BDB, 1002b; *HALOT,* 4:1444b; Delitzsch, Terrien, de Wilde, RSV, GNB. (2) "Wealth"; cf. שׁוֹעַ "noble, eminent" (*HALOT,* 4:1444b), and Arab. *wasi'a* "be wide, spacious; be prosperous; be noble, generous" (Freytag, 4:465a; Lane, 3052c; Wehr–Cowan, 1067b), and *sa'atun* "amplitude, wealth" (Lane, 3053b; and cf. also ישׁע hiph "deliver," perhaps in the sense of "make spacious"), as in Isa 32:5; Job 34:19; 34:20 (emended). So Driver–Gray, Gordis, Sicre Díaz, Gray, KJV, NIV, NJPS, NEB. (3) "Deliverance," a word not otherwise attested but equivalent to יֵשַׁע and יְשׁוּעָה "deliverance," as proposed by Hartley.

With the first meaning, the colon would be "Will your cry set you outside of affliction?" (thus Delitzsch, Budde). With the second meaning, it would be "Will your wealth draw up a line of battle (ערך) (for you) (so that you are) not in affliction?" See further on next *Note.* With the third meaning, the translation "Can one arrange your deliverance without distress or without all kinds of mighty efforts?" is offered by Hartley. ערך, however, never seems to mean "arrange" in the sense of "effect," but only in the sense of "arrange in order," which would be inappropriate if "deliverance" were the obj.

Among emendations of the whole colon as well as of the word itself: (1) Budde reads שַׁוְעֲךָ "your cry." (2) Duhm and Beer (*BH*[2] *al*) read שִׂיחֲךָ לוֹ "your complaint to him" (cf. 23:2). (3) Fohrer and de Wilde read היערך שַׁוְעֲךָ לוֹ "can your cry be a match for him?" or "can you with your cry compete against him?" (the form שַׁוְעֲךָ is not attested, but שַׁוְעִי occurs at Ps 5:2 [3]); but whether Job can compete against God seems far from the topic of Elihu's speech. (4) Beer (*BH*[2] *frt*) reads יִשְׁעֲךָ "your safety," but it is hard to see what this might mean in the context. (5) Terrien translates "Would you attack him with your cries of distress?," presumably reading הֲתַעֲרֹךְ שועך בְּצַר לוֹ (unless שועך is taken as the subj of יערך). This would make for a very disjointed sequence of thought in this strophe.

(6) Kissane emended to הוֹעֵד כְּשׁוֹעַ כְּלֹא־בֵצֶר "Arraign the rich as well as the penniless," but the proposal is forced: יעד hiph "arraign" occurs only rarely (BDB, 417a; *DCH,* 4:241a), and should Job be "arraigning" the rich? Furthermore, שׁוֹעַ means "noble, independent" (BDB, 447b; *HALOT,* 4:1444b) rather than "rich"; and לֹא־בֶצֶר, lit. "no-gold," is an unparalleled term for "penniless," even if we have לא־כח "no-strength" for "weak" at 26:2 and לא חכמה "no-wisdom" for "foolish" at 26:3. (7) Kissane also offers an alternative reading הַעֲרֵךְ שׁוֹעַ כְּלֹא־בֶצֶר "treat alike the rich and the penniless," but while ערך can sometimes mean "compare" (BDB, 789b, §2a; *DCH*, vol. 6, *s.v.*; but not *HALOT,* 2:885a), there is no parallel to a meaning "treat alike," and the same difficulties with שׁוֹעַ and לֹא־בֶצֶר apply here as already mentioned. Above all, there is no rationale for these generalized moralisms addressed to Job at this point.

(8) JB "Prosecute the rich, not merely the penniless; strong-armed men as well as those who are powerless" (NJB "Take the powerful to law, not merely the penniless, those whose arm is strong, not merely the weak") follows Larcher, who appears to have adapted Kissane's proposal and read הַעֲרֵךְ עָשִׁיר כִּבְלֹא בֶצֶר וְדַלִּים וְאַמִּי צִי־כֹח "compare the rich to the one without gold, and the poor to those with a powerful arm." (9) To similar effect Lévêque, 587, read הַעֲרֵךְ שׁוֹעַ כְּלֹא בֶצֶר וּכְדַלִּים אַמִּיצֵי־כֹחַ "consider (ערך hiph impv) the noble as equal to the one without gold, and the poor to the powerful" (correcting Lévêque's וּכְדַלִים).

19.b. ערך has four main senses according to *HALOT,* 2:884b: "lay out in rows; get ready, set in order; draw up a battle formation; confront." ערך appears elsewhere in Job as "(of the terrors of God) array in battle formation" (6:4), "marshal (words) as in a battle line" (32:14; 33:5), "set out (a case) in order" (13:18; 23:4; 37:19), and "equal, compare (gold, etc.) with wisdom" (28:17, 19). The most appropriate sense here is the military one, wealth being pictured as potentially drawing up a line of defense around Job, while Elihu denies that is possible when the attack comes from God as his punishment. RSV has "will your cry avail to keep you from distress," and NJPS, NEB "avail," NIV "sustain you," so perhaps they take the same view of ערך, except that their translations are rather loose and do not bring out the military metaphor.

Other senses are proposed: (1) Pope is attracted by the "juridical" sense and translates "avail with him"; but the juridical sense is "lay out (arguments) in order," while "avail" is more the military sense. (2) The sense "equal, compare" is drawn upon for the translation "suffice" (RV; cf. Driver–Gray "be equal [to it, *i.e.* suffice to do this]," who are tempted to add a suff יַעַרְכֶהָ "be equal to it"). (3) KJV "Will he esteem thy riches?" derives from the hiph of ערך "assess" (Buxtorf, 585, rendered *aestimavit*), at Lev 27:8, 12, 14; 2 Kgs 23:35 (so Gesenius, *Thesaurus,* 1069b; BDB, 790a; *HALOT,* 2:885a). The translation perhaps invites a slight emendation to the hiph form יַעֲרִיךְ. It is a not unattractive rendering, though not considered by modern commentators. Hölscher takes a similar view of ערך as "esteem" or rather (intransitively) "be sufficient."

Various emendations have been proposed: (1) Tur-Sinai reads הֲיְעִירְךָ, from עור hiph "stir up," thus "should thy wealth stir thee up, induce thee to pervert judgment?" The trouble with this is that Elihu's point here does not seem to be Job's execution of justice, but how he will respond to the challenge of divinely imposed suffering. Gordis adopts Tur-Sinai's emendation, but understands the verb to mean "watch, guard" (which he argues it means at 8:6 and Deut 32:11). This is not, however, a recognized meaning of the verb. It is presumably Tur-Sinai's emendation that is referred to by Gerleman (*BHS prp*). (2) Gray reads יַעֲרֹךְ "[will all your wealth] be comparable [to what you have lost]?" (3) Bickell, followed by Budde, emends the first colon to הֲיַעֲרֹךְ שַׁוְעֲךָ לוֹ "can your cry be set forth before him?"

19.c. לֹא בצר, lit. "not in distress," may be explained as "a condition of not being in distress" (cf. Gordis), and so in the context of the colon "defend you (so that you are) not in distress." The "distress" is of course the suffering Job is experiencing at God's hand; it contrasts with the צר "distress" from which Job in his former life had been protected (v 16). Driver–Gray simply understand לא בצר as "without affliction" (similarly Moffatt), meaning that suffering is indispensable; the phrases

לא בחכמה "without wisdom" (4:21), and לא ביד "without human agency" (34:20) are compared for the unusual position of the prep.

Alternatively, צר may be "adversary" rather than "distress." Thus Habel takes לא בצר as an independent sentence, "Not against the Adversary!," an allusion to Death as in v 16.

Emendations: (1) Another approach is to take בצר as בֶּצֶר "gold" (noted by *HALOT,* 1:149a; *DCH,* 2:247a). KJV has "Will he esteem thy riches? no, not gold, nor all the forces of strength." Hölscher makes בֶּצֶר the first word of the second colon, "will fine gold and all kinds of expenditure (suffice)?" Kissane, followed by JB and NJB, translated "the penniless" (lit. "no gold"); but see further *Note* 19.a above.

(2) Yet another possibility is to see בצר as a verbal form. Bickell, followed by Budde, reads לא as לוֹ "to him," attached to the preceding words, and vocalizes בָּצֻר "cut off," thus "[before him] (who is) cut off from (i.e., inaccessible to) [all exertions of strength]." This seems a somewhat strained interpretation of בָּצֻר. (3) Gray reads לְבָצְרְךָ "to what you have lost," lit. "what you have had cut away" (בצר; cf. also on 42:2, but it may be a different verb there). (4) A number of scholars prefer to read לא as לוֹ (so Bickell, Budde, Duhm, Dhorme, Hölscher, Fedrizzi, Sicre Díaz); thus, for example, Pope "Will your opulence avail with him in trouble?" (5) A final solution to the problem of the phrase לא בצר is to delete it as a gloss (so Fohrer).

19.d. וכל מאמצי־כח, lit. "and all exertions of strength" (מַאֲמָץ occurs only here [BDB, 55b; *DCH,* 5:119b], but it is a normal formation from אמץ "be strong"). Contrary to Tur-Sinai, Hölscher, Pope, Fedrizzi, Gordis, there is no reason to think the word means, or also means, "wealth."

Kissane read וְדַלִּים וְאַמִּצֵי־כֹחַ "and the weak and the mighty in strength," which is appropriate only if his understanding of the first colon is adopted; he is followed by JB, NJB.

20.a. NEB transposes vv 20 and 21, with no very evident improvement. Beer (*BHK*) thinks v 20 is doubtful, while Bickell and Friedrich Delitzsch delete it.

The whole verse is unexpected (why should Elihu imagine that Job is longing for the night?), and it is likely that the MT is corrupt. None of the proposals made for emendation of it, however, is convincing enough to be adopted: (1) Duhm emended the verse to אַל־תַּשְׁאֲךָ הֹלֵלֹת לַעֲלוֹת עִם מִתְחַכֵּם "let not folly deceive you, to exalt yourself (עלה piel inf constr) with one who thinks himself wise," which is more ingenious than persuasive; it has nothing to do with the present context; it is, however, followed by Moffatt. (2) Hölscher adopted Duhm's first colon, אַל־תַּשְׁאֲךָ הֹלֵלֹת "let not folly deceive you," and then emended to לַעֲנוֹת עֲמִיתְךָ תַּחְתֶּיךָ "to oppress your fellow [beneath you]," which is equally irrelevant to the context.

(3) De Wilde also takes a hint from Duhm, rewriting the line to אַל־תִּשְׁמַע הֹלְלִים לעלות עִמָּם אָרְחוֹתָם "Listen not to fools, to go with them in their paths." This piece of generalized sententiousness ("a commonplace of wisdom," as de Wilde himself allows), however, makes no sense at this point; what is more, שמע would need to be followed by ל or אל since with a direct obj it means "hear" (as at Gen 27:6; Num 11:10; Jer 20:1; 26:7; Dan 8:13; Eccl 7:21) rather than "listen to." הֹלְלִים is not attested for "fools" (the word would be *hōlălîm,* not *ḥōlălîm,* though the ptcp הוֹלְלִים apparently means "arrogant" at Ps 5:5 (6); 73:3; 75:4 (5), and there is a הוֹלֵל and הוֹלֵלָה "folly"; and לעלות אָרְחוֹתָם is a strange way of saying "to go in their paths." (4) Lévêque, 587, proposed ("without enthusiasm") אַל־תִּשָּׂא פְּנֵי פְּלִיל לַעֲנוֹת עַם מִתַּחְתָּיו "do not show partiality to a judge, lest the people be oppressed under him"; but there is no reason why Elihu should be offering this advice to Job at this point. (5) Fedrizzi suggested אל־תשאף הֹלֵלוֹת לְהַעֲמִיס תַּחְתָּם "Do not long for folly so as to burden yourself under it." Like so many of the other proposals, it seems irrelevant to the context; as well, תַּחְתָּם fails to agree with הֹלֵלוֹת, עמס is not elsewhere attested in the hiph, and it is uncertain that if it did it would mean "burden oneself" since in the qal it means "load" or "carry a load."

20.b. For שאף, BDB, 983b, notes two verbs: שאף I is "gasp, pant after" (cf. 5:5, and especially 7:2 where a slave "pants after" the evening shadow [צל]). שאף II, however, means "crush, trample on" (e.g., Amos 8:4); so Kissane, and Larcher, adopting Kissane's emendation of לילה "night" to בְּלִי לָךְ "not belonging to you." NEB "Have no fear if in the breathless terrors of the night you see nations vanish where they stand" is hard to decipher as a translation of the Heb.; perhaps שאף is understood as "pant with fear," but "breathless terrors" seems to repeat that.

20.c. For לילה "night," Kissane reads בְּלִי־לָךְ "[oppress not them that] belong not to thee," an awkward phrase, and feasible only if his emendation in the next colon is also accepted. בְּלִי־לוֹ "what is not his" (18:15) is an apparent parallel, but the text there is questionable. Larcher follows him, and so too do JB "do not trample on those you do not know" and NJB "do not crush people you do not know."

20.d. עמים seems plainly "peoples, nations." But emendations are proposed: (1) Kissane reads עַמֶּיךָ "your kinsfolk" in place of עמים "peoples"; he does not attempt to justify this sense of the pl of עַם, and it is not recognized by BDB or *HALOT* (but cf. *DCH*, vol. 6, *s.v.* §4, and the separate word עַם II "kinsman," which is perhaps how it should be analyzed), but we could compare Gen 17:14; 25:8, 17; 35:29; perhaps 49:10; Exod 30:33, 38; 31:14; etc. He is followed by Rowley and by JB, NJB "your relations." The resultant translation, however, is far from plausible: "Oppress not them that belong not to thee, That thy kinsmen may mount up in their place." But it is followed by Larcher, BJ, JB, NJB. (2) De Wilde reads עִמָּם "with them." (3) A minimal emendation which changes the sense of the second colon radically is proposed by Davidson: reading עָבִים "clouds" for עמים "peoples" yields "Pant not for the night, for the thick clouds to rise in their place"; the only difficulty with this is that תחתיו is on this reading not very well explained; do clouds have a place where they rise?

20.e. עלה can mean "go up, depart" (as in Isa 5:24), or in the hiph "take away (from life)" (as in Ps 102:24 [25]); cf. NIV "to drag people away." BDB, 749b §2c, also takes לַעֲלוֹת here as hiph inf (i.e., הַעֲלוֹת plus ל)." Gordis and Hartley take it as a qal, thus "go up, vanish."

20.f. תחתם, lit. "under them," i.e., "in their place" (as RSV), "where they stand" (NEB); for this sense of תחת, cf. BDB, 1065b §2, and Exod 16:29 שבו איש תחתיו "each of you stay in his place." NIV "[to drag people away] from their homes" could only be justified with an emendation to מִתַּחְתָּם (which Beer [*BHK prps*], Sicre Díaz, and Gray in fact propose). It does not seem likely that Elihu imagines Job has a longing to drive people out of their homes.

21.a. Kissane moves the verse to follow v 17, as the conclusion to the strophe.

21.b. כי־על־זה, lit. "for on account of this." It seems incorrect to understand "this" as "iniquity" (as do most), since iniquity (עול) is a choice that still lies ahead of Job, not exactly the cause of his present sufferings. It is in order to see whether Job will turn to iniquity that he is being tested; "this" (זה) refers to the words immediately following.

Among emendations, we should note Dillmann's אָוֶן "iniquity" for על־זה "because of this," i.e., "you have chosen iniquity rather than affliction," and, to the same effect, עַוְלָה "iniquity" (Budde, Duhm, Beer [BH^2], Peake, Strahan, Driver–Gray, Beer [*BHK frt*], Fohrer). But such a reading, however rhetorically effective (Moffatt "you prefer sin to suffering!," Gordis "you would rather sin than suffer," Hartley "evil, which you seem to prefer to affliction"), cannot be right, since Elihu is not setting himself up as Job's judge, but as his adviser, laying before him the doctrine of the two ways (vv 11–12). Moreover, since Elihu believes that iniquity leads inevitably to affliction, it is hard to see how he can imagine these as the two choices that have been lain before Job. In any case, what is the point of warning Job in the first colon not to turn to iniquity if in the second colon he has already made his choice (cf. Dhorme)?

Two philological proposals may be noted: (1) NAB "you have preferred carousal to affliction" apparently follows Guillaume in reading עֲלִיזָה, an otherwise unattested noun from עלז "exult" (cf. Arab. *'aliza* and Heb. עליץ "exult"; cf. *DCH*, vol. 6, *s.v.*; the Arab. is, however, elusive); similarly Gray, translating "you have preferred exultation to affliction." A less plausible charge against Job is hard to imagine. (2) Guillaume also offers the quite attractive translation "you have preferred impatience to resignation," reading על־זה as עֲלָזָה "impatience" (cf. *DCH*, vol. 6, *s.v.*; cf. Arab. *'aliza;* but this Arab. word also cannot be found in the standard lexica) and finding a new word עֳנִי "resignation" (cf. Arab. *'aniya* "be resigned"); but that Arab. verb means rather "suffer difficulty, contend" (Lane, 2180c), and "be resigned" is not among the renderings offered by Lane.

21.c. בחר is usually "choose," and many translate "this you have chosen rather than affliction" (RSV), "which you seem to prefer to affliction" (NIV); cf. also Gray, NAB "preferred." However, בחר is never followed by the prep על (2 Sam 19:39 is a special case, where על seems to mean "on [my] account"). It is much preferable to emend the vowels and read בֻּחַרְתָּ pual "you have been tested" (so Rowley, Gerleman [*BHS frt*], Sicre Díaz [*vel*], van der Lugt; Dhorme, Hölscher, Kissane, Larcher, Pope, Fedrizzi, de Wilde, Sicre Díaz [*vel*], NEB [Brockington] make it בֹּחַרְתָּ), whether "refine, test" is regarded as a separate sense of בחר (BDB, 104a; *HALOT,* 1:120a) or as a separate verb (בחר III, according to *DCH,* 2:139b; cf. Aram. בחן; and cf. G. R. Driver, in B. Gemser, *Sprüche Salomos,* 2d ed., HAT 1.16 [Tübingen: Mohr (Siebeck), 1963] 111–14 [112]). Thus NRSV "because of that you have been tried by affliction," JB "for such has been the true cause of your trials," NJB "for this is why affliction is testing you now," NEB "for that is why you are tried by affliction"; and similarly in the *Translation* above. It must be admitted, though, that בחר does not occur elsewhere in the pual (the reference in BDB, 104a, is an error, as Gordis points out).

21.d. מעני "by affliction," the מן signifying the "efficient cause" (GKC, §121f), though admittedly ב would be more usual.

22.a. ישׂגיב is the only example of the hiph of שׂגב "be high." BDB, 960b, translates "[God] acts exaltedly," and Delitzsch likewise "acteth loftily," Driver–Gray "showeth loftiness, doeth loftily." The English versions, however, are content with "is exalted" (RSV), "sublime" (NAB, NJB), "towers in majesty" (NEB), "is pre-eminent in majesty" (REB). NJPS "God is beyond reach in His power" perhaps takes a hint from BDB's gloss "be (inaccessibly) high," but although what is high is frequently inaccessible there is no reason to think that inaccessibility is part of the meaning of שׂגב. KJV "God exalteth by his power" regards the hiph as a true causative.

Ehrlich, noting the frequency of the niph in reference to God (Isa 2:11, 17; 33:5) and his name (Isa 12:4; Ps 148:13), proposes to read נִשְׂגָּב כֹּחוֹ "his power is exalted" (niph ptcp), but the change is unnecessary. So too is the reading of Beer (*BH*[2] *frt*), יַשְׂגִּי "is high" (from שׂגא), the final ב being a dittograph; יַשְׂגִּיא, however, is adopted by NAB (*Textual Notes,* 378).

Guillaume would rather see here a new שׂגב "doom to destruction" (cf. Arab. *šajaba* "perish" [Lane, 1505b], not *sajaba,* as Guillaume writes).

22.b. KJV has "by his power," but other versions take ב as "in."

22.c. Dahood reads וּמִי "and who?," presuming כחו ומי had been written כחו מי by haplography (*Psalms III,* 22).

22.d. מוֹרֶה is normal, though rare, for "teacher" (elsewhere in the Heb. Bible only Prov 5:13; Isa 30:20 [of God], though common in DSS). The connection of the two cola is not obvious, and it is interesting that LXX has δυνάστης "ruler," perhaps representing מָרֵא, Aram. for "master, ruler" (though LXX may be only an interpretation rather than reflecting a different Heb. *Vorlage*). If this were the original, it would have to be called an Aramaism (which is not a great problem, for שׂגיא in v 26 and 37:23 is an unquestioned one). This reading is adopted by de Wilde, Gray, NJPS "who governs like him?," and NEB "who wields such sovereign power as he?," reading מָרֶה as a Heb. equivalent of Aram. מָרֵא (Brockington). Dhorme translates "Who is a master like Him?," but in his note says it is unnecessary to change מורה to מָרֵא; the French *maître* is a proper translation of מורה, but not so the Eng. "master." Driver–Gray translate "Who is a teacher like unto him?," but comment that the LXX reading gives a far better parallel to the first colon. Hölscher translates "Who is a master like him?," but does not say he is emending the text (perhaps he means "teacher" by *Meister*). Fedrizzi, translating *maestro,* explains מורה as "one who makes known his will," but that is by no means a correct interpretation of the term. מורה is sometimes connected allusively to תורה "law, instruction" (so, e.g., Gordis), but such a connection can only be misleading in the present context, where law is entirely out of the frame. Tur-Sinai asserted that the word means not "teacher," but one who makes rulings in a court; but he does not advance any evidence.

Dahood derived מורה from a new מרה "be strong," which he explained as a byform of מרר "be strong" (*Psalms III,* 21–22; cf. מרה IV, *DCH,* 5:481b). He translates "puissant" but does not suggest, as he might well have, that it is this term, rather than מרא, that lies behind LXX. I. Eitan ("Studies in Hebrew Roots," *JQR* NS 14 [1923–24] 31–52 [31–34]) similarly understood the term as "governor, ruler," but on the basis of a supposed connection with Arab. *'imra'* and *'imru'* "man" (Wehr–Cowan, 901b); Eitan gives the form as *'amrun*; *'amīr* "prince, emir" (Wehr–Cowan, 27a) would be a better cognate.

Ehrlich read מוֹרָא "object of fear" (cf. Isa 8:13), and Guillaume presumably the same, translating "Who is so terrible as he?"

23.a. פקד is "pay attention to, visit (in blessing or punishment), appoint." Unlike 34:13, where פקד meant "assign, entrust," here it must be "direct, prescribe," but parallels are hard to find (but see *DCH,* vol. 6, *s.v.* §4).

NJPS "Who ever reproached Him for His conduct?" and Hartley "Who has held him accountable for his way?" attempt to create more of a parallel with the second colon, but there is no evidence that פקד can mean that (though it can mean "visit to test," as in 7:18; Ps 17:3). Kissane thinks it is "call to account." It is no objection to this interpretation (against Rowley) that Job has never claimed the right to punish God, for the statement is much more than a reproof of Job.

23.b. דרך "way" is also "way of life, behavior," as in 4:6; 13:15; etc. M. Dahood ("Some Northwest-Semitic Words in Job," *Bib* 38 [1957] 306–20 [320]) takes דרך as "power" (cf. on 26:14; and cf. *DCH,* 2:472b), and translates "Who gave him his power?," no doubt understanding פקד as "assign." Similarly Gray "Who has prescribed his government for him?" Pope wonders if the poet intended both "power" and "conduct," an unlikely supposition.

23.c. Habel translates פעלת עולה "you created the wrong way," but there is no need to make the language so specific.

24.a. Fedrizzi strangely moves 36:1 ("and Elihu added and said") to this point, as signifying the beginning of the hymn (which he defines as 36:24–37:24).

24.b. תשגיא "you should declare (his work) to be exalted," the hiph being declarative. Tur-Sinai's emendation to הַשְׂגִּיא "[remember that] he worketh great things" is unparalleled and has nothing to recommend it.

24.c. שׁררו, lit. "have sung" (שׁיר polel, though Gordis says שׁור is "a metaplastic form for שׁיר"). Fohrer translates "(constantly) sing," feeling the verb needs some strengthening. KJV "which men behold" derives the word from שׁור "see" (as in 7:8; 17:15; not, however, elsewhere in polel unless שׁוֹרֵר "enemy" is a polel ptcp, as BDB, 1004a); in this it followed the rabbinic tradition of Rashi and ibn Ezra, which is also supported by Tur-Sinai. Guillaume invokes a new שׁרר "rejoice" (cf. Arab. *sarra* [Lane, 1337a]), as at 33:27, translating "whereat men rejoice."

25.a. Budde omits vv 25–26.

25.b. בו "on it" seems plainly to have פעלו "his work" as antecedent (so too Sicre Díaz); REB "all mankind gazes at him" is implausible since the idea of looking at God is problematic in the Heb. Bible. Some think that the verb implies looking "with delight" (so Delitzsch, Duhm, Driver–Gray, Dhorme, Rowley, Fohrer, Fedrizzi, Moffatt "all men love to see") or "with amazement" (Hölscher), but there is nothing in either the word or the context that suggests that.

NEB "All men stand back from him" depends on the proposal by G. R. Driver of a חזה "be opposite" (cf. Arab. *ḥadhā* "urge on," V "vie, contend, pursue" [Lane, 532b; Wehr–Cowan, 163b]), which he finds also in 8:17, where he translated it "run against" ("Studies in the Vocabulary of the Old Testament VI," *JTS* 34 [1933] 375–85 [381]; "Problems in Job and Proverbs Reconsidered," *JTS* 40 [1939] 391–94 [391]; cf. Thomas, 8:110–11; Gray "face him [from a distance]"; *DCH,* 3:181b). None of these renderings of the supposed Heb. cognate is supported by the Arab. *ḥadhā,* however.

25.c. מרחוק "from afar" (as in 2:12; 36:3), not "from the most distant days" (Ehrlich).

26.a. Budde, Duhm, Beer (*BH*^{2}), Moffatt, Hölscher omit the line as irrelevant to the context, or too like v 22a. Driver–Gray think the second colon out of place or corrupt.

26.b. שׂגיא "great," only here and at 37:23 (שׂגיא־כח "great in power"), though common in Aram. Ehrlich, however, translated "very old," comparing גדול "great" for "older" (brother); similarly Blommerde. But, despite the parallelism, there is no evidence that the word itself means "old."

26.c. מספר שניו ולא־חקר is lit. "the number of his years and no finding out," the ו "and" being out of its normal place at the beginning of the clause (similarly at 4:6; 20:18; 23:12). A variant reading, which does not presume ו is out of its usual place, is that of M. Dahood ("Hebrew-Ugaritic Lexicography V," *Bib* 48 [1967] 421–38 [428–29]), מְסַפֵּר, lit. "from numbering" (piel inf), i.e., "[his years are] without number(ing)"; so too at 16:22 (*q.v.*). He is followed by Pope in both places. Gray deletes the *waw.*

Duhm thought the whole line probably inauthentic, but proposed anyway that we should replace מספר שניו "the number of his years" with מַעֲשָׂיו "his deeds"; it is a prosaic suggestion. Tur-Sinai too thought the reference to the number of his years was "inapposite," attributing it to the formulaic language.

27.a. On the ground that vv 27–28 and 31 belong together, de Wilde moves vv 29–30 to precede them.

27.b. גרע occurred recently, at v 7, where God did not "withdraw" his eyes from the righteous; JB rather improbably follows this sense with "keeps the raindrops back," and Kissane "withholdeth the drops of water," i.e., he stops it raining, "dissolving the showers into mist, which otherwise the clouds would spill in floods over all mankind" (similarly Guillaume).

Preferable is the translation "draw up" (RSV, NIV, Dhorme, Hölscher, Gordis, Habel), presumably from the sea and earth into the clouds; it is not strictly drops that are "drawn up" (though the water vapor will become drops), but נטף may well refer to "exudation" as well as to formed drops (Moffatt thought to evade the problem in this translation of the verb by rendering "he draws up water from the sea," but נטף does not mean "water").

Simply "draw," as Pope's and Hartley's "He draws the waterdrops" (similarly Terrien), is quite unsatisfactory since no clear idea is given of what such "drawing" would consist of. Others think the word means "restrain" (BDB, 175b, cites Job 15:4, 8 in this sense, but that is doubtful); thus NAB "he holds in check," but the sequel is truly difficult to comprehend: "the waterdrops that filter in rain through his mists." Less credible are JPS "He draweth away the drops of water" (from where?), Fohrer "he takes out" (the drops from his storehouse or from the heavenly ocean), NJPS "He forms the droplets of water," Delitzsch, Davidson "he draws down" (from the waters above the firmament), and Budde "he gathers" (from the atmosphere), for there is no evidence that גרע can have any of those meanings.

In 15:8 גרע had meant "limit," and there are good examples of a sense "diminish, reduce" (Exod

5:8; 21:10); cf. 15:4 where it means "reduce in significance, slight." Thus KJV "he maketh small the drops of water," NJB "makes the raindrops small." This would produce an acceptable sense, though it would not suggest the process of evaporation, which does seem to be in view here.

Among philologically based suggestions, we may note: (1) Another גרע is proposed by F. Perles ("The Fourteenth Edition of Gesenius-Buhl's Dictionary," *JQR* 18 [1906] 383–90 [384]), meaning "sip, suck in" (cf. Arab. *jara'a* and *jari'a* "swallow" [Lane, 410c]); Gesenius–Buhl, 149a; *DCH,* 2:377a (where it is wrongly glossed as "drip"); he has the odd idea of God sucking in the water drops and then giving them forth purified in the form of rain. (2) Tur-Sinai also invoked Arab. *jara'a,* which he glossed as "swallow water" (cf. *jur'a* "draught"), but then translated גרע as "filter." His understanding is that God filters the water of the clouds as through a filter in the mouth of a bottle, and that is why rain falls in drops; he translates "he maketh drip the drops of water." (3) *HALOT,* 1:204a, and Ges[18], 1:230b, note a גרע II "draw up," comparing MH "hold water, drip" (Jastrow, 271b "form globules, drop"; P. Reymond, *L'eau, sa vie, et sa signification dans l'Ancien Testament,* VTSup 6 [Leiden: Brill, 1958] 205–6 has "attracts") and Arab. *jari'a* "slurp, gulp" (cf. B. Jacob, "Erklärung einiger Hiob-Stellen," *ZAW* 32 [1912] 278–87 [287]). But the MH senses are not close to that of the Arab., and the sense "drip" is not well supported. (4) It may be in reference to this MH word that Gerleman says (*BHS*) that גרע means "drip, drop, distill" (Lat. *stillare*), but it is doubtful that the root in Semitic ever signifies anything but the *intake* of moisture. It is the next verb, זקק, that should be considered for the sense "distill." (5) E. F. Sutcliffe ("Notes on Job, Textual and Exegetical: 6, 18; 11, 12; 31, 35; 34, 17. 20; 36, 27–33; 37, 1," *Bib* 30 [1949] 66–90 [79–81]), explaining well the sense "form globules" as merely an adaptation of the Gk. κάρυον, argues that גרע is really a byform of גדע "cut" and that its true sense is "separate"; since this is not particularly suitable here, he thinks a form of פרע "let go unrestrained" is perhaps the original reading.

Among emendations, we may note that of Duhm, Gesenius–Buhl, 149a, Driver–Gray, Beer (*BHK*), Gerleman (*BHS prps*), Lévêque, 588, Habel, Gray to נְטָפִים מִיָּם "drops from the sea," which NEB followed with "He draws up drops of water from the sea" (so too *HALOT,* 2:695a); but "drops" *tout court* is perhaps strange (Dhorme), so NEB would also accept נִטְפֵי־מַיִם מִיָּם "drops of water from the sea" (cf. Brockington), a reading that Dhorme too contemplates.

27.c. נֶטֶף "drop" occurs only here (נָטָף "incense," perhaps "stacte," is a different word; cf. BDB, 643a; *HALOT,* 2:694b–95a; *DCH,* 5:678b), so Dhorme's belief that "one says drops of water, oil, etc." and not just "drops" is hard to justify.

The verb נטף is usually "drip," but not necessarily in the sense of discrete drops (as with a leaky roof). In Judg 5:4 נטף is used of the heavens "pouring" (נטף) with rain (also Ps 68:8 [9]), and in Joel 3:18 (4:18) and Amos 9:13 of the mountains "running" with wine. So (against de Wilde) the noun could well mean "exudation" or "vapor," even though the usual term for the mist that rises from the sea is נשׂיא (Jer 10:13 || 51:16; Ps 135:7; Prov 25:14).

27.d. זקק is used for refining (gold, 28:1; Mal 3:3; 1 Chr 28:18; silver, Ps 12:6 [7]; 1 Chr 29:4) but also for filtering (wine, Isa 25:6). These are quite different processes, so we may assume that the word has a rather general sense (not specifically "strain, filter through," as Driver–Gray), such as "purify," which would perhaps allow the translation "distil/distill" (as RSV, NIV, NEB) as a kind of purifying process. The making of rain is analogous to distillation.

Other explanations of the word are: (1) Less appealing is JB's interpretation "dissolving [the showers into mist]," since dissolving cannot be related to purifying. (2) Hölscher has "he sprays the rain into mist," thinking that זקק means "blow," like Akk. *zaqâqu* (now written *zâqu* [*CAD,* 21:64a]), Arab. *ziqq* "bellows"; but Arab. *ziqq* means rather "receptacle of skin" (Lane, 1238b, Wehr–Cowan, 379b), and has nothing to do with blowing. (3) NJB "pulverizes the rain into mist" is an attempt to create a close parallel for גרע understood as "make small," but there is no evidence that זקק has anything to do with breaking into pieces. (4) NJPS "the droplets of water, which cluster into mist" likewise ignores the semantic range of זקק, which is far other than gathering together. (5) De Wilde's "he thickens his mist into rain" does not seem to retain the image of זקק at all. (6) KJV "they pour down rain" depends on the seventeenth-century understanding of זקק as "pour out, wash" (cf. Buxtorf, 195, where "refined" gold, for example, is understood as "washed" gold). (7) Kissane finds yet another זקק "bind," with cognates in Aram. and Arab., and reads יָזֹק "He bindeth up [rain for his mist]"; Aram. זקק is well attested (e.g., Jastrow, 410a), but there is no evident Arab. cognate (*zaqqa* is "feed" [of a bird; Lane, 1238a], though *HALOT,* 1:279a, claims a meaning "maltreat," which does not appear in the standard Arab. lexica). Whatever זקק means exactly, it is never used absolutely, so translations like "waterdrops that filter in rain through his mists" (NAB) or "the drops of water, which distill as water to the streams" (NIV) cannot be adopted (unless of course they presuppose emendation to the passive).

יזקו is "they refine, distill" (qal as in 28:1), but drops can hardly refine or distill water (Delitzsch, awkwardly, "they distil as rain in connection with its mist"). It is not very plausible that the pl is impersonal (Gordis, Hartley), still less that it is merely a phonetic addition after the ק (Tur-Sinai, Gerleman [*BHS frt*]), and we should therefore adopt an emendation to יֻזְּקוּ "they are refined as rain" (Hoffmann, Budde) or, preferably, to יָזֹק "he refines, distills," God being the subj as in the first colon (so too Duhm, Beer [BH^2 *prps* יָזֹק or יֻזְּקוּ], Hölscher, Lévêque, 588, Gerleman [*BHS prp* יָזֹק], de Wilde, Sicre Díaz, RSV, and NEB [cf. Brockington]); so also Dhorme, translating "he volatilizes the rain into mist" (but if it is mist that is the final product, it can hardly be rain that it is the raw material). This emendation is adopted in the *Translation* above. Driver–Gray, Beer (*BHK*), Gray add a suff יָזֹקֵם "he filters them," but the obj can just as easily be the rain. Terrien "he filters them in his mist so as to make from them the autumn rain" is not very easy to square with the Heb.

27.e. The second colon seems to read "he refines (see previous *Note*) rain to his mist," but that does not make sense. It would make more sense to have mist being refined into rain, and that would harmonize well with the first colon, where we have fine drops of water at the beginning of the process. Perhaps we should emend לאדו "to his mist" to מֵאֵדוֹ "from his mist," mist then being thought of as the substance from which rain is made, by a process akin to the refinement of metals. Thus NEB "and distils rain from the mist he has made." Duhm, followed by Strahan and Beer (*BHK frt*), offered this emendation, which is followed in the *Translation* above (though reading simply מֵאֵד "from the mist," as noted below); it would be possible to achieve the same translation by taking ל as equivalent to מן (so Pope, Hartley), but that sense of ל is poorly attested. Less probable is the idea that ל means "at the time of" (Driver–Gray; cf. BDB, 516b §6a), since a regular time for אד is hardly in view (contrast Gen 3:8 לרוח היום "at the breeze of the day").

אד was traditionally interpreted as "mist" (KJV, RSV). Its only other occurrence is at Gen 2:6 (perhaps also at Job 36:30 [*q.v.*]), where an אד in Eden would rise from the ground and water the earth. Since J. Skinner (*A Critical and Exegetical Commentary on Genesis* [Edinburgh: T. & T. Clark, 1910] 55), W. F. Albright ("The Babylonian Matter in the Predeuteronomic Primeval History [JE] in Gen 1–11," *JBL* 58 [1939] 91–103 [102 n. 25]), and E. A. Speiser, "*Ed* in the Story of Creation," *BASOR* 140 (1955) 9–11 (cf. also Otto Kaiser, *Die mythische Bedeutung des Meeres in Ägypten, Ugarit und Israel*, BZAW 78 [Berlin: Töpelmann, 1959] 101–7), it has generally been agreed the term is cognate with Akk. *edû* (*CAD*, 4:35b), from the Sumerian ID, the subterranean reservoir. It is now usually translated "stream" (NRSV, NAB; NJPS "a flow would well up from the ground," NJB "water flowed out of the ground," Pope "flood," Gray "[rain for] the abyss"). Proponents of this view, however, often overlook the fact that an underground reservoir is not likely to be the source of rain. Things might be different if the אד is conceived of as a reservoir that encircles the earth, being both below and above it (as Hartley), but there is nothing to show that was the conception. If the word here is to be connected with the Akk., it would have to refer to a heavenly storehouse of water (cf. *HALOT*, 1:11b "the celestial stream"; M. Dahood, "Eblaite *i-du* and Hebrew *ʾēd*, 'Rain Cloud,'" *CBQ* 43 [1981] 534–38). Fohrer seems to understand אד as rain (*Wasserstrom*), translating "they seep through as rain for his water-stream." The Qumran Tg reads this second colon as "and storms of rain go forth [?]" (וזיקי מטר יהכן); cf. Sokoloff, *Targum*, 82–83, 140–41. Sutcliffe's proposal to see here (written defectively) אֵיד "destruction," thus "downpour, destructive rain," is not very likely ("Notes on Job," 77–79), but it is followed by P. P. Saydon ("Miscellanea Biblica," *CBQ* 23 [1961] 249–57 [252]). More plausible is the suggestion of Houbigant to read לְנֹאדוֹ "[he encloses rain] into his water-bottle" (so too Beer [BH^2 *al*]).

אדו is "his mist/stream," but there does not seem to be much point in emphasizing at this moment that it is God's mist/stream, so perhaps we should read simply אֵד "stream." It is hard to believe Pope, Andersen, and Gray that the final ו represents the final vowel of the Akk. word. M. Dahood reads instead אֵדוֹ, which he takes as equivalent to יָדוֹ "his hand," rendering then לאדו as "from his hand" ("Ugaritic and the Old Testament," *ETL* 44 [1968] 35–54 [48–49]). In "Eblaite *i-du* and Hebrew *ʾēd*, 'Rain Cloud,'" 536–37, Dahood translated "from his raincloud," understood as the heavenly storehouse of rain, the waters above the firmament of Gen 1:6–7 (followed by Habel).

28.a. Terrien's reading of the verse as a wish ("May the storm clouds overflow and gush forth over the human multitudes") has no support in the Heb.

28.b. אשר "which" is read by NEB as אֶשֶׁר "torrent" ("the rain-clouds pour down in torrents"; cf. Brockington). אֶשֶׁר is unknown to the lexica, but *HALOT*, 1:93a, notes a verb אשר cognate with Aram. אשר "pour out," possibly the root of אֶשֶׁד "slope."

28.c. שחק is a normal word for "cloud," not specifically "storm cloud" (as Terrien).

28.d. נזל qal is often intransitive, "flow, trickle" (e.g., of water, Num 24:7; of teaching, Deut 32:2), but also transitive, "flow with, pour out, rain down" (of eyes running with tears, Jer 9:18 [17]; of skies raining down salvation [צדק], Isa 45:8; of a spring flowing with water, Ecclus 14:10; cf. *DCH*, 5:650a);

emendation to hiph יַזִּילוּ "they pour down" (as Beer [*BH*² *frt*]) is needless. Here the clouds (שחקים) pour down rain (מטר, v 27b), which is presumably the obj of נזל. Pope argues, perhaps correctly, that all apparent objs of נזל are in fact acc of material, but his translation "that trickle from the clouds," is not defensible since שחקים cannot be "an adverbial accusative"; Gray's explanation may be preferable, that שחקים "clouds" is the subj, and נטפים "drops" is an "internal accus." Tur-Sinai fancies that the rain is thought to trickle down through holes in the worn-out clouds (cf. on 37:16).

28.e. רעף qal "overflow with" is usually transitive, of pastures (מעגל III; cf. *DCH*, 5:380b) overflowing with fatness (Ps 65:11 [12]), and of clouds dropping down dew (Prov 3:20); once no obj is expressed but may be understood (Ps 65:12 [13], of the pastures [נאה] of the wilderness overflowing with fatness [cf. v 11b (12b)] or joy [cf. v 12b (13b)]). In Isa 45:8 (רעף hiph) skies overflow with salvation (צדק understood from the next colon). Here the obj seems to be the relative pronoun אשׁר, referring to "rain" (מטר) in v 27b.

28.f. M. Dahood ("Zacharia 9,1, *'ên 'ādām*," *CBQ* 25 [1963] 123–24) argues that in a few cases, including the present passage, אָדָם is to be understood as a byform of אֲדָמָה "earth" (so Gen 16:12; Jer 32:20; Zech 9:1; 13:5; Prov 30:14; Job 11:12). He is followed by *HALOT,* 1:14b (אָדָם IV), Lévêque, 588, Fedrizzi, Pope, de Wilde, Sicre Díaz, Gray, and REB "they descend in showers on the ground." Others simply emend to אֲדָמָה "the ground" (e.g., Sutcliffe, "Notes on Job," 81). The proposal makes good sense, but is not preferable to the MT. Ernst Jenni disputes the existence of an אדם "earth" (*TLOT,* 1:42).

28.g. אדם רב might seem at first to mean "many humans" (so JPS "the multitudes of men," Davidson "the multitude of mankind" [similarly Delitzsch], Driver–Gray "many men," Hartley "numerous people"), but that is impossible, partly because אדם refers to humans in general and so cannot be qualified with "many" (Pope), and partly because רב does not mean "many" in the sg. *HALOT,* 3:1171a, does indeed offer "numerous, many" as a translation of רב in the sg, "esp., with collectives which consist of several units" such as עם־רב "numerous people" (Gen 50:20) or קָהָל רָב (Ezek 17:17) "numerous assembly"; but in all the cited cases it would be better to understand רב as "great." The Qumran Tg has עם שׂגיא, but does this mean "a great people" or "numerous people" (as Pope; Sokoloff, *Targum,* 83)?

BDB, 913a, suggests רב means "abundantly" at Ps 18:14 (15); 123:3; but both passages are questionable. Sutcliffe ("Notes on Job," 81–82) adopts this sense (with some support from Szczygiel), and points to Gen 33:9. It may be enough evidence for this view that the form רַבָּה does seem to mean "abundantly" at Ps 62:2 (3); 78:15. KJV, RSV have "abundantly"; similarly NIV "and abundant showers fall."

The *Translation* above follows Wright in taking רָב as a byform of רביבים "showers" (so too Beer [*BHK frt*], Pope, Lévêque, Rowley, de Wilde, Sicre Díaz, Gray; cf. Moffatt "dropping in showers on men"). We may compare Ugar. *rb* and *rbb* (*DUL,* 730). NAB (*Textual Notes,* 378) actually reads רְבִיבִים. רב, being sg, should be construed not as the subj of ירעפו "they trickle down" but as its predicate; cf. Pope "pour on the ground in showers."

Tur-Sinai's proposal to read עלי אֻדָם רב "(pouring) from above (על) their rich stream" is strained; his parallels for על meaning "from above" are Gen 27:39; 49:25, where the form is not על but מֵעַל, which really does mean "from above."

31.a. V 31 is moved to this place for reasons explained in the *Comment.* The transposition is made also by Peake, Dhorme, Kissane, Larcher, Rowley, Lévêque, 588, Fedrizzi, Sicre Díaz, Whybray, and Gray, and among translations, by Moffatt, JB, NJB, NEB, and NAB (*Textual Notes,* 378).

31.b. בם "by them" is explained in the *Comment* as referring to the clouds. Blommerde, following Dahood (*Psalms I,* 122, though there the form is בָּהֶם), rather unpersuasively argues that בם can mean "then" (for other examples, cf. Blommerde, 19).

31.c. ידין has usually been taken as "he judges" (so KJV, JPS, RSV; NRSV, NIV "governs," NJPS "controls," Terrien "directs," Habel "judges"; similarly Davidson, Tur-Sinai, Newsom), the lightning serving to overwhelm his enemies (Ps 18:13 [14]), the rain to bring blessing (Isa 55:10).

However, an emendation to יָזוּן "feeds, nourishes" (Houbigant, Graetz, Budde², Driver–Gray, Dhorme, Beer [*BHK*], Kissane, Larcher, Fohrer, Lévêque, 588, Fedrizzi, de Wilde, Sicre Díaz, Hartley, Gray) has been widely adopted as more in keeping with the topic of the rain (so too JB, NAB "nourishes," NJB, NEB, Moffatt "sustains," GNB "feeds"). It is adopted in the *Translation* above. זון occurs only at Jer 5:8, but its noun מָזוֹן "food" is attested at Gen 45:23; 2 Chr 11:23; and in Aram. at Dan 4:12 [9], 21 [18]).

M. Dahood, however, thought that there is no need to emend and that דין is here a dialectal form of זו hiph ("Northwest Semitic Philology and Job," 71–72); similarly Pope, Blommerde, Gray. But more recently he reverted to the traditional reading, on the ground of some analogies to a parallelism between "judge" and "feed" ("Is the Emendation of *yādîn* to *yāzîn* Necessary in Job 36, 31?" *Bib* 53 [1972] 539–41).

Alternatively, ידין has been thought to be from a new word דון "be abundant, enrich, feed" (cf. Arab. *dāna* V "be abundant" [Freytag, 2:73–74; Lane, 938b]; cf. *DCH,* 2:426b; and cf. the proposal of דִּין II "food" in v 17 above), hence in the hiph "provide abundance" (so G. R. Driver, "Problems in the Hebrew Text of Job," 89–91). But this is a dubious proposal, since *dāna* usually means "be low, vile," the sense "enjoy abundance" being restricted to Form V, and also because "make abundant" is semantically not the same as "feed," which is what the present context seems to require. Guillaume also found the sense "feeds" here, but by postulating a new verb דין II (not in *DCH*) on the basis of an Arab. noun *zuwān,* which he allows usually means "the refuse in food that is discarded," and which must therefore be explained here as an *'aḍdād* (reversal of meaning) with the sense "food" ("Arabic Background," 123; *Studies,* 127; see also *Notes* on v 17 above). Such a labored account carries little conviction, and even less so when it appears that the standard Arab. lexica do not support the idea of the word as a general word for "food" (Lane, 1207c, recognizes *zuwān* as "bitter grass" and, at 1273a, *zân* as "darnel").

31.d. אכל is accepted by all as "food," with the exception of Tur-Sinai, who argues that it means "shouting" (cf. Aram. אכלי, aphel of כלי "roar, shout" [Jastrow, 642a]), and translates "and raiseth thunder as a judge." He finds the corresponding verb אכל in Ezek 18:6, 11, 15; 22:9; and sees the phrase נתן אכל as parallel to נתן קול "utter one's voice" (2 Sam 22:14 || Ps 18:13 [14]; 77:17 [18], in these texts also of thunder).

31.e. למכביר "in abundance" is hiph ptcp of כבר "be great, many" (כבר hiph occurs only elsewhere in Elihu's speech at 35:16). For examples of the hiph ptcp used as a noun, cf. GKC, §85m. לָרֹב would be more usual for "in abundance" (cf. 26:3).

Tur-Sinai believes that מכביר means "judge," as also at 34:17, 24; 36:5, as distinct from the מפגיע (v 32) "prosecutor."

29.a. Budde and Hölscher delete vv 29–30. NAB declines to translate v 29, though strangely they attribute the הן "Lo!" of v 30 to it.

29.b. אף אם is lit. the emphatic particle "surely" with אם the interrogative particle expecting the answer "no" (cf. BDB, 50b §2; so too Gray). Most translations ignore the אף, but NJPS attempts to reproduce it with "Can one, indeed, (contemplate) . . . ?"

Many think that a little feeble and prefer to read אף מִי "who indeed?" (so Siegfried, Budde, Duhm, Kissane, Larcher, Gerleman [*BHS prp*], de Wilde) or, with Pesh, deleting the אף, just וּמִי "and who?" (so Driver–Gray, Beer [*BHK*]) or מִי (Dhorme, Hölscher, Fohrer, Lévêque, 588, Fedrizzi). The alternative proposal noted by Gerleman (*BHS vel*), אָמְנָם "indeed," seems mistaken, since the line would then affirm that one can understand the expanse of the clouds.

Tur-Sinai argues that אף אם must be equivalent to אַף אָמְנָם, the double asseverative found in 19:4; 34:12. Gordis and Hartley follow, but there is no reason to equate אם with אָמְנָם.

29.c. Instead of בין "understand," Gordis postulates another verb בין "go between, among" (a denominative of בֵּין "between," which he finds also in Deut 32:10 polel), translating "he soars midst the spreading clouds"; he is followed by Hartley. Whatever "soars" means (Gordis seems to be thinking of his riding the clouds, as in Ps 68:4 [5]), it seems rather irrelevant to the present subject, which is the production of thunder and lightning.

There is a problem, however, with the usual interpretation of יבין as "understands": how or why is the spreading out of the clouds something no one can understand? NJB sees there is a problem, but "who can fathom how he spreads the clouds" is not a very convincing solution. NJPS tried "Can one, indeed, contemplate the expanse of clouds?"; but that is quite unsuccessful since obviously anyone can *contemplate* the clouds, and the answer expected by the particle אם is "no one." NEB tries even harder, with "Can any man read the secret of the sailing clouds" (REB "anyone . . . billowing clouds"), but we are still left in the dark about what the secret might be.

Tur-Sinai's proposal, that יבין is not the qal but the hiph of בין, i.e., "he teaches," does nothing to resolve the problem, for he fails to suggest what God may be teaching by the spreading of the clouds. The emendation of Graetz to יָכִין "[who] establishes [the spreading of the clouds]" is worth consideration.

29.d. מפרשׂ is (1) "spreading out, expanse" (מפרשׂ שחקים "expanse of the clouds," i.e., skies in 1QM 10:11), (2) "place of spreading" (1QH fr. 3:4), (3) "sail," as spread out (Ezek 27:7). Clouds are "spread out" in Ps 105:39 פָּרַשׂ עָנָן לְמָסָךְ "he spread out a cloud as a covering." In the light of such a text, Terrien's translation "who can understand the secret of the dispersal of the clouds?" is not very probable.

Torczyner postulates a מִפְרָשׂ "carpet" (cf. Arab. *mifraš* "quilt" lying upon a saddle [Lane, 2371c]), and reads יָכִין מִפְרָשׂוֹ "prepares his carpet" (see further *Note* 29.e). So too NAB translates vv 29–30 as "Lo! he spreads the clouds in layers as the carpeting of his tent," reading הֵן פָּרַשׂ מפרשׂי־עב תַּשׁוֹת סכתו and omitting אַף אם־יבין from v 29 and עליו אורו ושרשי הים כסה from v 30 (*Textual Notes,* 378); the noun תַּשׁוֹת "carpets" is apparently intended as a form of the new word תַּשְׁוִית "ottoman" proposed by Torczyner (see next *Note*).

It is emended to מִפְלְשֵׂי "poising, balancing of" by Ehrlich (*frt*), Hölscher, Fohrer, Peters (מִפְלְשֵׂי, but that seems a mistake), Sutcliffe ("Notes on Job," 82), as in the phrase מִפְלְשֵׂי־עָב "balancings of the cloud" in 37:16 (and it is attested for this place in one Heb. MS, Kenn 245). Gordis, however, thinks that מפלשׂי is no more than a phonetic variant of מפרשׂי.

It remains unclear why either the "spreading" or the "poising" of the clouds should be a matter for *understanding* (see further, *Comment*). It would be more intelligible if מפרשׂי referred in some way to the creation of thunder (which indeed no ancient human could understand); so perhaps the word is from פרשׂ "break, divide," a byform of פרס (BDB, 828a; Delitzsch denies it), or from an otherwise unattested פרשׂ "break forth" (cf. Aram. פרת, Syr. *prat*; BDB, 831b, offers also Arab. *faraša* as a cognate, defining the Arab. meanings, rather sensationally, as "IV *rip open* stomach, *and scatter* contents [cf. VII]"; from what source this view is derived I cannot say, for it is not in Golius, 1781b, nor Freytag, 3:333a, nor Lane, 2370a); *faraša* is simply "spread"), or from פרר "break, shatter" or פרם "tear, rend" or פרץ "break open," thunder being conceived of as the sound of clouds being broken. In 26:8, in a variant image, clouds could be "broken" or "torn open" (בקע) by the weight of rain water in them.

29.e. תְּשֻׁאָה is "loud noise," of shouts of a crowd (Isa 22:2; Zech 4:7), of a donkey driver (Job 39:7), or of the noise of a storm (Job 30:22 K [*q.v.*]), here apparently of thunder. Thus RSV, NJPS "thunderings," NJB "why such crashes thunder," NIV "how he thunders," KJV "noise," JPS "crashings" (similarly Gray).

Alternative readings include: מַשְׂאוֹת "liftings up (?)," which occurs elsewhere at Isa 30:27, where it may mean "clouds" (NAB) or "rising smoke" (RSV). So Beer (*BHK prps*), Gerleman (*BHS prp,* translating *elationes* "liftings up"), Fedrizzi "the high position [of his tent]," and Tur-Sinai "the heights [of his curtain]," the clouds being a curtain behind which God hides from humans. Sutcliffe ("Notes on Job," 82–83) reads עָבֹת שְׂאֵת "[the poising of] the clouds, the exaltation of [his pavilion]."

Torczyner sees here the word תַּשְׁוִית (cf. Aram. תַּשְׁוִיתָא "bed, mattress, carpet" [Jastrow, 1703a]); it is registered by KBL, 1043a (but merely mentioned by *HALOT,* 4:1799b), and adopted by NAB (see *Note* above), NEB "spread like a carpet under his pavilion" (Brockington), and Fohrer. Perhaps תַּשְׁוִית should be translated "cushioned couch, ottoman" (cf. *HALOT,* 4:1799b), in which case the clouds are understood as the heavenly couch on which God reclines. The recommendation of Beer (BH^2) to read a noun from the verb שׁוה "be equal," in correspondence with Theod's ἰσότητα "equality, impartiality," makes no sense in the context, and there is no Heb. noun available (שָׁוֶה "level plain" will not fit).

29.f. סכה "booth," which is generally a temporary lodging, e.g., for soldiers (2 Sam 11:11) or workers in a vineyard (Isa 1:8), but in 2 Sam 22:12 of darkness as a permanent dwelling for Yahweh (in the parallel Ps 18:11 [12] it is dark clouds). The reference here appears to be to the dark storm clouds.

Tur-Sinai, however, derived the term not from סכך "weave" (as, e.g., BDB, 697b) but from סכך "hide," thus "curtain," equivalent to מָסָךְ "covering, screen" (BDB, 697a); cf. Ps 18:11 (12), where סכה is parallel to סתר "hiding place." His explanation, that when it rains God spreads his reprimand (v 30a) on the cloudy curtain under the sky, is forced.

30.a. This verse is entirely obscure, although all the words are quite well known. In the absence of a satisfactory interpretation, a merely literal translation has been offered.

30.b. הן is commonly "behold," but also well attested as "if" (BDB, 243b §2), which can amount to "when, whenever" (for further examples, see *Note* 23:8.b). Clearly, the phenomenon of sheet lightning over the sea is no hypothetical occurrence, but well known, so the particle "if" could be misleading; hence the translation "when."

30.c. פרשׂ "spread out," as in מפרשׂ (v 29); Dhorme "He has unrolled His mist," explaining that "[I]t is because God unfolds his mist over the sea that the depths of the abyss become veiled"; but it is hard to see what all this has to do with the ostensible subject, viz. the lightning.

30.d. אורו "his light" is explained by Driver–Gray as the "blaze of light" that was supposed to surround Yahweh in the thunder cloud (cf. Ps 18:12 [13] נֹגַהּ נֶגְדּוֹ "the brightness before him"), not the lightning flashes (Budde). But several modern versions have "his lightning" (RSV, NIV, NJPS; and it is so understood by Gray), and אור seems to be "lightning" in 37:3 (but probably not in 37:11 [*q.v.*]). F.

M. Cross (*Canaanite Myth and Hebrew Epic: Essays in the History of the Religion of Israel* [Cambridge, MA: Harvard UP, 1973] 147 n. 4), however, insists that אור is "bright cloud," which he finds also at 37:11, 15, and in Ugar. *'ār*, as in the epithet *pdry bt 'ar* (Baal V iii 21 [*CML*, 87a]; 3 A 23 [*CML*², 46a]; *CTA* 1.3 I 23).

Some read אֵדוֹ "his mist" or "his stream" (as in v 27), which some LXX MSS support (reading ηδω, a transliteration rather than a translation of אדו). Thus Duhm, Beer (*BH*² אֵידוֹ), Driver–Gray, Dhorme, Hölscher, Kissane, Larcher, Guillaume, de Wilde, JB, NJB, NEB (Brockington). But this seems inappropriate here. Tur-Sinai sees here his proposed word אוֹר "condemnation" (from ארר "curse"), as also at 25:3; 36:32; 37:3, 11, 15, 21.

30.e. עליו "over it," referring to the sea in the next colon, or else "over himself" or "about him" (Duhm, RSV, NIV, REB), "around him" (Davidson, NRSV), "before him" (NJB). Alternatively, NJPS has "over it" (apparently in reference to "his pavilion" in v 29, though סכתו is fem and עליו is masc), and NEB "[unrolls the mist] across the waters" (though there is no masc sg antecedent for עליו).

Pope emends to עָלִי and translates "'Aliy spreads his light," עָלִי "'Aliy" being a title of Baal in the Ugaritic texts, and here supposedly also of Yahweh; so too Dahood (review of *Job et son Dieu,* 438) and Blommerde, vocalizing the name as עֵלִי "the Most High"; for other examples, see *Note* 29:4.c. Gray reads, less controversially, עֶלְיוֹן "the Most High."

Lévêque, 588, reads עֲלִיּוֹתָיו "his upper chambers" (as in Amos 9:6; Ps 104:13), פרשׂ being "spread out (a tent)" as in Exod 40:19.

30.f. כסה is unambiguously "cover" (as KJV, RSV), but it hard to see sense in this reading. GNB thinks it means "cover with darkness," in contrast to the sky, which is covered with light: "He sends lightning through all the sky, but the depths of the sea remain dark" (noted also by Newsom); but in a strophe about the sky, why should the sea be mentioned? Fedrizzi insists that it means here "cover with water," but that is too banal; with what else would the roots of the sea be covered? Davidson thought it meant that God covered *himself* with the masses of water in the clouds, in which case there would be a contrast between the light that surrounds God and the inner darkness in which he dwells. If God is indeed "covering" the roots of the sea, it must be with light, as the lightning penetrates to the bottom of the sea. Thus "he covers the roots of the sea *with it,* i.e., with the light" (cf. Delitzsch); so too apparently NIV "bathing the depths of the sea" (with light), and NJPS "it [the lightning] fills the bed of the sea." But even so, it does seem unnatural to speak of such an event as "covering."

Rather than כסה "cover," Budde read גִּלָּה "uncovers, lays bare," כסה being a slip of the pen because of its presence in v 32 (followed by Peake). Gordis, followed by Hartley, reaches the same conclusion by arguing that כסה is an *'aḍdad* (a word of like and opposite meaning), thus "reveal"; but his translation, strangely, reads "and covers the depths of the sea." To the same effect, by a different route, M. Dahood (*Proverbs and Northwest Semitic Philology,* Scripta Pontificii Instituti Biblici 113 [Rome: Pontificium Institutum Biblicum, 1963] 19; "Hebrew-Ugaritic Lexicography III," *Bib* 46 [1965] 311–32 [330]) claimed to have found a number of occurrences of the "privative piel" of כסה (Prov 10:11, 18; 26:26; Ps 143:9; Hos 2:11). This suggestion is adopted by Blommerde and Habel and in the *Translation* above.

An emendation is proposed: J. T. Marshall, *The Book of Job* (Philadelphia: American Baptist Publication Society, 1904), reads ושרשי הים כִּסְאוֹ "and the roots of the sea are his throne"; he is followed by Pope, who is delighted to find a reminiscence of the Ugaritic description of the dwelling of the Canaanite god at the source of the underground rivers (*mbk nhrm* [Baal II iv 21 (*CML,* 97; *CML*², 59) = *KTU* 1,4 IV 21]; see also 28:11; 38:16). But it is hard to see what the sea has to do with the heavenly phenomena that are the subject of the passage as a whole. Cross, however, also adopting this emendation, sees the divine throne on the tops of the mountains since he understands the "roots of the sea" as the primordial mountains, presumably rising far into the sky and going down deep into the sea (*Canaanite Myth and Hebrew Epic,* 147 n. 4).

30.g. NEB "its streamers cover the sea" reads וּשְׁרָשָׁיו (Brockington), apparently from שַׁרְשְׁרָה "chain" (a form without the second ר is found also at Exod 28:22); REB "its rays cover the sea" seems to follow the same interpretation. G. R. Driver had read וּשְׁרָשָׁיו "and its roots" ("Hebrew Studies," *JRAS* [1948] 175–76 [176]). "Streamers" is apparently intended in the sense of "a long, narrow strip of vapor, etc." (cf. *OED,* §2.e).

30.h. שרשי הים "roots of the sea," though intelligible for the bottom of the ocean, is a term not found elsewhere (though cf. the reference to the root [שׁרשׁ] of mountains, 28:9). It can hardly mean the water at the bottom of the sea that is drawn up into the thunder clouds: RVmg "and covereth it with the bottom of the sea" (similarly Ewald "the darkest water-clouds which seem to be drawn from the foundations of the sea," Dillmann). More worthy of consideration is the idea that the sea in question is the heavenly ocean, whose waters fill the clouds and obscure the light (Hitzig; similarly Tur-Sinai), though ים is never used for this ocean. Less plausibly, Cross avers that the "Roots of Sea" are the primordial mountains, comparing Ps 46:3 with its mountains in the heart of the sea (*Canaanite Myth and Hebrew Epic,* 147 n. 4).

Among emendations may be noted the following: (1) Very commonly, Duhm's emendation is followed. He reads אֵדוֹ "his mist" in the first colon, and here וְרָאשֵׁי הָרִים "and the tops of the mountains (he covers with it)," and he is followed by Budde[2], Ehrlich, Strahan, Davidson–Lanchester, Driver–Gray, Dhorme, Beer (*BHK*), Hölscher, Larcher, de Wilde, Gray, BJ, JB, NJB. (2) Kissane proposes וְשֶׁמֶשׁ בַּיֹּם "and [he covers] the sun by day," which at least leaves us in the realm of the celestial. Rowley seems inclined to this emendation. (3) Sutcliffe ("Notes on Job," 84), moving the *he* of הים "the sea" back to the previous word, reads שֳׁרָשֶׁיהָ יָם "he covered its root [apparently error for roots] with the sea"; but there is no evident noun to which the suff of שרשיה could refer (it is incredible that God's סכה "pavilion" should be conceived of as having "roots"), and such a covering would have been an act of creation, not connected with the sending of lightning, which is what the present context demands.

A philological proposal is offered by A. Guillaume, who sees here a new שֹׁרֶשׁ "mist" (he compares Arab. *šaršā'un* "thin white cloud," or perhaps rather *šarsâ'u* ("The Unity of the Book of Job," *ALUOS* 4 [1962] 26–46 [33–34]), translating "And he covers him with a mist from the sea," parallel to the first colon, "Behold he spreads his mist [reading אֵדוֹ] over him." These words, however, do not appear in the standard Arabic lexica.

32.a. In the *Translation,* v 31 has been moved to follow v 28, for reasons explained in the *Comment.*

32.b. כסה is "hide, cover" (as in v 30b); similarly Habel "envelops," Sicre Díaz "hides." If he covers the lightning with his hands, he may be said to "fill" his hands with lightning (as NIV), or lightning may be said to fill his hands (NJPS). However, the phrase is על־כפים כסה־אור "upon (his) hands he hides light," which is rather more difficult, and may be in need of emendation (see also next two *Notes*).

Two emendations of the verb are offered: (1) Dhorme, followed by Hölscher, Larcher, Fohrer, Lévêque, 589, de Wilde, Hartley, emends to נִסָּה (= נִשָּׂא) "he has lifted up" (cf. the same combination of על־כפים "on [their] hands" and נשא "lift up" in Ps 91:12); so too BJ, JB, NJB "He gathers up the lightning in his hands." (2) Pope emends to נָסְסָה "prances" from a new נסס (cognate with Akk. *nasāsu* "move to and fro, vibrate" [but this verb is not recognized by *CAD,* 11:23b]; cf. *DCH,* 5:701b *s.v.* נסס IV "suffer convulsions"; it is attested perhaps at Zech 9:16; Isa 10:18); he is followed by Gray, translating "flashes." The lightning that flickers from cloud to cloud would then be pictured as prancing on the palms of the deity.

32.c. כפים is usually taken as "hands." There are several other possibilities: (1) KJV "with clouds he covereth the light" follows Buxtorf, 372, which noted that some Jewish interpreters, including ibn Ezra, understood כף as "cloud" (as also at Exod 33:22; Lam 3:41). (2) Gordis sees here the MH כִּפָּה "arch (of heaven)" (Jastrow, 635a, *s.v.* כִּיפָּה), its dual form perhaps signifying a double arch. He renders, "the tent of Heaven He covers with lightning"; but it is not clear how the arch could be *covered* with lightning, and the image of lightning being hurled by the hand of the deity is much more probable.

(3) Tur-Sinai reads כפים as כֵּפִים "rocks, mountains" (as at 30:6; Jer 4:29); thus "he covereth the mountains with his condemnation" (see *Note* 30.d for אור "condemnation." (4) Szczygiel also reads כֵּפִים "rocks," emending the verb to כסס "count," thus "to the crags he calculates the lightning," apparently meaning that he apportions the amount of lightning that will strike the crags. (5) Peters, following an idea of Duhm's, thinks the כפים are the double hollow of a sling, but, as Sutcliffe points out ("Notes on Job," 85–86), in 1 Sam 25:29, the only other passage where כף can have this sense, the context makes it very clear that a sling is being spoken of. (6) NEB also reads כֵּפִים (Brockington), which it understands as "thunderbolts" ("he charges the thunderbolts with flame"), but the rendering is not explained.

32.d. על־כפים כסה אור seems to be literally "upon (his) hands he covered light," but Driver–Gray explain that אור is an acc defining that with which the hands are covered, thus "he covered his hands with light." Cf. Mal 2:16 וכסה חמס על־לבושו "and he covered his garment with violence." This is a different image from his "filling" his hands with lightning (as NIV), or from lightning "filling" his hands (NJPS). Sicre Díaz takes another direction in understanding "he covers the lightning with his hands"; but how is על to be rendered "with"?

Though אור is usually simply "light," most understand it to refer to lightning here, as also at 37:3, 15; 38:24. Thus here RSV "he covers his hands with the lightning," NAB "in his hands he holds the lightning," JB "he gathers up the lightning in his hands," NJPS "lightning fills his hands," GNB "he seizes the lightning with his hands." KJV, however, translated "with clouds he covereth the light"; see previous *Note.* Tur-Sinai sees אור "condemnation" again here; see on v 30. NEB reads אור as אוּר "flame" (BDB, 22a), translating "he charges the thunderbolts with flame."

32.e. ויצו עליו "and lays a command upon it" (צוה piel) is emended by G. R. Driver to וַיַּצְלִיעָהּ (= וַיַּצְלִיעוֹ) "and he caused it to come forth," postulating a צלע hiph cognate with Arab. *ṣalla'a* "emerge" ("Problems in the Hebrew Text of Job," 90). Hence NEB "launches them straight (at the mark)" (Brockington). There does not, however, appear to be an Arab. verb *ṣala'a* (*ṣalla'a* would be Form II); there is a *ḍala'a* "incline, deviate" (Lane, 1799a), but it is not cited for the sense "[the sun] emerged [from the clouds]," which Driver avers. Gray prefers to read וַיַּקְלִיעֶהָ "and he slings it"; but קלע does not elsewhere occur in hiph.

32.f. עליה "(lays command) upon it," אור "light" being, exceptionally, fem, as also in Jer 13:16 (so Dhorme, Pope, Gordis, Gray). Some, however, prefer to read the masc suff, with some Heb. MSS, עָלָיו (so Beer [*BHK frt*], Fohrer, Guillaume, NAB [*Textual Notes,* 378]). Tur-Sinai is alone in explaining it as an Aramaic-like masc suff (as עדיה at 6:20 and בניה at 39:16).

32.g. מַפְגִּיעַ has been variously understood. (1) Since פגע is "meet, light upon" the hiph ptcp מַפְגִּיעַ might be "one who lights upon, i.e., assailant" (so Dillmann, RVmg, Tur-Sinai "accuser," Guillaume "oppressor"); but this would be the only such use of the verb, which would be more likely to mean "one who entreats." (2) "One making it fall upon, hit," thus בְמַפְגִּיעַ "as [*beth essentiae*] a sure aimer" (Delitzsch, Pope). (3) KJV, understanding it as "one who interposes, entreats," translates "commandeth it *not to shine* by *the cloud* that cometh betwixt" (adding the words in italics for the sake of the sense). (4) Dhorme thinks מפגיע is a verbal noun "hitting" (cf. מכביר "abundance" in v 31), with the *beth* introducing the content of the command; thus "[has commanded it] to hit a mark." (5) For Gordis it is simply "target," an alternative form of מִפְגָּע.

A minor emendation is most often preferred, to מִפְגָּע "target, mark," as at 7:20 (Bickell[2], Budde, Duhm, Peake, Driver–Gray, Beer [*BHK*], Fohrer, Lévêque, 589, Gerleman [*BHS prp*], de Wilde, Gray, RSV, NAB [*Textual Notes,* 378], JB, NIV, NJPS, NEB). This proposal is adopted in the *Translation* above.

Duhm, Beer (*BH*[2] *prps*), thinking a "target" implied slinging, emended very ingeniously עַל־כַּף יְפַלֵּס הָאוֹר וַיְקַלְּעֵהוּ בְמִפְגָּע "upon the sling [כַּף "sling" as in 1 Sam 25:29] he balances the light, and slings it at the mark." But there is no reason to think specifically of a sling here.

33.a. רֵעַ is apparently a noun from רוע hiph "shout, give a blast (with trumpet or horn)," elsewhere at Exod 32:17; Mic 4:9; but in both places the text is questionable. It is not a natural word to use for the sound of thunder, and RSV, NJB "crashing," KJV, NJPS, Delitzsch "noise" are not very exact representations of the term. But many have no problem with "thunderclap" or "thunder" (Pope, Fedrizzi, Gordis, Habel, Hartley).

Other philological proposals include: (1) There is no likelihood that רע is here "friend" (with suff it is usually רֵעֵהוּ, though רֵעוֹ occurs once, at Jer 6:21), though that is how Pesh, Tg, Vg take it (so too Ehrlich, Peters). (2) Guillaume suspects רעו might be "his brightness" (cf. Arab. *ray'* [Lane, 1201b]), but *ray'* means "increase," then "best part of something"; one phrase is quoted in which its sense is "the whiteness, and beautiful splendour, of the first part of the day after sunrise," but that does not amount to evidence of the sense "brightness" for the noun. (3) Gray thinks rather that רע itself means "thunder," like Arab. *rāghā* "rumble (as thunder)," Ugar. *r'* "thunderbolt" (but "thunder" in *DUL,* 727). But *rāghā* is attested as "grumble, utter a cry" (Lane, 1114c), without any reference to thunder.

Among emendations, (1) Budde suggested instead רַעְמוֹ "his thunder," which is followed by NAB (*Textual Notes,* 378), BJ, JB (though not by NJB), and apparently by NIV, GNB (unless perhaps they are translating רֵעַ as "thunder"); so too Driver–Gray (*vel*), Beer (*BH*[2] *frt*), Kissane, Larcher, Fohrer, Pope, Rowley (*frt*), Lévêque, 589, de Wilde. This reading is adopted in the *Translation* above. Beer (*BHK*) and Driver–Gray (*vel*) prefer רַעַם "the thunder."

Other, less appealing, emendations are: (2) Dhorme emended to רֹעוֹ "his shepherd," translating "the flock [understood from מקנה in the second colon] has warned its shepherd." It should be noted that נגד hiph with a person as a direct obj is very rare (*DCH,* 5:600b, cites only seven cases); it is also unusual to postpone the subj to the second verb of a sentence. (3) Sutcliffe ("Notes on Job," 89) read לְרֹעִים "[it cuts down] the shepherds"; it is hard to see why the prep ל is inserted since גדע piel takes direct objs (*DCH,* 2:326a). (4) Tur-Sinai reads רִעוֹ "his wickedness," i.e., he tells humans of their wickedness, רֹעַ (BDB, 947b) being parallel to עַוְלָה "iniquity" in the next colon. (5) Strahan translates "his mercy announceth him," without saying how he reads the text; perhaps he emends to רַחֲמָיו "his mercies."

33.b. יגיד "declares" (נגד hiph impf) is accepted by most. JB "his thunder gives warning of its coming" (similarly Larcher, NJB) is a somewhat loose rendering, in that there is no word for "coming" (it is not following the proposal of Driver mentioned in the next *Note*). Sutcliffe ("Notes on Job," 89), however, proposes an emendation to יְגַדֵּעַ לְרֹעִים "it cuts down the shepherds" (see further in *Note* 33.d).

33.c. עליו is as it stands "concerning him," and it might be possible to interpret the line as "his thunder declares concerning him that he is passionately angry against iniquity."

Among philological suggestions are: (1) G. R. Driver proposes for עליו "concerning him" a new word עֱלִי "coming up" from עלה "come, go up," vocalized עֱלְיוֹ or עַלְיוֹ "its coming up" ("Problems in the Hebrew Text of Job," 90–91). Inverting the two cola, he reads קָנָה אַפּוֹ עַלְעוֹל וְיַגִּיד עַלְיוֹ/עֱלְיוֹ רַעְמוֹ "he creates (in) his anger the storm and announces (by) his thunder its coming"; thus NEB "in his anger he calls up the tempest, and the thunder is the herald of its coming." He claims 16:9 and Isa 42:25 as parallels for the omission of the prep before "anger," but both cases can be otherwise explained (the one as subj, the other as obj of the verb). It is not one of Driver's more inspired suggestions, but Gray follows it for the first colon of the MT, translating "thunder announces his coming." (2) Stier saw here a new word עַוְלָה "anger" (cf. Arab. *ghulwā'* "violence" [Lane, 2288a, and Wehr–Cowan, 682b, "excess," but not "violence") or another word עִוְלָה "hatred" (cf. Arab. *ghill* "hatred"). (3) Pope sees here again the divine name 'Aliy (as in v 30) as the subj, "'Aliy speaks with his thunder" (similarly Sicre Díaz, "the Most High"; cf. for many other examples, L. Viganò, *Nomi e titoli di YHWH alla luce del semitico del Nord-ovest,* BibOr 31 [Rome: Biblical Institute Press, 1976] 37–45).

Emendations: (1) Driver–Gray propose זַעְמוֹ "his wrath," reading יגיד זַעְמוֹ רַעַם "the thunder declareth his indignation"; so too Beer (*BHK frt*). This emendation is adopted in the *Translation.* (2) Sutcliffe ("Notes on Job," 89) reads for אף על־עולה "(?) anger against iniquity" פָּעַל עֹלָה "it makes [the flock] a holocaust," which seems an awkward use of פעל "do, make."

33.d. מקנה is "cattle," as KJV, RV, NIV ("even the cattle make known its approach"), GNB, ibn Ezra, Ewald, Delitzsch; Davidson translated "[it telleth] unto the cattle." The thought would be that the cattle have a presentiment of the coming storm (cf. Virgil, *Georgics* 1.375–76). T. H. Gaster (*Myth, Legend, and Custom in the Old Testament* [London: Duckworth, 1969] 799) notes some parallels in popular belief. But something more climactic might be expected at this point, and a reference to cattle seems out of place to many. The position of אף "also" after the noun מקנה also seems strange and apparently unparalleled.

An emendation seems required, and some form of קנא "be jealous, be angry" will be appropriate (as Tg also suggests). Reuss, Hitzig, Dillmann (*vel*), Fohrer, Terrien, Gerleman (*BHS prb*), Sicre Díaz read מַקְנֶה (hiph ptcp). Dillmann (*vel*), Budde, Duhm, Hölscher, Gray read מְקַנֵּה or מְקַנֵּא (piel ptcp) "one jealous with anger." Kissane likewise has מְקַנֵּא "as he exciteth wrath against iniquity." Pope reads מַקְנִיא "one who incites passion" and translates "venting his wrath against evil" (the same reading is followed by NAB [*Textual Notes,* 378]). G. Sauer points out that the semantic range of קנא is rather broad, including jealousy (e.g., Num 5:14), religious zeal (2 Kgs 10:16), sexual passion (Cant 8:6), envy (Eccl 4:4), hostility between nations (Isa 11:13), and personal anger (Job 5:2) (*TLOT,* 3:1145–47 [1146]). For parallels to the combination of קנאה "passion" and אף "anger," cf. Deut 29:20 (19); Ezek 35:11; Zeph 3:8. מְקַנֵּא אף (or one of the other proposed forms of the verb) could perhaps best be translated "one who shows passionate anger"; for the syntax, cf. Zech 8:2 וחמה גדולה קנאתי לה "and I am jealous for her (with) great anger." But with what is the קנא word to be connected? (1) God, so RSV "concerning him, who is jealous with anger," Peake "kindling his anger against iniquity"; (2) anger, so NJB "anger flashes out against iniquity"; or (3) the thunder, so NAB "(his thunder) incites the fury of the storm," JB "his thunder gives warning of its coming."

According to Tur-Sinai, followed by Gordis, Habel, Hartley, Newsom, מִקְנֶה is a noun, "wrath," equivalent to קִנְאָה "jealousy, anger"; Gordis sees the word also at Ezek 8:3 (emended). Though this word is not found in any lexicon, the case is well argued, and the view is adopted in the *Translation* above. Tur-Sinai had pointed the way with his proposal of a new word מִקְנֶה "wrath." Fedrizzi similarly proposes מְקַנֵּא as a noun, "zeal"; cf. NJPS "the kindling of anger."

Other emendations are: (1) מְקַדֵּם "herald" (de Wilde; NEB "the thunder is the herald of its coming" does not follow such an emendation); קדם piel is "be in front, meet." Though the ptcp is not attested, it would mean "one going in front," thus perhaps a herald. This is perhaps the reading of Larcher and BJ, who translate "approaches" (*la colère s'approche*), and perhaps also JB "wrath overtakes iniquity." (2) Beer (*BHK*) proposes וִיחַוֶּה "and [his anger] shows [his wrath]." (3) Lévêque, 589, reads קֹנֶה "creates" (cf. *HALOT,* 3:1112b), i.e., "[in his anger] he creates [the storm]." (4) Beer (*BH*[2] *frt*) suggests קֹרֵא "calling," which seems rather feeble.

33.e. אף "anger" (as RSV, NJB, NJPS; cf. NAB "fury"; Duhm, Budde, Driver–Gray, Hölscher, Kissane,

Terrien, Fohrer, Pope), not "also, even" (as KJV, NIV). Perhaps it should be vocalized אַפּוֹ "his anger" (Beer [*BHK*], Gordis). Lévêque, 589, would read בְּאַפּוֹ "in his anger."

Dhorme emends to שֹׁאֵף "sniffs, smells," of the flock of cattle that sniff the approaching storm; he takes his clue from the passage in Virgil cited above (*Georgics*, 1:370–72) where the heifer sucks in the wind with its nostrils.

33.f. עַל־עוֹלֶה is, as it stands, "against one who comes up" (עלה ptcp); cf. Davidson "concerning Him that cometh up," i.e., approaches in the thunder cloud. NIV "even the cattle make known its approach" presumably understands it as "(declares) about it as it comes up." KJV "concerning the vapour" (i.e., what goes up) suggests another way of construing the phrase. JPS "concerning the storm that cometh up" supplies "the storm" in explanation of "that cometh up" (it does not adopt the emendation mentioned in the next *Note*).

An interesting emendation is to עִלְעוֹלָה (or עַלְעוֹלָה, Beer [*BHK*], or עַלְעוֹלֹה "his whirlwind," Beer [*BH*²]) "whirlwind," not otherwise attested in Heb., but cf. MH עלעול and Aram. עַלְעוֹל (Jastrow, 1085a); so Graetz (apparently misspelled as אלעולה), Perles, 37–38, Driver–Gray, Dhorme, Beer (*BHK*), Lévêque, 589, Gordis, de Wilde, Sicre Díaz, Habel, Hartley, van der Lugt, Newsom. This could be parallel to רֵעְמוֹ "his thunder" in the first colon. But what would מקנה mean then? Beer (*Text*) suggested we read קֹרֵא אַף עַלְעוֹלֹה "his whirlwind also proclaims." In *BHK* he proposed וִיחַוֶּה אַפּוֹ עַלְעוֹלָה "and the whirlwind shows his anger." The difficulty is that we have not heard of the whirlwind in this strophe, and it seems somewhat out of place with the thunder and the lightning. Perhaps, though, עַלְעוֹלָה means more generally "storm" (as NAB [though *Textual Notes*, 378, say, apparently by mistake, that they read עַל עוֹלָה], and Gordis, translating the second colon as "His mighty wrath, the storm [proclaims]"; similarly Hartley).

Guillaume also reads עַלְעוֹלָה, but understands it as "mischief, disturbance" (cf. Arab. *'ulūl* [Lane, 2125b, "evil, mischief, commotion, fight"]) and translates "when his wrath provokes disaster."

A much more attractive emendation, adopted in the *Translation* above, is that of Böttcher, to עַוְלָה "iniquity"; thus BJ, JB, NJB, NJPS (there is support in Aq, Theod). It is followed by *HALOT*, 2:798a, Hitzig, Budde, Duhm, Hölscher, Kissane, Larcher, Tur-Sinai, Fedrizzi, Gerleman (*BHS*), Andersen, Gray. But there remains a difference of opinion over the subj of מקנה if it is understood as a verbal form: Is it (1) God (RSV "he is jealous with anger against iniquity," Fohrer, Pope, Gray), (2) wrath (אף) (JB "wrath overtakes iniquity," NJB "anger flashes out against iniquity," Terrien), (3) "what arouses" (מַקְנֶה) (Tur-Sinai "what arouses anger because of iniquity"), or (4) "kindling" (מקנה) (NJPS "the kindling of anger against iniquity"). The view taken in the *Translation* above is that מקנה is a second obj of יגיד "declares," parallel to אף "anger" in the first colon.

37:1.a. אף is usually "also," but because there has been nothing previously that has made Elihu's heart tremble, it is more likely to be the emphatic "indeed" (for examples, see *DCH*, 1:352b, though it is there understood as "also"); so too Gordis, Hartley. See also 15:4; 19:4; 34:17. Driver–Gray note Ps 16:6, 7, 9 as examples of אף introducing emphatically a new thought. KJV, RSV, NJPS, NEB understand it as "also," while NJB "my very heart" seems to take it as an emphatic, and NAB ignores it altogether. Emendations to אַךְ "indeed" (Graetz) or הֲלֹא "does it not?" (Bickell, Duhm, Beer [*BH*² *prps*]) have the same effect. Both Ball and Sutcliffe ("Notes on Job," 89–90) remove the "colourless" אף־לזאת "also for this," and find here the noun פַּלָּצוּת "horror," i.e., "with horror my heart trembles" at the thunder and lightning.

1.b. Duhm and Beer (*BH*² *frt*) emended לבי "my heart" to לִבְּךָ "your heart," on the ground that "it must be a matter of indifference to his hearers whether Elihu fears the storm or not, if they do not fear it" (so too Moffatt "Does it not make you tremble?"). But to mention one's own reaction to bad news is a normal trope in Heb. (cf. D. R. Hillers, "A Convention in Hebrew Literature: The Reaction to Bad News," *ZAW* 77 [1965] 86–90). Further, if Job is addressed here, we must also emend שמעו "hear" (pl) to שְׁמַע "hear" (sg) in v 2 (as Duhm does).

1.c. נתר is usually understood as "spring, start up, leap" (BDB, 684a [נתר I]; *HALOT*, 2:736b [נתר II]; *DCH*, 5:817b [נתר II]). G. R. Driver ("Difficult Words in the Hebrew Prophets," in *Studies in Old Testament Prophecy*, FS H. Robinson, ed. H. H. Rowley [Edinburgh: T. & T. Clark, 1950] 52–72 [71–72]; cf. נתר IV, *DCH*, 5:818a), however, postulated another נתר "fall away," cognate with Arab. *natara* "drag violently, tear" (Lane, 2761c); NEB, with "start from its place," does not follow this suggestion of Driver's, contrary to its custom. Gray would derive it rather from נתר "be free, loose" (as in 6:9), thus "be dislocated." Dhorme and Tur-Sinai both proposed a root תרר "tremble, quake" (cf. Akk. *tarāru* "palpitate").

Thinking the second colon too short, Beer (*BHK*) makes the unsupported suggestion to read קִרְבִּי "my inner self" instead of לבי "my heart" and to make לבי the subject of ויתר in the second colon (Driver–Gray are attracted by this too, and Hölscher adopts it).

2.a. שמעו שמוע is the familiar idiom of the finite verb with the inf abs to express emphasis (NRSV, NIV, NEB "listen, listen," NJPS, REB "just listen," KJV "hear attentively"). NAB omits שמעו as a dittograph, while Beer (*BHK*) omits שמוע for the sake of the meter. Dahood read שְׁמַע מָע "hear, pray" ("Northwest Semitic Philology and Job," 72), suggesting a new word מָע, cognate with Ugar. *m'* "please" (after an impv; see *DUL*, 519). Theod had "listen" as a sg (ἄκουε), as if addressed to Job, but Job does not appear to be addressed until v 14. Duhm, Beer (*BH*² שְׁמַע), and Hölscher, however, emend to שְׁמַע "hear" (sg). Aq had ἤκουσα "I heard," by assimilation to the verbs of v 1. It is improbable that any allusion is made to Job's own use of the same idiom in 13:17; 21:2 (against Strauss).

2.b. The noun רגז seems best translated "raging" in its seven occurrences (plus one in Aram.); so in 39:24 it is paralleled with the רעשׁ "shaking" of the war horse, while in 3:17 it is the "raging" of the wicked (see *Comment* on 3:17). NAB "his angry voice" captures the idea. It is not a generic term for "noise" (as KJV, NJPS), still less specifically for "thunder" (RSV, NEB), "blast" (NJB), "roar" (NIV, Hartley), "rumbling" (Driver–Gray), or "rumble" (Habel). Gray remarks that Arab. *rajaza* VIII means "thunder," but this is not quite right, for the verb means "recite, make a continuous sound," which may be used of wind or thunder or the sea but does not specifically mean "thunder" (Lane, 1036a).

2.c. קולו is "his voice." קול sometimes clearly means "thunder" rather than "voice" (e.g., Exod 19:16; 1 Sam 12:17), but never with the suff קולו "his voice," even though the referent may well be the thunder.

2.d. Though the noun הֶגֶה occurs elsewhere only in two other places, of mourning (Ezek 2:10) and of sighing (Ps 90:9), the verb הגה is a generic word for repetitive or continued sound of various kinds: the growling of a lion (Isa 31:4), the moaning of a dove (Isa 38:14), the groaning of mourners (Isa 16:7), the sound of speech (e.g., Isa 59:3) or of verbally expressed meditation (e.g., Josh 1:8). Both noun and verb are always of the sound of animate beings, so it seems preferable to use a term applicable to a person (as against RSV, NIV, NEB, Moffatt, Hartley "rumbling," similarly NAB; GNB "thunder"); KJV, NJB, NJPS have simply "sound." "Muttering" (Driver–Gray) is not a very attractive suggestion. Habel has "growling," as in the *Translation* above.

3.a. תחת is lit. "under," but the sense must be "across" (NJB, GNB, NAB "everywhere under the heavens"; similarly Hölscher); the parallel is "to the corners of the earth."

3.b. The verb is usually taken to be שרה "let loose" (so BDB, 1056a; *HALOT*, 4:1652b; RSV "lets it go," NRSV, NJPS "lets it loose," NIV "unleashes," NAB "sends," NEB "lets it roll," JB "hurls," Moffatt "sends it pealing"), cognate with Aram. שרא (with Arab. *saruwa* "throw off" [Lane, 1353a], according to Guillaume). It hardly means "hurl," which is how Dhorme and others would like to translate it (NJB "is hurled"). But this would be its sole occurrence in Biblical Heb. (its use in the Qere of Jer 15:11 is doubtful). KJV "directeth it" derives the verb from שרה, understood as a byform of ישר "be straight" (cf. Buxtorf, 847).

A preferable suggestion was made by H. L. Ginsberg ("נוספות לעלילת אַלאִין בעל [Addenda to the Epic of אלאין בעל]," *Tarbiz* 4 [1933] 380–90 [385]; "The Ugaritic Texts and Textual Criticism," *JBL* 62 [1943] 109–15 [109 n. 1], though with less assurance than in his 1933 article), who connected it with Ugar. *šrh* "flash," used in Baal II.v.9 (*CML*, 97 = Baal 4.v.71; *CML*², 61 = *KTU* 1.4.V.9; *CTA*, 19a), which is precisely of causing lightning to flash. So too Pope, Blommerde, Fohrer, Habel, Hartley, and Cohen (*Hapax Legomena*, 124); Andersen is tempted. Whether the verb has a 3 masc sg suff or is an old *yaqtulu* form (as A. Schoors, "Literary Phrases," in *Ras Shamra Parallels: The Texts from Ugarit and the Hebrew Bible*, ed. L. R. Fisher [Rome: Pontifical Biblical Institute, 1972] 1:1–70 [24–25]) can be left open. Gray also follows Ginsberg's proposal, but understands the word as a noun, שְׁרֵהוּ "[under the whole sky is] his flashing."

Other philologically based solutions, less persuasive than the foregoing, are: (1) Another verb שרה "multiply" is proposed by P. Wernberg-Møller ("Two Notes," *VT* 8 [1958] 305–8 [307–8]); he appeals to Arab. *šr'*, finding the verb also at Isa 57:9; Ezek 27:25. But it hard to see what verb he intends since Arab. *šarra* is "be bad" (Lane, 1524a). (2) Also without great merit is the view of Tur-Sinai and Gordis that ישרהו is the noun יֹשֶׁר, meaning "approval" (Tur-Sinai) or "strength" (Gordis), not "uprightness" as it does usually. But we would expect the first vowel to be *qāmeṣ qāṭān* (cf. יָשְׁרוֹ at 33:23), and the suff to be וֹ rather than הוּ־.

Earlier emendations, such as that of Ehrlich, to read יְשׁוּרֻהוּ "they perceive it" (Aq and Vg also saw the verb שור here) are rendered unnecessary by the proposal of Pope.

3.c. אורו, lit. "his light," i.e., lightning, as in 36:30. The word אורו "his lightning," which belongs to the second colon, is anticipated by the obj suff in the verb ישרהו; in the *Translation* it has been transferred to the first colon for the sake of intelligibility (so too Dhorme). That the whole line refers to lightning is accepted by NIV, NJB, NJPS, GNB. Others think the first colon refers to the thunder of v 2 (e.g., RSV "under the whole heaven he lets it go," Moffatt "He sends the sound pealing across the sky").

Tur-Sinai saw אור "condemnation" here (see *Note* 36:30.d), in contrast to ישר "approval" in the first colon.

3.d. על "upon" seems equivalent here to אל "to" (as Beer [*BH*²] noted).

4.a. Dhorme has "behind Him," but it seems more likely that the picture is of the thunder following the lightning; cf. Habel "in its wake."

4.b. It is קול "a sound" (not "a voice," as Dhorme), rather than קולו "his voice," as emended by Bickell², Budde (קֹלוֹ), Duhm, Beer (*BHK*), Hölscher, Sicre Díaz, Hartley (possibly), NAB (*Textual Notes*, 378) with the support of two Heb. MSS, or קוֹלִי "his voice," the *yodh*, a 3d-person suff, being omitted by haplography (as Blommerde; for other examples, see *Note* 21:16.e). At 28:26 (which is also Elihu's, on the view taken in this commentary), קול seems to mean "thunder" (חֲזִיז קֹלוֹת "lightning of thunders"); see also *Note* 37:2.c above.

4.c. שאג is commonly of the roaring of a lion (Judg 14:5; Amos 3:4, 8; Ps 104:21), and of Yahweh's roaring, presumably in the thunder, at Jer 25:30; Amos 1:2; Joel 3:16 (4:16).

4.d. יַרְעֵם is hiph impf juss (cf. BDB, 947a), a poetic usage, and does not need to be altered to יַרְעִים (as Beer [*BHK*]). Duhm and Hölscher add (*frt*) אֵל "God [thunders]" (as in v 5).

4.e. קול גאונו, lit. "the voice of his majesty." The term may, however, mean simply "his uplifted, mighty voice" (cf. *HALOT*, 1:169a); and see *Note* on 38:11. Duhm read גְּרוֹנוֹ "[he does not restrain the voice of] his throat," but the phrase does not occur elsewhere. The *Translation* above, following NEB, transposes v 4c to follow v 6.

5.a. On the reasons for regarding this colon as not original, see *Comment*. It is deleted by Driver–Gray, NAB, NJB.

Among emendations, (1) Duhm attractively reads יַרְאֵנוּ אֵל נפלאות "God shows us wonderful things," deleting בקולו "with his voice" (so too Strahan, Beer [*BHK frt*], Hölscher, Fohrer, Terrien, Lévêque, 589, NJB "Yes, certainly God shows us marvels"). The acc of both the person and the thing is well attested for ראה hiph (e.g., Gen 12:1; Exod 9:16). (2) Budde reads עשה נפלאות וְאֵין חֵקֶר "he does wonderful things past finding out," adding וְאֵין חֵקֶר as in 5:9 (cf. 9:10; so too Driver–Gray). (3) Dhorme has "God by his voice works [יַעֲמֹל for ירעם] wonders" (followed in part by de Wilde, who, however, deletes בקולו); but the verb עמל always seems in Heb. to mean "labor," not simply "do, work," and it never takes an obj (except the noun עָמָל "labor"). NEB "God's voice is marvellous in its working" emends ירעם "thunder" to יַעֲמִיד (Brockington), presumably in the sense "establish."

5.b. Rather than "thunder" for רעם, Fedrizzi made the interesting suggestion that in the qal the verb means "be dismayed, disconcerted, agitated" (of the sea at Ps 96:11; 98:7; 1 Chr 16:32; of persons at Ezek 27:35); he would render here "God makes marvelous things lowly with his voice." Gray reads יִפְעַל "[God] does [wondrous things]," omitting קולו "his voice," but the suggestion is a little weak.

5.c. The *Translation* takes נפלאות עשה "he does wonderful things" together, against the Masoretic accents (similarly Larcher, JB "reveals wonders," NJB "shows us marvels"). The Masoretic punctuation would suggest that נפלאות is the obj of ירעם "thunders," but Gordis understands קולו נפלאות as "with his wondrous voice" (so too M. Dahood ["The Phoenician Contribution to Biblical Wisdom Literature," in *The Role of the Phoenicians in the Interaction of Mediterranean Civilizations,* ed. W. A. Ward (Beirut: American University in Beirut, 1968) 123–52 (140)], Blommerde, Sicre Díaz), the suff being attached, unusually, to the nomen regens in the construct chain. נפלאות might perhaps be an adv acc, "(acts) wonderfully" (so Strauss; cf. GKC, §118p), but it seems rather to be a noun parallel to גדלות. It is a noun in the acc case also in v 14.

5.d. NAB attractively reconstructs v 5 thus: עשה גדלות ולא נדע "he does great things beyond our knowing," followed by נִפְלָאוֹת וְלֹא נַעְקְבֵם "wonders past our searching out," lit. "and we cannot search them out" (*Textual Notes,* 378). Gray thinks לא נדע "we do not know" is a relative clause, and wants to remove the *waw,* but the MT is perfectly satisfactory.

6.a. שֶׁלֶג "snow" is here spelled שֶׁלַג by Codex Leningradensis (the base text of *BHS*).

6.b. אמר is usually "say," but Gray thinks it here has the nuance "command," like Arab. *'amara* (Lane, 95b).

6.c. הוא is sg impv of הוא "fall" (BDB, 216b), cognate with Arab. *hawâ* (Lane, 3046b); elsewhere the verb has been recognized at 1 Sam 1:18 and Prov 14:35 (G. R. Driver, "Problems in Aramaic and Hebrew Texts," in *Miscellanea orientalia dedicata Antonio Deimel annos 70 complenti,* Analecta orientalia 12 [Rome: Pontificio Istituto Biblico, 1935] 46–70 [48–49]), and perhaps in Eccl 5:16 if emended (see *DCH*, 2:493b, Guillaume, Gray). It is an alternative form for הוה "fall" (*HALOT,* 1:241b; *DCH,* 2:502a). It is not the verb הוה "be, become," equivalent to היה, which occurs some five times. KJV, thinking it is, has "Be thou on the earth," but most modern versions have "fall."

Emendations have been proposed: (1) To רַוֵּה or רַוֵּא "saturate," by Graetz and Beer (*BH*² *frt; BHK prps*); rain and snow are said in Isa 55:10 to saturate (רוה hiph) the earth. But the Masoretic text, though exceptional, may stand. (2) Tur-Sinai has the idea to read הוא רֻץ "Ho! Run!"; he compares הוא (which he does not vocalize) with Syr. *hwâ'*, Arab. *hayâ* (Wehr–Cowan, 1044b, has *hīh* "hey"), and Heb. הוֹי. The reading רֻץ "run" presupposes that the initial *aleph* of ארץ is a dittograph of the last letter of הוא. But it is hard to believe that "run" would be the verb of command for the *snow.*

6.d. MT has וגשם מטר וגשם מטרות "and a shower of rain and a shower of rains," a simple duplication that cannot be right (though KJV tried to make sense of it with "to the small rain, and to the great rain," while NRSV has "the shower of rain, his heavy shower of rain," NJPS "the downpour of rain, his mighty downpour of rain"; similarly Habel). Budde, Driver–Gray, Dhorme, Hölscher, Kissane, Tur-Sinai, Guillaume, Gordis, de Wilde, Hartley, van der Lugt, Strauss, NAB omit the first phrase, וגשם מטר; in that case, מטרות needs to be revocalized as an absolute, מְטָרוֹת, and the phrase needs to be prefixed with ל, thus וּלְגֶשֶׁם מְטָרוֹת "and to the rain of showers," which is adopted in the *Translation* above. מטר, which is always "rain" in the Hebrew Bible, happens to be used of snow at Ecclus 43:18, and it is tempting to think that this might be so here too, making the line concern snow alone. But then the two cola would be almost identical in meaning, which is unlikely. Others omit the second phrase, and read, for example, וְלַגֶּשֶׁם וּמָטָר "and to the shower and the rain" (so Beer [*BHK*], Fohrer, Lévêque, 590, Gerleman [*BHS prb*], Gray); so too RSV. NEB also omits the second phrase from v 6b, and reads וגשם מטר "and [to] the rainstorms" (Brockington); it transfers גשם מטרות to a newly constructed v 6c: (ו)כי ישמע קולו גשם מטרות (ו)לא יעקבם "And when his voice is heard, the floods of rain pour down unchecked."

Though some seek to distinguish גשם as "downpour" and מטר as "rain" (so Hölscher; cf. Dalman, *Arbeit und Sitte,* 1:144), their usage in the Hebrew Bible does not permit it.

Sicre Díaz proposes a small emendation, וְגֶשֶׁם מַמְטִיר "and he sends the rain [and the rain of his powerful showers]." Good reads לַגֶּשֶׁם מְטַר "and to the rain, Rain."

6.e. עזו is, as it stands, "(of) his strength," which is reflected in KJV "and to the great rain of his strength," NRSV "his heavy shower of rain," NJPS "his mighty downpour of rain," NAB "to his heavy, drenching rain," Habel "his mighty torrential rain"; similarly Tur-Sinai, Good, Strauss. But most prefer to revocalize the word to עֹזּוּ "be strong" (עזז impv pl), parallel to the impv command to the snow; so Dhorme, Beer (*BHK*), Hölscher, Kissane, Larcher, Fohrer (עֹזּוּ), Guillaume, Lévêque, 590, Fedrizzi, Gerleman (*BHS prb*), de Wilde, Hartley, van der Lugt, Gray (עֱזּוּ), NEB "Be fierce," REB "Be violent," NJB "Now rain hard!," RSV "Be strong." Not so attractive are the suggestions of Duhm, Beer (*BH*[2] *vel*), תָּעֹזּוּ "you shall be strong," of Gordis (followed by Sicre Díaz), עוּזוּ "flow down," from עוז, which he argues means "flee, run" rather than "take refuge" (as BDB, 731b; *HALOT,* 2:797a), or (mentioned by Beer [*BHK*]) עֲרֹפוּ "drop down (rain)" (cf. Deut 32:2). The pl impv calls for a pl subj, hence the preference in the preceding *Note* and the *Translation* for the phrase וּלְגֶשֶׁם מְטָרוֹת "and to the rain of showers."

4c.a. With NEB, the colon v 4c is transferred to this point, for the line in its usual place is repetitious and anticlimactic. See further, *Comment.*

4c.b. Taking the colon in its Masoretic place, NJB has "He does not check his thunderbolts until his voice resounds no more." This sounds impressive, but can the poet really be saying that God does not stop the lightnings until there is no more thunder? It would be more meaningful to say that he does not stop the thunder until there is no more lightning. Strauss thinks the כי introduces a consecutive clause ("he does not hold them back, so that his voice is heard"), comparing GKC, §166b; but the examples given there (a fuller list in *DCH,* 4:386a) do not inspire confidence for such a rendering here (most examples are following an interrogative). Duhm reads מִפִּיו "from his mouth" instead of כי "when," i.e., "from his mouth his voice is heard" (noted by Beer [*BHK*]); it is, however, too banal. Gray reads מִפִּי יִשָּׁמַע קולו "as peal upon peal is heard," taking מפי as equivalent to כְּפִי or לְפִי or עַל־פִּי "in proportion as"; but this seems impossible, since such idioms are followed by a noun or verbal noun.

4c.c. Lit. "he does not delay them." יעקבם is often understood as "he restrains them." If the colon is left in its Masoretic place, there is no antecedent for the suff "them," and, although the lightning must be meant, the term אוֹר used for it in v 3 is sg, and we cannot brush aside the discrepancy as Gordis does (Kissane emends to יְעַקְּבֶנּוּ "he [does not] hold it back," and Pope thinks the final letter is enclitic *mem*). Hence many propose we read יְעַקֵּב בְּרָקִים "he [does not] restrain (his) lightnings" (so Budde [בְּרָקִם], Peake [*frt*], Beer [*BHK prb*], Dhorme, Driver–Gray, Hölscher, Larcher, Fohrer, Terrien [בְּרָקָיו "his lightnings"], Lévêque, 589, de Wilde, BJ, JB, NJB). RSV does not emend, but feels obliged to translate "does not restrain the lightnings" (similarly NJB). NIV "he holds nothing back" does not represent the pl suff. NJPS "No one can find a trace of it by the time His voice is heard" takes its clue from עקב "follow the heels, track, trace," but what is it of which no trace can be found? The lightning, which has disappeared when the thunder sounds? Or the sound of the thunder? Habel adopts the latter interpretation, with his "Once his voice is heard, none can track it down"; but the thought of tracking down the sound of thunder remains strange. Moffatt had a good idea, that what is restrained is the rain ("Nor does he hold the downpour back"), but there is unfortunately no word for rain in the text (though Gray reads יְעַקֵּב מַיִם "he does [not] restrain the water"). NEB, which transfers the colon to the end of v 6, also understands עקב as "restrain," translating "And when his voice is heard, the floods of rain pour down unchecked" (the "floods of rain" having been referred to in the previous colon, v 6b).

It is questionable, however, whether עקב really does mean "restrain." If it is indeed connected to עָקֵב "heel," it can mean "attack at the heel" (Hos 12:4) or "overreach" (Gen 27:36; Jer 9:3) (so BDB, 784a; *HALOT,* 2:872a), but "restrain" is a rather different idea. Gordis regards it as a byform of עכב "detain, prevent," well attested in MH (Jastrow, 1077b), a much better solution (followed by Pope); Gordis, however, continued to translate "nor does He restrain the lightning bolts." Hartley, following Gordis's proposal, translates more appropriately "one cannot stay them when his voice is heard," explaining that humans cannot stay the lightning or keep back the thunder. Perhaps that is too obvious, though. Pope's interpretation, "Men stay not when his voice is heard," is not likely, for the only evidence for עקב is that it is a transitive verb. Guillaume understood the verb as "delay," comparing Arab. *'aqaba,* but that verb means "follow" (Form IV "cause to follow") rather than "delay" (Lane, 2097c, 2099b).

7.a. ביד־כל־אדם יחתום is lit. "on the hand of every human he sets a seal" (RSV "he seals up the hand of every man"), which could comfortably mean "the activity of every human he seals up, i.e., prevents." Many, however, thinking of 9:7 (ובעד כוכבים יחתם "and upon the stars he sets a seal," so that they do not appear above the horizon), emend ביד "upon the hand of" to בְּעַד "upon" (Graetz, Beer [*BHK*], Duhm, Ehrlich, Dhorme, Fohrer, Pope, Fedrizzi, Gerleman [*BHS prp*], Sicre Díaz, Hartley, NEB [Brockington], NAB [*Textual Notes,* 378]); this is followed in the *Translation* above. Gordis agrees that is the meaning, but argues that יד is nothing but "a divergent phonetic orthography" for עד (cf. his "A Note on *Yad,*" *JBL* 62 [1942] 341–44). The idea is of humans being confined indoors by the snowfalls or by the downpours of rain; thus NJB "he brings all human activity to a standstill," NIV "he stops every man from his labor," NEB "he shuts every man fast indoors," Moffatt "that keep men within doors."

NJPS "the downpour of rain . . . is as a sign on every man's hand" can be understood only by reference to 33:16, which it renders "Then He opens men's understanding, and by disciplining them leaves His signature," the idea being that both discipline there and the snow and the rain here are signatures of the divine presence (so too Habel); but it seems a somewhat fanciful view. Strauss also retains the MT by understanding "What is in every human's hand he seals up," an abbreviated object clause in initial position; but this is a little awkward.

Tur-Sinai suggests an emendation for יחתם "he seals," יַחְתֵּם "he sends them down" (from נחת "go down"), understanding ביד as "for." The form יַחְתֵּם, however, cannot be well supported, and the parallels he alleges for ביד (8:4; 12:6; 15:23) are completely unconvincing.

7.b. The colon is omitted by NAB as a dittograph of vv 5b, 7a (*Textual Notes,* 378).

7.c. אנשי is constr, "men of," but that does not make good sense. אנשי מעשהו "men of his deed," though odd, could mean "men whom he has made" (cf. RV; so too Strauss). But it is far preferable to emend to אֱנוֹשׁ "(every) human" (so Perles[2], 26, Beer [*BHK*], Kissane [*vel*], Fohrer, Sicre Díaz; and the *Translation* above) or אֲנָשִׁים "humans" (so Beer [*BHK vel*], Dhorme, Hölscher, Kissane [*vel*], Pope, Gerleman [*BHS prp*], Hartley, van der Lugt), the final *mem* having been lost by haplography. Gordis, less convincingly, agrees that אֲנָשִׁים is intended, but argues that the form is an abbreviation or due to "phonetic elision." אֲנָשִׁים for "humans" is especially typical of the Elihu speeches (33:15, 16, 27; 36:24; 37:24; the word appears in Job outside the Elihu speeches only at 4:13). Beer (*BH*[2] *frt*) thinks כל "all" should perhaps be deleted.

7.d. לדעת . . . מעשהו, lit. "to know his deed." Though it is not very clear what exactly is meant by God's "deed," the line of thought does seem to match Elihu's argument that nature is a divine revelation. D. W. Thomas ("Note on לָדַעַת in Job xxxvii. 7," *JTS* NS 5 [1954] 56–57), on the other hand, found here a further example of the root ידע II "be quiet, be at rest; be humiliated," cognate with Arab. *wadu'a* "be quiet" (Lane, 3051a; see *DCH,* 4:110b, 586a [bibliography]); he proposes לדעת כל־אֱנוֹשׁ מִמַּעֲשֵׂהוּ "so that every man might rest from his work [in the fields]" (מעשה meaning "husbandry" also at Exod 23:16; Judg 19:16). This suggestion is followed by Guillaume, Rowley, de Wilde, Gray, and in part by NEB "and all men whom he has made must stand idle" (REB "and all whom he has made are quiet"). On the supposed root ידע II, the existence of which has been challenged, see *Note* 33:24.c.

A possible emendation is עֹשֵׂהוּ "his maker, creator" for מעשׂהו, restoring the *mem* to the end of אנשׁים (so Reiske, Hirzel). Not so persuasive is Ehrlich's reading מְעַטֵהוּ "[so that every human may know] his littleness" (inf of מעט, with suff), which is doubtfully supported by LXX τὴν ἑαυτοῦ ἀσθένειαν "his weakness."

8.a. חיה is collective, "beasts," as in 5:22, 23; Gen 1:25. Tur-Sinai has the novel idea that חיה refers to the cherub on which God rides, and translates "the storm-beast," but he does not explain why it is retiring into its lair during the rain.

8.b. ותבא must mean "and enters," but it breaks the rules of the *waw* consec; hence NAB reads תָּבֹא, without the copula (*Textual Notes*, 378). Watson, 345, notes this example of "reversed ballast prepositions," in which the usual prep *beth* comes second and the fuller form במו comes first (another example at 34:26).

8.c. עֶרֶב "lair" of a wild animal; the noun occurs only here and at 38:40. Though the verb means "lie in wait, ambush," the noun does not convey any thought of attack in these two passages.

8.d. מְעוֹנָה is a "dwelling place," of Yahweh (e.g., Ps 76:2 [3]), humans (Jer 21:13), wisdom (Ecclus 14:27), light (1QH 12:5), and, often, wild animals (Amos 3:4; Nah 2:12 [13]; Ps 104:22; Job 38:40). The form מָעוֹן is more common.

9.a. Kissane moves to this point vv 21–22a.

9.b. Duhm, Beer (*BH*[2] *frt* תֵּימָן) added תמן to חדר (deleting also the ה of החדר), reflecting the phrase חדרי תמן "chambers of the south" in 9:9. Thus RV "out of the chamber of the south," NJB "from the Mansion of the South," though these translations do not necessarily accept the emendation (nor does Gray). The חדר of the winds is not elsewhere thought of as a prison (unlike the winds of Aeolus; see *Comment*), so NEB's "The hurricane bursts from its prison" is hard to justify.

9.c. סופה is "storm" (BDB, 693a; *DCH*, vol. 6, *s.v.*) or "gale" (*HALOT*, 2:747b), so "tempest" (NAB, NIV), "storm wind" (NJB, NJPS), or "hurricane" (NEB), but not "whirlwind" (KJV, RSV, NRSV); see *Comment.*

9.d. The term מזרים, found only here, is usually taken as "the scattering ones," "the scattering winds" (RVmg), piel ptcp of זרה "scatter" (so RSV, Hölscher, Fohrer, Pope). The view that the reference is to a constellation Mazzarim, the rising of which heralds the onset of the cold (as NJPS "the cold from the constellations"), goes back to Hoffmann.

Proposed emendations are (1) מְזָוִים "storehouses" (from מָזוּ, as at Ps 144:13) (so Budde, Duhm, Beer [*BH*[2] *prps*], Driver–Gray, Beer [*BHK*], Kissane, Habel), or (2) זֶרֶם "downpour" (apparently N. Herz, "The Astral Terms in Job ix 9, xxxviii 31–32," *JTS* 14 [1913] 577), or (3) מַזְרִים "the one that brings rain [זֶרֶם]" (Mowinckel, cited by Hölscher). (4) Tur-Sinai suggests מְזָרִים is "the press" (cf. זור "press"; *DCH*, 5:212b, מְזָרִים I; Levy, 2:22a), in which water is squeezed from the clouds; he is followed by Good. (5) G. Schiaperelli (*Astronomy in the Old Testament* [Oxford: Clarendon Press, 1905] 69–72) reads מִזְרַיִם "the two winnowing-fans" (from מִזְרֶה), a term for the constellations of the Greater and Lesser Bear (the Big and the Little Dipper), thought of as the origin of the south wind; so too de Wilde.

10.a. קֶרַח is both "frost" (Gen 31:40; Jer 36:30) and "ice" (Job 6:16; 38:29; Ps 147:17; Ezek 1:22 is dubious). Implausible in the context is Tur-Sinai's proposal that it is a word for "tempest" (cf. Syr. *qarḥā* [J. Payne Smith, 518b]).

10.b. יִתֵּן is "he gives," but it would be strange that "God" should be the subj when we have just had מנשמת־אל "by the breath of God." Many therefore read יֻתַּן "is given" (so Beer [*BH*[2]], Dhorme, Hölscher, Kissane, Pope [*frt*], de Wilde, Gray); it is not always clear whether versions, ancient and modern, read the Heb. differently or simply smoothed the clause with a translation in the passive. Thus Symm δοθήσεται, Pesh *ntyhb*, Tg יתיהב "will be given"; KJV, RSV "is given," NJPS, NEB "is formed." The subj of the qal יִתֵּן could of course be indefinite (Gordis; cf. GKC, §144b), which is probably the best solution.

Ehrlich would read יֻתַּךְ "is melted" or יַתֵּךְ "he melts," understanding the line as "by the breath of God the ice is melted, or, he melts the ice, and the breadth of waters turns into a flow," מוצק being derived from יצק "flow." But it would be strange to hear of the ice melting without hearing of its being formed.

10.c. במוצק, lit. "as a hardened thing," the *beth* being *beth essentiae* (as also de Wilde, Gray), and the noun מוּצָק "hardened, solid thing," from יצק "pour out" (מוּצָק I in BDB, 427b; *HALOT*, 2:559b; *DCH*, 5:185a; so too de Wilde); cf. מוצק as a solid mass of earth in 38:38. Cf. NEB "frozen hard as iron," GNB "turns to solid ice." There is no ground for Tur-Sinai's concept of a storm (see *Note* 10.a on קרח) driving the abundance of waters behind "a solid dam," the firmament.

Less probable than the connection with יצק "pour out" is a derivation from צוק "narrow, constrain," thus a "narrowing" or "straitening" of the waters as solid ice forms where there had previously been water, as KJV "the breadth of the waters is straitened"; so too *HALOT,* 2:559b, Driver–Gray, Good. But it is possible that "in constraint" means "frozen" (מוּצָק II in BDB, 848a; *DCH,* 5:185b).

11.a. אַף "also," not emphatic (as Gordis), unlike 37:1.

11.b. טרח occurs only here, but the noun טֹרַח is plainly "burden" at Isa 1:14; Deut 1:12. So "loads" (RSV, NIV, NJPS), "weighs down" (NJB), or "he gives the dense clouds their load of moisture" (NEB) are good translations; KJV had "he wearieth." Hontheim, however, followed by Budde², Beer (*BH*²), Dhorme, finds a different root טרח, cognate with Arab. *ṭaraḥa* "fling, hurl" (Lane, 1837a) (similarly Tur-Sinai, Pope); this is followed by REB "he hurls lightning from the dense clouds."

11.c. עב "cloud" and ענן "cloud" are both sg, but collective; they are translated here with pls only to satisfy the needs of v 12, where we cannot easily ascribe wheeling round and round to a collective "cloud." Pope implausibly translates "he hurls lightning from the nimbus," taking עב "cloud" as an adv acc, as also ענן "cloud" in the next colon.

11.d. רי, occurring only here in BH (though it has been proposed also for 33:21), is generally understood as "moisture" (so RSV, NEB, Hölscher, de Wilde), from רוה "be saturated" (BDB, 924a; *HALOT,* 3:1223b); the word occurs in the form רְאִי in Ecclus 31:28. This interpretation is accepted in the *Translation.* KJV's "by watering he wearieth the cloud" is called "bizarre" by Rowley. One can see how they came to the translation, but what does it mean? Does God "water" the clouds as one waters a garden, until the cloud is completely saturated?

Among alternative interpretations, (1) Hoffmann thinks רי a writing of רֳאִי "spectacle," i.e., the rainbow, or of רְאִי "reflection." (2) Ehrlich (following Tg) takes the word as ברי rather than רי, thus בְּרִי "sunshine" or "brightness," from ברר "purify." (3) Dhorme proposed that ברי was Boreas, the name of the north wind in Greek mythology ("Un mot aryen dans le livre de Job," *JPOS* 2 [1922] 66–68); though he later foreswore this view in his commentary, it remains plausible. (4) Ancient versions were baffled by the term, and saw in it either בַּר "corn" (as Vg) or "chosen" (Theod).

Emendations: (1) Hontheim, Budde², and Beer (*BH*² *frt; BHK*) read בָּרָק "thunderbolt" (thus Dhorme "at times the cloud hurls [see *Note* 11.b on טרח] a thunderbolt," REB "he hurls lightning from the dense clouds"; Driver–Gray, Pope). This may fit better with the second colon, if it is thought to be about lightning (in the *Translation* above it is taken to be about rainstorms). (2) Duhm, Beer (*BH*² *al*) read בָּרָד "hail"; hence NAB "With hail, also, the clouds are laden." (3) O. Komlós ("אַף־בְּרִי יַטְרִיחַ עָב" [Job 37:11], *VT* 10 [1960] 75–77 [77]) implausibly reads אַף בּוֹרֵא "the nose of the creator [hurls the cloud]"; even allowing that God's "nose" could hurl anything, it is not cloud but wind or lightning that can be hurled. (4) Tur-Sinai reads בֹּרוֹ "his innocence," which he takes to mean "his declaration of innocence," parallel to אורו "his condemnation" in the second colon (see *Note* 36:30.d); the sense is forced. (5) Gray reads בָּרוֹ "his bright (sun)."

To similar effect as that of the last mentioned suggestion, M. Dahood ("Hebrew-Ugaritic Lexicography II," *Bib* 45 [1964] 393–412 [412]; *Psalms I,* 123), followed by Blommerde, vocalizes בָּרִי "his shining one (the sun)," the suff being 3d person (for other examples, see *Note* 23:14.b), and translates "And his shining one dispels the mist, and his sun scatters the clouds"; but such a sentence is out of place here where the rains of winter are being described.

The issues relating to רי and טרח are discussed by Grabbe, 114–16, and A. Robinson, "The Meaning of *rî* and the Dubiety of the Form *harrê* and Its Variants," *VT* 24 (1974) 500–504.

11.e. יפיץ is universally taken as פוץ I hiph "scatter," but this does not seem an entirely suitable verb to use of lightning or light (אור); it is not the same thing as "spread" (RV, NEB) or "radiate" (NJB). It seems more likely that we have here פוץ II "flow, overflow" (BDB, 807a; *DCH,* vol. 6, *s.v.*), cognate with Arab. *fāḍa* "overflow, pour forth" (Lane, 2471c; cf. Kopf, "Arabische Etymologien," 191) (*HALOT,* 3:918b, conflates פוץ I and II).

11.f. ענן אורו is in the Masoretic vocalization "his cloud of light," which Gordis takes to be the lighter clouds that are driven away by the denser rain clouds. If we take these two nouns together in a construct chain, God must be the subj of the verb יפיץ "scatters," as of the verb יטריח "loads" in the first colon (so KJV "he scattereth his bright cloud," NIV "he scatters his lightning," NJPS "[He] scatters His lightning-clouds"). The *Translation* above agrees that God is the subj of the verb, but it understands פוץ as "overflow" and emends ענן to אֵדוֹ "his mist." Cross (*Canaanite Myth and Hebrew Epic,* 147 n. 4) sees here another example of אור as "bright cloud."

Many, however, prefer to take עָנָן, so vocalized as an absolute, as the subj of יפיץ "(the cloud) scatters (its light, or, lightning)" (so many Heb. MSS, RSV, NAB; similarly NJB, NEB, REB; Beer [*BHK*], Driver–Gray, Kissane, Pope, Hartley [*frt*]).

A reference to lightning, however, seems out of place at this point, and we may well suspect that

אורו is corrupt. NEB (but not REB) has "and the clouds spread his mist abroad," reading אֵדוֹ "his mist," as Tg. This seems an excellent idea, all the more so if we take אד as "flood" or the like (see *Note* 36:27.e), as is done in the *Translation* above, since then the whole strophe will have as its theme the winter downpours and would not be reverting to the topic of the lightning. De Wilde less plausibly reads אַכְפּוֹ "[the cloud pours forth] its load, store" (אֶכֶף "pressure" is attested at 33:7). Dahood has "his light [i.e., the sun] scatters the clouds," arguing that אור means "sun" also at 31:26; 37:21; 41:10; Hab 3:4; Ps 37:6 ("Hebrew-Ugaritic Lexicography II," 412; *Psalms I,* 228; cf. also *DCH,* 1:161b §2 "luminaries"). Of these, only Job 31:26 is a clear example; the main difficulty with this suggestion, however, is that the *dispelling* of the clouds does not seem to be the subject matter at this point (contra Gray, who translates "its [the sun's] light dispels the cloud").

12.a. In the Masoretic vocalization the first colon (והוא מסבות) seems too short, and there is no main verb in the sentence, so Budde, Beer (*BHK*), Hölscher insert יִתְהַלֵּךְ "it goes hither and thither" at the end of the colon (followed by Driver–Gray, Gerleman [*BHS frt*], de Wilde); Duhm, followed by Dhorme, inserts it after מתהפך. Beer (*BH*²) inserts יְסוֹבֵב "goes about" at the end of the first colon. Pope, by contrast, virtually eliminates the first colon by deleting מסבות as a gloss on מתהפך.

NAB radically rewrites vv 12–13: והוא מְסִבּוֹתָם הֹפֵךְ בְּתַחְבּוּלֹתָיו "He it is who changes their rounds, according to his plans"; לפעלם על־פני תבל ארצה "in their task upon the surface of the earth"; אם לשבט אם לחסד יצום "whether for punishment or mercy, as he commands" (*Textual Notes,* 378).

12.b. והוא "and it." Is "it" the lightning (אור), as Budde, Peake, Driver–Gray, Strauss, or the cloud (ענן), as Dillmann, Duhm, Guillaume, Gordis? It is improbable that הוא refers to God, though NAB has "it is he who changes their rounds," reading מְסִבּוֹתָם הֹפֵךְ; and cf. NJB "he himself guides their wheeling motion," though it is not clear what their Heb. is, and similarly NJPS "He keeps turning events by His stratagems." In the *Translation* above, the clouds (ענן as a collective) are taken as the subj, hence "they." The fact that in Gen 3:24 הפך hithp is used of the whirling fiery sword is no proof that here it should refer to the lightning. Beer (*BH*²) inserts, without any apparent reason, יְסוֹבֵב "[the clouds] circle about," noting יִתְהַלֵּךְ "go about" as an alternative reading; in *BHK* he adopts the latter reading. Gerleman (*BHS frt*) is also inclined to insert יִתְהַלֵּךְ; so too Gray "it goes its course [in its circuits]."

12.c. מסבות is "circles" (*DCH,* 5:359b; *HALOT,* 2:604a; BDB, 687a [*s.v.* מֵסַב]), used as an adv acc (Gordis), i.e., "in circles." Budde read מִסָּבִיב "round about"; but that word refers to the space about a person or thing, not to motion round about (Driver–Gray). Kissane reads מֵסֵב אוֹתָם "he makes them go round about" (hiph ptcp of סבב), which seems to be followed by Larcher, and JB, NJB "he himself guides their wheeling motion." הפך hithp is "turn this way and that." Hartley thinks that מסבות should probably be deleted as a gloss on מתהפך, as also לפעלם as a gloss on בתחבולתיו and ארצה as a gloss on תבל.

12.d. תחבולה "counsel, direction" from חבל "cord," presumably through the use of a cord to change direction when steering a boat or directing an animal. K is sg, "at his direction"; Q בְּתַחְבּוּלֹתָיו "at his directions" is perhaps to be preferred since the word occurs elsewhere only in the pl (Hölscher, de Wilde, Strauss read K). NJB "presiding over their seasonal changes" is hard to understand. Kissane reads תְּהַפְּכֵם תַּחְבּוּלֹתוֹ "His guidance maketh them change," but the sense is awkward. N. Shupak ("Stylistic and Terminological Traits Common to Biblical and Egyptian Literature," *WO* 14 [1983] 216–30 [222–26]) argues that the word means rather "knot," a term used in Egyptian wisdom literature for a tightly phrased maxim, but such a sense fits the context here poorly.

12.e. לפעלם "for their deed, for their doing" could perhaps be taken as a way of saying "so that they may do" (so Gordis). Others prefer to emend to לִפְעֹל "(in order) to do" (Budde, Beer [*BHK*], Driver–Gray, Sicre Díaz, Gray). In any case, the word should be more closely connected with what follows, "all that he commands them" (כל אשר יצום) being its obj, rather than with what precedes, as in the Masoretic punctuation. To explain the presence of the final *mem* of לפעלם, some have proposed that what follows was originally מִכֹּל אשר יצום "(to do) [anything] of all that he commands them [or יְצַוֵּהוּ commands it (Budde)]" (Budde², Beer [*BH*²], Guillaume). Hartley is inclined to delete the word as a gloss on בְּתַחְבּוּלֹתָיו "at his directions."

12.f. כל אשר יצום "all that he commands them"; the pl suff of the verb is unexpected, since the reference is to the sg cloud (עב, and probably also ענן) of v 11, resumed by the הוא at the beginning of the present verse. But variation in number is a common phenomenon, and emendation to יְצַוֵּהוּ "he commands it" (as Beer [*BHK*], Gray) is not obligatory. Pope thinks the final *mem* is enclitic *mem.*

12.g. NIV connects על־פני תבל ארצה "upon the face of the earth" with מתהפך "swirl around" rather than with כל אשר יצום "all that he commands them," which is possible. ארצה is a poetical form of אֶרֶץ "earth" (BDB, 76a; Gerleman [*BHS frt*]), not to be read אַרְצֹה "his earth" (as Budde,

Beer [*BHK*], Driver–Gray, Dhorme, Hölscher, Larcher, Pope, Gerleman [*BHS prp*], JB) or emended to אַרְצוֹ "his earth." The phrase תבל ארצה "the world of the earth" seems strange, but it is attested at Prov 8:31 (תבל אַרְצוֹ "his earth"). Duhm, followed by Beer (*BHK prps*), attractively emended ארצה to כִּרְצֹנוֹ "according to his pleasure."

13.a. Budde and NEB delete the verse. It was absent from the Old Greek, the present LXX text being derived from Theod.

13.b. שבט, lit. "rod," symbol of punishment. Guillaume read לְשַׁבֵּט "to bring heavy rain" (cf. Arab. *sabuṭa* "rain heavily"), parallel to "to promote spring growth he directs it" (see below on ארץ and חסד; his translation [*Studies,* 67] by oversight does not include this word). The root *sabuṭa,* however, means "be profuse" (of hair, or of rain, etc.) but is not itself a word for "rain" (Lane, 2194b). שבט can also be "tribe," but it does not make sense here (against Good).

13.c. אם־לארצו, lit. "or for his land." Some (e.g., Dhorme) find this phrase troublesome, because it is not abstract like the polar terms "correction" (שבט) and "love" (חסד). Numerous emendations are suggested: (1) If אם "if, or" is deleted, we would have "whether for correction for his land" (so Bickell[2], Dillmann, Budde, Beer [BH^2], Fohrer). (2) Hoffmann proposed לְ(א)רְצוֹ "for favor" (inf abs of רצה, equivalent to רָצוֹן, the *aleph* being prosthetic). (3) Duhm, followed by Beer (*BHK*), Driver–Gray, Moffatt, proposed וְלִמְאֵרָה "and for a curse." (4) Dhorme, followed by Hölscher, Terrien, Lévêque, 590, and apparently Rowley, read יְמַלֵּא רְצוֹנוֹ "he accomplishes his will"; but that makes for a very heavy line: "Whether it be for punishment that He accomplishes His will, Whether it be for mercy that he brings it to pass." (5) Hitzig read אם לא רָצוּ "if they are not content, willing," i.e., to obey, followed by Tur-Sinai, Gordis, Hartley, van der Lugt. (6) Peake and Kroeze, followed by de Wilde, delete אם לארצו altogether as a dittograph; Hartley thinks ארצו may well be a gloss on תבל "world." (7) De Wilde proposed in the place of that phrase some verb such as יְלַאֲכֵהוּ "he sends it out," parallel to the verb at the end of the line. However, a verb לאך, though it may be presumed as the root of מלאך "messenger," does not actually occur. (8) Gerleman (*BHS prp*) noted אֻמְלַל אָרֶץ "[if] the land languishes [because of the rod]"; but why is the verb not fem? (9) Beer (BH^2 *frt*), rather improbably, suggested יְרִיצֵהוּ "he makes it [the cloud, v 11] run." (10) Kissane reads עַמֵּי־אֶרֶץ וְ "[the chastisement of] the peoples of the earth, and," which is graphically attractive, but throws the verse out of balance. (11) Following Kissane, Larcher apparently reads לְעַמֵּי־הָאָרֶץ "[to punish] earth's peoples," as does NJB (similarly JB).

Without emending the text, Dahood ("Northwest Semitic Philology and Job," 72), followed by Pope, thought of another word אֶרֶץ meaning (not "earth" but) "grace" (from the root רצה "be pleased," with a prothetic *aleph*). That seems a rather desperate solution, though Grabbe, 117–18, seems attracted by it, and Andersen ("or for pleasure") and Newsom ("or for acceptance") adopt it. Cf. Hoffmann above, and also on 39:24. To similar effect, Gray proposes a new word אַרְצוֹ "favor," cognate with Aram. רְצוֹ, Arab. *raḍwu* (Wehr–Cowan, 344b, have the forms *riḍwān* and *riḍā';* cf. Lane, 1100a). Guillaume found here a verb ארץ "be fruitful" (cf. Arab. *'aruḍa* [Lane, 47c]), thus לְאַרְצוֹ piel "to make it fruitful."

There is really no problem with the line, however; though KJV's "whether for correction, or for his land, or for mercy" (RSV "love") is a little cryptic, these are three very plausible reasons for God to send rain; see further, *Comment.* There seems little reason to adopt the translation of Habel, "Whether for a scourge—even on his own earth—or for a blessing," or that of Strauss, "whether as a rod—if it concerns his earth," or that of NIV "or to water his earth and show his love." It is much more likely that the three nouns are syntactically parallel.

13.d. On חסד "loyalty," see *Comment.* Guillaume, however, reads לְחַסֵּד "to promote spring growth," comparing Arab. *ḥaṣad* "early growth," which he finds also at Isa 40:6 (cf. his interpretation of שבט and ארצו above). The words *ḥaṣād, ḥaṣd,* and *ḥiṣād,* however, mean "time of reaping" or "harvest," and *ḥaṣīd* "crop, harvest," without any specific reference to "early growth" (Lane, 582a; Wehr–Cowan, 81a).

13.e. מצא hiph is "cause to meet, deliver up" or "cause to befall, cause to overtake, cause to come" (*DCH,* 5:441b). The 3 masc sg obj in ימצאהו will most naturally refer to the last masc sg, which has been clearly marked (with הוא) as the subj of v 12, viz. the (collective) cloud, עב and ענן. Similarly, NJB has "he despatches them," NIV "he brings the clouds." Alternatively, the obj could be indefinite, and the verb would mean "he brings it to pass, he causes it to happen" (so RSV; cf. KJV "he causeth it to come"). It would be very strained to imagine with Gordis that the suff refers all the way back to אדם "humans" in v 7a. If the implied obj is the lightning, then a translation like "he makes it find its mark" (Pope; cf. Good) is appropriate; but, as Pope admits, it is hard to see how the lightning can be a sign of God's mercy (unless, as he says wryly, the mercy is for those it misses). Peake had a better solution: "The O.T. theophanies, in which lightning frequently plays a part, were often merciful to Israel, because destructive to its foes." Thunder and lightning are merciful in *1 En.* 59:1–3. But it is better still to regard the clouds and not the lightning as the obj.

Duhm offered an emendation, noted also by Beer (*BHK prps*) and followed by de Wilde, to יַצְאֵהוּ "he brings it out" (or, says Duhm, יוֹצִאֵם "he brings them out," i.e., sends them out, followed by Larcher, JB, NJB [though *yotzi'am* is incorrect]). Since מצא does not really suit the context, the emendation is adopted in the *Translation* above. An emendation to יְאַמְּצֵהוּ "he strengthens it" is noted by Gerleman (*BHS prp*) (also in *DCH*, 5:441b).

14.a. זאת "this," looking forward, as previously in v 1.

14.b. Beer (*BHK*) recommends deleting either איוב "Job" or עמד "stand still." If עמד is retained, he says, it had better be moved to the first colon of the verse.

14.c. עמד "stand" may be used in the sense of "stand still" as at 32:16. For BDB, 764a, this is the only place where it means "be attentive."

14.d. בין hithpo "consider," as at 11:11; 23:15; 26:14; 30:20; 31:1; 32:12; 38:18.

15.a. There is a classic sequence of four rhetorical questions in vv 15–16 (cf. Watson, 339, for other examples).

15.b. שׂים על is generally said to mean "lay a charge upon" (RSV "how God lays his command upon them," NJB, Hartley "controls them," Habel "orders them," NJPS "what charge God lays upon them," Pope), but parallels are difficult to uncover; an obj for the verb would be expected. It is hardly likely that some word for "decision" or "command" is understood (even though Tg adds גזירתא "a decree," and Hölscher, for example, thinks that is implied). Job 34:23 (mentioned by Dhorme) needs emending (*q.v.*); Exod 5:8 (mentioned by Gordis) is not parallel, since an obj is stated. Some have thought "his heart, mind" (לִבּוֹ) is understood (so Delitzsch, Zorell, 706b, Good), but that seems rather weak. Nor is it clear what the "them" of the suff of עליהם "upon them" refers to: it could be the "wonders" (נפלאות) of the previous colon except that they are fem and the suff is masc; so it must be the clouds of v 11, which is some way back. Driver–Gray fudge the issue with "the natural agencies just described." Gray reads עֲלֵיהֶן "upon them (fem.)."

An emendation seems called for, which Bickell and Duhm supply, reading אֵל פְּעָלָיו (Bickell אלוה), "[do you know how] God ordained his works?" following LXX ὅτι ὁ θεὸς ἔθετο ἔργα αὐτοῦ "that God set his works" (so too Strahan, Driver–Gray, Beer [*BHK*], de Wilde); this suggestion is adopted in the *Translation* above. Less persuasive is G. R. Driver's suggestion ("Hebrew Homonyms," in *Hebräische Wortforschung*, FS W. Baumgartner, VTSup 16 [Leiden: Brill, 1967] 50–64 [61–62]) that here we have a new Heb. עַל "deed" (he compares עֲלִילָה "[wanton] deed"; Aram. עִלָּה "cause"; cf. *DCH*, vol. 6, *s.v.*), which he finds also in v 16, "the cause of the poisings of the clouds"; Ezra 1:6; Prov 14:14; Jer 32:31 (wrongly written as Jer 37:3). NEB "how God assigns them their tasks" follows this suggestion, but it is still not clear what the referent of "them" is, and it is questionable whether the same word can mean "cause" and "task."

Viganò (*Nomi e titoli*, 55) reads עֶלִי הֵם "[how] the Most High [orders] them"; the effect is clumsy.

15.c. אור is "light," but the only light that comes from clouds is lightning, so we should understand the term with the special sense it has in 36:32; 37:3; 38:24 (but probably not 37:11 [*q.v.*]). Cross (*Canaanite Myth and Hebrew Epic*, 147 n. 4) sees here yet another example of אור as "bright cloud," which seems implausible syntactically. De Wilde, not unreasonably, thinks that yet further reference to lightning would be excessive here, and reads אוּר "heat," translating "how he makes his heavens radiate heat"; the difficulty lies with his understanding of ענן (see *Note* 15.e).

15.d. יפע has two objs: lit. "causes the cloud to shine lightning out." The inf prefixed with a prep is, as so often, followed by a pf verb with simple *waw* (cf. GKC, §114r).

15.e. De Wilde understands ענן as "heaven" rather than "cloud," comparing שחק "cloud, heaven" in v 18; but there are no other examples of ענן with such a sense.

16.a. ידע "know" is never elsewhere followed by על "about," and it is unsatisfactory to say, with Gordis, that nevertheless it is "perfectly comprehensible." It would be more correct to say that the text is suspect. The *Translation* above is *faute de mieux*. Beer (*BHK*) reads למפלשׂי, deleting the *ayin* of על as a dittograph of the last letter of התדע (so too Driver–Gray). But that is not much improvement, since even ידע followed by ל of the direct obj seems attested only in one place (Ps 69:5 [6]); see *DCH*, 4:105b. Dhorme argues that ידע על means "know something about" (so too Lévêque, 590), the noun after על being "the thing which is the subject of discussion or talk," but that seems like special pleading. It can hardly be, as Beer (*BH*[2] *frt*) suggests, that we should read הֲתִדְאָה "do you dart?"

J. Reider ("Etymological Studies in Biblical Hebrew," *VT* 4 [1954] 276–95 [293–94]) quite attractively reads, instead of על מ׳, a new word עֶלֶם "secret" (cf. עלם "conceal"), "[do you know] the secret of [the swaying of clouds]?" Less persuasive is Driver's proposal ("Hebrew Homonyms," 62) to find a new עַל "cause," thus "do you know the cause of the poisings of the clouds" (see *Note* 15.b, and cf. *DCH*, vol. 6, *s.v.*).

Blommerde revocalized עַל to עֲלִ "Most High" ("Do you recognize the Most High by his outspread clouds?"), parallel to the divine epithet "Perfect in Knowledge" (as he thinks it) in the second colon. But there is no question here of whether Job "recognizes" God or not, and it would be a strange idea to recognize God by his clouds (it is not correct that "the outspread cloud is a sign of God," as Blommerde alleges). For other examples of the supposed name 'Aliy "God Most High," cf. *Note* 29:4.c.

16.b. Unless, as Gordis suggests, מפלשׂי־עב is nothing but a phonetic variant on מפרשׂי־עב at 36:29 (or unless we should emend the form here to the form there, as Budde), whatever it means there ("spreading"?), the word here would be connected with פלס "weigh, make level" (BDB, 814a); *HALOT*, 2:618a, offers "floating, hovering," connecting it with פלס II "observe" and its noun פֶּלֶס "scales," presumably as a means of observing or measuring rather than expressing any idea of balancing. *DCH*, 5:432b, has "poising, balancing," from פלס "weigh" (similarly Terrien, Fohrer, Habel, de Wilde, Gray).

Since the idea of the clouds being "balanced" seems intuitively difficult (even if picturesque, according to Driver–Gray), it is perhaps best to adopt the equation of the term with the מפרשׂי "spreading (?)" of 36:29. NAB "how the clouds are banked" (cf. Pope "do you know about the cloud banks?") perhaps means "how they are balanced on one another," but it is not too easy to see what the ancient writer would have found so marvelous about that. Blommerde, on the other hand, suggests we read מִפְּלָשָׂיו "from his spreadings out," from פלשׂ, which he takes to be "strew, sprinkle" (as M. D. U. Cassuto, "מותו של בעל [לוח I* AB מכתבי ראס־שמרה] [The Death of Baal (Table I* AB from Ras-Shamra)]," *Tarbiz* 12 [1940–41] 169–80 [179]; G. R. Driver, "Ezekiel: Linguistic and Textual Problems," *Bib* 35 [1954] 145–59 [157–58]) rather than "wallow, roll in" (as BDB, 814a; *HALOT*, 3:835b); the final *yodh* is, according to him, a 3 masc sg suff (for other examples, see *Note* 21:16.c). Driver ("Notes on the Psalms," *JTS* 36 [1935] 147–56 [151]) had earlier related מִפְלְשֵׂי to Arab. *palaša* "unfold" (apparently a Syrian Arab. spelling [Hava, 574] of the more usual *paraša* "spread out" [Lane, 2369c]), thus "the unfoldings of the clouds."

Tur-Sinai developed a theory that the waters were thought to be held through the summer in clouds conceived as waterskins (נבל, 38:37) that would gradually become tattered and let rain drip through and finally become a downpour. God would then patch up (רקע) the waterskins, which would last until the next autumn (H. Torczyner [Tur-Sinai], "The Firmament and the Clouds, *Rāqîa'* and *Sheḥāqîm*," *ST* 1 [1948] 188–96). Here he translates פלשׂי as "the piercing" of the clouds, claiming (Tur-Sinai, 319) a verb פלשׂ equivalent, by metathesis, to שׁלף "pierce" (cf. also Aram. פלשׁ "divide, go through," Syr. *plaš* "break through," Akk. *palāšu* "dig hole"), as also at 20:25. The view is too speculative.

16.c. מפלאות occurs nowhere else, though it must mean "wonders, marvels," from the verb פלא "be wonderful." Very possibly it is a miswriting of נִפְלָאוֹת with the same meaning (so Siegfried, Budde, Beer [*BHK*], Driver–Gray, Hölscher, Fohrer, Ravasi, Strauss [or a free variant], Gray). Blommerde thinks it should be revocalized as מִפְּלָאוֹת "from (his) wonderful acts," the 3 masc suff of פלשׂי doing double duty for this noun also.

16.d. The phrase תמים דעים, lit. "perfect of knowledge," is very questionable, partly because it is a phrase Elihu has used of himself (with the slight variation of the fem form דֵעוֹת) in 36:4, and partly because this epithet for God is not at all well motivated here. Can it really be true that the poet thought of the balancing of the clouds as "a miracle of consummate skill" (NJB)?

It will not help to suppose that the phrase is an ironic address to Job ("O thou perfect in knowledge"), as Ehrlich. Among emendations, (1) Duhm rather extravagantly proposed מַפִּיל תְּהֹם מֵרַעַם "making a waterflood pour down at the thunder" (or would it be better to translate "laying the deep prostrate by thunder"?). "This is not to be preferred," Rowley drily remarks; but Strahan accounted it "very clever." Beer (BH^2) reports the proposal, but not inappropriately adds two question marks. (2) It is even more difficult to understand how the extraordinarily banal פִּתְאֹם מפלות רְעִים "suddenly the wicked fall" could ever have been proposed (Beer [BH^2 *prps*]), even though LXX ἐξαίσια δὲ πτώματα πονηρῶν "and the extraordinary calamities of the wicked" has something like it. (3) The other emendation, mentioned by Reider ("Etymological Studies," 293–94), rather drastically emends to מֶמַד עִים "[the wonders of] the measurement of clouds," מֵמַד being known from 38:5, and עִים being a new word cognate with Arab. *ghaym* "cloud" (Wehr–Cowan, 691b; and cf. MH עמם and עמעם "darken"). Is it conceivable, though, that the measurements of clouds could be called "wonderful"?

Pope thinks דעים probably does not mean "knowledge" but "utterance," from דֵּעַ "word" (דֵּעַ II in *DCH*, 2:456a; following Ginsberg), as at 32:10, but he retains "perfect in knowledge" in his translation.

17.a. De Wilde moves the line to follow v 15; understanding v 15b to concern the day's heat rather than lightning, he connects its content with the hot clothes of v 17. NAB "You, whom the streams of water fail" follows a credible but needless emendation to אשר בְּגָדוּךְ נַחֲלֵי מים (*Textual Notes*, 378). Tur-Sinai, in developing his thesis about the leaking clouds, reads בִּגְבֹר כֹּחַ מַיִם "[when] the force of the waters becomes strong" (cf. גבר of the waters at the flood, Gen 7:18–20, 24), continuing "when they let fall their wet clay (מִדְרָם) to the earth (אַרְצָה = ארץ)."

17.b. An implied 2d-person pronoun is the antecedent of the relative אשׁר, as also at Hos 14:4. NIV renders attractively "you who swelter in your clothes." But אשׁר might also mean "when" (as, e.g., Josh 4:21; Isa 31:4); so Duhm, Strauss.

17.c. שׁקט is "be quiet, still, inactive, undisturbed"; the hiph should be "show quietness" (BDB, 1053a, Driver–Gray), but that nuance does not seem relevant here. KJV "he quieteth the earth by the south wind" has a lot to recommend it. Most, however, do not see God as the subj: NIV "the land lies hushed" is perhaps not exactly the sense of שׁקט here. NJPS "the land is becalmed" raises the question of whether land, or only sea, can be becalmed. NEB "lies sultry" is good.

17.d. דרום (seventeen occurrences) is elsewhere always "south" (*DCH*, 2:461b), but here apparently "south wind." De Wilde suggests that it means "heat from the south," but מדרום "from, or, because of, the south" would be a strange way of saying that. His further argument that the land would not be "still" (שׁקט) if a wind was blowing is countered by the descriptions of travelers mentioned in the *Comment.*

Tur-Sinai (see *Note* 16.b) takes מדרום as a later spelling for מִדְרָם "their wet clay" from מֶדֶר (MH; cf. Arab. *madr* "mud brick" [Lane, 2698c, and Wehr–Cowan, 898b, spell it *madar* and gloss it "clod of earth"]; Eth. *mədr* "earth"; see *DCH*, 5:149b).

18.a. LXX omits this verse. Duhm and Beer (*BH*[2] *frt*) move it to precede v 21; Ehrlich moves it to before 38:4.

18.b. עמו is lit. "with him," i.e., as his companion (KJV, NAB; cf. NIV "can you join him?," NJPS "can you help him?," Pope, Hartley); Job 9:26 may suggest that it means "like him" (RSV, NJB; cf. NEB "as he does"; so too Terrien, Strauss), but, if creation is being referred to (see *Comment*), "with him" would make better sense. E. Zurro Rodríguez ("Valor comparativo de la partícula *'im,*" *EstBíb* 56 [1998] 251–60 [258]) sees this as the עם comparative (for other examples, see *Note* 29:18.c); Gray too thinks it implies contention or comparison.

18.c. רקע is literally "stamp, beat out, beat down." The word alludes to the רקיע "firmament" (Driver–Gray). If the verb is impf, it would suggest repeated (daily) action, but it might well be a preterite, denoting a single action in the past.

Gordis, however, while deriving the word from the same verb, understands it to mean "soar (to the heavens)," as in Modern Hebrew. Tur-Sinai (see on v 16) has it mean "patch" (he compares Aram. רוקעא [though the word is not in the standard lexica], Syr. *rûq'e* "piece of worn cloth, rag," and Arab. *ruq'a* "patch" [Lane, 1137b]), translating "will you patch up the tattered clouds," with reference to his theory about the clouds as waterskins that gradually get worn out (see *Note* 16.b).

18.d. לשׁחקים "the skies," prefixed by the well-attested, though not common, *lamedh* indicating the direct obj (BDB, 511b §3; *DCH*, 4:483b §12). שׁחק is usually "cloud" (as at 35:5; 36:28; 38:37), but is found also in the metonymic sense "sky" (as at Ps 89:6 [7], 37 [38]). Dhorme and Habel, exceptionally, think it is the clouds here, translating "spread forth clouds," "spread out the clouds," the verb רקע depicting "the clouds extended in the sky like a firmament." But how can clouds be said to be "solid as a mirror of cast metal" (Habel)? Habel thinks of spreading a "solid mass" of clouds across the sky to give relief from the heat, but a "solid" mass of clouds seems a far cry from a solid piece of metal.

Tur-Sinai finds in the cognates to שׁחק (Arab. *saḥq* "worn out garment," "thin cloud like such a garment" [Lane, 1319b; Tur-Sinai does not mention the citation here of thin clouds being likened to a worn-out garment], *saḥaqa* "grind" [Lane, 1318c], Aram. שׁחק, Syr. *šḥaq* "pulverize") support for his thesis that the clouds were thought to become tattered and worn out, and that רקע refers to their patching up. But clouds may be called "thin things" (like worn out clothes) without themselves being thought to be worn out; and since clouds are not always allowing rain to leak out, it would be strange to give them the standing sobriquet of "the tattered ones."

18.e. חזק is usually "strong," but the point of comparison must be the hardness or firmness of a mirror, which is not notably strong; חזק is "hard" of a face (Ezek 3:8) or forehead (Ezek 3:8, 9) or heart (Ezek 2:4). Most versions have "hard," NJPS "firm"; "strong" (KJV, Pope, Good; cf. *DCH,* 3:191a) is inappropriate, as also is "tempered" (NJB).

18.f. מוּצָק "a solid thing," from יצק "pour out," last occurred in v 10 in reference to ice. Here it is a mirror of "cast metal" (NJB, NJPS, NEB); no doubt the metal in question is bronze, but the Heb. word does not specify (though NAB has "brazen mirror," NIV "cast bronze"). It is difficult to see why KJV separated חזקים "hard" from ראי "mirror" ("which is strong, and as a molten looking glass"). The use of "molten" in the sense of "formerly melted and now solidified" (as KJV, RV, RSV, NRSV, Hartley) is probably now archaic (cf. *OED*), and should be avoided; its more normal current sense is "liquefied by heat."

18.g. ראי "mirror," the form occurring only here; but מַרְאָה is found elsewhere (Exod 38:8; 1QH 5:5, 11; cf. *DCH,* 5:474b). Tur-Sinai sees a new word רָאִי "likeness, aspect" (as in MH; cf. Jastrow, 1436a), thus "looking like a solid thing." His theory of the tattered clouds is very weak at this point, since patching the clouds is hardly likely to make them look "strong as a solid dam."

19.a. Duhm and Hölscher, among others, have felt that the sequence of thought in vv 19–22 has been much disturbed in transmission. Duhm thinks the original order was vv 22a, 21b, 22b, 23a, and Hölscher vv 21a, 21c, 19, 20, 22a, 21b, 22b—which is to say, a verse about the clouds (v 21a, c) followed the verse about the sky as a mirror (v 18), and the cola about the golden gleam (vv 22a, 21b) were related to those about the glory of God (vv 22b, 23). The origin of the dislocation may have been the ambiguity of בהיר (v 21): is it "bright" or "dark"?

19.b. הוֹדִיעֵנוּ "teach us," but many MSS and the oriental K have הוֹדִיעֵנִי "teach me" (followed by Dillmann, Bickell, Duhm, Beer [BH^2], Driver–Gray, Dhorme, Hölscher, NJB).

19.c. The transition from God's direction of the natural order to the old subject of legal debate with God is indeed abrupt, and it is not surprising that some have attempted to show that the former subject is continued here. Thus Tur-Sinai "Tell us what we shall say to it," i.e., to God's expression of disapproval revealed in the dark clouds. But such an explanation is very awkward.

19.d. ערך "put in order, arrange" has no expressed obj, but, as at 33:5 (*q.v.*), some term for "words," such as מלין, is no doubt understood, as at 32:14; KJV "order our speech," RSV, NIV "draw up our case," Hartley "prepare our case," NJPS "argue," NEB "marshal our thoughts" are preferable to "make our plea" (NAB). NJB "but better discuss no further" is not explained.

19.e. חשך "darkness" is perhaps a little surprising at this point, and it is understandable that emendation is considered. Perles ("The Fourteenth Edition of Gesenius-Buhl's Dictionary," 384; review of *Das Buch Hiob,* by K. Budde, *OLZ* 17 [1914] 178–79 [179]) proposed a word חֹשֶׂךְ "lack" or "hindrance" (cf. חשך "refrain" [BDB, 362a]; so too Fohrer, de Wilde, Gray; Fedrizzi is tempted), but such a word would not necessarily mean "lack of words" (though de Wilde translates "speechlessness" and Gray "silence"), and Dhorme remarks that not to speak because of a lack of words would be a rather banal idea. Pope's translation "we cannot argue from ignorance" inappropriately draws upon a specialized idiom in English. Lévêque, 590, offers the excellent emendation פִּינוּ נַחְשֹׂךְ "we restrain our mouth," the same phrase as in 7:11 (Elihu has used the verb in 33:18); its only weakness is that it makes the second colon rather heavy.

20.a. Duhm's rewriting of the line yields a good sense in itself, but does not form a very good sequel to v 19: הֲיִסּוֹר לוֹ כִּי יְדַבֵּר "Has he [God] a reprover [the form occurs also at 42:2] when he speaks [or does a man say that he (God) is confused]?" (also Beer [*BHK prps*]). Moffatt represented this finely with his "What! Man to cavil at his word? Man to charge him with confusion?" Gray makes an independent attempt at the line with "Is it said to Him, 'Nay, but I will speak'? Has anyone ever said, 'Nay, but he *will* be told'?" But the point at issue seems to be not so much the impossibility of speaking to God, but of offering him any knowledge or advice he does not already have (as the *Translation* above suggests).

20.b. אדבר "I speak" is emended to יְדַבֵּר "he speaks" by Duhm, Beer (*BHK prps*), de Wilde, NEB "Can any man (REB anyone) dictate to God when he is to speak? Or command him to make proclamation?" This latter rendering does not follow well from the previous verse. It seems preferable to keep the MT, though its exact sense is not certain. The wording may suggest a courtier reporting (or failing to report) to God when an address has been made by a human; thus, e.g., KJV "Shall it be told him that I speak?," RSV "that I would speak," NRSV "that I want to speak," NAB "Will he be told about it when I speak?" NIV has another thought, with "Should he be told that I want to speak?" (similarly Pope, Hartley); but it is hard to justify this.

20.c. יספר is almost universally taken from ספר piel "tell." Ehrlich postulated another ספר "disperse" (cf. Arab. *safara* [Lane, 1370a, "sweep, take away, disperse"]; and cf. ספר II, *DCH,* vol. 6, *s.v.*), as also at 38:37, and understood vv 19–20 in reference to the clouds; but he has no followers. NEB

"Can any man (REB anyone) dictate to God" emends to הֲיְסַפֵּר (Brockington). NJB "will he take note?" presumably emends to הֲיִסְפֹּר "will he take account of, or, carefully observe?" (qal, as BDB, 707a), and deletes לוֹ "to him" (similarly Guillaume).

20.d. אם "if" is deleted by NAB, translating "or when a man says."

20.e. Understanding כי as the emphatic (for other examples, see *Note* 22:26.b). Gordis explains it as the sign of a question, as in 2 Kgs 18:34 || Isa 36:19; 2 Sam 9:1 (הֲכִי), and commonly in MH.

20.f. בלע is usually understood as "swallow, engulf"; see *Comment.*

But we should also reckon with a verb בלע II "communicate, announce" (cf. Arab. *balagha* II "reach; afflict; make known, inform" [Lane, 251b]; first proposed by Jacob, "Erklärung einiger Hiob-Stellen," 287; cf. KBL, 131a; *HALOT,* 1:135a; *DCH,* 2:180b [בלע III]); it occurs at 2 Sam 17:16; Prov 19:28. So Dhorme "is he informed?," JB "do man's commands reach his ears?," NJB "does he take it in?" So also Hölscher, Fohrer, Lévêque, 591, Gordis, Sicre Díaz, de Wilde, van der Lugt, Gray. This is the verb adopted in the *Translation.* NEB "Can any man . . . command him to make proclamation?" emends to יְבַלַּע piel (Brockington).

The other sense of Arab. *balagha,* i.e., "afflict," is invoked by A. Guillaume ("A Note on the √בלע," *JTS* NS 13 [1962] 320–23); he cites 2 Sam 17:16 "lest disaster befall the king," and finds this sense of בלע also at Job 2:3; 10:8; Pss 35:25; 55:9 (10); Prov 19:28; Eccl 10:12; Isa 28:7; 9:15; 19:3. He notes that Arabic lexicographers say it is a synonym of *'āniya,* but such a sense is not acknowledged by Lane, 250b, or Wehr–Cowan, 73a. For the present verse, Guillaume offers "Would a man wish that he should be afflicted?"

Yet another בלע (בלע III in *HALOT,* 1:135a; בלע II in *DCH,* 2:180b; Gesenius–Buhl, 101b, sees it as related to בלל; and cf. בֶּלַע "confusion" [Ps 52:4 (6)]) "confuse" is sometimes invoked (NJPS "Can a man say anything when he is confused?"; Duhm, Habel, Hartley), but this seems less likely. We could also consider בלע IV "touch, strike" (*DCH,* 2:180b; see G. R. Driver, "Hebrew Notes," *ZAW* 52 [1934] 51–56 [52]; "'Another Little Drink'—Isaiah 28:1–22," in *Words and Meanings,* FS D. W. Thomas, ed. P. R. Ackroyd and B. Lindars [Cambridge: Cambridge UP, 1968] 47–67 [52]).

21.a. Many observe that "[T]he return to natural phenomena here is curious" (Rowley). Kissane removes vv 21–22a to precede v 9, but there is nothing here that belongs unequivocally with the winter scene depicted in vv 1–8. Pope moves v 21 to follow v 18, but his interpretation of the resulting sequence of thought is questionable. He claims that "the blazing sun above the dust clouds which obscure it" is what makes the sky like a brazen mirror, but acknowledges that vv 17–18 do not actually refer to the sun.

A quite different approach to the interpretation of this line is taken by others. NJPS "Now, then, one cannot see the sun, though it be bright in the heavens, until the wind comes and clears them [of clouds]"; but this requires supplying "clouds," and it is perhaps questionable whether a Hebrew poet would think of the sun as being bright even when it is invisible. NIV "Now no one can look at the sun, bright as it is in the skies after the wind has swept them clean" (similarly RSV); but this does not seem to be linked to the context in any way. Rowley thought the point was that if the clear sky is too bright for human eyes, "the dazzling brightness of God's presence would be even more unbearable" (similarly Habel, Whybray); but it is hard to see v 22 as being about the brightness of God's presence. Pope thinks the point is that when the wind clears the sky of clouds, the sun is too bright to look at; but the sun is always too bright to look at, and when it is obscured by clouds no one says that they are looking at it.

The key may well lie in the opening word ועתה "and now" (see next *Note*).

21.b. ועתה "and now" has puzzled many; Driver–Gray note that it could be understood temporally, contrasting the present with either the past or the future, or logically, drawing a conclusion from what has just been said. It may be better to understand it dramatically, as focusing the eye on one moment, which will be superseded by another very different moment; so Hölscher, NEB "at one moment," linking to "then" (simple *waw*) at the beginning of v 21c. The pf verbs ראו and עברה (followed by a *waw* consec ותטהרם) are not easy to explain on this interpretation, it must be admitted.

21.c. אור is of course usually simply "light," but at 31:26 it plainly stands for the sun itself, and the "great lights" are the sun and the moon at Ps 136:7. There is no contrast between "light" and darkness here, but a contrast between sunlight and shade. And it is not the lightning, either. For Tur-Sinai, אור is once again "disapproval, condemnation" (cf. *Note* 36:30.d).

21.d. לא ראו "they have not seen," or rather, the verb being used impersonally, "it is not seen" (so too Gordis, de Wilde). Budde reads רָאִנוּ "we see," Beer (*BHK*) רָאוּי "is seen" (qal passive ptcp), comparing LXX ὁρατόν "seen," and Gray רָאֹו "one does [not] see" (inf abs, indefinite subj).

21.e. בהיר occurs only here. It is often connected with בַּהֶרֶת "brightness, bright spot" on the skin

(BDB, 97b); so too Hölscher, Fohrer, Lévêque, 591, Gordis ("But now, after men saw no light, the skies grow bright"), KJV, RSV, NIV, NJPS. But the context, as here understood, speaks rather for the sense "dark" (cf. Syr. *bahîr* [J. Payne Smith, 36b]), as also *HALOT,* 1:111a, NEB "being overcast with cloud," NJB "behind darkening clouds," NAB "obscured among the clouds"; so too Friedrich Delitzsch, Budde, Driver–Gray, Dhorme, Beer (*BHK*), de Wilde, Sicre Díaz. Tur-Sinai's emendation to בִּרֹה "his approval" is unsatisfactory, since בֹּר means "innocence" and not "approval" (cf. also *Note* 37:11.d).

21.f. V 21 is usually regarded as a tricolon, but in the interpretation offered here a new bicolon begins at this point (so also NEB). Fohrer (followed by Lévêque, 591) deletes this colon as a gloss expanding on שחקים "clouds."

21.g. Instead of ותטהרם "and it clears them away," Gray reads וַתְּטַהֲרֶנּוּ "and it clears it [*sc.* the sun]."

22.a. "Golden splendor" is the traditional translation (RSV, NIV, Hartley; cf. NEB "a golden glow") for זהב "gold." See also *Comment.* Many, however, follow the suggestion of Graetz to read זֹהַר "brightness" (followed by Duhm, Budde[2], Driver–Gray, Beer [*BHK*], Hölscher, Larcher, Rowley, Fedrizzi, de Wilde, Gray; so too JB, NAB [*Textual Notes,* 378], but translating "splendor"); cf. the elaborate description of the presence of Yahweh in Ezek 1, where נֹגַהּ "brightness" occurs four times (vv 4, 13, 27, 28). KJV "Fair weather cometh out of the north" is not "surprising" (Rowley); it is explained by Buxtorf, 181, that "gold" is metaphorically "serenity" or "golden light" (*aurescens lux*), which comes when the north wind blows away the clouds leaving the purest serenity. Buxtorf quotes ibn Ezra, who glosses the Joban phrase as זוהר השמים, the brightness of the sky, which is like the color of gold.

Guillaume ("Arabic Background," 109; *Studies,* 129) sees here another זָהָב, which he explains from the cognate Arab. *ḏihbat* "light rain (shot through by the rays of the sun)" (Lane, 983b, gives "light rain" or "copious rain" and has nothing about the rays of the sun, though the word is related to *ḏahab* "gold"); but he retains the translation "golden splendour." Tur-Sinai continues his independent line with "out of the hiding [a new צָפוֹן from צפן "hide"] it [human innocence] comes forth like gold"; he is followed by Gray.

22.b. The *Translation* follows NEB's interpretation of the colon as a explanatory marginal note; in its footnote it has "Hebrew adds *this refers to God, terrible in majesty.*" The על "upon" will be the signal that what follows is a gloss.

Among alternative suggestions, (1) the על may mean "upon," in the sense that awesome majesty is upon God as clothing (so RSV, NJB, Hartley), or else "around" him (as NRSV; cf. NJPS; cf. also KJV "with God"). NAB "From the North the splendor comes, surrounding God's awesome majesty!" no doubt implies, more literally, "around God, awesome of majesty." NIV "Out of the north he comes in golden splendor; God comes in awesome majesty" appears to ignore the על altogether. (2) D. W. Thomas suggests that we have here a new verb עלל "enter," as in Aram. עלל ("Job xxxvii 22," *JJS* 1 [1948–49] 116–17), thus "God enters, terrible in majesty" (cf. *DCH,* vol. 6, *s.v.*); but Fohrer thinks this spoils the sequence of thought, and it is none too clear what God is supposed to be entering. (3) Blommerde revocalizes על to עֵל "(God) Most High" (Andersen is tempted to follow him), but he does not explain how the second colon can mean "The Most High God, awful in majesty" when the first colon means "From Zaphon comes gold." For other examples of the supposed name 'Aliy "God Most High," cf. *Note* 29:4.c.

22.c. נורא is evidently "awesome," but the word order of נורא הוד is a little strange for "upon (or, around) God is awesome majesty." One would expect rather הוד נורא, and Budde proposed we reorder the text (taking purism too far, says Dhorme). Keeping the Masoretic order, Driver–Gray rendered "upon God majesty is terrible," which is too awkward. Gordis has the remarkable suggestion that נורא is really the niph ptcp of ירא = ירה "shoot, throw," thus "upon God, majesty is poured forth." No one else knows of a verb ירא with this meaning, and ירה does not elsewhere mean anything like "pour."

Dhorme curiously advises to read with Houbigant נִרְאָה "[glory] has been seen, appears" (so too Beer [*BH*[2] *frt; BHK*]) instead of נורא, but does not take his own advice; even more curious, he translates "Around Eloah lies a crushing glory" without explaining that "crushing."

23.a. The Masoretic punctuation divides the line into two overlong bicola, the first ending after שגיא־כח; but that leaves the next word, ומשפט "and justice," without syntactic connection in its colon. So it is better to divide the line into three cola (so too Dhorme, Pope, RSV), and better still if we move "mighty in righteousness" into the second colon, as in the *Translation* above. Fohrer deletes ורב־צדקה לא יענה as an explanatory gloss on משפט "justice."

23.b. M. Dahood vocalizes לא "not" here in the second colon and in the next verse as לָא "the Omnipotent One" (review of *Giobbe,* by P. Fedrizzi, *Bib* 55 [1974] 287–88 [288]).

23.c. מצא is usually "find," but Gray thinks it has here more an Aram. sense "attain" (often identified as the sense "reach," as, e.g., by *DCH*, 5:435a §4).

23.d. רֹב "abundance," but Dhorme (followed by Beer [*BHK*], Hölscher, Lévêque, 591, de Wilde) reads רַב "a master [of righteousness]," "the Lord [of righteousness]," parallel to שׂגיא־כח "great of power." Beer (*BHK*) moves רב־צדקה to follow כח and consequently takes משפט "justice" as the obj of the final verb (cf. Moffatt "he violates no right"; similarly Sicre Díaz). Both these suggestions are adopted in the *Translation*.

Gordis strangely takes רב־צדקה as referring to humans, translating "The man abounding in goodness he does not torment," but the use of the abstract רֹב "greatness" instead of the concrete רַב "great one" is odd (the alleged parallel at 11:2 is not very convincing). Perles[2], 67, followed by Gray, reads רִב־צדקה "the just cause" (so too Dahood, review of *Giobbe*, by P. Fedrizzi, 288), but such a phrase occurs nowhere else.

23.e. The piel יְעַנֶּה is apparently from ענה III "afflict." But many renderings do not observe the usages of this term. It is rarely, if ever, used with an abstract obj (Ps 102:23 [24] seems to be "he has broken my strength"). And while it means "humiliate, do violence to," it does not mean "violate" or "oppress" or "torment"; even in a sexual sense, it probably does not mean "rape' (E. van Wolde, "Does *'innâ* Denote Rape? A Semantic Analysis of a Controversial Word," *VT* 52 [2002] 528–44). So RSV "abundant righteousness he will not violate" (similarly de Wilde) can be faulted on more than one ground. And the verb is not used without an obj, so "he does not oppress" (NIV; cf. NJB "yet no oppressor," KJV "he will not afflict"; so too Dhorme, Terrien, Pope, Hartley, and Hölscher [with "right" understood]) and "He does not torment" (Gordis) are equally hard to defend.

Given these difficulties, the emendation to יְעַוֵּת "and he does not pervert [the abundance of (his) righteousness]" begins to look very attractive (so Driver–Gray, Beer [*BHK*]); it is adopted in the *Translation* above. It has been used at 8:3 with משפט "justice" and צדק "righteousness" as the obj, and at 34:12 with משפט as the obj, where Elihu himself says that Shaddai (as here) will not pervert justice. To similar effect, Gray emends to יְעַוֶּה "distorts."

The verb ענה I "answer" has been seen here, though the verb is not used elsewhere in the piel, and revocalization is required. NAB "his great justice owes no one an accounting" depends upon an emendation to וְרַב צדקה לא יֵעָנֶה, lit. "and the master of justice will not be answered" (niph of ענה I) (*Textual Notes*, 379), presumably on the basis of the gloss in *HALOT*, 3:852b, "allow oneself to be moved to answer"; but that rendering is suggested only for Ezek 14:4, 7, and it is by no means certain. Habel reads יַעֲנֶה "he does (not) answer" as a counterpart to "we cannot reach him" at the beginning of the verse.

24.a. Fohrer deletes the line as a later moralizing addition. Terrien encloses it in square brackets and does not comment on it.

24.b. יראוהו is pf, "have feared him" (i.e., as an established fact, say Driver–Gray), but we should expect an impf ייראוהו or יְרָאוּהוּ (as apparently read by LXX; so too Beer [*BHK* יְרָאוּהוּ] and the *Translation* above), expressing either a fact, "fear him" (as KJV, RSV, NAB, NJB, NJPS, NEB), or, with a modal use of the verb, a wish, "should fear him"(Budde, Duhm, Pope, Gray).

24.c. This colon, lit. "he does not see all (or, any) who are wise of heart," has proved a difficulty. It has been taken to mean: (1) "he does not look even upon the wise" (ibn Ezra, Hölscher, Pope, Rowley, Lévêque, 591, Whybray; cf. KJV "he respecteth not any that are wise of heart") or (2) "he does not look upon those who are wise in their own conceit" (Vg *qui sibi videntur esse sapientes* "who seem wise to themselves"; Rashi, Driver–Gray, RSV). Gordis has, however, convincingly shown that חכמי־לב cannot mean this, since it is always used in a positive sense (as in 9:4; Exod 31:6; 35:10; 36:1, 2; Prov 10:8; 11:29; 16:21), whereas the negative is expressed by חכם עיניו "wise in one's own eyes" (Prov 3:7; 26:5, 12, 16; 28:11). (3) NIV makes the colon a question: "for does he not have regard for all the wise in heart?" This explanation for why all fear God is totally implausible.

Among emendations, some retain the verb ראה "see": (1) NAB reads יִרְאוּהוּ (though the form does not occur in the Hebrew Bible) "though none can see him, however wise their hearts" (*Textual Notes*, 379); similarly Habel "but even the wise of heart cannot see him," Strauss (but without emending). It is not a natural way of taking the Heb., and the issue of whether God can be "seen" seems somewhat out of place here. NJPS "men are in awe of Him Whom none of the wise can perceive" must also depend on revocalization of the verb to the pl; the supposition that the second colon is a relative clause is hard to justify. (2) NEB revocalizes לא to לוֹ "to him" (Brockington) and, presumably, יראה to יִרְאוּ "look" to yield "all who are wise look to him" (so too de Wilde); the sense is weak, and REB is preferable (see below). (3) Hartley takes the לא as asseverative (for other examples, see *Note* 21:16.a) and reads יִרְאוּהוּ (not יְרָאֻהוּ as his note says) to yield "indeed, (all the wise of heart) see him."

(4) An alternative emendation, which is accepted in the *Translation* above, finds rather the verb ירא "fear." Thus Gordis revocalizes יִרְאֶה "he sees" to יְרָאֻה (= יִירָאוּהוּ) "they fear him" (Kissane יְרָאֻהוּ); so already LXX φοβηθήσονται δὲ αὐτὸν καὶ οἱ σοφοὶ καρδίᾳ "and the wise in heart also fear him." It is necessary at the same time to take the לא not as the particle "not" but as asseverative (see suggestion [3] above and *Note* 21:16.a; see also *DCH*, 4:495a [לא II], 610a [bibliography]). Thus Gordis translates "Yes, all the wise-hearted stand in awe"; similarly Moffatt ("and thoughtful men revere him"), REB ("and all who are wise fear him"), JB ("hold him in awe"), Larcher, Hartley, Newsom. F. I. Andersen has pointed to other examples of repetitive parallels, where the same word occurs in both cola of a line, noting that in such cases the word tends to be spelled *plene* the first time and defectively the second, as here ("Orthography in Repetitive Parallelism," *JBL* 89 [1970] 343–44).

In a less attractive variation on the foregoing, some have proposed here the noun יִרְאָה "fear," thus לוֹ יִרְאַת "to him is the reverence of [all those wise in heart]" (Terrien, Fedrizzi).

Form/Structure/Setting

The *structure* of the speech is fairly plain: it contains two roughly equal Parts: 36:2–25 (twenty-four lines), continuing the theme of the justice of God, and 36:26–37:24 (thirty-two lines), exploring the purposes and instruction of God in nature. Part 1 is introduced by the topic sentence "to ascribe justice to my Maker," Part 2 by "Who is a teacher like him?" Job is focalized much more in the first Part, where he is addressed directly in 36:2–4, 16–21, 24. In the second Part, Job is not addressed until three-quarters of the way through: from 37:14 to 37:19 every verse is directed to Job, but elsewhere he is no more than an audience for Elihu ("we" at 36:26; 37:5, 23 refers to humanity in general, and not specifically to Job), who even alludes to his own feelings, something he has not done since chap. 32.

There is an evident *strophic structure,* even if the strophes, of three, four, five and (in one case) six lines, are not very regular nor always easy to identify (textual and exegetical decisions often determine where the dividing line between strophic divisions is drawn). In this commentary, thirteen strophes are identified.

Part 1	strophe 1	36:2–4	3 lines
	strophe 2	36:5–7	3 lines
	strophe 3	36:8–12	5 lines
	strophe 4	36:13–15	3 lines
	strophe 5	36:16–21	6 lines
	strophe 6	36:22–25	4 lines
Part 2	strophe 7	36:26–28, 31	4 lines
	strophe 8	36:29–30, 32–33	4 lines
	strophe 9	37:1–4b	4 lines
	strophe 10	37:5–6, 4c, 7–8	4 lines (v 6 is bracketed; v 6 + v 4c a tricolon)
	strophe 11	37:9–13	5 lines (v 12 a tricolon)
	strophe 12	37:14–18	5 lines
	strophe 13	37:19–24	5 lines + a pendant

There are some clear markers of strophe divisions: "behold" (הֵן) at 36:5, 22, 26; "indeed" or "also" (אַף) at 36:29 and 37:1; and "hear this, O Job" at 37:14. The division between strophes 3 and 4 of Part 1 is assured by the content distinction between the righteous who fall into suffering (vv 5–12) and the truly godless (vv 13–14). The division between strophes 4 and 5 of Part 2 is suggested by the unusual word order at the beginning of v 9 ("out of its chamber"), as well as by the transition in topic. The division between strophes 6 and 7 of Part 2 is marked by the resumption in v 19 of the imperative address to Job that also began v 14.

Among the versions, NAB presents a strophic structure close to that outlined above, except that it offers no translation of 36:16–20, it links 37:5–13 together, and it splits 37:19–24 into two three-line cola (vv 19–21, 22–24). RSV's divisions differ somewhat: in Part 1, however, it links strophes 2 and 3 together, and it joins vv 22–23 to strophe 5; in Part 2, it joins vv 24–25 to strophes 1 and 2, which it links; it links strophes 3, 4, and 5; and it attaches vv 19–20 to strophe 6 rather than strophe 7. NIV's strophes are 36:2–4, 5–15, 16–21, 22–26, 27–33; 37:1–13, 14–18, 19–24. NEB does not apparently concern itself with strophic structure, though it makes certain divisions: 36:2–4, 5–15, 16–21 (omitting 20), 20+22–37:12 (a unit of twenty-five lines, which can hardly be a single strophe!), and 37:14–24. REB splits 36:5–15 into vv 5–12, 13–15, and NEB's long unit into 20+22–31; it still treats 36:29–37:13 as a single unit (seventeen lines!).

Among commentators, Terrien demarcates two poems, 36:2–25 ("The Divine Educator") and 36:26–37:23 ("The Lord of the Seasons"). The first poem contains four strophes, vv 2–7a (3+2 lines), 7b–12 (4+2 lines), 13–17 (3+2 lines; v 18 is omitted), 19–25 (3+4 lines). The second has six, in three pairs: (1) "The Lord of the Autumn": 36:26–30 (3+2 lines), 36:31–37:3 (3+3 lines); (2) "The Lord of the Winter": 37:4–8 (2+3 lines), 9–13; (3) "The Lord of the Summer": 37:14–18 (3+2 lines), 19–23 (2+3 lines; v 24 is omitted). The structure is very similar to that adopted here.

Several scholars see strophes that are mostly couplets. Fohrer, deleting 36:1, regards 36:2–26 as part of Elihu's third speech, analyzing strophes as 35:16+36:2–4, 36:5–10, 11–15, 16–21, 22–26; thereafter he sees a "Hymn to the Power of God in Nature" (36:27–37:13, entirely in couplets) and a "Conclusion to the Speeches of Elihu" (37:14–23, with two strophes, vv 14–18, 19–23). De Wilde names the two Parts of the speech "The Fourth Speech of Elihu" (36:1–25) and "Elihu's Concluding Hymn" (36:26–37:24); he sees only couplets (except for the triplet 36:2–4 and two isolated lines 37:1 and 24). Van der Lugt identifies three units after the introduction in 36:2–4: (1) 36:5–25, with three strophes: vv 5–12 (3+3+2 lines), 13–21 (3+3+3 lines), 22–25 (2+2 lines); (2) 36:26–37:13, with five strophes: 36:26–29 (2+2 lines), 30–33 (2+2 lines), 37:1–5 (1+2+2 lines), 6–10 (2+3 lines), 11–13 (2+2 lines); and (3) 37:14–24, with two strophes: vv 14–20 (1+2+2+2 lines), 21–24 (2+2 lines).

The *genre* of the speech is a mixture of *wisdom instruction* and *admonition*. Unlike Elihu's previous speech, which was predominantly disputation, with only a single sentence of wisdom instruction, this speech is very largely instruction, with occasional elements of warning and advice. The first major unit of *instruction* concerns God's just treatment both of the wicked and of the righteous who have fallen into sin (36:5–15). The second concerns the works of God in the natural sphere, the themes being the power of God and God as a teacher (36:26–37:24). These units are long and carefully constructed. The first begins with a line that contrasts the wicked and the righteous (v 6); vv 7–12 then concern the fate of the righteous, viz. those of them who go astray, vv 13–14 describe the fate of the wicked, and v 15 finally summarizes aphoristically the experience of the righteous. The second unit is apparently structured according to the three seasons: autumn (36:26–37:4), winter (37:5–13), and summer (37:14–24, with some admixture of an instructional element in v 14, rhetorical questions in vv 15–18, and wisdom sayings in vv 23–24).

Between these two units there is an address to Job (36:16–25), in the genre of the *admonition* typical of the wisdom literature (rather than of the prophetic books); its characteristic features are the negative imperatives (with אל) at vv 18b, 20a, and the imperatives השמר "take care" at v 21 (cf. also v 18a) and זכר "remember" at v 24.

The *function* of the speech is to invite Job to "stop" his complaint against God and marvel rather at the divine justice and self-revelation.

The *tonality* of the speech is determined for many readers by its apparently sarcastic questions and appeal to Job near its end (37:15–20): "do you know?," "will you hammer out the sky?," "teach us what we shall say to him." They remind us, as second-time readers of the book, of the sarcasm of the divine speeches soon to come. But it would be better to start with other examples of Elihu's tone in the speech. In 36:2 he is quite deferential, betraying a consciousness of how long he has been speaking and asking Job to be "patient" with him. In vv 5 and 15, though he speaks in generalizations, he is entirely positive toward Job's position, assuring him that God will not reject the pure of heart and that he delivers the afflicted by their affliction. In v 16 he depicts Job as enjoying God's blessing. On a less positive note are his warnings to Job in vv 18–21, but they have no edge to them, being generalizations (against mockery, trust in wealth, despair, and temptation to wrongdoing) unrelated to Job's life or situation, almost as if he had forgotten it was Job he was addressing (the same was apparent in chap. 35; see *Form/Structure/Setting*). His direct addresses to Job in 36:24 and 37:14 call on him to "remember to extol [God's] work" and "stop and consider the wonderful deeds of God." None of this is remotely hostile. Admittedly, "Teach us what we shall say to him" (37:19) is ironic, since he does not truly believe that he has anything to learn from Job about how properly to address God; but his purpose is not disparagement of Job but rather to express the gulf between humans and God (cf. vv 19b–20, which focalize "us," humans, rather than Job). Rather than attack Job, he wants to stress that Job and he are in the same boat: "we cannot order our thoughts because of the darkness" (v 19), "As for the Almighty, we cannot find him" (v 23). And as for the ironic questions of vv 15–18, there is a world of difference in the tonality of a "do you know?" that means "you do not know, but I do" (as in the divine speeches) and "none of us knows." Elihu certainly thinks he has a lot to teach Job, and that Job is in the wrong in his attitude to God, but he keeps far from an oppositional stance toward Job. The tonality of the speech then is generally supportive, as Elihu's previous speeches also have been.

There are two *nodal verses* in this speech, reflecting its twin concerns: Job 36:3 "I will range far and wide for knowledge to ascribe justice to my Maker" headlines the material of the first Part of the speech (36:2–25), while Job 36:22 "Behold, God is exalted in his power; who is a teacher like him?" enshrines the dual themes of the instruction on the phenomena of nature: God's power, to which Job's response should be wonder, and God's teaching conveyed through nature.

Comment

36:1–37:24 Elihu's fourth speech consists of two not quite equal Parts: 36:2–25, continuing the theme of the justice of God, and 36:26–37:24, an instruction on the theme of the God of nature. How these two Parts fit together, if at all, is a difficult question. They are "so distinct in tone and content as to give the impression that they are independent compositions and could have been separate speeches" (Andersen). It is unlikely, however, that the theme of Part 2 is simply the power of God, for that is a subject deeply irrelevant to God's justice, which has been the overriding theme of all Elihu's interposition. There are enough hints that the power of God in creation and nature is for Elihu not a subject of praise in its own right, but somehow connected with the matter of God's justice. God's creatorial energies and world governance are not displays of power, they are the vehicle of his righteous judgments. The sending of clouds and rain, for example, is for Elihu not some evidence of supreme power but an exhibition of divine justice (37:13; cf. also 36:31; 37:23).

36:1 This opening verse is deleted by a number of scholars (e.g., Hölscher, Fohrer, Ravasi) on the ground that the wording "and Elihu added and said" (ויסף אליהוא ויאמר) differs from that of 32:6, 34:1, and 35:1, "and Elihu answered and said" (ויען אליהוא ויאמר [אליהו in 35:1; in 32:6, Elihu's patronymic is added]). This is thought to be evidence that the heading here is a secondary addition. But vv 2–4 are clearly the proem of a speech (de Wilde), and if v 1 disappears, vv 2–4 must also be moved (as Fedrizzi sees).

2–4 Elihu's speeches have contained more than their fair share of introductory material (cf. 32:6–22; 33:1–7; 34:2), and the wordiness of Elihu as a character must be ascribed to the intention of the author. But we should not jump to the conclusion that he is making fun of Elihu as a pompous and immodest young man. For all we know, his elaborate language could have been regarded as an ingredient in politeness.

Unlike all Elihu's previous speeches, this one contains no quotation of Job's words (contrast 33:8–11; 34:5–6; 35:2–3), no doubt an indication that Elihu is now attempting a summary statement of his own position rather than a refutation of Job.

3 He will "lift up" or "bear" (נשׂא) his knowledge from afar. נשׂא is an unusual word for "bring," but we can compare "bring tribute" (נשׂא מנחה, 2 Sam 8:2) or "carry treasure" (נשׂא חיל, Isa 30:6); Delitzsch compares the fleet of Hiram that carried (נשׂא) gold from Ophir in Solomon's days (1 Kgs 10:11). Elihu seems to be envisaging his knowledge as a valuable object he bears or imports from foreign parts. He is presumably referring to the range of "scientific" knowledge he is about to set forth in the second Part of the speech (36:26–37:24). He will not trade in commonplaces (Strahan), but, Solomon-like (Habel), will let his researches range over the world of natural phenomena in order to introduce new proofs of the divine justice. Some see in the term למרחוק "from afar" an allusion to heaven as the source of his knowledge (so ibn Ezra, Fohrer, Hartley), but this view is not probable.

He says he will bear his knowledge from afar *and* ascribe justice to God, his meaning being that he will deploy his knowledge *in order to* declare God just. This is an important signal that the depiction of the fates of the righteous and the wicked in vv 5–15, the address to Job in vv 16–21, and the poem describing the workings of God in nature in 36:26–37:24 are all essentially about God's justice. Elihu is still concerned to refute Job's criticism of God's justice.

Why does Elihu here refer to God as his "Maker"? We have heard him say in 32:22 that he will not give flattering titles for fear that *his Maker* might soon put an end to him, and just recently he has suggested that the reason why the oppressed are sometimes not answered by God is that they do not address *their Maker* (35:10). It must be that he views right behavior and the practice of justice as a fundamental part of the world order, set up at creation by its author.

4 This sentence gives many commentators, often naively pre-critical in their representations of the other, yet another welcome opportunity to sneer at Elihu as a "stranger to modesty" who "frequently finds it necessary to certify his own genius" (Rowley), or even "in attempting to vindicate God, falls into the trap of playing God" (Habel). By his braggadocio, it is said, he spoils his vision of a divinely ordered universe (Good), or even, it is claimed, his "presumption reached an apex with this verse" (Alden). His claim is extravagant, presumptuous, and absurd (Strahan). It is "extravagant self-praise, even for an Oriental, the more pitiful that the speeches themselves give the lie to his claim" (Peake), though "as an Oriental speaker he is allowed a certain licence which would never be conceded in the West" (Strahan). "It is impossible to acquit Elihu of overweening arrogance" (Gibson). It is a "stupendous claim . . . not only ludicrous, underlining Elihu's egregious self-conceit, but also close to blasphemy" (Whybray). "Elihu is giving himself such a certificate of genius, as if the brash young man is all unaware of its presumption" (Andersen). A question that is never asked by these writers is why the author, whose creature Elihu is, would have wanted to portray such a ludicrous character. Does the author not have some sympathy for the ideas he puts in the mouth of Elihu? If he does not, why does he think it worth inventing him?

As it turns out, Elihu's language is by no means as self-important as it sounds in many of our translations. In saying that his words are "not false," Elihu assures Job of his honesty and integrity rather than strictly of his accuracy (as "not false" of RSV, NIV, and NJPS, and Habel's "flawless," might suggest). שקר is "deceit" rather than "lie, falsehood." It is the opposite of reliable personal relations rather than of objective truth. M. A. Klopfenstein sees it as essentially signifying an aggressive breach of faith (*TLOT,* 3:1399–1405 [1401]).

In referring to himself as תמים דעות, often translated "one perfect in knowledge" (KJV, RSV, NAB, NIV; Habel "perfect in reasoning"), he is not being as self-important as it may seem. Some versions try to soften the tone by translating "you have a man of sound learning here" (NJB), "a man of sound opinions is before you" (NJPS), "before you stands one whose conclusions are sound" (NEB), "here stands a man whose insight is unerring" (Moffatt). More correctly, תמים means morally upright, sincere (Gordis), as Job describes himself in 12:4; the same is true of the similar word תם at 1:1 (*q.v.*), 8; 2:3; 8:20; 9:20–22. Newsom also recognizes that the term is "merely a claim to 'sound,' 'wholesome' knowledge." Cf. the phrase "in sincerity and faithfulness" at Josh 24:14 (בתמים ובאמת; the reverse order at Judg 9:19). It is curious that the same phrase is apparently used by Elihu in 37:16 of God (the noun differs slightly, being דֵעוֹת here and דֵעִים there), but we should not imagine that the language is appropriate only for the divine (no one is scandalized by the term "just" being applied both to humans and to God; perhaps the text of 37:16 is corrupt anyway). It is worth recalling as well that the Hebrew term ידע "know" includes also what we would call "think" or "have an opinion," so Elihu may not be more self-regarding than any of our contemporaries who says, I believe my opinions are sincere.

5–21 In this section, Elihu does not merely revert (as against Strahan) to his earlier theme of the educational value of suffering (as in 33:12–30), but combines that theme with the one he has just now handled, the fact of transgression in the righteous.

5–15 The theme of this section is how God treats those among the righteous who do wrong in comparison with how he treats those who are really wicked. The fate of the wicked, that they are not kept alive (6a) but die in youth (14), more or less frames the depiction of the righteous who fall into sin (7–12, 15). Because they are righteous, they are watched over by God (7a) and raised to positions of importance (7bc). But if they subsequently find themselves in an unhappy state (8), that will be for a reason, and God will tell them what the reason is (9) and instruct them in what they must do to escape from their misery (10). If they comply, they are restored to happiness (11), but if they do not they die in ignorance (12)—as if they were godless from the start. The wicked, on the other hand, do not appeal to God for deliverance from their misery (13), and their fate is to die young, in shame (14). The righteous, by comparison, receive instruction when they are suffering, and so find deliverance from their suffering (15). These generalizations will be followed by an address to Job personally in vv 16–21.

The point of the comparison of righteous and wicked at this moment in Elihu's speech seems to be a further justification of God and proof that he is righteous in all that he does—which Elihu has proclaimed as the purpose of the speech (v 3b). Although he does not affirm explicitly in these verses that God is just, his purpose seems to be much more than simply to sketch the varying fates of the two classes of people: the way they are treated is for him further evidence of the outworking of the justice of God in human affairs.

Interestingly, Elihu here goes beyond the traditional classification of people into two classes, good and bad. It is a refinement in his theology that he reckons with the reality of good people who go to the bad and need rescuing from the consequent misery they find themselves in. In fact, they are the only kind of good people he seems to know about. It is a more realistic view than that of the wisdom literature and the Psalms, where the world often seems simply divided into two undifferentiated classes, the good and the bad.

A number of commentators do not recognize that the righteous who go wrong are the principal theme of this section, and think rather that much of the focus is on the case of kings who become prisoners (taking v 7bc and v 8 together, usually with some emendation of the text); thus, for example, de Wilde. Such kings would be an illustration of the choices that lie before a person who is suffering: either they listen to God's instruction and find happiness (v 12), or they do not listen, and come to a violent end (v 13). This would be a more conventional scenario than that sketched above, and it is hard to see why the case of kings in particular who are imprisoned should be chosen.

5 This is a particularly difficult verse, and many emendations have been offered (see *Notes*). The solution adopted in the *Translation* is to take the second half of the verse to mean that "God will not reject the pure of heart"; this involves moving כח "strength" from the second colon to the first, and emending כביר "strong" in the second colon to בְּבַר "to the pure." Such a sentence would signal that what will follow, the cameo of the righteous who fall into sin but are rescued through obeying God's instruction, will show God's justice in preserving (i.e., not "rejecting") those who are "pure" (i.e., righteous).

As for the clause with which the verse begins, "Behold, God is mighty," the sense seems to be that God is indeed mighty but his power does not override his sense of justice. The two cola are simply connected with "and": God is mighty *and* he will not reject the pure. But it seems best to understand the first as concessive: "though God is mighty, he will not reject the pure." His grandeur might suggest he cares for nothing on earth; not so, says Elihu, he positively upholds the pious (on the litotes, see below). God's own power does not imply contempt for the powerless. Less appropriately, Hartley thinks that God's might is the reason why he acts justly: because no one can threaten him, he never acts from fear. And equally out of place is Habel's suggestion that כביר "mighty" means "courageous," i.e., he is one who "does not shrink from executing justice according to the laws of his cosmic order."

"Pure of heart" (בר לב) recurs in Pss 24:4; 73:1 (לֵבָב in both); cf. Matt 5:8. The idea of God "rejecting" (מאס) the perfect person (תם) occurs also in 8:20. מאס seems essentially to mean "esteem or treat lightly" (cf. S. Wagner and H.-J. Fabry, *TDOT,* 8:47–60 [49]), but that sense must be just a token for what is really meant, which is something like "disregard the rights of." In any case, "does not reject" is a litotes (Dhorme) for "actively maintains the rights of," just as "he does not let the wicked live" is a litotes for "he slays the wicked."

6 The two aspects of God's just dealings are mentioned: he slays the wicked, he gives justice to the afflicted. This is headline stuff, for Elihu himself knows that reality is much more complicated. On the one side, the wicked are obviously very much in evidence (cf. 34:7, 18, 22, 26–28), and clearly not all have been instantly put to death. And on the other side, just now Elihu has been explaining how there is more than one kind of afflicted person: there are the deserving and the undeserving (35:9–13). So it is not true, as a blanket statement, that the "afflicted" (עניים) get "justice," in the sense of deliverance, for some at least of the afflicted do not deserve to be heard. Maybe not being delivered is justice of a sort, but a disregarded cry (35:13) is not what Elihu means by "justice" (משפט) here.

The afflicted who have their "right" asserted are those who, being righteous, fall into sin but learn from their suffering and so in some sense deserve their deliverance. Elihu is not thinking of a poor afflicted but righteous man who rises to prominence like Joseph (against Hartley), nor of an imprisoned king like Manasseh (against Dhorme) or others (cf. de Wilde).

7–12 Focusing now on the righteous, he develops a little cameo of how God's care for them operates. The picture of them being set on thrones with kings, and then bound in fetters, may be intended to be illustrative of how their lives may falter, or the language may be more metaphorical. In the former case, the narrative is literally true only of some of the afflicted, though they may be representative of all; in the latter case, the language will be metaphorically true of all the afflicted.

7 God does not "withdraw" (גרע) his eyes from the righteous; it is another litotes, for Elihu means that God has them constantly in view. It can hardly be literally meant that the righteous are enthroned as kings, for that does not often happen. Rather, God's justice for the righteous ensures that they rise to positions of importance, or, at least, that they find their own kind of success in life. For the phrase "cause to sit (on a throne)" (ישב hiph), cf. 1 Sam 2:8; 1 Kgs 2:24; 2 Chr 23:20.

Many commentators see a change of subject in v 7b, as if the matter of the righteous has come to an end, and a different topic begins, that of kings who fall on hard times and are then offered a choice of futures by the almighty deity (vv 7b–12) (so, e.g., Strahan, Dhorme, Terrien, de Wilde). Such a picture would, it is true, serve to illustrate the workings of the divine justice, but it would not be relevant to the question of how the righteous are treated by God—which seemed to be announced in v 5 as the theme of this section. For the kings who become imprisoned in v 8 are neither good nor bad to begin with—we hear nothing of them before their decline into bondage; so they cannot be an example of the vicissitudes of the righteous. All in all, it is much better to see the contrast in vv 5–16 as between the truly righteous who fall into sin and may or may not escape, and the truly wicked who come to an early grave.

8 The second phase in the life story of these righteous folk is that, after their elevation to places of prominence, they find themselves in fetters and cords, no doubt metaphorical of affliction in general (though Delitzsch thinks the fetters are literal and the cords metaphorical, as with those "imprisoned in misery and iron" in Ps 107:10). There is nothing very novel in the book of Job about the idea that suffering may be disciplinary (Eliphaz had already said so in 5:17; and cf. Elihu in 33:16–22). What is different here is the affliction of those who have already been the beneficiaries of God's justice: for their righteousness they have been elevated to power, and now they have overstepped the mark and have been brought low. It is not the story of Joseph that is being alluded to (against Andersen), for Joseph is not said to have brought his imprisonment on himself. On suffering as discipline, cf. J. A. Sanders, "Suffering as Divine Discipline in the Old Testament and Postbiblical Judaism," *Colgate Rochester Divinity School Bulletin* 28 (1955) 28–33.

It is not said by whom they have been bound (unless we adopt the emendation of אסורים "bound" to אֲסָרָם "he has bound them" [see *Note* 36:8.b]), and it is not to Elihu's point here to make God the author of their affliction (against Habel), since the issue is not so much how the affliction has come about but how the afflicted should behave in their affliction. Nevertheless, we may be sure that what happens to the righteous happens at God's instigation, and so we may appropriately speak of a theme of "redemption through affliction" (Newsom).

"Fetters" (זק) is a generic term for any means of physical restraint, whether for the neck, hands, or feet; they appear in the Hebrew Bible as devices for detaining captives (Isa 45:14; Nah 3:10; Ps 149:8). For illustrations, cf. *ANEP,* figs. 10, 49–51, 55, 57, 325–26. Metaphorically, bonds signify affliction (מוֹסֵר in Isa 28:22; 52:2; Jer 30:8; Nah 1:13; Ps 2:3), as do, for example, yokes (עֹל in Gen 27:40; Lev 26:13; 1 Kgs 12:4; Isa 9:4 [3]; 10:27; etc.). Cf. also the "stocks" (סד) of Job 13:27 (*q.v.*); 33:11. "Cords" (חבל), as what restrain, are cords of death (2 Sam 22:6; Ps 116:3) and of Sheol (2 Sam 22:6); only here is affliction spoken of as cords, but the imagery is plain. With the idiom "cords of affliction" we may compare "days of affliction" (ימי עני, 30:16).

9 We may be sure, says Elihu, that if righteous folk find themselves in fetters, that is where they deserve to be: their deeds (פעל, a neutral term for "what they have done") have amounted to "transgression" (פשׁע, a negative term for "what they have done wrong"). See further, *Note* 36:9.b. They have been behaving "arrogantly" (גבר hithp)—at least that is how the word is translated. Now arrogance is not the only fault wrongdoers may be culpable of; this particular sin is itself no doubt also metaphorical, like the throne and the fetters, since it is the sin to which kings and princes on thrones are especially prone. The verb גבר is "be strong," and the hithpael form suggests "display oneself as strong." Being strong, or showing oneself as strong, especially if one is a king or a prince, does not seem to be much of a fault (it is God himself who has set them on thrones with kings so that they are high [גבה, v 7], which does not sound so very different from גבר "be strong"), and in fact most uses of the verb have no negative connotations. But here it is a "transgression," and that must mean that it is intrusive on God's authority and calls into question his power in some way.

Unlike 33:23, where the key knowledge is conveyed to the sufferer by an angel, here it is God himself who declares to the afflicted the significance of their deeds, i.e., how they have erred. The means God uses for making the sufferers aware of their misdeeds is not alluded to here; in 33:14–28 Elihu had spoken of dreams and of illness as methods of divine communication, and no doubt he also thinks of himself as a bearer of a message of instruction.

10 It is characteristic of Elihu (Fedrizzi) that he sees God as the great Instructor (see also 33:14–16), and not surprisingly he envisages the divine response to transgression (v 9b) as the delivery of corrective "instruction" (מוסר; cf. on 5:17). Perhaps there is a reminiscence in the word מוּסָר *mûsār* "instruction" of the term אָסוּר *'āsûr* "bound" in v 8 (Good): suffering is discipline, bondage is instruction. But, unlike "instruction" in the wisdom tradition, which may as easily be physical punishment as words of reproof, here it is plainly speech (not chastisement, as Tur-Sinai) that serves as instruction, for the ears are open to receive it.

On the phrase "uncover the ear" (גלה אזן), cf. on 33:16; it seems no different from "open the ear." An open ear is one that is ready to receive instruction and be obedient (cf. Isa 50:4–5). To "turn" (שׁוב) from iniquity is traditional prophetic language for "repent" (cf. J. A. Soggin, *TLOT,* 3:1312–17), but the term never seems to mean that in Job. Here, as at 22:23 (*q.v.*), the idea is that of turning away from practicing iniquity.

11–12 We need to remember that here Elihu is still speaking of the righteous of v 7a. When they have fallen into sin, they have had set before them two scenarios: either they "hearken" (שׁמע "hear," thus "obey"), or they do not "hearken" (שׁמע again). Either they "return from iniquity" (v 10b) and live out their days in happiness (v 11bc), or, in not hearkening, they perish and die in ignorance (v 11). The two ways are signaled by very similar-sounding verbs (Andersen, Good): either they hearken and "serve" (עבד *'ābad*), or they fail to hearken and "cross over" (עבר *'ābar*) to the underworld. No doubt the same options are set before every person, but (as against Andersen) it is not Everyman who is here in view, but still that particular group of people, the righteous who have fallen into sin.

The depiction of the two futures, prosperity and pleasantness on the one hand, and death without knowledge on the other, is reminiscent (Dhorme, Good) of the prophetic disjunction: "If you are willing and obedient, you shall eat the good [טוּב, equivalent to טוֹב here] of the land; but if you refuse and rebel, you shall be devoured by the sword" (Isa 1:19–20 NRSV). But, nearer to hand, it is very similar to the picture painted by Eliphaz in 22:21–28 of the happy future that awaits Job if he will "return" (שׁוב) in repentance to God. What we read here is just another instance of the common doctrine of the "two ways" (cf. Deut 30:15–20; Jer 21:8–9; Ecclus 15:14–17; *T. Asher* 1:3–9; Matt 7:12–14; *Didache* 1).

To die without gaining wisdom is for Elihu, the pedagogue, a most calamitous end (cf. also Eliphaz at 4:21). "They pass ignorantly into the region where there is no knowledge to be gained" (Andersen). On the river of death, which the non-obedient cross prematurely, see on 33:18.

13–15 A further contrast is drawn here, between the ultimate fate of the godless (חנף, vv 12–14) and that of the afflicted (עני, v 15). It is the same contrast as we saw in v 6, between the fates of the wicked (רשע) and of the afflicted (עני). It is not at all the same contrast that has occupied us from v 7 to v 12, which was between two kinds of righteous people: those who respond to the message contained in their affliction (v 11) and those who do not (v 12).

In v 16, Elihu will turn directly to Job and address him as "you," but there is no need to doubt that Elihu has Job in view all the way through his depiction of the fates of the righteous. Though Elihu's chief purpose is to justify the ways of God as righteous, explaining how there may be good reasons why even the righteous afflicted are not always delivered, and even though he is not thinking of Job principally, Job must be for him a prime example of a righteous man in danger of dying "without knowledge" (v 12) if he does not accept the divine instruction that lies inherent in his suffering.

13 The term now is חנף "godless" rather than רשע "wicked" as we had in v 6, but they are the same people. Most agree that חנף should be translated "godless" (RSV, NIV) or "impious" (NAB, NJPS) (cf. BDB, 338a; *DCH*, 3:277a). R. Knierim has argued that it really means "perverted" (*TLOT*, 1:447–48), but K. Seybold thinks rather that it suggests "deceptive, dissimulating, hypocritical" (*TDOT*, 5:36–44 [43]), a sense that Dhorme also proposed (KJV also had "hypocrites in heart"). NEB's "proud" no doubt depends on the suggestion that there is a חָנֵף II "haughty" like Ugar. *ḫnp* (also used in the phrase *ḫnp lb* "haughty of heart," as here). But the most likely understanding is that it has no very specific meaning but is a generic term for wrongdoers.

Even if we could be confident about the text, that it says such wrongdoers "lay up anger for themselves" (see *Note* 36:13.c), it is not entirely clear what this would mean. Perhaps it means that they are forever increasing the store of divine anger that is due to them. Less probably, they harbor the anger roused in them by their suffering (Habel), cherishing angry thoughts about God's discipline (Peake).

Whereas the first colon of v 13 apparently depicts the divine reaction to their unceasing wickedness, the second colon is more evidently one of the reasons why they attract the divine wrath (or perhaps even why they are called "godless" in the first place). It is that they do not "cry out" (שׁוע piel) when God "binds" (אסר) them with affliction. The very same language of "binding" had been used in v 8 of the experience of some of the righteous, viz. those who become arrogant when they have been raised to positions of importance by God. Here we are not dealing with righteous people at all, but that is no reason why the poet should not use the same term. It is strange, however, that the wicked should be faulted for not "crying out" in their suffering when Elihu has been at pains to explain that "crying out" of itself is not good enough for God: merely to "cry out" (זעק) without explicitly calling upon God will ensure that God will not listen (35:9–12). Should not the error of the godless here also be, not that they do not cry out, but that they do not also say, "Where is God our Maker?" or some such words? It does seem an inconsistency, but it would be rash to blame Elihu; the difficulty may be entirely due to the corrupt textual state of these verses.

14 It is characteristic of retributionist theology in the Hebrew Bible that the wicked are said to die prematurely: Zophar, for example, says that "the triumph cry of the wicked has been of the briefest, the rejoicing of the godless has lasted but a moment" (20:5), and Eliphaz that evildoers are "shriveled up before their time" (22:16). But nowhere in Job is it suggested that evildoers are cut off "in their youth" (נער), as Elihu here alleges. It does not seem a very plausible position to hold, to tell the truth, for even a hardened retributionist must know of middle-aged or even elderly wrongdoers who have plainly not "died in youth." Once again, it is a little difficult to believe that Elihu has said quite what stands in the Masoretic text (for the difficulties of the text, see *Note* 36:14.b).

The second colon of the verse is, however, much more difficult. At face value, the text says that "their life [dies] among prostitutes" (קדשים is usually said to mean "male prostitutes," and moreover male prostitutes attached to temples and shrines, but in both respects this view is questionable; see *Note* 36:14.b). This seems a strangely specific end for the godless in general, and it is difficult to see how either Elihu or the poet could have imagined it could be true of the godless as a class. It is argued, of course, that prostitutes are among the most despised members of society, and that it is the shameful end of the wicked that is the point at issue. On the other hand, since there appears to be evidence of brothels within the Jerusalem temple in monarchic times (cf. 2 Kgs 23:7), can we be so sure that prostitution was such a shameful occupation? Some authors stress that Elihu is referring to "pagan" shrines (so Terrien), but Elihu of course, like the rest of the book of Job, knows nothing specifically Israelite.

Some have thought that there is a closer connection between the two cola of the verse: if in the first colon the wicked die "in their youth," in the second colon dying "among the prostitutes" should perhaps also refer to an early death. "[T]hese male devotees to unchastity," say Driver–Gray, "... must, worn out by their excesses, have died, as a rule, at an early age, so that they became proverbial as victims of an untimely death" (similarly Peake). "[I]t is likely that sexually transmitted diseases claimed the lives of many, then as now" (Alden). There is, however, not a shred of evidence for these beliefs.

A partial solution to the problem may be offered by the LXX, which reads "and their life is wounded by angels," understanding the consonantal text קדשים as a reference to the "Holy Ones" (קְדֹשִׁים), who have appeared previously at 5:1 and 15:15. In Ps 78:49 there is a reference to destroying angels who execute God's wrath upon rebellious Israel, and Elihu has already referred to their work at 32:33. It would make much more sense of the verse if these godless people should die in their youth at the hands of heavenly beings (so the *Translation* above) rather than "among prostitutes." A fuller examination of the question (see *Note* 14.b) comes to no certain conclusion, but questions whether the Masoretic text is in order.

On the much debated question of prostitution and especially of cultic or temple-associated prostitution, see: P. E. Dion, "Did Cultic Prostitution Fall into Oblivion during the Postexilic Era? Some Evidence from Chronicles and the Septuagint," *CBQ* 43 (1981) 41–48; W. Fauth, "Sakrale Prostitution im Vorderen Orient und im Mittelmeerraum," *JAC* 31 (1988) 24–39; K. van der Toorn, "Female Prostitution in Payment of Vows in Ancient Israel," *JBL* 108 (1989) 193–205; idem, "Cultic Prostitution," *ABD*, 5:510–13; D. A. Garrett, "Votive Prostitution Again: A Comparison of Proverbs 7:13–14 and 21:28–29," *JBL* 109 (1990) 681–82; P. A. Bird, "The End of the Male Cult Prostitute: A Literary-Historical and Sociological Analysis of Hebrew *qadeš-qedešim*," in *Congress Volume: Cambridge 1995*, ed. J. A. Emerton, VTSup 66 (Leiden: Brill, 1997) 37–80; J. Day, "Does the Old Testament Refer to Sacred Prostitution and Did It Actually Exist in Ancient Israel?" in *Biblical and Near Eastern Essays*, FS K. J. Cathcart, ed. C. McCarthy and J. F. Healey, JSOTSup 375 (London: T. & T. Clark, 2004) 2–21.

15 By contrast with the "godless," the "afflicted" (עני) are delivered. The term (already in 24:4, 9, 14; 29:12; used by Elihu in 34:28; 36:6) refers to any oppressed, that is, underprivileged, persons in Israelite society; they are of course typically the economically poor, but they include other types of oppressed persons, such as the chronically ill and prisoners (cf. further on 24:14ab). It is a nice crystallization of Elihu's view of suffering as a means of salvation when he says that the "afflicted" (עָנִי *ʿānî*) are delivered by "affliction" (עֳנִי *ʿonî*), the aphorism being signaled further by the wordplay on "delivers" (יְחַלֵּץ *yeḥallēṣ*) and "distress" (חַלַץ *ḥalaṣ*) (cf. Watson, 240).

The aphorism is of course paradoxical, for it is God who delivers, and he delivers because the afflicted person accepts the proffered instruction about the meaning of the suffering; the affliction does not itself deliver, and, truth to tell, it is never anything else but what one needs to be delivered *from*. All the same, if understanding the reason for one's affliction leads to salvation, one could say, at a pinch, that one is delivered *by* the affliction, and Elihu is certainly operating at the extreme of what the language can tolerate. The second colon, that God "opens their ears by their distress," corresponds exactly to what Elihu has said in vv 9–10, even including the phrase "open the ear" (גלה אזן; cf. on 33:16).

16–25 The boundaries of the present section are not certain. Did the previous section conclude with the aphorism of v 15, or with the application of his theory of God's justice to Job personally at v 16 (as the strophic structure would suggest)? In any case, a definite change comes about at v 16, where Elihu begins to speak to Job directly again for the first time since v 4. He will address him as "you" (with personal-pronoun suffixes or second-person verbs) in vv 16–21, 24. Only vv 22–23 and v 25 lack direct reference to Job, and it is possible that the present section could be ended with v 21 or perhaps v 24. On the other hand, v 26 seems to begin a new section, with its initial "Behold, God . . ." (הן־אל), the same phrase that began the section starting with v 4. So it is reasonable to take vv 16–25 as one of the principal sections of the speech.

In this section, Elihu offers his personal advice to Job. It would be too much to say that he applies the lessons of vv 5–15 to Job, for he seems to go off into quite different directions, and it is in any case hard to be sure that we understand the Hebrew correctly, since the text is very uncertain.

Dhorme relates the verses differently: he regards the generalization of v 15 as a preamble to vv 16–17, which he understands as an encouragement addressed to Job for the future ("He will remove you from the jaws of trouble . . ."). Peake similarly thought v 16 described God's present endeavors with Job: "Yea, he allureth thee out of distress" (similarly Terrien). There is no reason, however, why Elihu should be offering Job encouragement at this point; his purpose rather is to warn Job to accept the instruction being given him by God through his suffering.

More attractive is the interpretation of RV, which took v 16 as a depiction of where Job could be now if he had heeded the divine advice: "Yea, he would have led thee away out of distress into a broad place, where there is no straitness.... [17] But thou art full of the judgement of the wicked."

16 Elihu begins his words of advice to Job by reminding him of God's past care for him. His life as a whole has been marked by "spaciousness" (רחב) rather than "constraint" (לא־מוצק), and he has always enjoyed what life had to offer him ("what is set on your table is full of fatness"). The "narrowness" (צר) from which he has been delivered all his life is "distress"; cf. Pss 31:7 (8) "you know my adversities," lit. narrownesses, of life (צרות נפש); 4:1 (2) "You gave me room (הרחבת) when I was in distress (צר)." The opposite of narrowness is spaciousness (רחב in the next colon), a familiar concept for ease (cf. J. F. A. Sawyer, "Spaciousness [An Important Feature of Language about Salvation in the Old Testament]," *ASTI* 6 [1967–68] 2–34). His table is "full of fat," which may jar somewhat with today's slimline reader. In Job's day, however, fatness was a mark of strength, prosperity, and sound health (cf. on 15:27; 21:24).

17–18 But now Job finds himself in the position of the wicked, being punished by God. He is "full of the judgment due to the wicked," and the justice that comes to the wicked has fallen upon him. What is he to do? Certainly not what he has been doing, complaining about the injustice of his suffering. Far from it; he has before him an opportunity to discover God's instruction and so to be restored to prosperity and happiness (v 11). But it is a risky situation to be in, for Job can so easily let his suffering lead him further away from God: that very judgment that God intends as warning and instruction can become "mockery" (ספק, if that is what the word means; see *Note* 36:18.d), the occasion for insult of God. Job is all too capable of thinking too highly of himself, and his wealthy lifestyle has to be considered a real hindrance to a humble piety. The "ample ransom money" (רב־כפר, lit. "abundance of ransom") he has always had at his disposal has perhaps persuaded him he can buy his way out of any difficulty; but that is a terrible mistake (it could "lead him astray" [נטה hiph]) when his current difficulty is a matter of suffering imposed from on high. He has no resources now that can be used to alleviate his suffering; only obedience to the divine teaching will suffice. In 33:23 a "ransom" found by the mediator angel was perhaps not money but simply an unspecified means of redemption from death; here too the point is that Job has no such means (other than, of course, a willingness to learn from his suffering).

Such a reading of these verses seems far preferable to one that finds here only unreasonable criticism of Job's past life (17) and jejune advice to Job about making just decisions and not being swayed by bribes (18). NJB, for example, has "you did not bring the wicked to trial and did not give fair judgement to the orphan" (17) and "Beware of being led astray by abundance, of being corrupted by expensive presents" (18). On the one hand, it seems highly improbable that Elihu would attack Job on the very matter of social responsibility, where Job feels so certain of his innocence (29:12–17; 31:16–21), and, on the other, Job is surely of all people least in need of warning against expensive presents.

To be "full of the judgment of the wicked" seems to mean to suffer judgment that rightly falls on the wicked, not "to join the wicked in their judgment of God when He afflicts" (Davidson).

19 Continuing the thought of v 18, Elihu advises Job that there is no escaping the divine justice. Job's wealth will never keep him from the "distress" (צר) of divine punishment, nor will any strenuous "effort" (מאמץ) he might make to resist it.

A question arises, with Elihu's talk of Job's wealth (כפר "ransom money," v 18; שוע "sufficiency, wealth," v 19), whether indeed Job still possesses any wealth, or whether he has lost everything in the tragic events of chap. 1. Plainly Job's wealth had consisted mainly in livestock and servants, all of them now gone; but there is in one place a reference to Job's possession of other wealth, when he avers that he has not made gold his trust (31:24), and in 31:39 he has obviously been paying his workers money wages; when disaster strikes, he is not without resources, and he does not behave like a poor man. Of course, when his sufferings are over, he will be showered with gifts of money and gold (42:11), but even now in his sufferings he is not destitute.

20 This is a most difficult verse to make sense of in its context. Gordis explains persuasively that Elihu is warning Job "not to hope for the shelter of night as do other evildoers (cf., e.g., 24:13–17) because whole nations are destroyed by God overnight (cf. 34:20, 25)." That is to say, no more than in his wealth can Job find refuge from the divine reproof in the shadows of night; for the night is a dangerous time for individuals and nations alike (it is not, against Habel, that Job is tempted to join forces with the dark forces of the night whom he had earlier summoned to curse the day of his birth, 3:8). It is ironic that Elihu should imagine Job longing for the night, when Job himself knows so much of "nights of misery, or, toil (עמל)" (7:3), nights that are too long and full only of wakefulness (7:4), and nights that pierce his bones (30:17). It cannot be that Elihu is warning Job not to long for death (as Budde), for Elihu knows only of death as a punishment for wrongdoing, not as a blessed relief.

21 Finally, in what is effectively his final address to Job personally (since the remainder of this fourth speech will be largely occupied with the doings of the creator God), Elihu summarizes his whole position on the meaning of Job's present experience. In his suffering, Job has before him two possibilities, either to learn from the divine displeasure and come to enjoy God's favor (as in v 11), or to remain stubbornly in the guilt that has brought down upon him divine punishment and so come to an early end (as in v 12). Job's final fate has not been settled, and even at this juncture Job can decide to "turn" (פנה) toward iniquity or away from it. It is for the sake of that very choice that Job has been brought into the affliction that now overwhelms him: "that is why you are being tested, or, refined, by affliction."

These verses, from v 13 to v 21, have been among the most difficult and controverted in the book, and the proliferation of variant renderings and proposed emendations is bewildering. Some, like NAB, give up the task of translating vv 16–20 altogether. But there is no need to panic, for by keeping the already stated position of Elihu clearly in view and rejecting proposals that deviate from his present purpose or descend into banality or generalized advice, a reasonably coherent sense can be attained.

22–25 The focalization of these verses (perhaps v 26 belongs with this and not the following strophe; so Fohrer) changes from that of the previous strophe (vv 16–21). There it was Job, now it is God. "Behold, God . . ." (הן־אל) begins the strophe (as it will the next strophe also), and although Job is still addressed, he and his situation are no longer the primary theme. In vv 16–21 the issue was the choice that confronted Job, whether or not to accept the divine instruction he was being offered through suffering. Now the topic has changed to God, and we find in vv 22–25 a generalizing introduction to the celebration of God in creation that will run from v 26 to the end of chap. 37. Job is indeed addressed in the imperative "remember" (זכר) of v 24, as he will also be included in the "we" of v 26 who are incapable of comprehending God, but the matters of Job's choices, his complaints against God, and his sufferings have all disappeared. Job will, incidentally, be addressed again in 37:14–19, even by name in 37:14, but he will no longer be the focus, any more than Elihu himself who appears as "I" in 37:1, 20 and among the "we" of humanity in general in 37:23.

There is passion here, as Elihu begins to expatiate on the divine teaching that is embedded in the cosmic order. Terrien is impressed by how "the pedantic orator, the grotesque conversationalist" is gradually "molting" into a psalmist; on the contrary, Elihu's poetic gifts and religious sensibility go to show how shallow the common judgments about his pedantry are.

22 At first sight there are two unrelated topics in this verse: the might of God, and the fact that he is an unrivaled teacher. Both are great themes of Elihu, but what does he mean by putting them together in one sentence? It must be that the power of God has some connection with his teaching. And the connection may be suggested to be this: every demonstration of the power of God is itself instruction, every aspect of his ways in creation, for example, is itself pedagogy. For Elihu, God is not some heavenly dictator who runs the universe by remote control, but humankind's great Instructor who brings them enlightenment through every evidence of his working.

Elihu begins with a sentence that sounds commonplace, "God is exalted in his power"; who ever in the book of Job denied it? But even that verb שׂגב hiphil has more in it than a mere abstract statement of God's supreme status (elsewhere of God or his name at Isa 2:11, 17; 12:4; 33:5; Ps 148:13): the hiphil voice suggests "deals loftily," "acts sublimely" (cf. Driver–Gray), as a hint that the greatness of God will, in what follows, be shown to consist in his deeds rather than in his nature.

And his deeds are themselves his teaching. It has been a reiterated theme of Elihu (33:14–18; 34:32; 35:11; 36:9–10) that God communicates with humans as their teacher, but here Elihu goes well beyond anything he has previously said. Hitherto, God's teaching has always been thought of as conveyed through the suffering he imposes (or the nightmares he sends), but now Elihu widens his scope in order to present the whole created universe as the vehicle of divine instruction. Only in certain particulars is that point made explicit in what follows (36:31–32; 37:13, 23–24), but it underlies everything that he says about the created order.

The concept of God as a teacher is rare in the OT, though see Isa 28:26; 30:20–21; Pss 25:8, 9, 12; 94:12. Habel suggests indeed that the notion of God as a counselor is in fact a "major tradition of wisdom theology," and wonders whether there is not in the background here an "ancient apologetic against speculation about the various roles and relative status of the gods." We should certainly compare Isa 40:12–15, where Yahweh needs no counselor to advise him on the creation of the world, a probable allusion to an ancient Near Eastern myth of a divine counselor (see also R. N. Whybray, *The Heavenly Counsellor in Isaiah xl 13–14: A Study of the Sources of the Theology of Deutero-Isaiah,* SOTMS 1 [Cambridge: Cambridge UP, 1971]). But Elihu goes further than affirming that God needed no advice from a counselor: not only did he not need to be instructed, he himself is an instructor (Newsom).

"Who is like him?" (מי כמוהו) is a common formula of praise of God that occurs in both cultic (especially hymnic) and prophetic language (Fohrer; cf. Exod 15:11; Pss 35:10; 71:19; 89:8 [9]; and cf. כמוני "like me" in Isa 44:7; Jer 49:19; 50:44; in Deut 33:29, exceptionally, in reference to Israel).

A very interesting alternative reading of the second colon is provided by the Septuagint, which reads "Who is a ruler (δυνάστης) like him?" (see *Note* 36:22.d). Though there are some problems with this reading (it presumes the text had the Aramaic מָרֵא "lord" rather than the Hebrew מוֹרֶה "teacher"), it would easily solve the immediate difficulty of the relation between the two cola of the verse by making them simple parallels. But it would make it more difficult to relate all that follows (36:27–37:24) to what Elihu has previously been saying; for he has never made the power of God a principal part of his argument. His interest has always been rather in the *relation* between divine power and justice and, especially from the beginning of chap. 36 onwards, in how divine power effects justice among humans through teaching and instruction. So there is everything to be said for retaining the Masoretic text at this point.

23 Whether in prospect or retrospect, God is not subject to direction or audit; that is the significance of these two rhetorical questions. No one gives him directions in advance on how to conduct himself; no one assesses his performance after the event. Elihu leaves out of account, of course, all those critics of the divine like Job who are not loath to comment on the quality of God's activity, for Elihu does not acknowledge their standing as assessors.

God's "way" (דרך) may refer specifically to his creative work, as it does in Prov 8:22 (so Whybray), where God created wisdom as the beginning of his "way." But the thought here is very general, and the reference may well be to any of God's doings.

When Elihu affirms that no one says, "You have done wrong," he is not thinking so much of charges against God such as Job has uttered (e.g., 19:7; 24:12; 27:2), but of evaluation of the divine works by a superior authority. No one says to God, "You have done well," either; that would be equally inappropriate. God himself is pictured in the Psalms as reviewing the performance of the lesser gods and, effectively, saying to them, "You have done wrong" (Pss 58:1–2 [2–3]; 82:1–4).

For parallels to the language of reproach to God, cf. 9:12 (Job); 11:10 (Zophar); 23:13 (Job). It would in principle be possible to translate "Who ever visited (punishment) on him for his behavior?," taking פקד in its common sense "visit for punishment." That would make the two cola more closely parallel, and one could compare 21:31, where no one declares to the wicked their "way" (דרך, as here). For פעל עולה "do wrong," cf. 34:32 (פעל און "do iniquity" in 31:3; 34:8, 22).

24 What is the "work" (פעל) of God, and why should Job (and presumably other mortals) need encouraging not to "forget" it? Allusion to Yahweh's "work"

(פֹּעַל twelve times, always in the singular) belongs to the language of prayer (J. Vollmer, *TLOT,* 2:1014–18 [1017]). The term can refer to God's acts in Israel's history (e.g., Pss 44:1 [2]; 95:9) or to acts of deliverance in the future (Ps 90:16) or to his righteous rule in general (Deut 32:4; Ps 92:4 [5]). In Isa 45:11 the "work of my hands" refers to God's creation both of the world and of humankind. Only here does it refer to the created order primarily (so it is a little too presuming to translate with "his creation" here, as Habel). All this means that the reader does not know for sure what Elihu is referring to when one has read only to v 24. The mystery in which he clothes his thought is continued with the vague but suggestive allusions to God's work as the subject of song (v 24b), and to it as the object of human gaze from afar (v 25).

"Remember" (זכר) is a request frequently addressed to God in the language of prayer (cf. on 7:7; 10:9; and see W. Schottroff, *TLOT,* 1:381–88). More rarely, humans are called upon to remember (the days of old, Deut 32:7; Isa 46:9; Israel's creation by God, Isa 44:21; one's creator in youth, Eccl 12:1; Yahweh in a distant land, Jer 51:50; God's wonderful works, 1 Chr 16:12; the teaching of Moses, Mal 4:4 [3:22]). Only in Job is the idiom זכר כי, lit. "remember that," but in the sense "remember to (do something)," "take care to do something" (Delitzsch), to be found (7:7; 10:9). Elsewhere זכר "remember" with a direct object can often be "not so much a caution not to forget to do so as a command to do so" (Whybray); cf., e.g., Exod 20:8 "Remember the Sabbath day." In all these cases of people being urged to "remember," the implication is that they are forgetting, or overlooking, or failing to do, something important. It is certainly true in the case of Job that he has not been spending a lot of time extolling God's creatorial activity.

How exactly would Job "extol" (שׂגא hiph, "declare to be great") God's work in creation? Presumably by joining the universal choir (Terrien), the singing of praise that is already going on (v 24b). Though there is no direct reference to the Hebrew psalms, hymns like Pss 8, 19, 29, 65:6–13 (7–14), 104, 147, 148 would fit the description well. Peake (following Duhm) opined that the author of Job "was very likely a Psalmist himself," and Strahan that Elihu's fondness for allusions to the Psalms (cf. 33:27; 35:10) "suggests that his creator may have been of the singers of Israel." If that were so, this would be the author's modest self-advertisement for his own productions. And why should Job now be extolling God's work, according to Elihu? Because to praise God's work requires one to become occupied with it, to research it and come to know it; if Job were to do that, he would learn the lessons that God, the unrivaled teacher (v 22b), has imprinted in the book of nature.

It is men (אנשׁים, plural of אישׁ "man") who have sung of the works of God, since temple choirs seem to have been wholly male (professional female singers are attested in 2 Sam 19:35 [36]; Eccl 2:8; Ezra 2:65 || Neh 7:67; 2 Chr 35:25, but never in a cultic context). On the other hand, as v 25 will say, all humans, regardless of gender (which is what אדם "humans" signifies), have gazed upon it, and every human, equally without reference to gender (which is what is implied by אנושׁ "person"), has beheld it from afar. On אדם "human, humanity" as a non-gendered term, see D. J. A. Clines, "אדם, the Hebrew for 'Human, Humanity': A Response to James Barr," *VT* 53 (2003) 297–310.

On "singing" in praise of God, cf. J. W. Kleinig, *The Lord's Song: The Basis, Func-*

tion and Significance of Choral Music in Chronicles, JSOTSup 156 (Sheffield: JSOT Press, 1993). The singing in 33:27 is a hymn of thanksgiving such as we meet with frequently in the Psalms (e.g., 13:6; 28:7; 98:1), not the kind of hymn here in praise of the creator God.

25 Gradually the reader becomes aware that the work of God that Elihu will speak of is of universal significance, not something special to Israel but something in the past, and something that is remote from humans. But as yet we do not know what this work is. Only from v 27 onward will we discover that it is the work of creation of the natural order.

Is it because humans can behold the work of God only from afar that they cannot understand it completely (Rowley)? Fohrer thinks that the clause is concessive, "though humans can see it only from afar" (similarly Gordis). Davidson and Peake thought that it is not possible to see it except from afar, for it is too great to see close at hand. But perhaps, more prosaically, "from afar" (מרחוק) refers only to the distance from the earth to the sky, where many of the phenomena described in the following hymn occur (Tur-Sinai, Whybray).

36:26–37:24 Given all that we have heard so far from Elihu, we would not expect him to turn now to descriptions of the created world. Although he has seasoned his didactic poetry with little narrative cameos (33:15–28; 34:24–28; 35:9–12; 36:7–12), they have always depicted the world of humans. He has not before drawn upon the marvels of nature to illustrate his argument.

This section, with its thirty-two verses, is by far the longest of Elihu's excursions away from his theological exposition, and it clearly comes at a climactic position in the series of speeches. As the book of Job stands, it is the end of Elihu's intervention, and the author will have wanted his character to leave the stage with an impressive rhetorical flourish. If the argument advanced in this commentary is correct, that the Elihu speeches (chaps. 32–37) properly and originally stood after the last speech of the third cycle (chap. 27) and that chap. 28, the so-called poem on wisdom, was originally the end of this fourth speech of Elihu's, we would be encountering an even more marked transition in the Elihu material, a transition from a more didactic to a more lyrical style (for 36:26–37:24; 28:1–28), adumbrating the lyricism of the divine speeches. See further, D. J. A. Clines, "The Poetic Achievement of the Book of Job," in *Palabra, Prodigio, Poesía: In Memoriam P. Luis Alonso Schökel, S.J.,* ed. V. Collado Bertomeu, Analecta Biblica 151 (Rome: Editrice Pontificio Istituto Biblico; Jávea [Alicante]: Huerto de Enseñanzas [ALAS], 2004) 243–53.

Terrien has the interesting idea that this section can be typified as a hymn of praise to the Lord of Autumn (36:26–37:5), the Lord of Winter (37:6–13), and the Lord of Summer (37:14–24). What of spring? Gordis thinks that the section devoted to that season may have dropped out of the text, but do we know that the Hebrews thought of the year as having four seasons rather than three, or two? De Wilde saw here the autumn rains, which give food (v 31), in 37:6–10 the winter, in 37:11–13 the spring rains, and the summer in 37:14–18. On the emotions called forth by the clouds, cf. Dalman, *Arbeit und Sitte,* 1:114–15.

26 One cannot be sure whether this verse concludes the strophe that began at v 22, with the same "Behold, God," or whether it is the start of the new strophe that runs to v 33. Either way, it is another verse where the connection of its parts is not transparent. How is God's greatness related to the "number of his years"?

If the number of God's years is beyond discovery, does this mean that he has no age and "his work is therefore not limited by time" (Dhorme)? That seems too abstract a thought. Ps 102:27 (28), that God's "years will not end," is no real parallel, since it only means that he is immortal. If the number of God's years cannot be counted or found out, it can only be because he is so very old. He is like the hoary El of the Ugaritic literature, "king, father of years" (*ab šnm, Baal* VI.iii.24 [*CML*, 75b] = 4.iv.24 [*CML*², 59] = *KTU* 1.4 IV 24), and he is himself the "ancient of days" of Dan 7:9, 13, 22, his hair white as pure wool. Now his age must be related to his wisdom. If God is infinitely old, he must also be infinitely wise (as also de Wilde, alone of modern commentators, recognizes). Ironically, Elihu has been at pains to assert that age is no assurance of wisdom (32:9), but the burden of tradition about the number of God's years is evidently more than he can throw off. Wisdom is, in a traditional pedagogy, the principal attribute of a teacher, and for Elihu, it is God's wisdom in creating and sustaining the world that is his greatness, and never simple power or might. The whole description of the natural world from here to the end of chap. 37 can be seen as focusing on the divine wisdom rather than divine strength.

"Beyond finding out" (ולא חקר, lit. "and there is no searching") has no exact parallel; at 34:24 לא חקר means "without investigation." The very similar phrase ואין חקר occurs at 5:9; 9:10 (of God's great deeds), Isa 40:28 (of God's understanding), Ps 145:3 (of God's greatness), and Prov 25:3 (of the mind of kings).

The same question of the relation of the parts arises also for the first colon in itself. The two clauses of this colon are linked by "and," which invites us to consider their relation: God is great *and* we know it not. But when we attempt to state the connection, it cannot help but sound prosaic: thus NEB "God is so great that we cannot know him," "the greatness of God exceeds our knowledge" (NJB), "God is great and we do not know how great" (Dhorme). It is better to leave the translation sounding more like the Hebrew and oblige the reader to consider how the parts are to be connected. Obviously we humans do know that God is great; otherwise the poet cannot be saying so; presumably what we do not know is the extent of his greatness, but "this perceived limitation does not invalidate what we do know" (Andersen). The term "know" (ידע) does not have an expressed object, and we may be tempted to supply "it" or "him." It amounts to much the same thing, for if we do not comprehend the extent of God's greatness, we do not "know" him. Looking at the two other passages in Job where the same phrase "and we do not know" (ולא נדע) occurs, however, we might wonder whether a better translation still might not be: "and we know nothing." In 8:9 Job had said that we are of yesterday and "know nothing," and in 37:5 Elihu will say that God does great things and "we know nothing." This would be an even more radical negation of the value of human knowledge. He would not mean that we can know nothing at all about God, but that the sum of what we know amounts to next to nothing when set beside the reality.

27–28 What appears to be no more than a proto-scientific description of the formation of rain very probably serves a more theological purpose as well. Elihu's theme, though it has only been hinted at in v 22, may well be "wisdom in the clouds," a suggestive phrase that RSV offers us at 38:36 (even if the Hebrew means something quite different). The God who devised the order of nature is humankind's great Teacher (36:22), and has built into the creation of the world lessons for the improvement of humans, "tongues in trees, books in the running brooks, sermons in stones" (*As You Like It* 2.1.18–19).

The production of rain must be among the least dramatic of the works of God in creation, but it is the example with which Elihu begins his account of the deeds of God that have been hymned in song (cf. v 24). It is a creative work that is current, perpetual, beneficial for humans, even essential. It is a mysterious process also, for it is obvious, to the ancients as well as to ourselves, that salt seawater is destructive while fresh rainwater is life-giving; how is the one changed into the other? We apparently have here an account of the complete cycle of rain formation, from the evaporation of water from the sea to the creation of clouds and the falling of rain from the clouds. It begins with God "drawing up" (if that is the meaning of גרע) "drops," i.e., vapor, from the sea. He next "distills" that vapor into drops held in clouds, which are then poured out (נזל, רעף) as showers of rain upon humans. The whole process seems to be reflected also in Eccl 1:7 and perhaps also in Amos 9:6. In an alternative understanding of the Hebrew, the focus is simply on the process in the sky, where God makes very fine drops of water (גרע being understood as "make small, minimize"). On this view, evaporation is not in mind (Sicre Díaz even thinks it unlikely that the author knew about it).

The reference to humans (though it is possible that the word אדם may here signify "land" rather than "human"; cf. *Note* 36:28.f) is a hint of Elihu's orientation throughout the whole poem: nature does not exist for its own sake, or (as contemporaries of ours might say) as a self-regulating system, but as a human-related network. It operates largely for the sake of humans (it will be a very different perspective on the universe in the divine speeches), and they may draw inferences from its workings about its creator. For it is all the work of the great Teacher, who intends the universe as instruction.

Duhm made the ingenious observation that whereas rain is here understood to be produced by evaporation of water from the earth, in the divine speeches rain is thought to be stored in heavenly reservoirs (cf. 38:25–27, 37–38); the author of the Elihu speeches, he inferred, lived later than that of the divine speeches, and was influenced by Greek science. It is not a fanciful idea (as Pope), and there is indeed a difference between the two portrayals, though the difference is not due to the date of the composition; it is simply that in chap. 38 the depiction is less analytical (de Wilde "less physical").

According to the modern scientific explanation of rain, when moisture-laden air is heated by the sun it begins to rise. As the bubbles of air containing the moisture rise, the surrounding air pressure and temperature decrease, the air bubbles expand, and the moisture condenses into clouds. As the cloud cools further, the droplets that make up the cloud combine, some of them becoming so large and heavy that the currents of air in the cloud can no longer support them and they begin to fall as rain.

Bibliography: G. Rendsburg, "Hebrew *rḥm* = 'rain,'" *VT* 33 (1983) 357–62; G. M. Tucker, "Rain on a Land Where No One Lives: The Hebrew Bible on the Environment," *JBL* 116 (1997) 3–17; E. F. Sutcliffe, "The Clouds as Water-Carriers in Hebrew Thought," *VT* 3 (1953) 99–103.

31 This verse should no doubt be transferred to this point, for a number of reasons. (1) Where it stands, the giving of food seems connected to the topic of the lightning (vv 29–30); while it is true that lightning generally accompanies rainstorms, it would seem more appropriate if the giving of food were connected with the account of the rain in vv 27–28. (2) A referent is needed for the phrase "by them" (בם): by what does God "judge" or "nourish" humans? It must be the clouds (שחקים) of v 28, since there is no suitable plural noun in all of vv 29–30 (the "spreadings of the clouds [מפרשי־עב]" can hardly be what produces food). (3) A further reason, though it would not be determinative, is that by moving v 31 to this place two parallel strophes become evident: vv 26–28, 31 (four lines) on the rain, vv 29–30, 32–33 (four lines) on the lightning; each of the strophes would end with an explicit statement of the impact of the heavenly phenomena on humanity.

It would be very interesting, and highly relevant to Elihu's main theme, if the text said that God uses the giving of rain as a means of judging nations (as RSV "by these he judges peoples"). Elihu is not only concerned in this speech to ascribe justice to his Maker (36:3) but also to argue that God is the great Teacher, who is always engaged in instructing humans for their improvement. If some cities are rained upon, and others suffer drought, that could well be a sign of divine pleasure in the former and displeasure in the latter (cf. Amos 4:7, where the same thought is explicit). The giving of rain could itself be a judgment, and those in the rainless city would have the opportunity of learning a lesson. A corresponding translation such as "by these he judges nations" is offered by KJV, JPS, RSV, Habel; cf. NRSV, NIV "governs," NJPS "controls."

On the other hand, with this translation it is hard to make sense of the two cola of the verse. For if the first colon speaks of the use of rain to discriminate between the deserving and the undeserving, it is strange that the second colon speaks only of the *abundance* of rain and not of the selectivity with which it is apportioned. It becomes very attractive then to adopt the emendation "he nourishes peoples" (reading יזון for ידין) in the first colon, which would create a rather exact parallel with the next colon, "he gives food in abundance." This emendation is accepted by many scholars, and among modern English translations, NAB, NJB, NEB, and GNB, as well as in the *Translation* above. For further details, see *Note* 36:31.c.

The most important feature of the verse (which does not depend on the translation of the first colon) is its assertion that in his establishment of the cosmic order God has in mind human needs. The phenomena of the clouds are not just signs of the majesty of God, nor are they here tokens of the divine warrior (cf. Ps 68:34 [35]), but they represent divine beneficence (cf. also Ps 104:13).

29–30, 32 In this strophe the accent changes from the rain to the phenomena of thunder and lightning. Electrical storms occur in Palestine and the western deserts especially in the spring and autumn, when moist air moving in from the sea is heated up and rises rapidly into the cold upper air (cf. R. B. Y. Scott, "Thunder and Lightning," *IDB,* 4:637). Lightning occurs after particles in a cloud become electrically charged, possibly through collisions, the smaller particles becoming positively charged and rising to the upper regions of the cloud, the larger negatively charged and located in the lower portion of the cloud. Lightning is an electrical discharge between the positive and negative regions of clouds, or between clouds and the ground. The air along the path of the lightning is heated to 20,000 degrees centigrade (three times the heat of the sun's surface). This sudden heating compresses the surrounding clear air, producing a shock wave that then decays to the acoustic wave we experience as thunder.

29 No one can understand the "spreading" (מפרשׂ) of the clouds, says Elihu in this rhetorical question; but what is it about their spreading that is difficult to understand, or, indeed, that *can* be "understood"? Anyone can easily *observe* the clouds spreading across the sky, but what is there to *understand*? Elihu may mean only that the movement of clouds is a mysterious thing (it is hardly the "balancing" of the clouds, as Fohrer thinks, comparing 37:16), but he must know that they are driven by winds, so where is the mystery? Can it have been a matter of speculation in Elihu's world how clouds were formed, sometimes being "no bigger than a man's hand" to begin with (1 Kgs 18:44), and then spreading across the whole sky? It is understandable that no one knows how and when thunder will be produced ("the thunderings from his pavilion," תשׁאות סכתו; see *Note* 36:29.e), and it may be that the first colon originally spoke not of the "spreading" of the clouds but of the production of thunder through the "breaking open" of the clouds (see *Note* 36:29.d).

God's pavilion (סכה) is referred to elsewhere in 2 Sam 22:12, where it is darkness that is a dwelling (סכה) for Yahweh (in the parallel Ps 18:11 [12] it is clouds dark with water). Clouds are the dwelling of Yahweh or his manifestation in Exod 16:10; 20:21; Lev 16:2; 1 Kgs 8:10; Ezek 10:4.

30 Along with the thunder goes the lightning, called here simply "light" (אור), rather than the more common ברק "lightning" (once לפיד "torch" also is used for lightning [Exod 20:18]). If it is "spread out" (פרשׂ, which does not mean "scatter," as RSV, NIV, REB), it must be sheet lightning that is in view (though other commentators do not notice this); sheet lightning is not different in its nature from any other lightning, but because it occurs within a cloud, it can light up the whole sky (other references to sheet lightning may be Pss 77:18 [19]; 97:4 where God's lightnings [ברק] "light up" [אור hiph] the world; and perhaps Dan 10:6, of the facial appearance of a visionary figure). Elihu pictures such lightning as illuminating even the most hidden and inaccessible parts of the earth, of which the bottom of the sea often figures in Hebrew poetry as a prime example; cf. Ps 68:22 (23); Isa 51:10; Mic 7:19. Nowhere else, it is true, do we hear of the "roots" (שׁרשׁ) of the sea, though 28:9 has spoken of the "root" of the mountains, and the text may be questionable. The closest parallel may be Ps 18:15 (16), which speaks of the "channels" (אפיק) of the sea being seen and the foundations of the world being laid bare when God sends out his lightning. Ps 46:2 (3) envisages the mountains shaking in the midst of the sea, so perhaps it is the mountains' roots in the sea that are here uncovered.

It is a greater difficulty that the lightning is said to "cover" (כסה) the roots of the sea. The context seems rather to call for the meaning "uncover," and three suggestions have been made that would yield such a sense: (1) we could emend כסה "cover" to גלה "uncover," explaining כסה as a scribal error due to its presence just two verses later (or, rather, just three words later if v 31 originally followed v 28); (2) we could argue that כסה is one of those words attested in some Semitic languages that can bear an opposite meaning to their usual sense, thus "cover" *and* "uncover"; or (3) we could regard the piel voice of the verb as functioning as a negative or privative, thus "uncover." See *Note* 36:30.f for details.

Bibliography: J. P. Brown, *Israel and Hellas,* BZAW 276 (Berlin: de Gruyter, 2000) 2:62–64; F. M. Cross, *Canaanite Myth and Hebrew Epic: Essays in the History of the Religion of Israel* (Cambridge, MA: Harvard UP, 1973) 147–94; M. Futato, "A

Meteorological Analysis of Psalms 104, 65, and 29," diss., Catholic University of America, 1984; E. L. Greenstein, "YHWH's Lightning in Psalm 29:7," *Maarav* 8 (1992) 49–57; I. Singer, *Muwatalli's Prayer to the Assembly of Gods through the Storm-God of Lightning (CTH 381)* (Atlanta: Scholars Press, 1996).

32 Attention turns now to "bolt" lightning, which travels beyond the edge of the cloud itself and from the cloud to earth. God is pictured as holding this lightning in his hands and aiming it at a target on earth, just like an arrow. Such lightning is even more dramatic than sheet lightning, since it seems to be deliberately directed at an object, or even a person, on earth; its crooked, zigzag path to earth only accentuates its inescapability. In 2 Sam 22:15 the lightning bolts are Yahweh's arrows (|| Ps 18:14 [15]), in Ps 144:6 they are parallel to arrows, in Zech 9:14 his arrows are like lightning, in Nah 2:4 (5) chariots dart like lightning, in Ezek 21:28 (33) a sword flashes like lightning. In Semitic art, lightning is frequently depicted in the hands of warrior gods (e.g., *ANEP,* figs. 501, 519, 520, 521, 532, 533, 537, 538, 651, 703). In *Enuma Elish* (4.39), Marduk is equipped with lightning as a weapon, as is also Baal: "Seven lightning bolts he casts, eight magazines of thunder; he brandishes a spear of lightning" (*Ugaritica* V 3 [RS 24.245] = *CML*², 138a).

The image of the deity with a thunderbolt in his hand is familiar also from the classical world, where Zeus is often so represented. So Horace, *Odes* 1.2.2–3, where Jupiter smites the hill-tops "with his red right hand"; 3.5.1–2 "we believe Jupiter reigns in heaven because we hear him thunder." Zeus is "Lord of the bright lightning" (Homer, *Iliad* 19.121); "even he [the ocean] hath fear of the lightning of great Zeus whenso it crashes from heaven" (*Iliad* 20.197–98). Pliny distinguished between "thunderbolts" (*fulmina*) that come from the three stars (especially Jupiter) (*Natural History* 2.18), and lightning, caused by the friction of clouds (2.43).

33 The lightning is the effective weapon, directed precisely to its goal; but it is accompanied by thunder, which does not itself carry out God's sentence of punishment but makes plain God's anger against offenders. While the lightning executes God's justice, his thunder (רעו "his noise," or perhaps רעמו "his thunder" by emendation; see *Note* 36:33.a) declares (נגד hiph) it.

The second colon of the line (lit. "the cattle also declare concerning what goes up"; cf. NIV "even the cattle make known its approach") is almost certainly corrupt. Of the many possibilities for emendation that have been suggested, perhaps the most attractive is that adopted in the *Translation,* "the passion of his anger against iniquity," as a further definition of "his wrath" in the first colon. Whether we translate with RSV "he is jealous with anger against iniquity," or with NJB "anger flashes out against iniquity," it is reasonably certain that we should read the last word עולה, apparently "what goes up," with only a change in the vowels, as עַוְלָה "iniquity" (see further, *Note* 36:33.c). The important point is that the lightning and thunder are viewed as yet further examples of God's acts of justice and of instruction. Anyone struck by a thunderbolt is clearly a great sinner being punished by the divine wrath, and all those who see the lightning from heaven strike the earth may learn the lesson that God is dispensing justice.

37:1–4 After a strophe mainly about the lightning, Elihu turns to the thunder, without, it must be said, having a great deal that is interesting to say about it.

He may seem to have forgotten for the moment his key theme of nature as a vehicle of divine instruction (cf. on 36:26–37:24; 36:33), or his larger project to "ascribe justice to [his] Maker" (36:3), but see on "listen" in v 2.

The theme of the thunder as the voice of the gods is richly illustrated in ancient Near Eastern and classical literature (e.g., Baal's voice that causes earth to quake [*Baal* II.vii.29–32 (= *CML,* 101b); 4.vii.29–32 (*CML*[2], 65); *KTU* 1.4 VII 29–32; *ANET* 135a]; Homer, *Odyssey* 20:103–4; Horace, *Odes* 3.5.1–2; Brown, *Israel and Hellas,* 2:64–65).

1 This is the only time that Elihu lets his own feelings about the natural order he describes show through. Though he himself presumably has nothing to fear from the thunder and lightning, since he is not one of the wicked, he is nevertheless alarmed by it: his heart "trembles" or "throbs" (Dhorme) and, hyperbolically speaking (Watson, 318), "leaps" (if such is the meaning of נתר; see *Note* 37:1.c) out of his chest or to his mouth, as we might say (cf. Moffatt). His reaction is reminiscent of Jeremiah's, whose heart beats wildly when he hears the sound of the battle trumpet (4:19).

It is a nice question whether the particle אַף, with which the verse and the strophe open, means "also" or "indeed." If it is "also," Elihu would mean that as well as signalling God's displeasure at the wicked (36:33), the lightning and thunder evoke awe and fear in Elihu himself, who is an innocent bystander. If it means "indeed," it denotes rather the start of a new topic.

2 He wants his audience (Job and the three friends, no doubt; not "humanity in general" [Whybray]) to share his experience. Usually he addresses the others when he has some argument he wants to impress on them; but here it might seem he wants them only to agree with his sense of the majesty of the storm. And yet "[God's] thunder is not a mere noise" (Whybray), and Elihu cannot just be summoning the friends to listen to a sound they cannot help but hear. What is to be heard in the thunder is the voice of God, and the inarticulate and wordless thunder is therefore yet another of his manifold ways of communicating with humans—a leading theme of Elihu's speech.

There is much of the language of the theophany in these verses. For רגז "rage, quake" in the context of Yahweh's appearance, cf. 9:6; 1 Sam 14:15; 2 Sam 22:8 = Ps 18:7 (8); Isa 13:13; Jer 33:9; Amos 8:8. The thunder as the "voice" (קוֹל) of God is frequent in descriptions of a theophany; cf. 1 Sam 7:10; Isa 30:30; Pss 18:13 [14]; 29:3–9. שׁאג "roar" (v 4) is another theophanic term (Jer 25:30; Amos 1:2), as is רעם "thunder" (Isa 29:6; Pss 18:13 [14]; 77:18 [19]; 104:7; Ecclus 46:17). The thunder here is nevertheless not descriptive of a theophany, but a metaphor of a theophany.

3 Traditional renderings of this verse (e.g., RSV "Under the whole heaven he lets it go") have now been superseded by recognition of the verb in a comparable Ugaritic text about the onset of the rains: "Now Baal will begin the rainy season, the season of wadis in flood; and he will sound his voice in the clouds, flash his lightning to the earth (*šrh larṣ brqm*)" (*Baal* 51.v.68–71 = *Baal* II.v.9 [*CML,* 97b] = *Baal* 4.v.71 [*CML*[2], 61] = *KTU* 1.4 V 9). The verb for "flash" (*šrh*) is exactly the Hebrew שׁרה that we have here.

What the verse has in view then is how the thunderstorm dominates the whole sky ("across the whole heavens"); Strahan may even be right that "a local thunderstorm was believed to be universal." Although the focus in this line is on the lightning, it is not on the lightning as exposing and revealing (as in 36:30, 32–33), but as the precursor of the thunder (v 4).

The concept of the corners of the earth derives from thinking of the earth's surface as a cloth, a garment, or perhaps a carpet (as also in 38:13; Isa 11:12; 24:16; Ezek 7:2); כנף is first "wing," and then "extremity." See also C. Houtman, *Der Himmel im Alten Testament: Israels Weltbild und Weltanschauung,* OTS 30 (Leiden: Brill, 1993) 221–22. The parallelism of "under the whole heaven" and "to the ends of the earth" is found also in 28:24 (though there it is the "ends" [קצות] rather than the "corners" [כנפות] of the earth), perhaps another indication that chap. 28 belongs with this speech of Elihu (see on chap. 28); "under all the heaven" is also found at 41:11 (3).

4 After the lightning comes the thunder, which is a token of God's "majesty" (גאון). That term is often used with the pejorative sense of "pride" (e.g., 35:12; Ps 59:12 [13]; Prov 8:13), but here it obviously has the positive sense of "majesty, excellence" (as at 40:10; Exod 15:7; Isa 60:15).

The third colon of the verse, "And he does not delay (not "restrain"; see *Note* 37:4c.c) them when his voice is heard," is difficult to understand. There is no antecedent for the "them" (the lightning has been referred to in the singular in v 3), and it is unclear what it can be that God does not delay. The solution adopted here is to suppose that the colon has been misplaced from its original position at the end of v 6 (so too NEB); in that location the "them" would refer to the snow and the rains just mentioned, and the colon would mean that so soon as God gives his commands to the snow and rain, they begin to fall.

5–8 This strophe concerns the snows and rains of winter, which water the earth (v 6), keep people indoors (v 7), and drive the animals to take refuge in their dens (v 8). These phenomena are on the one hand mysterious, "great things that we cannot comprehend," and on the other a further communication of the divine, "so that all may know his work," recognizing in the rhythms of nature the design of the creator.

While with the thunderstorms of vv 1–4 we are probably still in the sphere of autumn, since thunder is a feature of the autumn climate of Palestine and the inland deserts, with v 6 we are clearly in a winter landscape.

5 As a preface for the strophe, Elihu typifies these natural phenomena as "wonderful things" (נפלאות), which is the nearest Hebrew gets to a word for "miracle"; it is noticeable that in the Hebrew Bible "miracles" are not, as they often are in current discourse, violations of natural law, but precisely the outworkings of what we call nature (see also on v 14). The term, according to R. Albertz, "indicates an event that a person, judging by the customary and the expected, finds extraordinary, impossible, even wonderful. [It] never hinges on the phenomenon as such but includes both the unexpected event as well as one's astonished reaction to it" (*TLOT,* 2:982). But what is it about the snow and rain that we cannot understand, or "know" (ידע), as the text has it? It is not the mechanics of their production, or the science that explains them, for the Hebrews would not have been puzzling about such matters. What we do not know is God's purposes and plans. Why does he sometimes withhold the rain, and sometimes create floods with it? Is he trying to tell us something? What? We can never know the totality of what the world means, indeed Elihu might even say that compared with the totality what we do know is nothing at all (cf. *Comment* on 36:26). But he does not wish to negate human knowledge, not least because all his speeches are themselves instructions aimed at increasing human knowledge. As in 36:26, where he had said that we do not "know" God (the same ולא־נדע "and we do not know" as here), he does not literally mean that we know nothing at all, for then what would he have to talk about, and how will the peasant sheltering from the rain come to "know" (the same verb ידע) God's work—which is the whole point of his being kept indoors?

The opening colon, "God thunders wonderful things with his voice" (ירעם אל בקולו נפלאות), is problematic, and should probably be bracketed as not being original. It is suspect textually on three grounds: (1) it is repetitious of the material of v 4b, (2) the verb רעם "thunder" is not elsewhere used transitively (1 Sam 1:6 is questionable), (3) the verse appears to be an introduction to the following strophe about the snow and rain (as the opening כי "for" shows), so the reference to the thunder seems out of place. The phrase is omitted by, for example, Driver–Gray, NAB, and NJB.

6 Torrential rains can elsewhere in the Hebrew Bible be the accompaniment of a theophany (Ps 68:8 [9]; Judg 5:4–5). Though Elihu speaks here of the normal winter rains, they too are a kind of revelation of the deity; for while humans are perforce idle during rainstorms and snowstorms, they have the leisure to observe, perhaps not so much the power of God (as Fohrer, Whybray), but God at work in the fields, commanding his minions snow and rain to saturate the soil in readiness for the season of growth.

Snow is not unknown in Israel, falling in Jerusalem, for example, three days a year on average. Conditions are harsher in the eastern deserts, where Job's Uz is no doubt set. Heavy rain is also a feature of the Palestinian winter (cf. for winter rainstorm, Isa 25:4; for heavy rain in the ninth month [December] in Jerusalem, Ezra 10:9); typically, in the rainy season rain falls for periods of two or three days at intervals of a week or so (W. S. La Sor, "Palestine," *ISBE,* 3:642). See R. B. Y. Scott, "Palestine, Climate of," *IDB,* 3:621–26; J. Ben Yoseph, "The Climate in Eretz Israel during Biblical Times," *HS* 26 (1985) 225–39; K. U. Mané, "A Severe Rainstorm in the Coastal Plain of Israel," *IEJ* 6 (1956) 115–19; D. Nir, "Whirlwinds in Israel in the Winters 1954/55 and 1955/56," *IEJ* 7 (1957) 109–17.

7 The poet speaks of a world in which agricultural labor, not industry or home work, is the primary form of production. If it should cease, humans risk their livelihood. Yet even the capacity to work for a living is subject to the will of the deity, who may have other plans. The peasant farmer will reflect on that fact while he is confined indoors, yet not so much simply to acknowledge the greater power of God (as Fohrer) as perhaps to recognize that his interests and God's do not necessarily coincide.

The effect of winter storms on the peasant farmer in the ancient world is well attested: Homer and Virgil also speak of such storms that make humans cease their work (*Iliad* 17.549–50; *Georgics* 1.259).

The mysterious line "on the hand of every human he sets a seal" sounds as if God stamps a seal on everyone's hand (so Good), but it is hard to see what the meaning of that would be in this context. It is better to assume that sealing up the hand is an idiom for preventing a person from acting or working, as it was when God "set a seal" on the stars so that they would not shine (9:7). The line has been used as a foundational text for palmistry, with the inference that secrets about each individual's destiny are sealed up on the palm. Much less mystical, though still very poetical, is the implication in the Hebrew that human activity can take place only when God releases human hands for work.

G. Fuchs (*Mythos und Hiobdichtung: Aufnahme und Umdeutung altorientalischer Vorstellungen* [Stuttgart: Kohlhammer, 1993] 75ff.) argues that חתם "seal" is a technical term from the myth of the struggle against chaos; but that idea seems out of place in this context.

8 It is a nice touch that the animals too are depicted as locked up in their dwellings by the storms (it is not their winter hibernation, against Rowley). Their "hand" or activity also is "sealed up," though v 7 thinks only of the humans' cessation from their normal activity. The animals have no idea why they cannot go out hunting for food (some animals adapt to the cold by huddling together and keeping still to conserve energy); humans on the other hand are supposed to be reflecting on the significance of their enforced idleness for what God may be teaching them through it. Elihu would see it as another example of God "teach[ing] us more than the beasts of the earth, mak[ing] us wiser than the birds of the heavens" (35:11). And yet human comprehension too has its limits, as these very verses underline: the "wonders" and "great things" that God does, such as the direction of these meteorological phenomena, are things that "we cannot know" (v 5). See also for the image of wild animals in their lairs, 38:39–40.

9 In this cosmology, meteorological elements are located in specific places. Just as hail and snow are kept in heavenly storehouses (38:22), the winds too are housed in their own chambers, under the auspices of various constellations of stars. When they are needed, they are brought out of their storehouses by God (Ps 135:7; Jer 10:13 || 51:16). Perhaps there is a thought here too that everyday winds are no mere natural occurrence, but, originating in a sphere beyond the mundane, bring something of the otherworldly, the mysterious, and the unknowable with them (cf. R. Mosis, *TDOT,* 4:222–25 [224]). The "chamber" (חדר) of the tempest is no doubt the same place as the "chambers of the south" (חדרי תמן) in 9:9, which seem to be the southern constellations of stars viewed as the storehouse for winds. In comparative mythology, El is depicted as dwelling in seven (or eight) chambers (*ḥdrm,* the same word as in Job), which may or may not be equivalent to the storehouses for the seven winds in Mesopotamian cosmology (H. and J. Lewy, "The Origin of the Week and the Oldest West Asiatic Calendar," *HUCA* 17 [1943] 1–152c [8–10, 15–21]). See also M. H. Pope and J. H. Tigay, "A Description of Baal," *UF* 3 [1971] 117–30 [123–24]; C. Houtman, *Der Himmel,* 253–59). On the chamber of the winds, cf. Homer, *Odyssey* 10.1–12 (the sons of Aeolus in their dwellings); Virgil, *Aeneid* 1.52–63 (the winds kept in prison by Aeolus).

From the south comes the סופה, customarily translated "whirlwind," but that term is properly defined as "a body of air moving rapidly in a circular or upward spiral course around a vertical or slightly inclined axis which has also a progressive motion over the surface of land or water" (*OED*)—or a tornado. True whirlwinds are said to be rare in Palestine, and occur mainly near the Mediterranean coast (R. B. Y. Scott, "Whirlwind," *IDB,* 4:841). סופה, however, is a more general word for a gale or storm or tempest; the reference here is to the winter gales that blow from the south, more severely in the eastern deserts.

The "scattering winds" (מזרים) is a well-attested ancient name for the bitter north winds (cf. Qur'an 51.1); NIV has "driving winds." Other versions add comment to the translation: NAB, NJB actually translate "north winds." NJPS "the constellations" follows the suggestion that מזרים, or Mazzarim, is a name for the constellation otherwise known by the feminine form of the word, Mazzaroth (as at 38:32).

10 It is still winter. Winter winds from the south are reputedly tempestuous (Isa 21:1; Zech 9:14; Ps 78:26), while those from the north are icy (cf. Ecclus 43:20, "Cold northern blasts he sends, that harden the ponds like solid ground. He spreads a crust over every body of water, and clothes each pool with a coat of mail" [Skehan–Di Lella, *Wisdom,* 486]).

The "breath" (נשמה) of God has been referred to at 4:9; 32:8 (cf. also Isa 40:7; Hos 13:15). It usually refers to a hot blast, but here it is wintry.

11 Though the Hebrew is very difficult, it seems that we have here a description of the functioning of the clouds. How, and why, do clouds get to be full of water, and how, and why, do they release that water? The answer is that God keeps on "loading" (טרח) the clouds with moisture, and so eventually, as if they were containers that become overfull, he causes them to "overflow" (פוץ II) with their streams of water. Many translations, however, think that the second colon concerns the production of lightning, in which case what God does is "scatter" (פוץ I) the lightning from the clouds (see further, *Note* 37:11.e).

12 The topic here remains the clouds, as it was in v 11. Despite the many versions and commentators who think it is the lightning, the language of "wheeling round and round" (מסבות "circles," and הפך hithp "turn this way and that") is much more suitable for the clouds. Nature, in brief, is an exhibit of divine programming.

13 V 7 left us with the peasant shut fast indoors by a downpour and pondering its divine significance. Now, at the end of the next strophe, we see what Elihu has in mind as the meaning of rain. It is not a univocal meaning, and those who contemplate the matter may find at least three possible significances, he suggests. Rain, if it is excessive, may be a punishment for those whose property is destroyed by it. It may, on the other hand, if it is welcome, be an act of God's loyalty (חסד) toward his creation. Or, it may have nothing to do with the deserts or otherwise with humans: it may be simply a manifestation of God's care for his own land, as when he makes rain fall on a land where no human lives (38:26). Whatever meaning is found in the coming of the rain, the key thing is that rain, like all the phenomena of nature, is a form of divine communication—which has been Elihu's great theme. Even if humans only imperfectly interpret its significance, it is plainly a resource God has at hand for delivering justice (we have not forgotten that to "ascribe justice to [his] Maker" is Elihu's stated project at 36:3).

The word translated "loyalty" (חסד) has been met with earlier at 6:14 (of the loyalty of a friend) and 10:12 (of God's loyalty); it is not a general or diffuse word for "love" (RSV, REB) or "mercy" (KJV, NAB), but usually denotes beneficent action within a broader commitment. The object of God's loyalty may be either humans or the creation in general; so we may see here an allusion to some undertaking by God to sustain his universe, which, disappointingly, Elihu does not further elaborate.

Does Elihu mean that some clouds, with their rain, are sent for "correction" and others for "loyalty" and that we can know which is which? Or is it that there may be many reasons in God's mind for sending rain, though we cannot know which is operative at any one moment? Probably the latter, since nowhere in these depictions of the seasons is the weather a means of discriminating between the righteous and the wicked.

It is doubtful whether 1 Cor 4:21, "Shall I come to you with a rod, or with love?" is a reminiscence of this verse, as some think; but see C. Spicq, "Une réminiscence de Job XXXVII, 13 dans I Cor IV, 21?" *RB* 60 (1953) 509–12.

14–24 This conclusion to Elihu's fourth speech has several odd features. (1) After the passages on the autumn (26:26–37:4) and the winter (37:5–13), we are not surprised to find lines about the summer (vv 15–18, 21–22); but the description of the natural phenomena is very different here, being overshadowed by Elihu's projection of himself and his concerns. (2) Unlike in the previous passages, the wonders of nature are here not portrayed as divine instruction to humans; they are simply "wonders," as if there were nothing to be learned from them and they were only to be marveled at in silent adoration. (3) Elihu adopts a new style in addressing Job, the kind of ironic questioning more familiar from the divine speeches (e.g., 38:4–6, 12, 16–18; 39:1). "Do you know," he asks Job, knowing that no human could (v 16); "teach us," when he knows Job has nothing to say (v 19); "can you hammer out the sky?," when he already knows the answer (v 18). Elihu has never spoken to Job like this before. He has been blunt and challenging, but not ironic. (4) Yet it is not irony, but a different and unparalleled mood altogether, when he allows that "we cannot arrange our thoughts because of the darkness" (v 19b), and when he wistfully acknowledges that no one can have anything to say to God that he does not know already (v 20). It is a deeply pessimistic thought, and out of character for the self-confident, if not brash, Elihu. (5) He concludes on the note of the "fear of God" (v 24), as if recommending it were the purpose of the whole speech; and yet he has never alluded to "fearing" God before.

Added to the problem of discerning the train of thought in these verses is the extreme textual difficulty, which no amount of rearrangement of the verses can solve. It may well be that this passage has suffered so badly in transmission that it is now beyond satisfactory repair, and we must just make the best of what can be understood without claiming to comprehend what exactly is going on here.

Terrien, who sees better than anyone the movement from season to season since the middle of chap. 36, blithely entitles vv 14–24 the "Third Tableau: The Lord of the Summer." The first strophe (vv 14–18) he can label "The Heat of the Sky," but what of vv 15–24? Here Terrien sees an "epiphany," which prepares for the self-revelation of God in the divine speeches. And yet there is so very little in the text about epiphany, apart from a golden glow in the north (v 22a), that we must question whether this can be the central theme of the whole section.

There is certainly a transition to a new element of the speech beginning at v 14. Elihu's disquisition on the three seasons as revelatory of their creator (36:26–37:13) has come to an end. There was a quite comprehensive sentence of closure in v 13, and now there is a new address in v 14 directly to Job, whom we have almost lost sight of during the twenty verses from 36:27 to 37:13; Elihu has not spoken to him specifically since 36:24.

And if the theme of the seasons seems the same, it is only the same with a difference. Now Elihu's theme is not only how God communicates with humans through the phenomena of nature (a theme reiterated at climactic moments, 36:31, 33; 37:7, 13; and see also v 14), nor is it the underlying theme of ascribing justice to his Maker (36:3), but the "wonder" of God's orchestration of the ever changing weather of summer. How God "arranges" (שׂים) his works, deciding that now is the time for a lightning storm (v 15b), now for a sky overcast with clouds (v 16a), now for a sky like brass (v 18), now for clouds (v 21a, b), now for wind (v 21c), now for sunshine (v 22a)—that is a marvel, and one that displays a wonderful God. Autumn and winter have their hidden messages for the receptive soul, but summer reveals a variegated disposition of natural forces that Job cannot understand (vv 15–16), that leaves the garrulous Elihu at a loss for words (v 19a) and even in despair at human knowledge (v 19b), that typifies the Almighty as incomprehensible (v 23a). This God who balances conflicting cosmic forces is equally adept (it may be inferred) at controlling the tug-of-war between power and justice (v 23b); being supreme in both, he cannot pervert the "righteousness" that consists in making right decisions and having the power to execute them (v 23c).

14 Elihu has previously made a formal appeal to Job to "listen" at the beginning or end of a unit of his speech, with "hear" (שׁמע) at 33:1, 31, 33 (also 32:10; 34:1, 10, 16 to others), and "give ear" (אזן hiph) at 33:1 (also 34:2; 34:16, to others). Here it is the language of a new beginning, introducing vv 14–24; the "this" (זאת) also looks forward. "Stop" is an unusual meaning for the common verb "stand" (עמד). We have seen it of standing still in silence (32:16) and of (apparently) standing to plead one's case in 30:20. But here it seems more likely to summon Job to stop what he is doing (such as appealing for justice) and spend some time in contemplation; עמד means to stop doing something at Gen 29:35; 30:9; 2 Kgs 13:18; Jonah 1:15. בין hithpolal is "consider, ponder," as at 11:11; 23:15; 30:20; 31:1; 32:12 (and even at 26:14; 38:18), rather than "understand," as the simple בין usually means. Pondering is meant to lead to an insight; Job has much to learn, Elihu implies, from the wonderful deeds of God he is about to portray. Elihu is still occupied with the theme of nature as revelation of the divine.

The "wonders" or "wonderful deeds" (נפלאות) of God are in the Hebrew Bible overwhelmingly his historical acts of deliverance of Israel (cf. R. Albertz, *TLOT,* 2:981–86 [983]), and the only times the term is used of natural phenomena seem to be at Ps 107:24 (God's wonders in the deep, i.e., the amazing sea creatures [cf. Ecclus 43:24–25]) and in this chapter (also v 16, if the unique word מפלאות is a miswriting of נפלאות; the occurrence in v 5 seems to be an error; see *Note* 37:5.c). The term is used in this sense also at Ecclus 42:17 and perhaps at 43:29.

15 What is it that Job does not "know"? What Job does not know, and what Elihu ironically questions him about, is not the science of meteorology, but the divine disposition of the forces of nature, i.e., "how God arranges them" or, better, with a small emendation, "arranges his works" (see *Note* 37:15.b). Only one example of such a "marvel" is given before Elihu reiterates his "do you know?" in v 16a: the lightning. We have heard a lot about lightning already in 36:30, 32; 37:3, but the uncanny marvel about it that has not been mentioned is that there is no predicting it. No human can know when an electrical storm will suddenly develop in a cloudy sky.

It is true that the verb יפע hiphil "shine out" is a typical term within a description of a theophany or divine self-revelation (Deut 33:2; Pss 50:2; 80:1 [2]; 94:1; it is used ironically of theophany at Job 10:3) (cf. F. Schnutenhaus, "Das Kommen und Erscheinen Gottes im Alten Testament," *ZAW* 76 [1974] 1–22 [8–9]; E. Jenni, *TLOT,* 2:560–61; C. Barth, *TDOT,* 6:220–25); Ravasi, among others, thinks this a sign that we are dealing here with more than an atmospheric phenomenon. But it has been used in Job twice in the physical sense: at 3:4, where no light should shine on the day of Job's birth, and at 10:22, where the light that shines in the underworld is as darkness; in the present context, where the natural order is foregrounded, it is unthinkable that it should not refer to some kind of earthly light. It is conceivable that Elihu refers to the sun shining *through* the clouds, but the Hebrew has "makes his cloud shine light," which suggests rather the lightning (as אור "light" means at 36:32 and 37:3).

Many have compared the style of Elihu's questions here (and in vv 16, 18) with the ironic divine speeches (e.g., 38:4–6, 12, 16–18; 39:1), some seeing them as a prelude or anticipation or foreshadowing or even an undercutting of the divine questions. It is easy to overestimate the significance of such parallels, however, and we may note that the questions of vv 15 and 16 (introduced by התדע "do you know?") have no exact parallel in the divine speeches, where it is the perfect tense (הידעת) rather than the imperfect that is used, and that only in 38:33 and 39:1. Elihu has been using rhetorical questions such as "Who is a teacher like him?" and "Who can understand the spreading of the clouds?" earlier in this speech (36:22, 23, 29; cf. also 34:7, 13).

16 In asking, "Do you know the spreading of the clouds?," Elihu cannot be asking Job if he knows *how* the clouds are spread over the face of the sky, for he must have seen as well as we have clouds being carried along by the wind. His question seems rather *why* the clouds should form now, and not at some other time, what plan or purpose there may be in their spreading. To ancients and moderns alike the formation and movement of the clouds is an unpredictable marvel. Some commentators think the word is not "spreading" (מפלש understood as the equivalent of מפרש as in 36:29; see *Note* 37:16.b) but "balancing" (מפלש being connected with פלס, "weigh"), in which case perhaps the question is how the clouds can float freely in the air when they are so heavy with rain (v 11) (so Fohrer; cf. Ravasi). Strahan indeed thinks the line contains "one of Elihu's best phrases, expressing his wonder that the apparently unsupported clouds, bearing their burden of blessing for the earth, are poised aloft in air." J. Ruskin has a delightful meditation on the wonder of the clouds in his chapter "The Cloud-Balancings," in his *Modern Painters* (Orpington: Allen, 1897) 5:113–20. But this interpretation would make the science of clouds the matter for marveling, which seems to be beside the point here.

If indeed Elihu describes God as "perfect in knowledge" (see *Note* 37:16.d), he does not, as Habel rightly points out, refer to any divine omniscience but to "his capacity to comprehend and hence operate the meteorological mysteries of the cosmos."

17 Job is a mere mortal who is helplessly subject to the divinely arranged weather, whatever it may be. So far is he from taking control of the sky and beating out the heavens into a thin sheet of bronze (v 18) that he cannot even control the temperature of his own clothes. "This sensation of dry hot clothes is only experienced during the siroccos," averred the nineteenth-century traveler W. M. Thomson. The sirocco, the hottest wind, is usually called the east wind (קדים), but, since it blows from the east and southeast it can apparently also be called the south wind, as it is in Luke 12:55 (RSV): "When you see the south wind blowing, you say, 'There will be scorching heat.'" In Thomson's description, "There is no living thing abroad to make a noise. . . . No one has energy enough to make a noise, and the very air is too weak and languid to stir the pendent leaves even of the tall poplars" (*The Land and the Book, or, Biblical Illustrations Drawn from the Manners and Customs, the Scenes and Scenery of the Holy Land* [London: Nelson & Sons, 1883] 536). Cf. also Dalman, *Arbeit und Sitte,* 1:470–72.

18 The picture here is typical of Hebrew cosmology. The sky is viewed as a solid, but thin, sheet of beaten metal (a "firmament," רקיע), as in Gen 1:7. Above it are storehouses for the rain, snow, and hail (38:22) that descend to the earth through the "windows of heaven" (Gen 7:11). In the firmament are fixed the sun, moon, and stars (Gen 1:14, 15, 17), so we can read of the "shining of the firmament" (Dan 12:3). The beating out of the firmament is most likely conceived of as an act at creation (cf. KJV "Hast thou with him spread out the sky?"), though most apparently envisage it here as a daily task of God's (the imperfect verb תרקיע may suggest repeated action, but it could equally well be a preterite of a single past action), which Job, naturally, is incapable of cooperating in. Metals are several times said to be "beaten out" or "hammered out" (רקע) (gold leaf in Exod 39:3; Isa 40:19; silver in Jer 10:9; bronze censers in Num 16:38–39 [17:3–4]). Metaphorically, the earth, viewed as a flat disk, is elsewhere spoken of as having been "hammered out" at creation (in parallel to the "spreading out" [נטה] of the sky, presumably like a curtain or tent; cf. on 26:7), at Isa 42:5; 44:24; Ps 136:6. It is here the sky that is "hammered out" (Fohrer, however, thinks it must be the clouds, since only they can be hammered out afresh from day to day; but it is hard to see how the clouds can be "hard as a metal mirror").

A metal mirror is manufactured quite differently, usually from casting molten bronze; hammering it after it had been cast would ruin its reflectiveness, which can be improved only by polishing. The image of hammering out the sky must be kept distinct from that of casting a mirror. The point of comparison between a mirror and the sky is not the mirror's reflectiveness nor its strength, but its firmness. "Hard as a mirror" may seem a strange expression since a mirror is perhaps not the first thing that would come to mind as an image of hardness; but in a world in which ceramics and textiles predominated in a domestic context, the hardness of bronze, not very commonly attested in such a chunky object as a mirror, must have been quite striking. Bronze is copper hardened by the addition of tin.

Mirrors in the biblical period (referred to in the Bible only here and at Exod 38:8; Ecclus 12:11, where wickedness is compared to the rust that forms on a mirror after it is wiped) were typically a circular piece of polished bronze, often with an ornamented handle of wood or ivory. Other metals used in the ancient Mediterranean world for mirrors, but less well attested, are copper, silver, gold, and electrum. Glass mirrors were not known until late Roman times. On metal mirrors, see G. A. Barrois, *IDB,* 3:402–3, with an illustration of a bronze mirror from 'Athlit (fifth century B.C.E.); F. W. Danker, *ISBE,* 3:382–83; L. Y. Rahmani, "Mirror-Plaques from a Fifth-Century A.D. Tomb," *IEJ* 14 (1964) 50–60; J. F.

Strange, "Late Hellenistic and Herodian Ossuary Tombs at French Hill, Jerusalem," *BASOR* 219 (1975) 39–67 (62); Y. Israeli, "A Mirror Plaque from the Clark Collection, Jerusalem," *IEJ* 24 (1974) 228–31 (Byzantine, containing glass).

For the image of a sky like brass, cloudless and rainless, cf. Deut 28:23. Cf. also the Homeric epithet "brazen heaven" (*Iliad* 5.504; 17:425; *Odyssey* 3.2; also in Pindar, *Pythian Odes* 10.27; *Nemean Odes* 6.3).

19 Why is Elihu (ironically) inviting Job to offer him words for addressing God? He has not been thinking of doing that on his own account, has he? Nor does it seem very likely that Elihu is thinking of the weather here, as if he and Job should be making a joint request to God for less insupportable weather (as Andersen, tongue in cheek, one supposes). Those who are truly wise, according to Elihu, know their limitations, and do not expect to be able to argue with God. Job, however, he teasingly suggests, moves on a higher plane, and has undertaken to debate questions of divine justice with the deity; perhaps he can pass on a few pointers to others, like Elihu, should they ever find themselves in Job's position.

It is an unexpected touch when Elihu comprehends humanity within a realm of "darkness." In fact, his language is cryptic: we cannot marshal our thoughts (NEB), he says, "because of the darkness"; no doubt that means "since we are in the dark" (NJB), but it is a strangely pessimistic thought for this bright young man, who believes in thinking positively and praises God as the great educator and enlightener, to admit that, in some global sense, "all is dark" (NEB). "Dark is the world to thee; thyself art the reason why" (Alfred Lord Tennyson, "The Higher Pantheism"). It is unlikely that Elihu is alluding to the darkness in which God is traditionally said to dwell (contrast Rowley), since that would not be a reason why "we" cannot put our thoughts together. It would be a pity to dispense with the image of (mental and metaphorical) "darkness" and replace it with "ignorance" (as Pope).

20 The sentence is (except for the last word) in the simplest Hebrew, but its meaning is open to many interpretations. In the *Translation* above, it is assumed that the thought follows closely on that of v 19: there Elihu had invited Job, ironically, from his greater knowledge of the universe, to instruct other humans on the arguments they should prepare when confronting God. He himself, in this scenario, despairs of being able to order his thoughts, or of having anything worth saying to the deity: "If I speak, will he be told something?" For what can I say that he does not know already? The same is true for everyone else as well: "If anyone says anything, is he (God) better informed?" Not only can humans not rightly arrange their thoughts should they find themselves in converse with the deity; anything they would have to say would be of no consequence, for no one can tell God a thing. In so saying Elihu implicitly denies any value to Job's desire to speak to the Almighty (e.g., 9:35; 13:22; 23:4; 31:37).

The Hebrew says simply "Will it be told to him when (or, if) I speak? If a man speaks, will he indeed (if כִּי means that here) be informed?" (if that is the meaning of בלע here; see *Note* 37:20.f). The second colon is very much more uncertain than the first, but is presumably in close parallel with it. The image in the first colon could be of a courtier reporting (or failing to report) to God when an address has been made by a human (thus, e.g., KJV "Shall it be told him that I speak?"). But it might be more simply that human speech adds nothing to the divine knowledge; perhaps NJPS is along this line when it has "Is anything conveyed to Him when I speak?"; cf. Gordis "You tell us what to say that will make an impact upon Him."

If the final verb is understood differently, as connected with בלע "swallow up, destroy" (so, e.g., Rowley, Good), a range of alternative renderings is opened up. Thus KJV "if a man speak, surely he shall be swallowed up," RSV "Did a man ever wish that he would be swallowed up?," NIV "Would any man ask to be swallowed up?" (similarly Pope), NAB "when a man says he is being destroyed." (However, "wish" or "ask" as a translation of אמר "say" can hardly be justified, though "think" or "ponder," i.e., "say [in one's heart]" is acceptable; cf. BDB, 56b §2; *DCH,* 1:324a §7.)

21–22 According to the *Translation* offered above, we are suddenly back in the realm of meteorology, the emphasis being on the change from one kind of weather to another. At one moment the sky is completely overcast and then suddenly the clouds are swept away by the wind and the sun breaks through. Dalman (*Arbeit und Sitte,* 1:508–9) observes how on a summer's day the sky can be at one moment heavily overcast and at another completely cloudless.

The theme is so much like that of vv 15–18, where the topic sentence "Do you know how God arranges his works?" (v 15a) led into a description of the changing from storm to clouds to cloudless sky, that we are tempted to suppose that these verses (21–22) have been incorrectly transposed from their original place (see *Note* 37:21.a). The one hindrance to reassigning their place is that it would spoil the balance of the otherwise neat final strophes of the chapter (vv 14–18, five lines, and vv 19–24, five lines plus a pendant). It remains probable, however, that the theme here is the same as that of vv 14–18: the dramatic changes in the sky are orchestrated by God, who always has his purposes. Here the change is from an overcast sky, when the sun cannot be seen, to the golden light that follows rain.

21 Some commentators (e.g., Fohrer, Terrien, Ravasi, Strauss) think we are reading here about a theophany, and indeed the language contains a number of parallels with descriptions of divine epiphanies. For darkness, cloud, and fire, cf. Deut 4:11–12; cloud, with brightness and fire, cf. Ezek 1:4; brightness like the sun, cf. Hab 3:4; fire and darkness, cf. Ps 18:8–9 (9–10); a fire advancing before him, cf. Ps 50:3; clouds, darkness, fire, and lightning, cf. Ps 97:2–3. See also the language of the "north" in v 22.

But does this scenario really suit the language? "The light cannot be seen, or, looked at" could fit either an epiphany or a skyscape, though it is never said that the light of an epiphany is too bright to look upon; "it is bright in the clouds" could be said of the light signifying the presence of God (as in Deut 4:11), but if the translation is "it is dark with clouds" (see *Note* 37:21.e), that cannot apply to the divine light. Finally, "the wind blows and clears them away" can only refer to a skyscape, since there is no parallel to winds clearing away the clouds that surround the deity (Fohrer, who thinks there is a theophany here, is compelled to delete this third colon). If there is really talk of theophany here, it could be a very important element of Elihu's whole intervention, aligning personal revelation of God beside the other forms of divine communication he has depicted (dreams, suffering, the natural order). But the language here is so allusive, and so unlike the formal pedagogy of Elihu that we have met before (e.g., "For God speaks in one way, and in another," 33:14), that we can hardly make of it Elihu's climactic statement. Elihu is not the precursor of the divine epiphany in chaps. 38–41 (against, e.g., Ravasi: "The final personal theophany would be nothing else, in the eyes of Elihu, than the formal . . . confirmation of Elihu's teaching").

22 Since we are still in the realm of meteorology, "out of the north comes gold" cannot possibly be about mineralogy, despite evidence from Herodotus (3:22) and Pliny (cf. Pope) for the north as the source of gold. The "gold" (זהב) must be something to do with the appearance of the sky; Dhorme thought it described "the state of the sky when the golden rays of the sun border the clouds which are being dispersed by the wind (v. 21)." Less probably, Driver–Gray saw a reference to the aurora borealis in the north, which "may well have been supposed to be an effulgence from the presence of God Himself" (cf. Rowley), "gleams from the inner glory of heaven" (Strahan).

Then, if the gold is the color of the sky, what is the significance of the "north" (צפון)? Pope thinks the reference is mythological, to the palace of gold, silver, and lapis lazuli built for Baal on the heights of Mount Zaphon ("Mount North") according to the Ugaritic texts (*Baal* II.v.55 [*CML*, 99a] = 4.v.117 [*CML*², 62] = *KTU* 1.4 V 55 = *ANET*, 134a); cf. also R. J. Clifford, *The Cosmic Mountain in Canaan and the Old Testament*, HSM 4 (Cambridge, MA: Harvard UP, 1972) 55–79; C. Virolleaud, "La montagne du nord dans les poèmes de Ras Shamra," *Babyloniaca* 17 (1937) 145–55. Habel thinks of a gold aura or stream of rays surrounding the deity (cf. Ps 104:2, where God is covered with light as with a garment; and the Hymn to Aton [*ANET*, 369–71]).

Certainly, there is a lot of evidence in the OT that the north was viewed as the dwelling place of God. The chariot in Ezekiel's vision came out of the north (1:4). The "mount of assembly" of God and the heavenly beings is, according to Isa 14:13, "in the recesses of the North." The same phrase is used in Ps 48:2 (3) where Zion, as the city of the Great King, is said to be "in the far north"—which can only be true by mythological, not geographical, standards.

But there is not necessarily any reference here to the dwelling of God; the "north" may mean no more than "the highest heavens," as it apparently does in 26:7 (*q.v.*), the "golden glow" being nothing more mysterious than the sun itself.

Bibliography: A. Causse, "Sentiment de la nature et symbolisme chez les lyriques hébreux," *RHPR* 1 (1921) 387–408; J. Hempel, "Die Lichtsymbolik im Alten Testament," *Studium Generale* 13 (1960) 352–68; S. Herner, *Die Natur im Alten Testament*, Kungl. humanistiska vetenskapssamfundet i Lund, Årsberättelse 1940–1941 (= Bulletin de la Société royale des lettres de Lund, 1940–1941) (Lund: Gleerup, 1941) 27–122; A. Lauha, *Zaphon: Der Norden und die Nordvölker im Alten Testament*, AASF B49/2 (Helsinki: Finnische Akademie der Wissenschaften, 1943) 47–48; S. Moscati, "The Wind in Biblical and Phoenician Cosmology," *JBL* 66 (1947) 305–10; E. C. Rust, *Nature and Man in Biblical Thought* (London: Lutterworth, 1953) 45–47.

The second colon of the verse is here regarded as an explanatory gloss (see *Note* 37:22.b).

23 There is an apparent tension here, between the incomprehensibility of God, whom we cannot "find" (מצא), and a knowledge of his power and justice, and especially of their being in perfect equilibrium. The book of Job, however, does not preach the incomprehensibility of God, but rather the impossibility of humans fully comprehending him. When it is said that he or his wisdom cannot be "searched" (with the root חקר), it is not meant that nothing can be known about him, but that the limits of his being or his wisdom cannot be reached. So with his "unsearchable" deeds (5:9; 9:10) and with the mystery that cannot be "reached" or "attained" (מצא, 11:7 *q.v.*). The unknowability of God is for Elihu a doctrine that sets limits to human pride, and that can halt a Job in his tracks and make him marvel at divine wonders (v 14b); but for all practical purposes Elihu acts and speaks as if God *is* knowable, and in the very verse in which he declares we cannot "find" him he nevertheless affirms central truths about him.

Elihu thinks, no doubt, with his dogma of "we cannot find him" (he speaks for all humanity, we observe) that he has negated Job's desire, "O that I knew how I might find him" (23:3); but "find" will mean as much as the speaker wants it to: if Elihu wants to deny the total comprehensibility of God, it will suit, and if Job wants to enter into dialogue with God, it will suit. But the two of them will not be able to communicate with one another if they define key words to their own taste.

For the idea of God being "unreachable," cf. 1 Tim 6:16, where he "inhabits unapproachable (ἀπρόσιτος) light."

24 The proper human attitude toward the deity is to fear him. This seems a strange conclusion for Elihu to arrive at, since he has never spoken before of the fear of God (the reference in v 22 to God being "awesome [i.e., fearful] in majesty" has been understood as a gloss; even if it were not, it is such a traditional term that it would not contribute much to the elucidating of Elihu's thought). Fohrer simply regards it as a later moralizing addition in the spirit of 28:28 (cf. his *Studien zum Buche Hiob [1956–1979]* [Gütersloh: Mohn, 1963] 107; [2d ed., Berlin: de Gruyter, 1983] 113; similarly Terrien, Lévêque, 651, Ravasi).

But an ending is not necessarily a conclusion. The theme of Elihu's speeches remains the forms of God's communication with humans, and God is still essentially the great Educator, whose aim it is to instill wisdom in his creatures. What they can learn about God is manifold, but, not surprisingly, it is the wonderfulness of his being and of his acts that stands in the climactic position (cf. "marvels" in recent verses, 37:5, 14, 16). While there are many proper human responses to God's various messages, there is only one appropriate response to his absolute perfection and supremacy: it is fear, which is a recognition of the enormous gulf between the human and the divine. This is not only a natural human reaction to the divine; it is also the emotion felt by the "wise" or "everyone thoughtful" (NJB), those who have busied themselves with learning all that can be known about the ways of God. To accept Elihu's teachings about God does not domesticate God or make his presence more comfortable; God remains fearsome.

Why is Elihu saying all this to Job? He must mean that Job has been too free with God in demanding answers from him, and even more so in charging him with wrong. What we know of God, says Elihu, should lead us to tremble at his majesty, not to conceive of him as a legal opponent or a military enemy, and it would be wisdom for Job to learn that lesson.

The "fear of God" does not refer, as many think, to a religious attitude or to a sense of reverence, for the term "fear" denotes nothing other than the emotion of fear. Terrien rightly remarks that "It would be a grave error . . . to soften the meaning of the expression ['fear of the Lord'] and to ignore its central element of *mysterium tremendum*.... [T]he fear of the Lord is not merely to be equated with reverence, piety, or religion because it is impossible today to revaluate and again charge these terms with their ancient—but now largely lost—connotation of awesomeness" (*IDB*, 2:258). See further, D. J. A. Clines, "The fear of the Lord is wisdom' (Job 28.28): A Semantic and Contextual Study," in *Job 28: Cognition in Context*, ed. E. van Wolde, Biblical Interpretation Series 64 (Leiden: Brill, 2003) 57–92. At the end of the day, Elihu shows himself deeply inconfident of human capacity if he concludes that "fear" is the appropriate human attitude in the presence of God.

On the view taken in this commentary, Elihu's speeches are not yet over. It is argued here that originally chap. 28 was the end of the Elihu discourses, and that chaps. 32–37 were wrongly moved into their present position during the course of transmission of the text. The poem about wisdom in chap. 28 would on this understanding fill out further Elihu's views on wisdom and the fear of God. If for him God is the great Teacher, it is in order that humans may become learners, which means to say, wise. And acquiring wisdom about God is not an accumulation of knowledge, but a development of insight within a context of proper feeling toward God: the feeling of human fear in the presence of the divine. It is a remarkable confirmation of the theory about the relationship of chap. 28 and Elihu's speeches in chaps. 32–37 that chap. 28 comes to rest on the same note as this last verse of chap. 37: "The fear of the Lord, that is wisdom" (Andersen has already noted that with 37:24 "we come full circle to Job 28:28," and Ravasi that it is an "antiphon" to 28:28).

Explanation

In this his fourth speech Elihu excels himself. Despite many difficulties in the Hebrew, no doubt the result of errors in scribal transmission, the poetry is surefooted and its design is grand. The depiction of the differing fates of the wicked and of the righteous who fall into sin (36:5–17) is as fine a piece of expository verse as anything in the book, and the cameos of the three seasons (36:26–37:24) reach new heights of lyricism. Elihu shows himself again quite a phrasemaker: with kings on a throne God seats the righteous (36:7), he delivers the afflicted by their affliction (36:15), to the snow he says, Fall on the earth, and to the downpour of rain, Be strong (37:6), in his winter storms he seals up the hand of every mortal from activity, and the beasts too take refuge in their lairs (37:7–8), whether for correction, or for his land, or for loyalty, he dispatches the clouds (37:13), can Job, like God, hammer out the sky, hard as a metal mirror? (37:18), we cannot order our thoughts because of the darkness (37:19), out of the north comes a golden glow (37:22).

But it is Elihu's conceptions that are the most impressive thing about this speech. The first comes in his exposition of the righteous and the wicked in 36:5–17. In this he transcends the old distinction between the righteous and wicked that is the staple of the wisdom and psalmic literature and that constrains the thinking of the other friends. Eliphaz, it is true, has allowed that the innocent never suffer permanently, and that Job's calamity must therefore be shortlived (4:3–6), but it is Elihu's special contribution to have thought through a whole philosophy of God's treatment of those among the righteous who find themselves in the toils of suffering because of their wrongdoing. If they are bound with fetters, he says, God declares their transgression to them, and opens their ear to instruction. At that point, two roads open up before them: either they can hearken, in which case they complete their days in prosperity, or else they fail to hearken and they must cross the river of death (36:8–12). This recognition that even the righteous can fall into sin is of course a much more realistic view of human nature than the old bipolar structure that made a sharp division between the righteous and the wicked.

The second attractive element of Elihu's thinking in this speech is his conviction that the workings of the universe are a channel of divine communication: in casting his eye over the round of the seasons, he notices everywhere divine messages. Rainfall is God's gift of nourishment (36:31), thunder the declaration of his wrath (36:33). By winter storms he grants to mortals an opportunity to reflect on the divine activity (37:7), while the stormclouds may signify his correction of evil, his covenanted loyalty to humans, or his beneficence to the physical world he has created (37:13). All in all, meteorology is chock full of significance, a revelation of God's power (36:22; 37:23), a profusion of wonders (37:5, 14) from which humans may learn to fear the Almighty (37:24). Suffering, Elihu had said early on, is a form of divine communication (33:19–28), as also are nightmares (33:15–18); now we find that weather too is charged with theological meaning.

Yet each of these interesting features in Elihu's speech has its downside: even though Elihu distinguishes among sufferers between the basically good and the basically wicked, he still operates within the traditional framework of suffering as punishment. Innocent or inexplicable suffering is outside his whole range of experience. And on the second point, while it may be uplifting to consider the universe as testimony to the wonder of the deity, it could be a retrograde step to imagine that the weather is an instrument of divine self-revelation. It will not do much harm to hear in the thunder the sound of the divine wrath (36:33), or find in enforced idleness during winter storms a heaven-sent opportunity to contemplate the divine activity (37:7), but if for a moment Elihu thinks that a lightning strike is a mark of divine judgment, or that the coming or the withholding of rain signifies the pleasure or displeasure of the deity, he is a poorer theologian than he seems. Another Hebrew sage knew that God sends rain on the just and unjust alike (Matt 5:45), still recognizing a religious significance in rain, but not a discriminatory one. Elihu, to be fair, does not ever say explicitly that the natural phenomena separate out the righteous from the wicked, though 37:13 might at first suggest this.

Finally, according to the argument advanced in this commentary, Elihu has not yet finished speaking. It is suggested that in the original book of Job the speeches of Elihu were made after those of the other three friends had ceased, i.e., after chap. 27. The unassigned poem on wisdom, chap. 28, would then fit well as the finale of all Elihu's speeches. It is interesting that the note on which the present chapter ends, that those who are wise fear God (37:24), is exactly the same as the sentence that concludes chap. 28: the fear of the Lord is wisdom (28:28).

Elihu's Fourth Speech Concluded (The Poem on Wisdom) (28:1–28)

Bibliography

Aitken, J. K. "Lexical Semantics and the Cultural Context of Knowledge in Job 28, Illustrated by the Meaning of *ḥāqar.*" In *Job 28: Cognition in Context.* Ed. E. van Wolde. Biblical Interpretation Series 64. Leiden: Brill, 2003. 119–37. **Baldauf, C.** "Menschliches Können und göttliche Weisheit in Hiob 28." *TVers* 13 (1983) 57–68. **Barton, G.** "The Composition of Job 24–30." *JBL* 30 (1911) 66–77. **Budde, C.** "Die Capitel 27 und 28 des Buches Hiob." *ZAW* 2 (1882) 193–274. **Busslinger-Simmen, H.** "Gesucht—doch nicht zu ergründen: Das Lied der Weisheit (Hiob 28)." In *Hiob: Ökumenischer Arbeitskreis für Bibelarbeit.* Ed. R. Berger-Lutz. Bibelarbeit in der Gemeinde 7. Basel: Reinhardt, 1989. 244–60. **Byington, S. T.** "Hebrew Marginalia II: Job 28." *JBL* 61 (1942) 205–7. **Clark, D. J.** "In Search of Wisdom: Notes on Job 28." *BT* 33 (1982) 401–5. **Clines, D. J. A.** "'The Fear of the Lord Is Wisdom' (Job 28:28): A Semantic and Contextual Study." In *Job 28: Cognition in Context.* Ed. E. van Wolde. Biblical Interpretation Series 64. Leiden: Brill, 2003. 57–92. **Conti, M.** *La sapienza personificata negli elogi veterotestamentari (Pr 8; Gb 28; Sir 24; Bar 3; Sap 7).* Spicilegium Pontificii Athenaei Antoniani 36. Rome: Pontificium Athenaeum Antonianum, 2001. **Cook, J.** "Aspects of Wisdom in the Texts of Job (chapter 28)—Vorlage(n) and/or translator(s)?" *OTE* 5 (1992) 26–45. **Cyss-Wittenstein, C.** "Reading Job 26–31 with Bakhtin." *Gravitas* (Graduate Theological Union) 1/2 (2000). **Delriu, T.** "Un recuerdo para los mineros de hace treinta siglos" [Job 28]. *CB* 14 (1957) 113–22. **Dhorme, P.** "Les chapitres XXV–XXVIII du Livre de Job." *RB* 33 (1924) 343–56. **Dick, M. B.** "Job xxviii 4: A New Translation." *VT* 29 (1979) 216–21. **Driver, G. R.** "Birds in the Old Testament: I. Birds in Law." *PEQ* 87 (1955) 5–20. ———. "Problems in Job." *AJSL* 52 (1935–36) 160–70. **Elbourne, D. A., Jr.** "The Grammar of Poetics and the Contextual Function of Job 28." Diss., New Orleans Baptist Theological Seminary, 2002. **Elwolde, J. F.** "Non-Contiguous Parallelism as a Key to Literary Structure and Lexical Meaning in Job 28." In *Job 28: Cognition in Context.* Ed. E. van Wolde. Biblical Interpretation Series 64. Leiden: Brill, 2003. 103–18. **Fiddes, P. S.** "'Where shall wisdom be found?' Job 28 as a Riddle for Ancient and Modern Readers." In *After the Exile.* FS R. Mason, ed. J. Barton and D. J. Reimer. Macon, GA: Mercer UP, 1996. 171–90. **Geller, S. A.** "Where Is Wisdom? A Literary Study of Job 28 in Its Settings." In *Judaic Perspectives on Ancient Israel.* Ed. J. Neusner, B. A. Levine, and E. S. Frerichs. Philadelphia: Fortress, 1987. 155–88. **Giesebrecht, F.** *Der Wendepunkt des Buches Hiob, Capitel 27 und 28.* Diss., Greifswald, 1879. **Graetz, H. H.** "Die Integrität der Kapitel 27 und 28 im Hiob." *MGWJ* 21 (1872) 241–50. **Greenstein, E. L.** "The Poem on Wisdom in Job 28 in Its Conceptual and Literary Contexts." In *Job 28: Cognition in Context.* Ed. E. van Wolde. Biblical Interpretation Series 64. Leiden: Brill, 2003. 253–80. **Guillaume, A.** "The Arabic Background of the Book of Job." In *Promise and Fulfilment.* FS S. H. Hooke, ed. F. F. Bruce. Edinburgh: T. & T. Clark, 1963. 106–27. **Habel, N.C.** "The Implications of God Discovering Wisdom in Earth." In *Job 28: Cognition in Context.* Ed. E. van Wolde. Biblical Interpretation Series 64. Leiden: Brill, 2003. 281–98. ———. "Of Things beyond Me: Wisdom in the Book of Job." *CurTM* 10 (1983) 142–54. **Hadley, J. M.** "Wisdom and the Goddess." In *Wisdom in Ancient Israel.* FS J. A. Emerton, ed. J. Day, R. P. Gordon, and H. G. M. Williamson. Cambridge: Cambridge UP, 1995. 234–43. **Harris, S. L.** "Wisdom or Creation? A New Interpretation of Job xxviii 27." *VT* 33 (1983) 419–27. **Hecke, P. J. P. van.** "Searching for and Exploring Wisdom: A Cognitive-Semantic Approach to the Hebrew Verb *ḥāqar* in Job 28." In *Job 28: Cognition in Context.* Ed. E. van Wolde. Biblical Interpretation Series 64. Leiden: Brill, 2003. 139–62. **Hulsbosch, A.** "Sagesse créatrice et éducatrice: I. Job 28." *Aug* 1 (1961) 217–35. **Hung, C.** "An Independent Poem in the Book of Job" [ch. 28]. *ColcTFu* 85 (1990) 357–60. **Japhet, S.** "מסורת וחידוש בפירוש רשב"ם לספר איוב איוב פרק כח" [Tradition and Innovation in the Commentary of Rabbi Samuel ben Meir (Rashbam) on Job: The Hymn to Wisdom (Job 28)]. In *Tehillah le-Moshe: Biblical and Judaic Studies.* FS M. Greenberg, ed. M. Cogan, B. L. Eichler, and J. H. Tigay. Winona Lake, IN: Eisenbrauns, 1997. 115*–42* [Heb]. **Kamp, A.** "World Building in Job 28: A Case of Conceptual Logic." In *Job 28: Cognition in Context.* Ed. E. van Wolde. Biblical Interpretation Series 64. Leiden: Brill, 2003. 307–19. **Küchler, M.** "Gott und seine Weisheit in der Septuaginta (Ijob 28; Spr 8)." In *Monotheismus und Christologie: Zur Gottesfrage im hellenistischen Judentum und im Urchristentum.* Ed. H.-J. Klauck. QD 138. Freiburg i. Br.: Herder, 1992. 118–43. **Löhr, M.** "Hiob c. 28." In *Oriental Studies.* FS P. Haupt, ed. C. Adler and A. Ember. Baltimore: Johns Hopkins UP, 1926. 67–70. **Lugt, P. van der.** "The Form and Function of the Refrains in Job 28: Some Comments Relating to the 'Strophic' Structure of Hebrew Poetry." In *The Structural Analysis of Biblical and Canaanite Poetry.* Ed. W. van der Meer and J. C. de Moor. JSOTSup 74. Sheffield: JSOT Press, 1988. 265–93. **Michel, W. L.** "*Slmwt,* 'deep darkness' or 'shadow of death'?" [Job 28:3]. *BR* 29 (1954) 5–20. **Müller, H.-P.** *Das Hiobproblem: Seine Stellung und Entstehung im Alten Orient und im Alten Testament.* 3d ed. ErF 84. Darmstadt: Wissenschaftliche Buchgesellschaft, 1995. 129–34. **Muraoka, T.** "Words of Cognition in Job 28: Hebrew and Greek." In *Job 28: Cognition in Context.* Ed. E. van Wolde. Biblical Interpretation Series 64. Leiden: Brill, 2003. 93–102. **Newsom, C. A.** "Dialogue and Allegorical Hermeneutics in Job 28:28." In *Job 28: Cognition in Context.* Ed. E. van Wolde. Biblical Interpretation Series 64. Leiden: Brill, 2003. 299–305. **Niccacci, A.** "Giobbe 28." *SBFLA* 31 (1981) 29–58. **Nielsen, E.** "Homo faber—sapientia Dei" [Job 28; Prov 8)]. *SEÅ* 41–42 (1976–77) 157–65 [Danish]. **Oorschot, J. van.** "Hiob 28: Die verborgene Weisheit und die Furcht Gottes als Überwindung einer generalisierten חכמה." In *The Book of Job.* Ed. W. A. M. Beuken. BETL 114. Leuven: Leuven UP, 1994. 183–201. **Pascual Recuero, P.** "El poema de la sabiduría en el libro de Job (Notas exegéticos sobre el capitulo 28)." *MEAH* 5 (1956) 249–60. **Passoni dell'Acqua, A.** "La Sapienza e in genere l'elemento intermedio tra Dio e il creato nelle versioni greche dell'Antico Testamento: Giob. 28 e 38." *EphLtg* 98 (1984) 270–322. **Regnier, A.** "La distribution des chapitres 25–28 du Livre de Job." *RB* 33 (1924) 186–200. **Settlemire, C. C.** "The Meaning, Importance, and Original Position of Job 28." Diss., Drew, 1969. DissAb 30 (1969) 2142A. ———. "Meaning, Importance, and Original Position of Job 28" [diss. abstract]. *Drew Gateway* 41 (1970) 34–35. ———. "The Original Position of Job 28." In *The Answers Lie Below.* FS L. E. Toombs, ed. H. O. Thompson. Lanham, MD: Univ. Press of America, 1984. 287–317. **Steck, O. H.** "Israels Gott statt anderer Götter—Israels Gesetz statt fremder Weisheit. Beobachtungen zur Rezeption von Hi 28 in Bar 3,9–4,4." In *Wer ist wie du, HERR, unter den Göttern?* FS O. Kaiser, ed. I. Kottsieper, J. van Oorschot, D. Römheld, and H. M. Wahl. Göttingen: Vandenhoeck & Ruprecht, 1994. 457–71. **Tournay, R.** "L'ordre primitif des chapitres XXIV–XXVIII du livre de Job." *RB* 64 (1957) 321–34. **Tsevat, M.** "Some Biblical Notes." *HUCA* 24 (1952–53) 107–14. **Waterman, L.** "Note on Job 28 4." *JBL* 71 (1952) 167–70. **Wolde, E. van.** "Wisdom, Who Can Find It? A Non-Cognitive and Cognitive Study of Job 28:1–11." In *Job 28: Cognition in Context.* Ed. E. van Wolde. Biblical Interpretation Series 64. Leiden: Brill, 2003. 1–35. **Wolde, E. van,** ed. *Job 28: Cognition in Context.* Biblical Interpretation Series 64. Leiden: Brill, 2003. **Wolfers, D.** "The Stone of Deepest Darkness: A Mineralogical Mystery (Job xxviii)." *VT* 44 (1994) 274–76. ———. "The Volcano in Job 28." *JBQ* 18 (1989–90) 234–40. **Zamodi, J.** "הימנון החכמה ומקומו בספר איוב" [The Wisdom Hymn and Its Place in the Book of Job]. *BMik* 28.94 (1982–93) 268–77, 310. **Zimmermann, R.** "Homo Sapiens Ignorans: Hiob 28 als Bestandteil der ursprünglichen Hiobdichtung." *BN* 74 (1994) 80–100.

Bibliography on Mining and Smelting

Forbes, R. J. *Studies in Ancient Technology.* Leiden: Brill, 1957, 1958, 1963, 1964. 5:110–231; 6:66–86; 7:104–243. **Guillaume, A.** "Metallurgy in the Old Testament." *PEQ* (1962) 129–32. **Kessler, R.** "Silber und Gold, Gold und Silber: Zur Wertschätzung der Edelmetalle im Alten Israel." *BN* 31 (1986) 57–69. **Merkel, J. F.** "A Laboratory Reconstruction of Late Bronze–Early Iron Age Copper Smelting in the Arabah." In *Midian, Moab and Edom: The History and Archaeology of Late Bronze and Iron Age Jordan and North-West Arabia.* Ed. J. F. A. Sawyer and D. J. A. Clines. JSOTSup 24. Sheffield: JSOT Press, 1983. 125–28. **Rothenberg, B.** "Ancient Copper Industries in the Western Arabah." *PEQ* (1962) 5–71. **Rothenberg, B.**, ed. *The Ancient Metallurgy of Copper: Archaeology—Experiment—Theory.* Researches in the Arabah 1959–1984, vol. 2. London: Institute for Archaeo-Metallurgical Studies, 1990. **Rothenberg, B.**, and **J. Glass.** "The Beginnings and the Development of Early Metallurgy and the Settlement and Chronology of the Western Arabah, from the Chalcolithic Period to Early Bronze Age IV." *Levant* 24 (1992) 141–57. **Van Leeuwen, R. C.** "A Technical Metallurgical Usage of יצא." *ZAW* 98 (1986) 112–13. **Weeks, L.** *Early Metallurgy of the Persian Gulf: Technology, Trade, and the Bronze Age World.* American School of Prehistoric Research Monograph Series 2. Leiden: Brill Academic Publishers, 2003. **Wilsdorf, H.** *Bergleute und Hüttenmänner im Altertum bis zum Ausgang der römischen Republik.* Freiberger Forschungshefte, Beihefte der Zeitschrift "Bergakademie," Reihe D, Kultur und Technik 1. Berlin: Akademie, 1952. **Winnett, F. V.** "Metallurgy." *IDB* 3:366–68. ———. "Mining." *IDB* 3:84–85.

Bibliography on the Fear of God (28:28)

Alonso Schökel, L. "Temer o respetar a Dios?" *CB* 33 (1976) 21–28. **Balz, H. R.** "Furcht vor Gott? Überlegungen zu einem vergessenen Motiv biblischer Theologie." *EvTh* 29 (1969) 626–44. **Bamberger, B. J.** "Fear and Love of God in the Old Testament." *HUCA* 6 (1929) 39–53. **Barré, M. L.** "'Fear of God' and the World View of Wisdom." *BTB* 11 (1981) 41–43. **Becker, J.** *Gottesfurcht im Alten Testament.* AnBib 25. Rome: Pontifical Biblical Institute, 1965. **Beentjes, P. C.** "'Full wisdom is fear of the Lord': Ben Sira 19,20—20,31: Context, Composition and Concept." *EstBíb* 47 (1989) 27–45. **Berthold, F.** *The Fear of God: The Role of Anxiety in Contemporary Thought.* New York: Harper, 1959. **Blocher, H.** "The Fear of the Lord as the 'Principle' of Wisdom." *TynBul* 28 (1977) 3–28. **Boularand, E.** "Crainte." In *Dictionnaire de spiritualité, ascétique et mystique.* Ed. Marcel Viller et al. Vol. 2. Paris: Beauchesne, 1937–1995. Cols. 2463–2511. **Bowman, J.** "The Fear of the Lord." In *Studies in Wisdom Literature: Papers Presented at the 15th and 16th Congresses of the Ou-Testamentiese Werkgemeenskap in Suid-Afrika Held in 1972 and 1973.* Ed. W. C. Van Wyk. Hercules, South Africa: NHW Press, 1981. **Brongers, H. A.** "La crainte du Seigneur (Jir'at Jhwh, Jir'at 'Elohim)." *OtSt* 5 (1948) 151–73. **Catanzaro, C. J. de.** "Fear, Knowledge, and Love: A Study in Old Testament Piety." *CJT* 9 (1963) 166–73. **Cate, R. L.** "The Fear of the Lord in the Old Testament." *Theological Educator: A Journal of Theology and Ministry* 35 (1987) 41–55. **Coles, D. R.** "The Fear of the Lord from the Perspective of Christianity and Islam." *Stulos* (Bandung) 2.2 (1994) 135–45. **Cox, D.** "Fear or Conscience? *Yir'at yhwh* in Proverbs 1–9." In *Studia Hierosolymitana.* Vol. 3, *Nell'ottavo centenario francescano (1182–1982).* Ed. G. C. Bottini. Studium Biblicum Franciscanum, Collectio maior 30. Jerusalem: Franciscan Printing Press, 1982. 83–90. **Derousseaux, J.** *La crainte de Dieu dans l'Ancien Testament: Royauté, alliance, sagesse dans les royaumes d'Israël et de Juda; recherches d'exégèse et d'histoire sur la racine yârê'.* LD 63. Paris: Cerf, 1970. **De Vries, S. J.** "Note concerning the Fear of God in the Qumran Scrolls." *RevQ* 5 (1964–66) 233–37. **Di Lella, A. A.** "Fear of the Lord as Wisdom: Ben Sira 1,11–30." In *The Book of Ben Sira in Modern Research: Proceedings of the First International Ben Sira Conference, 28–31 July 1996, Soesterberg, Netherlands.* Ed. P. C. Beentjes. BZAW

255. Berlin: De Gruyter, 1997. 113–33. **Engelbrecht, B. J.** "Die betekenis van die begrip 'Vrees van die Here' in Spreuke, Job en Prediker." *HvTSt* 7 (1951) 191–223. **Fuhs, H. F.** "יָרֵא *yārēʾ*; יָרֵא *yārēʾ*; יִרְאָה *yirʾâ*; מוֹרָא *môrâ*." *TDOT* 6:290–315 [originally *TWAT* 3:869–93]. **Gruber, M. I.** "Fear, Anxiety and Reverence in Akkadian, Biblical Hebrew and Other North-West Semitic Languages." *VT* 40 (1990) 411–22. Reprinted in *The Motherhood of God and Other Studies,* South Florida Studies in the History of Judaism 57 (Atlanta: Scholars Press, 1992) 193–208. **Hänel, J.** "Die Ehrfurcht vor Gott." In *Die Religion der Heiligkeit.* Gütersloh: Bertelsmann, 1931. 106–34. **Hempel, J.** "Die Furcht vor Jahve." In *Gott und Mensch im Alten Testament: Studie zur Geschichte der Frömmigkeit.* 2d ed. Stuttgart: Kohlhammer, 1936. 4–33. **Janzen, J. G.** "The Terror of History and the Fear of the Lord." *Enc* 42 (1981) 369–78. **Joüon, P.** "Crainte et peur en hébreu biblique: Etude le lexicographie et de stylistique." *Bib* 6 (1925) 174–79. ———. "Etudes de sémantique hébraïque: 4. Locutions pour craindre de (que) en hébreu." *Bib* 2 (1921) 336–42, esp. 340–42. **Kaiser, W. C., Jr.** "Wisdom Theology and the Centre of Old Testament Theology." *EvQ* 50 (1978) 132–46. **Klostermann, A.** *Die Gottesfurcht als Hauptstück der Weisheit: Rede beim Antritt des Rektorates der Königlichen Christian-Albrechts-Universität zu Kiel am 5. März 1885.* Kiel: Toeche, 1855. **Loretz, O.** "'Il meglio della sapienza è il timore di Jahvè' (Prov. 1, 7)." *BeO* 2 (1960) 210–11. **Louis, B.** "'Die Furcht des Herrn ist der Anfang der Weisheit': Psychologische und geistliche Erwägungen zur Gottesfurcht." *GuL* 58 (1985) 280–93. **Marböck, J.** "Die Furcht des Herrn ist Anfang der Weisheit: Erinnerung an ein Paradigma des Glaubens Israel." In *Metamorphosen des Eingedenkens: Gedenkschrift der Katholisch-Theologischen Fakultät der Karl-Franzens-Universität Graz 1945–1955.* Ed. M. Liebmann, E. Renhart, and K. M. Woschitz. Graz: Styria, 1995. 113–23. ———. "Im Horizont der Gottesfurcht: Stellungnahmen zu Welt und Leben in der alttestamentlichen Weisheit." *BN* 26 (1985) 47–70. **Murphy, R. E.** "The Fear of the Lord: The Fear to End All Fears." In *Overcoming Fear between Jews and Christians.* Ed. J. H. Charlesworth. Philadelphia: American Interfaith Institute; New York: Crossroad, 1992. 172–80. **Nagel, G.** "Crainte et amour de Dieu dans l'AT." *RTP* 33 (1945) 175–86. **Olivier, B.** *La crainte de Dieu comme valeur religieuse dans l'Ancien Testament.* Etudes religieuses 745. Brussels: La Pensée catholique, 1960. **Oorschot, J. van.** "Hiob 28: Die verborgene Weisheit und die Furcht Gottes als Überwindung einer generalisierten חכמה." In *The Book of Job.* Ed. W. A. M. Beuken. BETL 114. Leuven: Leuven UP, 1994. 183–201. **Pfeiffer, R. H.** "The Fear of God." *IEJ* 5 (1955) 41–48. Originally published in *ErIsr* 3 (1953) (Cassuto Memorial Volume) 59–62. **Plath, S.** *Furcht Gottes: Der Begriff yara im Alten Testament.* AzTh 2.2. Stuttgart: Calwer, 1963. **Schmid, H. H.** "TIMOR DOMINI INITIUM SAPIENTIAE." In *Ernten, was man sät.* FS K. Koch, ed. D. R. Daniels, U. Glessner, and M. Rösel. Neukirchen-Vluyn: Neukirchener Verlag, 1991. 519–31. **Vigouroux, F.** "Crainte de Dieu." *DB* 2:1099–1100. **Wilson, L.** "The Book of Job and the Fear of God." *TynBul* 46 (1995) 59–79. **Zatelli, I.** "Yir'at JHWH nella Bibbia, in Ben Sira e nei rotoli di Qumran: considerazioni sintattico-semantiche." *RivB* 36 (1988) 229–37.

Translation

1 [a]*Surely*[b] *there is a mine*[c] *for silver,*
[d]*and a place for gold that will be refined.*[e]
2 *Iron is taken*[a] *from the soil,*[b]
rock[c] *that will be poured out*[d] *as copper.*[e]
3 [a]*An end is put*[b] *to darkness,*
and[c] *to the furthest bound they*[d] *seek*[e] *the ore*[f]
[g]*in gloom and deep darkness.*[h]
4 [a]*A foreign race*[b] *cuts*[c] *the shafts;*[d]
forgotten[e] *by travelers,*[f]
[g]*far away from humans*[h] *they dangle*[i] *and sway.*[j]

5 [a]*That earth from which food*[b] *comes forth*
is underneath[c] *changed*[d] *as if by fire.*[e]
6 *Its rocks are the source of lapis,*[a]
with its flecks[b] *of gold.*

7 [a]*There is a path*[b] *no bird of prey*[c] *knows,*
unseen[d] *by the eyes of falcons.*[e]
8 *The proud beasts*[a] *have not trodden*[b] *it,*
no lion[c] *has prowled*[d] *it.*
9 [a]*The men*[b] *set their hand against the flinty rock,*
and overturn[c] *mountains at their roots.*[d]
10 *They split open*[a] *channels*[b] *in the rocks,*[c]
and their eye lights on any[d] *precious object.*
11 [a]*They explore*[b] *the sources*[c] *of rivers,*[d]
bringing to light[e] *what has been hidden.*[f]

12 [a]*But*[b] *where*[c] *is wisdom to be found?*[d]
And where is the place of understanding?
13 *Humans do not know the way to it;*[a]
it is not to be found in the land of the living.
14 [a]*The ocean deep*[b] *says, "It is not in me,"*
and the sea, "Not with me."

15 [a]*It cannot be bought with refined gold,*[b]
and its price cannot be weighed out in silver.
16 *It cannot be valued*[a] *against gold*[b] *of Ophir,*
against precious cornelian[c] *or lapis lazuli.*[d]
17 *Gold and glass*[a] *cannot*[b] *equal it,*[c]
and jewels[d] *of gold cannot be exchanged for it.*
18 *Coral*[a] *and rock crystal*[b] *are not worthy of mention*[c] *beside it;*
a pouch[d] *of wisdom fetches more than rubies.*[e]
19 [a]*The olivine*[b] *of Cush cannot compare*[c] *with it,*
it cannot be valued against pure gold.

20 *But whence comes wisdom?*
And where is the place of understanding?
21 *It is hidden*[a] *from the eyes of every living being,*[b]
concealed from the birds of the sky.
22 *Abaddon and Death say,*
"We know of it only by hearsay."

23 *But God understands*[a] *the way to it;*[b]
it is he who knows its place.
24 [a]*For*[b] *he looked*[c] *to the ends of the earth,*
and beheld everything under the heavens,[d]
25 *so as to assign*[a] *a weight*[b] *to the wind,*
and determine[c] *the waters by measure,*[d]

[26]*when he made a decree*[a] *for the rain,*
and a path for the thunderbolt[b]—
[27]*then*[a] *he saw*[b] *it and appraised*[c] *it,*
established[d] *it and fathomed*[e] *it.*
28 [a]*And he said to humankind,*[b]
Behold, wisdom is to fear the Lord,[c]
understanding is to shun evil.

Notes

1.a. Some would insert at the head of the poem the refrain of v 12, "where shall wisdom be found?" (so Duhm, Beer [*BH*²], Peake, Strahan, Moffatt, Fohrer); but it is not immediately obvious how the existence of mines for metals could be the reason for asking "Where shall wisdom be found?"

1.b. כי is usually "for," but its use as an asseverative "surely" is well attested (cf. BDB, 472b §1e; *DCH,* 4:388a; Hölscher, Gordis, Habel, Gray), thus "surely" (KJV, RSV), "indeed" (NAB). Most translations simply omit the word. An example of its use at the beginning of a unit may be Isa 15:1. כי here can hardly mean "for," even if we accept that chap. 28 was originally preceded by chap. 37 since there is nothing there for which the material of chap. 28 could be the reason.

1.c. מוצא has a wide range of meanings, such as "exit, departure, export, growth, utterance." It is commonly "spring, source" of water, and taken by most as, by analogy, and here only, "mine" (so most modern versions, though KJV has "vein"). M. Dahood (*Proverbs and Northwest Semitic Philology,* Scripta Pontificii Instituti Biblici 113 [Rome: Pontificium Institutum Biblicum, 1963] 52), however, understands it as "smelter" (*DCH,* 5:185a), from a new word יצא II "be pure, shine," parallel in sense to the place (מקום) for refining gold in the second colon; smelting is, on this view, understood as the process that makes silver shine; so too Pope, Fedrizzi. On יצא II "be pure, shine," see further *Note* 23:10.e; *DCH,* 3:265a. The connection with a יצא II is forced, but it is worth considering, nevertheless, whether מוצא does not refer to the place of smelting rather than to the mine (as R. C. Van Leeuwen, "A Technical Metallurgical Usage of יצא," *ZAW* 98 [1986] 112–13); but since vv 2–6 concern mining rather than smelting, it is best to retain the reference here to mining. See, further, *Comment* on vv 1–2.

Among emendations, P. Joüon ("Notes philologiques sur le texte hébreu de Job 1, 5; 9, 35; 12, 21; 28, 1; 28, 27; 29, 14," *Bib* 11 [1930] 322–24 [323]) reads מִמְצָא "place of finding," a word that seems unexceptionable but does not otherwise occur.

1.d. Obviously there is a relative clause in this colon, though no relative pronoun is used. The colon is probably to be understood as "[a place for silver,] (which) they (later) refine" (cf. RSV; similarly NAB, Habel, Guillaume), i.e., its focus is on the mine rather than on the refinery, "[a place] (where) they refine gold" (as Dhorme, Fohrer, Gordis, Hartley, Good), זהב "gold" being prefixed by *lamedh* of the direct obj; for the focus throughout vv 1–2 is on the natural location of the four metals.

1.e. זקק "refine, purify" has as its obj silver (1 Chr 29:4; Ps 12:7) and gold (1 Chr 28:18) and also wine (Isa 25:6) and rainwater (Job 36:27). It is not that the use in reference to liquids is secondary (Dhorme, Pope) but that the term is a general one for purifying (cf. *Note* 36:27.d). There is no evidence that it can be used for washing the ore to reveal the gold (against Strahan, Driver–Gray, Fohrer, Hölscher, de Wilde, Strauss). Against Pope's claim that the term refers especially to the bellows of a forge, see J. Kaltner, *The Use of Arabic in Biblical Hebrew Lexicography,* CBQMS 28 (Washington, DC: The Catholic Biblical Association of America, 1966) 39–40. Other terms for the smelting of silver and gold include צרף "smelt, refine" and טהר "purify" (cf. Mal 3:3). The pl subj here is impersonal.

2.a. יקח "is taken"; emendations to יִקַּח "he takes" (Duhm, Beer [*BH*² *frt,* יִקַּח]) or יִקְחוּ "they take" (Tur-Sinai) are possible, but not necessary.

2.b. עפר is loose earth, "dust (Habel), mud, soil"—not "the earth" as most versions have—here in contrast to (solid) אבן "stone."

2.c. The idea is, as Gordis shows, that the rock was regarded as becoming metal in the course of being heated; cf. also Deut 8:9 "a land whose rocks are iron." If אבן "rock" is the subj of the verb יצוק, it must be masc, as perhaps in 1 Sam 17:40 (but see also proposed emendations in the next *Note*). Others assume, less probably, that the מ "from" of מעפר "from the earth" is understood before אבן also; so RSV, NIV, NEB "copper is smelted from (the) ore," NAB "copper is melted out of stone," Blommerde "from stone is the smelting of copper."

2.d. יצוק is either qal passive ptcp of יצק "pour," i.e., "rock is poured out," or impf of צוק "pour out, melt" (as in 29:6), i.e., "one melts rock into bronze" (BDB, 848a, Driver–Gray, Sicre Díaz). One cannot tell how the Eng. versions understand the term, but they agree in translating "molten" (KJV), "smelted" (RSV, NJPS, NIV, NEB), or "melted" (NAB). Other possible readings are יוצק hoph of יצק "is poured" (Budde, Beer [*BHK*], Fohrer, Gerleman [*BHS prp*]; so too *HALOT,* 2:428b) or יֻצַּק pual "is poured," or else, to avoid making אבן masc, יָצוּקוּ (Budde) or יִצְקוּ (Tur-Sinai) "they pour, smelt," or יָצוֹק "one smelts" (Duhm, Beer [BH^2 *frt*], Driver–Gray, Hölscher), or יָצִיק (hiph) "one makes [stone] exude [copper]" (Gray). Dhorme takes יצוק as an adj, "hard," but a verb seems necessary for the sense "a hard stone *becomes* copper." Blommerde read, awkwardly, יְצֹק inf constr "[and from stone is] the smelting of [copper]."

Since the other cola in vv 1–2 have been about the mining process, it is unlikely that v 2b should concern smelting (e.g., RSV "and copper is smelted from the ore"); of course the raw products are destined for the smelter, but it would be best to understand the second colon as another description of the raw material, thus "and rock, which will be smelted into copper, is [also] taken from the earth."

2.e. נחושה "(into) copper," acc of product.

3.a. It is unusual to find a tricolon that is not in a climactic position, and Duhm may be on the right track in editing the line to create just two cola: בִּקֵּשׁ בחשך תכלית חָקַר אבן אפל וצלמות "he searches through the darkness to the furthest bound, he seeks the stones of thick darkness and the shadow of death" (so too Moffatt). Driver–Gray were much tempted by this emendation, though they did not adopt it in their translation. Wolfers, 350, 495–96, on the other hand, attempted to solve the problem by making three couplets out of the six cola: "(1) An end (man) puts to darkness / as he explores to every frontier. (2) The very stone of the Underworld / erupts a stream from near some vagrant exile. (3) These forgotten ones, off the beaten track / they languish; they wander away from humankind." The result is less than persuasive.

NAB moved the first two cola to follow v 24.

3.b. The verb שׂם is active, "he puts, one puts." But because no subj is stated, it is natural to translate it as a passive. Eng. versions often insert "men" as the subj (RSV; "man" in NJB, NIV), while NRSV and GNB insert "miners" to clarify the subj. Budde, Beer (*BHK frt*), and Gray add אָדָם "humans" as the subj after שׂם "set"; Bickell added אֱנוֹשׁ.

שׂם is no doubt the ptcp, not the pf, of שׂים "set," in parallelism with the ptcp חוקר "seeks" in the second colon; the ptcps signify recurring events (Driver, *Tenses,* §135.2 Obs.), i.e., what happens whenever a mine shaft is opened.

De Wilde offers the interesting emendation to קֵץ שָׂמַל חשך "darkness cloaks the end," i.e., of the shaft. It is not an important objection that a verb שׂמל does not occur elsewhere in Heb., for שִׂמְלָה "mantle" is well known, and a cognate *šamala* "wrap up" occurs in Arab. (Lane, 1699a). The problem rather is that the mine shaft has not yet been mentioned (נחל is first in v 4), and without that term the sense of קץ would be entirely obscure.

NEB has "the end of the seam lies in darkness," reading שָׂים for שׂם (Brockington), but not explaining how the translation is achieved. Habel offers "Some seek to establish the extremity of darkness," the verb being conative, "seek to set," and קץ being "extremity" (parallel to תכלית "end") rather than "cessation." But such an ambition is hardly in the mind of the miners.

3.c. Beer (BH^2 *frt*) suggests omitting the *waw* "and," with the support of two MSS.

3.d. The subj is הוא "he," translated above by the indefinite "they." It is strange that the pronoun should refer to the unnamed subj of the previous verb שׂם (Driver–Gray), so some omit הוא (Duhm, Beer [BH^2 *frt*]; see next *Note*]), and others insert a subj after שׂם (see *Note* above).

3.e. The ptcp חוקר "seeks" is emended to חָקַר "he, one sought" by Duhm, Beer (BH^2 *frt*), with the omission of הוא. NEB has "and it [the seam] is followed to its furthest limit," reading חָקוּר "is sought" (Brockington).

3.f. אבן "stone, ore" is here transferred from the third colon to the end of the second, against the Masoretic punctuation. So too RSV, NRSV, REB, NIV. Otherwise we should understand that the obj of the miners' quest is "the stone of darkness and gloom" (cf. Dhorme "[he searches for] the stone hidden in darkness and shade"; similarly Guillaume, Hartley). NJB has "he digs the black rock in shadow dark as death," but it is inconceivable that אפל should be in constr relation with אבן and at the same time צלמות should be an adv phrase. Good's "through dim and gloomy rock" leaves חקר without an obj; his translation "digs" is moreover a bit loose. Moffatt's "in the pitchy gloom for stones they grope" can hardly be right, for miners are not searching for "stones."

Wolfers (495–96; "The Stone of Deepest Darkness: A Mineralogical Mystery [Job xxviii]," *VT* 44 [1994] 274–76) thought אפל וצלמות "darkness and the shadow of death" was the Underworld, as it is in 10:21–22, and the stone of the Underworld must be lava, which can properly be said to "erupt a stream" (פרץ נחל); see also Gordis on v 4. But one cannot imagine what part the lava plays in the scenario.

3.g. Fohrer, NAB, and NEB omit the third colon (in the Masoretic punctuation), אבן אפל וצלמות "the stone of gloom and deep darkness."

3.h. On the meaning of צלמות, lit. "darkness of death," see *Note* 3:5.a.

4.a. Duhm thinks מעם־גר a variant of מני־רגל, and הנשכחי a variant of אנוש נעו; so he reads פרץ נחל מני־רגל דלו בְמַשְׁכָה נעו "one breaks open a shaft away from [human] feet, one sways below, swinging from a rope"; Moffatt follows, except that he reads נֵר; see below. NAB omits the whole of the verse as corrupt.

4.b. מעם גר is lit. "from with one who sojourns," which could, with difficulty, be understood as "away from where men live" (RSV; similarly NIV, NJPS), "from near some vagrant exile" (Wolfers).

An emendation seems required, of (A) מעם, or of (B) גר, or of (C) both מעם and גר, or by (D) an insertion or relocation.

(A) Emendations of מעם: (1) Ehrlich read מֵעַם גר "from a foreign people"; Pesh and Vg had seen עם "people" here already. Dhorme transfers the initial *mem* to the previous word, reading נְחָלִים עַם גֵּר "a foreign people [has pierced] shafts," in reference to foreign slaves working in the mines. Similarly Graetz, Hölscher, Larcher, Pope, Gerleman (*BHS prp*), de Wilde, Sicre Díaz, Strauss, NJB, NEB; and G. R. Driver, "Problems in Job," *AJSL* 52 (1936) 160–70 (162); M. Tsevat, "Some Biblical Notes," *HUCA* 24 (1952–53) 107–14 (114); M. B. Dick, "Job xxviii 4: A New Translation," *VT* 29 (1979) 216–21. This emendation is accepted in the *Translation.* (2) A. Guillaume, "The Arabic Background of the Book of Job," in *Promise and Fulfilment,* FS S. H. Hooke, ed. F. F. Bruce (Edinburgh: T. & T. Clark, 1963) 106–27 (117–19), reads עַם "covering" (of chalk) (cf. Arab. *ghamma* "cover" [Lane, 2289a]); cf. *DCH,* vol. 6, *s.v.*

(B) Emendations of גר: (1) Some read גֵּר "foreign"; see (A) (1) above. The proposal is adopted in the *Translation.* Gray observes that גֵּר may have already acquired the connotation of "slave," as in 1 Chr 22:2; 2 Chr 2:16. (2) Others read גִּר "chalk, limestone," following LXX κονία "dust" (so Dillmann, Guillaume, "Arabic Background," 117–19). J. Reider ("Contributions to the Scriptural Text," *HUCA* 24 [1952–53] 85–106 [105–6]) reads מֵעִמְקֵי גִיר "[a torrent bursts forth] from chalk valleys," but it is hard to see what this has to do with the depiction of mining. (2) גר may be emended to נֵר "lamp, light," מעם נר being "from the light" (Ley[2], Peake), "far from daylight" (Moffatt). Or else we may read, ingeniously, עַם נֵר "the people of the lamp," meaning miners (L. Waterman, "Note on Job 28 4," *JBL* 71 [1952] 167–70); so too JB "lamp folk." (3) Gordis, following Yellin, reads גָּר "crater" (cf. Arab. *jawrat* "deep hole" [Lane, 488a]), translating "from within the crater" (מעם as in Gen 48:12; Ruth 4:10).

(C) Emendations of מעם גר: (1) Beer (*BH*[2] *frt*) reads מֵרְגָבִים "from clods" (as in 21:33), a very implausible suggestion. (2) Merx reads מֵעָפָר "from the earth," and Siegfried בְּעָפָר "in the earth," appealing to LXX (see above). (3) Tur-Sinai reads וּמַעְיָן "[he broke open rivers] and fountains."

(D) Emendations with insertions or relocations: (1) The word אוֹר may be added, מֵעַם גָּר אוֹר "from a people living in the light" (Bickell[2] [except that he reads מֵעַם], Budde, Beer [*BHK frt*], Driver–Gray "away from them that sojourn in the light"). (2) Kissane moved the last three words of v 3 to the beginning of v 4, and read פֹּרַץ נְחָלִם מעם־גֶּבֶר "[the stone of darkness and death-shade] is pierced [פרץ pual] with channels by man's agency"; it is an intelligent proposal, though there is a difficulty with the sense of פרץ, as the next *Note* will show.

4.c. פרץ is "break through, burst open," but not usually "cut, break open" with the obj being the thing cut or broken open (BDB, 829a, gives this as the only occurrence of the sense "break open"; so too *DCH,* vol. 6, *s.v.*). There are some examples of the sense "breach," with a wall as the obj: Isa 5:5; Pss 80:12 (13); 89:40 (41); Eccl 10:8; Neh 4:3 (3:35); 2 Chr 26:6; the idiom פרץ פֶּרֶץ "break open a breach" (Gen 38:29; 2 Sam 6:8 || 1 Chr 13:11; cf. Job 16:14) is perhaps a special case. None of these is closely analogous with the idea of cutting a shaft, for which the technical term seems to have been נקב "bore" (as in the Siloam inscription; cf. *DCH,* 5:747a). Other Eng. versions translate "cut" (NIV), "open" (RSV), "open up" (NJPS), "bore into" (NJB), "sink" (Good), idiomatically "they run a shaft down" (Moffatt), though none of these is really suitable for פרץ. KJV "the flood breaketh out from the inhabitant" (similarly RVmg) is faithful to the Heb., though the sense is unintelligible.

Gray offers a small emendation to פָּרְצוּ "they have opened [shafts]."

Because of the difficulties with פרץ as "open," Driver ("Problems in Job," 162) suggests we have another פרץ, cognate not with Arab. *faraṣa* "cut, slit" (Lane, 2372a) but with *faraḍa* "notch, incise" (Lane, 2373b; cf. *DCH,* vol. 6, *s.v.*; *HALOT,* 3:971b, seems to relate the usual פרץ to *faraḍa*); thus NEB "[strangers] cut [the galleries]," REB "[foreigners] cut [the shafts]"; a mining gallery is horizontal, a shaft is vertical, so the translation will depend on how the mining technique is envisaged. A. Guillaume ("Arabic Background," 118), however, connects פרץ with Arab. *faraṣa* "cut, slit," translating "he cuts a shaft through the covering of chalk."

Other solutions to the problems of this verse are: (1) S. A. Geller, followed largely by Newsom, reads "They spread out through wadis far from habitation, they wandered through [wadis] forgotten by travelers, poor in population" ("Where Is Wisdom? A Literary Study of Job 28 in Its Settings," in *Judaic Perspectives on Ancient Israel,* ed. J. Neusner, B. A. Levine, and E. S. Frerichs [Philadelphia: Fortress, 1987] 155–88 [179 n. 9]). (2) M. B. Dick ("Job xxviii 4," 216–21) reads פֶּרֶץ נחל, פֶּרֶץ being a noun "breaking out, breach" and נחל being חלל "pierce" in the niph; he translates "An excavation is carved out by the foreign work-force, Stooped over by disease / Nergal, Weakened by illness, they stagger about." Though the suggestion is attractive to Sicre Díaz, פֶּרֶץ is not attested in the sense "excavation" (but mentioned in *DCH,* vol. 6, *s.v.*), and חלל "pierce" is not elsewhere found in the niph.

4.d. נחל is usually "torrent," and thus the "wadi, valley" in which the stream runs or else its dried up bed. This is the only case where BDB thinks the word has a different meaning ("miner's shaft," p. 636b), but some have seen the sense "grave trench" at 21:33, and "tunnel" in Neh 2:15 (cf. *DCH,* 5:659b). Gray proposes we read the pl, נְחָלִים "shafts."

Driver ("Problems in Job," 162) proposed another נַחַל "excavation, shaft" (cf. Akk. *niḫlu*) (נַחַל VI in *DCH,* 5:659b); but *niḫlu* is not known to von Soden, and it appears in *CAD,* 11:219b, only as attested in a lexicographical list in the sense of "sifting." Guillaume related נַחַל "wadi" to Arab. *ḫalal* "gap," *ḫallat* "hole" (Lane, 779b), and so argued that the meaning "mine shaft" was an appropriate sense (*Lexicography,* 4:10; נַחַל IV in *DCH,* 5:659b). For the explanation of נחל as "pierced" (from חלל), see preceding *Note.*

4.e. הנשכחים "those forgotten" does not appropriately refer to נחלים "shafts" (against Dhorme, NJB "ravines in unfrequented places") but rather to the collective עַם "people." Guillaume ("Arabic Background," 117–19) has "those who are swept off their feet," supposing a new word שכח "sweep away" (cf. by metathesis Arab. *kasaḥa* [Lane, 2610a]). Dick ("Job xxviii 4," 216–21) proposed a new שכח "bend, curve" (cf. Ugar. *ṯkḥ* "curve, incline"), thus "bent over, weakened [by illness]," following others who have also seen this root in Heb.: W. F. Albright, "Anath and the Dragon," *BASOR* 84 (1941) 14–17 (15 n. 3) (for Pss 102:5; 137:5); Dahood, *Psalms I,* 190 (Ps 31:12 [13]); *Psalms II,* 72, 228 (Pss 59:11 [12]; 77:9 [10]); *Psalms III,* 11, 271 (Pss 102:4 [5]; 137:5); J. J. M. Roberts, "*Niškaḥtî . . . millēb,* Ps. xxxi 13," *VT* 25 (1975) 797–801 (though insisting on the sense "bend down, droop" rather than "wither"). Gray emends to נִשְׁפָּחִים, from שפח "pour," thus "poured out" or, of a rope, "paid out"; he translates "let down [without foothold]." The root שפח does not occur in Heb., though שִׁפְחָה "maid" and מִשְׁפָּחָה "clan" are perhaps derived nouns; it would be cognate with Arab. *safaḥa* "pour" (cf. also BDB, 1046a; *HALOT,* 4:1620b).

4.f. מני רגל is lit. "by foot." It is impossible to see how anything can be "forgotten by foot" (as KJV, though NIV has "forgotten by the foot of man" and Dhorme "forgotten of human feet"); a song being "forgotten by the mouth" (Deut 31:21) is not a very close parallel. It is usually assumed therefore that רגל means "foot travelers" or is equivalent to רַגְלִי "pedestrian, foot soldier" (RSV "travelers," NJPS "wayfarers"). De Wilde actually reads רַגְלִים "pedestrians, travelers."

Ehrlich had the interesting idea that רגל was another word, meaning "man," cognate with Arab. *rajul* (Lane, 1045a), thus "forgotten by man." So too Tsevat, "Some Biblical Notes," 114. The Arab. word comes from the verb *rajala* "go on foot."

Another approach is to connect the phrase with the following verb דלו "[they dangle] without foothold" (Driver, "Problems in Job," 163; cf. NEBmg "languishing without foothold," REB "suspended without foothold"; JB "in places where there is no foothold" does not, however, see here the verb דלו; NEB deletes the phrase). But there is no parallel for such a sense of רגל, though Fedrizzi also accepts it. Wolfers also connected the phrase with דלו, translating "off the beaten track they languish," but the languishing of miners can hardly be the point here.

HALOT, 2:598b, understands the מן as "without," and translates "without using the foot"; but what would they be using their feet for, anyway?

4.g. Beer (BH^2) deleted this colon as irrelevant to the context.

4.h. The מ of מאנוש appears to be the מן of separation, i.e., "away from humans." Fedrizzi took it to mean "unlike [humans]." Duhm read בְּמֹשְׁכָה "by a rope"; the form is a possible sg of מֹשְׁכוֹת, attested only at 38:31 and usually registered as מֹשֶׁכֶת (BDB, 604b; *DCH,* 5:531a; *HALOT,* 2:646b, has the form מֹשְׁכוֹת).

4.i. דלל is said to be "hang, be low, languish" (BDB, 195b), but it is better to distinguish a דלל I "be low, diminished" from דלל II "hang down, dangle" (as *DCH,* 2:440), which is the verb identified in the *Translation* above. Gordis argues that דלל here is "be lifted up," i.e., "be removed," and translates "bereft [even of men who have wandered far]"; if that were the meaning, it would be better to suppose a דלל III "be high," as proposed for Isa 38:14 (cf. *DCH,* 2:440b; G. R. Driver, "Linguistic and Textual Problems: Isaiah i–xxxix," *JTS* 38 [1937] 36–50 [47]). Kissane, thinking the verb referred to the underground streams, read דַּלּוּ (from דלל I) "diminish."

Others read דָּלוּ "they dangle," from דלה (Hölscher, comparing the verb in Prov 26:7; similarly, Beer [*BHKfrt*], Larcher, BJ, JB, NJB).

De Wilde suggests we read חֲדֵלֵי מאנוש "forsaken by humans" (cf. Isa 53:3 חדל אישים "forsaken by men"), though חדל is perhaps better understood as active, "withdrawing from humans" (cf. D. W. Thomas, "Some Observations on the Hebrew Root *ḥdl,*" in *Volume du Congrès, Strasbourg 1956,* VTSup 4 [Leiden: Brill, 1957] 8–16; "A Consideration of Isa LIII in the Light of Recent Textual and Philological Study," in *De Mari à Qumran. L'Ancien Testament, Son milieu. Ses écrits. Ses relectures juives. Hommage à Mgr J. Coppens,* ed. H. Cazelles, BETL 24 [Gembloux: Duculot; Paris: Lethielleux, 1969] 119–26 [122]).

4.j. נוע is "sway, stagger, wander"; though the *Translation* above adopts the view that the miners are suspended by ropes, it must be admitted that neither this verb nor the last explicitly refers to hanging from ropes, and מאנוש נעו would perhaps most naturally mean "they wander far from other humans" (so too Tur-Sinai, de Wilde).

Gordis offers a wholly different explanation of the verse, which he begins with the last three words of v 3: "The lava dark and pitch-black (אבן אפל וצלמות, lit. the rock of darkness and gloom) cleaves a channel for the crater (נָר; see above), forgotten by men's foot, bereft even of men who have wandered far." But he does not connect this phenomenon with the mining of metals in vv 1–3, and his proposal does not therefore fit with the general view adopted here. Kissane, believing that the colon refers to underground streams, reads נֶעֱווּ "are diverted" from עוה "bend, twist" (נֶעֱווּ is a correction of the misprint נֶעֱוּו; the form נַעֲוּו would seem better supported).

5.a. Budde deletes vv 5–6.

5.b. לחם is "food" in general; though it can sometimes mean specifically "bread," there is usually some contextual hint of such a sense, which is absent here. Nevertheless RSV, NRSV, NAB, NJB have "bread," NEB "corn," REB "grain." Moffatt has the very interesting rendering, "A harvest comes out of the earth below, when the miner blasts it underground," thus removing the contrast between the surface of the earth and what lies beneath it. But can לחם mean "harvest," or, rather, would the miners' spoil of minerals and gems be called לחם?

Gordis unpersuasively proposed a different word לָחֶם "heat" (he compared the לחום "anger, heat" he found at 20:23), for the sake of creating a parallel with fire in the next colon. Tur-Sinai's יֵאָצֵל חם "heat emanateth" (from אצל "withdraw") is strained. Houbigant reads לַהַט "flame." Andersen (followed by Hartley) suggests we read לוּחַ־ם "stone(-tablet)" (with enclitic *mem*), to match the other minerals in v 6.

5.c. תחתיה "its underneath" is taken as the subj of נהפך by Gordis, and so too apparently NEB "what lies beneath," but it is better not to create the conflict of gender between the noun and the verb. Most understand תחתיה as an adv, or an adv acc (with a passive verb, as GKC, §121a, b), "underneath" (RSV, NAB), "underground" (NJB), "below" (NJPS).

5.d. הפך niph "changed" (NJPS), "transformed" (NIV) (see *Comment,* and *DCH,* 2:580–81), not "turned up" (RSV), still less "ravaged" (NJB), "convulsed" (Gordis). NEB "raked over like a fire" is an attempt, though not a very successful one, to imagine how "like a fire" could be applied to הפך; REB has simply "is turned over." Gray would read נֶהְפְּכָה "is turned into," the fem to agree with the subj ארץ "earth."

5.e. כמו־אש "like fire" is understood by most as "as (if) by fire" (other examples of the omission of a prep when another is present in GKC, §118w). Some think, however, that there is a reference to actual fire, and read בְּמוֹ־אֵשׁ (cf. Vg *igni* "by fire"; so Merx, Hölscher, Larcher, Fedrizzi, Gordis, Habel, BJ, JB, NJB). Gordis sees here further evidence of a volcano (cf. on vv 3, 4).

Among philological suggestions, Ehrlich proposes a new אשׁ "foundation" (cf. אָשְׁיָה "buttress," Aram. אָשַׁיָּא "foundations"); but it is rather too obvious to say that the underneath parts of the earth are its foundations. Among emendations, de Wilde proposes we read מֵאֱנוֹשׁ "by humans," which would yield a sense that is true but not at all revealing.

6.a. ספיר is "lapis lazuli" (as RSVmg, NEB; see further, *Comment*), not "sapphire" (as KJV, RSV, NAB, NJB, NIV, GNB, NJPS), which apparently was unknown before Roman times.

מקום־ספיר אבניה is usually understood as "its stones are the place of sapphires" (RSV; similarly KJV), but Gordis (followed by Hartley) translates "a place whose stones are sapphires," in apposition to ארץ in v 5. This is not only awkward, but most implausible on Gordis's own showing of a strophic break between vv 5 and 6.

6.b. עפרת is lit. "dust" (in pl). It is not the earth that contains gold (as KJV, RSV, NAB, NJPS), not only because gold has already been mentioned in v 1, but mainly because gold belongs to it (לו, masc), which must be in reference to the lapis (NEB "lapis lazuli, dusted with flecks of gold," Driver–Gray), not to the earth (ארץ, v 5, fem; de Wilde reads וַעֲפָרָהּ זהב לו "and its dust is gold"), nor to the rocks (אבניה, as NIV), nor to מקום "place" as Dhorme, Gordis, nor to the miner (RVmg "he winneth lumps of gold," Moffatt "he picks up lumps of gold," Ewald, Hitzig, Good). Beer (*BHK frt*), NAB read וַעֲפָרָהּ "and its dust [is gold]." For the view that עפרת זהב is "gold nuggets" (like עפרת תבל "dirt clods" in Prov 8:26), see G. Wanke, *TLOT,* 2:940.

7.a. Duhm, followed by Beer (*BH*²), Fohrer, repeats the refrain of vv 12, 20 before this verse to make clear that it is the path to wisdom that is in view; but that is mistaken, since here it is the path cut by miners (see *Comment*). Peake and Strahan, not realizing that vv 7–8 are also about mining, transfer them to follow v 12. Kissane, thinking that the path is the way to wisdom, moves the verses to follow v 13. NAB moves the verses to follow v 21. Gray moves to this point vv 9–12.

7.b. נתיב is not to be explained syntactically as *casus pendens* (GKC, §116u) but as a noun clause, "(there is) a path (that)."

7.c. עיט "bird of prey" (BDB, 743b; *HALOT,* 2:816b; *DCH,* vol. 6, *s.v.*), from עיט "scream," is apparently a generic term, for it is not included in lists of unclean birds in Lev 11 and Deut 14 (W. S. McCullough, *IDB,* 4:440). G. R. Driver, "Birds in the Old Testament: I. Birds in Law," *PEQ* 87 (1955) 5–20, posits that all birds were divided into two classes: עיט "screamers," the birds of prey, and צִפּוֹר "twitterers," passerine birds. KJV's "fowl" is too general, and GNB's "hawk" too specific.

7.d. Lit. "the falcon's eye has not seen it." שׁזף occurs only here and at Cant 1:6, where it apparently means "scorch." There, however, it would seem to be a byform of שׁדף (Gen 41:6, 23, 27), and שׁזף here may be a different word. BDB, 1004b, offers no derivation for שׁזף, but for שׁדף compares MH שׁדף "scorch, blight," Aram. שׁדף "burn," Arab. *sadafa* "be dark" (995a). KBL, 959, 950b, distinguishes the senses "catch sight of" and "make brown, burn," and regards both occurrences of שׁזף as equivalent to שׁדף, which it likewise compares to MH and Arab. *HALOT,* 4:1456a, follows suit, and offers a fanciful explanation of how the one word can have such different meanings. The Arab. cognate *sadafa* should probably be left out of account, since it means both "become dark" and "become light" (Lane, 1332c), and it is not used of burning, scorching, or tanning. Guillaume thinks שׁזף here should be compared with Arab. *sadaf* "object seen in the distance" (Lane, 1333b), but the idea of "seeing" is not contained in this word, which means "the corporeal form or figures or substances of men or other things which one sees from a distance," which is connected rather with the senses "be dark, be light." In the end, while MH שׁזף "blacken, tarnish" (Jastrow, 1545a) is good evidence for the meaning "darken," there is no evidence for the meaning "look"—though that must clearly be the meaning here. Only the context can offer a reasonable sense.

7.e. איה is the falcon (Driver, "Birds in the Old Testament," 11; *DCH,* 1:208a; RSV, NIV, NJPS, NEB), or perhaps some other bird of prey (hawk, falcon, kite, according to BDB, 17a; black kite, according to *HALOT,* 1: 39a; vulture, KJV, NJB; hawk, NAB).

8.a. בני־שׁחץ is lit. "sons of pride" (also at 41:34 [26], of the beasts of which Leviathan is king). שׁחץ "pride" occurs only in these two places, but the meaning is confirmed by MH שׁחץ hithp "be lofty, proud" (Jastrow, 1550a). The term is generally understood to refer to lions as "the proud ones" (as is attested in the Talmud at *b. Sanhedrin* 95a), though most Eng. translations do not specify and simply have "proud beasts" (as RSV, NAB, NIV, NJPS; similarly Larcher, BJ). Despite the parallelism with lions in the next colon, the reference is most probably to "wild beasts" in general (so Dhorme, Fedrizzi, Habel, though Newsom thinks they may be lizards). KJV "the lion's whelps" understood שׁחץ as "wild" (cf. Buxtorf, 796), and followed Tg בני אריון "sons of lions." S. Mowinckel thinks that the "sons of pride" (like the שׁחל; see *Note* 8.c below) were mythological creatures; but we are in a realistic world here, even if we are reading of heroic activities.

8.b. דרך is clearly "tread," but Tur-Sinai and Gordis unnecessarily suppose it means "reach, attain" (following Yellin; cf. *DCH,* 2:464a), though Gordis's translation has "trodden."

8.c. שׁחל is generally recognized as "lion" (BDB, 1006b) or perhaps "young lion" (cf. *HALOT,* 4:1461a), but S. Mowinckel ("שַׁחַל," in *Hebrew and Semitic Studies,* FS G. R. Driver, ed. D. W. Thomas and W. D. McHardy [Oxford: Clarendon, 1963] 95–104 [95–96]) thinks that it was a mythological creature, a serpent or wyvern (so too Pope, Grabbe, 91–93; Geller, "Where Is Wisdom?" 179–80; NEB;

but REB has "lion"). Mowinckel finds this sense of שחל also at 10:16; Prov 26:13. Dhorme and Terrien take it as "leopard."

8.d. עדה is a rare word, "pass on, advance" (BDB, 723b; *HALOT,* 2:789a; *DCH,* vol. 6, *s.v.*), "run" according to Tur-Sinai, only here and at Prov 25:20 (hiph "take off [garment]"), if indeed it is the same word.

9.a. NAB moves vv 9–11 to follow v 3. Gray moves vv 9–12 to follow v 6.

9.b. The verb שלח "he sent out" has no expressed subj, but the miners of vv 3–4 must be in view.

9.c. There can be no doubt about the meaning of הפך "overthrow, change," but some versions find it hard to accept and translate "lay bare" (NIV, NEB), which is not a possible sense.

9.d. משרש is lit. "from the root," which may mean "by the root(s)" (as KJV, NJB, NJPS), as if the roots are seized, or "at their foundations" (NAB). Blommerde, following H. D. Hummel ("Enclitic *Mem* in Early Northwest Semitic, Especially Hebrew," *JBL* 76 [1957] 85–107 [103]), sees an enclitic *mem* here and reads הָפַךְ־ם שֹׁרֶשׁ "he overturns the base [of the mountains]"; cf. *DCH,* 5:101b.

10.a. בקע is "split, break open," not usually "cut" (NJB, NEB), "cut out" (KJV, RSV), "carve out" (NJPS), or "tunnel" (NIV, GNB). Perhaps we should translate "split open" (NAB "split," Good "cleave"); see further, *Comment.*

10.b. יאר is normally "stream" or "channel," of the Nile, and, less often, of the Tigris at Dan 12:5, 6, 7, of watercourses in general at Isa 33:21, and only here of channels or tunnels in the rock, not for water, but for the miners to access the minerals. The semantics are the same as those of נחל "wadi" at v 4, where it means (mining) "shaft." Here the "channels" seem to be horizontal (against Hartley), so NEB's "galleries" is more exact (so too Driver–Gray, Larcher, Fedrizzi, de Wilde, BJ, JB "tunnels"). NJB "canals" does not seem plausible.

10.c. בצורים is unproblematically "in the rocks," but Tur-Sinai sees here a noun בָּצוּר "strength, wealth, treasure" (cf. בֶּצֶר "gold"), as also at 22:24, thus "He broke through to the treasures of the rivers."

10.d. כל is "every" or "any"; perhaps it can be said poetically that the miner's eye sees "every" precious thing (so KJV, RSV, NJPS, Hartley), but it cannot be literally true, and "gems of every kind meet his eye" (NEB), "on the watch for anything precious" (NJB) are more attractive translations.

11.a. Beer (BH^2 *frt*) transposed this colon to follow v 10a.

11.b. חבש is "bind" (so KJV, RSV, Gordis, Sicre Díaz, Good, Newsom, Strauss; NEB, NJPS "dam up"), but it is far from clear how miners could restrain underground rivers, presumably to prevent the mine from being flooded. Much more probable is the small emendation to a new word חבשׂ "seek" (*DCH,* 3:157a; proposed also at 34:17), a byform of חפשׂ "seek," all the more so once מבכי is recognized as a word for "sources" (see next *Note*). It is questionable, however, whether "dig" (as GNB "they dig to the sources of rivers") is an appropriate translation. חבשׂ "seek" is to be credited to M. Dahood ("The Phoenician Contribution to Biblical Wisdom Literature," in *The Role of the Phoenicians in the Interaction of Mediterranean Civilizations,* ed. W. A. Ward [Beirut: American University in Beirut, 1968] 123–52 [126–27]); it is adopted by Pope, Blommerde, Hartley, van der Lugt, NAB "probe," NJB "explore," NIV "search." Grabbe, 96–98, seems unduly negative about the supposed interchange between the consonants *b* and *p.*

Prior to that suggestion, an emendation to חִפֵּשׂ "searched" was often adopted by those unhappy with חבשׁ "bind"; so Houbigant, Graetz, Dhorme, Beer (*BHK*), Hölscher, Kissane, Larcher, Gray (Vg, Aq, and Theod also had understood the verb as "search"). Tur-Sinai, who views all the activity of vv 9–11 as God's, reads הֹבִשׁ "dried up" (from יבשׁ hiph).

11.c. מבכי has traditionally been understood as מן "from" plus בְּכִי "weeping," i.e., "so that they do not trickle" (RSV); but בכי is never used in a metaphorical sense, and it is far preferable to see here a new noun מַבָּךְ "source of waters, fountain" (*DCH,* 5:127a; cf. Ugar. *nbk*) as the obj of חבשׂ "seek" (so NRSV, NAB, NJB, NIV, NJPS, NEB, GNB, Pope, Gerleman [*BHS*], Blommerde, Fedrizzi, Sicre Díaz, Hartley, van der Lugt; *HALOT,* 2:542b [though it understands "water-source" as "trickle of water in a mine," which is derived entirely from seeing בכי "weeping" here!]). Cf. H. L. Ginsberg, "The Ugaritic Texts and Textual Criticism," *JBL* 62 (1943) 109–15 (111); G. M. Landes, "The Fountain at Jazer," *BASOR* 144 (1956) 30–37 (32); M. Mansoor, "The Thanksgiving Hymns and the Massoretic Text (Part II)," *RevQ* 3 (1961–62) 387–94 (392–93). The word was already conjectured by Hoffmann, Beer (*BHK vel*), Budde; to similar effect Graetz, Hölscher (*vel*), Gerleman (*BHS vel*) read נִבְכֵי "springs of." Dhorme, Hölscher (*vel*), Kissane, Larcher (apparently) read מַבְכֵי "the sources [Kissane "beds"] of [rivers he searches]," NEB מִבְּכֵי (*vel*), Beer (*BHK vel*), NEB (Brockington) (*vel*), Gray מַבְּכֵי. For the *Translation* above, the emendation to מַבְכֵי "the sources of" is adopted. Less probably, Fohrer, following Peters, proposed a new word מִבְכִּי "the dripping of [the streams he dams up]," a formation from בכה "weep."

11.d. Duhm has the interesting suggestion that the "rivers" (נהר) are the mining galleries themselves; already two terms for streams have been used (נחל "wadi" for the shafts in v 4, and יאר "[Nile-] channels" for the galleries in v 10). The colon would then mean that the miners prevent seepage from flooding their galleries ("weeping" is used in Eng. precisely of water seeping into a tunnel; cf. *OED*, "weep," §4b).

11.e. אור can be explained as an acc of motion (Gordis). Dahood, followed by Blommerde, translates "he makes dark places shine with light," from יצא II "be pure, shine" (as also in Pss 17:2; 37:6; 73:7; Isa 13:10; cf. *DCH*, 4:265a). But this does not seem very appropriate for the work of the miners: even though they "put an end to darkness" (v 3), the success of their work lies in what they can bring out from the mine, not in their illuminating of the mining galleries. NAB reads הוֹצִיא pf rather than MT יצא impf.

11.f. תַּעֲלֻמוֹת are "secrets" at 11:6; Ps 44:21 (22); the *mappiq* in the final letter of the sg here, תַּעֲלֻמָהּ, is either for euphony (Gordis) or to be omitted (Beer [*BHK*], Hölscher, Fohrer, Gerleman [*BHS*], Gray; so too for the *Translation* above).

Duhm, followed by Beer (*BH*[2] *frt*), Fohrer, moves to this place v 24, though it is hard to believe that looking "to the ends of the earth" and seeing "everything under the heavens" can possibly describe the miners.

12.a. De Wilde regards this as the last line of the first strophe (vv 1–12), just as its repetition in v 20 is the last line of the second strophe (vv 13–20). But the sharp change of subj makes it better to see the beginning of a new strophe here.

12.b. The initial *waw* is adversative, "but" (*DCH*, 2:596b).

12.c. מאין is "whence?," which does not fit with the verb תמצא "shall be found." Either we must read אַיִן "where?" or we must emend the verb (see next *Note*). The above *Translation* adopts the emendation of מאין.

12.d. תמצא "shall be found" is inappropriate with מאין "whence?" Unless מאין is to be emended (as in the *Translation* above), we should read תָּבוֹא "comes" (as in v 20, with the support of one MS here; so Duhm, Beer [*BHK vel*], Gray) or perhaps תֵּצֵא "comes out" (as one MS here; so Dhorme, Beer [*BHK vel*], Hölscher, Larcher [apparently], and Fedrizzi). This latter reading would form a verbal link to v 1 (Driver–Gray), but there is otherwise little connection between the language of mining and that of the quest for wisdom. Fohrer defends the MT, pointing to the use of מצא with מן at Hos 14:9; but the case is not comparable (other examples at *DCH*, 5:438b). Tur-Sinai attempted to retain the MT by supposing a new verb מצי "reach, attain, come" (cf. Aram. מטי), thus "whence shall Wisdom come?" He found the same verb in 11:7 (*q.v.*), where a מצא "reach" has been accepted on the basis of Aram. מטה, following M. J. Dahood ("Northwest Semitic Philology and Job," in *The Bible in Current Catholic Thought: Gruenthaner Memorial Volume*, ed. J. L. McKenzie, St. Mary's Theological Studies 1 [New York: Herder & Herder, 1962] 55–74 [57]; "Hebrew Lexicography: A Review of W. Baumgartner's Lexikon, Volume II," *Or* 45 [1976] 327–65 [355]). The problem here is that "come" is not a very natural extension of the meaning of מצא/מצי "reach, attain."

13.a. עֶרֶךְ is "order, row, valuation," and here most probably "worth" (NIV), "price" (KJV), or "value" (NJPS); similarly NAB. The MT is retained by Andersen, Sicre Díaz, van der Lugt. The *Translation* above, however, follows the common emendation to דַּרְכָּהּ "its way," i.e., the way to it (so too RSV, NJB, NEB, Dillmann, Hitzig, Budde, Duhm, Peake, Strahan, Driver–Gray, Dhorme, Beer [*BHK*], Hölscher, Kissane, Fohrer, Terrien, Pope[1], Rowley, Fedrizzi, Gerleman [*BHS prp*], Habel, de Wilde, Gray; cf. LXX ὁδὸν αὐτῆς "its way"), as in v 23. Gordis argues unsuccessfully that ערך here means "place"; his examples of the related מַעֲרָכָה "row" meaning "battle-line" do not support the sense "place." Tur-Sinai emended to עֶרְכָּהּ, inf constr of ערך, thus "how to provide an equivalent, how to value it"; but the issue at this point is not the *value* of wisdom, but its *location*.

M. Dahood ("Hebrew-Ugaritic Lexicography VII," *Bib* 50 [1969] 337–56 [355]; review of *The New English Bible*, *Bib* 52 [1971] 117–23 [119]) proposed another עֶרֶךְ "house, temple" on the basis of Ugar. *'rk* parallel with *bt* "house," thus "her [Wisdom's] home" (cf. *DCH*, vol. 6, *s.v.*). He is followed by Pope, Hartley.

14.a. Vv 14–19 were not translated in the original LXX, its present text deriving from Theod. NAB transposes v 14 to follow vv 20–21, 7–8. Kissane moves vv 7–8 to precede v 14.

14.b. תהום "the deep" is usually fem, but masc here and in five other places (BDB, 1062b) (Jonah 2:5 [6]; Hab 3:10; Ps 42:7 [8]). Some, however, emend the verb to אָמְרָה (fem) (Duhm [*frt*], Beer [*BHK*], Hölscher). Blommerde agreed, but spelled it אָמְרָ, retaining the Masoretic consonants. G. R. Driver took it as a fem noun treated as masc because it is such in form ("Hebrew Studies," *JRAS* [1948] 164–76 [167]).

15.a. Budde deleted vv 15–20, thus making the reply of the Deep and the Sea (v 14, plus v 21) to be followed directly by that of Abaddon and Death (v 22). The absence of vv 14–19 from the LXX lends only slight support to his proposal. Bickell deleted in addition vv 12–14.

15.b. סְגוֹר is, according to BDB, 689b, "enclosure" (as apparently at Hos 13:8), and, according to *HALOT,* 2:742a, "lock" (cf. *DCH,* vol. 6, *s.v.*). It is not attested as a word for "gold," but the phrase זָהָב סָגוּר, evidently meaning "fine gold," occurs at 1 Kgs 6:20, 21; 7:49, 50; 10:21, so most think we should emend to the form סָגוּר (so, e.g., Duhm, Beer [*BHK frt*], Hölscher, Fohrer, NAB [*Textual Notes*], NEB [Brockington], de Wilde). Gerleman (*BHS*) does not advise an emendation, but regards סְגוֹר as equivalent to זָהָב סָגוּר, which *DCH,* vol. 6, *s.v.*, then registers as סְגוֹר II "gold." As for the phrase זָהָב סָגוּר, the סגור is commonly thought to be qal passive ptcp of סגר "shut" (BDB, 689a), and the phrase זהב סגור is sometimes said to signify leaf gold (de Wilde), since in 1 Kgs 6:20, 21 the gold is an overlay, which "shuts in" or encloses the inner sanctuary. However, in 1 Kgs 7:49, 50; 10:21, the vessels of the temple are surely made of "pure gold" rather than being overlaid with it. NEB has "red gold," following G. R. Driver, "L'interprétation du texte masorétique à la lumière de la lexicographie hébraïque," *ETL* 26 (1950) 337–53 (352). See also M. Görg, "Ein Ausdruck der Goldschmiedekunst im AT," *BZ* 28 (1984) 250–55. Gray very attractively proposes that סָגוּר is qal passive ptcp of a new word סגר "refine," cognate with Arab. *sajara* "heat in an oven or crucible" (Lane, 1308b; see *DCH,* vol. 6, *s.v.*); hence the *Translation* above, "refined gold."

Other terms for "gold" in this chapter are כֶּתֶם, of Ophir in v 16 and "pure" (טהור) in v 19, זָהָב, the usual word for "gold," in v 17a, and פַּז, traditionally understood as refined gold, in v 17b (in Ps 19:10 [11] it seems to be superior to זהב).

16.a. סלה II "weigh" occurs in the Hebrew Bible only here and at v 19 (BDB, 699a), though a byform סלא occurs at Lam 4:2; *HALOT,* 2:756b, is not quite right with "be paid (*bezahlt*)"; for a possible Qumran occurrence, cf. *DCH*, vol. 6, *s.v.* Tur-Sinai saw here rather סלה I "make light of, toss aside" (BDB, 699a), which he prefers to gloss as "reject as dross" (cf. Syr. *sl'*). It is no doubt true that wisdom would become worthless dross if mixed even with gold of Ophir, but that does not justify Tur-Sinai's extension of the meaning of סלה to "mix" ("it should not be mixed with the gold of Ophir").

16.b. כֶּתֶם is here the word for "gold," as also in v 19; 31:24. The term is derived from the Egyptian for Nubia, as a source of gold.

16.c. שֹׁהַם was formerly identified as "onyx," "a variety of quartz allied to agate . . . used in cameos" (*OED;* so KJV, RSV, NAB, NIV, NJPS, Pope), but NJB has "agate," "a precious stone . . . the semi-pellucid variegated chalcedonies, with the colours disposed in parallel stripes or bands, or blended in clouds, and often with curious markings due to the infiltration of other minerals" (*OED*), while Dhorme and NEB have "cornelian," which is "a variety of chalcedony, a semi-transparent quartz, of a deep dull red, flesh, or reddish white colour . . . used for seals" (*OED*), otherwise known as "sard." De Wilde, however, thinks rather of (dull) green cornelian, colored by nickel oxide, and properly called chrysoprase.

16.d. ספיר is not "sapphire" (as KJV, RSV, NAB, NIV, NJPS, REB), but the semiprecious stone lapis lazuli (as NEB), referred to also in v 6.

17.a. זכוכית "glass," from זכך "be clear"; see further, *Comment.* Some prefer to read מְזֻקָּק "refined" (pual of זקק), which modifies "gold" (זהב) at 1 Chr 28:18 (Beer [*BHK prps*]).

17.b. The לא "not" does double duty in both cola. On "double duty" לא, see GKC, §162z, Blommerde, 27–28 (bibliography); other examples in Job have been suggested at 4:18; 30:20, 25.

17.c. ערך "rank, compare," as in v 19; Pss 40:5 (6); 89:6 (7); Isa 40:18 (it is not intransitive, as BDB, 789b §2b). Blommerde thinks the suff is datival here and in v 19 (ערך is followed by ל at Isa 40:18); for other examples of datival suffs, see *Note* 22:21.d.

17.d. כלי is a common term for "vessel" or "object" (as NAB, NJPS; NEB "work"), but it may here mean specifically "jewel" (as KJV, RSV, NIV). It is not clear why Dhorme, followed by NJB, has "a vase." Many (e.g., Kissane, Gordis, NAB [*Textual Notes*]) read כְּלֵי "vessels of" rather than MT כְּלִי "a vessel of" (as many MSS, and Theod, Symm, Tg, Vg); Driver–Gray argue, however, that the sg is a collective. Beer (*BH*[2] *frt*) thinks, not very probably, we should read בְּלִי "[it cannot be bought] without [gold]."

18.a. ראמות is usually understood as "coral" (e.g., Dhorme, Pope; BDB, 910b, "corals") or "black coral" (NEB), but others think it is "mother of pearl" (de Wilde); *HALOT,* 3:1164a, does not offer a meaning.

18.b. גביש is either the usually green "jasper" (NAB, NIV) or "crystal" (RSV, NJB, NJPS, Dhorme, Pope, BDB, 150b), i.e., the semiprecious colorless quartz "rock crystal" (de Wilde, *HALOT,* 1:173b), or else white or bluish-gray "pearls" (KJV), or the usually pure white translucent carbonate or sulphate of lime, "alabaster" (NEB). The term appears to be connected to אלגביש "hailstone" (Ezek 13:11, 13; 38:22).

18.c. זכר is normally "remember," and rarely "mention" (*DCH*, 3:105a). But "let it not be mentioned" is the only possible sense here. One might have expected another word for weighing or buying.

18.d. מֶשֶׁךְ was formerly connected with משׁך I "drag" and understood as "the drawing up, or fishing up, [of wisdom]" (so BDB, 604b); this leads to the translation "price" (KJV, RSV, Guillaume, Hartley) or "value" (de Wilde) or "excellence" (Kissane), and to NJB "better go fishing for Wisdom than for pearls!" It lies behind Driver–Gray's rendering "acquisition" (cf. Sicre Díaz; and also A. Cohen, "Studies in Hebrew Lexicography," *AJSL* 40 [1923–24] 153–85 [175]), Hölscher's "possession," and Dhorme's "extraction." Among emendations, (1) Beer (*BH*[2] *frt*) reads וּמְשֹׁךְ "and to fish up." (2) NAB reads וּמְשָׁכָהּ מִפְּנִינִים וּפִטְדַת כּוּשׁ "it surpasses pearls and Arabian topaz," lit. "and its price is more than pearls and topaz of Cush." These semantic relations seem forced, however.

Many now acknowledge a new word מֶשֶׁךְ II "pouch, bag" (L. Köhler, "Hebräische Vokabeln II," *ZAW* 55 [1937] 161–74 [161–62]; KBL, 575a; *HALOT*, 3:646a; *DCH*, 5:525b); thus NJPS, NEB, Fohrer, Terrien, Strauss, Gray, and the *Translation* above, though it must be acknowledged that "a pouch of wisdom" is a strange idea. It is less likely that we should recognize a מֶשֶׁךְ III "price" (*DCH*, 5:525b), as proposed by R. Gordis (309; idem, "Psalm 9–10—A Textual and Exegetical Study," *JQR* 48 [1957–58] 104–22 [116–17]), following N. H. Torczyner ([Tur-Sinai] הלשון והספר, כרך הלשון [Jerusalem: Bialik, 1948] 383–97).

18.e. It is uncertain whether פנינים is "corals" (BDB, 819b), "red coral" (NEB, S. T. Byington, "Hebrew Marginalia III," *JBL* 64 [1945] 339–55 [340–41], de Wilde), "rubies" (KJV, NIV, NJPS, GNB, Pope, Hartley), or "pearls" (RSV, NAB, Dhorme, Gordis, Sicre Díaz). *HALOT*, 2:946a, offers "pearls of coral" (*Korallen[perlen]*), apparently in reference to pearl coral (*Plerogyra sinuosa*), otherwise known as bubble coral or bladder coral, giving the appearance of a mass of pearls; this attractive and no doubt much-prized coral is found in the Red Sea (www.oceanlight.com/lightbox.php?sp=Plerogyra_sinuosa). The occurrence in Lam 4:7, however, "their bodies were redder than פנינים," suggests a red gem such as rubies.

19.a. NAB moves the words פִּטְדַת־כּוּשׁ "topaz of Cush" to the end of v 18 and deletes the remainder of v 19 as dittographs of vv 16a, 17a, and 18b. Beer (*BH*[2]) would delete v 19a as a variant of v 17a, and v 19b as a variant of v 16a. Fohrer deleted the whole of the verse for similar reasons. Duhm agreed that these were dittographs, but found himself unable to decide which were the originals.

19.b. פטדה is usually translated as "topaz" (KJV, RSV, NAB, NJB, NIV, NJPS, NEB), but that term is now restricted to the pale yellow stone that is an aluminum silicate. The gem referred to here would seem to be what is now called peridot, the translucent pale green gem form of olivine, an iron magnesium silicate; it was formerly known as "chrysolite" (KBL, 758a, de Wilde, NRSV, NEBmg, REB). "Olivine" has been preferred for the *Translation* as a more "poetic" word than "peridot" or "chrysolite." See also J. M. Grintz, "מונחים קדומים ב׳תורת כהנים," *Leš* 39 (1974–75) 8–10.

19.c. ערך "compare"; cf. on v 17.

21.a. Many delete the initial *waw* in ונעלמה "and it is hidden"; so Driver–Gray, Beer (*BHK*), Hölscher, Fohrer (which corresponds to LXX, Pesh, Vg). Gordis resists the deletion, arguing that it suggests "for," which seems unlikely. Blommerde, 29, thinks it an emphatic *waw*; for other presumed examples of emphatic *waw*, cf. 4:6; 8:13; 14:20; 19:23; 31:30; 34:20; 36:7; 39:28. A special use of emphatic *waw* is found when a word from the first colon of a line is repeated at the beginning of the second colon, prefixed with *waw* (as at 3:17; 13:7; 17:15; 34:28; 38:17, 22; 41:24 [16]).

21.b. On the reference of כל־חי "all living," see *Comment*. Beer (*BHK*) emends to כָּל־חַיָּה "every beast" (חַיָּה as in 37:8).

23.a. Though הבין "discerned" and ידע "knew" are pfs, they should be translated as present-tense verbs, for the question is not who *knew* the way to wisdom but who *knows* it (as against Dhorme "discerned... has known"). Tur-Sinai is surely incorrect to translate "taught it its way" and "made known the place thereof" (reading יִדַּע piel). The reading of some MSS, הכין "establish" (cf. Gerleman [*BHS*]), is not to be preferred.

23.b. דַּרְכָּהּ "its way" is understood by Andersen as "its realm," appealing to דֶּרֶךְ II "power, dominion" (*DCH*, 2:472b); vocalizing it דְּרֻכָּהּ, he finds it also in 26:14; Prov 8:22.

24.a. Budde, Hölscher, and Fedrizzi delete the line as a gloss; Duhm, followed by Beer (*BH*[2] *frt*) and Fohrer, moves it to follow v 11.

24.b. כי is of course usually "for," and here it introduces the reason why God knows the way to wisdom. It is tempting, however, to translate "when" (as does Dhorme), since vv 24–26 refer to the time of creation, which is when God performed the four actions of v 27 in regard to wisdom. Yet the sense "when" for כי seems restricted to two settings: (1) after ויהי "and it came to pass" and the like (BDB,

473a §2a), and (2) introducing a conditional clause, sometimes with a temporal aspect, "if, supposing that, in the case that, when," usually with an impf verb following (*DCH,* 4:386b §5). Neither is the case here (יביט "looked" and יראה "beheld" are no doubt preterites rather than impfs).

24.c. יביט, like יראה, is a preterite, referring to a moment in the past; it is so translated by Moffatt, Dhorme, Tur-Sinai, Pope, Gordis, Habel. On the reason for not seeing a present tense here (as KJV, RSV, NAB, NJB, NIV, NJPS, NEB), cf. *Comment.*

24.d. Lit. "saw under all the heavens," but most understand the "all" (כל) to be logically the obj of the verb (contrast KJV "seeth under the whole heaven"). Cf. 41:11 (3). Beer (*BHK*), Gerleman (*BHS prp*), and Gray read כל תחת שמים "everything under the heavens."

25.a. לעשׂות, lit. "to make," as the purpose of God's scrutiny of the world. Some have suggested בַּעֲשׂתוֹ "when he made" (Budde, Ehrlich, Hölscher, Fohrer, Fedrizzi, de Wilde), as in v 26; this would make no difference to the general sense, but it would remove the idea of purpose. Less probable is an emendation to הָעֹשֶׂה "he who makes" (Duhm, Gray), for this is not hymnic language.

25.b. משקל "weight" is translated "counterpoise" by NEB, but the Heb. is not so specific and it is hard to see what image is invoked.

25.c. תכן is a pf, "he determined," which is anomalous compared with the inf לעשׂות "to make, give" in the first colon. Most translations harmonize the two verbs by making them both pfs; thus, e.g., RSV "he gave . . . meted out," NAB "weighed out . . . fixed," NIV "established . . . measured." But it is important syntactically to recognize that לעשׂות expresses the purpose or consequence of God's "looking" in v 24, so it would be better to translate both verbs as infs (so too Dhorme "to give . . . and to gauge"). Parallels to an inf followed by a finite verb are to be found at 29:3; 38:7; cf. GKC, §114r; Driver, *Tenses,* §§117, 118.

תכן is "regulate" (Driver–Gray), "mete out" (RSV), "apportion" (NRSV), "measure out" (NIV, NEB), "set the measure" (NJPS).

25.d. מִדָּה is an abstract, "measure, measurement, size" (*DCH,* 5:143a), not a concrete "[with a] gauge" (NJB) or "[with a] measure" (Dhorme).

26.a. Most understand חק as "decree" (KJV, RSV, NIV), "rule(s)" (NAB, NJPS), "law" (NJB), "ordinance" (Kissane), or "limit" (NEB, Gordis). Pope, however, takes it as "groove," thinking of the usual meaning of the root חקק "cut, inscribe," and the parallel with דרך "path" in the next colon. But "groove" is not attested elsewhere as a meaning of חק, and examples of the sense "limit, bound" that he gives are not relevant.

26.b. חזיז קלות is lit. "the lightning of the thunder" (KJV, RSV, Tur-Sinai), i.e., lightning, which is accompanied by thunder. Lightning has a path (דרך; the same phrase דרך לחזיז קלות in 38:25), though thunder does not, so it seems preferable to leave קלות out of the translation, as do several modern translations, with "thunderbolt" alone (so NRSV, NAB, REB, Gordis, Moffatt "lightning flash"). Cf. also *Note* 37:4.b. On the other hand, Dhorme thought חזיז was "rumble" (cf. Arab. *hazîz* [Wehr–Cowan, 1027a]), while KBL, 286a, takes it as "storm-cloud" and *HALOT,* 1:302a, as "blast, squall" (but then it is hard to see how it can understand חזיז קלות as "thunderbolt"). Among modern translations, NJB, Good (similarly Hölscher) have "thunderclap(s)," NIV, NJPS, NEB, Kissane, Rowley, Habel, Hartley "thunderstorm(s)," Pope "thundershowers," GNB "thunderclouds," Fohrer, de Wilde "stormclouds."

27.a. אז "then" temporal (BDB, 23a §1), not logical (§2); so, e.g., Whybray.

27.b. רָאָהּ "he saw it" is emended by Yellin (*apud* Gordis) to בְּרָאָהּ "he created it."

27.c. ספר piel "reckon, take account of" (see further, *Comment*), "appraise" (Dhorme, Pope, Habel, Hartley, NAB, NIV), "evaluate" (Larcher, BJ, NJB), "assess" (Whybray), "take stock" (NEB), "reckon" (Kissane, Andersen), perhaps "gauge" (NJPS), rather than "declare" (KJV, RSV; cf. Zorell, 559b) or "recount" (Driver–Gray), since it is hard to know who the audience for such a declaration might be (Terrien's "praises" is even more improbable). Peake suggested a naming of Wisdom in the sense of expressing its qualities. Duhm, followed by Strahan, Moffatt, Beer (*BHK*), NEB (Brockington), took the verb as a denominative from סֹפֵר "scribe," thus "studied" (reading the qal וַיִּסְפְּרָהּ). Tur-Sinai thought its sense here and at 38:37 was "make full, complete" but the resultant meaning is obscure. J. Reider ("Etymological Studies in Biblical Hebrew," *VT* 2 [1952] 113–30 [127]), not very convincingly, proposes a new ספר "probe," cognate with Aram. סבר "understand" (Jastrow, 951b) and Arab. *sabara* (Lane, 1293b), and found also perhaps at 38:37 (cf. *DCH,* vol. 6, *s.v.* ספר IV); he is apparently followed by Fohrer with *zahlen nach,* "check." Larcher reads the qal יִסְפֹּר "he evaluated."

27.d. כון hiph "establish" (as RSV); other versions have "confirmed" (NIV), "prepared" (KJV), "gave it its setting" (NAB), "organized" (Andersen). "Measured" (NJPS) is hard to justify. Whybray suggested that it was close in meaning to "create" (cf. Pss 65:9 [10]; 74:16; Prov 8:27). Duhm thought it was "set up as a model" for his creative works. Gordis translates "marked," arguing that כון hiph can mean "arrange, set in order" or "delimit, mark, measure out"; but while BDB, 466 §4, suggests a sense "arrange, order," the examples given, and cited by Gordis (2 Chr 29:19; 35:20), would easily fit under §2a "fix, make ready." And there is no justification for an extension from "arrange" to "delimit, mark." Hartley follows Gordis, but translates with even less good cause "discerned." De Wilde's "took her into his service as a counselor" is too speculative. Moffatt's "worked with her" is hard to understand.

Many are attracted by the variant reading הֱבִינָהּ "he discerned it," which has the advantage of making all four verbs concern intellectual activities. It is adopted by Dhorme, Hölscher, Larcher, Pope, Fedrizzi, Gray, NJB "looked her through and through," NEB "considered."

27.e. חקר is "search, explore, examine thoroughly," "know it through and through" (NAB), "probe" (NJPS), "prove" (Moffatt), or "fathom" (NEB, Andersen). Less appropriate are "assess" (NJB), "test" (NIV), and "dig out" (Good).

28.a. The verse is deleted by Beer (*BH*²), Dhorme as an inappropriate addition, wisdom elsewhere in the poem being personified metaphysical wisdom inaccessible to humans. Similarly Pope: the verse is "appended as an antidote to the agnostic tenor of the preceding poem." Kissane supposed there were words missing between "And he said to humans" and the final couplet. For the view that the verse is an integral element in the chapter, see *Comment.*

28.b. Tur-Sinai insists that אדם is here "Adam."

28.c. יראת אדני "the fear of the Lord" is in numerous MSS יראת יהוה "the fear of Yahweh." Some emend to יִרְאָתִי "my fear," i.e., "to fear me" (Beer [*BH*² *prps*]).

Form/Structure/Setting

The *structure* of the chapter is fairly plain, being marked out by the refrain that is repeated at vv 12 and 20, "Where shall wisdom be found?" (with a variation in v 20). The first section of the chapter is evidently vv 1–11, the depiction of mining as a human quest for what is desirable and precious. The refrain (v 12) then introduces the subject of wisdom, and the second section (vv 12–19) compares its value with that of precious objects. The refrain (v 20) reiterates the question how wisdom is to be attained, and the third section (vv 24–28) explains that wisdom is part of the natural order designed by God and divulged by him to humans.

Others have seen the refrains as the end, not the beginning, of the strophes in which they occur (JB, NJB, de Wilde, van der Lugt; see also the latter's "The Form and Function of the Refrains in Job 28: Some Comments Relating to the 'Strophic' Structure of Hebrew Poetry," in *The Structural Analysis of Biblical and Canaanite Poetry,* ed. W. van der Meer and J. C. de Moor, JSOTSup 74 [Sheffield: JSOT Press, 1988] 265–93) or as the beginning and (almost) the end of the strophe vv 12–22 (Murphy). Fohrer thought the refrain so determinative for the poem as a whole that he supposed it also occurred originally before v 1 and v 7.

The *strophic structure* is also quite straightforward, especially if the refrain is understood as marking new directions in the poem.

Part 1	strophe 1	vv 1–6	6 lines (vv 3, 4 tricola)
	strophe 2	vv 7–11	5 lines
Part 2	strophe 3	vv 12–14	3 lines (starting with refrain)
	strophe 4	vv 15–19	5 lines
Part 3	strophe 5	vv 20–22	3 lines (starting with refrain)
	strophe 6	vv 23–28	6 lines (including two words *extra metrum* in v 28)

Among the translations, RSV follows the same strophic divisions except that it has no break between vv 14 and 15. NIV shows only the three sections. NEB has no divisions, REB has the section breaks plus a break at the end of strophe 5.

Among the commentators, Terrien less plausibly recognizes the three strophes as vv 1–13 (with substrophes of vv 1–2, 3–4, 5–8, 9–13), vv 14–21 (with substrophes of vv 14–16, 17–19, 20–21), and vv 22–28 (with substrophes of vv 22–24, 25–27, 28). Fohrer has four completely regular strophes, vv 1–6 (seven lines, including the addition of the refrain at the beginning and the division of the apparent tricola vv 3–4 into three bicola), vv 7–11+24 (seven lines, including the addition of the refrain at the beginning of the strophe), vv 12–18 (seven lines, v 19 being omitted), and vv 20–27 (seven lines, v 28 being omitted). Van der Lugt identifies a total of fourteen couplets, arranged as four sections ("cantos"), vv 1–4, 5–12 (with two four-line strophes in vv 5–8, 9–12), 13–20 (with two four-line strophes in vv 13–16, 17–20), and 21–28 (with two four-line strophes in vv 21–24, 25–28). De Wilde, omitting vv 1–4 as extraneous, also finds couplets throughout, constituting sections of vv 5–12, 13–20, 21–28.

The *genre* of the chapter is often stated loosely as a *poem* (German *Lied*), sometimes as a *hymn* in praise of wisdom. These identifications, however, seem more determined by the prior decision that it is an independent poem than by its intrinsic characteristics. If indeed the chapter forms the conclusion to the Elihu material, as is argued in this commentary, it is more appropriate to refer to it as a *speech*. The elements of the speech are overwhelmingly didactic, so its genre is that of *instruction*—like much of the rest of the Elihu speeches (elements in chaps. 34 and 35, but principally in chaps. 36–37), it may be added. Perhaps even, to be more specific, we should say that the instruction takes the form of an *extended riddle* ("a statement [question or proposition] that is worded in such an ambiguous or intriguing way that it provides conjectural interpretation or solution" [Murphy, 181]). The classic examples of the riddle in the Hebrew Bible are those in the Samson story, the second riddle being at the same time the answer to the first (Judg 14:14, 18), but these are of course quite brief, one-line questions, with possible one-word answers. Here, on the other hand, the key riddling question, "Where shall wisdom be found?" (v 12, with variation in v 20), is a poetic couplet, and it does not admit of a direct answer. Moreover, the remainder of the chapter is not cast in the form of a riddle, though it sustains the overarching riddle about the location of wisdom. It is riddling discourse when the chapter opens with "Surely there is a mine for silver" (v 1), for what doubter is addressed by that "surely," and why are we hearing about mining in the topic sentence of the first paragraph or strophe when the chapter as a whole will be about something quite other? It is a riddle that for the first eleven verses of the chapter the primary subject matter is concealed. The riddle becomes a little narrative when in vv 14 and 23 the cosmic beings respond, and yet fail to respond, to the question about wisdom. And there is something of the riddle even in the concluding sentence, which should be the answer to the riddle; for "wisdom is the fear of the Lord" is a statement by no means immediately intelligible, a statement that needs unpacking, almost another riddle, like the wedding guests' reply in Judg 14:18.

Fohrer, on the other hand, denies that the question about wisdom is a riddle, viewing it rather as an element from the disputation speech of the wise (cf., e.g., Prov 23:29–30; Eccl 8:1). The distinction is perhaps needless, since riddling belongs not only to the portrayal of real-life situations like that of the Samson narratives, but also to the argumentative conversation of the sages. Other wisdom instruction elements also are evident in the chapter. We note the list-like notations of five materials found in the earth in vv 1–2, 6, which belong to what is called "educational wisdom" (*Bildungsweisheit*). Similar is the cumulative list of examples in vv 15–19, analogous to the priamel form in classical literature (cf. W. Kröhling, *Die Priamel [Beispielreihung] als Stilmittel in der griechisch-römischen Dichtung*, Greifswalder Beiträge zur Literatur- und Stilforschung 10 [Greifswald: Dallmeyer, 1935]; U. Schmid, *Die Priamel der Werte im Griechischen von Homer bis Paulus* [Wiesbaden: Harrassowitz, 1964]; W. H. Race, *The Classical Priamel from Homer to Boethius*, Mnemosyne Supplements 74 [Leiden: Brill, 1982]). The depictions in vv 3–5 and 9–11 of the tasks of the miners seem to be wisdom poems, building example upon example. The only material in the chapter that does not have its roots in the wisdom tradition is perhaps (so Fohrer) vv 25–26, the defining of the time of God's determining of wisdom, which has a *hymnic* cast.

The *function* of the chapter, viewed as the conclusion to Elihu's fourth speech, is to reinforce the general theme of Elihu's whole interposition in chapters 32–37+28, the fact of God's communication with humans. God is essentially the great Educator, whose aim it is to instill wisdom in his human creatures; this present chapter looks at that position from the standpoint of the humans, asking how they are to attain that wisdom, and what shape that wisdom will have for them. The previous section of the speech, 36:26–37:24, had come to an end with the couplet "Therefore mortals fear him, / and the wise in heart are afraid of him." This section returns us to the same thought, reiterating that the wise are those that "fear" God.

If the chapter is not seen as belonging to the Elihu material, it is not so easy to tell what its function may be. Whether it is a secondary intrusion into the present book of Job, or intentionally located here by the author, it is sometimes regarded as a "meditative interlude" (so Newsom). Some say it serves as preparation for the Yahweh speeches, some even that it weakens their impact. Given the exegesis presented in the *Comment*, where the stress lies on the accessibility of wisdom to humans, it seems rather that there is little to compare between chap. 28 and the Yahweh speeches, where the incapacity of humans to understand the nature of the universe is in the forefront.

The *tonality* of this part of the speech is extremely difficult to discuss, since there is no address to an audience (though it is presumably Job if the chapter is indeed the conclusion of Elihu's fourth speech), and the speaker says nothing of himself and his own feelings. There is not even a "we" that might include the speaker and the addressee or that might associate the speaker with humankind generally. These twenty-eight verses are perhaps the longest passage in the book that is completely externalized; we might compare in the Elihu speeches the seventeen verses of 33:14–30, the ten verses of 34:21–30, the eleven verses of 36:5–15, and the twenty-one verses of 36:26–37:13 (though there is an occasional "we" and a striking focus on the speaker in 37:1). It is argued, under *Form/Structure/Setting* on chaps. 36–37, that this fourth speech is generally supportive of Job, as Elihu's other speeches have been, and there is nothing countervailing in its conclusion in chap. 28. Indeed, since v 28 ("the fear of the Lord is wisdom"), though addressed by God to humankind generally, is also addressed by Elihu as the speaker to Job, it can be taken as a great compliment to Job and his way of life that Elihu has nothing to recommend to him apart from the very characteristics that we first learned about Job in 1:1, that he feared God and shunned evil.

The *nodal verse* is without doubt the final verse of the chapter, the divine disclosure to which the whole chapter has been moving. It is rare that it is the last sentence of a speech that should be identified as the key or nodal verse, but we have seen it before in the powerful chaps. 3 and 31, which inexorably build to a climax (cf. also 27:5–6 in the truncated ninth speech of Job and the nodal verses [vv 25–27] near the end in chap. 19). In Elihu's speeches the same structure has occurred at 33:32.

Comment

As the book of Job stands, this chapter forms the second part of the speech assigned to Job in chaps. 27–28. But we have seen good evidence for doubting that chap. 27 as a whole is Job's, and have assigned vv 7–23 (with the exception of vv 11–12) to Zophar as his final speech (see *Comment* on 27:7–13). Likewise, chap. 28 is almost universally denied to Job (though Budde, Janzen, and van der Lugt dissent, and Good suggests that it should be treated as Job's even if it was not originally intended as such), mainly because there is no conceivable reason why Job should suddenly launch into a didactic speech about wisdom. The consensus of scholarly opinion is that chap. 28 is an independent poem, not set in the mouth of any of the speakers of the book of Job.

It is another question whether the poem is to be attributed to the author of Job. Most think it is not, but there are some who are unwilling to deny the authorship of such a masterpiece to the poet. Some have suggested that it is from the author of Job but not designed for this place (Dhorme, Rowley), others that it was an earlier sketch by the author of Job on the Joban theme (Gordis), and others still that though it was written by the author of Job it was not he but a disciple who included it in the book of Job (Terrien). It is a question to which we can have no satisfactory answer, and in fact the question is of less importance than others that should be raised.

There are two pressing problems, neither of which is generally considered by commentators: (1) Why should there be a poem within the book that does not appear to be spoken by any of the interlocutors? (2) Why should there be a poem about the acquisition of wisdom in this book that is otherwise devoted to issues of suffering and justice?

(1) Habel has neatly categorized explanations for the presence of an unattributed poem within the book: critics have understood it, he says, as "an erratic intrusion, an inspired intermezzo, a superfluous prelude, [or] an orthodox afterthought." Hartley calls it a "bridge," Terrien a "musical interlude," Newsom a "meditative interlude." All these metaphors for the chapter deflect attention from the fact that it is a text within a context of nothing but speeches prefaced by very brief prose introductions to those speeches. Is it a speech, or is it not? And if it is a speech, whose is it? If it is not a speech and is not attributed to one of the characters in the book, we should call it, rather than anything else, an aberration.

(2) Why should the question "Where shall wisdom be found?" be raised at all in the book of Job? Who among the characters is wanting to know the answer, which of them is supposed to be able to benefit from the answer, and what in any case has the acquisition of wisdom to do with the quest of Job for justice or the endeavor of the friends to expound to him the doctrine of retribution?

To meet these difficulties (and others), a new proposal is made in this commentary, to regard the Elihu speeches (chaps. 32–37) as having been wrongly transposed from their original position before chap. 28. Originally, the theory is, when all three friends had finished speaking (at the end of chap. 27), Elihu then interposed his own contribution—in agreement with the preface to Elihu's speeches, which says that it was when the three friends ceased to answer Job that Elihu intervened, having waited to speak until they had finished because they were older than he (32:1–6). Elihu's four speeches would have concluded with chap. 28, and that would have been followed by Job's final speech in chaps. 29–31. Job's concluding declaration of innocence (chap. 31) and his summons to the Almighty to answer him (31:35) would have been followed immediately by the speeches of Yahweh from the tempest (chaps. 38–41).

This proposal of course meets the first problem noted above by assigning the chapter to one of the interlocutors in the book. It also connects the theme of wisdom with the speaker who is most engaged with that topic in the book (Elihu uses "wise" [חכם] or "wisdom" [חכמה] twelve of the twenty-eight times the terms occur in the whole book of Job). It is a major theme of Elihu that God is the Great Teacher, who has designed the world as an instrument of his communication with humankind. All along what he has been saying is that what Job needs, and what, by extension, humans generally need, is *understanding*—of God's purposes and intentions, of how the world is ordered. They need wisdom more than repentance, and it is wisdom that God offers to those who are willing to accept his instruction (e.g., 36:8–10). The last of Elihu's speeches as they now stand in the book concludes on a very similar note, with those who are wise among humans "fearing" the Almighty because of his power and justice (37:23–24). Job 28 then states again Elihu's underlying belief that while humans cannot know God completely (cf. 36:26; 37:23), they have it within their grasp to know all they need to know about the divine: God has told humans what wisdom is (v 28).

How could the disarrangement of the Elihu speeches have come about? We cannot know what the actual cause was, but it is helpful to recognize the kind of accident that could have befallen the text in the process of transmission. We could take as our model for a copy of Job the great Isaiah scroll from Qumran, written in columns on sheets of sheepskin, sewn together edge to edge to create the scroll. Each strip or sheet of skin contains either 3 or 4 columns of text, and columns are typically 29 lines long. There are 53.6 columns, each containing on average 316 words. Now if the book of Job were written on such a scroll, it would occupy about 26.6 columns. Chaps. 1–27 (5,001 words) would have taken just 16 columns (on 4 sheets of sheepskin with 4 columns each, or else on 4 sheets with 3 columns each plus 1 sheet with 4 columns), chaps. 32–37 (1,284 words) 4 columns, chaps. 28–31 (913 words) 3 columns, and chaps. 38–42 (1,146 words) 4 columns, the last being 0.6 full. If by accident the sheet containing the 4 columns of chaps. 32–37 were sewn in *after*, instead of *before*, the sheet with the 3 columns of chaps. 28–31, the result would be the book in the form we now have. We would have to suppose that this disarranged manuscript became the ancestor of the Masoretic text, and so perhaps that the accident happened at an early stage in the transmission of the text. We should also need to suppose that in our putative manuscript 3 sheets began with the first verses of chaps. 28, 32, and 38, respectively. For further details, see D. J. A. Clines, "Putting Elihu in His Place: A Proposal for the Relocation of Job 32–37," *JSOT* 29 (2004) 115–25.

1–6 This lyrical depiction of the mining of metals, in particular of copper, gives no hint of the theme of the poem as a whole, the quest for wisdom. The poet is deliberately transforming the thematic quest into a narrative quest, beginning the poem at great remove from its real subject and gradually approaching closer to the proper theme. Another sign of the narrative quest is the triple, cumulative, attempt to locate wisdom: at vv 13–14, humans do not know the way to wisdom, while the deep and the sea deny it is with them; at vv 21–22, it is furthermore unknown to all living beings, while Abaddon and Death, though acknowledging that they have heard of it, nevertheless do not know where it is; climactically, at v 23, God does know where the place of wisdom is, but that in itself still does not help humans to gain wisdom; only with the last verse of the poem, where, quite unexpectedly, God declares to humans what wisdom is, is the quest successful.

1–2 By artful indirection, the poet does not say at first what his theme in this poem will be, or even what he is inferring from the opening scene of the mining of various metals (it would spoil the mystery to insist that the poem originally began with the refrain found in vv 12, 20, as Fohrer); Andersen calls v 1a "an intriguing riddle in the true Wisdom mode." It will become evident later that mining is a prime example of the human quest for what is desirable and precious, and, secondly, that wisdom is even more desirable than any precious object. It is only when we are reading the poem for the second time that we realize that, while there is "indeed" (כי) a place for silver and the other valuable metals, there seems to be no place for wisdom, which is even more to be desired. Newsom notes how the language of v 1 points forward to v 12, where wisdom cannot be "found" (מצא is reminiscent of מוצא "mine" here, and מקום is "place" of understanding there and of gold here).

This is the only depiction of mining in the Hebrew Bible, and much of the language is obscure. The mining of the four metals, silver, gold, iron, copper, is briefly described, each in its own colon. The focus in each case may be upon the mining itself, the "mine" for silver in v 1a, the "place" for gold, which will later be refined (v 1b), and the "taking" of iron from the earth (v 2a) and of the rock that will later be smelted (v 2b). Most translations, however, think the first colon in each of the first two lines refers to mining and the second to smelting, rendering "a place where gold is refined" (e.g., NIV) and "copper is smelted from ore." If that is so, the two cola are, as Gordis notes, in complementary parallelism: it is not that whereas silver and iron are mined, gold and copper are smelted; rather, all four metals are mined, and all four metals are smelted.

Silver precedes gold, as usual in the Hebrew Bible; strangely enough, however, in all the other cases in Job gold precedes silver (3:15; 22:25 [בצר]; 28:15 [סגור]). On this issue, see R. Kessler, "Silber und Gold, Gold und Silber: Zur Wertschätzung der Edelmetalle im Alten Israel," *BN* 31 (1986) 57–69.

Though the land of Canaan was said to be rich in iron and copper (cf. Deut 8:9), the West Bank was relatively poor in minerals, and many were imported into Israel. Iron ore existed in the plateau of Transjordan, and copper was mined in Edom. Asia Minor and Spain (cf. Jer 10:9; Ezek 27:12) were sources of silver, Nubia and South Arabia of gold. Copper is found in copper ore, here called "stone" (אבן is here not a piece of stone but stone as naturally occurring; see *DCH,* 1:110b). Such ore typically in the western Sinai and the Wadi Arabah contained about 10 percent, or in very rich seams as much as 40 percent, of copper and would be smelted in crucibles to extract the metal. With the addition of a small amount of tin, copper could be hardened to bronze. On the practice of mining and smelting, see the *Bibliography* at the beginning of the chapter.

3 It is almost as if the poet is deliberately using the most cryptic language imaginable, while the reader feels caught up in an elaborate riddle: "An end one (or, he) set to darkness, and to every extreme he searches stone of (or, in) gloom and deep shadow." What can this be about? Since we have just been reading of the mining of metals, and since in vv 7–8 we shall hear of a path that is unknown to animals, most interpreters suppose that we are reading here about the work of underground miners, though no subject for the verbs "set" and "seeks" is mentioned, and there is nothing to confirm that the darkness is because the scene is set below ground. Presumably it is the miners who "set an end to darkness" by opening up shafts in the earth, though at the same time their quest for the minerals seems to be carried out "in deep darkness" (or perhaps, what they are looking for is "ore" that has hitherto been *hidden* in darkness). The poet seems to be matching the mysteriousness of the quest with a mysteriousness of language. He does not want to mention the miners specifically (everything in vv 1–3 is grammatically passive or indefinite), since his theme is not the miners and their courage, nor the human ingenuity that discovers hidden treasure, but rather the fact that precious materials, though hidden—underground, in darkness, remote, dangerous of access, without any path to them—can be obtained by humans. Though the poet says nothing about wisdom here, the second-time reader recognizes that, by contrast, wisdom appears to be even more inaccessible.

Some of the language here is very heightened and might seem more appropriate for divine activity. Is setting an end to darkness and searching to the furthest limit something we would expect of humans, or not rather of God? See also on vv 5, 9–11; and cf. C. Baldauf, "Menschliches Können und göttliche Weisheit in Hiob 28," *TVers* 13 (1983) 57–68 (60–62). Tur-Sinai, following the Targumic tradition and Rashi, indeed thinks that vv 3–11 are all about divine activity, but he is then at a loss to explain how vv 1–2, which are clearly about mining, can be connected with what follows (he concludes, lamely, that something must be missing between v 2 and v 3). The point remains, however, and it may well be that the poet is describing the heroic task of underground mining in terms more appropriate to divine feats.

"Putting an end to darkness" sounds like what God does when he calls up the dawn (38:12), knowing as he does the way to the home of light (38:19). All it can mean of the underground miners is that they dispel darkness by bringing a feeble light into the darkness of the bowels of the earth, both by the opening up of their mining shafts (Driver–Gray, Rowley) and by their lamps. Miners' lamps, which they bind to their foreheads, are mentioned in the first century B.C.E. by Diodorus Siculus in his account of gold mining in Nubia (3.12.6). Ovid too (*Metamorphoses* 1.137–40) writes of the achievement of human civilization in not only learning to farm the soil but also delving below it, into the bowels of the earth, bringing to light the wealth that the creator had hidden deep in darkness.

Searching to the furthest bound also sounds quite cosmological: it is God who has set the limit or boundary (תכלית) between light and darkness (26:10), while the "limit" of the Almighty is elsewhere something that cannot be found by humans (11:7). The word תכלית itself does not have a theological sense (it is used in Neh 3:21 of the "end" of a house, and in Ps 139:22 of the "extreme" of hatred), but in combination with "searching" (חקר) it sounds very much like God's primeval overview of the universe (v 24) and his "searching out" of wisdom (28:27). Nevertheless, as far as we can tell, here it is more prosaic: it is the furthest limit to which the miner digs. And yet, from the viewpoint of the poet, this is an almost superhuman achievement and not at all prosaic. What is more, the miners operate at the boundary between earth and underworld, between light and darkness, between life and death; their quest "is fraught with both power and danger" (Newsom).

4 The mining is apparently done by foreign workers. The use of foreign slaves and prisoners of war was common in antiquity for such dangerous occupations as mining (cf. R. J. Forbes, *Studies in Ancient Technology* [Leiden: Brill, 1963] 7:223–32). For slaves as construction workers, cf. 2 Chr 2:18 (17).

If the Hebrew is correctly translated, the picture is of miners hanging by ropes (or perhaps baskets or cages, as Pope) as they descend shafts. A sense of the danger to which they expose themselves becomes explicit in Shakespeare's lines about gatherers of samphire (sea fennel) on sea cliffs: "half way down / Hangs one that gathers samphire, dreadful trade!" (*King Lear* 6.6.21–22).

5 The natural assumption is that the account of mining continues. While on the surface of the earth the well-known observable rhythms of the seasons ensure the steady production of crops, underneath all is secretly in turmoil if there are miners at work. The emphasis is not on the contrast between the seen and the unseen, or between the upper and the lower, but rather more on the surprising truth about what may be going on underneath the ground unbeknown to most humans.

The key word is "changed" (הפך niphal). While in the active (qal) the verb often means "overthrow, devastate" as well as "turn, change," in the passive (niphal), as here, it typically means "be changed, transformed," and only in Jonah 3:4, where there is wordplay on the two senses "change" and "overturn," does it mean "overthrow." Underneath the earth "it is changed, or, transformed, as [by] fire." The Hebrew says it is changed "like" (כמו) fire, but since it is hard to say how fire itself is changed, it is better to think that what is below the surface is changed "as if" by fire. The main change that fire creates is to reduce much to little, so perhaps we should think of the underground change as being the burning up or burning away of the earth, the transformation of the solid earth into a warren of interconnecting tunnels and shafts, as if it had been ravaged by fire. Once again, the language could easily be mistaken for that of divine activity: elsewhere it is God who "overthrows" (הפך) cities (Gen 19:25; Deut 29:23 [22]; Jer 20:16) and kingdoms (Hag 2:22) and mountains (Job 9:5)—which is how the poet has designed his depiction of the miners (cf. also on vv 3, 9–11).

Some have interpreted the text to mean that the earth is not changed "like" fire or "as if by" fire, but actually "by" fire, thinking either of underground blasting and explosions (heating the rock by fire and then pouring water on it; cf. Pliny, *Natural History* 33.21.71; M. Löhr, "Job 28, 5," *OLZ* 19 [1916] 178–79; Peake, Hölscher, Hartley), or else of the rocks as themselves produced by fire (cf. Pope), perhaps by volcanoes (Habel); cf. "stones of fire" (אבני־אש) in Ezek 28:14. As against this suggestion, de Wilde rightly observes that in the mining locations known to the author of Job, the use of fire to break open the rocks is unlikely, given the scarcity of wood (he says that ninety kilograms of wood are needed to produce one kilogram of copper).

The phrase "bring forth food from the earth" is used also in Ps 104:14, but there seems to be no literary connection (cf. also Isa 55:10; and the Homeric phrases, "the grain-giving plow land" [*Iliad* 8.486; *Odyssey* 3.3] and "the wheat-yielding plow land" [*Iliad* 12.314; 14.123]). In general, mining was carried out in the ancient world in remote locations, far from human habitation, so the image of the surface of the earth yielding food and the depths of the earth yielding minerals is perhaps a little forced.

6 The connection of this verse with the preceding is hard to grasp. V 5 seems to have been about mining in general, so why does the poet fasten now in v 6 specifically on lapis lazuli as a product of mining? Perhaps it is that mining uncovers not only the valuable metals of vv 1–2, but also precious gems and stones, lapis being chosen as one example. Certainly, "its rocks," i.e., the rocks of the earth, are the "source" (מקום, lit. "place," as in v 1) of lapis, the semiprecious blue stone flecked or spangled with particles of iron pyrites that glitter like gold and must often have been mistaken for it ("fool's gold"); it is referred to in ancient times by Theophrastus, *De lapide* 31, and Pliny, *Natural History* 37.39.120. Lapis was used for jewelry and in the ornamentation of manufactured objects; see further A. Hermann, "Edelsteine," *RAC* 4 (1959) cols. 505–52.

7–11 If vv 1–6 have been about the human quest for what is precious (the unspoken word "wisdom" lies in the background), vv 7–11 will concern the making or finding of a *path* to what is precious (only as late as v 23 will we hear of a path to *wisdom*).

7 Nothing has been said previously about a path, so translations such as "that path no bird of prey knows" (RSV), apparently referring back to something already mentioned, are inappropriate, and we should rather translate "There is a path that no bird of prey knows." As its initial position shows, the word "path" (נתיב) announces a new subject. This path to which we must now attend is not the path to the distant mines (against Dhorme, Pope, Gordis); still less is it the path to wisdom (Duhm, Peake, Strahan), which has not yet been mentioned. It is the underground path bored out by miners, and unknown to every other living creature but themselves (similarly Habel).

Falcons are renowned for their keen sight; cf. *b. Hullin* 63b. The point is not to assert the superiority of human insight to that of birds (as Terrien, Hartley), since the wisdom of birds and certain beasts proverbially outstrips humans' (this perspective recurs in Elihu's speeches, at 35:11), but to emphasize the hiddenness of this activity, even from the famed sight of the falcon (it is hidden even from the generality of humankind). The theme remains that of the effort that humans will devote to locating and uncovering what is precious.

8 The presumption is that the wild animals, in their wisdom, will know every path on the face of the earth; but this underground path is one they do not know, since it is beneath the earth, hidden from all.

9 Continuing the theme of the making of a path to what is precious, vv 9–11 depict the miners opening up tunnels in the mountainside; while v 4 seems to concern vertical shafts (נחל), here we seem rather to find horizontal "galleries" (יאר) (as NEB). Though no subject of the verbs in these verses is mentioned, they are plainly the same persons as those who "seek the ore" in v 3. It is misleading to state the subject as "man" (as RSV, NJB, NIV, NJPS, NEB, Dhorme, Gordis, Hartley), since the focus is not upon humankind and its accomplishments, but solely upon one specific group of humans. It is true that they stand for humanity at large as an extreme example of human determination to discover what is precious, but within the cameo of vv 9–11 they are nothing but miners.

These miners address themselves, as Gray notes, to the hardest of stones, flint (חלמש), and to the largest mass of stones, mountains (הרים). They "put forth their hand" (שלח יד) against the flinty rock, a phrase that suggests an aggressive act (cf. 1:11; Gen 37:22; Exod 3:20; Ps 55:20 [21]; Esth 2:21), as if the stone were an enemy from which the minerals are wrested (cf. NIV, Hartley "assaults," NJB "attacks," Good "forces his hand into the flint"). The language here is heightened, but the language of the next clause is even more extreme: it is almost mythological, representing the miners as "overturning" (הפך) mountains, which in 9:5 is evidently a divine activity (on the verb, cf. also on v 5). Boring a tunnel in a mountain may not seem much like "overturning" it, but it is apparently viewed as a kind of denaturing of it. It is not the first place in this chapter where the labors of the miners are depicted as superhuman and even godlike (cf. vv 3, 5). Once again, the underlying theme is not "the achievements of man" (as Rowley), but the lengths humans will go to in their quest for what they regard as desirable.

The שרש "roots" of mountains are heard of nowhere else; the nearest parallel is the reference in Jonah 2:6 (7) to the "(lower) extremities (קצב) of the mountains"; cf. also Job 36:30 (also Elihu's!) where mention is made of the "roots of the sea." The more usual phrase is the "foundation" (מוסד) of the mountains (Deut 32:22; Ps 18:7 [8]), of the earth (Mic 6:2; Isa 24:18; 40:21; Jer 31:37; Ps 82:5; Prov 8:29), or of the world (2 Sam 22:16 || Ps 18:15 [16]). To strike at the roots of a mountain is to touch it "at the point where it is firmly rooted in the ground" (Dhorme), and so to call its being into question.

10 "Splitting open" (בקע) the earth is another activity we might naturally ascribe to the deity, who elsewhere is said to have "split the earth with rivers" (Hab 3:9) and "split open springs and rivers" (Ps 74:15), the same verb being used. Humans, as represented by these dedicated miners, go to heroic and almost superhuman extremes in the quest for what is "precious" (יקר).

Though there is no other place where the term יאר "channel" is not a water-course (it usually refers to the channels of the Nile), it is improbable that it is such here (despite Gordis: "the miner needs to hew out a channel to wash away some rocks that impede his work"). For it makes better sense for the miner to be on the lookout for "any precious object" while he is involved in his major activity of cutting out the mining gallery than when he is engaged in the merely house-keeping role of tidying a drainage channel. Some have thought that the "channels" were cut in the mine to carry off the excess water (cf. Driver–Gray, Rowley), or to dam up a flow of water that prevented access to the desired minerals (Gordis), but it is more likely that the reference is simply to the underground origins of springs and rivers.

11 Here too the language verges on the mythological, for in Canaanite literature it is traditional to speak of the dwelling of the high god El as lying "at the sources of the two rivers" (*mbk nhrm*, equivalent to מבכי נהרות "the sources of the rivers" here); see *Baal* II.iv.21 = *KTU* 1.4.IV.21 (*CML*, 97a; *CML*², 59). It used to be said that the miners were defending themselves against the danger of a flooded mine (RSV "he binds up the streams so that they do not trickle"), but most now accept that the verb is "explore" (חבשׂ) rather than "bind" (חבשׁ) and that it is a matter of exploring "sources" (מבך) of streams rather than preventing the mine "from weeping, trickling" (מבכי); see further *Notes* 11.b, c.

The sources of rivers naturally lie underground, and while the miners have little interest in exploring them for their own sake, their subterranean activity inevitably leads them to such hidden phenomena.

Vv 10a and 11a are parallel in thought, and so are vv 10b and 11b; but to suppose that they have been mistakenly transposed (as Duhm, Strahan, Moffatt) is "an exaggerated concern for symmetry" (Dhorme; cf. Gordis).

The last colon, "bringing to light what has been hidden," again has mythological overtones, for that is a divine work in 12:22 (cf. Newsom). The phrase registers the success of the miners' work, but it should not be thought that its language is the key to the whole description of the mining activity. An ending is not necessarily a conclusion, and we should not infer that the strophe means "All hidden material things man can bring to light, but not Wisdom, the light of the world" (so Gordis). The tendency of the poem up to this point has rather been the human quest for what is precious, and the extremes to which the miners' desire drives them. In the next strophe wisdom will be explicitly mentioned for the first time, and the question will be raised how this most precious of all objects can be attained. Dhorme's remark is also somewhat beside the point: "Nothing that is hidden escapes man's eye. And yet he does not find Wisdom (v. 12)!" For v 11 does not concern humankind in general, but only miners in their underground workings; and it is not surprising that they do not find Wisdom, since that is not what they seek.

12–19 At last we learn what the real subject of the poem is: it is not about mining at all (despite vv 1–11), but about wisdom! Readers have been wondering what the purpose of this marvelous depiction of underground searches is. Now we learn that what wisdom has in common with precious stones and valuable minerals is its desirability (for the explicit language of desire, cf. Prov 3:15). Everyone wants wisdom, but how can they acquire it?

Given the analogy with the valuable objects that are mined, one answer could be, Go and find it. Another could be, since it is a precious thing, Go and buy it. These are no more than metaphors for the quest for wisdom, and so they have much in common, even though the languages appropriate to finding and to buying are quite distinct. When the poet thinks of "finding" wisdom, he invents for vv 13–14 a little narrative (reminiscent perhaps of Elihu's narrative in 33:15–28), perhaps following up on the logic of the rhetorical question, Where is wisdom to be found? For the rhetorical question sounds like a real question, with a person asking and a person replying. The poet does not specify who the person asking might be (for it could be any human), but he does imagine who might reply. Obviously, it must be some superhuman being or entity, since (v 13) humans themselves do not seem to know the answer (by the time we reach v 28, however, we will know that there was something faulty with the questions). Since the answer is mysterious or hidden, the questioner should ask beings that are famous for concealment: the ocean deep or the sea (v 14), or Abaddon and Death (v 22).

The other question, How can wisdom be bought?, is being answered in vv 15–19. Here the poet does not develop a little narrative (except perhaps for the matter of "mentioning" precious objects alongside it, in v 18). Rather, the question is answered by cataloguing numerous valuable items and affirming that none of them could possibly pay for wisdom (vv 15–19).

12 The poet launches us on an intriguing and tantalizing quest for wisdom. There is a playful and riddling misdirection in this quest, and a deliberate withholding of the knowledge the poet most wants to convey until the very end of the poem (v 28).

The first intriguing element in this strophe is: who is being asked the question, "Where shall wisdom be found?" It is not said. Two verses later, the Deep and the Sea reply (v 14), so we must infer that they are among those who have been asked. That then makes us think that the reason why we are hearing in v 13 about humans not knowing the way to it is because they too have been asked. It sounds as if the speaker, or the poet, has sent out a general enquiry through the length and breadth of creation to get an answer to his question.

But the answers he gets, at this point, are no answers: humans do not know, and the Deep and the Sea say that the secret of its location is not in their keeping. At vv 20–22 the question will be repeated, and there will be some little progress in reaching an answer: on the negative side, it is not just humans, but also all living creatures, from whom the answer is hidden (v 21); on the positive side, while Abaddon and Death do not know the answer themselves, they have at least heard a report of it (v 22). The whole poem is structured around deliberate reticence and a slow unveiling of the truth.

But there is more than one tease in all of this. First, the question, "Where shall wisdom be found?," sounds like a rhetorical question expecting the answer "Nowhere." We are being set up to expect to learn that wisdom is beyond human acquisition (only in the last verse of the whole chapter will we find that the opposite is the case, and even as late as v 23 it sounds as if God alone knows the answer). Secondly, asking where wisdom may be *found* and what is its *place* seems intended to mislead us, since wisdom plainly does not have a "place" in the way that precious minerals and gems have a place or find-spot. So when the Deep and the Sea say that wisdom is not with them, we are at a loss to know what they really mean. Do they mean that, though wisdom is located somewhere or other, they are the wrong place to be looking for it, or that looking for wisdom in *any* place is the wrong way to go about things? Even when it is said that God knows its "place" and the "way to it" (v 23), we cannot be meant to take that literally; for when he comes to tell humans what wisdom is (v 28) he drops the language of "place" and location and does not suggest that humans must go somewhere to find wisdom. Thirdly, to say that wisdom cannot be found in the land of the living misleads an innocent reader (Andersen even says that as generally understood it is "palpably untrue"). For wisdom as defined in v 28 is well known among humans, Job himself being a signal example of it, though by no means unique.

Wisdom (חכמה) and understanding (בינה) are paralleled also at Prov 1:2; 4:5, 7; 9:10; 16:16; Isa 11:2, and the terms always occur in this order. As M. V. Fox points out ("Words for Wisdom," *ZAH* 6 [1993] 149–69 [154]), חכמה, "wisdom," is a very general word for all kinds of know-how, while בינה, "understanding" or "insight," refers much more specifically to intellectual discernment. Newsom interprets the combination of the two terms as suggesting "the kind of understanding that would provide insight into the nature and meaning of the entire cosmos." And yet at v 12, as also at v 20, the reader is still left very much in the dark about what the wisdom may be that is being sought, the plot of the quest and its very language creating further mystification. In the end, the wisdom of chap. 28 is far less grand and far more banal than the drama of the poem may have suggested: wisdom turns out to be no more cosmic in its scope than appropriate fear of the deity and the avoidance of wrongdoing (v 28). It remains uncertain whether any distinction is intended between "wisdom" and "understanding," especially since "understanding" drops out of view entirely except for the refrain (v 20) and the concluding aphorism (v 28).

13 According to the Masoretic text, the strange response to "Where shall wisdom be found?" is that "Humans do not know its worth, or, value (ערכה)," as in KJV, NIV, NJPS. It is true that vv 15–19 will concern the value of wisdom compared with other precious objects, but as it stands v 13a does not make sense as a reply to the "where?" questions of v 12, nor is it parallel to the second half of v 13, which is a statement about where wisdom is not to be *found.* It is therefore necessary to accept, with most translations and commentators, an emendation to דַּרְכָּהּ "its way," i.e., the way to wisdom (see further, *Note* 13.a).

The phrase "the land of the living" occurs elsewhere at Isa 38:11; 53:8; Ezek 26:20; 32:23, 24, 25, 26, 27, 32; Jer 11:19; Pss 27:13; 52:5 (7); 116:9; 142:5 (6), but usually it means "among living humans" as distinct from the netherworld, the realm of the dead. Here, however, there does not appear to be an overtone of life versus death; the contrast seems to be between the world of humans and the inanimate world (the Deep and the Sea), elements of which, nevertheless, speak like animate beings (cf. also the underworld entities Abaddon and Death in v 22).

14 The Deep and the Sea are, exceptionally for the Hebrew Bible, personified. The ocean deep (תהום) is synonymous with the sea (ים); but the first term is especially used of the primeval abyss (as in Gen 1:2; 7:11; 49:25). The parallelism of the two terms (in the reverse order) is found also at 38:16. In ancient mythology the sea is a divine power; it is even one of the oldest entities in the world order (Prov 8:24, 28). But yet, says the poet, it has no special knowledge about wisdom and its acquisition. See also C. Westermann, *TDOT,* 3:1410–14.

Tur-Sinai saw here the style of a discovery legend in which a hero searches for hidden wisdom, traveling from one presumed authority to another. The antiquity of those who are asked for their advice is a significant feature, since in such tales extreme old age is correlated with wisdom (cf. also 36:26).

15–19 The train of thought now moves in another direction from the question of where wisdom may be found. To acquire wisdom is highly desirable, all agree. If we do not know where we may go to find it in its native habitat, may we then purchase it, as we can purchase other precious objects? A whole catalogue of valuable minerals (gold, silver), precious gemstones (cornelian, lapis lazuli, rubies, topaz), costly natural products (coral, rock crystal), and an expensive manufacture (glass) is reviewed, and every item, no matter how costly, is declared to be unequal to wisdom in value. Even though we cannot be sure that we have correctly identified all the items, the point of this encomium to wisdom (Fedrizzi) is not in doubt.

There is nothing dreary about this catalogue (known by the literary term, a "tour," of which it is a splendid ten-line example; cf. Watson, 249–50). Newsom observes the delight with which the poet rings the changes on five different words for gold, "a connoisseur's familiarity with rarities among rarities," and sees in the lengthy enumeration of precious items "a sensuous quality that suggests all the fabled riches coming from widely differing places in the world." Fedrizzi senses a dreamlike and surreal atmosphere; Whybray, a "kaleidoscopic series of changing images." Even the variety of terms for bartering and buying—"given" and "weighed out" (v 15), "valued" (v 16), "equaled" and "exchange" (v 17), "equaled" and "valued" (v 19)—conjures up the bustle of an eastern market (Ravasi is reminded of the bazaars of the Arabian Nights, Whybray of Aladdin's cave of treasures), while the tolling of the unvaried monosyllable "not" (לא) with which each line of vv 15–19 begins (though it is the third word of v 18) brings home the impossibility of finding a price for wisdom. We should not disregard the dazzling array of colors, from the reddish cornelian and the blue lapis lazuli to the red coral and the pale green olivine (peridot) and the varieties of glass, with gold and silver—all the more striking in a world where manufactured colors were rare.

Wisdom is in Proverbs several times compared with precious objects such as silver and gold and jewels; it is more valuable than such desirable goods (3:14–15; 16:16), and—in an unembarrassed adoption of the language of the marketplace—it is said to be the commodity one should "buy" and not "sell" (23:23). But never in Proverbs is the *impossibility* of buying wisdom with silver and gold a theme, as it is here (though a "fool" is said to have in his hand the price of wisdom, 17:16).

15 We are reading here not of the acquisition of gold and silver by mining (as in v 1), but of the use of them in purchase. Strictly, the gold is being thought of as exchanged for wisdom (נתן תחת, lit. "give in exchange"), while the silver is "weighed" (שקל *šāqal*)—normally against a standard shekel weight, about 11.5 grams (see H. Hamburger, "Money," *IDB,* 3:423–24).

16 Ophir is today usually identified with the land known to the Egyptians as Punt, somewhere in the region of Somalia (G. W. van Beek, *IDB,* 1:605–6; cf. D. W. Baker, *ABD,* 5:26–27). It is referred to on several occasions as a source of fine gold (e.g., 1 Chr 29:4; 2 Chr 8:18), as well as of spices, precious stones, and monkeys (1 Kgs 9:28; 10:11 || 2 Chr 8:18; 9:10). Gold of Ophir is mentioned also on an ostracon from Tell Qasileh, and in two Qumran texts, the *War Scroll* (4QM[a] frag. 11.1.18) and *Songs of the Sabbath Sacrifice* (4Q400 23.2.9; cf. *DCH,* 1:156b). In 22:24 "Ophir" alone meant "gold of Ophir."

The stone שהם (*šōham*) has frequently been identified as onyx, a precious stone with alternating bands of white and black, or perhaps rather cornelian, a reddish chalcedony (see further, *Note* 16.c), which is noted at Gen 2:11–12 as originating from the land of Havilah, perhaps understood as located on the west coast of Arabia; at Exod 25:7; 28:9, 20; 35:9, 27; 39:6, 13 it is one of the precious stones in the ephod and the breastplate of the high priest; at 1 Chr 29:2 it is used for ornamentation in Solomon's temple.

17 Glass (זכוכית), often colored, was in pre-Roman times a very expensive material, equivalent in value to precious stones and used as jewelry or for inlays, not as a container; it was perhaps manufactured in imitation of naturally occurring precious stones (de Wilde). On ancient glass, see especially R. J. Forbes, "Glass," in his *Studies in Ancient Technology* (Leiden: Brill, 1957) 5:110–231.

18 "Coral" (ראמות) apparently refers to the red coral of the Mediterranean and the Red Sea, which was used in jewelry. In Ezek 27:16 it is traded by the Edomites with Tyre. The second colon, "a pouch of wisdom fetches more than rubies," looks like a proverbial sentence that had an earlier existence within wisdom teaching and outside this present list of precious objects. Wisdom comes in pouches no more than it is found in mines, but for the general idea, cf. Prov 3:15; 8:11.

19 Cush (כוּשׁ) is an ancient name of Ethiopia; ancient Ethiopia usually coincides rather with the modern state of Sudan than with modern Ethiopia, but here the area would seem to include all the region south of Egypt as far as the Red Sea. The gem called פטדה, traditionally translated "topaz," is probably what is known now as peridot (the term is probably derived from *faridat,* the Arabic equivalent of פטדה), also called chrysolite, a variety of olivine, a greenish gem. Since ancient times it has been mined principally on the island of Zabargad (St. John's Island) in the Red Sea, known to the Greeks as Topazos, Topaz Island. Cf. Pliny, *Natural History* 37.8.32.107–8.

21 The phrase "every living thing" (כל חי) can apply to humans and beasts (as 12:10; Gen 8:21; Ps 145:16), to humans alone (as 30:23; Gen 3:20; Ps 143:2; Eccl 4:15; 9:4), to beasts and birds alone (Gen 6:19), and here, apparently, to beasts as distinct from birds (Dhorme). Others however think the reference here is to both beasts and humans (Kissane, Tur-Sinai, Rowley, Newsom), or to humans alone (Fohrer, Andersen). Cf. also H. Ringgren, *TDOT,* 4:324–44 (322). On the term "all flesh," see *Comment* on 34:15. For the knowledge of birds in virtue of their sharp eyesight and lofty flight (but probably not their supposed powers of divination, as Strahan), cf. also v 7; 35:11.

On the theme of divine wisdom being hidden from humans, cf. Bar 3:15–35; *1 En.* 42:1–2. See also O. H. Steck, "Israels Gott statt anderer Götter—Israels Gesetz statt fremder Weisheit: Beobachtungen zur Rezeption von Hi 28 in Bar 3,9–4,4," in *'Wer ist wie du, HERR, unter den Göttern?'* FS O. Kaiser, ed. I. Kottsieper, J. van Oorschot, D. Römheld, and H. M. Wahl (Göttingen: Vandenhoeck & Ruprecht, 1994) 457–71.

22 Abaddon (אבדון) is another name for Sheol; see *Comment* on 26:6. The phrase "we have heard of it with our ears" occurs also at 2 Sam 7:22; Ps 44:1 (2); cf. Job's phrase "I heard with the hearing of the ear" (42:5). The phrase seems to suggest secondhand, hearsay evidence (Pope).

It is hard to know why Abaddon and Death should have more knowledge of the location of wisdom, slight though that may be, than do the Deep and the Sea, but the sense that "There must be wisdom with great Death" (Alfred Lord Tennyson, *In Memoriam* 51) is unsurprising. Perhaps it is because humans are to be found in the underworld rather than in the oceans (Gordis suggests that it depends on a belief that humans gain deeper wisdom on the threshold of death).

23–28 The whole of this passage is one carefully constructed unit, vv 24–27 being a single sentence that brings the whole poem to a stunning climax—or almost so, since v 28 will upset all notions of climaxes. The complex syntactic connection of the verses can be analyzed thus: God knows what is wisdom for humans (v 23), because (כי), at creation, he comprehended the whole created order (יביט "looked" and יראה "saw," past-tense verbs [preterites] in reference to single actions) (v 24) in order (for example) to assign (לעשׂות) a weight to the wind (while, at the same time, he measured [תכן] the waters) (v 25), that is, at the time when he made (בעשׂתו) a decree for the rain and a way for the thunderbolt (v 26), then (אז), at that time, he did four things with this wisdom for humans (ראה "saw," ספר piel "appraised," כון "established" [or בין "discerned"; see *Note* 27.d], and חקר "knew to its limits") (v 27), and, subsequently, once there were humans to address, told humans what this wisdom was (v 28). In short, *when* he created the universe, *then* he determined the nature of wisdom. Its character is therefore ingrained in the fabric of the world, its reality is as fixed as a law of nature.

There is a sense of grandeur conveyed by this extended sentence. Newsom perceptively compares the beginning of the Babylonian creation myth *Enuma Elish,* "When on high the heaven had not been named . . . when no gods had been brought into being . . . then the gods were formed within [the waters of Apsu and Tiamat]." And similarly the Hebrew creation story of Gen 2 begins, "In the day that the LORD God made the earth and the heavens, when no plant of the field was yet in the earth and no herb of the field had yet sprung up . . . then the LORD God formed man from the dust of the ground" (Gen 2:4–7 NRSV). And likewise the autobiography of wisdom in Prov 8:22–31: "When there were no depths I was brought forth . . . when he assigned to the sea its limit . . . when he marked out the foundations of the earth, then I was beside him" (NRSV). No claims for literary dependence of one text upon another need be made; the sublime subject of the founding of the world calls forth in each case a dignified and stately sentence.

Wisdom is here, unlike in Prov 8, neither personified nor hypostatized (against Hölscher, Fohrer, P. A. H. de Boer, "The Counsellor," in *Wisdom in Israel and in the Ancient Near East,* FS H. H. Rowley, ed. M. Noth and D. W. Thomas, VTSup 3 [Leiden: Brill, 1955] 42–71 [68–69], S. Schroer, "Weise Frauen und Ratgeberinnen in Israel: Literarische und historische Vorbilder der personifizierten Chokmah," *BN* 51 [1990] 41–60 [48]). It is not implied that the wisdom here being spoken of is divine wisdom, or, as some would have it, the wisdom by which God created the world: all that is said is that God knows how wisdom is to be accessed (v 23), and that he defined its nature as long ago as the days of creation (vv 24–27).

23 Even so late in the poem, it is still being implied that wisdom is not accessible to humans and that God alone knows it. It is even being assumed, since God knows the "way" to wisdom and its "place," that wisdom *does* have a location. The "misdirection" of the poem is still in force; but the concluding verse (v 28) will show that all these presumptions are incorrect.

24 When does God's looking to the ends of the earth take place? The opening word of the next verse, לעשׂות "so as to make," i.e., "assign, a weight for the wind," as also the opening word of v 26, "when he made" (בעשׂתו), shows clearly that we are hearing not of a repeated action (as suggested by most modern translations; see *Note* 25.a) but of the time of creation, when the norms of the created phenomena were determined. So it is God's primeval scrutiny of the cosmic totality that is referred to here, and the verbs must be translated in the past tense, "looked . . . beheld" (so too Pope, Tur-Sinai, Gordis, Habel). This looking was not, however, a search for wisdom (as Gordis), or in order to allocate a place for it (as Tur-Sinai).

25–26 On the basis of perfect knowledge of the whole universe (v 24), God exercises complete control over it. Even the phenomena of nature, apparently so haphazard in their operations, are subject to detailed direction and measurement: the wind, the waters of the sea, the rain, and the lightning (or, the thunderstorms) are all ruled by law (Andersen thinks all these may be elements of just one phenomenon, the thunderstorm; similarly Fedrizzi). The language of control is "weight," "measure," "decree," and "path." Now that world order is the framework within which God identifies and establishes the nature of "wisdom." Wisdom may seem, when we get to hear just what it is in v 28, rather pragmatic and experiential, even adventitious; but vv 25–26 assure us that it is foreseen from the beginning of creation and designed into the fabric of the universe. It is not that wisdom is itself the "ordering principle of [the] creation process" (Habel), but it is as much a feature of the cosmic order as the winds and the rain.

25 What is the wind's "weight" (משקל)? Driver–Gray define it as the "maximum of force or weight when it blew which it might not exceed." The delightful phrase may be found also in the lines of the French poet Maurice Blanchard (1890–1960), "The trees, bending under the invisible weight of the wind, swung back. They had won once more" (*Les barricades mystérieuses* [Paris: GLM, 1974]), and of Algernon Charles Swinburne (1837–1909), "All the weight of the wind bore down on it [the sea]" ("A Channel Crossing," l. 15). In sailing, too, wind shear (differences in wind speed or direction relative to height, e.g., between the deck and the masthead) is known as the "weight of the wind." But perhaps something more paradoxical is intended: as Dhorme remarks, "The wind is the lightest of things, and yet God determines for it a weight." The same may be intended in the early Muslim prayer, *Sahifa,* where there is praise of God who knows the weight of the heavens, the sun and the moon, the darkness and the light, and "the weight of the wind, how many times it is greater than the weight of a dust mote" (Sahifa al-Kamilah, supplication 55, "Glorification of Allah"). Tur-Sinai and Fohrer say that the ancients believed the wind had no weight, which might mean that even its weightlessness was assigned by God.

And what are the "waters" (מים)? It is tempting to interpret them as the rainwaters (so Dhorme, apparently Pope), since the other cola of vv 25–26 concern only heavenly phenomena. But would not then the "measure" (מדה) of the rain be the same as the "decree" (חק) for the rain in the next verse? The term "waters" here would better refer to the sea (as GNB); cf. Isa 40:12, where מים are the waters of the sea that are "measured" (מדד) in the palm of God's hand, and especially Prov 8:29, where at creation God assigned the sea a limit (חק) so that the waters should not transgress his command, and Job 38:10–11, where bounds (חק) are fixed for the sea, with the injunction "Thus far shall you come, and no farther, and here shall your proud waves be stayed." Driver–Gray envisage God "mark[ing] out with a measure the extreme limit to which the sea might overflow the land."

26 The "decree" (חק) for the rain is presumably "how, when, where, how heavily" it should fall (Dillmann). See further, E. F. Sutcliffe, "The Clouds as Water-Carriers in Hebrew Thought," *VT* 3 (1953) 99–103.

27 The opening word "then" (אז), used in a temporal, not a logical, sense, is crucial, binding together as it does the time of creation (vv 24–26) with God's engagement with wisdom (v 27).

It is perhaps a little strange that the first thing God did with wisdom was to "see" (ראה) it, for that suggests that wisdom was already existing, whereas Prov 8:22, 25 regards wisdom as a creation of God's (an emendation here to בְּרָאָהּ "he created it" [Yellin] has not found favor). But perhaps the four verbs of this verse do not refer to a sequence of actions (even though they are joined with the *waw* consecutive), but to four aspects of the divine knowledge of wisdom. On the other hand, it is not necessary that Job 28 should agree in all respects with Proverbs, and it may be that here wisdom is regarded as coexisting with God (cf. also Duhm)—in which case God's "seeing" it would make sense as his first act.

The second verb used here of God's activity is "appraised" (so, e.g., Dhorme, NAB, NIV). ספר piel is usually "told," "declared" (RSV), but here no audience is in view that might be the object of a declaration. More probably, ספר is used in its sense of "reckon, take account of" (as in 14:16 [qal]; 38:37; Ps 22:17 [18]), which makes sense especially in the context of God's primeval assignment and measuring mentioned four times in vv 25–26.

The third verb, כון, is variously understood (see *Note* 27.d); in view of the uncertainty, it is perhaps best to use the vague and general word "establish."

The fourth verb, "search" (חקר), often implies, as here no doubt, a search to the utmost, thus "fathom." The term was used in v 3 of the miners "seeking" the mineral ore to the furthest limit. Habel suggests that the four verbs together constitute the image of a jeweler with a precious jewel: the stone is sighted, appraised, prepared, and probed to its depths. But it is far from clear whether any comprehensive image is intended. Newsom's suggestion (following Janzen) is that the range of verbs signifies that "wisdom is perceived and known fully only in the act of creation itself"; it is like the experience of an artisan: "the wisdom that makes the crafting possible is known only in the exercise of that skill." Perhaps this would also fit the concept of wisdom in v 28, that wisdom is not an object that can be obtained, but an experience one comes to through appropriate behavior in religion and ethics.

S. L. Harris ("Wisdom or Creation? A New Interpretation of Job xxviii 27," *VT* 33 [1983] 419–27) put forward a new suggestion, that the object of the four verbs was the creation (heavens and earth), not wisdom. But it would be strange for the focus to shift from wisdom in vv 23–26 to the creation in v 27 and back to wisdom in v 28.

28 Surprising as it may seem, this verse is the climax of the whole poem. Whether it is a secondary addition, as many think, will have to be discussed later. But as the text stands, it is in this verse that the primary question of the chapter is answered, and a bonus is offered besides. "Where shall wisdom be found?" was not fully answered by v 23, which said that God knows its place, for the reader still did not know where that place might be. Now we learn, though the language of "way" and "place" has been given up, that wisdom belongs to no supernal realm but is in the hands of humankind (v 28), to whom it has been delivered by God. What is more, and this is the bonus, the reader now knows, not just how to go about acquiring wisdom, but what exactly it consists of. The commonsense view of wisdom is that it is to be gained only by effort and long discipline, and that one becomes aware of its content only gradually. On the contrary, says v 28, anyone can know the complete content of wisdom on first inquiring: it is the fear of the Lord and the avoidance of evil. No doubt it takes effort to *be* wise, i.e., to carry out the requirements of wisdom, but to *know* what it consists of is simplicity itself.

Now it cannot be said that this is the climax for which the poem as a whole has been preparing us. The account of mining in vv 1–11 gave us to believe, once we had seen that it was the backdrop to the quest for wisdom (v 12), that wisdom was a precious object that would be attained only by extraordinary effort. The comparison with valuable minerals and gems in vv 15–19 perhaps even suggested that wisdom was in fact unobtainable. The answers of the supernatural beings in vv 14, 22 made us think that wisdom was a transcendental object. The direct statements of vv 13, 21, that humans do not know the way to it, that it is not found in the land of the living, that it is hidden from all living creatures, confirmed that view. And the assurance that it is God who knows the way to it (v 23), and the connection of wisdom with the creation of the universe (vv 24–27), seemed to put wisdom entirely beyond human reach. And now, after all that, we are told that wisdom is accessible, intelligible, and obtainable!

Looking back on the chapter, we might feel that its misdirection was a playfulness (Newsom too speaks of the teasing and tantalizing character of its language). It might be more correct to call the whole poem an extended riddle. Though we were certainly misled, we were never told a falsehood. From the perspective of v 28, it remains true that wisdom is desirable, as desirable as any product of the earth for which miners exert themselves (as in vv 1–11). Wisdom, without doubt, cannot be bought or exchanged for precious stones (as in vv 15–19). Wisdom is not to be found with the cosmic beings like the Deep or Abaddon (vv 14, 22), for it is to humans that it has been disclosed (v 28). It is certainly true that God knows wisdom and therefore how it is to be obtained, and his "fathoming" of wisdom at creation means no more, now that we come to think of it, than his decision about what wisdom would be, right from the beginning (as in vv 23–27). Only with the sentences of vv 13 and 21 could we complain that we have been deceived about this wisdom. Perhaps even here we are meant to recognize, on a second reading of the poem—from the perspective of v 28, that is—that all talk about a "place" where wisdom might be found, a "way" one could take to reach that place, was itself a misdirection: wisdom never did reside in a "place"; it never could be attained by a journey. Wisdom is not "located" anywhere, it is not something to be "found," for its nature has already been disclosed to humans by God, and every person is in principle already a possessor of the knowledge of wisdom.

Even v 28 itself may display a certain playfulness, in that the key words "and he said to humans" are not part of the poetical or metrical structure: they form an anacrusis, lying outside the metrical rhythm (*extra metrum*), as a kind of afterthought or prosaic addition or marginal note or stage direction (like "a voice cries" in Isa 40:3). They are by no means a secondary addition, for they are crucial to the meaning of the verse; but they are not integrated into the poetry, as if the key to the whole poem somehow stands outside it, as if the nature of wisdom is, far from being transcendental, essentially prosaic and hardly even poetic—an impression the remainder of the verse will not dispel.

So what exactly does wisdom consist of? Its two elements, according to this verse, are the "fear of the Lord" and a "shunning of evil." The "fear" (יראה) of God is often understood as awe of God, reverence for God, or simply religious behavior (so G. Wanke, *TDNT,* 9:197–205; H.-P. Stähli, *TLOT,* 2:568–78). It is more probable, however, that the term "fear" refers to the *emotion* of fear, which is what the word group regularly denotes in Hebrew (see D. J. A. Clines, "'The Fear of the Lord Is Wisdom' [Job 28:28]: A Semantic and Contextual Study," in *Job 28: Cognition in Context,* ed. E. van Wolde, Biblical Interpretation Series 64 [Leiden: Brill, 2003] 57–92). "Shunning" is lit. "turning aside from" (סור), a metaphor that belongs to the sapiential concept of life as a way along which one walks. Keeping to the right way implies not "turning aside" to evil paths, which are viewed as alternative and crooked paths. It is truly a *via negativa* in the description of the ethical to regard it as the avoidance of certain behavior rather than as executing or accomplishing good. See further, *Comment* on 1:1; and *Explanation* to this chapter. Wisdom thus consists of the correct response to the divine (a feeling of fear) and a correct ethical attitude (a shunning or avoidance of evil). It is interesting that these two elements in wisdom are precisely those attributed to Job in the first verse of the book (1:1); and it is ironic that the speaker here (who is recognized as Elihu according to the position taken in this commentary) should be recommending to Job as wisdom nothing other than the rules by which Job himself has always lived—and which have led, so it appears, to such sorry consequences.

Then what is being said about wisdom by defining these as the two elements in it? It would seem that knowledge in general is being identified with the emotion of fear (of God), while "understanding" is identified with the avoidance of unethical behavior. Can it really be meant that knowledge is a form of religious activity or that it lies in the realm of the ethical? It may be that the speaker (and this observation fits well if we correctly identify him as Elihu) refers only to wisdom in the religious and ethical domain, that is, that he is not propounding a view about epistemology. But it would fit even better if the statement that the fear of God *is* wisdom means not that wisdom consists of the fear of God or that wisdom and the fear of God are the same thing, but rather that to fear God is a very wise thing to do, an act that is full of wisdom. (This is a rather different assertion from that of Prov 1:7 and 9:10, "the fear of Yahweh is the beginning of wisdom," for that seems only to posit a religious attitude as a prerequisite for gaining wisdom, not as the essence of wisdom.)

Finally, the question whether this verse originally belonged to the poem must be raised. A majority of commentators actually think it is a secondary addition (so, e.g., Driver–Gray, Fohrer, and those cited below). The reasons advanced are these: (1) The whole sentence is prosaic, especially when compared with the quality of the rest of the poem (Duhm). (2) The words "and he said to humankind" are outside the metrical scheme and may be evidence that the sentence is an addition. (3) The view of wisdom in this verse, that it is accessible to humans and that it consists in right behavior rather than in any kind of knowledge, is at odds with the view of wisdom in the rest of the poem. (4) The term "the Lord" (אדני) occurs nowhere else in Job (Duhm). (It is very unusual for God to refer to himself as "the Lord"; Driver–Gray note Ezek 13:9; 23:49; 24:24; 28:24, where it is, however, the phrase "the Lord God.")

The adding of lines at the end of a document is a not unknown feature in the Hebrew Bible, even of lines that in some degree subvert the intentions of the work to which they are added (cf. perhaps Eccl 12:13–14). So there is no reason in principle why v 28 should not be a later addition to the poem. What makes that view extremely unlikely, however, is that two questions remain unanswered: (1) What is the meaning of the poem if it contains only vv 1–27? (2) Why does it stand at this point in the book of Job? For (1) without v 28 the poem says only that wisdom is unattainable and known only to God. If that is true, why should anyone think it is interesting? Such wisdom by definition does not affect humans and cannot be comprehended by them. So who wishes us to know about it? (2) A poem about the impossibility of gaining wisdom seems implausible in the mouth of any of the friends, who regard themselves as wise men with something to teach Job. It is equally implausible as an intentional addition to the book of Job, since it addresses none of the issues of the book about justice or suffering. Murphy thinks it serves as a rebuttal of the kind of wisdom advanced by the friends and by Job himself, underscoring the "bankruptcy" of the dialogue up to this point. Westermann also sees the chapter as delivering the reason for God's judgment on the friends (*Structure*, 106–7): wisdom is not to be manipulated as they have been doing. But if the only wisdom in the universe is the unattainable wisdom of God, what are humans to be doing when confronted with the problems of existence? Of course, if the chapter is an accidental insertion into the book, it contributes nothing to the book, but then, as suggested above, it is hard to see what it would have contributed to anything. It is more reasonable to suppose that the chapter strives toward a conclusion, and if v 28 is an unexpected conclusion, perhaps it is all the more effective for that very reason.

Explanation

It does not matter a very great deal for the general sense of the chapter whether we regard it as an independent poem without significant links to its context (as is the almost universal view) or as the conclusion to the speeches of Elihu (the view taken in this commentary). In either case, it propounds a view, in a marvelously intriguing way, of what it means for humans to be wise, of what the wisdom is that they should strive for. Wisdom, according to Job 28, is not the accumulation of knowledge, nor is it the uncovering of secrets. Wisdom consists in a certain way of being and behaving, which is within the capacity of humans generally. It may be difficult to be wise and to stay wise, but it is not difficult to know what counts as wise. Wisdom is to fear the Lord and to shun evil (v 28)—which is to say, it is correct behavior in religion and in ethics.

To reach this position, the poet takes us down an unforeseen and mysterious path. Considering where the poem will end, with the fear of the Lord, it begins in the most unlikely place, a silver mine, and leads us by way of a bazaar in which precious gems are being traded, an encounter with fearsome cosmic beings like the Deep and Abaddon, and a visit to God's primeval workshop for the building of the universe. Throughout, we are being convinced not just of the desirability of wisdom but, increasingly, of its inaccessibility, more difficult to attain than minerals and gems in a mine, more expensive than any precious object of the merchants, more remote and hidden than anyone can conceive, more a denizen of the divine realm than of the human. And yet all that tendency in the poem, though it had a kind of truth in it as well, was a grand misdirection, for the sum of the matter was that wisdom is within the grasp of all, since it has been infallibly disclosed to humans by God.

The wisdom propounded by Elihu in this chapter has seemed to some rather banal, couched in the conventional language of the schools. But it has its own surprises. In religion, the wise thing to do, says Elihu, is to be afraid of God (that seems to be the proper meaning of the "fear of the Lord"; see *Comment* on v 28). It is not to worship or bring sacrifices or praise; it is not to engage in religious practices or to participate in religious assemblies. It is to experience a personal, individual emotion of fear in the perpetual awareness of the deity, a primal sense of creatureliness.

And as for ethics, the wise thing to do is to shun evil. It is not to seek the greatest good for the greatest number; it is not to maximize justice or spread bounty. It is not even to do unto others as one would have them do unto oneself. It has no social dimensions. It is to keep oneself, even self-regardingly, from one's own temptations.

Together, these components of wisdom seem to amount to a recipe for a quietist, even antisocial, life. But in the case of Job, who, we cannot forget, is praised in 1:1 for precisely this kind of religion and this kind of ethics, such a concentration on the self leads to a scrupulous concern with sin and sacrifice, and to a lifetime of public service. The self has not been the boundary for his religion and ethics. At the same time, the focus on the private values in religion and ethics (the fear of God, the shunning of evil) leaves open for the individual all the space any libertarian could desire: religion and ethics are disclosed to consist not in the performance of rituals or deeds devised and sanctioned by others—by society and tradition—but in an inner stability that invests behavior with personal conviction.

Within the horizon of the book of Job as a whole, however, a different evaluation of Job 28 may be needful. Its concern with the acquisition of wisdom may be viewed as a distraction from a more important concern, the question of justice. Job's complaint is that he is being treated unjustly, and that by God; no amount of good advice about gaining wisdom can address that complaint. In fact, to turn a question of justice, which is a social and political question, into a question of wisdom, which is an intellectual issue and at heart a privatized matter, may itself be an injustice. Some commentators' accounts of the divine speeches have the deity making exactly this move—which is to say, they insist that the essential issue is the question of Job's wisdom (or rather, the lack of it) and ignore the outstanding issue of justice—which is, from Job's point of view, to add insult to the original injury against his person. In the name of justice, therefore, the tendency of the Elihu speeches, climaxing in this poem, and especially in v 28 within the poem, should be resisted.

Job's Final Speech (29:1–31:40)

Bibliography

Althann, R. "Job and the Idea of the Beatific Afterlife." *OTE* 4 (1991) 316–26. **Aytoun, R. A.** "A Critical Study of Job's 'Oath of Clearance.'" *Interp* 16 (1919–20) 291–98. **Baisas, B. Q.** "Ugaritic *'ḏr* and Hebrew *'zr* I." *UF* 5 (1973) 41–52. **Barr, J.** "Is Hebrew קן 'Nest' a Metaphor?" In *Semitic Studies.* FS W. Leslau, ed. Alan S. Kaye. Wiesbaden: Harrassowitz, 1991. 1:150–61. **Bellia, A. M.** "Giobbe 29: Una evangelizzazione sapienziale." In *Evangelizare pauperibus: Atti della XXIV Settimana biblica [dell']Associazione biblica italiana.* Ed. B. Antonini et al. Brescia: Paideia, 1978. **Blank, S. H.** "An Effective Literary Device in Job 31." *JJS* 2 (1951) 105–7. Reprinted in *Prophetic Thought* (Cincinnati: Hebrew Union Press, 1977) 65–67. **Blommerde, A. C. M.** "The Broken Construct Chain, Further Examples." *Bib* 55 (1974) 549–52. **Bogaert, M.** "Les suffixes verbaux non accusatifs dans le sémantique nord-occidental et particulièrement en hébreu." *Bib* 45 (1964) 220–47. **Caquot, A.** "Traits royaux dans le personnage de Job." In *maqqél shâqédh, La branche d'amandier.* FS W. Vischer. Montpellier: Causse, Graille, Castelnau, 1960. 32–45. **Ceresko, A. R.** *Job 29–31 in the Light of Northwest Semitic: A Translation and Philological Commentary.* BibOr 36: Rome: Biblical Institute Press, 1980. **Clines, D. J. A.** "Those Golden Days: Job and the Perils of Nostalgia." In *On the Way to the Postmodern: Old Testament Essays 1967–1998.* JSOTSup 292. Sheffield: Sheffield Academic Press, 1998. 2:792–800. **Cohen, J. M.** "An Unrecognized Connotation of *nšq peh* with Special Reference to Three Biblical Occurrences [Gen 41:40; Prov 24:26, Job 31:27]." *VT* 32 (1982) 416–24. **Cox, C.** "Job's Concluding Soliloquy: Chh. 29–31." In *VII Congress of the International Organization for Septuagint and Cognate Studies, Leuven 1989.* Ed. C. E. Cox. SBLSCS 31. Atlanta: Scholars Press, 1991. 325–39. **Cox, D.** "Structure and Function of the Final Challenge: Job 29–31." *PrIrB* 5 (1981) 55–71. **Coxon, P. W.** "[ ] ושיקו שמיא in 11Q tgJob XXXI, 7." *IEJ* 27 (1977) 207–8. **Cyss-Wittenstein, C.** "Reading Job 26–31 with Bakhtin." *Gravitas* (Graduate Theological Union) 1.2 (2000). **Dahood, M. J.** "Hebrew-Ugaritic Lexicography II." *Bib* 45 (1964) 393–412. ———. "Hebrew-Ugaritic Lexicography VII." *Bib* 50 (1969) 337–56. ———. "Hebrew-Ugaritic Lexicography XII." *Bib* 55 (1974) 381–93. ———. "Nest and Phoenix in Job 29,18." *Bib* 48 (1967) 542–44. ———. "Northwest Semitic Philology and Job." In *The Bible in Current Catholic Thought: Gruenthaner Memorial Volume.* Ed. J. L. McKenzie. St. Mary's Theology Studies 1. New York: Herder & Herder, 1962. 55–74. ———. "The Phoenician Contribution to Biblical Wisdom Literature." In *The Role of the Phoenicians in the Interaction of Mediterranean Civilization.* Ed. W. A. Ward. Beirut: American University of Beirut, 1968. 123–53. ———. "Qoheleth and Northwest Semitic Philology." *Bib* 43 (1962) 349–65. ———. Review of *Job et son Dieu: Essai d'exégèse et de théologie biblique,* by J. Lévêque. *Bib* 52 (1971) 436–38. ———. "Some Northwest-Semitic Words in Job." *Bib* 38 (1957) 306–20. ———. "Ugaritic-Hebrew Parallel Pairs." In *Ras Shamra Parallels.* Ed. L. R. Fisher. AnOr 49. Rome: Pontifical Biblical Institute, 1972. 1:71–382. ———. *Ugaritic-Hebrew Philology: Marginal Notes on Recent Publications.* Bib Or 17. Rome: Pontifical Biblical Institute, 1965. **Dick, M. B.** "Job 31: A Form-Critical Study." Diss., Johns Hopkins, 1977. ———. "Job 31, the Oath of Innocence, and the Sage." *ZAW* 95 (1983) 31–53. ———. "The Legal Metaphor in Job 31." *CBQ* 41 (1979) 37–50. Reprinted in *Sitting with Job: Selected Studies on the Book of Job.* Ed. R. B. Zuck (Grand Rapids: Baker Book House, 1992) 321–34. **Dolbeau, F.** "Une citation non reconnue de Job 31, 11 (LXX), dans un sermon d'Augustin." *REAug* 43 (1997) 309–11. **Doucet, D.** "Job: L'Eglise et la tribulation: Augustin, Adnotationes in Job 29–31." In *Le Livre de Job chez les Pères.* Cahiers de Biblia patristica 5. Strasbourg: Centre d'Analyse et de Documentation Patristiques, 1996. 31–48. **Driver G. R.** "A Confused Hebrew Root (דום, דמה, דמם)."

In פרסומי החברה לחקר המקרא בישראל, ספר ח׳, מוגש לכבוד פרופ׳ נ.ח. טור־סיני למלאת לו שבעים שנה [Sepher N. H. Tur-Sinai]. Ed. M. Haran and B. Luria. Jerusalem: Kiryat Sepher, 1960. 1*–11*. ———. "Problems in Job." *AJSL* 52 (1935–36) 160–73. ———. "Problems in the Hebrew Text of Job." In *Wisdom in Israel and in the Ancient Near East.* FS H. H. Rowley, ed. M. Noth and D. W. Thomas. VTSup 3. Leiden: Brill, 1955. 72–93. **Fohrer, G.** "The Righteous Man in Job 31." In *Essays in Old Testament Ethics.* FS J. P. Hyatt, ed. J. L. Crenshaw and J. T. Willis. New York: Ktav, 1974. 1–22. Reprinted from *Studien zum Buche Hiob (1956–1979)*, 2d ed., BZAW 159 (Berlin: de Gruyter, 1983) 78–93. **Fuchs, G.** *Mythos und Hiobdichtung: Aufnahme und Umdeutung altorientalischer Vorstellungen.* Stuttgart: Kohlhammer, 1993. 141–87. **Good, E. M.** "Job 31." In *Sitting with Job: Selected Studies on the Book of Job.* Ed. R. B. Zuck. Grand Rapids: Baker, 1992. 335–44. Reprinted from *In Turns of Tempest: A Reading of Job, with a Translation* (Stanford: Stanford UP, 1990) 309–18. **Grieshammer, R.** "Zum 'Sitz im Leben' des negativen Sündenbekenntnises." ZDMGSup 2 (1974) 19–25. **Griffiths, J. G.** "The Idea of Posthumous Judgement in Israel and Egypt" [Lev 19:36; Job 14:7–10; 16:19–22; 19:25–27; 29:11; 30:20; 31; Prov 16:2; 21:2; 24:12]. In *Fontes atque pontes.* FS H. Brunner, ed. M. Görg. AAT 5. Wiesbaden: Harrassowitz, 1983. 186–204. **Guillaume, A.** "The Arabic Background of the Book of Job." In *Promise and Fulfilment.* FS S. H. Hooke, ed. F. F. Bruce. Edinburgh: T. & T. Clark, 1963. 106–27. ———. "Hebrew and Arabic Lexicography: A Comparative Study." *AbrN* 1 (1959–60) 3–35. **Habel, N.** "'Only the Jackal Is My Friend' [Job 30,29]: On Friends and Redeemers in Job." *Int* 31 (1977) 227–36. **Hardenbrook, W.** "A Model for Manhood" [Job 29]. *Epiphany* 7.1 (1986) 12–19. **Heras, H.** "The Standard of Job's Immortality." *CBQ* 11 (1949) 263–79. **Hill, J. S.** "The Phoenix." *Religion and Literature* 16 (1984) 61–66. ———. "Phoenix." In *Dictionary of Biblical Tradition in English Literature.* Ed. D. L. Jeffrey. Grand Rapids, MI: Eerdmans, 1992. 611–13. **Holbert, J. C.** "The Rehabilitation of the Sinner: The Function of Job 29–31." *ZAW* 95 (1983) 229–37. **Jeshurun, G.** "A Note on Job XXX: 1 [read XXXI:1]." *JSOR* 12 (1928) 153–54. **Joüon, P.** "Notes philologiques sur le texte hébreu de Job 1, 5; 9, 35; 12, 21; 28, 1; 28, 27; 29, 14." *Bib* 11 (1930) 322–24. **Kautz, J. R., III.** "A Hermeneutical Study of Job 29–31." Diss., Southern Baptist Theological Seminary, 1970. **Kuhn, H.** "Why Are Job's Opponents Still Made to Eat Broom-Root?" *BT* 40 (1989) 332–36. **Kunz, A.** "Der Mensch auf dem Waage: Die Vorstellung vom Gerichtshandeln Gottes im ägyptischen Totenbuch (Tb 125) und bei Hiob (Ijob 31)." *BZ* 45 (2001) 235–50. **Kutsch, E.** "Unschuldsbekenntnis und Gottesbegegnung: Der Zusammenhang zwischen Hiob 31 und 38ff." In *Kleine Schriften zum Alten Testament.* Ed. L. Schmidt and K. Eberlein. BZAW 168. Berlin: de Gruyter, 1986. 308–35. **Lescow, T.** "Hiob 29–31." In *Das Stufenschema: Untersuchungen zur Struktur alttestamentlicher Texte.* BZAW 211. Berlin: de Gruyter, 1992. 159–80. **Lévêque, J.** "Anamnèse et disculpation: La conscience du juste en Job, 29–31." In *La Sagesse de l'Ancien Testament.* Ed. M. Gilbert. BETL 51. Gembloux: Duculot; Leuven: Leuven UP, 1979. 231–48. **Malchow, B. V.** "A Royal Prototype in Job 29." In *The Psalms and Other Studies on the Old Testament.* FS J. I. Hunt, ed. J. C. Knight and L. A. Sinclair. Nashotah, WI: Nashotah House Seminary, 1990. 178–84. **Michel, W. L.** "BTWLH 'virgin' or 'Virgin (Anath)' in Job 31:1." *HS* 23 (1982) 59–66. **Murtagh, J.** "The Book of Job and the Book of the Dead." *ITQ* 35 (1965) 166–73. **Oeming, M.** "Ethik in der Spätzeit des Alten Testaments am Beispiel von Hiob 31 und Tobit 4." In *Altes Testament, Forschung und Wirkung.* FS H. G. Reventlow, ed. P. Mommer and W. Thiel. Frankfurt a. M.: Lang, 1994. 159–73. ———. "Hiob 31 und der Dekalog." In *The Book of Job.* Ed. W. A. M. Beuken. BETL 114. Leuven: Leuven UP, 1994. 362–68. **Ortiz de Urtaran, F.** "'Cuando Dios era un íntimo en mi tienda' (Job 29,4)." *Lumen* 33 (1984) 289–309. **Osswald, E.** "Hiob 31 im Rahmen der alttestamentlichen Ethik." *TVers* 2 (1970) 9–26. **Remus, M.** *Menschenbildvorstellungen im Ijob-Buch: Ein Beitrag zur alttestamentlichen Anthropologie.* BEATAJ 21. Frankfurt a. M.: Lang. 1993. **Ruiz, G.** "El clamor de las piedras (Lk 19:40; Hab 2:11): El Reino choca con la ciudad injusta en la fiesta de Ramos" [Job 31.38]. *EstEcl* 59 (1984) 297–312. **Saydon, P. P.** "Philological and Textual Notes to the Maltese Translation of the Old Testament." *CBQ* 23 (1961) 249–57. **Selms, A. van.** "Job

31:38–40 in Ugaritic Light." *Semitics* 8 (1982) 30–42. **Silbermann, A.** "Soziologische Anmerkungen zum Buch Hiob." *ZRGG* 41 (1989) 1–11. **Skehan, P. W.** "Job's Final Plea (Job 29–31) and the Lord's Reply (Job 38–41)." *Bib* 45 (1964) 51–62. **Smith, W. C.** "The Function of Chapters 29–31 in the Book of Job." Diss., Southern Baptist Theological Seminary, 1992. **Sutcliffe, E. F.** "Notes on Job, Textual and Exegetical. 6, 18; 11, 12; 31, 35; 34, 17. 20; 36, 27–33; 37, 1." *Bib* 30 (1949) 66–90. **Tang, S. Y.** *The Ethical Context of Job 31: A Comparative Study.* Diss., Edinburgh, 1966–67. **Webster, E. C.** "Strophic Patterns in Job 29–42." *JSOT* 30 (1984) 95–109. **Wolfers, D.** "The 'Neck' of Job's Tunic (Job xxx 18)." *VT* 44 (1994) 570–72. **Yamaga, T.** "Can the Roots of the Broom Be Eaten? A Proposal for the Interpretation of Job 30.2–8." *AJBI* 10 (1984) 20–32. **Zurro Rodríguez, E.** "Valor comparativo de la partícula *'im.*" *EstBib* 56 (1998) 251–60.

Translation

1 [a]*Job continued his discourse and said:*

2 *Oh, that I were in*[a] *the months of old,*
in the days[b] *when God watched over me,*
3 *when he made his lamp shine*[a] *over*[b] *my head,*
when by his light[c] *I walked through*[d] *darkness,*
4 *when I was in the days of my prime,*[a]
when the protection[b] *of God was over*[c] *my tent,*
5 *when the Almighty was still with me,*
and my lads[a] *were*[b] *around me,*
6 *when my footsteps*[a] *were bathed*[b] *in curds,*[c]
and the rock flowed with[d] *streams of oil.*

7 *When I would go out to the gate of the town*[a]
and take my seat in the square,[b]
8 *the younger men would see me*[a] *and withdraw,*[b]
the older men would rise and remain standing,[c]
9 *the princes would refrain from speaking,*
and clap their hand to their mouth,
10 *the voice of the nobles would be hushed,*[a]
and their tongue would cleave to their palate.[b]

11 [a]*When*[b] *the ear heard, it called me blessed,*
when the eye saw, it testified for me.[c]
12 *For I rescued the poor who cried out,*[a]
the fatherless, and those with none to help.[b]
13 *The blessing of those in danger of death*[a] *came upon me,*[b]
and I made the widows' heart sing for joy.
14 *I clothed myself with righteousness, and it clothed itself with me;*[a]
my justice[b] *was like a robe and a turban.*[c]

15 *I was eyes to the blind,*
and feet to the lame.
16 *I was a father to the poor,*
I studied[a] *the stranger's cause.*[b]

17 *I broke the jawbone*[a] *of the unrighteous,*
and made him drop[b] *his prey from his teeth.*

18 *Then I thought,*[a] *"I shall die*[b] *among my nestlings,*[c]
and[d] *I shall multiply my days*[e] *like the phoenix,*[f]
19 *my roots open*[a] *to the waters,*
and the dew lodging[b] *in my branches,*
20 *my glory*[a] *fresh with me,*[b]
and my bow[c] *ever renewed*[d] *in my hand."*

21 [a]*Men would listen to me,*[b] *and wait;*[c]
they would keep silence[d] *for my counsel.*[e]
22 *When I had spoken,*[a] *they would not speak again;*[b]
[c]*my words had dropped*[d] *upon them.*
23 *They waited*[a] *for them*[b] *as for rain,*
they opened their mouths[c] *for them as for the late rains.*[d]
24 *When I smiled at them, they would not*[a] *believe it,*[b]
and they did not disregard my good favor.[c]
25 *I decided*[a] *their way*[b] *and presided as their chief,*
I lived[c] *like a king among his troops,*[d]
[e][*like one who*[f] *consoles mourners.*[g]]

30:1 [a]*But now they*[b] *deride me,*
men who are younger[c] *than I,*[d]
whose fathers I would have disdained[e]
to set with[f] *the dogs of my flock.*[g]
2 [a]*What use*[b] *was the strength of their hands*[c] *to me,*[d]
men[e] *whose vigor*[f] *was spent?*[g]
3 [a]*From want and barren*[b] *hunger*[c] *they gnaw*[d] *the dry ground,*[e]
[f]*on the brink of*[g] *destruction and desolation.*
4 *They pick*[a] *mallow*[b] *from bushes,*[c]
and the roots[d] *of the broom*[e] *to warm themselves.*[f]
5 *They are driven out from human society;*[a]
others shout after them[b] *as after a thief.*
6 *In the gullies*[a] *of the wadis*[b] *they must dwell,*[c]
in caves[d] *in the earth*[e] *and among the rocks.*[f]
7 *Among the bushes*[a] *they cry out,*[b]
under[c] *the thistles*[d] *they couple.*[e]
8 *Children of the ignominious,*[a] *children of the nameless*[b] *indeed,*
they are scourged out[c] *of the land.*

9 *And now I have become their*[a] *mocking song;*[b]
I have become a byword to them.[c]
10 *They abhor me, they keep far from me;*
at the sight of me[a] *they do not hesitate to spit.*
11 *Because [God]*[a] *has loosened my cord*[b] *and humiliated me,*[c]
they have thrown off restraint in my presence.[d]

12 [a]*On my right hand*[b] *the mob*[c] *rises;*[d]
[e]*they trip me up;*[f]
they build siege ramps[g] *against me*[h] *to ruin me.*[i]
13 *They tear down*[a] *my defenses;*[b]
they succeed[c] *in bringing me down;*[d]
they need no help.[e]
14 *They enter as through*[a] *a wide breach;*[b]
they come on in waves[c] *through the ruined wall.*[d]
15 [a]*Terrors are set*[b] *against me;*
[c]*like the wind they put*[d] *my honor*[e] *to flight;*
my hope of safety[f] *has vanished like a cloud.*

16 [a]*And now*[b] *my life*[c] *is poured out,*[d]
days of[e] *misery have seized hold of me.*[f]
17 [a]*The night*[b] *pierces*[c] *my bones,*[d]
and those who gnaw me[e] *take no rest.*
18 [a]*With great force*[b] *he grips*[c] *my garment,*[d]
he clasps me tight[e] *like*[f] *the neck of my tunic.*
19 [a]*He*[b] *has thrown*[c] *me into the mire,*[d]
and I have come to look like[e] *dust and dirt.*[f]
20 *I cry to you,*[a] *and you do not answer me;*
I stand up,[b] *but you only stare*[c] *at me.*
21 *You have turned*[a] *cruel toward me;*
with the might of your hand you persecute me.[b]
22 *You snatch me up*[a] *and make me ride on*[b] *the wind,*
you dissolve me[c] *with a downpour.*[d]
23 *I know indeed*[a] *that you will hand me over*[b] *to death,*[c]
to the meetinghouse[d] *of all the living.*

24 *Surely I never stretched out my hand against any needy person,*[a]
if they cried out in their calamity.[b]
25 [a]*Did I not weep*[b] *for the one whose day was hard?*[c]
Was my heart[d] *not*[e] *grieved*[f] *for the poor?*[g]
26 *Yet*[a] *when I looked for*[b] *good, evil came;*[c]
when I expected[d] *light, deep darkness came.*
27 [a]*My inner body*[b] *is in turmoil*[c] *and never rests;*[d]
days of affliction confront me.[e]
28 *I walk about in black,*[a] *comfortless;*[b]
I stand up in the assembly[c] *and cry out for help.*[d]
29 *I have become a brother to jackals,*[a]
a companion of ostriches.[b]
30 *My skin turns black,*[a]
and my bones[b] *are burned with heat.*[c]
31 *My harp*[a] *has been given over to*[b] *mourning,*
and my flute[c] *to the voice of those who wail.*[d]

31:1 [a]*I laid an injunction*[b] *on my eyes.*[c]
How[d] *then could I even look upon*[e] *a young woman?*[f]

2 [a]*What*[b] *is the portion*[c] *from God*[d] *from above,*
what the inheritance from the Almighty from on high?
3 *Is it not calamity*[a] *for the unrighteous,*
disaster[b] *for those who work iniquity?*
4 *Does he not see my ways,*
does he not number[a] *all my steps?*

5 [a]*If*[b] *I have walked with falsehood,*[c]
if my foot has hastened[d] *to deceit,*[e]
6 [a]*let him*[b] *weigh me in a just balance,*
and[c] *let God know my integrity.*[d]
7 *If my step has turned out of the way,*[a]
if my heart has gone after my eyes,[b]
[c]*if any stain*[d] *clings to my hands,*[e]
8 *then let me sow and another eat,*[a]
then let my crops[b] *be uprooted.*[c]

9 [a]*If my heart has been enticed to*[b] *a woman,*
and I have lain in wait[c] *by*[d] *my neighbor's door,*[e]
10 *then let my wife grind for*[a] *another,*
let others kneel over[b] *her.*
11 [a]*For that*[b] *is a crime,*[c]
a punishable offense.[d]
12 *For*[a] *that is a fire that consumes down to Abaddon,*[b]
that would burn to the root[c] *all my harvest.*[d]

13 *If*[a] *I have rejected*[b] *the cause*[c] *of my servant, man or woman,*[d]
when they had a claim[e] *against me,*
14 [a]*what shall I do when God rises up?*[b]
When he enquires,[c] *how shall I answer him?*
15 [a]*Did not he*[b] *who made me*[c] *in the womb make them?*[d]
Did not the same God[e] *fashion us*[f] *in the womb?*[g]

16 [a]*If*[b] *I have withheld what the poor desired,*[c]
or caused the eyes of the widow to fail,[d]
17 *if*[a] *I have eaten my crust*[b] *alone,*
and no orphan shared it
18 [a]*(for from my youth*[b] *I brought him up*[c] *as a father;*[d]
from my[e] *mother's womb*[f] *I guided*[g] *her*[h]*),*
19 [a]*if I have seen*[b] *anyone perishing*[c] *for lack of clothing,*
or a poor person without covering,[d]
20 *if*[a] *their loins*[b] *have not blessed me,*
and[c] *they were not warmed*[d] *with a fleece*[e] *of my lambs,*
21 *if I have raised*[a] *a hand against the fatherless,*[b]
when I saw my help[c] *in the gate—*
22 *then let my shoulder blade*[a] *fall*[b] *from my shoulder,*[c]
and my arm[d] *be broken from*[e] *its socket.*[f]

23 [a]*For I would have been*[b] *in terror before God;*[c]
I would not have been able to endure[d] *the fear of him.*[e]

24 *If*[a] *I have made gold my trust,*[b]
or said to fine gold, "You are my confidence,"[c]
25 [a]*if*[b] *I have rejoiced*[c] *because my wealth was great,*
or because my hand had gained[d] *much,*
26 *if*[a] *I have gazed with delight*[b] *at the sun*[c] *when it shone,*
or[d] *the moon moving*[e] *in splendor,*[f]
27 *and my heart has been secretly enticed,*[a]
and my mouth has kissed my hand[b]*—*
28 [a]*this also would be a punishable crime,*[b]
for I would have been false to[c] *God above.*[d]

29 [a]*If*[b] *I have rejoiced*[c] *at the ruin of one who hated me,*
and was excited[d] *when evil overtook*[e] *him*
30 [a]*(I have not*[b] *let*[c] *my mouth*[d] *sin*[e]
by asking for his life with a curse[f]*),*
31 *if*[a] *the men of my tent*[b] *have not said,*[c]
"Oh that[d] *there were someone not yet satisfied with his meat!"*[e]
32 [a]*(the sojourner*[b] *has not lodged*[c] *in the street;*[d]
[e]*I have opened my doors*[f] *to the traveler*[g]*),*
33 *if*[a] *I have concealed my sin like Adam,*[b]
[c]*by hiding*[d] *my guilt in my heart,*[e]
34 *because*[a] *I was in fear of*[b] *the multitude,*[c]
and the contempt of my kin[d] *terrified*[e] *me*
[f]*so that I kept silence*[g] *and did not go out of doors,*[h]
38 [a]*if my land has cried out against me,*[b]
and its furrows have wept[c] *together,*[d]
39 [a]*if I have eaten its yield*[b] *without payment,*
and have caused its workers[c] *to groan,*[d]
40 *let thorns*[a] *grow instead of wheat,*
stinkweed[b] *instead of barley!*

35 *Oh, that I had someone to hear me!*[a]
[b]*Here is my signature! Let the Almighty answer me!*[c]
[d]*Oh, that I had*[e] *the indictment*[f] *written*[g] *by my opponent!*[h]
36 *Surely*[a] *I would lift it up*[b] *onto my shoulder;*
I would bind it about my head[c] *as a turban;*[d]
37 *I would give him an account*[a] *of my steps;*[b]
like a prince I would approach[c] *him!*

40c *The words of Job are ended.*[a]

Notes

29:1.a. Beer (*BH*[2] *prps*) notes the proposal, accepted by Kissane, to replace this colon with the formula וַיַּעַן אִיּוֹב וַיֹּאמַר "and Job answered and said." See further, *Comment*.

2.a. The prep *kaph* for "in," as commonly in expressions of time (GKC, §118u). This seems better than taking *kaph* as "as, like," with the prep *beth* "in" being understood. Job is not so much wishing that his present existence were "as in" the months of old (as KJV, Moffatt, JPS, RSV, NAB, NJPS) as wishing that he were now actually "in" those months (cf. NEB "If I could only go back to the old days," JB "Will no one bring me back to the months that have gone?" [similarly Sicre Díaz], NIV "How I long for the months gone by").

2.b. כימי "in the days that," the constr before a relative clause (GKC, §130d), and the *kaph* for *beth* as in the preceding *Note.*

3.a. בהלו "in his shining," the suff being anticipatory (cf. GKC, §131k). הלל "shine" occurs only here in qal. Driver–Gray doubt the form and read hiph בְּהַהִלּוֹ (? error for בַּהֲהִלּוֹ, as Hölscher, Beer [*BH*[2] *vel*]; cf. Hartley) or בְּהִלּוֹ "when he caused his lamp to shine" (so Duhm, Beer [*BHK*], Dhorme, Fohrer, NAB, Fedrizzi, Gordis, de Wilde, Gray), with elision of ה. Sicre Díaz maintains the MT, and likewise Gerleman (*BHS*), explaining the form as a writing of בַּהֲהִלּוֹ. GNB completely misses the idea of preserving life (see *Comment*) by "God was always with me then"; it is not a question of God's *presence.*

3.b. It cannot be "upon," as KJV, RV, RSV, NIV, for that would mean that Job's head was the object of the illumination, or even, perhaps, that Job's head was the lampstand.

3.c. לאורו, with the *lamedh* of norm or standard, "according to his light" (BDB, 516a, §5j).

3.d. הלך "go" with acc, or rather the obj used adverbally, as not infrequently (for a full list, see *DCH,* 2:548b).

4.a. חרף is "harvest-time, autumn" according to BDB, 358a (so also Schultens, Delitzsch, Dillmann, Duhm, Driver–Gray ["ripeness"], Dhorme, Pope[1], Gray). It is questionable, however, whether "autumn" is a suitable translation, since חרף is more properly "winter" (it is contrasted with קיץ "summer" in Gen 8:22; Zech 14:8; Ps 74:17; בית חרף is "winter house" as distinct from "summer house" in Amos 3:15, while in Jer 36:22 Jehoiakim is sitting in a בית חרף in the ninth month, November-December, when it is snowing). And the verb חרף does not seem to mean "remain in harvest-time" (as BDB, 358a) but "spend the winter" (parallel to קיץ "spend the summer" in Isa 18:6); so too *HALOT,* 1:355b; *DCH,* 3:320b. *HALOT,* 1:356a, which offers the meaning "winter," is to be preferred (though it strangely offers "early time, youth" for this passage). Others, noting that the year begins in the autumn, have taken חרף "autumn" as a term for "youth" (thus apparently Theod and Symm νεότητός μου and Vg. *adolescentiae meae* "of my youth," Tg. חריפותי "of my early manhood"; so also Michaelis, *Deutsche Übersetzung,* 1:59 ["the course of life"], Rosenmüller ["vigor"]).

Others find here not חֹרֶף "winter" at all but a different word חֹרֶף meaning "youth" (so KBL, 336a, Fohrer, Blommerde, B. Landsberger, "Jahreszeiten im Sumerisch-Akkadischen," *JNES* 8 [1948] 248–72, 273–97 [282–84], *DCH,* 3:321a). חֹרֶף II would be cognate with Aram. חרף "be early," whence חֲרָפָא or חַרְפָּא "early" (of crops or clouds; Jastrow, 505a), Akk. *ḫarpu* "early" and *ḫarpū* "early harvest" (*CAD,* 6:105b, 106a), Old S. Arab. *ḫrf* "year" (J. Derenbourg, *Corpus Inscriptionum Semiticarum... Pars Quarta, inscriptiones ḥimyariticas et sabæas continens* [Paris: Klincksieck, 1889] 4:46.6 [p. 78]; 325.5 [p. 361]), and Arab. *ḫarûf* "young lamb" (Lane, 726a) (so too Pope, followed by Hartley, though they confuse matters by transliterating *ḥarûf* and by translating "prime," which is not the same as "young" or "early"); and Job cannot mean "early manhood," for he is referring to the time just before the calamities of chap. 1, a time when his sons were already adult. Ehrlich less convincingly connects the word with Arab. *ḥarf* "peak of mountain" (Lane, 550a), hence perhaps "vigor, peak of power."

It is not always clear what understanding the various versions have of the term; KJV, JPS have "my youth," RV "the ripeness of my days," Moffatt, NEB, NJPS, NIV, NRSV "my prime," NAB "my flourishing days"; only RSV and Good (cf. also Sicre Díaz) offer "autumn days," though JB comes near to that with "my days of harvest"—whatever they are. Terrien has "my summer," with no justification for the translation. Proposed emendations include חַסְדּוֹ "his loyal kindness" or חֶסֶד "loyal kindness" (Beer [*BH*[2] *prps*]), חֶפְצוֹ "his pleasure" (Beer [*BH*[2] *prps*]), פִּרְחִי "my flower" (Volz, Beer [*BH*[2] *prps*]), חֶלְמִי "my health" (Ball).

All in all, it is surprisingly difficult to be sure how חרף can be shown to mean what we know from the context it must mean, something like "prime," "peak of one's power."

4.b. סוד is "council" or "counsel," hence, according to BDB, 691b, "intimacy" (citing as parallels Ps 25:14 סוד יהוה ליראיו "intimacy with Yahweh is for those who fear him"; cf. Prov 3:32), *DCH,* vol. 6, *s.v.*; hence RSV, Andersen, Good "friendship," NIV "God's intimate friendship," JPS "converse," NJPS "company" (KJV "secret" comes from the idea of סוד as "secret counsel"). But in Ps 25:14 it is preferable to understand "the counsel, plan of Yahweh is for those who fear him" (cf. NEB), and in Prov

3:32 "the counsel [perhaps, the secret counsel] of Yahweh is with the upright." It is a further difficulty of the MT that the סוד of God is "over" (על) his tent. Gordis, followed by Hartley, takes סוד as inf constr, "when God was an intimate in my tent" (but he does not explain על). Among philological proposals, D. W. Thomas ("The Interpretation of בְּסוֹד in Job 29:4," *JBL* 65 [1946] 63–66) explains the MT as meaning "protection," from a new word סדד "protect" (cf. *DCH*, vol. 6, *s.v.*), cognate with Arab. *sadda* "close, stop up" (Lane, 1328b); he is followed by Terrien, and Gray is tempted by the proposal. A rather desperate attempt to preserve the MT is made by Pope and Blommerde, following M. Dahood ("Hebrew-Ugaritic Lexicography VII," *Bib* 50 [1969] 337–56 [342]), who read בְּסוֹד "in the founding of," inf. of יסד "found," translating "when [God Most High] founded my family"; on the supposed divine name עֲלִי, see *Note* 29:4.c. Though "tent" can mean those who live in it, one would hardly speak of "founding a tent" when giving Job a family is what is in mind. An emendation is therefore commonly accepted (and is adopted in the *Translation* above), on the basis of LXX ὅτε ἐπισκοπὴν ἐποιεῖτο "when he made oversight of"; this may reflect a reading of בְּסֹךְ or בְּסוֹךְ "when he covered, protected" (inf constr of סכך or of סוך [Peters]); thus Moffatt "was sheltering," NAB "sheltered," JB, NEB, GNB "protected," Houbigant, Duhm, Peake, Strahan, Driver–Gray, Beer (*BHK*), Dhorme, Hölscher, Kissane, Larcher, Fohrer, Fedrizzi, Gerleman (*BHS prp*), de Wilde, Gray, *HALOT,* 2:745b. סכך is construed with על at Exod 33:22; 40:3; 1 Kgs 8:7.

4.c. Dahood sees in עלי the supposed divine name עֲלִי "'Aliy" or "the Most High," here an epithet of אלוה "God" ("Hebrew-Ugaritic Lexicography VII," 342; review of *Job et son Dieu: Essai d'exégèse et de théologie biblique,* by J. Lévêque, *Bib* 52 [1971] 436–38 [438]). The name עלי, a short form of Elyon, has been proposed also for Job 7:20; 10:2; 32:35; 36:30, 33; 37:15, 16; 37:22 (cf. Pope also on 19:29, and Blommerde, 24, for bibliography).

5.a. For discussion of whether נערים, properly "lads" (as NJPS) or "boys" (Habel), can include daughters, see *Comment.* Most versions have "children," Good "youngsters," but this is not a normal term for children of both sexes. It is not impossible that the term should be translated "servants" (as NEB), but it would perhaps be strange if Job regretted the loss of his servants and did not mention his children.

5.b. Dhorme adds עָמְדוּ "stood" at the end of the verse, deleting עמדי, from which he thought it had been corrupted, from v 6. He is followed by Gray, and by de Wilde, who, however, puts the verb after סביבותי. Similarly NEB "and my servants stood round me" (cf. Brockington).

6.a. הָלִיךְ, occurring only here, is said by BDB, 237a, KBL, 232a, to mean "step" (so too KJV, RSV) or "footsteps" (NAB). But it would perhaps be more natural for Job to bathe something more concrete, i.e., his "feet," and both *HALOT,* 1:246a, and *DCH,* 2:544b, allow either "step" or "foot" for הליך (JB, NJPS also have "feet"; cf. Vg. *pedes meos* "my feet"; similarly de Wilde); less probable is his "path" (NEB, NIV). According to M. Dahood ("Hebrew-Ugaritic Lexicography II," *Bib* 45 [1964] 393–412 [404]), followed by Ceresko, הֲלִיכַי is a dual, "my two feet." Gray, on the other hand, regards הָלִיךְ as a byform of הֲלִיכָה "caravan" or "traveling company" of merchants in 6:9, and translates "my nomads had abundance of [see *Note* 6.b on רחץ] curds"; "nomads," however, are far different from traveling merchants, and it is hard to see how merchants on the move could have anything to do with farm produce like curds.

6.b. רחץ is pretty clearly "wash" (BDB, 934a). Gray proposes a new רחץ "be abundant," cognate with Akk. *raḫâṣu* "overflow" and Arab. *raḫaṣa* "be cheap, plentiful" (Lane, 1058b); but the resultant sense is inappropriate (see *Note* 6.a).

6.c. חמה cannot here be חֵמָה "anger," and must be an alternative (Gerleman [*BHS*]) spelling for, or a misspelling of, חֶמְאָה "curd, *leben,*" a substance like yoghurt, and defined by *OED* as "coagulated sour milk"; BDB, 326, renders "curd" (Driver–Gray, Hartley, Gray "curds"), KBL, 308a, strangely "sweet, new butter, still weak," but *HALOT,* 1:325a, inconsistently "sour milk, cream" (cf. Dalman, *Arbeit und Sitte,* 5:194; 6:307–11); de Wilde has "sour milk" (*Dickmilch*), Strauss "still liquid sour milk." It is not "milk" itself (Moffatt, RSV, NAB, NJB, NEB, GNB, Good); still less is it "cream" (JB, NIV, NJPS, Pope, Habel) or "butter" (KJV, RV, Dhorme, Kissane). Whereas "curd" or *leben* is the coagulated milk itself, produced either by its natural acids when milk is left to stand or by the addition of rennet, cream is no more than the oily part of the milk that floats to the top, and butter is its churned version. Curds are a staple of the ancient Palestinian diet (cf., e.g., Gen 18:8; 2 Sam 17:29; Isa 7:15, 22). See further on Job 20:17.

6.d. יצוק עמדי is lit. "poured out with me"; KJV has "poured me out," RSV, NIV "poured out for me." But since עמדי is difficult to construe and the colon seems overlong, perhaps it should be omitted (so Ley, Beer [*BHK*], Larcher, Fohrer, KBL, 396a, NAB, and in the *Translation* above); Gordis, however, points out that some 1st-person reference occurs in all the cola of vv 2–6, and it could perhaps be understood as similar to the "ethic" dative, as Merx ("around me"). As for יצוק, several suggestions have been made: (1) BDB, 848a, takes יָצוּק as impf of צוק II "pour out." (2) KBL, 396a, however, does not recognize this root and takes יָצוּק as qal passive ptcp of יצק "pour out." (3) Beer (*BHK*) prefers reading יָצַק "pours out" (so too de Wilde, NEB, NAB "flowed with," perhaps JB "poured [from the rocks]"; the emendation is adopted in the *Translation* above). (4) Not at all probable (bizarre, says Dhorme) is the proposal of Duhm, Beer (*BH*² *frt*), Hölscher to read יָצוּק עָמְדִי "my standing still, where I stood, poured out," omitting צור as a dittograph of יצוק and revocalizing עמדי; the resultant sense is too awkward. (5) Nor is Dhorme's proposal acceptable, that יצוק means "hard"; though מֻצָק at 11:15 means "cast, poured" (as of metal, from יצק) and so "hard," rock is of course not poured or cast. (6) M. Dahood (*Ugaritic-Hebrew Philology: Marginal Notes on Recent Publications,* BibOr 17 [Rome: Pontifical Biblical Institute, 1965] 60) reads ברחץ הליכי וְצֳרִי צוק עֲמוּדַי פגלי־שמן "when my feet were bathed with cream and balsam, when rivers of oil flowed over my legs"; צוק would have to be inf of יצק "pour" (though צֶקֶת is the only form that appears), but it would be strange that the *beth* of the inf רחץ should have to do double duty for this verb also; עמדי "with me" becomes, in Dahood's reading, עֲמוּדַי "my pillars," which we would have to allow can mean "legs," attested nowhere else, though Dahood finds it also in 23:10. Too many points need to be stretched to make this suggestion remotely possible, added to which is the fact, pointed out by de Wilde, that צרי "balsam" is a resin or gum and thus highly unsuitable for bathing in (fragrant balsam, בשם, is what is needed).

7.a. The Heb. is surprisingly difficult, though the words seem straightforward enough. בצאתי שער עלי־קרת is lit. "when I went out the gate upon the town," which makes little sense. There is no problem with יצא "go out" followed by a direct obj (יצא פתח "go out the door" in 31:34, יצא את־העיר "go out the town" in Gen 44:4; Exod 9:29), but how are we to understand "upon the town"? There are quite a few possibilities:

(1) Perhaps Job goes out the gate of his own house "to" the town (so Davidson, Dillmann, Strahan, Driver–Gray, REB; cf. Gibson); but this would be the only place where a house would have "gates" (the "house of Yahweh" has gates in Jer 7:2; 36:10; Ezek 8:14; 10:19; 1 Chr 9:23, but that is different); Job's house has "doors" (דלת) in 31:32 (פתח in v 34). And why should we suppose that Job lived *outside* the town?

(2) Perhaps he went "to" the gate and "to" the city (Delitzsch, RV "to the gate unto the city"); but the previous objection applies here too. In addition, why should it say "to the gate to the city"? For when he has reached the gate he is at the city.

(3) Perhaps the gate is "over" the town (as על can well mean); so Dhorme translates "the gate that towers over the city." But there seems little point in describing the gate when all Job is doing is walking through it to get somewhere else. Duhm even suggests that Job's council met in an upper chamber of the gatehouse, but how could it then be in the "square" (רחוב)?

(4) Perhaps he went out (of his house, in the town) "to" the gate (the prep being understood) "in" or "at" the town (Stevenson, Hölscher, Tur-Sinai, Gordis), a normal enough sense of על. But why say "the gate *at* the city" if one means "the gate *of* the city"?

(5) Perhaps he went "to" the gate "through" the town (so KJV). But I can find no other place where על means "through" in a physical sense.

(6) Perhaps he went out of the gate of a smaller town and up to (על) a larger city on a mound above the town (so Guillaume). Forced.

(7) Perhaps we should turn to comparative Semitic philology for a solution. What if על means "from," as it does in Moabite and Phoenician and allegedly Ugaritic? So Pope, Ceresko, and Hartley, following M. J. Dahood ("Northwest Semitic Philology and Job," in *The Bible in Current Catholic Thought: Gruenthaner Memorial Volume,* ed. J. L. McKenzie, St. Mary's Theology Studies 1 [New York: Herder & Herder, 1962] 55–74 [68]); so too NEB. The problem is that there is almost nowhere else where על has been claimed to mean "from" in Hebrew; on this supposed sense of the prep, see Blommerde, 23 (with bibliography); the only other examples claimed for Job are 30:2, 4 (other cases include Pss 4:6 [7]; 81:5 [6]; Zech 9:16; Dan 2:1; 6:19; see G. R. Driver, "Hebrew Roots and Words," *WO* 1 [1947–52] 406–15 [413]; review of *The Assyrian Dictionary of the Oriental Institute of Chicago,* by A. L. Oppenheim et al., *JSS* 9 [1964] 346–50 [348–49]). Dahood argues, following Hitzig, that the רחוב was *outside* the city gate, being a "broad open place" equivalent to a threshing floor (גרן); but are we to imagine town assemblies being held in such a place rather than in the shade of the city gate?

(8) Perhaps there is no gate at all, and שער "gate" is to be revocalized to שֹׂעֵר, ptcp of שׂער "storm, rage," thus "storming from the city" (Ceresko), supposedly signifying "his enthusiasm in hurrying out to work." But can such an executive tycoon belong to the same world as a Job who washes his footsteps in yoghurt?

(9) Perhaps after all the text needs emending. LXX had ἐξεπορευόμην ὄρθριος ἐν πόλει "I went out early in[to] the city," evidently reading שַׁחַר "[at] dawn" or perhaps שֹׁחֵר "rising early" (elsewhere in qal only at Prov 11:27). The Qumran Tg is similar, except that it translates *both* שער and שחר with its בעצפרין בתרעי קריא "in the mornings at the gates of the city." Emendation to שַׁחַר "early, at dawn" is adopted by Ewald, Merx, de Wilde.

(10) Perhaps Budde was right to think שַׁעַר nothing but a gloss on קָרֶת, and that עלי was a misunderstanding for לַעֲלוֹת, thus "I went out to go up to the city." But perhaps not.

(11) Or perhaps it is קרת "city" that is the problem. Rashi understood קָרֶת as "a high ceiling," under which the elders of the city would sit to do business.

(12) Less probably, Gray thinks קְרָת has nothing to do with "town," but is the inf constr of יקר "be honorable," translating "I want out to the gate in honour." Though the form is acceptable, the inf constr of יקר does not actually occur.

(13) If only עלי preceded rather than followed שער! Then Job would have gone out "to the gate of the town," and all would have been well. I suspect that, by whatever means, this is the meaning we should end up with (so also Terrien, Fedrizzi, Gordis, Sicre Díaz, JB, NIV), and so adopt the emendation עלי־שער קרת for the sake of the *Translation*—though I am also attracted by the emendation to שחר on the basis of the LXX. In the GNB the gate, the town, and the square have all disappeared—presumably because they are all too culture-specific for readers who know of no towns with gates, and the phrase is simply "whenever the city elders met"!

7.b. רחוב is always "square" in the sg, "streets" in the pl; see D. J. A. Clines, "Squares and Streets: The Distinction of רחוב 'Square' and רחבות 'Streets,'" in *On the Way to the Postmodern: Old Testament Essays, 1967–1998,* JSOTSup 293 (Sheffield: Sheffield Academic Press, 1998) 2:631–36.

8.a. The pf-tense verbs in vv 8–11 are frequentative, following the impf אכין "I would settle" (v 7).

8.b. חבא niph, lit. "was hidden" (KJV, RV, Driver–Gray "hid themselves," Pope, NJPS "hid"). Though the literal sense is no doubt not intended, it is hard to be sure what the best sense is. JB, NIV, GNB have "stepped aside," NEB "kept out of sight," REB "kept back out of sight," RSV, NAB, Stevenson, Gray "withdrew," Moffatt "fell back before me." Guillaume ("Hebrew and Arabic Lexicography: A Comparative Study," *AbrN* 1 [1959–60] 3–35 [23]; "The Arabic Background of the Book of Job," in *Promise and Fulfilment,* FS S. H. Hooke, ed. F. F. Bruce [Edinburgh: T. & T. Clark, 1963] 106–27 [119]; *Studies,* 111; cf. Lane 701a), followed by Fedrizzi, thinks חבא means "stand silent," comparing Arab. *ḫabi'a* "die out" (of a fire).

8.c. קמו עמדו, lit. "arose, stood," by asyndesis (Joüon–Muraoka, §177). Dahood ("Northwest Semitic Philology and Job," 68–69), followed by Ceresko and Fedrizzi, regards קום as an auxiliary verb, thus "began (to stand up)"; so too NJB "rose to their feet," Strauss "began to stand up." Gordis thinks that עמד means "be silent" here and at Job 30:20; 32:16; Zech 3:5. Emendation of קמו to כֻּלָּם "all of them" (Merx, following LXX πάντες) is no improvement.

10.a. נחבאו niph, lit. "were hidden" (the verb as in v 8), pl in agreement with נגידים "princes" rather than with its grammatical subject, קול "voice" (emendation to sg נֶחְבָּא "was hidden" [Reiske, Ehrlich, Perles[2], 22] is not mandatory). Dhorme argues, not very convincingly, that חבא itself can mean "be hushed," since it can also mean "be veiled." RSV, NJPS also have "were hushed," NAB "was silenced," REB "died away," Moffatt "became dumb," but we do not know how they arrived at those translations.

No doubt a voice can be "hidden," but the idiom does not occur elsewhere, and since the verb has already been used two verses previously (of the young men), various emendations have been proposed here: (1) Some have emended to נֶאֱלָם "was silent" (Siegfried, Budde, Driver–Gray, Beer [*BHK vel*], Stevenson[2]) (*lips* are silent in Ps 31:18 [19]). (2) Others read נִכְלָא "was restrained" (Duhm, Driver–Gray, Beer [*BHK vel*], *HALOT,* 1:284b), or כָּלְאוּ "[nobles] restrained [their voice]" (Hölscher, comparing Vg *cohibebant*). (3) Gray reads נֶחְכָּא "was tied up," from a new Heb. חכא "tie up" cognate with Arab. *ḥaka'a* "tie, tighten a knot" (Lane, 615b). But it seems even stranger to speak of a voice being "tied up" than of one being "hidden." (4) H. P. Chajes ("Notes de lexicographie hébraïque," *REJ* 44 [1902] 223–29) sees here another Heb. verb חבא, cognate with Arab. *ḫb'* "become extinct" (cf. Guillaume, on v 8). (5) Tur-Sinai thinks it is really a נחב "grow lean, dry up" (as in Syr.), translating "was hushed" (cf. *DCH,* 5:652b); but it is no better to have a voice "lean" or "dried up" than "hidden." (6) Stevenson, transposing v 21 to follow v 10, also transposes the verbs נחבאו (v 10) and וידמו (v 21), thus translating "fell silent" (from דמם "be silent").

10.b. More prosaically, REB has "every man held his tongue." Beer (*BH*[2]) removes vv 21–25 to this point.

11.a. Beer (BH^2), followed by Moffatt, NAB, NEB, moves vv 21–25 to follow v 10. Moffatt rearranges the verses in the sequence 21, 22b, 23, 22a, 24–25.

11.b. כי must here be "when" and not "for" (against Driver–Gray), since v 11 is not the reason for the silence of the councillors in vv 9–10. Gordis prefers to take it as an asseverative, "indeed." On the "emphatic" כי, see *Note* 22:26.b. Duhm, Beer (BH^2 *frt*), Hölscher unjustifiably want to delete it.

11.c. עוד hiph "be a witness for" (so BDB, 729b; *HALOT,* 2:795a; *DCH,* vol. 6, *s.v.*), somewhat strangely perhaps, since in 1 Kgs 21:10, 13 עוד את hiph is "testify against." The suff would be datival (as König, *Syntax,* §21, Joüon, §125b, Blommerde). For other examples of datival suffs in Job, see *Note* 22:21.d. Gordis therefore thinks it must be from another עוד "help," which *HALOT,* 2:795a, recognizes for Pss 146:9; 147:6 (polel); 20:9 (hithpo), offering as cognate Arab. *ʿāda* IV "bring back, restore, bring about" (Wehr–Cowan, 635); cf. also *DCH,* vol. 6, *s.v.* Gordis thus translates "gave me strength, encouraged me," which is a possible, though not a preferable, sense.

12.a. שׁוע piel "cry out for help" (BDB, 1002b; *HALOT,* 4:1443b) is well attested. But we may perhaps have here the term שׁוֹעַ "high-ranking (person)," as also at 34:19, 20 (if emended); Isa 32:5 (*HALOT,* 4:1444a); see P. Joüon, "Notes de lexicographie hébraïque: XIII. שׁוֹעַ 'grand' (socialement)," *Bib* 18 (1937) 205–6; V. Sasson, "Ugaritic *ṯʿ* and *ġzr* and Hebrew *šôwaʿ* and *ʿōzēr,*" *UF* 14 (1982) 201–8; M. Dietrich and O. Loretz, "Ugaritisch *ṯʿ/ṯʿy* und hebräisch *šwʿ*," *UF* 19 (1987) 33–36. We should have to vocalize מִשּׁוֹעַ "from the noble" (presumably as a collective); Strauss alludes to this possibility but rejects it.

12.b. יתום ולא־עזר לו, lit. "the fatherless, and no helper to him." Two classes of persons could be in view (so NAB "the orphans, and the unassisted," Moffatt "the fatherless and helpless"), or else the second phrase could merely be descriptive of the fatherless (so Delitzsch, Stevenson, Fohrer, RSV, JB, NIV, GNB), the *waw* being *waw explicativum* (Blommerde, Ceresko; on the *waw explicativum,* see GKC, §154a n. 1b; Blommerde, 29–30 [bibliography]; it has been suggested also for 1:6, 13; 3:19; 15:18; 32:3). Some MSS omit the "and" (so too Kissane), thus making the second interpretation obligatory. B. Q. Baisas ("Ugaritic *ʿḏr* and Hebrew *ʿzr* I," *UF* 5 [1973] 41–52 [47]), followed by Ceresko and Habel, observes that עזר sometimes has the sense "deliver" (cf. *DCH,* vol. 6, *s.v.*), and so may be exactly equivalent to מלט in the first colon (at Ps 37:40 it is parallel with פלט; other possible examples are Ps 72:12, a close parallel to the present text, Lam 1:7; 2 Chr 32:8; 1QH 5:6); here he translates "who had no acquitter."

13.a. אבד "die, be destroyed" can mean "be about to die, be in danger of death" in its ptcp אבד (cf. *DCH,* 1:99a §1b). The ptcp is rendered by KJV "ready to perish," RSV "about to perish," Moffatt "perishing," JB, NIV "dying," NJPS, NRSV "wretched," GNB "in deepest misery," NEB "threatened with ruin," NAB "in extremity," Pope "destitute." Fohrer and de Wilde suggest "discouraged," on the basis of the phrase אָבַד לֵב (as in Jer 4:9), but this is improbable since the term לב is not used here. Gordis (as also Budde, Sicre Díaz) has "beggar," understanding אבד as "wander about" as in Deut 26:5; but it is doubtful if אבד ever has that sense, the meaning "stray" of sheep in Jer 50:6 being in the sense of "be lost, disappear" (though cf. *HALOT,* 1:2b §2; *DCH,* 1:99b §4).

13.b. Pope, Ceresko, Fedrizzi want the phrase בוא על, lit. "come upon," to mean "enter the presence" (as Dahood, "Northwest Semitic Philology and Job," 69). על may mean "before" in other contexts, but it is normal to speak of blessing being "upon" (על) someone (as Ps 3:8 [9]) or as "coming upon" (בוא על) someone (as Deut 28:2; Prov 24:25).

14.a. P. Joüon ("Notes philologiques sur le texte hébreu de Job 1, 5; 9, 35; 12, 21; 28, 1; 28, 27; 29, 14," *Bib* 11 [1930] 322–24 [324]), followed by Ceresko, NEB, revocalized וַיִּלְבָּשֵׁנִי qal to וַיְלַבְּשֵׁנִי piel "and it adorned me." But the qal has the same sense, "put on, wear," with the acc of the garment (as at Deut 22:11; Zech 13:4) (see *Comment*). N. M. Waldman ("The Imagery of Clothing, Covering, and Overpowering," *JNES* 19 [1989] 161–70 [166–67]) suggests that the second use of the verb is in the sense of "overpower, overcome" (as in Judg 6:34), but that is not clearly a preferable sense here. Emendation to hiph is not necessary (against Pope). NEB inexplicably translates וַיִּלְבָּשֵׁנִי twice: "I put on righteousness as a garment and it clothed me; justice, like a cloak or a turban, wrapped me around."

14.b. משפטי "my justice" is not thought a problem by most, but it is arguable that since צדק "righteousness" in the first colon has no personal suff neither should משפט here; thus Beer (BH^2) reads simply מִשְׁפָּט "justice," claiming the support of LXX, Pesh; so too Gray.

14.c. Others think this a case of enjambment, of the sense running on from the first half of the line to the second (so Hölscher, Fohrer, van der Lugt).

16.a. חקר is "search, explore" (BDB, 350b). If Job "explored" the cause (ריב) of aliens, it means no doubt that Job "championed" (NRSV), "took up [the cause]" (NEB), "took up [the case]" (Moffatt,

NIV), "took [the side]" (GNB) of such strangers, and that "the stranger's case had a hearing" from him (JB). But NJPS "looked into" and NAB "studied" (like KJV "searched out") are perhaps the most precise translations. Blommerde suggests that the suff is datival ("I investigated for him"); for other examples of datival suffs, see *Note* 22:21.d. Tur-Sinai is unsatisfied by the usual translations, wondering how merely searching out someone's cause will help them (it seems an academic enquiry in the worst sense of the word); so he suggests that רב is not "cause," but is a new word רָב or רֵב "poor, helpless" (on the word, supposedly cognate with Arab. *rwb*, cf. *Note* 4:3.c), and so parallel to אביון "poor" in the first half of the line. But, we might ask, why would Job be "searching" for poor people? Are they lost?

16.b. רב לא־ידעתי could mean "the cause I did not know" (as Vg *causam quam nesciebam*; so too Good), but, as Dhorme says, that would be too commonplace a sentiment, and the extraordinary thing is his taking an interest in the cause of a *stranger.* It is better to understand "the cause of someone I did not know."

17.a. מתלעות is "teeth" according to BDB, 1069a, who suspect that the root תלע, though not attested, would mean "gnaw" (so too "fangs" in RSV, NEB, JB, NIV). *HALOT,* 2:654b, understands it rather as "jawbone," while "jaws" is the rendering in KJV (RVmg "Heb. great teeth"), Moffatt, NAB, NJPS, AS, 470a. *DCH,* 5:570a, offers "tooth or jaws, jawbone." The word is spelled מַלְתָּעוֹת at Ps 58:7. M. J. Dahood, "The Etymology of *Maltā'ôt* (Ps 58,7)," *CBQ* 17 (1955) 180–83, supports the sense "teeth" (as in 4:10; and cf. the idiom of breaking the teeth in Ps 3:8); whether the noun is to be connected with נתע "break, crush," as Dahood there supposed, or with לוע "swallow" or a byform ילע (as in his "Hebrew Lexicography: A Review of W. Baumgartner's *Lexikon,* Volume II," *Or* 45 [1976] 327–65 [359]) is not our concern here. J. A. Hackett and J. Huehnergard ("On Breaking Teeth," *HTR* 77 [1984] 259–75) argue that the phrase is derived from ancient Near Eastern legal language; here, however, the second colon makes it clear that the imagery is of wild animals, and in any case it is uncertain whether the term means "teeth" rather than "jawbone."

17.b. אַשְׁלִיךְ "I caused to drop" is emended by Beer (*BHK*), Hölscher, Fohrer, Gerleman (*BHS prp*), Gray to אֶשְׁלֹף "I dragged" and by NEB to אֲשַׁלֵּף piel, according to Brockington. But שׁלף is generally used of unsheathing a sword, or drawing off a sandal (Ruth 4:7), and there is no parallel to the sense "drag away." G. R. Driver ("Problems in Job," *AJSL* 52 [1935–36] 160–73 [163]) sees here a new שׁלך "save, rescue," cognate with Arab. *salaka.* But, as J. Kaltner (*The Use of Arabic in Biblical Hebrew Lexicography,* CBQMS 28 [Washington, DC: Catholic Biblical Association of America, 1996] 53–54) points out, Arab. *salaka* means rather "insert" (Lane, 1411c), and only the late usages in Dozy, 1:676–77, are used by Driver in support. NEB with "I rescued the prey" follows Driver, despite Brockington's textual notes, but REB (like NJPS) "wrested the prey" reverts to the usual meaning.

18.a. ואמר, lit. "and I said" (as in KJV), but אמר often enough means "think" (cf. BDB, 56a §2; *HALOT,* 1:66b §4; *DCH,* 1:324b §8); so too, e.g., Moffatt, RSV, NEB, NJPS.

18.b. אגוע "I shall die," from גוע "perish, die" (BDB, 157a), is unproblematic. But Siegfried reads אֶזְקַן "I shall grow old," following LXX γηράσει. Guillaume wants a closer parallel with "multiply days," so proposes another Heb. גוע, cognate with Arab. *'aswa'a* "remain" (followed by Fedrizzi); but the proposal is not successful, since living long and dying are not at all contradictory; the proposal that *gimel* in the Heb. replaces *sin* in the Arab., though paralleled, is far-fetched; and the Arab. *'aswa'a* means rather "be straight, erect, firm" (Lane, 1477b). Gray reads אֶנְגַּע "[like a reed-cane] I will thrive," from a new נגע "thrive," cognate with Arab. *naja'a* (but *naja'a* seems rather to mean "benefit, be wholesome" [Lane, 3028b; Wehr–Cowan, 945a]).

18.c. עם־קני, lit. "with my nest (קן)," but קן means "nestlings" (as a collective) in Deut 32:11 (less probably Isa 16:2), as Driver–Gray, BDB, 890a, AS, 662b recognize. Thus too Moffatt "among my brood," NJPS "with my family," NIV "in my own house." J. Barr has indeed argued that קן can mean "family, home" without any metaphorical reference to a "nest" (as also at Num 24:21; Jer 22:23; Hab 2:9; Obad 4; Ecclus 36:26 [31; 37:30 is not a genuine occurrence]); cf. his "Is Hebrew קן 'Nest' a Metaphor?" in *Semitic Studies,* FS W. Leslau, ed. A. S. Kaye (Wiesbaden: Harrassowitz, 1991) 1:150–61 (154–56). Duhm, Hölscher, Fohrer, and Grabbe, 98–101, argue that Job expected to die "with his nest," like the phoenix (see *Note* below) who in some forms of the myth is burned at its death, along with its nest. But there is no "nest" in Job's life that he could imagine dying along with him; he certainly did not in former days envisage his family dying when he did. The same goes for the translation of A. C. M. Blommerde, "I shall die with my flock" ("The Broken Construct Chain, Further Examples," *Bib* 55 [1974] 549–52), reading עִם־מִקְנֵי; it is a further weakness that the second colon is very awkward, "after having multiplied it as the sand of the seas." Blommerde earlier translated "though I perish like its [the phoenix's] nest," taking the final *yodh* as a 3d sg suff (for other examples, see on 21:16) and עם as "like," following M. Dahood, "Nest and Phoenix in Job 29, 18," *Bib* 48 (1967)

542–44. On עם "like" (עם comparative), see BDB, 767b; *DCH,* vol. 6, *s.v.*; Blommerde, 25 (bibliography); M. Held, "The Action-Result (Factitive-Passive) Sequence of Identical Verbs in Biblical Hebrew and Ugaritic," *JBL* 84 (1965) 272–82 (280 n. 36); E. Zurro Rodríguez, "Valor comparativo de la partícula *'im,*" *EstBib* 56 (1998) 251–60 (258); other examples have been proposed for 3:14, 15; 9:14, 26; 37:18; 40:15. עם "like" is also recognized here by Kissane.

N. Herz ("Egyptian Words and Idioms in the Book of Job," *OLZ* 16 [1913] 343–46 [345]) suggests another Heb. קֵן, like Eg. *ḳn* "strength." So too G. R. Driver ("Birds in the Old Testament: II. Birds in Life," *PEQ* 87 [1955] 129–40 [138–39]; "Problems in the Hebrew Text of Job," in *Wisdom in Israel and in the Ancient Near East,* FS H. H. Rowley, ed. M. Noth and D. W. Thomas, VTSup 3 [Leiden: Brill, 1955] 72–93 [85–86]), comparing Akk. *qannu* "rope, cord." Thus also Terrien *en pleine vigueur,* NEB "with my powers unimpaired." But *qannu* is now understood rather as "hem" (*CAD,* 13:83a).

Among emendations, (1) Merx, Bickell[2] (קָנַי "my reeds"), and Kissane, Gray emend to קָנֶה "[like] the reed" (following Syr.), i.e., the long-lasting aromatic reed. (2) Following LXX ἡ ἡλικία μου γηράσει "my age will grow old," Ehrlich emends to מִזֹּקֶן "from old age," i.e., not prematurely, Cheyne to בְּזִקְנִי "in my old age" (*EB,* vol. 3, col. 3765), and Pope apparently to בְּזָקְנַי "in my old age." (3) Larcher reads קַרְנִי, lit. "[in] my horn," i.e., "in my pride (*fierté*)," as also BJ; hence too JB "in honour." (4) Dhorme tamely emends to עִמִּי זָקֵן אגוע "[I said] to myself, I shall die old"; similarly Rowley, P. P. Saydon, "Philological and Textual Notes to the Maltese Translation of the Old Testament," *CBQ* 23 (1961) 249–57 (252). (5) Tur-Sinai offers the stilted emendation עָם קני אגוע "I shall die with my nest a nation" (we should read rather עַם).

18.d. Strauss explains the *waw* as *waw explicativum* (GKC, §154a n.1b); for further examples, see *Note* 29:12.b.

18.e. The proposal of Blommerde, "Broken Construct Chain," 550–51, to read יַמִּים "seas" for יָמִים "days," the constr chain חל ימים "sand of the seas" being supposedly interrupted by the verb ארבה "I shall multiply," has little to commend it.

18.f. כַּחוֹל "like the sand" (BDB, 297b; Zorell, 227a; AS, 235a; Ges[18], 330a), as KJV, RSV, NRSVmg, NEB "uncounted like the grains of sand," JB, Merx, Ehrlich, Driver–Gray, Dhorme, Tur-Sinai, Pope, Rowley, Fedrizzi, Andersen, Sicre Díaz, Hartley, Good. Barr ("Is Hebrew קן 'Nest' a Metaphor?" 150–61) has with good cause remarked that if קן were not translated "nest" no one would have any difficulty with "sand" for חול. But many now follow the small alteration (which may be no more than a phonetic variant, according to Gordis) to כַּחוּל "like the phoenix" (*HALOT,* 1:297b, vocalizes חוֹל, noting חול as a reading of Oriental MSS; cf. *DCH,* 3:172a); this interpretation was already adopted by the Talmud (*b. Sanhedrin* 108b), and by the Masoretic tradition of Nehardea; so NRSV, NEBmg, NJPS, Ewald, Hitzig, Delitzsch, Davidson, Budde, Duhm, Gibson, Peake, Strahan, Hölscher, Stevenson, Fohrer, Terrien, Gordis, Habel, van der Lugt, Newsom; see also Grabbe, 98–101; D. N. Freedman, review of *Job 29–31 in the Light of Northwest Semitic,* by A. R. Ceresko, *JBL* 102 (1983) 138–44 (141). Whether or not the phoenix appears in Ugaritic (see W. F. Albright, "Baal-Zephon," in *Festschrift für Alfred Bertholet zum 80. Geburtstag,* ed. W. Baumgartner, O. Eissfeldt, K. Elliger, and L. Rost [Tübingen: Mohr, 1950] 1–14 [3–4]; M. Dahood, "*Ḥôl* 'Phoenix' in Job 29:18 and in Ugaritic," *CBQ* 36 [1974] 85–88) is of no consequence here. Dahood's interpretation of עם־קני, "Though I perish like its nest" ("Nest and Phoenix," 542–44), followed by Blommerde, introduces a false note, as well as requiring subscription to his view that עם means "like" and that the suff of קני is really a 3d-person suff. For the meaning "like" for עם, see *Note* 18.c above. On the 3d-person *yodh* suff, see *Note* 21:16.e. On the phoenix, see further, *Comment.*

Ball, Beer (*BH*[2]), Kissane, Larcher, de Wilde, Gray, following LXX, Vg, read כְּנַחַל "like a palm tree" (so JB); but though the palm tree is long-lived, and Pliny even tells us that like the phoenix, with which it shares its name, it comes back to life after it has died (*Natural History* 13.9.42), the idea of multiplying one's days like the palm tree seems very far-fetched.

19.a. פתוח, lit. "open to," i.e., accessible to, not exactly "spread out to" (as RV, RSV, NAB, KJV "spread out by"), "reaching" (NJPS), "reach[ing] to" (Moffatt, NIV), or "thrust out to" (JB).

19.b. On לין "lodge, dwell," and not just "spend the night," see *Note* 41:22 (14).a.

20.a. Hoffmann and Beer (*BHK prps*) read כִּידוֹנִי "my javelin" for כְּבוֹדִי "my honor." M. Mansoor, on the basis of a Qumran usage of כבוד, proposed "victory" or "strength" for the term ("The Thanksgiving Hymns and the Masoretic Text [Part II]," *RevQ* 3 [1961–62] 387–94 [387–89]), a sense that he found also in Pss 3:3 (4); 24:8; 1 Sam 4:21; Isa 10:16, but this proposal is unnecessary. Ceresko, followed by Hartley, postulates a new כָּבוֹד "liver" (as in Ps 16:9, where it is parallel to לב "heart"; and cf. also Gen 49:6; Pss 7:5 [6]; 57:8 [9]; the word would be a byform of כָּבֵד "liver"), but the supposed parallel with "hand" is nugatory since it is "bow" that is parallel to כבוד.

20.b. Moffatt "fresh honours fall to me," JB "my reputation will never fade." There is perhaps something unexpected in parallelling כבוד "honour" with קשׁת "bow," and the justification of Driver–Gray, that "Job speaks, not as a warrior, but as a *moral* hero," falls short of convincing. NEB, translating "the bow always new in my grasp," follows Driver, "Problems in the Hebrew Text of Job," 85–86, in reading כְּבֵדִי "my bow-handle," cognate with Arab. *kabid* "heavy part, central piece" of a bow (Lane, 2584c). חדשׁ "new, fresh" may, however, be thought a strange adj to use of a bow-handle (for its uses, cf. *DCH,* 3:165a).

20.c. קשׁת is unquestionably "bow," so NEB "arrow" is inexplicable. Gray reads, for קַשְׁתִּי "my bow," קְשׁוּתִי "my strength," but the word (presumably קְשׁוּת) is unknown in Heb., and Gray may be proposing a new word like קְשִׁי "obstinacy" (BDB, 904b); he finds it also at Gen 49:24.

20.d. חלף hiph is usually "change" (as of garments); in 14:7 it was of a tree sprouting new shoots, but it can hardly be thought that a bow should "sprout" (against Budde, Hölscher, *HALOT,* 1:321b), perhaps like Aaron's rod (Num 17:8 [23]). But since "change" can often imply "exchange old for new," the verb can signify "renew" (as in Isa 40:31; 41:1, where כח "strength" is the obj). So it might mean here "renews itself, is renewed" (internal hiph), that is, his bow is always as good as new, as pliable (so too Driver–Gray, Gordis) as a new-cut bow; thus RSV, NJPS "ever new," KJV, Pope "renewed." NEB "the arrow ever ready to hand" is not what the Heb. says. JB "the bow in my hands will gain new strength" seems to borrow some of its sense from the eagles' wings of Isa 40:31, but כח "strength" is explicit there, and not here. The suggestion of KBL, 304b, "my bow throws arrow after arrow" (followed by Fohrer), is entirely implausible (even more so Tur-Sinai's wonder bow, which automatically replaces shot arrows with new ones—science fiction, says Sicre Díaz), since there are no arrows in the sentence (whether or not the thought is "too aggressive" for Job, as de Wilde thinks, is another matter). Since the bow is said to be a figure for strength, Moffatt has, reasonably enough, except for suppressing the metaphor, "I grow in might," and NJPS has "my vigor refreshed."

21.a. Beer (*BH*[2]), followed by Moffatt, Larcher, Gray, BJ, JB, NJB, NAB, NEB, moved vv 21–25 to follow v 10.

21.b. לי "to me" is in emphatic position, at the beginning of the sentence; so too KJV "unto me men gave ear."

21.c. ויחלו, lit. "and they waited" (יחל piel), is translated by some with an adv modifying "would listen"; thus "expectantly" by NEB, NJPS, NIV, "anxiously" by JB, "carefully" by Moffatt. The Heb. seems to say rather that after they "heard" Job, they "waited" in silence, just as, in the next verse, when he had spoken they would not speak again. We might of course have expected in that case that ויחלו would have been vocalized with *waw* consec. Duhm, Beer (*BH*[2]) inexplicably emend ויחלו "and they waited" to וְיֶחַכּוּ "and they waited" (from חכה piel).

21.d. Duhm and Dhorme reverse the positions of ויחלו "and they waited" and וידמו "and they were silent" on the ground that "for my counsel" is unintelligible after "they were silent" (similarly Beer [*BH*[2]], reading וַיִּדֹּמּוּ וַיְחַכּוּ; Driver, "Problems in the Hebrew Text of Job," 86); but the sense seems to be that, rather than speaking themselves, they would just wait until Job had some more of his wisdom to impart. דמם I has generally been recognized as "be silent, cease" (BDB, 198b; *HALOT,* 1:226a; *DCH,* 2:450b), but G. R. Driver has argued that this verb, with the Akk. cognate *damāmu* "groan" (*CAD,* 3:59b) (cf. Arab. *damdama* "hum, mumble" [Wehr–Cowan, 292a]) properly means "moan, groan." We should therefore, he says, read יִדְּמוּ "they were silent," from דמה niph "be silent" (recognized by *HALOT,* 1:225b; *DCH,* 2:448b). See his "Problems in the Hebrew Text of Job," 86–87; "A Confused Hebrew Root (דמם, דמה, דום)," in פרסומי החברה לחקר המקרא בישראל, ספר ח׳, מוגש לכבוד פרופ׳ נ.ח. טור־סיני למלאת לו שבעים שנה [Sepher N. H. Tur-Sinai], ed. M. Haran and B. Luria (Jerusalem: Kiryat Sepher, 1960) 1*–11*. In the notes to the NEB (Brockington, 112), however, it is said that NEB read וְיָדֹמּוּ, from דום "be silent," a verb not recognized by BDB and only alluded to by *HALOT,* 1:216b. *DCH,* 2:425b, mentions only the senses "stand still, cease, wait" for דום; cf. also Guillaume, "Hebrew and Arabic Lexicography," 21–22.

21.e. Reading either למו עצתי, or, with many MSS, לְמוֹעֲצָתִי "to my counsel" (Beer [*BH*[2]], claiming the support of the ancient versions).

22.a. אחרי דברי, lit. "after my word," which would equally well render an emended דַּבְּרִי "my speaking" (so Merx, Dillmann, Budde, Duhm, Beer [*BHK frt*], Hölscher [*frt*]).

22.b. ישׁנו "they would repeat" (שׁנה III, BDB, 1040a) seems unexceptionable as an impf of repeated action, but Beer (*BH*[2] *frt*) would read the pf שָׁנוּ, with the same meaning.

22.c. Moffatt moves vv 22b–23 to follow v 21, in an attempt to remove some apparent illogicalities in the MT sequence. V 22b seems logically to precede the silence of the counselors in v 22a, but there is no need to reverse the cola (as de Wilde).

22.d. נטף is "drip, drop" (BDB, 642b), in two places of clouds dropping water (Judg 5:4) and of the sky dripping (Ps 68:8 [9], without an expressed obj). So it is understandable that NRSV adds "like dew," NJPS "my words were as drops [of dew]," Moffatt "my words fell fresh on them like showers." But the word does not usually refer to rain (and dew does not, in any case, truly "drip" or "fall"): in Joel 3 (4):18 and Amos 9:13 mountains drip with wine, while in Prov 5:3 and Cant 4:11; 5:13 lips drip honey and myrrh, and in Cant 5:5 hands drip myrrh. So some such rendering as NEB "my words fell gently on them" (similarly NIV, Hartley), JB "my words dropped on them, one by one," NAB "received my pronouncement drop by drop" (similarly Rowley) may be more to the point. Yet the uses of the verb would suggest that the sense is more of *pleasing* with words than *refreshing*, and the image of *rain* is perhaps not present here but for the first time in v 23.

23.a. Duhm and Beer (*BH*²) argued that since v 23 develops v 22b, the verb here should be a *waw* consec וַיְּחַלוּ; but this must be wrong, since the waiting is not subsequent to the "dropping" (נטף). ויחלו "they waited" (from יחל) is unexceptionable, but Beer (*BHK frt*) suggests rather וַיְחַכּוּ, with the same meaning, from חכה.

23.b. לי is lit. "for me," but it is his words they are waiting for, so, without emending the text, we can translate "for them" (so too NEB).

23.c. Rather than ופיהם פערו "and they opened their mouths," Beer (*BH*²) reports the proposal כְּפִי הַמֶּגְרָפוֹת "[they waited] like the mouth of clods [for the late rains]." But it seems likely that מֶגְרָפָה means "shovel" rather than "clod" (see BDB, 175b; *HALOT*, 2:546b; *DCH*, 5:138a).

23.d. למלקוש, lit. "for the late rains," but the *kaph* of comparison is understood from כמטר, just as the *lamedh* here is assumed in כמטר; there is no need to emend to כַּמַּלְקוֹשׁ "like the latter, i.e., spring, rain" (as Duhm, Kissane [כְּמַלְקוֹשׁ]). Moffatt "like the dry clods in spring for rain" adopts the readings הַמֶּגְרָפוֹת "clods" and מַלְקוֹשׁ "spring rain."

24.a. Budde, Duhm, Peake, Beer (*BHK*), Hölscher, Fohrer omitted לא "not"; thus NEB "when I smiled on them they took heart" (similarly Moffatt, NAB). Beer (*BHK*) would also read וַיַּאֲמִינוּ "and they took heart." Predictably, Ceresko revocalizes לא to the alleged לֵא "victorious," translating "When I smiled on them, powerful"—a dubious suggestion. For other examples of the supposed לֵא "Victor, mighty one," see *Note* 21:16.a. Gray reads the emphatic particle לְ, prefixed to יַאֲמִינוּ, thus "then indeed they gained confidence" (for other examples of לא emphatic, which is the same word, see *Note* 21:16.a).

24.b. So NJPS, like KJV "if I laughed on them, they believed it not," JB "it was too good to be true"; similarly NIV, Dhorme, Terrien, Pope, Gordis, Hartley. Driver–Gray read differently: "I laughed at them when they believed not." Kissane's interpretation, "If I laughed at them, they believed not," meaning that everyone rejected views at which he laughed, is strained. RSV has "I smiled on them when they had no confidence" (similarly RVmg, Gibson, de Wilde), but, as Driver–Gray remark, אמן hiph means "believe" and it is בטח that means "be confident." Duhm reads niph וַיֵּאָמְנוּ, but that still does not mean "and they were encouraged," but rather "and they were confirmed"—which is not entirely appropriate.

24.c. ואור פני לא יפילון is lit. "and the light of my face they did not cast down." For the interpretation of the clause as in the *Translation* above (cf. Good "treasured"), "and they did not disregard my good favor," see *Comment*. Perhaps NIV "the light of my face was precious to them" understands the colon similarly.

There are several other possible interpretations of the clause. NJPS has "they never expected a sign of my favor," JB "they watched my face for the least sign of favour." RSV's "and the light of my countenance they did not cast down" (NRSV "did not extinguish") sounds as if they could not overcome Job's relentless cheerfulness. Moffatt similarly translates "my cheerful gaze put heart into the hopeless." Dhorme explains, tortuously, "they did not allow the light of my face to fall, i.e., be lost" as meaning "nor was my smile lost on them," i.e., in accepting his smile they did not ignore its significance (similarly Hartley). More attractively, Pope understands that they were eager to catch the beneficent light of his face and let none of it be lost (similarly Terrien).

Among philologically based suggestions, (1) Gordis, following Yellin, understands יפילון as a short form of יַאֲפִילוּן "they [did not] darken [my face]," i.e., they did nothing to provoke my displeasure. But this understanding is not likely, because Job is not so much reflecting on his own feelings as on the dynamics of his relationship with his inferiors. (2) G. R. Driver ("Problems in the Hebrew Text of Job," 87–88) similarly read ואור פְּנֵיהֶם לא יַאֲפִילוּן "and they did not darken the light of their faces," i.e., they showed no angry looks (so NEB "[when my face lit up,] they lost their gloomy looks"). But this does not explain why the participants in the town council should have had gloomy looks in the first place. (3) Hölscher takes אור as a verb, translating "if my face was bright," with no improvement to the sense. Gray adopts this suggestion, reading אָרוּ פני לְיַבְלִיגוּ "if my face was bright they beamed," emphatic *lamedh* being prefixed to יבליגו and the verb being בלג as in 9:27; 10:20. (4) Ceresko understands "in the light of my face they did not grow sad," יַפִּילוּן being elliptical for יַפִּילוּן פְּנֵיהֶם "they did not let their faces fall" (cf. Gen 4:6), and a בְּ presumably being supplied before אור. (5) NJPS has "they never expected," deriving the word from פלל, usually "pray" but "expect" in Gen 48:11; it would be necessary to emend to piel, יְפַלְלוּן.

Among emendations, NAB, following Beer (*BH*[2] *prb; BHK prps*), deletes לא יפילון and substitutes אבלים ינחם from v 25c; thus "mourners took comfort from my cheerful glance" (see further on v 25).

25.a. Andersen revocalizes to אֻבְחַר "I was chosen," "implying election rather than the imposition of authority," he says. Ceresko, translating "I convoked their assembly," takes בחר as "gather," following M. Dahood ("Qoheleth and Northwest Semitic Philology," *Bib* 43 [1962] 349–65 [361]), who compared Ugar. *pḫr* "assembly" (*DUL,* 669), supposedly also at 1 Sam 20:30 and Eccl 9:4; see also *HALOT,* 1:120a; *DCH,* 2:139b.

25.b. NEB "planning their course," Moffatt, not a little anachronistically, "fixed their policy." There can be no question here that the clause is only hypothetical, "if I chose their way" (as Budde). Some older commentators thought it was the way *to* them and their company that Job sought out (so Dillmann, Budde, Gibson "I gladly frequented their society"; cf. Vg *si voluissem ire ad eos* "if I wished to go to them"). But the analogies (see *Comment*) make this unlikely.

Ceresko wants to find here דֶּרֶךְ II "power, dominion" (cf. *DCH,* 2:472a) in the supposed sense of "assembly" as the place where power is exercised (as Dahood also claimed for Ps 1:1 [*Psalms I,* 2]). Though דֶּרֶךְ as "power" may well be acceptable, an extension to "assembly" is forced. Gray also sees here דֶּרֶךְ II, translating "I chose their government," but it is hard to see how choosing a government could have been an option for a tribal leader like Job. Andersen reads דָּרִיכָם "their governor," comparing Canaanite *dāriku.*

25.c. שכן, lit. "dwelled." Ceresko claims it is "tented," but there is no parallel to such a sense of this verb. Equally unparalleled is the sense proposed by Gordis, "I sat at their head in ease."

25.d. כמלך בגדוד, lit. "like a king with a troop," is rendered by NEB "like a king encamped with his troops," and by Moffatt "commanding as a monarch among men." Gray thinks, however, that we have here a new גְּדוּד "excellence, prestige," cognate with Arab. *jadd* (Lane, 385b); he translates "I lived like a king in prestige."

25.e. The colon should probably be deleted, as in the *Translation* (with Budde, Driver–Gray, Beer [*BH*[2]], Stevenson, Jastrow, Hölscher, Fohrer, Hesse, Moffatt, NEB). Peake moves it to follow v 24. Most modern Eng. versions, including REB, retain it, as do Kissane (as an appropriate summary of the whole chapter), Terrien, Habel. Budde, Beer [*BHK*] and Duhm, de Wilde, NAB delete אשר and move the other two words to v 24b. But mourners are almost as much out of place in v 24 as they are here (so Driver–Gray).

25.f. Ceresko contrives to find here "a happy man" (followed by Good), vocalizing כְּאָשֵׁר. The word is not otherwise attested, but there is a noun אֶשֶׁר or אֹשֶׁר "happiness," and the personal name אָשֵׁר "Asher" would have the same form as the proposed word.

25.g. אובלים is evidently "mourners"; but some endeavor to find a meaning that will better suit the context. Dhorme's "where I led them, they were willing to go," followed by Larcher, BJ, JB "I led them where I chose," adopts the ingenious suggestion of N. Herz ("Some Difficult Passages in Job," *ZAW* 20 [1900] 160–63 [163]), בַּאֲשֶׁר אוֹבִילָם יָנְחוּ "wherever I conducted them they were led [נחה]"; so too Sicre Díaz, Gray, and Pope, who vocalizes יָנְחוּ hoph. The sense is, however, something of a tautology, and it is hard to believe that this fine poem concluded on such a lame note. Less probably still, Gordis suggests that we read אבלים יַנְחֶ־ם "[like one who] leads camels," אבל being cognate with Arab. *'ibil* "camels" (Lane, 8b), יַנְחֶה being from נחה hiph "lead," and the final *mem* being an enclitic. On top of this set of implausibilities, his suggestion also requires us to transfer the colon to follow the first two words of the verse.

30:1.a. Beer (*BH*[2]), following Duhm, is inclined to delete the whole verse.

1.b. Some think the line too short and add a subj after עלי, perhaps מְתִים "men" (de Wilde) or אֱוִילִים "lads" (Houtsma).

1.c. צעירים "smaller, younger" is emended to צֹעֲרִים "shepherds" by Bickell, Beer (*BHK prps*) (after Zech 13:7); but it is more likely that the term there refers to sheep rather than to shepherds; so BDB, 858b; *HALOT,* 3:1043b.

1.d. ממני לימים "than me in days" is deleted by Merx, Siegfried, Budde, Beer (*BH*[2] *frt*)—a pure whim, says Dhorme.

1.e. מאס, lit. "reject"; "disdain" seems the perfect translation (as KJV, RSV, NJPS, NAB, NJB, NEB). Ceresko's "considered too poor" robs the term of its sharpness.

1.f. שית "set" is usually quite a physical act, rather than mental, so NAB "rank with" is inappropriate. שִׁית need not be parsed as a passive inf (as Blommerde, Ceresko, comparing שִׂים in 20:4). E. Zurro Rodríguez ("Valor comparativo de la partícula *'im,*" 258) sees this as another example of the עם comparative (as also at 9:26; 37:18).

1.g. לשית עם־כלבי צאני "to set with the dogs of my flock," more elaborately "Their fathers have always been so worthless that I wouldn't let them help my dogs guard sheep" (GNB), or better "to trust with a sheep-dog's task" (Moffatt).

2.a. Duhm, Beer (*BH*[2]), Fohrer regard vv 2–8 as a later addition disturbing the flow of the poem from 29:7 to 30:31; Moffatt removes the verses to follow 24:8. Gray regards vv 3–8 as secondary. Fohrer deletes the colon v 2a as an explanatory gloss to v 1b.

2.b. למה, lit. "for what?"

2.c. ידיהם is unmistakably "their hands." NEB "strong arms" seems strange, since the next colon says that their vigor had wasted away; REB "the strength of their arms" is not open to the same objection. כח ידיהם is *casus pendens* (cf. GKC, §143), thus "the strength of their hands, what is it to me?" (Ceresko). De Wilde arbitrarily adds before כח ידיהם "the strength of their hands" מְהֵרַת רַגְלֵיהֶם "the swiftness of their feet," thinking of Ovid's *regna tenent fortes manibus pedibusque fugaces* "the strong of hand and swift of foot hold power" (*Fasti* 3.271).

2.d. למה לי is lit. "for what is it to me?" Duhm's emendation to כָּמַהּ לוֹ "had become faint" (also Beer [*BH*[2] *frt*]), like that of Ball to רָפָה לוֹ "had become relaxed, drooped down," "deprive the passage of its personal note" (Dhorme); Duhm obviously does not want Job to say something so crass and cruel as the MT suggests.

2.e. Good can hardly be right that it is Job himself whose vigor has perished.

2.f. כלח has sometimes been understood as "old age" (KJV), "ripe age" (RV), but it is better to take it as "strength" or "vigor" (RSV, NIV, NJPS; "vigour" NEB; so BDB, 480b; *DCH,* 4:420a, distinguishes the two senses as different words; *HALOT,* 2:478b, glosses it both as "ripeness, ripe age" and as "vigour," which is unlikely); for full discussion see *Note* 5:26.a. There is no cause to believe that כלח is a composite word, formed by "congeneric assimilation" from כח "strength" and לח "freshness" (as Blommerde). Ceresko most improbably revocalizes כלח to כִּי לֵחַ "full vigor," understanding כי as "emphatic כי." Tur-Sinai's insistence that it means "harvest, crop" leads to no acceptable meaning.

Beer (*BHK*) notes the emendation to כָּל־חַיִל "all strength" (following Pesh), and Budde, Beer, *Text* (followed by Pope) to כָּל־לֵחַ "all freshness." Ehrlich ingeniously writes עֲלֵמוֹ אָבַד כֹּחַ "the youngest of them is already lacking in strength," but עויל "suckling" is manifestly inappropriate here, since sucklings are of course lacking in strength; what is more, אבד does not mean "lack" but "cease, vanish" (see next *Note*). Dhorme and Larcher emend to עֻזָּמוֹ אבד כָּלָה "their vigor had wholly perished"; thus JB "enfeebled as they were." Dathe reads כָּל חַי "all living." NAB reads כל "all" for כלח "vigor," thus "they were utterly destitute." All the emendations seem superfluous.

2.g. It is hard to reproduce in Eng. the force of עלימו, lit. "upon them"; it is an excellent example of the use of על "denoting with some emphasis the subj. of an experience" (BDB, 753b §II.1.d), otherwise known as the "pathetic" על; other examples are 30:16, 17, 30; and cf. *Comment* on 14:22. Dahood ("Northwest Semitic Philology and Job," 56–57), followed by Blommerde, Ceresko, Hartley, unnecessarily sees here על meaning "from" (on this alleged meaning, see *Note* 29:7.a).

אבד is, when used of abstracts, "cease, vanish, fade away" (*DCH,* 1:99b). The proposal of M. Dahood (followed by Ceresko) that it is an אבד II "flee," cognate with Akk. *abātu* B (*CAD,* 1:45a) is not well supported ("Northwest Semitic Philology and Job," 56–57; *Psalms III,* 318), though alleged also for Ezek 12:22; Prov 21:28.

3.a. Hölscher and Gray think that a colon has dropped out before these words.

3.b. גלמוד elsewhere means "barren" (BDB, 166b; *HALOT,* 1:194b; *DCH,* 2:356a) or perhaps "stony" (3:7; 15:34; Isa 49:21); it is a little strange to apply it to hunger, but perhaps it is a transferred epithet that more properly relates to the "dry ground" (ציה). Gray thinks it should be taken "in its Arab. nuance as 'hard'" (Lane, 445c). Dhorme has "dismal famine." Others make it an adj describing the outcasts; thus "gaunt" (RV, NEB, Moffatt, Driver–Gray, Pope, Gordis, de Wilde), "haggard" (NIV), or "wasted" (NJPS). KJV's "solitary" cannot now be justified, though it depends on ibn Ezra as cited by Buxtorf, 117; its margin "dark as the night" may derive from 3:7. It is unlikely that גלמוד suggests that these poverty-stricken people are literally barren without offspring (as Fohrer, Hesse), especially because we hear of their sons in v 1. The sg is a little odd, since the subj of the sentence, and indeed the next word (הערקים), are pl. Driver–Gray's "With want and with famine (each) is gaunt" is an awkward attempt to explain the sg.

Among emendations may be mentioned גָּלְמוּ "are coiled up, crumpled up" (Hitzig, Duhm, Beer [*BHK frt*]), but that, as Driver–Gray point out, is an odd way of expressing the effects of hunger on the body.

3.c. Pope insists that it is "famine," i.e., the objective lack of food (as with חסר) rather than "hunger," which is the personal experience. Dhorme, JB remove בחסר ובכפן to the end of v 2. Beer (BH^2 *al*) mentions the proposal to read בכפן מערקים ציה "in hunger they gnaw (apparently piel) the dry ground."

3.d. ערק, occurring only here and in v 17, is probably "gnaw," as Arab. *'araqa* (Lane, 2017c) (so most Eng. versions; BDB, 792a; *HALOT,* 2:888b; *DCH,* vol. 6, *s.v.*); but Aram. ערק "flee" (Jastrow, 1123a) is also a possible cognate (thus KJV, following Buxtorf, 588, NJPS "flee," NAB, "fled," NIV "roamed," Ehrlich, Tur-Sinai, Gordis, Hartley).

To gnaw the dry ground is a harsh image, and many follow Ball in inserting עִקְּרֵי "the roots of" (so NEB, JB "gnaw the roots of desert plants" [NJB "of the thirsty ground"], Dhorme, Hölscher, Larcher, Fohrer, Rowley, Fedrizzi, de Wilde, Gray). Duhm had proposed יֶרֶק "the vegetation of [the dry ground]," and Gray suggests also צֶאֱצָאֵי "the growth of." עִקַּר, attested in the Aram. of Dan 4:15 (12), 23 (20), 26 (23), would be a new word in Heb. (cf. *DCH,* vol. 6, *s.v.*). Though there is not much vegetation on dry ground (as Dhorme observes), it is interesting that the Qumran Tg has the word ירק (the term for "dry ground" is missing in the MS). But neither emendation is at all essential, and Sicre Díaz rightly observes that to add anything is to destroy an expressive metaphor.

3.e. Pope adds אֶרֶץ "land" before ציה, ostensibly because the colon is too short, but others do not think so. For ציה, Kissane reads צֵיד "the food of [waste and desolation]," i.e., צַיִד II "provisions, food" (BDB, 845a; *HALOT,* 3:1020b); the reference would be to the mallow and broom roots in the next verse.

3.f. RSV, NEB omit altogether this admittedly difficult colon. Beer (BH^2) omits אמש שואה as a dittograph of משאה, NAB as an "auditory duplication" of that word. Duhm removes it to follow v 4, rendering "they grope in waste and devastation, and are driven out from society." JB "and brambles from abandoned ruins" is explained by Larcher as an "approximate and conjectural" translation.

3.g. אמש is lit. "yesterday" (as at 2 Kgs 9:26) or "last night" (as at Gen 19:34; 31:29, 42; thus RVmg "which yesternight was"; so BDB, 57a; *HALOT,* 1:68b; *DCH,* 1:328b), but most are uncertain about its meaning here (*DCH* offers "evening, twilight"). The word means properly "the eve of," and so may perhaps signify "the edge of." Some think the poor are "gnawing" or "roaming" (see *Note* 3.d above on "gnaw") "by night" (Tur-Sinai, Pope, Sicre Díaz, Habel, Hartley, NIV "at night"), but it is hard to see why this activity should be specifically at night. Some think that "last night" or "yesterday" suggest, metaphorically, "olden times"; thus KJV "in former time." Others take "night" as a metaphor for "darkness"; thus Delitzsch, Peters, RV "in the gloom of," Terrien "twilight" (*crépuscule*) or "place of gloom" (NJB; BJ *ce sombre lieu*).

Among emendations we may note: (1) Gerleman (*BHS*) reported the reading of one Heb. MS, אֱנוֹשׁ "a man of [destruction and devastation]," which makes good sense, but it is obviously a *lectio facilior.* Kissane offers the same reading, but regards the word as misplaced from v 5, where, he says, we should read מִן־גֵו אֱנוֹשׁ "from the society of humans." (2) Duhm proposes יְמַשְׁשׁוּ "they grope," from משש (BDB, 606b); he is followed by Moffatt. (3) Gordis suggests יָמִישׁוּ or יָמוּשׁוּ (or perhaps a sg) "they move, wander off," from מוש "depart, remove" (BDB, 558b); it is not an objection that the idea of darkness is implied in the term (as Dhorme argues), for cf. Gen 27:12; 31:34. Schultens also thought of משש as the root, rendering "destruction and devastation that may be touched" (*palpabilem vastitatem et evastationem*). Inferior emendations are (4) to אֵם "mother" (Hoffmann, Ehrlich, Fedrizzi, Gray) or אִמָּם "their mother," thus "the mother of what is devastated and desolate" or "their mother was a devastated and desolate region" (Budde, Dhorme, Driver–Gray, Beer [*BHK prps*]), (5) to אֶרֶץ "land of" (Siegfried, Fohrer, Rowley), and (6) to גָּרְמוּ "destruction and devastation remain (?)" (Beer [BH^2 *al*]). (7) Ceresko ingeniously but quite unconvincingly reads אוֹ מַשׁ "or swamp," a supposed cognate of the dubious Ugar. *mšmš* (*DUL,* 592). (8) Hölscher and de Wilde think of Ugar. *'mt* "fodder" (of asses) and translate "briars, undergrowth (*Gestrüpp*)"; but such a Ugar. word is no longer recognized. (9) Michaelis, *Supplementa,* 102, thought it was "field," comparing Syr. *'myš'* (but Payne Smith, 19a, says this word means "pool, swamp"). Hontheim consequently renders "swampland," vocalizing the word אֶמֶשׁ (cf. Syr. *'amîšâ* "pool" [J. Payne Smith, 19b]). (10) Guillaume proposes אָמֹשׁ, inf abs of a new word אמש "chew," cognate with Arab. *hamaša* (Wehr–Cowan, 1034b). (11) The omission of the word as a dittograph of שואה ומשאה "destruction and devastation" (Beer [*BHK al*], NAB) is a counsel of despair.

4.a. קטף is "pluck off or out" (BDB, 882a) or "break off (ears of corn)" (*HALOT,* 3:1094a). KJV has "cut up," but modern versions prefer "pick" (RSV, NJB) or "pluck" (JB, NJPS, NAB, NEB).

4.b. מלוח, also translated as "saltwort" (RV, Moffatt, NEB, NAB) or "salt herbs" (NIV), a desert plant that grows in salt marshes; its name is evidently connected with מֶלַח "salt." See further *Note* 24:24.e on "mallows." Tur-Sinai emends to וּמְלֵחָה "[who flee into the wilderness] and the salt-land."

4.c. Lit. "upon a bush" (עלי־שׂיח). Dhorme, translating "from the bush," explains that the mallow grows on a bush. Driver–Gray has "by the bushes" (as also KJV), i.e., in their shadow (similarly Davidson, Hölscher). Or על could indicate the vicinity of bushes; thus NIV "in the brush," Moffatt "under bushes," Pope "among the scrub," Hartley "among the shrubs." Ceresko finds here another example of על meaning "from" (cf. *Note* 29:7.a), but it is impossible to distinguish this sense from "upon" in this context; if mallows are taken "from" bushes, they must have been "upon" bushes to begin with. Saadia understood "leaves of a tree," and thus Hontheim (followed by Beer [*BHK*], Kissane, Larcher, Tur-Sinai, de Wilde, Gray) proposed reading וַעֲלֵי שִׂיחַ "and the leaves of a bush" (from עָלֶה); hence JB "brushwood leaves," NAB "and shrubs." NEB "[they plucked saltwort] and wormwood" seems to read וְלַעֲנָה, without acknowledging it in their textual notes (Brockington); so too NJPS. Perhaps "the leaves of bushes" is understood as the specific "wormwood," properly the leaves of the plant *Artemisia absinthium,* known for the bitterness of its taste.

4.d. שֹׁרֶשׁ, lit. "root of." Ceresko insists that this is a defective writing for שָׁרְשֵׁי "roots of," but there is no real problem with the sg. It is no more than fanciful to suggest that the prefixed *waw* is emphatic *waw,* "the very roots" (Ceresko).

4.e. רתם "broom"; for details, see *Comment.* NEBmg "fungus on broom root" is not explained.

4.f. לַחְמָם "(as) their food"; thus KJV "juniper roots for their meat," JB "making their meals off roots of broom" (similarly NEB, NAB, NIV, Duhm, Dhorme, Terrien, Fedrizzi, de Wilde, Sicre Díaz). But לַחְמָם could also be the inf of חמם "be warm" (as at Isa 47:14; cf. GKC, §67cc; so too Hölscher, Tur-Sinai, Pope, Gordis; mentioned by Beer [*BHK al*]). Alternatively, we could emend to piel inf לְחַמֵּם or לְחַמָּם (Budde), or pual inf לְחֻמָּם "to warm them" (Richter, Fohrer, Gerleman [*BHS frt*], Gray); whether emending or not, REB has "for warmth," Moffatt "for fuel," Gordis "for firewood" (similarly RVmg, Gerleman [*frt*], Pope). The roots of the broom are "almost inedible" (Löw, *Flora,* 2:471), so there can be little question about the translation; Duhm's supposition that these people had discovered a means of abating the bitterness of the plant is wishful thinking. H. Kuhn ("Why Are Job's Opponents Still Made to Eat Broom-Root?" *BT* 40 [1989] 332–36) finds three equally plausible interpretations: (1) the inedible broom roots are used for burning; (2) their "food" is broom in the sense that they sell embers or coals of broom to earn a living; or (3) רתם is not "broom" but a fungus-like plant that grows in salt marshes, sometimes around the roots of the broom; it is scarlet cynomorium, *Cynomorium coccineum,* or "Dog's club" (*Hundskolben*), which is eaten in times of famine. See also T. Yamaga, "Can the Roots of the Broom Be Eaten? A Proposal for the Interpretation of Job 30:2–8," *AJBI* 10 (1984) 20–32.

Ceresko wants to revocalize לחמם to לֹהֲמִים defectively written, "devouring," in order to create a closer parallelism with קטפים—an unimpressive idea.

5.a. גו is apparently not גֵּו I "back" but גֵּו II "community, society" (so *HALOT,* 1:182a; *DCH,* 2:328b; Driver–Gray, Dhorme, Hölscher, Fohrer, Pope, Rowley, Gordis, Habel, Ceresko, Sicre Díaz, Hartley, Good, Gray, NRSV "from society," JB, NEB "from the society of men," REB "from human society," NJB "from human company"). Some older scholars understood גו here as another גֵּו "midst" (an Aramaism, so BDB, 156a), thus "from the midst [of humans]"; so KJV, RSV, NAB "from among men." It is not easy to tell what NIV "from their fellow men" reads.

Several emendations, none of them strong, have been proposed: (1) to מִן גּוֹי "from a nation" (Merx, Duhm, Beer [*BH*[2]]); the emendation is both forced and entirely unnecessary (NAB, for example, reads מִן גּוֹי גֹּרָשׁוּ "they were banished from among men" [lit. "from among a nation," which does not sound probable]). (2) Beer (*BHK frt*) reads מִן־גֵּו גּוֹיִם "from among nations," spelling גֵּו rather than גֵּו. (3) Tur-Sinai's proposal (מִגְּגוֹ "from the land"; cf. Aram.) is weak, since the form attested is נִגְוָון (Jastrow, 2:873a). (4) M. Dahood ("Some Northwest-Semitic Words in Job," *Bib* 38 [1957] 306–20 [318–19]) found here a גֵּו "voice" (cognate with Ugar. *g* [*DUL,* 290]; cf. *DCH,* 2:328b); thus "with a shout they are driven forth"; for other suggested examples, see *Note* 35:12.d.

Fohrer (following Ley) finds the line too short, and adds אֲנָשִׁים "men" after יגרשו as the subj of "they drive out"; so too Gray. Similarly Kissane reads מִן־גֵו אֱנוֹשׁ "from the society of humans," אנוש being miswritten אמש and misplaced in v 3b; NEB reads מִן־גו אִישִׁים "from the society of males," rendering "of men." REB "human society" can hardly represent אישים. Grimme writes מִן־גּוֹי אֶל־גּוֹי יגרשו "from people to people they are hunted."

5.b. JB turns this nicely with "raised hue and cry against them," and NAB poorly "with an outcry like that against a thief."

6.a. Taking ערוץ, occurring only here, as cognate with Arab. *ʿirḍ* or *ʿarḍ* "gully, valley" or "slope of a valley" (Lane, 2008a); so Michaelis (*Deutsche Übersetzung,* 61), Hitzig, Driver–Gray, Dhorme, Hölscher, Stevenson, Tur-Sinai "bed of a wadi," Gordis, Good, RSV, NEB, NJPS, NIV "in the dry stream beds"; cf. *DCH,* vol. 6, *s.v.* Such a sense was already known to KJV with their "clifts" (RV "clefts"); cf. Buxtorf, 588 (*ruptura, concavitas*). Others think rather of the sense "slope" (so *HALOT,* 2:883b, Dhorme, Fohrer, de Wilde, JB "on ravines' steep sides," NAB "on the slopes of the wadies," Gray [reading עֲרוּצֵי "slopes of"]).

For others, especially of an older generation (e.g., BDB, 792a; Zorell, 627b; AS, 587b), ערוץ is an adj "dreadful" (from ערץ "be shocked, tremble"), thus "in the most dreadful of ravines," and so too RVmg "in the most gloomy valleys," ASV "in frightful valleys," Moffatt "in dark ravines" (similarly Duhm, Peake, Ceresko, Sicre Díaz); the introduction of an emotive term here, in the midst of rather objective description, is not likely.

Emendations to חָרוּץ "hollow" (Ehrlich) or בְּנַעֲצוּץ "among thorn bushes" (Beer [*BHK frt*]) are no improvement.

6.b. נחל is properly a wadi, a usually dry river bed, and so NRSV, NJPS, NAB. KJV "valleys" is not exact, and RSV "torrents" is misleading, for people can hardly live "in the gullies of torrents."

6.c. לשכן, lit. "to dwell," i.e., they are driven out from human society (v 5a) and so forced to dwell (denoting the result of their expulsion; so too Dhorme) in gullies and caves. Alternatively, the inf with *lamedh* can be understood as the "periphrastic future" (Driver, *Tenses,* §204; GKC, §114k).

6.d. חר denotes various kinds of holes. Holes in the earth are usually called "caves" (as KJV, NAB, JB) rather than "holes of the earth" (RSV, similarly NJB, NEB) or "holes in the ground" (NRSV, NIV, REB). NIV unaccountably reverses "caves" and "rocks."

6.e. עפר is not only "dry earth, dust," but also "surface of the earth" (BDB, 779b); it appears with caves also in Isa 2:19.

חרי "caves of" could apply both to עפר "dust, earth" and to כפים "rocks" (so RV, RSV, NEB "holes in the earth and rocky clefts," NAB "in caves of sand and stone," JB "in caves or clefts in the rock," Tur-Sinai, de Wilde). For two gens, cf. GKC, §128a. Alternatively, the two kinds of dwellings in question could be "caves in the earth" and "the rocks" (so KJV, NRSV, NIV, NJPS, Moffatt, Driver–Gray, Stevenson).

6.f. כֵּף "rock" occurs only here and at Jer 4:29; Ecclus 40:14. It is generally assumed to be an Aramaism (Wagner, *Aramaismen,* §130). Guillaume, however, thinks of an Arab. cognate, *'akâfîf* "the tops of mountains" ("Arabic Background," 119); but although *kifāf* "border, edge" appears in Wehr–Cowan, 831b, *'akâfîf* does not seem to be registered in Lane or Freytag.

7.a. שיח is any bush or shrub (BDB, 967a; *HALOT,* 3:1320b), without specification.

7.b. נהק is elsewhere "bray" (BDB, 625b; *HALOT,* 2:676b; *DCH,* 5:631b), of a hungry ass (6:5); thus NEB "howled like beasts," NAB "raised their raucous cry," JB "wailing." Moffatt's "grunting" implies a sexual meaning; see *Comment.* Tur-Sinai, finding נהק "bray" inappropriate for humans, reads סְיָחִים ינהקו "[among] young asses who bray" (סְיָח "foal, young ass" in Jastrow, 2:978b; cf. *DCH,* vol. 6, *s.v.*).

7.c. Ceresko wants תחת "under" to mean "among," so that it is parallel to בין in the first colon (he finds other examples of תחת in this sense at 30:14; 34:26; Ezek 10:2); תחת has been understood as "in the place where" at 40:21.

7.d. חרול is defined in the lexica as "a kind of weed, perh. chickpea" (BDB, 353b), "weed in field or fruit garden" (*HALOT,* 1:351b), "nettles or thistles" (*DCH,* 3:314b); it is more probably "thistles" (Dhorme, JB, de Wilde, Gray; cf. Dalman, *Arbeit und Sitte,* 2:318) than "nettles" (RSV, NAB, NJPS); NEB "scrub" and NIV "[in] the undergrowth" are perhaps too vague.

7.e. For this translation (following Moffatt) of יספחו I pual "are joined," see the *Comment;* see also *DCH,* vol. 6, *s.v.* Others, like RSV, have "huddle together," "the *pu'al* bring[ing] out very well the passivity of these wretches" (Dhorme). Some prefer the niph יִסָּפֵחוּ (Budde, Duhm, Driver–Gray, Beer [*BHK*], Hölscher). RVmg "stretch themselves" (so also Davidson, rendering "fling themselves down") is from ספח II "pour out" (Delitzsch has "spread about in disorder"); cf. *DCH,* vol. 6, *s.v.* Tur-Sinai, to match his view of the previous colon, has "under the nettles that grow wild," understanding ספח II on the basis of סָפִיחַ "growth from spilled kernels"; but the sense is strained.

8.a. נבל, traditionally translated "fool," probably does not have a moral connotation or even denote lack of wisdom. It is rather a social term, whether with the sense "outcast, sacrilegious person" (W. M. W. Roth, "*Nbl,*" *VT* 10 [1960] 394–409) or of "low-class, ignominious" (P. Joüon, "Racine נבל au sens de *bas, vil, ignoble,*" *Bib* 5 [1924] 357–61). G. Gerleman ("Der Nicht-Mensch: Erwägungen zur hebräischer Wurzel *NBL,*" *VT* 24 [1974] 147–58 [153–54]), however, argues that נבל is a very generalized term, signifying simply "less than human." Gordis insists that נבל means "low-born," and is equivalent to בלי שם "without shame," but Prov 30:22 does not prove that. See further, *Comment* on 2:10.

8.b. בני בלי־שם, lit. "sons, or, children, of those without name," i.e., reputation or standing in the community.

The variety of translations in the Eng. versions reflects both the range of meaning of נבל and the propensity of translators to excel in vituperation. Thus KJV "children of fools, yea, children of base men." RSV "a senseless, disreputable brood," NEB "vile, base-born wretches," REB "vile, disreputable wretches," NIV "a base and nameless brood," NJPS "scoundrels, nobodies," NAB "irresponsible, nameless men," GNB "a worthless bunch of nameless nobodies," Moffatt "brainless creatures and base," Stevenson "an ignoble and nameless people."

Larcher, followed by BJ JB, reads בְּנֵי נָבָל גַּם בְּנֵיהֶם, lit. "sons of an outcast are their sons indeed," i.e., "their children are as worthless a brood as they were."

8.c. There are four possibilities for the meaning of נכא: (1) It is usually regarded as "smite, scourge," a byform occurring only here of the common verb נכה (BDB, 644b). RV has "scourged out of the land," RSV, Good "whipped out," NIV, NAB "driven out," Moffatt "routed out," NJPS "stricken," NEB "hounded from the haunts of men," REB "outcasts from the haunts of men" (? adopting an emendation; see below). The translation "thrust" cannot be justified on the basis of 1 Sam 2:14 (as Rowley, Ceresko). (2) Gordis, however, regards נכא as another word, "be low, depressed" (cf. *DCH,* 5:683b), comparing the phrase רוּחַ נְכֵאָה "a lowly, depressed spirit" (Prov 15:13; 17:22; 18:14), thus "lower than the ground" (followed by Hartley); cf. KJV "they are viler than the earth"—"vile" not in a moral sense but meaning "of little account." (3) Guillaume, 114, supposes another new word נכא "put to flight" (cf. Arab. *nakā,* but that seems to mean rather "harm" [Wehr–Cowan, 1000a]); cf. *DCH,* 5:683b. (4) Tur-Sinai thinks of an Aram. נכי piel "deduct," thus "subtracted, blotted out from (the accounts of) the land"; but he translates "thrown out from."

Among emendations may be mentioned: (1) Beer, *Text* (not Beer, *BH*², *BHK*), reads נִדְכְּאוּ "are crushed," and (2) P. Joüon ("Notes de lexicographie hébraïque [suite]," *MUSJ* 5.2 [1912] 416–46 [436]; mentioned in Gesenius–Buhl, 503b, *s.v.* נכא) נֶחְבְּאוּ "they hide themselves [far] from the [inhabited] land," but the Heb. does not naturally imply that rendering. If any emendation is required, (3) Torczyner's נִכְרְתוּ "they were cut off" will serve (so too Dhorme, NJB "the very outcasts of society").

9.a. NIV "And now their sons mock me in song" adds "their sons," since those in view are no longer the penurious parents of vv 2–8 but Job's taunters, the young men of v 1.

9.b. נגינה is properly "music for stringed instruments" and secondarily "[mocking] song" (BDB, 618b; *HALOT,* 2:668a; *DCH,* 5:607a), hence NEB "the target of their taunts," NJPS "the butt of their gibes," Moffatt "the butt of their songs," NAB "they sing of me in mockery," JB "sing ballads about me," NJB "make up songs about me."

9.c. ואהי להם מלה, lit. "I have become a word to them"; JB "make me the talk of the town." מלה is used only here in the sense of "derisive byword" (*DCH,* 5:291a). But emendation to the more usual מָשָׁל "proverb, byword" (Beer [*BHK*], Gray), as in 17:6, is unnecessary.

10.a. Driver–Gray argue that not to withhold spitting from his face means that they did not shrink from spitting *in his face;* thus too KJV, RV, NEB, NAB, NIV, JB, Delitzsch, Dhorme, de Wilde, Terrien, Habel, Hartley "spit in my face," NJPS "do not withhold spittle from my face," Good "at me." But if they stand aloof from him (v 10a), they cannot also be spitting in his face (so too Peake, Strahan); so a preferable rendering is that of RVmg, RSV "at the sight of me"; similarly NJB "on seeing me, they spit without restraint," Moffatt "at the sight of me spit in disgust" (similarly Duhm).

11.a. The sg verb פתח "loosened" seems to require God as subj (as in 16:7; 20:23; 25:2); so too Delitzsch, Duhm, Peake, Strahan, Driver–Gray, Dhorme, Terrien, Fedrizzi, Gordis, Sicre Díaz, Habel, Hartley. Because of the following ויענני "and he has humiliated me," it is more difficult to take it as an indefinite than was the case in 3:20 (*q.v.*). On the meaning of loosening the cord, see *Comment.*

Another approach is to emend the verbs to pls; thus Budde reads פִּתְּחוּ יְעַנֻּנִי "they have loosed my cord [my authority] so as to humiliate me"; so too Beer (*BHK frt,* with יֶתֶר "[their] cord" or יִתְרָם "their cord"), NAB "they have loosed their bonds," Pope, de Wilde (reading יֶתֶר), Moffatt "they have unstrung me," Tur-Sinai "they have loosed my cord." NEB "they run wild" reads יֶתֶר פִּתְּחוּ "they have loosened (their) cord," i.e., have thrown off all restraint.

11.b. Q is apparently יִתְרִי "my cord" (so KJV, RVmg, RSV), i.e., "my bowstring" (NRSV, NJB, Budde, Duhm, Driver–Gray, Beer [*BH*² (?)], Larcher, Fedrizzi, Gordis, Sicre Díaz, Habel, Hartley) or "tent-cord" (Gray); thus NIV "unstrung my bow," NJPS "disarmed me"; since the bowstring is a key element of the bow, JB, more loosely, has "unbent my bow." K is יתרו "his cord" (so LXX, Vg, RV, Dhorme, Hölscher, Good). LXX apparently takes the cord as that of the quiver (φαρέτρα). For the idea of the cord as what restrains the young men, with an emendation to יֶתֶר, see preceding *Note.* A totally different view is that God has "uncovered" (פתח) his own bowstring in order to shoot at Job (cf. Hab 3:9, where the bow is stripped naked; and cf. Gibson, Davidson).

Kissane suggests that we have here, not יֶתֶר II "cord," but, as also perhaps at 4:21; 22:20, יֶתֶר I "remainder, pre-eminence" (BDB, 451b; *DCH*, 4:344b; *HALOT*, 2:452a, does not offer "pre-eminence" as a meaning), rendering "He stripped off my excellency." פתח "open" is however not a natural verb for "strip off," and the parallels Kissane mentions (12:18; Isa 20:2; 45:1; Ps 30:11 [12]) seem to mean "loose" rather than "strip off."

M. Dahood ("Hebrew-Ugaritic Lexicography XII," *Bib* 55 [1974] 381–93 [386]; followed by Ceresko) goes his own way, reading יָתֻר פֶּתַח וִיעַנְנִי "they watch my door and eye me," with תור "spy out, explore" (BDB, 1064a) and עין "eye, see, look suspiciously at" (BDB, 745a; *HALOT*, 2:817b; *DCH*, vol. 6, *s.v.*); but of course this ignores the Masoretic vocalization, as well as leaving us with a lame parallelism.

11.c. ויענני, lit. "and he afflicted, humiliated me" (ענה III, BDB, 776a). RSV, NJPS "humbled me," JB "chastened me," KJV, NJB, NIV "afflicted me," Moffatt "undone me." Those who think the young men of vv 1, 9–10, 11b are the subj here also read וַיְעַנֻּנִי "and they afflict me"; so Beer (*BHK frt*), NEB "[they] savage me," NAB "they lord it over me." Tur-Sinai finds here another noun, וַעֲנָנִי "and reins," comparing Arab. *'inân* (Lane, 2166a); cf. *DCH*, vol. 6, *s.v.*

11.d. רסן לפני שלחו is lit. "have let loose the bridle before me" (KJV); similarly JB "cast the bridle from their mouth," NJB "throw off [Good: 'put off'] the bridle in my presence," Moffatt "with their unbridled onset."

Among emendations, Kissane proposes, quite satisfactorily, מִפִּימוֹ "[the bridle] from their mouth [they have cast away]"; Larcher, followed by JB, offers the same rendering, but one cannot tell if the Heb. presupposed is מִפִּימוֹ or מִפִּיהֶם. Beer (*BH*[2] *frt*), Dhorme, and Hölscher read מִפָּנָיו שִׁלַּח "he [God] has cast the bit from his face," supposedly paralleling v 11a, but there the rope was for Job's bow; here it is God's own restraint. Beer (*BHK frt*) reads רִסְנָן "their restraint" to harmonize with the pls he reads in the first colon. Duhm, Strahan, Driver–Gray, Beer (*BHK prps*) change the image, to rather good effect, by emending to דִּגְלִי מִפָּנַי שִׁלַּח (or שִׁלֵּךְ) "he has cast down my banner from before me," a conceivable element in a siege.

12.a. NAB omits על־ימין פרחח "on my right hand the mob" and adds לְנַתֵּץ נְתִיבוֹתַי from v 13a (emended); thus "to subvert my paths [they rise up]." Dhorme emends to על־ימין יקומו עֵדִים "on my right hand witnesses rise up," but a lawcourt image is very inappropriate here. Duhm more attractively reads עָלַי מַעַרְכֹתָיו "against me his battle-lines [rise up]," continuing the theme of warfare. Tur-Sinai emends drastically, creating a confused image, עָלֵימוֹ נָפַר חָח יָקוּמוּ רֶגֶל יְשַׁלֵּחוּ "the muzzle upon them is broken (פרר niph); they rise up, let loose their foot (cf. Isa 32:20)" (to go wherever they please).

12.b. Ehrlich interestingly (but unconvincingly) takes ימין "right hand" as equivalent to יָמִים "days," thus "against age youth rises up"; but Job would hardly speak of himself as "old" (Gordis). With some justification, Budde, Duhm, Driver–Gray, Peake, Hölscher (*frt*), Fohrer, Gray delete ימין and read simply עָלַי "against me." Emendation to עַל־יְמִינִי "on my right hand" (Beer [*BHK*]) is unnecessary.

12.c. פרחח is "brood" according to BDB, 827a, and *HALOT*, 3:967a (both supposing it may be connected to פרח "bud, sprout"); cf. *DCH*, vol. 6, *s.v.* Hence RV, RSV "the rabble," Moffatt "a rabble," NIV "the tribe," NEB "in a mob." There is perhaps some evidence that פרחח, which occurs only here, refers specifically to young men: אֶפְרֹחַ is a "young bird" in 39:30; Deut 22:6; Ps 84:3 (4), and Aram. פֶּרַח "blossom" can occasionally mean "youth" (Jastrow, 1224a); similarly too Aq, Theod, and Tg have בניהון "their sons." Thus KJV "the youth," NJPS "mere striplings," JB "that brood of theirs," NJB "their brats." Gordis and Hartley combine the two senses with "young rabble."

Among emendations, (1) Kissane's is simple, to פִּרְחָם "their brood," though פֶּרַח is elsewhere "flower, bud" rather than "offspring, brood." (2) Pope postulates a Heb. חָח "filth," cognate with Akk. *ḫaḫḫu*, thus פֶּרַח חָח "a vile brood"; the rendering should however be adjusted in view of the glosses offered for *ḫaḫḫu* by *CAD*, 6:28b, "spittle, slime" or "cough (as an ailment)." (3) Duhm, Driver–Gray, de Wilde emend to עָלַי מַעַרְכֹתָיו "against me his [God's] lines of warriors [rise up]." (4) Ceresko offers a desperate remedy, reading פְּרָחָה, being the alleged particle פְּ "and" (see *Note* 33:24.c) with a supposed רָחָה "hand," thus "and [on my] left hand," though Ugar. *rḥ* is no longer recognized. (5) Gray reads מִפְדְּחוֹת, a new word מִפְדָּח "battering ram" or "siege-ramp," cognate with Arab. *fadaḫa* "make a fracture" (Lane, 2351b, "break"); but it is hard to see how the semantics of a simple verb "break," without any apparent derived nouns, will have developed, and the suggestion, though attractive, must remain doubtful.

12.d. יקומו "they arise"; Pope connects the verb with what follows: "rise and trip my feet." Gray reads יָקִימוּ "they raise" (places for battering rams); see also previous *Note*.

12.e. NEB, NAB, Moffatt, Merx, Peake, Driver–Gray, Beer (*BHK frt*), Hölscher, Rowley, Fedrizzi, de Wilde, Sicre Díaz, Gray omit this colon (it could be a dittograph of רסן שלחו in v 11).

12.f. רגלי שלחו is lit. "they push away my feet" (KJV) or "thrust aside" (RV). Other renderings are RSV "they drive me forth," Gordis "sending me sprawling," NIV "lay snares for my feet," Habel "trip up my feet," BJ "make my feet slip" (*ils font glisser mes pieds*), NJPS "put me to flight." Delitzsch thinks they are pushing him on step by step, "contending one foot's breadth after another with him." Driver–Gray say the phrase should mean "my feet they send on," i.e., they hunt me from place to place (cf. שלח in 14:20; similarly Davidson), but they omit it as out of place (even in the next line his enemies are still only *approaching* him). Others who omit the two words are Merx, Wright, Siegfried, Budde, Duhm, Hölscher, Fohrer. It is hard to see what such an image has to do with a siege (but perhaps the siege imagery begins only in the next colon).

Other suggestions are these: (1) NJB "to see when I am having a little peace" finds here the verb רגל "spy" (BDB, 920a), emending to וַיְרַגְּלוּ שַׁלְוִי, lit. "and they spy upon my quietness." (2) Ceresko finds the same verb and reads רֹגְלַי שֻׁלְּחוּ "those who spy on me are unrestrained," שלח pual meaning "be let loose, be unrestrained." (3) Kissane thinks רֶגֶל is not "foot," but a new word "slander" (from the well-attested verb רגל "slander," as at Ps 15:3; 2 Sam 19:27 [28]; Ecclus 5:14). (4) Ehrlich unpersuasively emends to רֶגֶל יְשַׁלְּחוּ "they send their feet against me," i.e., kick me. (5) JB's "stones are their weapons" depends on an emendation, but Larcher (*me lance des pierres commes projectiles*) does not say what (perhaps אֲבָנִים שלחו "they cast stones"). (6) Dhorme emends to בַּפַּח רגלי שלחו "they have drawn my feet into a net" (פח having been corrupted into פרחח), but the image of hunting is out of place here (NIV, though similar, does not appear to depend on Dhorme). (7) Hartley moves אידם from the end of the verse to the second colon, thus "they send my feet to their ruin" (can feet be ruined?).

12.g. סלל ארחות "cast up, build, roads" is the technical language for throwing up a siege-ramp, as in 19:12 (where the noun is דרך "way"); so too NEB, NIV "their siege-ramps," NAB "approaches," Moffatt more loosely "they set on to besiege me."

12.h. עלי "against me" is deleted by Hölscher.

12.i. ארחות אידם "the ways of their destruction" (KJV), i.e., "their ways of destruction" (RV, RSV), but it is of course the ruin of *Job* that is in mind. The *Translation* agrees with NRSV, NJPS "build roads for my ruin" (similarly Habel). JB "they take threatening strides towards me" seems unnecessarily loose.

13.a. נתס "tear down" (BDB, 683a; *HALOT*, 2:735b; *DCH*, 5:815a "break up") occurs only here; it is presumably a byform of the common נתץ "pull down, destroy"; thus too KJV, RV "mar," RSV, NIV "break up," NJPS "tear up." JB takes the phrase to mean "they have cut me off from all escape," and Terrien "they cut off my retreat"; similarly Moffatt, Dhorme. Duhm prefers יְנַתְּצוּ piel "they tear down." Gordis postulates another נתס "place thorns," on the basis of an Arab. cognate *nats* "thorns" (cf. *DCH*, 5:815a), but this hardly suits the image of a siege, and the Arab. word does not appear in Freytag, Lane, or Wehr–Cowan.

13.b. Some MSS and the ancient versions have the pl נְתִיבֹתַי "my paths"; so too NEB, de Wilde. But it is hard to see how נתס or נתץ "pull down" can have "path" or "paths" as its obj. So G. R. Driver's proposal ("Notes on Isaiah," in *Von Ugarit nach Qumran: Beiträge zur alttestamentlichen und altorientalischen Forschung*, FS Otto Eissfeldt, ed. J. Hempel and L. Rost, BZAW 77 [Berlin: Töpelmann, 1961] 42–48 [48]) becomes attractive, of another נְתִיבָה "defense" (cf. Akk. *natābu* "cut off"), as also at Isa 58:12; cf. *DCH*, 5:783b. Hence NEB "they tear down my crumbling defences." The suggestion is tentatively adopted in the *Translation*, though the Akk. cognate is not to be found in von Soden or *CAD* (it may be, however, a form of *tabāku*).

13.c. יעל hiph "profit, avail" (the reference in *HALOT*, 2:420b, to "prayers" as the subj here seems a mistake). Thus KJV "set forward," RSV, NJPS "promote," NIV "succeed in." NJB "seizing the chance [to destroy me]" and Moffatt "determined [to destroy me]" seem to be looser renderings with the same understanding.

Bickell emended to יַעֲלוּ "they attack" (from עלה "go up") (so too NAB, NEB "scramble up against me," Larcher, BJ *ils attaquent* [though JB omits the word altogether], Dhorme, de Wilde, Gray). Duhm, Beer (BH^2 *prps* [יֶהֶרְסוּ]) read יֶהֶרְסוּ מַעְגָּלָי "they destroy my tracks," which leaves us with a wooden parallelism. Graetz read יָגִילוּ "they rejoice" (following Pesh), but it is more likely that Job's opponents are actively attacking him rather than looking on (Driver–Gray).

13.d. להותי "to my ruin." Against the Masoretic vocalization, it is also possible to take the words with the preceding; thus NEB "to my undoing," REB "to destroy me," Dhorme "with a view to ruining me," Pope, de Wilde. It is then easier to accept the emendation of יעילו "they succeed" to יַעֲלוּ "they go up, attack"; see previous *Note.* Gray, noting that the sg הַוָּה occurs only once elsewhere (6:2), reads לְהַוּוֹתִי "to make me fall," inf constr of the new word הוה II "fall" (*DCH,* 2:502b; הוה I in *HALOT,* 1:241b).

13.e. Is it they who have no helper (as KJV, Delitzsch "they who themselves are helpless"; similarly Tur-Sinai)? Or is it Job who has no helper (as NIVmg "without anyone's helping me," Terrien "no one comes to my aid"; similarly Habel)? The former is to be preferred (see *Comment*). NJPS takes "no helper for them" as "although it does them no good"; but that is never the meaning of this common phrase (also at 29:12; and with אין rather than לא at 2 Kgs 14:26; Isa 63:5; Pss 22:11 [12]; 72:12; 107:12; Lam 1:7; Dan 11:45). To similar effect Good reads עֵזֶר "help," thus "no help to him," but the same criticism applies. Hartley has "there is none to help against them," taking ל as "against" (following Blommerde).

Other verbs spelled עזר are sometimes invoked: (1) Dahood (*Psalms III,* 95–96) and, more fully, B. Q. Baisas ("Ugaritic *'ḏr,*" 43, 47) propose a עזר meaning "rescue, save" (like Ugar. *'ḏr* [*DUL,* 153]; cf. *DCH,* vol. 6, *s.v.*), rendering "there is no one to liberate from them," the *lamedh* being "from"; Habel adopts this view. Ceresko, rather, proposes on that basis a new noun עֵזֶר "escape, rescue" (cf. *DCH,* vol. 6, *s.v.*) for the present passage. (2) An alternative suggestion is of another verb עזר "hinder" (as Ehrlich, Driver, "Problems in Job," 163, followed by Pope, Guillaume, Gordis, comparing Arab. *'azara* "hinder" [Freytag, 3:150b]; cf. *DCH,* vol. 6, *s.v.* [עזר V]).

עזר "helping" is commonly emended to עֹצֵר "restraining" (Dillmann, Peake, Driver–Gray, Dhorme, Beer [*BHK prps*], Hölscher, Kissane, Larcher, Rowley, Gerleman [*BHS prp*], de Wilde, Sicre Díaz, Gray); thus RSV "no one restrains them," NAB "with none to stay them," JB "there is no one to check their attack," NJB "no one stops them," Moffatt "loose to all restraints," NEB "unhindered." Duhm, Beer (*BH*[2] *prps*) emend freely, on the basis of LXX βέλεσιν αὐτοῦ κατηκόντισέν με "with his arrows he has shot me down," אֵלַי עָטְרוּ רַמָּו "his marksmen surround me" (עטר as at 1 Sam 23:26); but that image is out of place in the picture of a besieged *city.*

14.a. כפרץ רחב יאתיו, lit. "like a wide breach they come"; strictly speaking the attackers do not enter "like a breach," but "as through" a breach (RSV, REB, NIV, NJPS, JB "as though through"). But that is a little awkward, and not surprisingly NEB has "they burst in through the gaping breach," Moffatt "they pour in at the open breach." Actual emendation to בְּפֶרֶץ "through a breach" (de Wilde, Ceresko, Habel) can be dispensed with.

14.b. פֶּרֶץ is well attested as "breach" (BDB, 829b). Gordis's suggestion (followed by Hartley), that it is "torrent," is very unlikely; his supposed parallel, פרץ מים "a breaking forth of waters" in 2 Sam 5:20, shows only that פרץ means "breaking out," not "stream, torrent." F. Perles ("The Fourteenth Edition of Gesenius-Buhl's Dictionary," *JQR* 18 [1906] 383–90 [390]) has "like the bursting of a flood"; cf. also *DCH,* vol. 6, *s.v.* Tur-Sinai read רַחַב "wide expanse (of water)," as supposedly at 37:10.

14.c. גלל hithpalpel "roll oneself," hence KJV "they rolled themselves *upon me,*" RSV "they roll on," NJPS "roll in," NEB, NIV "come rolling in," REB "come in waves," NAB "come on in waves," Moffatt "rushing upon me." Others think the verb should be 1st person, הִתְגַּלְגָּלְתִּי "I am rolled, overwhelmed" (cf. 2 Sam 20:12); hence, following Larcher, JB "I am crushed," NJB "I go on tumbling," Driver–Gray "I wallow" (it is a 1st-person verb in LXX); Kissane reads אֶתְגַּלְגַּל "I was rolled about." Ceresko prefers to derive the verb from a גלי "arrive, penetrate" (proposed by M. Dahood, "Northwest Semitic Texts and Textual Criticism of the Hebrew Bible," in *Questions disputées d'Ancien Testament: Méthode et théologie,* ed. C. Brekelmans, BETL 33 [Gembloux: Duculot; Leuven: Leuven UP, 1974] 11–37 [30]); other places where it is claimed גלי occurs are 3:22; 20:28; Ruth 3:7. These examples are doubtful, and in the present place the hithpalpel is not accounted for, and a striking image has been lost if the proposal is accepted.

14.d. תחת שאה, lit. "under destruction," thus KJV "in the desolation" (similarly Good). Driver–Gray posit that שׁאה is essentially a noise (BDB, 981a: "roar, din, crash, uproar"), here of the falling masonry of the breached walls; hence no doubt RSV "amid the crash," NAB "amid the uproar," NEB "at the moment of the crash" (following Driver, "Problems in Job," 163–64); NJPS's "like raging billows" understands שׁאה similarly, and introduces "billows" from the waves that may be implicit in גלל. *HALOT,* 4:1427a, offers "storm, trouble," and Gordis, comparing Ezek 38:9, where it is parallel to ענן "cloud," translates "storm" (similarly Pope). More probably, though, שׁאה refers rather to "the ruins heaped up in consequence of the breaking down of the wall" (Dhorme); thus RV "in the midst of the ruin," NIV "amid the ruins," Moffatt "through the ruined wall," Habel "amid the rubble."

If we take תחת "under" very literally, perhaps the invaders are envisaged as entering the city through a breach in the lower part of the wall; thus JB "beneath the rubble," Dhorme "under the ruins," Delitzsch "through the wall which is broken through and crashes above the assailants." Ceresko's claim that תחת *means* "among" is less defensible (for other examples, see *Notes* 30:7.c and 34:26.c). Hitzig unpersuasively maintained that תחת here means "like" (comparing 34:26; similarly Gordis), and שׁאה "torrent."

15.a. Hölscher and de Wilde delete the colon as a secondary gloss; the reference to the terrors may seem to be at odds with the image of the siege.

15.b. הפך hoph "are turned," the sg verb with pl subj being nothing remarkable (cf. *Note* 22:9.a; Ceresko's claim that it is a "Phoenician" sg is implausible). JB renders "turn to meet me." NEB, no doubt thinking of the related noun מַהְפֵּכָה "overthrow" (of Sodom and Gomorrah), translates "overwhelm," NAB "[over me] rolls [the terror]," NJPS "tumbles," NJB "rounds on me," Moffatt "are let loose on me," Gordis "are turned loose," Good "are dumped over me." Gray would emend to the pl הָהְפְּכוּ "they are turned." Since the hoph of הפך occurs nowhere else, Duhm would revocalize to niph תֵּהָפֵךְ "is turned" (as one Heb MS [Gerleman] and Beer [BH^2 *vel*] to נֶהֶפְּכוּ "are turned"); Ceresko's revocalization to הֵהָפֵךְ, niph inf abs, cannot be justified on the ground of Esth 9:1, where the form is נַהֲפוֹךְ.

15.c. De Wilde moves v 15b, c to follow v 11.

15.d. תִּרְדֹּף "one (fem) pursues"; thus NEB "it [terror] sweeps away [my resolution]" (similarly NJPS). Some read תֵּרָדֵף "[my honor] is pursued" (RSV, REB, NIV, JB, Moffatt, Siegfried, Budde, Beer [*BHK vel*], Kissane, Larcher, Fohrer, Gerleman [*BHS prp*], de Wilde, Sicre Díaz, Hartley). Terrien raises the possibility that we have here an address to God, anticipating the 2d-person address in vv 20–23; but the suggestion is unlikely. Pursuing honor might be thought "a poor and unsuitable idea" (Driver–Gray), and so an emendation to תִּנָּדֵף "is driven away" is sometimes adopted (Graetz [*vel*], Duhm, Beer [*BHK vel*], Driver–Gray, Gray, NAB ["vanishes"]; so too Gordis, maintaining תרדף is an alternative writing for תנדף). But רדף itself can mean "put to flight" (BDB, 922b §1b, though not acknowledged by *HALOT,* 3:1191b) or "drive away" (Lev 26:36), so it is perfectly acceptable here.

15.e. נדיבה is "dignity" (*HALOT,* 2:674a), "nobility of rank, honour" (BDB, 622a). Thus RV, NJPS, Habel render "honour," NAB, NIV, Pope, Hartley "dignity," Driver–Gray "nobility," Dhorme "nobleness," Gordis "lofty rank, princely position," Good "standing." Less acceptable are NEB "resolution," REB "noble designs." LXX has μου ἡ ἐλπίς "my hope"; hence Volz, Beer (*BHK prps*) תִּקְוָתִי and JB "confidence" (BJ *mon assurance,* though Larcher does not note any deviation from the Heb.). Moffatt's "happiness" probably follows the emendation to טוֹבָתִי "my good fortune" (Duhm, Beer [*BHK prps*]). KJV "soul," mg "my principal one," follows Buxtorf, 447, who glosses נָדִיב as *voluntarius, spontaneus, ingenuus,* and *princeps,* among others, and offers "soul" for this verse.

15.f. ישׁועה is customarily "salvation"; thus KJV, NAB, Driver–Gray, Moffatt "welfare," Hartley "well-being," RSV, Pope "prosperity," NEB "hope of victory"; but more appropriately NIV, Good "safety," JB "hope of safety." Gordis suggests that we have another ישׁועה, "my standing as a שׁוֹעַ, nobleman," "my high position"; thus NJPS "dignity," Habel "prestige"; for שׁוֹעַ, cf. 34:19; Isa 32:5. This makes a nice parallelism with נדיבה "dignity," but the price of creating a new homonym for this common noun is perhaps too high.

16.a. NAB puts vv 16a and 27b together, and makes them follow v 26, deleting v 16b as a doublet of v 27b.

16.b. ועתה "and now" is omitted by NAB, Beer (*BHK frt*), Hölscher, de Wilde, Gray, and others who rearrange verses in this chapter on an extensive scale.

16.c. נפשׁ "life, vitality, etc." can certainly mean "throat" (*DCH,* 5:724b §1), but not here (as Ceresko), since a throat cannot be "poured out."

16.d. תשׁתפך עלי, lit. "is poured out upon me," עלי being another example of the "pathetic" על (see *Note* 30:2.g). A literal translation, as KJV "my soul is poured out upon me," is unintelligible, as is Good's "poured out over me," while RSV "poured out within me" and Pope's "my soul within me is emptied" are not much better. Other renderings are NEB "my soul is in turmoil within me," NIV, REB "my life ebbs away," NAB "my soul ebbs away from me," JB "trickles away," Habel "drains from me," Hartley "is emptied from me," NJPS "runs out," Moffatt "melts with sorrow." It is not necessary to invoke the sense "from" for על (as Ceresko; see *Note* 30:2.g). Duhm deletes עלי on the ground of its similarity with Ps 42:4 (5).

16.e. ימי "days of." Duhm, Beer (BH^2 *prps*) would read אֵמֵי "terrors of."

16.f. NEB more loosely "misery has me daily in its grip," Moffatt "misery masters me." Tur-Sinai implausibly makes the terrors the subj.

17.a. NAB omits v 17a as a dittograph of v 30, and transposes v 17b to follow v 27a.

17.b. Taking לילה "night" as the subj of the verb (as RSV, NIV, Delitzsch, Dillmann, Hitzig, Duhm, Pope, Sicre Díaz). Others regard לילה as "at night" (so KJV, JB, NAB, NEB, Dhorme, Fohrer, Terrien, Andersen, Gordis, de Wilde, Gray), in which case the pl עצמי "my bones" is the subj of the sg verb נקר "is pierced" (cf. *Note* 22:9.a), or there is an impersonal subj (Fohrer), or God is the subj though not mentioned by name (Terrien, Gordis, Habel, Hartley, Good; and cf. Driver–Gray; cf. *Note* 24:22.b), or we should emend נקר (see next *Note*). Budde, Beer (BH^2 *al*) deleted לילה, and Peake also is inclined to do so as a "blundering contrast" to "days of affliction" in v 16.

17.c. נקר piel "pierce, bore." If לילה is omitted (see previous *Note*), the verb would have to be vocalized נִקַּר "is pierced" (Budde, Beer [BH^2 *al*], Driver–Gray [*vel*]), with the subj the pl עצמי "my bones"; Kissane would read the pl verb נִקְּרוּ "are pierced." JB, however, following Larcher, emends מעלי "from upon me" to מַחֲלָה "sickness" to create a subject for נקר, but it is not clear what it intends by "saps [my bones]" (BJ has *le mal perce mes os* "sickness pierces my bones," which is more intelligible). NJPS "by night my bones feel gnawed" is a little banal, and נקר, properly "pierce," does not seem to mean "gnaw" (or "chew at," as Habel), nor does it really mean "rives" (Pope), which is to split asunder, nor "scrapes" (Tur-Sinai). It is unclear too whether it can mean "the bones are rotting in my body" (Moffatt). Gray reads נִקְדוּ "are hotter [than a cauldron]," though יקד does not elsewhere occur in niph, the qal serving for the sense "be kindled, burn."

17.d. מעלי "from upon me," KJV "in me," no doubt another example of the pathetic על as in vv 2, 16. It would not do to take the preps too seriously, as Driver–Gray "[my bones] fall away from me" (the supposed parallel in Deut 8:4 is of old clothes falling off someone). Kissane reads וְעָלַי and attaches it to the next colon, thus "and the pains that gnaw me take no rest." Duhm deleted מעלי, and Dhorme, Hölscher (*frt*), de Wilde read נִקְּרִים "are pierced" for נקר מעלי. Dahood (*Psalms I,* 74), followed by Ceresko, Gray (and already in his "The Massoretic Text of the Book of Job, the Targum and the Septuagint Version in the Light of the Qumran Targum," *ZAW* 86 [1974] 331–50 [345]), emends מֵעָלָי to מֵעֲלִי "[my bones are hotter] than a caldron" (cf. Arab. *ǵalā [y]* "boil" [Lane, 2288c]), calling upon יקד niph "burn" (cf. LXX συγκέκαυται [Ziegler] "are burned," and Qumran Tg יקדון "burn"). He finds עֲלִי "caldron" also in v 30; Ps 12:7; Prov 27:22; cf. also *DCH,* vol. 6, *s.v.*

17.e. עֹרְקַי is "my gnawers," understood by RV, RSV as "the pain(s) that gnaw(s) me," JB "I am gnawed by wounds that never sleep" (similarly NIV, Moffatt, Duhm, Davidson, Peake, Fohrer; Pope "my torturers never relax"), ptcp from ערק, occurring elsewhere only in v 3 (BDB, 792a; *HALOT,* 2:882b; *DCH,* vol. 6, *s.v.*); see further, *Comment.* KJV, however, has "my sinews," following LXX νεῦρα; likewise Kimchi and ibn Ezra, who connected the word with *'irq* "vein" (Lane, 2019b); cf. also Aram. עַרְקָא "strap (of a sandal)" (Jastrow, 1123a); cf. *DCH,* vol. 6, *s.v.* Similarly NJPS ("my sinews never rest"), Dhorme, Tur-Sinai, de Wilde, Hartley, NEB "there is ceaseless throbbing in my veins," Gordis "my veins know no rest," and Hölscher, more loosely, "my pulse does not quieten down." Gray follows the same interpretation, but recognizes the noun as עָקָר rather than עֹרֵק.

Ehrlich had the interesting suggestion that we should read עֲרָקַי "my fleshless bones" (cf. Arab. *'arq* [Lane, 20018c]).

NAB omits v 17a as a dittograph of v 30, and translates ערקי לא ישכבון לילה as "my frame takes no rest by night," which it inserts between vv 27a and 27b. "My frame" is presumably a loose translation for "my sinews."

18.a. NAB makes vv 18–26 follow immediately on v 15.

18.b. רב־כח, lit. "greatness of strength." KJV has "by the great force *of my disease*" (the words in italic being supplied to make the sense), RVmg "by his great force." Duhm, followed by Beer (*BHK al*), imaginatively emends to ברב כַּחַשׁ "by reason of great wasting, leanness"; he is followed by Peake, Strahan. Beer (*BHK prps*) records the alternative emendation בְּרָקָב "with rottenness."

18.c. As MT stands, חפשׂ hithp is "disguise oneself," whether by a change of clothes (as in 1 Sam 28:8; 1 Kgs 22:30 || 2 Chr 18:29; 35:22), or by pulling a headcloth over the eyes (1 Kgs 20:38); since חפשׂ is properly "search," this sense is explained as "let oneself be searched for" (BDB, 344b; KBL, 322b). A disguise makes no sense here, though some think such a disguise could be a disfigurement; hence Delitzsch "my garment is distorted," RV, RSVmg "my garment is disfigured" (but hardly that because Job has lost weight his clothes are hanging badly, as Duhm, Gordis). NIV "God becomes like clothing to me," i.e., binding Job like the neck of his garment, presumably understands "he disguises himself (as) my clothing"—which is hard to believe; and why remove the idea of disguise, unless tendentiously? Tur-Sinai arrives at the amazing rendering "in my cloth he disguiseth himself as an attorney" (as he understood רב כח in 23:6, *q.v.*). KJV has "[my garment is] changed," following an older tradition that the verb means "change" in the hithp (so Buxtorf, 253); NJPS perhaps follows this tradition, but offers a banal rendering, "with great effort I change clothing [so that the neck opening fits about the waist]" (cf. GNB "twists my clothes out of shape").

Ceresko adopts the qal and piel sense of חפשׂ "search," but it is hard to think of any meaning for his translation "he rifles [i.e., searches] my garment" (following M. Dahood, "Ugaritic-Hebrew Parallel Pairs," in *Ras Shamra Parallels,* ed. L. R. Fisher, AnOr 49 [Rome: Pontifical Biblical Institute, 1972] 1:71–382 [249]); the suff would be datival (for other examples, see *Note* 22:21.d).

The difficulty of the MT inclines one to consider the emendation to יְחַפֵּשׂ "seizes" (as of catching hold of clothes in 1 Kgs 11:30), which is probably what LXX ἐπελάβετο "it took hold on" and 11QtgJob יאחדון "they seize" read. So Houbigant, Siegfried, Gibson, Ehrlich, Dhorme, Beer (*BH*[2] *frt*), Hölscher, Kissane, Larcher, Fohrer, Fedrizzi, Pope, de Wilde, Sicre Díaz, Gray, RSV "it seizes" (similarly JB); the suggestion is adopted in the *Translation* above. Probably God should be understood as the subj; thus NAB "one with great power lays hold of my clothing," NRSV "he seizes," NIV "he binds me," Dhorme, Rowley, Hartley. Habel has a different idea with "ties me up with my garment," but that is hard to extract from the Heb. Gordis (followed by Sicre Díaz [*frt*] and Hartley) avoids emendation as such by claiming that חפשׂ is a phonetic variant for חבשׁ "bind"; but that does not mean the same thing as "he grasps my garment," as Gordis argues, and his explanation of the hithp form as a conflate of 2d-person תְּחַפֵּשׂ and 3d-person יְחַפֵּשׂ is very lame.

Another marginal possibility is to find here the verb חפשׁ hithp "be freed" (occurring in the pual at Lev 19:20 and conjectured for the hithp at 2 Chr 35:22, where MT has חפשׂ; cf. *HALOT,* 1:341b); thus "[my garment] is loosed."

Alternative routes to a solution arise from cognates to the Heb.; thus NEB "my garments are all bespattered with my phlegm" follows the suggestion of J. Reider ("Some Notes to the Text of the Scriptures," *HUCA* 3 [1926] 109–16 [114]), for a new word כֹּחַ "phlegm," thus "because of the great amount of mucus (or phlegm) my garment is disfigured" (the noun may occur also in Ps 22:15 [16], and a corresponding verb in Job 20:18). Guillaume ("Arabic Background," 120) also thinks כח is "pus" (cf. Arab. *qayḥ* [Lane, 2576b]; *DCH,* 4:382a) and proposes that חפשׂ is "saturate" (cf. Arab. *ḥafaša* "run" [of water], "bring rain" [of clouds] [Freytag, 1:410b; not in Lane]), thus "my clothing is saturated with much suppuration."

Among emendations, Duhm, Beer (*BH*[2] *al*) emend freely to יִתְחַבֵּא לבושׁי "my garment is contracted" (so too Peake, Strahan), so that his garment clings to him like a vest (Peake); כחשׁ "leanness" is attested in 16:8, but חבא hithp cannot mean "be contracted" (see Driver–Gray).

18.d. לבושׁי is "my garment." Moffatt, following Friedrich Delitzsch, thinks the reference is to Job's skin: "my skin is wrinkled with the fell disease," but the "tunic" (כתנה) in the second colon is a literal garment, and so must be the לבושׁ in the first. Budde, Beer (*BH*[2] *prps*) actually emend to בְּשָׂרִי "my flesh [is disfigured]," but that leaves a problem with the subject of the second colon. Gray reads כִּלְבוּשִׁי "[affliction grips me] as my garment," parallel to the thought of the next colon.

18.e. אזר hiph "hold tight," KJV "bindeth me about" (similarly RSV). NRSV, Rowley, Gordis take God as the subj. NEB "[my phlegm] chokes me like the collar of a shirt" (did Job wear shirt collars? we wonder; REB at least has "garment"), JB "[sickness] clutching at the collar of my coat." NJPS, to match its rendering of the previous colon, has "the neck of my tunic fits my waist," but it is hard to see how that can be justified. Habel, matching his rendition of the first colon, has "strangles me with the neck of my tunic"—a difficult feat. Moffatt "[my skin is] drawn tight over my limbs" cannot be right. In line with his rendering of the first colon, Tur-Sinai has, equally willfully, "as my mouth he girds on my own coat."

Ehrlich, Pope, Sicre Díaz emend to יֹאחֲזֵנִי "he grasps me," to create closer parallelism with the first colon; but אזר hiph is already close enough. Ceresko, following Blommerde, reads יְאַזְּרֵנִי, supposedly a privative piel meaning "loosen from me [a datival suffix]"; but the suggestion is forced. Privative piels supposedly reverse the meaning of a verb; for examples in Job, cf. Blommerde, 17 (bibliography), and see also 12:18; 36:30.

18.f. כפי "like the mouth [of my tunic]," KJV "as the collar of my coat"; similarly RSV, REB; NEB "like the collar of a shirt." NAB, NRSV, NJB "by the collar" apparently silently emend to בְּפִי (as Larcher, Gordis, de Wilde, Sicre Díaz, Habel), as does JB "[clutching] at the collar." Ancient garments did not have collars, however, a difficulty not evaded by NIV's "binds me like the neck of my garment." NJPS "the neck of my tunic fits my waist" is an amusingly literalistic interpretation, thinking that Job has lost so much weight that his waist is no bigger than his neck; quite how the neck of Job's tunic slips over his shoulders to hang round his waist at the hips may be left to the imagination. Budde thinks כפי is simply a long form of כ "like" ("he holds me tight like a tunic"). Ceresko reads כַּפַּי "with his hands," allegedly a "third person yodh suffix." Andersen thinks כפי are the "paws" of the attacker, represented as a wild beast. D. Wolfers ("The 'Neck' of Job's Tunic [Job xxx 18]," *VT* 44 [1994] 570–72) observes that כפי usually means "in the same measure as" (cf. BDB, 805 §6.b) and infers, implausibly, that Job's garment, which is his righteousness (29:14), girds him as little as his undershirt does—now that his righteousness has been stripped from him.

19.a. Driver–Gray insert הִנֵּה "behold" at the beginning of the line; but the line needs no improvement.

19.b. RSV, NEB, Moffatt, Driver–Gray supply God as the subject; for other examples, see *Note* 24:22.b. Budde, Duhm, Beer (*BH*[2] *frt*, אֵל; *BHK frt*, הֵן אֵל), Pope, Hartley (perhaps) actually insert אֵל "God" because the line is so short; NEB inserts הוּא "he." JB makes the subject "sickness." Volz makes it a 2d-person verb, הוֹרִיתַנִי "you have cast me," anticipating the verbs of vv 20–23.

19.c. הרני "he has thrown me," from ירה. Duhm, Driver–Gray, Beer (*BHK frt*, הֹרִדַנִי), Hölscher (*frt*), Fohrer, de Wilde, Gray, however, propose הוֹרִדַנִי "he has brought me down [to the clay]." NJPS "he regarded me as clay" is unexplained. Tur-Sinai absurdly has "he teacheth me: '(thou art like) the clay.'"

19.d. Gray thinks the colon short and proposes, in balance with the wordplay in the second colon, לְחֹמֶר וּלְחָמְרִי "to the mire and Confusion," חמרי being explained as a reference to Ḥmry, the Ugar. city of Mot, the god of death.

19.e. משל hithp "show oneself like" (KBL, 576a; Dhorme, Habel "come to resemble") rather than simply "be like" (BDB, 605a) or "become like" (*HALOT*, 2:647b) or be "no better than" (NEB, JB); the hithp often carries the connotation of display. NIV, Moffatt "I am reduced to" and NAB "I am leveled" slightly miss the point. Terrien "as if I were dust and ashes" is interesting, but not what the Heb. says. Good has "I'm a cliché, like dust and ashes," thinking of משל as the verb of מָשָׁל "proverb" (though there are no parallels for such a sense of משל); but while Job hated being a מָשָׁל in the sense of a "byword" (cf. מלה, v 9), he is not enough of a metropolitan sophisticate to worry about being a cliché. Ceresko reads וָאֶתֹּם מָשְׁלָךְ "and I perish, flung [into the dust and ashes]"—which is no more than ingenious; and in any case, תמם "perish" is hard to parallel (Deut 2:15; Josh 8:24 are not close enough).

19.f. אפר is traditionally translated as "ashes," especially in the phrase עפר ואפר "dust and ashes" (occurring elsewhere at 42:6; Gen 18:27). Though it is clearly "ashes" at Num 19:9, 10, it is more likely a general word for "dirt, dust" in its other twenty-two occurrences, which is how indeed KBL, 79, translates it. For full discussion, see *Note* 42:6.e.

20.a. NIV, REB, GNB supply "God" as a vocative.

20.b. Driver–Gray, Dhorme, Terrien, Hartley think עמד is "stand (in prayer)," as in Jer 15:1. But more probably NEB is correct in seeing a forensic force here, rendering "I stand up to plead." Gordis maintains that עמד can mean "remain silent" (as in 29:8; 32:16); so too Good (cf. *DCH*, vol. 6, *s.v.*). Sicre Díaz, following Schultens, thinks it means "insist." Merx, Duhm, Hitzig, Budde, Beer (BH^2), Pope emend (with one Heb. MS and Pesh) to עָמַדְתָּ "you stand"; so too NAB "you stand off."

20.c. בין hithpo is usually "consider" (as BDB, 107a; *DCH*, 2:145a; "behave intelligently" according to *HALOT*, 1:122b). Here however it seems to mean "look, stare" (so Schultens, Rosenmüller, Delitzsch, Dillmann, Hitzig, Budde, Dhorme, Stevenson), as also at 31:1; 38:18; 1 Kgs 3:21; Isa 14:16 (perhaps also 42:15). RV renders exactly, "and thou lookest at me" (similarly Pope), but that does not make much sense; NIV, NRSV "you merely look at me" (similarly NAB) are better, and Delitzsch "look fixedly." Good's proposal has its merits: "I stand [silent], and you examine me," Job thus complaining about divine inconsistency: if he cries out, God ignores him; if he is quiet, God interrogates him. But the key seems rather to lie in the place where Job has been left in v 19a: on the floor (as we say in Yorkshire).

Many add לֹא "not" (with one Heb. MS, Vg); thus KJV, RSV, JB, NJPS, Bickell[2], Siegfried Beer (*BHK frt*), Driver–Gray, Dhorme, Hölscher, Kissane, Larcher, Fohrer, Terrien, Fedrizzi, de Wilde, Habel, Hartley, Gray. It is difficult to believe that the "not" in the first colon "does duty" for the second colon also (as Terrien, Gordis, Andersen), since there are two clauses in each colon (for examples of double-duty לֹא, cf. *Note* 28:17.b); but cf. Vg *clamo ad te et non exaudis me sto et non respicis me* "I cry to you and you do not hear me, I stand and you do not look at me." NEB "thou sittest aloof" (REB "you keep aloof") is presumably a loose rendering of "you do not look at me." More loosely still, Moffatt renders "thou hast ceased to care for me," while Tur-Sinai unjustifiably emends to תִּתְנַכֵּר "you make yourself strange to me." The proposal noted by Beer (*BHK al*), מֵהִתְבּוֹנֵן, would mean "you stand (aloof) from considering me."

21.a. ההפך niph "you have turned" (as NRSV; similarly KJV, RSV), since niph of הפך is commonly "turn oneself" (BDB, 245b; *DCH*, 2:581a; *HALOT*, 1253b, however, acknowledges only the sense "be changed"); thus also JB "you have grown [cruel]" (a similar construction at Isa 63:10). It is a change in God's disposition toward Job, rather than a "turning upon" Job in aggression, as in the renderings "you turn on me [ruthlessly]" (NIV), "you turn upon me without mercy" (NAB), or "thou hast turned cruelly against me" (NEB).

21.b. שׂטם is "cherish animosity" (BDB, 966a; *HALOT,* 3:1316a); so KJV "opposest thyself against me," RSV "persecute me," NJB "torments me," NIV "attack me," NJB "buffet me," NJPS "harass me." JB "your hand lies on me, heavy and hostile" is a periphrasis. But LXX με ἐμαστίγωσας evidently renders תְּשַׂטְּטֵנִי "you whip, scourge me" (the verb שׂוט is not attested, but the noun שׁוֹט "whip" is); this is adopted by Merx (תְּשַׂטְּטֵנִי), and hence Moffatt "thou layest thy heavy lash on me." Implausible is Ceresko's claim that we have here a shaphel form (otherwise unattested) of טמן "hide," thus "you make me take cover."

22.a. תשׂאני is lit. "you lift me up" (similarly KJV, RSV, NAB, NJPS), but some more dramatic term seems called for, such as "snatch up" (as NEB, NIV).

22.b. תרכיבני is lit. "you lift me up to the wind and make me ride [it]," and since רכב hiph does mean "cause to mount and ride," JB "you carry me up to ride the wind," NJB "you carry me away astride the wind" (similarly RSV) may seem correct. Yet NAB, NIV "drive me before the wind," Moffatt "tossest me" seem more appropriate, since it is God himself who rides on the winds (Ps 18:10 [11]). KBL, 891a (not *HALOT,* 3:1233a), would read עַל "upon" rather than אל "to." Less plausibly, Ceresko makes of אֵל a vocative, "O God." Tur-Sinai arbitrarily emends to תַּרְכִּיכֵנִי "it [the height] makes (my heart) weak" (as at 23:16).

22.c. מוג polel is "soften, dissipate" (BDB, 556a), "soften, dissolve" (KBL, 501a; *DCH,* 5:170b), or "soften, disperse" (*HALOT,* 2:555a), as in Ps 65:10 (11) of making soft the ground with rain. KJV has "dissolve" (so too Davidson), Delitzsch "vanish"; and presumably Moffatt "I break up under the blast." NJPS has "you make my courage melt," but there is nothing about courage in the text.

Other translations have recourse to a different sense of מוג "wave, sway" (so KBL, 501b, for niph; *HALOT,* 2:555a, for qal, niph, polel), which should preferably be derived from another מוג "wave, waver" (as *DCH,* 5:170b); so RSV, JB, NAB, NIV, Pope, Hartley "toss about," NJB "blow me to pieces," de Wilde "you make me into a game-ball" (!).

22.d. K תְּשֻׁוָּה is presumably a form of תְּשׁוּאָה or תְּשֻׁאָה "noise (of thunder, storm)" (BDB, 996b), "shouting, crashing" (KBL, 1042b), "noise, crash" (*HALOT,* 4:1799a), or, more broadly, the storm itself and its rain (we need a word for the water that will dissolve him); thus RV, NIV, Beer (*BHK*), Gordis "in the storm," JB "in a tempest," Pope "with a tempest," RSV "in the roar of the storm," NEB "the tempest tosses me up and down" (similarly NAB, Gray). Dhorme interestingly renders "a storm dissolves me, drenches me, in water." Kissane reads בְּשׁוֹאָה, which he renders "with a storm," paralleling רוח "wind" in the previous colon (|| ענן "cloud" in Ezek 38:9, and סופה in Prov 1:27, reading Q שׁואה); see *Note* 30:14.d for this meaning of שׁוֹאָה. Larcher also adds the prefix *beth* to the noun. The recommendation of Gerleman (*BHS*) to "read" K תְּשֻׁוָּה is misleading, unless he is proposing that such a word be added to the lexicon, for it does not exist otherwise. Q תֻּשִׁיָּה "wisdom, success" will make little sense here; Duhm can hardly be right that מִתֻּשִׁיָּה, which he reads, can mean "without continuance, help" (as also at 6:13), nor is Ceresko's explanation acceptable, which renders "you sweep victory away from me" (where does מוג mean "sweep"?), nor is Habel's persuasive ("then [you] made my success melt away"), since the parallelism is entirely lost. Good's reading תְּשַׁוֶּה "you level me" (from שׁוה I) is tempting, since it would provide a good parallel to תמגגני "you dissolve," but שׁוה piel is used elsewhere only in the senses of "smooth, quieten, account suitable," not "level [to the ground]."

KJV's "my substance" depends on an older interpretation of תּוּשִׁיָּה as "essence, substance" (so Buxtorf, 341, deriving it from a root ישׁה "be," from which יֵשׁ "there is" would also come).

Merx read תְּשָׁדֵּנִי "you destroy me" (from שׁדד "deal violently with," as BDB, 994a), which is insufferably weak. Tur-Sinai thinks the noun is תְּשׁוּאָה, which he understands as "height," though it is unattested elsewhere. Siegfried emended to מִתְּשֻׁעָה "(far) from help," which is rather feeble.

23.a. כי could perhaps be "for" (as KJV, Moffatt), giving God's ultimate intentions for Job as the reason for his present behavior toward him. But it is more likely that we have here the emphatic כי, according to RSV "yea," NJB "yes," NAB "indeed," Fohrer *ja wohl* (for other examples, see *Note* 22:26.b). NEB, NIV, NRSV, Pope do not translate the particle at all. Dhorme surprisingly claims that the כי "ought to follow" ידעתי "I know that."

23.b. תשׁיבני "you will return, deliver me"; so NEB "hand me over." שׁוב hiph is of course properly "cause to return," and it may seem a little strange that Job will be "returned" to death, where he has not been before. But we can recall that in 10:9 God "returns" (שׁוב hiph) Job to the dust, and death and the dust are not dissimilar (so too Pope "will return me to Death," viewed as the underworld ruler; similarly Delitzsch "wilt bring me back to death," Habel); and it is also possible to understand שׁוּב hiph as "relinquish, hand over," as it appears to be in 20:10 (see *Comment*). NAB "you will turn me back in death to the destined place of everyone alive" is complicated, but probably correct. All these are better renderings than "bring me" (KJV, RSV, NJPS) or "bring down" (NIV) or "take me" (JB), which miss the element of "return" in שׁוּב. Duhm, Beer (*BH*² *al*) needlessly emend to תֹּשִׁיבֵנִי "you will make me dwell."

23.c. מוּת "[to] death," an acc of place (Dhorme).

23.d. בית מועד, lit. "the house of meeting" (RVmg), "meetinghouse" (Pope, Hartley), "meeting house" (Habel), "meeting place" (Dhorme), "common meeting place" (JB). Since מוֹעֵד means not only "meeting" but also "appointment" (BDB, 417a), others have "house appointed" (KJV, RSV, NIV; similarly NEB, and NAB "destined place," NJPS "house assigned"), but the analogy is rather with the term אהל מועד "tent of meeting." Moffatt has "thou wilt house me with death," but בית "house" belongs with כל־חי "all living" rather than with מות "death." It is unnecessary to revocalize to וּבַיִת מוּעָד "and a house is appointed" (as J. Reider, "Contributions to the Scriptural Text," *HUCA* 24 [1952–53] 85–106 [102–3]).

24.a. This is one of the most unintelligible verses in the book. Literally it appears to read, "Surely one does not stretch out a hand to a ruin, or in his calamity a cry for help to these things [לָהֵן as a neuter]?" The older versions attempted to wrest a sense from these words; thus KJV "howbeit he will not stretch out his hand to the grave [which is how "ruin" is interpreted], though they cry in his destruction," RV "surely against a ruinous heap he will not put forth his hand; though it be in his destruction, one may utter a cry because of these things." RSV follows essentially their lead: "yet does not one in a heap of ruins stretch out his hand, and in his disaster cry for help?"

When the sense of the individual words is so vague or uncertain, it becomes all the more necessary to ask what is suitable to the context. The next verse has Job speaking of his care for the needy as the bitter backdrop to his present afflictions, and it would make sense to see v 24 also as portraying his generosity. The key image then must be the stretching out of the hand; elsewhere the phrase שׁלח יד (ב) means to assault, attack (as in Gen 37:22; Exod 3:20; 1 Sam 24:6 [7]; Esth 3:6; Ps 55:20 [21]). And Job must be denying that he ever did such a thing. We could then perhaps emend (with Wright, Dhorme, Rowley, Habel; similarly Gerleman [*BHS prp*]) בעי "against a ruin [?]" to בְּעָנִי "against a poor man" (as also Dhorme, Beer [*BHK al*], Kissane, Larcher, Pope, JB, NAB), ישלח "he sent" to אֶשְׁלַח "I sent" (with LXX, Beer [*BHK al*], Kissane, Larcher), and להן שוע "(?) to them a cry" to לִי יְשַׁוֵּעַ "[if in his calamity] he cried to me" (as also Gray). Such an emendation is adopted in the *Translation* above. This rendering is essentially identical to that of JB "have I ever laid a hand on the poor, when they cried out for justice in calamity?" Similar solutions, though without emending ישלח, are adopted by NRSV "surely one does not turn against the needy" (similarly Pope, NIV), NJPS "surely He would not strike at a ruin?" (retaining בְּעִי; similarly Good). The second colon is commonly interpreted in the same way; thus NRSV "when in disaster they cry for help" (similarly JB, RSV, NIV, NJPS). Alternatively, we could read לֹא יְשַׁוֵּעַ "does he not cry out?" (Bickell, Budde, Duhm, Peake, Beer [*BHK frt*, יְשַׁוֵּעַ], Hölscher, Fohrer, Gerleman [*BHS prp*, יְשַׁוֵּעַ (לֹא =) לֹה], Hesse, de Wilde), or לוֹ יְשַׁוֵּעַ or לֹה "one cries out to him" (Hartley). NEB reads לֹה נוֹשַׁע "was delivered (by me) in his distress."

The hostile sense of שׁלח יד ב rules out the translations of NAB "should not a hand be held out to a poor man?" (reading בְּעָנִי), NEB "yet no beggar [see below] held out his hand [but was relieved by me]" (REB "held out his hand in vain"), and Delitzsch "doth not one stretch out the hand in falling" (from עוה "bend, twist," thus "fall"); cf. also Andersen. Gordis's claimed support from Ps 144:7 for the sense "extend help" is illusory, since there it is Yahweh attacking the psalmist's enemies. For the same reason the common emendation of בעי to טֹבֵעַ "one who is drowning" (Moffatt "a sinking man will stretch his hand") by Dillmann (?), Bickell, Budde, Duhm, Peake, Strahan, Driver–Gray, Beer (*BHK frt*), Hölscher, Fohrer, Gerleman (*BHS prp*, בְּטֹבֵעַ), Hesse, de Wilde, Sicre Díaz cannot be accepted (quite apart from the presumable rarity of drowning in the land of Uz). Gordis's emendation is equally open to criticism; he reads אַךְ לֹא בָעֵי יִשְׁלַח יָד אִם בְּפִיד אֱלוֹהַּ יְשַׁוֵּעַ "if a man pleads, one must extend one's hand, if under the calamity of God he cries out," taking לֹא as "if" (though in that sense it elsewhere states "a case which has not been, or is not likely to be, realized" [BDB, 530a]—which is not what we have here), and בעי as ptcp of בעה (the nearest analogy to this sense being only Isa 21:12, where it is of "inquiring" of a prophet); further, the phrase פיד אלוה "calamity of God" is improbable, since פיד is elsewhere (21:20 [emended]; 31:29; Prov 24:22) calamity as suffered rather than calamity as inflicted; and finally, it is unlikely that the adjacent verbs בעי and ישלח should have different subjs (as Sicre Díaz also observes).

Emendation of לְהֶן שׁוּעַ to לֹא נוֹשָׁע "was he not saved?" (Beer [*BHK al*], Gerleman [*BHS al*], NEB "[every beggar] was relieved") is possible, but the point in vv 24–25 seems to be not so much Job's success in relieving the distress of others as his sympathy. The same applies to the view of G. R. Driver ("Problems in Job," 164–65), who proposes בֶּעָי "beggar," or בָּעָי (Brockington, 113), comparing Syr. *ba'āyā*, and rendering "surely no beggar would put out his hand if he had found no relief in his plight" (similarly NEB, REB). It applies to Gray's reading of בֹּעֶה "[to one who] made a request [I would put out my hand]"; he explains לֹא, not very successfully, as *lamedh* plus אַי "any," a new word cognate with Arab. *'ayy* "whoever" (Wehr–Cowan, 36b). And it applies also to the proposal by J. Reider ("Etymological Studies in Biblical Hebrew," *VT* 2 [1952] 113–30 [127–29]) and by Guillaume of an עַי "weakling," on the basis of Arab. *'ayy* "helpless, impotent" (Lane, 2205c; Wehr–Cowan, 660a); cf. *DCH*, vol. 6, *s.v.*

A more conservative reading would be "surely he [God] would not stretch out his hand against a ruin [such as Job]" (so NJPS); similarly Hartley "God does not stretch out his hand in destruction." Terrien also retains בעי as "in his ruin," rendering "in his extremity, will he not stretch out his hand"; similarly L. G. Rignell, "Comments on Some *cruces interpretum* in the Book of Job," *ASTI* 11 (1978) 111–18 (118). Grabbe, *Comparative Philology*, 101–3, understands עי as "destruction" and renders "let him not send his hand with complete destruction as in his calamity there is a cry for help." But with these renderings it is extremely difficult to discern a connection with the following verse.

24.b. NAB reads אם־בפידו לְהוֹשִׁיעַ "(or) to help [a wretched man] in his calamity," but the syntax of the inf is hard to understand. Kissane proposes לְדִין שִׁוֵּעַ "[if in his calamity] he cry out for redress," an attractive emendation that is followed by Larcher, JB "when they cried out for justice."

25.a. Terrien thinks vv 25–26 are out of place here, and that they originally preceded 31:1, as part of Job's oath of innocence.

25.b. The interrogative אם expects the answer "no," as in 6:12 (BDB, 50b). Strahan would prefer to read a 3d-person verb, בָּכָה, and to have נַפְשׁוֹ in the second line; thus "doth he not weep who is in trouble? Is not the soul of the needy grieved?"; similarly Moffatt; and likewise Beer (*BH*^{2} *frt*), Hölscher, de Wilde, reading בִּכִית "the weeping of" or בְּכִי, with the same meaning (Beer [*BH*^{2} *frt*]). But that is hard to connect with what follows.

25.c. קשה־יום, lit. "hard of day, i.e., "that was in trouble" (KJV), "whose life was hard" (NEB), "the unfortunate" (REB), or "the hapless" (Pope). Good's "for a difficult day" is hard to justify.

25.d. For נפשי "my heart" Beer (*BH*^{2} *frt*) suggests נַפְשׁוֹ "his [God's] heart."

25.e. The לא of the first line does double duty for the second line also; for other examples, see *Note* 28:17.b.

25.f. עגם "grieve," occurring only here, is no doubt a byform of אגם (BDB, 723a; *HALOT*, 2:785b; *DCH*, vol. 6, *s.v.*). Cf. the phrase אַגְמֵי נֶפֶשׁ "the sad of life" in Isa 19:10.

25.g. Duhm, Beer (*BH*^{2} *frt*), and Hölscher emend לאביון "to the poor" to לְאֹבֵד "to the perishing," but it is hard to see what is gained.

26.a. The disjunctive "yet" is added by NAB, NIV, REB. Duhm, Gordis regard the initial כי "for" as anticipatory, giving the reason for v 27. Beer (*BHK*), followed by Gray, thought it should perhaps be deleted (in correspondence with LXX, Pesh, Vg).

26.b. According to W. L. Michel, cited by Ceresko, קוה piel is not the usual "wait for" but a קוה II "cry out" (as supposedly also in 3:9; 17:13; Isa 59:9).

26.c. The two terms טוב "good" and רע "bad" are of course capable of variant renderings; thus JB "I hoped for happiness, but sorrow came," Dhorme "happiness, misfortune," NJPS "good fortune, evil."

26.d. Some correct the first vowel in ואיחלה to וָ (so Beer [*BHK*]), making it *waw* consec; but it is hard to believe that the "expecting" took place after the "looking."

27.a. NAB locates here vv 16a, 27b, 17b, 27a.

27.b. It is hard to find an Eng. equivalent for מעים, a general term for the internal organs, including the intestines, the stomach, the womb, and, probably, the heart (in Job only elsewhere at 20:14). The traditional rendering is "bowels" (as KJV, NEB, NJPS); NRSV, NAB have "inward parts," RSV "heart," JB "stomach." BDB, 588b, glosses it as "internal organs, inward parts," *HALOT*, 2:609b, "entrails, intestines; that part of the body through which people come into existence; inner being; stomach," and *DCH*, 5:382a, "genitals (of a man); womb; offspring; belly; internal organs; inner person, self; belly (from external perspective)."

27.c. רתח, lit. "boil" (as BDB, 958a, explaining the verb here as figurative of violent emotions) (as KJV), as also at 41:31 (23). RSV, NJPS "are in turmoil," NEB "are in ferment," NAB, JB "seethe," Moffatt "is hot," NIV "the churning inside me never stops."

27.d. דמם I "be silent, cease" or, if we emend to דָּמוּ, from דמה II "cease" or דום "cease" (*DCH*, 2:450b, 448b, 425b); so NEB "know no peace." See further, Driver, "Confused Hebrew Root," 1*–11*.

27.e. קדם "be in front, meet" (KJV "prevent"); NIV, NJPS, Dhorme, Pope "confront," Moffatt "faces me," NAB "have overtaken me," NJB "have struck me," JB too loosely "every day brings further suffering." "Stretch out before me" (as NEB, Good) is too tame.

28.a. קדר is "be black" (BDB, 871a; *HALOT*, 3:1072a), not infrequently of the somber dress of a mourner (*HALOT* specifically offers the sense "be dirty, untidy, in mourning garb," citing E. Kutsch, "'Trauerbräuche' und 'Selbstminderungsriten' im Alten Testament," in *Drei Wiener Antrittsreden*, by K. Lüthi, E. Kutsch, and W. Dantine, Theologische Studiën 78 [Zürich: EVZ, 1965] 23–42 [= his *Kleine Schriften zum Alten Testament*, ed. L. Schmidt and K. Eberlein, BZAW 168 (Berlin: de Gruyter, 1986) 78–95]); so also 5:11; Jer 8:21; 14:2; Pss 35:14; 38:6 (7); 42:9 (10); 43:2. It is strange then that only KJV and Peake seem to understand קדר as "mourning." RSV, NIV have "blackened," NRSV "in sunless gloom," NAB "I go about in gloom" (similarly Pope), JB "sombre," NEB "dejected"—translations that offer either a literal sense of "black" or, what cannot be substantiated, a metaphorical sense of "gloomy, dejected." Dhorme is certain that it means "I have walked about all tanned when there was no sunshine," but he does not explain how Job comes to be "tanned" without the benefit of sunshine, or in what part of the world Job was living that he could avoid sunshine. The very same phrase, קדר הלכתי "I go about blackened," i.e., with the dark clothes of a mourner, occurs in Ps 38:7, where there is no reference to the sun. Some see here a reference to the black skin of a leper, but leprosy does not make the skin black (see *Comment*), and Budde rightly observes that with the verb "walk about" (הלך piel) "blackened" should refer to the clothing, not the skin; and of course the clothing is not affected by the sun! Rowley, Gordis, and Hartley think Job's face is black because of his illness, but they do not say what illness makes the face black. It is much better to see here the dark clothing of the mourner.

28.b. חַמָּה is certainly "sun" at Cant 6:10; Isa 24:23; 30:26, though it is "heat" in Ps 19:6 (7); so BDB, 328b. *HALOT*, 1:326b, thinks it is "glow" rather than "heat" at Ps 19:77 (6), and raises the possibility that the word is חֲמֹתוֹ "its sight" (from a new word חמה "see"); *DCH*, 3:250a, adds to examples of the sense "heat" Ecclus 43:2 (Bmg). If חמה here means "sun," the phrase בלא חמה "without sun" will probably mean "without the sun (being the cause of my black countenance)" (Gordis); so RSV "blackened, but not by the sun," NRSV "in sunless gloom," NAB "in gloom, without the sun," BJ "sombre, without the sun" (*assombri, sans soleil*); JB and NJB lack any reference to the sun. At a pinch, it could mean "without the benefit of the sun," i.e., miserable (Fedrizzi), but hardly that even the sun had clothed itself in black mourning (Delitzsch).

Two other new words have been proposed: (1) D. Winton Thomas, in his unpublished *Lexicon* (1970), 8:236, suggests a חֵמָה "protection," which has been followed by NEB "friendless" (cf. Brockington, 113; *DCH*, 4:251b). (2) Ceresko proposes a new word חֲמָה "answer," on the basis of M. Dahood's supposition ("The Phoenician Contribution to Biblical Wisdom Literature," in *The Role of the Phoenicians in the Interaction of Mediterranean Civilization*, ed. W. A. Ward [Beirut: American University of Beirut, 1968] 123–53 [125–26, 144]; "Hebrew-Ugaritic Lexicography XII," 382) of another verb חמה "answer" (also at Zech 10:2), cognate with Ugar. *tḥm* "word" (*DUL*, 865), its noun תַּנְחוּמָה "reply" being proposed for 15:11; 21:2; the sense is good, but the foundation is weak.

A very plausible emendation, adopted in the *Translation* above, commends itself: for בלא חמה "without the sun" read בְּלֹא נֶחָמָה "without comfort" (the noun at 6:10; Ps 119:50); so Duhm, Peake, Strahan, Driver–Gray, Beer (*BHK frt*), Hölscher (*frt*), Larcher, Fohrer, Gerleman (*BHS prp*), Hesse, de Wilde; among translations, the emendation is adopted by JB "yet no one comforts me," NEB "friendless," REB "comfortless," Moffatt. The combination of "mourning" and "comfort" more or less clinches this proposal. Other emendations are less attractive, e.g., בְּלֹא חֶדְוָה "without joy" (Voigt), בְּלֹא חֶמְדָּה "without desire" (Beer [*BH*²]), וְלֹא אֶחֱשֶׁה "and I am not silent" (Beer [*BH*² *prps*]), and especially בְּלֹא חֵמָה "without butter" (Kissane), i.e., without affluence (חמה being a form of חֶמְאָה "curds," as it is at 29:6).

28.c. בקהל is "in the assembly." Gordis, however, cannot accept that Job can really be in the assembly when he says this, and so argues that קהל is an Aramaism for קוֹל "voice," thus "in a loud voice." But such a קהל is not attested (though there is perhaps a קְהִלָּה in Neh 5:7, according to F. Zimmermann, "The Root *Kahal* in Some Scriptural Passages," *JBL* 50 [1931] 311–12, rendering it "rebuke," and NEB), and the argument that in v 29 "his loneliness is clearly indicated" rests on a misunderstanding: Job is not out in the wilderness with jackals and ostriches; he only means that he would be a suitable member of their families because he makes the same mournful sounds as they do. The suggestion of Beer (*BH*² *frt*) בְּקוֹל "with (my) voice" or בְּקוֹלִי "with my voice" is weak, since without the presence of the term קהל "assembly" Job's standing up is unmotivated; if he is not in the assembly, why should he stand up in order to cry out?

28.d. The impf ישוע following the pf קמתי suggests the subordination of the second verb (GKC, §120c), in this case almost as a purpose clause; thus NEB "only to appeal to help." שׁוע is "cry for help" (BDB, 1002b), not "weep," as against Tur-Sinai "I burst into tears," NAB "I rise up in public to voice my grief," JB "if I rise in the council, I rise to weep." For בקהל אשוע "in the assembly I cry out," Duhm, thinking it impossible that Job should now be in the assembly, read בִּקְהַל שׁוּעָל "in the company of the jackal" (followed by Peake and Strahan, and by Moffatt "fit company for howling jackals"); but this does not correspond well with the first colon, and it lessens the impact of v 29.

29.a. תַּנִּים is "jackals" (BDB, 1072a; *HALOT,* 4:1759a), as most translations (e.g., RV, RSV, JB, NIV, NJPS), though Moffatt and NEB have "wolf." KJV "dragons," following Vg, confuses this word with תַּנִּין "serpent, dragon, sea-monster."

29.b. בנות יענה, lit. "daughters of greed" or "daughters of screeching" (see further *Note* on 39:13), the usual term for ostriches (so RV, RSV, JB, NAB, NJPS); Moffatt's "screaming ostriches" alludes to the supposed derivation of the word from ענה IV "sing" (BDB, 777a). The old view that they are owls persists; thus KJV, NIV, while NEB has "owls of the desert."

30.a. Heb. adds מעלי, lit. "from upon me," another example of the "pathetic" על (see *Note* 30:2.g); it overinterprets to render "and falleth from me" (RV; similarly RSV, NAB, NIV, NJPS, Moffatt, Delitzsch, Duhm, Terrien, Rowley, Sicre Díaz, NEB "my blackened skin peels off"; similarly Pope, Hartley). Dhorme rightly recognizes that מעלי is "quite simply 'on me'" and that it is unnecessary to assign it a more subtle meaning; likewise Hölscher, Gordis, de Wilde.

Dahood (*Psalms I,* 74), followed by Ceresko, emended מעלי to מֵעֲלִי "[my skin is blacker] than a caldron" (the new word עֲלִי, which he finds also at v 17). Caldrons however are noted for features other than their color, and the phrase does not ring true. Gray thinks rather, in view of the parallel "with heat," that עֲלִי should be a verbal noun, "scorching."

30.b. The sg עצמי "my bone" could stand for his bones in general (as עצם sg in 2:5; 19:20; Ps 102:5 [6]; Prov 15:30; Lam 4:8) or for his whole body (as in Lam 4:7; perhaps Prov 16:24; Exod 24:10 [the "body" of heaven]).

30.c. ועצמי־חרה מני־חרב, lit. "and my bone burns because of the heat," חֹרֶב being "dryness, drought, heat" (BDB, 351a; *HALOT,* 1:350a; *DCH,* 3:310a); thus NEB "my body is scorched by the heat," NJPS "my bones are charred by the heat," JB "my bones are burnt with fever," NIV "my body burns with fever," Moffatt "my limbs burn with the fever."

31.a. כנור is a stringed musical instrument, a lute, a lyre (RSV, NJPS), or a harp (KJV, NEB, NAB, JB, NIV). See also *Comment* on 21:12.

31.b. היה ל, lit. "become for," signifying "serve the purpose of," as in Gen 1:14; 17:7; 28:21 (BDB, 226a, §II.2.e). NJPS "my lyre is given over to mourning," or, a little more loosely, "is tuned to mourning" (NIV), "tuned to funeral wails" (JB), "tuned to dirges" (NJB; similarly NEB), are preferable to "is turned to" (as KJV, RSV, NAB).

31.c. עוגב is an aerophone, i.e., a pipe (RSV, NJB, NJPS; NAB "reed pipe") or flute (NEB, JB, NIV), not a stringed instrument (as RSV, REB "lyre"); cf. BDB, 721b; *HALOT,* 2:795a; *DCH,* vol. 6, *s.v.* KJV "my organ" followed Vg *organum* (LXX had ὄργανον at Ps 150:4). See also *Comment* on 21:12. The Edinburgh Hebraist Strahan believed the עוגב was the bagpipe, citing the authority of W. Nowack, *Lehrbuch der hebräischen Archäologie* (Freiburg i. B.: Mohr [Siebeck], 1894) 1:277.

31.d. בכים "weepers" is not very probably an abstract noun "weeping" (as Gordis), though that would create a stricter parallelism with אבל "mourning."

31:1.a. Vv 1–4 were not present in the original LXX, and some question whether they belong here. Beer (*BH*[2]) would delete them altogether, while Moffatt would move them to precede v 9. NEB moves v 1 to follow v 5, and NAB to precede v 9, translating "if I have made an agreement." Terrien moves 30:25–26 to precede v 1. For other transpositions, see *Comment.*

1.b. ברית כרתי לעיני is often translated "I made a covenant with my eyes" (e.g., RSV); JB "pact," NJB "agreement," NEB "I have come to terms with." But, as Driver–Gray and Gordis point out, the prep is not עם but ל, which implies the imposition of an obligation by a superior on an inferior (Exod 23:32; 34:12, 15; Deut 7:2; Josh 9:6, 7, 11, 15, 16; Judg 2:2; 1 Sam 11:1; 2 Chr 29:10 is an exception that proves the rule [against Dhorme, Rowley]; cf. also M. Weinfeld, *TDOT,* 2:253–79 [259]). Moffatt correctly has "laid an interdict," Pope "put a ban on." For the idea of ברית, conventionally translated as "covenant," as "obligation," see E. Kutsch, "Der Begriff בְּרִית in vordeuteronomischer Zeit," in *Das ferne und nahe Wort,* FS L. Rost, ed. F. Maass, BZAW 105 (Berlin: Töpelmann, 1967) 133–43.

1.c. Ceresko unconvincingly interprets as "in his eyes," the suff being explained as 3 masc sg.

1.d. Dhorme, Hölscher, Pope, Andersen, Ceresko, Habel, Hartley take מה as a negative particle equivalent to Arab. *mā* "not" (Lane, 3016b; see on 16:6), hence "that I would not look upon folly"; but there is no need to postulate this word.

1.e. אתבונן is hithpo of בין "discern," thus "shew oneself attentive, consider diligently" (BDB, 107a) or "consider, examine, look at" (*DCH,* 2:145a). In the context, some such translation as NEB "take notice of," REB more realistically "never to let my eyes linger" (similarly JB), NJPS, Ceresko "gaze (up)on" is appropriate; the word itself does not contain the idea of desire, as in Moffatt's "look with longing," NIV's "look lustfully," and GNB's "look with lust" (an echo of Matt 5:28?). NAB, seeing the sense as part of an "if" clause, has "and entertained any thoughts against a maiden." Duhm, Beer (*BHK frt*), Gerleman (*BHS prp*), Gray unnecessarily emend ומה אתבונן "and how should I look?" to מֵהִתְבּוֹנֵן "so as not to look."

1.f. בתולה is traditionally translated "virgin," as RSV (KJV "maid," Moffatt, NJPS "maiden," NEB, NIV, GNB "girl"), but the term means only a young woman of marriageable age, and could refer to a married or unmarried woman, though the former sense is rare (cf. *DCH,* 2:289b). Peake, Pope, de Wilde would emend to נְבָלָה "wickedness," and Kissane to בְּהָלָה "[why must I contemplate] calamity."

2.a. Gordis regards this verse as another of his "virtual quotations," rendering "For I thought, 'If I sinned, what would be my portion.'" The point of this suggestion is obscure, and it is hard to see the justification for adding "if I sinned."

2.b. ומה, lit. "and what?" KJV "for what?"

2.c. חלק is "the portion, a portion." RSV has "my portion" (similarly Moffatt), but Job is perhaps thinking not specifically of himself but of humans in general (see *Comment*).

2.d. In חלק אלוה, lit. "the portion of God," the gen is subjective (the portion that God allots), though elsewhere is it usually objective (the portion of the person to whom it is allotted), as is also the case with נחלה "inheritance."

3.a. Larcher adds at the end of the first colon נָכוֹן "fixed," i.e., "Is it not the misfortune he reserves for the unjust?" The omission of נכון is explained as due to haplography, the next word being נכר. Hence NJB "disasters appropriate to the wicked."

3.b. נֵכֶר is only here (נֹכֶר at Obad 12); BDB, 648b (misspelling it נֶכֶר), and *HALOT,* 2:700a, render "misfortune"; it appears to be connected with נֵכָר "alien," but only in the sense of "other," thus "alteration [of fortune]," RSV "disaster." KJV's "strange *punishment*" attempted to preserve the overtone. Ley added נָכוֹן "is established" before נכר, thinking the colon too short; the addition tempts Duhm, Beer (*BHK ins ?*), and Hölscher (*frt*).

4.a. NJPS, REB strangely "take account of."

5.a. Moffatt and NAB reverse the order of vv 5 and 6.

5.b. NEB, understanding the initial אם (lit. "if") as the opening of an oath, renders, "I swear." Gordis thinks it an interrogative particle expecting the answer "no," hence "have I walked with falsehood?," but there is no reason not to take it as "if." Ceresko translates "whether," and connects it with v 4.

5.c. Falsehood is personified by the use of עם "together with"; so NEB "have had no dealings with falsehood," JB "have I been a fellow traveller with falsehood?," NJPS even more concretely "with worthless men" (similarly Andersen). M. Dahood (*Ugaritic-Hebrew Philology,* 31, 32; similarly at Ps 78:37 in his *Psalms II,* 51–100, 243), followed by Pope, claimed that עם here was "toward," but the normal sense of עם is much preferable. Dahood (*Ugaritic-Hebrew Philology,* 31), followed by Ceresko, saw in שוא and מרמה more concrete senses, "an idol," "a fraud," but the language seems much more general than that. Two MSS, followed by LXX and Pesh, have מְתֵי שוא "men of falsehood" (Gerleman [*BHS*]), whence Bickell מְתֵי שוא and Beer (*BH*^{2} *frt*) אַנְשֵׁי שוא "men of falsehood," avoiding the personification of falsehood as a companion to Job.

5.d. וַתַּחַשׁ "and [my foot] hastened." Many emend to a more regular form וַתָּחָשׁ, from חוש "hasten" (so, e.g., Beer [*BHK*], Hölscher), but the present form is not without parallels (GKC, §72ff). Gray prefers to postulate a new word חשה II "hasten," a byform of חוש.

5.e. NEB more blandly "have not embarked on a course of deceit," a translation redeemed by REB with its "gone hotfoot after deceit." על is perhaps used in the sense of אל "to" (as Beer [*BH*^{2}] notes).

6.a. Several versions take this verse parenthetically (so RSV, NIV). Strahan is tempted to place it before v 5, where it would make "an admirable exordium to Job's magnificent *apologia pro vita sua.*"

6.b. KJV and RSV take the subj as indefinite and so render with a passive "let me be weighed," because the name "God" has not yet been mentioned. Dillmann thinks the subject of the first verb is by implication God, and so too NEB. Ceresko, following Blommerde, has "should he weigh me," a conditional clause—which spoils the sense.

6.c. וידע with simple *waw,* not "that God may know" (KJV). JB is a little strained: "being God, he cannot fail to see my innocence."

6.d. תמה "innocence, integrity." But M. Dahood ("Congruity of Metaphors," in *Hebräische Wortforschung,* FS W. Baumgartner, VTSup 16 [Leiden: Brill, 1967] 40–49 [47–48]), followed by Blommerde and Ceresko, wants it to be "my full weight," presumably another metaphor for Job's perfect integrity.

7.a. Duhm and Beer (*BHK*) read מִנִּי דֶרֶךְ, "from (the) way," without the article, or מִן־הַדֶּרֶךְ (Beer [*BHK vel*]), presumably on grounds of rhythm.

7.b. JB, since there is some call for an indication of impropriety, "if my eyes have led my heart astray."

7.c. The line is omitted by Duhm, Beer (*BH*² *prb*), Strahan, Moffatt, Hölscher, Fohrer, Hesse, de Wilde.

7.d. מאום "blemish, defect" (BDB, 548b), but in the Leningrad MS, reproduced in *BHS,* it is written מְאוּם. NAB, JB rightly translate "stain," since the word has something of a ritual flavor (as in Lev 21:18; Deut 17:1; cf. NIV "my hands have been defiled," NJPS "a stain sullied my hands"), rather than "blot" (KJV), "spot" (RV, RSV). Driver–Gray read, with one MS and the Oriental K, מְאוּמָה "anything" (so too Fedrizzi, Sicre Díaz, Gray).

7.e. דבק is "cling, cleave, keep close" (BDB, 179b). NEB is more down to earth, "or any dirt stuck to my hands."

8.a. Beer (*BH*²) prosaically inserts (though with a question mark) כל "[let another eat] everything."

8.b. צאצאים is elsewhere in Job "offspring, descendants," as at 5:25; 21:8; 27:14 (thus Duhm, Pope, Ceresko, Habel, Good); but perhaps it is here "produce, crops" as at Isa 34:1; 42:5 (as BDB, 425b, and *HALOT,* 3:993b [though thinking it could include animals], against KBL, 790a). RV took it as "produce of my field," RSV "what grows for me," Moffatt, NEB, NIV "crops," NAB "my planting," JB "my young shoots," NJPS "the growth of my field"; so too Delitzsch, Davidson, Gibson, Peake, Dhorme, Fohrer, Rowley, Gordis. Beer (*BHK*) reads וְצֶאֱצָאֵי שָׂדַי "and the produce of my field."

8.c. Instead of ישרשו "let them be uprooted," Beer (*BH*² *frt*) reads יְרוֹשְׁשׁוּ "let them be impoverished," but the emendation is tame.

9.a. NAB transposes vv 38–40, followed by v 1, to precede this verse.

9.b. פתה על niph, lit. "deceived in respect of." BDB, 834b, thinks rather "enticed unto" (so too RV; similarly RSV, NAB), and Delitzsch "befooled about," Good "been fooled over a woman," Terrien *séduit pour une femme* (not *par une femme*). These are all acceptable renderings, but others are not (see *Comment*): KJV, blaming the woman, has "deceived by a woman," and similarly NEB, REB, NRSV, NIV, Hartley "enticed by," NJB, Habel "seduced by," NJPS "ravished by the wife of my neighbor," Moffatt "enticed by women," Pope "lured by." על does not mean "by," though Ceresko indeed wants to argue for that translation as a specialized sense. JB "lost my heart to any woman" unfortunately removes any note of blame from Job. On the niph of פתה "be (successfully) deceived," as contrasted with piel "(attempt to) deceive," an illocutionary verb as contrasted with a perlocutionary, see D. J. A. Clines and D. M. Gunn, "'You tried to persuade me' and 'Violence! Outrage!' in Jeremiah xx 7–8," *VT* 28 (1978) 20–27; reprinted in D. J. A. Clines, *On the Way to the Postmodern: Old Testament Essays, 1967–1998,* JSOTSup 292 (Sheffield: Sheffield Academic Press, 1998) 1:285–92.

9.c. ארב "ambush, lie in wait" is usually in a military context (cf. *DCH,* 1:365b), but not here. JB, REB, NIV render well with "lurked," Moffatt less successfully "haunted my neighbour's door."

9.d. Driver–Gray point out that על should mean "by, about" the door, not "at" the door," which usually needs no prep (e.g., Gen 19:11; 43:19); see also *Comment.* It is "her" door in GNB.

9.e. פתח is obviously the house door. The idea of a sexual connotation in this word, i.e., the genitalia of the woman (as Gordis, followed by Habel, Hartley [perhaps]) is most improbable.

10.a. תטחן לאחר "let her grind for another." KJV, RV "grind unto another" is obscure. Most versions understand the grinding as the normal domestic activity: NIV "grind another man's grain," Dhorme "turn the millstone for another"; but GNB "fix another man's food" is nowhere demeaning enough, while JB "grind corn that is not mine" rather misses the point. NEB "be another man's slave" does not apparently imply another reading, since REB notes "lit. grind corn for another"; similarly Moffatt "be a slave to strangers"; but the daily necessity of grinding grain, though a servile enough task, has been the duty of freeborn women in many cultures, and by no means implies slave status.

However, for the curse to have teeth, there ought to be a marked difference between a woman's drudgery in her husband's house and drudgery in someone else's, and so some have seen here a sexual sense (as already Tg, Vg, *b. Soṭa* 10a ["טחן is everywhere in Scripture of (carnal) transgression"],

Rashi, ibn Ezra; similarly Beer [*BHK*], Pope, Andersen [perhaps], Sicre Díaz, Habel, Hartley). The difficulty is that "grind" is not an entirely appropriate term for the woman (in *Midrash Rabbah Genesis* §48 it is used of the man's sexual activity), unless perhaps it signifies "serve him as it were as a nether mill-stone" (as Delitzsch). The parallelism in the second colon, where sexual activity is clearly spoken of, would incline one to this option, nonetheless. Hoffmann, Beer (*BH*[2] *frt*), Hölscher, Fohrer proposed to mend matters by reading תִּטָּחֵן "may she be ground," the following ל being the *lamedh* of agent (GKC, §121f); so too NEB (Brockington), but it merely translates "may my wife be another man's slave," as if there were no sexual reference at all.

10.b. The verb כרע "bend" (as in 4:4), "crouch" (as in 39:3), "kneel over" (NJPS, NRSV), "bow down upon" (so KJV) is indisputably used here of sexual activity. NEB, prudishly, has "let other men enjoy her"; still too tame are NAB "cohabit with her," NIV "sleep with her," NJB "let others have intercourse with her!," Moffatt "a concubine to other men." GNB "let her sleep in another man's bed" totally removes the coarseness of the original. JB "let her sleep between others' sheets" is an unspeakably bad translation.

11.a. NEB (but not REB), Fedrizzi, and Sicre Díaz put parentheses around vv 11–12; Hölscher deletes both verses. Dhorme and Kissane delete v 11 as a gloss, and Terrien and Pope are inclined to agree.

11.b. Read with Q הִיא זמה "it is a crime" and הוא עון "it is an offense" (so Beer [*BH*[2]], NEB [Brockington]).

11.c. זמה is, except for 17:11, where it means simply "plan," either an evil mental act or, more often, an evil act (BDB, 273a; *DCH*, 3:115b). So NEB "a wicked act," RSV, NAB, REB, Hartley "heinous," NIV "shameful," NJPS "debauchery," Pope, Habel "licentiousness," Good "an intended crime" (thinking more of its connection with זמם "purpose, intend"). JB "a sin of lust" and Moffatt "adultery would be an infamous offence" say more than the Heb. Ley arbitrarily prefixes חֵטְא "sin of" or דְּבַר "matter of" to זמה (for the sake of the meter), and Duhm adds וְסָרָה "and a betrayal" (taking a clue from LXX), thinking the line too short.

11.d. עון פלילים, lit. "a crime, judges," is rendered by NEB "an offence before the law," NAB "a crime to be condemned," NIV "a sin to be judged," NJPS, NRSV, Habel "a criminal offense," JB "a crime punishable by the law," Moffatt "a crime that calls for punishment," Pope "criminal iniquity," Hartley "a punishable iniquity," Good "an actionable offense"; GNB goes well beyond the Heb. in saying "Such wickedness should be punished by death." פליל "judge" occurs elsewhere only in Deut 32:31 and (if the reading is right) Exod 21:22.

Instead of MT עָוֹן פלילים, which is strictly unintelligible, we should no doubt read עֲוֹן פלילים "offense of the judges" (as Merx, Hitzig, Siegfried, Good) or עֲוֹן פְּלִילִי "judgeable offense" (as Budde, Duhm, Beer [*BH*[2]], Dillmann, Hölscher, Fohrer, Larcher, Gerleman [*BHS*], de Wilde, with several MSS and with v 28); but it will not be פלילי plus an enclitic *mem* (as Pope and Gordis are tempted to believe). D. R. Ap-Thomas ("Notes on Some Terms Relating to Prayer," *VT* 6 [1956] 225–41 [233]), taking פלל to mean "cut off, break off," understood the word as "outlawing from the community" or more probably "common, low-class." E. A. Speiser ("The Stem *pll* in Hebrew," *JBL* 82 [1963] 301–6 [304]) argues that פליל means "assessable"; cf. *DCH*, vol. 6, *s.v.*

12.a. כי emphatic, "indeed," according to Gordis. For other examples, see *Note* 22:26.b. Duhm simply deleted it as a thoughtless repetition; so too Beer (*BHK*), Gray.

12.b. עד־אבדון is "to the place of destruction" (BDB, 2a), Abaddon being a name for Sheol. Simply "to destruction" (KJV, de Wilde) is inadequate, whereas RV "unto Destruction," NIV "to Destruction," NAB "down to the abyss," or RSV, NJPS "down to Abaddon" are all acceptable. JB "[burning] till Perdition" gives the wrong idea of Perdition as a moment rather than a place, though Gray also thinks the phrase may simply mean "for ever" (as also D. Yellin, "Some Fresh Meanings of Hebrew Roots," *JPOS* 1 [1920–21] 10–14 [11]). NEB has, too tamely, "a consuming and destructive fire" (cf. GNB "a destructive, hellish fire"), Moffatt far too loosely "a fire that burns life to a cinder."

12.c. שרש, as a denominative of שֹׁרֶשׁ "root," ought to mean "root out" (KJV), "uprooted" (NIV), "uprooting" (Good); but fires do not uproot. In this case, though there are no parallels, it must be "burn to the roots" (so BDB, 1057b, RSV). JB "would have devoured" and NAB "consumed" follow Duhm, reading תִּשְׂרֹף "would burn" (so too Peake, Strahan, Driver–Gray, Dhorme, Beer [*BHK*], Hölscher, Larcher, Kissane, Fohrer, de Wilde, Hartley, KBL, 1012a). NJPS "consuming the roots" gives the impression of combining שרש and שרף. NEB "raging among my crops" follows G. R. Driver ("Problems in the Hebrew Text of Job," 89) in emending to תְּרַשֵּׁשׁ "scorch," the new word רשש being cognate with Akk. *rašāšu* "be red-hot" (von Soden, 960b); so too Gray.

12.d. תבואה is "product, revenue" (BDB, 100a), thus NAB "possessions," NJB "revenue," Pope,

Habel "income," Good "produce." In the closely parallel Deut 32:22, תבואה means the produce of the land, and so it should here too. Gordis however thinks it is "offspring" (cf. צאצא in v 8), though there are no parallels.

13.a. אם, according to Gordis, is here not "if," but introduces a question; but the usual rendering is to be preferred.

13.b. מאס can be variously rendered "despise" (KJV), "reject" (RSV), "brush aside" (NJPS), "dismissed" (Habel), "ignored the rightful claim" (Moffatt), "refused justice" (NAB), "denied justice" (NIV), and "infringed the rights of" (JB).

13.c. משפט is probably best understood here as "cause, case to be judged" (*DCH*, 5:558a §1.c) rather than the abstract "justice" (*DCH*, 5:559b §2) or even "legal right, entitlement" (*DCH*, 5:564a §5).

13.d. Traditionally, עבד is translated "(man)servant" and אמה "maidservant," but since male and female servants will have been of the same age range, it is necessary to find terms in Eng. that do not infantilize the women servants, as do, for example, NEB "my slave and my slave-girl," NAB "my manservant, my maid," RSV "manservant, maidservant," NIV "menservants and maidservants," NJPS "my servants, man or maid." GNB removes the female servant altogether. It is rare to find a socially sensitive translation such as NRSV "my male or female slaves," Moffatt "any servant, man or woman." Beer (*BHK*) makes ואמתי "and my woman servant" part of the second colon.

13.e. ברבם עמדי, lit. "in their controversy with me." NAB's "when they had a claim against me" is adopted for the *Translation* above; cf. NIV "had a grievance against me," NEB "brought their complaint to me." RSV, REB "brought a complaint against me" and NJPS "made a complaint," and even more so JB "in legal actions against me," sound as if it was possible for Job's slaves to arraign him formally in a court, which of course would not have been possible. Beer (*BHK*) emends בְּרִבָם "in their claim" to בְּרִיבָהּ "in her complaint," in reference to the woman servant.

14.a. Duhm, Beer (*BH*²), Peake, and de Wilde remove v 14 to precede v 18.

14.b. יקום is "arises," hence NEB "if [God] appears," NIV "confronts me," Habel "rises in court." LXX ἐὰν ἔτασίν μου ποιήσηται "if [the Lord] prepares my trial" suggested to Beer (*BH*²) and Ehrlich an emendation to יִקֹּם "avenges"; so too M. Dahood, "Hebrew-Ugaritic Lexicography IX," *Bib* 52 (1971) 337–56 (346), Ceresko. But the image is of a law court (note "answer"), not of an act of revenge.

14.c. פקד is capable of a wide range of renderings (cf. *DCH*, vol. 6, *s.v.*), such as "visit" (KJV), i.e., "intervene" (NEB), "demanded an account" (NAB), "holds his assize" (JB), "when [I am] called to account" (NIV), "calls me to account" (NJPS), "took me to task" (Moffatt).

15.a. Moffatt inserts here v 23. Hölscher deletes the verse on the technical ground that the masc sg suff seems to overlook the woman servant of v 13; but Gordis wonders whether the real reason was that the verse's statement of human rights was too unpalatable for the commentator in Germany in 1937. If he is right, how to explain the same omission by Fedrizzi in Italy in 1972?

15.b. Ceresko predictably reads הֲלֹא as הַלֵּא "the Victor" (but surely it should be spelled הַלָּא?), an alleged divine title; for other examples of לֵא "victor," from a לאה II "be strong," see *Note* 21:16.a and *DCH*, 4:495b.

15.c. Gordis emends בַבֶּטֶן עֹשֵׂנִי עשׂהו "my maker made him in the belly" to בַּבֶּטֶן עָשָׂנִי עשׂהו "he made him in the belly in which he made me"; but it is hard to see how this yields "an incomparably better sense," especially when it cannot be literally true that Job and his slaves are children of the same mother.

15.d. עָשָׂהוּ "made him"; but there are *two* others in question, the male and the female servant, so we should translate "make them" (as NRSV, NEB, NIV; Larcher reads עָשָׂם "made them").

15.e. אחד "one," the subj of the clause, with reference to God. The term is understood as a divine title, "the Unique," by Dahood (review of *Job et son Dieu*, 438) and Ceresko (comparing 23:13; Deut 6:4; Zech 14:9); they are followed by Habel. See also C. H. Gordon, "His Name Is 'One,'" *JNES* 29 (1970) 198–99, for an argument that "One" is sometimes an epithet of Yahweh. Some would prefer to read בְּרֶחֶם אחד "in one womb" (Beer [*BHK al*]).

15.f. וַיְכֻנֶנּוּ (for יְכוֹנְנֶנּוּ; cf. GKC, §72cc) is lit. "and prepared him," which is acceptable on the analogy of עָשָׂהוּ "made him" in the previous colon (Duhm emends to יְכִינֵנוּ [hiph] "and made him"). But, for the sake of the sense, the Eng. versions unanimously render "create us" or some such phrase, and it is no doubt best to emend to וַיְכֻנֵנוּ "and made us" (so GKC, §58k, Beer [*BH*² *vel*], Driver–Gray, Fohrer, Gordis, Gray; Beer [*BH*² *vel; BHK*] וַיְכוֹנְנֵנוּ), a reading adopted in the *Translation* above. NEB reads rather וַיְכִנֵנוּ hiph (Brockington), with the same sense, "create us." It is just possible that the suff נּוּ־ is itself the 1st-person pl suff and that the verb means "fashioned us" without any emendation (so, e.g., Sicre Díaz).

15.g. JB, NIV "within our mothers"—just to avoid repetition of "the womb."

16.a. Sicre Díaz moves v 18 to this point. Larcher and Gray move vv 38–40b to this point.

16.b. Dhorme regards אם "if" as an interrogative, translating "Did I refuse to the poor?"

16.c. One can מנע "withhold" something from (מן) someone (like bread from the hungry in 22:7), or a person from something (like someone from honor, as Num 24:11; cf. also Eccl 2:10). Here it is no doubt the latter (less probably "withheld some of [מן partitive] the desire of the poor," as Ceresko; cf. Driver–Gray); thus "withheld the poor from their desire" (as KJV); RVmg "aught that the poor desired" (similarly RSV), NEB "their needs from the poor" (similarly REB), NIV "denied the desires of the poor," NAB "denied anything to the poor," NJPS "deny the poor their needs," JB "Have I been insensible to poor men's needs?," Moffatt "I never grudged a poor man anything," but hardly "have kept the poor from pleasure" (Good). M. Dahood reads אם אֲמַנְעֵם חֵפֶץ דלים "If I have withheld the poor's need from them," explaining the suff on the emended verb as a "dative of disadvantage" ("Some Rare Parallel Word Pairs in Job and in Ugaritic," in *The Word in the World,* FS F. L. Moriarty, ed. R. J. Clifford and G. W. MacRae [Cambridge, MA: Weston College Press, 1973] 19–34 [27]); the suggestion is not implausible, but it is a little strange to have both "them" (as the suff) and "the poor" (in the constr chain) in the same colon.

16.d. כלה piel is "complete, cause to fail" (BDB, 478a), but what does it mean to cause or let someone's eyes to fail? The "eye" (עין) here must be the "agent of affect and emotion" (as F. J. Stendebach puts it, though not in reference to this passage [*TDOT,* 11:34]); the widow whose eyes have failed has lost her desire for living. Many Eng. versions are unsatisfactory, thinking they must find some idiom containing the word "eyes"; thus NEB, for example, has "let the widow's eye grow dim with tears." JB's "let a widow's eyes grow dim" (without reference to tears), and similarly NIV "let the eyes of the widow grow weary" (NAB "languish"), and Good's "exhausted the widow's eyes," are well-nigh unintelligible, since weary eyes do not have a metaphorical meaning for us. Much better is Moffatt's "I never made a widow pine in want," NJPS "let a widow pine away," and Pope "made to pine." The *Translation* above contents itself with a purely literal rendering.

17.a. Dhorme regards the verbs of this verse also as interrogatives (as in v 16). NJPS "by eating my food alone" (similarly Habel) attempts to connect this verse with the preceding, but it seems improbable that Job means that his way of giving the poor what they needed or of keeping the widows' hopes alive was to share his food with the fatherless.

17.b. פת is properly "fragment, bit, morsel (of bread)" (BDB, 837b), variously rendered by KJV, RSV with "morsel," NAB "portion," NJB "my bit of bread," Moffatt "my bite of food," REB "portion of food," and NEB, exactly right for the occasion, "crust," in the sense defined by *OED* (§1.c) as "applied slightingly to what is much more than crust." It refers to his "food" (NJPS), "bread" (NIV), "share of bread" (JB), of course, but implies it is humble and meager. Why does Job downplay his no doubt sumptuous meals by calling them "a morsel"? Is it the same impulse that leads to speaking of a house as a "tent" and an estate as a "pasture" (see *Comment* on 5:24)?

18.a. Duhm, Beer (BH^2), and de Wilde transfer v 14 to this point. Gray transfers vv 19–20 to this point. Hölscher deletes the verse. Sicre Díaz moves this verse to follow v 15.

18.b. מנעורי is taken by M. Bogaert ("Les suffixes verbaux non accusatifs dans le sémantique nord-occidental et particulièrement en hébreu," *Bib* 45 [1964] 220–47 [240–41]), M. Dahood (review of *Il Semitico di Nord-Ovest,* by G. Garbini, *Or* 32 [1963] 498–500 [499–500]; "Hebrew-Ugaritic Lexicography II," 397), Blommerde, Ceresko (מִנְּעוּרֵי) as a 3d-person *yodh* suff, i.e., "from his youth." For other examples of the supposed suff, see *Note* 21:16.e.

18.c. גְּדֵלַנִי is perhaps to be explained as having a datival suff, "he (the orphan) grew up to me [as to a father]" (so GKC, §117x, Fohrer, Gordis, Hesse, Habel, Hartley); for other examples of datival suffs in Job, see *Note* 22:21.d. The word can be rendered KJV "he was brought up with me," RV, NJPS "he grew up with me," or, amounting to the same thing, RSV, NIV "I reared him," NRSV "I reared the orphan." In support of the latter sense, some read the piel אֲגַדְּלֶנּוּ "I brought him up," as in the *Translation* above (following Graetz, Dhorme, Beer [*BHK*], Pope, Gerleman [*BHS al*], Good [perhaps]) or גִּדַּלְתִּיהוּ "I brought him up" (Siegfried).

An alternative reading is גִּדְּלַנִי, "[God] raised me," thus "though like a father God has reared me from my youth"; so Merx, Duhm, Beer (BH^2), Peake, Strahan, Driver–Gray, Beer (*BHK al*), Hölscher, Kissane (גְּדֵלַנִי), Terrien, Gerleman (*BHS prp*), de Wilde, Sicre Díaz, Gray (similarly NAB, JB, Moffatt). However, God need not be the subj; REB has "[the boy who said, 'From my youth] he brought me up.'" And NEB "from boyhood honoured me like a father" adopts the same emendation but understands גדל piel as "magnify, esteem highly, honor" (as at 7:17; Pss 34:3 [4]; 69:30 [31]); cf. Olshausen, Delitzsch. Dahood ("Hebrew-Ugaritic Lexicography II," 397), followed by Ceresko, proposes גֻּדַּלְנִי, which allegedly means "he was raised by me."

18.d. כאב is lit. "a father," thus RSV "as a father," NIV "as would a father," NJPS "as though I were his father." But this is not suitable unless Job is the subj of the verb. KJV, taking the orphan as the subj, renders "as with a father." In that case, we could see here the contraction of two preps, כאב standing for כְּבְאָב "as with a father" (so Gordis); but it would be better to regard this phenomenon not as a contraction but as the omission of ב after כ (as GKC, §118s–w). In any case 29:2 is not a real parallel (see *Note* 29:2.a).

18.e. אמי is "my mother." It seems strange that prenatal Job should already have been a guide to widows, and so RSV and NEB read אִמּוֹ "his mother" (which will imply an emendation of the verb as well; see *Note* 18.g), while Dahood ("Hebrew-Ugaritic Lexicography II," 397), followed by Ceresko, offers the same translation by claiming that the suff of אמי is really a 3d-person *yodh* suff. NAB continues the thought with God's "guiding me from my mother's womb" (similarly JB, Moffatt, Driver–Gray). Fohrer and Hesse have "and as a brother I guided her," lit. "as one from the womb of my mother." Siegfried emends to אִמָּהּ "her (the widow's) mother's womb"—but no woman is a widow from birth. REB "or the girl who claimed that from her birth I guided her" must be adopting the same emendation but assuming that the obj is not the widow but a female orphan, whose presence is not otherwise signaled.

18.f. Pope alleviates the difficulty, but only seemingly, with the looser rendering "from infancy."

18.g. אַנְחֶנָּה is "I guided her," the widow of the previous verse (as also KJV, NRSV, NJPS, NIV). Those who read גִּדְּלַנִי "he reared me" in the first colon, usually read here "he [God] guided me," whether נְחָנִי (as Merx), הִנְחַנִי (as de Wilde, NAB), נָחַנִי (Duhm, Beer [*BHK*], Kissane [*vel*], Gerleman [*BHS prp*]), יַנְחֵנִי (Hölscher), יַנְחֵנִי (Terrien, Fedrizzi), אַנְחֵנִי (Gray), or אֻנְחָה "I was guided" (Kissane [*vel*]). Those, however, who think that the obj is the orphan read אַנְחֶנּוּ "guided him"; so Beer, Gerleman (*BHS al*), Sicre Díaz, Habel, RSV, NEB (אַנְחֶנּוּ = אַנְחֶנָּה). Dahood maintains, nevertheless, that the suff of MT אַנְחֶנָּה is actually 3 masc sg ("Hebrew-Ugaritic Lexicography II," 397), thus "I guided him."

18.h. אַנְחֶנָּה has only "her" as the obj, but Dhorme, NRSV, NIV, NJPSmg specify "the widow."

19.a. Gray moves vv 19–20 to follow v 17.

19.b. Fohrer, following M. A. van der Oudenrijn (*Angelicum* 13 [1936] 235), thinks ראה has a special sense, "watch calmly."

19.c. אבד is "die, perish" (BDB, 1a); it is used, rarely, of sheep straying or produce disappearing or being lost (*DCH*, 1:99b), but not of persons "wandering about" (as Fohrer, Fedrizzi, NAB "a wanderer"), despite the famous phrase "a wandering Aramean" (Deut 26:5), erroneous for "an Aramean on the point of death"; see further on 29:13. The translation "a wretch" (NJPS, JB) is unsuitable, since it does not mean a person in danger of dying.

19.d. כסות is probably an abstract term, and not a word for a garment (as NIV), or "coat" (Dhorme), though Deut 22:12 might suggest that. JB has "a beggar going naked."

20.a. Duhm, Driver–Gray, Beer (*BHK prps*) prefer וְלֹא "and not" to אם לא "if not." Dhorme again thinks the אם has interrogative force (as in v 17). G. R. Driver ("Problems in Job," 164–65) takes "if not" as an Aramaism meaning "but, except" (like Aram. אלא) and renders "without his loins having blessed me."

20.b. חלצו "his loins," חֲלָצַיִם denoting strictly the part of the body between the waist and the upper thighs, apparently by way of metonymy for the whole person; hence NEB "his body," NAB "limbs," NIV "his heart." It would be a pity to lose the Heb. idiom altogether, as in JB "without his having cause to bless me," and perhaps it is better to retain the idiom, however awkward in Eng. Gray reads חֲלָצָם "their loins," since v 19 envisages two different people. Even without emending, we probably need to translate "their."

20.c. We should make a close connection between the thought of the two lines; thus NIV "for warming him," NEB "because he was not kept warm," NAB "when warmed," JB "as he felt the warmth" (similarly NJPS)

20.d. יתחמם is lit. "he was warmed." We may suppose that the לא "not" of the first colon is to be supplied here too (as KJV, ASV, RSV, NEB), on the principle of "double duty" לא (for other examples, see *Note* 28:17.b). Less probably, the *waw* that begins the second colon may be emphatic (Blommerde), i.e., "they were indeed warmed"; but this would make the colon parenthetical. For other examples of the emphatic *waw*, see *Note* 28:21.a.

20.e. גז, from גזז "shear," is (as in *DCH*, 2:339a) the act of reaping (Amos 7:1; not understood by *HALOT*, 1:185b), the grass that has been mown (Ps 72:6), and here the "fleece" (as most versions) that has been shorn, though NJPS has "the shearings" (an unusual term for a fleece).

21.a. נוף is usually "wave" (as NEBmg), but sometimes with "hand" as the obj it signifies hostility (*DCH*, 5:645b §2); cf. Good "shaken my fist." A good case, however, can be made for postulating a different verb נוף V "raise" (cf. Arab. *nāfa* "be high" [Wehr–Cowan, 1011a]); see *DCH*, 5:647a, 898b [bibliography]).

21.b. Instead of עַל־יָתוֹם "against the fatherless," who have already been mentioned in v 17, Duhm, Peake (possibly), Strahan, Driver–Gray, Beer (*BHK frt*), Hölscher, Larcher, Fohrer ("peaceful"), Gerleman (*BHS prp*), Hesse, de Wilde, Sicre Díaz, Gray, NAB, NEB read עֲלֵי תָם "against the innocent," JB "guiltless" (but NJB "orphan"), Moffatt "if ever I sued unoffending men" (a similar case in 6:27). But it is not obvious that the innocent belong necessarily to the class of the underprivileged, with which these verses are dealing.

21.c. עֶזְרָה "help" is always elsewhere used as an abstract, but it is possible that it could refer here to personal helpers, as in NRSV, NAB "because I saw I had supporters" (similarly NJPS), NEB "knowing that men would side with me in court," REB "knowing that those who would side with me were in court." A more abstract sense is offered by NIV "knowing that I had influence in court," Pope "when I had the advantage," JB "presuming on my credit at the gate"; Moffatt "because I knew the verdict would be mine" is too loose.

Gray understands the word rather as עֶזְרָה II "strength" (cf. *DCH*, vol. 6, *s.v.*; connected with עֵזֶר II "hero, warrior," on which see *DCH*, vol. 6, *s.v.*). Here he would give it a concrete meaning as a collective, "warriors," translating "because I saw my bullies in the gate"—which adds a new but not-so-welcome dimension to the portrait of Job!

Dahood, "Ugaritic-Hebrew Parallel Pairs," 46, and Ceresko, following B. Q. Baisas ("Ugaritic *'ḏr*," 41–52), suggest that עזרתי is "his acquittal," but there is no reason to see a specific meaning of "rescue, liberation" in עזרה here. There is no evidence that עזרה can have a technical legal meaning of "acquittal," it does not make much sense to have Job threatening the orphan *after* he has seen him being acquitted, and in any case the suggestion suffers from the invoking of the alleged 3d-person *yodh* suff.

22.a. כתף is strictly "shoulder-blade," i.e., the scapula, the large flat triangular bone on the side of the shoulder, as distinct from שכם the "shoulder" proper, which is the scapula and the collarbone (clavicle) together; but כתף is also used loosely for "shoulder, back, side" (cf. *DCH*, 4:476a). If the collarbone is broken, the shoulder is broken, and the whole shoulder sags. That is presumably what RSV intends with "let my shoulder blade fall from my shoulder." RV's "let my shoulder fall from the shoulder blade" seems impossible, since either the shoulder blade is part of the shoulder or is below it (if the shoulder is loosely regarded as the clavicle), so the shoulder cannot fall from the shoulder blade. JB "let my shoulder fall from its socket" (similarly Moffatt, Pope) is physiological nonsense; the clavicle and scapula form a shoulder socket into which the arm fits, but the shoulder cannot fall from that socket. KJV, NIV, NAB, NJPS, and Good rather too loosely have "arm," though R. T. O'Callaghan ("The Word *ktp* in Ugaritic and Egypto-Canaanite Mythology," *Or* 21 [1952] 37–46 [43]) argues that the כתף is in fact the "upper arm," and thus parallel to אזרע in the next colon.

22.b. יפול is obviously "fall," but NEB thinks it an improvement to dramatize with "be torn"; but that is a different image.

22.c. משכמה should be vocalized as מִשִּׁכְמָהּ "from its shoulder," as the *raphe* on the following ה shows (GKC, §91e).

22.d. אזרוע occurs only here and at Jer 32:31, and in a few places in Dead Sea Scrolls, as a byform of זרוע "arm." Some say it can mean specifically "forearm" (*HALOT*, 1:280b; *DCH*, 1:172b; 3:136a), hence NAB, NJPS, Good "forearm," but there is no reason to invoke that sense here.

22.e. שׁבר is simply "break," so there is no call to follow NEB with "be wrenched out of," or Pope with "be wrenched off."

22.f. קנה is usually "reed," and only here of the socket or point into which the arm fits, presumably because it, like a reed, is hollow. KJV has "from the bone," mg "from the chanel-bone" (i.e., collar bone, clavicle), no doubt with special reference to the usual meaning of קנה. Moffatt too has "from the collar-bone," RSV "from the socket," JB, NIV "at the joint" (similarly Fohrer). There is little reason to translate, as NAB, NJB, NJPS, "at the elbow"; Pope's curious translation "above the elbow" is explained as the lower arm being broken off from the upper arm. NJPSmg has "from its shaft, i.e. the humerus," and Dhorme explains: קנה can be the beam of the balance (Isa 46:6), and if in the human body the arms are stretched out, the humerus corresponds to the beam and the hands to the scales. This seems rather far-fetched. Nor can it be a matter of one shoulder falling away from the other shoulder (as Tur-Sinai). מקנה should be vocalized מִקָּנָהּ "from its socket," as the *raphe* on the following ה shows (GKC, §91e). Ceresko interestingly proposes we read מִקִּנָּהּ "from its armpit, socket," from קֵן "nest."

23.a. Duhm and de Wilde remove this verse to follow v 28, Bickell to follow v 14, and Gray to follow v 34. Hölscher deletes it altogether.

23.b. That is, if I had done such things.

23.c. פחד אלי איד אל is lit. "a terror to me [was] the calamity of God," or perhaps "there was terror for me, the calamity of God" (as Delitzsch). KJV "for destruction from God was a terror to me," RSV "I was in terror of calamity from God," NIV "I dreaded destruction from God," NJPS "I am in dread of God-sent calamity."

Among emendations and other proposals we may note: (1) NAB emends אלי איד אל "to me the destruction of God" to אֵל עָלָי "[the dread of] God [will be] upon me." (2) Duhm, Beer (BH^2), Dhorme, Hölscher (*frt*), Kissane, Larcher (apparently), Fohrer, Fedrizzi, Hesse emend to פחד אֵל יֶאֱתֶה לִי "the terror of God would come to me" (following LXX φόβος κυρίου), JB "God's terror would indeed descend [NJB fall] on me." פחד is the subject of אתה also in 3:25. (3) Ceresko proposes יַד אל "the hand of God" for איד אל "the destruction of God." (4) Driver–Gray, Beer (*BHK*), Stevenson[2], de Wilde read עֲצָרָנִי "restrained me." (5) I. Eitan ("Two Unknown Verbs: Etymological Studies," *JBL* 42 [1923] 22–28 [22–24]; *Contribution*, 29–31) and G. R. Driver ("Problems in Job," 165–66) read יָאִיד "was strong," from a new word אוד "be strong," cognate with Arab. *'āda(y)* "be strong" (Lane, 37b); so too Gray. NEB follows this proposal, translating "the terror [REB fear] of God was heavy upon me" (though reading the verb as pf אָד [Brockington]). But this does not appear to be a regular word for "be strong," but specifically for "be equipped with weapons." (6) P. K. McCarter ("The River Ordeal in Israelite Literature," *HTR* 66 [1973] 403–12 [410]), understands איד אל as "the river (ordeal) of El" (see on 21:30), and sees here a self-curse by Job that, if he is not telling the truth, "Then let the River of El be a fearful thing to me, and let me not be stronger than its rising up."

23.d. לא אוכל is lit. "I am not able," hence NEB "I could do none of these things," NIV "I could not do such things." Dhorme has "I could not stand" (similarly Fohrer), and JB "how could I hold my ground?"

23.e. שאת is commonly taken as the inf constr of נשא "lift up," hence "excellency, majesty" (see *Note* 13:11.a); so KJV "by reason of his highness I could not endure," RSV "I could not have faced his majesty," NEB "for fear of his majesty," REB "because of his majesty," NIV "splendour," JB, Dhorme "majesty," NAB "his majesty will overpower me." But it is preferable to read, with NJPS "I cannot bear his threat," וּמִשְּׂאָתוֹ "and from (in the presence of) his fear," as in 13:11, where also שְׂאָה is parallel to פחד "terror." Gordis would revocalize מְשֹׁאָתוֹ "his destruction," i.e., the destruction coming from him. Ceresko revocalizes to מַשֵּׂאתוֹ "the raising of it [God's hand]." Good's translation "I cannot bear his partiality," taking משאתו as elliptical for מַשְּׂאֵת פָּנָיו "the lifting up of his face, i.e., partiality" is totally unsuitable for the context. McCarter takes the term in reference to the "rising up" of the river (see *Note* 23.c).

24.a. Dhorme and NJPS take the אם as an interrogative. But S. H. Blank ("An Effective Literary Device in Job 31," *JJS* 2 [1951] 105–7; reprinted in *Prophetic Thought* [Cincinnati: Hebrew Union Press, 1977] 65–67) maintains that a condition without an apodosis, such as we have here, is equivalent to an oath (but v 28 *is* the apodosis). Sicre Díaz actually prefaces the sentence with "I swear."

24.b. כסל is "confidence" (BDB, 492b), as well as, strangely, "stupidity." KJV has "hope," NAB, JB "trust," NEB "put my faith in," Moffatt "relied on."

24.c. The direct 2d-person address in the Heb. is retained by KJV, NIV; so too NJB "saying to fine gold, 'Ah, my security.'" Others, regrettably, level the sentence to match the first line: NJPS "regard fine gold as my bulwark," NAB "called fine gold my security," Moffatt "rested everything on solid gold." NEB's translation "my trust in the gold of Nubia" derives from the fact that כתם "gold" is Egyptian for Nubia, a source of gold; but there is no reason to think that Nubia is always in mind when gold is spoken of, any more than all china is from China or varnish from Berenice.

25.a. Hitzig deletes the verse as a prosaic repetition of v 24.

25.b. Dhorme and NJPS take the אם as an interrogative.

25.c. שמח is simply "rejoice," so "gloated" (JB, Pope, Ceresko) is gilding the lily.

25.d. מצא, lit. "find," is here "gain," as in 1 Sam 10:7; 25:8 (cf. Isa 10:10; Eccl 9:10; see *DCH*, 5:435a §8). Though מצא may mean "reach" in 3:22, there is no good reason to think so here (against Ceresko).

26.a. Dhorme and Gordis think the אם is interrogative.

26.b. ראה is of course "see," but Job does not mean that he has never looked at the sun; he can only mean "look with pleasure," as ראה plainly signifies in 20:17 (see *Note* a); 33:28; Pss 54:7 (9); 106:5; 128:5 (BDB, 908a §8.a.5; *HALOT*, 3:1158b §7.a.II.iii).

26.c. אור "light" (as NJPS, Pope, Good) is usually understood as the "sun" (see also on 37:11), though Duhm thinks that it means the light of the heavenly bodies, and Strahan that it includes the stars and the dawn. Ceresko has the attractive idea that this is a case of what he calls "delayed identification" and Dahood "explicitation" (*Psalms III,* 100–150, 52, 56, 57, 115, 128, 201, 232, 245, 260), and I call "the parallelism of greater precision" ("The Parallelism of Greater Precision: Notes from Isaiah 40 for a Theory of Hebrew Poetry," in *New Directions in Hebrew Poetry,* ed. E. R. Follis, JSOTSup 40 [Sheffield: JSOT Press, 1987] 77–100; reprinted in *On the Way to the Postmodern: Old Testament Essays, 1967–1998,* JSOTSup 292–93 [Sheffield: Sheffield Academic Press, 1998] 1:314–36). In that case, "light" would be a general term, which would be specified further in the second line as "moon," and there would be no reference to the sun at all. The verb הלל "be bright" does refer to the moon in 25:5, though to the sun in Isa 13:10. If we allow that הלל here could be connected with Ugar. *hll* and Arab. *hilâl* "crescent of the moon," we could have a reference to the moon brightening or waxing; on the Ugar. word, cf. *DUL,* 339; W. G. E. Watson, *DDD,* 392–94; on the Arab., cf. Lane, 3044b.

26.d. The *waw* would be *explicativum* if Ceresko's interpretation of "light" is correct, thus "namely the moon"; for further examples, see *Note* 29:12.d.

26.e. הֹלֵךְ is "walking" in KJV, "as it walked the sky" in JB, "moving" in RSV, NEB, "marching" in Pope, "on its course" in NJPS, "in the splendor of its progress" in NAB. Ceresko renders "waning," parallel to הלל as "waxing," and compares LXX σελήνην φθίνουσαν; other possible parallels to such a sense are 7:9; Hos 6:4; Cant 2:11.

26.f. יָקָר, lit. "as a glorious one," יקר in an Aram. sense rather than its usual Heb. meaning of "precious" (BDB, 430a); Good has "the gorgeous moon." Gordis rather unconvincingly argues that "rare, precious" is a term for "full" moon. Gray rather eccentrically proposes that the word be vocalized יָקֵר, i.e., קרר hiph "be cool," "the coolness of the moon being complementary to the brightness of the sun"; he translates "the moon on its cool course." Dhorme reckoned that LXX read יקר "precious, splendid" as ירק "pale," but that word is not attested in that sense in Heb.

27.a. פתה is, in the qal, "be simple," and thus, here and at Deut 11:16, "be enticed" (as KJV, RSV, NAB; cf. BDB, 834b; *DCH,* vol. 6, *s.v.*). Freer translations are NJPS "I secretly succumbed," JB "stolen my heart," Moffatt "and let my heart go out to them," Good "my heart is fooled."

Beer (*BHK frt*), Hölscher, Gray read וַיִּפֶּת niph "and was deceived" (niph also in v 9); on the sense of the niph as distinguished from the piel, see *Note* 31:9.b on "enticed to."

27.b. ותשק ידי לפי is lit., in "the prettier Heb. idiom" (Strahan), "and my hand has kissed my mouth" (as RVmg), "because the hand is more noticeable in the act of throwing a kiss" (Gordis). Most versions prefer the Eng. idiom (so KJV), though NJPS cleverly has "my hand touched my mouth in a kiss." NIV "offered them a kiss of homage," NAB "to waft them a kiss with my hand" (similarly Moffatt), JB "blew them a secret kiss." Pope, followed by Ceresko and Hartley, would take the prep ל as "from" rather than "to," thus "my hand kissed from my mouth." J. M. Cohen ("An Unrecognized Connotation of *nšq peh* with Special Reference to Three Biblical Occurrences [Gen 41:40; Prov 24:26; Job 31:27]," *VT* 32 [1982] 416–24 [423–24]) thinks to solve the difficulty by understanding נשק as "seal (the mouth)," i.e., maintain reverent silence. While kissing does indeed require a prior sealing of the mouth or pursing of the lips, it is hard to believe that putting one's hand to one's mouth is an act of homage (of astonishment at Isa 52:15). Tur-Sinai unnecessarily emends to וַתִּשַּׂק (= וַתִּסַּק) from סלק "rise," thus "my hand was lifted up to my mouth"; the same suggestion is offered by NEB "and raised my hand in homage" (cf. Brockington), though REB has "kissed."

28.a. The verse is deleted by Hölscher as a repetition of v 11, and by Fedrizzi as a marginal gloss. It is moved to precede v 23 by Beer (*BH*[2] *frt*). Kissane omits the first colon.

28.b. On פלילי, see *Note* 31:11.d. Of course, he means "a punishable crime *on my part,*" and Gordis's difficulty that pagan worship would still have been a punishable offense even if Job had not committed it is easily surmounted. Gray, following Pesh, reads גַּם הוּא עַיִן (כָּל־)עֲלִילוֹתַי "he also sees all my misdeeds," or better, נַפְתּוּלוֹתַי "my tricks," though there is no parallel to such a use of פתל "twist."

28.c. כחשתי is translated by KJV, RVmg, NJPS, NAB, JB, Moffatt as "denied," by RV as "lied to," by NEB and NIV as "been unfaithful to," by Pope as "betrayed." The pf is like a pf subjunctive, "would have been" (GKC, §106p). We may, following a hint of Delitzsch, be able to draw a distinction between כחש ל "be a hypocrite towards" (as here and 1 Kgs 13:18, though Deut 33:29 is a problem) and כחש ב "deny, disown" (as 8:18; Isa 59:13; Jer 5:12; though Lev 6:2 [5:21] is a problem). Delitzsch remarks that "his worship of God would have been hypocrisy, if he had disowned in secret the God whom he acknowledged openly and outwardly."

28.d. אל ממעל is lit. "God from above," which seems a little strange, but is adequately paralleled by Exod 20:4. JB, following Larcher, has "the supreme God."

29.a. De Wilde adds v 23 at this point.

29.b. Dhorme, Gordis think the אם is interrogative, Duhm an "indicative denial."

29.c. שמח "rejoice," as in v 25. Strangely, in view of its translation there, JB's "taken pleasure" here is tamer than the Heb.

29.d. התעררתי is from עור hithpo "be excited, aroused" (also at 17:8); thus KJV "lifted myself up," Ceresko "been elated." Many propose we should read, with Tg, וְהִתְרַעְתִּי "and I shouted in triumph," from רוע "raise a shout" (Beer [*BHK*], Driver–Gray, Fohrer, Gerleman [*BHS prp*], Gordis, Hesse, Gray); thus NAB "exulted." Others suggest that we have here a new verb, cognate with Ugar. *ġdd*, עוד palil (Dahood, "Some Northwest-Semitic Words," 319–20; cf. *DCH,* vol. 6, *s.v.*) or עדד (Gerleman [*BHS frt*]; cf. *HALOT,* 2:789a; *DCH,* vol. 6, *s.v.*) "rejoice"; we should, however, note that Ugar. *ġdd* is now said to mean "swell" rather than "rejoice" (*DUL,* 317). Since the senses are so alike, we cannot easily tell which of these proposals is followed by the versions: NRSV, NJB, Moffatt have "exulted," REB "been filled with glee," NIV "gloated," JB "made merry," NJPS "thrill." NEB "been filled with malice" is unexplained.

29.e. מצא is usually "find" (as KJV), but it can also be "meet, reach" (cf. *Note* 31:25.d). Cf. a similar phrase that occurs in Gen 44:34, "lest I see the evil that would come upon (מצא) my father."

30.a. Hitzig deleted the verse because of the logical difficulty of its relation to v 29.

30.b. Pope reads לא "not" as לו "if" (for a condition contrary to fact). Some have suggested that the *waw* of ולא is emphatic, thus "I have never let" (L. Prijs, "Ein 'Waw der Bekräftigung'?" *BZ* 8 [1964] 105–9 [107]; Blommerde, Ceresko).

30.c. נתתי, lit. "I have [not] given," נתן "allow" as in Gen 20:6; 31:7; Exod 3:19 (cf. GKC, §157b, note; *DCH,* 5:810b §7).

30.d. חקי, lit. "my palate" (as RVmg, NJPSmg).

30.e. ולא־נתתי לחטא חכי לשאל באלה נפשו, lit. as NEB "even though I did not allow my tongue to sin by demanding his life with a curse" (REB "laying his life under a curse"); similarly NAB; Moffatt delightfully "practised the sweet sin of cursing him and praying for his death."

30.f. לשאל באלה נפשו is lit. "to ask with a curse for his life," rendered by NIV "invoking a curse against his life," JB "by cursing them or vowing them to death," NJB "lay his life under a curse," NJPS "by wishing his death in a curse."

31.a. Dhorme takes אם as interrogative.

31.b. אהלי "my tent" (as KJV, RSV, NAB, JB, using the nostalgic term [see *Note* 31:17.b on "my crust"]). Is it not better to keep it in translation, unlike NJPS "my clan," NEB, NIV, Moffatt, Pope "my household," GNB "all the men who work for me"?

31.c. אם־לא אמרו "if [the men of my tent] have not said" (as, e.g., RSV)—whether it is a conditional clause resolved by the apodosis in v 40, or a conditional clause without any apodosis—means that according to Job they *have* said it. NEB "Have the men of my household never said" (similarly NIV) amounts to the same thing, though REB "have indeed said" (similarly NJPS) puts it more straightforwardly. So too JB "did they not say?" On the other hand, NRSV "if [they] ever said" assumes the omission of לא "not"; similarly Gordis "Did my kinsmen ever say?" or perhaps the revocalizing of it as לָא (= לוּ) "if" (Pope). Sicre Díaz understands אם לא as "I swear," continuing, "When the men of my tent have said..."

31.d. Duhm, Beer (*BH*[2], with a question mark), Strahan, and de Wilde (perhaps) would delete יתן "[who] would give," reading simply "who has not been satisfied?"

31.e. Though all the words are very simple, this is a very problematic line. The key elements are these: (1) מי יתן "O that," lit. "who will give?," which elsewhere in Job always introduces a hopeless wish (6:8; 11:5; 13:5; 14:4, 13; 19:23; 23:3; 29:2 [מִי יִתְּנֵנִי]; 31:35). (2) מבשרו "from his flesh," probably meaning "some of his flesh" (מן partitive), which could mean "his meat" or "his body" (whether or not in a sexual sense). (3) נִשְׂבָּע could be niph ptcp "satisfied" or niph pf "is satisfied" or 1st-person impf qal "we are satisfied." (4) The verse could be connected with what precedes, Job's refusal to gloat over the misfortune of his enemies (vv 29–30), or with what follows, his hospitality (v 32).

The best solution, though the thought is admittedly a little strained, is to understand the men of Job's household lamenting (wryly or a little ironically) that there is no one left whom Job has not showered hospitality on. They would be saying, "O that there were someone not yet sated with his meat"—no doubt so that Job "might be gratified by finding yet another recipient of his hospitality" (Driver–Gray). This reading is to be preferred because it takes מי יתן as a hopeless wish, as it is elsewhere. Several versions approximate to this rendering, but fail to convey the sense of מי יתן; thus RV "Who can find one that hath not been satisfied with his flesh?," NJB "Will anyone name a person whom he has not filled with meat?," JB "Is there a man he has not filled with meat?," or more loosely, NAB "Who has not been fed with his meat?," Dhorme "Who can be found who has not been satisfied with his meat?" (similarly Fohrer, who denies that מי יתן here introduces a wish, and de Wilde), NIV "Who has not had his fill of Job's meat?," Moffatt "Who is not satisfied with his provision?" REB's "Who has eaten of his food and not been satisfied?" seems to put the accent in the wrong place, on the liberality of Job's provision; it should rather be on its universality.

Other interpretations of "flesh" (בשׂר) are: (1) The flesh of enemies. Thus Gordis, thinking the sentence means that Job's kinsmen never said, "If only we had his flesh (i.e., our foe's flesh), we would never be satisfied (i.e., we could never gorge ourselves enough)"—which is to say that Job's kinsmen, and not only Job himself, were "free from virulent hatred of their enemies." This interpretation is exceedingly strained. Differently, Ehrlich understood "May we be never satiated with his (the enemy's) flesh," i.e., may we never have too much of it.

(2) Job's own body. Some versions leave open the question whether it is Job's meat or Job's own flesh that it is in view: thus KJV, RVmg, "Oh that we had of his flesh! we cannot be satisfied," NRSV "O that we might be sated with his flesh," NJPS "We would consume his flesh insatiably!" LXX has the delightful idea (Delitzsch thought it in bad taste) that his women servants (reading אַמְהֹתַי for מתי אהלי "men of my tent") wished they could eat him up, since he was so very kind (λίαν μου χρηστοῦ ὄντος).

(3) Job's body as a sexual object, or specifically his penis. Pope and Sicre Díaz, following Tur-Sinai, thought that homosexual rape is in view here, on the analogy of the incidents in Gen 19 and Judg 19, rendering "O that we might sate ourselves with his flesh," understanding בשׂר as "phallus." Similarly Dahood (*Psalms III,* 100–150, 15), Ceresko, and Fedrizzi. But it is only in the next verse that reference to a stranger is made, and here it is much more naturally the meat on Job's table that is in mind.

(4) Others think בשׂרו "his flesh" means "his kin," thus "Is there none of his kinsfolk who has not been satisfied?" (so B. Jacob, "Erklärung einiger Hiob-Stellen," *ZAW* 32 [1912] 286–87 [287]).

(5) A totally different approach is to take the idiom "to eat the flesh of" as "to slander" (as in Aram. in Dan 3:8; 6:25; cf. also Akk. *akālu qarṣi* [von Soden, 27b §10], Arab. *akala laḥmahu* "he ate his flesh" [cf. Lane, 71b]); thus NEB "Let none of us speak ill of him!"

32.a. Hitzig thought this verse a later addition. NEB takes the line as spoken by the "men of the household" (v 31).

32.b. גר is strictly "resident alien," occupying an intermediate legal position between a native (אזרח) and a foreigner (נכרי); cf. D. Kellermann, *TDOT,* 2:433. "Stranger" (as KJV, NRSV, NAB, NIV, JB, NEB, Moffatt) will not do as a translation, since that could mean a native-born traveler from another town (like the ארח in the next colon), who would not be a גר. Though the term "sojourner" is old-fashioned, it will have to serve (as also ASV, RSV, NJPS).

32.c. לין is both "spend the night" and "dwell, remain" (*HALOT,* 2:529a; *DCH,* 5:543a; BDB, 533b, however, does not clearly distinguish the two senses); here it is plainly the former sense, as REB "has had to spend the night in the street" (similarly NIV), JB "ever had to sleep outside," Moffatt "had to sleep in the streets."

32.d. חוץ, when it does not mean "outside" or "the open country," is everywhere "street" (BDB, 300a §2; *HALOT,* 1:298b §A.b; *DCH,* 3:175a §1), and not "square." On רחוב "square," see *Note* 29:7.b. It could perhaps mean "in the open" (NJPS) or "outside" (JB).

32.e. NIV inserts "for"—which is certainly implied.

32.f. NEB "I have kept open house," JB, NIV "my door was always open."

32.g. אֹרַח is "way" (so KJVmg), which makes little sense here, though NJPS has "opened my doors to the road," and Delitzsch "open to the street," comparing *Pirqe Aboth* 1.5 "Let your house be open to the square (רווחה)." Most emend, with LXX, Vg, to אֹרֵחַ "traveler" (KJV, NEB, NIV, JB, Moffatt), "wayfarer" (RSV, NAB, Good) (so Budde, Duhm, Peake, Driver–Gray, Dhorme, Beer [*BHK*], Hölscher, Kissane, Larcher, Fohrer, Rowley, Fedrizzi, Gerleman [*BHS prp*], Hesse, Sicre Díaz, Gray). Some avoid actual emendation: Habel thinks אֹרַח is a "contraction" of אֹרֵחַ, and Hartley that it is a variant spelling, while Ceresko maintains that אֹרַח is itself a ptcp form.

33.a. אם is taken as an interrogative by NEB, NJPS, Dhorme, Gordis.

33.b. כְּאָדָם "like Adam"; see *Comment.* Some understand "like humans, like ordinary people" (so Ewald, Davidson, Budde, Hesse, Hartley). Others emend, to בָּאָדָם "among humans" (Duhm, Beer [*BH*[2], with a question mark], Strahan, Peake, Hölscher [*frt*]), or to מֵאָדָם "from humans" (so JB, Moffatt "from men," NJB "from others," Graetz, Beer [*BHK prps*], Hölscher [*frt*], Larcher [apparently], Fohrer, de Wilde, Gray). Fedrizzi thinks "like Adam" is an interpretive gloss.

Dahood made the forced suggestion that כאדם be revocalized to כֶּאֱדֹם "like blood," which is supposed to be דָם "blood" with a preformative *aleph* ("Phoenician Contribution," 127–28). Subsequently, he preferred reading כאדם as "like the ground" (see W. Kuhnigk, *Nordwestsemitische Studien zum Hoseabuch,* BibOr 27 [Rome: Biblical Institute Press, 1974] 283), אָדָם supposedly being a variant of אֲדָמָה (though we might well ask whether the ground usually conceals sins), or else כְּאֹדֶם "like a jewel, precious stone" (see Ceresko, 173 n. 638). Ceresko's explanation is, if anything, even less plausible: he reads אִם־כִּסִּיתִיךָ אָדָם "if I have hid [my sin] from you in the earth," the *kaph* being a dative suff, and אָדָם "ground" sharing the prep of the parallel term בְּחֻבִּי, while בחבי itself does not mean "in my bosom" but "in Hades." Quite apart from the piling of linguistic oddity on linguistic oddity, he does not stop to explain how Job would have been concealing his sin "in the ground" or "in Hades." Blommerde's explanation, that כאדם is really כְּאָדָם "as in my hands," אַד being a northern (!) dialectal form of יָד "hand," need not detain us further.

33.c. Duhm omits the line (as does Beer [*BH*² *frt*]), and makes v 34a into v 33b.

33.d. לטמון "in hiding, by hiding," lit. "to hide"; for this use of the inf (not to express purpose), cf. GKC, §114o.

33.e. חב "bosom" occurs only here in BH (though it has been conjectured also for 33:2 [*q.v.*], and it occurs in the Qumran Hymns Scroll; see *DCH,* 3:147a), though it is obviously cognate with Aram. חֻבָּא. The "bosom" (usually חֵק) is the fold of the garment at the chest, used normally as a pocket (thus for carrying a lamb [2 Sam 12:3], or as of Moses carrying the people [Num 11:12], or of carrying insults [Ps 89:50 (51), emended] or for keeping things safe [Job 23:12]). We would more naturally speak of keeping secrets hidden in one's heart, but the "bosom" is not really a term for a part of the body. NEB renders "keeping my guilt to myself," Moffatt "covering up my guilt," REB "hidden within my breast," NAB "buried my guilt in my bosom" (similarly NJPS), JB "keeping my iniquity secret in my breast." Pope has "in a covert," connecting it with חבא "hide"; but how could Job hide his guilt in a covert? Ceresko thinks it an epithet for the underworld, comparing the name of a Ugar. deity or demon *Ḥby*; but that is an entirely ad hoc speculation.

34.a. כי is omitted by KJV "Did I fear a great multitude?" NJPS has "[bury my wrongdoing] that I (now) fear the great multitude." Ceresko argues that it is "if," but it is most probably "for," introducing the reason why he might have concluded his sin (v 33).

34.b. ערץ qal is usually "cause to tremble," but occasionally "fear, tremble" (as at Deut 1:29; 7:21; 20:3; 31:6; Jos 1:9; cf. BDB, 791b; *HALOT,* 2:888b; *DCH,* vol. 6, *s.v.*). Only here would it have a direct obj; so Fohrer would insert עַל "because of."

34.c. המון is both "sound, roar" and "crowd, multitude" (BDB, 242a; *HALOT,* 1:250b; *DCH,* 2:568b). Some versions try to incorporate both ideas (JB "common gossip," NAB "the noisy multitude," Pope "the rabble clamor," similarly Sicre Díaz), but it is more likely that it means just "multitude" (thus NIV, Moffatt "the crowd"). רב "great" is the adj applied to "multitude," as at Isa 16:14; Dan 11:11, 13; 2 Chr 13:8; 20:2, 12, 15 (המון is fem only here, and perhaps at Eccl 5:9 [Gordis]), but some English purists with a classical education are unhappy about putting the two words together, since "multitude" already means "a great crowd" if we have regard to its etymology. המון is elsewhere masc, so many emend רבה fem to רב masc "great" (Driver–Gray) or רָב (Beer [*BHK*], Fohrer); but the emendation is not strictly necessary.

Ehrlich thinks רבה is an adv, thus "I greatly dreaded the crowd" (likewise RSV "great fear"), but the clause does not need this degree of emphasis.

Several propose an emendation, from המון "sound, multitude" to הֲמוֹן "the din of" and understanding רבה as "capital" (as in, for example, the name Rabba as capital of the Ammonites), comparing המון קריה "the noise of the city" (39:7) and המון עיר "the noise of the town" (Isa 32:14). Thus Dhorme renders "the din of the capital," Tur-Sinai "the hum of the city," and NEB "the gossip of the town." So too H. P. Chajes, "Note lessicali," *GSAI* 20 (1907) 301–30 (307), Kroeze. But there are no true parallels to רבה as "capital," and it is entirely unexplained why the "din of the capital" should make Job afraid or why, especially, it should have led him to conceal iniquity in his heart. The proposal has to be judged unsuccessful.

34.d. משפחות are strictly "clans," or, more correctly, "phratries," which have been described as "the most important single group in Israelite society" (F. I. Andersen, "Israelite Kinship Terminology and Social Structure," *BT* 20 [1969] 29–39 [35]), the primary division of the tribe, consisting of several "fathers' houses" or "extended families" (בית אב). An Israelite male would be known first by the name of his father, and secondly by the name of his phratry. Only NIV ("the clans") acknowledges here this specialized meaning; traditionally the term has been translated "families" (as KJV, NJPS; similarly JB); NAB "the tribes" is actually wrong, because a tribe is an aggregate of משפחות. NEB "my fellow-citizens" and Moffatt "public opinion" unfortunately ignore the notion of tribal Israelite society organized by clans.

34.e. חתת is lit. "shatter" (thus NJPS), hence "dismay, terrify"; here it is hiph, in 7:14 piel.

34.f. The line is deleted by Volz, Duhm, Jastrow, Fohrer, Fedrizzi, Hesse as an explanatory gloss. NEB transposes it to the end of v 35.

34.g. ואדם "and kept silence," from דמם (*DCH,* 2:450). Tur-Sinai, followed by Pope, emends, improbably, to וְאָדָם לֹא אֹצִא פתח "and I brought no man out to the door" (for sexual attack), thinking of Gen 19:5, 6; Judg 19:22; but how would the "families" despise him for that?

34.h. Gray moves v 23 to this point.

38.a. Vv 38–40b are transferred in the *Translation* above to this point (as also by Dillmann, Driver–Gray, Beer [*BHK*], Fohrer, Gordis, de Wilde). NAB, Peters, Hölscher, Pope, Rowley transfer them to follow v 8, Budde to follow v 12, Larcher and JB to follow v 15, Stevenson to follow v 20, Moffatt to follow v 22, Siegfried, Sicre Díaz to follow v 23, NEB to follow v 28, and Merx, Duhm, Dhorme, Kissane to follow v 32. Volz deletes v 39, and moves vv 38 and 40 to follow v 22.

38.b. עלי is more likely to be "against me" (JB "calls down vengeance on my head") than "on account of me, because of me" (Ceresko).

38.c. בכה is simply "weep" (as RV, RSV, NJB, NJPS), but other versions think to improve on that with "complain" (KJV, NAB), "are wet with tears" (NIV), or even "every furrow runs with tears" (JB).

38.d. יחד can be "altogether" (as in 3:18; 21:26) or "all together," which is the sense to be preferred here (that is, together with one another [Gordis], "in concert" [NJB] rather than "together with the land" [as Dhorme]). Fohrer insists that יחד means "at the same time as."

39.a. The verse is deleted by Duhm as an attempt to explain v 38. The verse seems to be subordinate to v 38, though whether that is indicated by the pf tenses in v 39 as against the impfs in v 38 (as Dhorme) is hard to say.

39.b. כחה, lit. "its strength" (as KJVmg), obviously "its yield" (RSV, Gordis), "its produce" (NEB, NAB, NJPS), or "the fruits thereof" (KJV), "fruit grown on it" (JB)—as in Gen 4:12.

39.c. בְּעָלֶיהָ, lit. "its lords," i.e., its owners (as בעל of the owner of a house in Exod 22:8 [7]; Judg 19:22, 23). Some think we have a pl of majesty here, as is plainly the case with בעלים in Exod 21:29; Isa 1:3; thus "its owner" (so Dhorme, Fohrer, Rowley). Larcher proposes an emendation to פֹּעֲלֶיהָ "its workers"; hence BJ *ses ouvriers,* JB "those who toiled there," and perhaps NAB "its tenants," GNB "farmers"; so too Gray.

Without emending the text, however, it seems preferable to adopt the suggestion of M. Dahood (review of *Le Livre de Job,* by J. Steinmann, *Bib* 41 [1960] 303; "Ugaritic Studies and the Bible," *Greg* 43 [1962] 55–79 [75]; "Qoheleth and Northwest Semitic Philology," 361–62; "Phoenician Contribution," 144 n. 20), followed by Blommerde, de Wilde, Ceresko, Sicre Díaz ("day-laborers"), and *HALOT,* 1:142b, and proposed independently by A. van Selms ("Job 31:38–40 in Ugaritic Light," *Semitics* 8 [1982] 30–42), that we should understand בעל as a byform of פעל "do," and thus בעליו as "its workers" (cf. *DCH,* 2:237b, for several other places where the verb בעל II "do, work" may be suggested; for a contrary view, see Grabbe, 97). For Job has said in v 38 that he is speaking about "my" land (אדמתי), and it is hard to see how the same land could have other "owners" or "lords."

NEB "disappointed my creditors," REB "left my creditors to languish" must depend on an emendation to בַּעַלֵי, though it is not mentioned by Brockington, and the sense "creditor" is not justified.

39.d. נפח is "breathe out," in hiph lit. "cause to breathe out." The hiph is elsewhere only in Mal 1:13 "sniff" (in contempt). In 11:20 the phrase מפח נפש "breathing out of life" means "despair" rather than "death"; and cf. Jer 15:9. Here it may be grief or distress rather than despair specifically. This sense is perceived by a number of versions, as in LXX ἐλύπησα "I grieved"; and NAB "grieved the hearts of its tenants," NIV "broken the spirit of its tenants," NJPS "made its rightful owners despair," Gordis "brought its owners to despair" (similarly Habel), JB "given those who toiled there cause to groan" (similarly de Wilde), Good "made gasp." So too Driver–Gray, Dhorme ("distress or grief"). NEB "disappointed" is surely too weak, and REB "left to languish" is not much better. KJVmg offers a more literal translation, "caused to expire, breathe out."

Others think it is death that is in view; thus KJV has "caused the owners thereof to lose their life," RSV, NJB "caused the death of [its owners]," Rowley. But Job cannot mean that if he had wrongfully appropriated someone else's land, and they had *not* died as a result, he would have been guiltless.

Guillaume (*Lexicography,* 3:5) sees here a new נפח "beat, afflict" (cf. Arab. *nafaḥa,* though it has a wide range of meanings [Lane, 2820b]).

40.a. חוח is, according to BDB, 296a, "brier, bramble," according to *HALOT,* 1:296b, "thorn-bush" or "thorn," and according to *DCH,* 3:170a, "thorn, brier, bramble." In other words, we do not know precisely what the word means, so various renderings are acceptable: KJV, NEB, NAB "thistles," RVmg, Gordis "thorns," NIV "briers," JB "brambles," NJPS "nettles."

40.b. באשׁה is understood as "stinking or noxious weeds" (BDB, 93a), "cockle (*Lolium temulanetum*)" (*HALOT,* 1:107b), and "stinkweed" (*DCH,* 2:89a; NJPS, Good; cf. M. E. Weichselfish, הצמחים איזמא, "אגא וּבָאְשָׁה [The Plants איזמא, אגא and באשׁה]," *Leš* 34 [1969–70] 270–77; and cf. Akk. *bu'šu* [von Soden, 143b]; *CAD,* 2:353a, registers the word as the name of a plant but offers no identification). Stinkweed (באשׁה), taking its name from באשׁ "stink," is a plant with pale yellow flowers; it gives off a bad smell when crushed. According to Dhorme, באשׁה is "annual mercury, called dead nettle or malodorous nettle," a plant with poisonous sap. Fohrer and de Wilde regard it as "darnel" (German *Taumellolch*), *Lolium temulentum* (Dalman, *Arbeit und Sitte,* 1:407–9), a plant that grows up to two feet high, with black poisonous berries. Terrien (following H. N. and A. L. Moldenke, *Plants of the Bible* [New York: Ronald Press, 1952] 29–30) takes it as *Agrostenna githago,* a wild vine whose leaves are covered with a whitish excrescence, which produces irritation on the skin; its smell is disgusting. KJV "cockle" is very rare in Palestine, and was probably not found there in ancient times (M. Zohary, *IDB,* 2:297). Others, including Zohary, think it just a general term for weeds; thus KJVmg "noisome weed," RSV, JB, Gordis "foul weeds," NEB, NIV "weeds," REB, NAB "noxious weeds," NJB "rank weeds."

Ceresko emends באשׁה to בָּאָה אִשָּׁהּ "let fire come upon it," professedly in the interest of achieving "[b]etter balance with the first colon"; for this to be so, we should have to accept that the pf tense can express a wish, that אִשָּׁהּ "its fire" contains a "datival suffix" signifying "fire upon it," and that the fem suff refers back as far as the word אדמה in v 38a.

35.a. שׁמע לי, lit. "(someone) hearing me," but it is clear that the hearing is in a legal context, thus NAB "hear my case," NJPS "give me a hearing." NEB "Let me but call a witness in my defence!," JB "Who can get me a hearing from God?," NJB "Will no one give me a hearing?," Moffatt "here I enter my own plea of innocence. Oh for a hearing!"

Some are (needlessly) unhappy about the repeated לי "to me" in this colon; Gerleman observes that some MSS omit the first, and Beer (*BH*[2]) follows their lead, claiming the support also of Theod and Pesh; so too Gray. Others would emend לי שׁמע to אֵל יִשְׁמַע לִי "that God would hear me" (Ball, Houtsma, Driver–Gray, E. F. Sutcliffe, "Notes on Job, Textual and Exegetical: 6, 18; 11, 12; 31, 35; 34, 17. 20; 36, 27–33; 37, 1," *Bib* 30 [1949] 66–90 [71–72], Larcher, Terrien, Fedrizzi, de Wilde; JB "who can get me a hearing from God?"). Ceresko less persuasively emends to מי יתן לִי שָׂם עֵלִי "O that the Most High would pay attention to me!" supposing that there is an ellipsis of לב "mind, attention" after שׂים "set, pay," that the ptcp שָׂם can represent the impf for "that he might pay," and that there actually is in Heb. a divine title עַל "Most High" (for other alleged examples, see *Note* 29:4.c).

35.b. NAB removes this line to follow v 37b, and thus to form the very last line of the whole speech.

35.c. Lit. "behold my mark, let Shaddai answer"; תו is commonly explained as the sign *taw,* the last letter of the alphabet. It is variously rendered: KJVmg "my sign," RV, RSV "my signature," NIV "I sign now my defence," JB "I have had my say, from A to Z," NJB "I have said my last word" (similarly Kissane). NJPS, NAB, NEB do not appear to render the word at all.

The word has sometimes been understood as a form of תַּאֲוָתִי "my desire" (cf. Buxtorf, 857); thus Vg *desiderium meum,* Tg רגוגי "my desire" (רגוגי), KJV "my desire is, that the Almighty would answer me" (so too Gordis); de Wilde proposes that תַּאֲוָתִי actually be read. G. R. Driver ("Problems in Job," 166; *Semitic Writing from Pictograph to Alphabet* [London: Oxford, 1948] 209), however, proposes a new word תָּוָה "desire," cognate with Syr. *twâ* "incline," thus "my desire is that the Almighty should answer me." NEB "Let the Almighty state his case against me!" seems to manage without either "mark" or "desire," even though Brockington's notes say that תוי is equivalent to תַּאֲוִי "or a similar form from √אוה." Driver is followed by Sutcliffe, "Notes on Job," 71–72; Saydon, "Philological and Textual Notes," 252; Gray.

35.d. Duhm, Beer [*BH*[2] *frt*], Driver–Gray, Hölscher, Fohrer, Hesse assume the loss of a colon before v 35c. NEB transposes v 34c to this point. Duhm supplies, entirely conjecturally, the missing line as מִי יִתֶּן־לִי מְגִלָּה "O that I had the scroll [and the document]," and de Wilde apparently as יַרְאֶ לִי מְגִלַּת שִׂטְנָה "he shows me the scroll of (= with) the accusation" (his transliteration *jær'ā* seems a misprint).

35.e. It is implied that מי יתן־לי "who will give me," "O that I had" (as RSV) is repeated—a hopeless wish, as elsewhere (cf. on v 31). It is not at all likely that what is implied is the repetition of הן "behold," thus "behold my signature . . . and the document" (as Delitzsch, Merx). But it is not impossible that the line is *casus pendens* to v 36, thus "And as for the document that my adversary has written, upon my shoulder I would carry it" (as Hitzig, Budde).

35.f. סֵפֶר is "writing, document"; KJV "book" is anachronistic, and "indictment" (RV, RSV, NAB, NIV, NEB, Moffatt) or "bill" (NJPS) or "writ" (JB) is more appropriate.

35.g. כתב "[that] he has written" (pf); see *Comment.* KJV, RSV recognize that the indictment is already written. But NJPS does not see this, rendering "[O that] my accuser draw up a true bill," and NAB "[Oh] that my accuser would write out his indictment." NEB too thinks Job is merely wishing that it would be written ("If my accuser had written out his indictment, I would not keep silence and remain indoors" [transposing v 34c to here]); cf. JB "When my adversary has drafted his writ against me..."

Emendations are otiose, such as that of Grimme, יְיַשְּׁרֵנִי כְּתָב "let my written document justify me!" Even that of Gordis, to יִכְתֹּב "may he write out," is unnecessary.

35.h. איש ריבי "my adversary" (as KJV, RSV, JB) or "my accuser" (NEB, NIV, NJPS), in a legal setting, like אנשי ריבך "your adversaries" (Isa 41:11). Sometimes איש ריב is an obj gen, "the man of dispute" meaning the one with whom I am in dispute (as in Judg 12:2; Jer 15:10); but here it must be subjective, the one who is in dispute with me (so Dhorme). There can be no doubt that the adversary here is God (against Delitzsch). Kissane unusually reads איש רִיבוֹ "his [God's] adversary," rendering "behold my last word... and the scroll which His adversary hath written!" But Job does not describe himself as God's adversary, even though that is what he is.

36.a. The last example of a clause introduced by the particle אם "if" in the chapter is not followed by an apodosis. The protasis is not of course a self-curse, but a strong affirmation. There could be an *implicit* curse, but that is the same as saying that אם לא is an asseveration, "surely" (as KJV, RSV, NAB, NIV); similarly NEB "No!" Dhorme takes it as a yet another example of an interrogative, "Shall I not wear it?," which of course also amounts to the same thing. Moffatt, JB, NJPS ignore אם אל in translation.

36.b. נשא is "lift up, carry"; KJV has "take it upon [my shoulder]," RV, NJPS "carry it," Moffatt "bear it," NAB, NIV, JB "wear it," NEB "flaunt it on my shoulder."

36.c. אענדנו עטרות לי is lit. "I would bind it to me as a crown," best rendered by JB "bind it round my head," Moffatt "upon my head," less attractively NAB "put it on me," NIV "put it on," NEB "wear it," NJPS "tie it around me."

36.d. עטרות "crowns, turbans" (pl). The pl may refer to the tiers of the crown (Driver–Gray), or rather the windings of the turban (as also at Zech 6:11), or else may be emended, with two MSS (Gerleman) to עֲטֶרֶת "crown" (Beer [*BHK*], Hölscher, Gray) or עֲטָרָה "crown" (Duhm). KJV, RSV, NIV, Moffatt, Gordis have "crown," NAB "diadem" (as also Larcher), JB "royal turban," NJPS "for a wreath." There is no reason to invoke a Phoenician fem sg ending *-ôt* (as Blommerde, Ceresko), or to suppose an archaic sg ending *-ot* (as E. Lipiński, "Recherches sur le livre de Zacharie," *VT* 20 [1970] 25–55 [34–35]). Gray intriguingly imagines Job keeping God's indictment *in* his turban, "as the Scottish barons in the Isle of Arran kept their title deeds given by King Robert the Bruce in their bonnets."

37.a. אגידנו "I would declare (to) him," a dative-like suff (GKC, §117x); cf. also Bogaert, "Les suffixes verbaux," 229. For other examples of datival suffs in Job, see *Note* 22:21.d. But the double acc with נגד hiph is questionable; Duhm emends to אַגִּיד "I would declare" (without suff). On the nuance of נגד hiph as "declare, reveal," and especially in a quasi-legal sense, see *Comment* on 42:3.

37.b. מספר צעדי אגידנו can be rendered "I would declare unto him the number of my steps" (KJV), "I would plead the whole record of my life" (NEB), "telling every detail of my life" (Moffatt).

37.c. אקרבנו, piel of קרב, ought to mean "I would bring it near"; thus RVmg, Driver–Gray "I would present it," NJPS "offer it [the account of my steps] as to a commander," NEB "and present that in court as my defence." Most, however, think קרב hiph can mean "come near"; thus "I would go near unto him" (KJV), "approach" (RSV, NIV, Gordis), "go as boldly as a prince to meet him" (JB), "entering his presence like a prince" (Moffatt)—though apart from Ezek 36:8 there do not seem to be any suitable parallels. On the other hand, it is natural to take the 3 masc suff of אקרבנו as referring to God, as that of אגידנו does. NAB's "present myself before him" is difficult to justify.

40c.a. On the view that these words are a later, editorial addition, see *Comment.* Hölscher, Kissane, and Hesse would delete the words. LXX connects the words closely with the next chapter, and Budde also, rendering "the words of Job were ended, and these three men..." So too de Wilde, and Moffatt, rendering "Eyob ended, and the three men said no more to him." If, as is proposed in this commentary, the speeches of Elihu were originally located before this final speech of Job, their dislocation must have occurred earlier than the LXX translation of the book.

Form/Structure/Setting

This speech has a clear tripartite *structure,* corresponding to the three chapters, 29–31. The three movements are differentiated by their temporal focus: chap. 29 looks entirely to the past ("Oh, that I were in the months of old"), chap. 30 looks to the present as a contrast to that past, with the repetition of its key word "and now" (vv 1, 9, 16), while chap. 31, in returning to the past, has the future more in mind, both as the realm where Job's imprecations could come into being and as the sphere of the longed-for response from God.

The *strophic structure* of this long speech, the longest in the book, is varied but not especially complex. In chap. 29, there seem to be six strophes of normal length, ranging from three to five lines. It is quite different in chap. 30, where the writing is more elaborated and extensive; here we seem to have just four strophes. In chap. 31, there is less of an ordered pattern, strophically speaking. Here we should perhaps identify eight strophes.

Part 1	strophe 1	29:2–6	5 lines
	strophe 2	29:7–10	4 lines
	strophe 3	29:11–14	4 lines
	strophe 4	29:15–17	3 lines
	strophe 5	29:18–20	3 lines
	strophe 6	29:21–25	5 lines
Part 2	strophe 1	30:1–8	9 lines
	strophe 2	30:9–15	7 lines (vv 13, 15 tricola)
	strophe 3	30:16–23	8 lines
	strophe 4	30:24–31	8 lines
Part 3	strophe 1	31:1–4	4 lines
	strophe 2	31:5–8	4 lines (v 7 a tricolon)
	strophe 3	31:9–12	4 lines
	strophe 4	31:13–15	3 lines
	strophe 5	31:16–23	8 lines
	strophe 6	31:24–28	5 lines
	strophe 7	31:29–34, 38–40b	9 lines (v 34 a tricolon)
	strophe 8	31:35–37	3 lines (v 35 a tricolon)

The strophes, as usual, are to be distinguished from one another by a combination of criteria: formal repetitions (as in 30:1, 9, 16), changes of subject matter (as in the transition from the general picture of God's protection in 29:2–6 and the specific picture of Job at the city gate in vv 7–10), unity of subject matter within a strophe (as in 31:9–12), a continuing sentence that cannot be broken off by a strophic division (as in 31:16–23, a long, eight-line strophe).

The strophic structure envisaged in this commentary may now be compared with that of others. Among the versions, RSV adopts the same scheme, with only two differences: it recognizes only two (very unequal) strophes in chap. 29 (vv 2–20, 21–25), which is not very acceptable, and it makes 31:29–37 one strophe (which would not be the case if we rearrange the order of the verses; see *Comment* on 31:34–37). NIV differs from the present scheme only in regarding 29:7–17 as one strophe, and of course in the way it treats 31:34–37. NEB, although it marks certain divisions, does not seem to be working with the usual concept of strophes: it distinguishes 29:2–10+21–25, 11–20; 30:1–19, 20–31; 31:2–4, 5+1+6–28+38–40, 29–37; one cannot see what its principle of division here is. JB marks as strophes 29:2–6, 7–10+21–25, 11–17, 18–20; 30:1–15, 16–19, 20–23, 24–31; 31:1–15+38–40, 16–23, 24–34, 35–37, thus of 5, 8, 7, 3, 15, 4, 4, 8, 18, 8, 11, and 3 lines, respectively—which is virtually to abandon the idea of strophic structure.

At the other extreme, Terrien proposes a much more rigid structure, in which most strophes consist of two substrophes and all but two strophes are five or six lines: 29:1–6 (2 lines + 3), 7–11 (2+3), 21–25 (2+3), 12–17 (2+4), 29:18–30:2 (3+3), 3–8 (3+3), 9–14 (3+3), 15–19 (2+3), 20–24 (2+3), 27–31 (3+2), 30:25–26+31:1–4 (2+4), 5–8 (2+2), 9–12 (2+2), 13–18 (3+3), 19–23 (2+3), 24–28 (2+3), 29–34 (4+2), 35–40 (3+3). This scheme, however, cuts across some important sense divisions: thus 29:11 should rightly belong with what follows, not with what precedes, 30:1–2 is better suited to the subject matter of chap. 30, his proposed strophe 30:13–18 ignores the important divider "and now" at the beginning of v 16, 30:24 goes better with the following than the preceding verses, and 30:13–18 has no principal verb in it.

Fohrer's scheme differs from that adopted in this commentary in these respects: he concludes 29:7–10 with the addition of 29:21, he transposes 29:22–25 to precede 29:11, and he takes 29:12–17 as a single strophe; he makes 30:1+9–10 the first strophe, regards 30:2–8 as an addition, and sees strophes of 30:11–14, 15–19, 20–23, 24–27, 28–31; in chap. 31 he finds strophes of mostly four or three lines throughout, splitting 16–23 into 16–19, 20–23, and 29–34+38–40 into 29–32, 33–34+38–40 (5 lines).

Webster is in agreement with the structure outlined here, except that he would break 30:1–8 into smaller strophes of vv 1–2, 3–5, 6–8, 30:9–15 into 9–11, 12–15, 30:16–23 into 16–19, 20–23, and 30:24–31 into 24–26, 27–31, 31:16–23 into 16–18, 19–22 (connecting v 23 with 24–25), 31:24–28 into (23+)24–25, 26–28, and 30:29–34+38–40 and 30:35–37 into 29–31, 32–34, 35–37, 38–40.

Van der Lugt adopts the same structure, noting especially the importance of ועתה "and now" in the structure of chap. 30, but he can hardly be followed when he connects 29:18 with what precedes, for that splits Job's three-line speech to himself (vv 18–20) across two strophes. In chap. 31 he maintains that the key to the structure is that there are three strophes (vv 1–12, 13–28, 29–40), each with two substrophes; in each of the concluding substrophes within each strophe there is reference to an explicit punishment (vv 10, 22, 40).

Skehan, followed in detail by NAB, argued that the first movement of the speech is 29:2–30:8, in which he saw eleven strophes of three lines each (removing 29:21–25 to follow 29:10). He claimed that "and now" in 30:1 did not really belong with the two other uses of that term in 30:9, 16, since vv 1–8 is really about the past condition of the fathers of his young mockers, in the time depicted in chap. 29—a view that is certainly arguable (see *Comment* on 30:2–8). The second movement of the speech (30:9–31) consists of six three-line strophes and one four-line strophe (vv 23–26; it may be questioned, however, whether v 23 belongs with what follows). Skehan proposes quite a few alterations in the sequence of verses, which are reported in the *Notes* to the *Translation* above; the four strophes that need no adjustment are vv 9–11, 20–22, 23–26, 29–31. In chap. 31, having removed v 1 to precede v 9, v 5 to follow v 6, and vv 38–40 to follow v 8, he finds the following pattern: (1) an introduction of four lines (vv 2–4, 6), (2) three groupings of eleven lines (vv 5+7–8+38–40+1+9–12; 13–23; 24–34), made up entirely of substrophes of two or three lines, (3) a conclusion of three lines (vv 35–37). Given the adjustments to the order that he proposes, the scheme is attractive. The major divisions he suggests are in any case quite widely agreed to. Further details about how commentators divide the strophes can be found in van der Lugt, 330–31.

The poetic lines in the speech are overwhelmingly in the form of the *bicolon*. The only *tricola* appear at 29:25 (it is not uncommon to find a tricolon at the end of a strophe, as here, but is impossible to make sense of the third colon), 30:12 (here the second colon is unusually short, and many delete it as a repetition), 30:13 (all three cola are short, but the text does not seem defective), 30:15 (at the end of a strophe), 31:7 (though many delete the last colon), 31:34 (the last colon is perhaps questionable), 31:35 (a key line, perhaps the most significant in the whole speech).

The *genre* of the speech as a whole has been identified as a *soliloquy* (so Murphy), on the grounds that Job is no longer addressing the friends and that the speech thus stands outside the dialogue proper. On the other hand, near the center of the speech Job addresses God directly (30:20–23), which is strange for a soliloquy. That address raises the question whether the whole speech should not perhaps be understood as directed to God, even though second-person forms are not much in evidence. We certainly need to distinguish here between the *genre* of a unit and its *function*, since the latter is of more consequence for interpretation (see below).

The speech is striking form-critically speaking for its novelties. In chap. 29 the first-person *description of an experience*, the predominant form, is almost unparalleled in the Hebrew Bible. The nearest examples are in the mouth of the woman lover in Cant 3:1–4 and 5:2–7, where she describes her search for her beloved in the streets of the city, in one case finding him and in the other not; in both cases we may have the report of a dream. In Job we have of course a much longer description, which extends over twenty-four verses. There are of course Psalms in which Israel's historical experiences are recounted (e.g., Pss 105, 106), but in such cases it is the community who speaks, not an individual, and the subject matter is God's deeds, not the circumstances of life, as it is here. Fohrer sees the form as the counterpart of the wisdom poems on the fate of the wicked in 18:5–21; 20:4–29; but they are not first-person accounts and they focus upon the future end of the wicked, unlike Job's description here, which concerns several aspects of his happy past. It is part of the freshness of the poet's art that at this climactic moment he is able to develop his portrayal of Job by means of a narrative-like form he has not elsewhere drawn upon.

The other distinctive form in this speech is the *oath of purification*, sometimes called an "oath of clearance," which dominates chap. 31. This form can be paralleled in the Psalms (7:3–5 [4–6]), though in nothing like such an elaborated shape, nor with the motive clauses we find here (vv 11–12, 23, 28), nor with the delay or absence of the apodosis of the "if" clause (e.g., in vv 29–34+38–40, where a self-curse might be expected after vv 30, 32, and 34 but occurs only after v 40). In Exod 22:7–11 (6–10) there is reference to an oath between neighbors concerning theft or trespass, which would perhaps have taken a similar form; but the form itself does not appear (a similar reference appears in 1 Kgs 8:31–32 = 2 Chr 6:22–23). An oath has also been taken by Job in 27:2–4, but it is not in the form used in chap. 31, and it does not deal with any particulars, being only a general affirmation that he tells the truth. This oath of purification then is a quite unusual form, which has been extensively elaborated into a powerful rhetorical poem. See further, M. B. Dick ("Job 31, the Oath of Innocence, and the Sage," *ZAW* 95 [1983] 31–53), who shows in some detail how the straightforward legal form of the oath of innocence, which would have been spoken after the failure of pre-trial arbitration, has here been strongly influenced by the wisdom tradition.

Chap. 30 is composed in a more traditional form, that of the *lament*, which is sustained throughout the chapter, with the exception of vv 2–8, 24–25. The two types of lament, the "enemy" lament and the "I" lament (see *Form/Structure/Setting* for chaps. 16–17 and 19), are both employed, the former at the beginning of the movement in vv 1, 9–15, 18–23, the latter more toward the end, in vv 16–17, 27–31. It is noticeable that the enemies in the lament are both human (Job's mockers, vv 1, 9–14) and divine (vv 18–23; cf. also God's authorization of human assault in v 11); there is also assault by demonic powers (the "terrors," v 15). Within the lament proper, there is the element of the *accusation* (of God, vv 11, 20–22). Other formal elements in this chapter are the *pathetic description* (of the poverty-stricken outcasts from society, vv 2–8; cf. 24:5–8, 10–12) and the *avowal of innocence* (vv 24–25; cf. 23:10–12).

Motifs and language are borrowed from *psalmic literature*: for example, of God's "keeping" the pious (29:2), of God as a lamp (29:3), of the ruler's responsibility for protecting the underprivileged (29:11–17; 31:16–21), of the wicked as animals (29:17) and as "workers of iniquity" (31:3), of the "roots" of the righteous reaching to the waters (29:19), of the lamenter being the butt of mockery (30:9), of the absence of a "helper" (30:13), of his life being "poured out" (30:16), of his bones burning (30:30), and of the image of riding on the wind (30:22). From *wisdom literature* comes the language of his steps being open to God's eyes (31:4, 7), of the weighing of the heart (31:6), of sowing without reaping (31:8), of sexual misconduct leading to death (31:12), of the folly of trusting in wealth (31:24–25), of not rejoicing over an enemy's misfortune (31:29). The language of the *law* is drawn upon principally at the end of the speech, when Job offers his "signature" to his deposition and an "account of all his steps" and calls for God as his "adversary" to "answer" him and produce a written legal "document" (31:35, 37).

Noticeable too is a *traditional and old-fashioned language,* as when he speaks of his house as his "tent" (29:4), of God being "with" him (29:5), of milk and wine as symbols of plenty (29:6), of the underprivileged as typically the blind and the lame (29:15), the poor, the fatherless, the widow and the stranger (29:12–14, 16), of the blessing of the light of his face (29:24), of his speech dropping like rain or dew (29:22–23). Allusion to the myth of the phoenix (29:18) occurs only here in the Hebrew Bible, but it too belongs to the text's construction of an antique world.

As far as *function* is concerned, even if the speech is formally speaking a soliloquy, it does not mean that Job has lapsed into an inner world. Even without the presence of the second-person address in 30:20–23, it is evident that he speaks in order to be heard. At the critical moment of the conclusion to the speech, his words are "Here is my signature! Let the Almighty answer me!" (31:35), and that deposition of his legal case and call for a formal reply must be the goal to which the whole speech has been tending. Thus understood, the speech is the last step in Job's preparation of a "dispute" (ריב) against God, a "final statement before a judge" (Murphy); it is the last phase of a process that will force God into reply, a legal procedure that will indeed shortly prove entirely effective when God actually responds in chaps. 39–41.

The *tonality* of the speech is not uniform, but neither is it disjointed. The air of nostalgia in chap. 29 is persuasively introduced by the opening wish, "Oh, that I were in the months of old" (v 2), and sustained throughout the chapter, climaxing in Job's report of his former thought, "I shall die among my nestlings . . ." (vv 18–20). Everything in this first movement is sweetness and light, his footsteps bathed in curds (v 6), and his young people about him—with the lone exception of the passing reference to breaking the jawbone of the unrighteous (v 17). The speech takes on a much sharper tone, however, when in the second movement (chap. 30) Job turns to contrast his present state with that idyllic and no doubt over-idealized picture of the past. His depiction of the outcast poor in vv 2–8 is notable for the absence of venom, but once he turns to the attacks of the "mob" who deride him (vv 9–14, anticipated by v 1), his language is full of vigor as he portrays them as military enemies who are determined to defeat him. It is the same with his picture of the hostility of God toward him as he snatches him up to ride the tempest and then hurls him down into the mire (vv 18–23). There is more than a hint of self-pity in this movement, with the repeated pathetic keyword "and now" (vv 1, 9, 16), his sense of oppression by demonic "terrors" (v 15), and his physical and mental torments (vv 16–17, 27–31). If the speech were to end here, the misery would sound more bitter, but from the vantage point of the conclusion of the speech it loses something of its edge. The third movement (chap. 31) transforms the whole speech by modulating it into a key we would never have thought of when we began to read chap. 29. Almost obsessively, and with a pace that never slackens, Job asserts his innocence on every count he can think of, doggedly calling down such vengeance on himself if he is a liar that we sense that he is no longer a victim but is taking control of his situation. The climax, in which he demands that God give him a satisfactory and legally proper response, is the most positive and forthright of his statements in the entire book; it has been perfectly prepared for throughout the speech.

Three *nodal verses* in the speech, for each of its three movements, may be detected. In the first movement, the opening line, "Oh, that I were in the months of old!" (v 2), is evidently the key to all that follows. In the second, there is not so obviously one nodal verse, but the last verse (v 31) enshrines the theme of the movement perfectly, with its contrast between the former days and the present: "My harp has been given over to mourning, and my flute to the voice of those who wail." In the third movement, there can be little doubt that the key verse is that which brings together the whole of the chapter and calls for future action: "Here is my signature! Let the Almighty answer me!" (v 35).

Comment

1 There has been throughout the dialogues a standard formula for introducing a new speech: "Then X answered and said." The different formula here, "Then Job again took up his discourse (משל) and said," we have met with already at 27:1; both there and here it introduces a speech of Job that, in the present form of the text, follows immediately upon another speech of Job. Since, as has been argued in this commentary, the end of the third cycle of speeches has fallen into disarray in the course of transmission of the text, it seems reasonable to conclude that the present formula is a secondary creation, inserted into the text at 27:1 and at 29:1 after the disarrangement had taken place.

The idiom, "to take up a discourse" (נשׂא משל), elsewhere has a rather formal meaning, as Habel points out. It does not mean to "continue a speech," but is used to introduce the solemn refusals of Balaam to curse Israel (Num 23:7, 18) and his other oracles (24:3, 15). In Isa 14:4, Mic 2:4, and Hab 2:6 it introduces a taunt song or woe oracle. Habel thinks that in Job 27:1 it refers to the solemn oath that Job takes and that here it introduces a speech that will culminate in the oath of chap. 31. But it could simply be that a traditional formula is being used secondarily in a weaker sense.

2–6 In this last speech Job brings to a climax all his utterances. He wants one thing, and one thing only: the days of old, his old innocence and his old standing in the community. In this chapter he rehearses in loving detail what that old life has been; in the next chapter he portrays the pathetic contrast between that life and his present existence; and in the following chapter he binds himself by a solemn oath of purification that he is innocent of any crime that could account for his downfall from his earlier state to his present.

Much of the charm of these verses lies in their almost naive interweaving of the literal and the metaphorical, the way the simplicity of an image like "my young ones about me" (v 5) gives place to the exotic extravagance of a phrase like "my feet bathed with curds" (v 6). And much of its force comes from its composition as one unbroken sentence, from v 2 to v 6, clause piled upon clause and image upon image in a "tender elegaic strain" (Strahan) (NJPS alone of the standard versions reflects this structure by its repeated "when" at the beginning of most of the cola; JB, NEB, NIV obliterate the structure by making a new beginning at v 4).

2 This last speech of Job begins as powerfully as it will continue, for it comes immediately to the point. What Job wants, what he has always demanded, is a *restitutio in integrum,* a restoration to exactly the place where he was before the hand of God struck him in chap. 1. He does not long that he were "*as*" in the months of old (so KJV, RSV), but that he were actually "*in*" them again, as if they had never ceased (see *Note* 29:2.a). His only wish is that he should enjoy again the favor of God, the presence of his children, and his life of ease. But it is a forlorn wish, and he knows it. Every wish in the book of Job that opens in this way, "Who will grant that . . . ?" (מי־יתן), is a hopeless one (cf. on 23:3). With each of his memories of the past "there are unspoken associations with Job's vehement opposition to the way God treated him in recent times" (Habel).

It is a frequent trope in literature of many periods that every memory of a blissful past has a special bitterness of its own, "a sorrow's crown of sorrow is remembering happier things" (Tennyson, "Loxley Hall," l. 146). So too Boethius, "In every adversity of fortune, to have been happy is the most unhappy kind of misfortune" (*In omni adversitate fortunae infelicissimum genus est infortunii fuisse felicem; De consolatione philosophiae* 2.4). And Dante: "There is no greater sorrow than to remember in misery happier times" (*Nessun maggior dolore / che recordarsi del tempo felice / ne la miseria; Inferno* 5.121–23). And Chaucer: "For of fortunes sharpe adversitee / The worste kynde of infortune is this, / A man to han ben in prosperitee / And it remembren, whan it passed is" (*Troilus and Criseyde* 3.1625–28).

Job calls the time of his former existence the "months of old" (ירחי־קדם); the phrase does not occur elsewhere, but it is closely similar to the common phrase "the days of old." The days of old, however, are always far distant times, the time of the patriarchs (Mic 7:20), of the exodus and conquest (Isa 63:11; Ps 44:1 [2]), or of creation (Isa 51:9), for example (cf. also 2 Kgs 19:25; Isa 37:26; Lam 2:17). Never are they the former days of a person's life; but for Job those days, though perhaps no more than weeks or months ago, are as distant as if they had been ancient history. Elsewhere the "days of old" are usually times of God's beneficent activity (only in Isa 23:7, Jer 46:26, and Lam 1:7 is the phrase not connected with God), and that is the resonance here too, for what Job first recalls when he thinks of his former life is the protective presence of God (vv 2b–5a).

This idea of God's "keeping" (שמר) Job has been somewhat ambivalent in the book hitherto. In a positive sense, at 2:6 God has charged the Satan to "spare" (שמר) Job's life, no matter what; and at 10:12 Job has allowed that God's attention has "preserved" (שמר) his life. On the whole, though, the term has a sour tone in

Job: at 10:14 he charges God with the malevolent intention of keeping him alive only in order to be "watching" (שׁמר) him for signs of guilt; at 13:27 he complains that God watches (שׁמר) all his paths, keeping him under as close surveillance as if he had imprisoned him in the stocks; and at 14:16 his vision of impossible bliss includes God *not* watching (שׁמר) him. In the months of old, however, God's attentions had been only for good; he had "put a hedge about him and about his house and about all that [was] his on every side" (1:10; see the *Comment* there). For the use of "keeping" in the pious language of blessing and prayer, see Num 6:24; Pss 16:1; 91:11; 121:7–8.

What is this "keeping" by God? What does it consist of, what are its effects? On the most basic level, it is a keeping alive, so that if Job is alive it is evidence of God's "keeping" him. But "keeping" generally means more than that, and implies life with good fortune. In the days when God watched over him, Job was prosperous; and his prosperity is what he means here by God's keeping him. It is the same as in 1:10, where God's "putting a hedge" about him is parallel to, and essentially means the same as, God's "blessing" him so that his possessions increase. No doubt we should recognize that Job is expressing a gratitude to God when he attributes his wealth to God's blessing (as Hartley); but is he now expressing gratitude for God's taking his wealth away? In 1:21 he blessed the God who had given and who had taken away; but that does not seem to be his attitude now. Rather, he feels he has been abused by God.

3 A "lamp" (נר) is normally used metaphorically for human well-being and good fortune, and so the lamp is usually the lamp of humans (18:6; 21:17; 2 Sam 21:17; Ps 132:17). But sometimes it is God's commandment that is said to be a lamp to the feet (as in Ps 119:105; Prov 6:23), and God himself lights the psalmist's lamp in Ps 18:28 (29); so God can be regarded as the source of light, itself a metaphor for life (God is never the light himself, for 2 Sam 22:29, by comparison with its parallel Ps 18:28 [29], seems defective). If in the olden days God made his lamp shine over Job's head, it meant that he ensured Job's continuing life. The image is of the lamp suspended from the roof of the tent (cf. on 18:5–6). It is a ceramic lamp, like all those found in Palestine (cf. R. W. Funk and I. Ben-Dor, *IDB,* 3:63–64); KJV's "candle" is incorrect, since candles were unknown in biblical times.

In the second colon, the metaphor of the lamp as life merges with that of the traveler's lamp that shows the path in the darkness (חשׁך), which is the prime metaphor for danger (as also with the lamp to the feet in Ps 119:105; cf. also Ps 23:4); on "darkness," see H. Ringgren, L. A. Mitchel, H. Lutzmann, and L. T. Geraty, *TDOT,* 5:245–59. God's light has been for Job, as well as the life God has sustained, the life that God has preserved from danger. On the image of the lamp, cf. D. Kellermann, *TDOT,* 10:14–24.

4 These months gone by are called by Job the days of his "vigor" or "prime" (חרף); they are not his salad days, not his young manhood. Youth as such holds no attractions for him; it is in the maturity of his life that he found satisfaction, fulfilled in his consciousness of divine protection, in his domestic happiness, and in his enjoyment of surplus wealth. Today, as he speaks these lines, he is barely weeks or months older than he was when he was in his "prime," but he has aged dreadfully—and not just physically.

In the second colon, the Hebrew has "when the council, *or* counsel, of God was upon my tent." Many think that the term סוד *sôd* must here mean "intimacy" or "friendship" (so RSV; NIV "God's intimate friendship"), but there are no satisfactory parallels to this sense (see *Note* 29:4.b), and it would be strange to speak of the intimacy of God being "upon" (על) his tent. A minor emendation (of סוד "council" to סֹוךְ, the infinitive of סכך "protect") yields the much more satisfactory sense "when God protected my tent" (JB; similarly NEB, NAB, GNB). The phrase means the same as "when God watched over me" (v 2). Job does not of course live in a tent; he is not a nomad or a seasonal nomad, but a settled farmer who ploughs with oxen (1:14), and he lives in a house in a town (though Terrien envisages him living in a tent *and* in a town, in the dry season). But he and his friends use the old-fashioned ancestral language of living in a tent by way of a kind of solemn naïveté (as also in 5:24; 8:22; 11:14; 12:6; 15:34; 18:6, 14, 15; 19:12; 20:26; 21:28; 22:23; 31:31). Like "house," "tent" signifies not only the structure but also the existence of those who live in it; Job is referring to the divine protection of himself and his family from any disaster—ironically enough, disasters such as those that afflict them at the beginning of the book.

5 For the Almighty (שדי Shaddai) to be "with" (עמדי) Job does not signify some "spiritual" relationship between himself and the Almighty, some supernatural or extrasensory awareness of the divine presence, but a more pragmatic assurance of the divine favor displayed in his domestic happiness and material possessions. So also in Gen 28:20, where God's being "with" Jacob is expressed by giving him food and clothing, and in 31:5–9 where it is displayed in giving him cattle; in Pss 23:4 and 46:7, 11 (8, 12), likewise, God's being "with" the psalmist is a matter of protection from enemies. Now Job knows that God is no longer "with" him because he no longer enjoys that divine protection. It is not that he experiences the absence of God, for, in one sense, he is all too aware of the constant assaults of God upon him, and God is if anything not distant but too close for comfort. On the other hand, to find God so as to be able to argue his case with him is an impossibility, for God is too remote and his dwelling place inaccessible (23:3, 8–9). The language of presence and absence is obviously a defective one for speaking of God; what matters here is that, as far as Job can tell, God has removed his protective blessing from him. The "yet" (עוד) strikes a note of pathos, as if to say, All my life long, God was unceasingly my defense against disaster, my supplier of goods; now, that history has come to an end.

When he recalls the days when his "children" were still "around" him, Job is not thinking of his offspring as infants, for his nostalgia is for the days of his prime (v 4a), when his children are all adults and the seven sons at least are each living in their own house (1:4). So he calls them his "young ones" (נער), a term used occasionally of infants (e.g., Exod 2:6; 1 Sam 4:21) but more commonly of young men (e.g., Joseph is a נַעַר when he is seventeen years old, Gen 37:2). Job's daughters are not necessarily excluded by the language from his thoughts, for the term "young ones" (pl נערים) includes them at 1:19 (there is a separate word, נערה, for a young woman when females alone are in view; cf. on 41:5 [40:29]). No doubt, however, it was being surrounded by vigorous young men who would continue his family that gave Job the assurance of divine favor. We have little hint of what his daughters meant to him (though see *Comment* on 42:14); and the narrator tells us nothing of them except that they were not as numerous as the sons; we may well believe that if Job had had three sons and seven daughters he might not have felt so certain that God's blessing was on him. An alternative interpretation is worth considering, that the "young ones" in question are the four groups of "lads" (נערים), Job's servants, who died in each of the disasters in chap. 1 (vv 15, 16, 17, 19) (so Habel). Job's wife is strangely absent from his account of his former blessings.

6 He says that he did not merely have ample to satisfy his family; he had a superfluity of food, with curds (sour milk like yoghurt) enough to wash his feet in and oil flowing in "streams" or "rivers" (פלג) from his olive presses. There is a kind of innocent rejoicing here in the abundance of nature that is hard to cavil at; but there is also a callous disregard of the waste of human labor and natural resources that go into the production of such surpluses. We need of course to reckon with the fact that Job is drawing upon conventional language in speaking of his excessive wealth; cf. 20:17 where Zophar speaks of streams (פלג, as here, together with נהר "river") flowing with honey and curds (חמאה, here spelled חמה); Gen 49:11, where Judah washes his clothes in wine; Deut 33:24, where Asher dips his foot in oil (the lover's eyes "bathed in milk" in Cant 5:12 is a different image); and of course the stereotypical phraseology of Canaan as a land flowing with milk and honey (Exod 3:8; Deut 6:3; and eighteen other places). Cf. also the Ugaritic picture of the heavens raining oil and the wadis running with honey as a sign of abundant fertility (*Baal* III.iii.6–7 [*CML*, 113b] = 6.iii.6–7 [*CML*^{2}, 77] = *KTU* 1.6.III.6–7 = *ANET*, 140b). "The prose of it is that his milch-kine were numerous," says Strahan; but that it is not the real truth of it. For Job is not speaking here about natural superabundance; his curds and olive oil are the products of agribusiness, and there is an economic connection, which he of course does not recognize, between his overproduction and the poverty of the farm laborers he had so graphically and sympathetically (if also exaggeratedly) depicted in 24:10–11. Excessive wealth is to him a sign of God's blessing; to the poor who starve as they carry the sheaves it is a sign of God's curse upon themselves.

On "curds" (חמאה), properly a fermented milk product known today in the Middle East as *leben,* and akin to yoghurt, see on 20:17, and cf. Dalman, *Arbeit und Sitte,* 6:293–96. The "rock" (צור) that flowed with streams of oil is most probably the olive press: "A thick, vertical stone wheel, operated by a long, pivoted wooden bar, was rolled over the olives on another flat, circular stone, grooved to carry the oil to a basin at one side" (J. C. Trever, *IDB,* 3:596, with line drawing; see also R. Frankel, *Wine and Oil Production in Antiquity in Israel and Other Mediterranean Countries,* JSOT/ASOR Monograph Series 10 [Sheffield: Sheffield Academic Press, 1999]). There is apparently similar language in Deut 32:13, where Israel sucks honey and oil out of the rock, and in Ps 81:16 (17), where God feeds his people with honey from the rock; but these images do not seem to be related to the present one, for they represent Canaan generally as a rocky place, which nevertheless produces ample food. Others think, less probably, that the term here indicates that even the stony parts of his land were fertile (GNB "my olive trees grew in the rockiest soil"), or that the stony hillsides where his olives grew produced rich yields.

It is especially interesting that in this picture of his former happy domestic existence Job simply puts side by side various memories of his past, without categorizing or prioritizing them. Even if he thinks it, he does not want to say that any one of them is the key or the source of the happiness; he is not in the business of accounting. But commentators are. They insist on saying things like "Naturally the first element in Job's happiness . . . was the presence of his children. . . . The second, though a less, element of his happiness was his overflowing abundance" (Davidson). "[T]he presence of his children . . . constitute[s] God's blessing par excellence" (Gordis). "[God's] presence is the highest blessing he bestows on a person" (Hartley). "The companionship of God was his highest good, then the companionship of his children" (Peake). "The sum of his happiness had been his sure untroubled sense of the divine presence. . . . The second element of his happiness had been his domestic gladness" (Strahan). Job, on the other hand, is overwhelmed by a mixture of disparate memories, which are related in some way he does not wish to explore. Each has its charm and each its bitterness.

7–25 Job here turns from the picture of domestic bliss he has painted in vv 2–6 to describe his former state of social worth. Typically for a male in his society, the principal ingredient in his social happiness was that of honor, the regard paid to him by other males.

7–10 Job pictures what was probably his daily routine. Leaving his house in the town, which he pictures as fortified with a wall, he would head for the open place just inside the town gate where nonproductive upper-class males would gather for gossip, business, and law. When he appeared, all conversation would come to a standstill, such was the respect paid to him by young and old alike.

7–8 The "square" (רחוב) is an open place inside the gate of the town. When רחוב is in the plural it means "streets," as in, e.g., Amos 5:16; Prov 22:13 (see *Note* 29:7.b); but the parallelism with "gate" shows that we are dealing here with the main open space (surprisingly small). At Beersheba, for example, the Iron IIc city (Stratum II) had a square inside the gate, measuring about twenty by ten meters, and at Megiddo the Iron IIc city (Stratum III) had such a square about forty by twenty-five meters in size (see town plans in J. E. Stambaugh, "Cities," *ABD,* 1:1031–48). In Jerusalem, we read of a square before the temple (Ezra 10:9), of one before the Water Gate (Neh 8:1, 16) and one before the Ephraim Gate (Neh 8:16), of an East Square (2 Chr 29:4), and of "the square of the gate of the city" (2 Chr 32:6). In Susa, we hear of a square before the palace (Esth 4:6). The town square was the main center of (male) social life; while boys and girls play in the "streets" (רחובות, plural) and old men and old women sit in them (Zech 8:4–5), the main "square" (רחוב, singular) is the place for the conduct of the town's business. In Isa 59:14 truth is fallen in the square, so justice cannot enter the gate. In Ps 55:11 (12) fraud and oppression are in the square of the wicked city. Quite often the term "gate" (שער) is used for the square itself (e.g., Deut 21:19; Ruth 3:11; 4:10; Lam 5:14); it is in the gate that unfortunate people may be wronged (5:4) or conspiracies drawn up (31:21).

Each day, we may suppose, Job would go out of his house to the gate of the city (see *Note* 29:7.a) and take up his regular seat in the town square. His right to be seated signifies his status in the community (see also v 25; on the "sitting" of a king, see M. Görg, *TDOT,* 6:420–38 [430–31]), higher than that of other elders, who would rise to their feet as he approached and remain standing, presumably until he has taken his seat (Davidson, Driver–Gray, Fohrer) or invites them to sit down (Dhorme). Lev 19:32 prescribes the gesture of standing up in the presence of an old man; though Job is not old, he accepts the deference due to the aged.

In the town square there would be both young and old men; the two terms must include (by merismus) men of all ages, so the *Translation* suggests "younger" and "older" men. Job himself is apparently a man of middle years, and he is accorded the greatest respect by all his fellow citizens. The younger men, on noticing his approach, would "hide themselves," that is, respectfully withdraw into the background, regarding themselves as unworthy to participate in conversation while Job was present, or (Delitzsch) fearing his salutation. The older men, who would in other circumstances be those dispensing wisdom and justice, feel themselves so outranked by Job that they take on the same role as the young men. Cf. the picture of the elders in the council making way for Telemachus as he took his father's seat (Homer, *Odyssey* 2.14).

9–10 The two terms for leaders of the community, "princes" (שׂרים) and "nobles" (נגידים), are not to be differentiated; they are loose terms for the highest-ranking men in the town. "Prince" (שׂר) is commonly a term for social rank and "noble" (נגיד) for high office (both are often used of military commanders), but here they are obviously the members of the town council. See R. de Vaux, *Ancient Israel: Its Life and Institutions* (London: Darton, Longman and Todd, 1961) 69–70. They are already in conversation when Job arrives, but "a sudden hush falls on the assembly" (Strahan); their talk must stop and his agenda must be deferred to. They do not set their hand to their mouth in horror or amazement, as in 21:5 (*q.v.* for bibliography; cf. also Isa 52:15), and the gesture here is probably entirely metaphorical: they simply do not speak (cf. also Wis 8:12), but restrain (עצר) their words, as one restrains a prisoner or a plague or rain (Jer 33:1; Num 16:48 [17:13]; Job 12:15; Eliphaz could not restrain his words in 4:2; a similar idiom in Virgil, *Aeneid* 2.1). The voices of the leaders are "hidden," just as the young men in v 8 became "hidden" (both חבא). The image of the tongue sticking to the palate represents silence or dumbness, as in Ezek 3:26 and Ps 137:6 (if the psalmist forgets Jerusalem); but it signifies thirst in Lam 4:4 (cf. Ps 22:15 [16], where it sticks to the jaws). The language for their suppression of speech is strong: they restrain and hide their words, they are struck dumb. To Job their silence is a mark of respect; but the terms hint at a kind of psychic violence, imposed ultimately by Job's power (as Good also notes). We do not forget that he is wealthiest of the Easterners (1:3), and money talks.

Many commentators and some versions transfer to this point vv 21–25, which continue the scene of Job's reception by the men gathered at the city gate (so JB, NAB, NEB, Moffatt). But it can just as well be argued that vv 7–10 and 21–25 frame the scene of Job's humanitarian actions in vv 11–24. The order of the strophes does not matter very much, except for the question of the note on which the chapter ends. Does Job's depiction of his former happy state conclude with his thought that he would "multiply [his] days as the sand . . . [his] glory fresh with [him] and [his] bow ever new in [his] hand" (vv 18–20), or with his recollection that in the town council he "chose their way and sat as chief" (v 25)? The former is the more wistful and personal note on which to end, but the latter is perhaps nearer the nub of the matter: in his former days, it was not just the assurance of a long and prosperous life that Job relished, but rather the experience of being in control and being honored. He can face death (indeed, he has often expressed a longing for it), but dishonor and disgrace he cannot bear.

11–17 Job's presence in the council of city elders was an honored one, but it was not for the sake of the honor that he would take up his seat in the square. His chief function as the leading man of his town, so he says, was to protect the underprivileged—the poor, the orphan, the dying, the widow, the blind, the lame, the stranger (vv 12–16)—and to prevent them from being wronged (v 17). All who saw or heard of Job in action (except presumably the unrighteous of v 17) applauded everything he did. The populace at large was the witness to Job's integrity and philanthropy (v 11). Though Job does not address Eliphaz explicitly, his claim here serves no doubt as a rebuttal of Eliphaz's charges against him of gross inhumanity in 22:6–9.

Job's acts of positive discrimination in favor of the marginalized were enjoined on him as a man with power by Israelite ethics and indeed by the ethical values of the ancient Near East generally. See F. C. Fensham, "Widow, Orphan and the Poor in Ancient Near Eastern Legal and Wisdom Literature," *JNES* 21 (1962) 129–39; Hammurabi, rev. xxiv (*ANET,* 178a); Kilamuwa, *ANET,* 654b–55a. Danel in the Ugaritic epic of Aqhat "judges the cause of the widow, adjudicates the case of the orphan," an evidently formulaic line for the duties of a ruler (*Aqhat* II.v.5–7; I.i.24–25 = *ANET,* 151a, 153a), while Keret's son accuses him of failing as a ruler on this very point (*Keret* II.vi.33–34 = *ANET,* 149a). In the Egyptian tale, *The Protests of the Eloquent Peasant,* an official is flattered as "father of the orphan, husband of the widow, brother of the divorcee, apron of him that is motherless" (*ANET,* 408b). J. G. Griffiths ("The Idea of Posthumous Judgement in Israel and Egypt," in *Fontes atque pontes,* FS H. Brunner, ed. M. Görg, AAT 5 [Wiesbaden: Harrassowitz, 1983] 186–204 [199–200]) has pointed out the resemblances between Job's claim to good deeds and Egyptian texts of self-certification, for example the words of Harkhuf inscribed on his tomb: "I gave bread to the hungry, clothing to the naked; I brought to land him that had no ferryboat." See also T. Krapf, "Traditionsgeschichtliches zum deuteronomischen Fremdling–Waise–Witwe-Gebot," *VT* 34 (1984) 87–91.

Job's picture is a totalizing one, of a past that was cloudless, entirely without doubt or disappointment. One of his rhetorical devices for expressing this seamless totality is to conjure up a whole catalogue of bodily parts denoting his self—mouth (vv 9, 10), tongue (v 10), palate (v 10), heart (v 13), eyes (v 15), feet (v 15), jawbone (v 17), teeth (v 17). But the list carries with it a message, which is no doubt hidden from Job himself—that these are all external manifestations, just as his clothing in v 14 is, and there is in the background another more self-critical story about his life that he represses. Andersen notes that all Job's acclaim was "not just the obsequious honour given to a rich man because of his economic power and political influence"; that is true, but the word "just" must be noted. For Good, even more sharply, there is behind Job's self-satisfaction "an arrogant man's testimony to the successful exercise of his arrogance."

It should not go without notice that Job's sense of responsibility to the needy has the effect of making him into a near royal figure (cf. A. Caquot, "Traits royaux dans le personnage de Job," in *maqqél shâqédh, La branche d'amandier,* FS W. Vischer [Montpellier: Causse, Graille, Castelnau, 1960] 32–45; B. V. Malchow, "A Royal Prototype in Job 29," in *The Psalms and Other Studies on the Old Testament,* FS J. I. Hunt, ed. J. C. Knight and L. A. Sinclair [Nashotah, WI: Nashotah House Seminary, 1990] 178–84; L. G. Perdue, *Wisdom in Revolt: Metaphorical Theology in the Book of Job,* JSOTSup 112, Bible and Literature Series 29 [Sheffield: JSOT Press & Almond Press, 1991] 189–93; see also on vv 23, 25). In the Psalms, the one who has the duty of judging the poor and delivering the needy, the one who has blessings showered on him for his deeds of philanthropy, is the king (cf. Ps 72:1–4, 12–14, 15–17). Job's benevolence is sincere enough, but he benefits from it in self-esteem and in the regard of others.

Where is Job when he is carrying out these acts of kindness and justice? He could be anywhere, of course; but perhaps we are meant to infer that the primary location for his benevolence is that very town council he has pictured in vv 7–10. Business, gossip, and justice are conducted in the square by the gate, and that is where Job is normally to be found, clothed in righteousness (v 14), studying the stranger's cause (v 16), and breaking the jawbone of the oppressor (v 17). Most of the good that Job does he does by word, seated in dignity.

11 Job's philanthropy was no doubt an end in itself for him, but the public recognition that flowed from it was indispensable for his well-being—so signifies his headlining of vv 12–17 with this assertion of the approval of his neighbors. The text distinguishes between those who merely "heard" of his kind deeds and those who "saw" them for themselves; both the beneficiaries and an applauding public are in view.

Those who heard of him called him blessed "as one whom blessing and prosperity must follow because of his benevolence" (Davidson), "naïvely believing that his prosperity proved his goodness" (Strahan). Those who saw his deeds were eye-witnesses to his goodness (not, to his wealth, as Driver–Gray).

12 The "poor" (עני) and the "fatherless" (יתום, not "orphan"; cf. on 22:9) are among the stereotypically underprivileged persons in ancient Israel. The two terms occur in this order in Isa 10:2, and in the reverse order in 24:9; Zech 7:10; Ps 82:3. The wording of Ps 72:12 is also very similar to the whole verse. Habel remarks on the irony in the fact that when Job himself "cried out" for "justice" from God, he himself was not heard. On שוע "cry out," cf. on 19:7; 30:20.

13 The blessing of the dying, which in many cultures is especially potent, came upon Job in that, presumably, he rescued them from death (so too Delitzsch), just as he delivered the poor in v 12; but perhaps it means that Job's benevolence made the death of the dying easier for them, or perhaps they blessed him for all the favors they had received from him (Fedrizzi). The cry of delight or triumph (רנן, as previously in 3:7; 20:5) he evoked in widows will have been due essentially to his gifts of food or clothing or, perhaps more to the point, depriving their creditors of their hold over them. It is a metaphorical "cry" of the heart, greeting a relief from a situation of despair, not an inspiration to hum a happy tune (as Hartley); it is the heart and not the mouth here that sings. A widow was evidently at risk from money-lenders, since though she may still have had the possessions of her husband she may not have had the means of earning an income (see on 24:3). Eliphaz has specifically charged Job in 22:9 with sending widows away "empty," without the satisfaction of their need, and Job is implicitly responding to him here (and in 31:16).

14 Job "clothed" himself with righteousness (cf. Isa 59:17; 61:10; Ps 132:9); he adorned himself with this quality, and it brought honor to him, as a costly garment would. Evildoers are sometimes said to be clothed with shame (8:22; Ps 132:18); that is the opposite of the honor that accrues from right behavior. In

40:10 Job is challenged by God to clothe himself with glory and splendor if he is to be any match for the Almighty; it is implied that God himself is decked in the most glorious clothes imaginable. Here Job is thinking not so much of being surrounded by righteousness as one's body is surrounded by its clothes, but more as being noticed by others for the quality of his benevolence, as one is noticed for the quality of one's clothing. His right dealing with others serves like a mantle and a turban, clothing him entirely, and projecting the persona he desires. On the "mantle," a garment worn by persons of distinction or by others on special occasions over the everyday tunic, see on 1:20; 2:12. The turban, a cloth wrapped around the head, perhaps like the Arab *kufiyeh,* was especially the clothing of priests and kings (Zech 3:5; Ecclus 11:5; 40:4), and thus, like the mantle, no everyday article of apparel but a token of the wearer's honor, power-dressing indeed (see also on 31:36). On the mantle, see E. Haulotte, *Symbolique du vêtement selon la Bible* (Paris: Aubier, 1966) 21–43. For an illustration of a Syrian turban, see *ANEP,* pl. 61.

With a rhetorical flourish, Job improves on his claim that he clothed himself with righteousness with the conceit that righteousness "clothed itself" with him, which can only mean that he was an adornment to righteousness. It is not so much that righteousness filled or possessed him (Driver–Gray), as a person fills their clothes, and less that righteousness became incarnate in Job (Peake); it is rather that righteousness itself became more glorious, more noticeable and acclaimed, through adopting Job as its outward form, making itself visible in Job (Strahan). In Judg 6:34, where the spirit of Yahweh "clothed itself" (RSV "took possession of") with Gideon, it evidently took Gideon as its outward manifestation.

Job's righteousness (צדק) is not, as so often in the book, his own integrity, which is subject to perpetual challenge (as צדק or צדקה in 6:29; 27:6; 31:6), but rather his benevolent acts toward the underprivileged; this is a sense that the term often carries in Second Isaiah, for example, where it can be equivalent to "salvation" (cf. Isa 41:10; 45:8; 46:13). Justice (משפט) in Job is more commonly "lawsuit" (as in 9:32; 14:3; 19:7) or "justice" as what is owed to Job (as in 27:2; 34:5). But sometimes this term also has a more beneficent sense, in that what is owed to the poor is not some abstract justice of a balancing kind, but positive discrimination in their favor; it is a kind of redistributive justice (as also in 36:6).

15–17 Four more underprivileged persons—the blind, the lame, the poor, and the stranger—who figure frequently in the stereotypical lists of marginal persons in Israelite society, are the focus in vv 15–16, and then the focalization shifts to their typical oppressor, the unrighteous who feeds on them like a wild beast.

15 The terms "blind" (עור) and "lame" (פסח) are often linked, in that order at Lev 21:18; 2 Sam 5:6, 8; Jer 31:8; Mal 1:8; and in the reverse order at Deut 15:21; 2 Sam 5:8. Elsewhere, Moses tells Hobab that he will be "as eyes for us" (Num 10:31), and cf. Euripides, *The Phoenician Women* 834–35 (ὡς τυφλῷ ποδὶ ὀφθαλμὸς εἶ σύ "you are an eye to my blind foot"). Job may well include the physically handicapped in his depiction, but the language is no doubt essentially metaphorical, just like that of the heart of the widow (v 13) and the jawbone of the wicked (v 17).

16 In a patriarchal society, it is a father that the underprivileged need, for it is fathers who have the power. In Ps 68:6 it is God who is father of the fatherless and protector of widows, and Job, as we have observed before, in all sincerity shows no compunction in taking upon himself the responsibility of the most powerful. It is not so common in the Hebrew Bible for "father" to be extended in meaning beyond its literal sense of that of ancestor, but for parallel usages, see Gen 45:8; Judg 17:10; 18:19; Isa 9:5; Ecclus 4:10 (cf. *DCH*, 1:91a). Hammurabi proclaimed himself a father to his people (25.21, *ANET,* 178a). The ninth-century Syrian king Kilamuwa said, "[T]o some I was a father. To some I was a mother" (*ANET,* 654b). Job's language is proverb-like (as Duhm also notices); there is an assonance in *ʾāb* "father" and *ʾebyôn* "poor" (Delitzsch) that hints at a stylization of thought as well as of language here.

Job has "studied" or "examined" (חקר; cf. also at 5:27) the case of injury done to a stranger, who is not a member of his own community. This is an act of benevolence that goes beyond the call of duty, Job means to say (Proverbs explicitly warns against becoming legally involved on behalf of a foreigner [11:15; 20:16]). Strangers have always been liable to ill-treatment, especially when some disaster befalls a community; but, counterbalancing some strong expressions of xenophobia, there are some surprisingly firm provisions in biblical law to ensure their rights; see Exod 12:49; 22:21 (20); 23:9, 12; Lev 19:10, 33, 34; etc.; and cf. D. Kellermann, *TDOT,* 2:439–49; C. van Houten, *The Alien in Israelite Law: A Study of the Changing Legal Status of Strangers in Ancient Israel,* JSOTSup 107 (Sheffield: JSOT Press, 1991); M. Sneed, "Israelite Concern for the Alien, Orphan, and Widow: Altruism or Ideology?" *ZAW* 111 (1999) 498–507.

17 No doubt the unrighteous are being represented here as wild animals with "fangs" (מתלעה), used of lions at Joel 1:6 and Ps 58:6 (7) (the form there is מלתעה) and apparently of humans at Prov 30:14. For parallels to the wicked as beasts of prey, especially lions, see on 4:10. Job does not deal with these beasts on a piecemeal basis, but in breaking their jawbone he prevents further acts of depredation against the defenseless. In line with his self-assurance—not to say arrogance—in this depiction of his former state, Job expresses no misgiving about the use of violence in the interests of justice. Indeed, his assaults on those he identified as the perpetrators of injustice form a climax in his catalogue of memories of the past; it has been otherwise a totally pacific picture, in which he has figured as a leader who is respected rather than feared. This last sentence, however, shows that—not entirely unlike the "dreadful dominion" of God himself as portrayed by Bildad (25:2)—Job's acts of benevolence are the velvet glove over an iron fist. These animalistic opponents of Job, whose jawbones he shatters, are, we must recall, in all probability fellow citizens of his, with whom he does business at the town gate. His language makes them into almost demonic, and certainly subhuman, figures; but that is nothing but his decision about them, however justified in part it may be.

18–20 This triplet distinguishes itself from the surrounding verses as Job's remembrance of what he felt entitled to expect so long as he lived his life of wealth and privilege. In the days when God watched over him, when the protection of God was over his tent, and the Almighty was still with him (vv 2, 4–5), he had every reason to expect that his good fortune would continue for ever and that he would come to his grave only at a ripe old age. He believed he was living in a fairy tale, and why should he not? For by the end of the book of Job we find that his expectations are fulfilled to the letter: he dies an old man and full of days (42:17), surrounded by his family.

18 Some of our versions have Job multiplying his days "as the sand" (so RSV), and sand is certainly a frequent metaphor for huge quantity (e.g., Gen 22:17; 32:12 [13]; Josh 11:4; Judg 7:12; Ps 139:18; in Job 6:3 it symbolizes weight; see *Comment*). But an alternative reading is very attractive: it has Job multiplying his days "like the phoenix," the legendary bird that lives for 500 years (others say, variously, 540, 600, 1,000, 1,461, or even 12,994). There was a Greek saying, "to live the years of a phoenix" (Lucian, *Hermotinus* 53), and it is perhaps more realistic for Job to imagine living 500 years like a phoenix (he actually lives 200 years or so, according to 42:16) than an almost infinite number of years like sand. The legend of the phoenix was known to the Greeks and Romans, and it is encountered also in the rabbinic literature (*Genesis Rabbah* 19; *b. Sanhedrin* 108b), as well as in early Christian texts (e.g., *1 Clement* 25.2; Tertullian, *De resurrectione* 13). See in general, R. van den Broek, *The Myth of the Phoenix according to Classical and Early Christian Traditions* (Leiden: Brill, 1972); H. Heras, "The Standard of Job's Immortality," *CBQ* 11 (1949) 263–79; M. R. Niehoff, "The Phoenix in Rabbinic Literature," *HTR* 89 (1996) 245–65. It is objected against seeing the phoenix here that the myth of the phoenix also tells of its rebirth after its death, and Job of course is not thinking of any afterlife for himself. But the sole point of comparison here could well be its immensely long life, whether or not it is subsequently reborn.

It is ironic that the future Job envisaged for himself, surrounded throughout a long life by a large family and in the end going down to Sheol in peace, is exactly what he has described in 21:7–13 as the experience of the wicked. Now his observation of the prosperity of the wicked has not been made only since the reversal of his fortunes; he has long been aware of their well-being, so why did he never make a connection between his own hopes and the evidence of his senses?

19 In a land where rain is seasonal and scarce, the main sources of moisture for vegetation are dew and river water. If the roots of a tree can spread down to underground water or as far as a stream, the tree thrives—as we know from the image of the psalmist "planted by streams of water" (Ps 1:3; cf. also Jer 17:8; Ezek 31:4, 7; 1QH 8:7). Other references in Job to the need of plants for water are at 14:8–9; 18:16. For the parallel of "root" (שׁרשׁ) and "branch" (קציר here), cf. 18:16; Ezek 17:6, 7, 9; 31:7; Mal 4:1 (3:19).

Dew is a great blessing (see Gen 27:28, 39) and often mentioned along with rain (Deut 32:2; 2 Sam 1:21; 1 Kgs 17:1) or by itself (Gen 27:28, 39; Deut 33:13, 28; Hag 1:10; Zech 8:12) as a principal condition for life. Though dew soon evaporates in the morning sun (Hos 6:4; 13:3), if it has "lodged, spent the night" like a guest (לין, as in 24:7) or has lain all night, the vegetation will have had the benefit. It is most important because it occurs principally during the summer months (May to September) in which rain is rare (see F. S. Frick, *ABD*, 5:124–25, with charts of dew nights and quantity of dew, which can amount to as much as four millimeters in a month).

By thinking of his roots being "opened" (פתח) to the waters and of dew "lodging" (לין) on his branches, Job is, interestingly enough, regarding the waters that sustain his life as the active principle and himself as a somewhat passive recipient of their beneficence. He has only to be in the right place, like a tree planted by streams, for his life to enjoy its accustomed vigor. It is not at all an ugly picture, but he shows that he cannot imagine that life can be a struggle.

20 Long life is, according to proverbial wisdom, a reward for righteousness; as Prov 21:21, for example, has it, "The one who pursues righteousness and mercy will find life and honor" (Hebrew adds "righteousness and" before "honor"); cf. also Deut 5:33; 1 Kgs 3:14; Prov 10:27. But Job is perhaps not thinking so much of what he is owed because of his deeds of benevolence to the underprivileged, since he gives no hint that he is thinking of recompense; it is rather his natural assumption that his present state of life will continue unbroken.

As we have already noted, the key ingredient in Job's former life was "honor" (כבוד). It was not his exercise of power, it was not the satisfaction of bringing help to the needy, it was not his consciousness of the divine presence. They were all factors that contributed to the quality of his life, but what he really enjoyed, and what he so desperately lacks now, is honor. Honor is an acknowledgment of worth by one's society; though it may be always open to contestation, to gain it and to keep it is in traditional societies the primary goal of an adult male (see J. Plevnik, "Honor/Shame," in *Biblical Social Values and Their Meaning: A Handbook*, ed. J. J. Pilch and B. J. Malina [Peabody, MA: Hendrickson, 1993] 95–104 [96]; H. Moxnes, "Honor and Shame," *BTB* 23 [1993] 167–76; U. Wikan, "Shame and Honour: A Contestable Pair," *Man* NS 19 [1984] 635–52). What Job craves, and what he once enjoyed, was honor perpetually "fresh" (חדש "new"), new signals of approval and recognition by his peers.

There is a darker side to this honor, though. Not many would begrudge Job, or anyone, all the honor they can get, if honor means merely praise for adhering to socially approved values. But, as in v 17, we see that there is a cost in acquiring and keeping honor. Along with fresh honor goes an ever-pliant "bow" (קֶשֶׁת). Job does not represent himself in his speeches as a warrior (as, for example, the psalmists commonly do), and all the fighting he does is metaphorical. But his language is a reminder that in the quest for honor there are winners and losers; just as on the battlefield those who retire with "honor" are the victors and those with "shame" the vanquished, so in the social jockeying for position those who are not honored but dishonored or shamed are indeed the vanquished, even if the force of arms against them is entirely metaphorical. Job's "bow" is not his strength he merely keeps in reserve (against Fohrer) but the power that must be constantly in service to sustain a man of honor in his standing. For the bow as a symbol of strength, cf. Gen 49:24; and for breaking the bow as signifying defeat, cf. Jer 49:35; Hos 1:5; Ps 37:15; and the curse in the Vassal Treaty of Esarhaddon, "May [the gods] break your bow and make you crouch at the feet of your enemies" (*ANET,* 540a §77). It is wrong to speak of the bow as a symbol of "manliness" (Delitzsch) or "manly vigor" (e.g., Hartley) or "strength and resilience" (Alden) or sexual vigor (Fedrizzi, Good) and the like, without recognizing that bows are used only for inflicting injury and death on other people (or animals). There is nothing innocent about this image, which symbolizes not just internal strength but power over the life of others. (On bows, see J. P. Brown, "Archery in the Ancient World: 'Its Name Is Life, Its Work Is Death,'" *BZ* 37 [1993] 26–43; W. W. Hallo, "More on Bows," in *Eretz-Israel,* ed. A. Ben-Tor, J. C. Greenfield, and A. Malamat, Archaeological, Historical and Geographical Studies 20, Yigael Yadin

Memorial Volume [Jerusalem: Israel Exploration Society (= *ErIsr* 20), 1989] 68*–71*; O. Keel, "Der Bogen als Herrschaftsymbol," *ZDPV* 93 [1977] 141–77; K. L. Younger, *NIDOTTE,* 3:1004–6.)

21–25 The scene of this chapter has been since v 7 the town council (see on both vv 7–10 and 11–17), but here we return more directly to the dynamics of Job's relation with the other members of that assembly. Vv 10–17 have been about the righteousness he dispensed at the city gate—to all and sundry but especially to the underprivileged—but now we see again the interaction between him and the councillors, the spotlight shifting constantly between him and them. They listened, they waited, they kept silence, he spoke, they did not speak, his word dropped on them, they waited, they opened their mouths, he smiled on them, they did not believe it, they did not disregard his favor, he chose their way, he sat as chief, he dwelt as a king. Moffatt, among others (see *Note* 29:11.a), thinks the sequence of sentences has been disturbed into an illogicality; not so, for the theme here is neither Job nor his fellow citizens but precisely their interrelationship. On the suggestion to transfer these verses to follow v 10 (as in JB, NAB, NEB, Moffatt), see *Note* 29:11.a.

21–22 We learned in vv 9–10 that when Job would arrive in the town square to take his seat there would be a deathly hush; now we read that Job would speak his mind, the assembly would listen until he had finished—and then they would still be silent, as if he had spoken a divine oracle (Rowley). After he had spoken, they did not speak again! They would have "no alteration or improvement to suggest, no desire to hear anyone else" (Driver–Gray). This is a truly incredible picture, but it is what Job wants to remember. He seriously cannot remember anyone else having anything to say, and he can only recall everyone being immensely impressed with his wisdom and deeply grateful for it. He was never challenged, never put in the wrong, and, equally, never supported, never instructed, never stimulated. No town council in the world ever worked like that—not unless there was a dictator in their midst, not unless there was a hidden violence and an unexpressed fear. It is not a pretty picture, and it tells us more about Job than we would really like to know. But it sheds a welcome light on the enormity of his affliction: from being a man who is always in the right he has been turned overnight into a man who is wholly in the wrong—and always really has been. If he is being punished by God for his sinfulness—and that is what the town council now thinks—it cannot have been some crime lately committed; he must have been for years a secret sinner who has now had his wickedness exposed. What remains of all his wisdom in the assembly now?

And where do the three friends fit into this picture of Job? They seem to have no compunction about contradicting Job, and the only trace of respect lay in the first sentence of the first friend (Eliphaz in 4:2–4). A man who cannot be contradicted in Uz clearly needs friends like these, friends of his own standing who can speak frankly. But perhaps even for them it is only Job's suffering that has loosened their tongues.

"Waiting" (יחל) in "silence" (verb דמם or דום, noun דומם) is what the pious person does for God (Ps 37:7; Lam 3:26). The poet may be hinting that Job's fellow citizens, in his account of them at least, accord him extravagant honors. As for his words "dropping," the verb (נטף) is always used of heavens or clouds dropping rain (Judg 5:4; Ps 68:8 [9]) or, metaphorically, of other things letting things fall in droplets (like mountains dropping wine in Joel 3:18 [4:18]; Amos 9:13, or like hands or lips dropping honey or myrrh in Cant 4:11; 5:5, 13). Prophets drop their words in Ezek 20:46 (21:2); 21:2 (7); Amos 7:16; in Mic 2:6, 11 there is no object, and prophets simply "drop," as does the foreign woman in Prov 5:3. In all these cases except those about prophets, where the use is no doubt ironic, what is "dropped" is greatly desired by the one receiving it, whether it is rain or wine or honey or myrrh or pleasant words. Job's words, he imagines, were received by his hearers as delightful morsels; the age of the soundbite had already dawned. It is not meant that Job's discourse was very lengthy (against Dhorme who says that "fall drop by drop" implies that Job "had plenty of time to expound his ideas"; so too Rowley), nor especially that his words were gentle as the rain (as Hartley), nor that like rain they penetrated to the heart (Delitzsch).

23 For speech like rain, cf. Deut 32:2 (Homer, *Iliad* 3.222, has words like snowflakes). The rain here is both the usual term for rain (מטר, as in 5:10; 28:26; the verb in 20:23), and the "latter rain" or "spring rain" (מלקוש), which falls in March and April, and on which the harvest especially depends (see Jer 3:3; Zech 10:1; Prov 16:15; it is coupled with the "early rain" [יורה or מורה] in Deut 11:14; Jer 5:24; Hos 6:3; Joel 2:23, which falls in autumn and winter, and which softens the ground for plowing). In Prov 16:15 it is the king's favor that is like the cloud that brings the latter rain, and in Ps 72:6 the king is like rain on the new-cut crops; perhaps the phrase is another token of Job's presumed royal status (cf. above on vv 11–17).

The "gaping" mouth is in 16:10 that of the wild beast; nearer to the present point is the psalmist's mouth, which he opened (פער), panting for God's commandments (Ps 119:131). His hearers remain agape at his words as though they are some beneficent shower (Dhorme).

24 The meaning of this verse is much disputed. The key issues are: Did Job smile (whether in approval or encouragement) or laugh at his fellow citizens? The verb שחק could mean either. Did they "not believe" he smiled at them because he was usually so strict and solemn, or was it that he smiled on them because they were "inconfident" (לא יאמינו)? And what does "the light of my face they did not drop" mean? It is hard to say, but the best interpretation (see *Note* 29:24.c) seems to be that when he smiled on them in approval they could hardly believe their good fortune, since they never expected any opinion of theirs to merit his acceptance. It is unlikely that the friendlier, but tamer, interpretation of RSV, for example ("I smiled on them when they had no confidence"), is correct, since the verb אמן in the hiphil usually means "believe" and not "trust, be confident." Job represents his fellows as a very docile lot.

The "light of the face" must be one's favor, as the expression clearly means in Pss 4:6 (7); 44:3 (4); 89:15 (16); Prov 16:15 (and the phrase "to make one's face shine" [אור פניו hiph] in Num 6:25; Pss 31:16 [17]; 67:1 [2]; 80:3 [4], 7 [8], 19 [20]; 119:135; Dan 9:17). Only very important people, like gods or kings, who have something valuable to give or to withhold, have light in their face (e.g., Prov 16:15; Num 6:25); perhaps this is another facet of the quasi-royal depiction of Job (see on vv 11–17). To drop something or let it fall (נפל hiph) is to disregard it, as in the analogies in 1 Sam 3:19 and Esth 6:10, where Yahweh lets none of Samuel's words fall to the ground and Haman is to let none of his own words fall. That they did not disregard the importance of acquiring Job's favor is an understatement of course; to gain it was their supreme goal—that is what Job means to say.

Others interpret quite differently, seeing here a reference to Job's encouragement of the downhearted, and to the impossibility of anyone causing his happiness to falter (taking "cast down the light of my face" to mean "make me sad"). Thus, for example, Driver: "Job's clear-sighted counsel encouraged them, if they were despondent: on the other hand . . . their despondency never clouded his cheerfulness" (similarly Rowley); and Delitzsch "[He] did not allow anything to dispossess him of his easy and contented disposition."

25 This summarizing line portrays the extent of Job's control over his fellow citizens—or at least his memory of how he controlled them. Nowhere else in the Hebrew Bible does a person choose the way of another; humans choose their own way, whether for good (Pss 25:12; 119:30; Prov 3:31) or ill (Isa 66:3). Their way (דרך) is their destiny (see on 3:23) or, better, their conduct, how they should behave (see on 13:15). By Job's account of it, they had no freedom of decision or behavior. (This is a harsher picture of Job than that of many other commentators; Davidson, for example, finds here "the joy which he had in the fellowship of men.")

The hints of a royal status claimed by Job (see on vv 11–17, 23) now become explicit. He dwelt among the townsfolk like a king, he says; not like a king among his people, let it be noted, but like a king among his troops. In the army, there is much less room for debate and compromise; in the army, the king gives orders and his troops obey. The term for "sit" (ישׁב), i.e., to be settled, to be installed, also can have royal overtones (see above on vv 7–8), since it is the normal term for sitting enthroned (as in Pss 2:4; 9:7 [8]; 29:10; 61:7 [8]; Lam 5:19). On Job's royal status, see further Caquot, "Traits royaux dans le personnage de Job." The LXX additions to Job 42:17 actually make him a king of Edom. Hartley thinks, more democratically, of Job's being "appointed" by the people as their chief on account of his judicious counsel; and Andersen actually reads "I was chosen"; but not many kings, ancient or modern, have been "appointed" by their subjects, and the only clue the book provides to explain why Job is their chief is that he is the wealthiest man (1:3).

The last phrase in the Hebrew text, "like one who comforts mourners" (if that is the correct translation), does not simply seem out of place here; it is rather that it is impossible to make proper sense of it at all. Nothing that Job has said of himself in this chapter seems remotely like a comforter of mourners; everything that Job has been has been proactive, and what he remembers is his leadership (vv 7–10, 21–25) and his ability to change circumstances (vv 11–17). These are not the skills of a comforter. Hartley envisages Job addressing the assembly with consolation when they were mourning some disaster like famine or plague; but then he would have been a comforter, not "like" a comforter. Its presence in the text is a mystery, and there seems little choice but to omit it (see *Note* 29:25.e).

30:1–31 In this second movement of Job's final speech, the accent moves from his contemplation of his former existence in chap. 29 to his depiction of his present circumstances. It is suffused with strong feelings; almost every verse contains an expression of Job's present bitterness. In his former life, when the protection of God was over him (29:4), he was in control and he was honored. Today, now that God has thrown him into the mire (30:19) and has turned cruel to him (30:21), he is without power and he has become an object of scorn. Three times he begins this complaint, each time with "And now" (vv 1, 9, 16), as if the contrast is only now being borne in upon him.

This movement of the speech has three distinct sections: his account of his present dishonor (vv 1–15), a description of his inner suffering which turns into a direct address to God (vv 16–23), and a lament (vv 24–31).

1–8 Who is to say what the worst of it all is for Job? All we know is that the point at which he begins is the matter of his honor. That, as we have seen, was fundamental to his sense of well-being in chap. 29 (see especially vv 9–10, 14, 20), and that is what has now been lost. Now he is dishonored, derided even by his inferiors. It is, evidently, bad enough to be scorned by one's peers or one's superiors, but to be derided by one's inferiors is a double tribulation.

1 Job begins by speaking of those who scorn him. No doubt there are others besides these young men whom he refers to by way of example (Hesse), but it is especially galling to him that among his detractors are men "younger" than him. The phrase "smaller in days" unambiguously fits those of fewer years, but in using the term "smaller" (צעיר) he shows that for him it is primarily a question not of chronological age but of social status. By his standards, younger men are less significant, less entitled to form judgments; we recall the younger men at the town gate who would hide themselves when Job approached (29:8), knowing that Job had no esteem for them. It is galling to him to be the object of appraisal by men who have no right to an opinion.

But it is not just that they are younger; they are also the sons of worthless and despicable fathers. Job may be speaking in class terms, with "patrician pride" (Andersen), of men of humble origin without his status as a noble; but it is more likely that the worthlessness of the fathers is no more than a reflex from the behavior of the sons. If the sons mock Job, they must have low-class fathers. Job's sheepdogs (כלבי צאני, lit. "dogs of my flock") were trusty, as dogs go, for without them Job's great wealth in sheep (1:3) would have been very much at risk (for dogs as guardians of the flock, see Isa 56:10–11). But to compare a human with a dog is a grave insult (cf. 1 Sam 17:43; 2 Sam 3:8; 2 Kgs 8:13) or an extreme form of self-abasement (2 Sam 9:8); for Job to compare humans unfavorably with dogs, saying that he would have "despised" them as candidates for the duties of sheepdogs, is vicious language. The note struck is even sharper than our own culture might expect, which often thinks of the dog as "man's best friend." Tristram observes that "The shepherd's dog . . . is not the intelligent companion and henchman of his master; he is simply the guardian of the flock at night from wild beasts" (*Natural History,* 141). One suspects that Job is not talking about real people, but about the fathers he conjures up for these young men who despise him. (It is possible that Job means he would not have given such men the despised job of being in charge of his dogs, as Hartley thinks.)

There is a further indication that Job is inventing here. If his mockers are really the sons of social outcasts, who are chased away from the towns and villages (v 5), how can the sons themselves, who will have very little chance of coming up in the world from the abject state of their fathers, have come into some public place like the town square to deliver their insults against Job? Would the populace, however critical of Job, have stood with these marginal people and applauded their scorn for a Job who, however far he had fallen, was still one of their own?

What do these young men actually do?, we ask. We will hear a great deal more of them in vv 9–14, but at the moment, the chief of Job's complaints is that they "laugh at" or "smile at" (שחק על) him. We saw Job in 29:24 "laughing" or "smiling" at his fellow citizens, but there the preposition was אל "toward," not hostile like the preposition על "against" here (and in Ps 52:8; Lam 1:7; cf. also שחק ל in Job 5:22). But still we may wonder what exactly they did. Did they stand around pointing the finger at him and jeering like the scorners of Elisha in 2 Kgs 2:23–24, did they "make sport of" him (RSV), did they "laugh him to scorn" (NEB), did they "hold [him] in derision" (NAB), or did they just decide that he was a dreadful sinner who had been deceiving people with his claims to righteousness and perfection? Job is capable of calling that "scorn," just as he has called the friends' speeches mockery (21:3, לעג), and as they have called his (11:3).

On the term ועתה "and now," see A. Laurentin, "*Wĕʻattah*—Kai nun: Formule caractéristique des textes juridiques (à propos de Jean 17,5)," *Bib* 45 (1964) 168–97, 413–32.

The question has been raised whether the people in this depiction are themselves dispossessed and outcast Israelites or not rather desert-dwelling bedouin (as Budde and Volz suggest, and as is argued at length by S. Nyström, *Beduinentum und Jahwismus: Eine soziologisch-religionsgeschichtliche Untersuchung zum Alten Testament* [Lund: Gleerup, 1946] esp. 201–17). Since Job himself is not an Israelite, but a citizen of Uz, his tormentors are hardly likely to be Israelites; they seem very clearly to be members of his own society.

2–8 The connection of this picture of the desperately poor with the young men of v 1 is not evident, and it is not surprising that some have either regarded these verses as a later addition (so Peake, Fohrer, Hesse) or have moved them to another place in the poem (so Moffatt, removing them to follow 24:8). Duhm, Driver–Gray, and Fedrizzi omit vv 2–8. The difficulties with the present position of these verses are these: (1) It is not clear whether it is the sons (who are mocking Job) or their fathers who are the subject of the description; in v 2 it seems to be the fathers, who have most recently been mentioned in v 1c, but in v 9 the subject seems to be the sons, without any marker of transition. (2) If we consider vv 2–8 in themselves, "the impression it makes is not one of contempt for their abject condition, but of pity for their misery" (Peake)—unlike the evident note of contempt in v 1; so it becomes plausible to see these verses as misplaced from, say, chap. 24.

But equally there are difficulties with removing these verses. (1) If we remove vv 2–8, then two successive verses (vv 1, 9) would both begin with "But now" (ועתה), whereas it seems that the word is used in this speech as a strophe marker (it occurs next at v 16). (2) If we also regard v 1 as a later insertion (Duhm), then those who make Job a song and a byword in vv 9–10 are his fellow councillors of 29:21–25, and it is perhaps "not likely that those dignified senators would descend to such treatment of Job" (Peake). (3) If we have already removed 29:21–25 to follow 29:10, as many do (see on 29:9–10), it is an impossibly large jump from Job's thought about dying in his nest (29:18–20) to "But now I have become their song" (30:9); who are "they"? (4) The present verses *do* contain a note of contempt, in the reference to the poor as fools (v 8), and such a note would be out of place in chap. 24. (5) Above all, it seems that the poor who are described in chap. 24 are quite different people from those here. There they are farm laborers (vv 10–11), and the reference to their foraging in the wilderness is merely a metaphor for their scraping a living from their daily work (see *Comment* on 24:5). Here the poor are excluded from the towns and villages (v 5) and do not undertake any agricultural labor.

On the assumption then that these verses do belong here, we should no doubt suppose that it is the fathers of Job's youthful scorners who are here described. Job would then be attributing to those who dishonor him fathers who have no land or resources, nameless people (v 8), perhaps mentally disturbed (see *Comment* on v 8), who eke out a miserable existence on the edges of the settled land. We cannot possibly believe that the only people who "scorn" Job (whatever that means) come from the lowest orders of society, but that is how Job would like to represent things. His only mechanism for handling the dishonor he is suffering is to try to assign even greater dishonor to his opponents; he presumes that they come from disreputable backgrounds, and, moreover, that extreme poverty is itself a dishonor.

It is hard not to lose patience with Job at this point. His arguments are usually more compelling than this, but we seem to be encountering in these chapters a Job who is less attractive in several respects than the character we have become accustomed to

Job's rhetoric remains magnificent, of course; and it is less surprising than regrettable that many commentators are seduced by it into adopting Job's ideology and his tone. Rowley, for example, writes of the impoverished people here as "degenerate weaklings, unfit for honest toil," living in "squalor and degradation," and of the "ingratitude and arrogance of these worthless creatures"—which is if anything stronger than Job's language and does not reckon with the reality of abject poverty. Hartley speaks of them as "the dregs of society," "displaced desert rabble," "these desert rats," "these ruffians," "these scoundrels," "such riffraff," "these repulsive outcasts." Andersen comments: "Less than human, this gang is rightly expelled from where decent people live." Strahan sees them "becoming more and more degenerate." Alden speaks of them as "the scum of society," "malicious hoodlums," "worthless gangsters," and "undesirable criminal[s] banished from the community" and has Job depicting them as "coarse, wild animals, motivated by instinct and totally bereft of decency." Perhaps these authors are merely attempting to represent Job's point of view, and Hartley, for example, is not unaware of the problem, rightly reproaching Job that "his enlightened attitude toward the weak [in 31:13–15] has not been extended to include those viewed as social outcasts." But perhaps also their language is as much open to criticism as that of Job.

At such a point as this a reader who is outraged by the text cannot remain "objective" and distanced. It is interesting to notice, lest it be thought that having a social conscience about the text is a sign of fin de siècle trendiness and political correctness, a commentator of a much earlier age writing: "[T]he tone of disdain in verse 1 is unlike [Job], one might say unworthy of him, and leaves a painful impression" (Peake, a Manchester Methodist writing in 1904). Terrien also finds it strange that such a "model of generosity and civic responsibility should express himself now with such violent disdain for certain other human beings"; but he excuses Job's language by explaining how in ancient societies philanthropic duties were limited to those within one's tribal group. Going one step further, Strahan deduces from the attitude of the speaker that the verses must be the work of a later author: "That the humane poet himself should make his hero speak so contemptuously of bond-servants is inconceivable, as any one must feel who contrasts the verse with the exquisite language of 31:15." And in Duhm also it is evident that the commentator's judgment about the social attitude expressed here has been a factor in determining his decision about the authenticity of the verses; such a sentence as v 1, he says, cannot be harmonized with the nobleness of the poet, and for anyone to hold that these verses may be authentic shows eloquently how exegesis is a matter of the blind leading the blind.

There is perhaps a way in which the barb in Job's speech can be drawn. Gordis (followed by Habel) has argued that vv 2–8 are a virtual quotation, "a statement of Job's thoughts in the past." The Job who is speaking in these verses is the grand seigneur of chap. 29, who could afford to be disdainful of the lower orders of society. It was the wealthy landowner who would have judged the employability of these desert dwellers (v 1c). But now that he has been so reduced, he is much nearer to their lot than he could have imagined, and he would not now speak of them so haughtily; they are now his betters. And the Job who speaks now may be bitterly exaggerating the cruelty of the Job of earlier days. I doubt it, however.

2 Job's reasoning is: These opponents are so shameful that they must be the offspring of men who are worthless to society. Their fathers may be presumed to be so weak and incompetent that they are not employable, not worth their keep as sheepdogs earn theirs.

Needless to say, the logic is defective in at least two places. First, there is no reason to suppose that because people have made a judgment hostile to Job that any conclusion can be drawn about their parents. And in any case, we cannot help recall, anyone who judges Job a sinner is committing no worse a crime than adhering to traditional theology. Secondly, it is self-evident that the fathers in question are weak because they are starving. Either poverty and hunger are themselves a crime, in Job's eyes, or else he is callously disregarding the social causes of their weakness and holding them responsible for society's failure toward them.

In asking, What could I gain from the strength of their hands to me (lit. what is there for me)?, Job speaks like the coarsest of nineteenth-century mill owners, for whom people have no value apart from their productivity. Peake too is surprised by the "hard, commercial temper that Job displays."

3 These poverty-stricken men live in the steppe country, outside the limits of the cultivated land. There they must depend for their sustenance on the bushes and roots that grow in their dry and hostile environment.

4 Finding food and heat is the sole occupation of these miserable people. Saltwort is mentioned in the Talmud (*b. Qiddushin* 66a) as a food of the poor, and by Athenaeus as the diet of poor Pythagoreans (4.16); the small thick leaves have a sour salty taste "and would be eaten only in dire extremity" (Pope).

As for heat, they must rely on the roots of the broom (רתם, incorrectly translated "juniper" by KJV), the largest bush in the desert, often large enough to give shade, as Elijah found (1 Kgs 19:4–5). Its roots are bitter and inedible (Löw, *Flora,* 2:471), though its small berries can be eaten (Tur-Sinai), so while it is possible that the text depicts these starving people eating such food (so Strahan, Driver–Gray), it is more likely that the translation of KJV "juniper roots for their meat," JB "making their meals off roots of broom" (similarly NEB, NAB, NIV) is to be rejected. The verb (לחמם) can equally well be understood as "to become warm" (see *Note* 30:4.f), so we should translate "for warmth" (REB), "for fuel" (Moffatt), or "for firewood" (Gordis). The roots of the broom, "ruthlessly uprooted by the Arabs, who collect it wherever it is tolerably abundant, for the manufacture of charcoal" (Tristram, *Natural History,* 360), are attested also in the Bible as the source of good charcoal (Ps 120:4); see further Dalman, *Arbeit und Sitte,* 1:540; Str-B, 4:1079. For another ancient description of intolerable poverty, in this case among starving soldiers, see Lucan, *Pharsalia* 6.110–17.

5 What of their dealings with others? Like outcasts everywhere, these marginal people are the object of suspicion by those who are more socially secure. Whether or not they intend to pilfer from the villagers, whenever they come within sight they are chased away (גרש) and abused with the cry (רוע), "Thief!"—and are thereby both stigmatized and further isolated from access to the goods enjoyed by members of the settled community. To say "Thieves they were forced by want to be" (Peake), while sympathetic in intention, is unfortunately to adopt the perspective of the townsfolk who maltreated them.

6 And what of their dwellings? They must make do with natural shelters, whether caves in the earth (חר as in 1 Sam 14:11) or overhanging rocks. Lot lives for a time in a cave (Gen 19:30), as do David (1 Sam 22:1), prophets (1 Kgs 18:4), and the Israelites (Judg 6:2; 1 Sam 13:6) (all these texts have מערה for "cave").

7 It is not too difficult to imagine these poor people huddling together for warmth under nettles (RSV, NAB, NJPS) (חרול), or perhaps rather thistles (JB, Fohrer), which are tall enough to sit under, but it is hard to see why the subject of their warmth is being returned to after v 4b and why they are "braying" (נהק). Some have thought that the sound of animals is being ascribed to them ("hoarse cries of hunger," says Rowley; cf. Dhorme, Hartley), but this is the only place in vv 2–8 where they would have been likened to animals, and in any case why would they be braying "under nettles"? Much more probable is the view that it is their sexual activity that is described (so Duhm, Strahan, Driver–Gray, Peake, Fohrer, Hesse): lacking houses or privacy they groan or moan (Moffatt "grunt") in sexual pleasure among bushes in the open air, and couple upon beds no more delicious than beds of nettles. It is true that the terms "groan" (נהק; in 6:5 of a hungry wild ass) and "couple" (ספח, lit. "are joined," as in Isa 14:1) are not used elsewhere with these meanings, but language for sex is often quite allusive. In 3:7, for example, רננה "rejoicing" is used in that sense, but nowhere else among the fifty-seven occurrences of the noun and verb. It is not an objection to this interpretation that these people are said in v 2 to be lacking in vigor or that their hunger is "sterile" (גלמוד, v 3), since that term may not be meant literally.

8 These people who live outside the inhabited settlements are called "children of a fool" (נבל). A "fool" is often a godless person and a wrongdoer, as in Ps 53:1 (2), where the fool has said there is no God and has done iniquity. But it is possible also that a "fool" is a mad person (Duhm and Andersen: "idiot"), and that these social outcasts are regarded, rightly or wrongly, as mad. Their way of life marks them out as nonconformists to accepted behavior, and a corresponding "abnormality" of their state of mind is inferred by conventional people, especially the "wise" who are represented by Job and his friends. Job has already denigrated his wife's ideas as "like those of the mad women" (נבלות, 2:10).

Others argue that the "fool" here is essentially a godless person, the term expressing "deficiency, not of *intellect,* but of *moral* and *religious* sense" (Driver–Gray). Gordis thinks it is a low-class person. Good thinks rather of the ill-tempered Nabal, a "fool" by name and by nature, and translates "churls" (churls are mean-spirited and lacking in generosity, are they not, and what have these homeless people to be generous with?). A נבל is according to Dhorme "a branded creature, vile and abject," according to de Wilde "godless and unrespectable," according to Rowley "mentally and morally defective," according to Hartley "hardened fools [who] continually manifest their incorrigible folly." One senses that these poor people seem even more threatening to our commentators than to Job himself.

As for those who are "nameless," it is possible that what is meant is that from the perspective of the townsfolk these outcasts are unknown personally and have no known identity (much less likely that their names are not registered in any genealogy, as Duhm thought). But it is perhaps more likely that "name" is used in its common sense of "fame, reputation," and that these are people without honor (so Fohrer), people at the opposite end of the social spectrum from Job, for whom honor is his lifeblood (cf. on 29:20).

Because these people are deviants from the accepted norms of society, they cannot be tolerated, and so are rightly seen as expelled (נכא, lit. "struck, smitten") from the communities. In fact, they will have been subject to no formal expulsion, but, like homeless people everywhere, will have gravitated of their own accord away from centers of wealth and privilege to areas where the resources are so meager that no one else claims them. There will be enough bushes and roots for these marginal people to keep body and soul together, but they dare not show their faces in the villages. The townsfolk only encounter them as feared intruders, whom they frighten away with cries (v 5b).

Well-fed commentators rarely recognize that being homeless is not a moral fault. What are described in these verses are not wicked people but desperately poor people for whom there is no place in regular human society. Job, in order to taunt his youthful detractors (or perhaps, in order to make himself feel as bitter as possible about his present state), alleges that they are the sons of poverty-stricken outcasts, as if that somehow removed their right to make judgments about him. However arrogant his attitude, however class-ridden his outlook, he does not make the mistake of assuming that poor people are godless, and—apart from the term "fool" (נבל), which may or may not have a moral connotation for him—he does not say a word against those he describes in vv 2–8. By contrast, the venom of commentators against the outcasts is astonishing. Peake is an honorable exception, writing of them as "martyrs of civilization" and daring to compare them with the "heroes of faith" in Heb 11 who "wandered in deserts and mountains and caves, and the holes of the earth" (v 38).

9–15 We return to the scene with which the chapter began: Job is being scorned by young men who are far beneath him in social standing (v 1). His opponents here are thus not the outcasts of vv 2–8 (as against Delitzsch, Gibson, and others). They are no doubt the same young men who in 29:8 would in happier days retire in respectful silence when Job appeared at the city gate. Though in 30:2–8 Job has depicted their fathers as social outcasts, that is no doubt no more than his insult of them, not a piece of authentic reportage. These young men are of course not his only critics (as Hesse notes), but he fastens on them since the shame of being judged and mocked by one's inferiors is very bitter to him. In this passage we first encounter some professedly realistic description of their behavior (vv 9–10: they compose mocking songs and witty sayings against him, they shun him, they spit in disgust when they see him), followed by some frankly metaphorical pictures of their assaults on him (vv 11–14: Job likens himself, apparently, to a besieged city that is stormed by enemy troops), and finally a summary sentence that portrays his reaction (v 15: he experiences his critics as underworld demons who are free to savage him now that he has lost his honor and his health).

Job's extravagant language about the poverty-stricken fathers of these young men in vv 2–8 and his propensity for metaphor in vv 12–15 should alert us to the possibility that even in the more realistic depictions in vv 9–10 we encounter a heightened sensitivity rather than a transcript of social reality. Job is nothing if not paranoid about his loss of health and honor, and it would not be surprising if he were speaking here about what he fears rather than what he observes.

The behavior of his opponents, no matter how exaggerated Job's language, is no doubt ugly and despicable. But, just like their "fathers" in vv 2–8, they are still human beings, and, what is more, their condemnation of Job is entirely in harmony with the conventional theology of the day. To label such people "scum" (Andersen) or "desert dregs" (Hartley) or "constitutionally as well as morally degraded" (Delitzsch) is hateful and improper.

9 Job imagines that he and his misfortunes have become the subject of popular taunting songs (נגינה), such as we hear of in Lam 3:14, 63; Ps 69:12 (13); 1QH 2.11. He is not speaking of criticism or reproach or casual denigration; he is claiming that the young men in his community have been composing lyrics (no doubt observing the rules of Hebrew parallelism and other rhetorical devices) that make fun of him and dishonor him, not unlike the taunt songs we read in the prophetic books (see, e.g., O. Eissfeldt, *The Old Testament: An Introduction* [Oxford: Blackwell, 1966] 92–94). "The poets of the gutter compose lampoons about him which catch the general ear, making the great man whose sins have found him out an object of derision and contempt" (Strahan). He and his downfall have become the subject of a "byword" (מלה), some witty and insulting phrase or sobriquet. In 17:6 he had said he had become a byword (משל) in every land. See also Deut 28:37; 1 Kgs 9:7.

10 As he has said before about his family (19:19), he now says of these young critics also that they abhor or loathe (תעב) him. Like his brothers, who keep their distance (19:13), these young men keep aloof (רחק) from him. Isolation is hard for Job to bear. He does not like these opponents of his very much, but he is mortified when they keep their distance. Perhaps they spit in his face, as an insult against a man who has been shown up as a hypocrite and sinner (cf. Num 12:14; Deut 25:9; Isa 50:6; Matt 26:67; 27:30); but, since they are holding themselves aloof from him, it is more likely that they simply spit on the ground, in disgust at him (as is perhaps also the case in 17:6; see *Comment*).

11–14 His opponents are now represented as military enemies, attacking him as if he were a besieged city (the Hebrew of these verses is in several places very obscure); similar military imagery is to be found in 16:12–14; 19:8–13. It is important, but ultimately uncertain, whether God is being portrayed here as the author of all his misfortunes. His name is not mentioned, but in v 12 it is said that it is because "he" has loosened his cord and has humiliated Job that his human enemies are assaulting him, and we have elsewhere encountered passages in which God is equally present but not named (16:7; 20:23; 25:2; and perhaps also v 19 of this chapter); moreover, in vv 20–23 Job is addressing God directly. On the other hand, many scholars think the reference in v 11 is to Job's opponents, and that Job is not here speaking of God at all.

11 On the reading adopted in the *Translation,* Job means that once people have recognized that God has afflicted him, they themselves dare to take part in Job's public humiliation. While Job was still in control of the town's business, it would have been unthinkable for anyone to act insolently toward him; now there is no hesitation (חשׂך, v 10). So the blame for his dishonor rests principally with God. In former times, God's protection of him (29:4) kept at bay the hostility that now confronts him, and now that God has disarmed him he is powerless against his enemies. What Job does not admit to himself is that he has always had enemies, even if in his former existence their antipathy was muted or suppressed by his status. He is too important a man for the idyllic picture of chap. 29 to have been entirely true, and indeed even there the presence of the "unrighteous" (v 17) alerts us to a conflict that even then would from time to time come to the surface.

The Qere of the opening words is "he has loosened my cord" (יתרי פתח). If the cord (יתר) is a bowstring (as in Judg 16:7, 8, 9; Ps 11:2), to loosen a warrior's cord is to incapacitate or "disarm" (NJPS) him, since arrows can be fired only from a taut bow—such as Job had in 29:20 imagined his (metaphorical) bow would always be. Or the cord could be the cord from which the quiver hangs (so apparently LXX); loosing that cord would spill one's arrows onto the ground. A cord could also be used for girding one's clothes about one; loosing such a cord would be a symbol of humiliation and of loss of power (cf. loosing the belt in 12:18); so Habel. And of course a cord could also be a tent cord, and loosing a cord would signify bringing someone to death; we have already seen this image in 4:21 (where it was either the tent cord being loosed or a tent peg being pulled up); so Delitzsch, Hartley. In view of the military imagery of the subsequent verses, the first interpretation is preferable. Job is then disarmed by God, in the sense that his vital powers have been fatally weakened by God (Fohrer), and he has no longer the strength to resist the onslaughts of his critics (as he described them in v 9).

If we were to adopt the Ketiv reading, "he has loosened his cord" (יתרו), the sense would have to be that God had abandoned his own restraint and had let fly at Job with all his force. Job is quite capable of saying that, but the former reading suits Job's downbeat mood rather better. A yet further interpretation is that it is not God who has loosened the cord, whether Job's or his own; the second colon of the verse has Job's opponents casting off restraint (the term is רסן, lit.

"bridle," as in 41:13 [5]; Isa 30:28; Ps 32:9), so perhaps it is they too in the first colon who are loosing their own cord of restraint and attacking Job without reservation (so, for example, with a few minor emendations, NAB "they have loosed their bonds"); see further, *Notes* 30:11.b and 30:11.c.

12 It seems that the metaphor of the besieged city begins here. Casting up (סלל) paths or ramparts is the language of the siege; on the details, see *Comment* on 19:12.

Why does Job say that his opponents rise against him "on the right" (על־ימין)? The right is conventionally the stronger side (for right-handed people, of course), and Job would be meaning that even on his strong side he is no match for them. Some think that what is in view is a lawcourt, where the accuser would stand on the right (Ps 109:6; cf. Zech 3:1; so, for example, Fedrizzi).

The "mob" (פרחח), if that is the correct translation, would still seem to be the young men who are his opponents in vv 1, 9; many interpreters find in the term an explicit reference to the young (see *Note* 30:12.c). Fohrer, less convincingly, understands the "rabble" not as Job's mockers in v 9, but as the hosts of demons of sickness (as he had of God's troops in 19:12).

13 The metaphor of the attack on the city is apparently continued, though it is not easy always to see what the Hebrew means. NEB, of all the versions, attempts the most systematic account of the siege; it has Job's opponents "tear down [his] crumbling defences" and "scramble up against him unhindered." Though the Hebrew cannot be translated so precisely with any certainty, it does seem clear that the picture is one of preventing Job any exit from his beleaguered situation: his way is "broken" (נתס) and so impassable; he has no freedom of movement (cf. the image of blocking a path with a wall in 19:8). His opponents are, by general reckoning, not among the powerful in society: they are young men without a reputation of their own, men whose fathers can be alleged to be outcasts from society (vv 5, 8). But they, without any help, have managed to bring Job down (להותי־יעילו, lit. "they have succeeded at my fall"), the man who was the wealthiest and the most powerful of the Easterners. Saying that they had no helper is an irony on Job's part. Commonly an oppressed psalmist complains that there is none to help (Pss 22:11 [12]; 107:12; cf. Job 29:12), and the absence of a helper is a matter of regret; but here the absence of a helper is a matter of indifference, for these young men have all the power they need in themselves. Of course, it is not they who have actually brought Job low: it is God and his affliction of Job that have done that. What the young men have done is to rob Job of his honor in the public setting; it was one thing for all Job's fellow citizens to have drawn their own conclusions about Job's character; it is another thing altogether for his name to be dragged through the mire for sport.

14 The besiegers attain their goal when they break through the city wall with a "wide breach" (פרץ רחב; cf. 16:14); then the attacking army can come flooding in. The verb is "roll in" (גלל hithpalpel), as of water (Amos 5:24; and cf. the derived noun גל "wave") or perhaps of stones (Gen 29:3, 8, 10; Jos 10:18; 1 Sam 14:33; Prov 26:27). The imagery of breaching the wall of a city has been used already at 16:14, where also it was Job who was metaphorically the city; there, however, it was God who was his opponent, and not his human critics.

15 The metaphor of the city is over. What all these assaults on him by his critics and detractors amount to is the sensation of being set upon by the demons of the underworld, the Terrors (בלהות; see on 15:21; 18:11, 14; 20:25; 27:20). What they rob him of is honor and health. Here it is not just the honor he enjoys in the public eye, which is his כבוד; here it is his inner sense of nobility (נדיבה), his self-assurance, his sense of importance—such as he has been sketching for us in his picture of proceedings at the town gate (29:7–16, 21–25). And his health is not just his physical health, but his "salvation" (ישועה)—not in some religious sense but rather in the sense of his personal security, his "hope of safety" (JB). Job is not just distressed at the offensive behavior of his critics; he sees in their attack a cosmic assault upon him, in which malign superhuman forces are ranged against him (it is not that he has nightmares of being attacked by the desert dwellers of vv 2–8, with their "loathsome appearance and repulsive manners," as Hartley).

For the image of the wind driving objects away, see Ps 1:4; and for that of the cloud that vanishes, cf. on 7:9–10. It is usually insubstantial and light objects that are driven away by the wind, stubble (תבן, 21:18; קש, Ps 83:13 [14]; Jer 13:24) or chaff (מץ, 21:18; Isa 17:13; Pss 1:4; 35:5) or dust (עפר, Ps 18:42 [43]) or locusts (Exod 10:13, 19). And as for the cloud that vanishes, its significance is that it is never again seen (7:9; cf. Hos 13:3). Job can only mean that what he once prized so highly, his dignity and his security, were, in the end, of little consequence and no permanence.

16–23 The third "and now" (ועתה) of the chapter (cf. vv 1, 9) introduces a new movement in Job's contrast between his present and his former state. In the previous movement (vv 1–15) he has concentrated on the external dimension of his suffering—his loss of honor in society. The final sentence (v 15) has served as a transition to this new focus on his inner feelings, his bodily sufferings, and his reproach of God. In that verse, he had, for the first time in the chapter, spoken of the psychological effect of his shaming: it has not just been a loss, which might be experienced with regret, disappointment, and bitterness, but an assault of anxiety, such as we have noted before in 3:25. It is not just that his honor has been stolen from him, or that he suffers the opprobrium of public humiliation, being made a "byword" (v 9); it is, more fundamentally, that the "Terrors" have come upon him—which means that he feels assailed by these minions of the underworld ruler and in the grip of unwelcome cosmic attentions.

The transition from identifying his uppermost feelings to naming the cause of his anxiety is a swift one: by the time we reach v 18, he is already describing his inner afflictions (as in v 11 he had described his public humiliation) as God's torturing of him. God has picked him up by his clothes and thrown him into the mud (vv 18–19); he has ignored Job's cries, and even when Job raises himself to his feet God looks on coldly (v 20). Then God throws Job up in the air, to let the storm wind carry him about and "soften him up" (v 22). Such treatment can mean only one thing: God has in mind to hand him over to Death, to deposit him in the underworld assembly (v 23). The underworld Terrors that are already turned upon him (v 15) have their marching orders not only from Death, but from a higher command. Job will not here mention the name of his ultimate enemy, for, before he realizes it, he is already engaged in direct address to the deity (vv 20–23); as so often, he slips readily from complaint about God to accusation to God (e.g., 7:11–21; 9:27–31; 10:2–22; 13:20–14:22). This is almost his last address to God; only in 40:4–5 and 42:2–6, following the divine speeches from the tempest, will he speak directly to him, but his mood there is much altered. Here in these verses is his final direct accusation of God: God is the true cause of all Job's sufferings, and God's affliction of him is cruel and unusual punishment.

16 For Job's "life" (נפש) to be "poured out" (שפך) means that he has felt his life force running away like liquid out of a vessel, like the psalmist who was "poured out like water" (Ps 22:14 [15]). See also R. Dussaud ("La néphesh et la *rouaḥ* dans le 'Livre de Job,'" *RHR* 128 (1945) 17–30), who distinguished unpersuasively between two "souls," the vegetative (נפש *nepesh*) and the spiritual (רוח *rûaḥ*), and T. Collins ("The Physiology of Tears in the Old Testament," *CBQ* 33 [1970] 18–38, 185–97 [25]), who thinks of the life force being poured out in the form of tears. The phrase is used tellingly in Lam 2:12 where infants during the siege of Jerusalem cry out in faintness for food and their life is poured out on their mothers' bosom. By exhausting oneself in prayer or with grief, one can also pour out one's life (1 Sam 1:15; Lam 2:19; Ps 42:4 [5]). Job is like Jerusalem in Lamentations (1:7), which remembered in the days of her affliction (ימי עני, as here) all the pleasant things that were hers in the days of old (קדם; cf. Job's "months of old" [קדם] in 29:2).

17 His days are days of affliction; his nights are nights of pain ("nights of misery" in 7:3). The night, he says, bores or pierces his bones (elsewhere it was personified in 3:3, when it announced Job's birth). And his gnawers do not sleep. He does not say, prosaically, who his gnawers are, for the accent is on his experience of being mauled and gnawed as if by a wild beast. No doubt they are his pains, as many versions suppose (RV, RSV, NIV, Moffatt); and if his gnawers do not sleep (שכב), then of course neither does he (he speaks in 7:4 also of his sleeplessness).

18 The cause of his misery is of course God. With perhaps a single image, reaching from here to v 22, Job depicts God as a brute of a man, perhaps a wrestler (Dhorme) or a pursuing enemy (Siegfried), who picks up the puny Job and throws him about. In the Ugaritic myths, the goddess Anat apparently treats Mot in a similar way: she seizes him by the hem of his garment, takes hold of him by the corner of his robe (*Baal* 6.ii.9–11 [*CML*^{2}, 76]; by his shoe and his robe, according to Driver in *CML*, 111b [*Baal* III.ii.9–11] = *KTU* 1.6.II.9–11; *ANET*, 140b, differs). It is an image of his physical suffering in the first place, but it expresses also Job's sense of being a pawn in the hands of an angry God, and the experience of assault on many fronts (here, of being thrown down into the mud and being thrown up into the storm). At the center of Job's complaint lies not the fact of maltreatment itself but the deafness of God to his entreaties: "I cry to you and you do not answer me" (v 20).

In reading of Job's "garment" (לבוש) being "seized" (חפש, if the verb is rightly emended; see *Note* 30:18.c) we might think in the first place of his skin (as Moffatt, Fohrer, Hartley "the agony caused by the withering of his diseased skin"); but it is perhaps better to think of God picking Job up by his clothes. In 23:6 Job had doubted that God would use the "force of his power" (רב־כח, as here) to beat him into submission in a legal dispute; but Job is not sanguine here when he thinks of the effect of God's afflictions. He is conscious only of a superhuman force being exercised against him.

The parallelism between the two lines is not exact: in the first line God seizes Job's *garment*, in the second he holds *him* tight *like* a garment (specifically the neck of a tunic). We do not have to imagine a tight shirt collar (as NEB) or a "coat collar" (JB) to appreciate that the neck of a tunic is constrictive; God totally encompasses Job, giving him no room to maneuver, for he has determined to throw him to the ground.

19 There is no call to see here a reference to the appearance of Job's body, covered with scabs as if with the dirt of the ground (as Davidson, Peake). Nor is it that God has sullied him with dirt (as in 9:31). It is simply that God has utterly humiliated him, and thrown his honor to the ground. The "mire" or "muck" (Good) is strictly the clay (חמר), used in Job especially of the material of the human body (4:19; 10:9; 13:12; 33:6; 34:15). The nearest analogy to the present sense is "the mire of the streets" in Isa 10:6; the normal word for "mud" (עפר) can be dry "dust" or wet "mud," as in 10:9; Gen 2:7; 3:19. For "dust and dirt" (עפר ואפר *ʿāpār wĕʾēper,* conventionally translated as "dust and ashes," but see on 42:6) as a formula of self-abasement, cf. also Gen 18:27. We are not here dealing with Mire or Mud as names for the netherworld (cf. Michel, 159). If Job is to be pictured as still sitting on the city refuse heap (though there is other evidence that he still lives in his house; see on 2:8), then he has come to resemble his surroundings (Gibson).

20 Reciprocity has been Job's dearest desire, according to passages like 12:4; 13:3; 14:15 (though the claim has recently been subverted somewhat by Job's depiction of his one-sided conversational stance in 29:7–10, 21–22). But he gets no answer from God. Even if he stands in an attitude of prayer (as his friends had recommended [5:8; 8:5; 11:13]), perhaps he means to say, God regards him with impassive disdain; for the verb "stand" (עמד) signifying prayer, see 1 Sam 1:26; 1 Kgs 8:22; Jer 15:1; 18:20; Matt 6:5; Luke 18:11. Or perhaps he means that even when he raises himself from the mud where God has hurled him and stands upright (עמד), God merely looks at him, with a "malicious regard" (Peake), "with silent indifference, or in stern severity" (Davidson) (for בין hithpolel "stare, look closely at," cf. 31:1; 38:18; 1 Kgs 3:21; Isa 14:16; and perhaps also Isa 52:15), and does nothing. It is hard to tell whether שוע "cry out" refers specifically to his legal cries for justice as it did in 19:7 (so Habel) or to appeals for mercy.

21 Such an attitude on God's part is an about-turn from the days when God had watched over him and protected him (29:2–4). Now God has "turned himself" (הפך niph), made a change of direction, and become a monster, a cruel and unnatural deity (as in Isa 63:10, God "turned himself" to become Israel's enemy). The uncommon word for "cruel" (אכזר) is used in Lam 4:3 of the ostriches of the wilderness who are said to abandon their young (as in Job 39:14–16). In 41:10 (2) אכזר refers to the fierce courage of a person who contemplates stirring up Leviathan, and in Deut 32:33 to the cruel poison of asps. (It is rather too forced to see here a reference to Death as the Cruel One, as Michel urges, which has been sarcastically applied to God; so too Habel.) This cruel and unnatural behavior, carried out with the full force of the divine vigor (עצם יד, as in Deut 8:17), as though Job were being singled out for special attention, is a hatred of Job (שטם, as of Esau for Jacob [Gen 27:41], or of the hatred Joseph's brothers feared he would bear them [Gen 50:15]). Job has called God his enemy in 16:9, using this same word, and has charged that God counts him as one of his enemies in 13:24; 19:11.

22 It is not only the young men of his town who make sport of Job, but God too (Dhorme). First he throws him to the ground, then he snatches him aloft and lets the storm winds batter at him. Elsewhere it is God himself who rides on the wind (Pss 18:10 [11]; 68:4 [5], 33 [34])—but that is for the deliverance of the psalmist who calls out to him (Ps 18:3 [4], 16–17 [17–18]). Making Job ride the wind (רכב hiph) is a sardonic gesture of God's, as if he elevated him to near-divine status, only to let him bear the full brunt of the forces of nature. "God in His might and majesty may ride on the wind, but for man it is a giddy adventure, the prelude to destruction" (Driver–Gray). It is not entirely clear what the storm does to Job; elsewhere the verb מוג refers to the action of the rain in making the ground soft (Ps 65:10 [11]) or to the hills flowing with wine (Amos 9:13) and, metaphorically, to people or objects flowing or melting with terror (e.g., Exod 15:15; Jos 2:9; Nah 1:5; Ps 46:6 [7]). Here it is perhaps that the storm rains "dissolve" Job (cf. KJV); Dhorme pictures Job being carried along in the clouds and then suddenly "dissolved" by a cloudburst (it is not a question of being "tossed about" in the storm, as RSV, JB, NAB, NIV), but "dissolve" could signify more generally "destroy" (as Davidson). In any case, the term does not stay lodged within the metaphor; it conveys at the same time the sense of Job's loss of stability and, above all, the anxious terror he experiences. We are still at the point he reached in v 15a.

23 What Job "knows" (ידע) is that God's intention is to hand him over to the king of the underworld; his death has already been determined by God. We have often encountered Job's "I know," a statement of his deepest convictions. In 9:28 he knows that God will not count him innocent, in 10:13 that God's purpose was to mark him down as a sinner, in 13:18 that he is in the right, in 19:25 that he will ultimately be vindicated, in 42:2 that God can do everything. Some of what Job "knows" is actually wrong, but, right or wrong, these are the conclusions to which he feels driven. From his experience he now concludes that God purposes to "deliver" him (שׁוב hiph) to death; the term is literally to "cause him to return." While he might be thinking of a "return" to the underworld, in the sense of "dust to dust" (as in Gen 3:19), perhaps implying that life on earth is no more than a brief reprieve from Death (Habel)—and he has spoken elsewhere of a return to his mother's womb, whether the womb of mother earth or the underworld precisely (see on 1:21)—it is perhaps better to think of God as "delivering up" and "handing over" Job to death (as שׁוב hiph seems to be in 20:10). Death is then no doubt personified, as the ruler of the underworld (as in 18:13; 28:22; Hos 13:14). The name of the underworld, "the meetinghouse of all the living" (מועד כל־חי), is an ironic use; for its inhabitants are by no means "the living," and their rendezvous in Sheol is entirely accidental and involuntary (the underworld is elsewhere depicted as an assembly in Job at 3:13–19). In Eccl 12:5 it is the "eternal house" (בית עולם).

24–31 This middle movement (chap. 30) of Job's final speech draws to a close on the kind of downbeat note we have often enough heard before, flagged by key words like death, Sheol, darkness, restlessness, mourning, judgment (3:26; 7:21; 10:22; 14:22; 19:29). Here it is "mourning" and "weepers" (v 31), for the focus in this movement has been not upon Job's ultimate destiny as a citizen of the underworld (though we glimpsed that in v 23) but upon the loss of his former days of privilege. The keynote of the whole chapter has been that repeated "and now" (ועתה, vv 1, 9, 16), focusing our attention on the present, but always hinting at a very different background. So it is right that in the end Job should fasten upon the theme of "mourning," for what he laments is a bereavement.

In this long and fluent strophe he moves from his recollection of his constant deeds of generosity (vv 24–25) to a sense of bitterness that he has not been properly rewarded for his goodness (v 26), to a portrayal of the resultant inner feelings that overpower him (vv 27–31). Among them there is the sense of anxiety as fresh waves of affliction constantly confront him (v 27), there is the misery of his social standing that has turned him into a suppliant (v 28), there is the sense of being dehumanized (v 29), there are the bodily torments (v 30), there is in sum the sense that all the music of his life must now be in a minor key (v 31).

24 If this most difficult verse is rightly understood in the *Translation*, Job brings to the surface the contrast between the generosity he showed others and the cruelty he must now himself suffer. He never put forth a hostile hand toward any needy person, he says; the phrase (ב) שלח יד "put forth the hand to, against" means everywhere else "assault, attack" (as in Gen 37:22; Exod 3:20; 1 Sam 24:6 [7]; Esth 3:6; Ps 55:20 [21]), and we must assume it has the same meaning here. If there was any hostility on Job's part, it was only against those who stood to profit from the plight of the needy (29:17).

25 And not only did he perform deeds of philanthropy; there was behind his actions a fellow feeling for the unfortunates of this world. Those who are "hard of day" (קשה־יום) find all their days difficult (Hannah in 1 Sam 1:15 is "hard of spirit" [קשת־רוח], which the LXX read as our phrase here). Commentators compare the Pauline injunction "weep with those who weep" (Rom 12:15). Job does not mean "I wept for the sorrow of others, why should I not then for my own?" (Peake); he is not justifying his feeling sorry for himself, but expressing his bitterness that he has not received a fitting reward.

26 "While Job disputes the view of the friends that virtue leads to happiness, he shares with them the view that it ought to" (Rowley). His goodness gave him the right, so he reasons, to expect reward; but the reward he has is "evil" (רע), not in the moral sense, but "harm" (as in 2:10), and "deep darkness" (אפל), such as pervades Sheol (cf. on 3:6). There is no divine lamp shining over him now, no heavenly light to guide him through darkness (as in 29:3). The contrast is bitter and starkly expressed; the proverb-like rhetoric of contrast is especially familiar from Jeremiah (8:15; 13:16; 14:19; and cf. Isa 5:7; 59:9).

27 There is a physical reaction to his awareness of injustice; Job as always is a psychosomatic man. His bowels or internal organs (מעים; see *Note* 30:27.b), he says, are "seething" (רתח), choosing a verb for the boiling of meat in a pot (Ezek 24:5) or for the churning up of the sea by Leviathan (Job 41:31 [23]). For the bowels as affected by the emotions (not "as the seat of the emotions"), cf. Jer 31:20; Cant 5:4 (with המם "be in turmoil"); Lam 1:20; 2:11 (with חמר "be in ferment"); and Isa 16:11; 63:15; Jer 4:19. Shakespeare has "seething brains" (*A Midsummer Night's Dream* 5.1.5). We notice that Job does not experience his bitter disappointment as a weight that burdens him or as a drying up of his life force or as the assault of acute pain, but as *turmoil.* In the same way, he had brought his soliloquy of chap. 3 to a close with his avowal of "turmoil" (רגז) in 3:26; there as here it is not the fear that he may soon meet his death nor the anxiety that fresh disasters may be on their way that disturb him, but rather an existential and intellectual disequilibrium, the overturning of his moral universe. Though there are not many today who would hold to Job's view of exact retribution, the idea of living in a random universe would be no less unsettling to us than to him.

28 Whether or not Job's skin has literally turned black (see on v 30), it is not that of which he speaks here. Here he says that he is going about in the dress of a mourner, in black sackcloth (16:15). The term קדר "be black" is used of the sky, stars, sun, and moon in 1 Kgs 18:45; Ezek 32:7, 8; Joel 2:10; 3:15 (4:15); Mic 3:6, and of a wadi in Job 6:16; it is not used of persons in a literal sense. Of persons it means always "be dressed in black," i.e., "be in mourning," as in Jer 8:21; Pss 35:14; 42:10 (9); 43:2; Job 5:11. In Jer 4:28 the literal and the metaphorical senses merge, the heavens being personified as "black" and thus in mourning, while in 14:2 the gates of Judah are simply personified as mourners clad in black. We do not need to believe that Job is speaking literally, of course, for his concern is with his inner feelings rather than with his appearance. Nonetheless, we should not lose the metaphor by tamely translating the word as "sad."

This verse has something of a surprise in store. When we hear that he stands up in the assembly to plead for help, we learn something we have not known before, but something that we have perhaps already long suspected. Job may have taken himself to the ash heap outside the city to bewail his sufferings (2:8), and his friends may have found him there (2:12–13). But he is not *living* outside the city; he is still in his house with his wife and his household servants about him (19:15–17), he is still eating, and he is still, apparently, frequenting the town gate and the assembly he pictured so graphically in chap. 29. Now, of course, he says that he "stands up" (קום) in the assembly, whereas in 29:7 he had taken his seat of honor. Now, he says, he must crave the attention of the assembly as a mere suppliant, like one of the underprivileged persons it had been his pleasure to assist. But perhaps this image too, of Job's being unseated and having to stand upright in the assembly, is itself a metaphor of the loss of honor he experiences. A man of honor does not "cry for help," a president of the assembly has no need of sympathy and assistance; and if that is what Job now finds himself in need of, his world is truly in disarray. (Duhm, followed by Hartley, unconvincingly argues that Job would have been barred from the assembly, and that his language here is figurative of his public lamenting on the ash heap. Delitzsch, Duhm, Hesse, and others believe that Job has become a leper and would therefore have been disbarred from the assembly; but there is nothing of that in the text [see further on v 30]. It is equally special pleading when Fedrizzi claims that the "assembly" here is simply the group of Job's friends, or that "in the assembly" means "openly," as Delitzsch.)

29 It is not loneliness and isolation that put Job in the company of jackals and ostriches, and he is certainly not roaming the desert as they are (Ps 44:19 [20]; Jer 9:10 [11]). It is his miserable cries that parallel him to these creatures: if he rises in the assembly, it is only to "cry out" (שׁוע), like the jackal with its "doleful, mourning sound," like the crying of infants, say some (A. Musil, *Arabia Petraea,* vol. 3, *Ethnologische Reisebericht* [Vienna: Hölder, 1908] 18), producing "dejection and shuddering in all who hear it" (Delitzsch), or like the ostrich with its "hissing moan" (Gordis), "as if they were in the greatest agonies" (T. Shaw, *Travels, or Observations, Relating to Several Parts of Barbary and the Levant* [Edinburgh: Ritchie, 1808] 2:348–49), "like the hoarse lowing of an ox in pain" (Tristram, *Natural History,* 234), its "shrill cry varied by wailing tones of deep melancholy" (Delitzsch) (for the mourning cries of the ostrich, cf. Mic 1:8; and see also on 39:13–18). For the use of family terms like "brother" for other close relationships, cf. on 17:14, where Job calls the pit and the worm his father, mother, and sister.

30 His skin has grown black, he says. The verb שחר "be black" occurs only here, but the corresponding adjective שָׁחֹר is used in Cant 1:5 of skin, in 5:11 of the hair of the head, in Lev 13:31, 37 of the hair of the body, in Zech 6:2, 6 of horses, and in Cant 5:11 of ravens; and the noun שְׁחוֹר in Lam 4:8 apparently means "soot." Now it is sometimes said that blackness of skin is a symptom of leprosy (so Fohrer), and that Job is depicting himself as a leper, whether real or metaphorical. This is however a mistake, since if leprosy changes the skin color, it is to make it paler. What is more, it is improbable that true leprosy was known in the ancient Near East. The skin disease known in the Hebrew Bible as *ṣāraʿat* (צרעת), and traditionally translated "leprosy," whatever it is precisely, is also never associated with the blackening of the skin. There is a real symptom of leprosy, which some translations see in this verse, the falling off of the skin (so, e.g., NEB "my blackened skin peels off"). But this view misunderstands the Hebrew: it says, literally, "my skin is black from upon me," but that means only that his skin upon him is black (see *Note* 30:30.a), not that the skin is falling off. On "leprosy" in general, see D. P. Wright and R. N. Jones, "Leprosy," *ABD,* 4:277–82; and for further bibliography, see *Comment* on 2:8. So why is Job's skin black? Delitzsch thinks it is jaundice that turns the skin dark brown (especially in the tropics), Peake that it is the black crust of his ecthyma, but we really do not know.

His other symptom is that his "bone" burns with "heat" (חרב, elsewhere of the heat of the sun, Gen 31:40; Jer 36:30; Isa 4:6; 25:4, 5). We are no doubt not to take this too literally, for the singular "bone" (עצם) means his whole body (see *Note* 30:30.b); in any case, fever is not usually felt in the bones. For burning bones, see also Ps 102:4.

31 We have previously encountered the music of harp and flute in 21:12 as accompanying the merrymaking of children. But Job's instruments are now permanently dedicated to the service of lament (אבל is the funeral lament in Mic 1:8); they have been "given over" to (היה ל, lit." become for") funereal music, "tuned for a dirge" (NEB), or, as Moffatt has it, "my dances turn to dirges, my lyrics to laments." In Lam 5:15, the same trope appears: "our dancing has been turned to mourning (אבל)." On the instruments, the harp (כנור) and the flute (עוגב), cf. on 21:12. For the flute as mourning music, cf. Jer 48:36; Matt 9:23.

Job has been mourning his dead children, so the sounds of lament and of weepers have been echoing through his house. But the music that has changed its key is more than the sound of instruments: it is the music of his life.

31:1–40 As Job's final speech now moves into its third movement, the tone changes dramatically. In the first movement (chap. 29) he had been nostalgic, in the second (chap. 30) bitter, but now in the third he rises again to the challenge his treatment by God has set him. Here the tone is from the beginning a more confident, more aggressive one. Now he will take matters into his own hand with an oath of exculpation, which will testify that there is no reason in himself for God's attack on him, and that, by implication, God has acted arbitrarily or even unjustly toward him. He may have been robbed by God of all he owned, but he is still a prince, and it is "like a prince" that he will approach him (v 37)—with dignity and self-assurance. On the oath form, cf. S. H. Blank, "An Effective Literary Device in Job 31," *JJS* 2 (1951) 105–7; reprinted in *Prophetic Thought* (Cincinnati: Hebrew Union Press, 1977) 65–67.

From the point of view of the controlling metaphor of the lawsuit, what is happening in this movement of the speech is that Job is summoning God to a lawsuit. This fact is not always sufficiently recognized by commentators, who often regard it as essentially Job's protestation of innocence. It is that, and its content is overwhelmingly his testimonial to himself, but when we consider the purpose of this protestation, it is clear from "Here is my signature! Let the Almighty answer me!" (v 35) that the chapter serves as a formal if indirect address to God.

As a protestation of Job's innocence or oath of clearance, this is his last and his climactic statement; we have previously heard sentences in the same spirit in 9:21; 12:4; 13:15–16; 16:17; 19:25–27; 23:10–12; 27:2–6. For some concrete examples of the use of an oath of exculpation, cf. Exod 22:9–10; Num 5:20–22; 1 Kgs 8:31–32. The oath here has the form of a curse upon oneself that is meant to come into effect if the person swearing it is telling a lie. The punishment Job calls down upon himself does not always correspond very closely to the crime in question, but there is in general a concept of retribution underlying the principle of such an oath.

There is a formulaic and cataloguing quality to this movement, which lends it much of its torrential (Andersen) power. On the principle of repetition in Hebrew style, see, e.g., J. Muilenburg, "Hebrew Repetition and Style," in *Congress Volume, Copenhagen 1953,* VTSup 1 (Leiden: Brill, 1953) 97–111. By reviewing one area of his conduct after another and giving himself a clean bill of health in every respect he can think of, Job means to convince God—and us—that his charge of injured innocence is unassailable. The seven areas he treats are: deceit (vv 5–8), adultery (vv 9–12), disregard of servants (vv 13–15), disregard of the poor (vv 16–23), trust in wealth (vv 24–28), rejoicing at the misfortune of others (vv 29–34), and assault on the land (vv 38–40b).

Job is of course not an Israelite in the story world of the book, and we should not imagine that he lives by pentateuchal law. But the author of the book is an Israelite, and we cannot be meant to abjure comparing Job's standards of conduct with the formal ethical norms of Israelite society such as the Ten Commandments (note for example the apparent allusion to three of the commandments in 24:14–16). All the same, adultery is the only sin that Job's list here has explicitly in common with the Ten Commandments (covetousness does not seem to be specifically referred to in vv 7–8), and even in that case Job's language suggests that he is referring rather to an act of deception rather than to a physical act. In general, the sins he absolves himself of are not external acts but inner dispositions or intentions; some of them have external dimensions (e.g., deceit, disregard of servants and of the poor), but others seem to be wholly internal (e.g., trust in wealth, rejoicing at the misfortune of others). Not surprisingly, some Christian commentators have seen in Job's ethical values an anticipation of the moral standards of the Sermon on the Mount (so, e.g., Fohrer), the "high point of OT ethics" which would be better than the Ten Commandments for Christianity to adopt as an ethical foundation (Duhm). Job, however, must not be misunderstood as saying that it is the internal disposition that matters, or that external acts are of little consequence, or that the truly moral person makes a close connection between motivations and actions. Job is not in the business of promulgating ethical principles, and the function of Job's protestation here is to claim that if he is innocent even of internal flaws, he must be much less guilty of outward acts. There is an implicit argument from less to greater here.

There is some debate over the exact number of sins Job declares himself innocent of. Fohrer finds twelve: lust (vv 1–4), deceit (5–6), greed (7–8), adultery (9–12), injustice towards slaves (13–15), hardheartedness toward the poor (16–23), trust in possessions (24–25), false worship (26–28), hatred of an enemy (29–30), inhospitability (31–32), insincerity (33–34), and exploitation of the land (38–40). De Wilde also has twelve, but by a different method of counting: he omits lust and adds injustice in the gate (21–22). Gordis has fourteen, adding lack of pity for the traveler (19–20) and perversion of justice for the widow and orphan (21–23) (he headlines vv 5–6 cheating in business, and 38–40 the expropriation of the land of others). Hartley also finds fourteen sins, a numeric symbol of double perfection, by adding lust (1–4) and failure to clothe the poor (19–20). Hölscher too has fourteen, and Andersen can see sixteen different crimes, Ceresko, ten. Good would rather speak of fifteen curses. The number of the sins, and the distinction of one from the other, are of little consequence; what really matters is the sense of comprehensiveness the listing conveys.

Though the chapter is formulaic, it is not predictable. For, first, the seven areas of conduct are not treated at the same length; though the strophes on deceit and adultery are each four verses, leading us to expect that the subsequent ones will be similar, in fact the following strophes are three, eight, five, six, and three verses, respectively. Secondly, though each strophe has an opening "if" clause, only some strophes contain a subsequent oath against himself such as we have in the first strophe about deceit ("then let me sow and another eat"): it is to be found also in vv 10, 22, and 40, but not in the third, fifth, and sixth strophes. Thirdly, though some strophes have a "for" clause following the self-curse (vv 12, 23), others do not (Pope thinks they are moralizing additions of pietists). Fourth, the sixth strophe breaks off without a proper syntactic conclusion. Fifth, as the text stands, the seventh strophe seems to be misplaced, since we would expect the appeal in vv 35–37 to be the climax of the chapter and not the seventh strophe (vv 38–40). Sixth, it is not clear what the function of the opening verses 1–4 are, since they do not share the structure of the other strophes, and they seem to be quite general, and yet they contain a very specific self-exculpation about "virgins."

Many have compared, with good reason, the "avowal of integrity" in this chapter with the Declaration of Innocence (also known as the Negative Confession) in Spell 125 of the Egyptian *Book of the Dead,* which has been called the *locus classicus* for the idea of posthumous judgment; cf. Griffiths, "Idea of Posthumous Judgement," 200; A. Kunz, "Der Mensch auf dem Waage: Die Vorstellung vom Gerichtshandeln Gottes im ägyptischen Totenbuch (Tb 125) und bei Hiob (Ijob 31)," *BZ* 45 (2001) 235–50; P. Humbert, *Recherches sur les sources égyptiennes de la littérature sapientale d'Israël,* Mémoires de l'Université de Neuchâtel 7 (Neuchâtel: Secrétariat de la Université, 1929) 91–96. Humbert mentions the similarity in the two texts on the themes of the rights of servants and slaves, the poor, adultery, hospitality, and respect for the land of others. The Egyptian texts lay somewhat more stress on sins of ritual; and though they do not mention widows and orphans, they do refer to sins against infants, lower-ranking persons, and the dead. On the relationship of the chapter with the Ten Commandments, see M. Oeming, "Hiob 31 und der Dekalog," in *The Book of Job,* ed. W. A. M. Beuken, BETL 114 (Leuven: Leuven UP, 1994) 362–68. For a comparable confession of innocence, see J. S. Kselman, "Psalm 101: Royal Confession and Divine Oracle," *JSOT* 33 (1985) 45–62.

Several commentators and translations feel constrained to rearrange the order of the verses. Thus NEB makes v 1 follow v 5, NAB makes it precede v 9. Moffatt moves vv 1–4 to precede v 9. NEB moves vv 38–40b from the end of the chapter to follow v 28, NAB, Hölscher, and Pope to follow v 8 (because of the connection with sowing), Budde to follow v 12, JB to follow v 15, Moffatt to follow v 22, Siegfried and Sicre Díaz to follow v 23, Merx and Duhm to follow v 32, Driver–Gray and Fohrer to follow v 34. Moffatt also moves v 23 to follow v 14. I have moved vv 38–40 to follow v 34 so that the climactic verses 35–37 (plus 40c) should come at the very end of the speech.

1–4 In this preface to his oaths against himself, Job sets out the principles by which he has lived. He works entirely with the expectation of just retribution: calamity befalls the unrighteous (v 3). He does not mean, presumably, that he has done what is right only to avoid punishment; he must mean that he is not such a fool as to lay himself open to divine wrath for misconduct. If God sees everything—indeed, if he "counts" Job's steps—Job cannot afford to have anything in his life that needs to be hidden. Job is not complaining that he has no privacy from the divine gaze; he has no quarrel with the principle of accountability, only with God's failure to implement what has been given out as his own policy.

1 If this verse rightly belongs in this place, it must stand as an extreme example of Job's scrupulous behavior. Generally speaking, Job counts on being judged by his actions: has he committed adultery, has he refused charity to the poor, has he offered illicit worship to heavenly bodies? But he begins his catalogue of exculpations by claiming that his eschewing of wrongdoing went deeper than actions; he not only controlled his conduct but also his desire. He takes as his evidentiary example his sexual desires, which he says he suppressed. He has laid an injunction upon his eyes, he maintains, forbidding them even to "look upon" a young woman (בתולה, a "young woman of marriageable age"; see *Note* 31:1.f). The term is בין (hithpolal), meaning to "consider, contemplate"; he does not mean that he compelled himself to avert his eyes when he passed young women in the street. In Job's culture there is nothing wrong with men, even married men, looking with pleasure, delight, longing, or even lust upon young women. How is a man of Job's social standing ever going to acquire a second wife or concubines otherwise? (Delitzsch, on the other hand, believed that Job is portrayed as consistently monogamous in the book.) It is only if he acts on his desires that trouble could arise, but not necessarily even then. If the woman is already married or engaged, he runs a risk of social sanctions, even death, if he follows his desires (Deut 22:23–27), and if she is a virgin he must pay her father a fine and undertake to marry her (Exod 22:16–17 [15–16]; Deut 22:28–29). But if she is not, or is for example a prostitute, there is no social shame. Job keeps himself so far from any misconduct on this score, he says, that he simply proscribes his desire. He lays a covenant obligation on himself (כרת ברית), the preposition (ל) indicating that it is not a covenant between equals, him and his eyes, but the kind of requirement a suzerain will make of a vassal (see further, *Note* 31:1.b). The example is deliberately trivial, in Job's view; he means to make an a fortiori argument. If he so rigorously repressed an impulse that could just possibly lead to sin, how much more would he have been careful to avoid any deliberate act of wrongdoing.

The idea is common in the Hebrew Bible that sin proceeds from the eyes; cf. Gen 3:6; 2 Sam 11:2; Ps 119:37; Ecclus 14:10. Ben Sira advises his reader to entertain no thoughts about a virgin, but his reason is wholly prudential: it is "lest you be enmeshed in damages for her" (Di Lella's translation). We are still some way from Matt 5:28, where the look itself is already sinful.

There is no likelihood that the "virgin" is a term for the goddess Ishtar or for Anat, who is commonly referred to as such in the Ugaritic texts (so Ceresko and Good, following G. Jeshurun, "A Note on Job XXX: 1 [read XXXI:1]," *JSOR* 12 [1928] 153–54, who had found here a reference to Virgo, the constellation of the Zodiac; support is also lent by W. L. Michel, "BTWLH 'virgin' or 'Virgin (Anath)' in Job 31:1," *HS* 23 [1982] 59–66, by Pope, and by D. N. Freedman, review of *Job 29–31 in the Light of Northwest Semitic,* by A. R. Ceresko, *JBL* 102 [1983] 138–44 [143]). Such an allusion (though not in itself implausible in view of vv 26–27) is unlikely to form the headline of this chapter, which by no means centers on legitimate and illegitimate worship.

There are in these lines not a few places where Job depends on a distinction between himself and his body. Here, he, the "real" Job, has imposed an injunction on his eyes; in v 5 he imagines that his "foot" may have hastened to deceit, in v 7 that his "heart" may have followed his "eyes" and that some blemish may have attached itself to his "hands." In v 9 his "heart" could have been enticed to his neighbor's wife, or in v 27 to false worship. In v 30 he could have let his "mouth" sin. All this is not just picturesque poetic language, although of course it is all metaphorical. What it bespeaks is a worrying disjunction between the person and the body, that can enable, in other circumstances, an offloading of guilt from the person to the body; see further, D. J. A. Clines, "The Disjoined Body: The Body and the Self in Hebrew Rhetoric," in *Biblical Interpretation,* ed. G. A. van der Heever and S. W. van Heerden (Pretoria: University of South Africa, 2001) 148–57. Since Job does nothing but affirm his innocence, the question of culpability does not arise; but it is a hostage to fortune that he offers here.

2 Speaking now in generalities, Job asks what "portion" (חלק) or "inheritance" (נחלה) is given by God to humans. Though Zophar had used the same terms of the destiny of the wicked in 20:29—"portion" in the sense of the life viewed as a whole, "inheritance" in the sense of life in process of becoming—Job cannot have suddenly capitulated to Zophar. He is speaking, of course, of the principle by which he has lived his life; though all the evidences are against it now, what Zophar believes is what Job himself too has always believed. He has taken for granted that human destiny is divinely apportioned, and apportioned in strict relation to merit. (It is difficult to believe, with Fedrizzi and Hartley, that Job is incidentally refuting Eliphaz's accusation in 22:12–14 that Job thinks God's dwelling "in the height of heaven" makes him incapable of seeing what is going on below. And allusion to a so-called "cry of secession" in 2 Sam 20:1 and 1 Kgs 12:16 [Pope] is far-fetched.)

3 He had always believed that the wicked were punished for their wrongdoing, and the fear of divine retribution had always been in his mind. It does not seem that Job is here protesting that in fact he, the innocent man, is receiving the fate deserved by the wicked (against Dhorme), as he often has elsewhere, but simply that he has lived his life on the principle that wrongdoing would be punished. The "wrongdoer" (עול, as in 18:21; 27:7; 29:17; עויל in 16:11) is a favorite term of Job's, whereas the term we have here, the "workers of iniquity" (פעלי און), is more commonly met with in the Psalms (5:6 [5]; 6:9 [8]; 14:4; 28:3; and thirteen other places).

4 Moving from the general to the particular, and from the universal principle to his own case, he recognizes, without rancor, that his conduct (his "ways," דרכים), like that of everyone, is subject to the divine scrutiny (cf. 23:10; and 4:6; 13:15; 22:3). So untroubled is he by the idea that he had long ago imagined a dream scenario in which God would indeed count his steps, though he would not find any fault with his conduct (14:16). That God's recent scrutiny has been too close for comfort has been due entirely to the divine misjudgment of him, finding him at fault even when he knows nothing to be ashamed of.

The idea of the steps or way of humans being open to the sight of God is common especially in the wisdom literature; cf. Pss 33:13; 69:5 (6); 94:11; 119:168; 139:1–4; Prov 5:21; Jer 23:24.

5–8 In the first of his oaths of exculpation, he affirms that he is guiltless of the sin of deceit.

5 Already in 27:4 Job had sworn that he speaks no "wrong" (עולה, as here) and no "deceit" (רמיה there, equivalent to מרמה here), but there he had been speaking specifically of his claim that he is suffering undeservedly at God's hands. Here he speaks much more generally, of the whole course of his life, that he has not "walked" (הלך) "in the company of" (עם) "falsehood" (שוא) and that he has not hurried to "deceit" (מרמה). There is no specific reference to cheating in business (against Gordis, JB footnote "fraud in barter or in the market"). The metaphor of walking, with the associated terms of the way and of feet, for ethical behavior is of course common in wisdom texts; see on 23:11, and cf. Ps 119:59, 101; Prov 1:15–16; 4:26; 6:18. "Falsehood" (שוא) is properly "emptiness, vanity, worthlessness" (as, e.g., Pss 60:11 [13]; 127:1), but it often appears in the context of lying, as in 11:11; Exod 23:1; Deut 5:20; Isa 59:4; Ps 24:4; see further J. F. A. Sawyer, *TLOT,* 3:1310–12. Job has "lived by the same standard as that required of those about to enter the temple precinct" in Ps 24:4, where also the terms שוא and מרמה occur (Hartley).

6 The idea of God weighing the human being in the scales is reminiscent of (but not necessarily derived from; cf. Pope) the Egyptian picture of the underworld judgment of the dead. There the heart of the recently deceased is weighed against a feather (the symbol of Maat as truth) in the presence of Osiris in the "hall of truth" (*Book of the Dead,* chap. 125; for illustration, see *ANEP,* fig. 639). In the Hebrew Bible, the testing is, by contrast, a this-worldly one, as the allusions in Prov 21:2; 24:12 to God weighing the heart show (the spirits in 16:2; cf. also Dan 5:27; Ps 62:9 [10]). Here too Job invokes a weighing in the here and now, since God does not seem to know or recognize that he is dealing with an innocent man. His תמה "innocence" or "integrity" has been attested already in the prologue (2:3; cf. also 27:5). Job's insistence that he be weighed in "just balances" (מאזני־צדק "balances of righteousness") is not a cynical reference to divine dishonesty (as Terrien), but his confidence that if God truly considered his case instead of throwing his weight about he would find that Job is the innocent man he claims to be.

The postmortem examination of the heart was surely dreaded by most of those who believed in its reality; but it is hard to see how Job could do anything other than welcome an investigation of his heart, since it would vindicate his reputation. So to him being weighed in the balances could hardly be a punishment or a self-curse; it is very unlike the curse of v 8 that others should eat what he has sown. So we should, with several versions (e.g., RV, RSV, NIV), regard this verse not as a self-imprecation but as merely a parenthesis as the sentence moves toward its climax in v 8 (as against Fohrer). Pope rightly observes that the sentence is not a self-imprecation but a challenge to God to judge him justly and thus exonerate him.

7 The language is still of the most general kind; we cannot say that it is specifically about coveting and taking movable property, for example (against Gordis). Any detailed examination of Job's life—as distinct from mere allegations against him—would show that he is spotless ("stain" [מאום] is also in 11:15; the language is reminiscent of Deut 13:18). He uses the language of the psalms and of wisdom when he speaks of his "step" (אשׁר, as in Pss 17:5; 37:31; 40:2 [3]; 73:2; Prov 14:15) not having deviated (נטה, as in Ps 44:18 [19]), "turn aside") from the "path" (דרך, as in Pss 18:21 [22]; 25:9; 27:11; 37:34; 119:3, 15), that is, God's way, the path of life laid down by God (see further on 23:11). On the idea that sin proceeds from the eyes, see on v 1 above, and on the heart (לב) as the seat of intelligence and intention, cf. 8:10; 11:13; 12:24; 15:20; 17:4; 23:16. Cf. also W. G. E. Watson, "The Unnoticed Word Pair 'eye(s)' || 'heart,'" *ZAW* 101 (1989) 398–408 (elsewhere in Job at 15:12). The language of following (הלך אחר, lit. "go after") one's eyes is found also in Num 15:39. For the hands as showing signs of sin or innocence, cf. 11:14; 16:17; 22:30; Isa 1:15.

8 In this self-curse, Job invokes the loss of his means of survival; it is a kind of death wish. Had he been specifically referring to coveting the property of others (as Gordis and Andersen think), the self-curse would be especially appropriate: if he has enjoyed their goods, may they now enjoy his. But the thought is probably a much more general reference to deceit of any kind. The idea of sowing without reaping is a common proverbial one (as in Jer 12:13 [sowing wheat, reaping thorns]; Deut 28:38 and Hag 1:6 [sowing much, reaping little]; Amos 5:11; Mic 6:15; Zeph 1:13); here it is finding one's crops harvested and eaten by others (as in Lev 26:16; Deut 28:30; Isa 65:22). In John 4:37 the saying "one sows and another reaps" is cited as a "proverb" (λόγος), though it is used in quite a different sense. In the context, Job's "produce" (צאצאים) is more likely to be his crops (as in Isa 34:1; 42:5) than his offspring or descendants (as elsewhere in Job, at 5:25; 21:8; 27:14). It would be strange for Job to wish that his children should be "rooted out" when in fact they are already dead. To be "uprooted" (שׁרשׁ) is of course most naturally applied to crops, but it is used of humans in Ps 52:5 (7) and perhaps also at Job 31:12.

9–12 Job declares his innocence of the sin of adultery. He speaks reticently of what his own part in such a matter might have been (he would have been "enticed" or "deceived" and he would have lurked by another man's door) but violently of the punishment he conceives as appropriate. What he would have deserved is public humiliation, he thinks, and he knows of no worse humiliation than a disgrace to his wife; for a woman of his household to be shamed is the worst blow his own honor can suffer.

Commentators have long recognized the offensiveness of Job's concept of a just punishment. "It does not satisfy our ethical sense that for Job's offence his wife who had no share in it, but was rather the sufferer by it, should bear the greatest part of the punishment" (Duhm, cited by Driver–Gray). And Good comments that "For a speech full of high-flown ethical principles, this one falls with a crash to earth." Hartley, on the other hand, simply observes that it is "strange to a modern audience." Not a few commentators offer some "explanation" by way perhaps of excuse; Duhm, for example, thought it was because a wife counted as a man's property, and Gordis found it "entirely comprehensible in terms of the ancient doctrine of corporate responsibility and family," while Hartley remarks that "his disgrace is as great as hers for letting this grave injustice happen to her."

There is something strange here. According to Lev 20:10, the punishment for adultery is death by stoning for both parties. If that is the custom in Job's society, he is not free to invoke a punishment that touches only his honor and not his life (so Hartley's remark that "the court would render a stiff judgment against him" is hard to understand). Job is of course, as we have observed earlier, no Israelite, yet it is unimaginable that he lives in a society where there are no social or legal consequences for an act of adultery, and where the only dishonor a man can suffer is that which he might bring upon himself by invoking a self-curse like Job's. He says himself that it is a crime punishable by law (v 11), and it is surely the adulterer whom the punishment must strike. Job cannot be evading punishment, though here he focuses solely on the effect of the sin upon the wife.

9 Job has not watched outside a neighbor's house for the husband to go out and the wife to be accessible. Obviously he would not have "lain in wait" (ארב; for a neighbor also at Deut 19:11) "at" the door (as KJV, RSV, JB, NIV, NJPS have it), where he would have been all too visible, but "by" or near the door. We are perhaps to think of the would-be adulterer lurking in the shadows at twilight (as in 24:15).

It is very plain in the Hebrew that Job speaks of being "persuaded" or "deceived" or "seduced" (פתה) "in respect of," "in the matter of" (על) a woman. It is perhaps not surprising, though it is certainly improper, that many versions speak of being seduced or deceived "by" a woman, as if it were the woman's fault and the woman's responsibility—though the Hebrew preposition על cannot mean that. Among the English versions, KJV has "deceived by a woman," NEB, REB, NRSV, NIV "enticed by," NJB "seduced by," Pope (Anchor Bible) "lured by," and NJPS even "ravished by." Among the commentators, Dhorme actually writes "seduced by a woman, literally 'on a woman,' i.e. 'on account of a woman,'" implicitly admitting that his rendering goes against the clear sense of the Hebrew. If Job or anyone else in his position is seduced, he is seduced by himself or, as Job would say, by his heart or his eyes. But it is traditional, and convenient, for men (translators, commentators, and others) to blame women for their own sexual desires.

It does not occur to Job that his advances to his neighbor's wife might not have been welcomed. And it is not clear whether he distinguishes between consenting intercourse and rape (Hartley assumes it is a matter of violation).

10 Since in Job's world a man's adultery with a married woman is not an offense against his own marriage but an offense against the woman's husband, the punishment Job would have envisaged for himself is the adultery of other men against himself. Or, we could say, since adultery is regarded as primarily an infringement of property law (Terrien), Job's self-curse for robbing another man of his property is to hand over his own property to other men. Grinding grain is the occupation of the most lowly household servant; cf. Exod 11:5; Isa 47:2; Judg 16:21; Matt 24:41; Homer, *Odyssey* 20.105–8. There is a class aspect here, for Job's wife is not likely to have been a domestic drudge; he wishes for her a degradation in status. Some have seen in the term "grind" a sexual connotation, but this is unlikely without an emendation of the text (see *Note* 31:10.a). The fact that a woman slave would very likely also be used as a concubine of her master (so, e.g., Davidson) does not mean that such is the connotation of the term.

The second half of the verse envisages a savage fate for his wife: it is not that she is to become the wife or even the concubine (secondary wife) of another, but that she is to be a prostitute, with other men, in the plural, bending (כרע) over her (the term is as explicit and coarse in Hebrew as it in English). Commentators are united in shutting their eyes to this inescapable meaning of the plural verb (Job is assuredly not contemplating a string of serial marriages for her); see further, *Note* 31:10.b. That they do not rise up against the wickedness of any ideology or social structure—or poetic genius, for that matter—that would sentence, even rhetorically, a woman to prostitution for her husband's act of adultery is a black mark on their permanent record.

11 The term for crime or "wickedness" (זמה) is especially used of sexual offenses such as incest and prostitution (e.g., Lev 18:17; 20:14; Judg 20:6; Jer 13:27), though not exclusively (Hos 6:9; Prov 21:27).

12 There is another dimension to the punishment Job envisages. It is not just a matter for the society to handle; the sin brings its own retribution along with it, a kind of cosmic disorder. It is itself a "fire so fierce that it would not burn itself out till it had burnt down to Sheol" (Driver–Gray), a fire that would destroy all the man's possessions. The act of adultery, Job means to say, is not a self-contained or containable incident, but the initiation of a process of annihilation; there is a "destructive evil inherent in the act" (Habel). Fohrer, comparing other references to adultery as a fire (Prov 6:27–29; cf. Ecclus 9:8; 23:16), urges that the fire here is not the punishment but the act itself. The thought is, however, clearly not that of the fire of passion but of the consequences of it, as the second colon shows.

On Abaddon as a name for Sheol, see on 26:6. For the belief that sexual misconduct leads to death, cf. Prov 2:18; 5:5; 7:27; 9:18. In Ecclus 6:2–4; 9:3–9; 19:2 and 1QH 3.31–32 there are other harmful consequences. The idea of a fire that burns as deep as Sheol and devours the increase (תבואה here, equivalent to יבול there) of the earth is found also in Deut 32:22; our verse seems to be literarily dependent on Deuteronomy.

13–15 Job has never dismissed out of hand a call for justice by one of his servants or slaves. He would not have dared risk God's calling him to account over such a matter, he says. In any case, slaves also have their rights, according to Job: they are as much human beings as he is, created by the same God.

On the other hand, given Job's authoritarian manner in the public assembly in the city square (29:7–10, 21–22), which we have had attested from his own lips, it strikes us as faintly incredible that many of his domestic or agricultural slaves would have had the nerve to approach him with a grievance, let alone with a personal complaint against him (if that is what רבם עמדי means in v 13). However, that is how it seems to Job, and he cannot know how many injustices his slaves suffer in silence—like, for example, the inexcusable injustice of being a slave in the first place. It is inconceivable that any slave asking for freedom from slavery on the basis of the common humanity that Job here professes would have been granted it forthwith; Job's oath of protestation rings very hollow at this point. Nevertheless commentators, who have never been slaves themselves and have not allowed themselves the experience of reading against the grain or with the hermeneutic of suspicion, miss this fundamental point altogether and are rapt in their praise for Job as an enlightened humanitarian.

13 Slaves do not in general have rights against their masters, and it is inconceivable that they could take their masters to court, that is, to the assembly in the town square that Job has described in chap. 29. In acknowledging that slaves could have a "cause" or "suit" (the sense of משפט also in 13:18; 23:4; 40:8; cf. also *DCH,* 5:558a §1.c) against him, he is already out of line by the standards of slave-owners the world over. In not "despising" (מאס) their cause, he means that he has not ignored it or brushed it to one side.

Slaves had few rights in the ancient world and certainly not the right of taking their masters to an industrial tribunal (despite the impression given by JB's "infringed the rights of slave or maidservant in legal actions against me"). The principal part of Ben Sira's advice to masters on the subject of slaves is that they should work them hard, since idleness will turn their thoughts to the matter of their own freedom (Ecclus 33:25–30). Job must be claiming that he goes far beyond his obligations in admitting that slaves have rights at all, in allowing them to question the justice of how they are treated, in regarding male and female slaves as equally entitled to pursuing a grievance against their master, in believing that God might take him to task for not giving them rights, and in founding his conception of their rights upon his common humanity with them. Job's attitude certainly outstrips the norms of his day (Peake: "a most remarkable advance on the ethics of antiquity"), and contains at least the seeds of a very revolutionary social order.

14 When, did Job imagine, would God "rise up" (קום) to judgment (as in Ps 76:9 [10]) on behalf of wronged slaves, whether as a judge or a witness, calling their masters to account, "inspecting" them (פקד, as in 7:18, in its negative sense of "visit to execute judgment")? He is certainly thinking not of a postmortem judgment, but more, in the ideology of the psalmists, of God's capacity to intervene at any time on behalf of the oppressed. Perhaps Job means that since slaves had no recourse to a human tribunal their appeals to God are all the more likely to be investigated from on high (Rowley). Job is of course speaking of his earlier life, when he still believed that the world is governed justly; now he has concluded that God does not keep assize days for righting wrongs (24:1), so it is a bit of a puzzle to discern what Job really has in mind.

For "arising" to speak in a legal setting, see also 16:8; 19:25; 30:28 (and Deut 19:15, 16; Mic 6:1; Pss 27:12; 35:11; 74:22; 76:9 [10]; 82:8; 94:16), and for "reply" (שׁוב hiph) in the sense of responding to legal charges, cf. 13:22.

15 Job has, since the onset of his suffering, come to believe that all the intricate care expended by God upon the infant in the womb (see 10:8–11) had a cynical purpose; but in happier days he had gladly acknowledged the divine fashioning in the womb. If all humanity has been created by God, "what God has fashioned with care must be treated with care and respect by God's other creatures" (Driver–Gray). Job, we should note, says nothing of human equality, which he does not believe in: he only says that he and slaves have also been created by the one God, and implies that that fact gives them some basic human rights, not that all humans should be treated alike or that they are "equal in rights" (Gordis). The doctrine of creation, although a useful support for human rights (see also 33:6; Mal 2:10; Prov 22:2; Ecclus 33:31; it is different in Eph 6:9; Phlm 16), is by no means adequate for them, quite apart from the fact that it is not universally subscribed to. Not many observe that the logic of Job's position is not unassailable: God is also the creator of animals, but that does not entitle them to human rights.

The term בטן "belly" meaning "womb" has been used in 3:10; 10:19; 15:35 (of men, metaphorically). "Make" (עשׂה) and "prepare, fashion" (כון) are used in parallelism in reference to creation also in Deut 32:6; Ps 119:73.

16–23 "After the works of justice, those of mercy" (Dhorme). Job now turns to his humanitarian deeds toward the underprivileged of his society. Among them he names the poor, widows, fatherless, those lacking clothing. Protecting the rights of the poor is an especial duty of the ideal ruler, not only in the Hebrew Bible but in other ancient Near Eastern texts (cf. Kilamuwa's self-description, *ANET,* 654b; the Babylonian *Counsels of Wisdom, ANET,* 426d; the complaint of Keret's son against his father, *ANET,* 149a); in all these literatures there is a certain propagandistic element, and we should not too readily infer social realities from the self-advertisements of powerful men.

Eliphaz had alleged in 24:6–9 that Job had stripped his kinsfolk of their clothing, refusing water to the weary, denying bread to the hungry, sending widows away empty, and letting the strength of the fatherless be crushed. Though Job uses much of the same language as Eliphaz, it is not at all clear that he is offering a riposte to him. Job has spoken in similar terms already in 29:12–16, and although his words there too constitute a reply to Eliphaz's charges, they are not explicitly addressed to him.

The structure of this strophe seems to be a long series of five "if" clauses, from v 16 to v 21 (the "if" is implied at the beginning of v 17), interrupted by a parenthesis in v 18 and concluded by a self-imprecation in v 22 and a motive clause in v 23.

16 On the "poor" (דל), cf. on 20:19. For the eyes to fail (כלה) means for them to wear out by looking in vain for help and thus to lose hope (as in 11:20; Ps 69:3 [4]). No doubt Job is a kind-hearted man, but, to judge by his language here, he is also a self-deceiving one. He has withheld nothing from the poor—so long, that is, as they remain poor and he remains rich. He has totally accepted a social system in which some people, like himself, are extravagantly wealthy, and others are in need of basic necessities like food and clothing. While he does something to alleviate their misfortune, he deceives himself if he thinks that his individual acts of charity are sufficient and that nothing systemic needs to be done, or that his own position in his society and his extreme wealth are not very questionable.

17 Though it would by most ancient standards have been thought eccentric to eat alone, without the company of others, it is not that precisely that Job speaks of. He means: without the company of the fatherless, who will stand here for dependent persons of all kinds. Putting it positively, what he means is that he always had at his table less fortunate people than himself; or perhaps the picture of a large group of socially disparate diners is no more than a metaphor for his generous support of the needy. But once again, those who think, like Job, that individual acts of charity, like giving bread to the poor (Prov 22:9), are the appropriate response to a social system that marginalizes people without husbands and fathers, are politically naive.

Job speaks of his daily food as a "morsel" (פת) or portion, presumably of bread, since the term mostly occurs in the phrase "morsel of bread" (פת־לחם, Gen 18:5; Judg 19:5; 1 Sam 2:36; 28:22; 1 Kgs 17:11; Prov 28:21; cf. Ruth 2:14). It is hard to imagine the plutocrat Job dining on hard rations, morsels of bread; it is a self-deprecating deception if he thinks so, and it will not do to infer that "he was never a gourmand" (Strahan). His will be the grandest of dinners in the land of Uz, and if, as one suspects, he does not admit waifs and strays of all descriptions to them, but says he does, his rhetoric verges on the hypocritical. And yet the words have their own power. Says Strahan: "The simplest words become revolutionary when they touch the heart or the conscience of humanity; and this line of an ancient drama . . . has perhaps had more power to slay the sins of the epicure and the egoist than a hundred ancient sumptuary and modern socialistic laws."

18 There is more than a touch of hyperbole here. From his earliest youth, says Job, he has played the role of father to the fatherless, and, even more extravagantly, he began acting as "guide" of widows even before he was born. The Hebrew is strained, but no more than the thought. Literally, it says that the orphan grew up regarding Job as a father even when Job was only a youth (see *Note* 31:18.b), and that he guided the widow from his mother's womb. Needless to say, some commentators want to amend the text: Merx, Duhm, Driver–Gray, NAB, JB, Moffatt think it must be God who is the subject, and that it is God who has reared Job from his youth. But it takes some contortions to make a connection between God's raising Job and Job's care for the fatherless, and it is better to leave the Hebrew as it stands, awkward as it is. The text cannot be smoothed by the gratuitous supposition that Job learned to care for the unfortunate from his earliest youth because his father was accustomed to raising orphans alongside his own children (Hartley), and he had inherited "the traditions of a great and benevolent house" (Davidson).

Leading or guiding (נחה) is almost always in the Hebrew Bible a divine activity (as, e.g., in Gen 24:27; Exod 13:21; Pss 5:8 [9]; 23:3; 31:3 [4]). It is not the most natural word to use for the protection of a widow, though the picture may perhaps be of "a faithful child leading its sick or aged mother" (Delitzsch). We should also compare the self-description of Kilamuwa, king of Samal: "To some I was a father. To some I was a mother. To some I was a brother" (*ANET,* 654b).

19–20 The picture here is very much more realistic: if Job ever saw someone in danger of dying (אבד pctp, as in 29:13) from lack of clothing (לבוש) or covering (כסות, as in 24:7), he would offer such a person a fleece of wool from his flock. The loins (חלצים), which are in modern English, more narrowly, that part of the lower back between the ribs and the pelvis, in Hebrew include the waist and the genitals. Sometimes in the Hebrew Bible they are the place of procreative power (as in Gen 35:11; 1 Kgs 8:19 || 2 Chr 6:9), but here they are obviously the part of the body that is especially warmed by having a sheepskin tied about the waist. Nowhere else do loins *do* anything; it is a strange metaphor to have them "blessing" Job (though elsewhere bones are said to speak, Ps 35:10). In 29:13 also the blessing of those in danger of death comes upon Job.

For the combination of feeding and clothing the poor (always in that order) as charitable acts, cf. also Isa 58:7; Ezek 18:7; Tob 4:16; Matt 25:35–38. The "fleece" (גז, lit. "shearing") of the flock is mentioned also in Deut 18:4 (גזה in Judg 6:37–40); cf. also Prov 27:26, where lambs are for clothing.

21 Not only is Job active in caring for the underprivileged: he also makes sure that he does not harm any poor person. Though he could have the support of his fellows in the town council (the "gate" as in 29:7), he would not use his power to injure an orphan, he says. One should hope not. If he means that he protected orphans from revenge or punishment even when they deserved it, that is one thing; but if he means that it was only out of charity that he supported orphans, even when justice required that they be supported, this is not much of a boast. Within the velvet glove of his generosity there is the hint of a fist that is the front for a powerbase of patrician and influential men. Rowley comments that "Job could easily have exploited his power to secure a verdict against the weak in the court"; the fact that he "never stooped to this" is creditable, but it is alarming that the thought could have occurred to him.

It is not entirely clear what the meaning of the gesture of "shaking" (נוף) the hand against someone might be, but it is obviously not friendly (as also in Isa 10:32; 11:15; 13:2; 19:16; Zech 2:9 [13]; 1QM 17:9; Ecclus 36:3; 47:4). Andersen thinks of a fraudulent business deal, Fedrizzi of the gesture of the presiding judge prior to passing sentence, and Pope of a custom of "parties to a dispute having an escort to shout down, or, if necessary, beat down the opposition" (so too Hartley), but none of them cites any parallel evidence.

22 The principle of retaliation seems to be invoked here: if Job had lifted his arm (in order to shake his hand) against an orphan (v 21), may his shoulder blade (כתף) fall from his shoulder (שכם) and may his arm be broken from his body. If his shoulder, probably meaning here his collarbone, is broken, his arm hangs down and he cannot lift it again (on the physiology, see *Note* 31:32.f). As for the arm, the image of breaking (שבר) an arm (זרוע, here אזרוע) is a metaphor of destroying strength; it is used also in 38:15 (cf. also Jer 48:25; Ezek 30:21, 22, 24; Pss 10:15; 37:17). This punishment has of course a verbal relationship only to the last of the crimes mentioned.

23 As in v 14, Job founds his ethic upon fear of divine punishment. That need not mean that he has acted justly and charitably only through fear of suffering if he did not, but rather that the divine displeasure has always been a consideration, perhaps the ultimate sanction, in guiding his behavior. We are inescapably reminded of Bildad's conception of God's "dread dominion" that governs the world (25:2). There is a real note of terror here. It is not just a matter of Job's general conformity to the wisdom principle that the "fear" of God, or reverence for God, is the beginning of wisdom (Prov 1:7; cf. Hartley), for the language here, of "terror" (פחד, as in 13:11; 25:2) and "fear" (שאה; see *Note* 13:11.a) and "destruction" (איד, as in 18:12; 21:17, 30; 30:12), the lot apportioned for the wicked (v 3), is very much stronger than the conventional language of wisdom.

Given the possibility of divine scrutiny (v 14) and his fear of divine retribution, he was powerless and incapable (לא יכל), he says, of acting oppressively toward the poor.

24–28 In this strophe there are mentioned two apparently unrelated sins, of confidence in one's wealth and of worship of the heavenly bodies. It seems that a connection is being made between two forms of false worship: trust in wealth rather than in God for security, and reverence for sun and moon rather than for their creator. The latter is the only non-ethical sin in the entire catalogue, according to Gordis. But the ethical dimension is that for Job sin is not simply external acts, but intentions and inward desires.

The catalogue of sins does not pall, for the poet has introduced all kinds of variety into the chapter; this strophe, for example, has no self-imprecation, but concludes with a one-line adjudication (as against the two lines in v 11, which it partly repeats), and a one-line motive clause (as against the two lines in v 11 and v 23).

24–25 In denying that he has made gold (זהב) or "fine gold" (כתם; cf. on 28:16, 19) his "confidence" (כסל), he is no doubt implicitly asserting that God is the only appropriate source of hope for humans, as in Prov 3:26; Ps 78:7 (in a negative sense, of the confidence of those who forget God at Job 8:14). The same may be said of "trust" (מבטח) in God, which is a common word in expressions of Hebrew piety (cf. Jer 17:7; Pss 40:4 [5]; 65:5 [6]; 71:5; parallel with כסל also at Job 8:14). It is interesting that Eliphaz had told Job in 4:6 that his piety should be a source of "confidence" (כסלה, an alternative form of כסל) for him, so it is not entirely true that God alone is the ground of hope, as a rather simple piety has it (as in the Bach cantata, *Gott allein soll mein Herze haben*). And in a way the very idea of "confidence" deconstructs itself, for confidence and "stupidity" are both כסל (cf. Eccl 7:25; Ps 49:13 [14]; כסלה in Ps 85:8 [9]). Confidence itself is neither good nor bad, neither pious nor foolish. The question has to be: What is gold being relied on for, and is it suitable for such reliance? Rather than jumping to a moralistic conclusion, we may ask: is wealth really so unreliable? Job will not have had much benefit out of being a wealthy man if he has not realized that he *can* rely on his gold for many things: to provide him with a square meal and a roof over his head, to maintain his domestic establishment, to fund the parties of his children, to support his social esteem in the town council. A rich man's wealth is his strong city, as Prov 18:11 has it. And there is no point in riposting that wealth can disappear overnight; for if all one's confidence is in God, he too can turn bitter overnight, as Job has found to his cost. And even though Job has lost all his livestock and most of his servants, he has not lost his silver and gold; they have survived the tragedies of chap. 1.

Job here interestingly conjures up the picture of a personal relationship with wealth, the possibility that he could have addressed his money as a sentient being. It is not unlike his conception of walking with falsehood as with a human companion (v 5). This rhetorical move is not just "to vary the style" (Dhorme), but to express the sense that Job is indeed half in love with his wealth, and that trusting in it is a real temptation. Trusting in wealth rather than in God is the subject of typical wisdom reproaches (see Pss 49:6–7 [7–8]; 52:7 [9]; 62:10 [11]; Prov 11:28; Ecclus 5:1, 8; 11:24; 31:5–7; 40:25–26). They must stem from the idea that the truly pious person is poor, having nothing on which to rely but God; as

Duhm said, while "poor" does not mean "pious" in the book of Job, its poet would have understood the saying that it is hard for the rich to enter the kingdom of heaven (Matt 19:23–24)—and, we might add, "You cannot serve God and mammon" (Matt 6:24 RSV). Nevertheless, it is difficult to see how trusting in God and trusting in one's wealth are mutually exclusive, or what God and wealth have so much in common that they can be rivals. Why does Job not see God as the source of his wealth, as Eliphaz had urged him to in 22:24–25 (see *Comment*)—as so he should if his name really means "my God is fine gold" (cf. on 2:11)—and refuse the dichotomy between them? Ben Sira managed it: "Gold and silver make one's way secure, but better than either, sound judgment. Wealth and vigor make the heart exult, but better than either, fear of God" (Ecclus 40:25–26, translated by Di Lella). In opposing wealth and God as antithetical, Job displays his nervousness about a sin he has felt inclined to but has resisted nevertheless.

It is equally hard to see what is wrong, according to Job's standards, in rejoicing because his wealth is great. If God has given him his wealth (1:21; cf. 29:4–6; 42:10), and he is thankful for it (though he never says so directly), should he not "rejoice" (שׂמח) in it? There is no sinister meaning for שׂמח (despite the rendering "gloat" in JB and Pope); it appears elsewhere in Job at 21:12, where children (admittedly those of the wicked) make merry to the sound of the flute, in 22:19, where Eliphaz pictures the righteous being glad at the downfall of the wicked, and in 31:29, where Job denies that he has ever felt such pleasure. Outside Job, the word is used overwhelmingly in a positive and approving sense; rarely is it used of the rejoicing of enemies (e.g., 2 Sam 1:20; Jer 50:11; Hos 7:3; Obad 12; Ps 35:15, 19, 24), but that does not make rejoicing sinful any more than it makes eating sinful because bad people do it. So what has Job against rejoicing?

Gordis thinks that trusting in one's possessions means feeling free to act oppressively, and rejoicing in wealth means gloating over it like a miser—but Job does not say that. "Free from the narrowing lust of gold," remarked Strahan, "he used riches as a means of doing good to others, but never regarded it as his own chief good"—which is no doubt true, but not what the words mean.

26–28 Job evidently regards reverence to sun and moon as a form of illegitimate worship; to worship them is to deny God above (v 28). But his depiction of the heavenly bodies shows that, even with that conviction, he does not take a purely functional attitude to them (as Gen 1:14–18 does, for example, calling them reductively the big light and the little light): they are already for him objects of delight, for he fastens on the way the sun flashes forth light (הלל, as also in Isa 13:10, in Job 25:5, of the moon, and in 41:18 [10], of the sneezings of the crocodile), and how the moon moves in splendor (יקר, often used of precious stones and the like). His heart is already deeply involved in his regard for the sun and moon; how much further would he need to go for his heart actually to be enticed (פתה, as in v 9)? How enticed is the commentator who writes, "The moon moving in stately splendour across the wonderful Eastern sky is so majestic a spectacle that the thrill of homage it inspired is not hard to understand" (Peake), or the one who visualizes Job "lost in wonder beneath the Syrian stars" (Strahan)? May Job not waft a kiss (NAB) to it, as one might to a lover or a child, without denying God his rights? (Therapeutae and Essenes, and older generations referred to in the Mishnah [see references below], had no trouble in reconciling homage to the sun with their monotheism.)

There is a repression already in progress here. Job will call the sun simply the "light" (אור, as the sun is called also in 37:21; Isa 18:4; Hab 3:4; cf. Homer, *Odyssey* 3.335), putting a fence about his lips. He knows that any enticement must be a secret one, for reverence for sun and moon will not be approved in his society. That his heart would have been "secretly" (בסתר, as in 13:10) enticed seems, as Driver–Gray observe, "rather otiose, since the movements of the heart are essentially secret"; his act of homage would have been nothing more gross, nothing more public and demonstrative, than a furtive thrown kiss. He recognizes the urge to worship as arising from within himself as a person ("The old chords were in his nature to respond to the touch of the old faith," says Peake), not as a participant in some formal and regulated state cult. And yet he thinks he would have laid himself open to punishment by the judges, who would not wait for God to take up his own cause, but who would act peremptorily on his behalf. That would be a punishable crime, he says, for I would have been false to God above. His mind has run rapidly on, from a secret thought to a modest gesture to a public prosecution to an open apostasy (perhaps he even thinks of a capital punishment, like the death by stoning prescribed for worship of heavenly bodies in Deut 17:2–7). He is not guilty, but he knows intimately what guilt would feel like. Terrien also has sensed the "force of character needed to resist the fascination of the surrounding religions," offering as they did "a most insinuating attraction to his inmost impulses." "Outwardly a monotheist, he yet knew the seductiveness of this worship" (Peake).

Habel has pointed out how many correspondences there are between this illegitimate worship and adultery. The "heart" is "seduced," the deed is done "in secret," there is the "kiss," and the whole act is "a punishable crime," a "betrayal." "He has 'looked' with lust neither on a woman nor on the heavens," Habel comments.

The idea that the worship of forbidden deities can result only from enticement and deception appears also in Deut 11:16 (where also פתה appears); in the same way sinners "entice" a good young man (Prov 1:10). For the prohibition of worship of sun and moon, see Deut 4:19; 17:2–7; cf. 2 Kgs 21:3, 5; 23:5; Jer 7:18; 8:1–2; 44:17–18; Zeph 1:5; Ezek 8:16; and see Qur'an 41.37; cf. 6.76–80.

On sun and moon as deities in ancient Near Eastern religions, cf. E. Lipiński, *DDD*, 764–68; B. B. Schmidt, *DDD*, 585–93. Among the Egyptians, see the Hymn of Aknaton to the sun god Aton (*ANET*, 369–71). According to Tacitus, *Histories* 3.24, it was a Syrian custom to salute the rising sun. Herodian (4.15.1) says the same for the Parthians, but he may be simply imitating Tacitus. Procopius says the same of the Persians (*The Persian War* 1.3.20). The Nabataeans, according to Strabo, honored the sun, with altars in each house and daily libations. The Greeks, according to Lucian (*The Dance* 17), would kiss their hands to the sun as it rose, while the Indians, he says, would welcome it with dancing. The Essenes, according to Josephus's report (*Jewish War* 2.128 [2.8.5]), offer at dawn prayers to the sun "as if beseeching it to rise." For beliefs about the moon among Palestinians of a century ago, see Dalman, *Arbeit und Sitte*, 1:10–12.

For references to "denying" (כחש) God, which means to ignore him, have nothing to do with him, see Josh 24:27; Isa 59:13; Jer 5:12; Prov 30:9. That God is here called God "on high" (ממעל, lit. "from on high," as in v 2; 3:4) recalls, by contrast, the commandment that prohibits the worship of anything in heaven above (ממעל) (Exod 20:4).

Since "the kiss-throwing hand was obviously the most important gesture of worship in Sumerian, Babylonian and Assyrian religion" (S. Langdon, "Gesture in Sumerian and Babylonian Prayer: A Study in Babylonian and Assyrian Archaeology," *JRAS* [1919] 531–56 [549]), it is likely that other biblical references apparently to kissing statues (1 Kgs 19:18; Hos 13:2; and cf. Ps 2:12) are rather to blowing kisses. For the gesture of throwing kisses to statues of deities, with the palm inward and the fingers bent near to the lips, see Langdon, "Gesture," 546–49. Kisses are of course thrown when the object of affection or devotion is distant. On the subject of star worship, see I. Zatelli, "Astrology and the Worship of the Stars in the Bible," *ZAW* 103 (1991) 86–99. J. Ruskin uses this language of Job elegantly to illustrate the attractions of classical learning for a nominally Christian European culture (*The Stones of Venice,* vol. 11 of *The Works of John Ruskin* [London: Allen, 1904] 129).

29–32 Three sins that Job has forsworn are linked together in this strophe: hatred of enemies, lack of hospitality, and concealment of wrongdoing.

29 Loving one's neighbor is part of common Israelite morality (Lev 19:18)—which wisdom writers take to include forgiveness of a wrong done by a neighbor (Ecclus 28:1–7). Loving the stranger also is required by the law (Lev 19:34), and in one place even an enemy deserves compassion, for Exod 23:4–5 urges an Israelite to help an enemy with a straying or overburdened animal. Job goes a step beyond that, in claiming he has treated his enemy as a neighbor. He has followed, so to speak, the rule of Prov 24:17, "Do not rejoice when your enemy falls, and let not your heart be glad when he stumbles" (RSV; cf. 17:5; 25:21–22 is not so altruistic). Job lays claim to a very scrupulous ethic; for Andersen testifies that "It is impossible for even the most spiritual to avoid a momentary surge of pleasure at the ruin of an enemy, sanctified by gratitude to God for His justice." Perhaps it is a little cruel of the commentator to remark that "[h]ere then is either a very clean conscience or a very calloused one"; for we have no reason to think of Job's conscience as insensitive.

There is more than one view in the Hebrew Bible about *Schadenfreude,* rejoicing at the downfall of an enemy. On the other side to Job, there are many examples in the Psalms of rejoicing at the destruction of the wicked: 52:6 (8); 58:11 (10); 107:42; 109:6–20; 118:7; 137:8–9; Wisdom laughs at the calamity of the foolish in Prov 1:26; and Jeremiah is not averse from calling for vengeance on his persecutors (11:20; 12:3). In the book of Job itself we have heard from Eliphaz how the righteous laugh when they see the downfall of the wicked (22:19–20), as well as the curse (on Zophar's lips) that his enemies should be "like the wicked," that is, cut off from life by God (27:7); Zophar's speech in general has had more than a touch of *Schadenfreude* about it (see 27:13–23 *Form/Structure/Setting*).

30 There is a world of difference between being glad when enemies meet with disasters (v 29) and actively seeking the death of enemies by cursing them (v 30). If Job has never even been glad when suffering has befallen them, why does he need to say that he has never actively wished fatal suffering upon them? The former seems more a fleeting sin of bad taste than a truly vicious act; the latter is a deliberate, heartless, and essentially murderous act (not just a wish for their harm, as Rowley thought). It can hardly be that he was so far from gloating over his enemy that "he had never permitted himself in hasty anger to throw out an imprecation against him" (Davidson), for the offense in v 30 is surely more serious than that in v 29.

Perhaps Job means to say that he has never rejoiced over the troubles of his enemies; and, on the principle of *qal wahomer* (Latin *a minore*), how much less will he have cursed anyone or uttered a wish for their death. Job, we recall, has been calling down curses upon *himself* throughout this chapter, so he is no stranger to the language of cursing; but he has never allowed himself to think of doing it to the harm of anyone else. Fohrer compares the Egyptian saying, "It is better to bless another than to wrong someone who has offended you" (Papyrus Insinger 23.6; see F. Lexa, *Papyrus Insinger: les enseignements moraux d'un scribe égyptien du premier siècle après J.-C. Texte démotique avec transcription, traduction française, commentaire, vocabulaire et introduction grammaticale et littéraire* [Paris: Geuthner, 1926]). "If the writer of Job knew such prayers as 'In Thy lovingkindness destroy all them that afflict my soul' (Ps 143:12), 'Send out Thy arrows and destroy them' (144:6) . . . he kept his lips closed while others sang them. . . . But his heart would have burned within him if he could have listened to Matt 5:43–48" (Strahan).

The palate (חך) has appeared earlier in Job as the organ of discernment (6:30); here it is simply the organ of speech (it does not seem to be that the cursing of one's enemies is thought of as a dainty morsel [so Peake, Rowley], though cf. Moffatt "practised the sweet sin of cursing him"). For allowing one's mouth to sin, cf. Eccl 5:5.

Asking for the "life" (נפש) of someone is really asking for their death (as in 1 Kgs 19:4; Jonah 4:8). Solomon is praised by God for not having asked for the life of his enemies (1 Kgs 3:11).

31 As against the more negative duty Job has imposed on himself not to gloat over his enemies, far less to curse them, he now mentions a more positive duty: the common ancient and oriental obligation to show hospitality to strangers ("From Zeus are all strangers and beggars," Homer, *Odyssey* 6.207–8; and cf. Matt 25:35). The Hebrew family was scarcely complete without the stranger, notes Strahan, and Job is foremost among Hebrew hosts. This is no piece of Job's private higher morality (as perhaps vv 1, 13, 29 have been), but he mentions it here as a count upon which he could have been charged with neglecting his duty. Such an obligation is of course closely tied up with notions of honor and shame (it is difficult for the modern reader to appreciate, for example, the shame incurred by Jael in assassinating Sisera when he has taken refuge in her tent [Judg 4:17–21; 5:24–27]). Davidson recounts how in the story of the Banker of Baghdad in *The Arabian Nights* a rich man's servants, who are thin "like moons on their fourteenth night," are overheard remarking, "Would Heaven some guest would seek admission this day! My master will not eat but with guests and we are come to this hour and I have not yet seen a soul" (959th night). One of the sentences in the *Sayings of the Fathers* (*Pirqe Aboth*) states: "May your house be open to the square; and may the poor be your guests" (1.5).

It redounds not only to Job's righteousness, but also to his honor, that people say, no doubt with good-humored irony, "If only we could find someone who has not eaten their fill at Job's table!"—admitting the utter hopelessness of finding a person who has not benefited from Job's hospitality. And it is not just run-of-the-mill fare that Job's guests enjoy: those who dine with him eat meat, "flesh" (בשׂר), which in ordinary Israelite society seems to have been reserved for high days and holidays (it is mentioned in connection with festivities in 1 Sam 25:11 and 1 Kgs 1:19, and it is absent from Ben Sira's list of the ten necessities of everyday life in Ecclus 39:26). "The peak of generosity is to kill sheep in honour of the guests" (Dhorme). At Job's table, of course, there could have been lamb or beef on the menu every day of the week (he has seven thousand sheep and one thousand oxen in 1:3; and cf. Solomon's menu in 1 Kgs 4:23 [5:3]). We are to imagine Job entertaining guests on the pattern of Abraham in Gen 18:2–8. On hospitality, see further, V. H. Matthews, "Hospitality and Hostility in Judges 4," *BTB* 21 (1991) 13–29; idem, "Hospitality and Hostility in Genesis 19 and Judges 19," *BTB* 22 (1992) 3–11; J. E. McKinlay, *Gendering Wisdom the Host: Biblical Invitations to Eat and Drink,* JSOTSup 216, Gender, Culture, Theory 4 (Sheffield: JSOT Press, 1996); T. R. Hobbs, "Hospitality in the First Testament and the 'Teleological Fallacy,'" *JSOT* 95 (2001) 3–30.

Strictly speaking, the men of Job's tent (אהל) are those who live with Job, his extended family. But of course, this being poetry, and Job being a rhetorician, he could be alluding to all those who are near to him, including fellow citizens. And Job does not live in a tent, as we have noticed before (on 29:4); "the men of my tent" is a formal, no doubt old-fashioned, phrase.

32 Strictly speaking also, the "sojourner" (גר) is a resident alien who is neither native born (אזרח) nor purely a foreigner (נכרי) (cf. J. R. Spencer, *ABD,* 6:103–4). But the parallelism with אֹרַח "traveler" (see *Note* 31:32.g; the two words also in Jer 14:8) suggests that the גר here is no more than a passerby (who is an ארח in 2 Sam 12:4; Jer 9:1), like the Levite of Judg 19:13–15, who plans on settling down for the night in the town square because no one has invited him home (cf. too Gen 19:2; Luke 24:29). True sojourners have their own homes, and do not need overnight accommodation with Job; travelers would be in need of some such invitation. Despite the narratives of Gen 19 and Judg 19, it is by no means likely that sleeping in the street would have been "a sure invitation to abuse by the local degenerates," as Pope fears.

33–34 Job has not previously been admitting to any sins on his part—except for a passing reference to the "sins of my youth" (13:26), presumably committed before an age of responsibility and thus wrongs for which he is not morally responsible. So it is strange to find him here denying that he has concealed his "sin" (פשׁע)—all the more so within this chapter whose purpose is solely to attest his innocence. So he does not mean that whenever he has sinned he has frankly admitted it and not hidden it, but rather that he has not sinned at all, far less sinned and concealed his transgression. So while this is in a way an oath that he has not acted hypocritically (Driver–Gray), the emphasis is not on his frankness but on his total innocence. He simply means that he has had nothing to hide. (Andersen's view does not seem correct, that "Job never pretends to be sinless" and that "Job's candour in admitting to *transgressions* in verse 33 is a bit startling in view of his claim to virtual sinlessness sustained through the rest of the chapter.")

The "multitude" whom he might have feared are much the same as the "clans" whose contempt would have terrified him; the second line specifies both who the multitude are and why he would have been afraid of them. Those he would have feared are "families" (משׁפחות), by which he can only mean the "clans" or "phratries" represented in his town and among his acquaintance. He refers to all those he mixes with, "all that constituted society in those days" (Strahan), his fellow townsfolk as well as his own clan or phratry (משפחה) who were his blood kin. And why would he have been afraid of their contempt (בוז) (since he is not afraid that they would have lynched him, as Duhm thought)? There are various reactions people can have to the news that another has committed a sin; why, in the case of Job, would his townsmen have "ridiculed" him? It can only be because he has laid such a claim to righteousness. If he had been an ordinary man, the "multitude" might have been ashamed or angry if he had committed some dishonorable act; but, being Job, he must count on ridicule if his behavior does not live up to his professed ethic.

In not hiding sin he distinguishes himself from Adam. כְּאָדָם is most naturally taken as "like Adam" (so KJV, NJPS, *DCH,* 1:129b, Delitzsch, Gibson, Terrien, Pope, Gordis, Sicre Díaz, Habel) or "as Adam did" (NIVmg); it is beside the point that Adam hid his sin from God and not from other humans (as Driver–Gray note). Dhorme thinks that "like Adam" is "too Jewish in tone" (whatever that might be), and many others also think that we should translate "as men do" (NEB, NIV), "as others do" (NRSV, REB), "after the manner of men" (RVmg), "like the common herd" (Dhorme), which is to say "out of human weakness" (NAB). But, as Driver–Gray point out, such a sense "would cast a quite uncalled for reflection on the rest of mankind."

The language of "hiding" (כסה piel) a fault (עון) occurs also in Ps 32:5 (cf. Prov 28:13, where the sin is פשע, as here). If he had not taken his place in the public assembly day after day (cf. 29:7–17, 21–25) people might have suspected that he had something to hide; but his public appearances showed that everything in his life was above board. We in our age might not be so trusting. It is a cruel irony that Job's affliction by God enables everyone to draw the opposite conclusion—that he has indeed been a secret sinner.

35–37 For *Comment,* see after v 40b. As the text stands, at this point Job makes his final appeal to God, then in vv 38–40 resumes his catalogue of oaths of innocence. We cannot of course be certain that this was not the original sequence of the chapter; there could be a kind of force in having his very last words be yet another negative confession, as if he could go on forever certifying his innocence (see also Davidson, Gibson), and it would not be out of character for the poet of Job to place the climax of a speech not at its very end, but just before it (as Terrien notes, comparing 3:23; 7:20; 10:20; 14:15; others who retain the traditional order of the verses are Fedrizzi, Andersen, Ceresko). Nonetheless, it seems on balance more likely that the original text would have concluded with his words of appeal in vv 35–37. The explanation of Gordis, though it can never be proved, that vv 38–40b were omitted by accident and then later restored at the end of the chapter rather than in their proper place, is not far-fetched; he argues that the same situation occurs also in Isa 38:21–22, which belongs after v 6, where it is found in the parallel passage in 2 Kgs 20:6–7; similarly Hos 2:1–3 might have been originally at the end of chap. 2.

Among those who believe that these verses originally stood as the conclusion of Job's final speech are the following: Moffatt, JB, NAB, NEB, Delitzsch, Duhm, Strahan, Driver–Gray, Dhorme, Fohrer, Pope, Gordis, Hesse, de Wilde, Hartley.

Not all think the dislocation of the arrangement "disastrous," ruining the effect, as Peake did.

38–40 The final sphere in which Job asserts his innocence is that of the land. It is not entirely clear what the crimes he might have committed could be. They might be crimes against former owners of the land, or against those who work on it now, or they could be crimes against the land itself.

38 If the crime that Job has not committed is specifically against the land itself, it could be that of exhausting it by not allowing to it its sabbatical rest (as in Exod 23:10–11; Lev 25:2–7), or perhaps the violation of some taboo, like sowing the ground with two kinds of seed (Lev 19:19; Deut 22:9); another possible analogy is the Egyptian Protestation of Innocence, where the pious person avers that he has not diminished or falsified the measure of land (*ANET,* 34b). This is more than a hint that the ground has rights of its own, a kind of environmentalist charter. It is noticeable that in other cases of a cry for justice (צעק or זעק), it is the person or thing itself that is suffering injustice that cries out, not someone else on behalf of the sufferer; thus the blood of Abel cries out (Gen 4:10), the oppressed strangers and underprivileged (Exod 22:21–23 [20–22]), the poor day laborer (Deut 24:15), or stones in a building (Hab 2:11), or Job himself (16:18). On the other hand, it is a little strange to have Job defending his adherence to a specifically Israelite law, whether about sabbath rest or about mixing seeds. Although Job does little that a pious Israelite of his type would not do, it is noticeable that the author of the book makes some attempt to sustain the portrayal of Job as a foreigner to Israel, especially by avoiding the use of the Israelite name for God, Yahweh (only in 12:9 within the dialogues). Perhaps we should think not so specifically of Israelite law about sabbatical rest for the land as of a more naive and popular concept of resting the land, which the Israelite law subsequently enshrines (so Duhm).

Alternatively, if we connect this verse more closely with the following, the land is personified as crying out against Job, whether as a person who has removed its rightful owners or as one who has withheld wages from those who work on it, whether with or without the support of the law. Job is aware that the law protects the strong rather than the weak, and that the weak can be injured lawfully. So he does not necessarily imagine himself violently and illegally throwing peasants off their land, still less shedding the blood of former owners (as Peake), acts for which he would no doubt have incurred public opprobrium if nothing worse, but as forcing peasants into debt and so eventually off their land. The practice of latifundium, buying up the land of others to increase one's own holdings, is referred to in Isa 5:8; Mic 2:2 (see also D. N. Premnath, "Latifundialization and Isaiah 5:8–10," *JSOT* 40 [1988] 49–60; J. L. Sicre Díaz, "Diversas reacciones ante el latifundismo en el antiguo Israel," in *Simposio Bíblico Español [Salamanca, 1982],* ed. N. Fernández Marcos, J. Trebolle Barrera, and J. Fernández Vallina [Madrid: Universidad Complutense, 1984] 393–412; H. Bardtke, "Die Latifundien in Juda während der zweiten Hälfte des achten Jahrhunderts v. Chr. [zum Verständnis von Jes 5, 8–10]," in *Hommages à André Dupont-Sommer,* ed. A. Caquot and M. Philonenko [Paris: Librarie Adrien-Maisonneuve, 1971] 235–54).

To none of the land he farms or grazes, in other words, do others have moral rights; his land (אדמתי "my land") does not cry out with a call for justice (זעק, with the same meaning as צעק; cf. 19:7; 27:9; 34:28; 35:9), as it does when innocent blood has been shed on it (16:18; Gen 4:10). For the idea of the furrows weeping, cf. the image in Hab 2:11 of the stones of a building crying out because of injustice. The land is personified also in Jer 12:4; Joel 2:21.

39 There is more than one way of taking this verse: if v 38 concerned injustice done to the land itself, we have in v 39 a further kind of wrong Job forswears, a wrong against the rightful owners of the land or against those who earn their living from working on it. But if v 38 was about them anyway, what we have in v 39 is the reason why the ground might have cried out for justice against him (the "if" here would then be subordinate to the "if" of v 38): that is to say, if he had taken its produce without paying its rightful owners or producers for it, or if he had wronged them in some other way.

The Hebrew text seems to speak of the "owners" (בעלים) of the land; but since Job has spoken of the land as "his" land (אדמתי), this rendering is questionable and it is perhaps preferable to accept the suggestion that the verb בעל here is an alternative spelling of פעל "do, work," and to render the term "workers" (see *Note* 31:39.c). The kind of injustice Job might have done to such "workers" is to withhold or delay payment for their produce; such a practice is expressly forbidden by Lev 19:13; Deut 24:15; Mal 3:5; Jas 5:4 (which speaks also of the "cries" [βοαί] of the harvesters defrauded of their wages).

Although Job depicts the final result of such theft as causing the owner of the land to "breathe out his life" (נפח נפש hiph), that does not necessarily mean the physical act of death; for a person's life or *nephesh* can depart when one is faint for lack of food (Lam 1:11; cf. Jer 15:9). In 11:20 also the "breathing out of life" (מפח־נפש) is a term for despair. Here it is more likely to be grief or distress rather than despair specifically (thus NAB "grieved the hearts of its tenants" and NIV "broken the spirit of its tenants"). Job, to his credit, does not dwell always on the plane of honor and reputation, but also can see the importance of money (כסף, lit. "silver"), and the timely payment of money, as life and happiness to wage earners like farm workers.

The owner or owners of the land are its human owners, not the *baalim,* the spirits that protect the fields and the crops (as against, e.g., S. Mowinckel, *Psalmenstudien,* vol. 2, *Das Thronbesteigungsfest Jahwäs und der Ursprung der Eschatologie* [Kristiania: Dybwad, 1922] 95; Good). Hartley defines eating its yield without payment as not paying tithes or not leaving gleanings for the poor, but it is unlikely that we should be so specific.

40ab Job's imprecation, if he should have been guilty of offenses against the land or have committed theft against the land of others, is that the land should become useless, and revert to its unsown nature, which produces only thorns and weeds (as in Gen 3:18, where the terms are קוץ "thorn" and דרדר "thistle"; cf. also Isa 5:6; 34:13; Hos 9:6; Prov 24:30–31). The "thistle" (חוח) is described as a noxious weed that chokes other plants; it is three to four feet high, prevalent in grain fields and fallow land. It has a stem with spiny wings, green leaves with white patches and veins, and yellow flowers in spiny heads (M. Zohary, "Flora," *IDB,* 2:283–302 [297]; I. and W. Jacob, "Flora," *ABD,* 2:803–17 [816]). Terrien, however, following Löw, *Flora,* 1:406, and H. N. Moldenke and A. L. Moldenke, *Plants of the Bible* (Waltham, MA: Chronica Botanica, 1952) 153, regards it as *Notobasis syriaca,* a prolific plant with itchy leaves and very sharp thorns. Wheat (חטה) and barley (שׂערה) are by contrast staple crops that support life (the two terms are coupled also in Deut 8:8 and Joel 1:11). See further, M. Zohary, *Plants of the Bible* (Cambridge: Cambridge UP, 1982) 74–76; Tristram, *Natural History,* 439.

Job is so wrapped up in the question of his own innocence that the rhetoric drives out any other perspective. His thought tends toward the cataclysmic and the catastrophic if he thinks a wrong done to the land can be righted by laying that land under a curse, or if his failure to pay for the produce he has wrested from its rightful owners (if that is the sense of the verses) can be compensated for by preventing them from ever making a living from their property, destined to bring forth only weeds now that Job's curse lies on it.

35–37 For an explanation of why these verses have been moved to this place, see the *Comment* after vv 33–34 above.

Job's long speech now reaches its climax, and we see unmistakably what its whole tendency has been. His longing here is that the Almighty would answer him. Once he had determined—early on in the book—that his suffering had been unjustly inflicted upon him, he realized that he had a case against the God who had wronged him. The image of a legal dispute had then slowly developed into the controlling metaphor of the whole poem. In 9:16 he had envisaged calling God to account, though there he almost abandoned the idea as soon as he thought of it, for he could have no confidence that his voice could be heard above the roar of the divine anger. In his next speech he said directly, without qualifications, "It is to the Almighty that I would speak; it is with God that I crave to enter dispute" (13:3). In the following speech, he affirmed that he already has a witness to his innocence stationed in heaven, his "cry" that is his "spokesman" in God's presence (16:19). Thereafter, while he becomes convinced that sooner or later—perhaps even after his death—he will be cleared of all suspicion against him, his chief desire has been that he should embark on a face-to-face disputation with God, "to see him for myself" (19:27). If only he could find the way to God's court, he has become convinced that "he would surely listen to me" (23:6). His final speech is an attempt to force God's hand: these chapters (29–31) are a document attesting Job's innocence and, metaphorically speaking, lodged in the heavenly court; God cannot surely fail to respond, by producing his own written document of charges against Job that justify (in his eyes) the way he has been treating him. "His claim cannot perish; it is greater than himself" (J. Pedersen, *Israel: Its Life and Culture* [London: Oxford UP, 1926] 2:366).

35 The one who Job desires would listen to him is of course none other than God himself. He does not want some sympathetic human ear (as Peake is tempted to think), and the time has passed (against Habel, and M. B. Dick, "The Legal Metaphor in Job 31," *CBQ* 41 [1979] 37–50 [47]; reprinted in *Sitting with Job: Selected Studies on the Book of Job,* ed. R. B. Zuck [Grand Rapids, MI: Baker Book House, 1992] 321–34) for the intervention of an arbitrator (as Job desired in 9:33). Job here represents his protestation of innocence as a written legal document. It is of course, within the world of the story, a purely oral statement, like all the speeches in the book; but it has also become, in the book of Job, a written text. So, though the character Job does not know it, his oral text that is metaphorically a written text has become eventually a written text literally, and his signature, which was originally no more than a gesture, is now a physical reality, an appendage to a written text.

His "signature" may not be exactly his name, as it is for us, but his "sign." The word is *taw* (תו), the name of the last letter of the Hebrew alphabet, in the form of an X in the old Hebrew (paleo-Hebrew) script. Presumably illiterate people marked documents with their X. Whether the character Job is represented as illiterate or not is of little account; perhaps he simply refers to his signature poetically as a sign. For the sign of *taw* marking the foreheads of those who are to be spared punishment, see Ezek 9:4, 6 (and cf. Rev. 7:3; 13:16). Though *taw* is the last letter of the alphabet, Job does not mean that this is his last word (as JB "I have had my say, from A to Z," NJB "I have said my last word"; see further *Note* 31:35.c); though indeed his speeches have drawn to a close, his emphasis here lies rather on the formality with which he certifies his innocence, and his attestation that he stands by what he has said in this speech.

In turn, Job challenges God as his legal opponent (as he is in 9:15–16; 10:2; 13:3, 18–22; 23:4–7) to "answer" (ענה) him as his respondent: he requires God to do that by delivering to him a document, the bill of charges against him, which might correspond to Job's own affidavit of innocence. (Diodorus Siculus speaks of both accuser and accused in Egypt presenting a written document to the court [1.75.6]; see also H. Richter, *Studien zu Hiob: Der Aufbau des Hiobbuches, dargestellt an den Gattungen des Rechtslebens* [Berlin: Evangelische Verlagsanstalt, 1959] 38, 90–92). Job calls the document he demands from God a ספר, generally translated, anachronistically, as "book," but also the term for a legal document at Deut 24:1, 3; Isa 50:1 (a deed of divorce) or at Jer 32:11–12, 14, 16 (a deed of purchase); here it is an indictment. It is a document already written (as the perfect tense suggests), for, to continue the metaphor, God has already made his judgment against Job on the basis of that bill of indictment, and has by now been long in the process of executing it. It is not a document that Job hopes will soon be written (as NIV "let my accuser put his indictment in writing"), nor is it a document of acquittal (as Pope) or writ of release (Habel, comparing the "deed of renunciation" in the Elephantine papyri [A. E. Cowley, *Aramaic Papyri of the Fifth Century B.C.* [Oxford: Clarendon, 1923] 16–18 [6.22; *ANET,* 491]).

The metaphor is perhaps not wholly self-consistent. As Driver–Gray point out, "protestations of innocence do not naturally demand an answer, they are rather themselves answers to a charge." Job could of course have made his final speech an indictment of God, a catalogue of the injustices he has suffered at God's hands (we have read such charges already in 10:16; 16:7–17; 19:6–20; 27:2). His claims to innocence, though they are not formally speaking such an indictment, already function as such. And it can be noted that self-imprecation, which is what chap. 31 has been from a formal point of view, is not a bill of indictment either; it could be argued that "the natural 'answer' of God to an imprecation would be to inflict the ill imprecated" (Driver–Gray). But Job has to leave open, theoretically at least, the possibility that there are other charges God has against him, which he himself has not thought of; so it makes sense that he should demand that God give an account of what he has against him.

On the adversary (איש־ריב, lit. "man of dispute"), cf. B. Gemser, "The *Rîb*- or Controversy Pattern in Hebrew Mentality," in *Wisdom in Israel and in the Ancient Near East,* FS H. H. Rowley, ed. M. Noth and D. W. Thomas, VTSup 3 (Leiden: Brill, 1955) 120–37.

36 Job has the most outrageous idea of what he could do with God's indictment. He will not whimper over it, or study it line by line, or invent elaborate rebuttals of its charges. He will go public with it. He will announce it to all the world, openly displaying it day by day as he goes about his business. Job would carry the bill of indictment on his shoulder so as to make it conspicuous, as in Isa 22:22 where the key of the house of David is laid by God on the shoulder of his servant Eliakim. Job would be proud for all the world to see the bill of particulars against him—for it would contain no charges whatsoever and be entirely blank (or else, perhaps, its charges would all be patently false)! And "far from blushing at the accusatory document," as Dhorme puts it, Job would roll it up and wind it about his head as a turban, as a testimony to his honor and innocence, somewhat like the teachings of father and mother, which the young man in Proverbs is urged to "bind (ענד, as here) . . . upon your heart always; tie them about your neck" (6:21 RSV). In 19:9 Job had said that God had stripped his "crown" or "turban" (עטרה, as here; cf. on 29:14) from him, that is, his honor or reputation as a righteous man; if God would deliver to him his indictment against him, that would restore his honor. A crown or turban is an image often used in wisdom texts for what brings honor; see Prov 4:9; 12:4; 17:6; Ecclus 6:31; 25:6. On the role of honor here, cf. C. A. Muenchow, "Dust and Dirt in Job 42:6," *JBL* 108 (1989) 597–611 (605–6).

In being upon Job's "shoulder" (שכם, "shoulder, back of the neck"), it is not that the scroll on which the indictment is written is to be read by those who come up behind Job (as Driver–Gray) rather than by those who meet him; it is that the scroll is blank, as any who encounter Job can see with their own eyes. And it is not that he would "pin it upon his breast like some decoration of honour" (Gibson), for the chest is not the shoulder. Nor is the idea that the scroll is an easy burden, being so short a document (as BDB, 1014a). Still less does there seem to be any remnant of an idea that a written curse would kill the one who bore it if he were guilty (as Fohrer, de Wilde [perhaps]). Fohrer thought that by exhibiting the document in public Job would effectively be submitting himself to a trial by ordeal, and counteracting the power resident in the document (G. Fohrer, "The Righteous Man in Job 31," in *Essays in Old Testament Ethics,* FS J. P. Hyatt, ed. J. L. Crenshaw and J. T. Willis [New York: Ktav, 1974] 1–22 [3]; reprinted in *Studien zum Buche Hiob [1956–1979],* 2d ed., BZAW 159 [Berlin: de Gruyter, 1983] 78–93 [79]). Peake thought, perhaps too subtly, that the indictment Job desires would not indeed be blank, but would contain in words what God had said of him in deeds; thus, Peake imagines, "He would bind God's accusations to him, transfiguring the shame into glory by the radiant glow of conscious innocence."

37 Job has nothing in his life to be ashamed of, and so he refuses to be cowed by the prospect of a written indictment from God. And it is not just that he is prepared to report on his every move; he is proud of his uprightness, and would present an account of himself "like a prince" (כמו־נגיד), his head held high, and "approaching" (קרב) God with assurance—like Frederick II who would "think, live, and die a king" (letter to Voltaire, 1751). "How different from Adam," remarks Delitzsch, "who was obliged to be drawn out of his hiding-place, and tremblingly, because conscious of guilt." We hear no Kyrie eleison here, for Job is no miserable sinner but a man justifiably proud of his innocence. On the term נגיד "prince," see J. de Fraine, *L'aspect religieux de la royauté israélite: L'institution monarchique dans l'Ancien Testament et dans les textes mésopotamiens* (Rome: Pontifical Biblical Institute, 1954) 98–100; G. F. Hasel, *TDOT,* 9:187–202.

His very last word, "I would approach him" (אקרבנו), is rich with resonance. The deprivations Job has suffered, at God's hands as he believes and as we are assured, might have made many mortals turn their back upon God, or be filled with a bitterness that made the thought of approaching God distasteful. Job indeed has almost nothing good to say about God, though he clings to the idea of some sense of justice deep down in the divine personality (23:6–7); but he has no fear of him and no trembling of confidence in the rightness of his own cause. It has been a long uphill path from the opening words of his first speech, "Perish the day I was born!" (3:3), but he stands triumphant now, as if he has been awaking from death. Nothing has changed, truth to tell; his bereavements are as real as they ever have been, his physical sufferings still torment him, and to this moment he is shorn of his honor and stigmatized by all who know him as the chiefest of sinners. Yet in himself he is still the prince, and that even before God. This final utterance, as Strahan says, is "rhetorically magnificent as it is morally audacious, and leaves the imaginative reader in breathless suspense."

40c The note "the words of Job are ended" is the author's formal conclusion (it is not an editorial addition, as Duhm, Gibson, Driver–Gray, Fohrer, Pope, Rowley, Fedrizzi [perhaps], Gordis, Hartley say). The similar formulas of conclusion in Jer 48:47, 51:64, and Ps 72:20 can more properly be called editorial or redactional. If, as is suggested in this commentary, the speeches of Yahweh immediately followed this sentence (before the Elihu speeches were misplaced here in the course of transmission from their original place before chap. 28), this note, with 38:1, forms the sole narrative transition from Job's last speech to Yahweh's reply (chaps. 38–41).

Explanation

Beginning where it does, this final speech of Job gives no hint of how it will end. It would not be unforgivable if Job were in the end to resign himself to his fate and bring his speeches to an end on a note of disappointment for how his life has turned out, of nostalgia for former happy days. But we are not surprised, once we have reached the end of chap. 31, with how he has moved in this his last speech. He has gone further backwards in time than anywhere else, but he has also looked forward more confidently, and insisted on his rights more unashamedly, than anywhere else in the book.

This is Job's longest speech, and it follows his shortest (27:1–6). That speech had been constituted by a single intense oath, that all he has said about his innocence has been true; and the oath, with dramatic fervor, had been sworn by the life of God. This speech is much more expansive and, especially at first, not so intense.

As it begins, his speech is wrapped in nostalgia, in a conjuring up of blissful days when the protection of God was over his tent (29:4). It is not a chapter in salvation-history, for Job's eye lights upon too many facets of his past—his children, his wealth, his esteem in the town, his deeds of generosity, his sense of security—for this to be simply a paean of praise to the Almighty. But neither is it the hymn of a self-made man, for Job takes an innocent, almost naive pleasure in his comfortable, carefree, and thoroughly patriarchal existence. He never thinks or speaks of how he got to his exalted status in society, and he never considers whether he deserved to be there. There he was, and he enjoyed it, not selfishly but honorably and with public spirit.

He speaks of a society in which others did not have his chances or his success: there are widows and fatherless, blind and lame, poor and unprotected strangers. His mission was not to change the system but to improve the lot of those within it. And they thanked him for it; when the ear heard, it called him blessed, and when the eye saw, it testified for him (v 11). He speaks too of a society that needed leadership, of people who wanted decisions to be made for them, of old men and young who wanted a "chief" (v 25). Job did not disappoint them: in the town council they gave him their enthusiastic support and their unwavering allegiance, opening their mouths for his words as for the spring rains (v 23). If there is a shadow in this portrait, it lies solely in a single reference to the "unrighteous," who are squeezed to the margin as less than human, wild animals who can be contained and subdued, their jawbones broken, by a man of quality (v 17).

In its second movement (chap. 30), this sunniest of pictures is fatefully overcast when it is set alongside the present scene. In the world of today, the man of honor is reviled—and that by his inferiors, men younger than himself (30:1), the mob (v 12), whose derision feels like the assault of an enemy on a walled town (vv 12–13). The worst of it is, God himself has authorized their insults: it is because God has slackened Job's bow cord that they have been able to throw off restraint in Job's presence (v 11). And God too has turned cruel to him (v 21), joining in the sport of Job-baiting: like a monstrous giant, a cruel Brobdignagian, he picks Job up by his clothes, throws him down into the mud, then snatches him up and hurls him into the air, dissolving all his vital energies (vv 18–19, 22). Job feels his life force has been poured out like water on the ground (v 16); he is in constant psychic torment (v 27); he knows only how to cry out in anxiety and pain, a brother to doleful jackals and a companion of shrieking ostriches (v 29).

It is something of a miracle then when in the third movement (chap. 31) Job can find in himself such vigor, such self-assurance, such determination that he can sustain a rigorous review of his life, its manifestations and its motivations, can allow himself a clean bill of moral health, and, above all, can demand from God sight of any charge sheet that would incriminate him. Job has never been more compelling on the matter of his innocence than he is here, never more unflinching before the divine presence. The cumulative effect of his oath of clearance is to convince us, if we have never been persuaded of it before, that he is in the right and God's hounding of him is in the wrong. He has behaved "like a prince," and like a prince he is entitled to approach God, not with a request but with a demand, that his case be heard, and that God should give him justice.

It does not undermine the dramatic logic of the poem if in the course of this last speech we come to modify our view of Job the man. In his previous speeches we have seen him in the midst of his grief, and the figure he has cut has been hugely sympathetic as he has tried to wrest justice from a distant and unresponsive God. Now in these chapters we are given more than a glimpse of the Job of the days before the book opened, and heard from his own lips what it was like to be "blameless and upright," as the opening sentence of the book had certified him. Perhaps he lets slip more than we would really like to know. For though he is not a bad man, by standards of our own time he stands condemned out of his own mouth on many a count, and we may come to hesitate, as we never did before, to assent to the judgment of the narrator that this is a perfect man. We see him in the town council, taking his own authoritarian attitude for granted, listening to no one else's opinion and brooking no interference with his decisions (see on 29:7–10, 21–25). We see his attitude to his youthful opponents, whom he despises for their youth and to whom he ascribes social outcasts as fathers (see on 30:2–8), we hear his rhetoric of assault (30:1, 9–13) with new ears, wondering if he is truly capable of distinguishing criticism and evaluation by others from unprincipled character assassination, and we listen to his catalogue of oaths with a growing suspicion that Job may be in several respects the victim of his own self-deceptions. He is so concerned for his honor that he can wish for the disgrace of his wife if he himself has offended the sexual code (31:9–10); he has convinced himself that his slaves are in every respect treated fairly and properly by him while discounting the fact that they remain slaves (31:13–15); he congratulates himself on his support of the underprivileged (31:16–22) while never questioning the system, and his complicity in it, that makes and keeps them underprivileged; he has denied any participation in the disallowed worship of the heavenly bodies but has let slip his heartfelt attraction to it nevertheless (31:26–28).

Different readers will react differently to these observations. Some will insist that Job be judged only by his own standards and the standards of his time, and will be deeply impressed by his emphasis on the importance of motivation in ethics, an emphasis that seems to go deeper than conventional morality of his own time or ours. Others will feel that they have no other standards to judge by except those to which they themselves are committed, and will regretfully decide that the Job whose part they have been taking throughout the dialogues is a flawed character, even if still a remarkable and attractive personality.

Not many will deny, however, that with this speech we have reached the high point of the book, with its hero taking control of his own life, at the same time making it impossible, whether theologically or narratively, for the character God not to comply with his demands. If, as is being argued in this commentary, in the original book of Job this speech of Job was followed immediately by the divine speeches of chaps. 38–41 (the Elihu speeches of chaps. 32–37 having originally preceded chap. 28), Job will have had his demand for a divine response met immediately. But even if the more usual view is taken, that the divine reply is delayed until the speeches of Elihu are concluded, it is still only a short time to wait until Job will have his answer. Or will he? Will he hear from the tempest anything like he expected? And will his cry for justice be heard?